TEXTBOOK OF CRIMINAL LAW

AUSTRALIA AND NEW ZEALAND
The Law Book Company Ltd.
Sydney : Melbourne : Perth

CANADA AND U.S.A.
The Carswell Company Ltd.
Agincourt, Ontario

INDIA
N. M. Tripathi Private Ltd.
Bombay
and
Easter Law House Private Ltd.
Calcutta and Delhi
M.P.P. House, Bangalore

ISRAEL
Steimatzky's Agency Ltd.
Jerusalem : Tel Aviv : Haifa

MALAYSIA : SINGAPORE : BRUNEI
Malayan Law Journal (Pte.) Ltd.
Singapore

PAKISTAN
Pakistan Law House
Karachi

TEXTBOOK

OF

CRIMINAL LAW

SECOND EDITION

BY

GLANVILLE WILLIAMS, Q.C., LL.D., F.B.A.

Honorary and Emeritus Fellow of Jesus College, Cambridge;
Honorary Bencher of the Middle Temple;
formerly Professor of Public Law and Quain
Professor of Jurisprudence in the University of London,
and Rouse Ball Professor of English Law
in the University of Cambridge

LONDON
STEVENS & SONS
1983

First edition 1978
Second impression with Supplement 1979
Second edition 1983

Published by
Stevens & Sons Limited of 11 New Fetter Lane,
London, Computerset by Promenade Graphics
Limited, Cheltenham, and printed in Scotland

British Library Cataloguing in Publication Data
Williams, Glanville
Textbook of criminal law.—2nd ed.
1. Criminal law—England
I. Title
344.205 KD7869

ISBN 0–420–46850–1
ISBN 0–420–46860–9 Pbk

PREFACE

In the preface to the first edition I briefly explained the main unconventional feature of this book, namely the conversational, thrust and parry method of presentation. Explanations of this kind are included in prefaces chiefly by way of defence against possible objections from reviewers, and I am glad and relieved to say that the reviewers of the first edition approved and even welcomed the method (with the notable exception of Mr. Richard Buxton).

As before, the book is designed to be read at two levels. The text in larger print is sufficient for readers who wish to keep to the highroad, at any rate on first reading. It states the principles, with some explanatory detail and discussion of fundamentals. This gives more than enough information for passing an examination. The additions in small print are for practitioners, or are optional extras for students who wish to delve more deeply.

As a second means of helping the beginner to view the wood in isolation from the trees, the book contains summaries after all the chapters except the first. I would suggest that the student should read the summary for each section after reading the section, and then the summary for the chapter as a whole after reading the chapter. The practitioner may find the summaries useful as a quick guide to the book.

The text has been heavily revised and in many places rewritten to take account of new developments. Chief among the statutes since the first edition are the Theft Act 1978, the Criminal Attempts Act 1981 and the Forgery and Counterfeiting Act 1981; but these are eclipsed in general significance by the twin decisions of the House of Lords on recklessness in *Caldwell* and *Lawrence.* Further statutes and important cases on the criminal law appeared with embarrassing frequency while the book was going through the press, but I have managed to deal with all of them up to the date of this preface, including *Miller* on arson, *Seymour* on motor manslaughter, and *Sullivan* on automatism, in the House of Lords; *Kimber* on mistake, *Wilson* on inflicting actual bodily harm, *David Morris* on appropriation in theft, and *Gilmartin* on postdated cheques, in the Court of Appeal; *Winzar* v. *Chief Constable of Kent* on liability without an act, *Elliott* v. *C.* on recklessness, and *JJC* v. *Eisenhower* on wounding, in the Divisional Court; *Gillick* v. *West Norfolk AHA* (Woolf J) on consent to treatment; and the Mental Health Act 1983.

Having mentioned the reviewers of the first edition I should like to acknowledge my indebtedness to them for their constructive suggestions—sometimes, very courteously, communicated to me by private letter additional to the review. My grateful thanks are due also, for assistance on various points, to Dr. Ashworth, Professor Griew, Dr. B W Napier, Mr. Justice McCullough, Mr. A T H Smith, Mr. D G T Williams (who called my attention to the animadversions of the Royal Commission on

Environmental Pollution on the decision *Smedleys Ltd.* v. *Breed*), and above all to Mr. Glazebrook, who subjected my text to detailed and penetrating criticisms, to my great profit.

Jesus College, Cambridge GLANVILLE WILLIAMS
August 1983

CONTENTS

PART ONE: GENERAL CONSIDERATIONS

PART TWO: THE PROTECTION OF THE PERSON

TABLE OF CASES

Cases tried on indictment are listed under defendants. Bold figures indicate the main references.

TABLE OF STATUTES

TABLE OF GOVERNMENT ORDERS

ABBREVIATIONS

Nearly all the abbreviations employed in the footnotes are standard. Important statutes are frequently cited by their initial letters, *e.g.* CLA 1977 = Criminal Law Act. The references to Stephen, *HCL (History of the Criminal Law)*, Pollock and Maitland, Holdsworth, *HEL (History of English Law)*, and Radzinowicz, *HECL (History of English Criminal Law)*, are to well-known historical works. Note also:

BMJ British Medical Journal
CA Court of Appeal
CCCR Court for Crown Cases Reserved
CLJ Cambridge Law Journal
CLRC Criminal Law Revision Committee
HLR Harvard Law Review
JPN Justice of the Peace (Newspaper)
LQR Law Quarterly Review
MLR Modern Law Review
Model Penal Code Model Penal Code of the American Law Institute (ALI). References are to the Tentative Drafts (TD) and the Proposed Official Draft (POD).
NLJ New Law Journal
PC *Pleas of the Crown* (classical works under this title by Hale, East, Hawkins etc.).
Russell, 12th ed. Russell on *Crime*.
Smith and Hogan. *Criminal Law,* 4th edn. For preference, reference should be made to the current, 5th, edition.
The General Part. Glanville Williams, *Criminal Law: The General Part,* 2nd ed.

Part One

GENERAL CONSIDERATIONS

CHAPTER 1

CRIME AND THE CRIMINAL LAW

Whatever views one holds about the penal law, no one will question its importance to society. This is the law on which men place their ultimate reliance for protection against all the deepest injuries that human conduct can inflict on individuals and institutions. By the same token, penal law governs the strongest force that we permit official agencies to bring to bear on individuals. Its promise as an instrument of safety is matched only by its power to destroy. Nowhere in the entire legal field is more at stake for the community or for the individual.

Herbert Wechsler, *The Challenge of a Model Penal Code*.

§ 1.1. SCOPE OF THE STUDY

THIS first chapter is not an essential part of the book for examination purposes. Examiners on the criminal law tend to be severely professional, concentrating on the intricacies of subjects like complicity and burglary. They do not usually ask about the nature of a crime, the justification of criminal punishment, the reasons why one offence often includes another, the arguments for and against having widely drawn offences, and the strategic considerations leading the police to charge one offence rather than another. So if examination credit is the object of your study, reader, you may lose no marks if you pass over these preliminary remarks.

All the same, I trust you will read the chapter, even though quickly, because it will help you to understand the working of the law, including the procedural and sentencing details of the cases in the law reports. Some knowledge of these matters is part of the mental equipment necessary for an intelligent approach to problems of substantive law.

If you are in too much of a hurry to read the whole chapter, you will not lose the thread, though you will miss some information, if you skip the fine print; and the same applies to the rest of the book. Alternatively or additionally, if you wish to keep in step with lectures you can, if necessary, postpone the reading of this chapter and of Chapter 2 for the time being.

To begin with territory: the subject of our study is the criminal law in force in England and Wales, the Scots being a law unto themselves.

Parliament legislates for the whole of the United Kingdom, but it frequently needs to distinguish betwen Scotland on the one hand and England and Wales on the other, since the legal systems are largely different.

We refer to "England and Wales,"[1] because they are felt as two countries (at any rate by many of my Welsh compatriots), but what is called English law applies equally to Wales. For practically all legal purposes the territory is a single unit. It would be wrong to speak of "English and Welsh judges," because although we have both English and Welsh High Court

[1] The Interpretation Act 1978 s.25 and Sch. 3 repeals the Wales and Berwick Act 1746 under which the word "England" included Wales.

and circuit judges they were not appointed on that basis. "English and Welsh law" would be even worse, since there are not two systems. One is compelled to say, therefore, that the Welsh are governed by English law, just as Americans and Australians have to express themselves in the English language. Occasionally, for convenience, I will even use the word "England" to stand for the orthodox and diplomatic expression "England and Wales," simply because the latter expression is too cumbrous.

The law of Northern Ireland, and indeed of the Republic of Ireland, is basically much the same as in England, though there are various statutory divergencies. Also, many of the underlying concepts of the criminal law are still recognised in other countries that started from the English common law, such as the United States, Canada, Australia and New Zealand, and African States too numerous to mention. Overseas decisions based on the common law have persuasive authority in our courts.

§ 1.2. THE PROSECUTION OF OFFENCES

The police are charged with enforcing the criminal law in respect of the major crimes against the person, property and public order, and in respect of driving offences and miscellaneous minor offences. Prosecutions may also be instituted by the Director of Public Prosecutions (DPP), particularly in the more serious or difficult cases.

Revenue offences are prosecuted by officers of the Inland Revenue and Customs and Excise. Other administrative or public welfare offences are prosecuted by inspectors and other officers of the Departments concerned, for example the Department of Trade (in respect of parts of the law within its purview, such as company law), health and safety inspectors of the Health and Safety Executive, and trading standards officers of the local authorities. Local authorities may prosecute in matters like public nuisance and offences against planning regulations and bylaws; some charges can be brought only by local authorities. Then there can be private prosecutions. Any queries so far?

Do the police bring a charge whenever they have enough evidence?

They will nearly always bring proceedings for a major crime, provided that there is a reasonable prospect of conviction; but they exercise discretion in lesser cases, and in offences by youngsters. They may content themselves with warning or cautioning the offender, even when they have evidence sufficient for a conviction. The same policy is followed by Government inspectors. It is not always wise, or even just, to let the heavy hand fall, and anyway the volume of offences is so large that charges have to be selective. To prosecute too often would cause the courts to fall even more into arrears than they are now, and would soon lead to a collapse of the edifice of justice. But the consequence of the present policy of selective crack-down is that many regulations, even safety regulations, are inadequately enforced. Moreover, it is not entirely to be commended that enforcement policies should differ markedly between one Chief Constable and another, as they sometimes do.[1]

[1] See D G T Williams in *Crime, Criminology and Public Policy*, ed. Hood (London 1974) 161.

When can a private prosecution be brought?

In general, anyone can prosecute: the greatest fetter is that legal aid is not available. Traders sometimes prosecute for theft, and members of pressure groups and vigilante groups occasionally prosecute for such offences as stage obscenity and cruelty to children. Private persons can prosecute even for murder and other serious offences against the person or property, and very occasionally do so when they can afford the expense. Exceptionally, the consent of some central officer like the DPP or Attorney-General is sometimes required.

Why?

The requirement is put in as a safeguard against over-enthusiastic prosecutions. The Government Department or other body that devised the legislation may have been afraid that it had cast too wide a net, and may have relied on the discretion of the specified officer to confine charges to clear and flagrant cases. Or the legislation may be controversial, so that the requirement of an officer's consent is a compromise between the opinions of those who would have an unfettered offence and those who would support only a greatly restricted offence or none at all. It is even possible that the legislation is passed merely to satisfy those who wish Parliament to state what they consider to be a moral principle, without wanting to see many prosecutions brought under it. In other words, the law's bark is to be worse than its bite. Such considerations explain why, for example, the consent of the DPP is required for a charge of abetting suicide.

But if the DPP can fix criteria to govern the giving of his consent, the same rules could have been incorporated in the offence.

It is hard to deny that leaving the decision wholly to the DPP is to delegate an essentially legislative decision to an executive officer.[2] The matter would stand differently if the DPP's consent were required merely to protect the individual against flimsy charges.

What if the defendant admits guilt; must there be a full trial?

On a plea of guilty there is no trial, only sentence (or other disposal).

Can a prosecutor drop the charge on condition of the defendant's paying a fine?

Generally not. Fines must be imposed by the court. But there are exceptional provisions whereby various officials may accept payment of a penalty in minor cases without court appearance.

The Inland Revenue operates a system of "civil penalties" for breaches of the tax code; these can be collected, by agreement, without legal proceedings. The obdurate non-payer must be proceeded against before the General Commissioners or the High Court, but the proceeding for a civil penalty is civil, not criminal.[3]

Customs and Excise officers[4] and local vehicle licensing officers can also allow an offender

---

[2] See D A Thomas in *Reshaping the Criminal Law*, ed. Glazebrook (London 1978) 30–31.
[3] Taxes Management Act 1970 s.100.
[4] Customs and Excise Management Act 1979 s.152. See *Patel v. Spencer* [1976] 1 WLR 1268.

to buy himself out of the court process.[5] There are "fixed penalty" offences relating to vehicles (including parking, speeding, various vehicle defect offences and failing to comply with traffic directions) which retain their criminal character even though they need not come before the court; the payment to a magistrates' court of the penalty stated on the ticket saves a court hearing.

A ticket-tearer can be prosecuted for the offence for which he was given the ticket. The owner of the vehicle is also made liable for the fixed penalty offence if the penalty is not paid, even though he was not driving at the time.[6] This may appear harsh, but it has been found to be necessary because the police can be led a merry dance in trying to find a driver who is not the owner.

The spot fine system is still fragmentary. For example, there are no spot fines for littering, fouling by dogs, free-loading on public transport, or breaches of social legislation generally (like offences under the Health and Safety at Work Act). However, a procedure in magistrates' courts allows a defendant to plead guilty by post, thus saving himself the trouble of appearance.[7]

These time-saving devices are likely to be extended in the future. A growing body of opinion would support the "decriminalisation" of minor offences, which would then become "contraventions" attracting a civil penalty. The penalty would be assessed in the first instance by the enforcing agency; in the event of a dispute it would be assessed by a court in civil proceedings.[8] Such a procedure would be an enormous relief for the courts and make for better enforcement.

Aren't spot fine provisions objectionable as reducing the awesome system of justice to a commercial transaction?

This criticism has, of course, been made. Lady Wootton said that such provisions are "frank and final confessions that we have abandoned all hopes of enforcing the law, and that it is open to anyone with sufficient means to buy a right to lawbreaking in the same way as he might purchase a pound of cheese."[9] The criticism overlooks the fact that even where spot fines are not operated, magistrates's courts operate a tariff of fines that in effect enables the rich to buy "impunity" cheaply. Moreover, it is because ticket penalties are almost commercial transactions, so that the conduct in question is in effect decriminalised, that some people (like the owners of vehicles) can be made to pay penalties for the misbehaviour of others. They are induced to help in bringing pressure to bear on the real offenders to behave, and the efficacy of the law is increased without a strong sense of injustice building up. Looked at in the aggregate, lawbreaking can be prevented far better by streamlining enforcement procedures for minor infractions than by trying to give such consideration to the individual case that the whole machinery fouls up.

§ 1.3. WIDE AND NARROW OFFENCES

I should like you to imagine for a moment that you are engaged on a legislative exercise.

---

[5] For a cogent criticism of the way in which these powers are sometimes exercised see 145 JPN 452.

[6] Road Traffic Act (hereafter referred to as RTA) 1974 ss.1–5; Transport Act 1982.

[7] Magistrates' Courts Act (hereafter MCA) 1980 s.12. The provision does not apply in respect of offences carrying a possible prison sentence of 3 months or more.

[8] See David Tench, *Towards a Middle System of Law* (Consumers' Assn 1981).

[9] Barbara Wootton, *In a World I Never Made* (London 1967) 235.

Suppose that you are parliamentary counsel compiling a criminal code for a newly-settled country (perhaps one day you will find yourself actually drawing one up for England and Wales, since we have none at present). You will obviously wish to include a provision punishing rape. Would you define the offence as one of rape, or would you leave rape as one example of the wider law of assault? Or would you have, perhaps, an even wider offence of "public mischief," covering not only assault but an indefinite number of other forms of misbehaviour? Either of the two latter solutions (assault or public mischief) would make a special law of rape unnecessary. What considerations would move you to define the offence one way or the other?

Calling it "public mischief" would be too wide. Rape is public mischief, but no one could tell what else a judge might regard as public mischief.

That is an important consideration. The law should tell us with reasonable clarity what it expects of us. Complete precision cannot be achieved, but very nebulous prescriptions should be avoided, because they give insufficient guidance to the citizen and correspondingly too wide a discretion to law-enforcement agencies. The practical way in which law is administered would depend too much on the decisions of the police and other prosecutors, taken in private and without effective control.

There used to be a common law (i.e. judge-made) offence of causing a public mischief, which allowed the courts to punish any conduct of which they disapproved. It was strongly criticised by commentators, and in practice prosecutors did not make much use of it; eventually the House of Lords overturned the previous learning on the subject and declared that the offence did not exist.[1] The notion of an offence of public mischief infringed the principle of legality—the proposition that there should be no criminal offence except one specified in pre-existing law (*nulla poena sine lege*, or *nullum crimen sine lege*).

Some statutory offences are open to the same objection of vagueness, though when they are only lightly punishable the objection has less force than for the common law offences just mentioned. An example is the offence of selling an article of food not of the nature, substance or quality demanded by the purchaser.[2] Under this provision the courts formerly had to decide in every particular case whether a thing sold as a sausage was in truth a "sausage" or virtually a packet of bread crumbs. Now, however, regulations require a pork sausage to contain at least 65 per cent meat, and a beef sausage at least 50 per cent.[3] Obviously a strong case can be made for settling such a point uniformly by legislation, after consultation with manufacturers and with consumers' organisations. To leave the question What is a sausage? to impressionistic decision by different magistrates when prosecutions are brought is inefficient, as well as unfair to manufacturers and traders who want to keep within the law if they can find out what the law is. Yet there are many articles of food (*e.g.* minced meat[4])

---

[1] *Withers* [1975] AC 842.

[2] Food and Drugs Act 1955 ss.2, 106, 108; Amendment Act 1982.

[3] Sausage and other Meat Products Regs., SI 1967 No. 862 as amended.

[4] See *Goldup* v. *John Manson Ltd* [1982] QB 161; Stephenson in 132 NLJ 553; R G Lawson in 146 JPN 200.

where magistrates still have to find whether they are of proper quality without receiving any help from the law.

So, coming back to the question, the law should be reasonably precise. Opinions may differ about what is reasonably precise, but we rule out having an offence of public mischief. Then what is the case for having an offence of rape? I think you will agree that your code must have an offence of assault (in the sense of a physical attack upon another person). So would you include an offence of rape as well?

Rape is much more serious than an ordinary assault, and needs a more severe punishment. So it must be a special offence.

Your reasoning expresses the present legal position. Rape can be treated as a kind of indecent assault, but the maximum for an indecent assault (sexual assault) on a woman is two years. Rape is therefore made an offence on its own, punishable with life imprisonment. (Of course, this does not mean that every rapist gets "life." The specification of a punishment in a statute is a maximum, so a rapist may be imprisoned for a fixed period of years or—theoretically—simply fined. In practice he is likely to get perhaps three or five years depending on the circumstances. The life sentence is reserved for a few people who are regarded as very dangerous—and does not usually last for life).

We have here an illustration of the fact that the same conduct sometimes amounts to two or more offences of different gravity. The graver offence (rape) carries a relatively high maximum punishment. If for some reason the defendant cannot be convicted of that, he may be convicted of the lesser offence (indecent assault) carrying a lower maximum, this lesser offence being defined more broadly than the graver offence.

Other examples of such two-tier offences are murder and manslaughter; wounding with intent and unlawful wounding; robbery and theft; reckless driving and careless driving. The more serious offence includes some circumstance of aggravation that is not necessary for the less serious offence: perhaps a special mental element; or a higher degree of damage, injury or alarm caused or likely to be caused by the offence.

It can be argued that the two-tier (or multiple-tier) arrangement is not strictly necessary. We could continue to use the name of the low-grade offence while attaching to it the maximum punishment of the more serious offence. So it would be theoretically possible to provide a maximum sentence of life imprisonment for any indecent assault, which would mean that the special offence of rape could be abolished; and this has been seriously suggested. The court would be left to work out the right punishment in each case, with the safeguard of an appeal.

This could be regarded as not involving a radical change, since the courts already operate a customary "tariff" of punishment which is generally well below the maximum allowed by Parliament for the offence. If the two-tier system were abolished the law would be simplified. Murder could be merged in manslaughter, reckless driving in careless driving, and so on. Some very serious cases of indecent assault, such as using threats to compel a woman to submit to "oral sex," could be punished as severely as rape.

We have already had some law reform along these lines. The Criminal Damage Act 1971 abolished many offences of damage carrying different maxima and substituted broadly defined offences with a scale of maximum punishments that do not (in general) depend on the gravity of the harm done (§ 41.1). The Theft Act 1968 abolished a number of special offences of theft carrying special penalties, leaving basically a single offence punishable with a maximum of 10 years' imprisonment. Theft covers everything from treating the boss's tools as a kind of "perk" to a highly organised raid upon a mail train; from the employee who cannot bring himself to disclose that there is too much in his pay packet to the bank clerk who embezzles tens of thousands of pounds to make good his betting losses. In practice thieves rarely get as much as 10 years, and the great majority are not imprisoned at all. When the courts are given a wide discretion in sentencing they can take account of many circumstances of aggravation and mitigation. It is generally best this way. Singling out some circumstances of aggravation and putting them into special offences not only complicates the law but often makes it look arbitrary. The worst instances of the lesser, general, offence are often more anti-social and reprehensible than the most excusable instances of the serious special offence. Moreover, complicated provisions increase the possibility of morally guilty people escaping on technicalities.

I am beginning to see the possibility of dispensing with the offence of rape. If we can cover criminal damage and theft by wide offences without subdivision, we might as well rest content with a wide offence of indecent assault.

I have given you only one side of the argument. There are two persuasive reasons for not relying too much on "broad band" offences.

1 The first reason is historical and psychological. Crimes like rape and murder are established in the public mind as special offences. There would be serious misunderstanding if a proposal were made to abolish them. The public would regard the effectiveness of the criminal law as being lessened, even though rape and murder might in fact continue to be punished in the same way under more general names. Words like "rape" and "murder" incorporate immemorial taboos, and if these words were not attached to the offence the force of the prohibition might be weakened.

2 Widening the scope of serious offences reduces the function of the jury in the trial and may deny them the opportunity to decide the most important issue. To continue the previous example, whether the defendant raped the complainant or did not go beyond indecently assaulting her will be of great importance for sentence under any system of rules. If the question does not enter into the definition of the crime the judge will have to decide it on his own. To some extent the judge is bound to decide questions of fact for the purpose of sentence; but very important questions, if they are capable of succinct and rational formulation in the definitions of offences, should be decided by the jury. What is the point of having a jury as the tribunal of fact if we do not allow it to adjudicate the most important questions?[5]

So, as always, there is a golden mean. The law is a pragmatical compromise between opposing considerations. Strong arguments can be found for not simplifying its structure too radically. The grading of offences

[5] For an important criticism of some modern legislation on the ground that it reduces the function of the jury too greatly see D A Thomas in *Reshaping the Criminal Law*, ed. Glazebrook (London 1978) 21.

both limits and assists the judge; it also settles the function of the jury, helps to control the forum, and assists plea-bargaining. These points may be expanded.

- *Limiting the judge.* Although the courts do not generally use to the full the Draconian powers that Parliament may give them, it is accepted that judges ought not to be set completely free from statutory fetters. Imprisonment for "life," *i.e.* for an indeterminate period, is acceptable as a possible sentence for multiple rapists, but it would not be acceptable as a possible sentence for indecent assault (which includes such comparatively minor—though strongly resented—interferences as touching the breasts of a woman in a crowd).

  The judge is limited not only by the legal maximum set by Parliament but by the generally lower scales known as the "tariff" devised by the appellate courts. The theory is that the maximum sentence was intended only for the worst offence of its kind, and the judge must award less than that for other cases.[6]
- *Assisting the judge.* In the ordinary trial in the Crown Court, the evidence is listened to by the jury, for the purpose of deciding whether to convict, and by the judge, for the purpose of deciding what the sentence is to be in the event of conviction. It is the judge who decides whether there are aggravating or mitigating circumstances affecting the question of punishment.[7] But where there are two or more charges, and the jury acquit on the graver charge while convicting on a lesser charge, the rule is that the judge in sentencing for the lesser offence must pay due respect to the acquittal; hence he must assume (whatever his own opinion may be, and however clear the evidence) that the circumstances of aggravation necessary for conviction of the graver charge were not proved.[8]

  Many cases do not reach the jury. The defendant pleads (*i.e.* pleads guilty), and there is no trial. In legal parlance he is convicted on his plea, not by verdict. ("Plea" for lawyers always means a plea of guilty; when we refer to a plea of not guilty the whole phrase is used.) The defendant may plead to a lesser charge, and if the plea is accepted by the prosecution the judge will (after considering matters relevant to sentence) proceed to sentence; but he must honour the implied bargain and not sentence on the basis of any circumstances of aggravation that would have to be established for the graver charge.[9] So far is the principle carried that that even when only one offence is charged, if an aggravated form of the offence could have been charged the judge must not sentence on the basis that the offender committed the aggravated form.[10]

  It will be seen that having different grades of offence assists the judge because it helps to reduce the scope of his problem in choosing the proper sentence. This is not a very strong point, because even if two offences are charged and the defendant is convicted only of the lesser offence, this may still leave the judge with a wide range of discretion. Also, there are extreme cases, where the offender is looked upon as dangerous, that force the court to disregard the fact that a more serious charge has failed.[11]
- *Giving power to the jury.* The jury cannot take any part in sentencing as such, and this

---

[6] *Mills* (1982) 146 JPN 266; Thomas, *Principles of Sentencing* 31. But Thomas's studies have demonstrated that many statutory maxima are purely arbitrary or traditional, and make a poor guide to sentence.

[7] The CA generally discourages trial judges from questioning the jury as to matters not necessarily covered by the verdict. One reason is that the jury may not have reached agreement on such other matters. See note to *Stosiek* [1982] Crim.LR 615.

[8] See the commentary to *Craig Davies* [1982] Crim.LR 243, deploring an isolated departure from the rule.

[9] An example is *Twomey* [1964] Crim.LR 419: the prosecution accepted a plea of not guilty to robbery with violence, guilty to simple robbery; held, that it was improper for the judge in sentencing to refer to the violence that had caused the victim's injuries, and the appellate court reduced the sentence accordingly. Cp. *Denniston* [1977] Crim.LR 46; *Fisher* [1982] Crim. LR 191 (attempt).

[10] *Foo* [1976] Crim.LR 456. The rule is clear where the two offences are part of the same hierarchy, the prosecution charging the lesser offence and not the aggravated form. Where this is not strictly true, the application of the rule is more complicated. See notes to *Ribas* [1976] Crim.LR 520 and *Rubinstein* [1982] Crim.LR 614.

[11] *McCauliffe* [1982] Crim.LR 316.

imposes a considerable strain upon their consciences. Are they to convict this nice-looking young fellow on a serious charge, if it means that that unbending character on the Bench will send him to prison for many years? Giving the jury the opportunity to convict of a lesser offence means that they can fetter the judge in his sentencing power. More important is the fact that by convicting of the lesser offence the jury send up a smoke signal that they want the offender to be treated fairly leniently. Indirectly, therefore, the jury are given some small measure of control over sentence, which may make the fact that they cannot directly control sentence more palatable to them. It is generally more in the public interest that the defendant should be convicted of the lesser offence than that he should, when guilty, escape with an outright acquittal.[12]

- *Controlling the forum.* Another result of the grading of offences is that it helps to govern the selection of the court of trial. Graver offences are triable in the Crown Court, perhaps only there; lesser offences are triable in magistrates' courts, perhaps only there.
- *Assisting plea-bargaining.* The defendant through his advocate may offer to plead guilty to the lesser charge if the prosecution will withdraw the graver charge. For example, magistrates sometimes commit on the serious charge of "wounding with intent" when the facts only doubtfully warrant it. In that case, defending counsel may ask his opponent informally whether he will accept a plea (that is, a plea of guilty) to the lesser charge of unlawful wounding.[13] If the two sides reach agreement, counsel for the Crown will explain the facts to the judge, and state why he would find difficulty in proving the more serious charge. The judge, if he approves the arrangement, will give leave to withdraw the count in respect of the graver charge, and will take the plea of guilty to the lesser. This saves the time of the court, the time of witnesses and the strain upon them of giving evidence, and avoids the possibility that the defendant may succeed in getting off altogether. The defendant benefits on sentence.

It may be a matter of considerable difficulty for defending counsel to decide whether to advise his client to offer a plea. If he thinks he has a sporting chance of getting him off altogether, as on a defence of accident or self-defence, he may fight the case. If the defendant has a bad record, or the facts are black against him, counsel may think it wiser to attempt the compromise, for this will protect his client from the possibility of a conviction by the jury of the more serious charge, which may in turn lead to a stern sentence by the judge; and, quite apart from this, it is the custom to allow a "discount" for the mere plea of guilty, which saves the time of the court.

There is a darker side to plea bargaining. It is generally the police who first make the charge, when the defendant is before the magistrates, and although the charge may be varied later they retain considerable control over it. The police often overcharge, perhaps because they are not sure of the facts and wish to preserve all their options. So they may charge attempted murder, or wounding with intent, when it later transpires that the case amounts only to unlawful wounding. The fact that a very serious charge is included in the indictment is a source of grave anxiety to the defendant, and a powerful inducement to him to try to settle the case by pleading to a lesser charge. If the lesser charge alone had been included, he might have been encouraged to adduce his evidence and perhaps win an acquittal. Sometimes the result is injustice.[14]

§ 1.4. THE JUDICIAL DEVELOPMENT OF THE LAW

The criminal law, like all our law, rests for the most part on statutes, but also, to a considerable extent, on decisions of the courts.

---

[12] For a criticism of some modern legislation on the ground that it unduly reduces the function of the jury see D A Thomas in *Reshaping the Criminal Law*, ed. Glazebrook (London 1978) 23–24.

[13] The defendant is allowed to plead guilty to an included offence: Criminal Law Act 1967 s.6(1)(*b*). For included offences see § 7.8.

[14] See John Baldwin and M McConville, *Negotiated Justice* (London 1977).

Hold a moment. When you speak of a decision, who decides the case, judge or jury?

At a trial in the Crown Court the judge instructs the jury on the law, and the jury then pronounce a verdict on the case as a whole. But when we speak of decided cases as one basis of the law we are generally referring to the decisions of the appellate courts, where there is no jury. (The direction to the jury given by a trial judge may be cited as an authority, but it is low in the hierarchy. What the jury decide, whichever way it is, is of no importance as a legal precedent.)

The non-lawyer who turns his attention to the law naturally begins by supposing that the law is a body of rules laid down in advance to govern people's conduct, and that these rules also govern the courts in deciding whether a breach has occurred. The reality is somewhat different. Many decisions as to what the law is are in reality only statements of what the law is going to be after the decision. "That's not a regular rule," said Alice to the Queen; "You've just made it up." Not only is there inevitable uncertainty in applying the abstract rules to concrete facts, but even when the law is clear and capable of precise application the judges are smitten from time to time with the desire to change it in the act of adjudicating it.

Most decisions are, of course, routine. The judge functions in the way that is expected of him, ascertaining what the law is and applying it. Nevertheless, the judge has a measure of freedom to make law under the guise of exposition. He will often not be completely bound by a precedent. He may be able to overrule it or refuse to follow it, according to the rank of the court that decided it; and even if he supposed to be bound by it, he may "distinguish" it by finding some real or quibbling point on which the precedent differs from the case before him. Lawmaking is, therefore, as we shall have much opportunity to observe in this book, part of the art and craft of deciding cases.

It is somewhat the same with statute interpretation. The courts cannot manufacture statutes as they manufacture precedents, but they can "interpret" them. They can cut them down, or expand them. Courts still pay lip-service to the ancient principle that in case of doubt a criminal statute is to be "strictly construed" in favour of the defendant; but the principle is rarely applied in practice, if there are social reasons for convicting. Indeed, we may make bold to say that the looser the defendant's conduct, the more loosely the judges construe the statute designed to control him. When the defendant has acted immorally, nothing short of the most powerful reasoning based on the wording of the statute is likely to dissuade the judges from holding that the statute applies to him.[1]

The law of prostitution supplies examples of both the legitimate and the illegitimate

---

[1] Consider the massive argument that had to be mounted in the House of Lords in *Bloxham* (§ 39.4) to persuade it to reverse the plainly erroneous decision of the CA, and the equally powerful argument that failed to persuade the House to uphold the plainly correct judgment of the CA in *Lambie* § 34.2 n. 9.

interpretation of criminal statutes to cover peripheral cases. It has been held that the word "prostitute" includes a "masseuse" who, for hire, gives men manual stimulation.[2] This is not the usual idea of prostitution, and the court certainly did not apply "strict construction" to the penal statutes in which the word occurred. The court proceeded entirely upon a purported interpretation of the word, and did not express any reasons of policy. However, such reasons could well be found. The ostensible "massage parlor" is open to some of the objections to a regular brothel, besides tempting some women into full prostitution. The police could not well control prostitution if they had to prove exactly what sexual practices went on in private. And although the decision stretches the meaning of the word "prostitution," it does not do so to breaking-point. For this reason I do not criticise the decision, but merely give it as an example of the court preferring the wider to the more usual narrower meaning of a word used in penal legislation when the meaning was in doubt.

The other decision passes from reasonable though wide interpretation to what is in reality covert legislation. It is not a representative specimen of the interpretation of statutes; on the other hand, it is not unique.

> A statute makes it an offence for a prostitute to solicit "in a street." The courts hold that if a prostitute solicits by gestures when standing at the window of a room fronting the street, her gestures being directed at men in the street, she solicits in a street.[3]

Most people would, I think, be surprised at this interpretation. It rests on the following reasoning (which the court did not spell out as clearly as I am about to do.)

1 The statute forbids a prostitute to solicit in a street.
2 "Soliciting" refers to soliciting a man.
3 Therefore the statute forbids a prostitute to solicit a man in a street.
4 Here the prostitute solicited a man in a street.
Therefore she solicited in a street.

The fallacy should be obvious. The last premise (4) has implied hyphens in it: the prostitute solicited a-man-in-a-street. It does not follow from this that her solicitation was in a street. (If a woman sang in her room for the benefit of someone in the street, we would hardly say that she sang in the street.)

There are, in fact, indications in the statute that Parliament did not intend the Act to apply as the court said. In particular, the statute expressly defines "street" to include doorways, which shows that it was not intended to include rooms fronting the street.

Although the Court of Appeal has said that its own precedent is not binding on it when the precedent is "against the liberty of the subject," this rule is hardly ever applied in practice. Almost all errors of understanding or reasoning on the part of the judges, however flagrant, are healed by the miraculous powers of the doctrine of precedent. So every judicial extension of the law forms a firm base from which further sallies may be mounted. When the courts had decided that a prostitute in a room can solicit in a street, they proceeded to hold that she "solicits" if she displays herself passively at her window (scantily clad, however, and bathed in red light).[4] It is true that the prostitute's object in exhibiting herself was to attract custom. But in its ordinary meaning the word "solicits" implies an act of soliciting, not a mere appearance in a place. A provocatively-dressed prostitute in a bar who hoped for custom but made no sexual approach to any man by word or gesture would not be said to solicit.

The decisions I have just mentioned are supported by general public opinion, and save us from sources of offence. The doubt is not whether the rules they establish are good in their effect but whether the last two decisions I have mentioned are justifiable exercises of the judicial function.

---

[2] *Webb* [1964] 1 QB 357, following earlier authority.

[3] *Smith* v. *Hughes* [1960] 1 WLR 830, 2 All ER 859; see *Crime, Proof and Punishment* (ed. Tapper) (London 1981) 71. A brief account of the doctrine of precedent, the sources of law in general and the structure of the courts will be found in my *Learning the Law*.

[4] *Behrendt* v. *Burridge* [1977] 1 WLR 29, [1976] 3 All ER 285.

So the judges concoct the law as they go along?

That is an exaggeration, even though it has a considerable measure of truth.

It is an exaggeration because judges tend to be conservative and traditional. They like to think of themselves as administering a system of law, not merely "cadi justice," justice under a palm-tree.

It is true because the common law is made, and statutes are interpreted, and therefore moulded, by the judiciary. Parliament is a legislature that intervenes only occasionally, and only in matters that it (or, more usually, some Minister) regards as of pressing importance. The day-to-day task of adjusting the law to present needs falls on the courts. In doing this they are strongly influenced by their own ideas of what conduct should be allowed. The tendency of the courts to create new criminal law is so pronounced that it is generally almost impossible to say with assurance what antisocial conduct (or conduct that the judges will regard as antisocial) is not criminal: only what is.

In some ways the continuous creation of law by the courts is a tremendous advantage for the legal system. It is particularly welcome when the judges create a new defence required by justice or social policy, as they very occasionally do (witness the celebrated direction to the jury by Macnaghten J in *Bourne* § 13.4.) But judges rarely invent restrictions on the criminal law. Their creative capacity goes in extending it. And the image of the judge as a clandestine lawgiver, achieving his result by the cunning manipulation of words, rules and precedents, consorts ill with the image of the judge as an impartial adjudicator between State and subject.

We must keep a sense of proportion. Most judicial hawkishness is directed against people who would be accounted pests in any society. It is far removed from the tyranny of totalitarian regimes. Nevertheless, it constitutes a departure from the ideal of law as a pre-established and knowable body of rules of behaviour. Villains, and others who threaten the social order, and some people who are merely nonconformist, sexually or otherwise, can rarely be sure that the law will not be "reinterpreted" against them.

I should have thought that the law would quite clearly provide for the conviction of villains, at least.

The only way of making sure that the courts can convict all evilly disposed persons would be to have offences without firm limits. But, as was said before, a vague penal law is an evil for citizens who want to know how they stand. It may catch people who were not meant to be caught. So the modern tendency is to have laws defined with relative precision. Nevertheless, the more precise the law, the easier it is for evil-doers to skate around it. Some people commit "the oldest sins the newest kinds of ways," and judges want to deal with them, which they can do by reinterpreting the law. So the administration of criminal justice is the result of opposite pressures: the pressure to make the penal law certain, and the pressure to make it adaptable.

The argument for the second view is encapsulated in Shakespeare's vivid metaphor.

> We must not make a scarecrow of the law,
> Setting it up to fear the birds of prey,
> And let it keep one shape, till custom make it
> Their perch and not their terror.

The argument for adaptability—that is, for judicial expansion of the law, where this is thought to be necessary—has been powerfully supported by judges in the past, and still has adherents; but to most commentators the contrary position now seems the more persuasive. The law ought not to be open-ended, and the judges should not break through its boundaries. The classical expression of this opinion was by Francis Bacon (Lord Chancellor Bacon).[5]

> "Judges ought to remember that their office is *Ius dicere*, and not *Ius dare*; to interpret law, and not to make or give law."

Notable support was given to the Baconian principle by Stephen J—the revered Sir James Fitzjames Stephen, greatest criminal lawyer of his age, author of *A History of the Criminal Law* and of the *Digest of the Criminal Law*; principal author of the Draft Code of 1879, by means of which Britain presented a criminal code to various other parts of the world while rejecting it herself.

> "A considerable part of the law of England consists of judicial decisions, and in the very nature of things this must be so. Every decision upon a debated point adds a little to the law by making that point certain for the future. Indeed, whichever way this case may be decided, it will settle the law upon the precise point involved, and it is this which gives to judicial decisions their great importance.
>
> It seems to me, however, that in exercising the narrowly qualified power of quasi legislation which the very nature of our position confers upon us, we ought to confine ourselves as far as possible (there may be cases in which such a course is not possible) to applying well-known principles and analogies to new combinations of facts, and to supplying to general definitions, and maxims, or to general statutory expressions, qualifications, which though not expressed, are, in our opinion, implied. . . . If we go further and extend the law upon considerations of general expediency, we are, I think, invading the province of the legislature."[6]

In this passage Stephen J did not draw certain distinctions that he might well have drawn.

The objections to judicial legislation are much less (and therefore are much more easily counterbalanced) in the civil law than in the criminal. The civil law does not generally lock people up or otherwise punish them. Even in the criminal law, there is no reason why the judges should not expand excuses for crimes, for reasons of justice, or alter technical rules of procedure and evidence established at common law, when they impede the quest for truth. These are not matters on which people try to understand the law for the purpose of conforming their conduct to it. The issue concerns the expansion of the range of the substantive law of crime—the extension of criminal prohibitions. Here the Baconian principle has much stronger claim to recognition.

I think that your argument against the judges expanding crimes is too much a counsel of perfection. When judges make the law more efficient they have general public support. No one wants to be governed by antiquated law. People generally don't know the law, but they do know when they are being knaves or brutes; so there is no harm in the judges manipulating the law to catch them. Brutes do not take legal advice in advance; knaves may, but the lawyer in advising will take the attitude of the judges into account when predicting their action.

There is much force in what you say. But prediction is not so easy as you

---

[5] *Essay of Judicature.*

[6] *Coney* (1882) 8 QBD at 550–551.

imply. Because judges vary in outlook, it is often hard to know in advance whether they will change the law or not. In the case of the prostitute at the window, if she had sought my advice beforehand I would have given my opinion that what she proposed to do did not fall within the statute, since all the legal arguments went that way, though I would have warned her of the possibility that the judges might take a different view. People do sometimes act upon an interpretation of what appears to be the present law, only to be confounded by a judicial decision that not only changes it but changes it retrospectively to their disadvantage.

Whatever the arguments, judicial legislation continues. Some common law crimes are so vaguely defined that it is easy to extend them when purporting to apply them. This is particularly true of public nuisance, a heterogeneous group of offences bearing a single name, which gives some signs of taking the place in the judicial armoury formerly occupied by public mischief.[7] The administration of justice, also, is protected by the amorphous crimes of interfering with justice, obstructing the police and contempt of court. Almost any misbehaviour in relation to legal trials, and many in relation to the prosecution of offences, can be punished under one or other of these open-ended headings, without its being always clear in advance what the judges will regard as misbehaviour.

> An example of how the law of contempt can involve controversial applications at the discretion of the judges is *Home Office* v. *Harman*,[8] where the House of Lords held (against the notable dissents of Lords Simon and Scarman) that it was a civil contempt of court for a solicitor to supply to a journalist copies of documents that had been disclosed in legal proceedings, even after they had been read out in open court during the trial.

Generally, the expansion of the law is unavowed, and takes place by small steps, the judges keeping up the pretence that they are mere mouthpieces of the law, *lex loquens*. A judgment will marshall the authorities in a manner suggesting, to the uninitiated, that the court is ineluctably bound to reach the conclusion it does reach, when to the discerning eye it is often no more than what is popularly called "special pleading"—that is, rationalisation accompanied by misdirection and legerdemain. The legal pros and cons are not fairly stated. (They cannot be, if the authorities are against the decision and if the court is not prepared to admit that it is changing the law.) The court selects the arguments and authorities leading to the conclusion it desires, and minimises or ignores the weight of authority or force of argument going the other way. Ordinary lawyerly reasoning, as generally employed in civil cases, may be rejected in favour of fallacious and shallow arguments. The unavowed premise is that those who break fresh ground in the annals of crime cannot rely upon any previously-established rule of law being maintained in their favour. If the law were so-and-so, the court says, it would be absurd, and would fail to give sufficient protection to the public interest; therefore (the conclusion immediately follows) the law is *not* so-and-so.[9]

It would be wrong to give the impression that courts always construe the law against the defendant. We enjoy a blessed degree of political liberty, and part of the credit for this is due

---

[7] See *Norbury* [1978] Crim.LR 435; *Soul* (1980) 70 CAR 295, criticised in [1980] Crim.LR 233, and by Spencer in [1982] Crim.LR 275.

[8] *Home Office* v. *Harman* [1982] 2 WLR 338, 1 All ER 532.

[9] An example is *Instan* [1893] 1 QB at 454, where Lord Coleridge said that the failure to punish a niece who was living with her aunt and who let her aunt die "would be a slur upon and a discredit to the administration of justice in this country;" *therefore* the failure must be manslaughter.

to the judges. From time to time some doubtful matters are resolved in favour of the defendant, even though he is a scamp. In matters of procedure and evidence the courts generally apply technical rules of the common law with great rigidity in favour of defendants, guilty or innocent, although these rules are of far more assistance to the guilty than to the innocent.

Of course, judges differ in temperament. A few will, when stirred to action, play fast and loose with the authorities. Most, however, will genuinely try to follow the authorities except in an extremely provoking case. So whether the defendant is acquitted or convicted may depend on whether he is tried before a judge of orthodox or adventurous views.

These facts are well known to lawyers, though they do not often find expression in forensic discussion. A rare example of judicial frankness is an utterance of Bridge LJ (now Lord Bridge) speaking for the Court of Appeal.

> "It is right, we think, to shun the temptation, which sometimes presses on the mind of the judiciary, to suppose that because a particular course of conduct, as was this course of conduct, was anti-social and undesirable, it can necessarily be fitted into some convenient criminal pigeon-hole."[10]

Accordingly, the court quashed the conviction. But mark the sequel. On further appeal the House of Lords succumbed to temptation and restored the conviction.[11]

You wouldn't argue, would you, that in case of doubt the law should always be construed in favour of the rogue?

Notwithstanding all the arguments against judicial legislation, it must be tolerated to some extent. The social interest in having an effective criminal law is great enough to justify some extensive interpretations of it. If the argument for conviction is supported by legal reasoning and authority (even though not so weighty a body of authority as the argument against), and if, in addition, it accords with clear social policy, and is not contrary to authority binding on the court, the court may properly decide in favour of conviction.

I would add this qualification: when the decision rests largely on considerations of policy, and particularly when a precedent in the defendant's favour is overruled, or distinguished virtually out of existence, the judges should, in honesty, admit that they are newly extending the law. The consequence that would inevitably follow from such candour would be that they would not be able, as now, to impose punishment on the person who occasions the extension of the law, and on others who offended before the new departure took place. They would have to give such persons at least an absolute or conditional discharge; and preferably they should acquit. Where the extension relates solely to the grade of the offence, or where the defendant intended to break the law, different considerations may apply.

As has already been intimated, the major cause of the trouble is that we have suffered centuries of neglect of the criminal law by the legislature. Parliament has been industrious in multiplying offences, very inartistically drawn, but it is slow to remedy clear absurdities and deficiencies in the law as they come to light, and it has not bothered itself much in providing necessary defences. Under present arrangements both Government and Parliament are inadequate to meet all the demands made upon them.

Many Commonwealth countries have a code superseding the ramshackle creations of history; but proposals to this end have always been resisted in England. Two great efforts to produce a criminal code were made in the 19th century, one from 1833 onwards on the initiative of Lord

---

[10] *Charles* [1976] 1 WLR at 256C, 1 All ER at 666A.

[11] See § 34.2 n.8.

Brougham and another from 1878 by Stephen;[12] the reason for their failure was largely the opposition of the judges themselves, who wished to retain their discretionary powers.

But isn't a statute a kind of code? You say that most of the criminal law is in statutes.

A statute generally does not embody the common law, where much of the uncertainty in the criminal law occurs. Statutes, which are generally drafted by Government officials, often neglect juristic principles and often fail to define fundamental concepts. A well-drafted code should be the product of open government using the best brains of the legal profession. Not the least of its advantages for everybody except the lawyers would be that, by settling foreseeable difficulties in the law, it would save the taxpayer large sums spent on legal aid in appealing technical points. Moreover, a code would enable the whole body of law to be regularly checked by a supervisory commission.

New machinery for reform was introduced with the setting up of the Criminal Law Revision Committee ("CLRC") in 1959 and the Law Commission in 1965. While the former confines itself to proposing changes in rules that have been found to be unsatisfactory, and steadfastly refuses to codify even the branches of law on which it is working, the latter is now making a fresh effort to draft a code;[13] but the prospects are doubtful. The Commission has drafted parts of the proposed code; they are valuable in themselves and are suitable for adoption by Parliament (even though in some respects they could be improved upon); but they have met not with reasoned consideration and consensual amendment but with ministerial and bureaucratic indifference, passive resistance, and outright opposition.[14] The same fate has befallen important legislative proposals of other Government committees, like those of the Butler Committee pertaining to criminal responsibility. The community at large is uninterested, and even within the legal profession as a whole there is no burning passion for rationalising the criminal law.

§ 1.5. THE CLASSIFICATION OF OFFENCES

The word "offence" is another name for a crime. Crimes in the broad sense include not only the major crimes (indictable offences) but summary offences. The latter regulate many trades and special activities (the so-called "regulatory offences"), as well as the conduct of ordinary people in their daily life.

---

[12] Also, an excellent code was produced by R S Wright in 1874; this failed because of Stephen's ungenerous opposition. See Friedland in 1 Oxford Jrnl of Leg.Stud.307.

[13] For a survey of progress consult the latest annual report of the Law Commission.

[14] See Sir Michael Kerr in 96 LQR 515.

In practice, a summary offence would not usually be referred to as a crime, which is felt to be too strong a description of it. Indeed, we have become a bit squeamish about the word "crime" altogether. Just as we are now chary of blaming people or of saying that they have done wrong (which may have been one of the reasons for the increase of criminality), so we do not seem to like saying that they have committed crimes. Even vile crimes like murder and rape are now termed "offences" in the statute-book. But it is not technically incorrect to call them crimes as well. Certainly we have no substitute for the expression "criminal law" (except "penal law," which is not much used); and the word "offence" happens not to yield a suitable adjective. In this book "crime" will continue to bear a generic meaning.

Summary offences are legion. If you are not an air pilot you may fondly believe that the Air Navigation Order is no concern of yours; but you may be summoned under it if you take a child to fly a kite within five kilometres of an airfield (or, of course, fly it yourself).[1] It is a summary offence to export antiques without a licence;[2] to sit idly listening to fire brigade messages on the radio (or even listening to pirate radio stations);[3] to charge for supplying addresses of houses to let;[4] to collect from house to house for charity without a licence;[5] to allow a dog to be on a highway without a collar inscribed with the owner's name and address (even if it is on a lead[6]); to allow a dog to be on a "designated road" without being on a lead;[7] and for a driver to fail to sign his driving licence.[8] The phlegmatic Englishman is embodied in the rule that when traffic-snarled (or otherwise stationary) he may not relieve his frustration by hooting;[9] the taciturn Englishman receives due acknowledgment in the rule that one must not converse with a bus driver.[10] Do you ever park in a street when you shouldn't? If you do, you commit an offence; but don't think you can mitigate the offence by drawing up partly on the pavement. That will land you in liability for a second offence.[11]

Employers are a special target of the law, and they are expected to be specially active with words and figures. An employer commits a summary offence if he fails to make a record of an accident,[12] and it is not only a summary but an indictable offence for him to fail to write a statement of his policy for safety at work, for his employees to read (unless he is exempted).[13]

We must not make fun of the law. One or two of these offences may look like over-ebullience on the part of Parliament and the Government, but most have good reasons, or some sort of reason, when you come to think about them. Most summary offences are the result of prosaic efforts to improve safety standards, or to prevent petty fraud or oppression.

Many occupations are regulated by statute, and it is generally made an offence to carry them on unless one is licensed, registered or otherwise qualified. Which occupations are thus favoured (or aimed at) often depends upon the accidents of political pressure. We went until 1975 (long after the age of horse traffic was over) before it was thought necessary to enact that only qualified blacksmiths can shoe horses;[14] but there is no law

---

[1] Air Navigation Order 1976 art. 64.

[2] Export of Goods (Control) Order 1972 No. 1536.

[3] Wireless Telegraphy Act 1949; see *Paul* v. *Ministry of Posts* [1973] RTR 245, Crim.LR 322.

[4] Accommodation Agencies Act 1953 s.1(1)(*b*).

[5] House to House Collections Act 1939; see *Hankinson* v. *Downland* [1974] 1 WLR 1327, 3 All ER 655.

[6] 143 JPN 321.

[7] Road Traffic Act 1972 s.31.

[8] Motor Vehicles (Driving Licences) Regulations 1976 reg. 11.

[9] Motor Vehicles (Construction and Use) Regulations, SI 1978 No. 1017 reg. 118.

[10] Passenger Service Vehicles (Conduct of Drivers, Conductors and Passengers) Regulations, SR & O No. 619 reg.9 (vi).

[11] RTA 1972 ss.36(1), 36A; RTA 1974 s.7(1). There are exceptions for heavy vehicles in certain situations of necessity, including loading and unloading *where the vehicle is attended throughout*. See 145 JPN 697.

[12] Social Security Act 1975 s.88.

[13] See *Osborne* v. *Bill Taylor of Huyton Ltd* [1982] Crim.LR 305.

[14] Farriers (Registration) Act 1975 s.16, as amended in 1977.

to stop anyone claiming to be a chiropodist and treating the feet of human beings.

Most licensing provisions are a response to proved needs, particularly on grounds of public health and safety and the prevention of fraud. They can be of value in ensuring that standards are laid down and generally maintained, particularly where work is supervised by inspectors reporting to a supervising body. The licensing authority is frequently empowered to impose conditions and to withdraw the licence for misbehaviour; or a court on convicting of an offence may be authorised to order the revocation or suspension of a licence or registration—the best-known example being disqualification from driving.[15] (Even when an activity does not need a licence, the court on convicting of certain offences is sometimes empowered to make a disqualification order in respect of it. For example, the convicted persons may be disqualified from managing companies for up to 15 years.)[16]

What I have been saying about summary offences represents the lower reaches of the criminal law. You may at this point suppose that as this book proceeds it will give you further information on what people may and may not lawfully do. In fact, like every other discursive work on the criminal law, it will say little on this score that you do not know already. "Be honest and refrain from violence": these two commandments are almost the sum of it. Detailed and systematic information about the mass of regulatory offences is outside my purview. But dishonesty and violence and the legal structure erected to deal with them are sufficiently large topics for one book: too large to be dealt with except selectively. In addition, we shall be concerned with the general principles governing liability for crimes whether serious or trivial.

What exactly is a summary offence?

An offence triable only[17] in magistrates' courts, which sit without a jury. In the clipped language of lawyers, a person charged with a summary offence has no "right of trial," i.e. by a jury. His trial, if he contests the case, is by magistrates.

In contrast to summary offences, indictable offences committed by adult offenders are in principle triable in the Crown Court by jury. (The explanation of "in principle" will be given presently.) Cases tried in the Crown Court are said to be tried on indictment, the indictment being the formal document of accusation on which a trial by jury is based. The important characteristics of a trial on indictment are that it is always by jury and always in the Crown Court.

The term "summary offence" is now established, and is used in legislation; but it is somewhat inappropriate, since what is summary is not the offence itself but the mode of procedure. Even as applied to the procedure, "summary" is an infelicitous adjective, because

---

[15] On licensing generally see Harry Street, *Justice in the Welfare State,* 2nd ed.; 20 Current Leg. Prob. 81. See also § 1.8 n. 14.

[16] Companies Act 1948 s.188 as amended by CA 1981 ss.93–94.

[17] Interpretation Act 1978 s.5 and Sch. 1 as amended. For the single exception see § 14.3 at n. 4.

the procedure of magistrates' courts is supposed to be as careful and formal as trial by jury. The chief differences between so-called summary trial and trial on indictment are that the latter is preceded by "committal proceedings" (the magistrates committing the defendant for trial in the Crown Court), and, of course, that there is no jury on summary trial.

Indictable offences used to be divided into *felonies* (the graver class) and *misdemeanours* (graver than summary offences but not so grave as felonies). The distinction, at first of great importance, became eroded by various reforms, and the law was updated in 1967 by the simple expedient of applying the law for misdemeanours to felonies as well.[18] In consequence, we need no longer use either word. Not "felonies," because they no longer have distinctive features, and not "misdemeanours," because the whole point of that expression was to make a distinction from felonies. Besides, to designate murder as a misdemeanour would make it sound like a peccadillo.

How does one know whether an offence is indictable or summary?

Summary offences are entirely the creatures of statutes. If Parliament has intended to make an offence punishable summarily, it should have made this meaning clear in the statute. If Parliament prohibits an act without saying how a violation is to be tried, it becomes an indictable offence.[19]

Some indictable offences exist at common law. But the great majority now rest on statute, even though some were originally judge-made.

So the beaks try summary offences, while the Crown Court tries indictable offences?

Yes as regards the first part of your proposition, but the second part is over-simplified. Magistrates' courts can try some indictable offences, in addition to summary offences.

To explain: practically every criminal case starts in a magistrates' court. The first step when proceedings are contemplated is to bring the suspect before the magistrates, either by arresting him or by serving him with a summons to attend.

- If the charge is of a summary offence the magistrates will normally try it themselves ("summary trial").
- If the charge is of an indictable offence the magistrates may nevertheless have power to try it summarily. An indictable offence that can be tried summarily is said to be "triable either way." For such an offence, the magistrates first decide whether the case is suitable for summary trial. If it is not, they proceed to act as "examining magistrates" conducting "committal proceedings." Their duty is to consider whether a *prima facie* case has been established. If they find in the affirmative (as they almost always do), they send ("commit") the defendant for trial before a jury ("trial on indictment").[20] There is a modern form of committal on

---

[18] Criminal Law Act 1967 s.1.

[19] Cp. 142 JPN 689. But where a statute imposes a "penalty" for an offence, the court may find an implication that the penalty is to be recoverable only in a magistrates' court: see *Johnson* v. *Colam* (1875) LR 10 QB 544.

[20] Cp. 142 JPN 689. The proceedings were formerly called also the "preliminary examination" (or "enquiry"). "Commitment" or "committal" in its original meaning refers to imprisonment by order of court; the word is generally confined to (1) imprisonment pending trial (as here), and (2) imprisonment for contempt of court. By an extension, we now speak of commitment on bail (which means freedom) as an alternative to commitment in custody.

written statements, in which the magistrates need not consider the evidence if the defendant does not ask them to.[21] Committal proceedings can be held by one magistrate.

If the magistrates decide that they can suitably deal with the case themselves, they can do so, subject to a qualification (as to the defendant's consent) to be mentioned presently.

You say that some but only some indictable offences are triable either way. Which are they?

I will tell you how to find out. "Either way" offences are (*a*) those expressly stated to be triable either way in the legislation creating them, plus (*b*) the offences listed in the Magistrates' Courts Act 1980 Schedule 1. There would be little point in reproducing the list here. All other offences are either only summary or triable only on indictment. Let us call the latter "purely indictable" offences; they include all offences punishable with life imprisonment.

Who decides how an offence triable either way is in fact tried? Is it the prosecutor?

Neither the police nor private prosecutors can insist upon one form of trial rather than the other. The case will be tried on indictment if:

1 the magistrates consider the case more suitable for this form of trial, or
2 (although the magistrates consider it more suitable for summary trial) the defendant elects to "go for trial."

Otherwise the case will be tried summarily.

It will be seen that ordinary charges of "either way"[22] offences (those brought by the police or private prosecutors) are tried on indictment unless *both* the magistrates *and* the defendant are agreeable to summary trial.[23] This means that the defendant has an overriding right to be tried by jury. There is an elaborate—indeed, over-elaborate—procedure for informing him of his rights in this matter. Magistrates for their part will generally be prepared to try the case if the defendant will let them and if it is not too serious.

Don't the magistrates listen to what the police have to say on this point?

The police may be happy to have the case tried summarily; it will save them time. It they want the defendant to be sent down for a good stretch they may try to persuade the magistrates that the offence is too grave for summary trial. (The police are dissatisfied by the excessive leniency of magistrates in some cases, particularly those involving violence against themselves.) But the only way in which the police can be sure of getting the case to the Crown Court is by charging a purely indictable offence. This is

---

[21] Magistrates' Courts Act 1980 s.6(2).

[22] To avoid this uncouth phrase I used the name "dual offence" in the first edition of this book. Alas, no one took it up, so I now return to the accepted name, under protest.

[23] For more details see MCA 1980 ss.17–28; 142 JPN 381, 384.

when the police are prosecuting on their own: the defendant's right to go for trial of an either way offence is excluded if the prosecution is brought by a Law Officer of the Crown (the Attorney-General or Solicitor-General) or (as much more commonly happens) the DPP.

The effect, then, is that on any serious 'either way' charge a defendant who wants trial by jury will normally get it?

Yes, and also on some charges that are not so serious. Possession of a single cannabis reefer or the unauthorised possession of a few amphetamine tablets, although not for the purpose of supply, is an either way offence. So is theft. The defendant can insist on trial in the Crown Court even though it is only a charge of theft of cigarettes worth £1 and the case is going to saddle the public with a bill of £4000 in costs. If he is eventually convicted he may be ordered to pay the costs, but of course he may not have the means to do so.

Couldn't the law be rationalised?

The law, like life in general, is a compromise. A section of opinion would strongly disapprove if people were deprived of their right of trial for theft, conviction of which is regarded as stigmatic. On the other hand, a number of very stigmatic offences are triable only summarily.

Generally the defendant will accept summary trial if offered, because he thinks the case will be heard more quickly by magistrates (though this is not always so). Also, magistrates' courts are less terrifying. On summary conviction the maximum punishment is generally 6 months' imprisonment and a fine of £1000,[24] and even within that limit offenders are likely to be treated more leniently by the magistrates than if they elected for trial in the Crown Court. (Judges and recorders regularly impose punishment on a scale that most magistrates would regard as monstrous.[25] And conversely, changing the adjective to "derisory.").

Occasionally the defendant will opt for the panoply (and expense) of the Crown Court because he wishes to air his defence before a jury (and more would do so if they were better advised). He has a better chance of being given legal aid for the Crown Court than for the magistrates' court; he has the advantage of seeing the full Crown case in advance;[26] and juries are apparently readier to acquit than magistrates.[27] Also, opting for jury trial will probably put off the evil hour when he is convicted. (He will probably get bail and be free for perhaps a year, by which time, he may hope, the witnesses for the prosecution will have forgotten their evidence![28]) If he is convicted by the Crown Court he can appeal against sentence with legal aid, whereas if he is convicted by magistrates he cannot appeal against sentence except by appealing the whole case to the Crown Court; the magistrates are quite likely to refuse him

---

[24] MCA 1980 s.32. But the court can in certain circumstances convict the defendant and commit him to the Crown Court for a sentence exceeding the powers of the magistrates (MCA s.38; 145 JPN 480).This power is given even for some summary offences: they do not thereby become offences triable either way. See, e.g., Bail Act 1976 s.6.

[25] See, e.g., 144 JPN 675. On the other hand, many magistrates are unduly lenient about serious offences like mugging and commercialised poaching; and the prosecution, unfortunately, cannot have such leniency corrected by appealing. See Thomas in 146 JPN 284.

[26] The CJA 1967 s.48 gives the defendant the right to know the prosecution evidence in advance of summary trial, but, scandalously, the Home Office has failed to bring the section into force.

[27] See 146 JPN 360. While the fact is undoubted, its interpretation is problematic. Perhaps juries acquit more often because innocent defendants, and those against whom the evidence is thin, are more ready to opt for jury trial.

[28] For fuller discussions of the pros and cons of "going for trial" and the anomalies of the present law see 144 JPN 675; 145 JPN 245, 402, 667, 736; 132 NLJ 73, 125, 579, 732.

legal aid for the appeal and bail pending the appeal, and the Crown Court may increase the sentence instead of reducing it. All these considerations may cause an inconvenient number of defendants to claim jury trial.

It sounds like the end of a game of chess in which only one player has any freedom of manoeuvre.

The game is not entirely one-sided. The police can sometimes forestall a claim to jury trial by charging what is theoretically a less serious offence. The same act may be both an indictable offence and a summary offence; and then there is nothing wrong in the prosecution choosing to pitch the charge at the lower level if the case is not grave.[29]

The selection of charges is an art that the police have to learn. For example, if there has been a fracas they may, according to circumstances, charge anything from an affray (which is purely indictable) to a summary offence of threatening behaviour under the Public Order Act (§ 9.9 at n. 19). An assault may be charged as a summary offence (if the charge is brought by the victim or if it is an assault on a police officer) or as an indictable offence triable either way. A football hooligan who needs a "short sharp shock"[30] would probably be charged with threatening behaviour instead of assault, to deprive him of jury trial; but if he had the forethought to brandish a half-brick and is charged in addition with possessing an offensive weapon, that charge will give him a right of trial. For this reason, the police will quite possibly decide not to add the offensive weapon charge. (And the defendant will not gain by informing the Bench that he was in fact carrying a half-brick; he has no right to be charged with that if the police do not want to.) Other summary offences which the police find useful as excluding trial on indictment are wilfully obstructing the police and wilfully obstructing the highway.

Similarly, a driver may be charged with excess alcohol, drunken driving, no insurance, careless driving, and failing to stop after the inevitable accident; all these offences are purely summary, and can generally be quickly despatched. Yet if the police decide to add a charge of driving while disqualified, the defendant can elect to go for trial on that charge. If he does, the magistrates will usually feel obliged to adjourn the summary charges pending the Crown Court trial; and if the defendant, after long delay, manages to secure an acquittal by reason of the staleness of the evidence the magistrates may feel it unjust to restore the other charges in view of the lapse of time.[31]

A number of offences may be charged either on indictment (under statute or common law) or as summary offences under bylaws. Many bylaws create summary offences duplicating offences triable either way. At first sight they may seem pointless, but for the police they have the virtue of enabling the offence to be charged in a way that involves no right of trial. Of course, the drawback is that the bylaw offence is only mildly punishable.

At the other end of the scale, if the police wish to prevent magistrates trying the case they can sometimes charge a purely indictable offence. The unreformed common law offences, such as public nuisance, unlawful assembly, riot and affray, can be useful in this way, since they are triable only on indictment and are punishable with fine and imprisonment at discretion (*i.e.* as the court thinks fit). However, some offences that originally existed at common law have been turned into statutory offences and have lost the characteristics just mentioned.

The above provisions relate to the trial of adult offenders (17 or over).

---

[29] *R* v. *Canterbury JJ, ex p. Klisiak* [1981] 3 WLR at 73, 1 All ER 950, 72 CAR 250. This was an application by a private person in the name of the Crown for judicial review of an order of justices in a criminal case; such an application is civil, not criminal, and for this reason I preserve the "*R v*" of the title.

[30] The origin of this phrase, which has passed into current use in penal matters, is now generally forgotten. It comes from *The Mikado*.

[31] See Eric Crowther's article in 145 JPN 245, which is well worth reading.

There are wider provisions for the trial of juveniles in the juvenile court (a special version of the magistrates' court); these are briefly set out in Chapter 28.

Apart from the question of jurisdiction, are there any differences in law between indictable and summary offences?

A few, but only one is important for substantive law. An attempt to commit an indictable offence is itself an indictable offence, but an attempt to commit a summary offence is not punishable in the absence of express statute. This difference is not accidental: summary offences are not sufficiently grave to make prosecutions for a mere attempt worth while.

Two procedural differences may be mentioned. First, indictable offences can generally be prosecuted after any length of time, but summary offences cannot generally be charged after the lapse of six months.[32] A person who is acquitted of a summary offence cannot be awarded costs out of central funds. For the purpose of these rules, as already indicated, an offence triable either way remains "indictable" even though it is tried summarily.[33]

§ 1.6. CRIMINAL AND CIVIL LAW

The layman tends to think of the law primarily as the criminal law; but most of it is civil, not criminal.

In principle there are two sets of courts: criminal and civil (though the same court often has both kinds of jurisdiction). Similarly there are two kinds of legal procedure: civil and criminal. The criminal law is administered by criminal courts following criminal procedure, and similarly with civil law.

An act can be either a civil wrong (wrongful by the civil law) or a crime; or it can be both.

The part of the civil law bearing the strongest resemblance to the criminal law is the law of tort. Its effect is primarily to give an action for damages (compensation).

Why are there two sorts of law?

The criminal law is concerned primarily with the question whether wrongdoers are to be punished (or compulsorily treated). The civil law is concerned with private rights: for example, enabling the owner of an article to get it back from someone who has gone off with it, or alternatively to get damages for its detention.

Is libel a crime or a tort?

Theoretically it is both; but it is now rarely prosecuted.[1]

---

[32] MCA 1980 s.127.
[33] CLA 1977 s.64(1).

[1] See J R Spencer in [1977] Crim.LR 383, 465; Law Commission, Working Paper No. 84, *Criminal Libel*.

But surely people who libel others do find themselves in the dock from time to time?

Not commonly in the dock, which is a feature peculiar to the criminal courts. A libeller can be sued for damages in tort, and the damages are likely to be heavy. He may find himself in the witness box, giving evidence as defendant in a civil action, but he is most unlikely to be in the dock.

What if the libeller can't pay the damages; does he go to prison?

No. To the bankruptcy court. This is a big difference between civil damages and the criminal fine: a fine defaulter can in certain circumstances be sent to prison.[2]

Can a criminal always be prosecuted for damages?

Hold on: your terminology is mixed. Actions (not prosecutions) for damages are a matter of civil law. One *sues* (brings an action for) the civil wrong, *prosecutes* for the crime.

No, every crime is not a civil wrong. Numerous offences under statutory regulations are not the subject of an action for damages.

If I am injured in an accident with a drunken driver, can I sue him for damages for the offence of drunken driving?

Not for the offence as such; you sue for damages for negligence, which is the tort.

But his drinking was wilful. It is not a case of negligence.

He drank intentionally (wilfully), but he did not injure you intentionally. Anyway, negligence covers cases of intention. In law we always speak of the *minimum* degree of fault necessary for liability, so a man who injures another intentionally is *a fortiori*[3] accounted negligent.

Can anyone be prosecuted for breaking a contract?

A few dangerous breaches of contract are criminally punishable,[4] and a few types of debt-frauds are crimes (Chap. 40), but on the whole the law in this area is weak and under-enforced. For the most part a breach of contract is not a crime. Incurring a contractual debt by deception is often criminal, but getting a contractual benefit and then dishonestly avoiding paying for it is generally not. The remedy of the aggrieved party is to bring a civil action for debt, damages, specific performance or injunction. (A contracting party who fails to comply with the court's order of specific performance or injunction may be sent to prison for contempt of court, but the commitment is regarded as "civil" rather than "criminal".)

---

[2] MCA 1980 s.76; PCCA 1973 s.3 as amended by CJA 1982 s.69. Cross and Ashworth, *The English Sentencing System*, 2nd ed. 28. The enforcement provisions in respect of fines apply also in respect of compensation orders (§ .8 n. 10) and costs.

[3] With stronger reason (generally anglicised in pronunciation as "ay forsheeohry").

[4] See Treitel in *Crime, Proof and Punishment*, ed.Tapper (London 1981) 83. The criminal law also imposes various obligations on certain parties to contracts or proposed contracts: *ibid.* 85–86.

But dishonesty in not paying contractual debts is rife. Many people nowadays delay payment of debts in order to profit by interest on the money retained, while others do their best to avoid paying at all. Why doesn't the criminal law reach such people?

The chief reason is the fear that the law might be used to re-introduce what would be in effect imprisonment for debt, as we had in Dickensian times.

When an act is both criminally and civilly wrong, is the wrongdoer punished twice?

The damages in the civil action are regarded as compensation for the victim, not as punishment for the wrongdoer.

If the same act can be both a crime and a tort, what is the difference between a crime and a tort?

To say that an act is a tort or other civil wrong means that it can be followed by a civil action for damages, or other civil redress. To say that it is a crime means that it can be followed by a criminal prosecution.

Not only the procedure and evidence but the outcomes differ.

The usual outcome of *civil* proceedings is:

a judgment for debt or
damages or
compensation or
restitution, or

an order for specific performance of a contract, or

an injunction to prevent the commission of a wrong, or its continuation, or

a declaration as to rights.

There are also civil remedies in relation to the dissolution of marriage, care proceedings in respect of juveniles, other proceedings for transferring parental rights, and the application for judicial review.[5] The latter asks the High Court to grant relief against improper conduct by public authorities and inferior tribunals; the relief may take the form of a declaration, injunction, damages, or one of the prerogative orders (mandamus, prohibition, certiorari), or the prerogative writ of habeas corpus. All these are distinctively civil orders.

§ 1.7. THE DEFINITION OF CRIME

We are now in a position to define a crime. A crime (or offence) is a legal wrong that can be followed by criminal proceedings which may result in punishment.

[5] Rules of the Supreme Court Or. 53.

Haven't you produced a circular definition? We don't know whether an act is a crime unless it can be followed by criminal proceedings; and we don't know whether the appropriate proceedings are criminal unless we know that the act is a crime!

The question is a thoughtful one and deserves an answer. The answer is no. My definition is not circular, even though it may appear to be so. Criminal proceedings, that is to say a prosecution, can be described in great detail without ever using the word "crime," or at any rate without requiring the word "crime" to be defined for the purpose of understanding what is said.

Let me essay an outline of criminal proceedings. A person who is suspected of one of certain types of legal wrong (that is to say a crime, but, knowing that you are ready to pounce, I am avoiding the word) may be brought before the magistrates in custody, as a result of having been arrested without warrant or arrested on warrant. Alternatively he may come to court as a result of an information leading to a summons directing him to appear.[1] Subsequent proceedings will depend upon whether the matter charged against him is indictable or summary. You will observe that so far I have not been obliged to use the word "crime" or "criminal." And so I could go on with a complete description of criminal procedure and evidence, which differ in many ways (though not in all) from civil procedure and evidence. The fact that the wrong can be followed by this type of proceeding shows that it is a crime.[2]

To give a few examples of the procedural differences between crimes and civil wrongs:

- A civil proceeding in the High Court is generally commenced by writ, whereas the document commencing a criminal trial in the Crown Court is an indictment. At magistrates' court level, a document commencing a civil proceeding is called a complaint, whereas a document commencing a prosecution is, as we have seen, called an information.[3]
- Civil proceedings are, in general, brought by the person directly affected. Prosecutions can, in general, be brought by anyone, whether he is affected by the offence or not, subject to the restrictions that have already been noticed (§ .2).
- The plaintiff in a civil action can abort the proceedings at any time, whereas they cannot be stopped by a Government officer. In contrast, no prosecutor except the Attorney-General and DPP can be sure of being able to stifle a prosecution once started. If the prosecutor changes his mind about the case he may withdraw with the leave of the court; but if he does so without that leave a police officer or anyone else may continue the proceedings on behalf of the public. The DPP may take over the proceedings even without the prosecutor's consent, either in order to conduct the case more efficiently or even to discontinue it[4]—though he will intervene only in the most exceptional circumstances, as where the trial is improper for technical reasons, or the Government desires to protect a

---

[1] Even when a person has been arrested the police have certain powers to release hion bail, or he may be given bail by the magistrates or by a High Court judge.

[2] See further 8 Current Legal Problems 107, commented upon by Graham Hughes in [1959] Crim.LR 239 and P J Fitzgerald in [1960] Crim.LR 256.

[3] For an example of a complaint on a public matter see *Worcestershire CC* v. *Newman* [1975] 1 WLR 901, 2 All ER 673. Confusingly, some statutes use the word "complaint" although the proceeding is intended to be criminal. See *R* v. *Newham East JJ, ex p. Hunt* [1976] 1 WLR 420, 1 All ER 839. Cp. 140 JPN 284.

[4] Prosecution of Offences Act 1979 s.4; *Raymond* v. *HM Attorney-General* [1982] 2 WLR 849, 2 All ER 487.

criminal who has "grassed" on his former companions.[5] The Attorney-General may stop any prosecution in the Crown Court by entering a *nolle prosequi*, though here again he rarely intervenes except when the trial is improper for technical reasons.[6]

Can I come in again? Your description does not explain what a crime really is. It only states the consequences of a crime.

The objection mistakes the purpose of definition. The object of a definition is to explain how words are used. Suppose that a Minister announces in Parliament that the Government intends to introduce legislation to make it a crime (or an offence) to join an unofficial strike. This means that a person who goes on unofficial strike will be subject to criminal proceedings (and we know what they are), the possible outcome being punishment (and we know what that is). So we know the meaning of saying that unofficial striking is to be a crime.

The definition of crime cannot tell us what sort of conduct is a crime. To answer that question there is, unfortunately, no escape from studying the criminal law. Lord Atkin:

> "The domain of criminal jurisprudence can only be ascertained by examining what acts at any particular period are declared by the State to be crimes, and the only common nature they will be found to possess is that they are prohibited by the State and that those who commit them are punished."[7]

If you are still not content, and go on pressing me to say what a crime "really" is, I can only reply that a crime is an act that is condemned sufficiently strongly to have induced the authorities (legislature or judges) to declare it to be punishable before the ordinary courts.[8]

§ 1.8. CRIMINAL DISPOSAL

The only crimes for which punishment is fixed by law (mandatory for the court) are murder (life imprisonment) and treason (death). Here the judge has no discretion. (Owing to the exercise of the prerogative of mercy, there have been no executions in peace time for treason for more than a

[5] See *Parl. Deb., H of C*, November 9, 1981, Written Answers col. *12*.

[6] The Attorney-General cannot stop a summary prosecution, but, as was said above, the DPP can take over any private prosecution in order to end it. See generally J Ll J Edwards, *The Law Officers of the Crown* (London 1964) Chap. 12.

[7] *Proprietary Articles Trade Assn* v. *Att.-Gen. for Canada* [1931] AC at 324. Lord Atkin's definition is a little too wide for English law; it should exclude offences against a code of law applicable only to a limited class of persons, like prisoners, which are not triable before the ordinary courts. See *R* v. *Board of Visitors of Hull Prison, ex p. St Germain* [1979] QB 425.

[8] The above definition, like Lord Atkin's, is inadequate for a federal system like that of Canada, which allocates legislative power in respect of criminal law to the Parliament of Canada, the federation, but allows the component Provinces to legislate in matters of a "local or private nature." Can a Provincial legislature pass an Act of a local nature that imposes penalties for breach of its provisions? The solution that the courts have reached is to say that "criminal law" in the constitution means only the criminal law relating to disorder and the major traditional crimes; so it is open to a Province to enact anti-noise legislation, for example, and to impose penalties. In substance, therefore, the Provinces can create criminal law, though the Canadian courts have to avoid saying this.

century.) In all other cases[1] the court (judge or magistrates) has a discretion as to the amount of fine or prison sentence, up to the limit (if any) provided by law.

All indictable offences are punishable by fine, and if the trial is on indictment the fine is now at large (at the discretion of the judge). For summary offences the maximum fine (or term of imprisonment) is stated in the statute.[2] Remember that every determinate (fixed) sentence of imprisonment is cut by one-third remission, and there is also the chance of parole.[3]

Young offenders, in place of prison, are either sent to detention centres for up to 4 months (ages 14–20) or sentenced to youth custody (in the former borstals) with supervision on release (ages 15–20). The power of courts to pass a custodial sentence in respect of young offenders is hedged about with conditions which are hoped to limit the use of this power to the irreducible minimum of cases.[4]

The court may treat the offender leniently by granting him an *absolute discharge*, if for example the offence was trivial or there were very strong mitigating circumstances. The defendant is technically convicted (for some though not all purposes), but no consequence follows. Alternatively, the court may give him a *conditional discharge*—conditional, that is, upon his not offending again for up to three years. Or it may put him on *probation*, which means that he will be under the supervision of a probation officer, but will not be punished for this offence if he complies with the terms of the probation order. (He may be required to reside in a probation hostel, or to undergo mental or other treatment, or to attend a day training centre (which provides remedial education of a simple kind) or a treatment unit for alcoholism (the so-called detoxification centre). For offenders below 17 probation is replaced by supervision, which may include an order to take part in specified community activities or subject the offender to a curfew.[5] Or the court may give the offender a *suspended sentence*, which makes a more specific threat of imprisonment for this offence if he offends again.[6]

Yet another possibility is to bind over the defendant to keep the peace or to be of good behaviour—not as a sentence, but because magistrates (including judges) have the remarkable power to bind over any person who appears before them. If the defendant refuses to be bound over he can be sent to prison. Another power of the court is simply to *defer sentence* to see whether the offender can evince a desire to change his ways.[7]

---

[1] Except in capital piracy, where the death penalty is obsolete in practice. See § 36.3.

[2] CJA 1982 ss.37, 46, establish a "standard scale" of fines for summary offences which may periodically be adjusted, and succeeding sections of the Act provide for certain increases in permitted fines.

[3] A prisoner may be released on parole when he has served one-third of his sentence or 12 months, whichever is later. There is power to reduce the period of 12 months by order: CJA 1982 s.33.

[4] See CJA 1982 Pt. I.

[5] CJA 1982 s.20.

[6] On the commission of another imprisonable offence during the operational period of suspension, the appropriate court must order the suspended sentence to take effect unless it is of opinion that it would be unjust to do so, and gives reasons for the opinion. The reasons may, however, be wide-ranging. A prison sentence may be partly suspended: CJA 1982 s.30.

[7] See amendment in CJA 1982 s.63.

The offender may regard these orders or expedients as a let-off, for the time being at least. But he may not view with such equanimity a *community service order* (for the over-17s) or an *attendance centre order*[8] (for offenders up to the age of 21, with the emphasis on discipline). The court may make a *hospital order*, sending him to a psychiatric hospital, but this is strictly without punitive intent. All these forms of disposal are subject to various rules and restrictions.[9]

The criminal courts seem to be concerned mainly to make an offender pay his debt to society. Perhaps it is more important to make him pay his debts to those whom he has injured.

Criminal courts have now been allowed to make a limited entry into the field of compensation (which traditionally belongs to the civil courts). Most offenders are not worth suing for damages; their assets are too small. So a criminal court, on convicting an offender, is empowered to order him to pay *compensation* in respect of personal injury and other loss or damage;[10] but the means of the offender are taken into account.

When the offender is a man of straw the victim of a crime of violence who has sustained personal injury will find it preferable to apply for compensation to the Criminal Injuries Compensation Board, which makes awards from State funds.[11] The police have to be informed without delay, but the offender need not have been prosecuted; so a patient in a psychiatric hospital, for instance, can get compensation if he is unlawfully attacked by a nurse, even though the authorities are not disposed to bring proceedings.

Another civil remedy that has been made available to the criminal courts is the order for *restitution* of stolen property or its proceeds;[12] and the Crown Court may, subject to certain conditions, make a *criminal bankruptcy order* against the offender.[13]

Civil actions can also play their own part in making criminals disgorge. The police can obtain an *ex parte* injunction to freeze a suspected fraudster's bank account until trial,[14] or to obtain possession of stolen goods.

Are there any ways of making it impossible for an offender to continue in his evil path?

The most complete form of incapacitation is imprisonment, but to some extent offenders can be "incapacitated on the outside." The court in convicting an offender may for example order the *suspension or revocation of a licence*. In the case of driving licences the order of disqualification is regarded as being partly punitive, and the making of the order is therefore governed by considerations of justice.[15]

---

[8] CJA 1982 ss.16–19.

[9] See Cross and Ashworth, *The English Sentencing System* , 3rd edn., read in the light of CJA 1982.

[10] Cross and Ashworth, *op. cit.* 64–68; CJA 1982 s.67. A compensation order may be made where there would be no civil remedy; see the criticism by Treitel in *Crime, Proof and Punishment*, ed. Tapper (London 1981) 88.

[11] Damage to property is not covered, but compensation can be claimed from public funds in respect of damage to buildings or the property therein (not cars parked on the highway) resulting from a riot. See Riot (Damages) Act 1886.

[12] Theft Act 1968 s.28 as amended; CJA 1972 s.6; see *Thibeault* [1983] Crim.LR 102. See also Police (Property) Act 1897. The police may seize goods reasonably suspected of having been stolen or obtained by deception: *Chic Fashions (WW) Ltd* v. *Jones* [1968] 2 QB 299.

[13] Powers of Criminal Courts Act 1973 ss.39–41. See 132 NLJ 330.

[14] *Chief Constable of Kent* v. *Verdon-Roe* [1982] 3 WLR 462. For defects in the law and its practice see The Company Lawyer 146.

[15] *Cooper* (1982) 146 JPN 564.

Again, the court may order the *forfeiture* of certain property illegally acquired[16] or possessed,[17] or make a *deprivation order* in respect of property legally possessed but used or intended to be used for the purpose of committing or facilitating the commission of an offence (the robber's getaway car).[18] Magistrates' courts may also, in some circumstances, make an order forbidding the continuation of a dangerous state of affairs, such as the breach of factory regulations, or they can make an order for the closure of filthy catering premises[19]; but these are regarded as civil remedies and the proceedings are initiated by complaint. Lastly, the court may recommend an adult alien (a person who is not a British subject) on conviction of an imprisonable[20] offence to be *deported*.[21] The order is probably not meant as a punishment, but is a way of relieving the country of a troublesome person.

§ 1.9. CIVIL LAW AND SOCIAL CONTROL

To some extent the civil law shares with the criminal law the aim of controlling conduct. This is one of the objects of the action for damages,[1] and the action for an injunction has no other purpose. The injunction orders the defendant not (for example) to continue a nuisance, or not to publish, or continue publishing, a libel; and if he disobeys he can be committed (sent to prison) for contempt of court.[2]

Oh ho! So civil courts can even send people to prison.

Yes for contempt of court. This offence is anomalous because there are both civil and criminal varieties. Civil contempt is committed chiefly where a person flouts an order of the court. Criminal contempt covers a miscellany of acts interfering with the work of the courts, ranging from contumely in court to the improper publication of matter that may influence the outcome of legal proceedings.[3] If a person is imprisoned for disobedience to a court order the court may order his discharge when he obeys.[4]

---

[16] The powers in this respect are fragmentary; an example is the Misuse of Drugs Act 1971 s.27. For the restricted ambit of the section see *Ribeyre* [1982] Crim.LR 538.

[17] Stone, *Justices Manual*, index *s.v.* Forfeiture.

[18] Powers of Criminal Courts Act 1983 s.43. A deprivation order is not technically forfeiture because the rights of third parties are not affected. These powers are not used for ordinary driving offences. See generally 138 JPN 690; Thomas in [1979] Crim.LR 796.

[19] See as to the latter Food and Drugs Act 1955 s.14.

[20] Police jargon, but a convenient word.

[21] Immigration Act 1971 s.3(6).

[1] See 4 Current Legal Problems 137; Williams and Hepple, *Foundations of the Law of Tort* (London 1976) 25. The civil law may also punish a person who makes an illegal contract by declaring that he cannot recover property otherwise due to him.

[2] Injunctions are not normally granted against apprehended personal injury. But a county court on the application of a spouse (or cohabitee) may grant an injunction forbidding the other party to molest the applicant or a child; or the injunction may exclude the defendant from the home: Domestic Violence and Matrimonial Proceedings Act 1976 s.1. By s.2, the judge may attach a power of arrest to the injunction if he is satisfied that the defendant has caused actual bodily harm to the applicant or a child and is likely to do it again, and the defendant can then be arrested by a constable who reasonably suspects him of breaking the injunction. Somewhat similar powers are given to magistrates' courts by the Domestic Proceedings and Magistrates' Courts Act 1978, but this Act does not apply to cohabitees, and there are other differences of detail (143 JPN 402).

[3] See Arlidge and Eady, *The Law of Contempt* (London 1982); Borrie and Lowe, *The Law of Contempt* (London 1973).

[4] By the Contempt of Court Act 1981 committal is for a maximum of two years (superior courts, including the county courts) or one month (inferior courts). The offender may also be fined.

Other people who can be jailed on civil process are those who are in default of payment of income tax, rates, and similar public dues[5] (but not council house rents), and men who default on payments of maintenance for a wife or children (including illegitimate children). However, the defendant goes to prison not as a criminal but as a civil offender, and he receives certain concessions in prison that are not extended to criminals.

Some statutes choose to use the arm of the civil law in preference to the criminal law to effect social change.

> "Recently an audience of nearly 100 law students and lecturers were asked which if any of the following were criminal offences: to refuse to serve a black man in a pub, to refuse to employ a man because he was a Jew, or to advertise a flat with the words: 'No Irish need apply.' Only about 10 per cent. of the audience answered correctly that each kind of conduct was unlawful but not criminal, since the Race Relations Act operated primarily through conciliation machinery rather than the criminal law."[6]

In the last resort a complainant may bring civil proceedings under the Race Relations Act in the county court or industrial tribunal, and the Commission for Racial Equality may assist him to do so.

The Sex Discrimination Act 1975 also avoids the use of the criminal law. The Equal Opportunities Commission can investigate discrimination against women or men (with power to require the attendance of witnesses or the production of documents). If discrimination is found it may issue a non-discrimination notice, against which the recipient may appeal to the county court or industrial tribunal, but, in addition, individuals have direct access to the courts and tribunals. Non-discrimination notices are enforceable in the courts by injunction.

The use of the civil law means that the police are not concerned with enforcement, but this does not matter when special enforcement agencies are set up. The civil law can pack a nasty punch in an order for the payment of compensation, and also in legal costs, which are never light. And the use of civil process means that the complainant can extract information from the defendant before the trial, which the criminal law would not allow.

What principle is followed by the legislature in deciding whether to give a criminal or a civil remedy?

The general policy is not to use the criminal law if the civil law is sufficient to keep the conduct in check. Generally the criminal law has to be used to protect the public interest because there is no one who can be relied upon to take civil proceedings on behalf of the public. Also, the civil law has few terrors for the thoroughly impecunious.

Can one say that the court order in civil proceedings is sought by and made for the benefit of a private individual, while the order of a criminal court is to protect society as a whole?

Alas, no, for an order of mandamus[7] (which is civil, or at any rate non-criminal) requires the defendant to perform his public duty, and is not intended to benefit one particular individual; while a criminal court can make an order for compensation which is intended to benefit an individual.

There are two particular ways in which the line between civil and criminal law is blurred.

(1) The practice of binding over straddles civil and criminal procedure.

---

[5] Including the payment of social security contributions. See 142 JPN 116.

[6] Albie Sachs in 36 MLR 100. See now the Race Relations Act 1976. For the sole penal provision see § 9.9.

[7] 'We command.'

As an example of its criminal use, suppose that a private citizen charges another before the magistrates for assaulting him, and the defendant says that the prosecutor provoked him. The magistrates may metaphorically knock their heads together by requiring both to enter into recognisances, with or without sureties, to keep the peace (or to be of good behaviour). The recognisance (whether of the person bound over or of his surety) requires the payment of a sum of money in the event of breach. Refusal by the person bound over to enter into the recognisance or failure to find the required sureties can result in an immediate sentence of imprisonment (even when the person in question has broken no law). Breach of the recognisance when entered into can be punished by the forfeiture of the whole or part of the sums promised to be paid.

The bind-over can also be used even when no criminal proceedings are in progress. If it is feared that a person will misbehave himself he may be brought before a magistrates' court in civil proceedings (*i.e.* by complaint) and bound over to be of good behaviour and to keep the peace. The recognisance may in appropriate cases be for a large sum. This procedure is sometimes used where a person has regularly flouted the law because the statutory fines are low; by binding him over the magistrates can mulct him in a heavier penalty next time.[8]

(2) The civil courts can sometimes grant an injunction or declaration to prevent criminal offences. This can be done under the express or implied authority of a statute.[9] Also, the Attorney-General may sue at common law for an injunction to prevent a public nuisance or other breach of public duty; and a private person may, with the Attorney's consent, sue for the injunction in his name. This last is known as a relator[10] action, because the Attorney acts on the relation (*ex relatione*) of the citizen who is the real plaintiff and who has to foot the bill of costs.

Is the relator action civil or criminal, and is it brought for a crime or for a civil wrong?

It is a civil action, but is brought on account of a crime or other breach of public duty.

That seems a rare muddle. I thought you were saying that crimes are matters for the criminal courts. But now you tell me that the civil courts can interfere.

Yes in respect of apprehended crime. The action for an injunction (or, as an alternative, for a declaration) is brought in the High Court, which has

---

[8] See *The General Part* 2nd edn Chap. 16.

[9] By the Fair Trading Act 1973 Part III the Director General of Fair Trading may apply for a court order to restrain a firm from continuing with malpractices. Where a statute gave an electricity board power to enter land, the board could sue obstructors for an injunction, and was not confined to the criminal proceedings provided: *R* v. *Chief Constable of Devon and Cornwall* [1982] QB at 466H. In *Pharmaceutical Society of Great Britain* v. *Boots* [1953] 1 QB 401, the plaintiff society was required by statute to take steps to secure compliance with the statutory provisions (see now Poisons Act 1972 s.9(1)), and instead of prosecuting for a summary offence under the Act it brought a civil action, apparently for an injunction or declaration. However, the House of Lords has now adopted a restrictive attitude in these actions: see authorities in § 33.3 n. 7. Actions for declarations by people who fear prosecution are noticed in § 20.1.

[10] Accent on the second syllable.

both criminal and civil jurisdiction; the proceeding is governed by the rules of a civil action and is not thought of as criminal because no question of punishment is involved.

What is the point of bringing a relator action? Why not just prosecute for the crime?

The crime may be threatened but not yet committed, and the injunction may prevent it from being committed. Or the criminal penalty may be only a modest fine, which is not enough to stop criminal activity from continuing, whereas disobedience to an injunction can land the offender in jail.

Why must the action be brought in the name of the Attorney-General when the real plaintiff is a private person?

Relator actions are brought when the defendant is in breach of his *public* duty, or threatens such breach. A barrow-boy obstructs the street with his barrow; or buses park in the road in which you live and cause congestion. No one has his individual rights infringed: the obstruction of the highway is an infringement of the right of the public to pass without hindrance, and is normally prosecuted as a summary offence. But the courts allowed the Attorney-General to sue in the interest of the public, and the Attorney in turn decided to allow his name to be used by members of the public. Since he only consents to a single action being brought, this saves the vexation and waste of money that would be involved if many people sued the same defendant.

What if the Attorney-General doesn't want the law to be enforced, and refuses his consent?

The courts accord him an absolute discretion, and will not interfere. The Attorney may refuse his consent, for example, if he thinks it unwise to antagonise a powerful trade union. Whatever his reasons, good or bad, he need not express them.[11] The only important exception to the Attorney's absolute control over the action to protect public rights is that, by statute, a local authority may sue to protect the interests of the local inhabitants.[12]

In short, the line between criminal and civil law is somewhat arbitrary. The broad point remains that all crimes can legally be followed by punishment, and that criminal courts *generally* punish (or sentence the defendant in a way that puts him under a special risk of being punished, as in the case of probation or suspended sentence), while civil courts are not oriented to punishment in the same way. I have to say it is the broad point, because sometimes a civil court punishes, as when it orders a penalty to be paid.

---

[11] *Gouriet* v. *Union of Post Office Workers* [1978] AC 435. See D G T Williams in [1977] Crim.LR 703; R C Simpson in 41 MLR 58; Feldman in 42 MLR 369. The case arose at a time when it was an offence for Post Office workers to strike. Parliament has since taken the easy way out by legalising these strikes.

[12] Local Government Act 1972 s.222; *Kent CC* v. *Batchelor* (No. 2) [1979] 1 WLR 213, [1978] 3 All ER 980. For another exception, under the Fair Trading Act, see n. 9 above.

§ 1.10. THE JUSTIFICATION OF PUNISHMENT

As the last of these preliminaries, consider the proper basis of punishment.[1] This has greatly exercised the minds of both jurists and philosophers. Why are people punished, do you think?

I can answer promptly. Because they have done wrong and so ought to be punished.

You have stated the theory of *ethical (moral) retribution* (otherwise called retributive justice, or desert), which holds that wrongdoers are punished in accordance with a moral law that requires this, or at any rate permits it. There is supposed to be some necessary moral connection between wrongdoing and punishment.

Both moral blame and legal punishment are social reactions to what may broadly be called aggression—*i.e.*, defiance of social standards or the moral code.

Retributive justice can be explained as a refinement of the primitive urge to take revenge for injury, which has a biological explanation. A judicious measure of retaliation in addition to self-defence is, in the long run, beneficial to the defender by dissuading or disabling the attacker from repeating his aggression. So retaliation, and not merely defence, has survival value. Both fear and anger are defence mechanisms. Human beings still have these emotions, but we have sublimated our anger into moral disapproval and the legal system.

Philosophers have analysed the notion of retributive justice into two propositions, negative and positive.

The negative side of the proposition is that people ought not to be punished unless they have done wrong (which must mean moral wrong). We have a strong feeling (which we tend to regard as intuitive, though it is largely cultural) that punishment should not be given to anyone who is not guilty. Many utilitarians would support this negative proposition, because it is peculiarly offensive to our moral feelings if an innocent person is punished.

But we never would punish the innocent, except by mistake.

That is not entirely true. We often quite deliberately punish people who have not been at fault. This is called "strict liability," and some think it unjust. It is largely, though not entirely, confined to minor offences, generally summary offences.

Anyway, a person wouldn't be sent to prison unless he has been in some way at fault.

Probably never nowadays, though the courts have not always kept to this principle in the past. It would now be generally agreed that a person should at least not be seriously punished unless he is at fault in breaking the law, and he should not be even mildly punished (as by fine) unless he is at fault or unless the offence is a minor one not involving much stigma. Qualified in this way, the negative side of the theory of justice can be regarded as agreed; and some would agree it without qualification.

---

[1] On which see generally Nigel Walker, *Punishment, Danger and Stigma* (Oxford 1980); Philip Bean, *Punishment* (Oxford 1981).

What is the positive side of the theory of justice?

The one you stated at the beginning. Wrongdoers ought to be punished. No wrongdoer should escape, if we can help it, because haphazard punishment would be unjust.

I hope you will not be offended if I say that lawyers and philosophers are now practically unanimous in rejecting this proposition. Even philosophers who support retribution no longer argue that wrongdoing is a *sufficient* condition of punishment (they do not argue that all wrongdoers must be punished); they say only that it is a *necessary* condition (no one can properly be punished who is not a wrongdoer). Perhaps it is always just to punish the guilty, because that is the meaning of "just" in this context. But whether or not this is so, we no longer think that it is always *justifiable* to punish the guilty. Since this opinion is generally accepted, we allow the police and other prosecutors a discretion whether to prosecute at all. Also, in practically all crimes except murder we give sentencers a discretion whether to punish the convicted person. He may, for example, be put on probation (which is designed to help him not to offend again), or be given an absolute discharge. In short, the theory of ethical retribution is now generally rejected by people who think about the subject, except as a limitation upon punishment.[2]

If we reject the demand for just punishment, on what basis do we punish?

The only possible answer is the utilitarian opinion that punishment is preventative. Utilitarians (who take the view that the whole of morality is concerned with maximising human happiness, or welfare) naturally conclude that offenders are punished for social reasons, looking to the future, not for metaphysical reasons, looking to the past. Bentham, the father of utilitarianism, wrote:

> "All punishment is mischief. All punishment in itself is evil. It ought only to be admitted in as far as it promises to exclude some greater evil."[3]

Punishment appears to look to the past, but for the utilitarian its real justification looks to the future. "Men are not hanged for stealing horses, but that horses may not be stolen" (George Savile, Marquis of Halifax). In other words, the utilitarian reason for punishment is either its effect upon the person punished (*particular deterrence*) or by serving as a warning to others (*general deterrence*).[4] In addition, the penal process can have a certain *educational* effect. Punishment can bring an offender to a realisation of the badness of his conduct.

Suppose a person does something wicked but it is quite certain that he will never repeat it. For example, a man murders his terribly spiteful and

---

[2] For a re-examination of retributive theory see Galligan in *Crime, Proof and Punishment*, ed. Tapper (Oxford 1981) 144.

[3] *Morals and Legislation*, Chap. 15 s.1.

[4] On deterrence see J Andenaes, *Punishment and Deterrence* (Ann Arbor 1974); Walker in [1979] Crim.LR 129; also Zimring and Hawkins, *Deterrence* (Chicago 1973).

nagging wife, and it is inconceivable that he will be such an idiot as to marry another such. Would he be punished, on utilitarian theory?

Obviously yes, for reasons of general deterrence. Similarly the spy in the Defence Establishment whose cover is blown is jailed in the hope of encouraging others in or under the Defence Ministry to resist any similar inclinations. If a prison officer helps a prisoner to escape by giving him an impression of the cell key for him to copy, the officer if discovered is dismissed, and will never be a prison officer again; but he is sent to prison all the same.

What you say sounds all cut and dried, but punishment doesn't work very well, does it?

No, but consider how much worse off we should be if we had no social provision for punishing evildoers.

To say that the rational justification of punishment is the prevention of crime is not to say that punishment always has this effect, or that it is wisely and moderately used. We have discovered that comparatively mild punishments often have the same effect as comparatively severe ones, and that non-punitive disposals of the offender are often better at preventing a recurrence, or not worse, than a punitive sentence.

Which theory do the courts act on in sentencing: the retributive or the utilitarian?

The courts accept the negative side of retributive theory as asserting the general principle that offenders should not be punished more severely than is proportionate to their guilt. Beyond that they have no clear philosophy and do not follow an entirely consistent line. Utilitarian theory implies that offenders should be punished or otherwise dealt with as stringently as is necessary to maximise crime prevention but no further; and it teaches that regard must be had to the evil effect of punishment on the offender and his family, and to the degree of evil attributed to the offence. Probably this is what the courts generally try to do, but there are great practical difficulties.

One factor influencing the courts more than can readily be explained on utilitarian theory is their desire to use the criminal trial by way of denunciation—that is, as a means of reinforcing society's feeling that the conduct is bad. Of course, this can be a utilitarian purpose, but everything depends on the way in which it is applied.

> In one case a man of low intelligence had buggered his 12 year old daughter, during a course of consensual intimacy that lasted for about a year. He used no coercion and the girl suffered no physical effects, though the court thought it almost certain that she would suffer psychologically. The man was unlikely to behave in this way with any other child, and would now be separated from his daughter, his marriage and home having broken up. The court said that a deterrent sentence was not needed for this sort of crime, because no one in his right mind was going to commit it, but a fairly long term was required to mark the revulsion of society. The man was sentenced to 5 years' imprisonment.[5]

---

[5] *Lorraine* (1982) 146 JPN 533. Cp. *Hitchcock* [1982] Crim. LR 541, where the objects of sentencing are stated as being punishment (i.e. retribution), denunciation (retribution again?), and deterrence, in that order. On denunciation see Walker, *op. cit.* n. 1 above, 109. It may be observed that if public opinion is divided or confused about the badness of the conduct, the criminal trial may reinforce the doubts and serve to call in question the law that it tries to enforce.

If, as is surely the case, public opinion is in general entirely healthy on this subject, is there really any utilitarian need to sentence a man with an IQ of 74 to prison for this length of time merely to mark the revulsion of society? In practice the "revulsion of society" seems to be a significant factor in sentencing only in offences of a sexual character. It looks like being positive retribution in another guise.

In summary, judges (including magistrates) generally sentence serious offenders on the basis of a rough assessment of what the offence is "worth." There is a customary tariff, the details of which are constantly being refined by the Court of Appeal; it is a mysterious mix of notions of ethical retribution, deterrence, reassuring the public, publicly repudiating the offence, and disabling the offender for a time. The tariff, it must be understood, is not a formal document, but has to be gathered from the appellate decisions.[6]

The tariff states not a definite sentence for a particular offence but the range of sentencing appropriate to ordinary circumstances, or to such special circumstances as may be specified in the tariff. The point at which the court fixes the sentence within the range depends in part upon the presence or absence of mitigating or aggravating circumstances. A bad criminal record, for example, is an aggravating circumstance, in the sense that it may dispose the court to sentence at the top of the scale—though the theory is that the court should not sentence *above* the tariff range on account of previous convictions,[7] or for the purpose of general deterrence.[8]

The weight given to the various factors probably varies with the type of offence and with the opinions of the age. Judges, however, are not good at explaining their own motivations. They sometimes say that the sentence they are awarding is a "punishment" and is not meant to deter others, apparently meaning by the latter phrase that the particular sentence is not set at the upper range of the tariff for the purpose of increasing general deterrence. Obviously, every tariff sentence contains an ingredient of deterrence.

For the most part the judges, when they have rejected the possibility of a "reformative" disposal of the case, appear to think in retributive terms. Paradoxically, this can result in a more lenient sentence than one conceived in terms of deterrence or incapacitation. In sexual offences, however, it results in greater severity.

In applying the tariff the courts may also take account of practical considerations, such as that there is not much use imposing anything more than a nominal fine on an unemployed offender, for whom the choice may therefore be either a prison sentence or no immediate punishment at all.

Sentencing is not an exact science, and great differences of approach exist between different judges and benches. Excessive sentences in the Crown Court[9] can be reduced on appeal, and the Court of Appeal does not merely enforce the tariff maximum but scrutinises the actual sentence within the tariff. This produces some degree of uniformity, but, since the

---

[6] The standard works are D A Thomas, *Principles of Sentencing*, 2nd edn, and the same author's *Current Sentencing Practice* (London 1982).

[7] See, e.g., *Queen* [1982] Crim.LR 56.

[8] D A Thomas, *Principles of Sentencing*, 2nd edn 35–37.

[9] The sentence of a magistrates' court can be reduced on appeal to the Crown Court. The Divisional Court cannot generally reduce magistrates' sentences. But some measure of High Court control over magistrates has now been introduced by the decision in *R* v. *St Alban's Crown Court, ex p. Cinnamond* (1980) 2 CAR(S) 235 (see [1981] Crim.LR 348, [1982] *ibid.* 651). This allows an application for judicial review where a sentence is regarded as violating legal principle.

prosecution cannot appeal against sentence, wholly inadequate sentences (which are of daily occurrence, particularly in magistrates' courts in respect of violent offenders) have to stand.

With the advent of Lord Lane as Chief Justice in 1980 an effort has been made to reduce the prison tariff. The courts now generally consider the least amount of punishment (within the tariff) that is necessary to deter offenders; partly, no doubt, they are motivated by utilitarian principle, but they also feel the need to reduce the gross overcrowding of the prisons. Even when it is thought that a prison sentence is essential, the defendant will whenever the judges think it possible receive a very short sentence such as 28 days, frequently coupled with a fine. Merely hearing "the clang of the prison gates" is thought to be almost sufficient warning in itself for for first offenders.[10] But ethical retribution still looms large for sexual offences against children. Whereas a first-time offender will often receive a sentence of only a few weeks or months for theft, thuggery or corruption, if he goes to prison at all, a man who interferes with small girls without any objection on their part is likely to lose his liberty for several years.

Sometimes the courts do not even approach the case in terms of the tariff. An initial choice is made between applying the tariff and "individualising the sentence" (giving such a sentence as is most likely to prevent this offender from offending again); and there are customary rules observed by the courts in making this difficult discrimination.[11] An individualised sentence is always given with utilitarian intent, and usually it means a less onerous sentence, with the hope of reform (*e.g.* ordinary probation, or probation with a community service order, or even a mere discharge).

When an arsonist or burglar is sent down for a good stretch, isn't the chief object to switch him off for a while?

The very gravest offences carry a possible "life" sentence, which the court will award if it regards the offender as being particularly dangerous.[12] But in theory determinate (fixed) sentences of imprisonment are not calculated with an eye to their disabling effect. The Court of Appeal generally insists that (unless the statutory provisions for what is called an "extended term of imprisonment"[13] are invoked, which is unusual) an offender must not be given a longer sentence than he deserves for the offence of which he now stands convicted, even though his past conduct shows him to be a pest to society, unless (a recent qualification) he is "dangerous" (whatever that means).[14] Nor will the court usually give a prison sentence exceeding the tariff range because the offender is a psychiatric case (where no suitable psychiatric accommodation can be

[10] So although an offender is not to have his sentence assessed above the tariff on account of his past transgressions, by falling outside the "clang of the prison gates" principle he may in fact suffer severely on account of them. See *Osborn* (1982) 146 JPN 223.

[11] See D A Thomas, *Principles of Sentencing* Chap. 1. An interesting example of individualised sentence is "last chance" probation where the court sees a glimmer of hope for a recidivist; see, e.g., *Hammond* [1982] Crim. LR 539.

[12] See *Barron* [1982] Crim.LR 318 and note thereto.

[13] Powers of Criminal Courts Act 1973 s.28. This applies to repeated offenders where certain conditions are fulfilled. The extended term may even exceed the maximum otherwise allowable for the offence.

[14] E.g. *Green* [1981] Crim.LR 655. Sentences out of proportion to the offence are sometimes given because there is no other way of incapacitating the offender for a sufficient period: see *McCauliffe* [1982] Crim.LR 316 and note thereto. A serious offender like a dangerous arsonist is likely to be regarded as deserving of a substantial sentence, which the court may also justify as being "for the protection of the public." Even a minor arsonist is sometimes treated in this way by a court that sees no alternative, though such a course is a departure from the principle usually stated. See note to *Walsh* [1982] Crim.LR 247. In sexual cases the judges sometimes express a strange view of desert—as when a man who indecently handled boys received a sentence of 4 years from the CA, not (the court emphasised) for the purpose of keeping him out of the way of small boys for a time, but purely because he deserved it: *Gooden* [1980] Crim.LR 251.

found for him).[15] If the generality of offenders were sentenced on the basis of protecting the public from their foibles, our prisons would be even more crammed than they are. Mentally disordered offenders may in very serious cases be packed off to a "special hospital" with the avowed object of keeping them safe, but, as already said, this is not regarded as a punishment. These rules show that retributive punishment can be more lenient and libertarian than a sentence based on "social defence."

Wouldn't it be better always to treat offenders than to punish them?

Yes if we could. Many attempts have been made to "treat" offenders, as for example in a "therapeutic community" where "group therapy" or "conversational therapy" is practised. Such methods have often been felt to be beneficial by the offenders themselves, but, strangely, they do not generally show any improvement in the reconviction rate when compared with the traditional methods of dealing with offenders.[16] There is no infallible psychological treatment (and if methods were developed they would probably be denounced as "brainwashing"). The roots of offending lie deep in the human personality (with some contribution from social conditions); they include greed, boredom, malevolence, and poor parental upbringing. Benefit has been found from some regimes, particularly community service schemes for young offenders. But the only general means we have of preventing offences is by threatening punishment.

[15] *Fisher* [1981] Crim.LR 578. But here again the courts sometimes depart from their own principles: see *Gouws* [1982] Crim.LR 187.

[16] For an interesting survey of changes in American opinion on this see Radzinowicz and Hood in *Crime, Proof and Punishment* (Oxford 1981) 127.

Chapter 2

JUDGE AND JURY

So prove it,
That the probation bear no hinge nor loop
To hang a doubt on.

Othello v. iii.

Before passing to the substantive law, we must consider a part of the law of procedure and evidence that is intimately related to the substantive law. This concerns the burden of proof on the issues before the court and the distribution of functions between judge and jury.

§ 2.1. THE INCIDENCE AND QUANTUM OF THE BURDEN OF PROOF

An indictment (or information before magistrates) gives what are called particulars of the offence charged. For example, on a charge of theft in the Crown Court the particulars will say that AB on the blank day of blank stole a wallet belonging to CD. This does not expressly state all the elements of theft. In particular, it leaves the mental element to implication, because the mental element is taken to be comprised in the word "stole." Nor does it state where the alleged offence took place, or the time of day. But the defendant is given formal notice, however briefly, of the charge against him.

Suppose the jury or magistrates cannot make up their minds on whether the defendant is guilty or innocent?

Then they must find him not guilty.

So an acquittal is not a certificate that the defendant is innocent?

The jury or magistrates must acquit even though they believe the defendant to be guilty, if the evidence leaves them with any reasonable doubt as to his guilt. The acquittal does not mean that the defendant leaves the court without a stain on his character. Whether it does so depends on the circumstances.[1]

The best-known statement of the burden of proof is in the celebrated case of *Woolmington*.[2] The old writers, notably Foster, had declared that every killing was presumed to be murder until the contrary was shown; and the statement was repeated in Archbold. It was decisively

[1] An acquittal is generally taken as conclusive in the criminal law (see § 7.8), but not for the purpose of later civil proceedings. See Mirfield in [1980] Crim.LR 343 n. 33.
[2] [1935] AC 462.

rejected by the House of Lords, who asserted the fundamental presumption of innocence in criminal cases. When a defence to a charge of murder is accident or provocation, the onus rests on the prosecution to satisfy the jury that the killing was intentional and not provoked. Viscount Sankey LC said: "If the jury are left in reasonable doubt whether the act was unintentional or provoked, the prisoner[3] is entitled to be acquitted," that is, of murder. (There can still sometimes be a conviction of manslaughter.) The Lord Chancellor also put the point more generally in words that have rung down the years: "Throughout the web of English criminal law one golden thread is always to be seen, that it is the duty of the prosecution to prove the prisoner's guilt, subject to the defence of insanity and subject also to any statutory exception."[4]

The burden of proof so placed upon the prosecution remains with them throughout the trial. Obviously it does not "shift" to the defendant merely because the prosecution make out a *prima facie* case.[5]

The criminal burden is contrasted with the civil one. In civil cases the burden of proof generally rests on the plaintiff, but he need only prove the case on the balance of probabilities.[6] The criminal burden is supposed to be heavier.

What is meant by reasonable doubt?

The phrase is virtually indefinable. It can be said to mean not a mere fanciful doubt but one to which reasonable men would give weight—but how does that help? The best course for the judge is to state the rule without comment.

Judges have tried to explain the phrase to juries, but often wrongly and convictions have sometimes been quashed inconsequence. In 1952 the Court of Criminal Appeal suggested that it would be better to ask the jury whether they were "satisfied so that they can feel sure," or some similar phrase.[7] The change did not work well, and in 1979 the Judicial Committee of the Privy Council recommended a return to the time-honoured formula.

> "Attempts to substitute other expressions have never prospered. It is generally sufficient and safe to direct a jury that they must be satisfied beyond reasonable doubt so that they feel sure of the defendant's guilt. Nevertheless, other words will suffice, so long as the message is clear."[8]

It is sometimes suggested that the degree of proof required varies directly with the

---

[3] Formerly the judges spoke of the defendant on a felony charge as "the prisoner," but this fell into disuse with the abolition of the special incidents of felony; it was in any case pejorative for a person who had not been convicted. Both judges and statutes generally refer to the defendant as "the accused." But it is again an emotionally loaded word: if you were on trial for a crime, would you rather be called "the accused" or "the defendant"? It seems to me that the latter expression is preferable, as the more neutral. Formerly the CLRC in its Reports used "the accused," but in its 14th Report it changed to "the defendant."

[4] The splendour of this passage was marred by an examination candidate who reproduced the word "web" as "cobweb."

[5] *Stoddart* (1909) 2 CAR at 241–242.

[6] In some exceptional civil cases the criminal standard (or at any rates something higher than the usual civil standard) is applied.

[7] *Summers* [1952] 1 All ER 1059, 36 CAR 14.

[8] *Ferguson* [1979] 1 WLR at 99A, 1 All ER at 882a (PC). For example, the judge may merely ask the jury whether they are (or feel) sure of the defendant's guilt. It is recognised as undesirable merely to ask them whether they are "satisfied" of guilt (instead of "sure" or "satisfied so that they feel sure" or "completely satisfied"), and such a direction may be accounted a misdirection (*Gourley* [1981] Crim.LR 336). A direction about being "reasonably satisfied" is even worse (*Kritz* [1950] 1 KB 82); yet trial judges go on making these mistakes from time to time.

seriousness of the charge;[9] but this is suspect doctrine and it is virtually never invoked in practice.

Occasionally the Court of Appeal has also laid down that it is not enough for the judge to say that the jury must be sure of the defendant's guilt beyond reasonable doubt (the quantum of proof), without adding that the burden of proof is on the prosecution (the incidence of proof). This view is hard to follow, because the second proposition is contained in the first. There is no point in telling the jury what is inevitably implied. At any rate, the position now is that if a judge directs the jury merely in terms of the quantum of proof, although the Court of Appeal may frown upon the direction as being unduly lax, an appeal may be nevertheless dismissed under "the proviso" (see below § .7) on the ground that no miscarriage of justice has actually occurred.[10] The appellate court is now much less ready to allow appeals on account of technical inadequacies in directions on the burden of proof than it used to be. Even positive misdirections are sometimes overlooked if no reasonable jury could have failed to convict on a proper direction.[11]

§ 2.2. THE SUBMISSION OF "NO CASE"

The direction on burden is not the only control over the jury. At the close of the case for the prosecution, you may hear counsel for the defence submitting to the judge that there is no case to answer. This is sometimes called an application for a directed verdict. If the judge (after hearing anything prosecuting counsel has to say) rules in favour of the submission, he will not leave the case to the jury's decision but will direct the jury to acquit.[1]

The submission is made after the jury have heard the prosecution evidence. There would be a danger of prejudice if they heard the submission being made, because if the judge rules that there is a case to answer the jury may say to themselves: "The police think he did it, and now the judge thinks he did it as well." Accordingly, the accepted practice is that if the submission is made on the ground that the evidence for the Crown is insufficient to be left to the jury (as opposed, perhaps, to a submission that there is a purely technical defect in the prosecution case), the submission should be made and argued in the absence of the jury.[2]

Why does the judge have to say that there isn't enough evidence? If the prosecution case is as pathetic as all that, the jury wouldn't take long in coming to the answer themselves.

The rule is a safeguard for the defendant. He may want to cut short the proceedings by convincing the judge that the prosecution are mistaken in their view of the law. He may want to win an acquittal because of the weakness of the prosecution's case, without revealing the weakness of his own defence. Or he may want to avoid the risk of a perverse jury deciding against him without any real evidence at all. True, a perverse verdict might

---

[9] *E.g. Bater* v. *Bater* [1951] P at 37.

[10] Criminal Appeal Act 1968 s.2(1); *Friend*, The Times, March 28, 1962, [1962] Crim.LR 568.

[11] *E.g. Hughes* [1963] Crim.LR 294; *Folley* [1978] Crim.LR 556. But see *Kwan Ping Bong* [1979] AC at 616H, where the Privy Council said that the proviso is seldom applicable to a misdirection as to the onus of proving an essential fact.

[1] See [1965] Crim.LR 343, 410.

[2] *Falconer-Atlee* (1973) 58 CAR at 354.

be set aside on appeal. But this procedure avoids the necessity for an appeal.

In other words, a submission of no case means "The prosecution have cocked it up, haven't they?"

Yes, but another translation of the submission is: "My client hasn't a dog's chance if you force him into the witness-box, so I hope you'll find that the prosecution case has collapsed before it is his turn to speak." Putting this in formal language, the submission, if successful, protects the defendant from having to give evidence, when he may be forced under cross-examination to admit facts that prove the charge. Although the law does not compel him to give evidence, he may in practice be unable to avoid doing so if the submission is rejected, because of the bad impression that his silence may make on the jury.

These two reasons for the submission of no case may be viewed with mixed feelings. The first reason, the desirability of putting an end to a mistaken prosecution (both to save public money and to save the defendant from needless worry and the risk of a perverse verdict) is wholly in favour of allowing the submission to be made. The second reason will not be looked kindly upon by those who do not favour the defendant's so-called "right of silence." It is a right that many offenders have had occasion to bless, since it has saved them from the practical necessity of having to own up; but that is not a reason why law-abiding citizens should look kindly upon it.

Can't the prosecution call the defendant as one of their own witnesses?

Dear me, no. It is the right of silence again. The defendant gives evidence only if he wants to, along with (almost always before) the other defence witnesses.

Why doesn't the judge stop the case on his own initiative? Is it that the defence prompt the judge in order to wake him up?

The judge does not regard it as his duty to attend to the sufficiency of the evidence at that stage, if counsel for the defence does not make a submission. He may let the case run, even if he detects deficiencies in the evidence for the Crown, if he thinks that the deficiencies may be made good by admissions extracted from the defence witnesses. However, if the defendant is unrepresented it seems to be the judge's duty to consider the point on his behalf.[3]

If the defendant submits no case and the prosecution realise at once that they have omitted to adduce evidence on something vital, can they make good the deficiency at that stage?

Yes if the court (i.e. the judge or magistrates) so allows, as in a proper

---

[3] See [1981] Crim.LR 276.

case it can.[4] If the defect is purely formal or technical the court generally *must* allow the additional evidence, granting an adjournment if necessary.[5]

Suppose the judge directs the jury to acquit but they are stiff-necked and want to make true deliverance on their own whatever the judge thinks?

If the foreman refuses to comply, the judge may tell him to stand down and may ask another juror to comply with his direction. If they persist in refusing he can empanel a more complaisant jury.[6] These are ridiculous subterfuges: we need a statute saying that the judge can enter an acquittal without having to overbear the jury.

What if the judge fails to accede to a submission of no case when he ought to?

If defence counsel has the courage to call no evidence, the Court of Appeal will quash a conviction if the judge ought to have accepted the submission. If, however, counsel continues with the case, practice has not been uniform. The Court of Appeal has on occasion looked at all the evidence to decide whether the verdict is "unsafe or unsatisfactory." On other occasions, however, the appellate court has taken the view that if the judge improperly rejected a submission on the evidence as it then stood, the impropriety is not cured by evidence given after the submission.[7]

The submission of no case and the possibility of an appeal mean that, in Lord Devlin's phrase, the jury are "limited at both ends"[8]—before they deliberate, and afterwards. Broadly speaking, they should not be allowed to decide a very shaky case (or rather a very shaky case of a certain type), and if they are allowed to decide it, and convict, the conviction may be quashed.

However, the test of shakiness differs at the two stages. At the final stage it is a broad test. The Court of Appeal is directed by statute to quash a conviction if it is "unsafe or unsatisfactory" (§ .7). A few years back there was authority for saying that the trial judge should apply the same test: would a conviction on this prosecution evidence be unsafe or unsatisfactory? But the Court of Appeal has now rejected this, and gone back to the traditional narrower rule, which is that on a trial by jury the judge is required to accept a submission of no case only if he decides that there is no evidence of guilt, or if the evidence is tenuous and the judge concludes that taken at its highest it is such that a properly directed jury could not properly convict on it.[9]

---

[4] *Doran* (1972) 56 CAR 429; *Matthews* v. *Morris* [1981] Crim.LR 495. The court can recall a prosecution witness on its own initiative.

[5] The permission may be granted even after the defendant has called evidence: *Doran*, last note. Cp. 145 JPN 233. But if the submission of no case is overruled, and the defending advocate announces that he will call no evidence and closes his case, the court cannot then allow the prosecution to call further evidence: *Saunders* v. *Johns* [1965] Crim.LR 49.

[6] 139 JPN 159.

[7] See *Juett* [1981] Crim.LR 113, 277; cp. [1965] Crim.LR 349; Archbold, 41st edn § 7–36.

[8] *Trial by Jury* (London 1956) 65.

[9] *Galbraith* [1981] 1 WLR 1039, 2 All ER 1060, 73 CAR 124.

The professed reason for wording the rule in this severely limited way is that the judge must not usurp the function of the jury. The credibility of witnesses is supposed to be a matter for the jury alone. Therefore, the judge in ruling on a submission must pretend to himself that he believes evidence that in fact he regards as a pack of lies, or evidence that contradicts itself and is contradicted by overwhelming evidence to the contrary.[10] The judge must also, it seems, assume that there will be no evidence to displace inferences that might reasonably be drawn from the evidence in the absence of explanation.

This professed reason offered by the Court of Appeal is wholly unconvincing. We are told[11] that the jury should be allowed to decide the case because they have heard and seen the witnesses. But that is equally true of the trial judge. Moreover, the Court of Appeal, which has not heard and seen the witnesses, is allowed by statute to set aside a conviction on the general ground that it is unsafe or unsatisfactory; and it may therefore seem on the face of things to be remarkable that the trial judge, who *has* heard and seen the witnesses, is not required to intervene at an earlier stage when he could save the vexation, risk and waste of public money involved in a mistaken or ill-advised prosecution. While it is good to have the Court of Appeal as one safeguard against an unsound conviction, it would be better still to have two safeguards. The danger to justice is heightened by the fact that even the Court of Appeal refuses to consider questions of credibility of evidence.

But in human affairs arguments are rarely all one way, and things are not always what they seem. There is one strong reason for the present view of the Court of Appeal, which the court may have had in mind but was too discreet to parade in public. The submission of no case, as already explained, gives powerful backing to the "right of silence," which is strongly supported by one body of opinion but at the same time causes failures of justice. If the judge is compelled to stop the trial on a submission of no case, the "right to silence" is fully protected. If he is allowed to reject the submission, the defendant may feel obliged to give evidence, and may be compelled in cross-examinaton to make admissions that defeat him. So those who think our criminal process is too indulgent are not keen on the submission of no case, except where the prosecution case is visibly misconceived. The difficulty hardly arises at the stage of appeal, because then all the evidence is generally in and the court can review it as a whole.

Some years ago the Criminal Law Revision Committee, in its Report on the Law of Evidence, proposed that the right of silence should be moderately curtailed by allowing the jury to take account of the defendant's failure to explain his conduct; but the proposal met with such an outcry from eminent persons and bodies (including the Magistrates' Association) that not only was it dropped but the whole Evidence Report was jettisoned. Yet no one notices when the judges chip away at the right of silence by restricting the submission of no case. The more the submission is restricted, the more the defendant is put under pressure to enter the witness-box to testify.

Suppose that there is no successful submission of no case and the trial runs on. Can the judge afterwards stop the case on his own initiative when he finds that the prosecution case has really broken down?

He has a discretion to do so at any time after the close of the prosecution case—even after all the evidence is in.[12] This is an important point, which is frequently overlooked. It means that the restrictive rules relating to submissions of no case apply only to the judge's duty to accept the submission, not to his power to do so if he pleases. There is no point in prolonging a trial at public expense if the trial judge, after hearing evidence

---

[10] There is authority for allowing the judge to stop the case if the prosecution evidence is inherently incredible: see Rosemary Pattenden in [1982] Crim.LR 562. This does not apply merely because the prosecution evidence is contradicted by weightier evidence.

[11] In *Galbraith*, n. 9 above.

[12] *Young* [1964] 1 WLR at 720, 48 CAR at 296.

from the prosecution (and also, perhaps, from the defendant, if he elects to give evidence), thinks there is no good reason for continuing.[13] The exercise of this discretion in suitable cases is much the best way of solving the problem of the half-baked prosecution.

Can a submission of no case be made in a magistrates' court?

Certainly.

The magistrates are judge and jury, but they rule on a submission by pretending that they are merely the judge, considering whether there is sufficient evidence or whether they should withhold the case from an imaginary jury.

The following peculiar situation can therefore arise: the defence advocate submits no case; the magistrates rule that there is a case to answer; the defence advocate then announces that he will call no evidence; the magistrates retire and decide to dismiss the charge! It may look like two inconsistent decisions, but the magistrates have acted properly in law. The first decision expressed not their opinion on the proper outcome of the case but a legal judgment.

There is, however, an important distinction between the powers of magistrates and those of the trial judge in the Crown Court. By a Practice Direction of 1962,[14] a submission in a magistrates' court that there is no case to answer may properly be upheld: (*a*) when there has been no evidence to prove an essential element in the alleged offence, or (*b*) when the evidence adduced by the prosecution has been discredited as a result of cross-examination or is so manifestly unreliable that no reasonable tribunal could safely act on it. Apart from these two situations "the decision should depend on whether the evidence is such that a reasonable tribunal might convict." This last is the same test as the Divisional Court uses on appeal from magistrates, so here the first- and second-stage controls coalesce, as they do not in jury trials. No satisfactory explanation has been given of the reason for the discrepancy,[15] but it probably is that at the time of the Practice Direction the law for jury trials was thought to be otherwise than it is now settled to be.

So what it comes to is that on a trial on indictment the prosecution must give enough evidence to take the case to the jury, and also give the possibly greater amount of evidence necessary to convince the jury?

Quite. These two burdens are now frequently called the *evidential* and *persuasive* burdens respectively, or the *burden of production* and the *burden of persuasion*.

The distinction has only gradually made its way into legal thinking, and various expressions are used to denote it. English judges sometimes speak of the persuasive burden as the "ultimate" burden or "legal" burden or burden "at the end of the day," while the evidential

---

[13] Pattenden, *op. cit.* at 565, says of this discretion that "the Court of Appeal has criticised its exercise on so many occasions . . . that it is difficult to envisage a case in which a trial judge would be justified in exercising the discretion." But she also gives as the reason for the objection a statement by Roskill LJ that "it is not proper for a judge to invite a jury to stop a case. If a judge has doubts whether the evidence is sufficiently strong to justify a verdict of guilty then it is his duty to stop the case. It is not his duty to shift that responsibility to the jury." This does not say what Pattenden appears to understand by it; it says the opposite.

[14] [1962] 1 WLR 227, 1 All ER 448. Cp. *Young* [1964] 1 WLR at 717, 48 CAR at 296.

[15] Archbold, 41st edn § 4–387 rationalises the rule by saying that magistrates, unlike trial judges, are judges of fact as well as of law; but this does not explain why the "right of silence" should be better protected in magistrates' courts than in the Crown Court. The editors add, darkly, that "in any event we know of no authority as to the issue of Practice Directions in criminal cases relating to questions of law as opposed to practice." This seems to imply an opinion that the Practice Direction has no effect upon the law; but the editors do not clearly state what they think the law is apart from the Direction.

burden is also called the "provisional" burden or "tactical" burden (both bad names[16]) or the "initial hurdle." However, the name "evidential burden" now has wide acceptance.[17]

Is there an evidential burden in respect of a question of law?

Burdens are in respect of facts; questions of law are decided by the judge, without any question of burden. But some questions, such as the question of reasonableness, are in an intermediate position. They are value-judgments marking the boundary between criminal and non-criminal conduct, and therefore are really decisions on law; yet they are made by the jury, except that there must be evidence that, in the view of the trial judge, would justify the jury in finding that there has been reasonableness or unreasonableness or whatever. For example, an allegation of negligence is not left to the jury unless there is evidence of negligence sufficient to support a conviction.

§ 2.3. RULES ASSISTING THE PROSECUTION

The prosecution's evidential burden is alleviated in two ways.

First, the judge can draw common-sense inferences from evidence; and some of these have hardened into propositions of law. An illustration is the presumption arising when a person is found in possession of goods that have recently been stolen. He may be indicted for theft or for handling stolen goods, or for both; and on proof that the goods had recently been stolen and that the defendant was found in possession of them, the prosecution are entitled to have the case left to the jury.[1]

Although this presumption assists the prosecution to have the case left to the jury, satisfying their evidential burden, it does not shift the persuasive burden, the burden of proof. The jury must still be told that the burden of proving the case so that they feel sure of guilt is on the prosecution. Therefore, if the defendant gives any explanation of his possession consistent with his honesty so that the jury are left in doubt, he is entitled to an acquittal.[2]

This is traditionally expressed by saying that the presumption is only a presumption of fact; it would better be called an *evidential presumption*, discharging the evidential burden. It is a rule for the judge, instructing him to leave the case to the jury, not a rule for the jury, directing them to find the defendant guilty. There is no occasion for the judge in directing the jury to refer to a "presumption" under that name, and it would be well for him not to do so, since an impromptu explanation of the meaning of a presumption is likely to muddle the jury

---

[16] "Provisional" is uninformative, and "tactical" misleading. Evidential burdens are imposed by law, not mere matters of tactics.

[17] The first judicial acceptance of the term appears to have been in *Gill* [1963] 1 WLR 841. Judges have sometimes made strange blunders in stating the theory of persuasive and evidential burdens. See 127 NLJ 156.

[1] See Griew, *The Theft Acts*, 4th edn 184. Hence the celebrated marginal note to the report of *Clement* (1830) 1 Lewin 113,168 ER 980: "Possession in Scotland evidence of stealing in England."

[2] *Schama* (1914) 11 CAR 45; *Aves* [1950] 2 All ER 330, 34 CAR 159; *Hepworth* [1955] 2 QB 600.

on the persuasive burden. The jury can be adequately instructed on common-sense inferences without referring to presumptions. Where the defendant has been found in possession of goods recently stolen, and gives a somewhat lame explanation ("I bought them from a man who said they fell off the back of a lorry"), the jury can be told that the burden of proof beyond reasonable doubt rests on the Crown; that they can use their common sense in drawing inferences from the whole of the evidence given, and can convict on the evidence of possession if no explanation is given; but must give the defendant the benefit of any reasonable doubt. Such a formula avoids the language of presumption, which would almost certainly conflict in the minds of the jury with what they have been told on the burden of proof.

Again, on a charge of rape or assault the burden is on the prosecution to adduce evidence that the complainant did not consent to the act.[3] But if the prosecution show that violence was used, this would be strong presumptive evidence of lack of consent, and the judge would certainly leave the issue of consent to the jury. On the rape charge the defendant may say that the woman was masochistic and liked to be physically forced; on the assault charge he may say that it was a friendly fight with mutual consent; the jury may or may not give sufficient credence to these defences to feel a doubt about the charge, but the question will be for them.

Another illustration relates to charges of careless driving (§ 14.2).

These are ways in which the prosecution's evidential burden can be discharged. But, secondly, there are certain respects in which the prosecution are wholly relieved of the evidential burden, which is imposed instead on the defendant. This raises the question of defences, a subject to which we now turn.

§ 2.4. DEFENCES

That a person does a forbidden act, even intentionally, does not mean that he is necessarily guilty of an offence. Various defences are recognised, quite apart from the defence of absence of the requisite mental element or degree of fault. Among the circumstances of justification or excuse are self-defence, public authority, and duress.

And alibi?

Yes and no. The word "defence" is used in two different senses, broad and narrow.

For the layman, in relation to argument, it means, *broadly*, anything that a person may urge to rebut a charge. Lawyers use the word in this way too. Yes, they speak of a defence of alibi; but an alibi is only a particular way of denying that the defendant did the act (he could not have done it, because he was elsewhere at the time). The defendant does not justify or excuse the alleged act, but denies that he did it.[1] Similarly a defence of accident, mistake or automatism usually denies that the defendant was at fault. Generally speaking, these defences do not introduce any further issue; they merely combat the allegations of the prosecution.

---

[3] *Donovan* [1934] 2 KB 498.

[1] The defendant does not bear any burden of proving an alibi: *Denney* [1963] Crim.LR 191. He must give notice of this defence, unless the court waives the requirement (CJA 1967 s.11). See Gooderson, *Alibi* (London 1977).

In the *narrow* (or, if you like, proper) sense a defence means a justification or excuse or one of certain technical points alleged by the defendant in order to avoid liability. It introduces a new issue into the trial.[2]

Some explanations please. You spoke of accident and mistake. What exactly is the difference?

An accident is an unintended or unforeseen consequence of conduct. Mistake means a false understanding. Although in itself it is a mental fact, it may have physical consequences, and may therefore cause an accident. As where a learner-driver presses the accelerator by mistake for the clutch.

And what is the difference between a justification and an excuse?

Very little. They are both defences in the full sense, leading to an acquittal. However, when the act is not justified but only excused it is still regarded as being in some tenuous way wrong, for certain collateral purposes. We shall come to this later (§ § 15.16, 23.1).

A little bit of history: the term "justification" was formerly used for cases where the aim of the law was not frustrated, while "excuse" was used for cases where it was not thought proper to punish. Killing a dangerous criminal who tried to avoid arrest was *justified*, since the law (if one may personify) wished this to happen, whereas killing in self-defence was merely *excused*. The distinction was important because justification was a defence to the criminal charge while an excuse was not, being merely the occasion for a royal pardon.[3] By the end of the middle ages (it is difficult to assign a fixed date) even excuses were recognised by the courts. After that it was frequently supposed that no occasion arose to distinguish between justification and excuse, but that is not entirely true. More of this anon. On the rare occasions when the point matters the courts would nowadays regard self-defence as a justification, not as a mere excuse.

I suppose the defendant bears the burden of proving defences in the proper sense?

Yes for some, but not all. He does not carry any burden of proof in respect of most of the common law defences, such as provocation (on a charge of murder), self-defence and duress. *Woolmington* and the cases following it show that the burden rests on the prosecution to negative these defences, not upon the defendant to prove them.[4] In common law matters the courts laudably adopt the attitude that although the defence has come from the defendant, what has to be decided is the single issue of guilt, the burden of proving which rests on the prosecution. Moreover, when such a defence is in issue, it is not enough for the judge to direct the jury in general terms that the charge must be proved so that they feel sure of guilt. "Where the issue of self-defence is raised, a specific direction should be

---

[2] For the proposition that the word "defence" should be taken to refer only to matters of procedure and evidence see § 6.8 at n. 6.

[3] Anglo-Saxon law did not clearly exempt those who inflicted harm by accident or in self-defence, or when of unsound mind, though these facts went in mitigation of the penalty, or, after the Conquest, were grounds for the exercise of the prerogative of mercy. Later, the courts took it upon themselves to accord a defence in these cases. Sporadic instances of acquittal for insanity in medieval times are recorded by N D Hurnard, *The King's Pardon for Homicide before AD 1307* (Oxford 1969) 166. The modern practice of acquitting on this account appears to date from 1505: Nigel Walker, *Crime and Insanity in England* (London 1968) i 25–26; below § 23.1.

[4] For self-defence see *Julien* [1969] 1 WLR 839, 2 All ER 856, 53 CAR 407.

given on the law of self-defence and on the burden of proof on the prosecution."[5]

How does the defendant raise a defence?

He is not required to put it in a formal written pleading. Even if the matter is a defence in the strict (narrow) sense of that word, he puts it in issue merely by adducing evidence upon it.[6]

The evidential burden in respect of defences (in the strict sense) rests on the defendant. For example, it is not enough for defence counsel to argue that the defendant may have been acting in self-defence, or under provocation, if he has not adduced some minimum of evidence to support the argument. The judge is not required to direct the jury on such a defence unless there is "*prima facie* evidence" or a "proper foundation in the evidence" for it.[7] In such cases:

> "though questions whether evidence should or should not be accepted or as to the weight to be attached to it are for the determination of the jury, it is a province of the judge to rule whether a theory or a submission has the support of evidence so that it can properly be passed to the jury for their consideration. . . . It is not every facile mouthing of some easy phrase of excuse that can amount to an explanation. It is for a judge to decide whether there is evidence fit to be left to a jury which could be the basis for some suggested verdict."[8]

Some judges have lately fallen into the habit of declaring that when a defence (such as self-defence or the prevention of crime) involves the question whether the defendant acted reasonably, "what is reasonable in the circumstances is always a question for the jury, never a point of law for the trial judge."[9] In terms of the traditional understanding of the law this is a misleadingly hyperbolic way of expressing the position. It is true that the question of reasonableness is for the jury, but only in relation to provocation (by statute[10]) is it *entirely* one for the jury. For all other defences the rule is subject to the important proviso that the judge is entitled to decide whether there is any evidence of reasonable conduct for the jury's consideration. Could any reasonable jury find in favour of the defendant on the evidence?

How can one tell what evidential burdens lie on the prosecution and what on the defence?

Basically (and with exceptions) the distinction is between elements relating to the core of the offence and elements relating to an exception from liability or other defence. We may call these the prosecution (or definitional) elements and the defence elements respectively. There are difficulties in the distinction, but some distinction has to be made in distributing evidential burdens between the prosecution and the defence.

---

[5] *Owen* [1964] Crim.LR 831; *Cameron* [1973] Crim.LR 520; *Folley* [1978] Crim.LR 556. For a suggested form of summing up see *Abraham* [1973] 1 WLR at 1273–1274, 3 All ER at 696.

[6] Therefore one should not, strictly, speak of a defendant to a criminal charge "pleading" insanity, self-defence etc., though this loose language is often used for convenience, even by judges. The strictly correct phrase is that the defendant "adduced evidence of" the facts constituting the defence, or "raised" the defence.

[7] *Bratty* [1963] AC at 413–414; cp. *Hill* v. *Baxter* [1958] 1 QBD at 284.

[8] *Per* Lord Morris in *Bratty* at 416–417.

[9] See § 22.6 n. 18.

[10] § 24.3.

In assault, for example, the basis of the offence is that the defendant went up to the victim and punched him on the nose?

Yes; the charge of assault implies an intentional or reckless attack, and both the evidential and the persuasive burden of this is on the prosecution. Distinguish the defence of self-defence, where the evidential burden rests on the defendant.

Well then, the defendant bears the burden of proof of defences.

Not necessarily. He generally bears the evidential burden, that is all.

What is the difference between evidence and proof? Surely evidence is proof.

Evidence becomes proof only when the jury accept it as being sufficient for proof. When the defendant bears an evidential burden of a defence, he must adduce (or anyway there must be) enough evidence in favour of the defence to persuade the judge to leave it to the jury; but the judge must still direct the jury to acquit unless they are sure that the defence is *not* established.[11] (See § .5 as to persuasive burdens on the defence.)

What's the point of putting an evidential burden on the defendant?

Whether the defendant bears an evidential burden or not, he is obviously going to adduce all the evidence he can on the issue. For this reason, the question whether he bears an evidential burden does not often arise. The point is that the judge may withdraw a merely fanciful defence from the jury, thus simplifying their task, and preventing the jury from accepting a defence where the defendant has made no sufficient efforts to back it up.[12] But even if the judge can withdraw the defence from the jury, it is rare in practice for him to do so, because he is not sure of himself and is aware of the risk that if the Court of Appeal thinks he was wrong a conviction will be quashed.

The more important result of placing an evidential burden on the defence is to prevent the defendant submitting no case if the prosecution have led no evidence on that issue. The task of the prosecution is therefore simplified. (The same result is, as we have seen, sometimes achieved by creating a presumption of fact in favour of the prosecution, an evidential presumption, without imposing an evidential burden on the defendant.)

Let us revert to the example where the prosecution on a charge of assault give evidence that the defendant hit the victim. Suppose that at the close of the prosecution case the defending advocate rises and addresses the court thus: "An assault in law is not committed by a blow struck in lawful self-defence. The prosecution have given no evidence to negative the possibility that this blow was struck in self-defence. For all we know it was; therefore they have not given evidence of an assault in law, and there is no

---

[11] Do not speak of an "evidential burden of proof" resting on the defendant. An evidential burden is not a burden of proof. See *Jayasena* [1970] AC at 624.

[12] *Critchley* [1982] Crim.LR 524.

case for the defendant to answer." The judge (or magistrates) will overrule this submission, because although the premises are correct the submission overlooks the rule that the evidential burden of self-defence is on the defendant. If the defendant is going to raise a particular defence seriously he must have some evidence of it, and that evidence should be given. It is not enough for his counsel to make up a tale.

But can't the defendant tell the tale instead of his counsel?

The defendant can give evidence to support his defence in the witness-box. The point is that what his counsel says in argument is not evidence.

And counsel can't say: "My client says so-and-so"?

Certainly not. The evidence must be given on oath (or affirmation), by the defendant or other witness.

Do the jury have to believe the defendant merely because he says something?

They are not bound to believe him. But if the defendant testifies, that is evidence on which the jury should act if they think it sufficient to raise a reasonable doubt in his favour.

And when the defendant gives evidence he can be cross-examined and perhaps tripped up?

Yes.

Aren't you forcing the defendant to convict himself? The poor chap is caught either way. If he gives no evidence his defence won't be left to the jury; if he does he can be shown up as a liar.

Putting the evidential burden on the defence does not necessarily mean that the defendant must give evidence. He may *adduce* evidence, by calling other witnesses to give evidence on his behalf. Or he may get the evidence before the court by extracting admissions from the prosecution witnesses under cross-examination.[13]

But if the prosecution witnesses deny it flatly, and the defendant has no other witnesses, he will have to give evidence.

In effect yes, but I think you are pushing your sympathy for the defendant to an extreme. If he cannot produce any evidence to support his defence, not even his own word, it is too bad for him. But if his tale is a plausible one and he stands up to cross-examination the jury are likely to give him the benefit of the doubt. I do not share the anxiety felt by some to protect a defendant from having to give evidence.

The test whether the evidence is sufficient is similar to that already stated in respect of prosecution evidence (§ .2): is there before the court evidence that, if believed, and on the

---

[13] It is sometimes said that when the prosecution witnesses supply evidence relating to a matter of defence, such as self-defence, no evidential burden in that respect rests on the defendant. Whether one puts it this way or says that there is an evidential burden that is discharged is purely verbal.

most favourable view,[14] could be taken by a reasonable jury to support the defence of provocation,[15] self-defence,[16] duress,[17] "reasonable excuse" under statute,[18] "or whatever it may be"? The duty of the judge is to assume that the defendant's evidence, in so far as it can be reconciled with the unchallenged evidence in the case, is substantially true, and to ask himself whether it discloses some material suggesting a valid defence.

There is, however, this important difference between the position of the prosecution and that of the defence, namely that the persuasive burden generally rests on the prosecution. All that the defendant has to do is to bring before the court that small modicum of evidence that might be taken by a reasonable jury to raise a reasonable doubt as to his guilt. In practice, the judge will never withdraw a defence from the jury if the defendant has himself given evidence in support of it, however unconvincing his evidence may appear.[19] It would almost seem as though the unavowed purpose of the law when it casts an evidential burden on the defendant is to put pressure on him to enter the witness box and submit himself to cross-examination. The only occasion on which the trial judge is likely to require more than the defendant's own evidence is when a medical question is involved, as when the defendant sets up a defence of automatism (Chap. 29). Here, he must generally call a medical witness.

If the defendant fails to support his defence to the extent just indicated, the judge may omit to mention the issue in his summing-up to the jury[20]; indeed, he may positively direct the jury that there is no evidence on the issue for their consideration.[21] Contrariwise, if the defence is clearly proved the judge can (and should) withdraw the case from the jury.[22]

In short, the rule imposing an evidential burden is applied by the judge, in deciding whether to leave an issue (the general issue or some specific question) to the jury. The rule imposing the persuasive burden is for application by the jury. Putting this in another way, the evidential burden governs what the judge *does*, in leaving the question to the jury or withdrawing it from them; the persuasive burden governs what he *says*, in directing the jury how they are to reach their verdict.

Suppose the defendant does not argue a particular defence, or mention it by name (e.g.self-defence), but there is evidence of it before the court?

If there is evidence to support a defence the judge should leave it to the jury even though the defendant has not argued it. Lord Morris:

> "It is always the duty of the judge to leave to the jury any issue (whether raised by the defence or not) which on the evidence in the case is an issue fit to be left to them."[23]

---

[14] The expression used by Viscount Simon in *Holmes* [1946] AC at 588. Cp. *Lee Chun-Chuen* [1963] AC 220.

[15] *Mancini* [1942] AC 1; *Hodges* [1962] Crim.LR 385.

[16] *Lobell* [1957] 1 QB 547; *Abraham* [1973] 1 WLR 1270, 3 All ER 694, 57 CAR 799; *Walker* [1974] 1 WLR 1090 (judge need not leave self-defence to jury if only evidence shows that it was unnecessary for defendant to act in self-defence); *Bonnick* (1977) 66 CAR 266; *Critchley* n. 12 above. See generally Chap. 23.

[17] *Gill* [1963] 1 WLR 841, 2 All ER 688, 47 CAR 166. See generally Chap. 27.

[18] See *John* [1974] 1 WLR 624, 2 All ER 561, where, under cover of the rule, the CA limited the kinds of excuse that could be taken to be reasonable (religious belief not a reasonable excuse for failing to provide a specimen under the blood-alcohol legislation). Cp. [1976] Crim.LR 482, 539. Normally a judge must hear the evidence for the defence before ruling on a defence (*Brown* [1974] RTR 377, Crim.LR 670), but perhaps that is not so where the defence of reasonable excuse raised by cross-examining the prosecution witnesses is incapable of being regarded as reasonable. See also *Leer* [1982] Crim.LR 310. See also § 23.3 at n. 10.

[19] This generalisation applies to questions of fact in the narrow sense, but not to matters of value-judgment like the issue of "reasonable excuse," where the courts exercise a considerable measure of control.

[20] *Mancini* [1942] AC at 12; *Walker* [1974] 1 WLR 1090; and see the cases on "reasonable excuse" (n. 18 above).

[21] *Bonnick*, n. 16 above.

[22] § 23.1 n. 9.

[23] *Palmer* [1971] AC at 823. Cp. *Walker* [1974] 1 WLR 1090.

The rule is particularly important where the defendant cannot raise the defence because it would be inconsistent with another defence (such as alibi): § 22.13).

§ 2.5. BURDENS OF PROOF ON THE DEFENCE

Harking back again to *Woolmington* (§ .1), it will be remembered that Viscount Sankey said that "it is the duty of the prosecution to prove the prisoner's guilt, subject to the defence of insanity and subject also to any statutory exception." This remark, which has been judicially approved on a number of occasions, makes no exception for presumptions. In civil matters there are certain rebuttable presumptions of law which place the persuasive burden on the other side, but it seems that in criminal cases they do not operate in favour of the prosecution, but merely discharge the prosecution's evidential burden. "The accused does not need to establish, in the generality of cases, any defence or fact in order to secure an acquittal."[1]

The defence of insanity will be dealt with in Chapter 28. Many statutes shift the persuasive burden. It has become almost a matter of routine for Parliament, in respect of the most trivial offences as well as some serious ones, to enact that the onus of proving a particular fact shall rest on the defendant, so that he can be convicted "unless he proves" it.[2] This type of provision is used particularly in respect of circumstances of excuse, such as the possession of a licence, and of mental states such as the absence of knowledge.

An example is provided by the Prevention of Corruption Act 1916 s.2.

> "Where . . . it is proved[3] that any money, gift or other consideration has been paid or given to or received by a person in the employment of His Majesty . . . by or from a person, or agent of a person, holding or seeking to obtain a contract from His Majesty . . . the . . . consideration shall be deemed to have been paid or given or received corruptly . . . unless the contrary is proved."

Suppose that the director of a company that has a contract to supply red tape to a Government Department is friendly with a civil servant and pays him a sum of money. He is prosecuted for corruption, and gives evidence that he paid the money in discharge of a debt, thereby leading the jury to doubt whether the payment had been made "corruptly." If the burden of proving this lay on the prosecution, as in the absence of express statutory provision it would, the jury should acquit. But since it is here for the defendant to prove that the payment was *not* made corruptly, the judge must direct the jury to convict if the evidence leaves them in doubt on the point.[4]

---

[1] *Sparrow* (1962) 46 CAR at 289.

[2] Another formula is: "it shall be a defence to prove. . . ." See *Thurrock District Council* v. *Pinch Ltd.* [1974] RTR 269, Crim.LR 425.

[3] These words are inept. If the defendant submits no case, on the ground that the consideration has not been proved to have been given corruptly, the judge is evidently intended to apply the section; yet before verdict nothing has been "proved"—only evidence has been given.

[4] *Evans-Jones* (1923) 87 JP 115, 17 CAR 121.

When a statute shifts the burden of proof, must the defendant prove the issue beyond reasonable doubt?

No: the courts alleviate his position by holding that he need only discharge the civil burden, establishing his case on a balance of probability.[5]

Do you mean possibility?

If you like, but the meaning would be the same either way.

The defendant has only to show that it could have been so?

No: that it was so on a balance of probability, or "on the preponderance of evidence"—that is, that the odds in his favour are better than evens.[6]

How do you work out the odds?

These things cannot be estimated with any nicety. All that one can do is to give the general instruction to the jury: is it more likely than not that the defence is true?

Why do statutes shift the burden of proof?

The answer, in part, is that it is the result of confused thinking in relation to the common law.

During the 19th century, and for a good time afterwards, the distinction between the persuasive and evidential burdens was not perceived; so it came to be held, as a rule of the common law, that when a matter was particularly within the knowledge of the defendant, the "burden of proof" was on him. This would have been a reasonable proposition if it had referred only to the evidential burden; but why, because the matter was peculiarly within the knowledge of the defendant, should he be deprived of the benefit of the doubt?

A contributory factor in forming the law was that many judges came to the criminal courts with their minds influenced by the civil law, which they assumed applied equally to criminal cases. They therefore held that the burden of proving any exception from liability fell on the defendant (which was the civil rule). These judges did not appreciate that the important difference between the criminal and civil law is that the civil law does not set out to punish, as the criminal law basically does.[7]

Anyway, this attitude of the judges influenced the legislature, and it is reflected particularly in legislation now represented by the Magistrates' Courts Act 1981, which places on the defendant in a magistrates' court the burden of proving all matter of exception, excuse or qualification.[8] On its face this would put the burden on the defendant in respect of common law defences like self-defence, but magistrates' courts assume that it applies only to exceptions to statutory offences and not to the traditional defences in criminal law.

Woolmington was a recognition of the principle that a criminal defendant should receive the

---

[5] *Carr-Briant* [1943] KB 607; *Morton* v. *Confer* [1963] 1 WLR 763, 2 All ER 765.
[6] *Public Prosecutor* v. *Yuvaraj* [1970] AC at 922.
[7] See George P Fletcher, *Rethinking Criminal Law* (Boston 1978) 524–532.
[8] See 2 Leg. Stud. 236.

benefit of the "presumption of innocence." As we have seen, the courts accept the logical consequence that in common law matters this applies to the whole issue of guilt. Unfortunately, our legislative masters (meaning, in reality, parliamentary counsel and the bureaucrats in Government Departments) continue in their bad old way, probably because they are not satisfied that merely placing an evidential burden on the defence will prevent a jury, or even magistrates, from swallowing a meretricious and meritless defence too easily. But surely it unjust for the judge to have to say in effect to the jury: "You have heard evidence on this from both sides, and if in the end you are left in a fog and don't know what to think you must convict the defendant, because English law presumes him to be guilty in respect of this issue unless he shows himself to be innocent."

The older attitude has also been preserved by some judges, who, blindly devoted to precedent, have continued to hold that the defendant, even in the Crown Court, must prove that he falls within any exception from the statutory offence on which he relies, even though the statute is silent on the burden of proof. For example, on a charge of selling liquor without a licence it is for the defendant to prove that he had a licence.[9] This rule, said the Court of Appeal in the leading case, *Edwards*,[10]

> "is limited to offences arising under enactments which prohibit the doing of an act save in specified circumstances or by persons of specified classes or with special qualifications or with the licence or permission of specified authorities."[11]

The "limitation" is so broadly worded that it may seem at first sight to be no limitation at all. But it means, for example, that where a statute penalises the doing of something without reasonable excuse, or lawful excuse, the burden of disproving the excuse rests on the prosecution, since the case does not fall within any of the excepted categories.[12] Also, the rule in *Edwards* does not apply to offences created by the judges. Whether there is any rhyme or reason in these complexities is a question.

So in effect the courts have added a third exception at common law to the two exceptions stated in Woolmington?

Yes.[13] That there were only two exceptions had been taken for granted in a number of cases since *Woolmington*, for example *Mancini*,[14] where Viscount Simon said:

> "The rule [in *Woolmington*] is of general application. . . . The only exceptions arise, as explained in *Woolmington's* case, in the defences of insanity and in offences where onus of proof is specially dealt with by statute."

It cannot plausibly be said that the onus of proof is "specially dealt with by statute" where a statute merely enacts a licensing provision. Moreover, *Edwards* is inconsistent with authority in respect of acts prohibited "save in specified circumstances," for sexual intercourse is prohibited (as rape) save in the "specified circumstances" of the woman's consent, yet the burden of disproving these circumstances rests on the prosecution.

An argument against shifting the burden of proof deserving more attention than it has received relates to the simplicity of the trial. If the evidential burden is placed on the

---

[9] *Edwards* [1975] QB 27.

[10] *Ibid.*. at 40. For criticisms see 2 Leg. Stud. 236–238; 126 NLJ 1032.

[11] This formula does not include a fault element. For example, the defence of belief in right under the Criminal Damage Act (§ 41.6) relates to the mental element required for the crime, and the burden of proving the issue clearly rests on the prosecution.

[12] Only an evidential burden rests on the defendant: *Cousins* [1982] QB 526. Cp. § .4 n. 18.

[13] And they have since added a fourth: the burden of proving a defence of previous acquittal or conviction rests on the defendant: *Martin Coughlan* [1976] Crim.LR 631; *Iremonger* v. *Vissenga, ibid.* 524.

[14] [1942] AC at 11.

defendant, the judge need not (and should not) direct the jury upon it; he himself decides whether the evidence is sufficient to take the defence to the jury, and if it is he merely directs the jury in the ordinary way that the burden of proof rests on the prosecution. But when the persuasive burden is on the defendant the judge has to direct the jury that on certain issues the prosecution must prove the case beyond reasonable doubt, while on one particular issue the defendant must prove his defence on a balance of probability. This is a difficult intellectual task for the ordinary jury.

The Criminal Law Revision Committee in its Evidence Report[15] proposed that a statute should be passed putting the persuasive burden on the prosecution on all issues, except where subsequent legislation makes it clear that a persuasive burden is to rest on the defendant, and except also in cases where a statutory defence depends upon the defendant successfully throwing the blame on a third person. The Committee said:

> "We are strongly of the opinion that, both on principle and for the sake of clarity and convenience in practice, burdens on the defence should be evidential only."

§ 2.6. LAW AND FACT

The basic rule is that in the Crown Court the jury are the "tribunal of fact." It is for the judge to direct the jury on the relevant law,[1] always remembering the principle stated by Diplock LJ (as he then was):

> "The function of a summing-up is not to give the jury a general dissertation upon some aspect of the criminal law, but to tell them what are the issues of fact on which they must make up their minds in order to determine whether the accused is guilty of a particular offence."[2]

The jury find the facts and apply the law to the facts by returning a verdict of guilty or not guilty; so they decide the case as a whole. The judge may review the facts and even suggest how the jury may find or regard them, so long as he says that the decision on the facts is for them.

So it is for the judge to interpret legislation and explain it to the jury?

The judge applies the principles of interpretation to the legislation in question, advises the jury which meaning is to be adopted in case of ambiguity, and advises them also as to the meaning of technical legal words. For example, if the judge thinks that the statute impliedly requires *mens rea* he tells the jury that they cannot convict unless *mens rea* was present. (Not that he is likely to use the Latin phrase.)

How do we know that the jury understand the judge's instruction on the law?

We don't. Authority has sternly set its face against any attempt, in

---

[15] Cmnd. 4991 of 1972, paras. 137–142.

[1] The judge may, even in advance of the trial, decide (on a motion to quash the indictment) whether the alleged offence exists in law, and for this purpose decide any relevant facts: *Goldstein* [1982] 1 WLR 804.

[2] *Mowatt* [1968] 1 QB at 426. The judge need not explain the whole of a section, for instance, if only part is relevant: *Alford* v. *Magee* (1952) 85 CLR at 466 (Aus.). It is not customary to give the jury copies of the statute, because they should accept its meaning as explained by the judge. Cp. *Tennant* (1975) 31 CRNS 1, 23 CCC (2d) 82 (Ont.).

Britain, to investigate how well the jury perform their allotted task. (To try to do so can even be a criminal contempt of court.[3]) It seems reasonable to assume that the jury make many mistakes. A law student is selected for above-average intelligence, and spends a considerable time studying the basic concepts of the criminal law under the guidance of a teacher. A judge is expected to convey the same information to a randomly selected jury, who, if they are to do their work properly, must not only understand the concepts but apply them to an intricate web of evidence.

This suggests that the criminal law should be made as simple as possible. But it is better to have good rules, even though they are rather difficult for the jury to understand, than to have rules that have no other merit than simplicity of statement. There is at least the hope that the good rules will, for the most part, be properly applied.

Where the facts are quite clear, can't the judge tell the jury so?

He may make the jury aware what his opinion is.

In *DPP* v. *Smith*,[4] a policeman clung to the defendant's car, trying to stop him, but the defendant drove on and the policeman fell off and was killed. The defendant said in evidence that he did not know the policeman was on the bonnet, and the trial judge directed the jury as follows.

> "There is a limit, is there not, members of the jury, to human credulity, and you may think that the accused man's unsupported assertion on this part of the case goes well past it, that the evidence is overwhelming, and he knew his car was carrying the officer up the road? The matter is one for you, but if you arrive at the conclusion that, of course, he knew, it is one which I would regard as abundantly right. Indeed, on the evidence I do not see how you could properly arrive at any other conclusion. If that be so the defence of pure accident goes."

When the case came before the House of Lords Viscount Kilmuir LC commented that the judge's remarks were fully justified.

Normally, the judge would not direct the jury so strongly as this, and, except where the facts are not in dispute,[5] he must never direct the jury to convict.

Can the judge say to the jury: I direct you that the law is such and such, so if you find the facts to be such and such, then you must convict?

Certainly, if the judge is merely telling the jury that they must take the law from him.

Apart from the judge's power to withdraw an issue from the jury, the only questions of fact decided by him in criminal cases are:

- questions of fact relating to the admissibility of evidence (e.g. whether a witness qualifies as an expert; and whether a confession was induced by promises, threats or oppression, in which case the jury are generally not allowed to hear evidence of it), and
- questions of fact in relation to sentence. While the jury are listening to the evidence for the purpose of convicting or acquitting, the judge is listening to it for the purpose of sentence in the event of conviction, and he may hear further evidence for this purpose after conviction. In sentencing, the judge acts on his own view of the facts.[6] If he wishes, he may

---

[3] Contempt of Court Act 1981 s.8.

[4] [1961] AC 290 at 324. Cp. Lord Devlin in *Chandler* [1964] AC at 803–804.

[5] As to which see n. 11 below.

[6] *Whittle* (1974), *Current Sentencing Practice* (ed. David Thomas) L2.1 (*b*). This is subject to the important qualification that the judge must not assume the defendant's guilt of an offence for which he has not been convicted, and in particular must honour an acquittal on another count: see § 1.3 at nn. 7–10.

ask the foreman of the jury whether the verdict was based on one view of the facts or another;[7] and if the judge does this he must accept the opinion expressed by the jury.

What is the line between fact and law? If the law refers to a "building," who decides whether a caravan is a building, judge or jury?

You may be surprised to know that the general answer is: the jury.

Lawyers inveterately assume that questions of fact (and only questions of fact) are for the jury, but this involves giving a wide meaning to the phrase "questions of fact." Four types may be distinguished, and it is convenient to give them names.[8]

1 *Questions of primary fact.* Primary facts depend chiefly on whether a witness is to be believed in reporting what he did or perceived or mentally experienced (did he see black marks on the road?).
2 *Questions of inferential fact.* These concern the proper factual (non-verbal) inference to be drawn from the primary facts (were the marks caused by the defendant braking hard?).
3 *Questions of evaluative fact.* These principally concern the legal assessment of the facts as reasonable or negligent (if the defendant had to brake hard, does that mean that he was driving too fast, and therefore negligently?). All value-judgments relating to matters of reasonableness, such as "reasonable excuse" under statute, or whether a person who made an arrest had "reasonable cause to suspect an offence," are left to the jury, provided that there is sufficient evidence to support a positive finding. They are not really questions of fact, but the equation of jury questions and questions of fact means that they have to be pushed into this category.[9]
4 *Questions of denotative[10] fact.* These concern the application of ordinary (non-legal) words used in legal rules—subject to the observations that follow. To take your example, is a caravan a building?

In general, all four questions of fact (primary, inferential, evaluative and denotative fact) are for the jury. But:

1 The judge need not leave to the jury a question of fact that is not in dispute[11] (though he will generally do so, for safety's sake). This proposition does not apply where, although the brute facts are agreed, it is disputed whether they fall within a particular legal classification which has to be adjudicated by the jury.

The fact that both sides agree that they are talking about a caravan

---

[7] See § 30.2.

[8] The following account is based on an article in [1976] Crim.LR 472, 532. See also D W Elliot in [1976] Crim.LR 707.

[9] See § 6.11.

[10] In formal logic, denotation refers to the aggregate of objects of which a word maybe predicated, while connotation means the qualities that define the word.

[11] *Goldstein* [1982] 1 WLR 804; [1976] Crim.LR 474–475. "Where facts are proved and accepted, then whether those facts amount to a crime or not must be a question of law, not of fact:" *Larkin* [1943] 1 All ER at 219H. But even though the evidence is all one way, a fact will be regarded as disputed if the defendant or his counsel has invited the jury to disbelieve the evidence: *Leer* [1982] Crim.LR 310. See also, as to causation, § 16.3.

and not a summer-house still leaves the jury to decide whether a caravan is a building. Another example is where it is disputed whether admitted acts went so far beyond mere preparation for the commission of the crime as to amount to a criminal attempt,[12] or whether admitted harm amounts to grievous bodily harm. Here the issue must be left to the jury.

2 The judge may withdraw an issue from the jury if there is no sufficient evidence to support a finding on it, as already explained. A conspicuous example is the defence of "reasonable excuse" under statute, which judges are disposed to control quite tightly.[13]
3 An appellate court may quash a conviction if the verdict is unsafe or unsatisfactory, whatever type of question of fact is involved (below § .7).

I still don't really see how you distinguish questions of law from questions of fact. Take the question whether D committed a burglary. That can involve both law and fact.

Whether D surreptitiously entered, say, a caravan while its normal inhabitants were away and stole something in it is a question of fact. Whether one can commit burglary in a caravan is a question of law, and the law answers it in the affirmative, provided that the caravan is inhabited. (Burglary can be committed in "an inhabited vehicle or vessel."[14]).

Although this distinction is clear, trouble can arise in applying the words of the law to facts. All words are to some extent imprecise, in the sense that difficulties can arise in applying them, and some words are very imprecise. A typical example is the question whether a particular injury amounts to "grievous bodily harm." Although this is a somewhat antiquated legal phrase, it merely means serious (or, some say, really serious) injury. Apart from that it has no specifically legal meaning. It involves a question of degree, and its application is chiefly one for the tribunal of fact. Similarly, the question whether a person is "driving" a car, within the meaning of a statute, is left to the jury. It is what we are calling a denotative fact. Philosophically speaking, of course, word-meanings are distinguished from questions of fact.

The jury wouldn't be allowed to find that a scratch was grievous bodily harm?

If that were the only evidence, the judge would not leave the case to the jury.

I can see that the jury must be left, within broad limits, to decide whether an injury is grievous bodily harm, because otherwise there would be nothing for them to decide. It is a question of degree, to be settled by a gut reaction. But whether a person can be said to be driving a car is different. It can depend on the shade of meaning you give to the word. Are you driving if you are being towed?

And is a passenger driving if he grabs the wheel in an emergency, when the driver has passed out? Or is a man driving if he releases the brake and

---

12 See § 17.5 at n. 21.
13 Above § .4 n. 18.
14 Theft Act 1968 s.9(3).

lets the car coast downhill? Or if someone else is pushing the car and he walks beside it, controlling the steering through the open window? These questions are left to the jury, though the judge may advise the jury of what he thinks.[15]

But surely the judge ought not to leave the meaning of the words of the law to be decided by vox pop? One jury may jump one way, another another.

For hundreds of years judges took the view that it was part of their function to define words in statutes for the benefit of juries, thus creating a "judicial dictionary" of words commonly used for legal purposes. Then, suddenly, the House of Lords announced a new rule: the meaning of "ordinary" words is a question of fact for the jury. Although the judge may instruct the jury on the meaning of terms of legal art, he is not supposed to lay down law on the meaning of ordinary words: *Cozens* v. *Brutus*.[16] (This was an appeal from magistrates on a case stated, but the decision was intended to apply equally to findings by juries.)

> The decision concerned the meaning of the word "insulting" in a statute making it a summary offence to use threatening, abusive or insulting words or language in a public place whereby a breach of the peace is likely (§ 9.9 at n. 19). Brutus was one of some demonstrators who invaded a tennis court when a match was in progress, by way of protest against the presence of a South African player. The magistrates held that his act was not insulting; the Divisional Court reversed, offering an obviously wrong definition of the word; then the House of Lords, disagreeing with the Divisional Court's definition, restored the decision of the magistrates—not because all of their lordships necessarily thought that the act was not insulting (though they probably thought it was not), but because they thought the question was for the magistrates. The opinions of the House make it plain that the same rule would apply where the application of the statute has to be made by a jury.

So the jury look the word up in a dictionary?

They have no dictionary. They can use only the information they get in open court or what they have in their own heads.

Can't they ask the judge for a dictionary?

They are unlikely to be given one. Dictionaries cannot define the word in its particular context, or pay attention to the questions of policy involved.

---

[15] For the chaos resulting from the absence of a legal definition of "driving" see Wasik in 145 JPN 247.

[16] [1973] AC 854. But see Rupert Cross, *Statutory Interpretation* (London 1976) 53–55, pointing out that the ordinary meaning of a word is not a question of fact in the usual sense, because evidence cannot be given upon it.

The statute may contain a definition of a word it uses, in which case the judge must explain the statutory definition to the jury, who are then left to apply it. In *Wheatley* [1979] 1 WLR 144, 1 All ER 954, 68 CAR 287, the judge was held to be entitled, in view of the statutory definition, to direct the jury in effect that the defendant had no defence. Presumably this was because the application of the statutory definition to the facts was not in dispute (above n. 11). *Wheatley* also illustrates the point that the definition need not be in the statute creating the offence; it may be in another statute dealing with the same general subject-matter (*in pari materia*), where the two statutes can be regarded as part of a legislative scheme. Further, Lord Reid in *Brutus* v. *Cozens* (at p. 861C) said that "if the context shows that a word is used in an unusual sense the court will determine in other words what that usual [unusual?] sense is."

The jury may go back into court, and the foreman may ask for further guidance on the meaning of the word, and then perhaps the judge may read out the relevant entry in the dictionary to them, with an appropriate explanation. Or the judge may just tell the jury to go back and use their common sense.

Lord Reid, who gave the fullest reasons for the decision in *Cozens* v. *Brutus*, said that a dictionary would define "insulting" by giving synonyms; but, he said, "few words have exact synonyms." The alternative would be for the court to frame a definition, "but the purpose of a definition is to limit or modify the ordinary meaning of a word and the court is not entitled to do that."

This remark does not carry conviction. The object of the court's definition may be not to modify the ordinary meaning but to state it. As a definition of "insulting" in ordinary speech I offer the following: language or conduct is not said to be insulting unless it is intended to show contempt or disesteem, or is understood by the hearer or observer to show this attitude. This was probably the meaning of the word that the magistrates had in mind, and they were right in holding that the defendant did not intend to insult the spectators of the game, even though his conduct was no doubt offensive to them. (Neither the magistrates nor the Law Lords seem to have considered the possibility that the demo was insulting to the South African player.)

The scope of the decision of the House of Lords is not entirely clear. Lord Reid said that if the context of the statute shows that the word is used in an unusual sense, the court will determine in other words what that unusual sense is. (He did not explain why the court could determine the unusual sense of words in a statute but not the usual sense.) Conceivably a judge might say that the usual sense of driving a car is driving it under its own power, but that the policy of, say, the drink-drive offence is to forbid people who are under the influence to have control of a vehicle while it is in motion, so that for this purpose the word has a wider meaning; and the judge might then, on Lord Reid's principle, instruct the jury in this wider meaning. But this still would not allow the judge to instruct the jury dogmatically on the ordinary meaning of an ordinary word like "insulting."

Suppose that this offence of insulting words were triable by jury, and the jury decided that a demo on a tennis court was insulting although the evidence was clear that it was not intended to express and was not understood to express any disrespect for anyone present, but was merely an offensive way of publicising political opinions. Would the conviction be set aside on appeal?

It might be. Lord Reid said that "the question would normally be whether the decision was unreasonable in the sense that no tribunal acquainted with the ordinary use of language could reasonably reach that decision." He was here presumably speaking of an appeal on law from magistrates. The formula he used does not apply to appeals from juries, where the question is whether the verdict is unsafe or unsatisfactory (§ .7)—though that probably gives the appellate court more control than the other.

I have been saving up a supplementary for you. If the verdict would be upset as being unsafe, wouldn't it be more sensible for the trial judge to warn the jury how they are to interpret the word, so as to save all the trouble of a wrong conviction and an appeal?

That seems common sense. But it is uncertain how far the Lords would go in saying that the question is wholly for the jury and is not subject to appellate control.

The main objection to the rule in *Cozens* v. *Brutus* is that an appeal to common sense and to the jury's knowledge of the English language is an over-estimation of the jury's abilities, and also shows a misunderstanding of the function of language and a lack of appreciation of the peculiar difficulty of interpreting the law. As to the first point, there is no educational qualification for juries; disgracefully, people are allowed to act on them without enquiry on whether they can read. No one even gives them a test to see whether they can understand spoken English.

It is true that anyone who knows English knows how to use common words. Whether words are used "properly" or not does not matter so long as information is conveyed. But to ask the jury to decide whether the words of a statute apply to a given situation is to set them a task to which they are wholly unaccustomed. Success in it depends not merely upon an ability to use the words correctly but upon a consideration of the context in which the particular words appear, the general policy of the statute, and the practical result of giving the words one meaning or the other.

What is the distinction between ordinary words and technical legal words? The House of Lords gave no examples to help us.

With rare exceptions, all words used in statutes are probably comprehensible in ordinary usage to every sixth-former, and the great majority of such words would be at least roughly understood by O–level pupils. (Not that it can be assumed that jurors fell into either category at any time in their lives.) Statutes use "ordinary" words (that is, words found in compact dictionaries and used from time to time in general contexts) to express specialised legal concepts; we do not generally use outlandish words for legal purposes. Literally applied, therefore, the rule in *Cozens* v. *Brutus* would leave almost every statute to be interpreted by the jury. Yet the fact that the ordinary man can understand a word in ordinary use does not mean that he can understand it properly when it is used in a particular context in an Act of Parliament.

The courts of first instance and intermediate appellate courts (Court of Appeal and Divisional Court) have on occasion shown a certain amount of healthy insubordination in respect of *Cozens* v. *Brutus*. (Even the House of Lords forgot it, or closed its eyes to it, on one occasion.[17]) The tendency is to hold that key words in statutes, the words on which legal issues often hang, are not "ordinary," although the uninstructed observer might think they are. At any rate, the law reports contain a number of examples of judges very sensibly asserting as a matter of law what such words mean.

So judges have ruled upon the meaning of the words "assist,"[18] "produce,"[19] 'reckless,"[20] and "retention"[21] in particular statutory offences. These are certainly important words in

---

[17] See n. 20.

[18] *Vickers* [1975] 1 WLR 811, 2 All ER 945, 61 CAR 48 ("In ordinary English one who assists knows what he is doing and the purpose with which it is done").

[19] *Nock* [1978] AC at 984E.

[20] Recklessness was defined by the CA in *Briggs* [1977] 1 WLR 605, 1 All ER 475. The particular definition there favoured was disapproved in *Caldwell* [1982] AC 341, where Lord Diplock announced (on behalf of the majority) that recklessness is not a term of art but bears the meaning it has in ordinary speech; having said that, he laid down in express terms the definition of recklessness on which the jury were to be instructed. See § 5.4. The two pronouncements cannot stand together. Either "recklessness" is not an "ordinary word" bearing the meaning that it bears in ordinary speech or its meaning is a question for the jury—unless (happy thought!) their lordships are now prepared to repudiate *Cozens* v. *Brutus*.

[21] *Pitchley* (1973) 57 CAR at 37; the CA stated the meaning of "retention" even while saying that it was an "ordinary English word."

criminal matters, but they are not exclusively legal words. If they are ordinary words, and if *Cozens* v. *Brutus* is followed, any conviction resulting from a positive direction by the judge on the meaning of the word should theoretically be open to attack on appeal; but often that is only theory, since the appellate court may be ready to dismiss an appeal under "the proviso" (see next section). The more cautious judge will leave the meaning of the word to the jury while giving them a strong intimation of his own opinion.[22] Some judges, with regrettable reticence, offer the jury no help.[23] If, as a result, the jury convict, having attached a wholly unreasonable meaning to the word, the conviction can presumably be quashed on appeal as being unsafe or unsatisfactory, as already said. But since the prosecution cannot appeal, this control over the jury works only one way: if the jury attach a foolishly benevolent meaning to the word and acquit, the law provides no remedy.

A striking example of the freedom that may now be left to the jury relates to the Sexual Offences Act 1956 s.32, whereby it is an offence for a man persistently to solicit in a street for immoral purposes. This prudish wording, studiously obscuring the conduct that Parliament meant to prohibit, has inevitably created problems. "Immoral purposes" was clearly intended to cover (and be confined to) sexual purposes, but what sexual purposes were to be regarded as immoral was left to the guesswork of those administering the law. After some vacillation the courts have now decided the point by not deciding it; they hold that the jury should be left to determine in each case whether or not the law covers a homosexual purpose! So whether a homosexual who seeks a partner is convicted or acquitted depends upon the moral views of the particular jury, on a question that plainly ought to be resolved as one of fixed law.[24]

What about magistrates? Are they in the same position as juries?

One is tempted to say that *Cozens* v. *Brutus* has been a *brutum fulmen* in relation to magistrates, even though it was decided on an appeal from magistrates. Although the Divisional Court is supposed to hear appeals only on questions of law, it exercises tight control over magistrates' courts (and over the Crown Court on appeal from magistrates). It is strange that a random collection of jurors, who have perhaps never been in a court before, should be given a free hand, while magistrates, who are carefully selected and given some training, and generally have considerable experience, are kept on a close rein; but that is how it is. The Divisional Court will readily say that a summary conviction is perverse and also (since even the prosecution can appeal) that a summary acquittal is perverse. It will say this even where the task of the magistrates was to interpret an ordinary word in a statute.[25] But there is a certain area in between where the Divisional Court does not take a strong view and allows the court below to have its own way.

---

[22] In *Att.-Gen.'s Refce* (No. 1 of 1976) [1977] 1 WLR 646, 3 All ER 557, 64 CAR 222, the CA said that, on an issue as to the meaning of statutory words, it is proper that the judge should indicate to the jury his view that the case is all one way.

[23] Examples of words that have been left unglossed for the jury to interpret are "appropriates" (*Hale* (1978) 68 CAR 415), "obtains" (*Hayat* 63 CAR 181, [1976] Crim.LR 508 and commentary), and "dishonestly" (*Feely*; see Chap. 32).

[24] *Gray* (1981) 74 CAR 325. The CA, in holding that the judge was wrong not to leave the question to the jury, nevertheless applied the proviso and affirmed the conviction on the ground that the jury, if properly directed, would inevitably have convicted. How far the section covers the soliciting of a woman by a man is doubtful, but it seems possible that a judge would be regarded as bound to leave this question, too, to the jury. See the full study of the legislation by Cohen in [1982] Crim.LR 349. Soliciting by female prostitutes is not within section 32, which is confined to men, but it is a summary offence under the Street Offences Act 1959 as amended.

[25] E.g. *Behrendt* v. *Burridge* [1977] 1 WLR 29, [1976] 1 All ER, 63 CAR 202; *Chief Constable of West Midlands* v. *Billingham* [1979] 1 WLR 747, 2 All ER 182; *Seamark* v. *Prouse* [1980] Crim.LR 240; *Jones* v. *Pratt* (1982), The Times, June 11 (driving); Wasik, *op. cit.* n. 15 above.

While the practice of the Divisional Court is socially beneficial (even if legally very questionable in view of the decision of the Lords), the contrast is strange with jury trial. The difference of treatment is particularly anomalous in the case of either way offences. The appeal court may tell magistrates (carefully selected, experienced in administering the law) in no uncertain terms whether a particular person was "driving" a vehicle or not; yet when the identical question arises before a jury (unqualified, inexperienced) the judge is supposed to leave the matter to their unfettered discretion.

§ 2.7. APPELLATE CONTROL OVER JURIES

Although the Court of Appeal (like its predecessor the Court of Criminal Appeal) has always had power to quash erroneous convictions, it has been remarkably disinclined to exercise the power where the rules of procedure and evidence have been complied with. One reason is the strong feeling of English lawyers that the responsibility for convicting rests with the jury.

But doesn't the Court of Appeal fall down on its job if it allows an obviously erroneous conviction to stand—or even one that is reasonably likely to be erroneous?

I share your view. So did Parliament, when it passed the Criminal Appeal Act 1968 s.2, requiring the Court of Appeal to allow an appeal if the conviction is unsafe or unsatisfactory. But even this enactment has not produced a revolution in judicial practice.

Lord Widgery, speaking for the Court of Appeal, has described the effect of this section in two different ways. In 1969[1] he stated a test much more liberal than anything that had gone before. The question for the appellate court, he said, is:

> "whether there is some lurking doubt in our minds which makes us wonder whether an injustice has been done. This is a reaction which may not be based strictly on the evidence as such; it is a reaction which can be produced by the general feel of the case."

But alas! in 1976 he ignored the language of the statute and went back to a more stringent test.

> "It is for the jury in each case to decide which witnesses should be believed. On matters of credibility this court will only interfere in three circumstances: first, if the jury has been misdirected as to how to assess the evidence; secondly, if there has been no direction at all when there should have been one; and thirdly, if on the whole of the evidence the jury must have taken a perverse view of a witness, but this is rare."[2]

The reason for paying special deference to the jury on the credibility of witnesses is that the appellate judges have not heard the witnesses and generally have not even read a full transcript of the evidence. The reason for this again is the vast number of appeals; restrictive practices have to be developed if the work-load is to be bearable.

Suppose that the appeal court takes the view that there was insufficient evidence on a count on which the defendant was convicted, but that he was

---

[1] *Cooper* [1969] 1 QB at 271, approved in *John Smith* [1973] 1 WLR at 1519.
[2] *Turnbull* [1977] 1 QB at 231D.

undoubtedly guilty of some other offence. Can the court substitute a conviction of that other offence?

Yes if it was one of which the jury could have convicted, on the indictment as it stood.[3] But if the proper charge was not expressly or impliedly included in the indictment, or if the jury have acquitted on the proper charge, the court is helpless.[4]

What if the conviction, though technically irregular, was substantially right? Can the Court of Appeal overlook the defect?

It can if it so chooses. Formerly, the practice was to quash a conviction if there were almost any procedural irregularity at the trial, but this is now less common. By the Criminal Appeal Act 1968 there must be a "material irregularity" before the appeal should be allowed; and even then, by section 2(1), the appellate court can apply what is called "the proviso"—the concluding words of the subsection, which allow an appeal to be dismissed although there has been a technical irregularity if "no miscarriage of justice has actually occurred."

The way in which this power is exercised depends to some extent upon the facts, naturally, but also upon the philosophy of the judges who happen to sit on the Court of Appeal.

- If there has been a breach of proper procedure (for example, when the defendant is clearly guilty, but of a crime different from the one charged against him) the Court of Appeal still generally quashes a conviction, notwithstanding the words of the Act, since it regards the trial as being vitiated. In practice the defendant is not put on trial a second time, even though he generally could be.[5] So, obviously guilty people escape. Although it has often been suggested that the Court of Appeal should have power in such circumstances to order a new trial, in order that the substantial question of guilt can be tried properly for the first time,[6] the "sporting theory of justice" has hitherto prevailed, and the proposal has not been accepted.
- If there has been a misdirection to the jury, the appellate court has again, on many occasions, evinced a reluctance to apply its curative power under the proviso, holding that a conviction should be upset if as a result of the misdirection the defendant has been deprived of his chance of acquittal by the jury. But the legal principle is supposed to be that the proviso should be applied if "a reasonable jury, after being properly directed, would, on the evidence properly admissible, without doubt convict."[7] The Court of Appeal may have no doubt about the defendant's guilt, but juries are known from time to time to give effect to fanciful doubts, and the Court of Appeal may for this reason refuse to cure the defect.

If the judge has usurped the function of the jury, e.g. by wrongly telling them that a particular fact has been proved, then if it is a question of primary or inferential[8] fact the proviso will not be applied, and the conviction will be quashed. However clear the evidence

---

[3] Criminal Appeal Act 1968 s.3.

[4] And there are other restrictions as well: e.g. the CA cannot convict on a count that the trial judge has erroneously quashed. See J R Spencer in [1982] Crim.LR 260 at 272–275. The court cannot apply the proviso (see below), because that only allows an appeal to be dismissed when the jury could have convicted.

[5] See Spencer, *op. cit.* 272 n. 43.

[6] See Spencer's splendid invective in the article cited.

[7] Viscount Simon LC in *Maxwell* v. *DPP* [1944] AC at 321; cp. *Pink* [1971] 1 QB 508. Sometimes the CA is disposed to limit the proviso even more by in effect adding: "unless there is something to indicate that this jury would have acquitted." See *Virgo* (1967) 76 CAR 323, discussed in [1978] Crim.LR 561.

[8] E.g. intent in carrying a weapon that is offensive in law only if carried with offensive intent. See the strong decision in *Leer* [1982] Crim.LR 310.

may be against the defendant, the jury have a sacred right to be perverse if they want to. But the appellate court has sometimes applied the proviso (and therefore upheld a conviction) where a judge has wrongly taken it upon himself to decide questions of denotative[9] or (more rarely) evaluative fact. The present temper of the court seems to be against applying the proviso on questions of evaluative fact, but the cases are not wholly consistent.[10]

SUMMARY

The burden lies on the prosecution to prove the guilt of the defendant beyond reasonable doubt (or, so that the tribunal feels sure of guilt). § .1

The evidential burden generally lies on the prosecution. This means that if (at the conclusion of the prosecution's case) the prosecution have not given sufficient evidence to take the case to the jury, the judge may rule that there is no case for the defendant to answer. He should do this when there is no evidence of guilt, or if the evidence is tenuous and the judge concludes that taken at its highest it is such that a properly directed jury could not properly convict on it. A similar practice, framed in wider terms, prevails in magistrates' courts. § .2

In ruling upon a submission of "no case," the judge may draw commonsense inferences from the evidence, and some of these have hardened into rules of law, e.g. the presumption arising from the possession of stolen goods recently after the theft. In addition, the evidential burden on issues that are regarded as defences is cast on the defence. § .3

The word "defence" in its narrow and technical sense refers to defences of justification or excuse, or technical points urged in order to deny liability. The defendant bears an evidential burden in respect of such defences, but not necessarily a persuasive burden. In particular, the persuasive burden (the burden of proof) when a common law defence is raised is generally upon the prosecution. § .4

A burden of proof proper (a persuasive burden) is placed on the defence (1) in respect of the defence of insanity, (2) by express statute, and (3) by judicial construction where the statute prohibits the doing of an act save in specified circumstances or by persons of specified classes or with special qualifications or with the licence or permission of specified authorities (*Edwards*). The defendant need only prove his defence on the balance of probabilities. § .5

There are four types of "questions of fact" for the jury: as to primary facts, inferential facts, evaluative facts and denotative facts (*Cozens* v. *Brutus*). The last applies only to "ordinary words," whatever those are. However, the judge may withdraw the case from the jury if there is insufficient evidence on any of these matters (if the evidential burden rests on the prosecution); correspondingly, he may withdraw a defence from the jury if the evidential burden on the issue rests on the defence. § .6

The Court of Appeal can allow an appeal against conviction if the verdict is "unsafe or unsatisfactory." On the other hand, the court is not always bound to allow an appeal on purely technical grounds, because it can dismiss an appeal under "the proviso" if "no miscarriage of justice has actually occurred." Unfortunately, the Court of Appeal interprets both formulas restrictively, so that from time to time meritorious appeals are dismissed and unmeritorious ones allowed. § .7

---

[9] E.g. on what facts constitute an attempt: *Stonehouse*, § 17.5 n. 23.

[10] See [1976] Crim.LR 481–482; *Leer* n. 8 above; *McIvor* [1982] 1 WLR 409; *Grey* [1982] Crim.LR 176.

Chapter 3

INTENTION

Desire and force between them are responsible for all our actions; desire causes our voluntary acts, force our involuntary.

Pascal, *Pensées*.

§ 3.1. ACTUS REUS AND MENS REA

The mere commission of a criminal act (or bringing about the state of affairs that the law provides against) is not enough to constitute a crime, at any rate in the case of the more serious crimes. These generally require, in addition, some element of wrongful intent or other fault.

Increasing insistence upon this fault element was a mark of advancing civilisation. In early law the distinction between what we now call crimes and civil wrongs was blurred, and liability in both was very strict. Little or no mental element was requisite: the law hardly distinguished between intentional and unintentional acts. In the animistic period of legal thinking "punishment" was inflicted even upon animals and inanimate objects.

The law has followed a development that can still be seen among our own young. Small children think of wrongness as any disobedience to rules, irrespective of intention. Later they learn the relevance of wrongful intent, and defend themselves by saying "I didn't mean to do it." Similarly, judges came to accept the maxim *Actus non facit reum nisi mens sit rea*[1] as a general principle (though one subject to exceptions) governing serious crimes. For example, assault involves an intentional or reckless interference with another. The requirement of a wrongful mental state is found not only in most common law crimes but also in nearly all statutory crimes if they are of any degree of seriousness. Thus criminal damage, a statutory crime, requires intention or recklessness. (Certain difficulties in the notion of recklessness will be discussed later.)

If a penal statute does not include a mental element expressly, the courts will sometimes, sporadically and without much discernible principle, imply the requirement, on the assumption that Parliament probably intended the new offence to be read in the light of a general *mens rea* requirement. The assumption ought to be made more regularly than it is. The operation of the criminal law in respect of offences traditionally regarded as serious ordinarily involves so drastic an interference with the liberty of the subject that it is not generally appropriate to those who are not deliberate offenders.

Do you mean that Oedipus did not commit incest, merely because he did not know Jocasta was his mother? What he knew made no difference to what he did. Surely he committed incest in fact.

The union was incestuous (it was subject to the genetic risks attaching to

---

[1] "An act does not make a man a criminal unless the mind be guilty": it may be anglicised in pronunciation as "actus non fasit reeum nysy mens sit reeah" (though nisi should properly be "nissy"). The brocard is of canonical origin; it is first found in the *Leges Henrici*, but goes back in one form to St. Augustine. It was not true for the run of crimes in Henry I's day.

incest), but Oedipus did not commit incest morally or (under English law) legally. The crime of incest, like nearly all serious crimes, has a mental component. If a driver accidentally kills a pedestrian, would you say that he commits murder "in fact"? He commits an act that would be murder if he had the necessary intent, which is however lacking. In lawyer's language, Oedipus and the driver commit the *actus reus* of a crime, without committing the crime.[2] This bit of legal jargon comes from the Latin maxim quoted above, which also gives us the corresponding term *mens rea*.

I have a brilliant idea. Why not omit fault from the definition of crimes, and leave the judge to mitigate or remit punishment where fault is absent?

The idea is not so brilliant, though you are not the first to think it is. The scheme would remove the question of fault from the consideration of the jury, thus simplifying their task. But would you, if you have unluckily killed a pedestrian by a pure accident when driving, appreciate being convicted of (or declared to have committed) unlawful killing? Would you be wholly comforted by the fact that the judge subsequently decides to remit punishment? Conviction without fault—that is, strict liability—gives no guidance to the police and others as to when they may properly prosecute, and imposes no limits upon the judge and magistrates as to whom they may punish. Also, our trial processes are not well suited to make full enquiry into matters of mitigation.[3]

I still do not know precisely what mens rea means.

In Latin it means a guilty mind, but in legal use it denotes the mental state (subjective element) required for the particular crime in question. Or it can refer to the mental states commonly required for serious crimes (and a number of lesser offences). *Actus reus* denotes the external situation forbidden by law—the external elements of the offence.

Normally, the required mental element is either:

— an *intention* to do the forbidden act, or otherwise to bring about the external elements of the offence (whether you know of the legal prohibition or not), or

— (in most crimes) *recklessness* as to such elements.

Intention includes knowledge.

---

[2] The criminal law does not accept the notion of what may be called *de facto* crime (crime in fact though not in law) for penal purposes, except for a limited purpose in relation to excuses. See § 15.16. However, a non-penal statute referring, say, to incest may for some purposes be construed to mean incestuous acts objectively regarded, rather than the commission of the crime. Cp. *R v. Secretary of State for the Home Dept., ex p. Khan* [1977] 1 WLR 1466, 3 All ER 538.

Lord Diplock expressed distaste for the customary latinisms in *Miller* [1983] 2 WLR at 542B, saying that in discussing statutory crimes it is better to speak of the conduct of the accused and his state of mind (meaning the conduct or state of mind required for culpability). But the Latin expressions are shorter. Lord Diplock's particular objection to *actus reus* was that it misleadingly suggests that a positive act is required; but the opinion may be held that liability for omissions is and ought to be exceptional: see § 7.3. (His lordship also criticised *actus reus* as "converting incorrectly into an adjective the word *reus* which was used [in the maxim] correctly in the accusative case as a noun." He overlooked the fact that the maxim, of very respectable antiquity even though post-classical, itself used *rea* as an adjective.)

[3] See Kadish in 26 CLJ 273; Wasserstrom in 35 U of Chic.LR 92; Thomas, *Principles of Sentencing*, 2nd edn 366–372 and in [1980] Crim.LR 248.

By "external elements" do you mean the parts of the offence that are not in the mind?

Those that are not in the defendant's mind. Rape, for example, is (1) sexual intercourse by a man with a woman without her consent, (2) the man knowing that she does not consent or being reckless whether she consents or not. The elements that I have put under (1) are the external elements, and they include lack of consent by the woman. The external elements are all the elements of the offence other than the *defendant's* mental element. They generally include some conduct by the defendant, and sometimes require a specified result to follow from his conduct.

You don't approve of my good ideas, but why not say that mens rea means wickedness or moral guilt?

My dear imaginary interlocutor, do not be offended if I put down your ideas. After all, it is I who have put into your mouth some of the not-so-good ideas that have occurred to brilliant minds in the past! The answer to your present suggestion is that *mens rea* is merely convenient shorthand for the mental elements that are legally required for the crime. To say that a person did the *actus reus* with *mens rea* does not mean that he acted immorally. One who breaks the law with a good motive, or for conscientious reasons, or from religious belief, still commits a crime. So also (in many cases) does a person who breaks the law in justifiable ignorance of its existence, or who misunderstands it.

> *Heron*[4] may stand as an example. By statute, "every person who falsely makes or counterfeits any coin resembling any current coin" committed an offence. (The particular statute is now replaced by another statute in slightly different words.[5]) Heron[6] made coins resembling half-sovereigns, and when prosecuted submitted, through his counsel, that the Crown had to prove a dishonest intention—an intent to pass the counterfeit coins off as genuine. The House of Lords upheld the trial judge in holding that such proof was not required. Parliament wished to prevent counterfeit coins being made, because of the obvious danger that they might get into circulation. The only intent necessary was what Lord Simon called the "basic intent" of doing the act, without any regard to its purpose.

Their lordships recognised that some crimes require more than a "basic" intent; they are crimes of "specific" (or, better, "ulterior") intent. The offence specifically requires some intent beyond the basic intent, or else it impliedly requires such an ulterior intent. (It is because the further requirement may be implied that the word "ulterior" is better than

---

[4] [1982] 1 WLR 451, 1 All ER 993, 73 CAR 327.

[5] Forgery and Counterfeiting Act 1981 s.14(2). Lord Scarman said in *Heron* (at p. 458H) that the decision had no bearing on this new provision, but the view may nevertheless be confidently held that the law is the same. See the editorial note in [1982] Crim.LR 431.

[6] In legal arguments and judgments the practice is to refer to the defendant by that title, or as the accused, and not by his proper name unless it is necessary to distinguish between joint defendants. In an appeal he is referred to as the appellant (accent on second syllable), except where the prosecution have been able to appeal in which case the defendant will become the respondent. But in my encapsulations of cases I customarily use proper names in the hope that repetition will assist the reader to remember the name of the case. Remembering the names of cases is not of great value in itself, but it is of some small utility in discussion.

"specific".) A crime of basic intent, in contrast, merely requires that the physical act be done knowingly or (sometimes) recklessly.[7]

An example of an ulterior intent expressly (specifically) required is the offence of delivering to another anything which is, and which the deliveror knows or believes to be, a counterfeit currency, intending that the person to whom it is delivered (the deliveree) shall pass or tender it as genuine.[8] Here the offender must have intentionally delivered the coin or note (basic intent) and must have had the further intent specified in the subsection as to what was to happen afterwards. The requirement of ulterior intention may also be indicated by the words "with intent to" or "dishonestly" or "fraudulent" in the definition of the offence.[9]

The requirement of an ulterior intent may be implied if the court thinks that that was the intention of the legislature. The section under which Heron was charged included the word "falsely," and this might in a different context have implied a requirement of dishonest intent—an intent to defraud. The books contain many examples of the courts implying such a requirement of intent to defraud, or of absence of claim of right, in statutory offences.[10]

Part of the discussion of the mental element in crime concerns the meaning of the relevant terms. What precisely is to be understood by the words intention, recklessness and knowledge? We need to have reasonably precise definitions, not too far removed from the ordinary meanings of these words, so that the legislature can use them in defining offences and so that a trial judge can explain them confidently to a jury.

The other part concerns the issue of policy. How far is it proper to make a mental element an essential ingredient of an offence? Ought a particular offence to require intention, or should it be capable of being committed by recklessness, or just by negligence, or even be an offence of strict liability, with virtually no element of fault? Primarily these questions are for the legislature to answer when it creates the offence. But some offences rest on the common law, and even statutes are often silent or ambiguous on the mental element. Here the views of the judges on the social policy are important.

Although the mental elements are basically simple, the courts have enveloped them in considerable confusion, partly because they feel a continual need to expand criminal liability on social or moral grounds. The easiest way to do this is to stretch the meaning of the words used to define the liability. As a result of this, doubts still remain about the legal meaning of the *mens rea* words. It is lamentable that, after more than a thousand years of continuous legal development, English law should still lack clear and consistent definitions of words expressing its basic concepts.

Doing the best we can to produce an intelligible scheme, we may say that legal fault[11] can be classified into mental elements (awareness, *mens rea*) and negligence. Negligence is legal fault although it is not (or is not necessarily) a mental element. The mental elements can be subdivided into

---

[7] See, further, § 21.4.

[8] Forgery and Counterfeiting Act 1981 s.15(1)(*b*).

[9] See, e.g. *Att.-Gen.'s Refce (No. 1 of 1981)* [1982] 2 WLR 875, 2 All ER 417.

[10] E.g. *Allday* (1837) 8 C & P 136, 173 ER 431 (see § 20.6). See also *Kemp* [1964] 2 QB 341; *Moore v Branton* [1974] Crim.LR 439; *The General Part* 156 n. 1, 219 n. 2, 305–341. However, offences of forgery and suchlike do not require selfishness: a person may forge a will from motives of altruism: *Draper* [1962] Crim.LR 107. For another counter-example see § 20.6 n. 10.

[11] "Fault" is a convenient generic term for *mens rea* and negligence, and it must be understood in this technical meaning. A person may break the law laudably or excusably and still be at fault in this sense.

intention and recklessness (subject to a confused piece of law as to recklessness, to be noticed later[12]). Offences not involving legal fault are those of strict liability.

This is a classification of positive mental states; but exceptionally a crime may require the *absence* of a particular kind of intention, knowledge or belief. This is so, for example, with crimes of dishonesty, like theft and obtaining by deception. These crimes require an absence of *honest* intent. A person who has intentionally taken money from another may defend himself against a charge of theft by saying that he took it in order to recoup a debt owed to him. His intention to obtain payment of the debt can be regarded as an honest intention which removes the criminality of his intentional taking of the money.

Mental states may be required by implication. For example, as we have seen, statutes creating an offence of false statement are sometimes held impliedly to require an intent to deceive or defraud, even though there are no words to that effect; but on other occasions (as in *Heron*) it is held that the offence is committed merely by knowingly doing something that in fact violates the words of the statute. Sometimes, as we shall see in Chapter 42, offences of false statement are held to be matters of strict liability. It is hard to see a consistent pattern.

§ 3.2. THE BASIC MEANING OF INTENTION

The general legal opinion is that "intention" cannot be satisfactorily defined and does not need a definition, since everyone knows what it means. This is largely true. Trouble has been caused in the past because when judges have provided the jury with definitions or tests of intention, they have used wide language going beyond the ordinary meaning of the word. The present practice is to leave the word without explanation, which in every case except one (to be discussed in § .5) is perfectly acceptable.

As a philosophical matter, however, intention is readily definable. With the one exception already mentioned, a consequence is said to be intended when the actor desires that it shall follow from his conduct.

I have many desires. Some I recognise to be too visionary; some I lack the energy to implement. But if I decide to try to achieve my desire and start to act to that end, the desire becomes the intention with which I act.

The end aimed at may be a desire only in the sense that it is the lesser of two evils. When I am sitting in the dentist's chair, the last thing I "really" want to do is to open my mouth to have my tooth filled, yet I "really" want to do so, because I wish to avoid toothache in future. The desire need not be an end in itself (certainly having a tooth filled is not that) but may be a medial desire—a step on the way to something else (freedom from future toothache). The desire may be conceived on the instant, not premeditated. It need not be formulated in "interior language." Judges sometimes reject a definition of intention in terms of desire, but one reason may be that they overlook these explanations of the meaning of "desire." It is true, however, that in one respect the definition in terms of desire is too narrow: see § .5.

---

[12] Recklessness is included among the mental elements because until recently it had an important mental component. But, as we shall see, the extent to which this component is still necessary for a finding of recklessness has been brought into doubt by decisions of the House of Lords.

The idea of intention is expressed in law not only by the words "intention" or "with intent to" but also by other words, such as "with the purpose of" or "wilfully." (But the latter word often includes recklessness.

Isn't the desire of a consequence the motive for acting, rather than intention?

It can be regarded as either. In ordinary speech, "intention" and "motive" are often convertible terms. For the lawyer, the word "motive" generally refers to some further intent which forms no part of the legal rule.

If we say that a man shot and killed his aunt with the motive of benefiting under her will, the immediate intent, which makes the act murder, is the intention or desire to kill, while the further intent or motive, which forms no part of the definition of the crime of murder, is the intention or desire to benefit under the will. Other motives are the desire to obtain the satisfaction of revenge, or to get rid of a rival, or to promote a political object. (Such motives may also be expressed in abstract terms: "he killed her from a motive of greed/revenge/jealousy." Motive in this sense is irrelevant to responsibility (guilt or innocence), though it may be relevant to proof, or to the quantum of punishment. The prosecution may prove a motive for the crime if it helps them to establish their case, as a matter of circumstantial evidence; but they are not legally bound to prove motive, because a "motiveless" crime is still a crime. Conversely, the defendant may adduce evidence of his good motive in order to reduce his punishment, perhaps to vanishing-point.

Exceptionally, the term "motive" is used in a sense relevant to responsibility in the crime of libel. Also, crimes of ulterior intent require two intents, one lying behind the other, and the second may be called motive. The crime of burglary is committed where a person enters a building or part of a building by way of trespass with intent to commit one of certain crimes therein. There is an intentional entry, with the ulterior intent of committing a crime in the house; this ulterior intent is the motive of the entry, and is sometimes referred to as such, yet here it forms part of the legal definition.

It is sometimes hard to determine from legislation what is to be regarded as an unlawful intention and what merely as irrelevant motive.

> In *Chandler*[1] a prosecution was brought against several persons who had organised a ban-the-bomb demonstration at a Royal Air Force station with the object of grounding all aircraft. They were convicted of conspiring to commit a breach of section 1 of the Official Secrets Act 1911, namely, to enter the airfield "for a purpose prejudicial to the safety or interest of the State." The trial judge had directed the jury to convict if they were satisfied that the defendants' immediate purpose was the obstruction of aircraft, and the conviction was upheld by the House of Lords. Their lordships rejected the argument that the defendants' object was to get rid of nuclear weapons and thereby, in their view, to promote the safety and interests of the State.

The various lords gave somewhat discordant reasons, but perhaps the clearest way of expressing the decision would be to say that the defendants had two purposes: an immediate one, which in itself was illegal, and an ultimate one, which, although thoroughly well-intentioned, did not exclude the illegality of the immediate purpose. Judges could not be

---

[1] [1964] AC 763.

expected to decide that demonstrators were entitled to blockade a defence airfield for a political end.

Notions of public policy can also be detected in the way the courts interpret the statutory offence of wilfully obstructing a constable in the execution of his duty.[2] It is held that obstruction can be by words and other inconvenient behaviour; so the offence can be committed by "tipping off" a speeding driver that the police are operating a speed check,[3] or similarly informing a publican that the police are operating in the vicinity to detect licensing and liquor offences.[4]

Suppose that the driver was not speeding at the time, and the landlord of the pub was not committing offences. Surely one can warn people not to commit offences. It cannot be an offence to try to prevent offences.

The courts were at one time of this opinion, but they have abandoned it because it would allow people to interfere seriously with the work of the police. Once the offender has been tipped off, it may be impossible for the police to prove that he was offending. If the defendant's motive was to frustrate the police, he is guilty of obstructing them.

But if I see a man driving carelessly, can't I warn him that if he goes on like that he will get copped?

Presumably. If your object was to prevent the offence being committed now *or ever*, you would be acquitted of obstruction.[5] You are then not intending to obstruct the police, because their duty is to prevent crime as well as to detect it. If your object was merely to prevent it being committed now, while the police are about, you would be convicted. The motive will generally appear quite clearly from the circumstances.

It will be seen that in defining the offence of obstructing the police one cannot eliminate questions of motive. Again, motive can make an appearance in crimes requiring fraud or dishonesty.

You have defined intention in relation to consequences. Don't we speak of an act itself as being intentional?

Yes. We may quite properly say, for example, that D intentionally trespassed on V's land,[6] or that D intentionally went through a bigamous ceremony of marriage—without referring to, or implying any consequence. We say that bodily movement (like speaking, writing, gesturing, walking) is intentional if it is conscious or heedful, meaning that the actor in a sense knows what he is doing when he does it. He need not consciously attend to his movements, but they are purposive and are under his control.[7]

The offence of wilfully obstructing the police may again be taken as a

---

[2] See § 9.7.

[3] *Betts v Stevens* [1910] 1 KB 1.

[4] *Green* v. *Moore* [1982] QB 1044. Since this decision, *Bastable v. Little* [1907] 1 KB 59 is unlikely to be followed.

[5] See *Green* v. *Moore* (last note). This is the only ground on which *Bastable* v. *Little* (last note) can now be supported, and it is a very unlikely interpretation of the facts.

[6] In the discussions in this book, D of course stands for defendant, V for the victim or alleged victim of an illegal act.

[7] Another element in the notion of intentional conduct will be considered in § 6.2.

practical example. In one case the police were engaged on lawfully arresting a man, and the defendant interposed to try to persuade them that the man was innocent. To attract an officer's attention he took hold of his arm, and persisted in this conduct despite being warned by another officer not to do so. It was held that he was guilty of wilfully obstructing the police in the execution of their duty, even though he acted in good faith, believing that the man was innocent, and whether or not he was correct in that belief.[8] The defendant presumably knew that he was delaying the officer in his task, and his good motive was no defence. He should have let the police get on with it and tried to persuade them afterwards that they were mistaken.

But perhaps the defendant did not know that the police were acting in the execution of their duty. He may have thought that since the man was innocent they had no right to arrest him.

The courts do not accept a defence of ignorance of the law of arrest, or ignorance as to the other powers and duties of the police (§ 23.5 n. 8).

How is the line drawn between an act and its consequence? If D shoots and kills V, is the killing D's act or its consequence?

As you like to regard it. Ordinary language tends to blur the distinction between bodily movement and its consequences, since a statement that a person has acted in a particular way sometimes implies a consequence of acting. A statement that D has killed V implies that D has caused V's death. From one point of view the death is a consequence; from another point of view it can be regarded as part of D's movement.

I perform the act of *crooking* my forefinger; since my finger is around the trigger of a loaded gun (a circumstance of my act of crooking my finger) I perform at the same time the act of *firing* the gun; since I have pointed the gun at a victim I also *wound* him; since he dies I also *kill* him; since his wife subsequently dies of a broken heart I *cause her death*. In all these examples, except the first and the last, a consequence can be spoken of as part of the act, because we happen to be provided with verbs (fire, wound, kill) that bring in the consequence. The last example must be excluded from the list of acts, because as soon as the word "cause" has to be used we do not regard the result as part of the act. But it is an accident that our language enables us to say "I killed him" rather than compelling us to say "I caused his death"; and similarly with all the other examples except the first and last. Only what I voluntarily do with my own body can indubitably be said to be an act and not the consequence of an act. Anything else *can* be called a consequence, though language may enable us to avoid calling it a consequence.

The way in which the accidents of language influence common notions of an act and its consequences may be further illustrated by considering wounding with a knife.

1 D, holding a knife, plunges it into V's body. Here we naturally say that D has stabbed V. We think of the wounding as practically a part of D's bodily movement; we speak of him as inflicting the wound rather than *causing* it.
2 D throws a knife at V and so causes a wound. Here we would probably not say that D has stabbed V, but rather that he has caused the wound. The wound is a consequence of his act of throwing the knife.

For legal purposes the situation is the same in both cases. In both, D has, in law, both

---

[8] *Hills* v. *Ellis* [1982] 2 WLR 234. Notwithstanding the doubts there cast on the earlier case of *Wilmott* v. *Atack* [1977] QB 498, this case should still be taken to stand for the proposition that a person who interferes with the police intending to help them is not guilty of a wilful obstruction.

wounded and caused a wound, and the wound is a consequence of D's bodily movement. There is no point in making a distinction, saying that the wound is a consequence of what D has done in the second case and part of what he has done in the first.

The only qualification of the above remarks is that a lawyer's use of language may be controlled by the definitions of particular words. An example is the word "kill," which is used in the definition of murder and manslaughter; this is given a wider meaning by the law than it perhaps bears in ordinary speech, because, as we shall see, it covers the causing of death by some omissions and by some indirect means.

Another ambiguity may be noticed. If D murders V by shooting him, we say that D "intended to do it," or "meant to do it." Do what? D might have intended to shoot V in a non-vital part merely as a warning for the future. It would be wrong to say that because he intended to shoot, therefore he intended to kill. If we are speaking precisely we ought to speak about intending the *consequence* (if the consequence is important) rather than about intending the *act*. Clearly, the act must be intentional as to the *relevant* fact, whether bodily movement or consequence as the case may be.

> Suppose that Winkle is out shooting partridges when his shot accidently hits Tupman. We can say that Winkle intentionally fired the gun, and that he hit Tupman, but not that he intentionally shot Tupman. It would be an unscrupulous use of language to argue that Winkle committed an "intentional act" and therefore an intentional crime. Yet sometimes, as we shall see, even the most eminent judges have made a mistake of this kind.[9]

The distinction between acts and their consequences has caused some judges (following a suggestion by Professor Smith) to classify crimes into two sorts: conduct-crimes and result-crimes. For the reasons already given the distinction, although sometimes useful, cannot be made perfectly precise.

Conduct-crimes (such as assault) are those that are completed by the bodily movement (or other conduct) itself, with any requisite intent.[10]

Result-crimes (such as murder) are those requiring some consequence to follow. Some require the result to be intended; these are crimes of ulterior intent in which the intent must be accomplished. Others are satisfied with recklessness or negligence as to the result, or even require no fault at all.

The distinction between conduct-crimes and result-crimes is unscientific because of the ambiguity of language already discussed. Murder is a result-crime if you think of it as causing death, but a conduct-crime if you think of it as the act of killing. Unlawful wounding is a result-crime if you think of it as causing a wound, but a conduct-crime if you think of it as the act of wounding.

A third class of crimes does not fit neatly under either heading. They are what may be called *crimes of pure intention* (the "inchoate" crimes like attempt and conspiracy). They are not conduct-crimes in the same sense as other conduct-crimes, because no particular conduct is interdicted; and they are not result-crimes, because the desired result need not be achieved. They are committed by doing any act that (within certain rules) manifests a sufficiently firm intention to bring about another crime.

It may sometimes be hard to determine whether Parliament meant to create a conduct

---

[9] See Lord Salmon's comments upon *Lamb*, discussed in § 12.6.

[10] Conduct-crimes may be subdivided into the two sorts that we know already. Their common characteristic is that no result is required. (1) Some are crimes of basic (or general) intent, in the sense that the only mental element required is an intention to go through the bodily movements, coupled (generally) with one of various kinds of mental elements as to the relevant circumstances. Examples of such conduct-crimes of basic intent are perjury, blackmail, incest, bigamy, and sexual intercourse with a girl under 16. (2) Other conduct-crimes, while not requiring the achievement of a forbidden result, require an intention to achieve such result, and are therefore crimes of ulterior intent. The definition of the crime contains two requirements: some specified criminal conduct, and an intention to produce a result. Examples are: theft (which involves dishonestly appropriating the property of another with intent to deprive him permanently of it), burglary (which involves trespassory entry upon property with one of certain forbidden intents), and wounding with intent to cause grievous bodily harm. Some so-called crimes of specific intent can be committed with recklessness instead of intention.

crime or a result-crime. In an offence of allowing or permitting someone to do something, is the offence committed by giving the permission, or only when the permission is acted upon? The courts say the latter.[11]

§ 3.3. THE PROOF OF INTENTION

As we saw in the last chapter, the burden of proving a necessary mental element rests upon the prosecution.

No presumption shifts the burden to the defendant. A defence that the defendant did not intend a consequence to follow from his act is frequently called a defence of accident, but this is merely a denial of intention and recklessness; and the burden of proving intention or recklessness rests on the Crown. In the same way, the prosecution must prove dishonesty and fraud, where these are required elements.[1] It makes no difference that the mental element is a matter lying peculiarly within the knowledge of the defendant.[2]

I don't understand how intention is proved. Suppose the evidence is that when V was ill D gave him a dose of arsenic. D says it was by mistake for a sleeping powder; at least, that is what he told the police, but he does not give evidence in court. Do you mean that the prosecution have the burden of proving that D did not make a mistake and intend to kill V? How can they do so if D does not give evidence and so lay himself open to cross-examination?

What D said to the police is not evidence in his favour. As the case stands, therefore, the evidence is only that D gave V arsenic. The courts do not generally impose an evidential burden on the defendant on the issue of *mens rea* (as perhaps they should), but the facts you put would certainly be held sufficient to discharge the prosecution's evidential burden. The jury must be directed that the burden of proving the intention to kill (where the charge is of murder) rests on the prosecution, and that such intention must be proved beyond reasonable doubt; but they may also be told that they are entitled to infer an intention from the evidence. In practice D may be bound to offer evidence of the alleged mistake if he wants it to be considered[3]; but any such evidence, however thin, must be left to the jury.

But aren't there many cases where a court of law could not possibly distinguish between "accidental" and "accidental on purpose"?

Maybe; but certain modes of proof are accepted as sufficient to distinguish between the genuine and the feigned defence.

Facts are proved by direct evidence (the evidence of witnesses—including the defendant himself—who perceived or experienced them) or by circumstantial (indirect) evidence (the evidence of witnesses as to other

---

[11] *Diggin* [1981] RTR 83, 72 CAR 204.

[1] E.g. [1958] AC 173; *Lusty* [1963] 1 WLR 606, 1 All ER 690.
[2] *Spurge* [1961] 2 QB at 212–213.
[3] Occasionally a mere statement of counsel as to the defendant's intention has been left to the jury as though it were evidence; but it should not be.

facts, from which the facts in issue are inferred). This is as true of the proof of intention as of the proof of other facts.

(1) Intention may be directly proved from what the defendant says. Evidence may be given of what he said contemporaneously with the act (by way of application of the so-called *res gestae* rule), or of his prior or subsequent admission of what he intended to do. Such evidence is, of course, not conclusive in itself; it may be overborne by stronger evidence the other way; but usually it will be sufficient for a finding of intention. A subsequent admission of guilt is called a confession, whether it is made before[4] or at the trial.

(2) If the defendant does not give the court this assistance, the jury (or magistrates) will have no direct access to his mind.[5] Therefore, unless the defendant confesses, the state of his mind at the time in question must be judged from his outward acts, whether they are contemporaneous or not.

- It may be gathered from *previous or subsequent* conduct on his part. There may be evidence of previous planning, or a subsequent flight from justice. An important part of the law of evidence relates to evidence of other offences. Normally, English law does not allow a charge of crime to be made out by showing that the defendant has committed other crimes; but if the various crimes exhibit striking similarities, so that it is impossible or difficult to imagine that they could all have been the result of coincidence, the other crimes (whether previous or even subsequent[6]) may be given in evidence in order to show that the defendant had a "system" of committing such crimes. This evidence may convince the jury not only that he did the act charged against him but that he did it with the requisite intent. Evidence of possible motive (e.g. an expectation under a will) will be of some weight in supporting other evidence.
- More frequently, the defendant's intention will have to be collected from the evidence of what he did *on the occasion in question*. If one man loads a revolver, points it at another, aims it carefully at the victim's heart and pulls the trigger, the jury will find that he intended to kill, because that is the only reasonable hypothesis to explain his conduct. They are not obliged to swallow a denial that is in common sense unswallowable.

Doesn't it boil down simply to the probability of the consequence occurring?

Not quite. Probability is a guide, but it is not conclusive.

This matter has a history. For many years the courts fudged the notion of intention. When a crime required intention and the judges thought this too narrow, they extended the law by the doctrine that a person was "deemed to intend the natural and probable consequences of his act." The

---

[4] There are certain restrictive rules. A confession out of court is inadmissible, in certain cases, if obtained by oppression or by a promise of a threat, the evidence and argument on this issue taking place in the absence of the jury; and even if the judge rules that the confession is admissible, its credibility may still be attacked when the jury return into court. The judge may also exclude a statement from evidence at his discretion if it was obtained in breach of the rules for police questioning known as the Judges' Rules. See CLRC, 11th Report, Cmnd. 4991 of 1972, pp. 34–47.

[5] There is a machine known as the lie-detector or polygraph which is supposed to indicate whether a lie is being told, by means of physiological changes resulting from the subject's emotional reactions; but this device is not used in the courts, partly because its scientific accuracy is disputed and partly because the tradition is that defendants to a criminal charge are not subject to compulsory interrogation. For a survey of opinion on the machine see Harnon in [1982] Crim.LR 340. Psychiatric evidence is not admissible from either side on the issue of intention or other mental state except on the issue of insanity, diminished responsibility, or automatism. See *Chard* (1971) 56 CAR 268; *Turner* [1975] QB 834. For the three exceptions see Chaps.28–30. The law is criticised by Samuels in [1981] Crim.LR 762.

[6] *Hurren* (1962) 46 CAR 323.

principal reason was the desire of the judges to procure and uphold the conviction of people who were public dangers or public nuisances.

A contributory factor was that lawyers spent no time reflecting on their fundamental concepts. They were slow in developing the concept of recklessness. When the only mental element they could think of was intention (or knowledge), they found that they needed to give it a wide definition which in effect covered recklessness. Unfortunately it then covered negligence as well.

But the maxim about intending probable consequences was always objectionable. It created a fictitious or "constructive" intention.[7] (A person who asserted that he knew that a driver who had had a nasty accident intended to cause it, when he knew full well that the driver had only taken a risk, would be regarded by everyone, except possibly a lawyer, as having told a lie.) It applied to some crimes but not to all, and when it did apply it turned negligence into intention.

The maxim gained some plausibility from the fact that it superficially resembled a common sense rule of evidence. Often one can judge whether a man intended a consequence only by asking whether anyone in his shoes would have realised that the consequence was likely *and whether there is any reasonable interpretation of his actions other than the hypothesis that he intended the consequence*. The maxim was erroneous because it omitted the emphasised words.

Change in the law came at last as a reaction to the decision of the House of Lords in *Director of Public Prosecutions v. Smith*,[8] the most criticised judgment ever to be delivered by an English court. The Lords there applied the probable consequence maxim even to the crime of murder. They held that not merely could intent be inferred from the probability of the consequence but that the presumption of intent in such circumstances was irrebuttable. In other words, the judge could say to the jury:

> "Members of the jury, in deciding whether the defendant intended this consequence you merely have to consider whether a reasonable man would have foreseen it as probable. Do not enquire whether the defendant foresaw it, or whether he intended it. You can find that he intended it although you are sure he did not."

This preposterous rule was overthrown, or was intended to be overthrown, by the Criminal Justice Act 1967 s.8.

> "A court or jury, in determining whether a person has committed an offence
>
> (*a*) shall not be bound in law to infer that he intended or foresaw a result of his actions by reason only of its being a natural and probable consequence of those actions; but
>
> (*b*) shall decide whether he did intend or foresee that result by reference to all the evidence, drawing such inferences from the evidence as appear proper in the circumstances."

---

[7] A word is used in a constructive sense when the ordinary meaning is replaced by an artificial, technical meaning as a method of extending rules beyond their plain scope.

[8] [1961] AC 290.

As will be shown, in cases involving intoxication the section is blatantly disregarded by the courts. Apart from that, however, it is accepted as establishing that intention is to be ascertained by a "subjective" investigation—an investigation into the mind of the defendant—even though one can generally make this investigation only by studying his outward acts.

Suppose the defendant says that he was in a blind rage, or in the grip of fear, and did not know what he was doing. Might that get him off, if the offence charged requires intention or knowledge?

Since the enactment of section 8 the defence would have to be left to the jury. But the judge would doubtless tell the jury that they are entitled to find that acts done in rage or fear can be found to be purposive, the emotional state overcoming the defendant's inhibitions rather than his awareness.[9]

Does section 8 get rid of strict liability?

The section applies only when the crime is one requiring *mens rea*. It tells you that if a crime requires a mental element, that mental element must be genuinely ascertained, so far as this can possibly be done; and if it cannot be done, then the prosecution, who have the burden of proving the mental element, must fail. The section is inapplicable if the crime does not require a mental element.

§ 3.4. AWARENESS OF PROBABILITY

It might have been thought that section 8 would have put an end to the mendacious definition of intention in terms of probability. Unfortunately, the section does not define intention, and this has given some judges of the old school the opportunity to fight a rearguard action. They continue to say that the definition of intention includes a reference to probable consequences, modifying this (in obedience to section 8) only by requiring that the defendant must have been aware of the probability of the consequence. They read the word "intend" in the section to mean "intend in law," not "intend according to the ordinary meaning of the word." If this is correct, intention in law still covers recklessness, or at least a large part of it.

The opposing view is that intention should now, at long last, be brought back to the natural meaning of ordinary speech, so that a consequence cannot properly be said to be intended unless the consequence is the doer's purpose, or is inseparably connected with his purpose (in a way to be explained presently).

The most powerful advocate of the fictitious definition of intention at the present day is Lord Diplock. His opinion is not merely that the known

[9] Fear is likely to be regarded more indulgently than anger. See *Att.-Gen. for Northern Ireland's Reference* [1977] AC 105, discussed in the 1st edn 63.

probability of the event is equivalent to intention but that the known *likelihood* is.[1] "Likelihood" is a looser word than "probable" (which is itself pretty loose). On one occasion Lord Diplock remarked that a consequence can in some contexts be regarded as likely if it is "on the cards."[2] So it seems that in his opinion a man can be taken to intend what he foresees as a merely possible outcome.

There are strong arguments against such an extension of crimes of intention.

- Extending words by giving them constructive meanings is tolerable in trivial matters, as when Parliament provides that a town square is deemed to be a street. That is merely using a word as shorthand for a group of words, as a matter of convenience. Constructive meanings should not be attached to words expressing moral and political concepts. Otherwise, moral and political positions can be captured not by argument but by Orwellian newspeak, in such a way that not merely discourse but thought in the old way becomes impossible.
- Section 8 distinguishes between intention and foresight. Lord Diplock's opinion would make them largely synonymous.
- Parliament now regularly enacts offences in terms of a two-part requirement of intention or recklessness; this clearly implies that recklessness is distinct from intention, and may fairly be taken to imply that mere foresight of probability or likelihood is not part of intention.
- The judges generally sentence much more leniently for reckless crimes than for intentional ones, even where the statutory maximum is the same in both cases, because they see a great moral and social difference between the two.[3] Crimes involving foresight of probability (or of likelihood, whatever that means) are not so bad as cases of true intention and should not be lumped with it.
- Some decisions specifically hold that when a crime can be committed only intentionally, and not recklessly, intention bears its ordinary meaning and not a fictitious meaning involving knowledge of probability. This is so in relation to:
  —wounding with intent[4];
  —theft[5]
  —all statutory offences of doing something "with intent to" do something else.[6]
  —The rule also held for the offence of attempt at common law, and doubtless the same rule now applies to statutory attempts.[7]

  These decisions show that when it comes to the point the courts do not accept the fictitious meaning of intention. The Law Commission, too, accepted the natural meaning,[8] and the CLRC followed suit.[9]
- Even if the fictitious meaning is worded in terms of foresight of probability and not likelihood, the notion of probability is too vague to be satisfactory in this context. "Likelihood" would be even worse. Statisticians treat "probable" as synonymous with "possible:" one can have a statistical probability of zero, or of one in a trillion. It may be tempting to say that for legal purposes "probable" means "more likely than not,"i.e. greater than a probability of 50 per cent. (0·5). This is so in some legal contexts in which probability is used. But a person who knowingly ran a one in three risk of killing a man

---

1 *Lemon* [1979] AC at 638 (dissenting opinion).
2 *Sheppard* [1981] AC at 405C.
3 § 6.10 n. 12.
4 § 9.1.
5 Chap. 32.
6 E.g. *Steane* [1947] KB 997.
7 § 17.4.
8 See [1978] Crim.LR 589.
9 See § 3.5 n. 9.

would certainly be regarded as risking a probable consequence. The law, when it speaks of probability in relation to fault, is interested not only in the degree of probability of the consequence but in the magnitude of the calamity if it occurs. This can be accommodated in the notion of recklessness as an unreasonable or unjustifiable running of risk, but not suitably within the notion of intention.

In *Hyam*[10] members of the House of Lords were somewhat divided between the two definitions, but the point was not directly before the House. In *Belfon*,[11] the next year, the Court of Appeal accepted Lord Hailsham's natural definition in *Hyam* and rejected the artificial definition; yet the year after that, in *Allsop*,[12] a differently constituted Court of Appeal accepted the artificial definition. It was unnecessary for the court in the last case to do this, since all that it was expressing was the fact that the particular offence before the court was not confined to an intention to cause harm, in the ordinary sense of the word "intention."[13]

§ 3.5. THE KNOWN SIDE-EFFECT

Even though a man's knowledge that a particular consequence will probably result from his act is sometimes an insufficient basis for saying that he intends it, there are strong reasons for holding that as a legal matter he can be held to intend something that he knows for sure he is doing. This is sometimes called "oblique" intent—not the result that is in the straight line of the defendant's purpose, but a side-effect that he accepts as inevitable.

Clearly, a person can be taken to intend a consequence that follows under his nose from what he continues to do,[1] and the law should be the same where he is aware that a consequence in the future is the certain or practically certain result of what he does. As Lord Hailsham said in *Hyam*,[2] "intention" includes "the means as well as the end and the inseparable consequences of the end as well as the means." (What he evidently meant was the consequences known to the defendant to be inseparable.) It is arguable that everyone would understand "intention" in this extended meaning; at any rate, the extension is not sufficiently great to depart seriously from ordinary ideas, while not to allow it would in some

---

[10] § 11.2 at n. 2.

[11] [1976] 1 WLR 741, 3 All ER 46, 63 CAR 59.

[12] (1976) 64 CAR 29.

[13] See further, on the authorities, my *The Mental Element in Crime* (Jerusalem and Oxford 1965) 25–35; J H Buzzard in [1978] Crim.LR 5; reply, J C Smith, *ibid.* 14; 1 Leg. Stud. 189. The artificial definition is still enthusiasticaly supported in Archbold, 41st edn para. 17–13.

[1] Mere knowledge is not, of course, enough to constitute intention if there is nothing that the defendant can do about it. This proposition is particularly important in relation to situational offences (§ 7.6). If a patient in hospital gets to know that his child at home is being neglected, he does not at that moment himself intentionally or wilfully neglect the child, if he cannot do anything to prevent the neglect continuing. See Glazebrook in *Reshaping the Criminal Law* (London 1978) 117–118. Similarly, a person who is non-culpably in possession of a contraband object is given a reasonable time to surrender it to the police: § 7.4 n. 3.

[2] [1975] AC at 74.

contexts make the concept of intention notably defective for practical purposes.

> To take a hypothetical case: suppose that a villain of the deepest dye sends an insured parcel on an aircraft, and includes in it a time-bomb by which he intends to bring down the plane and consequently to destroy the parcel. His immediate intention is merely to collect on the insurance. He does not care whether the people on board live or die, but he knows that success in his scheme will inevitably involve their deaths as a side-effect. On the theoretical point, common sense suggests that the notion of intention should be extended to this situation; it should not merely be regarded as a case of recklessness.[3] A consequence should normally be taken as intended although it was not desired, if it was foreseen by the actor as the *virtually certain* accompaniment of what he intended. This is not the same as saying that any consequence foreseen as *probable* is intended.

One specific argument in favour of recognising oblique intention is that sometimes it is only a verbal question whether one regards the intention as direct or oblique. D helps a friend to evade justice because the friend offers him payment. One can say that D intends to help his friend to escape (direct intention), his motive being to earn money (the motive being legally immaterial), or one can say that D intends to earn money, knowing that in doing so he is helping his friend to evade justice (oblique intention). The facts are the same either way, and how one verbalises them should make no difference.

This kind of intention should be sufficient to support a conviction of criminal attempt. Suppose that in the example of the bomb the villain were arrested as he was about to put the bomb on the plane. To account him guilty only of recklessness (which is not sufficient for an attempt) would make the notion of intention pedantically narrow. Whereas murder can be committed in some cases by recklessness, attempted murder requires an intent to kill and is not committed by recklessness as to death. Here the villain would properly be held to have intended to kill.

But is there a satisfactory line between foreseen certainty, which you say can be intention, and foreseen probability, which you deny is intention? The bomb might have gone off but the pilot might miraculously have brought the stricken plane safely to land.

Clearly, one cannot confine the notion of foresight of certainty to certainty in the most absolute sense. It is a question of human certainty, or virtual certainty, or practical certainty. This is still not the same as speaking in terms of probability.

The Law Commission in its draft Bill to clarify the mental element accepted the amplification of the definition of intention here proposed, to cover foresight of virtual certainty (without going as far as to allow it to cover all foreseen probabilities). The Commission proposed that the use in a statute of the word "intend" (or any of its direct derivatives, such as "intention") should imply the "standard test of intention," namely:

---

[3] Whatever the analysis, the culprit will be guilty either of murder or of manslaughter; these crimes will be discussed in the appropriate chapters.

> "Did the person whose conduct is in issue either intend to produce the result or have no substantial doubt that his conduct would produce it."[4]

The reference to "no substantial doubt" was thought (in my opinion, wrongly[5]) to be a clearer expression for the jury than "practical certainty."

The effect of the definition is not only to make it clear that intention covers cases of "no substantial doubt," but also to put an end to the idea that mere foresight of a probable or likely consequence is a form of intention.

While the general idea behind the Commission's draft is right, it would be well to qualify it by giving the court the right not to extend intention to cases of no substantial doubt where it would be contrary to the purpose of the law or contrary to justice.

A Working Party previously set up by the Commission had recommended that the definition should be qualified by a proviso to the effect that the extension of the meaning of intention to foreseen certainties should not apply to the illegal conduct of other persons. The Working Party had in mind the decision in *Beatty* v. *Gillbanks*, which will be discussed later.[6] In that case, members of the Salvation Army foresaw that when they assembled they would be set upon, because they knew that this was the policy of their opponents; but that did not make them responsible for being set upon.[7] The reason for the limitation is partly the result of our notion of responsibility, which we attribute to the immediate wrongdoer, not to the innocent party who merely foresees the wrongdoing. It would be an intolerable extension of criminal responsibility if people who were exercising their lawful rights and liberties were to be made responsible for the acts of deliberate mischief-makers. The Law Commission rejected the Working Party's proposal on this subject without saying why.

It seems that there are other circumstances where the application of the doctrine of oblique intent would be undesirable, for which reason it would be better to give the court a general discretion.[8]

The Law Commission does not walk the corridors of power, and its draft Bill on this subject, like many others of its excellent recommendations, lies neglected. There is a strong suspicion that this particular report is blighted by failing to win the acceptance of officials in Government Departments, whose opinions Ministers tend to take in preference to anybody else's. The Commission's views of what the law should be are also studiously ignored by the House of Lords as the final judicial tribunal. However, as was mentioned before, the proposals were approved by the CLRC in its report on offences against the person, and the committee recommended that if not otherwise made law they should be enacted in the proposed new Offences against the Person Act, for the purpose of that Act.[9] This report, too, has not yet broken through the official wall of silence.

If the Commission's definition or something like it is enacted in the

---

[4] Law Commission, *Criminal Law: Report on the Mental Element in Crime* (Law Com. No. 89, 1978) 56. The draft Bill is reprinted in Smith and Hogan, *Cases etc.*, 2nd edn 97.

[5] See [1978] Crim.LR 588.

[6] § 15.4 at n. 8.

[7] See *The General Part* 2nd edn § 19. For a discussion of this distinction in relation to the notion of conditional intention see J C Smith in [1974] Current Legal Problems 113.

[8] See § § 7.5, 15.9.

[9] CLRC, 14th Report, Cmnd 7644 of 1980, paras. 6–11.

proposed code, this will not mean that the trial judge will always have to read it out to the jury in a case requiring proof of intention. Normally, intention means purpose, and it will be sufficient to tell the jury that, or indeed to leave the word without explanation.[10] The instruction about "no substantial doubt" need be given only where there was no desire to bring the particular event about.

This discussion has been chiefly concerned with intention as to consequences. Intention as to circumstances will be considered in § 6.2.

SUMMARY

Mens rea means the mental state required for serious crimes (and a number of § .1
lesser offences), or for some particular crime. *Actus reus* means the external elements of a crime. *Mens rea* can be present although the offender had a good motive or did not know the law. It may relate to the doing of an act (in crimes of basic intent, where the act is done intentionally or recklessly), or to the consequences of the act (in crimes of ulterior intent). Whether a crime is one or the other may depend, e.g. on whether or not a statute impliedly requires a fraudulent purpose. Some crimes require the *absence* of a dishonest or fraudulent intent.

Motive is ulterior intention; but lawyers generally use the word to denote an § .2
ulterior intention that is not part of the legal rule. Whether the court will interpret a particular intention as an illegal purpose or as an immaterial motive sometimes depends upon the court's perception of policy, as in the offence of wilfully obstructing a constable in the execution of his duty. To avoid errors in reasoning, acts should not be categorised as intentional in the abstract; they must be intentional as to a relevant fact, whether bodily movement or consequence as the case may be.

The Criminal Justice Act 1967 s.8 establishes that intention and foresight are to § .3
be ascertained by a "subjective" investigation; but the judge may tell the jury that they may infer these mental states from what the defendant did, provided that they look at the whole of the evidence.

In the past, a body of legal opinion has favoured a concept of fictitious or § .4
constructive intention, in terms of the defendant's knowledge that the consequence is probable. This should be regarded as abolished by section 8.

However, the definition of intention as actual intention must be modified or § .5
explained in one respect. Awareness that a consequence is certain or practically certain may be taken to be intention in law, unless this is contrary to justice.

---

[10] See *Belfon* [1976] 1 WLR 741, 3 All ER 46, 63 CAR 59.

Chapter 4

NEGLIGENCE

'Taint what men don't know that makes trouble in the world; it's what they know for certain that ain't so.

Josh Billings.

§ 4.1. THE DEFINITION OF NEGLIGENCE

Intention is clearly a mental state, and a type of legal fault. Another type of legal fault, not necessarily involving a mental state, is negligence.

Some accidents (or other events) are so unexpected that when they happen we can only say that they were unavoidable—in legal language, "inevitable." We cannot think of anything that a careful person would have done to avoid the evil result, if he had been in the shoes of the defendant.

Other accidents happen because of the neglect of some precaution that a reasonable man would have used. (The reasonable man is sometimes, and better, called a prudent man.) Such accidents are the products of what we call negligence, or carelessness.

Negligence, then, is failure to conform to the standard of care to which it is the defendant's duty to conform. It is failure to behave like a reasonable or prudent man, in circumstances where the law requires such reasonable behaviour. (In this context, of course, as nearly always in law, the word "man" includes "woman.") An employer may for example be negligent as to whether safety precautions are being used by his workpeople.

You mean the defendant was thoughtless?

Yes, or incompetent in a job (such as driving a car) in which he should have been competent. Or, worse still, he may actually have seen the danger and "chanced his arm." In the latter case he is advertently negligent, or in other words reckless. If he did not advert to the danger, or in other words realise there was a risk, when he ought to have, he is inadvertently negligent. Negligence means forbidden conduct where the defendant's liability depends on the fact that he failed to realise (foresee/know) what he ought to have realised, and failed to conform his conduct accordingly, or, *a fortiori*, that he did realise it and yet failed to conform his conduct as he should.

The test of negligence in terms of the prudent man is called an "objective" standard, because it does not depend upon a finding of what passed in the defendant's mind.

Why do you bring in the prudent man in defining negligence? Is it because otherwise the standard would vary for everyone?

There would be no standard at all. Every judgment of a man's conduct implies judgment measured against a standard external to him.

Who is this "prudent man"? Is he the man in the street?

The man in the street, that legendary combination of sage and ignoramus, does not quite represent the idea. The "prudent man" or "reasonable man" of the lawyer's imagining is the exemplary man: the cautious, circumspect, anxiously calculating paragon who is held up by the judges as a model of behaviour. Sometimes, it is true, he is described as the ordinary man, or the average man. But little effort is made at trials to find how ordinary men behave; and it would not be a cast-iron defence to a charge of negligence to show that other people are prone to do exactly as the defendant did. (At least, that is the position in the law of tort.) *Homo juridicus* is the ideal man, the moral man, the conscientious man—not setting the standard so high that life becomes impossible in ordinary terms, but nevertheless requiring the most careful consideration to be given, so that harm is avoided and the law obeyed.

Why not eliminate talk of reasonable men by asking simply whether the harm was probable?

Probability is a matter of varying degree. Negligence consists in taking a risk of harm with such a degree of probability as to be socially unacceptable. This depends on what it is that is at stake. A surgeon may, if there is no other way of alleviating his patient's suffering or prolonging his life, perform an operation that carries a very high risk of killing his patient, without being adjudged negligent. An employer who, in order to increase production and profits, takes what is, statistically, a much smaller risk with the lives of his workpeople may well be held to be so.

What should a prosecutor do to prove negligence?

In an action in tort for negligence the plaintiff must give particulars of the alleged negligence in his statement of claim. For example, in a running-down case he will say that the defendant drove too fast, on the wrong side of the road, without keeping a proper look-out, and so on. There are no similar pleadings in criminal cases, but the prosecutor who alleges negligence must be prepared to say what the defendant could and should have done (or refrained from doing) in order to avoid the accident or other occurrence.

The evidence given on the negligence issue is almost exclusively evidence of what the defendant did (or failed to do). After that, it is for the jury (or magistrates) to say whether the defendant's behaviour showed a lack of due caution. But occasionally experts called on behalf of the prosecution or defence are allowed to say that a mistake made by the defendant in a technical matter was an understandable one,[1] or that the defendant behaved as people do in the particular occupation.[2] As said before, it is not necessarily a defence to show that

---

[1] *Lamb* § 12.2 n. 5.

[2] Winfield and Jolowicz, *Tort*, 11th edn 88–89, 94; J Munkman, *Employer's Liability at Common Law*, 9th edn 43–47.

the defendant complied with the average standard of conduct, because the tribunal may still say that this average standard was negligent; but the evidence may help the defence all the same.

A person who, otherwise than in an emergency, undertakes a task that can be safely performed only if he has special skill will be negligent if he does not possess that skill.

The word "carelessness" as a synonym for negligence is misleading unless we realise that legal carelessness can be committed by those who care deeply. A man may take all the care of which he is capable, and yet be accounted "careless" or negligent for failing to reach the objective standard. He may honestly (or, to use another expression, in good faith, *bona fide*[3]) believe that the facts are such that he is not imperilling anyone; but he may be held to have been negligent in arriving at that belief. An incompetent driver may be convicted of driving "without due care and attention" even though he was doing his level best. The careless person is the person who does not *take* the care he ought to take: never mind whether he *felt* careful. He can be held to be negligent in making a perfectly honest mistake.

Almost the only crime at common law carrying responsibility for negligence, certainly the only one of importance, is manslaughter; and here the courts have developed the restriction that the negligence must be "gross" in order to found criminal responsibility. This means that a small lapse from reasonable conduct does not make a person punishable.

Several other offences of negligence have been created by statute. The legislature seems to prefer to speak of a failure to use care (as in the offence of careless driving) or of a requirement of due diligence or reasonable conduct; but these are only different ways of referring to the concept of negligence. Statutes creating offences of omission often involve responsibility for negligence, because the purpose of such statutes is that the defendant should move himself to take positive steps to bring about the situation desired by the legislature.

When statutes create new offences of negligence, they do not specify the degree of negligence requisite for penal responsibility; and it might perhaps have been thought that, by analogy with the rule developed in manslaughter, the judges would have required all criminal negligence to be "gross." The rule is proposed in the American Law Institute's Model Penal Code.[4] English judges have not taken this line, so that, with us, statutory criminal negligence generally means any departure, however small, from the standard of the reasonable man. If some courts act more leniently, that is not reflected in the theory of the law.

Do I gather that when considering negligence you entirely ignore the defendant's state of mind?

That would be going too far. One can imagine circumstances where an ordinary driver would not be careless in running a blind man down, if he did not know he was blind and had no reason to suppose he would proceed as he did. But a driver who knew that the man was blind might on such facts be guilty of careless driving.

Is negligence a form of mens rea?

Some judges assume this, but there are substantial arguments the other way.

- Negligence is not necessarily a state of mind, so it is not properly called *mens rea*.
- The most serious and severely punishable crimes are defined to require intention or recklessness. If it were allowed that negligence is *mens rea*,

[3] Generally pronounced "bohna fydee." Note that this means "in good faith." The noun "good faith," if you wish to speak Latin, is *bona fides* (generally pronounced "bohna fydeez").

[4] S. 202(2)(*d*).

the judges might extend the concept of recklessness to cover negligence (which some of them are in any event strongly inclined to do), and might hold that all crimes at common law can be committed negligently (which would result in a great increase of severity). The argument does *not* involve saying that negligence should not be punished: only that it should not generally be punished on a par with crimes requiring a mental element.[5]

§ 4.2. THE JUSTIFICATION OF PUNISHMENT FOR NEGLIGENCE

The reason for punishing negligence is the utilitarian one, that we hope thereby to improve people's standards of behaviour.

Isn't the question one of moral wrong? It is wrong not to exercise consideration for others.

If inadvertent negligence results from not caring about other people, it is a defect of character and may be regarded as morally wrong. But what lawyers call inadvertent negligence is not always of this kind. Negligence may be just a slip by a well-disposed person, and whether that should be accounted morally wrong is open to debate.

Even though the offender did not realise the danger on the occasion in question, he would have realised it if he had taken due precautions. So he was morally to blame.

I do not dissent; but we should keep our eyes open to the facts. Apply what you say to the particular case of a forgetful person. A man with a bad memory can often take steps to remedy his deficiency—by keeping a diary of his engagements and consulting it frequently, and so on. But his memory may be so bad that one day he forgets to look in his diary, or forgets an item recorded in it. Perhaps, to overcome this risk, he takes additional steps, such as asking his wife to remind him of a particular engagement. But one day he forgets to ask his wife. Is he to think of another device to remind him to look at his diary or to ask his wife to remind him? Is it moral fault not to do so? What we are faced with is the plain fact that on the particular occasion the thought of the engagement never comes into his mind. That is a deficiency in his mental make-up which he cannot help. To search back into his past for the purpose of finding some defect in the arrangements he made to remedy his failing, and blaming him on that account, often wears the appearance of being an unrewarding exercise in moralism.

---

[5] Fletcher in 119 U of Pa L Rev. 401 would like to make *mens rea* mean not the state of mind proscribed by law (given the other elements of the crime) but the normative concept of culpability. But if *mens rea* refers to culpability the term ceases to have any independent value. Fletcher's argument is also impaired by his false assumption that those who object to *general* penal liability for negligence would "excuse every inadvertent factual risk" taken by a careless person.

It is not only a question of memory. Many studies have been made of accident proneness; and it has been found that large categories of people are more accident prone than others. Old people are worse than younger people, men worse than women, unmarried people worse than married.[1] But some individuals are particularly accident prone. They are born negligent, so to speak, or become so through their experiences. A person has an innate temperament, which may in course of time be modified by many circumstances over which he has no control. The result may be that he is impulsive, unable to stop and consider the consequences of what he is doing, or too dull in mind to imagine them; that he is selfish, preferring his own convenience to the safety of others; that he is clumsy, unable to control his own movements (or those of a machine he is using) with due precision, or with a slow reaction-time in case of emergency.

If, as you say, the individual is unable to help these aspects of his mind or body, how can he be said to deserve punishment?

This objection to imposing liability for negligence appeals particularly to those who take the "determinist" position, according to which all events (including human acts) are governed by pre-existing events which are their causes. Everything we do is the product of our genetic constitution and personal history.

We need not go into the voluminous arguments for and against determinism. Sufficient to say that the determinist philosophy, though it may be true, is of little interest either to the lawyer or to the moralist. The question in law and morals is whether the offender could have acted otherwise *if he had willed*. If he could, he is morally and legally responsible.[2] The further question "Was he able to will?" may be speculated on by philosophers, but is eschewed in law and morals for a pragmatic reason. The object of the law and of a moral system is to influence our wills in a socially desired direction. Once this simple point is grasped, the apparent difficulty of reconciling the philosophy of determinism with ordinary moral attitudes disappears. However, malfunctioning of the will is given moral and legal significance when it is associated with childhood or is regarded as a symptom of mental disorder.

The notion of fault has a place even within the framework of the determinist philosophy. Whether fault "exists" or not, the plain man thinks that it does exist. He is prepared to acknowledge that punishment for fault is just, when punishment without fault would be unjust. Therefore, we secure the best acceptance for the operation of the criminal law if we limit it to cases perceived as ones of fault—that is, cases where most people, *properly conditioned*, would have acted otherwise.

Again, punishment for what is seen as fault can affect future conduct in a way that punishment without fault cannot. Punishment for fault assumes that the offender could have prevented the occurrence—or, at least, that there were no circumstances *outside the defendant's mental and bodily constitution* that he could not have modified to prevent the

---

[1] See K Knudsen in 18 Acta Sociologica 62.

[2] I do not, therefore, accept Fletcher's criticism (*Rethinking Criminal Law* (Boston 1978) 504–505) that an objective standard of negligence implies that negligence is not blameworthy.

occurrence[3]; and we may entertain a hope that such punishment may cause him to act better afterwards. The application of punishment is a way of conditioning the offender for the future.

The position is different if punishment is administered for inevitable accidents, when it is admitted that no ordinary person doing what the offender was doing would have been able to avoid a recurrence of the situation, otherwise than by ceasing altogether from the class of activity in question—which activity may be socially desirable. Here the offender is made to accept the risk of punishment as an unavoidable incident of the activity. This is the position with crimes of strict responsibility, but from the moral point of view strict liability is highly suspect doctrine.

Liability for negligence is a way of sanctioning (punishing) common sense rules that in themselves have no legal force. There are well-known rules of prudence relating to the management of firearms, that one should never leave them loaded, or point them at anyone even though believed to be unloaded, and so on. Again, it is only a rule of prudence, not explicitly one of law, that one should not pass on a blind corner (except that there is a law on the subject of not crossing double white lines). Failure to observe these rules (which will generally be an intentional or reckless failure) will readily be held to be negligence, founding a charge of careless driving or of manslaughter.

The reason why drivers do not pass on blind corners is because they apprehend a consequence much more immediate and terrifying than what may afterwards happen in a court of law.

That is true, but the law of reckless and careless driving can add to the pressure to make bad drivers change their habits and in the last resort to give up driving.

Carelessness with firearms is in a different legal position from careless driving. Such carelessness is not an offence in itself, and it is not an offence even if it causes severe injury, the reason evidently being that accidents with firearms are too uncommon to attract particular attention from the law. However, if the victim dies, a charge of manslaughter may be brought.

Paradoxically, the justification for punishing negligence is stronger in minor offences involving neither imprisonment nor odium than in major offences. "Regulatory offences" generally relate to the conduct of a business or other undertaking where the situation is a recurring one. Fines, and if necessary repeated fines, prod people into taking care. On the other hand, a substantial sentence of imprisonment would make little sense, since it would be disproportionate to the occasion. As regards the offender himself it would be more likely to destroy his occupation than to improve his standards. Even when the harm done is great, if the situation is one of only isolated occurrence there may be little or no social advantage in

[3] That is to say, could not have modified if he had had a normal make-up. A determinist would not agree with the test suggested by Hart in *Oxford Essays in Jurisprudence* (ed. A G Guest, London 1961) 44–49: could the the defendant, given his mental and physical capacities, have taken the precautions that a reasonable man would have taken? For, according to the determinist, no one, given his mental and physical capacities, could have acted otherwise than as he did. Even one who does not know what to think about determinism may see difficulties in Hart's thesis. It postulates that a person has the capacity to overcome his own mental incapacities. Sometimes one can (and does) "overcome" them for practical purposes, but sometimes well-intentioned people fail to do so. Is it not because on these occasions they lack the "overcoming" capacity? The whole investigation is much too dubious to be made the foundation of a legal principle.

inflicting heavy punishment on the inadvertent and unlucky offender. Such a sentence, passed for reasons of general deterrence, is unlikely to make ordinary people attend more anxiously to the consequences of their conduct, except perhaps in the cases already mentioned where compliance may be demanded with some identifiable rule of prudence.

In short, although there is little objection to fining the inadvertent offender, for reasons of general as well as particular deterrence, it seems right if possible to do so in summary proceedings for a breach of some specific regulation rather than by making negligence a serious and stigmatic offence. This is an objection to the crime of manslaughter as we now have it. Lord Radcliffe observed that "there is a certain virile attraction in the idea of making a man answer for the foreseeable consequences of what he has done without troubling to search his mind for motives or purposes: but it does not go well with the dock or the prison gate."[4] Responsibility for negligence is therefore exceptional for the more serious crimes. There would be much to be said for enacting that no one should be sent to prison on account of negligence.

§ 4.3. THE HANDICAPPED DEFENDANT

When comparing the physically handicapped (blind, maimed, etc.) defendant with the reasonable man, we suppose that the reasonable man suffers from the same handicap. The defendant need only do his best with the body he has. But it would generally be negligent for a handicapped man to undertake something that could be done safely only by an ordinary man, if he has the opportunity not to do it.

What if the defendant is substandard in abilities?

The reasonable man is not imagined to be substandard in intelligence or foresight.

But wouldn't it be more just to have different standards of care for experts at one end of the scale and people of poor intelligence at the other?

We were all born green. Some people remain that colour, but even dullards are not immune from the conditioning processes of life, including the law.

The jury or magistrates apply the negligence test, roughly speaking, by asking themselves: Was the defendant a bigger fool than I like to think I should have been in the same circumstances? That is a workable test, even though not very precise. But it would be impossible and impolitic to have an array of standards varying with position on an IQ scale. For example, an old man who has a driving accident may decide to give up driving as a result of having to answer a charge of a driving offence, quite apart from any disqualification that the court may impose upon him. It would be absurd to say: the older or more stupid the driver, the lower is the degree of care we expect from him.

Moreover, if the law's reasonable man is to be invested with the defendant's IQ, there seems to be no reason why he should not be invested with the defendant's emotional instability, and indeed with his whole character as resulting from his genes and environment. But if the reasonable man is given all the characteristics of the defendant, the standard of judgment wholly disappears, for we can then compare the defendant's conduct only with the (presumably identical) conduct of a fictitious construct who is like the defendant in every conceivable way.

---

[4] *Censors* (London 1961) 20.

However, where a person is mentally impaired (a technical term), this can introduce the question of mental responsibility. See Chapter 28.

If the defendant was drunk, do you suppose that the reasonable man was likewise?

Obviously, the "reasonable drunken man" would be an unworkable concept. The reasonable man is as sober as the proverbial judge. So on a charge involving negligence no allowance is made for the hallucinatory or disabling effects of alcohol or other drugs when taken voluntarily (§ 21.5). The rule is justified on social grounds, since the criminal courts need the power to control those who are given to drinking and who when in drink are dangerous.

If the defendant is a juvenile, do you compare him with the reasonable person of his age?

Yes. This is a modification of the usual rule requiring the mental characteristics of the defendant to be ignored.[1]

SUMMARY

Negligence is the failure to behave like a reasonable (or prudent) man, in circumstances where the law requires such behaviour. It should not be regarded as a form of *mens rea*, but may be said to be a form of legal fault. § .1

Negligence can also be said to be a form of moral fault, but punishment should be closely confined by utilitarian considerations. § .2

A person who is voluntarily intoxicated is judged by the standard of the sober man where negligence is in issue. But one who is physically handicapped, or a juvenile, is not expected to behave like a fit adult. § .3

---

[1] The modification is an inference from *Camplin* (§ 24.4 at n. 8) on provocation, and from the civil cases: see Winfield and Jolowicz, *Tort*, 11th edn 644.

CHAPTER 5

RECKLESSNESS

"It's a poor sort of memory that only works backwards," the Queen remarked.

The White Queen to Alice.

§ 5.1. RECKLESSNESS IN THE CRIMINAL LAW

WE learn as a result of experience and instruction, and our learning brings awareness of the dangers of life. We can guess at the probable present even when we cannot directly perceive it, and can project ourselves into the future by foreseeing the probable consequences of our acts. Our memories work forwards.

This is the foundation of the notion of recklessness. "Reckless" is a word of condemnation. It normally involves conscious and unreasonable risk-taking, either as to the possibility that a particular undesirable circumstance exists or as to the possibility that some evil will come to pass. The reckless person deliberately "takes a chance."

Other things being equal, this is evidently a less culpable mental state than intention, though worse than inadvertent negligence. Recklessness, like negligence, is unjustifiable risk-taking. It differs from simple negligence in that the risk is known (subject to an important qualification that is still to come). The culpability of recklessness depends on a number of factors, including the degree of known risk.

Some crimes can be committed only intentionally. But nearly all crimes requiring *mens rea* (which are, broadly speaking, the more serious crimes) now recognise recklessness as an alternative to intention. This proposition holds for most common law crimes[1]; and of late years parliamentary draftsmen have begun to include it in their formulations of offences, as by making it an offence to do something "knowingly or recklessly."

The courts were slow to develop the concept of recklessness. In relation to the consequences of conduct, they tended to think only in terms of intention, negligence and strict liability. Recklessness was accommodated within intention by two lines of reasoning, one now discredited and the other, though still occasionally found in judicial rhetoric, highly suspect.

- The presumption about intending probable consequences was used to make the notion of intention cover what we now term recklessness (and it covered negligence as well).[2]

---

[1] Even where a common law crime has been traditionally stated in terms of intention, the courts may redefine it in terms of intention or recklessness, as they did, with regard to rape, in *Morgan* [1976] AC 182 at 203D–E, 209G–H, 225F.

[2] See, e.g. *Pembliton* (1874) LR 2 CCR 119, [1874–80] All ER 1163, particularly the judgment of Blackburn J.

- The other technique was to speak of "intentionally creating (or taking) a risk,"[3] or 'intending to do something whether or not something else happened or was present."[4] The effect was again to lump recklessness with intention.

Nowadays the two ideas are generally differentiated, but much confusion remains.

Isn't recklessness just extreme negligence? Why not use only the general category of negligence?

The main answer is that even when inadvertent negligence is punishable, the law often treats it as a less serious offence than offences of recklessness. Moreover, whereas recklessness is now recognised as a mode of committing most crimes, many cases of inadvertent negligence are left outside the criminal law as a matter of policy. So we need to have suitable terms to distinguish between (1) recklessness and (2) negligence not necessarily amounting to recklessness.

Although we have general offences of recklessness causing injury to the person or damage to property, we have no such general offences of negligence (apart from driving offences and homicide). Both of the standing reform bodies, whose members are predominantly judges and practitioners, have made a pragmatic judgment in support of this position. The Law Commission decided against having an offence of negligent damage to property when it drafted what is now the Criminal Damage Act 1971, and Parliament accepted the decision. The CLRC decided against proposing an offence of negligent injury to the person when it considered the law of offences against the person.[5] Some Continental jurisdictions have general penal liability of this kind; but we have not hitherto found it to be necessary. Accepting negligence as a general mode of offending would either strain the overworked resources of the penal system or bring about highly selective and indeed capricious enforcement. In general, negligence causing injury or loss is best left to the civil law; if it is to be dealt with penally, this should be done by specific provisions dealing with common categories of negligence.

This leaves us, then, to define recklessness.

§ 5.2. SUBJECTIVE RECKLESSNESS

The subjective-objective controversy again rears its head. The courts have hovered between the idea of recklessness as gross negligence (the "objective" definition) and the idea of recklessness as advertent negligence (the "subjective" definition).

1 The idea of recklessness as gross negligence proposes that recklessness

---

[3] This reasoning was used by Lord Hailsham in *Morgan*, n. 1 above. The technique does not work well. If "intentionally creating a risk" of a result is equivalent to intending the result, then the doer will be guilty even though the risk was justifiable. So a surgeon who operates with a slim hope in a desperate case, and who, therefore, "intentionally runs a risk," would be guilty in the same way as if he had intended the patient's death if that occurs. If he intended the death when doing what he did, the patient's desperate condition would be no defence. In order to avoid this conclusion Lord Hailsham spoke of "exposing the patient to the risk without lawful excuse." There can indeed be a lawful excuse for exposing a patient to a justifiable risk, but not for intentionally killing him. This shows that the rules of law for risking a result and intending a result are not the same. In fact two of the Lords in *Morgan* (Hailsham, in one place, and Edmund-Davies) spoke in terms of recklessness, which is obviously the proper word in relation to conscious risk-taking. See further on this case § 6.6 at n. 4.

[4] § 6.6 at n. 14.

[5] Working Paper on OAP (HMSO 1976) para. 90.

is an extreme departure from the standard of conduct of the prudent man. Often the defendant will have adverted to the risk, but he may not have; and he can (on this view) be accounted grossly negligent whether he adverted or not. The tribunal of fact (jury or magistrates) does not attempt to look into his mind, but simply measures the degree of his departure from the proper standard.

2 The subjective definition, on the other hand, attempts to look into the defendant's mind. It asks whether he realised that there was a risk but carried on regardless.

Although this remains a cloudy area of law, it is probably safe to say that the subjective definition is now partly accepted, but major qualifications are imposed upon it which will have to be studied in due course.

It's perfectly true that we sometimes consciously run a risk. But how can it be proved? When the affair is over, whatever realisation the defendant had at the time leaves no trace. If he says he didn't think, who can contradict him?

One must admit that the subjective theory is an ideal imperfectly achievable. Even if it is accepted in theory, we have to use something suspiciously like an objective test. The jury may be instructed that if anyone would have realised the risk involved in the particular conduct, they may infer that the defendant did so. But:

- There is a difference of degree between saying that the risk was so obvious that the defendant must have appreciated it (subjective recklessness), and saying that a reasonable man would have appreciated it but all the same quite a number of people might not have (when, in the absence of additional evidence, subjective recklessness cannot be inferred, though the defendant will be liable if there is a relevant offence of negligence).
- If the jury are applying the subjective theory they should regard themselves as trying to assess what the defendant must have foreseen (that is to say, did foresee); and if there is something in the particular facts indicating that he may not have appreciated the risk, that will be overriding. If the facts show that the defendant was or may have been only momentarily careless, not appreciating the risk in what he did, he should be acquitted of recklessness on the subjective theory. (Whether he *will* be acquitted depends on how far the courts will go in applying the rule in *Caldwell*, to be considered presently.)

When the subjective definition refers to the defendant realising that there was a risk, what degree of risk are we speaking of?

If the subjective definition were fully adopted, the tribunal of fact would in theory enquire first what degree of risk the defendant foresaw, and would then determine whether that risk was a reasonable/justifiable one for the defendant to run. In practice the enquiry cannot be so fine-tuned. But the tribunal may ask itself whether there was any social justification for the defendant causing more than the usual accepted risks of life. If there was not, then if the tribunal believes that the defendant must at least have foreseen some small risk beyond these accepted risks in what he did, then he can be accounted reckless. In special cases the circumstances may be held to have justified him in running an appreciable degree of risk.[1]

Is a person reckless if he intended the result?

Certainly, *a fortiori*. And a person can be convicted of an offence of negligence if he was reckless or acted intentionally. The wider fault element includes the narrower one.

Nevertheless I can't help feeling that subjective recklessness is a very narrow concept. A person may properly be punishable although he cannot be proved to have been subjectively reckless.

The concept is narrow, but it is meant to be narrow. If the legislature wishes to create an offence of wider range, it can use the concept of negligence.

The fear you have expressed is the main reason why the subjective definition has met with resistance from the judges. They are apprehensive that the jury will acquit too readily. The objective definition, in contrast, enables the jury to express its indignation at the defendant's conduct without bothering about what went on in his mind. But against this it may be said that to ask the jury whether the defendant departed grossly from the reasonable standard leaves them to make a value-judgment with very little assistance.

Part of the trouble arises from the origin of the word "reckless." Etymologically, "recklessness" and "carelessness" mean the same; they refer to the state of mind of not caring, or recking. In the two cases of *Caldwell*[2] and *Stephen Lawrence*[3] (which are to be discussed later in the chapter), Lord Diplock assumed that this meaning still holds. Speaking of recklessness, he said: "The popular or dictionary meaning is: careless, regardless, or heedless, of the possible harmful consequences of one's acts;"[4] and he assumed that this is also the legal meaning. Lord Diplock's words were unexceptionable if he was using "careless" as well as "reckless" in its literal or etymological sense. The reckless person pursues an object without caring, or without caring very much, whether he is creating danger or not. But it has already been observed that the word "careless" does not now mean this, either in its legal sense or in general use; nor did Lord Diplock suppose that it does. A careless person is one who does not *take* care, not one who does not care. The careless driver certainly cares about having an accident, but for temperamental or other reasons is unable to drive in such a way as to avoid it. Lord Hailsham in *Lawrence*[5] remarked on this change in the meaning of carelessness and the consequent fallacy of identifying it with recklessness. He said: "Reckless has . . . almost always . . . applied to a person or conduct evincing a state of mind stopping short of deliberate intention, and going beyond mere inadvertence, or in its modern, though not its etymological and original sense, mere carelessness." He went on to say that the word retains its dictionary sense (the sense he had just explained) in legal contexts; but he also approved the "lucid legal interpretation" given to it by Lord Diplock—failing to perceive that Lord Diplock had accepted the possibility of finding recklessness without any state of mind. In the drowsy atmosphere of the committee room the other lords agreed both with Lord

---

[1] For a fuller discussion see the 1st edn 72–77.
[2] [1982] AC 341.
[3] [1982] AC 510.
[4] *Caldwell* [1982] AC at 351D.
[5] *Lawrence* [1982] AC at 520F.

Diplock, that recklessness means carelessness, and with Lord Hailsham, that it does not. However, the fact remains that the majority of the lords in *Caldwell* and all the lords in *Lawrence* concurred with Lord Diplock in the direction that he proposed should be given to a jury, and this direction appears on its face, as we shall see, to be very largely "objectivist" in approach.

The linguistic question is not merely one of ascertaining the meaning of "recklessness" in the ordinary, unconsidered language of every day. For legal purposes we need a word intermediate between inadvertent negligence and intention, to express the position of one who consciously runs an unjustifiable risk (whether the risk be as to the presence of a circumstance or as to the bringing about of a consequence). There is no word in the language more suitable than "recklessness." If Parliament means to refer to gross negligence, there is nothing easier than for it to say so. If it has specified recklessness, the courts should surely assume that the subjective sense is meant.

The subjective view of recklessness is socially superior to the definition in terms of gross negligence because the latter would subject clumsy or foolish people to the severe punishment intended for deliberate and wicked risk-takers. If the law does not distinguish in terms of possible punishment between crimes requiring a mental state and those not so requiring, some wrong-headed sentencers are going to treat some simpletons and bunglers with unreasonable severity.

I am not really convinced that there is a practical difference beween what you call the subjective and the objective definition. If a man is grossly negligent, then surely a jury is always going to find that he must have realised he was running a risk.

Generally that will be so, but not always. The circumstances may indicate that he did not realise it. The case of *Lamb*[6] is a perfect illustration of negligence without realisation of risk.

> Lamb had a revolver in which there were two bullets; but he ascertained that neither was in the chamber opposite the barrel. So it was safe to pull the trigger, wasn't it? You are wrong, just as Lamb was. He pointed the gun at a friend (who knew that he was acting only in jest), and pulled the trigger. The revolver fired and the friend fell dead.
>
> What Lamb had not realised was that when the trigger was pulled the chambers rotated and brought a bullet into the firing position; and three experts at the subsequent trial agreed that it was natural for a person without experience to make a mistake on this point. Indeed, two police officers gave evidence that they would have made the same mistake as Lamb. Lamb thought that revolvers work by revolving *after* the bullet is fired, when in fact they revolve when the trigger is pulled and *before* the bullet is fired.[7]
>
> Lamb was convicted of manslaughter, and sentenced to 3 years' imprisonment, but on appeal the conviction was quashed for misdirection. We shall return to the case later as a decision on manslaughter (§ 12.2); for the present it is enough to observe that Lamb's error amounted to negligence, not recklessness. To convict him of such a serious offence as manslaughter on these facts (as apparently he could have been convicted on a proper direction) was an over-assessment of his degree of fault. Manslaughter should be confined, in general, to cases of subjective recklessness.

---

[6] [1967] 2 QB 981.

[7] Gallyons the gun dealers tell me that in their experience all revolvers work like this, not just the particular revolver in the case.

I don't think I agree with your "poor Lamb" attitude, where the outcome is as terrible as in this case. People who have killed others by sheer stupidity must take the consequences.

They must live with the physical consequences. But legal punishment is imposed by man, and there must, surely, be a moral or social justification for it. It is not enough to use this cant phrase about taking the consequences.

Of course, Lamb did not behave like the lawyer's prudent man, or as any ordinary person would behave who had been instructed in the use of firearms. I do not deny that Lamb might have been regarded as justly punishable on the scale appropriate to negligence. But he was not reckless: before playing his "joke" he had carefully and correctly ascertained that no bullet was opposite the barrel. There will always be some dolt who plays with a firearm. Have we any reason to suppose that the occasional accident will be prevented by the sentence that Lamb would have served if a technical fault had not been found in the direction to the jury?

After many years of doubt, the subjective meaning of recklessness seemed to be settled by decisions of the Court of Appeal, particularly at the end of the 1970s, on the meaning of statutory "malice," which was held to cover recklessness.[8]

Early statutes had defined a number of serious assaults and also criminal damage in terms of "maliciously" assaulting a person or "maliciously" damaging property. Originally this word was apparently intended to bear its ordinary meaning of spite or ill-will; but Parliament quite possibly did not intend its colourful language to be taken literally, and anyway the judges came to the conclusion that the literal meaning would be too narrow. So they redefined the statutory word.[9] "Malice", it was held, merely meant intention, and never mind about a malicious motive. To say that a ship's passenger who carved his name on the woodwork as a memento of his trip acted "maliciously" was a notable extension of the meaning of the term; but it was necessary if the law of malicious damage was to be given the socially desirable meaning.

The next step was to make malice cover recklessness, but in the first decisions to this effect, and in nearly all the later cases, the courts clearly used the word "recklessness" in a subjective sense.[10] It is true that a few judges seem to have come to the conclusion that "malice"could be treated as a joker word, so that they could, like Humpty Dumpty, make it mean anything they chose; and accordingly they even extended it to cover negligence. But this opinion was never generally accepted, and in the 1970s, as already said, the Court of Appeal rejected it. The court was persuaded, largely perhaps by the influence of academic writers from Kenny onwards, that recklessness as a component of what the judges thought of as malice must bear a subjective meaning.

The Law Commission agreed that the word "reckless" should be interpreted in this way. The definition proposed by the Commission (substantially following the definition of the American Law Institute's Model Penal Code) runs in part as follows:

"The standard test of recklessness as to result is—Did the person

[8] See *Briggs* [1977] 1 WLR 605, 1 All ER 475, 63 CAR 215; approved in relation to the Criminal Damage Act 1971 by *Stephenson* [1979] QB 695; *Mullins* [1980] Crim.LR 37.

[9] Williams, *The Mental Element in Crime* (Jerusalem and Oxford 1965) Chap. 2.

[10] *Ibid.* 69–73.

> whose conduct is in issue foresee that his conduct might produce the result, and, if so, was it unreasonable for him to take the risk of producing it?"[11]

Although the Commission's legislative proposals have disappeared into the Home Office oubliette, its definition of recklessness, like its definition of intention, was approved in substance by the CLRC.[12] Moreover, the Law Commission's definition of recklessness accords with section 8 of the Criminal Justice Act (§ 3.4), which makes foresight entirely a subjective question; so there is a strong argument for saying that the definition is, or should be taken as, part of the present law, not a mere proposal for law reform. It is true that the section does not in terms refer to recklessness, but there is virtually nothing else that it could have been meant to refer to, since the criminal law does not speak of the defendant's foresight apart from recklessness.

We shall see in the next two sections that the opinions catalogued above have been drastically qualified by the House of Lords, which pays virtually no attention to section 8. But the extent of the qualification is not completely clear, and their lordships have not said that they reject subjectivism altogether.

§ 5.3. RECKLESSNESS AND VOLUNTARY INTOXICATION

The meaning of recklessness was reconsidered by the House of Lords in the two cases already mentioned, *Caldwell* and *Stephen Lawrence*.[1]

Both decisions were rendered on the same day in 1981; the majority opinion in *Caldwell* was delivered by Lord Diplock, and the opinions in *Lawrence* were delivered by Lords Hailsham and Diplock (on this occasion with all the other Lords concurring). The first case concerned reckless damage, the second reckless driving. Both cases gave recklessness a wider meaning than had been favoured in the preceding years; they aroused much perplexity and disquiet, but their precise effect upon the law is not yet established. The implications of part of the decision in *Caldwell* (relating to intoxication) can be disposed of before considering its more controversial aspects.

It has long been obvious that voluntary intoxication (alternatively called "self-induced intoxication") presents a problem for the subjectivists. A man may severely wound another, or set fire to a building, and when charged may say that he was so drunk (or so much under the influence of other drugs) that he did not know what he was doing.

But when he was consuming such a quantity of drink he must have known that he was impairing his self-control, and was therefore reckless.

I am not speaking of self-control. Failure of self-control through

---

[11] *Criminal Law, Report on the Mental Element in Crime* (Law Com. No. 89) 60.
[12] § 3.5 n. 9.

[1] Above § .2 nn. 2,3.

intoxication is clearly no defence. The problem arises when the intoxication brings about a failure to perceive risk.

In getting drunk the man knew there was a risk that he might injure someone, so he was reckless.

Your theory of recklessness in imbibing has been twice accepted by the House of Lords,[2] but it involves problems. Whether the man knew he was creating a risk by getting drunk is a question of fact in each case. Perhaps he has got very drunk many times before, and on all previous occasions has fallen peacefully asleep.

Then he should be regarded as being reckless nevertheless.

"Regarding" or "deeming" someone to be something when you do not know he is, or know he is not, is to create a legal fiction, and a fiction does not explain anything—it is merely a disguised restatement of the rule. What I wish to discuss at the moment is whether such a person falls within the definition of subjective recklessness, and I suggest he does not, if his defence is believed or not disbelieved.

Of course the jury may refuse to believe it. There is little to suggest that juries would be be unduly disposed to give credence to a drunkard's affirmation that he was unaware of an obvious danger to a person he was attacking or to property that he was apparently trying to destroy. Nevertheless, judges have feared the possibility of juries doing so.

Even if the drunkard's evidence is accepted, intoxication is so common an accompaniment of violent and destructive behaviour that it ought not be allowed as a let-out from criminal responsibility. Accordingly, trial judges have from time to time told juries that evidence of voluntary intoxication is no defence as a matter of law.

Two reasons may be assigned for taking this line.—First, although it may be unlikely that an intoxicated person is unable to realise what he is doing, the jury (or magistrates) may have difficulty in deciding such an issue.—Secondly, drink and (other) drugs being frequently matters of habit or addiction, there is a substantial possibility that the harmful conduct will be repeated if the offender is not made to alter his ways. If one could be sure both that the defendant did not realise the danger on the present occasion and that he would not inactivate his reasoning powers again, there would be no case for punishing him. But one generally cannot be sure, and anyway the question is best left to the judge in sentencing (or, at least, is best so left if we can trust the humanity and understanding of the judges). By holding the defendant liable, the court is able to consider whether to apply pressure to him to make him avoid becoming intoxicated in future, the pressure taking the form either of punishment for what he has just done or of some form of imposed treatment for his addiction.

Instead of departing from subjectivism in the major offences, why not provide for the dangerous drunk by a new offence of strict liability?

This has been suggested, but the objections to it have been thought to be too great.

The proposal was rejected by the CLRC partly because it was thought too difficult to draft

---

[2] See Lord Elwyn-Jones in *Majewski* [1977] AC at 474–475, cited with approval by Lord Diplock in *Caldwell*. Neither Lord recognised that the proposition could not be supported as an unqualified statement of fact, and that as a statement of legal fiction it could not afford a rational justification for any rule.

satisfactorily. It would complicate the trial by giving the jury another offence to consider. It might encourage lenient juries to go for the new offence instead of for the serious offence that has in fact been committed. And to deal with the very dangerous offender the maximum for the new offence would have to be high.

For these reasons the CLRC, in its report on offences against the person, followed the ALI Model Penal Code (MPC) in recommending legislation to make an exception from the ordinary subjective definition of recklessness. The Committee thought it should be provided that

> "in offences in which recklessness constitutes an element of the offence, if the defendant owing to voluntary intoxication had no appreciation of a risk which he would have appreciated had he been sober, such lack of appreciation is immaterial."

As we know, the committee's recommendations remain pigeon-holed, but in *Caldwell* the House of Lords decided upon instant law reform by judicial fiat. It established the MPC rule (which was a proposal for consideration by American legislatures) as a matter of newly-minted English common law.

> Caldwell was charged under the Criminal Damage Act 1971 section 1 (2) with arson, in that he had set fire to property intentionally or recklessly, being reckless as to whether the life of another would be thereby endangered. He did not deny that he was guilty of simple arson (intentionally or recklessly setting fire to property), but denied being guilty of the aggravated form of arson, saying that he was not reckless as to danger to life because he was so drunk that he never thought of such danger. The trial judge ruled that this was no defence, and Caldwell was convicted, his conviction being upheld on appeal by the House of Lords.

From one point of view the whole legal exercise was unnecessary, since the maximum punishment for simple arson (to which Caldwell confessed) is imprisonment for life, the same as the maximum for arson accompanied by recklessness as to danger to life.[3] However, the theoretical implications of the decision are important. Although it was immediately concerned with arson, the rule was stated as applying generally to the concept of recklessness in statutes.

The opinion delivered by Lord Diplock on behalf of the majority falls into two parts. It begins with a general consideration of the meaning of recklessness (in which respect it will be discussed in the next section), and then turns to the instant case. On the case itself the rule formulated is in terms of the MPC's proposal. It extends the notion of recklessness to circumstances where

> "the actor, due to self-induced intoxication, is unaware of a risk of which he would have been aware had he been sober."

This rule, which, as has been said, was proposed by the CLRC as a legislative solution, is generally acceptable in point of policy, though how (as a matter of present law) it can be reconciled with section 8 of the Criminal Justice Act (§ 3.3), which Lord Diplock did not even trouble to mention, has not been satisfactorily explained.[4] If it should happen that a person

---

[3] The courts normally sentence less severely for a lower-grade offence than for a higher-grade offence, even though the maximum punishment for both is theoretically the same. See, e.g. *Willder* (1973) (Thomas, *Current Sentencing Practice* L2.1(c)). It would, however, be illogical to apply this principle to a case of voluntary intoxication, where the prosecution have not proved otherwise than that the defendant's mind was a blank as to the circumstance of aggravation.

[4] Lord Diplock presumably thought that s.8 had been effectively neutered by the reasoning of Lord Elwyn-Jones in *Majewski* § 21.4 n. 6, but the assumption may be seriously questioned.

intoxicates himself to escape temporarily from the stress of life, and under the influence of the drug commits some mindless and dreadful act, of which he had no expectation or premonition,[5] there is no evidence upon which he may be said to have been in fact reckless as to the result. So the rule in *Caldwell* is not an application of the notion of recklessness to cases of voluntary intoxication (as Lord Diplock presents it to be). It merely makes a pretence of finding recklessness, for reasons of policy. His lordship could not avow this, because the statute under which the defendant was convicted required recklessness, so that it could not be said, without confessing a naked usurpation of legislative power, that as a matter of legal theory recklessness was not required. All that could be done was to deem recklessness to be present, and judges, of course, can deem anything, since there is no one to say them nay.

The limit of the intoxication rule, as stated by Lord Diplock, is that it applies only when the risk is such the defendant would have known of it if he had been sober.

In other words, if a reasonable man would have known of it?

Lord Diplock did not say that. His words were: "a risk of which he *would* have been aware," not "should have been aware."

The reasonable man represents an ideal, unvarying standard of behaviour. Actual people differ in their awareness and in the care they take to ascertain risks. The tribunal must be certain that *this defendant* would have been aware of the risk if he had been sober, which means that allowance must be made for the range of human foresight. To come within the rule the risk must, I suggest, be very obvious indeed. As where the defendant says he did not realise that fire on a floor might burn down the house, or that hitting a man a heavy blow on the head might injure him.

This limitation could keep the rule in *Caldwell* to reasonable proportions. There is, however, a distinct possibility that the courts will widen the intoxication rule by making it purely objective, using the test of what a reasonable man would have known (§ .5).

Suppose that the drunkard was not merely unaware of the risk but positively under the impression that he was acting safely?

We shall see in the next section that the general *Caldwell* rule for recklessness (apart from intoxication), which creates a concept of objective or constructive recklessness, does not apply where the defendant thought that what he was doing was safe. Here the subjective notion of recklessness is allowed to continue. It seems, however, that the special rule in *Caldwell* for intoxication applies even in these circumstances, provided that the tribunal is satisfied that if the defendant had been sober he would have appreciated the risk.

> For example, a man who is the worse for drink may do a silly thing when shooting, believing in his fuddled condition that his act is safe. He is presumably guilty of recklessness under the intoxication rule in *Caldwell*. See § 21.5.

You approve the intoxication rule as a matter of policy, but isn't it very harsh to say not merely that the drunkard is guilty of an offence but is guilty of even the gravest offences on the basis of fictitious recklessness?

Lord Edmund-Davies thought so, in his dissenting opinion in *Caldwell*. Everything depends on the circumstances, and on the humanity of the

---

[5] As in *Lipman*, § 21.3 at n. 10.

courts in sentencing. If they sentence as the judges did in *Lipman* (a case to be considered later), it would indeed be harsh. Murder should certainly stand outside the intoxication rule, as the CLRC proposed.

The subject of intoxication is further considered in Chapter 21. On automatism in relation to intoxication see § 29.6.

§ 5.4. FAILING TO STOP AND THINK

A second difficult case for the definition of recklessness in subjective terms is that of the man who says that he was acting in a blind rage. One may doubt whether there is in fact any such thing as a blind rage; what rage does is to destroy self-control, not awareness. Anyway, rage, like intoxication, is a common concomitant of aggression, and the law cannot look with sympathy on a defence that "I was so angry I didn't know what I was doing." Although no provision was made for blind rage by the Law Commission and the CLRC in the definition of recklessness they favoured, this was because these bodies thought that juries would be so likely to reject the defence that it was not worth legislating for. But in *Caldwell* Lord Diplock, although the case before him was one of intoxication, extended the intoxication rule to cases of rage; and for good measure he brought in other cases of excitement, and even other cases of "not thinking." According to Lord Diplock, whose opinion was concurred in by the majority of the Appellate Committee (and in *Lawrence* by the whole committee), the rule is that if you would have realised the risk if you had stopped to think, then you are held to be reckless for the purpose of a statutory offence of recklessness. Accordingly, in *Caldwell* he enunciated the following model direction to the jury on recklessness in criminal damage. (He was here speaking about recklessness generally, without reference to the particular problem of intoxication.)

> "A person is . . . 'reckless as to whether any such property would be destroyed or damaged' if (1) he does an act which in fact creates an obvious risk that property will be destroyed or damaged and (2) when he does the act he either has not given any thought to the possibility of there being any such risk or has recognised that there was some risk involved and has nonetheless gone on to do it."[1]

It will be seen that, starting with the idea that people who are intoxicated or angry should not on that account be allowed to get away with a criminal act, Lord Diplock saw no stopping place at that point, and reached a position that almost, though not quite, abandons subjectivism in relation to statutory recklessness. The direction was stated in relation to criminal damage because that was their lordships' immediate concern, but Lord Diplock intended a similar rule to apply to other charges of statutory

---

[1] [1982] AC at 354F. For critical discussions of *Caldwell* and *Stephen Lawrence* in relation to recklessness generally see J C Smith, [1981] Crim.LR 393,410; Griew, *ibid.* 743; Williams, [1981] CLJ 252.

recklessness, and the courts have applied it also to certain offences of recklessness at common law.[2]

Let us be clear that in the model direction Lord Diplock is not referring to two distinct classes of people, those within 1 above and those within 2. They are the same class of people. Conditions 1 and 2 must both be satisfied before a person is to be accounted reckless.

Condition 1 states the accepted rule that one cannot be reckless unless one is negligent. It does not state the rule well, because the fact that a person "creates an obvious risk" is not enough. For him to be negligent, which is a condition precedent to his being accounted reckless, the risk must be one that it is unreasonable (unjustifiable) for him to take.[3]

For our purposes we can strip away from the direction the last words of condition 2. These refer to the man who recognises the risk and unreasonably goes ahead. He is reckless on the subjective definition previously accepted. The new element in the definition, what one may call *Caldwell* recklessness, concerns the man who "has not given thought to the possibility of there being any such risk."

Doesn't the rule put the defendant in a cleft stick? Either he saw the risk, in which case he is subjectively reckless, or he didn't think, in which case he is Caldwell reckless.

Yes, except that there is a third possibility, a loophole in the new dispensation of *Caldwell*. The defendant may have given thought and decided that the act would be safe. Here subjectivism still reigns.

The passage quoted, and indeed the rest of Lord Diplock's opinion, does not expressly deal with the point. It does not tell us whether, supposing negligence, the act would be deemed to be reckless. The opinion contains several passages disparaging the subjectivist approach to questions of fault in the criminal law, and from this it might be hastily inferred that recklessness in our law is now negligence and nothing more. However, many reasons can be found for concluding that the opinion was not intended to go quite so far as this.[4] One of the reasons is that Lord Diplock spoke in terms of moral fault, and of people who "do not trouble" to consider risks; these words may possibly apply to those whose minds are a blank on the subject of risk, but not to those who believe that there is no risk because they believe that what they are doing is safe. A person who *has* given thought and has decided that there is *no* risk (whether because the act was inherently safe or because he has taken sufficient precautions to make it safe) is not *Caldwell* reckless even though he may have been negligent. So Lamb[5] and his like would not be regarded as being constructively reckless under the new rule.

It should not be necessary to state, as a corollary of this, that if a person firmly believes that a fact is present or will come about, he need not consider the risk that it is not present or will not come about. (And for this purpose, of course, a fact includes a negative fact—the non-occurrence of a fact.) If a man is convinced that what he is saying is true, and therefore does not consider the risk of its being untrue, it would be absurd to say that he is guilty of *Caldwell*

---

[2] In *Lawrence* he stated the same rule for "the adjective 'reckless' when used in a criminal statute." The rule was applied to rape in *Pigg* [1982] 1 WLR 762, 2 All ER 591, 74 CAR 352, and to manslaughter in *Seymour*; see § 12.2 at n. 9

[3] That Lord Diplock appreciated this appears from a passage elsewhere in his opinion in *Caldwell*: [1982] AC at 354B.

[4] I have enumerated the reasons in [1981] CLJ 280–281 and 132 NLJ 313, 336.

[5] § 5.2 at n. 6.

recklessness because he does not stop and think. If one believes a fact to be so, that is in itself a belief that there is no risk of the non-fact being so.[6]

So if I am charged with an offence of recklessness, I had better say that I believed there was no risk, or that I carefully considered the risk and decided that it was so slight as to be negligible, instead of saying that I did not think about it?

That might improve your chance of acquittal, but do not be cocksure. The jury or magistrates may decide that you were not justified in knowingly running even a small risk, if there was no sufficient social value in what you were doing to justify the small risk. And even if you said that you thought there was no risk, they may disbelieve you if they regard the risk as having been obvious.

Apart from this point, that *Caldwell* does not apply where the defendant thought his act safe, your "cleft stick" may seem to hold. If so, the effect is to treat every negligent person as reckless if he did not positively believe his act to be safe. If this conclusion is correct, it means that the Appellate Committee, contradicting recent policy decisions of reform bodies, has created general offences of negligence in relation to property and perhaps to the person. It has also made some people who previously committed only summary, finable offences liable to conviction in the Crown Court on charges carrying possible prison sentences. An example, relating to the negligent opening of car doors, will be given in a moment.

It is paradoxical that their lordships, who as members of the legislature consider the reports of reform bodies and legislate on the basis of them, should, as members of the Appellate Committee of the House, avert their gaze from the same reports in interpreting the resulting legislation. Had they looked at the Law Commission's report which led to the passing of the Criminal Damage Act, and which was referred to in the legislative debate, they would have seen a clear expression of intention that recklessness for the purpose of the Bill drafted by the Commission was to be understood in the subjective sense established by the Court of Appeal cases. A further paradox is that their lordships should be prepared to quote selectively from the Model Penal Code, an American policy document, emanating from an American professional organisation without official standing (though of high repute), while paying no attention to a policy document of our own Law Commission, itself a highly esteemed body established by Act of Parliament, from which the Act under consideration sprang. And, curiouser and curiouser, whereas the Lords were ready to cite and adopt the section of the MPC extending the notion of recklessness where the defendant was intoxicated, they suppressed mention of the section of the same document stating the subjective definition of recklessness in other cases.[7]

The House of Lords has decided that the courts should not look at the reports of committees merely to establish the meaning of legislation, but that they may look at such reports to establish the defect in the previous law that the statute was designed to remedy, and *per contra* the fact that there was no mischief in the law on a particular point calling for legislative intervention. There are examples of their lordships doing this in criminal cases,[8] which makes it all the more difficult to understand why they did not do so for the Law Commission's Report. Had the House of Lords looked at this, they would have found that the Commission was satisfied with the subjective definition of recklessness.

---

[6] The contrary is, however, maintained by Jennifer Temkin in [1982] Crim.LR 5. Her chief object is to develop an argument that will extend the scope of the law of rape.

[7] MPC s.2.02(2)(c) (POD).

[8] See *Lawrence* [1982] AC at 524E; *Bloxham* § 38.3 at n. 4.

Even paradoxes have reasons, and in this case the explanation of their lordships' inconsistencies must be that the section of the MPC thought deserving of quotation by their lordships accorded with their opinion, while the passage in the Law Commission's report and the neglected section in the MPC were passed over in silence because they did not support the meaning that their lordships wished to read into the Act. One would not advance this explanation if any other were available, but none is.

A simple illustration will show the extraordinary effect that the decision in *Caldwell* may have.

> Suppose that a car driver, momentarily forgetting that a cyclist may be passing, flings open his door to get out. There is an accident, and a cyclist is injured and his machine damaged. Incautious opening of vehicle doors is a summary offence punishable with a fine of £200 under the Construction and Use Regulations 1978.[9] But if the driver is held to be reckless under the rule in *Caldwell*, in not giving thought to the risk he is negligently creating, he can be convicted of the offence in the Criminal Damage Act 1971 s.1(2) of recklessly damaging property being reckless whether the life of another would be thereby endangered, and the possible punishment for that would be imprisonment for life.

He wouldn't get that, of course.

No; he would probably receive much the same sentence as under the Construction and Use Regulations. (Unless the fact that he has unluckily caused serious injury leads the court to view the case more severely, as may happen.) But even if the offender is leniently dealt with, the mere conviction of a crime of such gravity would be out of proportion to the facts. It could not have been the intention of Parliament to embrace a momentary act of carelessness within it. The difficulty is to see how the situation (and countless others of the same kind) can be taken out of Lord Diplock's model direction. This question will be explored in the next section.

§ 5.5 POSSIBLE LIMITATIONS ON THE RULE IN CALDWELL

There are various contradictory passages in the two cases under discussion, of which an advocate may make something in court.

(1) Lord Diplock said in *Caldwell* that the word "reckless" in the Criminal Damage Act "is an ordinary English word," not "a term of legal art,"[1] and it is to be noted that in saying this he used the present tense. Yet he directed that the jury were to be instructed on its meaning, which is a contradiction of *Cozens* v. *Brutus* (§ 2.6). If the latter case is still law, the jury should only be advised, not instructed, on the meaning of recklessness; and counsel could argue before the jury that they are entitled to accept Lord Hailsham's opinion, that recklessness bears a meaning "going beyond mere inadvertence" (§ .2 n. 5). If such an argument were disallowed by the trial judge, and the point again came before the House of Lords, it would be interesting to see which decision their lordships

---

[9] § 14.7 at n. 18.

[1] [1982] AC at 353H.

would prefer, if they were forced to choose between them: *Cozens* v. *Brutus* or *Caldwell*. The ideal, that they should disown both decisions, would of course be unattainable.

(2) Condition 1 in Lord Diplock's model direction refers to an "obvious risk," which may seem to mean a risk that is obvious to a reasonable man, or that is now with hindsight obvious to the jury. Condition 2, which refers back to "such risk," may seem to have the same reference. But elsewhere in the opinion his lordship indicates that for the purpose of condition 2 "obvious risk" means a risk that was obvious to the defendant, or that would have been obvious *to the defendant* if he had thought (assuming that he was in a position to think). For example:

> "Recklessness presupposes that if thought were given to the matter by the doer before the act was done, it would have been apparent to him that there was a real risk of its having the relevant harmful consequences."[2]

It will be remembered, too, that even Lord Diplock's intoxication rule carried this conditionally subjective meaning; it referred to a risk of which *the actor* would have been aware had he been sober. This is a very important point. It was suggested in § .3 that the drunkard is not to be accounted *Caldwell* reckless unless the jury are sure (the burden of proof being on the prosecution) that the defendant would have realised the risk if he had been sober. The test is not that of the reasonable man, who is a legal paragon, but what can confidently be said of this defendant; and the risk must be very obvious indeed to the ordinary man before a sufficiently certain finding can be made. If that is so for the drunkard, it must be so also for others. There would be no sense whatever in having a more lenient test of recklessness for the drunk than for the sober.

Unfortunately, this interpretation of *Caldwell* was rejected by a Divisional Court in *Elliott* v. *C.*[3]

> C, a girl of 14 who was in a remedial class at school, was acquitted by justices of recklessly damaging property under the Criminal Damage Act s.1(1). She had poured white spirit on the carpet of a garden shed and ignited it with matches. The fire immediately flared out of control. The justices found that while the girl realised that the white spirit was inflammable, she did not think of the risk of the fire destroying the property, and the risk would not have been obvious to her if she had thought. They reached this finding have regard to C's age and understanding, her lack of experience of inflammable spirit, and the fact that she must have been exhausted at the time. On appeal the Divisional Court reversed the justices' decision, on the ground that under *Caldwell* the question was whether the risk would have been obvious to a reasonable prudent person, not necessarily to the defendant if he had given any thought to it. Goff LJ, while concurring in the decision, did so unhappily and only because he felt constrained by the rule finally stated by Lord Diplock.

That C was technically guilty, even apart from *Caldwell*, seems obvious. If she knew she was burning the carpet she must have known that she was damaging it. The *mens rea* need not go to the whole of the damage. But the reason given for the Divisional Court's decision has remarkable

---

[2] [1982] AC at 351E.

[3] The Times, May 25, 1983. See further § 28.8.

implications. If read literally, it would make an insane person who kills not knowing what he is doing guilty of manslaughter on the ground of constructive recklessness, and would therefore nullify the traditional rule that such a killer is entitled to a verdict of not guilty on the ground of insanity. Also, it would mean that the intoxicated person is to be judged on a fully objective test, not Lord Diplock's semi-objective test.

Notwithstanding the criticism of *Caldwell* expressed by Goff LJ in the Divisional Court, the House of Lords refused C leave to appeal. It seems depressingly clear from this that their present lordships will not lend a ready ear to any suggestion that Lord Diplock's model direction to the jury should be modified, even when his words are in conflict with other passages in his speech.

It was suggested before (§ .4 at n. 4) that the rule in *Caldwell* does not apply to the person who considers whether there is a risk and rules it out in his own mind. He may, for example, have decided that there was no risk because he was dim-witted. Even if his failure to appreciate the risk was unreasonable, he is not guilty of recklessness. Now suppose that such a person does not think about risk, but the tribunal of fact comes to the conclusion that if he had thought about it he would have decided that there was no risk. Logically, the conclusion should be that he is not to be accounted reckless, because in these circumstances his failure to think did not have any effect upon his conduct. This is another reason for thinking that the decision of the Divisional Court should be accounted wrong, even if *Caldwell* is fully accepted.[4]

(3) Fearful, perhaps, that his opinion so far might be thought to be too clear-cut, Lord Diplock added a kind of postscript at the end of his opinion in *Lawrence*.

> "If satisfied that an obvious and serious risk was created by the manner of the defendant's driving, the jury are entitled to infer that he was in one or other of the states of mind required to constitute the offence [of reckless driving] and will probably do so; but regard must be given to any explanation he gives as to his state of mind which may displace the inference."[5]

No hint was given as to what "explanation" would be acceptable. Nor do we know whether such an explanation, whatever it is, would be allowed where the charge is of a crime other than reckless driving. (Incidentally, if the jury are to be told to have regard to the defendant's explanation, why are they not told to have regard to "all the evidence," as section 8 of the Criminal Justice Act directs? Lord Diplock did not mention section 8, although in *Caldwell* he was reminded of it by Lord Edmund-Davies, dissenting.)

Five other possible ways of limiting, without totally rejecting, the rule in *Caldwell* must be considered. I present them in small print out of consideration for the reader, who may now be forgivably tired of wrestling with this unhappy case and may therefore wish to exclude all further

---

[4] See Syrota in [1981] Crim.LR 658; [1981] CLJ 268–272; 132 NLJ 290, 314.

[5] [1982] AC at 527B. See [1981] CLJ 277.

arguments from his consideration until such time as the House of Lords has pronounced on them. Although some of these suggestions have seemed possibilities to me in the past my present opinion is that they are unlikely to lead anywhere much.

1 It may be argued that the door-opener in the previous hypothetical (§ .4 at n. 9) is outside the rule in *Caldwell* because, as has been shown, a person who believes his act to be safe is outside the rule, and at the time when the driver opens the door he believes his act to be safe. No one would open his car door in circumstances in which he thought that this would, or even might, cause an accident. Why should he? Causing an accident while he is stationary does not serve the driver's purpose in any way. A driver may knowingly take a risk while driving in order to travel more quickly, perhaps only for the joy of speed; but causing an accident when opening a car door is merely a nuisance, even from the most self-centred point of view.

While this line of defence may seem attractive at first sight, it has to face a serious difficulty. The door-opener "has not given any thought to the possibility of risk," and so falls literally within the model direction. There is good reason to say that *Caldwell* does not apply where a person has thought and has ruled out all risk in his mind, but the argument for distinguishing *Caldwell* becomes inadmissible when it has to be conceded that the case is one of not thinking.

2 Another possible argument, founded upon some expressions in Lord Diplock's opinion, is that his lordship was really concerned with the person who knows the danger but who does not focus upon it at the moment of acting, perhaps because he is more concerned with a nefarious purpose of his own.[6] The most obvious candidate for condemnation as being *Caldwell* reckless is the person who in a searing rage hits another over the head, gravely injuring him, and who then says in court that in his anger he did not think of the consequences. There is no contradiction in holding that such a person knew of the risk even though he did not think of it. I may be said to be intentionally walking to work even though my mind may be far away and I am thinking neither of my work nor of walking. Similarly with knowledge: it is true to say that I knowingly possess explosives even when I happen not to be thinking of the fact that I have explosives stacked in the garage (§ 6.3 at n. 6). Similarly, too, with recklessness. If, by excluding every consideration from one's mind except some illegal object like hitting a man over the head or committing a robbery, one could escape a judgment of recklessness, that concept would obviously be too limited to be legally usable. So the reasoning is this: that just as we may be said to "know" a thing because we can instantly recall it, even though it is not at the moment present in our minds, so it is not unreasonable to say that a person knows of a risk for the purpose of the law of recklessness if he would be aware of it the moment he attended to it, even though, being intent upon something else, he does not consciously attend to it. This would imply that a person who does not in any sense know of the risk is not reckless.

One trouble with the argument is that it again falls foul of the model direction, which expresses no such limitation. What the model direction asks in effect is not whether the defendant who failed to stop and think knew of the risk but whether he might have realised it if he had stopped and thought. Moreover, the argument based on ability to recall still leaves *Caldwell* to operate where it should not. Too much of the draconic rule in that case is still left to operate untouched. If our car-driver were cross-examined he would probably admit that he knew in a general way that it was dangerous to fling open car doors on the highway without paying regard to the traffic; but the fact is that he did not realise that his own act of flinging open the door was dangerous at the time when he did it. He simply did not think. He was inadvertently negligent. Are all inadvertently negligent people to be accounted reckless because they know of the risks of life in a general way, but fail to apply their knowledge at the moment of acting? We are back to the fundamental difficulty with the pronouncement in *Caldwell*, that it largely effaces the distinction between recklessness and negligence.

---

[6] See the argument stated at length by Syrota in [1982] Crim.LR 97, and the criticism by R A Duff in [1982] CLJ 273.

3 The third suggestion relates, in a way, to the defendant's character and motivation. Lord Diplock regarded recklessness as a "blameworthy" state of mind, involving "moral turpitude." The truly reckless person is a bad lot. He is indifferent to risk. He does not "care" about it, does not trouble himself about it, because he has some overriding purpose of his own. He may not be wholly indifferent to causing injury or damage, since he would almost certainly prefer (even if only for his own purposes) not to cause trouble than to cause it; but he is intent on some other aim by reason of which he takes the risk.[7] This suggests that if excuses can be found for the defendant's failure to think (e.g. shock, stress or fatigue) he may be accounted not reckless.[8]

The suggestion may have only limited scope: if read as confined to special excuses depending on special facts it would do nothing to protect our door-opener from conviction on account of recklessness. It is true that it might alleviate the rule in *Caldwell*. But it has to meet the objection that, once again, it is not mentioned in the sweeping terms of Lord Diplock's model direction.

Moreover, the third suggestion involves difficulties in its reliance on the factor of blameworthiness. It would make the law excessively difficult to have to distinguish between the blameworthiness of inadvertent negligence resulting from fatigue etc. and *Caldwell* recklessness. A person who does something dangerous when fatigued may be accounted negligent and blameworthy in carrying on when he might have stopped, and it would be strange to say that he is not blameworthy as regards *Caldwell* recklessness.

4 A fourth possibility is to limit the rule in *Caldwell* to cases where the "not thinking" arises from certain emotional states. Lord Diplock's initial proposition concerned a person who, "because his mind was affected by rage or excitement or confused by drink, did not appreciate the seriousness of the risk."[9] Had his final pronouncement been limited to these cases it would have been much less objectionable (though not completely free from objection); but it was not, and the Court of Appeal is unlikely to limit the decision along these lines. (Or the House of Lords either, since their lordships make a policy of neither admitting nor correcting their own mistakes in criminal cases.[10])

5 Fifthly, there is a possible argument founded upon a dictum in *Lawrence*. The model instruction in *Caldwell*, taken in isolation, is capable of being read as meaning that any negligence is equivalent to recklessness. It is true that Lord Diplock there said that the gravity of the possible harmful consequence is an important factor in the assessment of the risk as negligible or otherwise. But he made this remark on the basic requirement of negligence, which underlies any finding of recklessness. In negligence, the degree of probability of injury and the extent of the probable injury are inversely related requirements: the more there is of the one, the less is needed of the other. To run a very small risk of producing a very harmful outcome can be negligent.

However, in *Lawrence*, where Lord Diplock expressed much the same opinion as before, he modified it in one respect. He said that the risk had to be not only obvious but "serious."[11] This seemed in the context to express an overriding limitation that a person could not be reckless (within the artificial rule as to not thinking) except as to serious injury. The same limitation may perhaps be read into the *Caldwell* direction.

Against this suggestion, it may be said that the dictum in *Lawrence* was worded in that way to preserve the distinction between reckless and careless driving—a problem unique to driving cases. Moreover, if Lord Diplock intended his qualification to apply generally, it is surprising that he did not confess in *Lawrence* that the same qualification should have been expressed in the opinion he had just delivered in *Caldwell*, and was there omitted by mistake. Since he made no such confession, he must have intended to lay down different rules for the two cases. But to this it may be answered that the problem of distinguishing between recklessness and inadvertent negligence is not unique to driving cases but general

---

[7] For this opinion see R A Duff, *op. cit.* last note, and my own reply, *ibid.* 286.
[8] The point is made by Griew in [1981] Crim.LR 747.
[9] *Caldwell*, [1982] AC at 352A.
[10] See among several pronouncements *Cunningham* [1981] 3 WLR at 232E–H. It was made in the name of "commanding and retaining respect for the criminal law."
[11] § 14.4 at nn. 4–6.

in the criminal law, and that the limitation is just as necessary for the general rule in *Caldwell* as it is for the more specific rule in *Lawrence.*[12]

It will be seen that there are difficulties in the whole argument, and one has again to add the depressing postscript that even if the argument is valid it might not save some people from being wrongly classified as reckless. For instance, a driver who throws open the car door on a busy road is negligent both in respect of the high probability of causing an accident and in respect of the probability of doing great injury if an accident happens; yet, as said before, common sense suggests that he should not be accounted reckless if it cannot be inferred that he realised the risk.

If, patient reader, you have been waiting to hear my own solution to the problem raised by the decision in *Caldwell*, I can only say that, having pondered on the above suggestions, having felt the allure of some of them, but having finally discarded all of them, I now have no solution, other than a legislative one. It seems to me that the subjective definition of recklessness remains the most acceptable; but, speaking as a subjectivist, I would be prepared, by way of political compromise, to accept special rules for voluntary intoxication and rage, even though it has not been demonstrated that special rules are practically necessary. I think it is going too far to extend the *Caldwell* rule to any "excitement," as Lord Diplock did; a person who does a risky thing in the excitement of play should not be accounted reckless if he did not realise there was a risk.[13]

We have not yet done with the discussion of *Caldwell.* It will reappear in connection with mistakes (§ 6.6), assault (§ 8.1), crimes of malice (§ 9.3), and insanity (§ 28.8).

SUMMARY

After many doubts the opinion favoured by the end of the 1970s was that recklessness in law bears a subjective meaning: a person is reckless as to a consequence if he foresees the possibility (risk) of the consequence. This was the basis of the definition of recklessness favoured by the Law Commission and the Criminal Law Revision Committee. §§ .1, .2

In *Caldwell* the House of Lords adopted a rule proposed in the American Model Penal Code and held that a person is to be accounted reckless if "owing to self-induced intoxication he is unaware of a risk of which he would have been aware had he been sober." § .3

Caldwell and *Stephen Lawrence* also laid down the further rule for the purpose of statutory offences based in terms on recklessness that "a person is reckless if (1) he does an act which in fact creates an obvious risk and (2) he either has not given any thought to the possibility of there being any such risk or has recognised that there was some risk involved and has nonetheless gone on to take it." It seems clear that this does not account a man reckless if he has given thought and decided that there is no risk. Otherwise, however, it seems to turn negligence into recklessness. There are phrases or passages in the opinions in *Caldwell* and *Stephen Lawrence* (which followed it) on which arguments for limiting the rule may be based, but the only proposition that may be put forward with some assurance is that, despite the rule formulated in *Caldwell*, a person is not to be accounted reckless although he did not think, if he would not have perceived the risk even if he had thought. § .4

---

[12] While the proposition that recklessness by "not thinking" should be confined to cases of serious risk, i.e. high probability, is acceptable (because any argument limiting *Caldwell* is acceptable), the same argument is not acceptable for all cases of subjective recklessness. A person who *knows* there is a small degree of risk of bringing about a calamitous consequence may properly be held to be reckless.

[13] See the "haka skirt" hypothetical in § 21.4, text at nn. 5–6.

CHAPTER 6

FAULT AS TO CIRCUMSTANCES

> Doubtless it is the judicial unwillingness to make any case law at all which accounts for the sloppiness with which it is made, when it is. Discussion of general principle is not encouraged. Cases relating to *mens rea* as an element in crime live in a shambles from which academic writers try to rescue them.
>
> Lord Devlin, *The Judge*.

§ 6.1. THE CIRCUMSTANCES OF AN ACT

HITHERTO we have been primarily concerned with fault as to consequences, but similar problems can arise in relation to circumstances.

Could you give me a capsule definition of a circumstance? If a man seduces a French girl, is the fact that she is French one of the circumstances?

The circumstances are not all the facts surrounding the crime but the relevant circumstances—the facts existing at the time when the defendant acts, being facts specified in law as conditions of the offence. About the only offence that might be committed in the case you put is one of having sexual intercourse with a girl under 16. The facts (1) that it is a girl and (2) that she is under 16 are circumstances of the offence, being specified in the law; but her Frenchness is irrelevant. No consequence is required for this "conduct crime," only the act and the circumstances.

As another example, bigamy is committed where a man goes through a ceremony of marriage with a woman when he is already married to another (or similarly for a woman). The offence is committed by the act of saying "I will" in the marriage ceremony. The fact that the defendant is already married is a circumstance of the offence. It is something specified in the statute that is not a consequence.

But isn't the consequence the fact that you become married?

The bigamous ceremony is null and void, and does not marry anybody. It has no operation in the civil law, even though it is a crime. But in any case, when one is analysing the elements of a crime and speaks of the consequences, one means the physical consequences, not the legal consequences.

Bigamy is historically made an offence because it is "the profanation of a solemn ceremony." Nowadays it is comparatively rarely prosecuted, and comparatively leniently treated, the main objection now seen to it being the opportunity it gives to deceive the second "spouse," or perhaps third persons.

If the law were clear and rational, fault in relation to circumstances could be fairly easily stated. It would be this:

- An act is intentional as to a circumstance if the actor knows that the circumstance is present.
- An act is reckless as to a circumstance if the actor knows that the circumstance may be present and takes an unreasonable risk as to its presence (subject to a reservation as to "not thinking" to be discussed in due course).
- An act is negligent as to a circumstance if the circumstance, though perhaps not known, could have been discovered by reasonable enquiry.

We shall see that the courts have introduced doubts and difficulties into the first two of these propositions.

I don't understand about being reckless as to a circumstance. A circumstance is a present fact. You can be reckless as to something happening in the future, but not, surely, as to what has already happened.

The recklessness relates to the question whether or not the fact exists. You may throw a letter on the fire being reckless as to whether it contains a pound note.

Part of the following discussion will be concerned with the effect of mistake, and it may be mentioned here that there are three kinds of mistake, only two of which concern us as affecting liability.

1 Mistake as to a definitional fact (part of the definition of the offence). This is our concern at the moment, and the argument will be that such mistake is a defence if it negatives a required mental element forming part of the definition.
2 Mistake as to a matter of defence (e.g. mistaken belief in the necessity for self-defence); this is considered in § .8.
3 Mistake as to a jurisdictional or procedural fact, which does not affect culpability and so is no excuse (e.g. a belief that you were acting in Scotland, when in fact you were acting in England, or a mistaken belief that you have diplomatic immunity). Of this kind of mistake we shall have no more to say.

§ 6.2. INTENTION AS TO CIRCUMSTANCES

Intention was previously defined (§ 3.2) as relating to the result of an act, but we also speak of the act itself as being intentional. "The act itself" may mean *either* the bodily movement *or* the bodily movement plus the circumstances in which it was done.

As applied to bodily movement the notion of intention means that the movement was willed or volitional or purposive or done in a state of normal consciousness. (A sleepwalker does not intentionally walk, for legal purposes, because he is not in a state of normal consciousness.)

As applied to the circumstances of an act, the notion of intention, according to the usual understanding, means that these circumstances were known to the actor. If for example we say that D intentionally trespassed on an airfield, we mean more than that D went for a walk. We mean that he knew he was on an airfield, and knew he had no right to be there.

Suppose he didn't know that where he was was part of the airfield but suspected it might be, and took his walk regardless?

The proper language then, surely, would be to say that D recklessly trespassed on an airfield, if such it was. Or, more fully, that he took a walk, being reckless as to whether he was on an airfield. There is surprisingly little authority on the legal point, because most *mens rea* offences can be committed intentionally or recklessly, in which case all that the prosecution has to prove is recklessness. But the law should accept the ordinary use of language, so that an offence of intention (in the fullest sense of the word) should require knowledge of the circumstances, not just recklessness as to the circumstances. At the very least it should require one or the other.

As another example, take again the case of the man who held the policeman's arm in order to persuade him that the man he was about to arrest was innocent (§ 3.2 at n. 8). He was convicted of wilfully obstructing the constable because he knowingly obstructed the constable, even though only for a moment. He knew that he was, for that moment, hindering him. If you know what you are doing, you do it intentionally. (The word "wilfully" is sometimes construed to include recklessness, and a man might perhaps be convicted if he parked his car in a way that he knew might obstruct the police, and if in consequence he did obstruct them; but it would be pushing the offence very far.)

So much for the ordinary understandings of language. There is a body of judicial authority for saying that this is also the language of the law.[1] Unhappily, the cases are not entirely consistent. Some judges have said that a legal requirement of intention can be satisfied even if the defendant did not know the circumstances.

Take rape as an example. This was defined at common law as sexual intercourse with a woman without her consent. It has always been assumed that a mental element is required, but what mental element? Bridge J (as he then was) declared in the Court of Appeal in *Morgan* that the intention required for rape is simply to have sexual intercourse with a woman.[2] "Without her consent," he thought was not a part of the crime requiring a mental element. This strange idea was knocked on the head on appeal to the House of Lords,[3] which affirmed that rape does require a mental element, and not one that is merely confined to the act of sex.

The loose thinking of some judges on the subject of rape were not due to judicial bashfulness as to making law, as Lord Devlin suggests in the

---

[1] S. 8 of the Criminal Law Act does not expressly deal with the question of knowledge of circumstances as an ingredient of intention. The section was passed to alter the decision in the notorious case of *DPP* v. *Smith*; but even in *DPP* v.*Smith* the House of Lords recognised that intention requires actual knowledge of existing facts: see [1961] AC at 330–331, and J C Smith in [1974] Current Legal Problems 96. Regrettably, the Law Commission has refused to embody this rule in its proposed legislation on the mental element, notwithstanding representations on the subject. See [1978] Crim.LR 589–591. The Commission supposed that a statute wishing to speak of "knowing" a circumstance would always use that word, and would not seek to cover it by speaking merely of intention. Yet the Criminal Damage Act, which was the work of the Commission, used "intending" to cover a requirement of knowledge. See *David Smith*, n. 6 below.

[2] See the criticism by Lord Fraser in the House of Lords: [1976] AC at 236–237. Yet Lord Fraser perpetrated the same error in regard to bigamy; see at n. 4 below.

[3] [1976] AC 182.

passage at the head of this chapter. The courts, in my diagnosis, are far from unwilling to make law, if it is law extending offences and restricting defences. The reason why *mens rea* lives in a shambles—why judges incorrigibly defy the conventions of language and ordinary ideas of logic and justice, although their errors are continually being pointed out—is because they wish from time to time to exclude or restrict the *mens rea* doctrine.

Morgan concerned a crime the definition of which (at the time when the case was decided) rested on the common law (it has since been put in statutory form). Many other crimes are defined in statutes which do not expressly require a mental element. The traditional rule of the common law is that the requirement is nevertheless to be implied, but the courts frequently evade it. One technique is to say (as the Court of Appeal did in *Morgan*) that although the offence impliedly requires an intent, that intent need relate only to the doing of the forbidden act, omitting any reference to the circumstances of the act. This merely pays lip-service to the requirement of intent.

The drastic effect that such language can have on the *mens rea* principle may be illustrated by bigamy. Bigamy is defined by statute as marrying again during the the life of one's spouse. That is about all that the statute says on the basic requirements of the offence. The courts hold that the only mental element to be implied into the statute is an intent to do the forbidden act: in other words an intention to go through a marriage ceremony.[4] So everyone who gets married has the *mens rea* of bigamy! He is guilty of bigamy if, being already married, he is negligent as to the subsistence of the first marriage.

However, this severely restrictive attitude towards the mental element is generally found not in relation to technically serious crimes like bigamy but in relation to minor statutory offences, which are by this stratagem turned into offences of strict liability.

When a statute expressly requires a mental element, it seems that the courts will require the mental element to exist not merely as to doing the basic act but as to the circumstances of the offence. A mistake as to these circumstances can negative both intention and recklessness. In other words, if the actor believed that the required circumstances, the definitional facts, were not present, then his act was neither intentional nor reckless as to them. This proposition, which is the merest common sense, has been established for crimes of wilfulness by several decisions.[5] Nowadays the word "wilfully" is generally replaced in statutes by a requirement of intention or recklessness; and the same rule applies, as is shown by *David Smith*.[6]

---

[4] See the dictum of Lord Fraser in *Morgan*, § 6.7 at n. 8.

[5] *Eaton* v. *Cobb* [1950] 1 All ER 1016; *Wilson* v. *Inyang* § 20.6 at n. 5; *Bullock* v. *Turnbull* [1952] 2 Lloyd's Rep. 303; *Wilmott* v. *Atack* [1977] QB 498; *Ostler* v. *Elliott*, n. 12 below; *The General Part*, 2nd edn On the question of recklessness see § .6

[6] [1974] QB 354. In *Morgan* [1976] AC at 234, Lord Edmund-Davies said, mysteriously, that this "was a special case and at some future date the question involved in it may have to be reconsidered." This was a dissenting speech, and in fact the decision fully accords with the majority opinions in *Morgan*.

> Section 1(1) of the Criminal Damage Act 1971 provides that "a person who without lawful excuse destroys or damages any property belonging to another, intending to destroy or damage any such property or being reckless as to whether any such property would be destroyed or damaged, shall be guilty of an offence." Smith was the tenant of a flat who made some additions to it with the consent of his landlady. These additions, being "affixed to the soil," became the property of the landlady; but believing them to be his own property he superficially damaged them in order to remove certain wiring. A totally unmeritorious prosecution was brought against him for criminal damage, on the extraordinary argument that he had intentionally damaged property that in fact (though he did not know it) belonged to another; therefore he had intentionally damaged the property of another. This argument, believe it or not, was accepted by the trial judge, and Smith was convicted. James LJ, delivering the judgment of the Court of Appeal quashing the conviction, said that in construing section 1(1) "we have no doubt that the *actus reus* is 'destroying or damaging any property belonging to another.' It is not possible to exclude the words 'belonging to another' which describes the 'property.' Applying the ordinary principles of *mens rea*, the intention and recklessness and the absence of lawful excuse required to constitute the offence have reference to property belonging to another. It follows that in our judgment no offence is committed under this section if a person destroys or causes damage to property belonging to another if he does so in the honest though mistaken belief that the property is his own, and provided that the belief is honestly held it is irrelevant to consider whether or not it is a justifiable belief."

The judge says: "if the belief is honestly held." How could it be dishonestly held?

It could not be, of course. Judges in speaking of belief frequently say that it must be a genuine belief, an honest belief, a *bona fide* belief, a belief held in good faith. But such qualifiers are unnecessary, because one cannot believe ungenuinely or dishonestly or in bad faith.[7]

The decision in *David Smith* illustrates two important propositions.

(1) Where a statute uses a *mens rea* word, this word should be taken to control the whole provision unless the contrary is clearly stated.[8] "Intending to damage any property belonging to another" does not mean "intending to damage any property, such property in fact belonging to another." It means "intending to destroy any-property-belonging-to-another." The *mens rea* word governs the whole.

Unhappily there have been occasions when judges have acted like the trial judge in *David Smith*, defeating the plain intention of Parliament by construing an expressed mental element as applying only to a part of the offence. Even where the statute included a word like "wilfully," the word was sometimes not construed to require knowledge of the circumstances required for the offence.[9] A considerable weight of authority, exemplified by *David Smith*,

---

[7] See *per* Lord Fraser in *Morgan* [1976] AC at 236–237.

[8] Cp. the ALI Model Penal Code s.202(4): "Where the law defining an offence prescribes the kind of culpability that is sufficient for the commission of an offence, without distinguishing between the material elements thereof, such provision shall apply to all the material elements of the offence, unless a contrary purpose plainly appears."

[9] See, e.g. *Cotterill* v. *Penn* [1936] 1 KB 53 (statute now repealed), discussed in *The General Part*, 2nd edn 146; *McPherson* [1980] Crim.LR 654, criticised in [1981] *ibid.* 796.

now rejects this type of reasoning where the statute expressly requires *mens rea*. The defective authorities to the contrary relate to statutes now repealed, or are merely decisions by circuit judges, or have been reversed on appeal or overruled, or are obiter dicta; so there is nothing in them to bind even the humblest court at the present day. However, the old type of reasoning may still be employed when the statute does not expressly require a mental element. Here the courts can still interpret the statute as imposing strict liability, or liability for negligence.

(2) As a corollary of the first proposition, intention in relation to circumstances requires knowledge, and negligence in not acquiring knowledge is insufficient.[10] You can neither intend to damage property belonging to another nor be reckless as to damaging such property if you believe that the property does not belong to another.

Here again the decision supplies a valuable corrective to some earlier pronouncements. There has been a tendency to say that the meaning of the word "intention" and its grammatical variants (intent, intend etc.) is exhausted by requiring an act to be willed and a consequence to be intended or partly intended, so that no *mens rea* is required in respect of some of the circumstances or some of the required aspects of the consequences of the act. We may now assume that these remarks are wrong.

Another fallacy that is still distressingly embraced on occasion is that a person can be guilty of acting intentionally with respect to a particular fact even if he believes that the fact does not exist, if his belief is unreasonable. This remarkable opinion arises because of the tendency of judges, on both sides of the Atlantic and indeed throughout the common law world, to suppose that the word "belief" can never be allowed to stand nude. Sometimes, as we have seen, the judges think they have decently covered it by speaking of an honest belief. That adjective is harmless, if useless. More often they qualify the noun by the word "reasonable." But to hold that an unreasonable belief that a fact is not present can make a man punishable for a crime of intention in relation to that fact means that negligence, which often means stupidity, can be punished as a serious crime.[11] Once a phrase like "reasonable belief" becomes established, whether by an actual decision or not, lawyers tend to repeat it unreflectingly.[12]

Here is a particularly fine example of the self-contradictory nature of some assertions about reasonable belief.

> "Where the definition of the crime includes no specific mental element beyond the intention to do the prohibited act, the accused may show that though he did the prohibited act intentionally he lacked *mens rea* because he mistakenly, but honestly and reasonably, believed facts which, if true, would have made his act innocent."[13]

If the defendant made such a mistake, it would be untrue to say that he did the prohibited

---

[10] In *Morgan* [1976] AC at 215 Lord Hailsham said: "Though I get some support from what I have been saying from the reasoning of the decision in *Reg.* v. *David Smith*, I nevertheless regard that case as a decision on the Criminal Damage Act 1971, rather than a decision covering the whole law of criminal liability." It is difficult to know the purport of this reservation. Principle (2) in the text above, which can be extracted from *David Smith*, is the one eloquently supported by Lord Hailsham in *Morgan*. Principle (1) is supported by the whole trend of modern authority, for statutes in general not just one particular statute.

[11] That "unreasonable" means "negligent" was recognised by Hodgson J in *Albert* v. *Lavin* [1981] 2 WLR at 1076A, 1083H, 1 All ER at 633*a*, 639*e*. A number of eminent judges have failed to perceive that reasonableness introduces an objective test. Lord Fraser caught even Lord Reid out on this: *Morgan* [1976] AC at 239.

[12] The force of this particular linguistic habit may be illustrated by *Ostler* v. *Elliott* [1980] Crim. LR 584, where a Divisional Court, in delivering its judgment, said that a person could not be guilty of wilfully obstructing the police when he reasonably believed that the police were robbers come to attack him; the word "reasonably" was unnecesssary, since the authorities had clearly established that a mistaken belief could be a defence to a charge of wilful crime although the belief was unreasonable.

[13] *Morgan* [1975] 2 WLR at 921 (CA). The decision of the House of Lords in this case is discussed in § 6.6.

act intentionally, because "the prohibited act" must be taken to include the relevant circumstances. A mistake as to the required circumstances negatives the intention.

Judges who regularly speak in terms of reasonable belief rarely explain why they think that a belief in a fact (or in the non-existence of a fact) must be reasonable if it is to exclude liability. However, two judges of eminence have risked an explanation. Lord Simon in his dissenting speech in *Morgan* (a case to be considered later), quoted with approval the reason offered by Bridge J in the Court of Appeal:

> "A bald assertion of belief for which the accused can indicate no reasonable ground is evidence of insufficient substance to raise any issue requiring the jury's consideration."[14]

This explanation fails for three reasons. First, it confuses the question whether there is evidence for the alleged belief with the question whether the belief was negligently arrived at. The genuineness of an unreasonable belief may be abundantly proved.

> An example is a decision on bigamy[15] where the defendant, who was seeking a divorce, received a letter from his solicitors saying: "We have your telegram and hope to send you papers for signature in the course of a day or two." The defendant, a man of little education, jumped to a hasty and mistaken conclusion: he clapped his hands and said: "Thank God my divorce has gone through," and immediately remarried. He was convicted (though sentenced only to a nominal one day's imprisonment); and an appeal was dismissed, the appeal court saying that there was no evidence that he had *bona fide* and on reasonable grounds believed that he was liberated by divorce from his lawful marriage. Obviously there was evidence that he believed it, so the negative pregnant must have meant that the belief, if entertained, was unreasonable. Lawyers readily suppose that all mistakes as to the law and legal status made by laymen (including people who are illiterate or totally unversed in business matters) are unreasonable, but it is strange that the jury in this case took the same view.

The second objection to the reasoning of the two judges is that it conveys a *suggestio falsi* as to the evidential burden. It implies that the rule about unreasonable belief in some way saves the jury time or trouble. This might be true if the evidential burden rested on the defendant, but it does not. In respect of the issues of intention and knowledge the evidential burden almost always[16] rests on the Crown, so these two issues are necessarily before the jury, whether the defendant gives evidence on them or not. The failure of the defendant to give convincing evidence (and the fact that his denial of the mental element involves setting up a mistaken belief) does not entitle the judge to withdraw the issue of *mens rea* from the jury merely because the judge believes that the evidence is all one way. What the judge does is to direct the jury that if they find the mistake unreasonable (a question primarily for them), then, however satisfied they may be that the mistake was made, they must regard it as being no defence. This last direction may well bother the jury more than a simple direction to consider whether the defendant had the belief in question.

A third error made by the two judges is the logical fallacy already mentioned, of supposing that a person can be convicted of an offence of intention or recklessness when he has made an unreasonable mistake as to the circumstances required for the offence. Even if the doctrine of unreasonable mistake has some social advantage, the judges have no right to superimpose it on a statute requiring proof of *mens rea*. The logical point had been expounded by academic writers for many years before it found curial acceptance in *Morgan*,[17] by Lords Hailsham, Cross and Fraser.

Lord Hailsham's words in *Morgan* were as follows.

> "I cannot reconcile it to my conscience to sanction as part of English law what I regard as a logical impossibility. . . . Once one has accepted . . . that the prohibited act in rape is nonconsensual sexual intercourse, and that the guilty state of mind is an intention to commit it, it seems to me to follow as a matter of inexorable logic that there

---

[14] [1976] AC at 220H.
[15] *Wheat* [1921] 2 KB 119.
[16] One exception is in respect of the defence of automatism: § 29.2.
[17] [1976] AC 182.

is no room for a 'defence' of honest belief or mistake, or of a defence of honest and reasonable belief or mistake. Either the prosecution proves that the accused had the requisite intent, or it does not. In the former case it succeeds, and in the latter it fails. . . . Any other view . . . can only have the effect of saying that a man intends something which he does not."[18]

That's good. But why does Lord Hailsham use those quotes around the word "defence"? He seems to imply that an issue is not a defence (except by courtesy of quotation marks) if the prosecution carry the burden of proof. That can't be right. The prosecution have the burden of proof in respect of the defences of self-defence and provocation, but surely they are properly called defences nevertheless.

Agreed. Whether we need to trouble about what the word "defence" means is a matter we shall have to consider (§ .8).

After the decision in *Morgan*, following on that in *David Smith* and the cases on statutory wilfulness already referred to, it was confidently thought that we could at last regard the logical proposition as undoubted. Yet a more recent case in the Court of Appeal showed (though only in an *obiter dictum*) its continuing desire to follow the old ways.

The offending case is *Phekoo*,[19] which involved a charge under the Protection from Eviction Act 1977. This Act makes it an offence to harass a residential occupier "with intent to cause [him] to give up the occupation." Phekoo, a landlord, had harassed two men who (he said) he thought were squatters (squatters not being residential occupiers within the Act). The men were in fact subtenant's from Phekoo's tenant, and were therefore protected by the Act. The trial judge ruled that Phekoo's evidence, even if accepted, could not constitute a defence and he withdrew the defence from the jury, who accordingly convicted.

On appeal the Court of Appeal quashed the conviction for misdirection, since the jury had not been allowed to consider whether Phekoo held the belief he claimed. The actual decision is thus satisfactory: one cannot intend to cause a residential occupier to give up occupation if one believes that the person concerned is not a residential occupier. Unfortunately, the Court of Appeal added (while admitting that the opinion was only obiter) that if the jury had found that Phekoo had the belief but that it was unreasonable, he would have had no defence. On *Morgan*, the court simply said that that decision was confined to rape.

The court confined *Morgan* too narrowly; it could not have read the three speeches in *Morgan* already adverted to, otherwise one cannot believe that it could have expressed the opinion it did. But quite apart from the opinions in the House of Lords, authority should not have been needed to hold that a statute requiring intention means what it says, and must not be read as imposing liability for negligence.[20] Even if the court needed authority for the elementary proposition that intention requires knowledge, it could have found it in *David Smith*, which it cited but inexplicably refused to follow on this point. Moreover, on the policy question the court might have taken notice of the fact that the Law Commission, the CLRC[21] and the Heilbron Advisory Group on rape[22] have pronounced decisively against the view that a mistaken belief negativing the *mens rea* required for a crime must be reasonable. Since the remarks of the court were obiter, they have not overruled *David Smith* (a decision that in any event bound the court) or the cases on statutory wilfulness.[23] Moreover, the dictum in *Phekoo*

---

18 [1976] AC at 213–214. Cp. Lord Cross at pp. 203–204 and Lord Fraser at p. 237.

19 [1981] 1 WLR 1117, 3 All ER 84, 73 CAR 107.

20 The court relied in part on an obviously fallacious argument based on the wording of the Act. See Cowley in [1982] Crim. LR 200–201.

21 14th Report paras. 283–284.

22 Cmnd 6352 of 1975.

23 For a rebuttal of general arguments for the objectivist view of the defence of mistake see Cowley in [1982] Crim. LR 206–207.

was repudiated by a differently constituted Court of Appeal in *Kimber*,[24] where it was accepted that the decision in *Morgan* is not confined to the crime of rape.

We are now in a position to state the complete definition of intention. For legal purposes it means, or should mean:

1 (if we are speaking of the consequences of conduct) *the desire that the consequence shall follow from a bodily movement (or omission to move), or realisation that the consequence is virtually certain*, or
2 (if we are speaking simply of the act itself) *conscious movement (or conscious inactivity) with knowledge of the circumstances*.

If a crime is declared in general terms to require intention, that should relate to all three elements—the act, the circumstances and the consequences.

Other aspects of the defence of mistake are considered in the rest of this chapter; and the subject of mistake as to the victim or kind of harm is considered in § .9.

§ 6.3. REQUIREMENTS OF KNOWLEDGE

As has been seen, a statute may require knowledge by requiring intention, but it may also require knowledge by using that word, or one of its grammatical variants. An example of an express requirement of knowledge is the offence of knowingly possessing explosives.[1] In legislation of this kind the requirement of knowledge is generally interpreted as applying to all the circumstances of the offence, unless the statute makes the contrary meaning plain.[2] This is the same rule for offences of knowledge as *David Smith* (§ .2) illustrates for offences of intention.

> For example, an Act penalised any person who "knowingly makes any record without the consent in writing of the performers." The court regarded the word "knowingly" as qualifying not only the making but the absence of consent.[3] The *mens rea* word applies to all the elements of the offence. Unfortunately, as we have seen and shall see further, the courts do not always interpret statutes as this principle would require.[4]

Although the word "knowingly" is generally used in relation to circumstances, it is not incapable of applying to consequences. So a person who arranges for goods to be sent from Kenya to the United Kingdom can be convicted of being "knowingly concerned in the

---

[24] The Times, May 27, 1983.

[1] Explosive Substances Act 1883 s.4.
[2] Customs and Excise Act 1952 s.304.
[3] *Gaumont British Distributors Ltd* v. *Henry* [1939] 2 KB 711. Cp. *Cohen* [1951] 1 KB 505; *Bello* (1978) 67 CAR 288. The word "knowingly" can even extend to a question of age: *Groom* v. *Grimes* (1903) 89 LT 129; but see *McPherson*, § .2 n. 8.
[4] In the *Gaumont British* case, last note, the court applied "knowingly" to a qualifying phrase; but on one occasion the court refused (wrongly I think) to apply the word to an exception clause: *Brooks* v. *Mason*, § 42.2 n.7. On the position where a statute uses the word "knowingly" in some sections but not all see Smith and Hogan, 4th edn 103.

fraudulent evasion of a prohibition applicable to those goods" when they arrive in the United Kingdom.[5]

What if a person knows something but then forgets?

If he has truly forgotten, so that it is incapable of recall, he presumably no longer knows it. But if he can immediately recall it he knows it.[6]

How can knowledge be proved?

The prosecution of course bear the persuasive burden,[7] and they may have problems. The mere fact that the defendant *ought* to have known, i.e. that he was negligent in not finding out, is insufficient. But although the jury may swallow an incredible tale, on account of the defendant's frank blue eyes, they are not bound to do so.

In the first place, if any ordinary person would have known a fact, the jury may infer that the defendant knew it, simply because they cannot believe that he did not, in the circumstances, know it.[8]

Yet you say that it is not enough that the defendant was negligent in not finding out. I think the distinction is humbug. Whether the jury say that the defendant knew it because an ordinary man would have known it, or that he ought to have known it because a reasonable man would have known it, is merely a matter of words.

Very often there is no practical difference. But the point is legally important because it governs what the judge has to tell the jury. Besides, there are exceptional cases where the verdict can be influenced by evidence of: the sort of person the defendant is; his motives or lack of them in relation to the facts charged; his conduct before, at and after the time of the alleged offence; and so on. And even where particular evidence of this kind is lacking, the jury must be left free to decide how much weight to assign to the defendant's protestations of innocence. In short, the jury must be directed to consider all the evidence before drawing an inference of knowledge, as of any other mental state.

An important limitation on the evidence that can be adduced by the prosecution is the rule that, in general, no testimony can be called as to the previous convictions of (or other similar conduct by) the defendant.

> Suppose that D is charged with knowingly possessing explosives. It is proved that he was found in possession of a bag containing explosives. D's defence is that the bag was left in his custody by a friend from Italy, and he did not know what was in it. A hard-faced jury may refuse to credit this tale, and would undoubtedly be upheld in their refusal. But some juries may feel that D should be given the benefit of the doubt, and acquit him. They would not do this if they knew that D had a previous conviction for possessing explosives, but they are not allowed to know it.
>
> The CLRC proposed that when the *actus reus* was admitted by the defendant, evidence

[5] *Donald Smith* [1973] QB 924. The relevant statute is now Customs and Excise Management Act 1979 ss.68(2), 170(1).

[6] *Bello*, n. 3 above and commentary in [1978] Crim.LR 551.

[7] *Curgerwen* (1865) LR 1 CCR 1; *Cugullere* [1961] 1 WLR 858, 2 All ER 343.

[8] Cp. *Wilson* v. *Bird* [1963] Crim.LR 57.

of previous convictions should be admissible to prove a mental state like knowledge[9]; but the proposal met with determined opposition and has not been implemented.

In the second place (to revert to what I was saying), the strict requirement of knowledge is qualified by the doctrine of wilful blindness. This is meant to deal with those whose philosophy is: "Where ignorance is bliss, 'tis folly to be wise." To argue away inconvenient truths is a human failing. If a person deliberately "shuts his eyes" to the obvious, because he "doesn't want to know," he is taken to know.

While all the cases agree on this, they are at sixes and sevens on what wilful blindness means. The best view is that it applies only when a person is virtually certain that the fact exists. The Law Commission, in the report now gathering dust on a bureaucratic shelf, proposed the following formula.[10]

> "The standard test of knowledge is—Did the person whose conduct is in issue either know of the relevant circumstances or have no substantial doubt of their existence?"

This very limited doctrine can reasonably be said to be an explanation of what is meant by knowledge as a matter of common sense, rather than an illegitimate extension of the meaning of the term. If it does not give a sufficient extension to some particular offence, that is a matter for the legislature to consider when it is deciding between using the word "knows" and the words "knows or ought to know".

An example of wilful blindness in the proper sense is where an employer knew that his business was being run in an illegal way, and absented himself without having altered the arrangements; he was held to "know" that the law was being broken in his absence even though he had no direct information about what was happening then.[11]

Although the courts have sometimes seemed to use the doctrine of wilful blindness to embrace recklessness, they have also corrected the error.

In a case of handling stolen goods knowing or believing them to be stolen, the Court of Appeal said that "to direct the jury that the offence is committed if the defendant, suspecting that the goods were stolen, deliberately shut his eyes to the circumstances as an alternative to [directing them in terms of] knowing or believing the goods were stolen is a misdirection"; but "to direct the jury that, in common sense and in law, they may find that the defendant knew or believed the goods to be stolen because he deliberately closed his eyes to the circumstances is a perfectly proper direction."[12]

While this pronouncement is more satisfactory than some others, it would be much clearer to tell the jury that they may take a man to know a fact if they are satisfied that he was virtually certain that the fact existed, or (in other words) that he had no substantial doubt that it existed.

Why shouldn't one say that wilful blindness means recklessness? You agree that mens rea normally means intention or recklessness. Why not apply that principle here?

The courts sometimes do equate wilful blindness with recklessness, but they ought not to do so. If knowledge is judicially made to include wilful blindness, and if wilful blindness is judicially deemed to equal recklessness, the result is that a person who has no knowledge is judicially deemed to have knowledge if he is found to have been reckless—which is not what the

---

[9] 11th Report, Cmnd 4991 of 1972, draft Bill cl. 3 (4).

[10] *Report on the Mental Element in Crime*, Law Com. No. 89 p. 58.

[11] *Ross* v. *Moss* [1965] 2 QB 396.

[12] *Griffiths* (1974) 60 CAR at 18. See also § 38.8.

statute says. The word "knowing" in a statute is very strong. To know that a fact exists is not the same as taking a chance whether it exists or not. The courts ought not to extend a *mens rea* word by forced construction. If, when Parliament says "knowing" or "knowingly," it does not mean actual knowledge, it should be left to say as much by amending the statute. Parliament can quite easily say: "knowing that the fact exists or being reckless whether it exists."

The argument for giving the notion of knowledge a restricted meaning has particular point in relation to the offence of handling stolen goods. A trader may receive an offer of goods at a low price from someone who says that it is bankrupt stock. The trader realises that the man may be a rogue, but he is by no means certain. The offer is a tempting one, and the trader has no time or inclination to investigate it in depth; he must either accept or reject it. So he accepts it. The law is that the trader is not guilty of knowingly handling stolen goods if the goods turn out to be stolen. It would be vexatious to honest traders if the law were otherwise.

In one application, however, the notion of knowledge may justifiably be held to include recklessness. This is in relation to the consequences of conduct. Take again a statutory offence that has already been mentioned, of being knowingly concerned in the fraudulent evasion of a prohibition of the importation of goods. In *Donald Smith*[13]:

> the defendant with others sent cannabis by air from Kenya addressed to Bermuda. He knew that the most likely route to Bermuda was via London. On the arrival of the packet at London airport it was held that Smith could be convicted of being "knowingly concerned" in the offence.

The court made no reference to the doctrine of wilful blindness, which is normally used in relation to circumstances and is inapposite to consequences. It seems reasonable to say that, in relation to consequences, the notion of knowledge is capable of comprising recklessness, in the sense of knowledge of the risk. In relation to the future we never know for sure, as we often can do for the present; so "knowledge" in relation to the future must embrace knowledge of probability.

§ 6.4. OFFENCES OF PERMITTING

Minor offences are generally held to be of strict liability; but some statutory words are construed as impliedly requiring knowledge, even when they occur in minor offences. When a statute makes it an offence to "permit" something to be done, or to "allow" or "suffer" it to be done, many authorities require that the defendant should (basically) have known of the conduct or other event[1] in question, since a man cannot be said to permit what he does not know about.[2] This is one of the few *mens rea* rules on which the courts have shown consistency; and even this limited tribute has to be qualified. In expressing the fault element in offences of "permitting," the courts have used almost every variety of language. Sometimes they have required knowledge, sometimes knowledge or "wilful blindness" (expressing this doctrine in a considerable range of ways), sometimes knowledge or recklessness, sometimes even negligence.

---

[13] Above at n. 5.

[1] The rule applies both where the defendant is charged with having permitted a person to do something and where the charge is of having permitted a state of affairs to occur.

[2] For authorities see 1st edn 83 n. 1 *bis*.

It can now be said that negligence is rejected, subject to the aberrant decision that is always possible. Whereas the civil law of property has a doctrine of constructive knowledge (meaning knowledge that a man could have had if he had taken reasonable steps), no such doctrine is recognised in the criminal law. The classic statement is by Devlin J (as he then was).

> "The case of shutting the eyes is actual knowledge in the eyes of the law; the case of merely neglecting to make inquiries is not knowledge at all—it comes within the legal conception of constructive knowledge, a conception which, generally speaking, has no place in the criminal law."[3]

The best view seems to be that offences of permitting can be committed either knowingly or recklessly, and in no other way. The basis of the interpretation of the word "permits" is that a man cannot be said to permit what he does not know; he does not permit the use of a car in contravention of regulations if, although he permits the use of the car, he does not know that it is being used in contravention. But if he realises that the car may be used in contravention and yet fails to take reasonable steps to prevent this, he may well be said to permit the improper use.[4]

Although the law on this subject appears in general to be sweetly reasonable, the courts have not been able to save themselves from creating an anomalous exception on one point, namely in respect of offences of permitting the uninsured use of a motor vehicle. A person who permits the use of his vehicle is held to be strictly liable if the user happens to be uninsured.[5] So if you lend your car to a friend who says he has a driving licence when he has not, and in consequence your insurance does not cover him, you will be criminally liable even though you were not at fault.[6]

Where a statute makes it an offence to "cause" something to be done, this word is now often construed in the same way as "permit," to require knowledge[7] (or, presumably, recklessness).

---

[3] *Roper* v. *Taylor's Central Garage Ltd.* [1951] 2 TLR 284. The qualification "generally speaking" was perhaps a reference to the anomalous "licensee" cases discussed in Chap.43 § 3.

[4] In *Sweet* v. *Parsley* [1970] AC at 162, Lord Diplock said that "permit" connotes at least "knowledge or reasonable grounds for suspicion" that the prohibited act would be done, together with "unwillingness" to use available means to prevent it. At p. 165 he repeated this but transposed "reasonable" to "grounds for reasonable suspicion." But the word "reasonable" appears to be superfluous; if it could be proved that the defendant suspected, even though on "unreasonable" grounds, and was nevertheless unwilling to prevent the act, Lord Diplock would probably find that he permitted the act, while if the defendant did not suspect, although he had reasonable grounds for suspecting, it could hardly be found that he was "unwilling" to prevent the act. In *Souter* [1971] 1 WLR 1187, 2 All ER 1151 the Court of Appeal cited Lord Diplock with approval. Nevertheless, in *Sheldon Deliveries Ltd.* v. *Willis* [1972] RTR 217 MacKenna J left open whether recklessness was sufficient.

[5] In *Houston* v. *Buchanan* [1940] 2 All ER 179, 1940 SC (HL) 17, the House of Lords in a Scottish appeal held that this offence was of strict liability. The decision is theoretically binding on English courts, since it was decided on a statutory provision applicable both sides of the Border; and although it was in civil litigation, being concerned with liability in tort for breach of statutory duty, that fact does not deprive it of authority in criminal proceedings. The case is rarely, if ever, cited in criminal proceedings, but a line of criminal cases in fact follows it: see *Baugh* v. *Crago* [1975] RTR 453; *Ferrymasters Ltd* v. *Adams* [1980] Crim.LR 187, and other cases in 1st edn. 85 n. 5. There is a similar anomaly in the offence under the Sexual Offences Act 1956 s.26, as judicially interpreted; see criticism in [1981] Crim.LR 796.

[6] See *Baugh* v. *Crago*, last note. But the courts draw a subtle distinction: if you lend the car on condition that your friend obtains a licence, and if he does not, there is an exception to the exception; it is counted as a conditional permitting which (the condition being unfulfilled) is not a permitting, and you are not liable! See *Newbury* v. *Davies* [1974] RTR 367.

[7] Cp. § 42.4.

§ 6.5. NEGLIGENCE AS TO CIRCUMSTANCES

One can, of course, be negligent not only as to a consequence but as to a circumstance of one's act. In crimes requiring negligence, mistake of fact as to an element of the offence is no defence unless it is reasonable (i.e. non-negligent). Manslaughter, for example, is probably a crime of gross negligence, from which it follows that a grossly unreasonable mistake is no defence. An illustration would be where a man shoots at another mistakenly and grossly unreasonably believing that he is out of range.

§ 6.6. RECKLESSNESS AS TO CIRCUMSTANCES

That one can be reckless as to circumstances is again obvious. The Law Commission, in its Report on the Mental Element in Crime added the following to its proposed statutory definition of recklessness.

> "The standard test of recklessness as to circumstances is—Did the person whose conduct is in issue realise that the circumstance might exist and, if so, was it reasonable for him to take the risk of their existence?"[1]

As a statement of the present law this must now be read subject to the rule in *Caldwell* that failing to attend to an obvious risk is reckless. The latter rule was evidently intended to apply to recklessness in general, and has therefore been applied by the Court of Appeal to recklessness as to circumstances.[2]

Caldwell recklessness is not open to the same objection in relation to circumstances as it is in relation to consequences. This is because a failure to advert to the risk of a circumstance specified in the law will often be due to ignorance of the law, and such ignorance is no defence.

> Suppose that a man persuades a girl of 15 to come to live with him (though it cannot be proved that sexual relations took place). At the time when she was taken off the girl was, in the legal phrase, "in the possession of" her parents, but the man did not know this. He did not know about the law of abduction, and so did not know that the question of parental rights affected him; consequently, he made no enquiry on the subject. Suppose, further, that the offence of abduction is defined as taking a girl under 16 out of the possession of her parents without their consent, intentionally or recklessly. (The actual statute does not contain the last three words, but they probably represent the way in which the courts will construe it: § 9.12 n. 10). Although authority was exiguous, it seemed reasonable to say, even before the decision in *Caldwell*, that the man was to be regarded as reckless in respect of the risk of the legally-specified fact if he would have been regarded as reckless had he known the law, considered the risk and proceeded regardless. He is clearly deemed to be reckless under *Caldwell*.[3]

If the Law Commission's Report is ever disinterred from its mausoleum in Queen Anne's Gate and resuscitated for presentation to Parliament, and if the decision is made to restore generally the subjectivist definition of recklessness current before *Caldwell*, the Law

---

[1] The draft does not state, as it should, that the circumstance may be a negative circumstance—the absence of a positive circumstance. The draft provides in clause 6 for what it calls "exempting circumstances," but the commentary does not indicate that the Commission had in mind negative circumstances included in the main definition of the offence (Law Com. No. 89 pp. 64–65).

[2] *Pigg* [1982] 1 WLR 762, 2 All ER 591, 74 CAR 352 (rape).

[3] *The General Part*, 2nd edn § 55.

Commission's draft Bill should be amended to preserve the effect of that case whenever ignorance of fact results from ignorance of law. The point could conceivably arise even in respect of the unheeded risk of consequences, but is unlikely to do so, because everyone knows that the evils specified in the law of offences against the person and property are required to be avoided. If a person does not think that what he is doing may cause injury to the person or damage to property, it is not because of ignorance of the law.

Apart from the intoxication and "not thinking" rules, *Caldwell* does not affect the subjectivist view of recklessness expressed by the Law Commission. Notwithstanding *Caldwell,* a person who believes that a circumstance does not exist is not reckless as to that circumstance. Before *Caldwell*, the proposition was supported by *David Smith*, *Morgan* and the decisions on statutory wilfulness mentioned in § .2—since statutory wilfulness is taken to cover both intention and recklessness. These cases show that the same principles apply to recklessness as to intention.

An extract from the opinions in *Morgan*[4] has already been given; we may now add a statement of the facts. It concerned a prosecution for rape at common law.

> Morgan, an RAF sergeant, invited three other men belonging to the RAF to have intercourse with his wife. The three companions asserted (but Morgan denied) that Morgan told them that they must not be surprised if his wife struggled a bit since she was "kinky" and that in reality she would welcome intercourse. The men had intercourse with the wife by force, and immediately afterwards Mrs. Morgan drove to a hospital and complained that she had been raped. The three men were charged with rape, and Morgan was also charged as a party to the rape ("aiding and abetting" it) because he incited it. The three men advanced as a defence that Mrs. Morgan consented. (The *actus reus* in rape is sexual intercourse without the woman's consent, and her non-consent may be called a negative circumstance of the act.)
>
> The trial judge directed the jury that if Mrs. Morgan did not consent the fact that the defendants believed she consented (if they did so) would be no defence unless the belief were reasonable; and the jury convicted. Notwithstanding that the conduct of the men was abominable, the House of Lords by a majority of three to two disapproved the judge's direction. He should have asked the jury to decide whether the belief was honestly held, not whether it was reasonable. An honest belief in the woman's consent would negative both the intention to rape and recklessness as to lack of consent. However, the House felt able to uphold the conviction by applying the proviso.

The case appears on its face to lay down two propositions.

1 Rape requires a mental element.
2 The requisite mental element as to a circumstance is knowledge of or recklessness as to to the circumstance. If the defendant lacked this mental element he is not rendered guilty of the offence by negligence in not ascertaining the facts.

With the decision in *Morgan* the *mens rea* doctrine irrupted into the

---

[4] [1976] AC 182.

popular consciousness, and great was the consternation. Women demonstrated in the streets of Dublin and Canberra. Letters were written to newspapers complaining that no man could now be successfully prosecuted for rape; all he had to do was to "persuade himself" that he believed the woman consented. On the other hand, the decision on the point of law was greeted with approval by those lawyers who took a subjectivist position on the major crimes.

I rather sympathise with Women's Lib. A chap who forcibly rapes a woman ought not to be allowed to set up a cock-and-bull story about believing that she consented.

Granting your opinion for the moment, perhaps you will agree that the question should be one for Parliament. The courts should not turn rape into an offence of negligence on their own.

Some commentators agree with you on the policy.[5] But if you were persuaded of the truth of the defence—that the defendant believed the woman was play-acting in putting up a resistance, and was enjoying the affair immensely—would you really want to punish him as a rapist? Of course, you would be extremely unlikely to believe the defence, or even to think it might be true, but that is a different matter.

Perhaps you fear that the jury will be taken in. However, we have little evidence that juries are hard to convince that a man is guilty of rape where he has used force. Most judges and practitioners believe that acquittals of rape are almost invariably justifiable or understandable on the facts given in evidence. Remember that a judge is perfectly entitled to tell a jury that the unreasonableness of an alleged belief is *evidence* that it was not held—they may refuse to credit that anyone could have held the absurd belief that the defendant puts forward. The jury in *Morgan* were clearly of this opinion.[6] (And the person who tells the lie, and who is the chief author of the mischief, can in any case be punished under the rule in *Cogan*, to be discussed later.[7])

According to *Morgan* the defendant is guilty if he realised that the woman might not be consenting and took no steps to find out, as he could easily do. Even if he thought there was a faint possibility that she was not consenting, he would be reckless in going ahead without further enquiry, because there is no social value in what he does to justify him in running even a very slight risk of giving such a serious affront to the woman concerned. Moreover, the law is that the defendant's knowledge that the woman is acting under intimidation is automatically equivalent to knowledge that the woman does not consent.[8] The man cannot say he was drunk, without falling into the gently smiling jaws of *Caldwell*. So the law does not lack doctrines for dealing with dishonest defences.

It may be that, as some fear, these doctrines are insufficient to procure the conviction of a man who professes to believe that because a woman has some sexual experience or dresses provocatively, therefore she wants to have sex with him, whatever protests she makes to the contrary. If a law of "negligent rape" were necessary to deal with such a man, we should have to have it.

Finally, if it is desired to punish the man who negligently assumes the woman's consent, should this be done by the law of rape or by a special statutory offence? A man who has conceived one of the extraordinary ideas just mentioned can be corrected by a shorter

---

[5] For arguments in favour of extending the law to "negligent rapes" see Pickard in 30 U of Tor.LJ 75, 415; Celia Wells [1982] Crim.LR 213–216; R A Duff in 3 Liverpool L Rev. 49; Jennifer Temkin in [1983] Crim.LR 5.

[6] In *Cogan* (§ 15.16 n. 12), where a man terrorised his wife into submitting to sexual intercourse with the defendant, the jury found that the defendant believed that the woman was consenting but had no reasonable grounds for his belief. Details of the evidence have not been published.

[7] § 15.16 n. 12.

[8] See § 25.3.

sentence than is usual for rape. Moreover, indictable offences should be so worded that, if possible, the jury are given an opportunity to pronounce on the major issues going to culpability on which sentence will depend, and the distinction between an intentional rape and a "negligent" one is such an issue.[9]

To resume our history: attempts were made to have the decision in *Morgan* altered by legislation, but eventually all that emerged was a statute affirming the principle of the decision for the crime of rape. This was the Sexual Offences (Amendment) Act 1976, section 1(1) of which runs in part as follows.

> "A man commits rape if
> (*a*) he has unlawful sexual intercourse with a woman who at the time of the intercourse does not consent to it;[10] and
> (*b*) at that time he knows that she does not consent to the intercourse or he is reckless as to whether she consents to it."[11]

This wording is in one respect too lenient to the defendant, although the point has little practical importance. The theory of recklessness is that a person is entitled to ignore a slight risk if it is reasonable for him to do so; but it would never be reasonable for a man to ignore even the smallest risk that a woman is not consenting to sexual intercourse. He ought to satisfy himself beyond a doubt that she does consent. This should have been made clear in the Act, as could have been done if the Act had omitted the reference to recklessness and if paragraph (*b*) had been worded simply: "at that time he does not believe that she consents to the intercourse."

As the Act stands the judge must direct the jury in terms of recklessness, but he will follow *Caldwell* and tell them that the defendant was reckless not only if he was aware that the woman might not be consenting but also if he was indifferent and gave no thought to the matter in circumstances where if any thought were given it would have been obvious that there was a risk that she was not consenting.[12] In fact the latter of these alternatives will always be beyond belief. A man who has sexual intercourse with a woman may:

—believe that she consents, or
—know that she does not consent, or
—know that he is uncertain.

There is no other practical possibility, and *Caldwell* does not really expand the area of liability in this type of case. Instructing the jury on an inconceivable situation does not add to the effectiveness of the law.

As was mentioned before (§ .2 at n. 24), the Court of Appeal in *Kimber* accepted that *Morgan* is not merely a decision on the law of rape but is of more general application.

May an offence be so worded as to require intention as to consequences but to be satisfied with recklessness as to circumstances?

Yes, of course, if the law expressly says so. A problem arises only if the law requires intention as to the offence and does not provide for

---

[9] "Issues which are capable of reasonably precise definition, likely to be frequently contested, and usually considered to have critical importance for sentencing, should generally be reflected in internal distinctions between offences:" D A Thomas in *Reshaping the Criminal Law*, ed. Glazebrook (London 1978) 33. In *Morgan* Lord Cross said that if the defendant "was grossly careless then he may deserve to be punished, but not for rape."

[10] This refers to consent in fact. A girl under 16 who consents to sexual intercourse is not raped, but in such a case the man commits a special offence: § 10.9.

[11] Subs. (2) unnecessarily declares that the unreasonableness of an alleged belief in consent is evidence that it was not entertained.

[12] *Pigg*, above n. 2.

recklessness as to circumstances. There is a strong argument in point of principle for saying that in such a case knowledge of (or belief in) circumstances is required, not merely recklessness. An offence covering recklessness as to circumstances is naturally thought of as an offence of recklessness, or an offence with a mixed mental element, rather than as merely an offence of intention.

> To take a hypothetical example, if a statute makes it an offence to harbour an escaped prisoner intentionally, the offence should not be committed if the defendant gave shelter to a person whom he suspected to be an escaped prisoner but without anything like certain knowledge. If the defendant has committed an offence on these facts it is more naturally described as one of recklessly harbouring a convict than as intentionally harbouring a convict.

However, the courts nearly always choose to give the wider rather than the narrower meaning to penal legislation if this is at all possible, and there appears to be no authority in point that would prevent them doing this in the present instance. In fact, one case positively accepts recklessness as to circumstances as sufficient for a crime of intention; this bears on the law of attempt, and will be considered when we come to that topic.[13] There is a line of argument giving it theoretical support. Many cases of recklessness as to circumstances can be made to appear as offences of intention by the "whether or not" approach, which was used by Lords Cross and Hailsham in *Morgan*. These two lords sometimes spoke in terms of a rapist intending to have sexual intercourse and being reckless as to the woman's consent, and sometimes spoke of him as "intending to have intercourse whether or not the woman consents."[14] The latter formula makes the offence appear as entirely one of intention, not as an offence of mixed intention and recklessness. Going back to the hypothetical of the escaped convict, it can be said, according to this line of reasoning, that the man who gives him shelter without knowing for certain that his guest is a convict intentionally harbours a convict, because he intends to harbour him whether or not he is a convict. He thus offends against the statute, and it is unnecessary to consider whether the statute covers recklessness. The practical effect is achieved without talking of recklessness.

Attractive as this argument may appear at first sight, it is open to objection. It conceals the concept of recklessness beneath the concept of intention. Where the two differ, it puts cases into the wrong category. Whether the theoretical point will persuade a court not to extend the offence to a case that it considers should be covered as a matter of policy is another matter.

§ 6.7. MISTAKE UNDER STATUTES NOT EXPRESSING A MENTAL ELEMENT

We decided in § .2 that, notwithstanding some discordant authorities, an unreasonable mistake (or other failure to know) can negative intention, in § .3 that an unreasonable mistake (or other failure to know) can negative knowledge, and in § .6 that an unreasonable mistake can negative recklessness. What if the statute does not use words expressly or impliedly requiring intention, knowledge or recklessness?

It may be strongly argued that the same legal considerations apply as before. Many judicial pronouncements can be cited for the view that even without apt words the graver statutory crimes imply a requirement of a

---

[13] See § 17.4 at n. 7.

[14] For the latter phrase see [1976] AC at 203H, 209G.

mental element, which we now recognise as intention, knowledge or recklessness according to the context of the particular statute. As has been shown, these requirements imply that a mistaken belief inconsistent with the required mental element excuses from liability; indeed, this proposition being a tautology should not need saying. Nevertheless the law remains in doubt.

The cases stem from *Tolson* (1889),[1] where the court made contradictory pronouncements of the kind that will now be familiar to the reader, both requiring a mental element and saying that a mistake to be a defence must be reasonable.

Tolson is the most celebrated affirmation of the general need for *mens rea* in crime, or at any rate for proof of fault. The prosecution was for bigamy, an ancient offence reproduced in section 57 of the Offences against the Person Act 1861 (which is still in force). The gist of the section has already been given, but it may be set out virtually in full.

> "Whosoever, being married, shall marry any other person during the life of the former husband or wife, whether the second marriage shall have taken place in England or Ireland or elsewhere . . . shall be liable to [imprisonment] for any term not exceeding seven years. . . . Provided, that nothing in this section contained shall extend to any second marriage contracted elsewhere than in England and Ireland by any other than a subject of Her Majesty, or to any person marrying a second time whose husband or wife shall have been continually absent from such person for the space of seven years then last past, and shall not have been known by such person to be living within that time, or shall extend to any person who, at the time of such second marriage, shall have been divorced from the bond of the first marriage, or to any person whose former marriage shall have been declared void by the sentence of any court of competent jurisdiction."

The facts before the court were as follows.

> Mrs. Tolson was deserted by her husband, and as a result of enquiries she was led to believe that shortly after leaving he had been drowned at sea. She waited six years without having word of him, after which time she married again. Thereupon her husband reappeared; and some stupid person prosecuted Mrs. Tolson for bigamy. Literally she had violated the words of the statute. The case was tried by Stephen J, and in order to raise an issue for appeal, to settle the law, he directed the jury that a belief in good faith and on reasonable grounds in the death of the other party to a marriage was no defence to the charge of bigamy. On this direction (which Stephen J himself did not believe represented the law!) the jury convicted, and the judge passed a nominal sentence,[2] reserving for the Court for Crown Cases Reserved[3] the question whether his direction was right or wrong. He

---

[1] 23 QBD 168.

[2] Of one day's imprisonment, which meant the defendant's immediate discharge.

[3] This was a somewhat makeshift court of appeal in criminal cases. It was replaced in 1907 by a proper appellate court, the Court of Criminal Appeal, which in turn was superseded in 1966 by the Court of Appeal (Criminal Division). The position in 1889 was that the trial judge when convicting could take the initiative in reserving a point of law for the consideration of a large number of his fellow judges, constituting the Court for Crown Cases Reserved, which could quash the conviction. Since it was not technically an appeal, the trial judge could himself take part in the deliberations of the court.

similarly reserved the case of another woman who was convicted before him on closely similar facts. The appellate court held that the directions were wrong, and the convictions were quashed.

But the women did commit bigamy.

They committed the outward facts of bigamy, the *actus reus*; and the second "marriages" were nullities because of the subsistence of the earlier marriages; but these facts were held insufficient to constitute the crime.

Why not say that the women were guilty, and simply take the facts as a reason for not punishing them?

For a person who intended no harm it is terrible to be arrested, to face trial on a serious charge, and to be convicted, even though the conviction is not followed by punishment. The decision that the women were not guilty meant that if such facts recurred, and the prosecuting authorities were satisfied of the genuineness of the defence, there would be no prosecution.

The most admired of the judgments in the case is that of Stephen J himself. The learned judge commenced with some remarks upon the meaning of *mens rea* which were quoted in an earlier chapter (§ 3.1). He went on to state the view of the court that the bigamy section implied a requirement of fault even though none was expressed.

But is it right that the courts should add words to a statute that are not there? Shouldn't they regard themselves as bound to enforce the statute as it stands?

When a statute creates an offence, it does not recapitulate all the defences traditionally allowed by the criminal law; yet it must have been the intention of Parliament that these defences should apply. Similarly, since the requirement of *mens rea* is a traditional principle of law, for serious crimes, it is reasonable to suppose that Parliament meant it to govern the statute.

Stephen J stated this argument in a much-quoted passage.[4] It is too long to reproduce, but may be summarised. The judge begins by saying that "the full definition of every crime contains a proposition as to a state of mind." Then he spells this out again by saying that if the mental element is absent there is no crime; and he clearly means this proposition to apply to crimes created by statute as well as at common law, so that all alike require a mental element. There follows a series of instances showing that where a person does not know[5] a fact required for the crime he lacks the mental element and so cannot be guilty. Finally, however, the judge confines his proposition to cases where the defendant's belief that the facts were innocent was not merely in good faith but was based on reasonable grounds. This implies that if the defendant genuinely but unreasonably

---

[4] 23 QBD at 185 ff.

[5] At the present day we would generally want to add: "and is not reckless as to."

believed in the existence of justifying facts he has no defence, even though in that case he lacked the mental element that is supposed to be required. The reference to reasonable grounds departs from the purely subjective element that the judge has hitherto been propounding, and introduces an objective test. There is, therefore, a basic contradiction in the judgment.

Allowing a defence of belief in some circumstance of excuse, based on reasonable grounds, still allows for a mental element. Belief is a mental element. So I don't see how the judgment contains a contradiction.

You are going to see it. Stephen J is assuming that the mental element required for a crime is knowledge of a particular fact, which we may call A (e.g. "I am still married"). The defendant's defence is that he believed that the fact present was not-A ("I am not now married"). A defence of belief in not-A is of course the same thing as denying knowledge of A. But Stephen J says that belief in not-A is no defence unless it is reasonable. If it is unreasonable, the defendant is convicted although he believed not-A, i.e. although he did not know A. Yet the judge says that the defendant must know A. So he contradicts himself: QED. His judgment would make a person guilty of bigamy although the only mental element was that of intending to enter into a valid marriage—a state of mind that almost all of us possess at some time in our lives.

Although the question of reasonable belief was not before the court in *Tolson*, and although Stephen J and some other members of the court were clearly guilty of self-contradiction, the idea started in *Tolson* was perpetuated in later bigamy cases. Time and again the judges have said that a mistake of fact, to be a defence to a charge of bigamy, must be reasonable.[6] This evidently continues to be the law, and may apply to other criminal statutes besides.

The question turns on the extent to which the decision in *Morgan* affects that in *Tolson*. The lords in *Morgan* were split on the question whether the general principle was represented by *Tolson* or by that now announced in *Morgan* for the crime of rape. They all made it plain that they did not intend to make a clean sweep of the cases stemming from *Tolson*, but they differed as to the weight that they would continue to allow to the principle of those cases.

Of the three majority lords, Lord Hailsham went no further than to say that he was inclined to view *Tolson* as a narrow decision based on the construction of a statute,[7] an opinion that would not attach to it any significance outside the law of bigamy.

Lord Fraser's opinion may possibly be interpreted in the same way, but it was not clearly expressed. He distinguished *Tolson* from rape on the ground that "bigamy does not involve any intention except the intention to go through a marriage ceremony,"[8] but he did not

[6] E.g. *Gould* [1968] 2 QB 65, noted by Glazebrook in [1968] CLJ 177 (belief in divorce). But see *Beaver* [1957] SCR 531, 118 CCC 129, 26 CR 193, where Cartwright J, speaking for the Supreme Court of Canada, commented that the requirement in *Tolson* that the mistake should be reasonable must now he read in the light of *Wilson* v. *Inyang* (§ 20.6). This case, said Cartwright J, "rightly decides that the essential question is whether the belief entertained by the accused is an honest one and that the existence or non-existence of reasonable grounds for such belief is merely relevant evidence to be weighed by the tribunal of fact in determining that essential question."

[7] [1976] AC at 215D.

[8] At p. 238B.

explain why the *mens rea* requirement should be so restrictively interpreted. He pointed out Lord Reid's error in a previous case in supposing that the *Tolson* rule (that a mistaken belief as to required element must be reasonable to be a defence) could co-exist with the proposition that the *mens rea* required for crime involves a subjective test[9]; yet he did not criticise the judgments in *Tolson* for making the same mistake.

The most uncompromisingly pro-*Tolson* member of the majority was Lord Cross, who confined his opinion to the law of rape and was prepared to give wide effect to the *Tolson* rule by applying it to all statutory offences that are "absolute" on their face—i.e. not expressly or by clear implication requiring a mental element. (He found that the statute on rape impliedly requires a mental element because that was the rule at common law for rape.[10] Similarly, a statutory offence of assault impliedly incorporates the mental element required at common law for that offence: *Kimber* § .2 at n. 24.) The argument is that when a statute makes no mention of a mental element, directly or indirectly, and the requirement is merely implied by the judges, why then the judges can "imply" it in such truncated form as they please; and what pleases them is to have a general rule requiring mistakes to be reasonable. The logicians are fended off by interpreting the crime not to contain a general requirement of intention or recklessness. The fact that *Tolson* itself requires the graver crimes to incorporate a mental element, and that the *Tolson* rule contradicts that requirement, is of no moment.

The two minority lords, Simon and Edmund-Davies, were of course pro-*Tolson*, at least as a statement of the present law. They would make no exception from the *Tolson* rule, which they regarded as a universal principle, though the latter was in favour of legislative change.[11]

How one assesses the authority of these opinions depends upon whether one counts in the dissentients.

Taking the House as a whole, there was a clear majority (Cross, Simon and Edmund-Davies, at least) for the view that a mistaken belief cannot be a defence to a statutory offence absolute in its terms unless the belief is reasonable.

On the other hand, if we count only the lords who favoured the actual decision, it seems fair to say that the majority of the majority (Hailsham and Fraser) cannot be cited for anything more than that bigamy is to be regarded as special case, on which view *Tolson* does not lay down a principle of general application, and the counter-principle in *Morgan*, that a belief need not be reasonable to excuse, can be regarded as expressing the general principle.

What emerges is that although *Morgan* was a partial victory for subjectivism, the weight of precedent still hung heavily around their lordships necks. It seems clear that Lords Hailsham and Edmund-Davies, and probably Lord Fraser, would have shaken themselves completely free from *Tolson* if they had felt they could. No convincing reason was offered for continuing the rule laid down in that case.[12]

It remains to be noted that the language of reasonable belief and reasonable mistake has on various occasions been adopted by Parliament. When a statute expressly allows a defence of belief or mistake, the defence is generally qualified by inserting the word "reasonable."[13] This means that the crime is turned into one of negligence in respect of the ingredient in question, while the crime may require *mens rea* in other respects.

It is now common form in statutes making an offence dependent on the age of another person to provide that the defendant can defend himself by proving that he believed the other person to be over the age in question and had reasonable grounds for that belief.[14] An alternative formula is to word the offence as being committed only when the other person is or apparently is under the age in question.[15]

---

[9] At pp. 238–239.
[10] At pp. 202–203.
[11] At pp. 219–221, 234–235.
[12] See further, 2 Leg. Stud. 241–242.
[13] For example, to a charge of abducting a girl under 18 with intent that she shall have unlawful sexual intercourse, it is a defence that the defendant believed her to be 18 or over and had reasonable cause for the belief: Sexual Offences Act 1956 s.19. For another formula see Misuse of Drugs Act 1971 s.28. But occasionally a defence of mere belief is allowed: see the Abortion Act, § 13.4.
[14] E.g. Firearms Act 1968 s.24.
[15] E.g. Betting, Gaming and Lotteries Act 1963 ss.10, 21 and Sched. 4; Scrap Metal Dealers Act 1964 s.5(1).

§ 6.8. MISTAKEN BELIEF AND DEFENCES

During the nineteenth century there appears to have been no theory that an unreasonable belief as to a matter of defence could not excuse. Even the mistaken belief of a drunkard as to the necessity for private defence (self-defence) could excuse his attack on another person.[1] Later, however, the idea arose that the belief had to be reasonable, and this view has continued for all mistakes as to the elements of defences.

The House of Lords in *Morgan* did nothing to combat the opinion. The speeches were devoted to showing that the defendant's alleged mistake related to a definitional fact, and therefore could be a defence even if unreasonable. Nevertheless, there appears to have been no binding authority for the opposite rule in relation to defence facts before *Albert* v. *Lavin*,[2] where the court, overwhelmed by the mass of high-level dicta referring to reasonable belief, established the law that a mistaken belief in the necessity for private defence cannot excuse unless it was reasonable.

Anyway, you can't say that there is any logical fallacy in that, can you? One who wounds another in the mistaken belief that he has to act in self-defence has inflicted the wound intentionally. The question whether he was acting in self-defence or not does not bear on the question whether he was acting intentionally. So there is nothing illogical in saying that the wounding must be intentional but that an unreasonable belief as to self-defence is no excuse.

I hope to convince you that it *is* illogical.

Your argument assumes that no reference to defences is included in the definition of an assault, but I would put it to you that the assumption is untrue. Wounding another is not an assault in itself, or any kind of wrongful act. The wrong is in wounding another unlawfully, which implies an absence of a justification. Many definitions of assault (a common law offence) found in the books specify that an assault is an *unlawful* application of force, and this must be right. Now if the wounder believed that facts existed, and if, assuming those facts, then he would have been justified in causing the wound, he did not intend to cause the wound unlawfully. Yet in *Albert* v. *Lavin*[3] Hodgson J refused to accept the argument that the use of the word "unlawful" in the definition of an assault at common law impliedly imports into that definition the negative of defences.

There are several anomalies in the rule as now established in *Albert* v. *Lavin*. Arguments against it were listed in the first edition of this book[4]; Hodgson J pronounced them "cogent" and "extremely persuasive," but he thought that effect could be given to them only by legislation. Without repeating these former arguments, it is worth making four points.

- Murder requires an intent to kill (or to inflict grievous bodily harm); so it is not murder

---

[1] See 1st edn 454 n. 15.

[2] The point was dealt with in the judgments in the CA, [1981] 2 WLR 1070, 1 All ER 628, 72 CAR 178; see, on appeal, [1981] 3 WLR 955.

[3] Last note. The word "unlawful" is not in the Police Act 1964, but counsel argued that it is to be implied because the Act refers to an assault and unlawfulness.

[4] See Celia Wells in [1982] Crim.LR 214.

to shoot and kill another by negligence, however gross. But if a person kills another in the convinced but mistaken and unreasonable belief that he himself is about to be killed by the other, he is theoretically guilty of murder, even though on the facts as he believed them to be he would not have been guilty of any crime. Is not this a harsh rule? And (if it adds anything to the criticism) is it not illogical as well? Why should negligence be relevant in the one case but not in the other? Is public security appreciably improved by punishing the rare person who foolishly acts in supposed self-defence?

- A similar anomaly can be seen in the law of injuries to the person short of death. An acquaintance of mine shot his wife in the shrubbery, believing she was a rabbit. (Fortunately he only shot her in the leg.) This was a mistake as to a definitional fact (since the offences against the person are confined to action against a human being), and he could not have been convicted of any offence, even if gross negligence had been established. But if he had shot his wife in the dark in the woodshed, thinking she was a robber about to attack, he could, theoretically, be convicted of anything from murder downwards according to circumstances, if his mistake had been accounted unreasonable. Is this distinction sensible?
- Is it fair to apply criteria of criminal negligence to a fearful situation? A person who believes himself about to be attacked has to act on the instant, if he is to defend himself successfully; there may be virtually nothing he can do to test the validity of his fear before acting; yet he may be punished for an unreasonable mistake. In contrast, a man who has intercourse with a woman without her consent has plenty of time to satisfy himself as to her consent if he is in any doubt on the matter; yet according to *Morgan* his unreasonable belief in her consent can excuse him.[5] The courts proceed not upon an analysis of the various situations in terms of common sense or justice but by a mechanical application of an illusory distinction between offences and defences.
- No other rule of the substantive criminal law distinguishes between the definitional and defence elements of a crime, and it is a distinction that is impossible to draw satisfactorily.[6] A rule creating a *defence* merely supplies additional details of the scope of the *offence*. To regard the offence as subsisting independently of its limitations and qualifications is unrealistic. The defence is a negative condition of the offence, and is therefore an integral part of it. What we regard as part of the offence and what as part of a defence depends only on traditional habits of thought or accidents of legal drafting; it should have no bearing on the important question of criminal liability. For example, it is purely a matter of convenient drafting whether a statute says, on the one hand, that damaging the property of another without his consent is a crime, or, on the other hand, that damaging the property of another is a crime but that his consent is a defence. In fact we regard the non-consent of the owner as a definitional element, but there is no particular reason why this should be so, and the question of guilt or innocence should not depend on it.[7]

There is some hope of change. The CLRC has proposed legislation to provide that the issue for private defence should be one of belief only. The principle should be applied to defences generally. If the Law Commission's ill-fated Report is ever dragged forth from the vaults you know about, and prepared for presentation to Parliament, it should be amended to embody the sound rule in the Model Penal Code that "the elements of an offence" should be defined to include the negative of defences for all purposes of liability, except of course as may be specifically provided.

§ 6.9. MISTAKE AS TO THE VICTIM OR KIND OF HARM

A mistake as to the victim or as to the property concerned is legally

[5] With the exception of *Brooks* v. *Mason*, a very questionable decision. See § 42.2.

[6] Our notion of what issue is a "defence," in so far as we have any clear notion, seems to depend largely on whether we think that the defendant should be required to take the initiative in introducing it, i.e. on whether he should bear an evidential burden in respect of it. But there is no reason why the distribution of evidential burdens should affect the rules of liability. See 2 Leg. Stud. 255.

[7] For an elaboration of this see 2 Leg. Stud. 233. See also A T H Smith in 2 Ox. Jrnl. Leg. Stud. 429.

immaterial if it does not affect the category of the offence. So if a man makes a mistake as to the person he is assaulting, or the house he is burgling, the mistake does not let him out of liability. Even if the facts had been as he supposed, he would still have been guilty of an offence against the same legal provision.[1] Of course, if the mistake is relevant to guilt it is capable of negativing *mens rea*, as where a householder uses force against an innocent person thinking he is a burglar.

The fact that a mistake is immaterial as regards conviction does not mean that it is immaterial as regards sentence. For example, since the offence of criminal damage requires intention or recklessness, a person who mischievously sets out to damage property that he thinks has small value should not have his sentence increased by the fact that the property was much more valuable than he thought.

It goes without saying that the position is different if the mistake is material. Where a person commits the external elements of a *mens rea* crime, thinking that he is committing a different one, he generally cannot be convicted of either. He may, however, be convicted of an attempt to commit the crime that he thought he was committing.

> He may, for example, think he is looking after a box of cannabis for a friend, and it turns out to be a gun. He cannot be convicted of unlawfully possessing cannabis, because he did not do it; and probably he cannot be convicted of unlawfully possessing a firearm, because he did not know he had it (§ 42.5). The solution would be to convict him of attempting to possess cannabis.

As regards drug offences, when for example a man thinks he has cannabis when actually it is morphine, special provision is made for what may be called an interchangeable *mens rea*. The Misuse of Drugs Act 1971 divides drugs of abuse ("controlled drugs"), in descending order of dangerousness, into "Class A drugs," "Class B drugs" and "Class C drugs," as defined in Schedule 2. Morphine is a Class A drug, cannabis a Class B. Section 28(3) of the Act gives a person charged under the Act a limited defence of no *mens rea*, but not in such a way as to enable him to set up a mistake between the classes of drug.

Suppose a man is ignorant of the facts that make his act criminal (an actus reus), but all the same he knows that he is doing something morally wrong. You said that mens rea does not refer to knowledge of moral wrong, so I suppose he won't be convicted?

On principle you are clearly right. In the well-known case of *Prince*, which is to be discussed in § 9.12, a minority of the judges held that a person who knew he was committing a moral wrong could not set up the defence of mistake of fact, even though on the facts as he believed them to be his act would not have been a crime (but only a moral wrong). The

---

[1] In *McCullum* (1973) 57 CAR 645 a woman was convicted of assisting in the handling of stolen guns and ammunition, even though it was not proved that she knew what the property was; she would have been convicted in the same way even though she thought the articles stolen were spades, though her moral offence would have been much less. Ashworth has suggested that the courts should ensure that the wording of the conviction expresses the true degree of the offender's guilt, and I slightly elaborated the suggestion in [1983] CLJ 85. The court could have done justice in this instance by directing the conviction to be recorded merely as one of assisting in the handling of stolen *goods*.

idea resurfaces from time to time in the minds of the judges,[2] but that it is a confusion of thought can be proved by a multitude of examples.[3]

> To give only one: nearly everyone would call deer-stealing immoral, but if a person believes he is unlawfully shooting at a deer, when actually he is shooting at a man, he could not possibly be convicted of murder.

The subject of "transferred intention," where a person aims at V1 and hits V2, is considered in § 8.4.

§ 6.10. CHARGING A MENTAL ELEMENT

Modern statutes generally state the mental element by words expressing intention, recklessness or knowledge. Other expressions are found, particularly in older statutes, and unfortunately are still sometimes used.

The word "wilfully" is best regarded as meaning "intentionally or recklessly," but the courts have failed to attach a fixed meaning to it and the authorities are chaotic.[1] When the word bears the meaning just suggested, it follows that if a person acts under the mistaken belief (reasonable or not) that a relevant fact is absent, he does not act wilfully.[2]

Since the word "wilfully" is pejorative, judges have added that wilfulness connotes doing something that is not only intentional but without lawful excuse.[3] This has the practical effect of allowing the defence of claim of right in certain cases.[4] The proposition of law is, however, muddled for two reasons. (1) It introduces questions of the legality of conduct into the mental element, where they do not belong. The question whether there is or is not a lawful excuse for the act has nothing to do with the required mental element. Lawful excuse is an exception by law from the legal prohibition.[5] (2) If there is indeed a lawful excuse, it will operate whether or not the word "wilfully" is in the statute.

As has been seen, the antiquated word "maliciously" is interpreted in the same way.[6]

The term "wilful neglect," found in some statutes, has troubled the courts—understandably, since the two words may seem on their face to be contradictory. The meaning now favoured seems to be (at least approximately) "neglect with subjective recklessness."[7]

The word "purpose" is occasionally found, evidently as the equivalent of "intention."[8] It ought not to cover recklessness; but there is some authority for making it include a mere knowledge of probability.[9]

---

[2] A circuit judge in *McPherson*, § 10.9 n. 3, used the moral wrong doctrine as one of the grounds of his decision, which was clearly erroneous.

[3] See *The General Part*, 2nd edn 188–192; *Taaffe* [1983] 1 WLR 627, and important comment in [1983] Crim.LR 536. Leave has been given to appeal to the Lords. See also the rather tepid rejection of the moral wrong doctrine on the particular facts in *Morgan* [1976] AC at 238D–E.

[1] For a survey of the cases see J A Andrews in 1 Leg.Stud. 303 at 315 ff. On wilfully obstructing the police see § 9.7 at n. 3.

[2] See § .2 n.3.

[3] See, e.g. *Rice* v. *Connolly* [1966] 2 QB at 419.

[4] See §§ 20.5, 6.

[5] See R H F Austin in [1982] Curr.LProb. 192–193. (The author is wrong, however, in suggesting that the burden of proof of reasonable excuse is on the defendant: § 2.5 n. 12.)

[6] *Cunningham* [1957] 2 QB 396. See § 9.3 at n. 3. See § 9.3 generally on the problem created by *Caldwell*. This word, too, is interpreted to include an absence of excuse.

[7] See *Gittins* [1982] Crim.LR 584, and (on CYPA) § 9.9 n.4.

[8] White in 92 LQR 563 ff. points out some differences of usage, but I do not think they affect the point that in legal contexts intention in relation to consequences means purpose.

[9] The actual decision in *Chandler* § 3.2 at n. 1 need not be interpreted in this sense, but some dicta suggest it. See note, [1962] Crim. LR 786, and 1st edn 93.

The word "calculated" is conveniently mentioned here, though it does not belong to the subject of *mens rea*. In common speech it often refers to deliberate intent: a calculated risk or calculated insult means one that is deliberately taken or made. But its appearance in statutes is in the phrase "calculated to," as in "a statement calculated to deceive," and here its meaning has become debased to "likely." This meaning has been adopted by the courts.[10] It would be better if such a misleading word, pretending to indicate a mental state when it does not, were avoided by the legislature.

When an offence can be committed intentionally or recklessly, does the jury's verdict say which of the two they found?

The alternatives can be combined in the same count. The fact that the mental element is stated in alternative terms does not make the count "duplicitous."[11] When there is such a single count the jury need not specify in their verdict which alternative they have found. (Some jurors may have thought the one, some the other.) The point is, however, important for sentencing, because recklessness is generally punished much less severely than intention.[12] So since the judge has heard the evidence, he must make up his own mind as to the particular *mens rea*. Difficulty can be avoided if the prosecution charge intention and recklessness in separate counts, so that separate verdicts can be taken.[13]

§ 6.11. MENS REA, VALUE-JUDGMENTS AND STRICT LIABILITY

Where a rule of law involves the making of a value-judgment, the doctrine of *mens rea* does not generally apply in respect of the value-judgment.

On an issue of negligence, for example, the question whether what the defendant did was "negligent" on the one hand or "reasonable" on the other involves a judgment of value made by the jury (or, of course, by magistrates), and the question whether the defendant knew that he was being negligent is not controlling. Similarly a defence of self-defence is excluded if the jury think that the defendant reacted disproportionately, even though he considered that it was proportionate (§ 21.3); and a defence of necessity is excluded if the jury think that what the defendant had in mind to do was not socially justified, even though he thought it was (§ 24.12).[1] However, where the judge is of opinion that no reasonable jury would convict he should direct an acquittal.

The instances just given are all value-judgments, which are intermediate between questions of fact and questions of law. As with questions of law, the defendant's failure to foresee the decision of the court does not excuse him.

---

[10] *Davison* [1972] Crim.LR 786.
[11] Indictment Rules 1971 r.7. For the prohibition of duplicity in pleading see § 7.9.
[12] See D A Thomas, *Principles of Sentencing*, 2nd edn 99–100.
[13] *Hayter* [1981] Crim. LR 344.

[1] For exceptional cases where the law defines a value-judgment in subjective terms see §§ 37.4, 41.6.

The *mens rea* doctrine is equally excluded in cases of strict liability, even though a question of pure fact is involved. Here it is sufficient for the prosecution to prove the doing of the prohibited act, the existence of the circumstance or the happening of the consequence as the case may be.[2] In other words, any defence of ignorance, mistake or reasonable care is excluded unless the law allows it to some limited extent. The reason offered by some judges for construing an offence as one of strict liability is that the statute is silent on the question of *mens rea*; yet if there is in law an implied requirement of *mens rea* (as has from time to time been said), the fact that the Act does not express the requirement should not affect the matter.

Strict liability is sometimes called "absolute liability," but this, although accepted usage, is a misnomer, because all the usual defences are available except the defences of lack of intention, recklessness or negligence. For example, the defendant can set up a defence of duress,[3] automatism,[4] and perhaps impossibility in some circumstances.[5]

An offence may be of strict liability in one respect but require a fault element in another. Driving while disqualified is an offence of strict liability in respect of the disqualification (the driver is guilty although he firmly, but mistakenly, believed that he was not then disqualified), but it requires an intentional act of driving. We call it an offence of strict liability because that is its predominant feature.

When it is held that an element of a serious crime is a matter of strict liability, this is probably because the courts fear that the prosecution would find it too difficult to establish *mens rea* in respect of that element. Serious problems arise when the element in question is highly speculative.

> An example is the crime of blasphemous libel, commonly called blasphemy. This is a common law offence involving the publishing of matter that is "calculated to shock or outrage the feelings of Christians;" and here, as elsewhere, the courts distort the word "calculated" to make it mean something that is not calculated at all, but merely likely in the minds of the jury. The defendant must know that he is publishing something, and presumably he must know the meaning of the words he uses (lack of acquaintance with the English language could be a defence); but the question whether the words are calculated to shock involves only an objective question for the jury.[6] Likelihood of shock is a matter of strict liability or of negligence—the classification makes no difference.

The jury are allowed to find of their own knowledge that the publication would be likely to shock. Although the rule is worded in terms conveying the impression that the jury are to decide a question of fact, they are probably in reality deciding the evaluative question whether the publication is so scurrilous that its publication ought not to be allowed. (Nevertheless, it would doubtless be a misdirection to tell them this.)

Obviously, the issue in blasphemy is extremely debatable in the modern world. Christians differ in the details and strength of their religious belief, and in their degrees of tolerance of dissenting opinion. If questioned, some may profess shock about a particular publication (in the sense of strong disapproval), without being distressed otherwise than momentarily. The jury (who need not be Christians) are left to speculate, and the defendant is required, at the time of acting, to make an accurate forecast of the way in which they will decide.

Similar problems beset the crime of obscenity (the publishing of an obscene article, or

---

[2] It is preferable not to say that an offence requiring the prosecution to prove negligence is one of strict liability. Lord Diplock on one occasion said that careless driving is an offence of stfict liability (*Caldwell* [1982] AC at 00), but this would be inconvenient usage. For other aberrational uses of the term, which sometimes result in faulty conclusions, see [1967] Crim.LR 143–145.

[3] *O'Sullivan* v. *Fisher* [1945] SASR 337 (S Aus.).

[4] § 27.1 n. 5.

[5] § 24.13.

[6] *Lemon* [1979] AC 617; see the critical note by J C Smith in [1979] Crim.LR 312. See also Law Commission, *Working Paper No. 79, Offences against Religion and Public Worship.*

having an obscene article for publication for gain), under the Obscene Publications Act 1959, as amended by an Act of 1964.[7] The test of whether an article is obscene under the Act, as at common law, is whether

> "its effect . . . is, if taken as a whole, such as to tend to deprave and corrupt persons who are likely, having regard to all relevant circumstances, to read, see or hear the matter contained or embodied in it" (s.1(1)).

Here again the jury make the decision on the supposed question of fact without regard to what the defendant thought, and however reasonably he may have believed that the article would not deprave and corrupt.[8] The nebulous nature of the question gives the jury an extraordinary roving commission. As the courts have interpreted the legislation, the jury may find that the article tends to deprave if it encourages private sexual fantasies even without overt sexual activity[9] and the depravity need not relate to sex, since articles encouraging violence[10] or drug abuse[11] can be found to be obscene within the statutory definition. In short, it seems that the jury can condemn any publication tending to encourage a great departure from "current standards of ordinary decent people."[12]

The laxity of draftsmanship of the obscenity offence has been strongly, and justifiably, criticised.

> "Extensive jury discretion of the kind that is created by the use of a vague statutory formula requiring the jury to determine for itself what the relevant standard should be is discretion in its most objectionable form, because the chances of structuring the exercise of that discretion by other means, whether administrative guidelines or informal processes of discussion and consultation, are non-existent. . . . If the legislator wishes to use criminal sanctions to control behaviour of this kind he must accept the responsibility of defining the prohibited conduct more precisely, even if the resulting legislation makes distasteful reading, so that the jury is not required to go beyond the limits of its proper function."[13]

To wind up this discussion of *mens rea*, it was the judges who invented the doctrine, but we have seen (and shall see at greater length as the book proceeds) that some have fought a long rearguard action against it. The mental element has been virtually eliminated from many offences, while it has been watered down in others. There are distressing examples of a crime that expressly requires *mens rea* being held to require only what may be called half *mens rea—mens rea* as to some elements of the offence but not others. Sometimes the mental element has been qualified by insisting that lack of it (in cases of mistake) must be reasonable, which turns the offence into one of negligence. Even when intention was supposed to be required, there was for long a tendency (which some judges still cling to) to construe it "objectively;" and recklessness has also been given a semi-objective interpretation.

In short, the law on *mens rea* illustrates the eternal tension in the position of the judge. He is supposed to be an impartial adjudicator, applying the existing law and protecting the rights and liberties of the subject; but he is also a State instrumentality—in the wider sense, an organ

---

[7] See also Theatres Act 1968 s.2.

[8] Except that the defendant may prove that he had not examined the article and had no reasonable cause to suspect its nature: 1959 Act s.2(5); 1964 Act s.1(3). There is also a defence of public good under the 1959 Act s.4, as amended by CLA 1977.

[9] *Whyte* [1972] 3 All ER at 18.

[10] *Calder & Boyers Ltd* [1969] 1 QB at 172.

[11] *John Calder Publications Ltd* v. *Powell* [1965] 1 QB 509.

[12] The phrase used in *Knuller (etc.) Ltd* v. *DPP* [1973] AC 435. See generally Smith and Hogan, 4th edn 691–708.

[13] D A Thomas in *Reshaping the Criminal Law*, ed. Glazebrook (London 1978) 32.

of government. In general it is the second concept of the judge's role that shapes judicial attitudes on the issue of fault in the criminal law.

Some of the difficulties discussed in these chapters would be solved if the late lamented Report of the Law Commission were disinterred and resuscitated. But the Report itself is unduly timid in some respects: it would not apply to existing legislation (not even an important statute like the Criminal Damage Act), and the drafting is not sufficiently tight to be judge-proof.

SUMMARY

Circumstances are relevant facts existing when the defendant acts. § .1

To say that an act is intentional implies that the actor knows the relevant circumstances, or (in inchoate offences) believes that they exist. If he does not possess this knowledge or belief, the fact that he makes an unreasonable mistake or is in unreasonable ignorance does not make his act intentional. This was established in *David Smith* (CA), *Morgan* (HL) and various cases on statutory wilfulness. Correlatively, a statutory requirement of intention applies to all the elements of the offence unless the contrary is indicated. The courts now accept that the decision in *Morgan* is not confined to rape: *Kimber*. § .2

Similar considerations apply where an offence requires knowledge. As always, the defendant's state of mind can be inferred, it being permissible to assume that the defendant realised what any ordinary person would have realised, if that assumption is consistent with the evidence. A person knows a fact if he can instantly recall it. The strict requirement of knowledge is qualified by the rule that wilful blindness is equivalent to knowledge. Although the authorities are discordant, the best view is that of the Law Commission, that this doctrine refers to a situation where a person has no substantial doubt that the circumstance exists. § .3

The word "permit" and its synonyms, and also the word "cause," are generally taken to require knowledge, by implication, but the better view is that recklessness is sufficient. Anomalously, the defence of permitting the uninsured use of a motor vehicle is held to be of strict liability. § .4

An offence of negligence may be committed by negligence as to circumstances, e.g. by making an unreasonable mistake. § .5

The rules for recklessness are much the same as those stated above for intention and knowledge, and the authorities there given apply equally to recklessness. A person may be reckless as to the existence of a circumstance, but he is not reckless if he believed that the circumstance did not exist or if it was reasonable for him to take the risk of it. He may be guilty of *Caldwell* recklessness for not thinking. The circumstance may be a negative fact, like the non-consent of the woman in rape. The definition of rape now depends on the Act of 1976. In practice, though not in theory, the issue on the mental element in rape is whether the defendant believed the woman to be consenting. As always, the unreasonableness of the defendant's belief is evidence (but no more) that it was not entertained. § .6

According to the line of authority stemming from *Tolson*, a mistake, to be a defence to a statutory offence, must be reasonable, though the proposition can now apply only to statutes "absolute" on their face—i.e. not requiring intention, recklessness or knowledge expressly or by clear implication. It is uncertain whether the *Tolson* rule applies to all such statutory offences or only to bigamy. Parliament has sometimes expressly provided for a defence of reasonable mistake. § .7

An unreasonable mistake relating to a matter of defence (like private defence) does not excuse: *Albert* v. *Lavin*. § .8

A mistake as to the victim or kind of harm is legally immaterial if it does not affect the category of the offence. Where a person makes a mistake as to the type of *mens rea* crime he is committing, he generally cannot be convicted of anything except an attempt to commit the crime that he thought he was committing. A person does not become guilty of a crime because he believed his act to be morally wrong. § .9

"Maliciously" and "wilfully" generally mean "intentionally or recklessly and without lawful excuse." Where a statute provides that an offence can be committed intentionally or recklessly, the two states of mind should be charged in separate counts (or a choice made between them), even though in strict law they can be charged in one count. § .10

Where a rule of law involves the making of a value-judgment (e.g. negligence), the requirement of *mens rea* does not generally apply in respect of the value-judgment. Nor, of course, does it apply in respect of matters of strict liability. Although strict liability exempts the prosecution from proving fault, it does not preclude other defences. Some elements of an offence may be of strict liability, while others require fault. Serious problems arise when a value-judgment is highly speculative in nature, as in blasphemy and obscenity. § .11

CHAPTER 7

THE EXTERNAL ELEMENTS OF AN OFFENCE

He dreamed that he stood in a shadowy Court,
Where the snark, with a glass in its eye,
Dressed in gown, bands and wig, was defending a pig
On the charge of deserting its sty. . . .
"The fact of Desertion I will not dispute:
But its guilt, as I trust, is removed
(So far as relates to the costs of the suit)
By the Alibi which has been proved."
Lewis Carroll, *The Hunting of the Snark*.

§ 7.1. THE EXTENDED MEANING OF ACTUS REUS

ALTHOUGH lawyers find the expression *actus reus* convenient, it is misleading in one respect. As was said before, it means not just the criminal act but all the external elements of the offence.

Ordinarily, there is a criminal act, which is what makes the term *actus reus* generally acceptable. But there are crimes without an act, and therefore without an *actus reus* in the obvious meaning of that term. The expression "conduct" is more satisfactory, because wider; it covers not only an *act* but an *omission* (§ .3), and (by a stretch) a *bodily position* (§ 6). The conduct must sometimes take place in legally-relevant *circumstances*, and, as we have seen, in some crimes it must produce a legally-forbidden *consequence*. As a final complication, some crimes can be committed without any conduct by the defendant (§ .6).

All that can truly be said, without exception, is that a crime requires some *external state of affairs* that can be categorised as criminal. What goes on inside a man's head is never enough in itself to constitute a crime, even though it be proved by a confession that is fully believed to be genuine. English law has no instance of Orwell's "thoughtcrime," no equivalent of the adultery "in his heart" of the New Testament. Sir Edward Coke[1]:

> "No man shall be examined upon secret thoughts of his heart, or of his secret opinion: but something ought to be objected against him what he hath spoken or done."

The crime of attempt, for example, requires some kind of act directed towards the commission of the crime, going beyond mere preparation. It would be a great over-extension of the law to punish mere criminal fantasies which the defendant may lack the resolution to put into effect.

The proposition that there is no jail for thoughts will appeal to the civil libertarian, but it

---

[1] Co.Rep. 26, 77 ER 1308.

is in itself a rather hollow liberty, since a private resolve without external expression cannot be satisfactorily proved, and its external expression can be a crime. If you think it a good idea that the prime minister's house should be burgled, it is just as well not to express the thought to a cracksman, for you could then be liable for incitement or conspiracy, or as accessory to the burglary if it is committed. What is important to the libertarian is the fact that our law does not generally penalise the expression of political opinion.

The necessity for both criminal conduct and co-existing *mens rea* in the more serious crimes may be shown by two instances.

1 D, intending to steal V's umbrella, by mistake takes his own.
2 D, intending to take his own umbrella, by mistake takes V's.

In (1), D is not guilty of theft because, although he has the criminal state of mind, there is lacking the wrongful conduct required for this crime. Theft involves the dishonest appropriation of the property of another, and D has not done this. In (2) he is not guilty of theft because, although he has brought about the situation against which the law provides, he lacks the criminal state of mind.

Older expressions having the same meaning as *actus reus* are *corpus delicti* and "overt act." The latter means an act that is open to the world in the sense that it can be perceived by anyone placed to do so.

> "What's open made to justice,
> That justice seizes."[2]

The Treason Act 1351 (which, almost incredibly, is still in force) declares one form of treason to be "compassing or imagining" the death of the King. "It is really too hard upon human nature," wrote George Eliot "that it should be held a criminal offence to imagine the death even of the king when he is turned eighty-three."[3] But that is not what the statute is understood to mean; the judges require proof of an "overt act" evidencing an intention to kill the sovereign. However, an act done in secrecy is an overt act or *actus reus* if later it can be proved against the defendant (as if he confesses to it).

Although the term *actus reus* is convenient, it is in one respect misleading. The adjective *reus* does not imply that the act or other conduct must be obviously wicked or harmful in itself, apart from the intent that accompanies it. There may be an *actus reus* without any external consequence harmful to society. In the crime of conspiracy the fact of agreement is not in itself, and without more, harmful to society. Harm occurs only if the agreement is put into execution. But agreements are often acted upon, and so an agreement is punishable because of its tendency to result in harm. The same applies to the act necessary for attempt, and to the persuasion necessary for the crime of incitement.

Another point on the term *actus reus* is that when a crime requires *mens rea*, an *actus* cannot be legally *reus* (in the sense of involving criminal responsibility) unless there is *mens rea*. Therefore, it may appear self-contradictory to say: "There is an *actus reus*, but no *mens rea*." The solution of this difficulty is to define *actus reus* in a technical sense as meaning conduct that would be criminal provided that any necessary *mens rea* or other fault element were present. In other words, the *actus reus* is the conduct that is forbidden by the rule of the criminal law, on the assumption that any necessary fault is found to exist. When we get a criminal code it may be expected to refer to the external elements of the offence rather than to the *actus reus*; but *actus reus* is a conveniently concise exression when discussing legal problems.

§ 7.2. ACTS

Considerable confusion reigns, both in ordinary and in legal speech, on what is meant by an act, or a voluntary act. The most acceptable language

---

[2] *Measure for Measure* II. i.
[3] *Adam Bede*, Chap. 33.

is to say that an act means a willed bodily movement, so that if A pushes B against C and so causes C to fall over, we attribute the pushing of C to A, not to B. However, in a situation like this there is really no need to go into the meaning of an act. If B were charged with assaulting C, or with murdering C in the event of C's death, the obvious defence would be lack of the mental element, and there would be no occasion to discuss whether B had "acted."

Lawyers sometimes speak of a voluntary act, meaning only that it was willed. Since every act is by definition willed, there is no need to call it voluntary.

The element of volition in an act has greatly exercised the philosophers. Two of them, Ryle and Melden, have attempted to argue away the notion of will. They build their case upon the difficulty of identifying conscious volitions accompanying bodily movement. Certainly it would be false to assume that every act is the result of deliberation: I may scratch my nose while thinking, without knowing I am doing it or recollecting I have done it. Even when the act is conscious, introspection does not show a conscious exercise of will preceding conduct. When I move my arms, say in writing a letter, I do not consciously decide to move them before moving them. It is true that electrical impulses run from the motor nerve cells in the spinal cord through the nerve fibres to the muscles; and these muscles are under the control of the brain. But the mental functioning that controls movement is not conscious determination, and it takes place at practically the same time as the movement. Will is the mental activity accompanying the type of bodily movement that we call an act. It is, of course, possible to will the absence of an act, as when we sit still.

A bodily movement is said to be willed, generally speaking, when the person in question could have refrained from it if he had so willed: that is, he could have acted otherwise or kept still. Movements that are the result of epilepsy, for example, are involuntary or unwilled because the person concerned cannot by any mental effort avoid them. Whatever the difficulties in explaining what we mean by volition, everyone realises the important difference between doing something and having something happen to one; and this distinction is a basic postulate of a moral view of human behaviour.

Crimes are not generally defined by reference to the doing of an act in the abstract. A crime is committed in certain circumstances by appropriating property, or damaging property, or driving a vehicle, or killing someone. We can of course perceive a common element of an act in all these situations, but sometimes one has to look hard to find the voluntary conduct. For example: a person who takes an intoxicating drug, falls asleep and kills his bedmate thinking that he is struggling with a serpent is guilty of manslaughter,[1] yet he does not consciously kill a human being. The only voluntary conduct that can be found is in taking the drug in the company of the other person, which it is difficult in itself to describe as a killing.

§ 7.3. OMISSIONS

A crime can be committed by omission, but there can be no omission in law in the absence of a duty to act. The reason is obvious. If there is an act, someone acts; but if there is an omission, everyone (in a sense) omits. We

---

[1] *Lipman* § 23.2 at n. 10.

omit to do everything in the world that is not done. Only those of us omit in law who are under a duty to act.

When a statute expressly or impliedly creates an offence of omission, it points out the person under the duty by the wording of the offence.

This is true, for example, of the offence of failing to fill in one's income tax return, of not stopping after a traffic accident,[1] and of failing to fence dangerous machinery in a factory. The various offences of "permitting" something to be done can be committed not only by giving words of authorisation but by failing to prevent conduct when one is in control of the situation, and here again the person who must not permit is specified. Offences of possessing or retaining forbidden objects imply a duty to get rid of the object as soon as its nature is discovered (§ .4 n. 3). No general problem arises, except in deciding whether the offence was intended to be of strict liability or to require proof of negligence.

The law does not cast on us a general duty to play the Good Samaritan. Exceptionally, there is a statutory offence of failing to rescue those in peril on the sea.[2] Parents (and others who have the charge of children) commit a statutory offence if they wilfully neglect a child (§ 9.9 n. 3). A husband commits an offence if he persistently neglects to maintain his wife, and similarly a wife her husband, if public accommodation has to be found for them.[3] People are responsible if their premises become a danger to health or a nuisance.[4]

The difficulty arises where the offence is worded in terms primarily suggesting active conduct, yet considerations of policy seem to suggest the desirability of extending the offence to omissions. In such circumstances, omitting to prevent a result will sometimes be regarded by the courts as equivalent to activity bringing it about.

Murder and manslaughter are the most prominent examples. These are common law crimes traditionally defined in terms of "killing" someone. The judges reason thus:

> "Killing" means causing death. Agreed?
> Well, then, you can cause death by omitting to save a person, as much as by stabbing him.
> Therefore you can be guilty of murder or manslaughter by omission.

But that is conjuring with words: producing a rabbit from a hat that did not hold it. If I fail to warn a blind man that he is approaching a cliff, I may be morally guilty of "causing his death", or at any rate of letting him die, if he falls over, but I cannot in ordinary language be said to "kill" him. Besides, what if a whole crowd of people saw him walk to his death without intervening. Would they all "kill" him?

Let me ask a counter-question. If parents deliberately starve their child to death, wouldn't you say they have killed him?

That is an extreme case, and even there it might be truer to call it a bad case of child neglect rather than one of killing. Suppose parents fail to call a doctor to their sick child when they should, and the child dies in

---

[1] RTA 1972 s.25 as amended.

[2] Maritime Conventions Act 1911 s.6 (cp. Merchant Shipping Act 1894 s.680(1)); Merchant Shipping (Safety Convention) Act 1949 s.22.

[3] National Assistance Act 1948 ss.42, 51(1).

[4] See, e.g. *Coventry City* v. *Cartwrights* [1975] 1 WLR 845, 2 All ER 99, where however it was held that the deposit did not come within the statutory words.

consequence. It is harsh to say that the parents have killed their child. The disease killed; the parents culpably let the child die. They should be guilty of child neglect, not of killing.

Well put. The parents who bring about their child's death through want of medical treatment are regarded in law as killing the child, but it is stretching things.

Since the judges formerly assumed that they had the power to invent new crimes whenever they felt the need, it would have been better if they had invented a special offence of neglecting a duty to the helpless. But they preferred if possible to inflate crimes rather than create them; and extending the criminal law by attaching "constructive" meanings to words is one of the traditional weapons in the judges' armoury. So they made the word "kill," which primarily means killing by positive act, cover the causing of death by certain omissions.

The answer to your question, which I have not yet given, is no. You and the rest of the callous crowd in your hypothetical would not in law kill the unfortunate man, because you are not under a duty of care towards him. The lawyer takes straight the injunction in *The New Decalogue* which Clough meant as irony.

> Thou shalt not kill; but needs't not strive
> Officiously to keep alive

—exceptions apart. One such exception is the common law duty of parents to look after their children, which is held, as we have seen, to produce results in the law of murder and manslaughter.

In many legal problems one finds oneself on a slippery slope, which it is all too easy to slither down. In this case the judges extend the concept of killing by omission beyond parents who starve their children (where it might be regarded as common sense), and say that one who is in charge of any helpless person is under a duty, or can in certain circumstances be found by the jury to be under a duty, to take reasonable steps to preserve his life (for example, by summoning medical assistance when needed), and "kills" him if he dies through neglect of the duty (§ 12.3). To assert that if you fail to call a doctor to your sick lodger, and the lodger dies in consequence, you kill him is a colourful rather than a precise use of language; but it is the language the judges use in order to make the law of homicide apply.

What if the lodger did not die but suffered a severe illness that could have been prevented?

The case has not arisen. A statute makes it an offence to "cause" serious injury ("grievous bodily harm") (§ 9.1), and if the word "cause" is held to cover causing by omission then of course the landlord would be guilty of the offence. I would suggest that the law should not go beyond homicide, in the absence of express legislation.

When a court has to decide whether a particular statute applies to causing harm by omissions, its decision may well depend on the circumstances in which the question first arises. If a nursemaid maliciously allowed her infant protégé to fall over a cliff, from which he suffered serious injury, the court would doubtless stretch the statute on causing serious injury to cover the nursemaid; and then the statute would stay stretched even for landlords who do not call the doctor to their lodger, where the lodger suffers injury.[5]

Anyway, the general proposition at present (pending further judicial extensions of the law) is that the rules for murder and manslaughter are exceptional. People have not yet been held to be under a general duty to prevent calamities short of death, even in respect of persons under their care. However, parents and guardians commit an offence at common law if they cause injury to children by neglect,[6] and, as we have seen, there is a statutory offence to the same effect under which all the prosecutions in respect of children are now brought. Also, it is an offence at common law for a public officer to misconduct himself in his office, whether by act or by omission[7]; but this offence is practically never charged.

In short, the extensive construction of the word "kill" in murder and manslaughter is anomalous. Most statutes are aimed against bad acts, not bad omissions, and judges do not generally construe active verbs as covering omissions. They do not say, for instance, that a person "wounds" another by failing to save him from being wounded, or "damages" a building by failing to stop a fire.[8] At least, this has never been decided. It was held on one occasion that a statute forbidding the "doing" of something did not cover an omission.[9] Nor did an offence of "causing" something[10] or "assisting" the doing of something.[11] A draftsman who uses these words is obviously thinking of positive acts, not of failing to do something. The principle is, or should be, that words implying active conduct are not to be stretched by interpretation to include inactivity; and homicide should be regarded as highly exceptional. (It is not unique: another exception springs from the judicial tendency to increase the powers of the police: § 9.7.) One may suggest that except where these judicial manipulations are a settled part of the law, ambiguous words in statutes should never be interpreted to cover omissions; Parliament should be required to do the job expressly, if it is to be done at all.

But if a cat starts a fire in a rented house, by knocking over an oil lamp, shouldn't the tenant be guilty of arson if he lets the house burn down when he could have called the fire brigade?

The offence of arson is not *letting the house burn* but *burning* it

---

[5] The CLRC in its 14th Report, para. 253, expressed the opinion that the statute applies to omissions; but see *Price* v. *Cromack*, n. 10 below.

[6] Russell, *Crime*, 12th edn i 696.

[7] *Curtis* (1885) 15 Cox 746; *Dytham* [1979] 3 All ER 641, noted in Crim.LR 666.

[8] *Contra*, J C Smith in [1982] Crim.LR 527, 774, suggesting that one can destroy, damage, wound and even assault by omission in breach of duty.

[9] *Red House Farms (Thorndon) Ltd* v. *Mid Suffolk DC*, The Times, April 30 1980.

[10] *Price* v. *Cromack* [1975] 1 WLR 988, 2 All ER 113 (landowner does not "cause" polluting matter to enter a stream by failing to prevent such entry).

[11] *Brown* [1970] 1 QB 105. But see the questionable cases on becoming an accessory by omission: § 15.7.

(destroying or damaging property by fire). It would be unfair to describe a slack and ineffective tenant who lets premises burn as an arsonist. Courts quite frequently convict bad people of the nearest crime that can be found in the books, but they ought not to do so, when the act does not fall fairly within the offence. In the present instance, two undesirable consequences would follow from convicting your slack tenant.

First, the possibility would be increased that other verbs of action may be construed to include omissions, thus adding to the uncertainty of the law.

Secondly, if the judges were to declare it arson to omit to save someone else's house from destruction by fire, they would have to delimit the people who are under the duty. Is an aged and rather feeble tenant to be convicted of arson by omission, and his adult and able-bodied son who also resides on the premises acquitted? If the son is brought in, what about the tenant's wife or other bedmate? A lodger? A guest staying for the night? Is a trespasser under a duty to put out a fire started by another trespasser? What about a passer-by who sees flames? Judges should not allow themselves to construct general rules, extending the ordinary meanings of words, on the basis of rare and flagrant cases that may come to their notice. See, however, § .5 for a variant of the problem.

Although the courts do not generally impose criminal liability for omissions, they have sometimes construed apparently positive words to cover inactivity. One court, taking strong exception to the conduct of the defendant before it, held that a statute in terms referring to action applied also to an omission to prevent, where the defendant was well placed to do the preventing.[12] It is perhaps not accidental that this case, which will be discussed later, concerned a sexual matter, on which judges are notoriously sensitive.

Sometimes the defendant's conduct can be looked upon from one point of view as a forbidden act and from another point of view as an omission. Driving while too sleepy is an act, failing to stop and rest when sleepy is an omission. When, as in this instance, a person is pursuing an activity and performs it negligently by failing to take a precaution, his conduct is naturally regarded as a whole, so that we say that he is guilty of negligent activity (careless driving). One does not divide the conduct into bits in order to say that part was an omission.[13] Another case of liability attributed to a combination of act and omission will be considered in § .5.

However, liability for negligent activity is somewhat exceptional in the criminal law, outside the field of public welfare offences. The criminal law knows no general principle of liability for negligence (as the law of tort does), except where death occurs (§ 9.13). If, for instance, a sportsman forgets to unload the ammunition from his gun when leaning it against the wall, and someone is accidentally wounded, he is not guilty of an offence—not because the case is one of omission but because, traditionally, there is

---

[12] See *Speck*, § 10.5.
[13] See Helen Beynon in [1982] Crim. LR 22–23.

no criminal liability even for acts of negligence in these circumstances. (However, the courts may now regard the negligent sportsman as constructively reckless under *Caldwell.*)

What if the person charged with an omission was completely unable to act? We have seen that a physically compelled movement would not be said to be an act. Similarly, a person would not be convicted of an omission (intentional, reckless or negligent) if he was physically unable to act,[14] unless of course he had the requisite fault element at some prior time when he was within the wording of the offence.

§ 7.4. POSSESSION

The judges ultimately refused to recognise any offences of illicit possession as a matter of common law, saying that possession was not an act[1]; and such offences of the kind as we have are statutory.

The *acquisition* of possession usually involves an act (an act of grasping an object, for example), in which case there is no difficulty. Even when another person delivers goods to my premises without my touching them, I shall usually have ordered him to do so. However, one can instance cases where there is no relevant act. Take the statutory offence of "knowingly possessing explosives."[2] A man is in possession of a package which, when he first received it, he did not realise contained explosives, but he has later come to know that it does. There is no "act" on his part after he acquires the knowledge. The courts hold that he commits an offence if he retains the explosives, unless he does so only in order to inform the police.[3] In this respect, therefore, the offence is one of omission in breach of duty. The person who is under the duty to act is clearly pointed out by the statute, as being the person in possession of the property.[4]

It is sometimes hard to tell whether, when a particular person is in possession of contraband (an expression used in this book to denote any forbidden object), his possession will be treated in law as shared by another. The answer may sometimes depend on the particular offence charged, but the general principle is that a person may possess through another (particularly an agent or accomplice) if, though not in physical possession of the thing, he intends to exercise joint or sole control over it.

The courts are generally reluctant to hold that an employee possesses his employer's goods of which he is left in charge, for the purpose of convicting the employee of an offence of unlawful possession. The possession is generally regarded as being solely in the employer. This is so, for example, with regard to possessing unfit food for sale. But the attitude of the

---

[14] See Glazebrook in *Reshaping the Criminal Law* (London 1978) 116–118; §§ 3.5 n. 1, 26.10.

[1] *Dugdale* (1853) 1 El. & Bl. 435, 118 ER 499. See Glazebrook in 85 LQR 30.

[2] Explosive Substances Act 1883 s.4 (1).

[3] Similarly with the offences of handling stolen goods by retention: *Brown* § 39.3 n. 9; *Pitchley* § 38.4 n. 8. As to the qualification see *Wuyts* [1969] 2 QB 474: here the statute defined the offence as being committed only when the possession was "without lawful authority or excuse," but these words would anyway be implied. See *Selby* [1972] AC at 520F (possession of counterfeit coins). Cp. § 42.7.

[4] Whereas a person who consciously keeps a contraband object in order to inform the police is not liable, one who holds it not knowing its nature can, paradoxically, be liable for an offence of strict liability. See § 42.5.

court will naturally depend upon the offence charged, upon the degree of control exercised by the employer over the article, and upon the discretion given to the employee. The manager of a shop would readily be convicted of possessing contraband stock when he is effectively in sole charge of the business; and even more lowly employees may sometimes be held to have been placed in possession.[5] More about the doctrine of possession in the chapter on strict liability.[6]

§7.5 THE CONCURRENCE OF ACT AND INTENT

Normally, *actus reus* and *mens rea* must concur in point of time.

> If a person innocently acquires goods, he does not become guilty of receiving stolen goods by reason of subsequently finding out that they are stolen.
>
> Nor does a person who has been given goods become guilty of theft in acquiring them by reason of the fact that he subsequently finds that he has not obtained a good title to them.

But the rule is not so simple as it may at first sound. In the second hypothetical, the donee of the goods can become guilty of theft by dishonestly keeping them after he comes to know that they do not belong to him. The theft is not the original acquisition but the subsequent guilty retention, and this retention is an *actus reus* concurrent with the *mens rea* (§ .5).

Moreover, some criminal acts are regarded as continuing over a period of time. If the act is continuing, a guilty intent formed towards the end of this period can still make the actor guilty of the crime.

> A good example is false imprisonment (i.e. unlawful detention), which is committed for as long as the imprisonment lasts. If a library assistant locks me in the library by mistake, he does not at that moment commit false imprisonment. But if he subsequently perceives me through the window trying to get out, and decides to leave me in to teach me a lesson about something or other, he commits false imprisonment.

This point was involved, but not clearly perceived, in *Fagan* v. *Metropolitan Police Commissioner*,[1] the case of "parking on a copper's foot."

> Fagan, having accidentally brought his car to rest on the foot of a police officer, refused to remove it when asked to do so. After a short time he relented and moved the car. He could have been prosecuted for false imprisonment, but that is purely indictable, so he was brought before the justices on a charge of assaulting a constable in the execution of his duty. The difficulty was that an assault cannot be

---

[5] *DPP* v. *Brooks* [1974] AC 862 shows that an employee (in that case, a van driver) can be guilty of an offence of possessing a controlled drug even though he possesses only for his employer. Cp. § 42.5 n. 1.

[6] § 42.5.

[1] [1969] 1 QB 439.

committed by omission, and when Fagan drew up on the officer's foot he lacked *mens rea* for an assault. However, he was convicted.

On appeal the Divisional Court was quite clear that it wished to affirm the conviction, but took no pains to find a convincing reason. The court said that Fagan committed an *act* in keeping his car where it was, because he (1) remained in the car and (2) switched off the ignition. But was remaining in the car an act? And would the court have quashed the conviction if Fagan had left the engine running and got out of the car? If not, the reason offered was no reason. And, of course, the policeman's complaint was not that Fagan remained in the car and switched off the engine; his complaint was that Fagan did not move the car, which in itself looks like an omission.

The proper decision would have been that the offence of assault continued for as long as force was being applied to the policeman as a direct result of Fagan's act. That force was the force of gravity. The point is supported by civil cases.[2] On this view, Fagan's intent and unlawful act concurred in point of time.

Suppose a squatter smokes in bed and accidentally causes a small fire in the bed. He doesn't bother to put it out, so the fire spreads to and destroys the house. Can he be convicted of arson?

By a brilliant exercise of the imagination you have hit upon the very facts of the leading case of *Miller*.[3] The House of Lords affirmed the squatter's conviction, because he had created the danger by his own act and had then intentionally or recklessly failed to avert it.

The facts were intermediate between an act and an omission. There was an act on the part of the defendant: Miller dropped the lighted cigarette that started the fire. He burnt the house down: there is no fiction, no contortion of language, involved in saying that. So he certainly committed the act necessary for arson.

There was an element of omission in the case, but it was not one of mere omission. In a case of mere omission the brute facts do not point the finger of blame at one omitter rather than another (even though we may conventionally regard some people as under positive duties and not others), while here they did.[4] Lord Diplock, delivering the opinion of the House, said that the defendant would not have been liable if his role was at no time more than that of a passive bystander.

Of course, it is not enough to say that Miller burnt the house: arson also requires that the defendant should have intended or been reckless as to the

---

[2] The crime of assault stems from the old writ of trespass, which also gave us the tort of trespass to land. It is clear law that a man who places trespassory articles on the land of another is guilty of a continuing trespass as long as they continue there. There is no reason why the same principle should not apply where trespassory pressure is exercised upon the body of another.

[3] [1983] 2 WLR 539.

[4] Professor Smith and I differ on the proper ambit of the rule in *Miller*. Professor Smith would extend liability to cases where the facts do not single out the defendant as the positive causal agent, but where the court chooses to regard the defendant as responsible. See [1982] Crim. LR 527, 773.

burning. Here, Miller was at least reckless, in any meaning of the word, in letting the place burn down before his eyes. (Lord Diplock said that *Caldwell* recklessness would have been sufficient.) So there is both the *actus reus* and the *mens rea*.

The principle is that where a person accidentally creates a danger he can be liable for letting the danger eventuate. More technically, the rule is that where the law forbids a particular result (whether we call the crime a result-crime or not), then *mens rea* conceived after the act and before the result occurs (but at a time when the defendant could still have prevented the result) can (as the law is now established to be by *Miller*) lead to liability, provided that the defendant's conduct falls within the terms of the offence. The House of Lords stated the rule only for criminal damage, but it probably applies more widely. It can, for example, be regarded as applying to the facts of *Fagan*.

The most important question on the ambit of the rule concerns the hit-and-run driver who leaves the unconscious body of a pedestrian on a lonely road on a dark and freezing night. It may seem common sense that the driver should be guilty of manslaughter if he knowingly fails to take reasonable steps to avoid the death that results from his own act, even though the act itself was not negligent.[5] But would the victim of an attempted robbery who fells his attacker be obliged to summon an ambulance to him, or to give him the "kiss of life"? Although the question is difficult, it seems that the only possible answer in law is to say that the rule in *Miller* should apply.

Another observation is that although the judges in *Miller* spoke of the act as being either intentional or reckless in law, it would be too harsh to combine this rule with the doctrine of oblique intent (§ 3.5) to make the hit-and-run driver guilty of murder. The rule in *Miller* should not extend beyond liability for recklessness.

The foregoing discussion concerned cases where the intent supervened upon the commencement of the *actus reus*, or on the defendant's physical act that brings about the forbidden consequence. The converse situation is where the *actus reus* supervenes on the intent. If D tries to kill V and fails, and afterwards, when he has given up his plan, accidentally runs down V and kills him, it is obvious that his prior intent does not make him guilty of murder. But if D does something in pursuance of his intent, and his act brings about the intended result, it will not necessarily excuse him for him to show that he had repented before the result occurred. You cannot effectively repent while the bullet you have fired is on its way to the target. An illustration in the reports is *Jakeman*.[6]

> Jakeman booked two suitcases (containing cannabis) from Ghana to London, and they duly arrived. She was charged with being knowingly concerned in the fraudulent evasion of the restriction on the import of cannabis. She said in her defence that she had decided to abandon her part in the importation while the cases were still in transit, but, not surprisingly, the defence was rejected by the trial judge and on appeal.[7]

§ 7.6. OFFENCES WITHOUT RELEVANT CONDUCT

Parliament sometimes makes a person guilty by reason of his bodily

---

[5] Parliament, however, has not seen fit to deal with the question. Although the driver is under a statutory duty to stop after an accident (§ 7.3 n. 1), this is only to give his name and address to the other person involved, not to rescue such person from danger. The Act imposes no duty to summon an ambulance.

[6] [1983] Crim.LR 104.

[7] See also, on the general problem of the concurrence of act and intent, Marston in 86 LQR 221–226, and §§ 11.6, 12.7, 21.3 at n. 17, the doctrine of self-induced automatism discussed in § 29.4, and the doctrine of *With* v. *O'Flanagan* Chap. 34.

position, voluntarily assumed, as in the offence of being found on certain private premises for an unlawful purpose (§ 38.6). Some conduct can be seen, but the offence consists in the bodily position resulting from conduct rather than in the conduct itself.

On at least one occasion (which we have noticed before) the courts created such an offence by "interpretation".

> A statute makes it an offence for a prostitute to solicit in a street. A prostitute showed herself provocatively in a window fronting the street, without making a sign or other movement, but intending by her self-display to attract customers. It was held that she was guilty of soliciting in a street.[1] She had, of course, moved herself into the offending position, but it was her position and its accompaniments that was held to fall within the notion of soliciting.

What if there is no conduct at all—not even the conduct of taking up a position? Remarkable as it may at first appear, Parliament not infrequently imposes (or is interpreted as having imposed) penal liability upon people who have not in any relevant sense done anything, and who may not be at fault. To give this a distinguishing name, the term "situational liability" has been suggested.[2] Situational offences are committed by those who find themselves in a specified situation not involving any relevant conduct on their part. The most important illustrations turn on attributed (vicarious) liability (Chap. 43). Situational liability does not offend our sense of justice in "ticket" cases, when the penalty is light and imposed without court proceedings,[3] or when it requires fault by the defendant, but grave doubts arise when the liability is both situational and strict. Offences of this kind strike one as being particularly tyrannical. The criminal code of Stalin's Russia provided a scandalous example in the offence of being a "relative of an enemy of the people." In our law these offences arise partly because of the wording of some legislation and partly because of the failure of the courts to develop a liberal principle of interpretation.

> A case that is generally regarded as marking the extreme of severity in this country is *Larsonneur*,[4] where a Frenchwoman who went from England to Ireland was arrested by the Irish police and delivered by them in custody back to the Welsh police at Holyhead. The police charged her with the offence under the Aliens Order of being an alien who was "found" in the United Kingdom without permission; they had, of course, "found" her in their own custody when they received delivery of her protesting body from the Irish police. The London Sessions sentenced her to imprisonment for 3 days with a recommendation for deportation, and the conviction and sentence were upheld by the Court of Criminal Appeal.

---

[1] *Behrendt* v. *Burridge* § 1.4 n. 4.

[2] P R Glazebrook in *Reshaping the Criminal Law* (London 1978) 108. Mr Glazebrook includes offences of omission and possession under this heading.

[3] § 1.2.

[4] (1933) 97 JP 206, 24 CAR 774. Cp. *Chia Gee v Martin* (1906) 3 CLR 649 (Aus.); 21 MLR 379 n. 22: Colin Howard, *Strict Responsibility* (London 1963) 47. The decision of the Privy Council in *Lim Chin Aik* [1963] AC 160 may now be quoted *contra*.

The peculiar oppression of this decision did not lie in the mere fact that it imposed liability without any act or culpable omission. There are many offences of strict and attributed liability, to be studied in the last part of this book, which can also result in unjust condemnations; but they generally concern business matters, and result merely in a fine, so that, although they may be regarded as unjust, the injustice is perhaps not felt strongly. In *Larsonneur*, on the other hand, the events concerned the defendant's private life, and the sentence was one of imprisonment, even though for only a short time.

It is difficult to understand why the unfortunate woman was prosecuted, since she could simply have been sent back to her native country without prosecution. Nor was there any exegetical necessity for the court to read the Aliens Order as creating an offence in the absence of a culpable act or omission: the word "found" might well have been interpreted as meaning "found at liberty"—not "found" in police custody.[5] Alternatively, the court might have extended the defence of duress to include compulsion by law, or compulsion of circumstances.

Although the decision in *Larsonneur* has been roundly condemned by most commentators, a similar attitude was adopted by the court in a case of 1983.[5]

> The defendant was brought to a hospital on a stretcher; the doctor discovered that he was merely drunk, so the police were called. They removed the defendant to their car on the roadway, and then charged him with being found drunk in a highway. His conviction was affirmed by a Divisional Court.
>
> The proper mode of construing such legislation was exemplified by the Supreme Court of Alabama in a case where the police came to the defendant when he was sitting drunk in his house, carried him out on the street, and then arrested him for being drunk and disorderly in a public place. The statute under which the defendant was charged referred to "any person who, while intoxicated or drunk, appears in any public place . . . and manifests a drunken condition by boisterous or indecent conduct," etc. Literally the defendant had "appeared" on the street, but the court declared that "under the plain terms of this statute a voluntary appearance is presupposed."[6]

It was remarked just now that there is no objection on principle to convicting a person of a situational offence if he was negligent in bringing about the situation. So a man who creeps into someone else's house, drinks himself silly, is found by the owner and is ejected on to the street, could properly be convicted of being drunk in a public place because he might reasonably have foreseen that he would end up drunk in a public place. The conviction of Mlle. Larsonneur, likewise, has been supported on the ground that she had been ordered to leave the United Kingdom and did so by going to the Irish Free State; she should have foreseen that she might be expelled from Ireland back to the United Kingdom.[7] But this would be expecting great prescience of her. It was surely quite reasonable for her to think that even if she should prove to be as unwelcome to the Irish as she was to the English, she would be allowed to make her own way from Ireland back to France. Although situational offences may be unobjectionable if some kind of culpability is required, it would be strained to find any culpability in *Larsonneur*, and no such finding was in fact made.

---

[5] *Winzar* v. *Chief Constable of Kent*, The Times, May 28, 1983. *Contra*, *McKenzie* v. *Police* [1956] NZLR 1013.

[6] *Martin* v. *State* (1944) 31 Ala.App. 334, 17 So. 427. Cp. *O'Sullivan* v. *Fisher* [1954] SASR 33 (S Aus.), discussed by Roger S Clark in 14 Crim.LQ 413 (Can.). In *Kilbride* v. *Lake* [1962] NZLR 590 a regulation provided that "no person shall operate a motor vehicle . . . unless there is carried on the vehicle a current warrant of fitness." The defendant had a warrant but it was removed by some person unknown. Woodhouse J held that the defendant was not responsible. The case is discussed by R S Clark in *New Zealand Essays in Criminal Law* (Wellington, NZ 1971) 47; it has not been whole-heartedly followed in New Zealand.

[7] D J Lanham in [1976] Crim.LR 276.

§ 7.7. THE MISSING ELEMENT

Suppose a man thinks he is committing a crime, but a bit of the *actus reus* is missing. It goes without saying that the offence is not committed.

For example, a person who believes he has brought off a successful deception resulting in a profit cannot be convicted of obtaining property by deception if it turns out that what he said happened to be true.[1] And if a man who has been estranged from his wife thinks that he is marrying another woman bigamously, but it transpires that his wife had died just before the ceremony, he is not guilty of bigamy. The marriage that he thinks is bigamous is perfectly valid.

However, the would-be cheat could be convicted of attempting to obtain property by deception, and the would-be bigamist could be convicted of an attempt to commit bigamy—just as a man who shoots at a tree stump believing it to be a human being can be convicted of attempted murder. (In practice the question of attempt would be unlikely to arise, because the police would probably be satisfied with charging a firearms offence, or having the offender bound over, or perhaps just cautioning him. But it might arise if there was a prosecution for the completed crime and it was only discovered during the trial that the completed crime could not be established. In that case the prosecution might press the charge of attempt.)

But your would-be fraudster is only committing fraud in his heart, and the would-be bigamist is only committing bigamy in his heart. What he does is perfectly legal, so how can it be a crime? You said, didn't you, that our law does not go in for thought-crime.

It is not merely punishing for thoughts. These people have gone beyond thinking. They have taken steps. Yes, what they did was perfectly legal, *apart from the law of attempt*!

The act of attempt need not be illegal apart from its being the crime of attempt. If a man puts his own rat poison into his own bowl of soup and offers it to his wife with intent to murder her, he is guilty of an attempt even though, apart from the law of attempt, everything he has done is legal. It is not merely thought-crime: he has actually offered his wife what he believes is a deadly poison.

I still don't see why you should say that the intended bigamist commits an attempt. He has gone through what he imagined was a bigamous ceremony, and it wasn't. Why should he be guilty of attempted bigamy? So also the fraudster. They have done everything they intended to do, and it wasn't a crime. The question of attempt doesn't come into it.

Your difficulty is one that eminent judges have shared. As a result, the courts used to limit attempt at common law to cases where all the

---

[1] *Deller* (1952) 36 CAR 184.

circumstances required for the complete offence were present, or the forbidden consequences might happen. One could not "attempt the impossible." But the rule worked badly; it meant, for example, that the "dip" who tried to steal from an empty pocket could not be convicted of attempted theft, since one of the requirements of theft (property belonging to another as the subject of theft) was missing. Because of these and other problems the "impossibility" rule in the law of attempt was abolished by the Criminal Attempts Act 1981 (§ 17.4).

To return to where we started, whether a person is guilty of a completed crime when he mistakenly believes that a fact is present depends, of course, on what facts are needed for the crime. Difficulties can arise if a penal statute does not explain whether it is speaking of a mental state or of an external element. The point is illustrated by section 22(1) of the Theft Act 1968, which provides:

> "A person handles stolen goods if (otherwise than in the course of the stealing) knowing or believing them to be stolen goods he dishonestly receives the goods. . . . "

Here "believing them to be stolen" means "being almost sure that they are stolen, and being right, because they are stolen." So the subsection requires the goods to be stolen.

This point may not be immediately obvious. In some contexts the words "believing them to be stolen" could mean "correctly or mistakenly believing them to be stolen." The word "know" refers exclusively to true knowledge; we are not said to "know" something that is not so. Belief, on the other hand, can include a mistaken belief, a subjective conviction whether right or wrong. But this is not the only meaning; "belief" can refer to the degree of belief ("I do not *know* it is so; I am not 100 per cent. sure; but I believe it is so—with something less than complete certainty"). This must be the meaning in the subsection, because it opens with the words "a person handles stolen goods." It takes for granted as the *actus reus* the fact that the goods are stolen and are handled, and concerns itself only with the *mens rea*.[2] If the goods turn out not to be stolen, the would-be handler is guilty of an attempt.

Does the rule for offences apply similarly to defences? I readily see that a person cannot be convicted of an offence merely because he believed he was committing it. Can he be convicted of an offence notwithstanding that on the facts he would have had a defence, if he did not know the facts that gave him the defence?

Defences may be classified as excuses and justifications. In the former, the social mischief has happened but the defendant is allowed a defence on personal grounds. Examples of excuses are duress and (in murder) provocation. The essence of such a defence is that some pressure acted on the defendant's mind at the time. He must have been affected by the duress, or the provocation, and therefore must have known of it or believed that it existed.

Justifications are allowed by law where it is thought that, on the facts, the defendant was perfectly right in acting as he did. On principle, such defences should operate even though the defendant did not know the facts

---

[2] *Roger Smith* [1975] AC at 490, 497, 503. Although the meaning of the subsection is clear, the addition of "or believing" was unfortunate. If it refers to the doctrine of wilful blindness it was unnecessary, because the judges deem wilful blindness to be equivalent to knowledge without this having to be specially provided for. If it refers to some other degree of doubt, it introduces too much uncertainty into the law. For attempts see § 17.4.

creating the justification. For example, suppose that a statute makes it an offence to do something, but allows a defence where the defendant had a licence. If the defendant had a licence he is doubtless not guilty of the offence even though for some reason he did not know he had it.

However, difficulties arise in certain cases, which will be discussed when we come to defences.[3]

§ 7.8. MULTIPLE CHARGES

This almost completes the analysis of the external elements in crime, but we have some unfinished business on points of procedure, on questions relating to the dividing line between crimes, and on jurisdiction.

First of all, it is a cardinal principle that if the defendant is not proved to have committed the offence with which he stands charged, he must be acquitted of it, notwithstanding that he has evidently offended in some other respect.

We saw at the beginning of Chapter 2 that one reason for including particulars in the charge is to give the defendant formal notice of what is alleged against him. A second and more important reason, from the defendant's point of view, is to tie the prosecution to that charge.

But is the name of the game so important? What matters is whether the man offended on the facts proved against him.

Laxity in criminal proceedings would be regarded as unjust. The defendant comes prepared to meet the offence charged against him, not some other offence. However, the court has a discretion to allow the charge to be amended.

There is nothing to prevent the prosecution from charging two offences at the same time where the trial is on indictment. The indictment may contain several charges (subject to certain rules), each charge being in a numbered paragraph called a count. These may all be disposed of in the same trial.[1] (The rule does not apply to summary trials, since an information is not allowed to contain more than one charge. But two or more informations may be laid, and the magistrates may try them together if this course is fair.[2])

Express counts are not always necessary; sometimes an offence can be charged by implication.

Implication is allowed by various statutes, which provide the prosecution with a safety-net: if a person is charged on indictment with offence A, he can be convicted instead of the rather similar offence B, if it turns out that he committed that, even though B was not expressly charged.

These statutes apply only in respect of specified offences, but there are

---

[3] §§ 22.3 at n. 6, 23.2 at n. 11.

[1] Subject to rules as to what counts may properly be joined, and to the discretion of the court to order separate trials.

[2] *Chief Constable of Norfolk* v. *Clayton* [1983] 2 WLR 555.

also some general provisions. One is the rule that the jury can convict of an included offence.

To explain: where one offence has ingredients X, Y and Z, and another (lesser) offence has ingredients X and Y (Z being a matter of aggravation in the greater offence which is lacking in the lesser one), the jury on acquitting of the greater offence may convict of the lesser.[3] In other words, a "blue pencil" test is applied; if one can, by deleting ingredient Z, leave subsisting all the ingredients of the included offence, the included offence is impliedly charged in an indictment for the more serious and complicated one.

> An example is a charge of robbery, which involves all the ingredients of theft plus the use of force or threats as matters of aggravation. The jury when acquitting of robbery can convict of theft, even though theft has not been expressly charged.

Again, a count for a completed (consummated) offence is deemed by statute to include a charge of an attempt to commit the offence, so if the jury are not certain that the offence was completed (or are sure that it was not) they may still convict of the attempt.[4]

When two offences are charged, can the prosecution succeed if they prove that one of the offences must have been committed, without proving which?

The answer, regrettably, is no.

Couldn't the prosecution word the count as a charge that the defendant did A or B?

Each count must describe a single offence,[5] so it is generally supposed that a count in the form you suggest would be bad for "duplicity." (The same objection would apply to informations before magistrates.) The law on the point is in a difficult state, and the only safe course for the prosecution is to charge the different alternatives in separate counts, unless the statute makes it clear that only one offence is intended to be created. A conviction based on a duplicitous charge will be set aside on appeal.

Fortunate indeed is the guilty defendant who is charged duplicitously; his counsel can keep quiet about it at the trial (when the defect can be cured by amendment), and still have the conviction reversed on appeal. Even where the statute says in so many words that a person shall not do "A or B," the one sentence may be regarded as creating two offences which must be charged separately. Some statutes are so worded as to alleviate the embarrassment caused to the prosecution by these rules, but the law remains highly unsatisfactory.[6]

How does the judge sentence when there are convictions of several offences committed at the same time? Does he do simple addition?

No. Sentences of imprisonment are not made consecutive unless the various offences result from different incidents or transactions.

---

[3] This common law doctrine is now in statutory form: Criminal Law Act 1967 s.6(2) and (3). For the limitations of the rule see Spencer in [1982] Crim.LR 272–273. It was held in *McCormack* [1969] 2 QB at 446 that the judge is not bound to leave an included offence to the jury, but this rule may perhaps be reconsidered in the light of *Daley* § 12.1 n. 1. Magistrates are thought not to be able to convict of an included offence; there must be a new information. For the position where the jury cannot agree on the offence charged see *Collison* [1980] Crim.LR 591.

[4] § 17.2 at n. 6.

[5] Indictments Rules 1971 r.4.

[6] See Archbold, 41st edn paras. 1–59, 1–60; [1966] Crim.LR 255.

There are certain rules of practice on this point, all of them sometimes overlooked by the courts.

- An offender must not even be *convicted* of (let alone punished for) two technically different offences on account of what is in reality one offence. For example, he must not be convicted of both theft and obtaining by deception on the same facts.
- Where a minor offence is committed at the same time as a major offence, and would (even though it is not an included offence) be a factor in sentencing for the major offence, the conviction should be of the major offence only. There are other cases where the addition of a charge of a minor offence to one of a major offence would be frowned upon by an appeal court.
- Even when an offender is convicted of two different offences, the general principle is that where the offences were committed as part of a single incident or transaction, prison sentences should be concurrent, so that the offender serves only the longest sentence. This can result in great indulgence, for which reason the courts sometimes depart from the principle. On the other hand, it is sometimes applied even to offences committed on different occasions.
- Where none of these rules helps the offender, so that he is liable to consecutive sentences of imprisonment, it is still the duty of the judge to look at the total and to reduce it, or to make the sentences concurrent, if the total appears excessive.

§ 7.9 RES JUDICATA

The subject of multiple charges leads naturally to the subject of successive charges.

Suppose that a transgressor is tried, and is acquitted on a technicality or for lack of evidence. He cannot be tried a second time, even though on the second occasion the prosecution would be able to avoid the technicality and have better evidence. The defendant has what is termed, in legal Frenglish, the defence of autrefois acquit.

Similarly, if he is convicted, even if he is let off very lightly, he cannot afterwards be charged on fresh evidence, because he will have the defence of autrefois convict.[1] These inelegant phrases have never been superseded, though they might well be called the defence of "previous acquittal" and "previous conviction"; and *res judicata* (matter that has been decided) is a generic name for both.

A man is acquitted of murder and afterwards writes an article for a newspaper describing how he committed it. Would he be safe from being charged again?

He could not be charged again with murder. But if he had given evidence falsely denying the charge, he could be prosecuted for perjury. So held by the House of Lords in *Humphrys*.[2] The technical point is that, according to this decision, the criminal law knows no doctrine of "issue estoppel."

---

[1] Pronounced "ohterfoyz," with "acquit" and "convict" pronounced as in English.

[2] [1977] AC 1. For a critical discussion see Mirfield in [1980] Crim.LR 336.

After the acquittal, the Crown cannot charge the defendant with the same offence, but it is not estopped (prevented) from saying that he was guilty of *that* offence if it brings proceedings for a *different* offence (as perjury is). Neither the Crown nor the defendant in the later proceedings is estopped from disputing the decision in the earlier proceedings on a particular issue.

This is an example of the court making a law that is satisfactory on the facts before the court, but may be unsatisfactory in others. Where the allegation is one of perjury in the earlier proceedings, as was the case in *Humphrys*, the rule laid down in that case is common sense, but in other situations the absence of a doctrine of issue estoppel in our law may work hardship, and also may produce such inconsistent decisions as to bring the law into some measure of disrepute. It is hard on the defendant if, after he has at great cost in money and anxiety secured a favourable verdict from a jury on a particular issue, he must fight the battle over again when he is charged with a technically different offence arising out of the same facts. However, it is now recognised that the court has a discretion to stay the second proceedings as being vexatious or oppressive, and the use of this power can bypass the decision in *Humphrys* and achieve the same effect as if there were an estoppel.[3]

> Suppose a man is charged with driving a motor cycle with excess alcohol in his blood and also with riding a cycle (that is to say, the same motor cycle) without due care and attention, the two charges relating to the same incident. He elects to go for trial on the first charge, and is acquitted by the jury on his evidence that he was not in fact driving the vehicle. The police now restore to the list the summons for the summary offence of careless riding. If the case is heard, the police will be allowed to call evidence to the effect that the defendant was riding the cycle, notwithstanding his acquittal by the jury on this issue. On one occasion the defendant in such circumstances obtained a High Court order of prohibition directed to the justices, on the ground that it would be oppressive and unfair to restore the charge to the list. However, the High Court said that it made the order only because there was another outstanding charge against the defendant in the Crown Court.[4]

It is not at all clear, therefore, that the discretion of the High Court to stay proceedings will be used in such a way as to prevent the criminal process being used vexatiously. Although the House of Lords has now closed the door on issue estoppel in our law, there is much to be said for such a doctrine in circumstances like these.

Suppose a prosecution is started but the authorities make some awful technical mistake. Can they abandon the proceedings half way and start again properly?

Yes. The defence of *res judicata* arises only when there has been a conviction or acquittal. Some writers use the expression "double jeopardy" as another name for the *res judicata* doctrine, but it is misleading for English law. The defence is not given to a person merely because he was previously at risk of being convicted. The earlier proceedings must have gone to their conclusion.[5]

§ 7.10. THE TERRITORIAL SCOPE OF THE LAW

The general principle is that the criminal law and criminal jurisdiction are territorial, confined to acts done in England or Wales, with an extension

---

[3] *Dewhurst* v. *Foster* [1982] Crim.LR 582 (circuit judge).

[4] *R* v. *Cwmbran JJ., ex parte Pope* (1979), unreported; see 143 JPN 415, 568. On the power of the court to prevent abuse of process see note, [1982] Crim. LR 375.

[5] *Nasralla* [1967] 2 AC 238. There is a special rule for alternative charges: see this case at p. 251.

for British ships and aircraft. But the subject is complicated, because there are detailed rules specifying:

- what is meant by England and Wales;
- where a crime is held to be committed if part of its elements take place here and part somewhere abroad; and,
- the exceptional cases where our courts have jurisdiction over crimes committed abroad. (The most striking example is murder, which is punishable here if committed on land abroad, by a British citizen.[1])

The book being long enough without this subject, it is mostly omitted. But we can find room to add, on the second of the above three matters, that in the case of a result-crime, where the act is done abroad and the criminal effect is produced here, the crime is taken to be committed here.[2]

> For this purpose Scotland is treated as a foreign country. A wounding inflicted in Scotland is not triable in England. But if a person standing on the Scottish bank of the Tweed fires at and wounds a person on the English bank, he can be tried for the wounding in England. This is the "terminatory theory"[3] of the criminal act: the elements of the crime being split between two countries, it is regarded as being committed where the proscribed result takes place. Even if the attacker misses, he can be tried in England for the attempt.

What about the converse situation? Someone on the English bank wounds someone on the Scottish bank. Can he be tried for wounding in England?

It seems not. The existing authorities are against the assumption of "initiatory" jurisdiction, i.e. by the country in which the physical act is done.

> So if there is a conspiracy in England or Wales to do an act abroad that will be criminal under the foreign law, but will not be punishable under English law (because it is outside the jurisdiction), then the conspiracy is not punishable here either.[4] (Conspiracy to commit murder abroad is a statutory exception.[5])

Other authorities on other crimes are to the same effect.

While the rule for conspiracy will undoubtedly continue, this may be put on the ground that conspiracy is *sui generis* (unique);[6] the courts may perhaps come to claim initiatory jurisdiction for other crimes. But initiatory jurisdiction is subject to a special difficulty. It would be unjust for our courts to punish the act unless the defendant's object was to commit a crime against the law of the foreign country where the result occurs; so our courts would be involved in investigating the law of the foreign country, and perhaps also the degree of gravity of the crime according to that law. This difficulty is not pressing for ordinary cases of violence and fraud, where the approach of different countries is very largely the same. The usual procedure where a person within the jurisdiction has committed a crime abroad is to

---

[1] Offences against the Person Act 1861 s.9; British Nationality Act 1981. See on the subject generally M Hirst in [1982] Crim.LR 496.

[2] CLA 1977 s.1(4), reaffirming the rule in *Stonehouse* [1978] AC 55.

[3] [1978] AC at 66D.

[4] *Board of Trade* v. *Owen* [1957] AC 602; see 81 LQR 276, 395, 518, 534. See also *per* Lord Diplock in *Stonehouse* [1978] AC at 66E–F.

[5] Act of 1977, n. 2 above.

[6] *Per* Lord Salmon in *Stonehouse* [1978] AC at 79B.

extradite him to the foreign country for trial. There are also more expeditious arrangements for Scotland and Ireland.

SUMMARY

Actus reus in the wide sense means an occurrence constituting the external elements of an offence, or that would constitute such elements if there were *mens rea* or other required fault element. Some kind of external element is always necessary, but it need not involve bodily movement or be injurious in itself. It may, for example, be an act, an omission or a bodily position, all of which may be called "conduct." It may even be a mere "situation." § .1

An act means a willed movement. Sometimes a willed movement may be hard to find in offences like manslaughter, even though they appear at first sight to involve positive conduct. § .2

An omission implies the breach of a duty to act, the duty being imposed by law. Murder and manslaughter are common law crimes requiring a "killing," but the courts hold that killing may be by an omission to save life in breach of duty. Other common law crimes are not generally committed by omission, and the courts do not generally construe active verbs in statutes as covering omissions. However, in determining negligence, conduct may be regarded as on the whole an act, even though some component part is an omission. Where a person creates a dangerous situation and then intentionally or recklessly fails to avert the danger, he can generally be convicted on the basis of having done an act (*Miller*). Physical inability can negative a requisite fault element. § .3

Offences of unlawful possession are statutory; they can be analysed as involving either an act of acquisition or an omision to inform the police of the arrival of an unlawful object. A person may possess through another, and the other may also be regarded as being in possession; but there is room for flexibility in decision depending on such questions as the degree of control exercised over the object. § .4

Normally the act and mental element must concur in point of time. But there are exceptions and quasi-exceptions, notably in the case of continuing acts and under the doctrine of *Miller*. The latter case holds that where an act has accidentally caused a result, and the actor intentionally or recklessly failed to prevent the result, he can be held to have caused the result intentionally or recklessly, at any rate in loss of criminal damage . § .5

A statute may make (or be interpreted to make) a person guilty by reason of his bodily position, voluntarily assumed. There are also purely "situational" offences (without relevant conduct), an extreme example being *Larsonneur*. On principle the courts should strive to interpret such offences as requiring some kind of relevant act or omission involving fault, at any rate where the offence involves obloquy or may result in imprisonment. § .6

A person cannot be convicted of a completed offence if an external element is missing, but he can in appropriate circumstances be convicted of an attempt. On principle, a person should not be guilty if the facts constituting a *justification* are present, even though he is unaware of it; but he must know the facts constituting an *excuse*, or believe that they exist. § .7

Each count in an indictment must charge only one offence. An offence may be charged by implication under various statutes; in particular, the jury may acquit of the offence indicted for and convict of an included offence, or an attempt. In general, the prosecution cannot succeed if they can prove only that the defendant committed offence A or B, and a charge worded in these terms would be bad for duplicity. Where two crimes substantially overlap, the conviction is for one only. Even where it is possible to obtain a conviction on two or more serious charges, § .8

sentences of imprisonment are generally made concurrent if the offences are part of a single incident or transaction.

A person who is convicted or acquitted cannot be tried again; but the proceedings must have gone to their conclusion. The offender can be prosecuted a second time on a different charge, subject to the possibility that this prosecution will be stayed as oppressive. § .9

Jurisdiction in criminal law is generally territorial. One of the exceptions is murder on land abroad by a British citizen. Also, in the case of result-crimes and attempts to commit them, our law assumes terminatory jurisdiction even where the act itself was committed abroad. Conversely, our law does not assume initiatory jurisdiction where the intended result was to take place outside England and Wales, except that conspiracy here to murder elsewhere is, by statute, punishable here. § .10

Part Two

THE PROTECTION OF THE PERSON

CHAPTER 8

ASSAULT

A man's body and his mind, with the utmost reverence to both I speak it, are exactly like a jerkin and a jerkin's lining: rumple the one, you rumple the other.

Sterne, *Tristram Shandy*.

THIS and the next chapter are concerned with what may be called the right to bodily integrity: non-fatal injuries to the person (or threats of injury) of a non-sexual nature (or not necessarily of a sexual nature), brought about with an element of intention or recklessness. (How much intention or recklessness, we are to consider.) The basic offence at common law is assault, but this has been fortified by a number of statutory offences.

§ 8.1. THE TWO KINDS OF ASSAULT

The notion of assault enters into various crimes. In in its simple form, known as common assault (the subject of this chapter), it is punishable on indictment with (up to) one year's imprisonment,[1] and it is also punishable summarily.

The definition of assault and its sister offence battery are the same in crime as in tort, except that consent as a defence in tort is probably wider than it is in crime.[2]

The required mental element is intention or recklessness. An example of recklessness is where a man, lying on the ground, kicks out at random towards other people around him. He may have hoped to hurt someone, but anyway is reckless.[3]

The *Caldwell* extension of recklessness to "not thinking" (§ 5.4) should not apply to assault. Only in modern times was the idea of reckless assault accepted by the courts, and it was certainly not thought of as applying to cases of negligence.[4] If a person light-heartedly swings his walking-stick without thinking that someone may be behind him, his liability if any for hitting the other person should be for negligence, not recklessness; and it is a civil liability, not a criminal one. A difficulty is that in *Seymour* (§ 12.2 at n. 9), a case of "motor manslaughter," the House of Lords declared that "recklessness" should today be given the same meaning in relation to all offences involving recklessness unless Parliament has otherwise ordained. This dictum, however, went beyond anything calling for consideration in the case. Of course, the *Caldwell* rule for intoxication applies to assault.

---

[1] Offences against the Person Act ("OAPA") 1861 s.47. See 140 JPN 203, 231.

[2] In criminal law, consent is sometimes disregarded on grounds of policy (§ 25.14), but this is probably not so in the civil law. Formerly, a tortious battery (unlike a criminal one) could be committed negligently. But the courts now treat a negligent battery as being an instance of the tort of negligence, not of battery, though the point has no practical importance since anyway the defendant is liable in damages for negligence. See *Gorely* v. *Codd* [1967] 1 WLR at 25.

[3] *Venna* [1976] QB 421. That negligence is not enough was decided in *Ackroyd* v. *Barett* (1894) 11 TLR 115; indeed, the court there said that it was insufficient that the defendant acted "recklessly," but the word was evidently intended to mean "with gross negligence."

[4] In *Venna*, last note, the trial judge directed the jury in terms of knowledge of probability, and this was approved on appeal. See Griew in 146 JPN 146; [1981] CLJ 266.

Certain defences such as consent, self-defence, public authority, necessity and duress are of general importance in crime, and are therefore dealt with not here but in later chapters.

Ordinary usage creates a certain difficulty in pinning down the meaning of "assault." Etymologically, the word is compounded of the Latin *adsaltare*, to jump at. In popular language, it has always connoted a physical attack. When we say that D assaulted V, we have a mental picture of D attacking V, by striking or pushing or stabbing him.

In the middle ages, however, the terms "assault" and "battery" were given technical meanings which they have retained ever since. It became settled that though an assault could be committed by physical contact, it did not require this, since a show of force raising an apprehension in the mind of the victim was sufficient. Also, a "battery" did not require an actual beating; the use of any degree of force against the body would suffice. The acts of spitting on a person[5] and kissing without consent[6] are both batteries.

So an assault is a threatened battery?

An assault can consist of a threatened battery. But, unfortunately, lawyers have continued to use the word "assault" also in the sense of a battery.

Both in the interpretation of statutes and in ordinary legal discussions "assault" is regularly used to include or mean a battery—for example, in the statutory expressions "common assault"[7] and "indecent assault."[8] Also, the word "battery" is now almost out of use, except when the speaker tries to make his meaning abundantly clear by using the phrase "assault and battery." One could not talk of a "common battery" or "indecent battery" without being thought to use words oddly. The noun "battery" has never given an acceptable verb for expressing the range of the offence; we say that D assaulted V, but it would sound archaic and misleading to describe D's act in shooting or stabbing V in the words "D battered V," or "D beat V."

For these reasons, the word "assault" has to be recognised as covering not only an assault in the sense of an act causing apprehension but also what was formerly called a battery. Speaking of the statutory "indecent assault," Lord Goddard CJ said:

> "An assault can be committed without touching a person. One always thinks of an assault as the giving of a blow to somebody, but that is not necessary. An assault may be constituted by a threat or a hostile act committed towards a person."[9]

The last sentence gives examples of assaults, but it should be noticed that a non-hostile but unwelcome application of "force" can also be an assault.

The double meaning of "assault" creates a somewhat awkward linguistic situation. Assault in the wide sense means (1) a battery or (2) a threatened battery, according to context or circumstance. Kissing the Sleeping Beauty is an assault in the sense of a battery, while it is not an assault in the sense of an act causing apprehension. If a threatened battery is an assault, and a battery is an assault, it follows that a threatened assault is an assault!

The most convenient solution would be to recognise "assault" as the generic expression, consisting in certain kinds of unlawful interference with

---

5 *Smith* (1866) 4 F & F 1066, 176 ER 910.

6 *Dungey* (1864) 4 F & F 99 at 102, 176 ER at 487. In *Fagan* v. *MPC* [1969] 1 QB at 444F it was said that "assault may be committed by the laying of a hand upon a person."

7 OAPA 1861 s.42, marginal note.

8 Sexual Offences Act 1956 ss.14, 15.

9 *Rolfe* (1952) 36 CAR at 6.

another. This interference may be either (1) a physical assault, an unlawful bodily contact, that is to say a battery, or else (2) a psychic assault, an assault in the sense of a threatened battery. If this terminology is accepted, we can talk sense instead of paradox; we can say that a psychic assault is a threatened physical assault. Since physical assault is by far the commonest form of assault to come before the courts, it is usually referred to as an "assault" simply.

Although this suggested language may assist clarity of thought, it does not mean that assault in the generic sense is a single offence. The only offences are psychic assault and physical assault, and they are different offences.[10] There may be one without the other. An example of a psychic without a physical assault is a threatened blow. An example of physical without a psychic assault is giving a blow from behind, or giving a blow (or, as said before, a kiss) to a sleeping person, where there is no previous apprehension.[11] The general impression that there can be a conviction of "assault and battery" is therefore, strictly speaking, erroneous, for there cannot be a single conviction of two crimes. But a conviction in these traditional terms would be upheld as meaning a conviction of battery only.[12]

Is an insult a psychic assault?

No—not even if it is an insult by conduct. Nothing short of a threat is sufficient.

Is any threat a psychic assault?

A psychic assault is *a threat creating the apprehension of immediate force, made intentionally or recklessly*. The threat may be by conduct, or possibly by words; this will be discussed later. The force apprehended must be unlawful force to the body of the victim, and the victim must believe that the force is about to be applied to him.

It will be seen that there are two separate states of mind to be considered: that of the victim, and that of the actor.[13]

1 The victim must expect that force is about to be applied to him.[14] He need not experience fear, provided that he has that expectation.
2 The actor must intend to create the expectation or be reckless as to it. In other words, it is sufficient that he knows he is doing something from which the belief is likely to arise.

No blow need be struck. The actor need only do something inducing the victim to believe

---

[10] *Beasley* (1980) 73 CAR 44. The decision illustrates the anomaly of having two offences going by the same name. They should have different names, such as "assault" and "threatened assault."

[11] Hawkins, *PC* i 110, says that "every battery includes an assault," i.e. a psychic assault, but this is evidently a mistake. Cp. Russell, 12th edn i 655.

[12] In drawing an indictment or information the word "assault," if standing alone, will be taken to refer to a psychic assault or physical assault or both. So the charge will be valid whichever the evidence establishes. But if the draftsman contrasts "assault" and "battery," by charging that the defendant "did unlawfully assault or beat" the victim, the word "assault" will he read as meaning a psychic assault and the charge will then, for some baffling reason, be bad for duplicity: *Jones* v. *Sherwood* [1942] 1 KB 127.

[13] The term "actor" (or "doer") is a convenient general expression for the person doing the act in question. Usually it will be the defendant to a criminal charge, though occasionally it may be the prosecutor or some other person. For example, where the defendant claims that he acted in self-defence because the prosecutor had first assaulted him, if the issue is as to the alleged assault by the prosecutor, the prosecutor will be the "actor" within the rule stated in the text.

[14] It was once held that a mother's abandonment of her baby in a ditch was not an assault upon it, because the baby did not know what was happening: *Renshaw* (1847) 2 Cox 285. At the present day the charge of assault on such facts could be read as a charge of battery; but even then the charge ought to be dismissed as merely a legal ploy to treat what is really an omission to look after the child as a positive act. The proper charge is one of child neglect.

that he will instantly receive a blow (or other application of force) unless he does something to avoid it, as by striking in self-defence or retreating. It is immaterial that the actor is not at that moment within striking distance,[15] but he must, it seems, be sufficiently near to apply the force then and there, and he must do some act (or, as will be argued, utter some words) inducing the victim's apprehension.

> A case going to the limit of the law was one where the defendant entered a garden of a house and looked through the window of a woman's bedsitting room, intending to frighten her. When she screamed he went away. It was held that he was guilty of assault (and, in consequence, was guilty of being found on enclosed premises for an unlawful purpose). Yet the only movement he made was in going to the spot, and he could not have harmed the victim except by somehow getting into the house.[16]

Some of the old books define a psychic assault as an attempted impact,[17] but they are wrong. Psychic assault and attempted physical assault are two distinct offences. If D clenches his fist and threatens V, intending only to create apprehension, he is guilty of a psychic assault even though (since he does not intend to strike) he is not guilty of an attempted physical assault. Conversely, if D tries to strike V from behind, he is guilty of an attempted physical assault even though (since V does not know of his danger) there is no psychic assault.[18]

The confusion between psychic assault and attempted physical assault is responsible for the notion in some of the old cases that it is no assault to point an unloaded gun at another, even though the actor knows that the other thinks the gun to be loaded. Although the older authorities are in conflict,[19] it is now settled that such an act is an assault.[20] The reason is that the culprit has deliberately raised apprehension in the mind of the victim, which is precisely what a psychic assault is. The actor's belief that he can put the threat into execution is necessary for an attempted battery, but not for a psychic assault.

As will be shown in the next section, a conditional threat can be an assault.

§ 8.2. ASSAULT AND WORDS

To constitute a psychic assault the victim must apprehend immediate force.[1] It is not an assault if the defendant shows clearly in words that no immediate attack is intended, even if he makes a show of aggression. In the antique case of *Turberville* v. *Savage* (1669)[2]:

> Turberville and Savage exchanged quarrelsome words; Turberville laid his hand on his sword and said to Savage: "If it were not assize-time, I would not take such language from you." These words showed that Turberville's menacing gesture was pure bravado; so far from being a threat, the words were a reassurance. But Savage thrust at Turberville and put out his eye. Turberville sued for damages for

---

[15] *Martin* v. *Shoppee* (1828) 3 C & P 374, 172 ER 462; *Stephens* v. *Myers* (1830) 4 C & P 349, 172 ER 735.

[16] *Smith* v. *Superintendent of Woking Police Station* [1983] Crim. LR 323. A psychic assault can be committed on the other side of a locked door, if the victim believes that the attacker is about to break it down. Cp. *Beach* (1912) 76 JP 287, 23 Cox 181, 7 CAR 197, 107 LT 461. The conviction in this case was under OAPA 1861 s.20, which implies (according to the law as it was then understood to be) that an assault was committed. Query *Smith* v. *Newsam* (1674) 3 Keble 283, 84 ER 722, where a woman who, standing in a cutler's shop, shook a sword at the plaintiff across the street was held liable for assault.

[17] Hawkins, *PC* i 263; East, *PC* i 406.

[18] Cp. *State* v. *Wilson* (1959) 218 Ore. 575, 346 P 2d 115; *Doiron* (1960) 34 CR 188 (Brit.Col.).

[19] See 1st edn 138 n. 16.

[20] *Logdon* v. *DPP* [1976] Crim.LR 121; cp. *Kwaku Mensah* [1946] AC at 90–91.

[1] As in *Stephens* v. *Meyers*, § .1 n. 15.

[2] 1 Mod, 3, 86 ER 684.

assault; Savage pleaded self-defence because he feared an attack. It was held that Turberville had not opened the hostilities, because his words showed no present intention to do violence. Consequently, Savage was not entitled to claim that he acted in self-defence.

It will be seen that this case did not raise the neat question whether the plaintiff, Turberville, committed an assault. Quite possibly he did commit an assault when he made the menacing gesture of laying his hand upon his sword, if he did not utter his emollient words quickly enough to destroy the defendant's momentary apprehension. But, whether this was so or not, his words showed that he had no present intention of being an aggressor. Once he had uttered them, the defendant Savage could not claim that his retaliatory act was in self-defence.

The problem of the conditional threat arose again in *Light*.[3]

Light held a shovel over his wife's head and said: "If it were not for the policeman outside I would split your head open." The judges differed on the question whether this was a criminal assault, and the two reports of the case are not completely in accord on what the judges said. But it seems a fair inference from the various opinions expressed that the test is this: did Light's words so neutralise the menacing character of his acts as to prevent a reasonable woman from feeling apprehension?

It seems right to say that where the act is of a very menacing character, as it was in *Light*, the mere fact that words are spoken indicating no present intention to assault does not necessarily negative an assault in law. If a man raises a shovel to a position where he can bring it down on his wife's head, she will in all probability feel fear, and her fear will prevent her from listening carefully to what he says and coming to the calm conclusion that no assault is intended. Even if the reassuring words are heard and attended to, they may be wholly outweighed by the menace of the act. The victim may well fear that the aggressor will suddenly change his mind and attack notwithstanding the fact that the condition he has stated is not fulfilled.

Then what if one man says to another: 'Be quiet or I will blow your brains out,' pointing a gun at him a moment afterwards? Is this an assault?

Such a situation is clearly distinguishable from that in *Turberville* v. *Savage*, for there the words referred to an extraneous condition ("If it were not assize-time") which the victim knew was not fulfilled. There was, therefore, no present threat. But if the words fetter the victim's present freedom, an assault is committed.[4]

In these cases the requirement that the threat should be immediate is qualified: it need only be a threat of force to follow immediately upon disobedience, provided that obedience is required then and there. Were it otherwise, the highwayman who says "Stand and deliver," at the same time pointing a gun, would not be guilty of an assault—a conclusion that it is impossible to accept. The victim of the threat realises that he has to regulate his movements carefully if he is to avoid being shot. Even if he decides to comply with the demand, the fear of being shot, perhaps as a result of misunderstanding by the aggressor, is not absent from

---

[3] (1857) D & B 332, 27 LJMC 1.

[4] *Read* v. *Coker* (1853) 13 CB 850, 138 ER 1437 (threat, accompanied by conduct, to break the other's neck if he did not leave the premises); *Logdon* v. *DPP* (1976] Crim.LR 121. Cp. *Genner* v. *Sparkes* (1704) 1 Salk. 79, 91 ER 74. V came lawfully to arrest D; D kept him off by holding up a farm fork and retreating. The court said, *obiter*, that D's act was an assault. V had a right to advance, and D prevented him from doing so. The act of holding up the fork was in effect a conditional threat. See also [1957] Crim.LR 222–223; *Police* v. *Greaves* [1964] NZLR 295. *Contra, Blake* v. *Barnard* (1840) 9 C & P 626, 173 ER 985, where a quite inadequate direction to the jury is attributed to Lord Abinger by notoriously unreliable reporters.

his mind. Quite apart from this argument, it is a salutary rule that persons should not be allowed to constrain the conduct of others by threats of immediate physical force, and will be held guilty of assault if they attempt to do so.

Suppose you don't point a gun; can there be an assault by words alone?

It is said in most of the standard authorities on criminal law and the law of tort that words cannot constitute an assault, in the absence of accompanying gestures[5]; but the judicial authority for this supposed limitation is of the slightest. Ordinarily, perhaps, a spoken threat would not arouse an apprehension that violence is imminent, but some threats obviously may. There is no good reason for requiring a menacing gesture, if the words themselves are such as to arouse immediate apprehension.

Take again the case of the highwayman. Suppose that the highwayman is well known for his evil deeds, and that he stands in the road before a coachful of people, saying laconically "Your money or your life," but not troubling to pull out one of the weapons with which he bristles, because he is confident that his threat will exact compliance. There is no solid reason for doubting that this is a psychic assault, and the conclusion is supported by medieval and later authorities.[6] (In any case, the highwayman would be guilty of false imprisonment, attempted robbery, blackmail and a statutory offence of using threatening words.[7])

Another line of argument leads to the same conclusion. In the civil case of *Read* v. *Coker*,[8] D collected some men who mustered round V, tucking up their sleeves and threatening to "break his neck" if he did not leave the premises. V left, and successfully sued D for assault. In essence the assault was by words. There was, in a sense, some conduct in addition on the part of D and his men, for they tucked up their sleeves. But when a number of men propose to eject a single person from premises, it is not at all necessary that they should first tuck up their sleeves. This is merely a conventional way of conveying a threat, an alternative to words as a mode of expressing an intention. Symbolical gestures of this kind are logically the same as the utterance of words, for words are symbols. There would be no sense in attaching legal significance to the one that is not attached to the other.

Perhaps the reason for the common statement that assault cannot be by words is the fear that people would prosecute in trivial cases. The fear would be met if the notion of psychic assault were limited to threats that would make a reasonable person apprehend immediate hurt.

What of a threat by telephone?

This would normally lack the immediacy necessary for an assault. Besides, the assaults punished in the past have always involved personal presence; they have been what Roman lawyers called *corpore corpori* (by a body to a body). It is inconceivable that a threat by letter, for instance, could be an assault; and the same should apply to a threat by telephone. True, cases may arise in which the courts may be tempted to find an assault. If D calls V and says threateningly; "Get out of your house this moment: a bomb is due to go off in 30 seconds," the threat might have the

---

[5] The court inclined to this view (without deciding it) in *Springfield* (1969) 53 CAR at 612.

[6] See [1957] Crim.LR 219; cp. *Wilson* [1955] 1 WLR at 494, 1 All ER at 745. On the question of threatening more force in self-defence than once can lawfully use see § 23.3.

[7] Below § 9.9.

[8] (1853) 13 CB 850, 138 ER 1437. Cp. *Ansell* v. *Thomas* [1974] Crim.LR 31; *Logdon* v. *DPP* [1976] Crim.LR 121 (where it would merely have made no difference if the drawer had been lying open).

same psychological effect as if made by one who is present. All the same, it should not be regarded as an assault, because that would be getting too far away from the common understanding of the word. Conduct of this kind should be punished as a threat (§ 9.9).

§ 8.3. THE REQUIREMENT OF FORCE

It was said at the beginning that a physical assault requires some degree of "force" applied against the body of the victim. So poisoning a man's coffee, whereby he becomes ill, is not an assault.[1] It is, as we shall see, a statutory crime. Again, merely pulling away from one who seeks to arrest you is not an assault—even though the arrest is lawful.[2] It is the distinct offence of escape, assuming of course that the arrest has been properly effected and is lawful. Pulling an article from another's grasp is not an assault, even though it is with intent to steal.[3] But to push or strike the victim would be; and it seems clear that even a pulling of the article would be an assault if this is known to involve injury or pain to the victim, as where an ear-ring is ripped from the lobe of the ear.

As said before, the "force" used in a physical assault may be very slight. Unlawful touching is enough (§ .1 at n. 6).

According to an ancient maxim, the law does not take account of trifles (*de minimis non curat lex*), but this is a very misleading generalisation (§ 26.11). If the assault is trivial the court may grant an absolute discharge,[4] but, even so, the fact that an assault has been committed can have importance. It gives the person assaulted the right to act in reasonable self-defence, and where the assault is by a policeman it means that defensive force used to repeal the assault is not an assault upon the officer in the execution of his duty—either because the defensive force is reasonable and lawful, or, in any case, because the officer when he commits the unlawful act of assault is not acting in the execution of his duty(§ 9.7).

"Ordinary social contact" (tapping a man on the shoulder to attract his attention) is not an assault.[5] This rule may be based on the necessities of social intercourse. The exemption applies only to non-hostile acts, for, in the words of Holt CJ, "the least touching of another in anger is a battery," a physical assault.[6]

Is it an assault if a policeman puts his hand on my arm and says he wants to speak to me?

On principle, yes. The police have no general power to detain people for questioning, even those who are strongly suspected of crime. The police

---

1 See *Clarence* (1888) 22 QBD at 42; cp. *Hanson* (1849) 2 C & K 912, 175 ER 383

2 *Sherriff* [1969] Crim.LR 260.

3 *Ansell* v. *Thomas* [1974] Crim.LR 31.

4 OAPA 1861 s.44 gives magistrates the power to draw up a certificate of dismissal if the assault was so trifling as not to merit punishment. This power can now be regarded as an instance of the general power to grant a discharge, except that it has the peculiar property of barring a civil action.

5 *Coward* v. *Baddeley* (1859) 4 H & N 478, 157 ER 927; see also the cases in n. 8 below.

6 *Per* Holt CJ in *Cole* v. *Turner* (1705) 6 Mod. 149, 87 ER 907. The dictum does not mean that anger is required. See, as to indecent assault, § 10.3.

may of course ask people questions, just as you or I can, but they cannot require them to stop to be questioned.[7] If the person accosted is willing to answer questions, he can be spoken to without the necessity to lay hands upon him. If he is unwilling, the officer's laying a hand upon him in order to make him stop and listen should be accounted an assault.

However, there are indications that the courts are in process of changing to a rule more favourable to the police. Undoubtedly the police still lack power to detain anyone for questioning (apart from the law of arrest and certain powers of search); yet it has been held that a policeman commits no assault if he taps a pedestrian repeatedly on the shoulder after the person so accosted has expressed objection to speaking to the officer.[8] The point is important if the person accosted strikes the officer in order to prevent him continuing his unwelcome attentions. In the case just referred to the person accosted was held to have no right of self-defence, because in law he had not been assaulted.

The court did not make it clear why the officer was not regarded as committing an assault. It did not use the phrase "social contact," but something like that concept would seem to have been the officer's only defence. Nevertheless, it is extremely dubious whether an officious tapping on the shoulder by a person invested with the authority of a police officer can properly be so characterised. Perhaps a better way of deciding the case would have been to say that the officer was behaving (or proposing to behave) unlawfully, but that the use of anything but the gentlest force by way of defence was unreasonable when the apprehended assault was so trivial. Even so, a trivial bodily interference constantly repeated can be very irritating. If the citizen is not allowed to reply to it with some force, and if in addition he is held not even to have been assaulted (so as to have a remedy in the courts on that account), his right to freedom from physical interference by the police will lack effective sanction.

Must the attack be on the body? What about an attack on the clothes a person is wearing?

An attack upon clothes is certainly an assault if it causes the victim to feel pain, or apprehension in respect of his own safety. The better view is that it is an assault in any event, since clothes are so intimately connected with the wearer that offensive conduct against them is likely to be taken as

---

[7] *Rice* v. *Connolly* [1966] 2 QB 414; *Kenlin* v. *Gardiner* [1967] 2 QB 510; *Styles* v. *Sizer* (1980) 145 JPN 71; *Bentley* v. *Brudzinski* (1982), The Times, March 3, 11 (correction), [1982] Crim.LR 825. Although the outcome of the last case is satisfactory, it contains some regrettably misleading dicta. See next note. And see generally Lanham in [1974] Crim. LR 288.

[8] *Donnelly* v. *Jackman* [1970] 1 WLR 562, 1 All ER 987, 54 CAR 229; cp. *Squires* v. *Botwright* [1973] Crim.LR 106. See the powerful criticisms by Lanham, last note, and by J M Evans in 33 MLR 438; also Burton in 140 JPN 331. The court did something to retrieve the position in *Bentley* v. *Brudzinski*, last note. A police officer, having obtained answers to questions, still attempted to prevent the person questioned from leaving, by placing his hand on his arm; it was held that this was unlawful, being a more than trivial interference with liberty. But even a trivial physical interference would on traditional principles be unlawful; and the court also increased the doubts by mentioning that the officer had already obtained answers to his questions—as though, if he had not, he would have been justified. Cp. Bailey in [1982] Crim.LR 481–482. See also § 22.5.

an affront to the wearer. The basis of the crime of assault is the desire of the law to preserve the peace.[9]

Must the force be applied directly? What of the practical joker who balances a pail of water on a half-opened door? Or the reckless driver who strikes his passenger with a parked car?

The old law was that the force had to be applied "directly" (without intervening causation), and this is still so in theory. However, there is always the possibility of the offence, which lacks statutory formulation, being interpreted more widely. In your booby-trap case, traditionalists would see the victim's act in opening the door as the direct cause of his wetting, not the setting of the trap by the practical joker; but since the victim acted without knowing the circumstances and the foreseeing the consequence, the person who set the trap might now be regarded as having applied force directly. The same might be held for the case of the crashing driver, but the law is far from being completely clear.

The offence of assault at common law derived from the old writ of trespass, which has also given us the tort of assault. In general, an injury had to be direct and forcible before it (or the threat of it) came within the writ of trespass, and this limitation still affects the law of assault. It is true that some slight degree of delayed or indirect action is tolerated. A physical assault is held to be committed if the defendant sets a dog on a person, or strikes a horse to make it throw its rider,[10] or throws over a chair in which another person is sitting.[11] But, according to the old authorities, it is not a trespass, and so not an assault, to erect an obstruction that causes another person to fall, since here the injury is too "indirect" to come within the crime. The standard illustration was as follows: if a man throws a log of wood out of his window, and hits a passer-by, this is a trespass, and an assault; but if the log falls on the highway and a passer-by trips over it, it is not.[12] It made no difference that throwing the log on to the highway involved the use of force; the force was not direct. In general this must still be true. Similarly, if a person merely stands stock still, being "entirely passive like a door or a wall" as it was put in one case, it is not an assault, however inconvenient his presence at that particular spot may have been[13]; but it is a false imprisonment if the victim does not know that another exit exists.

If the old law is followed, it cannot be an assault to engineer the downfall of another by making use of his momentum. When a man trips over a log of wood on the highway, his momentum causes him to fall, yet it is not an assault—not even if the injury was intended. Logically, therefore, it cannot be an assault to cause injury by breaking the ice just in front of a skater,[14] or by stretching a wire to bring off a motor-cyclist, or by taking up the rails before an approaching train[15]; still less in your hypothetical of driving into a parked car. When the victim sees the danger ahead he may be very frightened, but is not psychically assaulted; and when the danger materialises he is not, on historical principles, physically assaulted.

---

[9] For the view in the text see *Day* (1845) 1 Cox 207; *Humphries* v. *Connor* (1864) 17 Ir.CLR 1. A civil case *contra* is *Pursell* v. *Horn* (1838) 3 Ad. & E 602, 112 ER 966, but this is of tenuous authority at the present day.

[10] *Dodwell* v. *Burford* (1670) 1 Mod. 24, 86 ER 703. There is, of course, no such thing as assaulting a horse: the point is the injury to the rider.

[11] *Per* Gibbs CJ in *Hopper* v. *Reeve* (1817) 7 Taunt. at 700, 129 ER 278.

[12] *Scott* v. *Shepherd* (1773) 2 W Black. at 894–895, 96 ER at 526. See § 9.5 n. 7.

[13] *Per* Lord Denman CJ in *Innes* v. *Wylie* (1844) 1 C & K at 263, 173 ER at 803. That assault cannot be committed by a pure omission was reasserted in *Fagan* v. *MPC* [1969] 1 QB 439. The court regarded the actual facts as constituting a positive act, but the reason given was very narrow (see 1st edn 143), and the court's result could now better be reached by invoking the doctrine of *Miller*. See §7.5.

[14] *Contra,* Kenny, *Outlines of Criminal Law*, 18th edn 209.

[15] *Contra, Jolly* [1923] AD 176 (South Africa).

Some of these acts amount to other offences: wilful obstruction of the highway, a railway offence,[16] or reckless driving. If grievous bodily harm is caused it is an offence under OAPA section 18 (§ 9.1). But the sousing of the skater is no offence if it is held not to be an assault and if the harm suffered is not serious.

If the skater case comes before the courts the judges will undoubtedly be strongly inclined to extend the law of assault. Judges do not like letting mischief-makers go scot free. There are already indications of this view being taken.

Two members of the court in *Clarence*[17] thought that an assault would be committed by "a man who digs a pit for another to fall into, whereby that other is injured," and one of these two thought that there was also an assault on the facts of *Martin*, to be considered presently.[18] But these remarks were obiter, and are open to criticism. Some of these cases could be prosecuted under the doctrine of *Wilson* (§ 9.5 at n. 4), if that decision is sustained in the Lords. In any case the courts would, it may be suggested, do better to preserve the law of assault in its traditional form, keeping the word close to its common meaning, while at the same time uttering a clarion call for the statutory creation of a new offence of causing bodily harm or discomfort intentionally or recklessly, whether by an assault or not.[19] At the same time the traditional law of assault should be put on a statutory footing.[20] It seems that even under the present law an assault can be committed by applying light, heat, electricity, gas, or odour to the victim, in uncomfortable quantities.[21]

§ 8.4. GENERAL AND TRANSFERRED INTENTION

If the defendant did not aim at anyone in particular, he is still liable on the basis of what is sometimes called "general malice"—better, "general intention." The most obvious example is the terrorist "bomber," though of course his crime is much graver than assault. An intention to hit anyone within range is always, in logic and law, an intention to hit the particular person who is hit.

Another possibility is that D aims at V1 but accidentally hits V2. This is an instance of what is traditionally called "transferred malice"—more precisely, transferred intention. Although D aimed to hit V1, since his blow took effect on V2 it is deemed at common law to be an intentional attack upon V2. The rule is that D is guilty to the same extent as if he had intended to injure the person whom he actually did injure. The intention in respect of one victim is transferred by a legal fiction to another.

---

[16] OAPA 1861 s.32.

[17] (1888) 22 QBD at 36, 45 (Wills and Stephen JJ).

[18] § 9.5. In *Fagan* v. *MPC* [1969] 1 QB at 444D a [psychic] assault was defined as "any act which intentionally—or possibly recklessly—causes another to apprehend immediate and unlawful personal violence." Perhaps the word "immediate" was meant to carry the sense of "directness"; in any case the violence before the court in *Fagan* was direct.

[19] This is so by OAPA 1861 s.18, but only where grievous bodily harm is intentionally caused. See § 9.1.

[20] There is no present prospect of this. The CLRC, the majority of whose members were antipathetic to codification, refused to recommend that the offence of assault should be statutorily defined: 14th Report, Cmnd 7844, para. 4.

[21] *Russell*, 12th edn 652–653.

The doctrine is a general one, and applies whenever a wrongful intention is formed in respect of a person or thing but it takes immediate physical effect[1] upon another person or thing, where the intended and the actual "victim" (person or thing) fall within the definition of the offence.[2] Returning to the specific case of an assault, the argument is that D had the requisite *mens rea* for assault, namely to hit someone, and he committed the *actus reus* of assault in hitting V2; therefore he has both the *mens rea* and *actus reus* for an assault on V2. The argument is of course fallacious, if D did not have *mens rea* in respect of V2.[3] Still, many will think that the doctrine of transferred intention does practical justice in this application.[4] It is closely similar to the case of mistaken victim (§ 6.9), even though it is analytically distinct from it.

Suppose an attacker aims at a dog and hits a man, or vice versa?

He cannot be charged either with an offence against the person or with an offence against property. There is no *actus reus* in respect of the dog and no intention in respect of the man.

The fuller reason is that there is no statute under which he can be charged with a consummated intentional offence. No law makes it an offence to injure an "animal" in a sense including both men and dogs. If there were such a law a charge would lie, the difference between the "animal" aimed at and the "animal" injured being immaterial. But under our law dogs fall within the Criminal Damage Act and the Protection of Animals Act while human beings fall within the Offences against the Person Act. On a charge of intentionally or recklessly damaging a dog under the Criminal Damage Act, *mens rea* would not be established by showing an intent to injure a man, because that would not be the *mens rea* required by the Act.[5] Similarly in the converse case. (But the attacker would be responsible if he were reckless in respect of the actual victim. And he can also be convicted of attempting to commit the offence that he tried to commit.)

The rule emerging from the above is that intention can be transferred only within the same crime, because the defendant must have the *mens rea* and commit the *actus reus* appropriate to the crime with which he is charged, even though they may exist in respect of different persons or objects. Combining the elements of two different offences is not allowed.[6]

One other point; defences are transferred with the intention. So if D was acting in self-defence against V1, he will be deemed to have been acting in self-defence against V2.

---

[1] In justice, the doctrine should not be applied where the immediate injury to V2 is non-physical, even though an injury intended for V1 causes fright and consequent injury to V2, as in *Towers* (1874) 12 Cox 530. D's liability in respect of V2 should be adjudged without reference to his intent against V1. The consequence of adopting the opposite rule was seen in the American case of *Ex p. Heigho* (1910) 18 Idaho 566, where D assaulted V1 and an onlooker, V2, died of fright; D was convicted of the manslaughter of V2! There is a danger that the mechanical reasoning adopted in *Mitchell* § 12. 6 n. 21 will lead English courts to the same conclusion.

[2] See *The General Part*, 2nd edn Chap. 4.

[3] The Law Commission's draft Bill on the mental element (Law Com. No. 89) does not deal with transferred intention, since the Commission erroneously thought this doctrine did not need statement.

[4] See more in § 17.3. The doctrine is, however, of doubtful merit in relation to offences against property. See § 41.3.

[5] This is the only logical interpretation of the decision in *Pembliton* (1874) LR 2 CCC 119, even though the rule does not clearly appear from the judgments in that case.

[6] Exceptionally, and quite logically, intention may be transferred betwen two offences differing only in that one has elements of strict liability. See §9.7 n. 6.

§ 8.5. THE PLACE OF ASSAULT IN THE LAW

Psychic assault is the only crime at common law in which the evil of the act consists merely in creating fear or apprehension in the mind of the victim. Historically speaking, the object of the law, in giving a remedy for this wrong, is to offer the victim some means of vindicating his own dignity and security without recourse to fighting. But nowadays the police rarely prosecute for psychic assault, or even for physical assault if no great harm is done. They take assaults as being of everyday occurrence, and cannot be bothered with them.

The police are most likely to make a charge for assaults occurring in a public place, but even then the charge is generally for insulting behaviour (§ 9.9) rather than for assault. The victim may bring a private prosecution, but probably the assaulter will only be bound over to keep the peace; and if the victim contributed in any way to the affair (as he often has) he will be lucky not to be bound over too. However, the law retains some importance because the notion of assault enters into the law of tort and also into some of the more serious criminal offences.

The dismissive attitude of the police towards complaints of assault results in part from the dismissive attitude of magistrates. Normally, a charge of assault is tried summarily,[1] and many courts are pretty lenient. An unprovoked attack with heavy blows to the face, perhaps breaking the victim's nose, is frequently followed by a paltry fine of £10 or £20—not a high price to pay for the satisfaction of giving vent to aggressive feelings. Another common outcome is an order binding the defendant over. Regarding small assault cases as a waste of their time, the chairman or clerk to the magistrates may warn both parties of such a possible outcome in order to promote a withdrawal of the proceedings. Even muggings, which, one would have thought, clearly need a prison sentence, often result in a fine (the attitude of the courts here being by no means shared by the public). Where the assault is by a person of substance the aggrieved party may be better advised to sue in a civil court and obtain damages, which may well be considerable, and will have the added attraction of going into his own pocket.[2]

SUMMARY

Assault requires intention or recklessness. It is of two kinds, which may be called physical assault (battery) and psychic assault. § .1

A psychic assault is a threat creating the apprehension of immediate force by way of a physical assault. The threat may be by conduct or possibly by words. Reassuring words can negative an assault. But threats intended to impose a restraint on the conduct of the victim will be an assault, even though they may be accompanied by an assurance that no harm will come to him if he does as he is told. § .2

---

[1] The offence under s.47 is triable either way. When charged on indictment this is generally as a count added to a charge of a graver offence. A charge of assault under s.42 (where the penalty is more limited) is purely summary. But the charge under the latter section can only be brought by the victim (*Nicholson* v. *Booth* (1888) 16 Cox 373), the reason being that the proceedings will bar the victim's civil action for damages (s. 45; see thereon A E Jones in [1959] Crim.LR 279; [1957] Crim.LR 44); P M North in 29 MLR 16. Justices cannot try a charge under s.42 if it involves title to real property (s.46 as amended). See generally, as to summary procedure, 94 JPN 326, 95 *ibid.* 487; 121 *ibid.* 834; 140 *ibid.* 203.

[2] In *Reynolds* v. *Comr of Police*, The Times, May 21, 1982, where the plaintiff was unlawfully arrrested and detained at a police station for one day, the jury were upheld in awarding £12,000 damages for false imprisonment.

A physical assault requires the application of some degree of unlawful "force" § .3
to the body of the victim. It may be very slight, but ordinary social contact is not an assault. The old law was that the force had to be applied "directly;" whether this is still so is not clear.

One who aims at persons in general can be convicted of assault on the basis of § .4
general intention. If he aims at V1 and hits V2, he is guilty on the basis of transferred intention. Intention can be transferred only within the same offence: combining the elements of two offences is not allowed. Defences are transferred with intention.

For minor assaults the civil remedy is often more satisfactory than the criminal § .5
one. But the notion of assault is important because it enters into the definition of more serious crimes.

CHAPTER 9

OTHER NON-SEXUAL INJURIES AND THREATS

Civilisation is nothing else but the attempt to reduce force to being the last resort.

Ortega y Gasset.

§ 9.1. WOUNDING WITH INTENT; OFFENCES AGAINST THE PERSON ACT SECTION 18

THE CRIMES that we are to consider are the major offence under section 18 of the Offences against the Person Act 1861 and the medium offences under sections 20 and 47, together with some miscellaneous offences against the person.

A rational legal system would probably grade attacks upon the person (not resulting in death) in three categories.

At a low order of gravity there would be assaults in which bodily harm is not an element; these were considered in the last chapter.

At the other extreme there would be the crime of intentionally (or perhaps recklessly) causing serious injury.

In between there would be attacks of medium gravity, where bodily harm (not necessarily serious) is caused intentionally or recklessly.

The Act of 1861 establishes something like the last two classes, but the crimes of medium gravity are expressed in language of unnecessary complexity. The luxuriant growth of decided cases on the Act makes it impossible to state the law in a clear and satisfactory way. Simplification has been recommended by the CLRC,[1] but at the time of writing there is no sign of legislation.

Section 18, as amended,[2] runs essentially as follows.

> "Whosoever shall unlawfully and maliciously wound or cause[3] any grievous bodily harm to any person, with intent to do some grievous bodily harm to any person, or with intent to resist or prevent the lawful apprehension of any person, shall be" punishable with imprisonment for life.

This section creates two offences, either of which can be committed with any of three intents.

Separating them out, they may be restated as follows.

Unlawfully and maliciously wounding any person:

---

[1] 14th Report, Cmnd 7844, paras. 149–157.
[2] By the Criminal Law Act 1967 Sched. 3 Pt. III.
[3] The word "cause" probably does not cover causing by omission (§ 7.3 n. 10). On causing otherwise than by assault see § 9.5 n. 8.

1 with intent to do g.b.h. to any person, or
2 with intent to resist the lawful[4] apprehension of any person, or
3 with intent to prevent the lawful apprehension of any person.

Unlawfully and maliciously causing any g.b.h. to any person:
1 with intent to cause it to any person, or
2 with intent to resist the lawful apprehension of any person, or
3 with intent to prevent the lawful apprehension of any person.

The section is compendiously referred to in legal discussions as creating the crime of "wounding with intent," but this is only half of it, since causing grievous bodily harm with intent is an alternative. The abbreviation "g.b.h." is frequently used in conversation, though not in court.

What is a "wounding"?

For a "wounding" the skin must be broken (the dermis as well as the epidermis),[5] and this need not amount to a grievous bodily harm. A scratch is not a wound; nor is an internal rupture. Generally, grievous bodily harm involves a wound, but it need not always do so—for example, where the skin is extensively bruised or burned, or a bone is broken.

Has "grievous bodily harm" a fixed meaning?

The phrase means "really serious harm"—a matter for the jury to decide. This equiparation was established by the House of Lords in *DPP* v. *Smith*, the well-known case on murder,[6] and has been followed for the offence under section 18.[7] The lack of any clear definition leads to the possibility that different juries apply different tests.[8]

Inflicting a deep wound in the head or trunk is indubitably grievous bodily harm because of the evident danger to life, unless the wound is in some non-vital part such as the ear or shoulder. But the test of danger to life, though a clear *positive* test of grievous bodily harm, is not a reliable negative one, since (as was held in *Smith*) harm can be grievous although it is not dangerous to life. For example, blinding a person or shooting him in the leg would be really serious harm, though there is no risk of death.

The suggestion has been made that juries can utilise the uncertainty of the meaning of "grievous" to regard the harm as grievous or not according to other circumstances, e.g. the degree of provocation if any. They are very likely to do this, and the judge need not stop them by telling them not to. But he is not supposed to encourage them.[9] Provocation is not in theory allowed to be taken into consideration by the jury, because it is feared that this would unduly lengthen trials.

What mental element is required under section 18?

A charge of wounding or causing grievous bodily harm with intent to

---

[4] In order for the defendant to be guilty of an intent to resist or prevent lawful apprehension the arrest must be authorised by law. If it is illegal, the defendant is not guilty under section 18 merely because of his intent to frustrate the arrest. (He will, however, be guilty under this section if his intent was to do grievous bodily harm.) Whether the arrest is illegal or not will depend upon the common law and statutory powers of arrest (Chap. 22).

[5] *JJC (a Minor)* v. *Eisenhower* (1983) The Times, May 3, [1983] Crim.LR 567.

[6] [1961] AC at pp. 333–335. Before *Smith* the judges had watered down the meaning of g.b.h. to the extent of holding that a mere interference with comfort was "grievous."

[7] *Metharam* [1961] 3 All ER 200, 45 CAR 304.

[8] For criticism see Hogan in [1980] Crim.LR 545.

[9] *Hamilton* [1980] Crim.LR 441.

cause g.b.h. clearly requires an actual intention, and not mere knowledge of the possibility of g.b.h.[10] Of course, intent may be inferred from conduct as a matter of fact.

It is well settled that "malice" in statutes means intention or recklessness (see § 6.1). In relation to the intent to do grievous bodily harm the word "recklessness" is surplusage, since the requirement of intent means that recklessness is not enough. But in relation to the intent to resist or prevent apprehension the word has a certain effect. Suppose that D, endeavouring to avoid being lawfully arrested by V, knowingly subjects V to a risk of serious injury, and V is in fact wounded or seriously injured. D did not intend V to be injured, but he is guilty under the section because he was malicious (reckless) as to the injury and he intended to resist a lawful arrest. (He would be guilty under the section even if the arrest that he was trying to prevent was the arrest of someone else.[11])

Can intention be transferred under the section?

The wording is clearly designed to allow this.

The doctrine of transferred intention applies to crimes at common law, such as assault and murder; but the courts have found difficulty in applying it to the construction of statutes unless the statute is aptly framed. Section 18 is an example of suitable wording. It repeats the phrase "any person" ("whosoever shall . . . wound or cause any grievous bodily harm to any person, with intent to do some grievous bodily harm to *any* person"—not "*such* person"). The object is to indicate that the intention can be transferred from the intended victim to the actual victim.[12]

§ 9.2. OFFENCES AGAINST THE PERSON ACT SECTIONS 20 AND 47

The statutory crimes of medium gravity are generally known as "unlawful wounding" and "assault occasioning actual bodily harm." They are created by sections 20 and 47 respectively. The penalty for each is the same—5 years' imprisonment.[1]

Section 20 creates two crimes: "unlawfully and maliciously *wound*[*ing*] or *inflict*[*ing*] *any grievous bodily harm upon* any other person." Section 47 penalises "any assault occasioning actual bodily harm."

The two sections are very similar, and the more one studies them the more similar they seem to become. The most obvious difference is in

[10] *Belfon* [1976] 1 WLR 741, 3 All ER 46, 63 CAR 59. On the position where the jury negative intent but find recklessness see § .5 at nn. 14, 15.

[11] If V goes to arrest D1, and D1 and D2 use force to thwart the arrest, it seems that Dl "resists" the arrest and D2 "prevents" it. D1 can also "prevent" his own arrest, it would seem, by rigging up a trap to incapacitate V.

[12] But it was ruled in *Monger* [1973] Crim.LR 301 that the indictment must be worded appropriately to cover the case. It must charge an intention against V1 and a wounding, etc., of V2. There was earlier (and higher) authority allowing the indictment to charge an intention against V2; see Ashworth in *Reshaping the Criminal Law*, ed. Glazebrook (London 1978) 84–85.

[1] The length of the term is stated in the Penal Servitude Act 1891 s.1. By the Firearms Act 1968 s.17 (2), it is an offence punishable with 7 years' imprisonment to be in possession of a firearm or imitation firearm at the time of committing or being arrested for a number of specified offences, including those under ss. 20 and 47 of the OAPA.

Whereas a charge under s.18 cannot be tried by magistrates, a charge under the other two sections can be. These two crimes are treated in practice as founding alternative charges, so that if there are counts for both, and the jury convict on one, they should be discharged from giving a verdict on the other: *Cowdell* [1962] Crim.LR 262. (The jury are not directed to *acquit* on the other of the two counts; it is left alive, so to speak, so that if, on appeal, the verdict on the one count is set aside, the appellate court can substitute a conviction on the other.)

respect of the outcome of the attack. Section 20 requires a wound or *grievous* bodily harm. Section 47 requires only *actual* bodily harm. Every wound (or almost every wound) must be actual bodily harm, and of course grievous bodily harm is an aggravated form of actual bodily harm. So section 47 is from this point of view the wider section.

The uncertainty about grievous bodily harm (§ .1 at n. 6) affects the notion of "actual bodily harm" in section 47 ("a.b.h." in police jargon). This is a silly expression—as though there were some kind of contrasting bodily harm that was not "actual"! Presumably it means "more than trifling." Transitory pain is obviously not enough, but a bruise is.[2]

"Actual" does not mean physical as opposed to mental, because the phrase has been ruled to include a hysterical and nervous condition resulting from an assault.[3] This ruling obviously presents some danger of an over-extension of the offence. That appreciable mental harm should be actual bodily harm is beyond doubt. Concussion, for example, is obviously bodily harm even where the injury to the skull is minimal. In such a case there is an injury to the brain, even though it is temporary. But the phrase "actual bodily harm" should surely connote something more than a trivial injury. Mental distress should not be regarded as sufficient unless there is psychiatric evidence of recognised mental disorder. However, there is no indication that the courts will recognise this limitation.[4]

§ 9.3. THE MENTAL ELEMENT UNDER SECTION 20

"Maliciously" in section 20 means, as we already know, that the act must be done intentionally[1] or recklessly, that is to say with foresight of the likelihood or possibility of the consequence[2]; it does not include inadvertent negligence in respect of the consequence. This appears plainly from *Cunningham*,[3] a case on poisoning, where the Court of Criminal Appeal laid it down that the word "malice" in a penal statute is a term of art meaning:

---

[2] In *Taylor* v. *Granville* [1978] Crim.LR 482 magistrates were held to be entitled to infer that "bodily harm, however slight," must have resulted from a blow to the face. But query whether the extension of a.b.h. to include very slight harm gives proper weight to the meaning of the word "actual" in the context. In *Christopher Jones* [1981] Crim.LR 119 the court said that to describe minor abrasions and a bruise on the face as a.b.h. "went to the very margin of what was meant by that term," and that to impose a term of imprisonment was incorrect.

[3] *Miller*, § .4 n. 2.

[4] There is no technical reason why the victim's mental suffering should not inflate the sentence if actual bodily harm has been occasioned. In *Maguire* (1982) 146 JPN 314 the defendant was convicted under section 47 where he had inflicted only slight bodily harm by a sexual assault (some grazing and bruising, but with severe shock). A sentence of 2 years' imprisonment was upheld, the CA assuming without firm evidence that the victim might suffer lasting psychological damage. Yet apart from the assumed psychological damage the evidence of bodily harm seems to have gone to "the very margin of what was meant by that term" (see n. 2 above).

[1] But the implied inclusion of intention in the section adds nothing to it, because of the practice of the courts in sentencing. See below § .6 n. 5.

[2] On "malicious" see also § 6.10 at n. 6.

[3] [1957] 2 QB 396 (below § 10 n. 14). Cp. *Solanke* [1970] 1 WLR 1, [1969] 3 All ER 1383, 54 CAR 30.

> "either (1) an actual intention to do the particular kind of harm that was done; or (2) recklessness as to whether such harm should occur or not (i.e. the accused has foreseen that the particular kind of harm might be done and yet has gone on to take the risk of it)."

Incidentally, this much-quoted passage shows that the judges recognise the difference of meaning between "actual intention" and "recklessness," even though the use of the adjective "actual" improperly suggests the possibility of some kind of legal intention that is not actual intention. Either intention is "actual" or it does not exist. The definition is also significant in clearly recognising the subjective meaning of recklessness.

But then it must be read subject to Caldwell.

That is not certain. There are arguments both ways.

For the view that the general *Caldwell* rule (as opposed to the special *Caldwell* rule for intoxication) does not apply to section 20, the point may be repeated that Lord Diplock did not apply his rule to statutory crimes of malice. In *Caldwell* he spoke only of the Criminal Damage Act,[4] and in *Lawrence* of "the adjective 'reckless' when used in a criminal statute."[5] In statutory crimes of malice the adjective "reckless" is not used in the statute; it is imported as a judicial interpretation of the meaning of the statutory word "malicious." Commenting upon *Caldwell*, Lord Diplock said that Kenny's parenthetical definition of recklessness in terms of foresight "has no bearing on the meaning of the adjective 'reckless' in section 1 of the Criminal Damage Act 1971."[6] This does not reject Kenny's definition for crimes of malice, but merely states that it has no bearing on the Criminal Damage Act. It is true that Lord Diplock added that Kenny's definition implied "fine and impracticable distinctions," but he did not say that these distinctions were not settled law for crimes of malice. In fact, after laying down the *Caldwell* rule for the Criminal Damage Act, he said only that "cases in the Court of Appeal *which held otherwise* should be regarded as overruled" (italics supplied). In other words, the cases are overruled only to the extent that they may be thought to conflict with the rule in *Caldwell* for the Criminal Damage Act. If the cases in the Court of Appeal are not overruled in respect of crimes of malice, then they continue fully binding on that court, unless and until they are overruled in the Lords.

This reading of *Caldwell* is confirmed by a consideration of the word "malicious." The word is nowadays too readily treated as a kind of empty symbol into which the courts can pour any meaning they please. In fact it has its own normal, dictionary, meaning in common use, and originally it was interpreted by the courts in something like this meaning (§ 5.2 n. 9). But then the judges, thinking this too narrow, took the legislative function upon themselves, and held that a person who did the forbidden act intentionally was malicious. Later they departed still further from the popular meaning by holding that subjectively reckless risk-taking was malicious in law. That is as far as the cases have gone. Perhaps even Lord Diplock sensed that it would be intolerable to hold that negligent injury is malicious. At any rate, we seem to be left with subjective recklessness as long as the offences of malice in the Offences against the Person Act remain.

That is the argument pro the interpretation of statutory malice in terms of subjective recklessness. The argument contra is that the House of Lords declared in *Seymour* that *Caldwell* recklessness applying throughout the criminal law unless Parliament has otherwise ordained (§ 8.1, text following n. 4). Moreover, it would be anomalous to have different definitions of recklessness for the purpose of the OAPA (subjective recklessness) and the Criminal Damage Act (*Caldwell* recklessness). It would mean that if a person without thinking what he is doing by the same act causes serious injury to a cyclist and damages his machine, the issue of recklessness on the charge of maliciously causing g.b.h. would be judged

---

[4] *Caldwell* [1982] AC at 354F.
[5] *Lawrence* [1982] AC at 525C.
[6] [1982] AC at 351G.

subjectively, while what is verbally but not legally the same issue on the charge of damage would be judged objectively (to the extent that *Caldwell* requires it to be judged objectively, which nobody knows for certain). The same jury would have to be instructed on the two meanings of recklessness in the same case.

Again, suppose that Parliament replaces the OAPA by a new series of statutory offences against the person which impose liability for recklessness. If Parliament merely puts the present law into statutory form, changing "maliciously" into "intentionally or recklessly" for the sake of modernising the language, this would not show any intention to change the law, since "maliciously" already means "intentionally or recklessly." Yet according to the argument pro considered above the mere fact of using the word "reckless" in a statute would alter the meaning previously attaching to the word, which is absurd.

The argument may be sharpened by pointing out that Parliament did in fact turn what was formerly called malicious damage into damage committed intentionally or recklessly. The pro view is that when it did this Parliament, according to *Caldwell*, changed the meaning of the word. The contra view must be that Parliament did not change the meaning of the word. The *Caldwell* meaning of recklessness always was "the law", and the cases in the Court of Appeal and the opinions of the Law Commission and the commentators saying the contrary were all wrong and never did state "the law." This further implies that *Caldwell* applies to statutory crimes of malice.

It may be suggested that, notwithstanding the absurdity of the position, the subjective view of recklessness expressed in *Cunningham* should be regarded as continuing to govern statutory crimes of malice. This is the most obvious interpretation of Lord Diplock's words, and the sweeping dictum in *Seymour* needs reconsideration.

Do I understand that, according to Cunningham, if a person intends to inflict actual harm and causes grievous harm, when his act was neither intentional nor reckless in respect of grievous harm, he cannot be convicted under section 20?

That would be the logical consequence of the decision. The courts tend to punish more severely under section 20 for grievous harm than under section 47 for lesser harm, and the logic of the *mens rea* requirement implies that it should govern the *extent* as well as the *existence* of criminal responsibility. A conviction under section 20 would not be possible if the rule in *Cunningham* were applied, in the absence of intention or recklessness as to grievous harm; and that would be the proper rule.

However, the courts have now veered away from *Cunningham* on this point. *Mowatt*[7] decides that a person may be convicted of maliciously wounding or inflicting grievous bodily harm although he did not intend to inflict such harm and was not reckless as to it—notwithstanding that "maliciously" is supposed to mean "intentionally or recklessly." According to *Mowatt*, foresight of some minor physical harm is sufficient. The decision has been subjected to reasoned criticism by commentators.[8] An argument against it (though one that falls on deaf judicial ears) is that the decision is contrary to section 8 of the Criminal Justice Act. Anyway,

[7] [1968] 1 QB 421.

[8] My own contribution to the criticisms will be found in the 1st edn 156–159. See also my *Mental Element in Crime* (Jerusalem and Oxford 1968), Chap.2.

the judges have rejected the criticisms (without offering any reasoned answer to them) and followed the decision.[9]

Happily, the CLRC has proposed the statutory reversal of *Mowatt*.[10] That decision was not necessary for the protection of the public against evildoers, because section 47 allows conviction of an assault occasioning actual bodily harm without the harm being grievous, and the section therefore imposes a lighter burden of proof on the prosecution than section 20. All that is required, to obtain a conviction without any legal problems, is to charge the offence under section 47. When prosecutors stupidly do not do this, the courts rescue them by distorting the accepted meaning of statutory malice.

Push it a stage further. The defendant did not intend to cause g.b.h., but he intended to give the other a severe fright, and did so in a way that created the risk of injury and actually caused serious injury. Couldn't the frightener be made liable under section 20?

The frightener may be liable under section 47, and he will be liable under section 20 if he was reckless as to causing harm (*Mowatt*). But, correcting some earlier pronouncements, the courts now hold, in accordance with principle, that an intention to frighten is not sufficient to create liability under section 20, in the absence of recklessness as to causing harm.

> So where a gamekeeper fired a shot towards a bush, thinking that a poacher might be there and wishing to "startle" him into coming out of hiding, but not believing that anyone was within range and not foreseeing the possibility of causing direct physical injury, but in fact caused g.b.h. to a man who was hiding in the bush, the gamekeeper's appeal against conviction under section 20 was allowed.[11]

But surely the gamekeeper was reckless. Would he have shot towards the bush if he had known that his wife or daughter was in it?

A good question to ask him in cross-examination. If the magistrates had found that the gamekeeper foresaw even a very small possibility of hitting someone, he would have been reckless as to causing harm, because no foreseen risk would be justifiable in the circumstances. But the appeal court was bound by the magistrates' finding of fact.

Before this case the judges had created a form of constructive intention, holding that the intent to frighten made the defendant automatically liable for harm resulting from the fright, even though the harm was not only unintentional but even unforeseen. The CLRC recommended that this rule should be reversed by statute; and although no statute has yet appeared, the courts by remoulding the common law (for once in the direction of restricting liability) have made the change theselves. It represents a minor success for the subjectivist approach to criminal liability, a small backwash in the general flow the other way.

One application of the old rule needs special mention. It was formerly held that if a person

---

[9] *Sullivan*, n. 11 below.

[10] 14th Report para. 6.

[11] *Flack* v. *Hunt* (1979) 70 CAR 51, followed in *Sullivan* [1981] Crim.LR 46. The negative finding in *Flack* v. *Hunt* quoted in the text above must be read as a colloquial way of saying that the gamekeeper positively believed that no one was within range and positively believed that there was no possibility of causing direct physical injury. If the gamekeeper had no belief one way or the other he could have been accounted reckless, both as a matter of common sense and under the rule in *Caldwell*.

did an act with intent to frighten, and the victim injured himself in trying to escape, the intention to frighten was sufficient for conviction under section 20 or 47, so that the doer could be punished for causing the injury even though he did not intend to cause injury and was not reckless as to it.[12] We can assume that these decisions are no longer law in respect of section 20. The frightener is liable under section 20 only for intention or recklessness as to injury. (See more below, § .5.)

You are not telling me that if one man scares the daylight out of another, who injures himself trying to escape, the first should not be accountable?

The frightener will generally be guilty of a (psychic) assault, and/or of a crime of uttering threats (§ .9). Often the tribunal of fact will be able to infer recklessness as to causing injury, which would be sufficient under section 20. According to the authorities the frightener can in any case be made liable under section 47 (§ .4). But the law now is that an intention to frighten is not in itself *mens rea* as to bringing about a wound or grievous bodily harm, which is the charge under section 20. Nor should it be so regarded. The CLRC, agreeing with this opinion, has recommended that the frightener should never be liable for an aggravated assault merely because he intended to frighten.[13]

Can intention be transferred under section 20?

Yes. There is nothing in the wording of the section to prevent such transfer.[14]

§ 9.4. THE MENTAL ELEMENT UNDER SECTION 47

Section 47 does not expressly state the mental element required, but it postulates an assault, and we have seen that an assault requires intention or recklessness. We have also seen that recklessness for this purpose should be taken in its pre-*Caldwell* sense (§ 8.1 at n. 4).

The Court of Appeal has held that an intention to frighten is sufficient. A person who assaults another physically or psychically, with the result that the other tries to escape and suffers actual bodily harm, is guilty under the section without proof that the assaulter foresaw the harm, at least if the harm was reasonably foreseeable.[1] Of course, *mens rea* is present as to the assault, but there need be none as to the harm. The crime is one of negligence as to the circumstance of aggravation, the occasioning of bodily harm.

Similarly, in *Miller*[2] a trial judge ruled that where D physically assaulted V, who was in consequence put into "a hysterical and nervous condition," the latter was "actual bodily harm" and D was liable for it under section

[12] See particularly *Halliday* (1889) 54 JP 312, 61 LT 701, 6 TLR 109. This was followed in a number of cases; see 1st edn. 155–156.
[13] 14th Report, Cmnd 7844, para. 6.
[14] See *Latimer* (1886) 17 QBD 259.

[1] *Roberts* §16. 8.
[2] [1954] 2 QB 282.

47; the judge did not direct his mind to the question whether it had to be proved that D realised the possibility of actual harm occurring, and for all that appears he regarded the outcome of the assault as a matter of strict liability, not even a question of liability for negligence.[3] On this view, a merely technical assault (pushing a person out of the way) can result in liability for the aggravated crime if the victim is injured in the most unforeseeable way. This reduces *mens rea* to little more than a bogus requirement. At the most, the crime becomes one of half *mens rea*.

Since an intention to frighten is no longer regarded as a sufficient mental element under section 20 (§ .3 n. 11), a court might possibly be persuaded to depart from the foregoing authorities in relation to section 47, so that both sections are construed in the same way on this point. On principle, the *mens rea* under both sections should relate to the specified harm. But if the court concentrates on the language of the section and does not trouble about legal principle, it may meet this argument with the reply that section 47 refers to an assault, and therefore that any harm resulting from an assault in either of its two senses is within the section.

The law is a shambles, admittedly, but I don't think you sufficiently acknowledge the difference between the two sections. Section 20 has an express mental element, section 47 hasn't. Parliament may well have intended that section 47 was to be an offence of strict liability in respect of the consequence. Section 47 implies a mental element as to the assault, but no more.

Let me explain why I do not agree with that view. Suppose that the statute had simply made it an offence to occasion actual bodily harm. If one accepts the *Tolson* principle, that every (major) crime implies a state of mind, this offence would require a mental element as to the harm. Now suppose that, as is the case with section 47, the statute specifies that the harm must be caused by an assault. This cuts down the ways in which the harm is caused, but why should it eliminate the mental element as to the harm?

In addition to this argument on principle, there is good authority for saying that a requirement of *mens rea*, once introduced into a statutory offence, governs the whole in the absence of an expressed intention to the contrary. Examples are *David Smith* (§ 6.2) and the cases on the word "knowingly" (§ 6.3).

Even if *Miller* and the other similar cases are wrong, so that section 47 carries a full *mens rea* requirement, it seems likely as a matter of general principle that when an attacker is reckless as to causing a particular type of bodily harm, he is liable under section 47 even though he caused some other type of bodily harm as to which he was not reckless. It would be pushing insistence on the mental element too far to require it to be as to the specific type of harm that was actually inflicted; what is necessary is that it should be as to the harm described in the section—actual bodily harm. Consequently, assuming that mental harm is

---

[3] *Roberts*, n. 1 above, is not inconsistent with this, because the reference to reasonable foresight in that case can he explained as going to the issue of causation. See § 16.8 at n. 1.

bodily harm, then if the defendant caused mental harm the jury may convict whether he intended or was reckless as to either bodily or mental harm.

§ 9.5. THE REQUIREMENT OF AN ASSAULT

There is a difference between the two sections in that section 47 on its face requires an assault while section 20 does not. Section 20 merely requires harm to be "inflicted." In the ordinary use of language harm may be inflicted without an assault (for example, by poisoning). But the courts have not found the question so simple.

For more than a century before 1983 it had been supposed that section 20, too, requires an assault, and this is still very largely true. The leading authority is the decision of the Court for Crown Cases Reserved in *Clarence* (1888).[1]

> Clarence, who had communicated venereal disease to his wife, was indicted under section 20. It was held that he was not guilty because an "infliction" under the section could only be by way of assault. "The words appear to me" said Stephen J (with whom three other judges concurred) "to mean the direct causing of some grievous injury to the body itself. . . . I think the words imply an assault and battery of which a wound or grievous bodily harm is the manifest immediate and obvious result."[2] Here there was no assault, because an assault presupposes lack of consent, and the wife had consented to the contact.

Obviously Clarence did not assault his wife. Her ignorance or mistake was as to the consequence of the act, not as to the act itself. The gravamen of the charge against Clarence was that he had communicated a disease. One can communicate a disease to another person without touching him or her.

Yes. We shall return to the disease point when we come to the law on administering noxious things (§ .10 at n. 20).

Would a psychic assault be enough under section 20? D moves to attack V, who in alarm jumps out of the window and is seriously injured. Can D be convicted under the section?

Yes and no. The cases to which reference has already been made (§ .3) show that he is liable even for the consequences of a merely psychic assault if he intended or was reckless as to causing injury, but only then. An

---

[1] 22 QBD 23, [1886–90] All ER Rep. 133.

[2] The concluding words of this quotation may perhaps be thought to embody a further limitation on the section: not only must there be an assault producing the harm as a consequence but the harm must be its "manifest immediate and obvious result." Probably, however, these words were inserted only to introduce the requirement of *mens rea* as to consequence. The importance of the result being "manifest" and "obvious" is that it can be assumed that the defendant must have foreseen such a result as a possibility—though it would be more in accordance with principle to word the question by reference to foresight (which should be a matter for the jury) than in the way chosen by Stephen J. In any case Stephen J's words were not attended to in *Miller*, § .4 n. 2.

assault, though generally a necessary, is not a sufficient condition of liability.

Why did the court in Clarence require an assault? It seems to me that Clarence did inflict g.b.h. on his wife. What did it matter whether it was by an assault or not?

Difficult to say why. The court in *Clarence* was partly following precedent, and partly, perhaps, giving effect to a notion of policy.

We do not know who decided to charge Clarence with a crime, but the charge was unprecedented. Millions of men and women must have infected their consorts with VD without being prosecuted. Perhaps the court in *Clarence* merely disliked the idea of bringing the marital bed into the criminal law. At the present day there is a recognised policy against prosecuting for infectious disease, because of the risk that prosecutions may inhibit people from seeking advice or reporting contacts. This policy is especially strong in the case of husband and wife. At the same time, it was unfortunate that the solution found by the court involved a general narrowing of the scope of section 20.

If *Clarence* was right (and until now it was always accepted as representing the law) both sections would require an assault, the one section expressly and the other impliedly by using the word "inflict." A consequence of the decision was that (as had, indeed, been held before *Clarence*) both assault and the offence under section 47 were wholly included within the offence under section 20, and therefore were impliedly charged when section 20 was charged.[3] However, in *Wilson* (1983)[4] the Court of Appeal, by an astonishing reversal of view, held that this is too narrow an interpretation of section 20. Although a section 20 offence can be committed by an assault, it can, in the alternative, be committed "by doing something intentionally,[5] which, though it is not itself a direct application of force to the body of the victim, does directly result in force being applied violently[6] to the body of the victim, so that he suffers grievous bodily harm."

The facts were that Wilson was driving a car when he had a "misunderstanding" with a pedestrian. The misunderstanding was unfortunate for the pedestrian, because the result of it was that Wilson punched him to the extent of seriously injuring him. Wilson was charged on an indictment containing a single count under section 20. The judge directed the jury that if they were satisfied that actual bodily harm was inflicted but no more, they might convict under section 47 as an included offence; and this they accordingly did. In giving his instruction the judge was faithfully following precedents dating from 1869 which were binding on him. On appeal, the Court of Appeal quashed the conviction. The judge had conducted the trial properly; the conviction was fair, and was in accordance with the law when it was rendered; but the judge, not being a clairvoyant, had failed to take account of the rule (stated above) that the Court of

---

[3] *Taylor* 1 CCR 194, followed in *Clarence*, n. 1 above; *Oakley* [1966] Crim.LR 287; *Snewing* [1972] Crim.LR 267. On included offences see § 7.8 at n. 3.

[4] *Clarence Wilson* [1983] 1 WLR 356.

[5] Or, presumably, recklessly.

[6] This word presumably means that the application of the force must be non-consensual, the limitation being the same as that for assault.

> Appeal now invented for the first time. The effect of the new rule is that assault and the offence under section 47 are no longer included offences on a charge under section 20.

But the jury found that Wilson committed an assault which occasioned actual bodily harm. Surely, therefore, they found all the essentials necessary for conviction under section 47.

That is so, but the law is technical. The question is not what the jury find but what has been expressly or impliedly charged. The relation of an included offence to the express charge may be visualised as a step (the included offence) leading to a platform (the offence charged), where the step must be mounted in order to reach the platform. If you can reach the platform by a straight jump, then the step is not an included offence. Since *Wilson*, the offence charged under section 20 can be proved without mounting the step (proof of an assault), so assault and the offence under section 47 are no longer included offences.

The decision in *Wilson* is under appeal to the House of Lords. However disastrous for the administration of justice in the particular case, it has the long-term advantage that it gives legitimacy to the old case of *Martin*, which had previously been in doubt.[7]

> Martin was one of the unfunny jokers who appear from time to time in the law reports. According to the special verdict of the jury he extinguished the lights in a theatre "with the intention of causing terror and alarm," and placed a bar across the door "with the intention of wilfully obstructing the means of exit." Persons were injured in the ensuing pandemonium, and the Court for Crown Cases Reserved held that Martin could be convicted of maliciously inflicting grievous bodily harm under section 20.

The court proceeded on the assumption that "maliciously" in the statute covered an act done with intent to frighten, and in that respect the case is no longer law. The more recent cases discussed in § .3 show that an intention to frighten is not sufficient under section 20. The jury should therefore have been directed to consider whether they were satisfied beyond reasonable doubt that Martin either intended to cause the bodily harm or was reckless as to it. If he foresaw even the slightest risk of causing harm (as he must have done), that would make him reckless. The lack of a direction along these lines was a flaw in the conviction, according to present ideas, but, applying the subsequent decision in *Clarence*, there was another and much more serious defect. As we have seen, section 20 was construed in *Clarence* to require an assault, and on traditional principles there was no assault in *Martin*. Assuming that Martin realised the danger he was creating, all he did was to set up a situation that he knew would cause panic, and then leave the members of the audience to injure each other. It cannot be said (if the decencies of language are observed) that he directly inflicted force upon the injured persons, so as to make him guilty of an assault. So he should not have been liable under either section.

---

[7] (1881) 8 QBD 54.

The court in *Martin* did not decide that Martin had committed an assault. It just did not consider that an assault might be necessary under the section. In *Clarence* Wills J expressed the opinion that in *Martin* there was a direct infliction of force, and therefore an assault.[8] But the other members of the court in *Clarence* did not deal with the matter, and Wills J's opinion stretches the notion of an assault, and of the direct infliction of force, well beyond its common legal understanding.[9] If Martin was guilty of a physical assault when the members of the audience injured each other, he was guilty of a psychic assault when a member of the audience was frightened on seeing the crowd surging towards him, but it is impossible to believe that such fright could properly have been held to make Martin guilty of a psychic assault.

The decision of the Court of Appeal in *Wilson* solves this problem for us, and gives a more reasonable ambit to the law. The formula favoured by the Court of Appeal wriggles between the conflicting decisions in *Clarence* and *Martin*. A person like Clarence would still be acquitted (because no non-consensual force was involved in communicating VD), and a person like Martin would still be convicted (because he caused members of the audience to inflict force on each other). However, in an ordinary case under section 20 the "force" would be inflicted by way of assault.

If the "inflicting" of section 20 requires an assault (or causing the application of force), does the "causing" of section 18 require an assault (or causing the application of force) also?

Remarkably, no. The law is that harm may be "caused" in any way conforming to the rules of causation, and need not involve an assault or force.[10] It is strange that section 18, which creates the more serious offence, should in this respect be more embracing than section 20. The result is that if D communicates a serious disease to V intending to cause V grievous bodily harm, he can be convicted under section 18 of causing grievous bodily harm with intent; but if his act is only reckless, he cannot be convicted of any crime, apart from the possibility of charging an offence of poisoning.

Suppose that D sends V a letter-bomb, which explodes injuring V. Will he be liable under section 20?

He was not liable before *Wilson*, but will be under that decision. (D is more likely to be charged with causing an explosion likely to endanger life or property.[11])

---

[8] 22 QBD at 36.

[9] As was said in § 8.3, the notion of assault is common to crime and tort, and sprang from the old action of trespass, which required an act of direct force or the threat thereof. In general, force was not direct if it was exercised by other people. The furthest that the courts went when they were governed by the "forms of action" in tort was to hold that it was a trespass to the person (a battery) to throw a lighted squib into a crowded market-place, the squib being in turn thrown by those at whose feet it fell, and eventually putting out the plaintiff's eye: *Scott* v. *Shepherd* (1773) 2 W Bl.892, 96 ER 525. The "force" was regarded as directly emanating from the defendant notwithstanding the conduct of the intervening throwers. But it was a civil case, turning only on the correct form of action (as the court observed); the squib could be regarded as force emanating from the defendant, the only problem being the conduct of the intervening throwers; Blackstone J dissented strongly and convincingly, and the majority reached their decision only on the assumption that the intervening throwers acted justifiably in self-defence or under necessity. This was a good way from the facts of *Martin*, who could not fairly be said to have used force himself at all.

[10] *Austin* (1973) 58 CAR 163; other authorities below n. 14.

[11] Explosive Substances Act 1883 s.2.

Where there was clearly an assault, isn't it best for the prosecution to charge under section 47, rather than section 20? The possible punishment under both sections is the same, and under section 47 the prosecution don't have to prove that the harm was grievous.

That is a misapprehension. Under present sentencing practice, remember, the court will not sentence for a graver offence that has not been charged.[12] It seems that section 20 is regarded as creating a graver offence than section 47 (notwithstanding that under the statute they have the same maximum punishment of 5 years), so if the case falls within section 20 it should be charged as such. If the conviction is under section 47 the court will apparently assume for the purpose of sentence that g.b.h. was not caused (however obviously this was in fact the case).[13]

A footnote may be added on included offences under section 18, for the benefit of those who will need to know it in practice. Suppose that on a charge under section 18 the jury think that the defendant was merely reckless. They can convict of unlawful wounding under section 20 if the express charge was for *wounding* with intent. Unlawful wounding is an included offence and is therefore implied in the indictment.[14] But if the express charge under section 18 was for causing g.b.h., it does not enable the jury to convict of unlawfully inflicting g.b.h. under section 20, or of occasioning a.b.h. under section 47, because the former section requires an assault or causing the application of force, and the latter section requires an assault, which the charge under section 18 does not.[15]

§ 9.6. THE WORKING OF THE LAW

A charge under section 18 is a serious matter for the defendant, because not only does he stand to receive a severe sentence if convicted, but he can be tried only in the Crown Court. In contrast, the offences of medium gravity are normally triable summarily with the consent of the defendant.

How is the decision made to charge an offence under section 18 or one of the offences of medium gravity?

All is not as it seems. In legal theory, the principal difference between sections 18 and 20 or 47 is that section 18 requires an intent to inflict the grievous bodily harm while the offences of medium gravity can be

---

[12] § 1.3 n. 9.

[13] D A Thomas, *Principles of Sentencing*, 2nd edn 102.

[14] See *Mowatt* [1968] 1 QB 421. However, the addition of a count under s.20 is desirable to guard against jury disagreement under s.18. See *Collison* (1980) 71 CAR 249.

[15] *Austin*, n. 11 above; *Nicholls* [1978] Crim.LR 247; *McCready* [1978] 1 WLR 1376, 3 All ER 967, 67 CAR 345. The decision in *Austin* was expressed to be confined to cases where the count does not particularise the way in which the harm was caused, thus suggesting that the decision would have been otherwise if the pleader had alleged that the defendant caused g.b.h. to V by an assault. Cp. *McCready*, above. But much the better view is that the addition of an unnecessary particular like this to the charge of an offence does not extend the number of included offences. The proper course for the pleader is to add a count under one of the other sections, or for an assault. See Archbold, 41st edn § 4–462. The judge can amend the indictment, at the prompting of the prosecution or on his own initiative, to add an express charge of another offence if no prejudice is likely to arise to the defendant and if the committal evidence supports the additional charge. Cp. *Collison*, last note. It is difficult to understand why the CA in *Wilson* thought that this could not have been done in that case.

committed recklessly, or with an even smaller mental element. This is not the way in which the distinction works in practice. In deciding whether to charge under section 18 the police will take into account such matters as the seriousness of the injury inflicted, the danger of the weapon used, the absence of provocation, and the defendant's previous convictions. In favour of the defendant, they may have regard to the availability of witnesses (a doctor who is to be called for the prosecution may be reluctant to face cross-examination), the close relationship of the defendant to the victim, and the possibility of a guilty plea to the lesser charge. A guilty plea at a magistrates' court to a charge under section 20 means much less writing and loss of time for the police officer in charge of the case than a trial under section 18.

Where the charge is under section 18, the magistrates in what are variously called "long" or "old style" committal proceedings[1] may of course refuse to commit the defendant for trial on this charge, and insist upon the charge being reduced to one under section 20 or section 47. But they rarely do this.

In deciding whether to offer the defendant summary trial of a charge under section 20 or section 47, magistrates are likely to pay attention principally to the injury and the weapon. If the injury was severe or if a weapon was used they are more likely to send the case for trial (that is, before a jury), but otherwise are more likely to offer to try it themselves. When a charge under section 20 or section 47 is tried summarily the sentence is often quite light—perhaps only a fine. If, after trying the case and convicting the defendant, the magistrates find that he has previous convictions, they may remand him for sentence in the usual way to the Crown Court, which can then sentence the defendant in the same way as if the trial had been on indictment; but the Crown Court is even then not likely to give quite so severe a sentence as if the case had been tried on indictment.[2]

It will be seen that the punishment the offender eventually receives may be determined partly by the police in deciding whether to charge under section 18 and, if they decide not to do so, partly by the magistrates in deciding whether to allow summary trial under one of the other two sections. If the case goes to the Crown Court, then the jury also play a part. They may have to consider a plurality of counts. Even if there is only a charge of wounding with intent under section 18 the jury can generally convict of the lesser offence under section 20 if they are leniently inclined, in theory because they have found that the act was done recklessly but not intentionally, actually because they realise that the lesser charge will carry a lesser sentence. (The judge does not tell the jury this, but he will probably intimate that the one charge is regarded as more serious than the other.) The practical difference between the sections in cases of wounding tends therefore to turn on the degree of violence used by the defendant, and upon any mitigating circumstances, rather than upon the difference between intention and recklessness.

Provocation is not a defence in law under either section, but in practice the judge will say to the jury: "If you think that in the heat of the fray, or because of his natural anger in the situation, the defendant did not think what he was doing, you may acquit him of the charge of wounding with intent and convict him of unlawful wounding." Conviction under section 18 frequently carries a sentence of between 3 and 5 years' imprisonment[3] (only very occasionally life), while conviction on indictment under one of the other two sections is unlikely to result in a sentence longer than 2 years, and it can be much less.[4]

---

[1] That is to say, where witnesses are heard and depositions taken.

[2] *James* [1963] Crim.LR 710.

[3] Account may be taken of various mitigating circumstances, such as provocation or even a mere "emotional relationship": *McPhillips* [1980] Crim.LR 450. Women offenders are regularly treated much more leniently than men.

[4] Illustrations are 144 JPN 401, 517; 146 JPN 516; [1980] Crim.LR 661.

Normally, as was said before, the judges regard an acquittal on a graver charge and conviction on a lesser charge (whether on plea or verdict), or even a failure by the prosecution to make a graver charge, as tying their hands to some extent, so that they do not award the sentence on the lesser charge that the undoubted facts may in themselves warrant.[5] Even so, the sentencer has such a wide measure of discretion that one cannot always be sure that these principles are fully operative. Some judges will give, say, 4 years' imprisonment under section 20 even though this is what the defendant would have got under section 18. Other judges, however, show considerable leniency.

Although the indictment may contain counts under all three sections, special steps are taken to ensure that he is not convicted twice for the same act. The judge will leave only one of the counts (that under section 18, if it is charged) to the jury to begin with. If the jury convict, the other counts will be ordered to "lie on the file," so that they will not be proceeded with unless perhaps there is a successful appeal against the conviction, in which case the Court of Appeal may substitute a conviction of the lesser charge. If the jury acquit on the first count the judge will direct them on another, unless he thinks that the acquittal on the first count implies that the defendant was not guilty on the other either. The same practice is followed for most other offences that are regarded as alternative, such as robbery and blackmail, robbery and being in possession of a firearm, and theft and obtaining by deception.

§ 9.7. ASSAULTING AND WILFULLY OBSTRUCTING THE POLICE

The Police Act creates an offence of assaulting a constable in the execution of his duty.[1] This is now a summary offence only, the reason for keeping it down to this lowly status being the desire to prevent the defendant having a right of trial. There is something of a paradox here, since a common assault, which in practice is a less serious charge, is indictable.[2] However, the reality is that whereas conviction of common assault is generally followed by a fine or bind-over, magistrates frequently send people convicted of assaulting the police to prison.

One particular feature of the above-mentioned paradox may be mentioned. Suppose an offender lays about him and causes serious injury to one police officer, A, as well as assaulting another, B. He is charged with causing g.b.h. to A under section 18 and with the summary offence of assaulting B in the execution of his duty. The magistrates commit him for trial in respect of the section 18 offence, since they cannot try it themselves. This means that there are two trials, one in the Crown Court and one before magistrates. This is an unfortunate consequence of our over-rigid distinction between indictable and summary offences. The

---

[5] These principles can have surprising consequences. On conviction under ss.20 or 47 the judge must assume that the defendant did not intend to cause g.b.h.: Thomas, *Principles of Sentencing*, 2nd edn 99–102.

[1] Police Act 1964 s.51 (1) as amended, replacing earlier legislation. Persons acting in aid of such constable are protected under the same provision. For the offence of assaulting bailiffs see CLA 1977 s.10; *Vaughan* v. *McKenzie* [1969] 1 QB 557. If a prisoner assaults a prison officer the usual sanction is that the offender is brought before the visiting justices who may order various minor punishments or loss of remission or even (with the confirmation of the Home Secretary, which seems no longer to be given) flogging: Prison Act 1952 s.18. Alternatively, assault on a prison officer can be prosecuted in the same way as an assault on the police: *ibid.* s.8.

[2] The penalty on summary conviction of assaulting a constable in the execution of his duty is 6 months and £1000 (see Sched. 1 to the CLA 1977); on summary conviction of common assault it is 2 months and £200 (Sched. 6); on conviction on indictment of common assault it is one year's imprisonment (OAPA 1861 s.47).

magistrates will, upon committing the defendant for trial, adjourn the hearing of the summary charge until after the case in the Crown Court is determined.[3]

Would it be a good riposte to the charge of assaulting a constable that the defendant did not know that the man he was hitting was a constable?

No. The defendant is allowed to say that he was not guilty of assault—for example, because he reasonably believed that he had to act in self-defence.[4] But, given the assault, he is not allowed to say that he did not know the person he hit was a policeman; so the offence is one of half *mens rea*. If, for example, the defendant assaulted a person who unknown to him was a plain clothes detective, he can be convicted of the offence under the Police Act even though he had no means of knowing the status of the person he was assaulting.[5]

Isn't that very unjust? If a detective in plain clothes wishes to receive the special protection given by the law to policemen, surely he should show his warrant card. If he chooses to remain incognito, there is no reason why the defendant should be convicted of the special offence.

The rule is a remnant of the principle, formerly advocated but now generally abandoned, that an intent to commit a moral wrong, or a lesser crime, is sufficient *mens rea* to convict of a crime.[6] The rule in respect of assaulting a constable is anomalous, and its abolition has been recommended by the CLRC.[7]

What is meant by "in the execution of his duty"? Does it mean that the policeman must be on duty?

The question is whether he is doing what he may lawfully do in his capacity of a policeman. He may be on duty and yet not acting in the execution of his duty, because he may be acting unlawfully. The courts have not yet had to decide the delightful converse question, whether an assault upon a constable who is off duty is an assault upon a constable in the execution of his duty if the constable would have been acting in the execution of his duty if he had been on duty![8]

If the court holds that the officer was acting outside his duty, because he was acting illegally, I suppose the defendant can still be convicted of a common assault on him if his hitting the officer was unjustified?

Yes, but the police are reluctant to add a charge of assault, because this gives the defendant the right of trial.

---

[3] For a criticism of the law see Coase in 144 JPN 441. If, however, the defendant in the case put above were resisting a lawful arrest, he could be charged with an assault upon B in order to resist lawful arrest under OAPA 1861 s.38. Unlike the charge of assaulting a constable this is an either way offence, so that magistrates could commit for trial upon it. See CLA 1977 s.16 and Sched. 2. According to the CLRC, the offence should not be charged where the summary offence is sufficient: 14th Report, para. 181.

[4] *Kenlin* v. *Gardiner* [1967] 2 QB 510; cp. *Mark* [1961] Crim.LR 173; Zuckerman in 88 LQR 246, 263. For self-defence see § 23.5.

[5] *Albert* v. *Lavin* [1981] 2 WLR 1070, 1 All ER 628, 72 CAR 178, following earlier authorities. Intention can even be transferred from a private citizen to a constable: *MacBride* v. *Turnock* [1964] Crim.LR 456.

[6] The rule was stated by Bramwell B, delivering the minority judgment in *Prince*, § .12 n. 13.

[7] 14th Report, para. 172.

[8] See 146 JPN 103.

Doesn't the reference to the policeman's duty mean what the policeman is bound to do, rather than merely what it is proper for him to do?

The courts give it the latter, and wider, meaning. The phrase is interpreted to refer to the functions of the police in arresting, searching, asking questions, setting traps, seizing evidence, maintaining the peace, directing traffic, and so on—anything lawful that the police choose to do as policemen.[9] The slightest act of interference with the police in these circumstances is likely to be held an obstruction. But the officer must not be acting unlawfully. He must not, for instance, be trespassing[10] or committing an assault.

Suppose the defendant admits that he knew he was belabouring a police officer, but says that he did not know the officer was acting in the execution of his duty?

What is the execution of duty by the police is, in the abstract, a question of law. It is taken to be part of the criminal law, and the citizen could not defend himself by saying that he did not know this part of the law.[11]

The rule about ignorance of the criminal law operates with great rigour in this application, because the legal powers of the police (in entering premises, seizing goods, interfering the person) are in doubt on many particulars—the courts themselves are uncertain about them.[12] In effect the position is that no one can safely use force against the police, because he cannot—or can rarely—be certain that the police have not the right to detain him, enter his premises, or seize his goods, as they claim to do—or will not be given that right *ex post facto* by the judiciary. Even if the defendant sets up a mistake of fact, such that if the fact had been as he believed the officer would have been acting outside his duty, still if the defendant is guilty of assaulting the officer he is, almost certainly, guilty also of assaulting him *in the execution of his duty*, this being as much a matter of strict liability as the fact that he is assaulting an officer.

It is generally regarded as oppressive to charge this offence of assaulting the police if the assault is technical or trivial; here the better practice is to charge the summary offence under the Police Act of wilfully obstructing a constable in the execution of his duty.[13] This offence is interpreted very widely. Although, under the statute, it is only summary, it extensively overlaps the common law offence of obstructing justice, which is indictable. The two offences have been developed by the courts into a barbed-wire entanglement protecting the operations of the police and the courts from all manner of interferences. They cannot be studied in detail here.[14]

The requirement of wilfulness for the offence of obstructing the police

---

[9] See the authorities collected by Gibbons in [1983] Crim.LR 25–28.

[10] *Davis* v. *Lisle* [1936] 2 KB 434; *Morris* v. *Beardmore* [1981] AC 446; Ross in [1977] Crim.LR 191.

[11] § 23.5 n. 7.

[12] See the article by Austin, n. 3 above.

[13] For the offence see Police Act s.51 (3). An indictable form exists at common law, but is now never prosecuted. On the statutory offence see [1975] Crim.LR 430 ff.; Ursula Ross in [1977] Crim.LR 187; R C Austin in [1982] Curr.LProb. 187; § 3.2 at nn. 2–5, 8. The obstruction offence does not give the police power of summary arrest, though this is often misunderstood: see Austin, *op. cit.* at 188.

[14] See [1975] Crim.LR 430, 479, 608; Law Commission, Working Paper No. 62, *Offences relating to the Administration of Justice*.

means that a mistake of fact by the defendant as to the official status of the person he is obstructing can be a defence[15]; but once again a mistake of law (e.g. as to what is the officer's duty) is not a defence.

Suppose that the police want to interview me about a crime, either because I am a witness or or because I am possibly the culprit, and I refuse to talk to them. Am I guilty of obstructing them in their constabulary duty?

No. Apart from certain powers of arrest and detention, to be considered later, the police cannot force themselves upon people in order to interview them, and they have no power to compel answers to be given to their questions.

But it is part of the duty of the police to investigate crime. How is it that I do not commit obstruction if I refuse to help them in their investigations?

The answer I would like to give you is: because an obstruction of the police means an active obstruction, not a failure to help them. Regrettably, the courts have developed a doctrine of obstruction by non-cooperation, so this is not the right legal answer.

It is clear that when the offence of wilfully obstructing a constable first appeared on the statute-book it was intended to deal only with physical obstructions, which is how the Scottish judges still interpret it. But the English judges conceived the idea that an obstruction can be non-physical, which means that they have been able to bring extensive new areas of conduct under control. For example, as we have seen, they are able to punish people who frustrate the police by warning offenders of their presence.[16] So the question was raised whether an obstruction can be brought about by an omission.

At first the courts held not, and this is shown by the much misunderstood case of *Rice* v. *Connolly*.[17] A Divisional Court there reached an impeccable conclusion for a reason that was slightly flawed but substantially sound. The impeccable conclusion was that a citizen who refuses to answer the questions of the police is not guilty of wilfully obstructing them in the execution of their duty.[18] The slightly peccable reason, contained in the leading judgment delivered by Lord Parker CJ, was that the offence requires wilfulness, which implies an absence of lawful excuse; and the citizen has a lawful excuse for not answering questions, presumably because of his "right of silence." The objection to this line of argument is, first, that questions of excuse have nothing to do with the mental state of wilfulness.[19] Secondly, the logical and proper reason why a failure to answer the questions of the police is not an obstruction is not because of any specific right the citizen has but simply because an "obstruction" must be taken to mean an active obstruction, not a mere

---

15 *Ostler* v. *Elliott* [1980] Crim.LR 584. On the requirement of wilfulness in general see Lidstone in [1983] Crim.LR 31.

16 § 3.2 at nn. 2–5.

17 [1966] 2 QB 498.

18 Cp. *Dibble* v. *Ingleton* [1972] 1 QB 480 at 488, where it was said that obstruction cannot be committed by a failure to act.

19 § 9.10 at n. 5.

failure to co-operate. If we are to be put under a legal duty to help the police, it must be by an Act of Parliament; and Parliament should say in what respects we are required to help the police on their request, and it should provide proper exemptions, and name the appropriate penalty for refusal. The job ought not to be done by judicial "interpretation" of the obstruction offence, which was obviously designed to do nothing more than prevent active obstructions.

To be fair to Lord Parker, although he started on the wrong foot he arrived at the right conclusion, because he said: "Though every citizen has a moral duty . . . to assist the police, he has no legal duty to that effect."

So far, all is fairly clear. Unfortunately, the courts in their anxiety to uphold the actions of the police are now using *Rice* v. *Connolly* to reach a result that is the reverse of Lord Parker's conclusion. They do this by taking a single sentence out of context, and not even reading it properly. Lord Parker said that "to 'obstruct' is to do any act which makes it more difficult for the police to carry out their duty." This does not mean, as is sometimes supposed, that everything making it more difficult etc. is an obstruction. For one thing, Lord Parker said "any *act*." For another, he was obviously speaking only of the lawful activities of the police. But the courts nowadays seem almost to say that because the police are doing something or other, therefore they must be doing it lawfully.

The following cases show the steady accretion to the powers of the police that is taking place by the judicial construction of this offence. They show that the police can require the active co-operation of the citizen in two important spheres of action: in preventing offences, and in protecting life and property, so that a refusal by the citizen to help them in these two matters is an obstruction.

> When a person obstructs the highway by congregating with others in a demonstration, and fails to go away when told by the police to move on, he may be charged with obstructing the highway or, alternatively, with obstructing the police, since it is the duty of the police to remove obstructions to the highway.[20] And when a person has the keys of a car that is obstructing the highway, and refuses to surrender them to the police who wish to move the car, he obstructs the police by refusing to give the keys up.[21]
>
> Since the police have the duty to prevent offences, and particularly breaches of the peace, an officer may lawfully require a person to desist from provocative (though lawful) behaviour, if this reasonably seems to be the only way of preventing a breach of the peace by others; and if the person so addressed refuses to desist he is guilty of obstruction.[22] Although it may seem right in the abstract that the police should have this power, they have sometimes been allowed to claim a fear of breach of the peace on indefensibly tenuous grounds, merely because the defendant was addressing a meeting or distributing pamphlets.[23]
>
> Quite apart from their power to prevent offences, the police are invested by the courts with a general power to protect life or property; and in the exercise of this power they may even direct the citizen to commit what would normally be a minor offence, and prosecute him for obstruction if he refuses.[24]

It may be thought that these cases generally produce a socially

---

[20] *Parkhurst* v. *Jarvis* (1910) 101 LT 946, 74 JP 64; cp. § 22.6 n. 1.
[21] *Stunt* v. *Bolton* [1972] RTR 435, noted in Crim.LR 562.
[22] *Humphries* v. *Connor* (1864) 17 Ir.CLR 1.
[23] *Duncan* v. *Jones* [1936] KB 218; *Dass* v. *Rennie* [1961] Crim.LR 396.
[24] *Johnson* v. *Phillips* § 26.5 at n. 8.

acceptable result, but the limits of the principle remain obscure. Since the notion of an omission makes no sense in the absence of a duty to act, one might have supposed that it was for Parliament to provide a list of these legal duties imposed upon people, not for the judges to make up the duties as cases come before them. Parliament has, in fact, provided some specific offences of failing to comply with the orders of the police,[25] which seems to indicate an opinion that specific legislation is necessary. This opinion is supported by the fact the giving of powers to the police involves sensitive issues of civil liberty. The courts recognise this in generally continuing to affirm that although it is an important function of the police to obtain evidence of offences, a person commits no offence in refusing to answer questions.[26] But on at least one occasion the principle was obscured.

> Two police officers attempted to question two men on the street. One of the men became abusive and tried to walk away. He was convicted of obstructing the officers in the execution of their duty, and the conviction was upheld on appeal.[27] No satisfactory reasons were given. If a man is not obliged to stay while he is being questioned by the police (which is undoubted law), it is impossible to see why his refusal to stay, accompanying his refusal by abuse and threats, makes him guilty of obstruction.[28] Whatever the defendant threatened, the police could not reasonably have believed that they were in danger of being assaulted, because they knew that all they had to do in order to close the incident was to cease pestering him with unwelcome questions. The decision seems to be the result of the confused idea that because the police are acting in pursuance of their general duty to enforce the law, therefore they have the right to interfere with the liberty of the citizen, as by compelling him to stop to answer questions. In fact the general "duty" of the police to enforce the law operates only within the legal powers and liberties allowed to them.

If the police can rope people in to prevent obstruction of the highway, could they organise a press-gang of passers-by to clear rubble from the street, prosecuting any recalcitrant person for obstructing them in the execution of their duty?

The decisions have concerned only people who were personally obstructing the highway or who (by possessing the keys of an obstructing car) were in a special position to prevent its continuance. Obviously the answer to your question is no. In general, the right of the police to require co-operation to prevent crime has been recognised only against those who

[25] E.g. Public Meeting Act 1908 s.1 as amended (failure to give a constable name and address on demand); RTA 1972 s.159 (driver failing to stop when so required by a constable in uniform; see McConnell in 133 NLJ 29.).

[26] *Rice* v. *Connolly*, n. 17 above; § 8.3 n. 7. On the question whether telling lies to the police in answer to questions is an obstruction see [1975] Crim.LR 481 ff.; Ross in [1977] Crim.LR 195; *George* [1981] Crim.LR 185. It is now held to be an obstruction to hinder the police in their questioning of a third party, e.g. by telling the third party not to answer questions (*Toomey* v. *Johnson* (1967), DC unreported), or by stepping between the police and the person they sought to question (*Rosato* v. *Wilson* (1978), discussed by Murphy in [1978] Crim.LR 474; cp. 128 NLJ 747).

[27] *Ricketts* v. *Cox* [1982] Crim.LR 184. See Lidstone's powerful attack upon the decision in [1983] Crim.LR 29 and 132 NLJ 953. See also *Donnelly* v. *Jackman* § 8.3 at n. 8.

[28] Bailey and Birch in [1982] Crim.LR 484 justify the decision on the ground that the full transcript shows that the defendant uttered threats; but this appears to be irrelevant, for the reason stated in the text above.

were in some way involved in the crime as fomenters or otherwise. But it is not at all clear how far the court's line of reasoning will be pushed; a new departure may be made at any time. The traditional rule, supported by many decisions, is that to justify interference with individuals the police must adduce specific legal authority. It is not enough for them to show that they were performing their general functions.

A special problem concerns trespass to land and buildings. It has always been assumed that although the police have the right to enter premises to prevent a breach of the peace or serious offence,[29] they generally have no such right merely for the purpose of obtaining evidence of past offences; and the correctness of this opinion was confirmed by a decision that it is not an obstruction to deny a police officer entry to premises to search for incriminating evidence when he has no warrant permitting him to do so.[30] Similarly, it has been supposed that a police officer cannot call upon people to help him to make an arrest (unless a breach of the peace has been committed in his presence by two or more persons[31]); and the correctness of this was confirmed by a case of 1861, where it was held that an occupier of premises is not guilty of obstruction if he refuses to help the police to find a criminal who is hiding on his premises.[32] Is this still the law? And does a landlord commit obstruction in refusing to allow the police to search his lodger's belongings for evidence to incriminate the lodger? It seems that in fact the offence of obstruction has never been extended to a person's failure to help the police to make an arrest or collect evidence of crime. So the courts have apparently, in an inarticulate and unsystematic way, arrived at a rough division of the functions of the police for the purpose of deciding what co-operation can be exacted from the public.

§ 9.8. AFFRAY

Affray (from the French *effrayer*, to frighten) is an aggravated physical assault. An ancient offence, it fell into desuetude for centuries, but was dusted off and refurbished by prosecutors and judges in our own time. The chief reason for the revival was that the offence, never having received the attention of Parliament, remains punishable as at common law, with complete discretion as to punishment, whereas conviction on indictment of common assault carries a maximum of one year. Moreover, affray cannot be tried summarily, however trivial the case may appear to the magistrates. Typically, the offence is committed by football rowdies who attack the supporters of a rival team, or by youths milling out of a club or dance-hall

---

[29] Hale, *PC ii 95; Handcock* v. *Baker* (1800) 2 Bos. & Pul. 260, 126 ER 1270; *Thomas* v. *Sawkins* § 22.6 at n. 22; *McGowan* v. *Chief Constable of Kingston-upon-Hull* [1968] Crim.LR 34 (an extraordinary decision upon the facts).

[30] *Syce* v. *Harrison* [1980] Crim.LR 649.

[31] It is an offence at common law for a person to refuse without lawful excuse to help a constable to quell a riot when he has seen a breach of the peace committed by two or more persons and there is a reasonable necessity for calling on for help: *Brown* (1841) Car. & M 314, 174 ER 522. Presumably the refusal could now be punished instead as an obstruction.

[32] *Green* (1861) 8 Cox 441.

late at night. A common sentence in a serious case is 3 years,[1] though in still more serious cases it has been as high as 8 years.

In a series of decisions the courts eliminated restrictions formerly thought to attach to the offence. It is now defined as an unlawful physical assault involving such a degree of violence that persons of reasonably firm character are likely to be terrified.

Formerly the offence was defined in terms of "fighting," but it is now held that it can be committed if one person attacks another person who merely defends himself (and therefore does not participate in the affray); or it can be committed by an attack that is not resisted, so that there is no "fight" at all.[2] The attack may take place in public or in private.[3]

Doubt surrounds the (potentially) terrified spectators in the definition. If bystanders are present, it is enough that, in the words of Lord Hailsham in *Taylor*,[4] the violence is "such as to be *calculated* to terrify (that is, might reasonably be expected to terrify)." Lord Reid added his concurring opinion, saying:

> "If people are present it is not necessary to prove by their evidence that they were terrified. It is enough if the circumstances are such that ordinary people like them would have been terrified. I say 'would' not 'might' have been."

If it need not be proved that anyone was terrified, it would seem to follow that no onlooker need be there, provided that there is a reasonable likelihood of a third party coming on the scene. This conclusion was drawn by a circuit judge.[5] The Law Commission, in its Working Paper on the subject, went further, and proposed legislation to the effect that the disturbance must be such as would reasonably have caused any other person, if present, to be put in fear of his personal safety; on this proposal it need not be shown that another person was reasonably likely to be present, and no mental element by the combatants as to the fear of a hypothetical bystander need be proved.[6] Even apart from legislation it is quite possible that the courts will continue along this road.

Thoroughly watered down in this way, the crime of affray comes to little more than a device for setting the courts free from any limit of punishment for major assaults.

However, a charge of affray gives the prosecution two technical advantages over the law of assault.

1 Where a general fight has arisen between opposing groups, an indictment in terms of assault would have to charge named persons with assault upon named persons (or upon persons unknown). If the indictment is to reflect the extent of the criminality, it would probably

---

[1] [1967] Crim. LR 490; [1973] *ibid.* 127.
[2] *Taylor* [1973] AC 964.
[3] *Button* [1966] AC 591.
[4] Note 2 above.
[5] *Farnhill* [1982] Crim.LR 38. Discordant provisional views had been expressed by Lords Hailsham and Reid in *Taylor*; see 1st edn 169–170. The actual or potential spectators must be persons not involved in the fight, whether as aggressors or defenders: *Farnhill*, above. Spectators of an unorganised fight are not guilty of participation unless there is evidence that they have encouraged the participants. See *Allan* [1965] 1 QB 130 and below § 15.7 n. 1.
[6] Working Paper No. 82 pp. 16–26, 55–86.

have to contain many counts charging different assaults against different groups of participants. The prosecutor might find difficulty in charging all the incidents with sufficient precision in advance of the trial, and the indictment would be unwieldy. Affray is a single offence for all the participants[7], and, provided it is shown that the defendant took part in the affray, the prosecution need not show what degree of injury, if any, he inflicted upon any particular person.[8]

2 Another procedural advantage of charging an affray arises when the fight is of long duration: an affray may be charged in a single count as continuing over a period of time, and it is immaterial that different persons join it at different times.[9] Assaults, on the other hand, would have to be charged separately in different counts.

Although the rules of affray might have some justification in an offence of low or medium gravity, they are remarkable in a crime punishable with life imprisonment. The Law Commission has proposed a statutory form of the offence which would impose virtually no restrictions on the prosecution and would still admit of very heavy punishment.[10]

The only real restriction on the offence at present rests on prosecutorial discretion. Having stripped the offence of most legal restrictions, the courts found that it was being charged for public-house brawls; and examining magistrates generally have no choice but to commit for trial at the Crown Court, even though the case does not justify it. The judges have now said that prosecutors should think hard before charging an affray, and should do so only in serious cases that are not far short of a riot.[11] This is a poor substitute for a proper legal definition.

The books suggest another form of affray: a display of force, in such manner that a person of reasonable firm character is likely to be terrified. The "display of force" is generally taken to mean brandishing a weapon. Both Lord Hailsham and Lord Reid accepted this form of the offence in *Taylor*,[12] though the point was not necessary for the decision. The Law Commission states that charges of this type are apparently not now brought, and proposes that it should be omitted from a statutory definition.[13]

§ 9.9. OTHER ASSAULTS, BREACHES OF THE PEACE, AND THREATS

Various other elements may affect the maximum punishment for assault and other similar crimes. Magistrates are given extra powers of punishment if a common assault is committed against a female or a boy under 14.[1] An

---

[7] As to the law of evidence see *Sidhu* [1976] Crim.LR 379.

[8] In *Chorley* (1978) 142 NLJ 519, where all the youths involved in an affray were sentenced to 3 years, the CA said: "Each must be prepared to accept what might be the uniform punishment for all, without measuring his respective contribution."

[9] *Woodrow* (1959) 43 CAR 105. But it seems that a single offence of affray is not committed where different fights take place in different parts of a crowd, in different streets, at different times, although the crowd continues together throughout: *John Jones* (1974) 59 CAR 120.

[10] See the critical discussion and valuable counter-proposals by A T H Smith in [1982] Crim.LR 487.

[11] *Crimlis* [1976] Crim.LR 693.

[12] Note 2 above. See the comment upon Lord Hailsham's words in 1st edn 171 n. 11.

[13] But see *Hamilton* (1980) 42 JPN 145, reported only on sentence. In *Meade* (1903) 19 TLR 540 a statute was invoked that has since been repealed. See J R Spencer in [1973] CLJ 186–187.

[1] OAPA 1861 s.43.

assault made with intent to rob is an indictable offence carrying a possible life sentence.[2]

Assaults may be charged under other names. There are statutory offences of attempting to choke etc. a person, or to chloroform etc. him, with intent to commit an indictable offence.[3] Assaults committed by the driving of vehicles are generally charged as driving offences. Cruelty to children may be prosecuted as an ordinary offence against the person, such as an assault or manslaughter or murder. But it is also covered by a special statute, the Children and Young Persons Act 1933 s.1 (as amended), creating summary offences of cruelty and wilful neglect.[4] The social and medical aspects of cruelty to children are of great importance, but limitations of space prevent them from being considered here. Mention may also be made of an offence of ill-treating a patient in a psychiatric hospital.[5]

The law reacts strongly against general public disorder, as we have already seen for the crime of affray. The offence of *unlawful assembly* may be briefly defined as an assembly of three or more persons who intend to commit a crime by open force.[6] It is a crime at common law, carrying a fine and imprisonment at discretion and not triable summarily. This is now rarely charged, but charges are still occasionally brought for the form known as a *riot*, where the unlawful assembly begins to carry out its unlawful purpose. Both offences are open to the same objections as affray, being far too heavy in maximum punishment when the requirements of the offence are so easily satisfied and when the guilt of a particular participant may be minimal. As with affray, the Law Commission has broached proposals for putting these offences on a statutory footing, but the Commission's ideas on the subject are too like the present law to allay the apprehensions of those who see danger in such provisions.[7]

Lesser charges may be brought for other offences arising out of public disorder. Particular mention may be made of the Prevention of Crime Act 1953, which makes it an either way offence where:

> "any person without lawful authority or reasonable excuse, the proof whereof shall lie on him, has with him in any public place any offensive weapon."

The terms used in this definition are themselves defined, both by the Act

---

[2] Theft Act 1968 s.8 (2). Other aggravated assaults, rarely charged, are in OAPA 1861 ss.36–37, 39–40; cp. Russell, 12th edn i 684 ff.

[3] OAPA 1861 ss.21, 22.

[4] See Clarke Hall and Morrison on *Children*, 9th edn 231 ff. On the offence of wilful neglect, *Sheppard* [1981] AC 394, overruling previous cases, attached a fairly reasonable meaning to "wilfully"; for a remaining difficulty see [1981] CLJ 257–258, 266; [1982] *ibid.* 288.

[5] Mental Health Act 1959 s.126; 24 JCr.L 93. A single assault can constitute ill-treatment: *Holmes* [1979] Crim. LR 52.

[6] *Per* Lord Denning in *R* v. *Chief Constable of Devon* [1982] QB at 471G. Some definitions of unlawful assembly include a meeting with intent to break the peace, and a meeting in such manner as to give reasonably firm and courageous persons reasonable cause to fear a breach of the peace. For the meaning of breach of the peace see § 22.2 at nn. 15–18. Lawton LJ said: "Comments . . . which seem to show that an unlawful assembly can occur without the fact of either violence or tumult do not accurately state the modern law:" *R* v. *Chief Constable*, above, at 474A.

[7] See A T H Smith in [1982] Crim.LR 490–494.

itself and by a considerable body of case-law.[8] The firearms legislation controls the possession of firearms and creates a number of serious offences in relation to their improper use.[9] A police officer who reasonably fears an immediate breach of the peace may arrest the person responsible, and wilfully to obstruct him in the execution of his duty is an offence.[10] Even when people commit summary offences the fact of riot may cause the punishment to be much more severe than it would normally be.[11]

A string of offences concerns the use of explosives for criminal ends.[12] The Post Office Act has a provision about dangerous things sent by post.[13] There are various offences of endangering passengers by rail[14]; and it is an offence maliciously to impede escape from wrecks or to impede one who is endeavouring to save the life of a person escaping from a wreck.[15]

Outside the law of assault, our law of threats is a thing of shreds and patches. It is an offence, punishable with 10 years' imprisonment, to threaten to kill the person to whom the threat is made or anyone else, without lawful excuse[16]; but this does not touch threats to torture or maim, which, if made merely by word of mouth or in writing, are generally no offence at all (unless assault can be committed by words, which is far from certain). Menaces over the telephone are an offence under the British Telecommunications Act 1981.[17] Threats in order to obtain property are blackmail (Chap. 37). Bomb hoaxes constitute an offence under the Criminal Law Act 1977 s.51. Picketing premises is an offence where it involves intimidation or "watching and besetting" a house or place of work[18]; but this is rarely invoked.

The Public Order Act 1936 s.5 (as amended) creates a summary offence of what may be broadly described as threatening behaviour. It is committed by a person who, in any public place or at any public meeting, uses *threatening, abusive or insulting* (not merely offensive[19]) words or behaviour with intent to provoke a breach of the peace[20] or whereby a breach of the peace is likely. The offence is much used by prosecutors, even for assaults. In an ordinary case the court is very ready (sometimes too ready) to find a likelihood of a breach of the peace. But where only the defendant and the police are present, it will refuse to do so, since it will not believe that the police will be provoked to illegal violence.[21] The Public

[8] See Brownlie in [1961] Crim. LR 19; Ashworth in [1976] *ibid.* 725; Smith and Hogan, 4th edn 392 ff.; below § 23.3. See also Public Order Act 1936 s.4. There is special legislation restricting the sale and possession of flick knives: Restriction of Offensive Weapons Acts 1959 and 1961; see *Gibson* v. *Wales* [1983] Crim.LR 113.

[9] See §19.6 n. 2.

[10] See § .7 n. 3.

[11] See *Munn* (1981) 146 JPN 191.

[12] OAPA 1861 ss.28–30, 64; Explosive Substances Act 1883 ss.2, 3 (as amended), 4.

[13] Post Office Act 1953 s.11.

[14] OAPA 1861 ss.32–34 as amended; Malicious Damage Act 1861 s.36 as amended. Cp. Russell, 12th edn Chap. 36.

[15] OAPA 1861 s.17.

[16] OAPA 1861 s. 16 as substituted by CLA 1977 Sched. 12. See *Cousins* [1982] QB 526.

[17] S. 49 (1). Presumably "heavy breathing" could be accounted a menace.

[18] Conspiracy and Protection of Property Act 1875 s.7. See A T H Smith in [1982] Crim.LR 494.

[19] See *Cozens* v. *Brutus*, § 2.6.

[20] On breach of the peace see § 22.2 at nn. 15–18.

[21] *Parkin* v. *Norman* [1982] Crim.LR 528.

Order Act 1936 section 5A, introduced by the Race Relations Act 1976 section 70, has a similar provision in respect of racial hatred (an indictable offence).[22]

Over-exuberant bus conductors and passengers are specially catered for by statutory regulations which provide a widely-drawn offence of disorderly conduct on public service vehicles.[23] It is an offence against these regulations to jostle in a bus-queue. There are several other statutes and many bylaws on disorderly conduct. Apprehended domestic violence can be dealt with by injunction.[24] Remember, too, the possibility of binding over.

We have two offences of harassment. It is provided by statute that a landlord commits an offence if he harasses a "residential occupier" with intent to cause him to give up occupation, or with intent to make him refrain from exercising a right that he has as tenant.[25] This covers not only physical "winkling" by locking the tenant out, but threatening him and his family with violence, or withdrawing services.[26]

The harassment of contractual debtors is also an offence.[27] It can be committed by over-frequent demands for payment, if they are calculated to subject the debtor or members of his family or household to alarm, distress or humiliation. Widely as the statute is drawn, the courts will probably administer it with due restraint, though the use of a van marked "Debt Collection" in visiting the debtor would undoubtedly call forth a penalty. Parliament has not yet found itself able to make harassment by journalists an offence.

§ 9.10. OFFENCES OF POISONING

The poisoner usually works in the traditional Borgia fashion, poisoning the chalice which the victim then unsuspectingly puts to his own lips. This does not involve an assault,[1] but it is one of two statutory crimes of poisoning

---

[22] For criticisms of the section as being ineffective in practice see Bindman in 132 NLJ 299.

[23] Public Service Vehicles (Conduct of Drivers, Conductors and Passengers) Regulations, SR & O 1936 No. 619 as amended, 1946 No. 457, continued in force by RTA 1960 s.267.

[24] § 1.9 n. 2.

[25] Protection from Eviction Act 1977 s.1. See *Phekoo* § 6.1 n. 17 and note, [1979] Crim. LR 167. The offence is triable either way, so if the landlord has used violence in order to enter it may be preferable (in order to stop him claiming jury trial) to charge the purely summary offence of violent entry under CLA 1977 s.6 (1), § 41.7. See generally Yell in 145 JPN 664. Cp., for caravan sites, Caravan Sites Act 1968 s.3.

[26] The landlord's success in *Westminster CC* v. *Peart* [1968] Crim.LR 504 was apparently due to a mistake made by the court as to the law of pleading: see *Abrol* [1972] Crim.LR 318. The Committee on the Rent Acts received "horrifying stories" of harassment of landlords by tenants to prevent them from pursuing their remedies (34 MLR 431), but no offence of this character was created.

[27] Administration of Justice Act 1970 s.40. In addition, subs. (1) (*b*) makes it an offence falsely to represent that criminal proceedings lie for failure to pay a debt; (*c*) penalises a false representation that one is authorised in some official capacity to claim payment; and (*d*) penalises false representations that a document has some official character. Unfair debt-collecting methods may be reported to the local trading standards officer, and the Office of Fair Trading may then put the debt collector out of business by revoking his licence under the Consumer Credit Act 1974.

[1] *Hanson* (1849) 2 C & K 912, 175 ER 383.

under the Offences against the Person Act 1861. Both specify an act of maliciously administering to any person (or causing to be taken by any person) any poison or other noxious thing.

The expressions "administering" and "causing to be taken" both mean that the poison must actually enter the victim's system: it is not enough that his food is poisoned, if he does not eat it. There is an "administering" even though the poison is unknowingly taken by the victim himself.[2] Generally, therefore, "administering" and "causing to be taken" are convertible expressions. But a possible small difference is that a poison is presumably administered if it is brought into injurious contact with the victim's skin,[3] although this is perhaps not causing it to be "taken."

What is a "poison or other noxious thing"?

Before answering this question we need to consider the more specific features of the two offences. Maliciously administering a noxious thing to any person:

1 so as thereby to endanger the life of such person or to inflict[4] upon him grievous bodily harm is punishable with imprisonment for 10 years[5] (s.23);
2 *with intent* to injure, aggrieve or annoy such person is punishable with imprisonment for 5 years (s. 24).[6]

The broad difference is that it is the graver offence when g.b.h. is actually inflicted, and the lesser offence when it amounts merely to an attempt to do harm (though with the actual administration of the poison). The lesser offence does not require that harm be actually done. Also, the lesser offence is committed where the intent is merely to annoy.[7]

To return to your question of what is noxious: if the drug has endangered life or inflicted g.b.h. under section 23 there can be no question but that it is noxious.

The interpretation of the word is more difficult if the drug has merely been administered with intent to annoy contrary to section 24. The rule as now settled in *Marcus*[8] gives the word a wide meaning.

> Until this case it had not been definitively settled that "noxious" covered ordinary sleeping tablets, administered for the purpose of

---

[2] *Harley* (1830) 4 Car. & P 369, 172 ER 744.

[3] In any case it is an offence under s.23 to use a corrosive or destructive substance with intent to burn or cause g.b.h. to any person. This provision was used in an unreported case of 1973 when a thwarted lover sprayed paint stripper on the crutch of his beloved's underclothes.

[4] Notice that the word "inflict" is here used in the Act to cover cases where there is clearly no battery. This is an argument against the decision in *Clarence*.

[5] If poison is administered (or even if it is merely mixed with food or drink that another is expected to consume), with intent to murder, this is an attempt to murder punishable with imprisonment for life under OAPA 1861 s.11. Also, if the intent is to cause grievous bodily harm short of death, and the poison has this effect, the administration is punishable with imprisonment for life under s.18.

[6] The punishment under s.24 now depends upon the Penal Servitude Act 1891. To administer or attempt to administer chloroform or other stupefying drug in furtherance of any indictable offence, even though no harm results, is punishable with imprisonment for life: OAPA 1861 s.22. The narrower offence under the Sexual Offences Act 1956 s.4 (1) seems to be unnecessary.

[7] Although s.24 is in effect an attempt provision, there is no reason why a person should not be charged with an attempt to commit it where the poison is not in fact administered.

[8] [1981] 1 WLR 774, 2 All ER 833, 73 CAR 49.

> making the victim fall into an unwanted sleep. In *Marcus* the Court of Appeal announced that a substance is noxious under section 24 even if it is merely "obnoxious, i.e. objectionable or unwholesome." (The word "obnoxious" as an equivalent for "noxious" appeared in a dictionary.) Consequently it was held that sleeping tablets administered in a normal dose are noxious; and the court said that even causing an unsuspecting victim to take a bottle of ginger beer with a snail in the bottom would constitute the offence, because of the revulsion that would be caused to the drinker on discovering the snail after drinking the ginger beer.

Can I have first pounce on the snail? Thank you. Noxious doesn't mean obnoxious, whatever the dictionary says. A nice lamb chop would be obnoxious to a vegetarian, but it would do him a power of good if someone got him to eat it by pretending that it was a clever concoction of soya. And an innocuous snail isn't noxious.

The last remark of the court, anent the snail in the bottle, certainly goes beyond anything that had been decided or even suggested before. Whether or not "noxious" sometimes means "obnoxious," it should be elementary that a dictionary only gives approximate synonyms for words, with perhaps an indication of the shades of meaning that they may possess in different contexts. If the court had paid attention to the present context it would have found that the statute not only makes "noxious" an alternative to "poisonous" (a strong word) but makes it alternative to "destructive" (also a strong word). One would have thought that in the context of the section "noxious" carries at least a whiff of the meaning of "poisonous" and "destructive." If this is so, a solution of decomposed snail doing no harm is not noxious.

Nevertheless, it was not an intolerable extension of the meaning of the word to make it cover sleeping tablets, which can induce an unwanted unconsciousness and therefore affect bodily (including mental) function. The idea that a harmless solution of snail is noxious merely because it is repugnant to the drinker goes too far, and the point was not before the court in *Marcus*. A thing should not be held to be noxious unless it either is harmful or interferes with bodily function (even though only slightly and temporarily).

What about lacing a teetotaller's lemonade with a couple of measures of gin?

It may be argued that the social acceptance of alcohol prevents it from being accounted noxious in law. But it interferes with bodily function, and here is known to be unwelcome to the recipient. Presumably the question would be left to the free discretion of the jury, turning them into *ad hoc* lawmakers.

Couldn't the joker say that in his opinion gin is a blessing to mankind and not noxious?

The court would undoubtedly hold that if the defendant knows what he is (or may be) administering, and knows that it has (or may have) the effect that makes the jury find it to be noxious, then he cannot say that in his opinion the effect is not noxious. Any mistake he makes is one of law.

It has sometimes been thought that a recognised poison is noxious even though administered in a harmless quantity.[9] This opinion always had its difficulties, and it seems now to be disapproved by a dictum in *Marcus* that the quantity of the drug must be considered.[10] Some recognised poisons are harmless (and even beneficial) when taken in very small doses. To administer a harmlessly small dose of a recognised poison is equivalent (for the purpose of section 24) to administering water, and it should not be an offence under the section. If the person who administers such a dose believes it to be harmful he would be guilty of attempting to administer a poison.

But he wasn't attempting to administer a poison, because it wasn't a poison.

It was a poison in his own mind. The type of argument you have advanced was successful when the "impossibility" rule held sway, before the Criminal Attempts Act 1981 (§ 7.6). The intention of the Act was to get rid of this rule.

A difficult intermediate case is where the would-be poisoner administers a first harmless dose of a poison that has cumulative effect, his intention being to follow this up with further doses in order to harm the victim. If the first dose is harmless it would seem that the poisoner's only guilt is for an attempt.[11]

It need hardly be said that the noxious thing need not be in solid or liquid form. Coal gas[12] and electricity[13] are noxious things within the sections.

It appears that a drug may be noxious in law although it is not likely to cause death or g.b.h. So suppose that D has administered something that he knew to be noxious, because of its soporific effect. He did not know that it was likely to cause death or g.b.h., but he unknowingly gave an overdose and so caused g.b.h. Would he be liable under section 23?

The difficulty is the familiar one of determining the elements of the offence to which a requirement of *mens rea* applies. It is possible to read section 23 as dividing into two distinct parts.

(1) "Whosoever shall unlawfully and maliciously administer to or

---

[9] There is a somewhat ambiguous dictum of Lord Cockburn CJ in *Hennah* (1877) 13 Cox 547 which may be read as meaning this; however, he also said that "unless the thing is noxious in the quantity administered, it seems exceedingly difficult to say that logically there has been a noxious thing administered." Cp. *per* Field J in *Cramp* (1880) 5 QBD 307 (a decision on the g.b.h. under section 23 there can be no question but that it is noxious.

[10] Cp. *Cato* [1976] 1 WLR at 119G, where Lord Widgery CJ said that "an article is not to be described as noxious merely because it has a portentiality for harm if taken in overdose." "Overdose" tends to beg the question, so perhaps the statement can be amended to read: "if taken in a larger quantity than that administered."

[11] For a conviction of attempt see *White* § 17.5 at n. 12.

[12] *Cunningham* [1957] 2 QB 396.

[13] *Donald*, The Times, May 9, 1955.

cause to be administered to or taken by another person any poison or other destructive or noxious thing, (2) so as thereby to endanger the life of such person, or so as thereby to inflict upon such person any grievous bodily harm. . . . "

On this reading, the requirement of malice applies only to the elements in (1), and the elements in (2) can be interpreted as being of strict liability. But the principle of construction contended for in previous chapters is that a serious crime should impliedly require *mens rea* as to all the external elements, in the absence of an expression of contrary intention, and that *a fortiori* a statutory requirement of *mens rea* should apply to all the other elements of the offence, again in the absence of a contrary intent (which is not expressed in the present section). It is not permissible to split a statutory offence in two and apply a requirement of a mental element only to the half in which the requirement happens to be expressed. Authorities for this proposition are *David Smith* (§ 6.2 n. 6) and some of the cases on offences of knowledge (§ 6.3). Unfortunately, the authorities on section 23 are in a difficult state.

The case of *Cunningham*,[14] was at first thought to settle all these problems in relation to statutory offences of malice.

Roy Cunningham wrenched away a gas coin meter to steal the contents, and left coal gas escaping from the pipe, which partially asphyxiated a woman who was asleep next door. The Court of Criminal Appeal held that, notwithstanding that Cunningham was engaged on a criminal enterprise, he was not guilty of maliciously causing a noxious thing to be taken, under section 23, in the absence of foresight that it would or might be taken. The court required proof that "the accused has foreseen that the particular kind of harm might be done and yet has gone on to take the risk of it. . . . The word 'maliciously' in a statutory crime postulates foresight of consequence."

This dictum is not as specific upon the mental element under section 23 as may appear at first sight. "The particular kind of harm" and the "consequence" referred to by the court may conceivably mean merely the harm and consequence of taking a noxious thing into the body. On this reading the court was considering only the defendant's foresight that the coal gas (which of course he knew to be noxious) might be inhaled by someone, and did not require foresight that the noxious thing would endanger life or might inflict g.b.h. But the more natural reading is that the court was referring to both elements: not merely to the noxious nature of the substance and its inhalation but to the harm and consequence specified in the section as a result of taking the substance, namely the danger to life or g.b.h.

If this is the correct interpretation of *Cunningham*, its effect, unfortunately, has been reduced by the later case of *Cato*.[15]

V produced heroin and syringes and invited Cato to have a "fix" with him. Each took a syringe, filled it to his own taste with a mixture of heroin and water, and was injected by the other. They did this several times during the night, and in the morning V died, there being evidence from which the jury could (and did) infer that the death was a consequence of the administration of the drug. Cato's conviction under section 23, and also of manslaughter, was upheld on appeal.

This was the first time that section 23 was held to apply to the administration of a drug with consent. The decision rests upon the principle that it is not competent to a person to consent to suffer death or grievous bodily harm.

---

[14] [1957] 2 QB 396.

[15] [1976] 1 WLR 110 at 120, 62 CAR 41. The report in [1976] 1 All ER at 269 is slightly defective. For a further discussion of the case in relation to consent see § 25.18 at n. 10.

There are considerable difficulties with it. All the previous cases under the section had concerned an administration without the recipient's consent, and the CLRC thought that the application of the poisoning offence to an administration with consent made in *Cato* should be rejected in any new legislation. The committee took the view that any offence relating to the consensual administration of drugs of abuse should be enacted in the drugs legislation.[16]

Even if the principle is accepted that the consensual administration of a drug can be an offence under section 23, the question remains whether heroin presents the degree of danger specified in section 23. Heroin addiction involves serious physical and mental consequences, but there appears to have been no evidence offered in *Cato* that a single dose, or a short series of doses, was necessarily dangerous, apart from the long-term danger of creating or increasing addiction. The injections did in fact endanger (and more than endanger) the friend's life; but the point as to the mental element remains. Should not conviction under section 23 require proof of a mental element beyond the mere intention to administer heroin?

The trial judge in this case had partly applied *Cunningham*, because he had required the jury to find whether the defendant knew that heroin was likely to do some harm. (This was not fully applying *Cunningham*, if we are right in our interpretation of that case, since *Cunningham* spoke of "the particular kind of harm," and, as already said, the particular kind of harm in section 23 may be thought to be the endangering of life or causing g.b.h.). The jury found that Cato had such knowledge (though on what evidence does not appear). On appeal the Court of Appeal not only affirmed the conviction but held that no direction as to foresight of harm was necessary

The court distinguished *Cunningham*, not (be it noted) as a case where the defendant may not have realised that the stuff would be "administered", but as a case where the injury to the victim was done "indirectly," the gas having escaped into an adjoining house or part of the house.

> "We think in this case where the act was entirely a direct one that the requirement of malice is satisfied if the syringe was deliberately inserted into the body of [V], as it undoubtedly was, and if the appellant knew that the syringe contained a noxious substance."

This is the worst kind of restrictive distinguishing, where an accidental factor present in the earlier case is regarded as part of the *ratio decidendi* merely for the purpose of disregarding the earlier case, although the factor has no logical relevance and the earlier court attached no significance to it. As the Law Commission has pointed out, criticising *Cato*, the distinction means that Cato would not have been regarded as "malicious" if he had offered his friend a glass containing the drug,[17] but was "malicious" because he injected it.[18] There is no rhyme or reason in such a rule. Its sole merit, if the word is appropriate, was that it served to uphold the conviction.

Apart from the common sense of the matter, there were authorities against the distinction. Section 23, in encompassing both administering and causing to be taken, shows that it is meant to cover both direct and indirect causation without discriminating between them. Further, the court took no account of *Mowatt* (§ .3 n. 7). In this case (which, it will be remembered, arose under s.20) the Court of Appeal held that, even in the case of a direct attack on the victim, statutory malice required an awareness of the possibility of causing some harm. It is true that in *Mowatt* the court

---

16 14th Report, Cmnd 7844, para. 190.
17 It is for this reason that secret poisoning is not an assault: above n. 1.
18 Law Com. No. 89 p. 15.

watered down *Cunningham* to the extent necessary to affirm Mowatt's conviction, but it did not go so far as to exclude the question of foresight altogether, even though the harm inflicted was direct. *Cato* waters down not only *Cunningham* but *Mowatt*, and the reason the court gave for distinguishing *Cunningham* did not distinguish *Mowatt*. Both *Mowatt* and *Cato* are open to the objection that they import a considerable measure of strict liability into a crime purportedly dependent on proof of "malice," as well as introducing complexity and artificiality into the law.

We are left in a state of some doubt as to the present law. The court in *Cato* might have decided that section 23 creates an offence of strict liability in respect of the danger involved, but it did not do this. It seemed content to accept that where the noxious thing is indirectly administered *Cunningham* requires that the defendant should have foreseen the danger specified in the last part of section 23. But when the noxious thing is directly administered, such foresight is not required. In view of the weakness of the reasoning in *Cato*, it may perhaps be reconsidered if the point arises again.

Consider the owner of a factory who knows that it is belching out noxious fumes in a populous area. Could he be convicted under section 23 if people suffer grievous bodily harm?

No reason why not. He recklessly causes the noxious thing to be taken. No such prosecution has yet been brought, but conservationists might like to take note.[19]

Could it be an offence under section 23 to communicate a disease?

It was said in *Clarence* (§ .5 n. 1) that "infection is a kind of poisoning. It is the application of an animal poison" (Stephen J). Yet it may seem rather forced to say that the communication of microscopic bacteria or viruses is the administration of a "noxious thing." If this extensive interpretation of "noxious thing" is accepted, it means that Clarence could have been successfully indicted under section 23, assuming that he was reckless as to the communication of venereal disease to his wife. But, as was remarked before, it is not the practice to prosecute in respect of this disease.[20]

Can intention be transferred under the sections?

Yes under section 23, but not under section 24.

This curious point may be elaborated as follows. Suppose that D puts a noxious thing into V1's lemonade, intending to injure him, and the liquid is actually consumed by V2, who suffers grievous bodily harm. D is guilty under section 23, which does not require the person injured to be the person aimed at. The section applies whenever one person maliciously

---

[19] However, if life is not endangered and serious injury is not caused no prosecution would lie under s.23; and none would lie under s.24, which requires intention (being in the nature of an attempt) and cannot be committed recklessly.

[20] The question of policy whether it should be an offence to transmit disease is discussed by Lynch in [1978] Crim. LR 619 ff.: but he does not mention the point in the text above.

administers a noxious thing to "any other person" (V2) so as thereby to endanger the life of "such person" (V2) or to inflict upon "such person" (V2) grievous bodily harm. This formula fits the above facts. The mental element is supplied by the word "maliciously"; but this word is to be interpreted in accordance with the general common law principle permitting of transferred intention, where this is not inconsistent with the wording of the statute. Therefore, it does not matter under section 23 that the intent was in respect of V1.

Contrast the position under section 24. Suppose in the case put that although V2 suffered harm, it was not grievous. Section 23 does not apply because the effects specified therein do not occur, and section 24 does not apply because it requires a malicious administration to "any other person" (V2) with intent to injure "such person" (V2), and here there is no intent to injure V2. The doctrine of transferred intention cannot be applied when this would be inconsistent with the words of the statute.[21]

§ 9.11. FALSE IMPRISONMENT

It is convenient to include this here, although false imprisonment need not involve any injury in the narrow sense of the expression. False imprisonment is the third traditional species of criminal trespass to the person, the other two being assault and battery (psychic and physical assault). Like assault, it is a common law offence; but it differs in that no statute puts a ceiling to the possible punishment. It is, therefore, punishable with imprisonment and fine at discretion. Proceedings for the offence are not brought lightly, because it is punishable only on indictment.

What is a "false imprisonment"?

This is an archaic name for the unlawful detention of a person. It usually involves an application of force to the body, when it amounts also to a physical assault. But false imprisonment is committed by a person who unlawfully turns the key on someone who is already in the room; and here there is no assault.[1] Logically, such an act should not have been regarded as falling within the notion of trespass to the person, but it was made to do so.

Does false imprisonment require physical detention?

False imprisonment is a total restraint of liberty, but it may be committed without physical detention—for example, by compelling the victim to go to a particular place.

Whenever a policeman (or other person) purports to make an arrest, even though it is only by using words of arrest, and the person so addressed submits to the arrest, this is an imprisonment in law; and if the arrest is not legally justified it is a false imprisonment. The reason is that an arrester impliedly threatens the use of force if his demand for submission is not complied with.[2] Similarly, if a policeman announces that he will arrest a person unless he

---

[21] If the point were free from authority it might be held that D's intent in respect of V1 was in law an intent in respect of V2. But the cases seem to be against this view. See Ashworth in *Reshaping the Criminal Law*, ed. Glazebrook (London 1978) 85; *The General Part*, 2nd edn § 46 nn. 10, 11; *Monger* [1973] Crim.L.R. 301. The opinion in the text is supported by the contrast in the wording of sections 18 and 24 (see § .1 at n. 11).

[1] *Linsberg* (1905) 69 JP 107; Russell, 12th edn 690.
[2] [1954] Crim.LR 11–12.

gives up a certain thing, and the other complies, this seems to be sufficient constraint upon the person to amount to an imprisonment.[3] The reason again is that the officer who makes such a threat is impliedly saying that the other must not go out of his presence until he complies with the condition. The threat becomes an imprisonment if the other party submits and remains with the officer while he complies with the officer's demand. Or perhaps the making of the demand, with the implied threat of force, is an assault in the absence of justification or excuse.[4]

The police evade restrictions on their powers of arrest by inviting suspects (or telling them) to accompany them to the police station, where they are questioned. The judges have remained quiescent on this practice. What is supposed to keep it legal is the free consent of the suspect to go to the police station and remain there. This is all very well if the voluntary nature of the expedition is made clear to him. But the ordinary person is likely to interpret a request made by a policeman in uniform, even if worded politely, as a command backed by the implied threat of force. It could well be argued that if the police use ambiguous language ("I want you to come with me to the police station") this is a deprivation of the suspect's liberty which can be justified only under the law of arrest. Either the police should arrest the offender, complying with the legal requirements of arrest, or they should make it plain that the suspect is not legally bound to accompany them.

There is no clear authority for saying that it is a false imprisonment (or kidnapping—see below) to cause a person by deception to remain in a place or to go to a place. The person who is deceived is caused to behave in a certain way but is not deprived of his liberty. However, it is quite possible that the courts will make this extension if the point arises. There are precedents for saying that an offence of doing something "against the will" of someone covers the getting of consent by fraud.[5]

You say that imprisonment involves a total restraint on liberty. Suppose there is an escape route, but a very awkward one? A man offers his dancing partner to drive her home, but deceitfully drives her to his own house. Then he refuses to drive her home. She stays the night because it would be a long and possibly dangerous walk home. Is that an imprisonment?

As I said just now, deceitfully taking the woman to the wrong place might be held to be a false imprisonment or kidnapping. Authority is lacking on whether the man's refusal to help the woman to get home would itself be an imprisonment. A court would certainly say that a dangerous escape-route is no escape-route. We do not know whether a judge would direct a jury to take extreme inconvenience or hardship in making an escape into account. Very likely he would. There is a case for having a statutory offence of fraud to cover a "marooning" of this kind.

Prosecutions for false imprisonment are uncommon because the damages obtainable in a civil action are likely to be far higher than the criminal penalty.[6] Another effective civil remedy is an application for a writ of habeas corpus, and anyone who impedes the process on habeas corpus can be committed to prison for contempt of court.

---

[3] *Grainger* v. *Hill* (1838) 4 Bing.NC at 220, 132 ER at 772–773.

[4] For a further discussion of false imprisonment see works on tort. There are also limited statutory offences of detaining adults: Habeas Corpus Act 1679 s.11 (sending prisoner out of England); Sexual Offences Act 1956 ss.17, 24; Merchant Shipping Act 1970 s.4 (marooning seamen).

[5] Rape, assault and abduction have included the words "against the will" as part of the definition, but this has not prevented the courts from extending these offences to cases of fraud. See § 25.5–9, particularly *Hopkins* § 25.8 at n. 1; *Wellard* § 25.9 n. 8. The CLRC recommended against any extension of the law, even by legislation, but the reason offered was unconvincing. See 14th Report, para. 231.

[6] A customer who was mistakenly arrested on a charge of theft in a supermarket was awarded £6,000 damages by a jury: The Times, January 20, 1978.

What about kidnapping?

There is a common law offence going by this name,[7] which is committed by carrying a person away without his consent. It is supposed to be a particularly serious form of false imprisonment, but over the years the courts have, in familiar fashion, attenuated the circumstances of aggravation, so that now the only distinguishing feature is that the imprisonment, to amount to an aggravation, must involve *either the secreting of the victim or carrying him away from the place where he wishes to be.*[8] It may be either by force or by the threat of force. (As was said before, the courts may perhaps extend it to a taking by deception.) Although the maximum punishment is the same as for false imprisonment, sentences for kidnapping are generally more severe; "life" imprisonment is not uncommon.

If an adult takes away a juvenile with his consent but without the consent of his parents, is this kidnapping?

No, according to a ruling of Lawson J.[9] But it can be one of a number of statutory offences, which are next to be considered.

§ 9.12. ABDUCTION

Some of the statutory offences of abduction are designed to safeguard the right of custody possessed by a parent or guardian. There is an ill-drafted section of the Offences against the Person Act making it an offence (sometimes known as child-stealing) to abduct a child under 14, male or female, by force or fraud.[1] The force or fraud may be against the child or against the parent,[2] but it must be one or the other; so where a child is induced to go voluntarily with the abducter, no fraud being used against either the child or the parent, no offence is committed against the section.[3] This result is at variance with its underlying purpose, though necessitated by its words.

Strangely, most abducters are men, who take older children rather than infants, sometimes from a sexual motive. The offence is not at all common. When committed by women, the offence of "baby-snatching" or "child-stealing" (in popular terms) is generally an attempt to

---

[7] *Reid* [1973] QB 299. There is a statutory form of the offence under the Taking of Hostages Act 1982, which is punishable wherever committed. On false imprisonment and kidnapping in general see Napier in *Reshaping the Criminal Law*, ed. Glazebrook (London 1978) 190 ff.

[8] *Wellard* [1978] 1 WLR 921, 3 All ER 161, 67 CAR 364, shows that carrying the victim away for 100 yards is enough. Lawton LJ seems to have regarded it as for the jury to decide whether the transporting of the victim went sufficiently far to be accounted a carrying away. But surely there must be some rule of law on the subject. In the old law of larceny, the least movement of an article constituted a carrying away, but that can hardly apply to kidnapping.

[9] *Hale* [1974] QB 819, following *Att.-Gen.* v. *Edge* [1943] IR 115.

[1] OAPA 1861 s.56; the section also applies to those who receive such a child after abduction. See notes to Halsbury's *Statutes*; *Pryce* [1972] Crim.LR 307.

[2] *Bellis* (1893) 17 Cox 660.

[3] *Mears* [1975] Crim.LR 155.

compensate for emotional deprivation or frustrated maternal feelings, and a real or imaginary miscarriage may be a predisposing factor. It is often associated with subnormality, schizophrenia or personality disorder; in the last case the woman may be attempting to influence a man by pretending that the baby is his.[4] Although the offence causes great anxiety to the natural parents, the woman looks after the baby well and it is generally soon recovered. On some occasions judges have punished the offence rather severely, only to find, probably to their surprise, that public sympathy (at any rate as publicly expressed) then moves to the side of the baby-snatcher.[5]

The section makes claim of right a defence, and there is clumsy wording that the courts take to mean that parents and guardians are exempt from the prohibition.[6] When parents fall out, and one or other of them spirits away the child, the matter is dealt with as an incident in custody proceedings. A judge in chambers can issue a warrant for the arrest of a parent who has gone off with a child after failing to get a custody order, and for the removal of the child from him or her; but this may take some days, by which time the delinquent parent and the child may be out of the country. (However, the Home Office will, on request referring to the court order, circulate ports and airports without waiting for a warrant.) If the order is made in time it can be enforced by the tipstaff of the High Court or his deputies—who include the police. A parent who ignores an order of the court to return the child can be punished for contempt of court. Another possibility is a proceeding for habeas corpus. Since this is a civil action, one spouse can be compelled to testify against the other (this is not generally possible on a criminal charge), and, once again, a person who assists the offender to avoid receiving service of the proceedings, or who harbours the child in defiance of the court's order, may be imprisoned for contempt of court.[7]

Apparently it is not now an offence against the person to take away a boy of 14 or upwards without the consent of the parent[8]; it will of course be false imprisonment if without the boy's consent, or a contempt of court if in breach of a custody order. Even a parent can be guilty of the statutory offence of taking a child who is in care of the local authority.[9]

Abducting an unmarried girl under 16 is an offence contained in the Sexual Offences Act 1956 (s. 20), though a sexual motive is not an element.

> "(1) It is an offence for a person acting without lawful authority or excuse to take an unmarried girl under the age of 16 out of the possession of her parent or guardian against his will.
>
> (2) In the foregoing subsection 'guardian' means any person having the lawful care or charge of the girl."

The section does not explicitly require a mental element, but on the other hand it contains no words to negative such an element if it is to be implied as a matter of general legal principle. It neither says that the defendant must know the facts, nor says that he need not. Nevertheless, the courts read it as requiring *mens rea* to the extent that the defendant must know that he is (or, presumably, may be[10]) taking a girl without her

---

[4] See d'Orbán in [1972] 2 BMJ 635 and 10 Brit.JCriminol. 275; Joan Hunter in 4 Social Work Today 266.

[5] An example of leniency is [1975] Crim.LR 400. But see [1979] Crim. LR 191.

[6] Also persons to whom the court has allowed some right of access. See *Austin* [1981] 1 All ER 374, 72 CAR 104. On the policy of the exemption see CLRC, 14th Report para. 246. Alas, the section, having exempted these parents from liability for taking the child, fails to exempt them from liability for wrongfully detaining the child; but presumably this exemption will be held to follow by implication, since otherwise the exemption provided by the section would invariably fail of practical effect. Those who snatch the child on the instructions of a parent are not protected: *Austin*, above.

[7] *Re T L H* (An Infant), The Times, April 19, 1968.

[8] So held by the Supreme Court of Eire in *Att.-Gen.* v. *Edge* [1943] IR 115; *Hale* [1974] QB 819.

[9] See *Johns* v. *Jones* [1978] Crim. LR 426.

[10] *Hibbert* (1869) 1 CCR 184 held that the abducter could not be convicted unless the jury found that he knew that the girl was in the possession of her father. But this was too narrow a rule; it is clear now that recklessness as to that possession would be sufficient.

parent's consent. Claim of right as such is not made a defence (as it is in the offence just considered of abducting children under 14), but only the possession of "lawful authority or excuse."[11] One may perhaps argue that claim of right is a defence under the general principles of the common law (§ 20.4), provided that the claim of right is not based merely upon the age of the girl.

The most celebrated decision on the section (as it appeared in earlier legislation) is *Prince*.[12]

> Prince won his toehold on immortality by abducting a girl who was under 16 but whom he reasonably thought to be over that age because she looked very much older. All the members of the Court for Crown Cases Reserved except Brett J held that he was guilty, but different reasons were given for the opinion. The majority, of 10 judges, in a judgment delivered by Blackburn J, did not question that the statute required *mens rea* in respect of taking a girl out of the possession of her parent against his will, but took the position that in respect of the girl's age the statutory prohibition was absolute, so that the defendant's mistake as to her age was no defence.[13] The reasoning was based partly upon the history of the section (i.e. previous legislation on the subject) and partly upon the absurdity that it was supposed would result from any other reading of the statute.

Prince illustrates a mode of interpretation that has been exemplified a number of times since. Legislation is interpreted to require a mental state only in respect of some of the elements of the offence (being a mental state that the defence will generally not be able to dispute), but not to require a mental state in respect of elements where it is frequently denied and hard or impossible to prove. In effect, the judges are satisfied with half *mens rea*. Important examples are some of the aggravated assaults that were studied earlier in this chapter: an intention to commit a common assault is sufficient to convict of some, but not all, of the more serious assaults.

Why did the judges allow a defence of mistake to Mrs Tolson (§ 6.7) but not to Prince?

The judgments are full of technical arguments purporting to justify the two decisions. But the real point was that the judges sympathised with Mrs Tolson but not with Prince. They strongly condemned Prince for taking a girl of any age out of the possession of her parents.[14] Probably they feared that if they allowed a defence of mistake as to age, this would prove to be a let-out for many defendants who might be charged in future. It is perhaps not without significance that the case was in a sense a sexual one (even though Prince was not shown to have seduced the girl). These are notoriously the occasions on which the law tends to be bent to give expression to feelings of moral outrage.

---

[11] See Card in [1969] Crim.LR 424. The excuse must be a lawful excuse, not just a good motive: *Tegerdine* [1983] Crim. LR 163.

[12] (1875) 2 CCR 154.

[13] Cross in 91 LQR 553 n. 28 made the interesting point that if the abducter of a girl believes her to be 18 he would now have a defence, not because of his mistake as to age simply (which is not a defence in itself) but because he would then believe the girl to have reached an age that, in law, puts her outside parental custody.

[14] The minority judges (*per* Bramwell B) voted for affirming the conviction on the ground that Prince had set out to commit a moral wrong or tort against the girl's father. But the opinion that this wrongful intention was sufficient to exclude a defence of mistake has not gained general acceptance. See § 6.9.

What was Prince's sentence?

Three months. In cases of strict liability judges sometimes mitigate the sentence to a fine or discharge, as they surely ought if fault has not been made out; but Prince has not been the only unlucky offender who has gone to prison without proof of legal fault.

What, then, is the ratio decidendi of Prince's case?

As often happens, either a wide or a narrow principle may be attributed to the majority decision under the doctrine of precedent. The narrow one is that a charge of abducting a girl under 16 is of strict liability in respect of the girl's age; this was the principle accepted by the majority of the court. But the reasoning was based on a wider ground, namely that references to the age of the victim of an offence in the Offences against the Person Act (now the Sexual Offences Act) are of strict liability as to age. The courts accept the wider rule, so that *Prince* is important outside the particular offence on which it was decided.[15] The point is clinched by the wording of the Sexual Offences Act. This Act creates a number of offences with regard to juveniles, and in some it expressly provides that reasonable mistake as to the age of the juvenile shall constitute a defence; but it does not say this for the offence of adbucting girls under 16. Consequently, the decision in *Prince* must now be taken, regrettably, to be affirmed by the legislature; and the case must be accepted as laying down a rule not merely for the particular offence with which the court was concerned but for all offences where the age of a juvenile is legally material and strict liability is not inconsistent with the words of the statute. The rule is capable of working substantial injustice, particularly since the use of cosmetics enables girls of 15 to make themselves appear much older.

The reference to girls under 16 means that girls of 15 are protected by the legislation, but not girls of 16. The protection ends on the 16th birthday.[16] If a girl is only a few days short of her 16th birthday, the court will in practice discharge the offender without punishment.[17]

Section 20. is aimed against abduction, not seduction: it does not require that sexual intercourse should have taken place, so it hits, for example, even a woman who takes away a girl under 16 without the permission of the parents. "Taking" does not mean that the act must be against the will of the girl; and it may be committed against the will of the parent by means of a fraud perpetrated on the parent.[18] Generally, nowadays, it involves not a ladder to the window but a car parked around the corner. It does not require a permanent deprivation[19], but a judge ruled that taking a girl for a short walk without her parents' consent does not amount to a taking out of the parents' possession within the section.[20] (The child-stealing offence, however, has been held to cover the briefest of takings.[21]) There is no

---

[15] *Maughan*, (1934) 24 CAR 130. For statutory exceptions see §§ 10.3, 10.9.

[16] In law, a given age is attained at the first moment of the anniversary of the date of birth: Family Law Reform Act 1969 s.9.

[17] For a useful note on sentencing practice see 127 NLJ 177–178.

[18] See § 25.8 at n. 1.

[19] *Baillie* (1859) 8 Cox 238 (where, however, the elopement was followed by marriage); *Timmins* (1860) 8 Cox 401.

[20] *James Jones* [1973] Crim.LR 621, criticised by the CLRC, 14th Report, para. 242.

[21] *Bellis*, above n. 2. Cp. *Mears* [1975] Crim. LR 155; *Dawson* (1976) 64 CAR 170, Crim. LR 692.

"taking" where a girl leaves her father's home and goes to the defendant without his persuasion, and the fact that the defendant then fails to restore her to her father does not make him guilty of the offence.[22] There are various other decisions on the interpretation of section 20, but this book does not attempt to give full details of all offences, and the reader who has a practical point on any particular statutory provision should consult the larger works—such as Archbold for indictable offences, Stone for summary offences, and the notes to Halsbury's *Statutes*.

Sections 17, 18 and 19 of the Offences against the Person Act create offences of abduction in respect of older women. These do not often come before the courts.[23]

§ 9.13. NEGLIGENT INJURIES TO THE PERSON

There is no general offence of negligently causing injury to the person. At common law, almost the only offence of this kind is manslaughter, which requires death to occur (by gross negligence or in certain other ways). Similarly, there is no *general* statutory offence of injuring by negligence. But provisions aimed against those who negligently create the risk of injury in particular circumstances have been seeping into the statute-book. The best-known is the offence of careless driving, but we now have in addition wide offences under the Health and Safety at Work etc. Act 1974.

Section 2(1) provides:

> "It shall be the duty of every employer to ensure, so far as is reasonably practicable, the health, safety and welfare at work of all his employees."

Section 3(1):

> "It shall be the duty of every employer to conduct his undertaking in such a way as to ensure, so far as is reasonably practicable, that persons not in his employment who may be affected thereby are not thereby exposed to risk to their health or safety."

This provision travels far outside the short title of the Act, and could be used if noxious factory chimneys injure the health of the surrounding population.

Section 4(1) imposes similar wide duties on persons concerned with work premises (including employees who have duties in relation to the premises), to ensure that the premises (and any plant or substance in the premises) are safe and without risks to health. Section 5 (1) is more specific on the subject of fumes:

> "It shall be the duty of the person having control of any premises prescribed by regulations to use the best practicable means for preventing the emission into the atmosphere of noxious or offensive substances."

Section 6 imposes a duty on any person who designs, manufactures, imports or supplies any article for use at work to ensure, so far as is reasonably practicable, that the article is designed and constructed as to be safe and without risks to health when properly used; and there are subsidiary provisions requiring testing and research, and similar provisions relating to the supply of substances for use at work.

---

[22] *Olifier* (1866) 10 Cox 402.

[23] s. 17 (abduction of woman for unlawful sexual intercourse) has been held to apply where a man forces a woman into a car, even though it is doubtful whether he hoped to rape her or to persuade her to accept intercourse: *Jones* [1973] Crim.LR 710. This is technically correct, but it illustrates the anomalous nature of the offence, since if the woman subsequently consents, the sexual intercourse would not itself be criminal. The proper charge in such circumstances is of assault or false imprisonment.

Section 7 shows an unusual lack of bias in this type of legislation by extending a general duty to employees. It is:

> "the duty of every employee while at work
> (*a*) to take reasonable care for the health and safety of himself and of other persons who may be affected by his acts or omissions at work; and
> (*b*) as regards any duty or requirement imposed on his employer or any other person by or under any of the relevant statutory provisions, to co-operate with him so far as is necessary to enable that duty or requirement to be performed or complied with."

Section 8:

> "No person shall intentionally or recklessly interfere with or misuse anything provided in the interests of health, safety or welfare in pursuance of any of the relevant statutory provisions."[1]

Penalties are provided by section 33 (as amended), which makes it an offence to fail to discharge any of these duties (or to contravene s.8). The offence is triable either way.[2]

These provisions are the most general of a mass of safety provisions in industrial legislation, failure to comply with which is an offence.[3] In addition there is a considerable body of law for the protection of consumers and the environment, which cannot even be touched upon here. When an activity involves risk, it is frequently confined to qualified persons—either those professionally qualified, or those with licences from public authorities; and it is made an offence for unqualified persons to act. For example, the Medicines Act 1968 ss.78, 84, create an offence of pretending to be a chemist; but the maximum fine is £100, even if many people have been negligently poisoned.

Why not have a general offence instead of all these detailed offences? If there is an offence of manslaughter by gross negligence, I don't see why there shouldn't be a general serious offence of causing injury by gross negligence, or indeed an offence of being grossly negligent. Liability should not depend on the accident of the outcome.

Some take this view, on logical grounds which I do not find persuasive. The offence of manslaughter by gross negligence has not worked satisfactorily, as we shall see. And even if it is thought worth preserving, we have got on well enough without a general offence of negligence not resulting in death. We have an embarrassing number of wicked people in prison and do not need to add incautious ones to them. If we are to have any offences of negligence they had better be summary, finable ones; and that is how nearly all the statutory offences just mentioned work in practice, even if most of them could as a matter of law be tried on indictment.

SUMMARY

OAPA s.18 creates two offences: wounding with intent, and causing grievous § .1

---

[1] The last phrase is widely defined in s.53 (1).

[2] See generally on the Act Kloss in [1978] Crim.LR 280.

[3] A wide provision in the Conspiracy and Protection of Property Act 1875 s.5 (as amended) has fallen into disuse. This makes it an offence maliciously to break a contract of service or of hiring, knowing or having reasonable cause to believe that the probable consequence will be to endanger human life, or cause serious bodily injury, or endanger valuable property. For painfully obvious reasons, no use has been made of the section in strikes by ambulance drivers, hospital personnel, electricity workers, etc. Yet Parliament went to the trouble in 1970 of specifically excluding seamen from the section.

bodily harm with intent. "G.b.h." means "really serious harm" (*DPP* v. *Smith*). Both offences require an intention to do g.b.h. or to resist or prevent lawful arrest. The intention can be transferred, because of the repetition of the phrase "any person" in the section. The offence is triable only in the Crown Court.

Sections 20 and 47 create offences of medium gravity. Section 20 creates two offences: unlawful wounding and unlawfully inflicting g.b.h. Section 47 creates the offence of assault occasioning actual bodily harm. The latter expression presumably means "harm more than trifling"; it includes a hysterical and nervous condition resulting from an assault (*Miller*). § .2

As to the mental element, section 20 requires "malice." Statutory crimes of malice are generally held to require intention or recklessness as to the particular kind of harm (*Cunningham*). Whether the redefinition of recklessness in *Caldwell* applies to this word as an element in statutory malice is unclear. An intention to frighten is no longer held to be enough, but, anomalously, an intention to cause injury falling short of g.b.h. is (*Mowatt*). The decision is out of accord with CJA s.8, and the CLRC has proposed its abrogation. Intention can be transferred under the section. § .3

Section 47 requires an assault, but the courts have declined to require a mental element as to the bodily harm. The trial judge in *Miller* apparently ruled that there need be no intention or recklessness as to causing harm, and the CA applied the same rule even where the defendant was guilty only of a psychic assault. These decisions fail to apply the general presumption that a serious crime requires *mens rea*. § .4

Section 47 requires an assault. The word "inflicts" in section 20 has been held to require by implication the application of non-consensual force, but this application may be either by an assault (*Clarence*), or by doing an act that directly results in force being applied violently to the body of the victim (*Wilson*). § .5

The gradation of offences in these sections enables the police, magistrates and jury to participate in influencing the sentence, and it also gives scope to plea bargaining. A defendant will not be convicted under more than one of the sections. § .6

It is an offence under the Police Act to assault a constable in the execution of his duty. This is of strict liability in respect of the victim and the execution of duty. But there must be an assault, requiring intention or recklessness in the usual way, so mistake as to the status of the victim can support a defence of belief in the necessity for self-defence. Another offence in the Police Act is that of wilfully obstructing a constable in the execution of his duty, which means intentionally (or perhaps recklessly) hindering the police in their lawful work as police officers. The offence is not committed by a person who simply refuses to answer the questions of the police (*Rice* v. *Connolly*), nor, apparently, by a person who refuses to help the police to obtain evidence of a crime, or to make an arrest (with one narrow exception by an old rule of the common law). But people have been convicted of obstruction in failing to comply with the directions of the police to prevent a crime in which they themselves played some part, as fomenters or otherwise, or to protect life or property. § .7

Affray is an offence at common law, punishable at discretion and not triable summarily. It means an unlawful physical assault involving such a degree of violence that persons of reasonably firm character are likely to be terrified. It may be committed by an attack by D upon V, or by a fight with consent. If spectators are present it is enough that the violence is such as might reasonably be expected to terrify (Lord Hailsham). This being so, the law perhaps is that no spectators need actually be present, or be likely to be present. At least, the Law Commission has provisionally proposed this rule as a matter of legislation; but the contrary has been ruled, for the present law, by a circuit judge. Parties to an affray may be indicted and tried together, and the affray may be charged as continuing over a period. § .8

There are various statutory offences akin to assault, and other offences designed § .9

to help preserve the peace. It is an offence to threaten to murder, but not to threaten to maim. It is a summary offence for a person, in any public place or at any public meeting, to use threatening, abusive or insulting words or behaviour with intent to provoke a breach of the peace or whereby a breach of the peace is likely.

OAPA ss.23–24 create two offences of poisoning. Maliciously administering a noxious thing to any person (1) so as thereby to endanger the life of such person or to inflict upon him g.b.h. is punishable with imprisonment for 10 years (s. 23); (2) with intent to injure, aggrieve or annoy such person is punishable with imprisonment for 5 years (s. 24). "Administering" includes deceiving the victim into taking the poison. It was held in *Marcus* that sleeping pills are noxious for this purpose, as, doubtless, is any other substance that interferes with bodily function. The court held that "noxious" means "obnoxious", but it remains undecided whether the covert administration of a substance comes within the section merely because it is known to be abhorrent to the victim. As to the mental element under section 23, *Cunningham* was at first thought to decide that "maliciously" in the section means "with foresight of consequence," i.e. intentionally or recklessly; but we are now told that this applies only when the consequence is caused indirectly, there being strict liability as to direct consequences: *Cato*. It was further held in *Cato* that the offence could be committed by an administration with consent, and that heroin could be accounted noxious for this purpose. The decision has been much criticised, but the courts follow it. Perhaps recklessly communicating a disease is covered by section 23. Intention can be transferred under section 23 but not under section 24, the distinction depending upon the wording of the sections. § .10

False imprisonment is a common law offence, punishable at discretion and not triable summarily. It requires a total restraint on liberty, but may be committed without physical detention. A variant is kidnapping, which is committed by secreting the victim or carrying him away without his consent. § .11

It is a statutory offence for anyone other than the parents, guardians or those with a right of access to a child to abduct a child under 14 by force or fraud. Claim of right is a defence. Abducting an unmarried girl under 16 out of the possession of her parent or guardian against his will is also an offence. *Mens rea* is required as to the possession of the parent or guardian, but not as to the age of the girl (*Prince*). This decision is held to be applicable to all offences referring to the age of the victim, unless the statute provides otherwise. § .12

There are many offences of negligence in labour law, consumer protection law and environmental law. § .13

Chapter 10

SEXUAL AGGRESSION

The freedom to reject or accept a man's advances is the most fundamental a woman can have.

Katharine Whitehorn

§ 10.1. THE CLASSIFICATION OF SEXUAL OFFENCES

To speak of sexual offences as a class is somewhat misleading, since there are important differences of types. The two main groups are sexual aggression and breaches of sexual taboo. In this book we are almost exclusively concerned with the first.

Those in the first group consist of injuries and affronts to a non-consenting victim, while in the second group the conduct is illegal whether or not the victim consents. The distinction is not precise, because of ambiguity of the word "consent." Misbehaviour by an adult with a consenting juvenile or severely impaired person may be assigned to either group, the consent of a protected person being disregarded for the purpose of certain offences. In the case of a very young victim it may in any case be unrealistic to speak in terms of consent.

The present chapter is concerned with those offences where the predominant motive of the law is to protect an innocent person against an aggressor. Offences that are predominantly consensual, such as homosexual[1] offences (buggery, and gross indecency between men)[2] and incest, are for the most part outside the scope of the book (even though they can be committed against a non-consenting partner).[3] The offences of abduction, which may have a sexual motivation, were considered in the previous chapter.

Even the general class of sexual offences is not clearly demarcated, because almost any crime can be committed from a sexual motive. Murder may have an overt or hidden sexual motive, ranging from the common case of jealousy or the desire to be rid of a sexual partner to the uncommon case of the necrophiliac. Sadism, another perversion of the sex instinct, may result in an offence of causing bodily harm. A fetishist may steal a sexual object (such as frilly panties from a clothes-line). The nuisance committed opportunistically by a peeper (one type of voyeur[4]) is in general so slight that it is not worth specially dealing with by law, and indeed the law does not do so. A peeper may enter a garden to spy on females undressing in a bedroom; he commits no offence, but by a misunderstanding of his motives he may find himself charged with being found on enclosed premises for an unlawful purpose (§ 38.5) or of attempted burglary; these charges are untenable if the true facts emerge, but by a stretch he may be bound over to be of good behaviour. A peeper in a women's public lavatory may be charged, again improperly, with insulting conduct under the Public Order Act,[5] or may be bound over to be of good behaviour (another abuse of the law). The transvestite (cross-dresser, who derives sexual pleasure from dressing and sometimes masquerading in the clothing of the opposite sex) commits no offence, but by a perversion of magisterial power is sometimes bound over.

---

[1] The word comes not from the Latin *homo*, man, but from the Greek *homos*, the same, and refers to an attraction to the same sex, whether male or female. There has never been a specific offence of female homosexual behaviour.

[2] Sexual Offences Act 1956 ss.12 and 13, as amended by SOA 1967. In general, the latter Act removes the prohibition from acts between consenting males over 21 in private. SOA 1956 s.16 (1) penalises assault with intent to commit buggery.

[3] For a brief account of homosexual offences see Tony Honoré, *Sex Law* (London 1978) 84 ff.

[4] See Paul H Gebhard and others, *Sex Offenders: An Analysis of Types* (New York 1965) 358.

[5] § 9.9 at n. 19.

If a sexual deviationist is convicted it is important to recognise the sexual motive at the disposal stage. Both fetishists and peepers appear to be underdeveloped sexually, and they may be helped by psychotherapy or by a probation officer to achieve a more satisfactory sociosexual adjustment. (Men who are not convicted but only bound over cannot be put on probation.)

§ 10.2. INDECENT ASSAULT

The law relating to indecent assault now rests on sections 14 and 15 of the Sexual Offences Act 1956, which is chiefly a consolidating statute, carefully preserving some ancient anomalies, though making a few minor changes in the law.

Subject to what is to be said in a moment, consent negatives an indecent assault just as it negatives a common assault. The prosecution frequently have a hard task in establishing lack of consent by the alleged victim, and the possibility of acquittal will naturally weigh with the police when deciding whether or not to prosecute in a doubtful case.

By the Sexual Offences Act s.14(1) and Sched. 2 as amended, an indecent assault by any person (man or woman) *on a woman* is an indictable offence and is punishable with 2 years' imprisonment (raised to 5 years if the offence is committed against a girl under 13[1]). "Man" in the Act includes a boy, and "woman" includes a girl: section 46.

The maximum is fully adequate for consensual acts, but inadequate for true sexual assaults where the act is of a serious kind and the offender presents a considerable danger to the public. In one case, where a man subjected a woman to prolonged and forcible penetration with a ginger beer bottle, the charge being indecent assault, he could be sentenced only to 2 years' imprisonment,[2] and the same remark applies to those who subject women to *fellatio* (oral sex committed on the man) under threat of violence,[3] which everyone would regard as more repulsive than rape.

A strange contrast with section 14(1) is presented by section 15(1) (read together with Sched. 2). This applies to an indecent assault by any person (man or woman) *on a man*, and lays down a maximum of 10 years' imprisonment.

It may be asked why the maximum for a male victim should be five times that for a female victim. The explanation, such as it is, is that an indecent assault upon a man is generally of a homosexual nature, which has in the past been viewed with great revulsion. In practice the sentences imposed for indecent assaults on males and females are quite similar, at any rate where the victim is 14 or over.[4]

§ 10.3. INCAPACITY TO CONSENT

The law of indecent assault has two effects. In the first place, it raises the maximum punishment to 2 years (or sometimes more) from the one year that would otherwise have been the maximum for a common assault. In the

---

[1] Indecency with Children Act 1960 s.2(1)(*b*).

[2] He could have been sentenced more severely if the prosecutor had had the wit to charge under OAPA ss.20 or 47, but then the conviction would not have recorded the sexual nature of the assault.

[3] In *Seaward* [1973] Crim.LR 642 the court found itself able to sentence such an offender to 7 years' imprisonment, but only because he had committed burglary.

[4] Walmsley and White, *op. cit.* 44,65.

second place, the law of indecent assault specially protects juveniles by disabling them from giving an effective consent.[1] Even when a youngster does not realise the significance of what is being done to him or her, and does not suffer harm, the law has to consider the alarm and annoyance caused to the parents. Consequently, section 14(2) of the Sexual Offences Act provides:

> "A girl under the age of 16 cannot in law give any consent which would prevent an act being an assault for the purposes of this section."

There is a similar provision in section 15(2) for a boy under 16, and severely mentally impaired persons are also protected.[2] These provisions apply only in respect of indecent assault, not common assault. A person under 16, and even a severely mentally impaired person, may, within limits, give an effective consent to what would otherwise be a common assault (§ 25.12, 13).

It may be questioned whether the common law notion of assault was properly applied by Parliament to an act done with consent. If one reads in the newspapers of a man having been convicted of indecently assaulting a girl of, say, 14, the picture that comes to mind is of an act done by force, not of fondling without resistance from the girl. To call the latter an assault is liable to evoke a misplaced emotional attitude. It would be an improvement if an act done with consent were given another name (such as gross indecency[3]), and it should be considered whether 16 is not too high an age for an offence of indecency.[4]

What if the offender is himself under 16?

It is an anomaly of the law of indecent assault that no exemption is provided for young offenders.[5] This is not because Parliament wanted schoolchildren who indulged in "petting" to be prosecuted (in practice they are not[6]), but, presumably, because it was too prim to make an express exception for them.[7]

---

[1] When a charge is based on the age of the "victim" the prosecution bear an evidential and persuasive burden in that respect unless the statute provides otherwise. Cp. *Dillon* [1982] 1 All ER 1017. There is no provision to the contrary for indecent assault.

[2] See ss.15(3), 45 and Mental Health Act 1959 s.4(2), as amended by MH(A)A 1982.

[3] This proposal was endorsed by a majority of the CLRC in its Working Paper on Sexual Offences (HMSO 1980) 32–33. While a rewording of the offence in terms of gross indecency would be an improvement, it would be better still if we had a more radical revision, the offence being described as "sexual misconduct" and being defined fairly narrowly. Cp. Card in [1981] Crim.LR 370.

[4] Particularly when 16 is the age for lawful *marriage*. My opinion that the age should be 15 for gross indecency (as opposed to sexual intercourse) was however rejected by the rest of the CLRC (Working Paper 31).

[5] *Brimilow* (1839) 9 C & P 366, 173 ER 891; *Williams* [1893] 1 QB 320 (conviction of a boy under 14). "Pupils at Stanground school, a mixed comprehensive near Peterborough, were warned yesterday about kissing and cuddling in the playground. A school spokesman said afterwards that any form of physical contact between the sexes could be construed in law as indecent assault." Guardian report reprinted in "This England," New Statesman, March 29, 1974.

[6] For prosecution practice, see A F Wilcox, *The Decision to Prosecute* (London 1972) 51.

[7] In any reform of the law, consideration should be given to confining the paedophiliac offences to cases where there is an appreciable disparity between the ages of the defendant and the victim. Cp. Proposed US Federal Code s.1645 (five-year age difference); ALI Model Penal Code s.213.3 (four-year age difference for unlawful sexual intercourse where the female is over 10). My proposal would be that it should be a defence to a man charged with gross indecency or sexual intercourse with a girl that he was not more than 3 years older than the girl; this would give partial recognition to prosecution practice. For the decision of the CLRC see its *Working Paper on OAP* 94.

To what extent does the offence require a mental element?

As was said before (§ 9.12), all sexual offences involving juveniles are construed as crimes of strict prohibition in respect of the age, unless the statute provides to the contrary. Certain exceptions are created by statute, but the only exception in respect of indecent assault on a girl under 16 relates to a particular point in the law of marriage. Where a man reasonably believes a woman to be his wife, but the supposed marriage is in fact invalid because she is under 16, he is given a statutory defence to a charge of indecent assault.[8]

On the point of mental impairment there is a more general relaxation: a person cannot be convicted of indecent assault on a severely mentally impaired person by reason of that impairment unless he (or she) knew of it or had reason to suspect it.[9] The concluding words ("had reason to suspect") would have been better omitted. The sole question should be one of knowledge, because the diagnosis of severe mental impairment and the distinction between that and mental impairment *simpliciter* requires an expert. No ordinary man, who does not know what diagnosis has been made, is likely to be able to tell the difference, at any rate in quite a broad band of marginal cases—even if he knew the statutory definition of severe mental impairment. To look for *mens rea* when a man in a cinema finds a mentally impaired girl next to him and has intercourse with her[10] is an impossible undertaking. For legislative proposals see § 25.12.

§ 10.4. THE NATURE OF AN INDECENT ASSAULT

Apart from the special provisions relating to the victim's consent, an indecent assault clearly supposes that there is an assault in the generic sense, accompanied by a circumstance of indecency. Since the word "assault" in statutory language means either a psychic or a physical assault, an indecent assault may be of the same two varieties.

> In *Rolfe*[1] Lord Goddard CJ, delivering the judgment of the court, said: "An assault can be committed without touching a person. One always thinks of an assault as the giving of a blow to somebody, but that is not necessary. An assault may be constituted by a threat or a hostile act[2] committed towards a person." It was therefore held that a man who indecently exposed himself and walked towards a woman with his person exposed, making an indecent suggestion to her, could be convicted of indecent assault. It may be questioned, however, whether the court paid sufficient attention to the requirement that the victim of a psychic assault must apprehend a physical assault.[3] If, in the case before the court, the woman was merely disgusted and disturbed by the behaviour, and did not apprehend that she would be

---

[8] Sexual Offences Act 1956 s.14(3).

[9] *Ibid.* ss.14(4), 15(3), 45 (the last as substituted by Mental Health Act 1959 s. 127(1)(*b*)).

[10] See *Hudson* [1966] 1 QB 448, where the court gave an indulgent interpretation to "had reason to suspect."

[1] (1952) 36 CAR 4.

[2] But the act need not be hostile: *Faulkner* v. *Talbot* [1981] 1 WLR 1528, 3 All ER 468.

[3] Cp. *Fissington* v. *Hutchinson* (1866) 15 LT 390.

touched, the case should not, on principle, have been regarded as an indecent assault, though it could be an offence of indecent exposure.[4]

The notion of assault does not require any knowledge on the part of the victim as to what is happening. A wrongful interference with a sleeping person or an infant would clearly be an assault. Such an assault, if indecent in nature, will also be an indecent assault.[5]

What indecency must there be to turn a common assault into an indecent assault?

"Indecent" may be defined as "overtly sexual," though it covers homosexual as well as heterosexual assaults. Two propositions may be advanced.

1 An assault is not indecent if it is neither intended by the defendant nor interpreted by the other party as having a sexual purpose. A doctor who makes an intimate examination of a girl of 15 for medical reasons is not guilty of indecent assault, because he acts from a non-sexual motive, though if it were an indecent assault the consent of the girl would be no defence.[6]

When a man photographed small boys (aged 11 to 13) in the nude, for the purpose of selling the photographs to magazines, not touching the boys except to arrange their poses, the touching was held not to constitute an indecent assault, not being indecent; and there was no common assault because the boys consented.[7]

Parliament responded to this decision by making it an offence to take indecent photographs of persons under 16, or to distribute or show or advertise such photographs.[8]

2 The mental state of the defendant and of his victim are not the only elements in an indecent assault. There must be an offence to customary standards of modesty. The offence may range in gravity from simulated intercourse—or, indeed, actual intercourse—to a comparatively slight case of manual interference. But there must, it seems, be a situation that would appear to the ordinary observer as an affront to modesty.

In a case at Lincoln Assizes,[9] the defendant was a shoe fetishist who

[4] Normally charged under the Vagrancy Act 1824 s.4; but it is also an indictable offene at common law.

[5] *Lock* (1872) LR 2 CCR 10. The decision in *Williams* v. *Gibbs* [1958] Crim.LR 127 is lenient; it can perhaps he justified on the ground that the acts alleged were somewhat trivial, but the court misapprehended the effect of the earlier decisions that it purported to follow.

[6] Similarly, a man who performs an illegal abortion upon a girl of 15, or who falsely pretends to do so for the purpose of obtaining money, should not be regarded as committing an indecent assault, even though, if it were an indecent assault, her consent would be no defence. It would be improper to use the law of indecent assault for the purpose of punishing what is in essence an offence of abortion or obtaining by deception. See, however, *Armstrong* (1885) 49 JP 745; *Pearson* (1908) 11 Gaz.LR 139 (NZ).

Indecent assault, it has been said, does not require a specific intent by the defendant to be indecent, so consensual activity with a person under 16 can be an indecent assault even though neither party regards it as indecent: *Mason* (1968) 53 CAR 12. While this is undoubted, it does not affect the proposition in the text.

[7] *Sutton* [1977] 1 WLR 1086, 3 All ER 476. There are questionable dicta in the judgment as to the nature of an indecent assault.

[8] Protection of Children Act 1978, applied to N.Ireland by SI No. 1047 of 1978.

[9] *George* [1956] Crim.LR 52. Cp. *Johnson* [1968] SASR 132 (Aus.).

attempted to remove a shoe from a girl's foot, the act giving him a perverted sexual gratification. It was ruled that this was not an indecent assault, because there were no circumstances of indecency towards the girl.

What of a kiss?

The judges have been divided on the point,[10] but the answer in common sense is clear. If kissing a woman against her will were an indecent assault, it would follow that for a youth to kiss a maiden of bashful 15 *with* her consent would be an indecent assault; but the conclusion would be absurd.

A kiss accompanied by carnal suggestions has been held to be an indecent assault,[11] but even this may be doubted. If a kiss (or the forcible removal of a shoe) is not in itself an indecent assault, it would seem that indecent words or suggestions should not be sufficient to create the indecency. This view is taken by the courts of New Zealand and South Africa, and apparently Australia. In Canada, on the other hand, words are held to be capable of being decisive.[12]

The above remarks apply to a heterosexual kiss. For a man to kiss and stroke a small boy has been held to be an indecent assault.[13] It is difficult to see on what principle this distinction between the sexes can be made.

Indecency can be constituted by the indecent behaviour of the defendant with his own body. In other words, the objective circumstances of indecency may relate to the conduct of the defendant and need not relate to the nature of his interference with the object of his attentions.

In *Beal* v. *Kelley*,[14] a man exposed his penis to a boy and then pulled the boy towards himself. It was held that this was an indecent assault, since indecency was offered towards the boy.

§ 10.5. INDECENCY WITH CHILDREN

An indecent physical assault requires that the defendant should have touched the victim, the "force" proceeding from the defendant to the victim. There is no assault if the defendant, without force or threats or touching with his own hands, induces a child to undress before him, or to touch him (the defendant) indecently.[1] The situation has now been covered by the Indecency with Children Act 1960, under which an offence is committed when "any person commits an act of gross[2] indecency with or towards a child under the age of 14, or who incites a child under that age to such an act with him or another."[3] The wording is wide enough to cover

---

[10] See 16 JCr.L 89; [1956] Crim.LR 530; *A.B.* (1955) 22 CR 353 (Alta.).

[11] *Leeson* (1968) 52 CAR 185.

[12] See the review of the cases by Mackesy in [1956] Crim.LR 531–533. Cp. *Coombes* [1961] Crim.LR 54, where the point was not discussed.

[13] *Kallides* (1976), referred to in [1977] 1 WLR at 1089.

[14] (1951) CAR 128. Cp. *Quinton* [1947] SCR (Can.) (attempted rape). Contrast the facts in *DPP* v. *Rogers* [1953] 1 WLR 1017, 37 CAR 137.

[1] *DPP* v. *Rogers*, § 10.4 n. 14.

[2] The use of the word "gross" would probably continue to exempt conduct like that in *Williams* v. *Gibbs* [1958] Crim.LR 127.

[3] The DPP's consent to prosecution under this section is no longer required: CJA 1972 s.48.

an indecent assault, but of course the object of the Act is to go beyond the law of indecent assault.

> A striking example of extensive interpretation of the Act is a case[4] where a man was sitting on a chair when a girl of 8 came up to him and put her hand on his penis. The extraordinary child kept it there for five minutes, during which time the man stayed passive and did nothing to encourage her. His appeal against conviction under the Act was dismissed.

The Court of Appeal held that the defendant's conduct amounted to "an invitation to the child to do the act," so that it "could fairly be said that what passed between him and the child constituted an act of gross indecency with or towards the child." Some might think it very unfairly said, since no self-respecting parliamentary draftsman would use the word "act" to cover inactivity without making his intention clear. The section, according to its terms, requires either an act or incitement; the court made no reference to the part of the section bringing in incitement, but held that the defendant's conduct amounted to an invitation to the girl to continue the act, this "invitation," so implied, being regarded as an act. This is an abuse of language, because there was no invitation in the ordinary usage of the word. (If my great-uncle George arrives uninvited from Australia and announces that he will give me the pleasure of his company for six months, I may permit him to stay and may even make him welcome but do not thereby invite him.) Also, there was no act. If an "invitation" implied from passivity is an act, there was no need for the section to refer to incitement, because that also would be an act. A draftsman who wanted to encompass the case before the court would surely have extended the offence to *permitting* an act of gross indecency to be performed upon the defendant; but no such words were included. The word "incites" carries a strong implication that a positive act of incitement was meant; and, as was said before (§ 7.3), there are good reasons why the courts should not construe apparently positive verbs in statutes to cover omissions unless the statute so indicates. Another remarkable feature of the case is that the court, while affirming the conviction of committing an act of gross indecency, carefully left open the question whether the act was grossly indecent.

§ 10.6. HOMOSEXUAL OFFENCES

Although this book is not supposed to embrace offences of sexual deviancy like homosexual offences, we should notice for completeness that it is an offence for anyone to commit buggery (anal intercourse) with man, woman or animal,[1] and for a male to commit gross indecency with another male (e.g. mutual masturbation).[2] These acts are generally committed with a consenting partner, but the former[3] is equally an offence if committed with a non-consenting one. When they are performed in private between two males over 21, and certain other conditions are fulfilled, the law is lifted.[4] For acts done to an under-16 these offences overlap indecent assault and indecency with children.[5]

---

[4] *Speck* [1977] 2 All ER 859.

[1] SOA 1956 s.12(1).
[2] *Ibid.* s.13
[3] Not gross indecency: *Preece* [1977] 1 QB 370.
[4] SOA 1967. For proposals to lower the age see CLRC, Working Paper on Sexual Offences 33.
[5] If a charge of indecent assault is brought when the evidence shows buggery, the court should sentence without reference to the buggery, in accordance with the general principle that a sentence should not be based on a graver offence if the conviction is of a lesser offence. See *Rothery* [1976] Crim.LR 640.

§ 10.7. SOCIAL ASPECTS OF CHILD MOLESTATION

Child molesters (termed paedophiliacs or paedophiles) and adult-seeking homosexuals form two distinct groups. Paedophiliacs are very rarely interested in sexual activities with adult males, and a substantial number (perhaps one-quarter) molest prepubertal girls as well as boys. Many of them are married though no longer having sexual intercourse with their wives. They are not violent, and their offence generally consists in indecent handling; only rarely do they perform buggery.[1]

Are offences with juveniles treated severely?

Some paedophiliacs make persistent nuisances of themselves and remain unaffected by short sentences, so that a longer term is justified simply for the sake of incapacitating them from mischief for a while. What is much more questionable is the practice of treating a child molester severely for his first offence.[2]

There is a noticeable, and paradoxical, tendency to sentence the molester more severely for acts done to boys than to girls.[3] Courts often fail to take account of the fact that the child took the initiative.[4] Schoolmasters and their school employees who fiddle with boy pupils (usually by masturbating them) are likely to be sent to prison (sometimes for the insensate term of 4 years on first conviction[5]). In addition to the humiliation of this punishment the schoolmaster will, at least for a time, have to leave the vocation for which he has been trained.[6] Men who are sent to prison for offences against children often have to suffer violence from other prisoners, who believe that they themselves rank above child molesters; consequently, child molesters frequently have to be placed on "Rule 43," which means that they are segregated in cells together and kept apart from ordinary prison life for their own protection.

Judges and magistrates, who often share with common criminals an extreme dislike of child molestation, seem to fear that it may do lasting harm to the victim, perhaps by imbuing a girl with an aversion to men, or a boy with an unhealthy liking for them. Whether the fear is well founded is still a matter of some difference of opinion. Studies of sexual deviants like prostitutes and homosexuals, and of adults suffering from depression or frigidity, show that some experienced genital touching by an adult when young.[7] But no firm conlusion can be

---

[1] Michael Schofield, *The Sociological Aspects of Homosexuality* (London 1965); D J West, *Homosexuality Re-examined* (1977) 214–217. Adults who take a sexual interest in adolescents are sometimes termed ephebophiliacs or ephebophiles; but many men will extend their sexual activities to adolescents if circumstances allow and if they are not deterred by law or the *mores*. Formerly, marriage could be contracted at the age of 12; this was not raised to 16 until 1929.

[2] A court presided over by Lord Lane CJ, which normally showed leniency for minor offences, thought 12 months a suitable sentence for a man (not in a position of trust) who handled young girls indecently: *Freeman* [1980] Crim.LR 737. For a similar decision by a court presided over by the equally enlightened Waller LJ see *Tipping* (1981) 145 JPN 656. In 1981 a first offender received a 5-year sentence: *Wheater* 145 JPN 263. See also *Ware* [1981] Crim.LR 653 (three and a half years to mark "public horror and revulsion").

[3] In 1973 the custodial rate for offenders aged 17–29 was 22 per cent. for indecent assault on boys under 14 and only 8 per cent. for indecent assault on girls under 13. See Walmsley and White, *op. cit.* 65. It seems, however, that the discrepancy was unusually large that year: *ibid.* 46 n. 14.

[4] The fact that the girl led the man on does not exempt him from a prison sentence: *Bernard Smith* (1978) 142 JPN 488.

[5] See [1968] Crim.LR 280, and cp. [1967] Crim.LR 548.

[6] The Department of Education circulates to schools a black list of teachers who are regarded as unsuitable for appointment by reason of misconduct, including conviction of sexual offences: The Times, August 14, 1974. The teacher can apply for reinstatement after three years.

[7] R Gundlach found that more than twice as many homosexual women as heterosexual recalled an early experience of rape or sexual assault: 40 Psychological Reports 250. This may indicate that early sexual abuse by men has a tendency to destroy a girl's respect for men and to produce lesbianism. But there is the possibility that lesbians adduce their memories in self-justification, and in any case the study does not show that genital touching does harm.

drawn from this, because many people who have developed normally were similarly interfered with. According to psychologists it is very rare for either girls or boys to be radically disturbed by a single event. Professor Ivor Mills wrote:

> "I cannot help wondering how many of the neo-Puritans who are pontificating on this subject have actually talked to children who have experienced touching of genitalia with an adult (without actual intercourse). How many have followed them as they grow up or talked to adults who had experienced genital touching as a child? When you do so you cannot help but be struck by how normally they develop."[8]

In the uncommon cases where harm appears to have been done one sometimes cannot be certain how much is to be attributed to family problems before the sexual incident, the reaction of parents to the incident, the trauma of taking part in legal proceedings, and anxiety or guilt at having been instrumental in sending the offender to prison, for perhaps several years. Sociological studies have failed to find any evidence that casual homosexual contacts with adults are liable to turn boys towards a homosexual orientation in later years.[9] Sometimes the initiative in the affair was taken by the child who, desperately needing affection, made seductive gestures to the offender. In one study, two-thirds of the child victims had been sufficiently willing participants to co-operate in the activity more than once with more than one man.[10] Children who have participated in sexual offences have frequently persuaded their friends to do likewise.

When a child has been molested, much will depend on the way in which the parents handle the situation. The important thing is not to involve the child emotionally in the sense of outrage felt by the parents, and particularly to reduce the disturbing effect for the child of being involved in legal proceedings.[11] The harm, if any, is done by insisting upon the child keeping the incident in mind and giving evidence upon it in court: still more if the offender is a person known to the child (perhaps an uncle), who in consequence is sent to prison. Unfortunately, as it must seem to the lawyer, these considerations argue against enforcing the law; but it would help if we could devise a special procedure for trying the case while protecting the child.

Whether to make a charge should depend on an assessment of the likelihood that the offender will repeat the offence. In the minds of many judges sex offenders are repeaters, but a Cambridge survey of 1,985 convicted sex offenders showed that 85 per cent. were not reconvicted during four years of freedom.[12] Men convicted of homosexual offences against boys were the most prone to offend again, but even with this group only 27 per cent. were reconvicted. First offenders show a distinctly lower reconviction rate, of about 10 per cent.[13] There is no general tendency for sexual offenders to progress in the seriousness of their offences.[14] A Canadian study found that adolescent paedophiliacs were shy and socially retarded youngsters who might be expected to develop normally in time. Among the older offenders, many had slowly developed a precarious sexual adjustment, which later gave way in the face of the stress of family or marital problems, or the feelings of loneliness and failing powers at the onset of old age. Only a minority were sufficiently compulsive to warrant custodial detention.[15]

These considerations indicate a great need for the courts to reconsider their sentencing policy for paedophiliacs, and the reconsideration would be helped if Parliament built safeguards into the law. The sentencing of first offenders for gross indecency with children should rest on the supposition that a conditional discharge or suspended sentence is sufficient for deterrence at this stage; and they should never be sent to prison for a first offence of this kind where the child is not attacked or frightened. A lenient treatment is particularly justified where the child

---

[8] Letter to The Times, February 15, 1978. Cp. Lindy Burton, *Vulnerable Children* (London 1968).

[9] M Schofield, *op. cit.* 154.

[10] T.C. N. Gibbens and J. Prince, *Child Victims of Sex Offences* (ISTD, London 1963).

[11] In an effort to lessen the harm, it is provided that in *any* legal proceedings the court may direct that the identity of the child or young person concerned in the proceedings shall not be published: CYA 1933 s.39.

[12] *Sexual Offenders*, ed. Radzinowicz (London 1957) 267.

[13] Mohr, Turner and Jerry, *Pedophilia and Exhibitionism* (Toronto 1964) 83.

[14] West, Roy and Nichols, *Understanding Sexual Attacks* (London 1978) 141–143.

[15] Mohr and others, *loc. cit.*.

precipitated the incident, because of the temptation to which the offender was subjected, the small likelihood of harm having been done to the willing child, and the increased likelihood of harm being done to the child by the severe punishment of one whom he regards as a friend.[16]

§ 10.8. RAPE

Rape is punishable with imprisonment for life.[1] The offence was not given a statutory definition until 1976, when the Sexual Offences (Amendment) Act put the decision in *Morgan*[2] on a statutory footing. The definition has already been reproduced.[3]

"A man" includes a boy.[4] The phrase "sexual intercourse" is used out of prudery, but it is a misleading way of stating the legal requirement, which is satisfied by the least degree of penetration.[5] The carnal act must be *per vaginam*; forcible buggery[6] and fellatio ("oral sex" simulating rape) are not included.

"Who does not consent to it" includes the woman who is unconscious and so neither consents nor consciously withholds consent. The subject of consent is more fully explored in Chapter 23.

Two classes of person are exempt from the law of rape. A husband is legally incapable of perpetrating rape upon his wife,[7] unless the parties are judicially separated,[8] or (probably) separated by consent,[9] or unless the court has issued an injunction forbidding the husband to interfere with his wife, or the husband has given an undertaking to the court in order to avoid the issue of the injunction.[10]

---

[16] A proposal that it should be a defence to a man charged with gross indecency towards a girl that the girl took the initiative and was not corrupted was rejected by the CLRC (the proposer dissenting). See *Working Paper on Sexual Offences* 94.

[1] Sexual Offences Act 1956 s.1 and Sched. 2. Rape, and unlawful sexual intercourse with a girl under 13, are triable only by judge (not recorder) and jury. If the jury are not satisfied that the woman was a non-consenting party, the man cannot be convicted of unlawful sexual intercourse with a girl under 16. A count for this offence must be added expressly if there is to be a conviction of it. But, by some highly technical and suspect reasoning, it is held that the defendant can be convicted of indecent assault if the girl is under 16, since this is a lesser included offence on a charge of rape: *Hodgson* [1973] QB 565.

[2] § 6.6 at n. 4.

[3] § 6.6 at n. 11.

[4] SOA 1956 s.46.

[5] Act of 1976 s.7(2), referring to SOA 1956 s.44. The latter merely says "penetration," but it is declaratory of the common law which declared that the least degree of penetration was sufficient. Emission is unnecessary. See *Dermody* [1956] IR at 32 (following earlier authority and departing from *Gammon* (1832) 5 C & P 321, 172 ER 994).

[6] *O'Sullivan* [1981] Crim.LR 406. The CLRC in its Working Paper provisionally accepted the existing definition of rape, which I think is right in respect of the *actus reus*. But some writers would like to see rape considerably widened to include such acts as fellatio procurred by threats. See Jennifer Temkin in 45 MLR 411–413; Card in [1981] Crim.LR 373.

[7] There was a division of opinion in *Clarence* (§ 9.5). The question was settled by the ruling in *Clarke* [1949] 2 All ER 448, 33 CAR 216, and *Miller* [1954] 2 QB 282; cp. English in 126 NLJ 1223. The Act of 1976 preserves the rule by declaring that rape is *unlawful* sexual intercourse; the word "unlawful" has always been held to exclude intercourse within marriage. See, e.g. Hawkins, *PC* i Chap. 41 s.1.

[8] *Clarke*, last note. Magistrates were deprived of the power to make separation orders by the Domestic Proceedings (Magistrates' Courts) Act 1978. A decree nisi has the same effect: *O'Brien* [1974] 3 All ER 663 (Park J).

[9] See *Miller* [1954] 2 QB at 290. Even this dictum does not provide for separation as a result of the husband's desertion.

[10] *Steele* [1977] Crim.LR 290.

The reason traditionally given for the general rule is the totally unconvincing one that the wife's consent is given on marriage, and she cannot revoke it.[11] It would be an understatement to say that this authentic example of male chauvinism fails to accord with current opinion as to the rights of husbands.[12]

As the law is now interpreted, it does not save the courts from investigating the difficult question of the wife's consent, because, although a husband cannot be prosecuted for rape, he can be prosecuted for assault in doing the self-same thing.[13] The law is thus inconsistent with itself, for if the rule for rape rests on the irrevocability of the wife's consent to sexual intercourse, it is illogical to treat the same act as an assault.[14]

The exemption of the husband does not prevent him from being convicted as accessory to the rape of his wife perpetrated by another.[15] And it has even been held that a husband can be an accessory to the *de facto* rape of his wife perpetrated by an innocent actor; this will be discussed in § 15.16.

The other person who cannot be convicted of rape is a boy under 14, the reason advanced being that he is irrebuttably presumed not to have reached the age of puberty.[16] This fiction is doubly silly. First, puberty may be attained before 14, and secondly, puberty is not necessary for rape. Rape requires only penetration, not fertilisation, so that it is only an ability to have an erection, not an ability to emit semen, that is physically necessary for the crime.

However, the rule has little practical importance, since a boy under 14 who commits what is in fact rape can be convicted of indecent assault.[17] He can be convicted as accessory to rape when he assists another to commit the offence.[18]

---

[11] *Per* Hawkins J in *Clarence* (1888) 22 QBD at 51. See Mitra in [1979] Crim.LR 558.

[12] The CLRC has provisionally recommended the abolition of the marital rape exemption: Working Paper 11; see thereon Jennifer Temkin in 45 MLR 407–411. For an opinion in support of the present law see Norval Morris and A L Turner in 2 U of Qd.LJ 256 ff.

The irrevocable consent rule is supposed to be the foundation of the exceptions noted above, relating to separation and court orders, where an event has happened that is supposed to revoke the irrevocable. Logically, the exceptions should be taken to be abolished by the Act of 1976, which confines rape to "unlawful" sexual intercourse, the word "unlawful" in this context being always taken to mean intercourse outside marriage. Consensual sexual intercourse by a husband with his wife is neither immoral nor illegal, even though it occurs after a separation or court order, because it is within marriage. It should follow that when consent it lacking it still cannot be rape. However, the court would probably say that it was not the intention of the Act of 1976 to abolish the common law rules.

[13] *Miller* [1954] 2 QB 282; cp. *Bourne* (1952) 36 CAR 125.

[14] The immunity of the husband under the common law is found also in some other countries, such as Belgium. But Sweden changed the rule by statute in 1962, and Denmark had changed it earlier. See *Sexual Offences*, ed. Radzinowicz (London 1957) 483, 493.

[15] *Lord Audley* (1631) 3 St.Tr. 401.

[16] *Groombridge* (1836), 7 C & P 582, 173 ER 256; *The General Part*, 2nd edn § 270. The rule is not restated in the Act of 1976, and the word "man" in that Act was clearly meant to include a pubertal boy. But there can be no doubt that it was not intended to include boys under 14.

A boy under 14 cannot be convicted of attempting to commit rape: see *Williams*, next note. The rule was extended so as to exempt boys from conviction of unlawful sexual intercourse in *Waite* [1892] 2 QB 600; see the next section as to this crime.

[17] *Williams* [1893] 1 QB 320.

[18] *Eldershaw* (1828) 3 C & P 396, 172 ER 472, *per* Vaughan B.

On a charge of rape, must the prosecution prove absence of the woman's consent, or is it for the defence to prove consent?

The burden rests on the prosecution, just as it does in cases of assault and indecent assault.[19]

Isn't absence of consent difficult to prove?

The facts of life make consent to sexual intercourse a hazy concept. It poses grave problems of proof and of justice.

1 Some (we do not know how many) complaints of rape are false, since the woman in fact consented. An adolescent girl who consents to intercourse may, to placate her parents, assert that she did not consent; the parents then complain to the police and the girl feels herself compelled to keep to her lie.[20] A girl who is ashamed of her part in the affair and perhaps fears that she is pregnant may even convince herself subsequently that she did not really consent. There is also the danger of a false allegation being made out of spite, when the man was in fact a lover who jilted the woman, or slighted her in some way, or for obscure psychological reasons.[21]

2 That some women enjoy fantasies of being raped is well authenticated, and they may, to some extent, welcome a masterful advance while putting up a token resistance.[22]

> A little still she strove, and much repented,
> And whispering "I will ne'er consent"—consented.

This is a sensitive subject, on which feminists understandably hold strong views. Byron used poetic licence: if the woman expressed her rejection of the man at the vital moment, then she did not consent. When brutal men assert a belief that a weeping or strongly resisting woman was really enjoying it, their defence deserves no attention. But the possibility that faint resistance and whispered protest were not seriously meant needs consideration where the man was well known to the woman and where it is clear that she was not intimidated. If in these circumstances the woman failed to use all means open to her to repel the man, including shouting for help if help was available, the jury may well think it unsafe to convict him. Obviously the argument has no weight where the man made an express threat or used real violence, for these are inconsistent with a merely pretended rape; and if the man was a stranger to the woman and knew that she might be in a state of fear the jury may be

---

[19] For indecent assault see *Donovan* [1934] 2 KB 498.

[20] See West, Roy and Nichols, *Understanding Sexual Attacks* (London 1978) 136. For an instance of a miscarriage of justice in Canada see *Young* (1970) 5 CCC 142. "Taken as a whole there are not a large number of cases of genuine rape, though there are many spurious and doubtful complaints alleging that offence": Lilian Wyles, *A Woman at Scotland Yard* (London 1952) 121. But this opinion was expressed before the present explosion of violence.

[21] Nicholas Fairbairn MP has suggested that a new peril of false complaints arises from the announcement of the Criminal Injuries Compensation Board that they value a proven rape at £2,250. In view of the serious difficulties of rape charges it seems of doubtful policy to attach such a financial inducement to the obtaining of a conviction.

[22] On rape and seduction fantasies in women see Helene Deutsch, *The Psychology of Women* (New York 1945) i 123–127, 256–257; and see Paul H Gebhard and others, *Sex Offenders: An Analysis of Types* (New York 1965) 178.

strongly directed that they can find not only that the woman did not consent but that the man knew it. One woman faced with a rapist intruder reported that her limbs seemed to go like jelly—though in the particular case she put up a resistance.[23] Another confessed that her abhorrence of violence was so great that she preferred to submit than to attack.[24] There is no evidence that juries are unduly prone to take the woman's non-resistance in such circumstances either as consent or as giving the man a credible defence of belief in consent.

3 As some kind of precaution the trial judge is required to warn the jury, on any charge of a sexual offence, of the danger of convicting on the uncorroborated evidence of one witness.[25]

Women who have been raped are reluctant to report it, partly because of the embarrassment of discussing the details with policemen, and partly because of the fear of the even greater humiliation of being a witness in court. So there is no doubt that many women victims do not go to the police, and even fewer would go if they knew what was in store for them.[26] The New York police now have a rape squad of women police, part of whose functions is to interview the victims of rape more sympathetically and effectively than a male officer could.

There is always a conflict between the effective enforcement of the law and the desire to safeguard defendants who may be unjustly accused. This is particularly pronounced in cases of rape. Rules designed to facilitate prosecution (as feminists strongly demand) almost inevitably reduce the safeguards for the defendant, while protecting the defendant diminishes the efficacy of a law that is at best difficult to enforce. The dilemma is particularly acute when the defence seek to cross-examine the woman complainant to show that she is free in her sexual behaviour. The evidence may lend credence to the defendant's evidence that she readily gave herself to him, but is of course bitterly resented by the complainant. The Act of 1976 attempted a solution in two ways. (1) By conferring anonymity upon the woman (unless the court gives leave to publicise her name). By way of partial *quid pro quo*, the defendant is allowed similar anonymity except after conviction. (2) By protecting the woman from having evidence given as to her "sexual experience" in all cases where the man pleads not guilty, unless the judge is satisfied that it would be unfair to the defendant to disallow the questions. (The restriction operates even when the defendant wishes to bring out the woman's bad character after conviction, in mitigation of sentence; but, strangely, it does not apply if he pleads guilty and offers the evidence for the same purpose.) In practice the judge will almost inevitably give his consent when the evidence is likely to weigh with the jury.[27] These provisions in respect of charges of rape apply also to attempted rape, incitement to rape and accessories to rape (but not, strangely again, to conspiracy to rape or burglary with intent to rape).

Is it a defence to a charge of rape that the woman took part in "heavy petting" before refusing consent?

No, but juries frequently acquit if the evidence establishes this. And it is of course a matter of mitigation.

---

[23] Tony Parker, *The Twisting Lane* (Panther Modern Society) 214.

[24] *Ibid.* 218.

[25] On the importance of this safeguard see R Brandon and C Davies, *Wrongful Imprisonment* (London 1973) 132 ff. The CLRC provisionally accepted the present law, in substance; but it is criticised by Jennifer Temken in 45 MLR 417–418. On the whole subject of consent in sexual offences see Koh in [1968] Crim.LR 81 150.

[26] The police in interviewing the complainant frequently "push" her hard, trying to break down her story, in order to see how it will stand up in court. See Barbara Toner, *The Facts of Rape* (London 1977) Chap. 7.

[27] See Adler in 45 MLR 664; note in [1982] Crim.LR 515.

§ 10.9. INTERCOURSE WITH YOUNG GIRLS

We have seen that, for the purpose of the law of indecent assault, girls under 16 are taken to need protection even against themselves; and the same rule of course applies to coition. The offence is termed "unlawful sexual intercourse" (sometimes informally abbreviated to USI). Intercourse with a girl under 13 (in effect, a prepubertal girl[1]) is punishable with imprisonment for life (the same maximum as for rape), under section 5 of the Sexual Offences Act; intercourse with a girl under 16 is punishable comparatively mildly with a maximum of 2 years' imprisonment under section 6 (as amended)—the same maximum, oddly, as for a mere indecent assault.[2]

The object of the law is to save young girls from their own inexperience, and presumably to protect the interest of parents in having a chaste daughter. But there are girls who develop young, who are sexually mature at 14 or even earlier, appearing to be much older, and who seek the attention of men. The man who is enticed into intimacy with such a nymphet may be more sinned against than sinning; yet a prison sentence may be imposed on him.[3] No defence is allowed that the girl was a wanton, or instigated the act, or was a prostitute, or that her parents consented, or even that the parties have married since. These mitigating factors are left either to the wisdom of the police in deciding whether to make a charge, or to the court in sentencing.

Although the police exercise considerable discretion in prosecuting,[4] their practices seem to vary considerably between different parts of the country. A young man who has a serious love-affair with an underage girl is often in greater danger of being charged than a young philanderer, either because it is easier to get evidence in the former case or because the parents are anxious to break up the match. Prosecuting a man who cohabits with an underage girl is particularly unfortunate if he is the father of her child. The sentencing policy of the courts is also very variable.[5]

Instead of bothering with these questions of justice and social policy, the substantive law is preoccupied with questions of age. Section 6, applying to girls under 16, is concurrent with section 5 in respect of girls under 13.[6]

---

[1] But this is only a rough translation. Many 12-year-old girls have attained puberty (even some 9-year-olds), and may not only willingly take part in coition but initiate it. In practice courts tend to attach special seriousness to offences with girls under 12, rather than with those under 13; but sentences are rarely for more than 5 years. See Walmsley and White, *op. cit.* 15–16, 64.

[2] The offence under s.6 became triable either way by CLA 1977 s.16 and Sched. 2. It is unusual for criminal prosecutions for indictable offences to be barred by lapse of time, but the SOA imposes a special time-limit of one year for prosecutions under s.6.

For the many adverse effects of early pregnancy see 280 BMJ 1061.

[3] As in *Taylor* [1977] 1 WLR 612, 64 CAR 183. However, in an even more extreme case where a nymphomaniac aged 11 used great determination to seduce a bus conductor, the latter's prison sentence was remitted on appeal: *Mellett* (1979) 143 JPN 610. If it is agreed that the man should not be punished on first conviction in such a case, why should he not be allowed a defence? Cp. Canadian Criminal Code s.146(3). It was held in *O'Grady* (1978) 66 CAR 279 that a custodial sentence should not be imposed where the parties "are both in the same age group." Why should not the relevant age group be specified by law?

[4] In 1973, for example, the police prosecuted in only 25 per cent. of known cases of USI with a girl 13–16; they cautioned in a further 18 per cent. and took no action in 57 per cent. It is commoner to take care proceedings in respect of the girl. See Walmsley and White, *Sexual Offences, Consent and Sentencing* (HO Research Study No. 54) 42; Card in [1975] Crim.LR 371, 373.

[5] There has latterly been an increase of leniency: in 1974 only 15 per cent. of adults convicted in respect of girls aged 13–16 were sent to prison. But in *McKay* [1982] Crim.LR 542 the CA refused to apply the "clang of the gates" principle where a mature man of exemplary character had sexual intercourse with a girl of 14. See also *Usher* and *Lawson* [1980] Crim. LR 601. A simple boy-girl affair usually ends in a police caution. Cp. Ashworth in 143 JPN 32–33.

[6] This is so as a result of the amendment introduced by the Criminal Law Act 1967. Formerly, s.6 applied only to girls between 13 and 16.

So if the girl has about reached her 13th birthday, a little more or less, any difficulty of proof of age can be circumvented by charging the lesser offence under section 6.

Suppose a man beds a girl under 13, believing her to be older?

He can be convicted under section 5, which, following *Prince* (§ 9.12) is taken to be an offence of strict liability in respect of the girl's age.

Suppose the girl is 14, and he believes her to be under 13?

He can be convicted under section 6. He has *mens rea* in respect of a girl under 16, and commits the *actus reus* in respect of a girl under 16. His mistake as to her precise age is immaterial.

Suppose the girl is between the ages of 13 and 15, and he believes her to be 16?

You have an excellent imagination. In general the offence under section 6 is a matter of strict liability, but a niggardly defence is given by section 6(3).

> "A man is not guilty of an offence under this section because he has unlawful sexual intercourse with a girl under the age of 16, if he is under the age of 24 and has not previously been charged with a like offence,"[7] and he believes her to be of the age of 16 or over and has reasonable cause for that belief."[8]

This is known in the profession as "the young man's defence." As will be seen, the concession is very grudging.

(1) It is given only to young men, under the age of 24, and (2) only in respect of a charge of the lesser offence—not in respect of a charge of intercourse with a girl under 13, which, paradoxically, remains a crime of strict liability in respect of the question of age, even though it is punishable with imprisonment for life. (3) The defendant must not merely believe the girl to be 16 or over but he must have reasonable cause for that belief, so that negligence in failing to make enquiries (even though his belief as to her age is clearly proved) deprives him of the defence.[9] (4) The defence is given only to first offenders; and the mere making of a charge under the section precludes the defence from being raised in future (even though the charge resulted in an acquittal). Parliament has, for once, acted on the slanderer's proverb, that "there is no smoke without fire." But, as a final paradox, it is of no account that the defendant has a string of convictions for indecent assault, rape, or even for sexual intercourse with a girl

---

[7] Including (as the subsection goes on to provide) an attempt to commit such an offence.

[8] See also s.6 (2): where a marriage is invalid because the "wife" is under 16, the man is not guilty of an offence of unlawful sexual intercourse under the section if he reasonably believes the marriage to be valid.

Where a man domiciled in another country marries a girl who is under the age of 16 and the marriage is valid by the law of that country, and he brings the girl here, the marriage will be recognised by English law, and, on principle, coition between the husband and wife could not be regarded as "unlawful" sexual intercourse: see *Alhaji Mohamed* v. *Knott* [1969] 1 QB 1, where however the last point was left open.

[9] The requirement of reasonableness is probably not a severe restriction upon the defence in practice. If the defendant sets up a grossly unreasonable belief as to the girl's age, he may fail, not because he has acted unreasonably but because the jury think that the defence is not an honest one. Lord Devlin, *The Enforcement of Morals* (London 1965) 21 states that in practice it is extremely rare for any youth who sets up the statutory defence that he had reasonable cause to believe that the girl was over 16 to be convicted; juries are easily satisfied of the reasonableness of the belief.

under 13. No evidence can be given of any of these matters, so that he will still be regarded as of unblemished character for the purpose of raising a defence of mistake of age if charged with an offence under section 6.

One of the ineptitudes of the legislation is that, while it gives the limited defence of mistake of age in respect of a charge under section 6, it does not give such a defence, even to a young man, in respect of a charge of indecent assault under section 14. Owing to the effect of the decision in *Prince*, the latter section, like all the other sections of the Act referring to age, is construed as being of strict liability in respect of the age of the woman, except to the extent that the Act expressly modifies this rule. Consequently, cases have arisen in which a young man is acquitted of unlawful sexual intercourse with a girl under 16, by reason of his belief that she was 16 or over, and yet is convicted of indecent assault on precisely the same facts. In some of these cases the Court of Criminal Appeal interfered, reducing the sentence to a nominal one, and strong remarks were made about the foolishness of the legislation and the impropriety of convicting of indecent assault.[10] Consequently, the general practice now is not to charge an indecent assault in circumstances where the real offence, if any, is under section 6, but where the defendant is a young man who has the statutory defence. Yet the law has never been changed, and sporadic cases occur in which there is still a conviction of indecent assault in these circumstances.[11]

What should be considered is whether the ordinary *mens rea* principle should not be applied by statute in respect of the girl's age—getting rid of *Prince*. That men do in fact mistake the ages of girls and women has been known for quite a time. Consider the sage remark of Cavendish CJ in 1376.

> "There is not a man in England who can rightly adjudge her under age or of age. Some women who are 30 years old will seem 18."[12]

The practice of teenage girls in wearing make-up and sophisticated dresses also bears upon the question of parental rights. Parents who abdicate all discipline and allow their 15-year-old daughter to pass herself off as an emancipated 18 can hardly complain if young men regard the girl as older than she is. Moreover, if the girl is of such precocity or of such borderline age that the man can mistake it, an acquittal of the offence is perhaps not of great consequence.[13]

It may be remarked at this place that the burden of proving all statutory exceptions under the Sexual Offences Act is placed on the defendant (s. 47); but, as usual, he need only establish the defence on the balance of probability.[14]

Is it a matter of aggravation that the USI was incestuous?

The legal maximum is not increased, but incest is a specific offence. The law regards it as serious; it is triable only on indictment, and the maximum punishment is 7 years' imprisonment (life, if with a girl under 13).[15] Sentences of imprisonment on men who have committed incest with their daughters are generally high (there are several reasons for thinking them much too high). Some forms of the offence can be committed by both sexes. Being primarily a consensual offence, it is not fully dealt with in this book; but it can be committed whether consent is given or withheld. The statute confines it to members of the nuclear family. A mother can commit

[10] *The General Part*, 2nd edn § 243 nn. 14, 15; Alec Samuels in 116 NLJ 1111.

[11] E.g. 135 JPN 25; 107 SJ 848; [1971] Crim.LR 299 (where a custodial sentence was imposed); [1977] Crim.LR 489; 142 JPN 472. In the latest instance, in 1982, the defendant was given an absolute discharge: 147 JPN 29. *McCormack* [1969] 2 QB 442 is also open to objection, notwithstanding that the alleged intercourse was not proved, for the statutory defence should apply to the preliminaries to intercourse.

[12] YB 50 Edw. 3 6 pl. 12.

[13] The CLRC provisionally proposed an alleviation of the law, but did not go as far as it might have done. See Jennifer Temken in [1981] Crim.LR 368.

[14] *Hudson* [1966] 1 QB 448.

[15] Sexual Offences Act 1956 ss.10, 11 and Sched. 2.

incest with her son (though this is very rare). So can a brother and sister with each other. But in all cases a girl under 16 who permits the offence to be committed with her is exempt.[16]

§ 10.10. DUTIES TO PREVENT SEXUAL OFFENCES

Not only parents but any person who has "custody or care" of a girl under 16 is guilty of an offence if he or she causes or encourages an indecent assault on the girl[1]; and such a person who fails to prevent an offence being committed in his presence "encourages" it in the judges' lexicon.[2] A non-parent is of course much more likely to be charged with this offence than a parent, because he has the enraged parents after him. By other provisions, the owner, occupier or manager of premises on which the act takes place is made guilty of an offence if he knowingly suffers it,[3] and this covers the parent who allows his daughter to misbehave at home.[4] Legislation aimed primarily against prostitution may also be used against persons who allow promiscuity on their premises, even by adults and even though no payment is made.[5] Finally, it is an offence for anyone to "procure" a girl under 21 to have unlawful sexual intercourse with a third person.[6] Not surprisingly, in our permissive age the police make little effort to enforce this legislation.

§ 10.11. SEXUAL OFFENCES BY WOMEN

It is not a specific offence for a woman to have sexual intercourse with a boy under 16, but she is guilty of indecent assault in such cases unless she is purely passive, refraining from indecently handling the boy in any way.[1] Also, if the boy is under 14 the woman is guilty of indecency with children under the Act of 1960.

SUMMARY

Some offences with a sexual motivation can be dealt with as ordinary offences, but there are also specific offences, most of which are in the Sexual Offences Act

[16] There is a large literature; particular mention may be made of Bailey and McCabe in [1979] Crim.LR 749. The CLRC made very modest proposals for the improvement of the law in its *Working Paper on Sexual Offences* 40–46.

[1] SOA 1956 s.28.

[2] *Drury* [1975] Crim.LR 655, where the owner of a house where a girl was baby-sitting was held to have the care of her. Cp. *Ralphs* (1913) 9 CAR 86. But see the discussion of accessoryship by omission in Chap. 13.

[3] SOA 1956 ss.25, 26. In one case (*McPherson*) a circuit judge refused to attach any effect to the word "knowingly" in relation to the girl's age, but it is an objectionable decision: see [1981] Crim.LR 796.

[4] *Webster* (1885) 16 QBD 134, decided on earlier legislation.

[5] SOA 1956 s.33 as interpreted in *Winter* v. *Woolfe* [1931] 1 KB at 555.

[6] *Ibid.* s.23. This requires the sexual act to have taken place: *Johnson* [1964] 2 QB 404. It is one of the sections aimed against the "white slave traffic." and applies where the intercourse takes place abroad, as well as where it takes place in this country. The section is not needed where the woman is taken off to prostitution, because that is an offence by s.22, which applies to women of any age.

[1] *Faulkner* v. *Talbot* [1981] 1 WLR 1528; see note, [1981] Crim.LR 705.

1956 (a consolidating measure). Under the Act, indecent assault has two effects: it raises the maximum punishment above that fixed for a common assault, and certain persons are disabled from consenting to an indecent assault. These are juveniles under 16 and severely subnormal persons. No exemption is provided for young offenders who commit indecent assaults.

The offence is of strict liability in relation to the age of the juvenile, with the § .1–3
following exceptions. (1) Where a man reasonably supposes a woman to be his wife, but the marriage is invalid because she is under 16. (2) Where the defendant did not know and had no reason to suspect that the victim was severely mentally impaired.

An indecent assault may be physical or psychic. The victim need not know what § .4
is happening. "Indecent" may be defined as "overtly sexual." An assault is not indecent if it is neither intended by the defendant nor interpreted by the other party as having a sexual purpose. Indecency involves an offence to customary standards of modesty. It has been held that male homosexual kissing is indecent; *sed quaere*. The element of indecency may arise because of indecency by the defendant with his own body.

By the Indecency with Children Act 1960, it is an offence for any person to § .5
commit an act of gross indecency with or towards a child under the age of 14, or to incite a child under that age to such an act with him or another. This has been held to cover a case where the defendant was totally inactive.

A homosexual offence and incest may be committed with a nonconsenting as well §§ .6, .9
as with a consenting partner.

Rape is committed where a man has unlawful sexual intercourse with a non- § .8
consenting woman, knowing that she does not consent or being reckless as to this (Sexual Offences (Amendment) Act 1976, affirming *Morgan*). The least degree of penetration *per vaginam* is sufficient. The husband is exempt, unless there is a court order forbidding interference or (probably) the parties are separated by consent; but the husband can be prosecuted for indecent assault although what he has done is rape in fact. Boys under 14 are also exempted from the law of rape and unlawful sexual intercourse.

The burden of proving non-consent rests on the prosecution.

Unlawful sexual intercourse with a girl under 16 is an offence; it is a more serious § .9
offence if the charge is stated to relate to a girl under 13. The age of the girl is, as usual, a matter of strict liability, except that a defence is given to a man under 24 who has intercourse with a girl aged 13–16 if (1) he has not previously been charged with a like offence, (2) he believed the girl to be 16 or over and (3) he had reasonable cause for that belief. Such a man can still be charged with indecent assault, though this is regarded as bad practice. The burden of proving all statutory exceptions under the SOA is placed on the defendant, but as usual he need only establish the defence on the balance of probability.

Various duties are placed on adults to prevent indecent assaults on and unlawful § .10
sexual intercourse with girls under 16, and not to allow promiscuity on their premises even by adults.

Chapter 11

MURDER

> There's the scarlet thread of murder running through the colourless skein of life, and our duty is to unravel it, and isolate it, and expose every inch of it.
>
> Conan Doyle, *A Study in Scarlet*

§ 11.1. THE PUNISHMENT FOR MURDER

KILLING a man, whether lawfully or unlawfully, is called "homicide," but this is only a literary expression. There is no *crime* of "homicide." Unlawful homicide at common law comprises the two crimes of murder and manslaughter. Other forms of unlawful homicide have been created by statute: certain new forms of manslaughter (homicide with diminished responsibility, and suicide pacts), infanticide, and causing death by reckless driving.

The classic definition of murder is that of Sir Edward (Chief Justice) Coke,[1] though its antiquated wording requires careful glossing.

> "Murder is when a man . . . unlawfully killeth . . . any reasonable creature *in rerum natura* under the king's peace, with malice forethought, either expressed by the party, or implied by law, so as the party wounded, or hurt, etc. die of the wound, or hurt, etc. within a year and a day after the same."[2]

"Any reasonable creature" means any human being (a demented person being protected), and "*in rerum natura*" (in being) excludes the unborn child. "Under the king's peace" covers everyone except the enemy killed in operations of war.

How are murder and manslaughter distinguished?

The requirements for both are the same except in respect of the fault element and mitigating circumstances. Murder requires, positively, the mental element traditionally known as "malice aforethought," and, negatively, the absence of certain mitigating circumstances that would turn the case into one of manslaughter.

During the formative period of the common law the distinction between murder and manslaughter was of great moment for the defendant, because murder was punished by death, unless the Crown respited the sentence, whereas a person convicted of manslaughter generally escaped that penalty owing to the indulgence known as benefit of clergy; when benefit of clergy was abolished the sentence was changed to a maximum of imprisonment

---

[1] Pronounced "Cook."

[2] *Inst.* iii 47.

for life. The death penalty for murder continued until 1965, when it was replaced by a mandatory[3] sentence of imprisonment for life.[4].

The reasons for abolition may be briefly stated. The mandatory death sentence for murder meant that an extra responsibility was imposed upon the Home Secretary in advising the Crown on the exercise of the prerogative of mercy. As the Royal Commission on Capital Punishment pointed out, there is no single class of offence varying so widely both in character and in culpability as murder. Most intentional killings are within the family, or are of a lover or cast-off lover, or are motivated by jealousy. The motivation is often strong, even to the eye of a detached observer, or else there is clear evidence of mental disorder. Even convinced advocates of the death penalty would agree that very many murders are unsuitable for it.

Consequently, the Home Secretary was faced with the task of examining every capital sentence, with the help of his advisers, for the purpose of determining whether the sentence should be commuted. So frequently had his intervention been called for during the 50 years before the Commission reported in 1953 that the death penalty had been exacted in little more than half the cases in which it had been pronounced.

Meanwhile, a movement had grown up throughout the world to abolish capital punishment, regarding it as an archaic survival of a purely retributive notion of punishment. By 1957, all the States of South America had abandoned it, and in Western Europe the death penalty survived only in the British Isles, France and Spain. It was not found in 7 of the United States, and had fallen into disuse in several others.

In England, a compromise of 1957 was intended to reduce the need for executive intervention, and also to go some way towards satisfying the opponents of the death penalty. The effect of the Homicide Act of that year was to divide murder into two classes: murder punishable capitally and murder not punishable capitally. Perhaps the details of the division could have been better devised, but as things were the compromise worked badly. It made the death penalty depend upon a variety of factors that were not necessarily connected with heightened moral guilt or even social danger. A person who happened to kill with a firearm, for instance, was punishable capitally, whereas one who chose a knife or a bludgeon was not. Eventually, in 1965, the abolitionist argument gained the day; whether rightly or wrongly, we need not discuss.

You referred to a mandatory sentence. Do you mean that under the Act of 1965 the offender must be sentenced to life imprisonment whatever the circumstances of the murder?

Yes if he is convicted of murder. However, provocation, for instance, is a defence to murder, reducing the charge to manslaughter.

But it isn't manslaughter. It's murder.

Killing by provocation is in fact mitigated murder, but in law it is called manslaughter. The purpose of calling it manslaughter was in the old days to escape capital punishment, and is now to give the judge a discretion as to sentence.

---

[3] A command to the court, leaving it with no discretion. Accent on first syllable.

[4] Murder (Abolition of Death Penalty) Act 1965 (subsequently made perpetual by resolutions in Parliament). A person under 18 at the time of the crime is sentenced to be detained during the Sovereign's pleasure: Children and Young Persons Act 1933 s.53, as substituted by the Act of 1965 s.1(5). Other persons under 21 are sentenced to custody for life: CJA 1982 s.8(1). Abolition was achieved in the face of strong popular objection, and opinion polls demonstrate that this feeling continues. For the virtual abolition of the death penalty in the Republic of Ireland see 128 JPN 674, and for Northern Ireland (where the death penalty is retained for murders of police officers or servants of the Crown) see [1967] Crim.LR 209.

The death penalty, though abolished for murder, remains on the statute book for certain offences against military discipline, for some forms of piracy, and for treason. Terrorists who kill for revolutionary purposes could still he convicted of treason and executed; it is only the climate of opinion (or the fear of provoking further terrorism) that prevents this.

What term do murderers in fact serve?

There is an ineradicable idea in the minds of the public that the term is 9 years, but this is only the average for all "lifers," whether murderers or others. Murder in the course of armed robbery, for instance, earns in practice about 15 years (which would be the equivalent of a fixed sentence of about 21 years), murder for gain, 12 years; but there are wide variations.[5]

What about the barmy ones? Must they too be sentenced for life?

Yes, if they are convicted of murder; but they will not be. A mentally disordered defendant (note the proper expression) can in appropriate circumstances set up either an insanity defence, resulting in a special verdict (§ 28.5), or a defence of diminished responsibility, resulting in a conviction of manslaughter (§ 30.1).

Why was the life sentence made mandatory? Why wasn't the judge given a discretion?

Several answers may be given. The most obvious is that murder was thought to be a bad crime that had to have a terrible punishment. The punishment for murder in the old days was a mandatory death sentence; now, by a quirk of language, it was to be a mandatory "life" sentence.

More realistically, the mandatory sentence was a political compromise arived at in order to get capital punishment abolished.[6] A subsidiary (but thoroughly unconvincing) reason for denying a discretion to the judge was that it was desired to keep murder separate from manslaughter. For manslaughter the judge has a discretion. He may sentence the offender to imprisonment for any term up to (and of course including) life; but on the other hand he may save the defendant from a prison sentence: for example, by merely fining him or putting him on probation or (conceivably) granting him a discharge. To make a distinction from manslaughter, the mandatory life sentence for murder was an obvious, if unsatisfactory, expedient. (In fact the two offences could have been retained without making any distinction in respect of sentencing powers.)

Yet another subsidiary reason was that it was thought unsafe for the judge to be allowed to sentence a murderer to anything less than "life"—the judge may underestimate the danger he presented to society. (This is made nonsense of by the fact that if the killer is suffering from mental disorder and gets a verdict of diminished responsibility, the judge has a complete discretion as to sentence. Mentally disordered killers are in general more dangerous and unpredictable than other killers.)

Those who are unpersuaded by the foregoing arguments for the mandatory life sentence may take more kindly to another reason, which is certainly not the official one. Murders often arouse strong emotion, and if a judge were allowed to sentence to any fixed term he might sometimes specify a very long one, such as 30 or 40 years. If an offender has to be kept in prison for a long time it is probably better that the sentence should be indeterminate, in order that it can be reviewed periodically in a state of detachment. (But this objective could be achieved by giving the judge a discretion to award life, or imprisonment up to say 10 years but not more, or any lesser sentence.)[7]

---

[5] John Staples in Prison Service Journal, April 1981.

[6] See D A Thomas in *Reshaping the Criminal Law*, ed. Glazebrook (London 1978) 25–29.

[7] The Butler Committee on Mentally Abnormal Offenders expressed itself as being against the mandatory sentence: Cmnd. 6244 of 1975, para. 19.11. The CLRC, after prolonged discussion, was equally divided on the subject: 14th Report, paras. 42–61.

On a conviction of murder, has the trial judge no control over the length of sentence served?

The Act of 1965 empowers the judge, when giving the life sentence for murder (not for any other crime), to recommend that the culprit (if over 18) should be kept in prison for a specified minimum term of years.[8] The idea was that the judge should be able to signal the seriousness of a particular murder and to satisfy the public that executive discretion would not be used to release the murderer after a relatively short time. Somewhat illogically, though fortunately, his recommendation was not made binding on the Executive.

Judges have used their power to make a recommendation sparingly, and not altogether consistently. Nearly all recommendations have been for substantial periods, ranging from 15 to 30 years,[9] and the Court of Appeal reinforced this tendency by laying it down that no recommendation should specify less than 12 years.[10] The 30-year recommendation is particularly severe: not only does it not, like an ordinary determinate sentence, carry one-third remission, but it does not imply the ordinary possibility of parole. (Although the Home Secretary *may* release the "lifer" on parole before the minimum period has expired, he is very unlikely to grant parole much before, and it is very rarely that he grants parole at all). If an offender is really to be kept in a penal institution for such a length of time, it might be better to have capital punishment.[11]

A curiosity of the recommended minimum sentence is that it seems unlikely that any prisoner will be kept in for longer than the minimum, since after he has languished in prison for perhaps 15 or 30 years, with his mind fixed on the minimum term, it would seem excessively harsh to detain him beyond it. But, if so, the judge's recommendation of a minimum is in fact an order of a maximum. Once it is realised that the judge is empowered in fact to put a limit on the sentence, the claim that the mandatory sentence is necessary as a safegurd against the over-lenient judge becomes even more difficult to maintain.

Some judges recommend a long minimum in very bad cases. Others make no recommendation even for the foulest murders, explaining that the offence is so heinous that no figure could be put upon it that would be appropriate to its gravity, and that the life sentence should mean what it says. Such an approach assumes that a minimum would be a maximum. Yet other judges make no recommendation and do not explain their reasons for not doing so. There is obviously the danger that two persons guilty of murders equally heinous will be treated differently, one receiving a recommended minimum and the other not, simply because the respective trial judges attached a different interpretation to the significance of the minimum.

In order to counterbalance any possible softness in the Home Office, it is provided that the Home Secretary shall not release a person sentenced to imprisonment for life (whether for murder or for any other crime) unless he is recommended to do so by the Parole Board, and first consults the Lord Chief Justice together with the trial judge if available.[12] The judges are

---

[8] For the origin of this see *Criminal Homicide in England and Wales 1957–1968: An Interim Report of the Homicide Research Project, Legal Research Unit, Dept. of Sociology, Bedford College, University of London* 65–68. For judicial practice see A M N Shaw in 15 Howard Jrnl 31. The CLRC recommended that the judge should state his reasons for a recommendation, and that if he is minded to make a recommendation he should so indicate and should invite the defence to make representations: 14th Report, para. 74. The Committee also recommended that there should be a right of appeal against the recommendation.

[9] On one occasion (the Guildford and Woolwich pub bombings) 35 years.

[10] *Flemming* [1973] 2 All ER 401, 57 CAR 524.

[11] Sometimes the judge recommended the full period of life as the "minimum." This recommendation is not within the terms of the Act, and is absurd. At the end of his life the prisoner may be a helpless invalid; is he still to be kept in because a judge said so, perhaps 40 years before? See CLRC, 12th Report, Cmnd. 5184, para. 30.

[12] CJA 1967 s.61.

evidently intended to stiffen the resolve of a possibly indulgent Minister; and judicial opinion is given further weight by the presence of judges on the Parole Board. The Parole Board now has a transcript of what the judge said in sentencing, and of the judgment on any appeal; so there is really no longer any need to consult the trial judge, who is unlikely to be able to add anything.

The judiciary are given another say in the duration of life sentences, but one that can be used in the direction of leniency as well as of severity. In 1965 the Home Secretary invited the judges to write to him after passing a life sentence for murder or manslaughter, setting out any special features of the offence or related to the offender that might be of assistance in the decision as to the treatment of the offender, the regime to which he should be subject, and his suitability for release on a review of his case. So the judge may in public wear a frightening mask, directing the jury in terms that lead them to convict of murder rather than of manslaughter; but then in private he may inform the Home Secretary that the offender was under great stress, is most unlikely to offend again, and should be released at the earliest possible date. It is important for defending counsel to realise the power possessed by the judge, and to bring out every possible circumstance in mitigation, addressing the judge in mitigation after the jury have returned their verdict. He is entitled to do this because of the judge's power to recommend a minimum; in a case where there is strong extenuation the judge will not exercise his power, but the effect of the argument may be to induce the judge to secure clemency by his private representations.

Still, the possibility of notable clemency must not be overrated. The practice is that life sentence prisoners are not looked at for parole until they have served between 3 and 4 years, and even then, very exceptional cases apart, the prisoner will not be considered by the Local Review Committee for several more years.[13] Where there are strongly extenuating circumstances the Home Secretary has very occasionally let out the offender after a year or even less.[14] But the minimum term served by a convicted murderer so far has been six months (and that was a highly exceptional case). It is, therefore, an egregious error to suppose that a person who is convicted of murder in circumstances arousing compassion is likely to be let out after a short time. In contrast, a killer who succeeds in a defence of provocation or diminished responsibility may be treated very indulgently by the court, as we shall see in due course. Many of those convicted of manslaughter do not receive a custodial sentence at all, and may indeed be given a virtual let-off.

It remains to be noted that every "lifer" who is given parole may be recalled to prison if he shows clear signs of continued homicidal tendencies.

§ 11.2. INTENT TO KILL

The mental element in murder is "malice aforethought," but this is a term of art, if not a term of deception. Murder does not require either spite or premeditation. Mercy-killing can be murder, and so can a killing where the intent is conceived on the instant. Malice aforethought is present in contemplation of law whenever there is

— an intent to kill, or
— an intent to inflict grievous bodily harm, or
— risk-taking of a certain (or, rather, uncertain) kind.

Starting with intention: since the enactment of section 8 of the Criminal Justice Act 1967 the courts have dropped the notion of an entirely "objective" intention that was expressed in in *DPP* v. *Smith* (§ 3.3).[1] As

[13] Keith Hawkins, *The Parole Decision* (Chichester 1977) 18.
[14] See CLRC, 12th Report, Cmnd 5184, Table B.

[1] *Wallett* [1968] 2 QB 367.

we have seen, the better view, and the predominant judicial view, is that intention now bears its natural meaning (§ 3.4).

Since the Criminal Justice Act the word certainly refers to the defendant's state of mind, but, even granted that, the persistence of a certain difference of judicial opinion on the subject of intention is evidenced by the speeches of the Lords in *Hyam*.[2] This was a charge of murder, and on appeal all five Law Lords agreed that consciously taking a specified degree of risk of causing death could be sufficient for the crime (see § .4). Lord Hailsham LC and Lord Cross reached this result by holding that intention to kill was not required for murder, which could also be committed by conscious risk-taking. They did not give an artificial extension to the term "intention." Viscount Dilhorne, the third member of the majority, inclined to hold that doing an act with knowledge that death (or g.b.h.) was a highly probable consequence amounted in law to an intention to cause it; but he recognised that the verbal question was unimportant for the decision. The two minority lords (who dissented because they thought the jury had been misdirected) showed by their language that they were using "intention" in its natural meaning, though Lord Diplock expressed his adherence to the artificial meaning. We may say, therefore, that apart from the hesitant language of Lord Dilhorne and a certain inconsistency between linguistic theory and practice on the part of Lord Diplock, *Hyam* represents a judicial acceptance of the natural meaning of "intention" and a rejection of the artificial meaning.[3]

§ 11.3. INTENT TO INFLICT GRIEVOUS BODILY HARM

The second form of malice aforethought at common law was an intent to inflict g.b.h. Its continued existence in modern law was reaffirmed by the House of Lords in *Anthony Cunningham*,[1] despite the fact that it involves anomalies.

Murder requires a killing, so the normal principle would be that the mental element in murder should refer to death, not to a harm short of death.

Moreover, a charge of attempt to murder requires an intention to kill, and cannot be established by proof of an intent to do grievous bodily harm.[2] It may seem remarkable that a person cannot be convicted of attempt to murder when he deliberately inflicts g.b.h. upon another, and yet can be convicted of murder if, as a result of the injury, the victim dies.

Lord Edmund-Davies in *Cunningham* pointed to another disquieting aspect of the rule in that it accounts a person guilty of murder although the harm he intended to inflict was unlikely to kill.

> "I find it passing strange that a person can be convicted of murder if death results from, say, his intentional breaking of another's arm, an action which, while undoubtedly involving the infliction of 'really serious harm' and, as such, calling for severe punishment, would in most cases be unlikely to kill."

An even more serious objection to the rule is that it leaves so much to prosecutorial discretion. In practice, deaths caused with this form of *mens*

---

[2] [1975] AC 55.
[3] See further, 1st edn 209–210.

[1] [1981] 3 WLR 223, 2 All ER 863.
[2] The rule goes back to *Donovan* (1850) 4 Cox 399; cp. *Grimwood* [1962] 2 QB 621. The defendant can, of course, be convicted of intentionally causing g.b.h., or of an attempt to do so, which are punishable as severely as attempted murder. In 1981 an armed robber who shot and paralysed a policeman when resisting arrest was acquitted of attempted murder but sentenced to imprisonment for life under s.18.

rea are generally treated as manslaughter, unless the defendant was engaged on a villainous enterprise. A parent who inflicts grievous harm on his child, so causing its death, is often charged with manslaughter only, and if the charge is murder juries regularly refuse to convict of more than manslaughter.[3] Or the judge may refrain from leaving the question of murder to the jury. So the rule in *Cunningham* is merely a rule that a person may be convicted of murder if he both falls within the rule and is unlucky in the choice of prosecutor, judge and jury.

Notwithstanding these objections, the rule was approved by the CLRC, though with the important qualification that it should be confined to cases where the act was known to the defendant to involve a risk of causing death.[4] The argument for the rule is that when a person shoots or stabs another, his act is sufficiently grave to justify a conviction of murder if death results, even though his intention was only to disable a person from whom he wished to steal, or to stop a pursuer when he was running away after a robbery, or to mutilate someone by way of revenge, or to stop a person giving an alarm. The human body is fragile, and a person who shows himself willing to inflict really serious injury to another, thus causing his death, is so little less blamable than the intentional killer that the law is right in not making a distinction.

There is also the argument that if the law were otherwise a truly intentional killer would be encouraged to run a false defence in the hope of bamboozling the jury. But this is unconvincing, because on a charge of attempted murder the jury must distinguish between false and true defences of lack of intent to kill.

§ 11.4. RISK–TAKING

Whether some degree of risk-taking suffices for murder was formerly in some doubt; all that we know for certain is that the cases on the subject were meagre. However, an affirmative answer was given by the House of Lords in *DPP* v. *Smith*, which lost its authority for a different reason, and then again in *Hyam*.[1] The facts of the latter case were as follows.

> Mrs Hyam, being animated by malice against Mrs B, poured half a gallon of petrol through Mrs B's letter box in the small hours of the morning and set it alight. Mrs B's two daughters died in the fire. Hyam was charged with murder. Her defence was that she had started the fire only to frighten Mrs B into leaving the neighbourhood. The judge directed the jury as follows. "The prosecution must prove, beyond all reasonable doubt, that the accused intended to kill or do serious bodily harm to Mrs B the mother of the deceased girls. If you are satisfied that when the accused set fire to the house she knew that it

---

[3] Thus presenting the judge with an embarrassing problem in sentencing. See § 12.1 n.2.

[4] 14th Report, para. 31. For Lord Wilberforce's objection to the proposal, and Professor Smith's effective answer, see [1981] Crim.LR 837.

[1] [1975] AC 55. For the previous authorities see 1st edn 213; D W Elliott in [1977] Crim. LR 76.

> was highly probable that this would cause death or serious bodily harm then the prosecution will have established the necessary intent. It matters not if her motive was, as she says, to frighten Mrs B."

It will be seen that this direction starts by requiring an intention to bring about the specified consequence, but then says that Hyam's knowledge that the consequence was highly probable would in law be an intention to bring it about. There was no need for the judge to use language in this way. He could equally have said that Hyam was guilty of murder if she either intended to cause death or serious bodily harm or knew that such a consequence was highly probable.

In the House of Lords, Hyam's conviction of murder was affirmed by three out of the five lords, and all five agreed that a person could be guilty of murder if he caused death as a result of consciously taking a specified degree of risk as to causing death. Differing views were expressed as to the precise rule of law.

I thought that people who killed as a result of deliberately taking a risk were guilty of manslaughter. If they are guilty of murder, how do you distinguish the two crimes?

Taking that as a rhetorical question, it is the most important argument against the wider view of murder. Everyone assumes that the reckless driver who takes a chance and causes a fatal accident is guilty at most of manslaughter, not murder. If recklessness is sufficient for murder such a driver must be guilty of murder. Since the conclusion is absurd the premise must be wrong, so that recklessness cannot rationally be regarded as sufficient for murder.

In *DPP* v. *Smith*, the House of Lords was pressed with this argument, and in order to answer it Viscount Kilmuir LC, who in effect delivered the judgment of the House, adopted an expedient. He said that the extended meaning of malice aforethought applies only when an "unlawful act" is "aimed" at someone; it is not enough that the defendant is reckless towards persons generally. This limitation, said the Lord Chancellor, is necessary "in order to eliminate cases of negligence or of careless or dangerous driving."[2]

The rule is stated in extremely loose terms. Only metaphorically can one aim an act. Does the rule require an intention to injure someone, and if so what is the necessary degree of injury?[3]

In *Hyam*, Viscount Hailsham LC thought that mere foresight of even a high degree of probability of harm was not intention, but he held that knowingly exposing a person to a serious risk of death or g.b.h. without lawful excuse amounted to an intention so to expose him, and was sufficient *mens rea* for murder. As to the degree of risk, he spoke of knowledge of: likelihood, probability, high probability, extreme

---

[2] *DPP* v. *Smith* [1961] AC at 327.

[3] It can be strongly argued that the alleged rule violates s.1 of the Homicide Act 1957, which forbids the courts to make a conviction of murder hinge on the commission of another offence.

probability, risk and serious risk. In his final formulation he settled for *serious risk*, but he (alone of the lords) qualified this by the "aiming at" doctrine of *DPP* v. *Smith*, which would presumably have the effect of removing some serious risk-takers from the ambit of murder. Viscount Dilhorne required knowledge of *high probability* of death or injury, while Lord Cross referred merely to knowledge of probability. He remarked of the trial judge's summing up that it was unduly favourable to the defendant in inserting the word "highly" before "probable." These were the majority lords.

Lords Diplock and Kilbrandon, the minority in respect of the actual decision, thought that the defendant must know at the time of doing the act that death is likely, though at another place in his speech Lord Diplock required that the defendant "must have foreseen as a likely consequence of his act that human life would be endangered," which postulates a double uncertainty: that implicit in the word "likely," and that implicit in the word "endangered." The reason for their dissent was that they required the risk-taking to be as to life, whereas the majority extended the law of murder to risk-taking as to grievous bodily harm. This particular divergence does not affect the significance of the minority views as to the degree of known risk.

None of the lords spoke of recklessness by that name and none of the expressions they used bears an exact meaning.

That there is a difference between the formulations may be illustrated by considering a case where a person places a bomb in a store and gives the people inside two or three minutes to get out before the bomb explodes. Suppose that, for some reason, one of these people fails to escape in time and is killed. (A deaf and arthritic person, who did not notice what was happening until too late.) Lord Hailsham's rule would (apart from the "aiming at" limitation) make the bomber guilty of murder if he knew there was a serious risk of death, which would be easy for the jury to find in these circumstances. Viscount Dilhorne's requirement of knowledge of high probability might be more difficult for the jury to find, if the bomber gave the public a "fair" chance to escape. Even Lord Cross's rule, favouring simple probability, might be more difficult to satisfy than Lord Hailsham's, because whereas a 30 per cent. risk of causing death would certainly be a serious risk, death would not be probable if "probable" means "more likely than not."

The "aiming at" doctrine creates a further complexity. In the case just put of the bomber who gives the public some opportunity of escaping from the store, he may say that he was not aiming at members of the public (as is shown by the fact that he gave warning), but wished only to damage the store. Even if it is found as a fact that he intended to alarm people, does one "aim at" a person by intending to alarm him but not to hurt him? Viscount Hailsham evidently thought so, because those were the facts of *Hyam*, but it is surprising that he did not discuss the point. Is it a proper use of language to say that one "aims at" a person if, in effect, one aims to miss, and intends only to frighten? In view of the fact that four out of five law lords in *Hyam* ignored this limitation of the law, it seems that Viscount Hailsham was stating a merely individual view—though it had the support of the whole House in *DPP* v. *Smith*.

All that *Hyam* decides is that a direction to the jury in terms of knowledge of high probability is valid. It does not decide (because the point was not before the House) whether a direction in terms of some lesser degree of probability may not be sufficient. Three law lords out of five favoured probability or likelihood, though whether these two terms are synonymous is anyone's guess.

We need not enter further into the difficulties of quantifying risk-taking for the purpose of murder.[4] Murder by risk-taking is in fact an example of Orwellian "doublethink"; it is a principle applied against those who are thought to deserve it, but is never contemplated in

---

[4] See more in 1st edn 215–216.

relation to those who do not.[5] Prosecutions based on it are rare. Killing by taking risks is the typical province of the law of manslaughter, not of murder. Even killing by a violent attack is often charged as manslaughter—particularly killing by parents of young children. Where a person whose life has been gambled with does not die, penalties are often very light. It is not at all uncommon for fleeing bandits or even ordinary motorists to drive recklessly at policemen and others to make them jump out of the way; if no death or injury occurs the driver is charged merely with reckless or careless driving and when convicted is often treated with astonishing leniency.[6] But if a policeman were killed in this way the driver would quite likely be charged with and convicted of murder.

On an ordinary charge of murder where there is clear evidence of intention to cause death or grievous bodily harm, the trial judge is well advised not to direct the jury on risk-taking, since this would complicate the issues unnecessarily.[7] The CLRC has recommended that the problems created by *Hyam* should be solved by abolishing the rule in that case.

§ 11.5. TRANSFERRED INTENTION

The doctrine of transferred intention applies in murder, an early example being *Gore* (1611).[1]

> Agnes Gore was a murderess, but not in the way that you might think. She mixed ratsbane with her husband's medicine. He took it, and, his condition suddenly worsening, the medicine was suspected. The apothecary who had compounded it, to prove there was nothing wrong with it, swallowed some himself and soon after died. Agnes was convicted of the murder of the apothecary, because "the law conjoins the murderous intention with the event which thence ensued."

A slightly different form of transferred intention occurred in the case of *Saunders and Archer* (1575),[2] dramatically reported by Foster as follows.

> "Saunders with intention to destroy his wife, by the advice of one Archer mixed poison in a roasted apple, and gave it to her to eat. She having eaten a small part of it gave the remainder to their child. Saunders at this dreadful moment made a faint attempt to save the child; but conscious of the horrid purpose of his own heart, and unwilling to make his wife a witness of it, desisted; and stood by and saw the infant he dearly loved eat the poison, of which it soon afterwards died. It was ruled without much difficulty that Saunders was guilty of murder of the child."

Saunders would have been just as guilty if his wife had passed the poisoned apple to the child in Saunders's absence and without his knowledge. But if the wife had come to know that the apple was poisoned,

---

[5] In *Att.-Gen. for Northern Ireland's Reference* [1977] AC 105, where a soldier shot at and killed a fleeing suspect, the judge in acquitting him of murder thought it sufficient to find that the soldier did not intend to kill or seriously injure the deceased, without considering the question of risk-taking. The decision passed without comment on this point in the House of Lords.

[6] In *Sheehan*, The Times, August 4, 1977, a man drove at speed for two miles in trying to shake another man off the bonnet of his car (facts very similar to *DPP* v. *Smith* except that the victim was not a policemen and was only bruised); he was merely fined for reckless driving etc. Cp. 142 JPN 460; *Phelan* [1978] Crim. LR 572; 1st edn 217 n. 10.

[7] *Beer* (1976) 63 CAR 222.

[1] Co.Rep. 81, 77 ER 853.

[2] Foster, *Crown Law* 371, 2 Plowden 473, 75 ER 706.

and had passed it to the child in his absence with the object of causing Saunders to feel remorse for the child's death, Saunders would not have been guilty of murder of the child, because the effective cause of the child's death would then have been the conscious act of the wife. (Saunders would, however, have remained guilty of attempting to murder his wife.)

The responsibility of Archer on the above facts will be discussed when we come to the subject of complicity.[3]

§ 11.6. KILLING A SUPPOSED CORPSE

Murder is committed by an act (or omission) causing death, and the question arises whether the mental element must exist at the time of the act causing death.

Suppose that D inflicts a series of knife wounds on V, intending to kill him. The medical evidence is that the last stab killed V, but at that time D was pretty sure that V was already dead, and delivered this last stab just to make sure. Clearly, he is guilty of murder, because when he delivered the last blow he had a conditional intention to kill—an intention to kill if the victim should still be alive.

Yes, but now suppose that, at the time of the act that killed, D fully believed V to be dead. D stabbed V intending to kill him. Believing him to be dead, D threw him over a cliff, or into a river, in order to conceal his crime; and the medical evidence is that V died from the fall or from drowning. Is this murder?

Although the authorities are not as precise as might have been wished, it can be said with some assurance that D's conduct will be viewed as a whole, and he will be guilty of murder.

The abstract principle is cumbersome to formulate, but it would run something like this. A person may commit two acts against another. (1) An unlawful act reducing him to a state in which the actor mistakenly believes him to be dead; this act is such that, if the victim had died as an immediate result, it would have been murder. (2) An act of disposal of the victim's body, which brings about the victim's death; this act is such that, if the actor had known the victim to be alive when he did it, the actor would have been guilty of murder. When these conditions are fulfilled, the actor is guilty of murder.[1]

Isn't there a problem? Normally, the defendant's act and his mens rea co-exist in point of time (§ 7.5). In the present situation, D had the mens rea before he committed the act that immediately caused the death (throwing

---

[3] § 13.9. Archer was held not guilty, and J C S Smith infers from this that Saunders's conviction did not rest on the law of transferred intention ([1983] Crim.LR 106), but this does not seem to follow. Archer was acquitted because Saunders, when he knowingly allowed the plan to miscarry, put the result outside the common purpose. This did not affect Saunders's liability as perpetrator on the basis of transferred intention.

[1] A similar principle would apply where (1) above is an unlawful omission.

If the omission occurs at the second stage (leaving the supposed corpse exposed so that the victim dies from exposure), obviously the case would again be classified as one of murder, since the death would be regarded as having been directly caused by the attack.

the body over the cliff); but when he committed this act he had no mens rea in respect of killing. In the ordinary case a person who thinks he is dealing with a corpse and who destroys it would not be guilty of murder even though the supposed corpse was alive, because there would be no intent to kill. Why should his prior and abortive intent to kill make any difference?

The courts have rejected this argument, though, as I said, not with the clarity of reasoning that might have been wished. They have reached their decisions by enquiring whether there was a preconceived plan covering what was done, or whether there was a continuing series of acts; but these enquiries are unsatisfactory substitutes for a basic decision of policy. The proper view is that this is a situation where the act and intent need not concur.

The first case in this country was *Meli*[2], before the Privy Council. A conviction of murder was upheld on the ground that the defendants had set out to do all the acts (including the disposal of the body) as part of a plan; and it did not matter that they thought that their purpose had been achieved (that the victim had been killed) earlier than it had been. An English case followed this and took the same position.[3]

But suppose that the defendant says that when he killed the victim he had no plan to dispose of the body, and only decided to do that when he had the "body" on his hands? The point arose in the Supreme Court of South Africa (Appellate Division), and also in the Fiji Court of Appeal; both courts held that the killer could be convicted of murder even though the disposal of the supposed corpse was not part of a plan conceived before the murderous attack.[4] There can hardly be any doubt that our courts would say the same if the point arose.[5] Policy requires this, because (1) there is no moral merit in the defence of lack of *mens rea* in these circumstances, and (2) acceptance of the defence would often impose an impossible burden on the prosecution of establishing the precise moment at which death occurred.

§ 11.7. AUXILIARY RULES

Contrary to the rule formerly prevailing, it is now permissible to include other counts in a charge of murder; and this is sometimes done.[1] But the judge has the usual discretion to order separate trial on any one or more counts; and if he thinks that in order to avoid unfairness to the defendant

---

[2] [1954] 1 WLR 228; *sub nom. Thabo Meli* [1954] 1 All ER 373.

[3] *Moore* [1975] Crim. LR 229. *Church* [1966] 1 QB 59 may seem on its face to be to the same effect, but the CA somewhat fudged the rule. Purporting to follow *Meli*, the court said, obiter: "The jury should have been told that it was still open to them to convict of murder, notwithstanding that the appellant may have thought his blows and attempt at strangulation had actually produced death when he threw the body into the river, if they regarded the appellant's behaviour from the moment he first struck her to the moment when he threw her into the river as a series of acts designed to cause death or grievous bodily harm." The obvious difficulty is that the disposal of the "body" was not one of "a series of acts designed to cause death etc." It lay outside any such series, because when it was done the defendant thought the victim was dead. For this reason, a direction in the terms suggested would be self-contradictory.

[4] *Masilela* 1968 (2) SA 558; *Tara Chand* (1967) (Fiji), discussed by I D Elliott in [1969] Crim.LR 512–513. In *Ramsay* [1967] NZLR 1005 the New Zealand CA held that the supposed corpse doctrine in murder applied only where there was an intention to kill, not where the murderous malice involved an intention to injure or risk-taking; but that limitation is unlikely to be accepted in England. See *Moore*, last note. For a suggested solution of the general problem in terms of causation, which however, seems to be open to objection, see 1st edn 220; Elliott, *op. cit.* 513–514. On the problem on manslaughter see § 12.7.

[5] See § 12.7.

[1] Practice Direction [1964] 1 WLR 1244; cp. [1958] Crim.LR 125, 466, 615; [1965] *ibid.* 663.

the murder charge should be tried by itself, he will order that the counts for the other crime or crimes shall lie on the file and not be proceeded with without leave. The same procedure is used if there is a second indictment.

Are there any other rules of law designed to prevent murder or to assist in its detection?

Of course there is elaborate control of firearms, explosives and poisons. Investigation into deaths is assisted by requirements of medical certificates of death or still-birth, by special requirements for cremation, and by requiring coroners' inquests and autopsies to be held or performed where the circumstances of a death are not satisfactorily explained by a medical certificate. A prominent purpose of these arrangements is to detect, and therefore to deter, criminal homicide; but they are by no means knave-proof. Where there is evidence of criminal homicide and a prosecution is likely to be brought, the coroner will adjourn the inquest until the prosecution has been concluded, in order to avoid a double investigation of the facts.[2]

SUMMARY

Murder is unlawfully killing a human being who has been born and is under the § .1
queen's peace, with malice aforethought, the death following within a year and a day. The same definition is supposed to apply to manslaughter, omitting the reference to malice aforethought. The punishment for murder is a mandatory sentence of imprisonment for life. The judge may recommend that the offender (if over 18) shall be kept in prison for a specified minimum sentence. There are special provisions relating to parole.

"Malice aforethought" has become a purely technical term, covering three § .2
different mental states. First, an intent to kill. The fictitious meaning of intention has been rejected since the Criminal Justice Act 1967 s.8.

Secondly, an intent to inflict grievous bodily harm (i.e. really serious harm): § .3
Cunningham.

Thirdly, consciously risking one of these outcomes. In *Hyam*, variant views were § .4
expressed as to the degree of risk, and Viscount Hailsham further said that murder by risk-taking could be committed only when the defendant aimed an unlawful act at someone. However, the "aiming at" doctrine is highly suspect, particularly as it was not mentioned by the other lords. In practice murder is rarely charged in a case of risk-taking; and on an ordinary charge of murder the CA has advised the trial judge not to direct the jury on this form of fault.

Intention can be transferred. § .5

Where D unlawfully attacks V with the mental element for murder and, thinking § .6
him to be dead, disposes of the supposed corpse in a way that in fact kills V, this is held to be murder.

Other counts may be added to a count for murder. § .7

---

[2] Coroners (Amendment) Act 1926 s.20, as substituted by CLA 1977 Sched. 10; 128 JPN 833.

CHAPTER 12

INVOLUNTARY MANSLAUGHTER

Crime is regarded as somewhat down-market by civil lawyers. Bankers and property developers are thought to be more desirable customers than indecent assaulters or petty thieves, or at least create a better impression when they are sitting round in the waiting-room. And yet, while civil law is nearly always about money, criminal law is concerned with more vital matters, such as life, love and the liberty of the subject.

John Mortimer, *Clinging to the Wreckage*

§ 12.1. THE KINDS OF MANSLAUGHTER

DEATH is not always the worst evil that can befall us, but we mostly so regard it. For this reason, various kinds of unlawful killing short of murder are grouped under what is legally the serious crime of manslaughter.

The definition of manslaughter is supposed to be the same as that of murder, except that the words "with malice aforethought either express or implied" are omitted. In fact the two crimes differ in a further respect, that certain exceptions from murder (provocation, diminished responsibility, suicide pacts), not stated in the traditional definition, reduce the offence to manslaughter.

Manslaughter is a built-in alternative to a charge of murder. All its essentials are supposed to be comprised in the charge of murder, so the jury may on the indictment for murder convict of manslaughter as an included offence. The theory is false, since it is not enough to convict of manslaughter merely to show that all the essentials of murder other than malice aforethought are present; but the result of the false theory is convenient, and it is confirmed by statute.[1]

If the jury return the lenient verdict, the judge in sentencing is bound to give effect to the view of the facts implicit in it. He must assume that the facts were not such as to justify a verdict of murder, even though in his opinion they were.[2] But he may sentence the defendant to life imprisonment for manslaughter (which would be the same as the sentence for murder) on the ground of the defendant's mental instability, this sentence not being governed entirely by punitive or deterrent considerations.

Assuming that the case is not one of murder, what precisely must be proved to make the killing amount to manslaughter?

The law-books recognise two forms of manslaughter, voluntary and involuntary, though the verdict of the jury does not distinguish between them.

---

[1] Criminal Law Act 1967 s.6(2). The judge was said in *Daley* [1980] AC 237 to be under a duty to direct the jury on manslaughter (so as to leave them with the choice) if there is evidence to make the propriety of a murder conviction at all doubtful. Previously the judge had an option except in cases of provocation, and the Privy Council does not seem to have been aware that it was requiring a change of practice; but the change is beneficial. Cp. § 7.8 n. 3.

[2] For this principle see § 1.3 n. 8. A departure from it was made in *Nuttall* [1968] Crim.LR 173; see criticism in [1968] Crim. LR 176–177, 398.

Voluntary manslaughter means an act of murder reduced to manslaughter on account of the mitigating circumstances already mentioned (provocation; diminished responsibility; suicide pact).

Involuntary manslaughter, the subject of this chapter, means the form in which there is (or need be) no intention (*voluntas*) to kill or do grievous bodily harm (a strange meaning of "involuntary"). There are two subspecies, both of them, as will be painfully seen in this chapter, exhibiting the common law at its worst. We cannot even give the first of them an uncontroversial name, since the courts have failed to settle clearly what fault element is involved; in this book it will be called "reckless manslaughter," though the word "reckless" will give us trouble. The other subspecies is constructive manslaughter.

§ 12.2. RECKLESS MANSLAUGHTER: POSITIVE ACTS

This form of manslaughter requires the prosecution to prove that the defendant *caused* the death in question by an act or omission, amounting in either case to what is called *recklessness* (in a special sense) in breach of a *duty of care*.

One is always under a duty of care not to cause the death of another by *positive acts* of negligence, so that nothing turns in practice on the requirement of duty in cases of this sort. The duty of care does, however, call for consideration in connection with manslaughter by omission (§ .3). The problem of causation is postponed to Chapter 16. This leaves us at this place to discuss the fault element.

At first the requirement was one of negligence. During the second half of the 19th century it came to be limited to gross negligence. The classic definition is in *Bateman*,[1] where the Court of Criminal Appeal said:

> "To support an indictment for manslaughter the prosecution must prove . . . that the negligence or incompetence of the accused went beyond a mere matter of compensation and showed such disregard for the life and safety of others as to amount to a crime against the State and conduct deserving punishment."

Isn't that a circular definition?

It is true that the definition serves to tell us little more than that the negligence necessary for the crime of manslaughter must be criminal—a fact that we knew to start with. It fails to express whether the defendant must have appreciated the risk, though perhaps this requirement is to be understood from the reference to a "disregard for the life and safety of others;" one cannot disregard a risk of which one is unaware. A minor objection is that the concluding words mistakenly suggest that it is for the jury to consider whether punishment is to be awarded. That is not their function. A conviction of manslaughter may be legally justified even though the judge afterwards grants a discharge.[2]

---

[1] (1925) 94 LJKB 791, 133 LT 70, 41 TLR 557, 19 CAR 8, 28 Cox 33.

[2] To avoid the second objection, it was proposed by the CCA in *Andrews* [1937] WN 69 that the concluding words should he altered to: "and to call for a conviction."

Whatever may be thought of the definition in *Bateman*, it has been frequently approved since. Not all judges have followed it exactly. Some have merely told the jury that the negligence must be of high degree, or must be "gross negligence" or "criminal negligence." Others have expressly required what they refer to as recklessness (without explaining it), or some kind of mental element. Previous practice is likely to be affected by the decision in *Seymour* (1983), to which we will come presently.

During the 1930s the view emerged that "recklessness" was a good word to use in explaining the fault required, but the cases favouring this word were most unsatisfactory. Sometimes the jury are instructed in terms of recklessness but are left to make what they can of it. ("After all," said Lord Widgery CJ , "recklessness is a perfectly simple English word. Its meaning is well known and it is in common use."[3]) Sometimes they are specifically told that they must find a mental element of recklessness, inadvertence not being enough. Sometimes the fault element is described in words so chosen that the reader or hearer is left in doubt whether it is objective or subjective, part of the judge's description fitting the one view, part the other—the judge apparently being unconscious that he is floundering between alternatives.[4]

The decision in *Lamb*,[5] the revolver case (§ 5.2 at n. 6), may be offered as a further example of the imprecision of judges' language.

> Much of the discussion on appeal in this case concerned the law of constructive manslaughter, which will be considered presently, but some remarks were made on manslaughter by negligence. The court laid it down generally that *mens rea* is now an essential ingredient in manslaughter, and proceeded: "When the gravamen of a charge is criminal negligence—often referred to as recklessness—of an accused, the jury have to consider among other matters the state of his mind, and that includes the question of whether or not he thought that that which he was doing was safe. . . . In the present case it would, of course, have been fully open to the jury, if properly directed, to find the defendant guilty because they considered his view as to there being no danger was formed in a criminally negligent way. But he was entitled to a direction that the jury should take into account the fact that he had undisputedly formed that view and that there was expert evidence as to this being an understandable view." The direction being at fault, the conviction was quashed.

What is one to make of this? The initial reference to *mens rea* and to a consideration of what the defendant thought suggests that the court has a subjective test in mind. Then this seems to be rejected, because we are told that the defendant can be guilty of negligent manslaughter although he thought that what he was doing was safe. So why were the jury bidden to enquire into the latter question? Well, the direction proceeds, they should take it into account. They take it into account, but it does not countervail evidence of negligence. So for what purpose is it to be taken into account? Some other decisions are more indulgent, at least in words. Consider *Cato* again.[6]

> A drug addict died as the result of an injection of heroin given him by the defendant. The judge directed the jury that it was manslaughter to cause death by an act that was "grossly negligent or, in other words, reckless"[7]—on its face, a similar equation to that propounded in *Lamb*. A conviction of manslaughter was upheld on appeal. One might have thought that the judge meant to convey to the jury that gross negligence (alternatively called recklessness) was sufficient. But the Court of Appeal seemed to understand the direction as meaning the opposite: that the gross negligence required had to involve subjective recklessness, so that it had to be shown that the defendant knew

---

[3] *Cato* [1976] 1 WLR at 119C, 1 All ER at 268*a*.

[4] The cases are collected in 1st edn 225 ff., and the speech of Lord Atkin in *Andrews* [1937] AC at 583, in particular, is discussed at p. 226.

[5] [1967] 2 QB 981.

[6] § 9.10 at n. 15. See the admirable note by Celia Wells in 39 MLR 474.

[7] See the report [1976] 1 WLR at 114H, 115A, 1 All ER at 264*c*.

that injecting heroin could give rise to death or grievous bodily harm.[8] The defendant in giving evidence had said that he had no idea that the injection could cause death or serious bodily harm, and on this the court commented that "of course in deciding whether the appellant had himself acted recklessly one would have to have regard to the fact, if it was accepted, that he did not know about the potentiality of the drug." Apparently the view of the court was that the jury had had their minds directed to the issue, and were free to find, notwithstanding the defendant's denial, that he was aware of the danger specified.

This is a very casual treatment of the matter. The heroin had been produced by the deceased himself, who had made up the syringe, and in these circumstances it is difficult to see how the defendant was reckless as to any special danger, other than the danger of producing an addiction. It is little use having a rule of law requiring a mental state if the jury are allowed to convict without any evidence of that state.

The theoretical law is one thing, practical realities another. Generally, a person who makes an honest mistake, who has not clouded his own judgment by taking drugs, and who has not undertaken an obviously risky course of conduct, is pretty safe from a conviction of manslaughter: and it is not normally the practice even to bring a charge in these circumstances. But if the defendant has taken drugs (including alcohol) and has killed otherwise than in driving, he is very likely to be charged and convicted, and he may be severely punished. See further on intoxication to Chapter 21.

Seymour[9] (referred to before) is a rare revival of the charge of "motor manslaughter," that is to say, manslaughter by driving. The usual charge in these cases is of the statutory offence of causing death by reckless driving, or of reckless or careless driving (Chap. 14). But in *Seymour*, on particularly flagrant facts, the House of Lords upheld a conviction of manslaughter, and felt compelled to wrestle once more with the fault element. The effect of the decision appears to be that manslaughter requires, in general, recklessness in the debased sense of *Caldwell* and *Lawrence*. Lord Roskill, delivering the opinion of the House, said that once it was shown that the statutory offence of causing death by reckless driving co-existed with the offence of manslaughter, it would be wrong to give the word "reckless" a different meaning according to whether the statutory or the common law offence was charged. Accordingly, the decisions in *Caldwell* and *Lawrence* applied to manslaughter. But their lordships qualified this in two ways. First, the recklessness required for manslaughter must be as to the risk of causing injury to the person.[10] Secondly, it must involve negligence of a higher degree than that required for a charge of causing death by reckless driving. "Parliament," said Lord Roskill "must be taken to have intended that 'motor manslaughter' should be a more grave offence than the statutory offence. The jury should be told that for manslaughter the risk of death being caused must be very high."

One would have thought that even on a charge of reckless driving the risk of death must be very high. If this is so, how are the two charges to be distinguished? The lame answer in

---

[8] *Ibid.* at 119B–D, 1 All ER at 268*a–b*, 62 CAR at 48. See § .4 as to knowledge of risk of a lesser degree of harm.

[9] The Times, July 22, 1983. See note on the court below in [1983] Crim.LR 260.

[10] See § 14.4 at n. 9.

effect given by their lordships is that the question is to be evaded by not requiring the jury to distinguish. Only very rarely should "motor manslaughter" be charged; if it is, it can be joined with a count for causing death by reckless driving, but the judge must require the prosecution to elect upon which of the two counts they wish to proceed.

In this way the jury are saved the embarrassment of making the choice between degrees of risk. But it seems remarkable that the choice is then left almost entirely to the prosecution. Suppose the prosecution elect to proceed on the charge of manslaughter, and suppose that the judge is of opinion, after the evidence has been heard, that the case does not come up to manslaughter; is he then to direct an acquittal, or can he allow the prosecution at that stage to reinstate the charge of the statutory offence? In practice, no doubt, if the prosecution go for manslaughter they will get a conviction, and the conviction will be upheld on appeal. From the defendant's point of view it is probably a matter of indifference whether he is convicted of one or the other. In *Seymour*, where the recklessness was extremely grave—so grave as to have justified a conviction of murder under the doctrine of *Hyam*—the sentence for manslaughter was only of 5 years' imprisonment, which would have been just as possible if the conviction had been of causing death by reckless driving.

The problem of recklessness in driving cases will be further considered in § 14.4.

§ 12.3. HOMICIDE BY OMISSION: THE DUTY

Omissions resulting in death can be regarded as either murder[1] or manslaughter according to the fault element. In practice charges are rarely brought, and even if a charge of murder might technically succeed the indictment is almost invariably for manslaughter.

If we had a statutory duty to render assistance to specified classes of persons in immediate danger, as there is in many European countries, it is to be expected that the penalty would be relatively light, reflecting the moral difference between killing and letting die. The prohibition of killing is the most urgent requirement of any society, whereas the intervention of the criminal law to promote the giving of assistance to those in distress is little needed for the general safety. Apart from the upbringing of children, it is only rarely that sick people are left without necessary assistance by their relatives and acquaintances, at least to the extent of informing the social services authorities of their plight.

Moreover, while killers transgress against a deeply-felt taboo, a person may neglect a child or invalid from his own inadequacy or selfishness rather than from malevolence. When a lodger (for example) falls ill, his landlord does not initiate his distress, but may merely fail to cope. Yet the courts, by extending the law of homicide to these omissions (§ 7.3), have at the same time caused such offences to be treated with something of the same severity as other cases of homicide; and the severity evokes no protest from a legal profession that has become habituated to the rule.

The courts first perceived a duty to act for the helpless as arising from status. Where a person was under a duty imposed by the Poor Law to maintain another, who was unable to look after himself, the neglect of that duty, where the other died in consequence, was manslaughter. The rule applied to husbands in respect of wives, and parents in respect of unemancipated children.

Did the Poor Law make it manslaughter to neglect wives and children?

No. It merely established financial responsibility for them. What the judges were really doing, of course, was to turn morality (or perhaps retributive instinct) into law; but they were chary about admitting this, and preferred to find some kind of legal basis for the conclusion even though it was not logically compulsive.

---

[1] *Gibbins* (1918) 13 CAR 134.

Once the concept of a duty to save life became established as the basis of a conviction of manslaughter, it was possible to expand the list of duties. Thus a duty was also imposed as a result of contract, where an employer received an employee or apprentice into his house. The employer was regarded as impliedly undertaking to provide the necessities of life if the other became incapacitated or was unable to withdraw from his control. In the second half of the 19th century the duty was extended to voluntary undertakings, as where the defendant had received a young child or a lunatic into his house. The undertaking was expressly or impliedly given to a relative or the previous custodian of the person received.[2]

The next step was to extend the duty to cases where there was no promise to care for the person received. At this point we must notice an ambiguity in the word "undertaking." It may mean either a promise to do something or actually doing it. If the defendant has received a foundling (like Tom Jones in Fielding's novel) there may be nobody to whom he makes a promise; yet he may still be said to have "undertaken" the child's care in the sense that he has actually taken its care upon himself. Such an ambiguity can be used as a cover for an extension of the law, as may be seen in *Stone*.[3]

> The two defendants were Stone, a man of 67, of "low average" intelligence, partly deaf and almost blind, and his mistress Mrs Dobinson, aged 43, who was ineffectual and somewhat inadequate. Stone's sister Fanny came to live with the couple as a lodger; she developed *anorexia nervosa* (a pathological condition involving an extreme disinclination to eat), became very weak, and refused to reveal the name of her doctor (because she was afraid of being "put away"). The defendants tried without success to find her doctor, walking a very considerable distance to do so (they were unable to use a telephone). They also tried unsuccessfully to find another doctor, but took no other steps, not even mentioning the problem to a social worker who used to visit Stone's mentally retarded son at his house. Meanwhile Fanny had taken permanentaly to her bed, eating only "biscuits and pop." When she died, in dreadful degradation because of the lack of nursing care, the two defendants were convicted of manslaughter, and their conviction was affirmed on appeal. The old man received an exceedingly unkind prison sentence of 12 months, "if for nothing else at least to mark the public disapproval of such behaviour." Mrs Dobinson had only a suspended sentence.

The Court of Appeal's idea of the function of a prison sentence is highly questionable, and in point of justice it insufficiently takes account of Stone's poor intelligence and his evident sense of hopelessness in the face of his sister's refusal to accept treatment.[4] The fact is that the problem was too big for him. Important as it is to maintain the principle that helpless invalids must be cared for, no great public harm would follow if indulgence

---

[2] On the history and generally see Glazebrook in 76 LQR 386; Dennis in [1980] Curr. L Prob. 255; George Fletcher, *Rethinking Criminal Law* (Boston 1978) 611–634.

[3] [1977] QB 354.

[4] Helen Beynon explains the harsh decision as an emotional reaction. "When a person dies in such abject squalor, a scapegoat has to be found" ([1982] Crim. LR 27).

were shown to inadequate people, and those who do not wish to force ministrations upon others; and Stone fell into both categories.[5] But what concerns us here is not the court's lack of human understanding but the principle upon which it found a duty of care to have been established. It was expressed in the following words.

> "Whether Fanny was a lodger or not she was a blood relation of the appellant Stone; she was occupying a room in his house; Mrs Dobinson had undertaken the duty of trying to wash her, of taking such food to her as she required. . . . [6] All these were matters which the jury were entitled to take into account when considering whether the necessary assumption of a duty to care for Fanny had been proved."

The observation that Fanny was a blood relation of Stone was surely irrelevant. Stone would *not* have been under a duty towards his adult sister if she had not been under his roof, and, contrariwise, we may be sure that he *would* have been regarded as under a duty to Fanny, a person under his roof, even if she had not been his sister.

I still don't understand in what way the defendants assumed a duty to Fanny.

The court found the language of assumption of duty in the precedents, so it sought somehow to apply it to the facts, but unconvincingly. If the idea is that when you allow your sister (or, surely, anybody else) to come to live with you, you impliedly promise to give her necessary aid if she falls ill, that is merely a "construction of law," and the court might as well state the reality of the rule, which is that the occupier of the house must take reasonable steps in these circumstances. The rule, as a rule, is a good one. (On that view of the law, however, it is strange that the judge should have left it to the jury to decide the question whether Stone was under a duty. If the matter was settled by law, as a conclusion from the mere fact that Fanny was incapacitated in Stone's house, the jury could and should have been explicitly directed on the point.)

All right: a man must look after someone who falls ill in his house. But what about Mrs Dobinson? It wasn't her house. She had "undertaken the duty" of trying to wash Fanny, in one meaning of the phrase, by reason of the fact that she did try to wash Fanny. But she undertook the duty only in the sense that she tried to perform a self-imposed duty, not in the sense that she promised Fanny or anyone else to perform it. Suppose that Mrs D did nothing for Fanny after Fanny took to her bed; would she then have been acquitted?

The judgment of the Court of Appeal on this point leaves the law quite obscure. The court is evidently seeking some fact that can plausibly be

---

[5] Generally they have no right to do so: see § .4.

[6] The words omitted from the quotation related to the defendants' knowledge of Fanny's condition and their failure to provide effective help. These matters are generally thought of as relating to the question of breach of duty rather than to its existence. It is strange that the court thought that such facts could serve to prove an *assumption* of duty by the defendants.

pointed to as an "assumption of a duty to care for Fanny." As you imply, to find such an assumption in the fact that Mrs D tried to wash her and took her food implies that if Mrs D had made no such efforts she would not have assumed the duty. But it is contrary to common sense to say that a person who voluntarily begins to help another is by reason of that fact subjected to a duty to continue the help, even though by giving the help he did (to say the least) no damage to the other, in comparison with his position if no help had been provided. It looks very much as though the court has hit upon an equivocal phrase and is proceeding to draw inadmissible conclusions from it.

The only reasonable ground for holding that Mrs D (who was not related to Fanny[7]) owed a duty to her would have been to say that she was an adult member of the household in which Fanny became ill, and as such was under the same duty (whatever it might be) as the occupier, Stone. That would be an acceptable rule (except that it is harsh to regard the breach of the duty as so grave a crime as manslaughter). There is no reason why the duty should be confined to the occupier. If a landlord suddenly falls ill in his house, why should not a duty be imposed on the lodger on his behalf, just as it is presumably imposed on the landlord on behalf of the lodger? But if Stone and Mrs D were legally on a par, as being members of the household, it is difficult to justify the distinction made between them in the matter of punishment. Mrs D would seem from the facts stated to have been the more competent of the two, and therefore the more responsible.

The legal development sketched in these pages leaves us with an assorted list of duties towards helpless persons based upon

— the defendant's status (marriage and parenthood),
— undertaking,
— the occupation of property, and, it seems,
— being a member of the household of a person who is under a duty as occupier.

In addition, the law still theoretically recognises duties owed to others (not necessarily helpless persons) arising in some cases from having given an undertaking to take safety precautions (a level-crossing gatekeeper); but the authorities are not wholly consistent, and anyway prosecutions on this ground, for a pure omission, seem no longer to be brought, though one is always possible where extreme recklessness is involved.

The law of manslaughter by omission remains one of the chief areas in which English law rejects the principle *Nulla poena sine lege*. Yet when the CLRC discussed the subject of offences against the person the majority were against having any statutory formulation of the duty to act, for the purpose of the law of murder and manslaughter, preferring to leave it to the courts to decide in each case whether there is a legal duty.[8] "The main reason for this view," said the committee "is that the boundaries of the common law are not clearly marked and there would be difficulty in setting

---

[7] Helen Beynon in [1982] Crim.LR 25 states otherwise, but the report does not bear her out.

[8] 14th Report, para. 256.

them out in statutory form." If the top lawyers in a Government committee find the law hard to state clearly, what hope have the Stones and Dobinsons of this world of ascertaining their legal position, in advance of prosecution, when they find themselves landed with a hunger-striking relative? Would the advice to Mrs Dobinson be: on no account do anything for the invalid? Would doing nothing save her from conviction, or merely make her position worse? The committee not only expressed satisfaction with the present law for homicide but even recommended that the courts should be entrusted with a similar roving commission to create positive duties in respect of certain other offences falling short of homicide.

§ 12.4. THE FAULT ELEMENT IN OMISSIONS

The authorities on the fault element in manslaughter by omission are in the same unsatisfactory state as for positive acts. In *Lowe*,[1] the Court of Appeal required recklessness for liability, and it seems clear that the term was used in the subjective sense. Phillimore LJ said that the jury had negatived recklessness, and added:

> "How then can mere neglect, albeit wilful, amount to manslaughter?"

If this is the rule, a corollary of it should be that the recklessness is required to be as to death, or at least as to grievous bodily harm. This is because the fault element in a crime should relate to the prohibited outcome, which in this case is death. The extension to g.b.h. can be regarded as a consequence of the law of murder; since an intention to inflict g.b.h. is sufficient for murder, it might be regarded as strange if recklessness (or gross negligence, if that is the chosen term) as to g.b.h. is not enough for manslaughter. However, in *Stone*[2] a differently constituted court rejected the opinion that the fault element in manslaughter was recklessness in the above sense. The court said:

> "The duty which a [*sic*] defendant has undertaken is a duty of caring for the health and welfare of the infirm person. What the prosecution have to prove is a breach of that duty in such circumstances that the jury feel convinced that the defendant's conduct can properly be described as reckless, that is to say a reckless disregard of danger to the health and welfare of the infirm person. Mere inadvertence is not enough. The defendant must be proved to have been indifferent to an obvious risk of injury to health, or actually to have foreseen the risk but to have determined nevertheless to run it."

The passage implies that one can be reckless and can disregard a risk without "actually" foreseeing the risk, if one is "indifferent to an obvious risk." But how can a person be shown to have disregarded a risk that he

---

[1] [1973] QB 702 at 709.
[2] § .3 at n. 3.

did not foresee?[3] Does "disregard" merely mean "fail to regard"? If so, it is an inappropriate and misleading way in which to use the word. Similarly, how can a person be proved to have been indifferent to a risk that he did not foresee?

Putting aside these problems, it is clear that the court regards the mental element as established if the defendant foresaw some "danger to health and welfare" resulting from his conduct. In a previous passage it categorically rejected the argument that "there must be an appreciation by the defendant of the risk of death or serious injury before a conviction for manslaughter in these circumstances can result." The reference to "welfare" is extraordinarily vague, but even the reference to "health" is an unnecessary extension of the crime of manslaughter. It would be a severe rule to say that a landlord is guilty of this crime if he knowingly fails to safeguard his incapacitated lodger's health, without realising that the lodger is in danger of death.

The attitude of the court in *Cato*[4] may be cited as coinciding with *Lowe* and opposed to *Stone*, for in *Cato* the court required (at least as a matter of words) knowledge of the risk of death or g.b.h. The case concerned a positive act, not an omission, but the fault required for an omission cannot be greater than for manslaughter by positive act.

One other question seems to me to need answering. Suppose that Stone had called a doctor to Fanny. What could the doctor have done, if Fanny had still refused food and treatment? Could she have been forcibly fed?

It is pointed out later (§ 26.7) that a sane adult cannot be subjected to compulsory medical treatment when he is ill. To interfere with a person by force without his consent and without authority of law is an assault; and there is no authority for allowing paternal interference except in limited circumstances that ought not to be taken as being present in this case. This freedom from a duty to submit to compulsory treatment is what is sometimes called the citizen's right of self-determination. If there is such a right, it should follow that the spouse or other person who refrains from obtaining medical treatment for the sufferer when he does not want it cannot be guilty of manslaughter if the sufferer dies, because the law does not impose a duty to commit an illegality.

There is one complicating factor. Statutory powers exist to remove to hospital or some other place people who are suspected of mental disorder or who are unable to cope (§ 26.8). But grave doubts are now felt, both by doctors and by social workers, about the compulsory uprooting of old people. If Fanny wanted to die at home in filth, and if the defendants were prepared to let her, their failure to put compulsory powers in motion should not have been accounted against them. Besides, even if Fanny had been institutionalised, that would not have given the institution the right

---

[3] Strictly, one should speak of foreseeing an event or of knowing a risk, not of foreseeing a risk, since the risk is present, not future. But the language of foreseeing risks is common.

[4] § .2 at n.6.

to force-feed her. So there is no assurance that the move would have saved her life. (Which is another argument against the conviction: a person cannot be convicted of manslaughter by omission unless it can be proved beyond reasonable doubt that action would have saved the life: § 16.2 n. 5).

Unfortunately, the notion that people have a right of self-determination, although inherent in the common law, seems still to be unfamiliar to English judges. In the later case of *Wilkinson*[5] a man of 66 was sentenced to 2 months' imprisonment and his daughter of 42 to 18 months for the manslaughter of the wife and mother, aged 72. She had taken to her bed ten years before out of a morbid fear of becoming geriatric, and violently resisted offers of medical help, so that, said the Court of Appeal, it was not surprising that her husband and daughter gave up. Yet the court refused leave to appeal against conviction. It altered the sentence to allow immediate release, but the defendants had been in prison for 5 months and remained with the reproach of the conviction.

The newspaper report does not state whether the right of self-determination was argued, but there appears to have been some discussion of it the next year in *Smith*.[6] Smith, a devoted husband, had not called a doctor to his deceased wife during her illness, but she had for a long time made known her firm decision not to have one. On a charge of manslaughter when the wife died the judge directed the jury that they had "to balance the weight that it is right to give to his wife's wish to avoid calling in a doctor against her capacity to make rational decisions. If she does not appear too ill it may be reasonable to abide by her wishes. On the other hand, if she appeared desperately ill then whatever she may say it may be right to override." The jury failed to agree.

The jury should have been instructed that a person has an absolute right to refuse medical assistance. Even a mental patient cannot be treated against his will, except to the extent authorised by statute or in certain extreme situations,[7] and an adult patient who is only physically ill cannot be treated against his express refusal in any circumstances. Even if a patient is *non compos* in the terminal stages of an illness, it would be wrong to give him treatment that he is known to have rejected when in full possession of his faculties. It would be a contradiction to say that people cannot be compulsorily treated against their will, even to save their lives, but that they can be compulsorily treated as soon as they are in a coma and near death, even though their previous opposition is quite clear.

The lamentable activity of prosecutors in this matter is further shown by a case of 1977,[8] where a man was charged with manslaughter of his wife on the ground that he had, in breach of his husbandly duty of care, failed to summon medical aid to her after she had taken an overdose of a drug, presumably intentionally. He was acquitted, but the brief newspaper report does not state the reasons. Since the judge left the case to the jury he presumably ruled that the husband could be convicted if the evidence against him were accepted. The question remains whether it is right to extend the duty to look after the helpless in such a way as to deny an adult's right of self-determination.

I have kept the best item till last. The CLRC has recommended that involuntary manslaughter should be confined to cases where a person causes death with intent to cause serious injury, or being subjectively reckless as to death or serious injury.[9] Unfortunately, the committee did not deal with the right of self-determination.

§ 12.5 CONSTRUCTIVE MANSLAUGHTER: DANGEROUSNESS

More technicalities. But first a historical note by way of explanation.

[5] The Times, April 19, 1978.
[6] [1979] Crim. LR 251.
[7] See § 26.8.
[8] *Osborne*, The Times, April 5.
[9] 14th Report, para. 124.

At one time it was held that a killing, though unintentional, was *murder* if it occurred in the course of any unlawful act; so an accidental killing while trying to steal a fowl was murder. This doctrine of constructive murder was limited in the course of time by judicial decision and statute; and the area progressively freed from the law of murder was simultaneously and automatically occupied by the doctrine of constructive manslaughter.[1] What had been murder became manslaughter. Hence, for several centuries, it was axiomatic that a killing in the course of an unlawful act was at least manslaughter by construction of law.

Just as the judges steadily diminished the law of constructive murder, so they came to whittle down the law of constructive manslaughter.[2] The present law contains some firm rules and some outstanding doubts. It may be summarised as follows. For the doctrine to operate:

— there must be an act (query as to an omission)
— which is unlawful, within certain rules, and also
— dangerous.
— The death must be a direct consequence of the unlawful act.

Two illustrations may be given of the working of the law.

> In *Newbury*[3] two 15-year-old boys pushed a piece of paving stone[4] from a railway bridge in the path of an oncoming train. The case for the defence was that they intended only to cause it to hit the roof of the driving cab or a coach, where it might have done some damage but not injured anybody (no reference to this defence is made in the report). Unfortunately the stone went through the window of the driving cab and killed the guard who was inside. The trial judge instructed the jury in terms of constructive manslaughter; the jury convicted, and the conviction was affirmed by the House of Lords.
>
> This decision was followed by the Privy Council in a case where the defendants threw stones at V who ran away from them. As he ran he tripped and was later found to be dead, it being possible that the death was caused by the fall rather than by hits with the stones. The judge in summing up said that "where one person causes in the mind of another by violence or the threat of violence a well-founded sense of danger to life or limb as to cause him to suffer or [and?] to try to escape and in the endeavour to escape he is killed, the person creating that state of mind is guilty at least of manslaughter." The jury convicted of manslaughter, and the conviction was upheld on appeal.[5]

In both cases the law of constructive manslaughter offered a short cut to conviction, but in neither was it socially necessary. In *Newbury* the lads were guilty of a statutory offence (of negligence or strict liability) in "endangering the safety of any person conveyed upon a railway."[6] Apart

---

[1] This pejorative but convenient expression assumes that manslaughter is first defined to require criminal negligence as to death or g.b.h., and is then extended by an irrebuttable presumption of criminal neglience in the case of an unlawful act causing death. The conviction is for "manslaughter" only; a separate crime of constructive manslaughter is not known to the law.

[2] For an account of the development see [1957] Crim.LR 299; Snelling in 30 Aus.LJ 382, 438.

[3] [1977] AC 500. See the criticism by J C Smith in [1977] Crim.LR 359.

[4] So the report. I am informed by counsel for the defence that it was in fact about a quarter of a paving stone.

[5] *Daley* [1980] AC 237.

[6] OAPA 1861 s.34.

from that, the jury would very probably have convicted of reckless manslaughter on a direction couched in terms of recklessness. The lads could even have been found subjectively reckless if they must have foreseen at least a slight possibility of the stone causing serious injury to someone. Conviction would have been even more likely if the prosecution had refrained from charging manslaughter and instead charged criminal damage to property intending to endanger life or being reckless as to such danger (§ 41.7). But not all cases of constructive manslaughter are as serious as the two just instanced.

We will commence to sort out the law by considering the definition of a dangerous act. Until quite recently the law of constructive manslaughter was operated with great severity. People were convicted notwithstanding that death would not have occurred but for some abnormal sensitivity of the victim of which the attacker had no reason to know.[7] A trivial physical assault or even a mere psychic assault resulting in death could amount to manslaughter, although the intention of the defendant was only to frighten or to perpetrate a stupid joke involving minor physical contact. The assault might be against a third party.

Nowadays the courts generally maintain that there must, at least, be a fault element as to the risk of causing some harm. The modern rule stems from *Church*[8], where the Court of Criminal Appeal said:

> "An unlawful act causing the death of another cannot, simply because it is an unlawful act, render a manslaughter verdict inevitable. For such a verdict inexorably to follow, the unlawful act must be such as all sober and reasonable people would inevitably recognise must subject the other person to, at least, the risk of some harm resulting therefrom, albeit not serious harm."

The correctness of this statement was recognised by the House of Lords in *Newbury*. Their lordships added the observation that the defendant need not know that his act was dangerous. Although this must be accepted, the point remains that there must be an unlawful act, which may involve a mental element. The requirement was unfortunately misunderstood and obscured by Lord Salmon, as we shall see in the next section.

The statement refers to "some harm." Presumably what is intended is the "actual bodily harm" of section 47 of the Offences against the Person Act.

But that may be a very small amount of harm: you gave the instance of a bruise (§ 9.2 n. 2). So, is the law much improved from the bad old days of which you spoke before?

Not much. But the whole point of constructive manslaughter is that it can arise from an unlawful act that was only likely to do minor injury. If

[7] 1st edn 238 n. 1.
[8] [1966] 1 QB at 70.

the act was likely to kill or do g.b.h. the doer would almost invariably be guilty of reckless manslaughter, so in that case there is no need for a doctrine of constructive manslaughter.

> An example of the potential severity of the law is the old case of *Towers*,[9] where the defendant assaulted a girl who was nursing an infant. The girl screamed, and this so frightened the infant that he became black in the face; later he had convulsions, and died. Towers was convicted of the manslaughter of the infant.[10]

Presumably all sober and reasonable people would inevitably recognise that assaulting a girl with an infant in her arms might lead her to drop and injure the infant; and if so a man like Towers could still be convicted of manslaughter, even though the particular mode of the infant's death was not reasonably foreseeable. No judge has explained on what ground of justice or policy a person who has made a minor assault should be rendered guilty of manslaughter by reason of an unknown weakness of the victim. All that can be said is that, the judges having invented the idea of constructive manslaughter, it is now part of the order of the universe and the judges are powerless to change it. (The courts often seem to treat the criminal law as a militaristic State treats its territory: something that can always be extended but must never be given back again.)

"All sober and reasonable people would inevitably recognise." Is that a gross negligence test?

One would have thought so, but the language of gross negligence is not used in relation to constructive manslaughter. Presumably the phrase means: consider the responsible and careful people you know. Do you think they would all say that this act carried a foreseeable danger of causing some injury? If you think they might be divided in opinion, constructive manslaughter is not made out. (But, of course, you do not sound the opinions of any actual people. And there is a whiff of begging the question about the test, because if a minority of the friends whom you imagine you are consulting report, in your imagination, that they do not think the act dangerous, you may rule them out of consideration as not being sober and reasonable people after all!)

If the test is gross negligence, then, according to what you said before (§ 4.3 at n. 1), the one to be applied in the case of juveniles is that of a reasonable juvenile of the defendant's age. Were the jury in Newbury asked to consider whether all reasonable lads of 15 would have known the act to be dangerous?

Presumably not. So far as we know, the point was not raised. It should have been put to the jury.

---

[9] (1874) 12 Cox 530. Cp. §§ 16.8, 16.11.

[10] There was probably an assault upon the child who died, because the defendant could have been found to have been reckless as to the child; but no point was made as to this, and the judge took the case merely on the assault on the girl. Cp. *Bruce* (1847) 2 Cox 262; *Re Heigho*, § 16.11 n. 2; *Mitchell* §12.6 n. 21, where, however, the question of foreseeability was not made an issue.

§ 12.6. THE UNLAWFUL ACT

The other main limit upon the doctrine of constructive manslaughter is that it applies only when the defendant committed an unlawful act, not including a merely negligent act. If what he did amounted to *Caldwell* recklessness, his liability is for reckless manslaughter.

Negligence is not an unlawful act for the purpose of constructive manslaughter even when it constitutes a specific statutory offence. This was settled by the House of Lords in *Andrews.*[1]

> It was there held that the mere fact that a person committed the offence of dangerous driving, and killed in consequence, did not make him guilty of manslaughter. Dangerous driving, though a statutory offence of negligence created for the protection of life, did not necessarily connote the same degree of negligence as that required for negligent manslaughter; and the commission of the statutory offence was not to be used to lay a foundation for a charge of constructive manslaughter. (The offence of dangerous driving has been abolished,[2] but the same proposition applies to careless driving.)

The general proposition that negligence is insufficient for constructive manslaughter is also illustrated by *Lamb*,[3] a case that we have had before. Since Lamb knew that his friend regarded the affair as a joke, he was not guilty of an assault on the friend, and committed no unlawful act, when he pointed the gun and pulled the trigger. The act was negligent; but negligent acts are not unlawful at the moment when they are done, even though they create liability in tort if they cause damage. This point was accepted in the Court of Appeal as a conclusive reason why Lamb was not guilty of constructive manslaughter. The court said:

> "[Counsel for the Crown] rightly conceded there was no evidence to go to the jury of any assault of any kind. Nor did he feel able to submit that the acts of the defendant were on any other ground unlawful in the criminal sense of the word. Indeed, no such submission could in law be made: if, for instance, the pulling of the trigger had had no effect because the striking mechanism or the ammunition had been defective no offence would have been committed by the defendant. . . . Unfortunately [the trial judge] fell into error as to the meaning of the word 'unlawful' in that passage [in *Church*[4]]. . . . The trial judge took the view that the pointing of the revolver and the pulling of the trigger was something which could in itself be unlawful even if there was no attempt to alarm or intent to injure"

and he was wrong in so doing.

This simple point was gravely misunderstood by Lord Salmon, stating the opinion of the House of Lords in *Newbury*[5]:

> "In manslaughter there must always be a guilty mind. This is true of every crime except

---

[1] [1937] AC 576, esp. at p. 585.
[2] § 14.4
[3] [1967] 2 QB 981. See § 5.2 at n. 6.
[4] § .5 at n. 8.
[5] [1977] AC at 509B. See the criticism by R D Taylor in 144 JPN 144.

> those of absolute liability.[6] The guilty mind usually depends on the intention of the accused. Some crimes require what is sometimes called a specific intention. . . . Other crimes need only what is called a basic intention, which is an intention to do the acts which constitute the crime. Manslaughter is such a crime. . . . *Reg.* v. *Lamb* is certainly no authority to the contrary. . . . The defendant was convicted but his conviction was quashed on appeal because, luckily for him, there had been a series of serious misdirections by the learned trial judge."

If this means that Lamb could have been convicted of *reckless* manslaughter on a proper direction, it may be true but is irrelevant. Perhaps he could have been, though improperly in my view. Lamb was not guilty of *Caldwell* recklessness or of gross negligence, notwithstanding the disastrous results. (On every charge of manslaughter the defendant has produced disastrous results, because he has caused death; that mere fact cannot turn tort negligence into gross negligence.) However, Lord Salmon was speaking primarily in the context of constructive manslaughter, and he was clearly in error in suggesting that on a proper direction Lamb's conviction would have been upheld *on the basis that he had committed an unlawful act.* Lord Salmon and the other lords who concurred with him were perhaps going upon a faded memory of the case; they could have corrected their mistake if they had re-read the headnote. (It correctly summarises the decision in these words: "manslaughter could not be established in relation to the first ground [the doing of an unlawful act] without proving that element of intent without which there could be no assault.") Besides, one does not need authority for saying that negligence is not an unlawful act for constructive manslaughter. If it were, constructive manslaughter would virtually[7] swallow up negligent manslaughter, whereas everyone agrees that they are separate concepts.

Lord Salmon's use of the notion of crimes of basic intention is also a most regrettable muddle. The misleading nature of the phrase "intention to do the acts which constitute the crime" may be shown by an example. When a driver "intentionally" drives in a certain way which the court regards as careless, he has, in a sense, an "intention to do the acts which constitute the crime," but this does not make him guilty of constructive manslaughter if his careless driving causes a death. It would be quite untrue in the ordinary understanding of words to say that the driver has intentionally committed an unlawful act. His offence is one of negligence, not intention. It follows that what can be said (in a strained and misleading sense) to be an intention to do the acts which constitute the crime is not necessarily sufficient for constructive manslaughter.

Lord Salmon was derailed by the language of "crimes of basic intention," which he found in cases on voluntary intoxication. It was there invented as what can only be called a piece of legal hocus-pocus in order to convict drunkards and evade section 8 of the Criminal Justice Act (§ 21.3–4). For this purpose, the courts say that assault is a crime of basic intent, in which all that is required for the drunkard to be convicted is an intent to do the acts constituting the crime. The falsity of the proposition that this is the only *mens rea* in assault can be seen from *Lamb*. Suppose for a moment that Lamb had wanted to frighten his friend, and had done so by pointing the loaded gun at him. Lamb would then have been guilty of an assault, and the "acts which constitute the crime" would be the pointing of the loaded gun. Now Lamb did indeed point the loaded gun. Let us imagine (contrary to the facts of the case) that his friend became frightened that Lamb was about to shoot him, though Lamb neither intended to do so nor realised that his friend would suppose the affair to be anything but fun. On such facts, Lamb would have done all the acts necessary to constitute the crime of assault. Nevertheless, he would not have committed an assault, and would not have committed an unlawful act, because he lacked the intent. Intending to do the acts which constitute the offence is *not* sufficient for the crime of assault. What is required is a further intent, to frighten or cause contact with the victim.

---

[6] Lord Salmon evidently took crimes of negligence to involve a guilty mind—a use of language that was deplored in § 4.1 at n. 4.

[7] The only case of negligent manslaughter that would be left outside constructive manslaughter would be one in which there is no "act," as where a woman carrying a baby negligently trips and drops the baby. But in such circumstances it would be rare for the negligence to be accounted sufficiently gross for negligent manslaughter.

The point that emerges is that an act is not unlawful for constructive manslaughter unless it satisfies all the requirements of unlawfulness. It is not unlawful as a lesser crime unless there is present the mental element required for that lesser crime.

Their lordships announced in *Newbury*[8] that the defendant need not have known that his act was unlawful; and the statement was given added weight by being repeated by the Privy Council on a subsequent occasion.[9] But why their lordships troubled to say it is a mystery. With rare exceptions the prosecution need never show that the defendant knew the law, and there was no occasion to state this elementary rule in the two cases in question. The statement in *Newbury* cannot be understood to mean that a mistake of fact is excluded. Lamb was not guilty of assault, and consequently was not guilty of constructive manslaughter, because, although he shot his friend, he believed that his revolver would not fire. For constructive manslaughter you need not know that your act is unlawful, but it must *be* unlawful; and when a mistake of fact negatives the required intention it also negatives constructive manslaughter.

The next qualification upon the "unlawful act" rule is that a tort (a civil wrong) is not an unlawful act for the purpose. The law of constructive manslaughter can operate to turn a minor crime into manslaughter if death follows, but it does not turn a tort into manslaughter. The only case directly in point is an old one: *Franklin*.[10] Although only a ruling by a puisne judge, it has been widely approved.

> Franklin took up a good-sized box from a refreshment stall on a pier and wantonly threw it into the sea; the box struck a swimmer underneath and caused his death. The prosecution urged that, death having been caused by an unlawful act, Franklin was guilty of manslaughter irrespective of negligence. Field J said: "The mere fact of a civil wrong committed by one person against another ought not to be used as an incident which is a necessary step in a criminal case. . . . I have a great abhorrence of constructive crime." He therefore left the case to the jury only on the basis of negligence. (Field J did not expressly notice that Franklin was also, presumably, guilty of theft of the box; but doubtless he regarded the offence against property as equally irrelevant.)

Franklin was approved in *Lamb*, where the Court of Appeal was laudably careful to speak not of an unlawful act simply but of an act that is "unlawful in the criminal sense of the word:"

> "When using the phrase 'in the criminal sense of the word' the court has in mind it is long settled that it is not in point to consider whether an act is unlawful merely from the angle of civil liabilities."[11]

Grateful as we may be for the clear and lucid reasoning in *Lamb*, it is a pity that the court chose the circumlocution instead of dropping talk of an "unlawful act" and speaking instead of "a crime."

Then where was the unlawful act, or the crime, in Newbury? The boys' act was not unlawful merely because it was negligent, and it was not unlawful

---

[8] [1977] AC at 507A.
[9] *Daley* [1980] AC 237.
[10] (1883) 15 Cox 163.
[11] [1967] 2 QB at 988D.

merely because it involved the tort of damage to the train (or, we suppose, criminal damage to the train).

Remarkably, the Lords did not endeavour to pinpoint the unlawful act committed by the boys. Lord Salmon merely said: "[Counsel for the defendant] did not and indeed could not contend that the appellants' act was lawful."[12] Of course it was not lawful (if that was the only question); the act damaged the train. But we cannot suppose that their lordships meant to overrule *Franklin* and to disregard the settled opinion in its favour without so much as referring to it. Nor can we suppose that they intended to depart silently from their own previous decision in *Andrews* (it was referred to in argument, but not in Lord Salmon's speech).

There is, however, one possible explanation of the decision in *Newbury*. The boys intended to frighten the crew and passengers in the train, or were reckless as to frightening or hurting them; and the jury could clearly have decided that were guilty of assault on this basis. Since the direction to the jury is not reported, we do not know whether they were directed in these terms. Obviously, a jury should not be left to find that the defendant's act was unlawful without being told the law.

One other case may be mentioned as an example of judicial laxity in finding an unlawful act. This is *Cato*,[13] the facts of which will now be familiar.

> The judge left the manslaughter charge to the jury on two alternative grounds: (1) that the death was caused by Cato's "recklessness or gross negligence"; and (2) that it was caused by the injection of heroin which, as Cato knew, was likely to do harm to the person injected. On appeal from conviction, it was argued that the injection of heroin is not an unlawful act for the purpose of constructive manslaughter. Possessing or supplying heroin is a statutory offence, but Cato did not supply it to the deceased, because he had received it from the deceased for the express purpose of administering it to him.[14] The prosecution had to show that the *administration* of heroin is an offence. The court held that it is, being an offence of administering a noxious thing so as to endanger life under OAPA 1861 s.23, the consent of the person injected being no defence. The court added that anyway there was the unlawful act of "injecting [V] with heroin which the accused had unlawfully taken into his possession."

Whether it was good law to hold that V's consent was no defence under section 23 will be discussed later (§ 25.18 at n. 12). The serious difficulty presented by the decision for the modern law of constructive manslaughter relates to the court's second ground (which in view of the first ground, relating to OAPA s.23, was unnecessary for the decision). The court acknowledged that there was no statutory offence of administering heroin. Even if Cato's momentary possession were regarded as sufficient for the statutory offence of possession, it was not his possession that killed. The illegality found by the court in the injection of heroin could therefore only be at common law. But the House of Lords had instructed the judges only the year before that they could not invent new crimes under the heading of public mischief[15]; and presumably they cannot invent them under any other name either. There was no authority, and the court did not assert that there was any authority, for saying that administering heroin is an offence at common law. The court merely expects us to accept its *ipse dixit* that the law is so. *Cato*, therefore, seems to stake a claim by the judges to extend the law of constructive manslaughter from time to time by inventing new kinds of illegalities on the spur of the moment.[16]

---

[12] [1977] AC at 507E.
[13] § .2 at n. 6.
[14] *Harris* [1968] 2 All ER 49.
[15] *Withers* [1975] AC 842.
[16] Notwithstanding the criticisms of commentators, *Cato* was followed in *Farr* (1982) 146 JPN 564.

Can a criminal omission be an "unlawful act"?

The answer, on authority, is no. The answer was given in *Lowe*,[17] where the Court of Appeal held, refusing to follow *Senior*,[18] that the mere fact that a parent is guilty of the statutory offence of wilful neglect of a child, whereby the child dies, does not make the parent guilty of manslaughter.[19] This was clearly right, because the law may impose low duties obliging to positive conduct (with a penalty of, say, a fine), and these ought not automatically to be translated into the far more serious duties implied by the law of manslaughter. In Fletcher's words, "if a rose is a rose is a rose, it does not follow that a duty is a duty is a duty."[20]

You said that the death must be a direct consequence of the unlawful act. What does this mean?

The rule was decided after *Newbury*, by the Court of Appeal in *Dalby*.[21] Unlike the House of Lords, this court was more disposed to limit constructive manslaughter than to extend it.

> Dalby, a drug abuser, obtained some tablets of a Class A drug and unlawfully supplied some of them to a friend. Both injected themselves with the drug intravenously. Shortly afterwards the friend died. The Court of Appeal quashed a conviction of manslaughter on the ground that "where the charge of manslaughter is based on an unlawful and dangerous act, it must be an act directed at the victim and likely to cause immediate injury, however slight." Dalby's act was not directed at the deceased, and the supply did not cause any "direct injury" to him (it will be observed that the court used the expressions "immediate" and "direct" as if they were identical). The decision reinforces the view that the conviction in *Newbury* must have depended on the supposition that the defendants directed their act against the passengers and crew of the train, i.e. intended or were reckless as to causing fright at least. One has pleasure in adding that in *Dalby* the House of Lords refused the prosecution leave to appeal.

Dalby does not affect the established rule that a person who secretly administers a dangerous drug to another and unintentionally kills him can be convicted of constructive manslaughter, because here the victim takes the drug unwittingly.

The court in *Dalby* did not find it necessary to comment on *Cato*, but the distinction apparently is that Cato himself injected his friend, whereas Dalby left his friend to inject himself.

The decision in *Dalby* may be taken to reinforce the opinion that a tort in respect of property, or simple criminal damage, is not an unlawful act for manslaughter. The aggravated form of criminal damage (damage intending etc. to endanger life: § 41.7) would still be sufficient unlawful act, but this crime requires proof of an intention or recklessness as to the

---

[17] [1973] QB 702. See 1st edn 90–91.

[18] [1899] 1 QB 283 (see 1st edn 88 and *Sheppard* [1981] AC 394).

[19] The court purported to follow *Andrews*; but that decided only that a statutory crime of *negligence* was not a sufficient foundation for a charge of constructive manslaughter. The crime of wilful neglect of children has a mental component. But the decision in *Lowe* can be explained, as in the text above, as a decision on crimes of omission. The court itself said: "We think that there is a clear distinction between an act of omission [*sic*] and an act of commission likely to cause harm."

[20] George P Fletcher, *Rethinking Criminal Law* Boston 1978) 621.

[21] [1982] 1 WLR 425, 1 All ER 916, 74 CAR 348. See note, [1982] Crim. LR 439. The decision does not affect a situation of transferred intention, where D assaults V1 and so causes the death of V2: *Mitchell* [1983] 2 WLR 938.

endangering of life; and proof of this mental element should be necessary, as requisite to the proof of the unlawful act, notwithstanding what was said in the Lords about the defendant not having to know that his act was dangerous.

Is it constructive manslaughter if an illegal abortionist accidentally kills his patient?

If the abortionist has supplied the woman with an abortifacient drug, which kills her, he may be able to defend himself against a charge of manslaughter by virtue of the rule in *Dalby*. But in the more usual case, where the abortionist has used an instrument on the woman and kills her, he is, anomalously, guilty of manslaughter, even if he was not negligent.

At one time this was murder, abortion being a felony. The judges mercifully reduced it to manslaughter, which it still is. But even a conviction of manslaughter is against principle, since the abortionist commits no crime against the woman. Abortion (in effect feticide) is not homicide, because in law *foetus* is not *homo*. It is somewhat artificial to hold that an intention to abort a fetus becomes manslaughter of the woman if she accidentally dies.

Some people would say that there is no moral difference between killing a mature fetus and killing a baby.

I am not debating the moral issue, but only the legal rule. Ever since the time of Coke it has been accepted that unlawful homicide (murder or manslaughter) is the killing of "a reasonable creature who is in being," and "in being "means" fully born alive." Many authorities demonstrate this limitation of murder and manslaughter. So, in abortion, there is certainly no intention to commit an offence against the person.[22]

The doctrine of transferred intention cannot be invoked, because that applies only when the defendant intends a particular crime, and commits the *actus reus* of that crime (though with a different victim). Here the defendant intends an abortion; what he does is, in addition,[23] to kill the woman; but the killing of the woman is a different crime—murder or manslaughter in some circumstances, but not abortion.

The judges have tried to explain the law by saying that abortion always involves considerable risk to the person, however carefully it is performed[24]; but this is palpably false. Abortion is dangerous in unskilled hands, but as safe as many another operation in skilled hands; and the law of constructive manslaughter is occasionally used even against skilled surgeons if they operate illegally and are unlucky enough to cause death. If the abortionist kills by gross negligence he is guilty of manslaughter for that reason. Otherwise, the law of abortion is sufficiently severe in itself.

Is there anything to be said for constructive manslaughter, ever? Why should punishment be increased simply because there is a corpse?

Some kind of answer can be made. Killings attract public attention, and

---

[22] Although abortion appears in the Offences against the Person Act, the name of the Act cannot be relied upon as a reason for departing from the established rule that a fetus is not a person. The OAPA also has a section on bigamy, which is clearly not an offence against the person in any reasonable meaning of those words.

[23] *Generally* in addition; but the abortion offence is worded as using "means" to procure a miscarriage, and it is committed even though the woman happens not to be pregnant.

[24] E.g. *Buck* (1960) 44 CAR at 219–220.

condign punishment may effect general deterrence, enabling other offenders who happen not to kill to be let off more lightly. But the counter-argument is the stronger: that the penal system should not be administered as a lottery.

Judges who compiled a memorandum on punishment as long ago as 1901 agreed that in manslaughter cases where death results from an assault the punishment should pay regard only to the injury that might reasonably be expected to result from the assault.[25] The logical conclusion is that there is no point in charging constructive manslaughter: the prosecution might just as well charge negligent manslaughter, or assault or other lesser crime. Some decisions on manslaughter seem to accept the principle stated in 1901; but in other cases, even of near-accident, the punishment is occasionally severe, apparently because different judges hold different opinions on sentencing policy.[26]

It may be that we shall not have to put up with this tedious, unnecessary and unjust part of the law for much longer. The CLRC has recommended the abolition of constructive manslaughter, on the ground that "the offender's fault falls too far short of the unlucky result."[27] All that constructive manslaughter really does is to make liability for manslaughter depend upon negligence as to slight harm, and that it should do so is wrong.[28]

§ 12.7. KILLING A SUPPOSED CORPSE

The problem involved where a person has killed another by getting rid of his supposed corpse has already been discussed in connection with murder (§ 11.6). The problem arises again for manslaughter. Although the killer will almost certainly not get off a charge of manslaughter by the "supposed corpse" argument, divergent legal theories have been invoked to justify this result.

The first is that the killer's attack on his victim and his subsequent disposal of the supposed corpse are a "series of acts" which the jury can regard as a single act. This principle was applied by the Court of Appeal in *Church* in relation to both murder and manslaughter. We have seen that the formulation of the rule, at least in relation to murder, was illogical because self-contradictory (§ 11.6 n. 3). However, in relation to manslaughter the court also quoted with approval the opinion that "if a killing by the first act would have been manslaughter, a later destruction of the supposed corpse should also be manslaughter."[1] This is the right rule, and the one required by policy. Contrary to the apparent opinion of the court, it does not involve any necessity to ask the jury to decide the metaphysical question whether there was a "series of acts."

The second line of approach was utilised in *Attorney-General's Reference (No 4 of 1980)*.[2] This was a case in which the prosecution were under the embarrassment of not being able to prove whether the death was occasioned by the attack or by the act of "disposal." The Court of Appeal held that the jury should be asked two questions. (1) Was the deceased's injury caused by an intentional act by the defendant which was unlawful and dangerous? (2) Was

---

[25] The memorandum is reprinted in R M Jackson, *Enforcing the Law* (London 1972) App. 5.

[26] See, e.g. *Stuart* [1979] Crim.LR 793 and commentary. See generally D A Thomas, *Principles of Sentencing*, 2nd edn 83; 1st edn of this book 245–246.

[27] 14th Report, para. 120. For other criticisms of the law see Lord Devlin in [1954] Crim.LR 671. The Model Penal Code of the American Law Institute does not propose its continuation.

[28] See § 16.8 on the special sensitivity rule.

[1] [1966] 1 QB at 71, quoting *The General Part*, 2nd edn 174.

[2] [1981] 1 WLR 705.

the defendant's treatment of the supposed corpse an act of gross criminal negligence? If the answer to both questions is in the affirmative, the defendant must be guilty of manslaughter, since he is guilty of that crime whether the death resulted directly from the attack in (1) or from the act in (2).

It seems to follow from the decision on (2)[3] that what the court thought of as negligent manslaughter can be committed in respect of a supposed corpse even when the defendant was not guilty of any act causing the victim's unconsciousness. The decision also implies acceptance of the opinion that such manslaughter does not require subjective recklessness, but it fails to examine the authorities on the point. A person would not be *Caldwell* reckless as to causing death if he believed that he was dealing with a corpse.

The decision in *Attorney-General's Reference* is slightly more indulgent to the defendant than the principle stated at the beginning which was approved in *Church*, because, unlike *Church*, it requires the jury to find that the defendant's dealing with the corpse was grossly negligent. Conceivably the jury may refuse to make this finding, in which case the rule in *Attorney-General's Reference* would acquit the defendant of manslaughter—a result of which few would approve.

Another difficulty with the principle stated in *Attorney-General's Reference* is that it cannot be successfully adapted where the facts leave the cause of death in doubt and the defendant had a *murderous* intent. D attacks V with murderous intent. Believing him to be dead, he throws the supposed corpse into the river. It cannot be established which act caused the death. On a charge of murder, the "either way" approach does not work, because a person who throws a supposed corpse into a river cannot by reason of that act alone be guilty of murder. If he is to be convicted of murder it must be because of his prior intent. The only practicable rule for murder is to say that in these circumstances the act and mental state need not concur; and if that is the rule for murder there is no reason why it should not also be the rule for manslaughter. It may be noticed that the court did not deny that the rule might be stated in these terms, but simply held that the case before it could be decided without going into the question. In so doing it put the law into unnecessary doubt.

§ 12.8. KILLING AND THE PROLONGATION OF LIFE

Exceptions apart, no one can treat a patient without his consent; so if a dying patient requests that no steps should be taken to prolong his life, we can assume (even though there are no cases) that the medical staff are bound to comply with his request, and therefore cannot be under a legal duty to ignore it.[1]

Suppose that the dying patient is unconscious and cannot express a wish?

On principle, the attending physician is entitled to give up treatment when he thinks that it is of no practical value.

More fully stated, the point is this. A doctor must never do anything actively to kill his patient, but he is not bound to fight for the patient's life for ever. His duty in this respect is to make reasonable efforts, having regard to customary practice and expectations, and in particular having regard to the benefit to the patient to be expected from further exertions. He need not and should not crassly fix his attention upon mere heart-beats. Hence the legal importance in this situation of the distinction between an act and an omission, between killing and letting die.

In an address to physicians in 1957 Pope Pius XII declared that when a patient was dying they were not morally obliged to use "advanced techniques" as opposed to "conventional

---

[3] This point was also an alternative ground of the decision in *Church*.

[1] The DPP will not in such circumstances institute a prosecution. See the Att.-Gen.'s statement in 284 BMJ 1562.

medical treatment" to save life. Some leaders of the Anglican Church have also accepted a distinction between acts and omissions, without insisting upon a subdivision into ordinary and extraordinary means.[2]

Support for the same view was given by Sir Roger Ormrod (who is not only a Lord Justice but a Fellow of the Royal College of Physicians), in an address to the Royal Society of Medicine in 1977. He pointed out that in recent years the medical profession has

> "recognised that it is concerned with something more than the maintenance of life in the sense of cellular chemistry, and so implicitly accepted the concept of 'quality of life' from which it has in the past always fought shy, for obvious reasons. It also has implicitly accepted that considerations of cost-benefit cannot be completely ignored. . . . Ten or fifteen years ago, mere mention of either was enough to precipitate an emotional response from most doctors. Now they are explicit and can be discussed and debated rationally—an important advance from many points of view."[3]

Suppose that a patient with brain damage is on a ventilator (a respirator); he is unconscious, but the machine keeps his heart and lungs going mechanically. The doctor decides that there is no chance of recovery, so he "pulls the plug." There is general agreement that he is entitled to do so. This is not a case where, by commencing to treat the patient, the doctor has put him in some peril to which he would not otherwise have been subject.

Three lines of argument can be used to exempt the doctor from liability. The first is by saying that the patient is already dead: on this view, turning off the ventilation does not kill him.

The problem of the time of death is important in various contexts.

1 *Property rights*. A corpse cannot have property or succeed to property. Suppose that X is an old man who has left Y a large sum in his will. Y is himself in a coma with a flat EEG (electroencephalograph) reading, but his relatives see that he is kept "alive" on a ventilator because they want X's money. As soon as X dies the ventilator is switched off and Y is buried. Will the dodge be successful, Y being regarded as still alive when X dies, so that his family become entitled to the property through him when the machine is switched off? Or is the patient with a flat EEG already dead, so that he cannot be entitled to property?

2 *Taking transplants*. Transplant organs are best used when fresh: is it permissible to take them from a decerebrate "donor" before the life-support system is removed?[3] Transplants cannot lawfully be taken from a living patient (if he cannot live without the part taken), but (subject to certain conditions[4]) can be taken from a dead one; so is the patient alive or dead?

3 *The responsibility of the doctor for switching off the machine*. He can be saved from responsibility if life is regarded as already extinct, for a corpse cannot be killed.

4 *The responsibility of an assailant for bringing the patient to such a pass*. Is the assailant guilty of murder or manslaughter in having caused the death when the ventilator is switched off, or is the cause of the death taking the patient off the ventilator? The question would arise

---

[2] In his Stevens Memorial Lecture, Dr Coggan, the Archbishop of Canterbury, suggested that, apart from the usual reasons, a relevant consideration is that the resources of the hospital services are limited, and "the extension of the life of a terminal patient may necessarily involve the suffering or even death of those who, if speedily admitted to hospital treatment, might have many years of useful life ahead" (70 Proc.Roy.Soc.Med. 76). This sensible remark was immediately criticised in an editorial in 3 Jrnl. Medical Ethics 1. See also George P Fletcher, *Rethinking Criminal Law* (Boston 1978) 606–610, 624. At the latter place Fletcher quotes the *Quinlan* court as saying that life-support can be considered "ordinary" for a curable patient but "extraordinary" for the irreversibly doomed patient. Generally, on the morality of omissions, see Jonathan Glover, *Causing Death and Saving Lives* (Penguin Books 1977) Chap. 7, and on the ordinary-extraordinary distinction see further Schwager in *Ethical Issues in Death and Dying*, ed. Beauchamp and Perlin (Englewood Cliffs 1978) 445–446.

[3] 46 Med. Leg.Jrnl 28.

[4] See Human Tissue Act 1961.

in another form if the assailant kept his victim "alive" on a ventilator in order to avoid a conviction of murder or manslaughter. Could there nevertheless be a conviction, when the victim's heart is still beating?

Formerly, the legal attitude was that death was something that could be left to the doctors to certify, but with the advance of science complications and doubts have set in. It used to be thought that death occurred when the heart stopped, but the French noticed that when an aristocrat or criminal was guillotined his heart continued to function for some seconds after his head was off. Was he still alive? The definition of death in terms of heart death was obviously suspect.

The doubts increased with the increase of medical skill. In open-heart surgery the patient's heart is temporarily stopped, but he is not regarded as dying. Conversely, when a hopelessly comatose patient is kept going on a ventilator, can he be regarded as dead? It has come to be realised that man's passing, like his creation, is a continuous process, and that there is no scientifically ascertainable moment of death. Different parts of the body die at different times (the skin remains alive for some time after the cessation of heart and brain activity, and hair goes on growing for another two days). So in attempting to pinpoint the death of the human person we are engaged in a verbal activity, a question of naming, and not primarily a scientific one.

Who is to do the naming? Not necessarily doctors. It was always a mistake to regard life and death as exclusively medical questions. Of course, in defining death judges will pay great attention to the state of medical science and the opinions of doctors, as well as to the practical consequences of choosing one definition rather than another. Moreover, it is the doctor who has to apply the legal definition by giving expert evidence. But the fact remains that although the diagnosis of death is medical, the definition must be legal. The law protects the living and ceases to protect the dead (at any rate, in the same way); and the line between the two has to be drawn by the law.

The doctors have now made up their minds in favour of brain death instead of heart death. The Conference of Medical Royal Colleges and their Faculties of the United Kingdom has resolved that when irreversible brain damage is diagnosed, and it is established by tests that none of the vital centres in the brain stem is still functioning, the patient is to be accounted dead, though the decision to cease artificial support should be taken by two doctors.[5] This has been circulated to all doctors by the Department of Health.

The pronouncement is important in relation to transplants. It will encourage doctors to remove kidneys while the patient is still on the respirator, thus increasing the likelihood that the organ will be an effective transplant. A surgeon who did this would be guilty of assault if the patient were not dead, but doubtless the courts will follow the medical lead. The law never fixed on heart death as the sole relevant point of time, because formerly it was not possible to distinguish for practical purposes between heart death and brain death. Now that the question has become a practical one, the courts are certainly free to adopt the definition of death in terms of brain death.

However, the Conference guidelines relate only to irretrievable death of

---

[5] [1979] 1 BMJ 332, and earlier report there referred to. Further guidelines for diagnosis were added later: [1981] 3 BMJ 505. See also Ian M Kennedy in [1977] Crim.LR 443; reply, *ibid.* 634. The notion of brain death was accepted by the trial judge in *Malcherek*, n. 10 below. See also 41 Medico-Legal Journal 18 ff.; David W Meyers, *The Human Body and the Law* (Edinburgh 1970) Chap. 5; S Gorovitz and others (eds.), *Moral Problems of Medicine* (Englewood Cliffs 1976) Chap. 3.

the brain-stem, through which messages to and from the body are routed. Acceptance of the guidelines would not settle the problem of "living death." A patient who has not yet suffered death of the brain-stem may be in a deep coma with irreversible brain damage, which means that he has merely a "vegetable" existence. If he is not being artificially supported, doctors do nothing, simply refraining from giving him medical treatment if, for example, he develops a fever. If he is on a ventilator they will eventually switch it off. The general view is that this cannot be justified by saying that the patient is dead, though some would extend the notion of death to all irreversibly comatose individuals.[6]

Couldn't you avoid the niceties of charnel knowledge by saying simply that the doctor who switches off the machine when the patient is in an irreversible coma is not guilty of murder because he does not perform an act of killing, but merely decides not to fight any more to save the patient's life?

This is the second of the possible solutions of the problem mentioned at the outset. It is capable of providing a defence to the doctor even where the patient has not suffered death of the brain stem but is irreversibly comatose all the same. The argument is that stopping the ventilator is in substance not an act but an omission to struggle. And the omission is not a breach of duty by the doctor, because he is not obliged to continue in a hopeless case.[7]

It has been objected[8] that this opinion would allow unauthorised strangers to interfere and kill the patient. The stranger owes no duty to prolong the patient's life, so if his conduct in stopping the ventilator is legally an omission, it could not be murder. The answer may be suggested that the intruder who switches off the machine may be held to commit an act (of murder), even though the doctor who does the same thing merely omits to continue to treat. The intruder has no responsibility for, or authority in respect of, the patient; he does not take part in the decision whether to continue medical treatment or not, so what he does is a positive act of intervention.[9]

Could one say that the doctor who switches off the machine does not cause the resulting death, which is caused by the illness or injury suffered by the patient in the first place?

This is the third possible line of argument. It would not help as regards

---

[6] See P D G Skegg in [1974] CLJ 130 and in 2 Jrnl. of Medical Ethics 190; reply, Kennedy in 3 *ibid.* 5; P J Pace in 126 NLJ 1232; Hillman and Aldridge in 116 Solicitors' Jrnl 323.

A different and even more puzzling problem of definition arises when a patient whose heart has stopped is afterwards resuscitated. If the doctor were to say that the patient was dead but has been restored to life the court would not accept his language, because the legal consequences would he too upsetting. On the death of the patient his estate would pass irrevocably to his executors and any life interest that he held in property would come to an end; so that if it were held that he was later restored to life, he would come back into the world a pauper. The law must say that the patient never died. This implies that the cessation of the heart beat, respiration and even brain activity need not signify death if the patient is afterwards resuscitated.

The problem is whether the possibility of resuscitation (when the patient is not in fact resuscitated) is to be taken as postponing the legal time of death. For example, the patient's legatee, to make sure that he is not resuscitated, plunges a dagger into his heart. Has an unlawful homicide been committed? The answer would seem to be that the legal moment of death is not to be postponed by reference to a possible resuscitation that does not take place, because the contrary view would create formidable difficulties.

[7] See the important points made by Helen Beynon in [1982] Crim. LR 19–23, 25–28; also the 1st edn of this work pp. 236–237.

[8] By P D G Skegg in 41 MLR 423.

[9] Dr Skegg tells me that he now agrees with this answer.

property rights and the taking of transplants, but it is a way of protecting the doctor from responsibility for stopping the ventilator. It is supported by the ruling in *Malcherek*,[10] where the trial judge refused to ask the jury to decide whether the fact that the doctors took the patient off the ventilator affected the defendant's liability for murder. On appeal the Court of Appeal similarly declined to hear alleged evidence that the doctors had not acted in accordance with approved medical practice.

Reviewing these arguments, all three have merit and there is no reason why the law should not adopt them all in order to promote a beneficial outcome. Brain-death, when it can be established, could well be taken as death for all legal purposes. No one could then gain a legal advantage by ventilating what is to all intents and purposes a corpse. Even when brain death cannot be established, but all efforts to restore consciousness have failed, the doctors should be entitled to turn off the respirator when this is the reasonable course; and they should be saved from liability for criminal homicide both by the doctrine of omission and by that of causation—and, indeed, by the doctrine of necessity, since medical resources cannot be deployed indefinitely for the preservation of a merely vegetable existence.

The first theory (brain death) involves the application of scientific criteria in virtually an automatic way. The others leave it to the doctor (at least in the first instance) to decide whether life has or will have any value for the patient. There is no way of escaping this, unless the doctor is to try to keep every creature alive indefinitely. It should be realised that the medical resources thus squandered will deprive other patients who would have benefited from treatment.

Isn't the distinction between an act and an omission, or the distinction based on the notion of causaton, in the case of the vegetative, etc., patient really a piece of moral cowardice? You want the poor chap to die, but haven't the courage to despatch him, so you withhold antibiotics, etc., and hope that nature will take him off. It would be kinder and more honest to give him a quick and easeful death.

Acting upon the distinction between acts and omissions, and upon there definition of death, is the furthest that doctors can safely go at present, with the law, theology and public opinion as they are. Moreover, most doctors reject active euthanasia. There is a strong culturally-induced resistance to the idea of interfering with the processes of human life except by prolonging its span.[11]

Would it be lawful for parents to decide against life-saving treatment for their handicapped infant?

They may certainly do this if the infant is so severely affected that he cannot have a life free from pain. Ormrod LJ, in the address before referred to, described the bitter sense of failure in the medical profession

---

[10] [1981] 1 WLR 690. Cp. § 16.3 at n. 10, 3rd ed.

[11] For a philosophical discussion of the difference between "passive" and "active" euthanasia see *Ethical Issues in Death and Dying*, ed. Tom L Beauchamp and S Perlin (Englewood Cliffs 1978) 240–258.

from its experience in treating many cases of spina bifida. He quoted Professor John Lorber's conclusion:

> "If today a surgeon is faced with a new-born baby with extensive myelomeningocele, he should not consider this as an immediate tactical problem, but should think of the life that lies ahead for the baby. If he would not like such a child of his own to survive, he should take the logical long-term strategic view and resist the temptation to operate."[12]

Ormrod LJ added his own more general conclusion: "The result of all applications of medical technology should be evaluated as soon as possible in terms of quality of life of the survivors and cost-effectiveness." The direction to the jury in *Arthur* was founded on this broader view of the right action.

> Dr Arthur, a highly respected paediatrician, had the care of a mongoloid baby, who died after Dr Arthur, at the request of the parents, prescribed "nursing care only." As a result of the activities of a moralist group the DPP was induced to prosecute Dr Arthur for murder. It transpired at the trial that the baby had serious physical defects, and it could not be proved that death was caused by withholding nourishment rather than by these defects; so the charge was reduced to attempted murder. Farquharson J directed the jury that doctors have no special dispensation in law to kill a child merely because it is handicapped or seriously defective. At the same time, he said, no one would say that a doctor was committing an act of murder by failing to operate on a mongol who has a physical defect from which he will die if not operated on. Similarly, if the mongol child gets pneumonia, and, the parents not wishing him to be kept alive, the doctor decides not to administer antibiotics, "by a merciful dispensation of providence he dies, once again it would be very unlikely, I would suggest, that you (or any other jury) would say that that doctor was committing murder." The question for the jury was therefore whether Dr Arthur merely prescribed a sedative as a holding operation, in order that the child might be comfortable while it was ascertained whether he might die peacefully from any organic defect or pneumonia. On this direction the jury acquitted. (The defence had not argued that one cannot, in any case, attempt to commit a crime by omission, though the point would seem to be open to argument.)[13]

It will be seen that this direction was wide enough to allow the withholding of all special measures to save the life of a mentally defective infant, even apart from its possessing any lethal defect. However, the attitude of the Court of Appeal in *Re B (A Minor)*[14] was less permissive.

> A child was born who was a mongol (suffering from what is clinically called Down's syndrome) and also had an intestinal blockage which would be fatal unless operated upon. The parents decided that the operation should not be carried out, but the local authority had the child made a ward of court, and the court (on appeal the Court of Appeal) authorised the operation. After the operation the local authority put the child out to foster care.

---

[12] 46 Med. Leg.Jrnl 29. Professor Lorber stated that more than 300 spina bifida babies suffering from serious handicap were allowed to die each year without public protest (The Times, August 13, 1981).

[13] The case is briefly reported in The Times, November 5, 1981. The above quotations are from the transcript.

[14] [1981] 1 WLR 1421. See 131 NLJ 1020.

The court, in overriding the parents' wishes and authorising the operation, acted in what it thought was the best interest of the child. The wishes of the parents were not regarded as being relevant. The evidence did not satisfy the court that the child's life would be "demonstrably awful" or "intolerable." The fact that the court thought the point relevant may suggest that different facts might have produced a different decision, but all that Templeman LJ said was that "there may be cases, I know not, . . . where the life of the child is bound to be so full of pain and suffering that the court might be driven to a different conclusion."

If the court feels entitled to take the line here faintly foreshadowed where the child is a ward of court, it seems obvious that parents and doctors would be entitled to act in the same way where the child is not a ward of court. Moreover, it must not be assumed that the parents and doctors concerned in *Re B* would have committed murder or manslaughter if they had not been superseded by the court and had allowed the infant to die. The court, having assumed the wardship of the infant, assumed that it had to take its own decision on the infant's future; but the court was not necessarily laying down a rule to bind parents and doctors where a judge has not issued a direction.

It may be thought to be wrong that doctors who have to take these difficult decisions, often in circumstances in which they must act quickly if they are to act effectively, should be subject to the law of murder if they are subsequently held to have broken the nebulous rules. A doctor who wants legal protection can have the child made a ward of court, but he should not be obliged to do so. Perhaps the doctor who obeys the parents could say in defence that when the parents refused consent to the operation he was discharged from responsibility for the child[15]; or perhaps he might say that his duty of positive action is limited to what is customarily to be expected of doctors.[16] Doctors and nurses have always exercised their judgment in deciding whether to keep severely handicapped neonates alive—even to the extent of refraining from giving such an infant the slap on the back that may be needed to start him breathing. There is, surely, a strong argument for keeping the law out of these cases. When a question is so much a matter of opinion, and when the good order of society in general is not at stake, the criminal law should stay its hand. Even if wardship proceedings are taken, the decision of the parents that a defective child should be allowed to die should prevail; and doctors generally recognise this.[17]

---

[15] See 131 NLJ 1040.

[16] See Helen Beynon in [1982] Crim.LR 27–28.

[17] Commenting on *Re B (A Minor)*, the BMA said: "All patients have identical rights—one right is to accept or reject medical treatment. A newborn baby has the right to accept or reject treatment. As the infant cannot take the decision personally it is the responsibility of the parents to take the decision. The decision will be based on consultation with the doctors, perhaps the GP, and perhaps the vicar or priest, but the *Handbook of Medical Ethics* quite clearly states, 'the parents must ultimately decide:' " [1981] 3 BMJ 567. See further, *Infanticide and the Value of Life*, ed. Marvin Kohl (1978); *Ethical Issues in Death and Dying*, ed. Beauchamp and Perlin (Englewood Cliffs 1978) 259–271; *Biomedical Ethics* ed. Mappes and Zembaty (New York 1981) 379–398.

§ 12.9. THE RATIONALE OF NEGLIGENT MANSLAUGHTER

The law of constructive manslaughter has been criticised, but it is not nearly so much open to objection as manslaughter by inadvertent negligence—which is what *Caldwell* "recklessness" can amount to. In constructive manslaughter there has at least been (in all probability) an intentional or reckless offence against the person, and all that the law of constructive manslaughter does is to set the court free from the limitation of punishment that would otherwise attach. In "reckless" manslaughter, on the other hand, as the offence is sometimes interpreted, the defendant may have had no idea of harming anybody.

Presumably, many deaths are caused by negligence or as the result of an assault. Yet they are rarely charged as manslaughter. It seems, therefore, that the enforcement of this part of the law is largely haphazard.

No precise figures can be given because the criminal statistics do not distinguish between manslaughter by provocation, manslaughter by negligence or recklessness, and constructive manslaughter. The figures of convictions for 1975 were as follows.

Murder	86
Manslaughter (s. 2[1])	74
Other manslaughter	185
Infanticide	35

The cases of "other manslaughter" included not only killing upon provocation but near-murders where there was an attack with a weapon, and cases of the latter type were probably the large majority. Judging from newspaper reading, cases of manslaughter by negligence like *Lamb* and *Stone* are exceptional. They may come before the courts in other ways, but not as manslaughter.

No one has studied how people become selected for the privilege of being prosecuted or manslaughter. Here are some more grisly figures. In 1975 there were 582,825 deaths in England and Wales from all causes, including the following (provisional figures).

Motor vehicle accidents	5,834
Accidents in factories	427
Accidents in the construction industries	182
Other accidents (home, rail, air etc.)	8,817

Some of these fatalities must have been caused by the negligence of other persons,[2] often (one may imagine) criminal in degree. If the culprits are charged at all, it is almost invariably with some more specific offence than manslaughter. Negligent drivers are proceeded against for a driving offence, and the outcome is generally lenient, even where death has been caused. Fatal "accidents" at work are charged as summary offences under the relevant legislation, if a breach has occurred. The average fine for all infractions (fatal or not) in factories and the construction industries in 1975 was £75; and the usual fine in fatal cases was not much higher: say about £200. Since the proceedings are almost invariably against companies, the individuals at fault are in effect shielded from liability. Inspectors regard it as their sole duty to bring a charge under the relevant legislation, not the more serious and cumbrous charge at common law. Similarly, when a man is killed at a poisonous waste tip, those responsible are likely to be charged with breach of regulations made under the Control of Pollution Act

---

[1] S.2 manslaughters are murders reduced to manslaughter by reason of diminished responsibility. See Chap. 30.

[2] A Health and Safety Executive Report on fatal accidents in the construction industry found that in 68 out of 100 the accident was "a reasonably foreseeable event which ought to have been seen by a member of management as a risk:" *One Hundred Fatal Accidents in Construction* (HMSO 1978). However, the HSE also emphasises the part played in accidents by the workers themselves.

1974 rather than with manslaughter. When a child is killed, by neglect or even by assault, the charge brought by the local authority or by the National Society for the Prevention of Cruelty to Children is a minor one under the Children and Young Persons Act, or other legislation, though very occasionally the police intervene to make it manslaughter.[3]

Can it be, therefore, that the few people who are indicted for negligent manslaughter each year generally suffer this fate only because there happens to be no other offence covering the case? It is noticeable that this was so with both Stone and Lamb (unless Lamb happened not to possess a certificate for his gun).

The better way of dealing with negligence is to have safety regulations that can be enforced by specialised inspectors. People are persuaded to improve their behaviour, but not by interfering with their lives to the extent of locking them up for a term of years.

Contrast the position when a manslaughter charge is brought for negligence. It cannot be tried summarily. It is heard in an emotional atmosphere because the defendant has been unlucky enough to have brought about a death, and the sentence in case of conviction is often severe. The prosecutions of Lamb and Stone were, presumably, exercises in public morality. But had they any useful purpose, even as exercises in morality?

The Criminal Law Revision Committee accepted this reasoning, and recommended that involuntary manslaughter should be committed only where the killer intended to cause serious injury, or was reckless as to death or serious injury.[4] The committee assumed that the subjective definition of recklessness would be accepted. However, if the rule in *Caldwell* is continued, it radically changes the effect of the recommendation, and would probably deprive it of most of its intended effect. In any case, decisions like *Stone* would not be altered by the recommendation unless the law of manslaughter by omission is reconsidered.

SUMMARY

The punishment for manslaughter may be anything up to imprisonment for life. On § .1
a charge of murder, manslaughter is an "included offence." Involuntary manslaughter (no *voluntas* for murder) includes what is here called reckless manslaughter and constructive manslaughter.

Reckless manslaughter requires what is variously called gross (or criminal) § .2
negligence or recklessness. The classic definition is in *Bateman*. Some definitions of gross negligence are ambiguous between objective and subjective meanings, and so also are definitions of recklessness in this context. In practice, convictions are sometimes upheld without proof of advertence; and in *Seymour* the House of Lords held that *Caldwell* and *Lawrence* recklessness in not thinking is sufficient, though the risk incurred must be very high.

Both murder and manslaughter can be committed by omission, but there must § .3
be a duty to act. The main example is the duty to save the lives of certain helpless persons. A parent is under such a duty towards his unemancipated child, and a husband towards his wife; presumably, also, a wife towards her husband. In practice an occupier will be regarded as under such a duty towards a person who resides with him and becomes incapacitated; but in *Stone* the judge left the question to the jury as though it were one of fact, and this was not disapproved on appeal. In the same case the jury were allowed to find that a duty fell upon the occupier's mistress as a matter of "undertaking," but the meaning given to the word was extremely loose.

The CA in *Stone* held that it is sufficient for liability if the defendant foresaw § .4
some "danger to health and welfare" arising from his omission; but this

---

[3] In *Horwood,* Daily Telegraph, March 19, 1971, parents whose child died as a result of what prosecuting counsel described as their "appalling neglect" were charged only with wilful neglect under the Ch. & YPA. In *Lovell*, The Times, June 17, 1971, a mother who hit and severely bruised her child, who died from asphyxia, was put on probation for an offence under OAPA s.47.

[4] 14th Report, para. 124.

may be questioned. There are also unsatisfactory cases that, like *Stone*, seem to overlook the right of self-determination.

Constructive manslaughter means killing as a result of certain kinds of unlawful and dangerous acts. "The unlawful act must be such as all sober and reasonable people would inevitably recognise must subject the other person to, at least, the risk of some harm resulting therefrom, albeit not serious harm" (*Church*). § .5

Limiting decisions on the "unlawful act" are, first, *Franklin* (tort insufficient: Field J), secondly, *Andrews* (statutory offence of negligence insufficient, HL), and thirdly, *Lowe* (crimes of omission insufficient, CA). In effect this seems to mean that there must be a criminal act directed at somebody. However, the CA in *Cato* apparently claimed the power to invent new unlawful acts, and the HL in *Newbury* neglected to incorporate the limiting decisions in its pronouncement as to the law. Indeed, dicta in the latter case would eliminate the need for a lesser offence; *sed quaere*. If the decision in *Newbury* is to be reconciled with the other authorities, it must be on the ground that the boys were at least reckless as to causing fright; but there appears to have been no finding of the jury to this effect. The CA subsequently decided, in *Dalby*, that the unlawful act must have been directed at the deceased and must have caused him direct injury; this reinforces the interpretation of *Newbury* just offered. Death caused by criminal abortion is said to be constructive manslaughter, though this is difficult to reconcile with principle. § .6

Killing a supposed corpse can be constructive manslaughter on the "series of acts" doctrine. It can also be regarded as manslaughter by gross negligence. § .7

On principle, a patient can refuse treatment, even to save his life; and a doctor is in any case not obliged to continue useless efforts to save life. Switching off the respirator in the case of a patient with brain damage can be justified, according to circumstances, either on the theory of brain death (death of the brain stem) or on the ground that switching off the respirator merely begins an omission where there is no longer a duty to act. There is also the possibility of justifying this course of action on a causal argument. It seems that parents and doctors can withhold life-saving treatment from an infant who is suffering from a lethal ailment, or (possibly) who is doomed to a life of suffering; but the court can overrule their decision in wardship proceedings. § .8

Prosecutions for involuntary manslaughter are sporadic; in practice other charges are nearly always preferred where they are available. § .9

Chapter 13

THE FETUS AND THE NEW-BORN CHILD

For Man to tell how human Life began
Is hard: for who himself beginning knew?
Milton, *Paradise Lost*, Book 8

§ 13.1. HOMICIDE AND THE NEW-BORN

The law protecting neonates and the unborn is not ordinarily met with in legal practice; but it is of importance for obstetric surgeons and is a matter of philosophical and human interest. It is also the subject of strongly-felt differences of moral opinion.

The definition of homicide (§ 11.1) requires the victim to be in *rerum natura* or "in being," which means that he must be 'completely born alive.'

Although injuries to a fetus[1] causing its death do not generally amount to homicide, there is a curious rule by which they can do so. If a fetus is injured in the womb and is subsequently born alive but dies as a result of the prenatal injury, this is murder or manslaughter according to the mental element.[2] So whether the offender is guilty of the crime will sometimes depend upon whether a doctor is able to remove the fetus from the womb while it is still alive, even though it is so premature that it is doomed to die almost immediately.

> In a New Jersey case, D shot a pregnant woman whose twin sons were then delivered by caesarean section (hysterotomy) but died a short time later. He was convicted of murder of the infants.[3] Had they died in the womb it would not have been murder.

The rule also applies to illegal abortionists. In this it seems to be over-severe, for it makes what may be a purely accidental fact turn the abortionist into a murderer. Mercifully, the judges have not extended it to cases where a mother neglects to take prenatal precautions for her child, so that it dies shortly after birth; this is not regarded as manslaughter, because the duty of care is held to commence only with the birth of the child.[4]

When exactly does birth take place?

The two requirements, birth and live birth, must be taken separately. The rule for birth is simple: the child must have been wholly extruded from the body of the mother. No part of the child must remain within the parts

---

[1] Often spelt "foetus," but "fetus" is now coming to be preferred in medical writing. The *e* is long.

[2] The rule depends on old authorities dating from Coke, and was accepted by the trial judge in *West* (1848) 2 C & K 784, 175 ER 329. It was held in Hong Kong that if D stabs V, a pregnant woman, whose child is born alive and then dies as a result of injury received from the weapon, D is guilty of murder or manslaughter of the child: *Kwok Chak Ming* [1963] HKLR 349, discussed by Cannon in [1963] Crim.LR 748. See also Atkinson in 20 LQR 157; Winfield in 8 CLJ 78–80; Russell, 12th edn 401.

[3] *Anderson*, The Times, July 17, 1975.

[4] *Izod* (1904) 20 Cox 690; D R S Davies in 1 MLR 210; Russell, 12th edn 406. The woman cannot be convicted of child destruction (see § .2), because that crime is limited to wilful *acts*. Customary attitudes are indicated by the fact that "during the 1956 Olympic Games in Melbourne at least six women athletes are known to have competed during the first four months of pregnancy. A recent high diving championship in Bulgaria was won by a woman six months pregnant." New Society, December 27, 1962.

of the mother if it is to be regarded as born. Even if the child is deliberately throttled when only its head is protruding, this is not murder.

Is it abortion?

Apparently not: abortion is committed only when the fetus is killed in the womb or caused to be prematurely born. Abortion is inapplicable to an act done when the child has left the womb during birth.[5] We shall see that the crime committed is child destruction. A fetus (or unborn child) is not a legal person, and so cannot (for example) own property; but its existence is recognised by law in some ways. The fetus becomes a legal person when it is born alive.

And when is that?

The question of live birth has given rise to confusion in the past, because of arguments on the question of "independent existence." Subject to what is to be said later, the law as now settled is that a child is regarded as born alive whenever it is fully born (as above defined) and is alive, the test of the latter being the functioning of the heart.[6] It does not matter that the umbilical cord, whereby the child is connected to the mother, had not been severed at the time when the defendant killed the child. Nor need the child have taken its first gasp, since this may not occur for some little time after birth.[7]

§ 13.2. CHILD DESTRUCTION

If a child is purposely killed in the process of being born, this should rationally be the offence of abortion. But it was thought that this offence did not apply to an act done during birth. Accordingly, the Infant Life (Preservation) Act 1929 created the additional offence of child destruction, punishable (like abortion) with imprisonment for life. The only situation for which the Act was required was where a baby was killed after being partially extruded; but it was given a wider ambit, overlapping the crime of abortion. The offence is committed

---

[5] Atkinson in 20 LQR 157.

[6] Suppose that a doctor, having fertilised an ovum in a test tube (*in vitro* in medical parlance), in order to produce a "test-tube baby," finds that it will no longer be required, and throws it/him/her away. Is this murder? The embryo has not been "born," but it has an existence independent of the mother; biologically it is alive, but is not legally alive if the law makes heart-beat the test! The sensible solution is to say that the embryo has not reached a sufficient stage of development to be "a reasonable creature" within the law of homicide.

[7] Some authorities lay it down that the child must have had a circulation independent of the mother, but this proposition is based on a biological misconception, since the "independent circulation" exists before birth. For several months the fetus has had a circulation independent of the mother in the sense that the embryonic heart maintains a fetal blood-stream, which does not directly communicate with the maternal blood. The two blood-streams are separated by a thin membrane, through which oxygen and nutrients pass to the fetus, and waste products back to the mother. When the child is born, if it does not breathe, its existence is dependent on the umbilical cord, through which its blood-stream is passing in both directions, and so long as the umbilical cord is pulsating in this way the child is dependent on its mother for life.

On the whole subject see Williams, *The Sanctity of Life and the Criminal Law* (London 1958) 19–23.

> "by any person who, with intent to destroy the life of a child capable of being born alive, by any wilful act causes a child to die before it has an existence independent of its mother."

This legislation is supposed to cover the last part of the period of gestation, namely, when the child is capable of being born alive—commonly, though perhaps misleadingly, called the time of viability. In order to determine the period more precisely, the Act provides a presumption that the child is capable of being born alive after the 28th week of pregnancy, i.e. the seventh lunar month.[1]

The statute expressly provides that no person shall be found guilty unless it is proved that the act was not done in good faith for the purpose only of preserving the life of the mother. This legalises an operation like craniotomy, designed to reduce the bulk of the mature fetus, which intentionally sacrifices the fetus in order to save the life of the mother.

Suppose a newly born baby is found dead. May not the prosecution find it hard to prove whether the baby was killed or not, and if so whether it was killed before birth or after?

The Act of 1929 does not help on this. It does not save the jury from the difficulty of making up their minds whether the child was fully born alive at the time when the criminal act was committed, because when the child is fully born alive (having an existence independent of its mother) the crime of child destruction becomes inapplicable and the crime of murder takes over. However, the indictment will contain counts both for murder and for child destruction, and the jury will be left to choose between them.

If the child destruction statute does not help with problems of proof, I don't really see why it was passed.

Because it was thought that abortion could not be committed during the birth. This was purely a technical diffculty: it would have been simpler to enact that abortion can be committed up to the moment when the child is born.

§ 13.3. CONCEALMENT OF BIRTH

The difficulty of proof of the unlawful homicide of new-born infants has led to an intervention by the legislature. It is an offence, punishable with 2 years' imprisonment, by any secret disposition of the dead body of a child

---

[1] Medical practice is to count pregnancy as commencing from the beginning of the woman's period before the conception, 40 weeks from this date being regarded as "full term." Assuming ovulation to occur about midway through the menstrual cycle, the actual length of pregnancy is probably at least two weeks less than 40. It is not clear whether the 28th week of pregnancy referred to in the Act is to be counted according to the medical fashion (*i.e.* the 26th week) or by reference to the reality. On principle it should refer to the reality, and since that cannot be established beyond reasonable doubt, it should be taken (in favour of the defendant) as referring to the latest date on which pregnancy could have commenced. There is an additional question as to what is meant by "pregnancy": see below § .4.

to endeavour to conceal its birth, and this whether the child died before, at or after birth.[1] The statute is of doubtful justice, because a woman who has given birth to an illegitimate child, which dies soon after, may wish to conceal its birth for reasons that do not indicate her responsibility for its death. The statute is not required in order to secure the public notification of births, because this is provided for in other legislation.

§ 13.4. ABORTION

Abortion (or miscarriage) may occur spontaneously, in which case it is of no interest to the criminal law; or it may be deliberately induced, when it is a serious crime.[1] For legal purposes, abortion means feticide: the *intentional* destruction of the fetus in the womb, or any untimely delivery brought about with intent to cause the death of the fetus. It is not criminal for a doctor to induce premature birth, when he has no intent to cause the death of the child; and he does not become criminally responsible even if he accidentally causes death.

Why do you keep on referring to the fetus? Wouldn't it be better to admit that we are talking about killing an unborn child?

There is a linguistic point, and a philosophical point. Ordinary language is uncertain: people used to speak of a pregnant woman as being "great with child," but on the other hand the woman might say that she has no child *yet*. She is "in the family way" rather than having a family. It is quite natural to speak of a mature fetus as an "unborn child," but it would be odd to refer to a microscopic fertilised ovum in that way.

The philosophical debate is whether there is a difference in moral status between the fetus and the born child. Only by stages do women come to regard the embryo as a separate entity from themselves. Most people agree that at some point of development a fetus has or should have rights, but not the full rights of a born child. We cannot go into the problem further,

---

[1] OAPA 1861 s.60. For cases see Halsbury's Statutes, 3rd edn 811–812. See also Atkinson in 20 LQR 137, 150; Davies in 1 MLR 213; Winfield in 8 CLJ 80; Williams, *op. cit.* 23. The courts in sentencing seem to take account of negligence contributing to the death: see *English* (1967) 52 CAR 119. The present tendency is to construe the statute restrictively: it does not apply to the concealment of a nonviable fetus: *Holt* (1937) 2 JCrL 69; *Matthews* [1943] CPD 8 (S Af.) It is not clear whether the abandonment of a dead child in a public place constitutes the offence: see Taylor, *Medical Jurisprudence*, 11th edn ii 40; *Bennett* (1938) 2 JCrL 530. On a charge of murder, the jury may convict of concealment of birth.

When there is no suspicion of foul play or negligence the outcome of the proceeding is usually indulgent. See 3 JCrL 38.

The CLRC thought that the offence was not properly regarded as one against the person, and decided not to include it in the projected new OAPA, recommending that it should be considered in relation to the legislation on the registration of births.

[1] Although "abortion" and "miscarriage" are now used by doctors as synonyms, the word "miscarriage" in medical usage formerly referred only to the miscarriage of a fetus of an appreciable degree of development, which is an argument for saying that this is its meaning in OAPA s. 58 (below). See Williams, *op. cit.* 139 n.1. Medical men frequently refer to an induced abortion as the termination of pregnancy.

and it is enough to say that the word "fetus" is here used to cover the product of conception before birth. A fetus is not a legal person, and so cannot (for example) own property; but its existence is recognised by law in some ways.

The early Church accepted, and transmitted to the Middle Ages, the generally held belief of antiquity that the soul entered the human fetus at some time *after* conception; this was called the theory of mediate animation, since "animation" was supposed to occur at some medial time in pregnancy. The common law absorbed this theory, and fixed the time of animation at the time of quickening, when the fetus moved in the womb, an event that usually occurs about half-way through the pregnancy (the 20th week), though at no fixed point. Abortion before quickening was not a crime punished at common law (though there are records of its being punished by ecclesiastical courts[2]); even abortion after quickening was not murder, because no "reasonable creature" was involved, but it was a common law misdemeanour, being the killing of a human being or potential human being presumably already possessed of a soul. Thus the common law distinguished between the moral status of the fetus and that of the child, according a lower protection to the former.

Men's thinking on this subject was confused, partly because the term "animation" might refer either to the entry of life (*animus*) or to the entry of the soul (*anima*). No one can prove when—or if—a "soul" enters; but to say that the fetus becomes alive only when it moves is a palpable error. The Roman Church had never regarded the time of quickening as decisive on the entry of the soul, and during the 19th century most Catholic theologians came to support the theory of immediate animation—that is, that the human soul enters at the moment of conception. Protestant theology paid virtually no attention to the question,[3] but the claims of logic or supposed logic were sufficiently strong to procure a stiffening of the common law. By a statute of 1803, attempting to procure a miscarriage even before quickening became a crime triable before the ordinary courts.[4]

Strangely, the law does not make the abortion itself a crime; the crime consists in an act done with intent to procure (cause) an abortion. It now rests on the Offences against the Person Act 1861 section 58.

> "Every woman, being with child, who, with intent to procure her own miscarriage, shall unlawfully administer to herself any poison or other noxious thing, or shall unlawfully use any instrument or other means whatsoever with the like intent, and whosoever, with intent to procure the miscarriage of any woman, whether she be or be not with child, shall unlawfully administer to her or cause to be taken by her any poison or other noxious thing, or shall use any instrument or other means whatsoever with the like intent, . . . shall be liable . . . to be kept in [imprisonment] for life."

It will be seen that the Act covers two cases.

First, where a pregnant woman uses any means with intent to procure her own miscarriage.

Although these words still stand in the statute book, women are not prosecuted for procuring abortion themselves, perhaps because of the difficulty of getting a jury to convict a woman for an act committed in extreme distress, and the unlikelihood that if convicted she will receive anything more than a nominal sentence. A further good reason for not prosecuting (whether or not it weighs with the police) is that a woman who has operated on

---

[2] See letter by Victor Tunkel in The Times, June 28, 1978.

[3] *Human Reproduction* (British Council of Churches 1962) 44. On the ethics of abortion see Jonathan Glover, *Causing Death and Saving Lives* (Harmondsworth 1977) Chaps. 9–11, and literature in bibliography therein.

[4] Though a distinction was still made in respect of punishment, abortion after quickening being capital.

herself, or taken drugs, will frequently have caused herself such injury as to necessitate medical attention; and it would be most undesirable that she should be deterred from seeking this attention through the threat of punishment.[5]

Secondly, where anyone else unlawfully uses means with such intent, whether the woman is pregnant or not. A woman who goes to an illegal abortionist becomes an accessory, but in practice she is not charged.

Legally, using means with intent is the full offence under the section. Presumably the Act was drafted like this in order to save the prosecution from having to prove that an abortion was caused.

Instances of means given in the statute are "poison or other noxious thing" and "any instrument." The statute is not confined to these two instances, and it has been held to apply to an abortion attempted by manipulation with the hand.[6] Where a drug is administered, the judges insist that it must be noxious in itself to be a "noxious thing" within the statute: a harmless dose does not become noxious because the drug in question would be noxious if taken in excess.[7]

Where exactly is the line drawn between contraception and abortion?

Formerly it was thought that the vital point of time was fertilisation, the fusior of spermatozoon and ovum, but it is now realised (although the point as not come before the courts) that this position is not maintainable, and that conception for legal purposes must be dated at earliest from implantation.

The legislation is unspecific. The abortion section does not expressly refer to conception; it speaks merely of a "miscarriage." There is, therefore, nothing to prevent the courts interpreting the word "miscarriage" in a way that takes account of customary and approved birth control practices.

After fertilisation the human egg stays in the uterine tube for three days, then descends to the uterus and on about the 10th day after fertilisation attaches itself to the uterine wall ("implantation" or "nidation"). The widely-used method of birth control called the intrauterine contraceptive device (IUD), such as the coil or loop, works by destroying the blastocyst (the developing egg) or preventing it from implanting itself.[8] If, therefore, conception refers to fertilisation, the IUD should be named post-conceptive rather than contraceptive. So-called oral contraceptives may also act in this way, for as well as suppressing ovulation there is evidence that they can prevent the fertilised ovum implanting or for long remaining implanted. That is certainly the mechanism of post-coital oestrogen and progesteron administration, these substances (the so-called "morning after" pill) being effective if used within 72 hours of coitus.[9] If these methods of birth control are abortifacient they are illegal, unless administered by a doctor with the specified opinions of two doctors and in a hospital or registered nursing home under the Abortion Act. But no one who uses or fits IUDs supposes that they are illegal or are governed by the Abortion Act. The only way to

---

[5] In 1977 a girl of 13 who was convicted of trying to give herself a miscarriage received a free pardon and an apology.

[6] *Spicer* (1955) 39 CAR 189.

[7] See *Hollis* (1873) 28 LT 455; cp. Russell, 12th edn 602, and *Marcus* § 9.10 n. 8. A poison is noxious even though it is not in fact an abortifacient: *Marlow* [1965] Crim.LR 35. For attempts see 1st edn 401–402, read in the light of the Criminal Attempts Act 1981 (§ 17.4).

[8] G W Duncan and R G Wheeler in 12 Biology of Reproduction 143. Although the IUD is normally inserted before coitus, it has been found to prevent pregnancy when inserted within three days of an unprotected coitus. This is regarded as a particularly valuable recourse for victims of rape. See 10 IPPF Medical Bulletin, No. 2.

[9] Colin Brewer in 11 World Medicine 33 quotes W Rinehart (ed.), *Population Reports* (1976) Series J No. 9 p. 147.

uphold the legality of present medical practice, to make IUDs contraceptives and not abortifacients, is to say that for legal purposes conception is not complete until implantation. An advisory group established by the British Council of Churches took this line.[10] Moreover, it has been accepted by the Department of Health and Social Security, and the Attorney-General has decided that pills designed to inhibit implantation are not abortifacient and their use is not criminal.[11] The legal argument is that the word "miscarriage" in the abortion section means the miscarriage of an implanted blastocyst.[12]

The line of argument would uphold the legality of a universal medical practice, and would therefore provide a partial solution to immediate problems. But our birth control methods have a devastating effect upon the anti-abortionist argument that there is something magical or divine about the moment of fertilisation which brings about a new "human person" who must be fully protected by law. If all abortion is a kind of murder, it must be recognised, in the words of Dr Colin Brewer, that uncounted thousands of human beings are slaughtered each day by widely accepted birth control devices, as well as by the pill. Those who are unwilling to denounce these forms of birth control cannot consistently argue for the prohibition of abortion from the moment of fertilisation.

Even dating the prohibition of abortion from implantation does not establish the legality of the gel and prostaglandin preparations, now being developed, which expel the fetus at an early stage after implantation. There is an argument for interpreting the word "miscarriage" to allow still a little more leeway on this question. "Miscarriage" may be interpreted to mean the miscarriage of a fetus when it has achieved a certain degree of recognisable human organisation. In particular, those whose objection to abortion depends upon belief in the soul may be impressed by the fact that until two weeks after conception it remains uncertain whether the egg will become twins (or quins) instead of a single person. Since theology has never contemplated the division of the soul, this implies that the soul cannot enter the body for at least a fortnight after conception. So this argument takes us back to "mediate animation."

Do abortionists ever get as much as life?

The maximum sentence is never awarded. In practice, 6 years is the utmost, even for the professional abortionist. Many receive much shorter sentences, and some are merely fined.

When did abortion come to be recognised as proper on medical grounds?

In 1929 Parliament perceived the need to qualify the child destruction statute by a provision for preserving the life of the mother, but crassly failed to add a similar exception to the abortion section. In 1861 (when the OAPA was passed as a consolidating measure) medical science was not sufficiently advanced to make it safe to terminate pregnancy, so this Act makes no exception for therapeutic (health) abortions.

With increasing skill it became medical practice to perform the operation on urgent medical grounds, and the legality of this was established in dramatic circumstances in *Bourne*.[13]

---

[10] *Human Reproduction* (British Council of Churches 1962). For a medical view in support see A J Parkes in 3 Jrnl. Reprod. Fertil. 159.

[11] The Times, September 15, 1981; *Parl. Deb., H. of C.*, vol. 42 cols. 238–239.

[12] The legality of IUDs would have arisen in *Price* [1969] 1 QB 541 if it had not been for the biological ignorance or kindness of heart of counsel for the prosecution. See Tunkel in [1974] Crim.LR 466–467; and see that article generally; also Tunkel in [1979] 2 BMJ 253.

[13] [1939] 1 KB 687. The judge's direction to the jury is reported presumably verbatim as delivered in [1938] 3 All ER 615. The variations between this report and that in the Law Reports are so great that the judge must have almost re-written his direction for the Law Reports version.

> An eminent gynaecologist aborted a girl of 14 who was pregnant as the result of multiple rape. He justified his action on health grounds, and was acquitted after a favourable direction by Macnaghten J. The judge rested his direction on the presence in the statute of the word "unlawfully," which he took to signify that some terminations of pregnancy were lawful. In itself this was not a strong ground, but he also referred to the choice of values or choice of evils that is generally known as the doctrine of necessity. He said: "The unborn child in the womb must not be destroyed unless the destruction of that child is for the purpose of preserving the yet more precious life of the mother."[14]

To expand this point: the woman is a developed human being, sensitive to pain and anxiety. She is established in the affections of her family, and upon her the welfare of other children and of a husband may depend. It is far more important to consider her life and health than that of an early fetus, representing only a child-to-be, which has not yet been fully formed, cannot feel pain, cannot live outside the womb, and has not entered the human community.

Bourne's acquittal did not at once produce a large increase in medical abortions. The attitude of the medical profession in general was hostile, and tragic cases continued to occur. A girl of 12, pregnant by her father, was refused an abortion. Special boarding schools were opened for expectant mothers aged from 12 upwards, in order that they might continue with their lessons while looking after their babies. Women who had been raped, women deserted by their husbands, and overburdened mothers living in poverty with large families, also failed to get a medical abortion. One "liberal" hospital in London and one in Newcastle performed the operation comparatively freely, and abortions could be readily bought in Harley Street; but in general the mass of women could only go to a "back-street abortionist," wielding a knitting needle, syringe or stick of slippery elm, or to a skilled operator acting illegally for large fees. Some unwilling mothers-to-be used dangerous methods on themselves,[15] or occasionally committed suicide. Although illegal abortions ran into thousands each year, convictions were comparatively few (less than a hundred a year), largely because women who had sought the help of an abortionist were unwilling to give him away, but partly also because the police themselves tended not to look upon abortion as a real crime.[16] The only people who were effectively deterred by the law were the doctors, who alone could operate safely. The problem was common to all Christian countries that started with an unqualified prohibition of abortion.

At the same time as these evils were beginning to be acknowledged, the opinion arose that a woman had the right to control her own fertility. But against the pro-abortionists was arrayed a powerful religious lobby basing itself upon the "sanctity of life."

The Abortion Act 1967 was a compromise measure which did not concede all the demands of the libertarians and feminists but substantially liberalised the law. In England and Scotland it supersedes the case-law, including *Bourne*.[17] Section 1:

---

[14] From the report in [1938] 3 All ER at 620. For some reason Macnaghten J excised the sentence from the Law Reports version.

[15] On one occasion a teenage girl who took quinine to produce a miscarriage became blind: letter by Dr. C Brewer in The Times, June 30, 1965. Other women became paralysed for life or gravely impaired in health.

[16] Ben Whitaker, *The Police* (London 1964) 36–37.

[17] Comparable legislation has heen passed in many other countries; but in the Republic of Ireland and Northern Ireland the legality of medical abortions still rests on the willingness of judges to act in the way that Macnaghten did. See generally M Potts, P Diggory and J Peel, *Abortion* (Cambridge 1977).

"(1) Subject to the provisions of this section, a person shall not be guilty of an offence under the law relating to abortion when a pregnancy is terminated[18] by a registered medical practitioner[19] if two registered medical practitioners are of the opinion, formed in good faith—

(*a*) that the continuance of the pregnancy would involve risk to the life of the pregnant woman, or of injury to the physical or mental health of the pregnant woman or any existing children of her family, greater than if the pregnancy were terminated; or

(*b*) that there is a substantial risk that if the child were born it would suffer from such physical or mental abnormalities as to be seriously handicapped.

(2) In determining whether the continuance of a pregnancy would involve such risk of injury to health as is mentioned in paragraph (*a*) of subsection (1) of this section, account may be taken of the pregnant woman's actual or reasonably foreseeable environment.

(3) Except as provided by subsection (4) of this section, any treatment for the termination of pregnancy must be carried out in a hospital vested in the Minister of Health or the Secretary of State under the National Health Service Acts, or in a place for the time being approved for the purposes of this section by the said Minister or the Secretary of State.

(4) Subsection (3) of this section, and so much of subsection (1) as relates to the opinion of two registered medical practitioners, shall not apply to the termination of a pregnancy by a registered medical practitioner in a case where he is of the opinion, formed in good faith, that the termination is immediately necessary to save the life or to prevent grave permanent injury to the physical or mental health of the pregnant woman."

§ 13.5. THE FETAL GROUND

The fetal ground (s.1(1)(*b*)) does not need extensive consideration. It is sometimes justified for eugenic reasons, but in fact the contribution that abortion is likely to make to the betterment of man's genetic inheritance is slight. No: the argument for abortion on the fetal indication relates to the welfare of the parents, whose lives may well be blighted by having to rear a grossly defective child, and perhaps secondarily by consideration for the public purse. That this is the philosophy of the Act is borne out by the fact that it allows termination only where the child if born would be seriously handicapped, not where it is merely carrying undesirable genes.

Whereas the health grounds recognised in the Act merely enlarge on the attitude of the

---

[18] Or, surely, attempted to be terminated. An attempt to terminate within the Abortion Act is not an attempt to commit a crime. This opinion was expressed by Lord Edmund-Davies and apparently also by Lord Diplock in *Royal College of Nursing* v. *DHSS* [1981] AC 800, but Lord Wilberforce differed. The Law Officers expressed the opinion in 1979 that a doctor who performs "menstrual aspiration" at a time when it is not known whether the woman is pregnant or not is protected by the Abortion Act if one of the grounds of termination specified in the Act is present.

[19] It is sufficient if the doctor makes the medical decision and performs such parts of the treatment as necessitate his particular skill, other parts being performed by nurses, even though in his absence: *Royal College of Nursing* case, last note.

judge in *Bourne*, that the health of full human beings is to be preferred to the interest of the fetus in being born where the two interests conflict, the fetal ground marks a new departure. The fetus is destroyed not necessarily in its own interest (the physician need make no judgment that life will be a burden for it), but in the interest either of the parents or of society at large, though of course only upon the request of the mother.

Although argument still rages on whether abortion should be permitted merely as a matter of convenience to the woman, the fetal ground is almost universally accepted. But it is of some interest to note that anyone who does accept the fetal ground for abortion commits himself to the view that the moral status of the fetus is not the same as that of a child. For we do not permit children to be killed because they are seriously handicapped.

Isn't the fetal ground abominably vague?

The physician must decide whether there is a "substantial" risk that the child if born would be "seriously" handicapped. Advances in knowledge and medical skills make it more and more possible to attach a precise mathematical weight to the chance of the fetus being affected by genetic defects or by what happens to it in the womb. But the doctor still has to decide whether the case is sufficiently grave to justify termination. He may, of course, take the view that a relatively low risk justifies termination if the risk is of a relatively serious handicap: in common sense, the two factors are inversely related. Even when the doctor thinks that the "fetal indication" is not itself sufficiently present, the fact that the patient is extremely depressed by worry that the child may be affected can itself be a reason for termination on the health ground.

§ 13.6. THE HEALTH GROUNDS

The health grounds subdivide in relation to the health of the woman and the health of existing children of her family.

Where a pregnancy is terminated on the ground of risk of injury to health, how great must the risk be to justify the termination?

When the Abortion Bill came before the House of Lords, much attention was given to this question. The adjectives "serious," "grave" and "substantial" were considered, but their lordships finally adopted Lord Parker CJ's suggestion (moved in his absence by Lord Dilhorne, a strong opponent of relaxing the law), which now appears in the Act. The risk of injury feared from allowing the pregnancy to continue must be "greater than if the pregnancy were terminated." Lord Parker said of his amendment that the doctor's decision was to be arrived at by comparing one risk with another, and only if the risk in continuation were greater than the risk in termination would a defence be created under the Act. If that was the test, he said, it would be unnecessary and wrong to talk about risk as being "serious" or "substantial."

In making this move some of the opponents of freer abortion were perhaps misled by propaganda emanating from their own side. It had been widely argued, against the practice of abortion, that it was a dangerous operation, and on this supposition the formula was a restrictive one. Even so, the formula was a doubtful advantage for the restrictionists, because no one knew how long it might be before the danger of the operation was reduced, thus extending its legality. But in any case the assumption that the operation was particularly dangerous was wrong even in 1967, at least in cases where the termination was performed early enough. Figures from Eastern Europe indicated that the operation, properly performed within the first trimester[1] (the first three months of pregnancy), was much safer (at least from the point of view of mortality) than normal childbirth. This has also been found in England, and experience in performing the operation has steadily increased its safety. There are, of course, other risks associated with medical termination of pregnancy besides death, just as there are other risks associated with childbirth.

The wording of the Act, then, suggests the argument that first-trimester abortions are now left to medical discretion in the sense that if the doctor comes to the conclusion that, as the figures firmly show, the general mortality risk of a first-trimester abortion is less than maternal mortality, and if he further believes[2] that the morbidity risk does not affect the general conclusion that abortion is safer,[3] and that there is nothing in his patient's condition to affect the application of the statistical argument to her case, he is entitled to terminate an early pregnancy without finding a more specific ground for termination. Although this argument has not been ventilated in court, and would doubtless be regarded with extreme reserve by the judges, there is no logical answer to it. The risks associated with normal maternity must be among the risks resulting from a decision not to terminate, so that they can enter into a calculation of the risks that are "greater than if the pregnancy were terminated"; and if these risks by themselves are greater than the risks of termination, no other question need logically be asked.[4]

But that would mean that we have abortion on demand, which Parliament never intended. So the Act ought not to be interpreted in that way.

Some would say so. The opposing view is that Parliament consciously settled for a certain test for the legality of abortion; that test is acceptable to very many people, and the courts should apply it according to its wording. It is not for the courts to speculate whether Parliament made some mistake of fact, and how it would have worded the Act if it had not made that mistake.

Some doctors (including hospital doctors) accept the above argument and assume that the Act enables them to terminate on the ground of hardship and distress, provided that they act early enough. Others, however, who disapprove of abortion, construe the Act restrictively;

---

[1] Accent on middle syllable.

[2] It seems that on the wording of the Act a doctor who terminates where there is a proper ground under the Act is technically guilty if he does not have it in mind to terminate on that ground. But this is against principle: see 2 Leg. Stud. 243 ff.

[3] The conflicting evidence on morbidity associated with abortion is largely explicable by the fact that the research is coloured by moral views. See Betty Sarvis and Hyman Rodman, *The Abortion Controversy* (New York 1973).

[4] A doctor would, however, not be protected if he has not examined the patient. See *John Smith* [1973] 1 WLR 1511, [1974] 1 All ER 376, where a doctor was convicted partly because of this fact. For objections to the use of the statistical argument see Bowles and Bell in 77 Law Society's Gazette 938.

so that a great variation of practice is found between hospitals in different parts of the country.

The argument that abortion is safer than childbirth (or may be held so to be by the particular doctor) applies to vaginal terminations performed in the first two or three months of pregnancy, when the operation is done without incision, by curettage of the womb or by the vacuum aspiration method. Ideally it should be performed within six weeks of pregnancy. Mortality and morbidity begin to increase after the second month, and are particularly associated with termination by hysterotomy.[5] Even the higher risk of a late termination can be medically justified in appropriate cases, but obviously it requires more serious grounds than does an early termination.

Can the doctor act at a very early stage, before it has been established whether the woman is pregnant?

No reason why not: the doctor may act on the ground that *if* the woman is pregnant it will be bad for the pregnancy to continue.

The point is important because of the practice of menstrual aspiration at an early date when the diagnosis of pregnancy may be uncertain. It may of course be argued, against the legality of operating, that the Abortion Act validates the proceeding only if the woman is in fact pregnant, because it supposes that "a pregnancy is terminated." But this would overlook the question of the *mens rea* required for an offence under section 58. Because of this consideration, the Law Officers of the Crown expressed the opinion in 1979 that menstrual aspiration is lawful.

Although the section makes it an offence to use means to procure the miscarriage of a woman who is not in fact with child, it obviously supposes that the defendant believed that the woman was or might be with child. Now the attitude of the doctor in the case we are considering is this. If the woman is with child, then what he does will result in an abortion, and it will be lawful under the Abortion Act. If the woman is not with child, then there will be no abortion. Either there will be no abortion, or it will be a lawful abortion. The doctor's intention being not to procure any abortion except a lawful abortion, it cannot reasonably be argued that an offence is committed.

What is meant by "the mental health of the pregnant woman"?

There is no case-law, but the phrase is capable of a wide interpretation.

Narrowly interpreted, it may require the doctor to fear that the patient will suffer from what is commonly called a mental illness, whether a psychosis or severe neurosis. This may include a depressive psychosis, and the British Medical Association recognises that termination may properly be advised on account of a "reactive depression," which is a pathological state of hopeless despair resulting from circumstances.[6] If the question is one of mental illness, the natural course would be to call in a psychiatrist, a specialist in mental disorder.

But "mental health" is susceptible of a wider meaning. The definition of health advanced by the World Health Organisation is that it is "the state of complete mental, physical and social well-being, and not merely an absence of disease or infirmity." Gynaecologists who take this broad view do not insist upon a psychiatric opinion, but are ready to act on their own opinion of the case, backed by the family doctor.

Can the doctor take account of the fact that the woman is a suicide risk?

A serious threat of suicide can clearly be taken into account, because it indicates the depth of the woman's depression. The BMA memorandum states that "the view that pregnant women never commit suicide is fallacious."

---

[5] Making an incision in the womb: a minor caesarean.

[6] [1968] 1 BMJ 171.

Can the doctor take account of a risk to the health of the woman arising not during the pregnancy but as a consequence of her having to rear the child if it is born?

The words of the Act suggest answers both ways.

The Act refers to "risk of injury to the health of the *pregnant* woman," and one may argue that when the child has been born the woman is no longer pregnant. Moreover, it must be "the continuance of the pregnancy" that produces this risk, and it is perhaps slightly strange, though not impossible, to say that the burden on a mother of having to rear a child was a result of "the continuance of the pregnancy."

On the other hand there are two clues in the Act making it reasonably clear that the wider meaning was intended by Parliament.

1 The words just quoted are used with regard to both the health of the woman and the health of existing children of her family. If one pays regard to the health of existing children, as the Act allows, it would be illogical to do this only during the time of gestation of the new addition to the family. What was evidently intended was that existing children might be adversely affected by the extra child being born and having to be brought up by an already overburdened mother.

2 Subsection (2) provides that "account may be taken of the pregnant woman's actual or reasonably foreseeable environment." This is not, as has sometimes been thought, a purely "social" ground for termination, since it is related to the question of health. It does not allow the operation merely because the patient will otherwise lose her job or her husband. Still, the statutory words make it clear that the question of health is to be considered broadly. There is not much point in directing the doctor to look ahead to the woman's future environment if he is to consider only the time of pregnancy. So it is really quite clear that the Act is intended to provide for the case of the overburdened mother.

The Act allows termination out of consideration for existing children of the family. How can existing children be affected in health by having another brother or sister?

Sometimes it may be reasonable to make this judgment. Consider the mother of a "problem family." She is living in poverty, with a large brood of children. Her husband has been in prison and has now been arrested again. Her existing children are badly cared for and play truant. Now she is pregnant once more. It may confidently be predicted that if the pregnancy is allowed to go to term, matters will be worsened for the existing children to the extent that their health may be affected. In practice, doctors who terminate on this ground generally tick it as an extra to the health of the woman.

Can the doctor take the poverty of the family into account?

Not directly, but he can if the woman's poverty, aggravated by the addition to her family, is likely to affect her health or that of her other children.

§ 13.7. LIMITATIONS OF THE ABORTION ACT

The Act does not provide for termination on the ground that the pregnancy was the result of rape.

In human terms there is a strong argument for this, but the proposal was successfully resisted in Parliament. The position generally taken was that abortion was immoral except when performed on health or eugenic grounds. Also, many doctors objected that they could not decide whether a rape had been committed. (This was really no argument against allowing the doctor to act where he thought the facts were clear.) All agreed, however, that the fact of rape could influence the decision of the doctor in invoking the health ground. In effect, doctors were encouraged to stretch their professional consciences, in order to enable the supposed moral principle to be preserved.

What if the woman is under the age of consent to sexual intercourse?

The position is much the same as for rape. There is no specific statutory provision. But the doctor can take the youth of the patient into account in judging the probable effect of a continuation of the pregnancy on her mental health. Here again the Act probably invites a degree of benevolent hypocrisy on the part of doctors, since the real argument for terminating in these cases may be social rather than medical.

The Act does not allow termination on the ground that the child would be unwanted, the woman having used a method of contraception that failed on the particular occasion. Again, it is no ground for termination that the mother has been convicted of baby-battering. The fact that the child when born is likely to be cruelly neglected or ill-treated is not considered. The only ground relating to the fetus is that of serious handicap.

Does the Act cut down the defence under Bourne?

It imposes two procedural restrictions, which did not exist for the common law defence.

1 The treatment must be given in an NHS hospital or approved nursing home. (Both nursing homes and pregnancy advice bureaux are inspected and tightly controlled.)
2 Two registered medical practitioners[1] must have formed the opinion in good faith that the case falls within section 1.

The reasonableness of the opinion is not in issue, though, of course, an alleged opinion that is grossly unreasonable may be held not to have been formed in good faith.

The doctor giving the treatment need not be one of those who gave the required opinion, though he may be. Nor is it required that both or either of the doctors be a consultant, and gynaecologists commonly rely to a considerable extent on the opinion of the woman's general practitioner as to her mental condition in relation to the pregnancy. It seems that in a suitable case one doctor would be justified in relying implicitly on the judgment of another; what he himself contributes to the case is his knowledge of the experience of his colleague. Owing to a defect in the wording of the Act, both doctors must act in good faith before either falls within the protection given by its wording.[2] But if a case arose in which one of two doctors alone acted in good faith, it could be argued in his defence that the general principles of *mens rea* save him from conviction. Believing that his companion acted in good faith, he would not have the necessary intent to commit an offence.

---

[1] For qualifications in respect of visiting forces, etc., see s.3.
[2] Contrast the common law: *Newton* [1958] 1 BMJ 1242, Crim. LR 612. The point was brought to the attention of the Home Office when the Bill was before Parliament, but nothing was done. The constant Government attitude is that any saving of words in a statute is pure gain, whatever trouble the saving afterwards causes.

The two procedural safeguards do not apply in serious emergencies, as specified in section 1(4) (though even in an emergency the termination must be by a doctor).

The draftsman evidently thought that by providing for an emergency he had rendered the common law wholly unnecessary, and section 5(2) accordingly provides that "for the purpose of the law relating to abortion, anything done with intent to procure the miscarriage of a woman is unlawfully done unless authorised by section 1 of this Act." This strikes down one of the reasons for the decision in *Bourne*, and was certainly intended to get rid of that decision in order to prevent the procedural safeguards from being circumvented. However, the total elimination of the defence of necessity, if that is what the subsection does, was of doubtful wisdom.

Another procedural provision in the Act relates to notification (s. 2). Non-compliance with this is a summary offence. Compliance is not a condition of the defence given by the Act to a charge of abortion.

Can an abortion be lawfully performed under the Abortion Act at any stage in the pregnancy?

Section 5(1) of the Abortion Act provides:

> "Nothing in this Act shall affect the provisions of the Infant Life (Preservation) Act 1929 (protecting the life of a viable fetus)."

It will be remembered that the Act forbids the destruction of a child capable of being born alive except to preserve the patient's life, and that the Act creates a presumption that a fetus of 28 weeks' gestation can be born alive. Medical practice, therefore, is to regard 28 weeks as the limit of time for legal terminations. Operating after this time limit, on a ground specified for lawful abortions, would not be the offence of abortion but would be child destruction.

The question arises whether the time limit is not earlier than 28 weeks of fetal age. It is said that babies that are as much as three months premature now have a 90 per cent. chance of survival under intensive care (though premature babies who survive have a high incidence of mental deficiency.) This fact is sometimes thought to have a direct bearing on the issue of legality as affecting the time of "viability" of the fetus and therefore the operation of the Act of 1929. The argument is that it is now illegal under the Act of 1929 to abort a fetus that is only 6 lunar months of age, because of the high probability that it can be reared. The logic of the argument is that all medical advances in the intensive care of premature infants extend the operation of the 1929 Act backwards in time. The argument the other way is that it would be absurd if advances in the rearing of premature infants should affect what was essentially a moral settlement made by the Abortion Act and the Act of 1929. The Act of 1929 should be construed as applying to infants who can be reared in the normal way without intensive care.

However, the argument for extending the operation of the Act of 1929 goes farther than this. The Act does not in terms refer to viability. It refers to a child "capable of being born alive" and does not state that it is concerned with viability in the sense of whether the infant can be reared, or whether it will live for any length of time. This would suggest that if it can be proved that the infant, however premature, would be alive at the moment of birth, the infant is "capable of being born alive" so that anything done to induce the premature birth must be judged on the strict criteria of the Act of 1929 and not on the more liberal criteria of the Abortion Act. The counter-argument, once more, is *ad absurdum*: it would be contrary to reason if the fact that the infant would be able to live for a few seconds or minutes after birth but would then be doomed to die makes it "capable of being born alive." The phrase must surely mean capable of being born with a reasonable chance of survival; and perhaps it means capable of survival with normal upbringing. This construction is borne out by the presumption established by the Act that a fetus of 28 weeks is capable of being born alive. The presumption was thought to be needed to solve difficulties of proof for fetuses of that age, because infants born at that fetal age would not (in 1929) long survive the premature birth. It was unnecessary if "born alive" referred merely to what the common law meant by a live birth, because in 1929 and for many years before it was possible to perform a hysterotomy and lift out a living (though non-viable) fetus of far less than 28 weeks' gestation. The presumption shows that viability, and not live birth in the narrow sense, was meant.[3]

However, this argument does not solve the problem of murder. Suppose that a doctor, intending to terminate a pregnancy on fetal grounds or on grounds relating to the patient's health, performs a hysterotomy and lifts out a baby of 24 weeks' gestation; he then severs the umbilical cord and the child dies. In law a child can be born alive even before the cord is severed, and the child need not breathe. It may be argued that here the child, though from the womb untimely ripped, and not "of woman born" according to *Macbeth*, is still "born" by artificial means, and is born alive. The doctor either knew that the child could be born alive by the means he adopted or was reckless as to this: so, the child having died after birth as the result of the injury, the doctor may be held to have committed murder.

The especially awkward feature of this argument is that it is not confined to the fetus of 24 weeks. A still earlier fetus (even one of 12 weeks) may be regarded as alive when removed from the uterus, and if so it may be held to be "born alive."

In order to avoid this remarkable conclusion, it may be argued that the doctor was intending in substance to perform an abortion, and should be protected by an analogical extension of the Abortion Act if he would have been protected in case of abortion by that Act. However, the point is sufficiently doubtful to make it inadvisable for a doctor to use this procedure. To avoid possible prosecution he should make sure that the fetus is destroyed in the womb.

When a live fetus is removed in the course of an intended abortion, the fetus upon being removed becomes a legal person and is fully protected by law. Therefore, reasonable efforts must be made to keep it alive, even by intensive care, if there is a chance that it can be saved and no undue risk that it will be seriously defective. The abortion may may have been performed because the woman was overburdened and would be affected in health by having to bring up another child; yet having produced a live child the obstetrician is required to try to keep it alive. As before, he would be legally well advised to make sure that the fetus does not emerge alive, because it is live extraction from the woman that endows the fetus with legal personality.[4]

§ 13.8. THE SUPPLY OF THINGS FOR ABORTION

Partly to put down abortions, and partly in order to prevent women who desire abortions from endangering themselves, it is made an offence unlawfully to supply or procure any noxious thing, instrument "or thing," with knowledge that it is intended to be used to procure a miscarriage,

---

[3] Further support for this argument can be derived from the Abortion Act, which (in s.5(1)) parenthetically refers to the Act of 1929 as protecting *viable* fetuses; this can be regarded as Parliament's own understanding of what the Act of 1929 means.

[4] Many second trimester abortions are now performed by intra-amniotic saline or urea injections, which generally (but not always) kill the fetus before delivery. Another technique is to bring down the umbilical cord through the cervix and cut it. This initiates abortion. Second trimester abortions are also performed through the vagina, destroying the fetus *in utero*.

The doctor's mode of proceeding in these cases has other legal consequences. If he extracts a live fetus, this is a live birth which must be notified, whether before or after 28 weeks' gestation, and maternity benefit and an income tax allowance may result. A still-birth after 28 weeks (but not before) must be notified, and maternity benefit is payable. See Lane Report (Cmnd. 5579 of 1974), para. 278. For legislative proposals see 1st edn 264 n. 9.

whether the woman be or be not with child.[1]

SUMMARY

If a fetus is injured, and, being born alive, subsequently dies, this can be murder or manslaughter. Killing a fetus that is not born alive cannot be either. Birth complete extrusion. Alive heart beat. § .1

The offence of child destruction under the Act of 1929 is committed by an act done with intent to cause and actually causing the death of a fetus/child when it is "capable of being born alive" and before it has "an existence independent of its mother." There is a presumption of the former after the 28th week of pregnancy. The offence is not committed if the act was done "in good faith for the purpose only of preserving the life of the mother." § .2

It is an offence "by any secret disposition of the dead body of a child to endeavour to conceal its birth" (OAPA). § .3

The offence of abortion protects the fetus up to the time when birth starts, and therefore overlaps child destruction. OAPA s.58 words it in terms of using "means" with intent to procure miscarriage. It covers, first, the woman herself if pregnant, and, secondly, anyone else whether she is pregnant or not. The DHSS has accepted the view that there is no "miscarriage" before the blastocyst has implanted. § .4

Whereas the Act of 1929 contained an exception for preserving the woman's life, the OAPA in defining the procurement of abortion did not. But an exception was read in at common law (*Bourne*), which is now superseded by the Abortion Act 1967. This recognises, first, the fetal ground (substantial risk of serious handicap). § .4, 5

Secondly, two health grounds, namely in relation to the health (physical or mental) of the (1) woman or (2) any existing children of her family. The risk of injury to the health of the woman if the pregnancy were continued must be greater than if it is terminated. The effect of these words has not been judicially tested, but they mean that almost all first-trimester abortions are now lawful, provided that the doctor is satisfied from his examination of the patient that no special features are present to affect his opinion based on the statistical evidence. § .6

Other grounds are not recognised. The Act imposes certain procedural restrictions. § .7

Since the Abortion Act expressly saves the Act of 1929, terminations cannot lawfully be performed in respect of a fetus capable of being born alive, except to preserve the patient's life. However, the courts may read the phrase "capable of being born alive" in such a way as to exclude the fetus that will survive only for a short time after a hysterotomy.

It is a statutory offence to supply things for abortion. § .8

---

[1] OAPA s.59. The woman need not be pregnant: *Titley* (1880) 14 Cox 502. It has been held that the supplier or procurer may be convicted under this section though he is the only person who has the criminal intent: *Hillman* (1863) Le. & Ca. 343, 169 ER 1424; *sed quaere*: see Archbold, 38th edn para. 2633. *Mills* [1963] 1 QB 522, noted in [1963] Crim.LR 187, gives a very limited meaning to the word "procure." A person may be convicted of an attempt at common law to commit an offence under s.59. If the noxious thing is taken by the woman, the supplier will generally be guilty under s.58, not merely s.59: *Turner* (1910) 4 CAR 203.

CHAPTER 14

TRAFFIC OFFENCES

In youth, by hazard, I killed an old man.
In age I maimed a little child.
Dead leaves under foot reproach not:
But the lop-sided cherry-branch—whenever the sun rises,
How black a shadow!

Kipling, *Arterial*

§ 14.1. ROAD SAFETY AND LEGAL CONTROL

FOR the ordinary legal practitioner the most important type of criminal liability for negligence relates to motor vehicles and other forms of transport. Only an outline of the law can be given; detailed treatment must be sought in works on the Road Traffic Acts and the transport of goods by road.[1]

The appalling casualty rate on the roads needs no emphasis. Nearly one-half of all male deaths in the 15–24 years age group are from road accidents, and road accidents are a major cause of permanent incapacity in the community. There are two main explanations of these casualties.

The first is that they are largely due to poor road design (and to a much lesser extent unsafe vehicles). The remedy, on this theory, must be better highway and mechanical engineering, for which there is still much scope. This approach has been triumphantly successful at particular danger-spots. The safety of vehicles can be further improved: we still permit cars to be made with flimsy side-walls, with steering columns that kill, and with plastic fascia boards that give inadequate protection from the engine when drivers' legs are flung against them. We also allow heavy lorries to be constructed in a way that permits cars to crash underneath them in an accident.

But these matters are of small concern to lawyers, who are in the business of driver behaviour modification and who see the prime cause of accidents in human wickedness and folly. Their opinion is borne out by governmental studies showing that human error is a factor in 95 per cent. of accidents. Among the causes of human error the one easiest to identify, and most readily admitting of remedy, is the demon drink. A third of the drivers killed (half of those between the ages of 20 and 24) have more than the legal limit of alcohol in their blood, and a Birmingham pathologist remarked that after some week-ends mortuaries stank like breweries. Two out of three fatal accidents at night are due to drinking. Yet pusillanimous Governments have refused to sanction random breath testing, or even the stationing of the police outside drinking places to test people who propose to drive away. Also, nothing has been done to relieve hospital doctors of the obligation of medical confidentiality in this matter of public interest.

It is true that the accident rate has been showing an encouraging improvement. In 1980, 6,010 people were killed on the roads: a stupendous figure, yet the lowest since 1958. Over the same period the volume of traffic rose threefold. The compulsory wearing of seat-belts in the front seats, under the Transport Act 1981, is expected to bring about a further improvement; and there is to be better control over the testing and licensing of motor-cyclists.

---

[1] G S Wilkinson, *Road Traffic Law*; Mahaffy and Dodson, *Road Traffic*. Kitchen, *Road Transport Law* is useful on transport regulations.

Most of the efforts of the police go in cautioning or prosecuting for careless driving and similar driving offences, but, depressingly, we have virtually no knowledge of whether the social cost involved is worth while in terms of accident prevention.[2] The vast majority of drivers do not need the prodding of the criminal courts to make them careful, the real penalty that they fear for great carelessness being natural and immediate. It would be counter-productive to force a driver into exaggerated caution, because this tends to create frustration in other drivers, which itself causes accidents. Another observation is that as a community we are indifferent to the numerous accidents in the home. For accidents in the air, on the railways, at sea and in industry the object is predominantly to investigate the causes with a view to prevention. It seems strange that only when accidents take place on the roads is our approach predominantly punitive. Nevertheless, we could not accept with equanimity that drivers could "jump the lights" without restraint, or drive at reckless speeds, or with glaring lights or otherwise unroadworthy vehicles. Some controls are obviously essential.

It is often thought that a supremely effective sanction can be applied to traffic offenders; disqualification.

For some traffic offences disqualification is obligatory (mandatory upon the court) in the absence of special reasons. Although Parliament left "special reasons" at large, the judges decided that these special reasons must relate to the offence and not to the offender.[3] (If, for example, you have committed an offence carrying obligatory disqualification, it is no use asking your employer to give evidence that he cannot continue your employment with him if you lose your driving licence.)

A much larger number of offences carry discretionary disqualification.

If the court decides not to exercise its discretionary power (or if in the case of obligatory disqualification it finds special reasons for not disqualifying), it will still order penalty points to be endorsed on the offender's licence. The points system is set out in the Transport Act 1981 section 19,[4] and represents a kind of obligatory disqualification for repeated offenders. Points (or a possible range of points, to be fixed by the court in the particular case) are assigned to various offences (sometimes called graded offences or scale offences). If the offender runs up 12 points within three years he is required to be disqualified from driving for at least 6 months unless the court is satisfied that there are grounds of mitigation; and the matters that can constitute mitigation are defined with stringently limiting conditions.

For example, the most serious offences, reckless driving and the intoxication offences, each carry 10 points, so that conviction of one of these is itself sufficient to put the offender in imminent peril of disqualification. Mercifully, it is provided that if the offender is convicted of several offences at the same time he is subject to penalty points only for the most serious one of them. (If, however, he *is* disqualified the court must take all the offences into account in fixing the period of disqualification.)

The trouble with a system of disqualification from driving is one of enforcement. The disqualified driver may respect the court order for a few days or weeks, but if the disqualification is for any length of time he is likely to relapse. A body of informed opinion now holds that disqualification for longer than six months is counter-productive.[5] It certainly makes little sense to disqualify an offender for a long time without compulsorily selling his vehicle.

Let us now look at the main offences. The present road traffic law depends principally upon the Road Traffic Act 1972 (a consolidating statute), as amended, and regulations thereunder. The law governs not only drivers but other people, such as the sellers of unroadworthy vehicles,

---

[2] A study in Israel found that more than 50 per cent. of drivers in a random sample committed at least one offence during the six-year period surveyed. *Severe punishment did not reduce either the number of later offences or their gravity*: rather the contrary. This was so, irrespective of the gravity of the offence for which the punishment was imposed. In contrast, 52·7 per cent. of the drivers who received only a warning did not repeat the offence. See Giora Shoham in [1974] Traffic Quarterly 61.

[3] For the difficulty of the distinction see, e.g. *Burgess* v. *West* [1982] Crim.LR 235.

[4] For problems see 146 JPN 658, 673, 701.

[5] Elliott and Street, *Road Accidents* (Harmondsworth 1968) 116 ff.

passengers (as well as drivers) who open car doors dangerously, and pedestrians who do not stop when directed by a constable regulating traffic, or who stray on to a motorway without excuse. (But jaywalkers who cross against the lights or who otherwise ignore crossings in busy streets commit no offence in this country, unlike several others.) We shall be concerned with the duties of drivers, and our interest in the matter will be chiefly in relation to the element of fault, since it is in this respect that the topic belongs to a study of the basic concepts of the criminal law.

In general, the driving offences are limited to the "driving" of a "motor vehicle" on a "road," and each of these constituents is the subject of a good deal of authority, which for the most part must be left, like much else, to specialised works.[6]

The first three sections of the Road Traffic Act, which (as amended) create what may broadly be described as offences of negligent driving of motor vehicles on roads, are of particular importance. They are stated in descending order of gravity.

> Section 1: causing death by reckless driving (triable only on indictment).
> Section 2: reckless driving (triable either way).
> Section 3: driving without due care and attention, and driving without reasonable consideration for other persons using the road (two[7] summary offences).

The following discussion will take the offences in their order of frequency, which is the reverse of the statutory order.

§ 14.2. CARELESS DRIVING

The offence of driving without due care and attention[1], which for brevity we may refer to as careless driving, is an offence of intention in respect of the *driving* of a vehicle, but of negligence in respect of the *manner* of driving. The negligent element being predominant, we naturally think of it as an offence of negligence.

The offence is committed if the driver fails to attain the standard of care and attention that is proper in the circumstances—in effect the tort standard, though the courts do not call it that.[2] Care is required in respect of property as well as the person, so the offence can be committed by

---

[6] For "driving" see § 2.6 n. 21. A person who drives a horse and cart, or who drives on a private way, may be charged under OAPA 1861 s.35 (§ .8).

[7] *R* v. *Surrey JJ* [1932] 1 KB 450.

[1] There is no authority on the relation of "care" to "attention," but "and attention" seems to be superfluous. Lack of attention when driving must be lack of care; and a person may be convicted of driving "without due care and attention" even though he was paying full attention. For a survey of case-law see Samuels in 129 NLJ 323.

[2] It has been judicially said that the criminal standard is not higher than the civil one: *Scott* v. *Warren* [1974] RTR 104, Crim.LR 117. Whether that is so or not, the courts have certainly put it extremely high. See, for example, the *Lyons* case, below n. 4. In *Lawrence* [1982] AC at 525A Lord Diplock called careless driving an "absolute" offence, but that was an idiosyncratic use of the expression.

denting the mudguard of a stationary unoccupied car.[3] The standard is objective. Even a learner-driver is required to conform to it, and cannot argue that he showed as much care as could be expected from a driver with his short experience[4] (a severe rule, if one considers the shortage of facilities for training drivers off the roads). The fact that the defendant made an "error of judgment" does not entitle him to an acquittal, since an error of judgment will be careless in law if it is one that a reasonable man would have avoided; but there may be cases where a driver makes an understandable mistake in the "agony of the moment" which is held not to be unreasonable and so not careless.[5] Failure to observe the Highway Code may be relied upon by the prosecution as tending to show carelessness, though the evidence is not necessarily conclusive.[6] For example, the Code requires the driver to leave sufficient space between him and the vehicle in front to enable him to pull up; but the courts do not insist strictly that the driver must be able to stop so as to avoid hitting the preceding vehicle in absolutely any emergency.[7] (All the same, the duty should be interpreted pretty strictly, because many fatal accidents are caused by "concertina crashes.") There are numerous other pronouncements on the duties of drivers in particular situations.

The question whether damage or injury was caused is irrelevant to responsibility, and in theory is irrelevant to punishment; but the fact that no untoward result occurred, or that it was contributed to by the victim, who bore a large part of the blame, may in practice be urged in mitigation.

How easy is it for the prosecution to establish careless driving when the facts are obscure?

There is a considerable divergence between the theory of the law, which regards motoring offences as ordinary criminal matters, and the practice of magistrates' courts working under pressure. Only 3 per cent. of motoring charges heard in magistrates' courts are withdrawn or dismissed. This is partly because defendants are generally unrepresented; partly because the prosecution evidence is often convincing; partly because magistrates are reluctant to reject the evidence of the police; partly because the Divisional Court insists upon magistrates' taking a fairly tough line; but also partly, of course, because very many charges are not seriously contested.

Turning to the rules of law: whereas, in the law of tort, the mere fact of collision between

---

[3] There is no reason why driving should not be careless in respect of the driver's passengers. The driver of a public service vehicle is under a duty to look after passengers when entering or alighting: Public Service Vehicles (Conduct of Drivers, Conductors and Passengers) Regs. 1936 (SR & O 1936 No. 619) reg. 4, continued in force by RTA 1960 s.267.

[4] *McCrone* v. *Riding* [1938] 1 All ER 157, 30 Cox 670, 102 JP 109; *R* v. *Preston JJ, ex p. Lyons* [1982] Crim. LR 451 and editorial note. See Wasik in [1982] Crim. LR 411, arguing convincingly that the care and skill required should only be that to be expected of a learner-driver, and that in any case the *Lyons* case was wrongly decided on the facts. Wasik points out that although learner-drivers are subjected to the full standard of care in tort law, this is to give compensation to people who are injured, a matter that has no relevance in criminal law.

[5] *Simpson* v. *Peat* [1952] 2 QB 24; *Taylor* v. *Rogers* (1960) 124 JP 217.

[6] RTA 1972 s.37(5).

[7] See *Scott* v. *Warren* [1974] RTR 104, Crim.LR 117.

two vehicles is some evidence that calls upon the drivers to give evidence of how the accident came to happen consistently with their care, the criminal law casts the usual burden of proof upon the prosecution, at any rate in theory. Consequently, it is not enough that there was a collision and that both drivers had a full view of the road. The prosecution may, however, be assisted by evidence of what a defendant driver said after the accident, or by detailed evidence as to the position of the vehicles, skid marks, etc.[8] Priorities at intersections may be determined by traffic signs displayed under statutory powers; and even where there is no sign the court may determine that a particular road has priority from the configuration of the roads; also, the judges recognise a convention that where there is doubt as to priority between approaching vehicles at an intersection, the vehicle that has the other on its right is the "give-way" vehicle.[9]

When the defendant appears to have been in sole charge of the situation, the courts seem to take a stricter view against him than when several vehicles are involved. They appear to act upon Sherlock Holmes's debatable aphorism that "when you have eliminated the impossible, whatever remains, however improbable, must be the truth." So if the defendant was alone on the road and ended up in the ditch, and if there is no evidence of unusual road conditions, mechanical failure, or physical ailment, and there is no other reasonable explanation of the accident consistent with due care having been taken, the High Court reaches the conclusion that the accident must have been the result of inattention or other misconduct by the driver, and does not allow the justices to accept a submission of no case.[10] Indeed, it generally requires them to convict. However, the defendant may offer an explanation that produces a reasonable doubt. It is not enough for him to "cull a suggestion out of the air,"[11] in other words to offer a purely fanciful or speculative explanation, such as that there might have been oil on the road[12] or that he might have had a dizzy spell or black-out.[13] This generally means that he must offer evidence in support of his hypothesis[14]; yet even if he goes into the witness-box, if all he can offer is speculation he may be convicted. Conversely, evidence is not essential if the facts proved are such as to make the defendant's explanation of what happened a reasonable one.[15] Notwithstanding the stern view taken in these cases, the courts acknowledge the continued validity of the principle stated by the Court of Appeal that "in cases of dangerous driving the onus never shifts to the defence."[16]

If the fault of a driver is clear, and it is merely a question of identifying the defendant as that driver, say, where it is known that the damage was caused by a lorry, the magistrates may infer that the defendant was the culprit from the fact that he appears to have been the only lorry-driver in the vicinity at the time.[17]

Is it necessarily careless to exceed a speed limit?

No. Although careless driving is capable of being committed by excessive speed alone,[18] the particular circumstances must be considered. Even a fast speed—as much as 65 m.p.h. in a 30 m.p.h. area—is not

---

[8] See Clarke in [1959] Crim.LR 492.

[9] *McIntyre* v. *Coles* [1966] 1 WLR 831 (a civil case).

[10] *Jarvis* v. *Williams* [1979] RTR 497. Cp. *Wright* v. *Wenlock* [1971] RTR 228, Crim.LR 49; *Rabjohns* v. *Burgar* [1971] RTR 234, Crim.LR 466; Wilkinson, 11th edn 253–254.

[11] *Scott* v. *Warren* [1974] RTR 104 at 108, Crim.LR 117.

[12] *Scott* v. *Warren*, last note.

[13] *Oakes* v. *Foster* [1961] Crim.LR 628; *Bensley* v. *Smith* [1972] RTR 221, Crim.LR 239; *Richards* v. *Gardner* [1974] Crim.LR 119; § 29.5.

[14] As in *Jarvis* v. *Fuller* [1974] RTR 160, Crim.LR 116 (collision with unlighted cyclist). Cp. *Gubby* v. *Littman* [1976] RTR 470, Crim.LR 386; *Webster* v. *Wall* [1980] RTR 284.

[15] *Butty* v. *Davey* [1972] RTR 75, Crim.LR 48. See also the surprisingly lenient decision in *Hume* v. *Ingleby* [1975] RTR 502, Crim.LR 396. It has been laid down that the magistrates should not themselves speculate on how the accident could have happened without fault, if the defendant does not suggest an explanation: *Bensley* v. *Smith*, n. 13 above; but that was probably in relation to the particular facts of the case. It is surely the duty of the magistrates to assess the evidence irrespective of the quality of the defence advocacy.

[16] *Spurge* [1961] 2 QB at 212, cited in *Bensley* v. *Smith*, n. 13 above.

[17] *Hampson* v. *Powell* [1970] 1 All ER 929.

[18] *Bracegirdle* v. *Oxley* [1947] KB 349.

necessarily careless.[19] There must be evidence, from the state of the road or the traffic or the particular way in which the vehicle was being driven, that the driving was careless.

Failure to observe a traffic sign (like a white line on the road) is evidence of negligence and is apparently enough to sustain a conviction of careless driving in the absence of explanation.[20] But such failure is an independent offence,[21] and one of strict liability, so the charge will usually be for that. A driver should not be convicted of both careless driving and some other offence on account of the same facts.

Is it careless to drink and drive?

A drink-driving offender will probably be charged with one of the specialised drink-driving offences (§ .6) rather than with careless driving, since the penalty for the specialised offences is higher (and can be imprisonment). However, if a charge is brought for careless driving it is permissible for the prosecution to support their case by giving evidence that the defendant had taken a quantity of alcohol that would adversely affect a driver, subject to the discretion of the court (the trial judge or the magistrates) to exclude the evidence if its prejudicial effect outweighs its probative value.[22] No guidance is given on the question when this is likely to be the case.[23]

Is it careless driving to drive a defective car?

If the facts are known to the police beforehand, they are likely to charge not careless driving but some more specific offence, particularly one under the Motor Vehicles (Construction and Use) Regulations 1978, as amended.[24] However, if the defendant is charged with careless driving, it will not advantage him to say that the accident was caused not by driving in a negligent manner but by driving a vehicle that it was negligent to drive. The case is one of what may be called "invisibly careless driving." The defendant's responses may appear to be careful, but when it is discovered that he has not properly maintained his car, or otherwise should have known of a dangerous defect, he can be convicted.[25]

Normally, the proper maintenance of a road vehicle is enforced under the Construction and Use Regulations already mentioned, which operate not only against the person immediately using the vehicle but also against his employer (who is taken to "use" in the broad sense of the word: §

---

[19] *Tribe* v. *Jones* [1961] Crim.LR 835, 59 LGR 582, where the defendant drove at this speed (in breach of a speed limit) at 7.20 a.m. on a major road bounded by common land and affording a clear view; traffic was very light, and the justices found that no one was in danger. An acquittal of the charge of dangerous driving was upheld.

[20] *Bensley* v. *Smith*, n. 13 above.

[21] RTA 1972 s.22 as amended.

[22] *McBride* [1962] 2 QB 167; *Sibley* [1962] Crim.LR 397; *Thorpe* [1972] 1 WLR 342, 1 All ER 929 (see note [1972] Crim.LR 240).

[23] See comment [1961] Crim.LR 626; Alec Samuels in 124 NLJ 1061.

[24] SI 1978 No. 1017. See Wilkinson, 11th edn 925.

[25] *Haynes* v. *Swain* [1975] RTR 40; *Simpson* [1981] Crim. LR 649. There were similar decisions on the abolished offence of dangerous driving: Spurge [1961] 2 QB 205; *Robert Millar (Contractors) Ltd.* [1970] 2 QB 54; *Atkinson* [1970] RTR 265. See, however, the conflicting authorities on illness: § 29.5.

43.5). Many vehicles are driven by employees who are not responsible for maintaining them; such employees are strictly liable under the Construction and Use Regulations, but will often escape liability for careless driving because they were not at fault in not knowing of the defect in the vehicle. If the driver is not guilty of careless driving, no one can be guilty as accessory—not even an employer who was personally at fault.[26] But such employer will be guilty under the Construction and Use Regulations.

Another kind of invisibly careless driving is where the defect relates to the driver's body. This is discussed later: § 29.5. For the penalty for careless driving, see the next section.

§ 14.3. INCONSIDERATE DRIVING

Driving without reasonable consideration for other persons using the road[1] (the other summary offence in s.3) is much less frequently charged, but occasionally it is needed because there is no carelessness. The driving is fraught with inconvenience rather than danger.

Instances of the offence are as follows.

(1) A motorist when driving stops his car (very carefully), continues again for a few yards and stops again (very carefully), for the purpose of annoying the driver behind.
(2) An old lady, without malicious intent, drives too slowly.
(3) A bus driver dawdles and holds back traffic because he is ahead of schedule.
(4) Drivers drive slowly in procession to make a demonstration.
(5) A driver pulls out of line to jump a queue.
(6) A driver drives too fast along a flooded road and soaks pedestrians.

It must be the *driving* that is inconsiderate; so a motor cyclist who rode alongside a cyclist and kicked him was acquitted.[2]

The penalty for inconsiderate driving, as for careless driving, is only a fine (up to £500) on first conviction,[3] but the offender may also be disqualified from driving.

Although both offences are summary, there is an exceptional provision whereby a jury in acquitting of reckless driving (or of causing death by reckless driving) may convict of careless or inconsiderate driving.[4] The Crown Court in sentencing will then pay regard to the

---

[26] Contrast *Robert Millar (Contractors) Ltd.* [1970] 2 QB 54.

[1] These "other persons" include the driver's own passengers: *Pawley* v. *Wharldall* [1966] 1 QB 373.

[2] *Downes* v. *Fell* [1969] Crim.LR 376.

[3] CLA 1977 Sched. 6, amending RTA 1972. On second conviction the penalty can be £500 and 3 months' imprisonment.

[4] RTA 1972 Sched. 4 Part 4 para. 3A, inserted by CLA 1977 Sched. 12. The same provision applies a similar rule in respect of the analogous cycling offences. Although these rules alleviate the rigidity of the distinction between indictable and summary offences, the rigidity remains in sundry other ways. Suppose that D is charged with driving while disqualified (triable either way),taking a motor vehicle without consent (ditto), excess alcohol (summary) and careless driving (summary). He elects for trial on the first two, and the magistrates adjourn the second two charges pending the determination of the first two by the Crown Court. At that court D is convicted and sent to prison. He must now be brought from prison to attend before the magistrates to be dealt with for the two summary offences even though he has indicated that he admits them. See 144 JPN 172, 441.

Magistrates who dismiss a charge of reckless driving may order a charge of careless or inconsiderate driving to be laid although 6 months have elapsed since the offence: *R* v. *Coventry JJ, ex p. Sayers* [1979] RTR 22.

sentencing guidelines drawn up by the Magistrates' Association and used in magistrates' courts.[5]

§ 14.4. RECKLESS DRIVING

Reckless driving differs from careless driving in being triable either way, and in carrying a possible sentence of 2 years' imprisonment even for a first offence. In order to understand the problem of defining the offence, which still besets us, something must be known of its history.

Before 1977 the relevant legislation created twin offences of reckless driving and dangerous driving, both being indictable offences carrying the same punishment. The original idea was that careless driving should cover any form of negligence in driving, while dangerous driving would be committed only by negligence of high degree. But the courts made nonsense of this scheme by construing dangerous driving as an offence of strict liability, with the result that a person could be convicted of the more serious offence, which was indictable and imprisonable, when he was not guilty of the minor, merely finable offence. Eventually the courts were persuaded to put dangerous driving on the more sensible basis of negligence; but then there was no substantial distinction between dangerous driving and careless driving. The courts failed to work out a theory of the higher degree of negligence for dangerous driving that would make sense of the distinction. So the police were left to decide on their own which offence to go for. Reckless driving (the alternative to dangerous driving) was infrequently charged, because it was more difficult to prove and offered little advantage to the prosecution over a charge of dangerous driving.

Whereas judges were largely on the side of the prosecution against the negligent driver, juries were largely on the side of the driver. Lord Devlin, in an address to the the Magistrates' Association in 1960,[1] pointed out that juries were extremely reluctant to convict of dangerous driving (suspecting that a conviction would be followed by imprisonment), unless the defendant was (in Lord Devlin's words) "a road-hog or a cad or an irresponsible youth who steals a car which he does not know how to drive."

The solution of the problem broached by Lord Devlin was that the distinction should be between bad driving, i.e. careless driving, and wicked driving. Bad driving should be tried by magistrates, with power to fine and disqualify; wicked driving could still go to the Crown Court.

The reasoning of the James Committee on the Business of the Courts[2] went on similar lines. Dangerous driving was to be abolished, and reckless driving should be triable either way. The committee described reckless driving as "deliberate disregard of the safety of others;" but it added, with prophetic insight, that "experience in this field suggests that however tightly the offence is defined, the definition is likely in time to become looser and to encompass offences of lesser gravity than was originally intended." Whether from a sense of the hopelessness of it all or for some other reason the Criminal Law Act 1977 which implemented the James Committee's recommendation made no effort to define reckless driving, notwithstanding the obvious danger that the courts would water down the concept to such an extent as to repeat the fiasco of dangerous driving.

There was also the opposite danger, unperceived by those concerned with the legislation, that reckless driving might be too restricted a category to embrace some drivers who deserved to come within the offence. As we have seen, in the later 1970s the Court of Appeal had begun to interpret recklessness in a subjective sense, which was eminently desirable for ordinary crimes of recklessness but doubtfully so for reckless driving. The difference arises

---

[5] *R* v. *Coventry JJ, last note.*

[1] In an address to the Magistrates' Association: 16 The Magistrate 143.
[2] Cmnd 6323 of 1975, App. K.

from the fact that while selfishness is a common human weakness, few people knowingly endanger themselves. In reckless injury to the person and reckless damage to property the offender who creates the danger generally does not put himself or his own property at risk. Therefore, when he creates an obvious danger for others it is relatively easy to come to the conclusion that he must have been aware of the danger and been prepared to subject someone else to it. In contrast, the danger for the allegedly reckless motor cyclist always includes a danger for himself as well as for others. He may, of course, accept it as the price of excitement. But another possibility is that he firmly believes in his own ability to avoid an accident; and the belief may receive some backing from the fact that he has on numerous occasions in the past succeeded in doing so. For this reason, the harum-scarum motor cyclist is unlikely to consider that he is running a serious risk, even though his driving seems to the observer to have all the characteristics of recklessness. If the driver really thought that he was going to have a bad accident he would very probably not drive like that. This argument may weigh with the jury, which may, therefore, be reluctant to convict the driver of recklessness, particularly if they are not given the assistance of a definition that modifies the normal subjective meaning of the word. Because of this difficulty it is unfortunate that the Ministry of Transport chose to perpetuate the name "reckless driving," instead of using some other expression, such as "irresponsible driving" or "wanton driving," which could more readily be given a distinctive meaning.

Let us try to visualise the drivers who should come within Lord Devlin's two categories. The typically careless driver is the stupid, muddled, forgetful, unobservant or clumsy driver, doubtless driving too fast for his own ability and the conditions of the road. Driving of this kind may cause dreadful accidents and may, because of the danger, be accounted gross negligence, but it is not reckless. It is adequately dealt with by a fine and possible disqualification, with a possible prison sentence on second conviction, all of which outcomes are provided for in the offence of careless driving.

The wickedly irresponsible driver, who may need a prison sentence even on first conviction, is rarely met with. He is, most conspicuously, the occasional motorway bounder and the offender fleeing from the police. He goes at an egregious speed, involving inordinate risk. He passes a line of traffic on a narrow road allowing himself only split-second timing to get by; he crosses a double white line to overtake a lorry travelling at speed; he tries to pass at an alarming rate when there are pedestrians on the road; he ignores traffic lights and pedestrian crossings. In short, he is the devil driver: one who pays little regard to the safety of others because he is out for thrills, or is prepared to subordinate everything to speed.

If this summary of the background of the legislation states its broad intention, the decision of the House of Lords in *Stephen Lawrence*[3] can only be regarded as a disaster. Their lordships interpreted the notion of recklessness in driving in much (though not entirely) the same way as they had for criminal damage in the immediately preceding case of *Caldwell*. Lord Diplock, speaking for the other lords as well as for himself, summed up his opinion in a model direction to the jury.

> "The jury . . . must be satisfied of two things:
> *First*, that the defendant was in fact driving the vehicle in such a manner as to create an obvious and serious risk of causing physical injury to some other person who might happen to be using the road or of doing substantial damage to property[4]; and
> *Second*, that in driving in that manner the defendant did so without

---

[3] [1982] AC 510.

[4] It is perhaps pedantic to criticise this wording by pointing out that it does not specifically state, as it should, that the driving must be negligent. One can conceive of cases where a driver is forced to take a serious risk in order to avoid an even greater risk for which he is not responsible, and where, in consequence, his driving cannot be accounted negligent and therefore cannot be reckless. Similarly, a driver may take a risk because he had some disability that he could not foresee and for which he was not responsible (e.g. the effect of a medicine of which he had had no warning).

having given any thought to the possibility of there being any such risk or, having recognised that there was some risk involved, had nonetheless gone on to take it."

Lord Diplock explained the first condition as the usual negligence requirement which is a presupposition of recklessness. He also pointed out that this condition goes to the *actus reus* (the manner of driving) as well as to part of the fault element in recklessness.

> "Since driving in such a manner as to do no worse than create a risk of causing inconvenience or annoyance to other road users constitutes the lesser offence [of careless driving] under section 3, the manner of driving that constitutes the *actus reus* of an offence under sections 1 and 2 must be worse than that; it must be such as to create a real[5] risk of causing physical injury to someone else who happens to be using the road or damage to property more substantial than the kind of minor damage that may be caused by an error of judgment in the course of parking one's car."[6]

This certainly makes a difference between careless and reckless driving, but in itself it still allows an undesirably large scope to reckless driving. Most errors of judgment in driving occur not in the course of parking one's car but in driving along the road, and here an error of judgment carries a real risk of causing injury to the person or substantial damage to property.

It follows that if the meaning of reckless driving is to be curtailed so as to make it substantially more limited than careless driving, in respect of ordinary road accidents (and not mere parking mishaps), this must be because of the second part of the instruction to the jury. But the second part would still allow many drivers who would ordinarily be thought of as merely careless to be accounted reckless.

> For example, a driver, talking to his passenger, does not notice that he is emerging on to a main road. He does not stop and look at the traffic, so there is an accident. Presumably he can be said not to have "given any thought to the possibility of there being any such risk;" and the risk is obvious (to a careful driver) and serious; so all the essentials of "*Lawrence* recklessness" are present. Yet the driver was not in any sense a deliberate risk-taker, and his fault does not deserve the appellation of recklessness in the ordinary meaning of the term.

The width of the rule in *Lawrence* is increased by the fact that the last part of Lord Diplock's second requirement refers only to the defendant's recognition "that there was some risk involved." Astonishingly, the defendant is not required to have recognised that there was a "serious risk" of causing physical injury or of doing substantial damage to property," as specified in the first requirement. It seems that his recognition of the smallest risk is enough. It is unnecessarily confusing for the jury to be instructed that the driver must have created an obvious and serious risk but is reckless if he merely realised that there was a small risk.

In a subsequent passage Lord Diplock introduced a reservation.

> "If satisfied that an obvious and serious risk was created by the manner of the defendant's driving, the jury are entitled to infer that he was in one or other of the states of mind[7] required to constitute the offence and will probably do so; but regard must be given to any explanation he gives as to his state of mind which may displace the inference."

What "explanation" the defendant is allowed to give remains mysterious. Could the driver in the hypothetical just given explain that he was talking to a passenger and so was not paying attention? But, if so, would any and every explanation of why the driver did not give thought serve to exclude "*Lawrence* recklessness"? Obviously, when a person fails to give thought, it is generally possible to offer some explanation of why he did not do so (he was thinking of or looking at something else, he was sleepy, he was just "slooming," his windscreen was

---

[5] In the model direction Lord Diplock spoke of a "serious" risk. He evidently meant "real" and "serious" to mean the same; both words refer to the degree of risk, not to the magnitude of the injury or damage that may result.

[6] Lord Diplock was here evidently referring to the minor cases of careless driving that do not amount to reckless driving. He was not saying that a more serious case of careless driving may not be so charged, instead of charging reckless driving.

[7] Here, as elsewhere, Lord Diplock supposes that "not thinking" is a state of mind.

fogged up), and if merely advancing an explanation for not thinking excludes the operation of the rule the rule is reduced to futility.

Notwithstanding these difficulties, a judge may perhaps use Lord Diplock's reservation as a way of enabling the jury to avoid too harsh a verdict when in fact the defendant has been merely careless and not reckless in the ordinary meaning of the word.[8] It is noteworthy that the reservation did not appear in Lord Diplock's opinion in *Caldwell*; why he made the resulting distinction between criminal damage and reckless driving does not appear.

Doubts as to Lord Diplock's meaning are increased by phrases in *Caldwell* suggesting that recklessness involves a "guilty state of mind," a "blameworthy" one, and in *Lawrence* that careless driving, unlike reckless driving, does not necessarily involve "moral turpitude."

It will have been noticed that Lord Diplock (in the passage cited at n. 6 above) contemplated that reckless driving can be committed by endangering property; but this had not previously been the general opinion of lawyers. There is now some authority against Lord Diplock's opinion. In *Seymour*[9] the House of Lords held that although the notion of recklessness was, in general, applicable to both the statutory offence of reckless driving and the common law offence of manslaughter, the trial judge on the charge of "motor manslaughter" before the House was right not to have referred to damage to property in his charge to the jury, since this was irrelevant. We may perhaps conclude, therefore, that damage to property is equally irrelevant to a charge of reckless driving.

If "*Lawrence* recklessness" is too wide because it improperly takes in some instances of merely careless driving, it is also too narrow in not embracing some situations that ought to be accounted reckless. This is because the direction does not refer to cases where the defendant thought that what he was doing was safe. The omission of such cases from the definition of recklessness was wise in respect of ordinary crimes of recklessness (for example, as we have seen, it would very rightly let out a person like Lamb,[10] who would not be accounted reckless in the ordinary meaning of the word). For driving offences, however, the omission was unwise. In common understanding a driver would often be accounted reckless even though he firmly believed he could "get away with" the risk he undertook. It perhaps cannot be said with confidence of such a driver that he has perceived risks in his own driving or has failed to give thought; consequently, he hardly comes within the *Lawrence* formula, and yet he ought to be accounted reckless for the purpose of the driving offence if he realised that his driving involved serious risks that are not generally inherent in driving.

The conclusion to which one is forced is that the rule in *Lawrence* is seriously defective. It seems to include that which it should not, and it fails to include that which it should. The trouble arises in part because their lordships failed to realise that the recklessness of reckless driving does not, as a practical matter, admit of the same definition as the recklessness of reckless damage. Although Lord Diplock sketched the history of the offence of reckless driving, and even cited the James Committee Report, he did not think it necessary to mention the committee's definition of reckless driving as involving "deliberate disregard for the safety of others," which was irreconcilable with his own idea of recklessness. It was,

---

[8] Cp. Griew in [1981] Crim.LR at 750: "It can be argued that evidence of what may be called 'conscientious incompetence' will be evidence of the appropriate kind."

[9] § 12.2 n. 9.

[10] § 5.2 at n. 6.

nevertheless, the James Committee's definition that was thought to have been the basis of the present legislation.

That definition should, it is suggested, be slightly elaborated. The notion of recklessness in relation to driving involves two elements. First, negligent driving creating an obvious and serious risk of causing injury or substantial damage to property, as Lord Diplock said. Secondly, a degree of fault going beyond mere error of judgment or failure of control or (*pace Lawrence*) momentary inattention. The driving must be of such a character that the driver can be confidently found to have known the risk involved (subjective recklessness in the ordinary sense), or it must show a *flagrant* rejection of (not merely a failure in the effort to observe) rules of prudence that are commonly accepted. Lawton LJ stated the second component in somewhat different language when he explained the kind of driving that called for a custodial sentence when it caused death: it is the driving of those who show "a selfish disregard for the safety of other road users or their passengers."[11]

The second positive component of the mental element now being suggested is confined to cases where the defendant has repudiated, cast off, deliberately flouted accepted standards of driving. His belief that he can "get away with it" may take him out of the first component of the mental element, but not out of the second. He is not allowed the cockiness of supposing that he can always accelerate out of tight corners.

The suggested definition of reckless driving does not cover the driver who, while in general driving temperately, fails to see a fast car, or fails to make a correct assessment of the speed of another car, or fails to control his own car, where he does not realise that he is creating an exceptional danger (one going beyond that inevitably incurred in using the roads) and does not repudiate rules of prudence. The fact that these modes of driving may involve great risk, and that in some of them the driver "gives no thought" to the possibility of risk in what he does (because he thinks that there *is* no unusual risk), should not be taken to make them reckless. Parliament having deliberately refrained from wording the more serious offence in terms of gross negligence, its decision should be respected by the courts. The obvious reason why a test of gross negligence was rejected was its imprecision, and also its too-embracing character.

The suggested definition of reckless driving leaves undecided the question whether a driver is to be deemed to know these rules of prudence without evidence to prove the knowledge. Some of the rules are in the Highway Code, but breach of them is not made evidence of recklessness, only of carelessness. Another difficulty is that the rules in the Highway Code are numerous, and not all of them are always observed even by drivers who would be thought careful. The adverb "flagrantly" in the suggested definition should be sufficient to solve difficulties in practice. If pushed to it, one would have to say, as the only practicable rule, that for the purpose of assessing reckless driving the defendant is to be taken to know the rules of prudence.

Would it be "invisibly reckless driving" if a person drives an old banger that is not fit for the road?

Presumably yes under *Lawrence*. Charges of "invisibly dangerous driving" were brought in respect of the abolished offence.[12] At the same time, it may be doubted whether a charge of reckless driving is

---

[11] *Guilfoyle* (1973) 57 CAR 549.
[12] See § 14.2 at n. 25.

appropriate. The charge would better be one of careless driving, or as a breach of one of the Construction and Use Regulations.[13]

There is a similar question whether a driver is guilty of reckless driving when he drives knowing that he is physically unfit; this is discussed in § 29.5.

§ 14.5. CAUSING DEATH BY RECKLESS DRIVING

When death is caused by reckless driving under section 1 (§ .1 above) the usual maximum of 2 years' imprisonment goes up to 5.

Why was this offence needed? Isn't it invariably manslaughter?

Juries are reluctant to convict fellow-motorists of a crime with so ugly a name as manslaughter, and so Parliament has diplomatically offered the euphemistic alternative. It is no longer the general practice to prosecute drivers for manslaughter in respect of reckless driving causing death.[1]

Whereas the other homicides are generally prosecuted by the Director of Public Prosecutions, causing death by reckless driving is normally prosecuted on the instruction of the local Chief Constable. It is said that the usual practice, at least outside London, is to reserve the charge under section 1 for flagrant cases, because this charge cannot be tried summarily. If the police are uncertain whether a jury would convict the charge will generally be reduced to one of careless driving.[2] The paradoxical result is that a driver who kills may stand a better chance of escaping being charged with reckless driving than one who does not. However, there is no legal reason why causing death by reckless driving should not be charged as reckless driving *simpliciter*, and this is done in the so-called "nearest and dearest" cases, where the person killed is the defendant's wife, etc.

Sentencing policy, too, is lenient. Three-quarters of those convicted are only fined and disqualified (at least, this was true before 1977, when the charge was usually of causing death by dangerous driving). The outcome does not seem to be significantly different from that where reckless driving alone is charged,[3] except that the fact of death makes disqualification from driving obligatory in the absence of special reasons, whereas when there is no death (and when it is not a second offence[4]) disqualification for reckless driving is discretionary. Even when an offender under section 1 is imprisoned, it is never for longer than the 2 years allowable under section 2.[5]

Recognition of these facts has brought about the opinion that section 1 is useless. If it were abolished, the prosecution would regain the freedom to have the charge tried summarily, unless the defendant claims to be tried by jury.[6]

---

[13] In *Simpson* [1981] Crim. LR 649 the defendant drove a lorry knowing that the brakes were not in perfect order; as a result, a motor cyclist was killed. He was convicted of careless driving. On the ordinary principles of recklessness in the criminal law the defendant was reckless, since he must have realised some possibility of causing injury; the reason why he was not charged with causing death by reckless driving was presumably that he was not regarded as creating the "real" or "serious" risk referred to by Lord Diplock as required in a case of reckless driving. Or perhaps it was that the more serious charge was in any case felt to be out of proportion to his fault.

[1] Notionally, however, manslaughter can still be charged against drivers. See *Seymour* § 12.2 n. 9.

[2] 130 JPN 124.

[3] See, e.g. *Brown* [1982] Crim.LR 242.

[4] For the precise provision see RTA 1972 Sched. 4.

[5] For an example of sentencing practice see *Matthews* [1981] Crim.LR 789.

[6] See Sir Brian MacKenna in [1970] Crim.LR 70; CLRC, 14th Report 64.

Suppose that what the defendant did was not the cause of the carnage?

We shall study the doctrine of causation in Chapter 16, but it may be said at once that problems rarely arise. The defendant sometimes argues that although he may have driven recklessly, one or two other drivers did the same, and that their recklessness was more "causative" than his. The judge may dispose of the problem by directing the jury that they can convict the defendant if his reckless driving was "a cause" of the death, being something more than a purely trivial cause (*de minimis*). It is now regarded as too lenient to ask whether the defendant's recklessness was a substantial cause of the death (§ 16.5). All the same, if the facts were that the deceased died because he negligently introduced dirt into a wound, for instance, the judge ought to consider the questions to be discussed in Chapter 16.

If the jury are not satisfied that the reckless driving caused the death, they can convict of reckless driving *simpliciter* under section 2.[7] Sir Brian MacKenna wrote: "I find that if juries are told of this power they usually exercise it."[8]

§ 14.6. DRINK OR DRUGS

The Act of 1972 s.5 provides two offences, informally called "impairment offences," relating to unfitness to drive. They are committed where a person:

1 drives[1] or attempts to drive, or
2 is in charge of

a motor vehicle on a road or other public place when unfit to drive through drink or drugs.

These charges were found difficult to prove except in extreme cases. So section 6[2] creates two further offences, commonly known as the "excess alcohol" or "breathalyser" offences. As these names indicate, they apply only to alcohol and not to other drugs. They are committed if a person:

1 drives or attempts to drive (or has driven or attempted to drive), or
2 is (or has been) in charge of[3]

a motor vehicle on a road or other public place, after consuming so much alcohol that the proportion in his breath, blood or urine exceeds the prescribed limit (35 microgrammes (μg.) of alcohol in 100 millilitres of breath, or 80 milligrammes (mg.) of alcohol in 100 ml. of blood, or 107 mg. of alcohol in 100 ml. of urine).[4]

The Criminal Law Act 1977, with somewhat surprising indulgence,

---

[7] CLA 1967 s.6(3).
[8] [1970] Crim.LR 69.

[1] On the question whether the notion of "driving" is affected by evidence of intoxication see § 29.5.
[2] As substituted by Transport Act 1981 s.25 and Sched. 8. The new section is not in force at the time of writing, but is expected to be brought into force early in 1983. See generally Amey in 146 JPN 480.
[3] For the defence that the defendant was unlikely to drive see s.6(2) as substituted.
[4] S.12(2) as substituted.

reduces all these to summary offences (the object, of course, being to exclude jury trial).[5] However, unlike careless driving, the drink-driving offences are punishable with imprisonment (for up to 6 months) and obligatory disqualification even on first conviction.

The offences under section 6 are governed by various procedural provisions, and are supported by ancillary offences, which need not be considered in detail. Suffice it to say that a constable in uniform may require a specimen of breath (the screening breath test) from a person who is or has been driving (or attempting to drive or in charge of a vehicle) where the constable has reasonable cause to suspect that the driver has alcohol in his body or has committed a moving traffic offence. A constable (not necessarily in uniform) may also require the specimen where the driver was driving or in charge at the time of an accident.[6] If the screening breath test is positive the suspect is taken to the police station for a more accurate electronic test.

Section 6 clearly creates strict liability,[7] and it is generally thought that section 5 does so too. An extreme illustration is *Armstrong* v. *Clark*.[8]

> Clark was a diabetic under insulin treatment. While he was driving, the insulin overacted and caused a deficiency of blood-sugar, so that he continued to drive in a state of semi-coma. He was convicted of driving under the influence of a drug, namely insulin. Lord Goddard CJ said that if people were in a condition of health that rendered them subject to coma, or the remedies for which might send them into comas, they ought not to drive because of the danger that resulted to the rest of Her Majesty's subjects.

One interpretation of this decision is that it imposes strict liability, but another is that it merely decides that a diabetic who is under insulin treatment is negligent if he drives. Either way, the result is unjust.[9]

The maximum prison sentence for the drinking driver being low, the prosecution may prefer to charge him with reckless driving when he has clearly been guilty of irresponsibly bad driving. (A charge under section 1 is particularly likely where death has been caused.) In that event the driver will, by reason of *Caldwell*, be unable to defend himself by saying that his abominable driving was due to drink. On the other hand, it is doubtful how far the prosecution can introduce evidence of excessive drinking to support the reckless driving charge.[10]

---

[5] See the amendments to the RTA in CLA 1977 Sched. 1.

[6] S.7. Although it has been generally thought that these rules prevent random checks, they do not do so. If a constable in uniform wishes to stop drivers at random in order to smell their breath, requiring a breath test if he smells drink, there is nothing in law to forbid him to do so (*Harris* v. *Croson* [1973] RTR 57; *Steel* v. *Goacher* (1982), The Times, July 8); but the police hold back because they lack public and governmental support.

The police may require the screening test to be taken either at the roadside, etc, or at a police station. They may enter premises to require the test to be taken only in the more serious cases (where the driver is suspected of having been impaired through drink or drugs or has been involved in an accident in which a person has been injured). For specimens of blood or urine in place of breath see s.8. If the lower of two readings on the breath test machine is not more than 50 μg. the suspect may opt for a blood test (or urine test if a blood test is not possible for medical reasons), this to allow for the physiological differences between individuals. For the protection of hospital patients see s.9.

[7] Lack of fault (e.g. in a "laced drink" case) is merely a special reason for not disqualifying.

[8] [1957] 2 QB 391.

[9] For an extended criticism see [1967] Crim.LR 205 ff.

[10] See 1st edn 432–433.

An awkward consequence of the present law is that if the reckless driving charge is tried in the Crown Court (as, indeed, it must be if it is a charge of causing death by reckless driving), the drink-driving charge will remain behind in the magistrates' court. Since it is important that this charge should be tried (particularly in order that a conviction on it should be on the driver's record for insurance purposes), some judges recommend magistrates to try the drink charge while the charge of reckless driving is still pending. The proper solution of the difficulty would be for Parliament to allow drink charges to be coupled with reckless driving charges when these are tried on indictment.

§ 14.7. STRICT LIABILITY

Virtually all traffic offences are held to carry strict liability unless they expressly require fault.[1] Examples of such strict liability are the offences of:

- failing to comply with a traffic sign,[2]
- exceeding a speed limit,[3]
- using an unroadworthy vehicle,[4]
- failing to have third-party insurance cover,[5]
- failing to exhibit a vehicle licence,[6] and
- driving while disqualified.[7]

Usually, of course, these offences will be committed knowingly or negligently, but it is quite possible to commit all of them without fault. A traffic sign may be obscured by bushes and posts. A car may be carefully maintained and yet the brakes may suddenly fail. The owner may be punished for the gross negligence of the driver in maintaining the vehicle, and the driver may be punished for the gross negligence of the owner. An owner may lend his car to a friend who he is credibly informed has a driving licence; if the friend has no licence, so that his use of the car is uninsured, the owner is guilty of "permitting" such use.[8] (We have seen that this is an anomalous exception to the usual rule for offences of permitting.) A driver may properly affix his excise licence but unfortunately it falls off when the vehicle is parked, and this is seen by a traffic warden. A driver may drive while disqualified because the period of disqualification has been wrongly marked on his licence.

It is impossible to see what social purpose is served by such decisions. A finding of negligence in failing to ascertain the true position might frequently be sustainable, but the courts do not investigate the issue. The fact that the courts are uninterested in the driver's explanation of why he failed to comply with the law contributes to the general disinclination to consider the prevention of road accidents rather than punishment.[9]

On one occasion, in deciding that an offence was one of strict liability, the court suggested that the police should not prosecute a person who was not at fault.[10] The police do from time to time take this consideration into account in deciding whether to bring a charge. But

---

[1] See *The General Part*, 2nd edn § 80. The New Zealand CA broke away from this principle in the important case of *Police* v. *Creadon* [1976] 1 NZLR 571, on the subject of failing to comply with a give-way sign at an intersection.

[2] *Hill* v. *Baxter* [1958] 1 QB 277.

[3] As happens with a number of offences, there appears to be no express decision that liability is strict, but this is so well understood that defendants plead guilty on the basis of strict liability and their plea is accepted. See, e.g. *Burgess* v. *West* [1982] Crim. LR 235.

[4] § 42.4. Also failing to produce a test certificate: § 26.10 n. 2.

[5] § 6.4 n. 6.

[6] *Strowger* v. *John* [1974] RTR 124.

[7] *Bowsher* [1973] RTR 202, Crim.LR 373; *Miller* [1975] 1 WLR 1222, 2 All ER 974, 61 CAR 182.

[8] *Baugh* v. *Crago* [1975] RTR 453.

[9] This point is made by J J Leeming, *Road Accidents: Prevent or Punish?* (London 1969) 189–190.

[10] *James & Son Ltd.* v. *Smee* [1955] 1 QB at 93.

prosecutions against drivers and owners who were not at fault still occur, and police forces seem to have no operational instructions to the contrary.[11]

Why do the courts exclude the issue of fault?

One reason, extraordinary as it may appear, is that the judges have confused a no-negligence defence with a defence of no *mens rea.*[12] Obviously, ordinary driving offences cannot require *mens rea,* but that is no reason why they should not require negligence.

The rule having been established, judges have said that it is not for them to speculate whether it would be better if it were different[13]—but it is they themselves who have adopted the present strict construction of the law. They have also said that traffic infractions are not truly "criminal"[14]; indeed, they tend to use a similar argument to justify strict liability for all minor offences. But it is difficult to attach much significance to the explanation. Magistrates may allow the traffic offender to preserve a modicum of his self-respect by standing in front of the dock instead of in it; yet he can often be tried on indictment, and he is subject to the same types of punishment as common criminals.

As we shall see in Chapter 44, many instances of strict liability have been alleviated by statute, but for some reason best known to those in authority Parliament has not been invited to intervene in this part of the law.[15]

There are only two traffic offences not expressly requiring a fault element that the courts have clearly construed as requiring fault. The first is failure to report an accident.[16] It has been held that the duty to report presupposes knowledge of the accident. "Unless a man knows that the event has happened, how can he carry out the duty?"[17] In view of this decision it is difficult to see how the judges assert that a driver can conform to a traffic sign that he cannot perceive because it is obscured.

In effect a defence of no negligence also succeeded where a driver was charged with an offence of opening his car door.

> By the Construction and Use Regulations it is an offence for any person (even a passenger) to "open any door of a motor vehicle on a road so as to cause danger to any person." But where a driver, having stopped on his near side, checked in both his rear view and wing mirrors and then opened his car door between six inches and one foot, thus striking another vehicle which was passing too close, he was acquitted under the regulation, the justices considering that since he had done all that was reasonable he had not caused danger. Their decision was affirmed on appeal, though the Divisional Court carefully avoided generalisation, saying that the facts did not raise any issue of what it called "*mens rea.*"[18]

---

[11] Elliott and Street, *Road Accidents* (Harmondsworth 1968) 42.

[12] See, e.g. discussion in [1967] Crim.LR 198; and see *ibid.* 142–145.

[13] *Bowsher,* n. 6 above.

[14] *Miller,* n. 6 above.

[15] Except that RTA 1972 Sched. 4 removes the court's power to impose disqualification for a construction and use offence under s.40(5) in the absence of fault. Parliament (or the Ministry of Transport which really does these things) does not mind that the morally guiltless offender is convicted and fined.

[16] RTA 1972 s.25 as amended.

[17] *Harding* v. *Price* [1948] 1 KB 695.

[18] *Sever* v. *Duffy,* The Times, June 23, 1977, [1977] Crim.LR 484.

Although the court purported to rest its decision on the narrow facts, the point remains that the word 'danger" must have been construed to mean "reasonably foreseeable danger" (which is its only reasonable meaning, since otherwise the mere fact of an accident would prove that there was "danger" of an accident, which would be completely out of accord with the ordinary understanding of the word). If one looks at the facts of the case, the defendant not only caused the danger of an accident but caused an accident. To say that he did not cause danger in law imports a requirement of fault via the doctrine of causation.

The terminological uncertainty that besets this type of case emerges particularly in pedestrian crossing cases. A driver commits an offence if he fails to give precedence to a pedestrian on an ordinary uncontrolled crossing.[19] In interpreting the regulations, the courts naturally and properly put the duty of the driver very high. The ordinary duty of the driver when there is no crossing is to use reasonable care to avoid pedestrians. But when a pedestrian is on a crossing the driver's duty is to give him precedence. It is no use the driver's saying that the pedestrian darted out under his wheels; the driver must be going so slowly that he can pull up even if the pedestrian does this, unless he himself has entered the stripes before the pedestrian does. Nor is it any use his saying that his view of the crossing was obscured by a lorry: if he sees that the crossing is there he must go slowly enough to be able to stop if there is someone on it, and if necessary he must stop to see if there is anyone on it. That is what is meant by saying that he must give precedence.[20]

While the actual decisions in these cases are perfectly sound, the courts have unfortunately fallen into the habit of saying that the driver is under a strict or absolute duty to comply with the regulation.[21] That this is going too far comes out in the type of case where the driver reasonably fails to see the crossing, because there is snow on the road and fog in the air,[22] or where he would normally be able to comply with his duty but fails to do so because of an unforeseeable defect in his vehicle or because he is affected by an unforeseeable illness.[23] Here the cases indicate that the driver is excused. The more recent cases in which the offence was said to involve strict liability have caused some commentators to suppose that the earlier cases accepting that negligence is in issue are no longer law. But the fact is that the more recent cases did not involve the point, and that the dicta on strict liability were unnecessary for the decisions. It would be illogical to argue: the driver must take infinite pains to see that no

---

[19] Road Traffic Regulation Act 1967 s.23; cp. Pedestrian Crossing Regs., SI 1971 No. 1524; "Pelican" Pedestrian Crossing Regs. and General Directions, SI 1969 No. 888 as amended; "Zebra" Pedestrian Crossing Regs., SI 1971 No. 1524 as amended.

[20] See, e.g. *Hughes* v. *Hall* [1960] 1 WLR 733, 2 All ER 504; and on the whole question, see [1967] Crim.LR 146 ff. ("Disreputable" on p. 147 is an unfortunate misprint for "disputable.") The authorities are reviewed in Wilkinson, 11th edn 436–438.

[21] [1967] Crim.LR 149–151.

[22] See *Leicester* v. *Pearson* [1952] 2 KB 668.

[23] See *Burns* v. *Bidder* [1967] 2 QB 277, noted in [1966] Crim.LR 396. In *Police* v. *Creadon* (n. 1 above) Richmond J accordingly expressed the opinion (at p. 571) that the NZ Pedestrian Crossing Regulations should be construed as imposing liability for fault only.

pedestrian is on the crossing; therefore his liability is strict; therefore he is liable even if he gets a heart attack as he is approaching the crossing.

§ 14.8. NEGLIGENCE WITH OTHER CONVEYANCES

Several statutes regulate conduct with conveyances other than motor vehicles. They may be briefly noticed for completeness.

The Road Traffic Act 1972 (as amended) contains offences of reckless cycling (s.17), careless and inconsiderate cycling (s.18), and cycling under the influence of drink or drugs (s.19).

There are also various odds and ends of legislation outside the Act. The OAPA 1861 s.35 has an offence of causing bodily harm by wilful misconduct with a carriage; this includes cycles[1] and horse-drawn vehicles, and it covers driving otherwise than on roads.[2] The Licensing Act 1872 as amended makes it an offence for a person to be drunk while in charge on any highway or other public place of any carriage, horse or cattle.[3] Negligent and drunken train drivers are dealt with extraordinarily leniently, the maximum punishment being 3 months' imprisonment or a fine of £200[4]; the court has no power to disqualify them, and no one breathalyses them. There is no offence of negligent navigation endangering other vessels at sea,[5] but such an offence is known on some of our rivers. In 1976 a canoeist was convicted by the Oxford magistrates of careless navigation in holing an Exeter College eight—under a private Act, the Thames Conservancy Act 1932 s.97.

SUMMARY

The Road Traffic Act 1972 ss.1–3 as amended create offences of bad driving of motor vehicles on roads. § .1

Section 3 creates two summary offences, of driving without due care and attention and driving without reasonable consideration for other persons using the road. The former offence is committed by the negligent driver. For the purpose of establishing carelesness evidence may be given that other road offences were involved, or that the Highway Code was not observed, but such evidence is not necessarily conclusive. The offence can be committed by driving a vehicle that has been negligently maintained by the driver, though in practice the charge would generally be for breach of the Construction and Use Regulations. § .2

The offence of inconsiderate driving is committed where the driving causes inconvenience to others. Like careless driving, it is punishable by fine, but not imprisonment on first conviction. Disqualification is usually discretionary. § .3

Section 2 creates an offence of reckless driving, triable either way, with possible imprisonment and discretionary disqualification. In *Lawrence* the House of Lords held that the offence has two components. (1) Driving so as to create an obvious and serious risk of causing physical injury or substantial damage to property. (2) § .4

---

[1] The word "cycle" is conveniently used (as in the Theft Act s.12) to cover not only bikes but trikes.

[2] See Wilkinson, 11th edn 270–271; *Cooke* [1971] RTR 11, Crim.LR 44. See also Highway Act 1835 s.78 as amended, which covers equestrians, and other legislation in Wilkinson, 10th edn 246–247.

[3] s.12: Wilkinson, 11th edn 236.

[4] Railway Regulation Act 1842 s.17, as amended, particularly by British Railways Act 1977 (c. xvii) s.13. Use does not seem to be made of OAPA 1861 s. 34, though there is no reason why not.

[5] But misconduct (including drunkenness) by master or crew endangering their own vessel is an offence under the Merchant Shipping Act 1970 s.27.

Failing to give any thought to the possibility of there being such risk, or, having recognised that there was some risk involved, going on to take it. This may be criticised as being both too wide and too narrow. It improperly includes the driver who is guilty of merely momentary inadvertence in traffic, and it fails to cover the driver who deliberately flouts accepted standards of driving if the jury or magistrates think that he may have believed he had sufficient skill to avoid risk.

Section 1 creates an offence of causing death by reckless driving, triable only on indictment; on conviction, disqualification from driving is obligatory in the absence of special reasons. On the causal question, the judge may ask the jury to consider whether the reckless driving was "a cause" of the death, being something more than a purely trivial cause. § .5

The Road Traffic Act as amended creates summary offences of driving or attempting to drive or being in charge of a motor vehicle on a road or other public place (1) when unfit to drive through drink or drugs (section 5) or (2) having consumed so much alcohol that the proportion in the defendant's breath, blood or urine exceeds the prescribed limit (section 6). These carry a possible prison sentence and also obligatory disqualification. Section 6 and (probably) section 5 crreate strict liability. § .6

Virtually all traffic offences are construed to carry strict liability unless they expressly require fault. However, a defence of no negligence can succeed on a charge of failure to report an accident or of opening a vehicle door so as to cause danger to any person. The Pedestrian Crossing Regulations impose a heavy duty on the driver to give precedence to pedestrians, but it is not certain that the duty is strict. § .7

Various other statutes create offences in connection with other conveyances, or with motor vehicles otherwise than on roads. § .8

Part Three

INVOLVEMENT IN CRIME

Chapter 15

COMPLICITY

For the sin ye do by two and two
ye must pay for one by one!
Kipling, *Tomlinson*

§ 15.1. THE DEGREES OF COMPLICITY: PERPETRATORS

Complicity in crime extends beyond the *perpetrator* to *accessories*.[1] Both the perpetrator and the accessories are regarded by law as participants in the crime, and are called *accomplices*. The perpetrator is an accomplice of the accessories, and they are accomplices of the perpetrator and of each other.[2]

An accessory (sometimes called a secondary party) may be either an *inciter* or a *helper*. He is one who incites or helps the commission of an offence by the perpetrator.

There is a small problem of terminology. At common law the person here called the perpetrator was called the principal in the first degree. Those who helped at the time of the crime ("aided and abetted") were termed principals in the second degree. Those who successfully incited ("counselled or procured") the crime were termed accessories (before the fact) in felonies, principals in misdemeanours and summary offences.

The Criminal Law Act 1967 abolished the distinction between felonies and misdemeanours, applying the misdemeanour rules to all indictable offences. The effect is to abolish accessories and make everybody a principal—if the old terminology is kept. But there is no point in continuing to speak of a principal if he is not contrasted with a non-principal.

Evidently, a new language is needed. The Law Commission Working Party proposed to speak of the doer as the principal and all the other accomplices as accessories.[3] Accessories, therefore, are both the former accessories in felony and the former principals in the second degree. While this extended notion of "accessories" is acceptable, there is one serious objection to the continued use of the term "principal" to denote the perpetrator. In the civil law (the law of contract and tort), where A directs B to do something on his behalf, A, the commander, is called the principal and B, the doer, his agent. It seems unfortunate to call B the principal in criminal law, when he is the agent in civil law.[4] Let it be known, therefore, that the name "perpetrator" is adopted in the present book.[5]

The "perpetrator" (or, if you will, the "principal") means, and means

---

[1] See further, *The General Part*, 2nd edn Chap. 9.

[2] The word "accomplice" is used chiefly in relation to the rule of evidence that the judge must warn the jury of the danger of convicting on the uncorroborated evidence of an accomplice.

[3] Law Commission, *Working Paper No. 43*.

[4] A further reason for abandoning the word "principal" in the criminal law is that it is liable to mislead when the older authorities are read. Before 1967 an abettor was a principal in felonies and all parties were principals in misdemeanours; since the misdemeanour rules have been generalised, all parties to all crimes are principals on the old terminology, but they were and are not all principals in the first degree (which is what we are now talking about). To abbreviate to "principals," simply, is capable of producing false reasoning.

[5] An incidental advantage of the word "perpetrator" is that it gives the verb "perpetrate;" the word "principal" yields no verb.

exclusively, the person who in law performs the offence. More precisely, the perpetrator is the person who, being directly struck at by the criminal prohibition, offends against it with the necessary *mens rea* or negligence (if either of these be required). He is normally indicated by the wording of the legal rule. In murder, he is the person who kills; in burglary, the person who trespasses with the requisite intent; in forgery, the person who makes or uses the forged document.

The perpetrator may do the deed by his own hand, or he may procure an innocent agent (or set up an instrumentality) to do it. In other words he may use a cat's paw to pull his chestnuts from the fire. He may, for example, get another to make false statements on his behalf by concealing the facts from him, or he may (keeping more closely to the fable) train a dog to steal meat. Also, an employer who is attributively responsible (that is, responsible for the act of his employee) is a perpetrator if the act amounts to an offence, because he is regarded as doing the act through his employee. So the full definition offered by the Law Commission Working Party on Codification is as follows. I quote it with an addition of my own in square brackets.

> "(1) A principal in an offence is one who, with any necessary fault element, [and possessing any qualification required for the offence,] does the acts constituting the external elements of the offence.
>
> (2) A person does such an act not only when he does it himself but also when he—
>
> (*a*) acts through an innocent agent; or
>
> (*b*) is otherwise responsible for the act of another which constitutes an external element of an offence."

Innocent agency and attributed responsibility will be studied later. At present we are concerned only with sub-rule (1).

The sub-rule as worded by the Working Party did not say, as properly it should have, that a person cannot be a perpetrator unless he possesses a qualification required for the offence. Bigamy, for example, can be perpetrated only by a married person ("Whosoever, being married, shall marry . . . "[6]), so if a married man goes through a bigamous ceremony of marriage with a spinster, the spinster cannot be guilty of bigamy as perpetrator, even if she knows of the bigamous character of the ceremony. (In the latter event she is guilty as accessory.)

Two persons may be guilty as joint perpetrators; and part of a crime may be committed by one perpetrator, another by another. Thus, in robbery, which involves the two elements of theft and threat, one person may steal while his companion makes the threat of force, and the two are co-perpetrators. The most common form of co-perpetration is where two join in committing an offence so that their respective contributions are indistinguishable. If two ruffians belabour a man about the head and he dies as a result of the combined blows, both are perpetrators of murder.

Suppose Dirk stabs a man while his companion Dastard pinions the man's arms so as to prevent him from defending himself. Are they joint perpetrators of the stabbing?

A perpetrator must himself do the criminal act, apart from the

---

[6] OAPA 1861 s.57.

exceptional cases in sub-rule (2) above. In your hypothetical the criminal act, the act of killing, is the stabbing. Dastard is an accessory.[7]

As another example, if D gives V a lethal pill to help V kill himself, V on taking the pill and dying commits suicide, but D is not guilty as perpetrator of a murder, because he did not do the act of killing. He is an accessory to the self-killing (suicide) by V, and commits a special statutory offence. If on the other hand D stabs V at V's request, and so kills him, he is guilty of murder.

§ 15.2. ACCESSORIES

The courts made accessories liable as a matter of common law, and this was put on a statutory footing by the Accessories and Abettors Act 1861.[1]

> "Whosoever shall aid, abet, counsel, or procure the commission of any indictable offence, whether the same be an offence at common law or by virtue of any Act passed or to be passed, shall be liable to be tried, indicted, and punished as a principal offender."

The four verbs used at the beginning of this section are the traditional way of expressing acts of accessoryship, and are still used in indictments (though there is no law compelling them to be used). Any one of the four verbs may be charged,[2] or all four may be charged together (with the conjunctive "and") in the same count. Charging all four is the safest thing to do, because the shades of difference between them are far from clear.[3]

Suppose you counsel someone to commit a crime, and he does not do it?

I should not be an accessory, because that supposes that the crime has been committed. I should be guilty of the inchoate crime of incitement.

Can the accessory be tried by himself?

Yes.

As a practical matter it is highly desirable that all the alleged parties to a crime should be indicted and tried together, as they can be. When they are jointly charged, a court is rarely well advised to consent to an application for separate trials. Still, if it is only possible to charge the accessory (e.g. because the perpetrator has escaped), there is no legal objection to it. Of course, the prosecution must establish the commission of the crime just as if the perpetrator were before the court. (But, as we shall see, "the commission of the crime" may have a peculiar meaning in this context: § .16.)

A few details of the law of evidence. Suppose the perpetrator has already been convicted. The conviction is not evidence against an alleged accessory to show that the offence was committed. It is *res inter alias acta*.[4]

Suppose the alleged perpetrator has already been acquitted. The acquittal will probably not bar the subsequent trial of the accessory, if the perpetrator's acquittal was merely the result

---

[7] A tendency to inflate the category of perpetrators, perhaps because of confusion arising from the old law, is visible in some judicial dicta, and is encouraged by Fletcher, who argues that all conspirators become co-perpetrators when the crime is committed. For a refutation see Lanham in 4 Crim.LJ (Aus.) 286–288.

[1] S.8, as amended. Cp. Magistrates' Courts Act 1980 s.44.

[2] Each word was said in *Attorney-General's Reference (No. 1 of 1975)* [1975] 1 QB at 779E to have a different meaning. In *Lynch* [1975] AC at 678A "aid" and "abet" were said to be synonymous; but see *ibid.* at 698F–G.

[3] See J C Smith in *Reshaping the Criminal Law*, ed. Glazebrook (London 1978) 120 ff.

[4] Cp. *Hassan* [1970] 1 QB at 426. The Latin expression means "a thing done between others."

of lack of evidence against the perpetrator, or other special ground which does not apply when the accessory comes to be charged.[5]

Suppose that D2 counsels D1 to commit a crime, and D1 complies. D2 confesses but D1 does not. D2's confession is admissible in evidence against him but not against D1; consequently, the case against D1 may break down for lack of evidence, but that is no reason why D2 should not be convicted on his confession. Similarly, if D1 is acquitted on some procedural ground, it is still possible to convict D2.[6]

The distinction between perpetrator and accessories does not, in law, control the punishment. Accessories are subject to the same maximum as that laid down by law for the perpetrator. On conviction of murder they are subject to the mandatory life sentence.

Except in murder, the court may of course differentiate between the accomplices in sentencing. The accessory may get more punishment than the perpetrator, as when he is the master-mind behind the crime; or he may get less, as when a stupid youth plays a subordinate part in a scheme initiated by another. That is a matter for the judge or magistrates. (One of the objections to the fixed penalty for murder is that the judge is not allowed to differentiate the sentence in this case.)

What about disqualification? Dan has had a number of stiff whiskies and his blood-alcohol content is obviously above the norm. Dare encourages him to drive, but does not drive himself, though he happens to possess a licence. If Dan is disqualified from driving by the court, can Dare be disqualified as well?

Yes. In the case of the perpetrator, disqualification is obligatory for this offence in the absence of special reasons. If there were no statute in point the court might say that disqualification applies only to the driver; but under the Road Traffic Act there is discretionary disqualification for the accessory.[7] So it is for the court to decide whether to disqualify Dare.

What if the prosecutor cannot be certain before the trial, or the jury cannot be certain at the trial, which of several people who were in cahoots with one another was the perpetrator and which were the accessories?

No problem. In contemplation of law, both the perpetrator and the accessories "commit" the offence, and there are procedural provisions

---

[5] *Remillard* (1921) 62 SCR 21 (Can.).

[6] This is borne out by certain old authorities and now seems clear since the decision of the HL in the conspiracy case of *Shannon* [1975] AC 717. The dicta in *Anthony* [1965] 2 QB 189 can safely he said to be wrong: see *Humphreys* [1965] 3 All E.R. 689 (Liverpool Crown Court); *Sweetman* v. *Industries and Commerce Dept.* [1970] NZLR 139; note, [1966] Crim.LR 98. As we shall see (§ .16), it has even been held in some cases that a person can be convicted as accessory although the alleged perpetrator is shown to have had a personal defence.

The remarks in the foregoing paragraph are certainly true when D1 is tried after or before D2, and there is no reason to doubt that they are true also where Dl and D2 are tried together. It must be admitted that on a charge of conspiracy the common law distinguished between these situations, but that was simply the spurious logic of the law of conspiracy; there is no need to extend it to complicity, and even for conspiracy the law has now been altered by statute, so that it is always possible to convict one alleged conspirator notwithstanding the acquittal of the other, if no argument of justice stands in the way. see § 18.8. The decision in *Davis* [1977] Crim.LR 542 is no obstacle; in that case the alleged perpetrator was acquitted and the alleged accessory convicted by the jury in the same trial, and the conviction was very properly quashed on appeal, since there was nothing in the law of evidence to explain the quirkish inconsistency. Cp. *Surujpaul* [1958] 1 WLR 1050, 3 All ER 300.

[7] Road Traffic Act 1972 s.93(6). See, however, *Ullah* v. *Luckhurst* [1977] Crim.LR 295.

whereby accessories can be charged and convicted as perpetrators and *vice versa*.[8]

> An indictment may allege that the defendant D2 on the blank day of blank *murdered* V, instead of alleging (as the fact is) that he counselled and procured D1 to murder V, or aided and abetted Dl to murder V. This saves the prosecution and the jury from embarrassment if it is not clear who perpetrated the offence and who incited or helped.[9]

In other words, the legal distinctions between perpetrator and accessories have been wiped out?

That is a tempting view, but it is not quite right. One can "commit" an offence as perpetrator or "commit" it as accessory, but the two forms of legal commission remain distinct.

- The chief distinction is that, as will be shown in § .4, the mental element for the accessory is not necessarily the same as for the perpetrator.
- *Someone* must be proved to have been the perpetrator; there cannot be an accessory without a perpetrator. This rule seems to have been qualified (§ .16), but it has not been entirely abolished.
- One can attempt to perpetrate a crime, but not, it seems, to be an accessory to it: § 17.6.
- Duress is a defence to an accessory in murder but not to the perpetrator (§ 27.2).
- The distinction is also relevant to a problem on self-manslaughter discussed in § 25.20.

You said that a husband can be accessory to a rape on his wife (§ 10.8 at n. 15). Can a woman commit rape, as accessory to rape by a man?

Certainly.[10] A person can be guilty as accessory although he could not commit the crime as perpetrator. Similarly, if a particular offence can be committed only by a person holding a licence to sell liquor, another person (such as his barman) can nevertheless be convicted of abetting him.

Reverting to the procedural point, although the wording of the charge generally does not matter, it is customary and wise for the prosecution to charge the perpetrator and accessories in appropriate terms where the evidence is clear.[11] The statement of the offence will give the name of the crime, but the particulars of the offence should, when possible, state that the defendant is charged with having aided, abetted, counselled or procured the crime, if such be the fact.

---

[8] See the statutes in n. 1 above. It is sometimes doubted whether an accessory can be indicted as a principal (e.g. 42 MLR 316 n. 8, quoting [1973] Crim.LR 225–227); but the courts are very unlikely to decide against the form of charge, except perhaps in the special cases to be mentioned presently. See *The General Part*, 2nd edn § 137.

[9] Cp. *Swindall*, below § .11 at n. 2. Of course, if it is only known that one or other of two people perpetrated the offence, and not clear that the other (whichever it was) helped him, neither can be convicted. But *Marsh* v. *Hodgson* [1974] Crim.LR 35 holds that in some cases an evidential burden lies on each person present to negative complicity (husband and wife jointly in charge of a child who was intentionally injured by one or other of them).

[10] *Ram* (1893) 17 Cox 609; cp. *Lord Baltimore* (1768) 1 Black. W 648, 96 ER 376.

[11] The high desirability of this was emphasised in *Maxwell* [1978] 1 WLR 1350, 3 All ER 1140, 68 CAR 142.

In bigamy, for example, where a married man has married a spinster who knows the bigamous nature of the ceremony, the spinster is an accessory and can be convicted of "bigamy," but it would be absurd for the particulars of offence to charge her that, being married, she has married again. In a case like this the accessory should be charged in express terms as accessory.[12]

Although the four traditional verbs are still used, the language is antiquated, and the Law Commission Working Party[13] proposed to simplify it into two words. Under the proposal, "aiding and abetting" will become "helping," and "counselling and procuring" will become "inciting." This simplified language will be used in the present book.

Does the rule that ignorance of the criminal law is no defence apply to accessories?

Yes.[14] In this application the rule is very severe. The perpetrator of one of the innumerable offences in relation to business or some other specialised activity such as driving can reasonably be expected to acquaint himself with the law relating to it. But he may use the services of many other people: suppliers, repairers, carriers, consultants, accountants, and so on. It is remarkable that they, too, are expected to learn the specialised law of all their customers and clients.

§ 15.3. INCITEMENT

The word "incitement" generally speaks for itself, but it includes advice, encouragement and authorisation,[1] as well as persuasion by threats. (The phrase used in the old books was "counsel, procure or command.") Encouragement may be given expressly or may be implied from conduct.[2]

So if a gang of rowdies proceed along a street, some members of it damaging property as they go, the others will very likely be found to have encouraged them by remaining part of the mob and moving with it. They will therefore be accessories, and all the mob can be charged with the offence without the prosecution being under the necessity of identifying the perpetrators.[3]

---

[12] But even if the indictment was glaringly at fault a conviction may be upheld on appeal. See *Cogan* [1976] QB at 224.

The points made in the text show that the distinction between perpetrators and others is recognised at common law. It is true that principals in the second degree (aiders and abettors) were lumped for many purposes with principals in the first degree (perpetrators); and Hale wrote that "if A be indicted as having given the mortal stroke, and B and C as present aiding and assisting, . . . in law it is the stroke of all" (*PC* i 437–438). But that was so only for the purpose of upholding an indictment as a matter of pleading, where the distinction was immaterial for the substantive law. Where the distinction was material, the stroke of the perpetrator was not the stroke of the helper.

[13] *Working Paper No. 43*.

[14] *Johnson* v. *Youden* [1950] 1 KB 544.

[1] For authorisation see *Derrick* [1970] Crim.LR 467.

[2] An example of implied encouragement was suggested in *Drake* v. *Morgan* [1977] Crim. LR 739 (agreeing to indemnify against a fine for a future offence).

[3] Cp. *Mackin* (1838) 2 Lew. 225, 168 ER 1136.

Hitherto it has not been customary to say that the accessory "incites" the crime; the verb has tended to be confined to the inchoate offence of incitement (i.e. where the offence is not committed). But the act is the same, whether the crime is committed or not, and there is no reason why the same word should not be used to describe what is done. Before the crime is committed, the inciter is called by that name; after the crime is committed he is called an accessory. Certain minor differences between the inchoate offence and accessoryship will appear in § 19.4.

Suppose D3 incites D2 to procure D1 to commit a crime, and all works out according to plan. Is D3 a party to the crime?

Certainly. He has incited at one remove.[4]

Can a man incite an indefinite series of crimes?

A person who exhorts another to commit a series of crimes will become an accessory to all of them when they are committed; but common sense is needed in applying this rule. If D2 persuades D1 to commit a series of murders for a political object, D2 will be inculpated in each of them. However, the position is surely different if D2 merely encourages D1 in his general criminal tendencies,[5] or even in the commission of crimes of a particular kind—as if he advises D1 that burglary affords a good opening. It would be too severe to say that such general encouragement makes D2 a participant in every crime that is thereafter committed by D1 within the terms of the encouraging words. There must be an element of particularity in the crime that is counselled in order to make the counsellor a party (§ .4 at n. 2).

Need there be an element of particularity in the people who are encouraged? What about an appeal to the general public to murder all members of the Cabinet?

Presumably the accessory must have communicated with an individual (or group of nameable individuals). He will not be an accessory to crimes committed by random members of the public. A person who incites the public generally to commit a particular crime is guilty of incitement to murder as an inchoate crime (§ 19.1), but no case decides that he becomes an accessory to all the murders that are carried out in consequence of his incitement. In common sense, there is a difference between incitement as an inchoate crime (which is fully committed as soon as the incitement is uttered) and incitement as making a person accessory to crime when it is committed.

Will you be an accessory if you do something that you know will encourage a crime, but without intent to encourage?

It depends on the circumstances. If I act in co-operation with someone, and my doing so encourages him in illegality, I shall not be heard to say that I did not intend to encourage. But if there is no co-operation between us I shall not be liable.[6] There must be an intention to encourage, a desire

[4] *Macdaniel* (1755) Fost, at 125–126, 168 ER at 62.
[5] See § .4 at n. 2.
[6] See *Swindall* and *Mastin* § .11 nn. 2, 3.

that the crime shall be committed. Even recklessness as to encouraging is not enough.

> The manager of a shop owned by a company sets out his wares on the pavement, where they may easily be picked up by a passer-by. He knows that some people will be tempted to steal articles from time to time. So he knows that he is (in a sense) encouraging people to steal (and also that he is making it easy for them to steal, and to that extent helping them to do so). But obviously when a theft takes place he is not an accessory to the theft from his employer, which he certainly does not want to encourage or promote.

There is authority for saying that every conspirator becomes a procurer in law when the crime is committed, and therefore becomes a party to the crime.[7] But this opinion should be rejected, because it inflates the notion of complicity beyond reason. However difficult it may be to formulate the rule, liability for complicity in crime should be confined to those who are in some appreciable way involved in the crime itself, either by encouraging the actual participants in some fairly proximate way or otherwise. It is noticeable, for example, that members of the Provisional wing of the IRA have not been charged with murder merely on the basis of their membership, though the conspiracy theory would suggest liability. The murderers are those who take part in the actual murder or who encourage the murderers with some realistic degree of proximity.[8]

§ 15.4. HELP

The accessory's help may be given before or during the crime. Examples of help given before the crime are supplying the tools or materials of crime, imparting the "know-how," and opening a bank account in a false name in expectation that a forger will pay into it the proceeds of forged cheques.[1]

> In *Bainbridge*[2] a thief broke into a bank with oxygen cutting equipment supplied by Bainbridge. It was held that Bainbridge was liable as accessory if he knew that a crime of breaking and entering premises (the former name used to describe offences like burglary) and stealing property therein was intended. It was not necessary that he should know when and where the offence was to be committed. As we shall see, a person like Bainbridge would now be liable even if he knew only that burglary was *one* of the crimes within the contemplation of the person he helped (§ .9 at n. 2).
>
> As another example, in a New Zealand case, where D2 wrote a letter to D1 at his request describing how to break open a safe with explosives, knowing that a crime was afoot, he was held to be a party to the crime committed by D1 in attempting to break open a safe with the information provided.[3]

Help also includes co-operation. So, as was said before, the other party to a bigamous ceremony is an accessory. If a statute forbids the selling of

---

[7] *Croft* [1944] KB 295.

[8] See *The General Part*, 2nd edn 363; Lanham in 4 Crim.LJ (Aus.) 283–286.

[1] On the bank account see *Thambiah* [1966] AC 37. Contrast *Scott* § .9 n. 4. *Farr* [1982] Crim.LR 745, on supplying premises for producing drugs, is not in accord with principle.

[2] [1960] 1 QB 129.

[3] *Baker* (1909) 28 NZLR 536.

something, a person who buys the thing can be liable as accessory, since there can be no seller without a buyer.[4]

The Law Commission Working Party proposed a partial definition in order to extend "helping" to cases that clearly need to be covered. (The primary purpose of the Working Party's propositions was to form the foundation of a code, but the propositions are sufficiently close to the present law to make them a useful basis of discussion.) The partial definition is as follows:

> "Help includes—
> (*a*) help given of which the principal was unaware[5]; and
> (*b*) conduct of a person which leads the principal to believe when committing the offence that he is being helped, or will be helped if necessary, by that person in its commission."

Paragraph (*b*) (to start with that) is declaratory of the present law. Examples are:

- Acting as a look-out. The look-out man is an accessory even though the gang are not in fact disturbed; he is ready to give a warning if necessary, and his presence is a comfort to them.
- Manning a get-away car. Here again the driver gives encouragement and psychological help even though all the accomplices are arrested before the car can be used.

Couldn't all these helpers be regarded as encouragers, and therefore as inciters, so that the category of helpers is not needed?

Many helpers can be regarded as inciters as well, but some cannot be.

> If D1 goes to D2 and asks for the loan of D2's gun for a robbery, and D2 complies, it is unrealistic to say that D2 has incited or encouraged D1. D2 said nothing by way of incitement or encouragement, but he helped, and he is an accessory.
>
> Again, one who, knowing that a person is going to be murdered, off his own bat lulls the victim's suspicions and directs him to the spot planned for the murder is an accomplice although he did not communicate with the actual murderer. He has purposely helped.

Another illustration of the same point is *Attorney-General's Reference (No. 1 of 1975)*.[6]

> A driver was convicted of having an excess of alcohol in his blood, and in order to persuade the court that there were "special reasons" for not disqualifying him from driving he offered evidence that his drink had been surreptitiously "laced" with spirits by a friend. Probably (although the report does not say so) the story was corroborated by his friend; at any rate the friend was then indicted for aiding and abetting the offence, on the basis that he knew that the driver would shortly be

---

[4] *Sayce* v. *Coup* [1953] 1 QB at 7–8.

[5] And, it may be added, help given to a person of whose identity the helper is unaware. On the question whether D2 is an accessory by reason of help intended to be given to X but actually used by D1 see Smith in *Crime, Proof and Punishment*, ed. Tapper (London 1981) 33–34.

[6] [1975] QB 773.

driving the car home. (One does not need to be told that the object of the prosecution was to reduce the popularity of the "spiked drink" excuse.) The judge ruled that there was no case to answer, and the Attorney-General referred the question to the Court of Appeal under section 36 of the Criminal Justice Act 1972. (Although the prosecution cannot appeal from an acquittal on indictment, this procedure allows them to obtain a decision of the Court of Appeal that the acquittal was wrong in law, so that the error is not perpetuated in future cases.) It was held that the ruling was wrong, the friend being an accessory because, in the words of the indictment, he "procured" the offence by reason of having caused it.

On its face the decision implies that a person can procure an offence by another when the other is unaware of the procurement; but this may be questioned. "Counsel or procure" in the Accessories and Abettors Act (§ .2) and in the indictment should be taken to mean what is here called incitement, and should presuppose that the counselling or procuring comes to the knowledge of the perpetrator. The indictment in this case had charged the friend in the usual blunderbuss language with aiding and abetting, counselling and procuring the offence, and the proper basis of the decision was surely that the friend had aided and abetted it, not that he had procured it. Lord Widgery CJ said:

> "It may very well be difficult to think of a case of aiding, abetting or counselling when the parties have not met and have not discussed in some respects the terms of the offence which they have in mind."

That is partly true for counselling (though an actual meeting is not necessary); but is it at all true for aiding and abetting? D1 and V are fighting, and D2, without prior agreement, holds V for D1 to punch or kick him. Is this not a clear case of aiding? And did not the defendant before the court also aid the offence by supplying the "material" by which it came to be committed? The offence was one of strict liability for the driver, but alcohol was necessary for its commission and the friend supplied the alcohol. It is settled law that a person who supplies the tools or materials of crime can be a party to it.

On the other hand, incitement means words or conduct operating on the mind of another person and intended to persuade him to adopt a line of conduct. There can be no incitement that does not come to the knowledge of the person incited. The same should be true of "procuring," at any rate where the procuring takes the form of inciting. If one calls every helping a "procuring," then it need not come to the perpetrator's knowledge, but such a use of language is not very apt.

In *Attorney-General's Reference* the defendant gave help and so caused the offence to be committed. (The only special feature of the case was that the "help" caused the person "helped" to commit an offence of strict liability of which he was unaware.) But no authority holds that the law of complicity extends to a person who causes an offence without inciting it or helping in its commission. The mere fact that a person is pursuing his lawful occasions,[7] not designing to bring about a crime or helping another to commit a crime in any way, does not make him a party to a crime committed by that other, even though the first knows that what he is doing will be made the occasion of crime by the other.

The leading authority for this proposition is *Beatty* v. *Gillbanks*.[8] The

---

[7] Or even unlawful occasions. The mere fact that A commits a crime parallel with the crime of B, and so causes B to commit his crime, does not make A an accomplice in B's crime. See *Mastin*, § .11 n. 3.

[8] (1882) 9 QBD 308. Cp. § 16.9 at n. 3; S A de Smith. *Constitutional and Administrative Law,* 3rd edn (London 1973) 493 ff. For an even stronger illustration of the rule see *Mastin*, last note.

Salvation Army was accustomed to hold Sunday meetings in Weston-super-Mare, and a hostile organisation, called the Skeleton Army, was formed to break it up. A Divisional Court held, on a case stated, that the leaders of the Salvation Army could not be convicted of a breach of the peace merely because of what the Skeleton Army might do. Field J said that there was no authority for the proposition that a man may be convicted for doing a lawful act if he knows that his doing it may cause another to do an unlawful act.

In so far as *Attorney-General's Reference* purports to decide that merely causing an offence can be said to be a procuring of it, it should be regarded as too incautious a generalisation. The decision is supportable, and supportable only, on the ground that the materials of the offence had been provided, so that its commission had been helped.

But the spiker did not merely provide the materials of the offence. He concealed the fact that what he did caused the offence. If he had not concealed it, he would not have been liable. If I throw a party with plenty of liquid refreshment, I am not my guests' keeper. All I do is to give a party. I am not responsible if my bibulous friends choose to drive home.

That is a reasonable view, but it is hard to see how you can avoid responsibility under the law as it stands. Your guests commit an offence in driving home, and you have supplied the materials for it, and you knew they were going to commit it.

In *Attorney-General's Reference* the Court of Appeal struggled with this question because it sensed the danger of extending the law too widely. Reasons were offered why the ordinary host could not be convicted, but they were somewhat obscure and unconvincing. It was suggested that where the host does not act surreptitiously he may properly leave the guest to make his own decision. But what if the host knows for a fact that the guest is becoming "tiddley" and yet does not withdraw the bottles, as he could legally do?

Granted that mere causation is not enough to make a person an accessory, would it be true to say that a person cannot be an accessory unless he caused the perpetrator to do as he did?

No. Incitement must come to the knowledge of the person incited, but the prosecution need not prove that it decisively affected his mind. Similarly the prosecution need not prove that the perpetrator would not have committed the crime if it had not been for the help given by the defendant. Such a requirement would present the prosecution with an impossible task.[9]

A different problem: one who supplies a tool for a crime, such as a burglar's jemmy, may know that it will be used for a large number of crimes. Similarly with know-how. Does he become implicated in every one of the crimes in which the tool or information is used?

This is another form of the problem discussed in the last section,

---

[9] See Smith in *Reshaping the Criminal Law*, ed. Glazebrook (London 1978) 131–134; *The General Part*, 2nd edn 381–383.

concerning complicity in an indefinite series of crimes. It may be suggested that the rule is that the helper is not an accessory unless at the time of the help (1) the perpetrator had a particular crime in mind (or one of a number of possibilities) and (2) the helper knew this. The helper will become a party only to this one crime (or a crime or crimes of the group).[10] However, it is not clear that the courts will restrict the law in this way.

But if my burglar friend writes to me asking for information on how to open safes, and I reply, I may not have the slightest idea whether he has a particular job in mind or simply wants to improve his own criminal education. Does my liability depend on the jury deciding whether I thought it was one or the other?

It can only be said that the law on this question is obscure.[11]

Need the helper have the mental state required for the perpetrator?

No. It is enough that he knows the perpetrator's intention (within limits to be discussed).

> For example, if D2 hands a knife to D1 knowing that he is going to use it for a section 18 offence, D1 must intend to do g.b.h., but provided that D1 has that intent, D2 need not share it. He can be an accessory even though he has no interest in the question whether g.b.h. is inflicted or not.
>
> That is a somewhat unlikely hypothetical, but less dramatic illustrations of the principle can be found in the reports. Where D2 lent a car to D1 knowing that the latter intended to use it to "break and enter," he was held to be a party to D1's offence[12]; and where D2 lent a car to D1 to drive, knowing that D1 was disqualified from driving, he became a party to D1's offence.[13] In neither of these cases did D2 have a personal interest in the offence.

You say that the accessory by helping must know the perpetrator's intention. Mustn't he also himself intend to help?

In no realistic sense was there an intent to help in *Attorney-General's Reference*. Such an intent, although sometimes postulated by the judges, is not necessary as a general rule. The accessory must know he is "helping;"

---

[10] I am indebted to P R Glazebrook on this point. The matter was touched upon by Lowry CJ delivering the judgment of the CA of Northern Ireland in *Maxwell* [1978] 1 WLR at 1375, 3 All ER at 1162. He said: "Such questions must, we think, be solved by asking whether the crime actually committed is fairly described as the crime or one of a number of crimes within the contemplation of the accomplice." This does not say that it must also be a particular crime (or one of a group) then contemplated by the perpetrator, but that was so on the facts of *Maxwell*, and it was on this basis that the House of Lords affirmed the conviction. See § .9 at n. 2.

[11] The Voluntary Euthanasia Society (formerly "Exit") published a booklet for its members describing methods of committing suicide. It is an offence to aid suicide (§ 25.15), and the Attorney-General sought a declaration that the supply of the booklet was unlawful: *Att.-Gen.* v. *Able* (1983) The Times April 29. Woolf J refused the declaration but also refused to declare that the supply was lawful. In his opinion a supplier could be guilty of the statutory offence if he intended to assist someone to commit suicide by means of the booklet and the person in question was assisted or encouraged to try to do so. It did not matter that the supplier did not know the state of mind of the recipient.

A similar (but morally very different) problem arises with regard to terrorist manuals describing methods of blowing up bridges etc. No prosecutions have been brought for these manuals.

[12] *Bullock* [1955] 1 WLR 1, 1 All ER 15, 38 CAR 151.

[13] *Pope* v. *Minton* [1954] Crim. LR 711.

he need not intend to help in the sense that he wishes to encourage the crime. See the next section. But there is one type of case where absence of an intent to help will negative liability, namely where a crime is facilitated without communication with the suspect and with intent to obtain evidence against him.

> The manager of a shop, suspecting an employee of theft, puts marked money in a cash box, leaves the box unlocked, and lies in wait. The suspect enters and steals from the box. Obviously, the manager is not an accessory to theft from his employers; yet he assisted the theft in fact.

§ 15.5. ORDINARY BUSINESS SUPPLY

The law of complicity constantly threatens to expand beyond reasonable bounds. One reason for this is the tendency of the courts to apply the rules mechanically, without considering the need to resolve the conflict between the necessary protection of society and the freedom of ordinary people to live their lives without harassment from the criminal law. This happened in *National Coal Board* v. *Gamble*.[1]

> The decision, shortly stated, was that when the seller of goods knew that the goods would overload a lorry in which the buyer intended to drive them away, the seller became a party to the buyer's offence of driving an overloaded lorry.

Presumably this means that a filling station attendant who fills up a car that he sees has worn tyres or is otherwise unfit for the road becomes a party to the offence of using an unfit car when the customer drives off. If he knows that the driver has no licence or insurance, he is a party to the offence of driving without a licence or insurance. If you help to pull a friend's car out of the ditch so as to put it on the road again, after noticing that it is decrepit to the point of illegality, you too will become a criminal by reason of your friendly act. A barman who supplies a customer till he is "over the limit," knowing that he intends to drive home, becomes an accessory to driving with excess alcohol. (We have already noticed this problem in the last section, in connection with the host at a party.)

But is this all really so? Will not, should not, a point be reached at which the assistance is too minor, or too much a matter of ordinary business or social practice, to be counted?

The fuller facts of the case just mentioned were as follows. The National Coal Board sold a bulk quantity of coal. A carrier's lorry was sent to fetch part of it; the lorry was loaded with a quantity of coal, and the NCB's weighbridge clerk (whose task was simply to find how much coal had been loaded in order to charge for it) then discovered that the load was in excess of what was allowed to be carried in the lorry on the highway. At that point he could have insisted that the lorry be relieved of sufficient coal to make it law-abiding. But all he did was to call the attention of the driver to the overload. The driver said he would risk it, and the clerk handed him the weighbridge ticket (this act passing the ownership of the coal to the

---

[1] [1959] 1 QB 11.

buyer), and allowed him to drive away with his load. It was held that the weighbridge operator, and through him the National Coal Board as his employer, became a party to the offence of driving the lorry when overweight.

The decision proceeded solely on the fact that the clerk knew of the intended offence and could have prevented it. The court did not consider the wider implications relating to the proper scope of the law of complicity.

The Board did not contest that they were liable if the clerk was liable, and the decision proceeded solely on the law of complicity. It has since become clear that the conviction of the Board was wrong, because it did not know of the offence.[2] This does not affect the decision on the question of the clerk's liability.

The argument in favour of the decision is that the clerk knowingly assisted in the commission of the offence. The offence could not have been committed without an excessive load, and the clerk knowingly allowed that excessive load to be carried. He contributed *more* to the offence than a person who lends a gun for a robbery contributes to the robbery, because a robbery can be committed without a gun, but a lorry cannot be driven overweight without an excessive load.

But the clerk's job was to weigh the coal for his employer's purposes, and he simply did this job. He did nothing exceptional or unusual to assist the offence. He was under no duty to investigate what load the lorry was permitted to carry. It was a pure accident, presumably, that he happened to know what this weight was. He called the driver's attention to the overloading as a good citizen, leaving the decision whether to commit an offence to him. It seems a strong thing to hold that a man who is simply pursuing his ordinary and lawful vocation, and takes no special steps to assist illegalities, becomes involved as a party to a crime committed by the customer merely because he realises that his customer will be enabled by what he himself does to commit such a crime.

The decision was a turning-point in the law of complicity. The dissenting judgment of Slade J shows that it was still possible at that date to hold the opinion that the prosecution had to prove that the abettor intended to aid the offence. Slade J read this as meaning that the abettor must act "with the motive of endorsing the commission of the offence." Lord Goddard CJ took the opposite view, quoting authority for holding that "if he knew all the circumstances and the circumstances constituted the offence . . . that was enough to to convict him of being an aider and abettor." The third member of the court, Devlin J (as he then was), held the balance between these two opposites with a judgment of unwonted indecision. He sided with Slade J in requiring not merely knowledge on the part of the abettor but an intent to aid, and said expressly that "proof that the article was knowingly supplied is not conclusive evidence of intent to aid." But then he turned over to the side of the Chief Justice by invoking the tired maxim that "*prima facie* a man is presumed to intend the natural and probable consequences of his acts." Since the consequence of supplying essential material was that assistance was given to the criminal, and the clerk had not given evidence of his real intention, he thought that the presumption stood and was enough to justify the verdict. We are left in the dark about what the outcome would have been if the clerk had given evidence. Devlin J did not suggest what the clerk could have said about his "real intention" that would have rebutted the supposed presumption. The only hint we have is Devlin J's statement that if it had been shown that the clerk was confused about the legal position and thought he was not entitled to withhold the weight ticket, he would not have been liable, since he would then have no intention to aid. In effect this allows a defence of claim of right or mistake as to the civil law. Apart from this point, the *NCB* case is theoretically inconclusive; but it is generally taken to settle that mere knowledge of the facts is enough to make aiding a crime itself criminal; and this is also borne out by other decisions.

Somewhat similar to the decision in *NCB* v. *Gamble* is the holding in another case that a criminal offence of offering contraband for sale is abetted by a publisher who publishes an advertisement of the offer for

---

[2] § .12 at n. 6.

sale.[3] The publisher has no interest in the commission of the crime, and merely accepts the advertisement as one of thousands of others that he publishes. But he knowingly assists in the offer for sale, and his assistance is much more positive than that given by the clerk in *NCB* v. *Gamble*, which amounted to little more than a failure to prevent the lorry from being driven away with its excess load.

In these cases it can at least be said that the defendant was directly implicated in the offence. In *NCB* v. *Gamble* the offending load was to be driven directly away from the defendants' premises. But suppose a person supplies goods or services in the ordinary course of his business, knowing that after they are supplied they will help the customer in some illegal activity, but the supplier does not adjust them to any special criminal requirements or charge an additional price to compensate for legal risks. The supplier knows that if he refuses to make the supply it will be obtained from some competitor (who may not know the facts as he does). There is no English authority for exempting the supplier, but well-known American cases do so. One case, for example, concerned a sugar retailer who made a normal sale to persons who he knew would use it for the illegal distillation of spirits. These cases exculpate the supplier from liability for both conspiracy and complicity.[4]

The difficulty is to formulate a satisfactory rule of exemption. One writer suggests that the defendant, to be liable, "must in some sense promote their venture himself, make it his own, have a stake in its outcome."[5] (As applied to English law the last phrase is inconsistent with the advertisement cases). The supplier must, in a different phrase, "intend to further the illegal activity;" but again this is too stringent a test for English law. (The supplier of a murder weapon may not care whether it is used for murder or not, but he would certainly be implicated if he knew the purpose.) The other suggested phrases do not sufficiently identify the activity that is to be regarded as criminal.

So it would seem that the only possible ground of exemption is that the defendant was acting in the ordinary course of a lawful business. If Parliament wishes to make exceptions from this exemption it should do so expressly, and there are instances where it has assumed the responsibility. There are statutory controls over the publication of advertisements[6] and the letting of premises to be used as brothels.[7]

The difficulty of the problem would be reduced if the grip of the criminal law were relaxed in respect of summary offences. Parliament decided in 1981 to keep summary offences out of the law of criminal attempts,[8] and there are equally strong arguments for removing them from the law of complicity.

§ 15.6. ACTS DONE UNDER LEGAL DUTY

It should need no demonstration that an act done in fulfilment of legal duty cannot be a crime. But this is an unreliable defence for a person charged

---

[3] *De Marny* [1907] 1 KB 388; cp. *Poultry World Ltd* v. *Conder* [1957] Crim.LR 803; *Ladbrokes Ltd.* v. *Perrett* [1971] 1 WLR 110.

[4] See *The General Part*, 2nd edn 378–379; Smith and Hogan, 4th edn 120–122.

[5] Fletcher, *Rethinking Criminal Law* 675.

[6] The publication of obscene advertisements is an offence under the Indecent Advertisements Act 1889 s.3.

[7] Sexual Offences Act 1956 s.35(3). By "wilfully" the Act seems to mean "knowingly." Such a landlord, if male, is also guilty, by judicial construction, of the statutory offence of being a male person living on the earnings of prostitution, but this is so, it seems, only if the premises are let exclusively for prostitution, and not for residence by the prostitute—unless, perhaps, the rent is exorbitant for such accommodation. See *Thomas* [1957] 1 WLR 747, 2 All ER 342 n., 121 JP 338, 41 CAR 121, as explained by Viscount Simonds in *Shaw* [1962] AC at 265–266.

[8] Criminal Attempts Act 1981 s.1.

as accessory, because the court can so easily nullify it by holding that there is no legal duty to participate in a crime. We are faced with two opposing arguments, each of them circular.

The law compels the performance of this duty; therefore doing it cannot be a crime.
To do this would be a crime; therefore doing it cannot be a legal duty.

The question has arisen when a person returns an article that he has been keeping for the owner, knowing that the owner means to commit a crime with it. It can also arise in other cases, as when a person who has sold a thing comes to realise after the sale and before delivery that the buyer has a criminal purpose. The cases are in a difficult state, but it may be said with some assurance that a person will not be an accomplice if he acts in the belief (correctly or otherwise) that he is bound by law to deliver the article, or if he is uncertain as to the legal position. If he believes that he is not bound to deliver the article, or has no opinion one way or the other, but nevertheless delivers it, he will very likely be made liable by a court of first instance, though the matter requires further consideration at a higher level.

The first case of importance on the subject is the jemmy case, *Lomas*.[1]

> Lomas had borrowed a jemmy from a burglar. He returned it to the burglar on request, thus restoring the *status quo ante*. He was held not to be implicated in a burglary subsequently committed with it.

There have been doubts as to the basis of the decision. Devlin J approved it in *NCB* v. *Gamble*[2] on the ground that (i) the owner had the right to demand his article back and (ii) Lomas in giving it back was not doing anything positive; he was simply refraining from using force to keep the article, which was only a "negative act," i.e. an omission. This was a broad-minded construction of the facts, since the verdict stated that Lomas handed the jemmy back to its owner—he did not merely permit the owner to retake it. As for the owner's right to demand his article back, Devlin J recognised that Lomas would have the right to detain the article forcibly "in the case of felony," apparently without noticing that burglary, the crime in question, *was* a felony. Although the special rules for felonies are now abolished, the Criminal Law Act 1967 section 3(1) allows the use of force in the prevention of crime (§ 22.6), which would presumably cover Lomas.[3] It is not clear from the judgment whether Devlin J put the main weight of his approval of the decision on the supposed fact that Lomas was bound the give the jemmy back (which the judge's own remarks contradicted) or on the fact that giving it back was regarded as being in substance a mere omission.

---

[1] (1913) 9 CAR 220, 78 JP 152, 23 Cox 765, 110 LT 239, 30 TLR 125. The headnote clearly misrepresents the decision. See generally the remarks in *Bullock* [1955] 1 WLR 1, 1 All ER 15, 38 CAR 151, and Smith in [1972B] CLJ 208–211; Smith and Hogan, 4th edn 124.

[2] [1959] 1 QB at 20 (where the words "former" and "latter" are inadvertently transposed).

[3] S. 3 in terms merely allows the use of force, and there is no indication that Lomas needed to use force; perhaps the lender did not know where his jemmy was. But presumably the right to detain a criminal article peaceably follows *a fortiori* from the right to use force to retain it.

Whatever the civil law may say on the duty or otherwise to give back property intended to be used for crime, Devlin J's instinct was surely right in approving the outcome of *Lomas*. It would be too severe to treat as an accessory a man who has done nothing to encourage the crime and whose only act of helping is to return property to its owner.

Lomas concerned a planned burglary, a serious crime. Even if the decision had been the other way, on the ground that Lomas had a right to detain a burglarious tool and should have exercised that right, it may be doubted whether there is a right to detain property from its owner in order to prevent him from committing a minor offence (withholding the key of his car because he is proposing to commit a parking offence, or because it is known that he always exceeds speed limits).

Unfortunately, the law was thrown into further doubt by the decision in *Garrett* v. *Arthur Churchill (Glass) Ltd.*[4]

> It was there held that when an agent who had bought a goblet for his principal handed it to his principal, the owner, at the latter's request on the termination of his agency, knowing that the owner intended to export it illegally, the (former) agent was not bound to hand it over for the illegal purpose, and was therefore himself guilty of being "knowingly concerned in the exportation of goods" with intent to evade a prohibition (a statutory offence) if by returning it he "lent himself to the idea of exporting it without the necessary documents." This was not a case of accessoryship, but the principle involved would appcar to have been the same. *Lomas* was not considered.

The meaning of the figurative phrase about "lending himself to the idea" was not analysed, and may involve the court in a delicate enquiry as to the defendant's motives. It seems that when the owner demanded the transfer of his goblet he had not at that time committed any offence. If the agent is entitled to detain the owner's property because he knows (or thinks he knows) that the owner intends to commit an illegality with it, for how long is he entitled to do so? If the owner assures him that he has now changed his mind, can he safely accept the assurance? Who pays for the insurance of the article while it is detained? What steps can the agent take to protect himself from an action in tort by the owner? To none of these questions did the court address itself in the goblet case.

A point made at the beginning of this discussion was that a person is not an accomplice if he believes that he is legally bound to do what he does. As was observed in the last section, this opinion was held by Devlin J in the *NCB* case.[5] Indeed, the judge's words may be taken to mean that the clerk's *doubt* as to the legal position would have been sufficient to justify him in refraining from taking strong action, and this would be common sense.

Much the same point appears from *Garrett's* case, where the justices were asked to decide the question of intent in the following terms. "Did he then only hand over because he felt that he had to as his agency was terminated, or did he at that stage lend himself to the idea of exporting this without the necessary documents?" The formula perhaps suggests that the

---

[4] [1970] 1 QB 92.

[5] [1959] 1 QB at 25. See further, on mistake as to the civil law, § 20.4.

defendant would be deemed to "lend himself to the idea" of illegality unless he believed that it was his duty to return the goblet.

Most people are hazy as to the law. (The courts themselves are hazy as to this point of law.) Suppose the buying agent says, when charged: "I had no idea as to the law, but I handed over the goblet because that was my business obligation" (or, "my moral obligation"). Should not that also be a defence? Or suppose he says: "I thought that perhaps I could have handed it to the police, or just detained it; but I don't agree with all these export restrictions." If the one defence is good and the other bad, does not this involve the criminal court going into the difficult question of the defendant's motive?

In short, the sensible rule would be that when a person acts in pursuance of either a legal duty (or what would be a legal duty if it were not for the law of complicity) or of a moral or business obligation, he should not be accounted an accomplice. If any exceptions are to be made from this principle because of the gravity of the crime they should be made by express legislation.

§ 15.7. WHEN AN OMISSION CAN BE HELP

The weighbridge clerk in *NCB* v. *Gamble* did a positive act: he handed over the ticket, which (the court held) gave the lorry driver a clearance. It seems plain from the judgments that if the clerk had done nothing at all, he would not have been liable. A person does not become an accessory merely by failing to prevent an offence; I am not my brother's keeper. This is so however morally culpable the defendant was. "It is no criminal offence to stand by, a mere passive spectator of a crime, even of murder."[1]

But may not a man's presence at the scene of a crime sometimes amount to an encouragement of the crime?

If a person, knowing that an offence is going to be commited, arranges with the intending perpetrator to be present, this will almost inevitably be construed as an encouragement. The question for the jury presumably is whether, by agreeing to be present, the defendant encouraged the perpetrator in the act and knew that he was giving this encouragement.[2]

Where there is no arrangement, presence should not generally be enough, even though the defendant went to the scene of the offence out of curiosity or otherwise. For he does not intend to encourage the offence, and generally has no reason to suppose that his mere presence encourages it.

In *Clarkson*[3] two men were charged as accessories to rape. They heard

---

[1] *Per* Hawkins J. in *Coney*, 8 QBD at 557–558. In *Allan* [1965] 1 QB 130 it was held that an onlooker's intention to join in an affray if his help were needed did not make him a party to the affray. Cp. *Smith* v. *Baker* [1972] Crim.LR 25 (remaining in car believed to be stolen).

[2] *C* v. *Hume* [1979] Crim.LR 328 is an indulgent decision, in respect of the charge of taking the vehicle. Had the defendant been older the conviction would surely have been upheld.

[3] [1971] 1 WLR 1402, 3 All ER 344.

> indications that a woman was being raped in another room, and they entered it and remained while the offence was committed. It was held by the Courts-Martial Appeal Court that the defendants could not be convicted if they had merely entered the room as voyeurs. To be guilty, they must have intended to encourage the act of rape, and have given actual encouragement. Since the direction was unsatisfactory on this, the conviction was quashed. So far the decision is to be welcomed; but at the end of its judgment the court said: "While we have no doubt that those inferences [as to encouragement] could properly have been drawn in respect of each defendant, so that verdicts of guilty could properly have been returned, we cannot say that the court-martial, properly directed, would necessarily have drawn those inferences."

On the facts reported it is diffcult to see what evidence there was before the court on which an inference of encouragement could properly have been founded.

But if a person deliberately goes to watch a crime being committed, isn't that evidence of encouragement?

It is very easy to slip from the proposition that A is evidence of B to the proposition that you only have to prove A to prove B. That merely creates a legal fiction that A = B. To constitute encouragement in these circumstances, for the purpose of complicity, the court should be satisfied both that the defendant intended to encourage the crime and that the perpetrator realised he had an approving audience. In any case, it may be doubted whether liability for a crime should be extended to mere spectators, whether they express approval of it or not. (See § .8.)

What if a person who is supposed to be in control of a situation neglects to prevent an offence by someone under his authority? Does the controller become an accomplice?

Yes, at least sometimes. This rule is particularly applied against the owner of a car who allows himself to be driven in an illegal manner, whether by his employee or by someone else: ownership is assumed to give sufficient control to entail responsibility.

> In *Du Cros* v. *Lambourne*,[4] the owner of a car who sat beside the driver was convicted of abetting him in driving at a dangerous speed, although there was no evidence of positive encouragement.
>
> Again, the supervisor of a learner-driver is assumed by reason of his position to have authority to control the learner, and can be convicted as accessory to the learner's traffic offences if he knowingly fails to take steps to do so.[5]

So if the car you drive happens to be in the name of your rich mother-in-law who is sitting in the back seat and cannot drive, she becomes responsible to try to control your driving?

In *Du Cros* v. *Lambourne* the owner was sitting in front, but the

---

[4] [1907] 1 KB 40. See on the whole subject of complicity in driving Lanham in [982] Crim.LR 419.

[5] *Harris* [1964] Crim.LR 54; *Carter* v. *Richardson* [1974] RTR 314, Crim.LR 190; Wasik in [1982] Crim.LR 415.

question is not where the owner is sitting but whether he or she knows that facts constituting offences are occurring or are about to occur.

It looks as though that is encouraging "back-seat driving"

Passengers in a car, even owner-passengers, are normally justified in leaving the driver to make decisions. The proposition seems to be that if the dangerous driving or other breach of law comes to the knowledge of the owner-passenger he must protest.

What about a passenger who is not the owner?

If he is the possessor of the car (e.g. a hirer) he is in the same position as the owner. If he is a mere passenger he has no right to control the driver and would not normally be liable. The responsibility for driving rests on the driver, and no social purpose is served by punishing the passengers. (It may be said that the argument based on social purpose applies equally where the passenger happens to be the owner.[6]) However, the passenger may be convicted where it can be inferred that he and the driver had set out with the intention of proceeding in a dangerous manner, or otherwise illegally.[7]

Suppose you find that you are being driven by someone who is the worse for drink?

The same principles apply. Normally you would not be liable,[8] but you might be if you were the owner of the car,[9] or if you had been drinking with the driver and so encouraging him to drink excessively before driving.[10]

The common law rarely pursues an undeviating course, and the stringent rule applied in the foregoing cases may now be qualified by the decision in *Cassady* v. *Reg. Morris (Transport) Ltd.*[11]; where it was held that an employer's failure to forbid an offence by his employee was evidence, but only evidence, of encouragement by the employer. Consequently, if on a summary charge the justices find that there was no encouragement or assistance the employer must be acquitted; and the rule was applied notwithstanding that the principal offence was one of omission.

This is certainly the right rule, but the appellate courts have failed to give any clear guidance on what is required, beyond the non-control, to constitute encouragement. The driving cases do not suggest that the owner's liability depends upon anything more than the fictitious

---

[6] See the remarks made upon *Du Cros* v. *Lambourne* in *Dennis* v. *Pight* (1968) 11 FLR 458 (Sup.Ct. of Australian Capital Territory).

[7] Cp. *Baldessare* (1930) 22 CAR 70, 29 Cox 193, 144 LT 185: two took a car unlawfully for "joy-riding," and a death was caused: both driver and passenger were convicted of manslaughter. But the fact that the car was taken unlawfully should not have been regarded as relevant. For evidence of association between driver and passengers in taking a car unlawfully see *Ross* v. *Rivenall* [1959] 2 All ER 376.

[8] Cp. *Smith* v. *Baker* [1971] RTR 350; *D (an infant)* v. *Parsons* [1960] 2 All ER 493 (a "joyriding" case). Parliament subsequently made express provision to bring in the passenger of a "joyrider:" § 29.9 n. 1b).

[9] Cp. *Tinsley* [1963] Crim.LR 520.

[10] Where two intoxicated persons set out in a car, each driving at different times, and killed a man, it was held in Manitoba that both could be convicted of criminal negligence causing the death, whichever of them was driving at the time of the accident: *Lachance* [1962] 132 CCC 202, 37 CR 65.

[11] [1975] Crim.LR 398.

encouragement held to result from non-control. At all events, it can be assumed that the person who has the right of control need do no more than is reasonable. The owner-passenger in a car must protest against illegality in driving, but is presumably not expected to require the car to be stopped so that he can get out and walk, if it would be unreasonable to expect this of him (as it usually would be).

The rule that a person who has some special legal right to stop an offence is an accessory on the ground of real or fictitious encouragement if he does not take reasonable steps to stop it is applied against a publican who fails to take steps to eject a customer at closing time. Owing to a quirk of legislative drafting, it is only the dilatory customer who perpetrates the offence of late drinking, but the courts use the law of complicity to bring in the publican as accessory, since the pub is his (or he is in control of it).[12] So, would a landowner be accessory to murder if he fails to try to eject a would-be murderer as a trespasser? Could Clarkson have been convicted of rape if he had owned the premises in which the rape was committed? If you find that your guest is in possession of cannabis, do you become an accessory to his possession if you do not endeavour to persuade him to flush it down the toilet? (An occupier is guilty of a statutory offence if he allows his premises to be used for smoking cannabis,[13] but that is a special offence and does not make him an accomplice in the illegality.)

The decision in the *Morris Transport* case puts the law on a better footing than previously, but it is doubtful whether it can be reconciled with the other cases, and to what extent it will be followed. At the same time, the decision is to be welcomed in point of policy. The Law Commission Working Party thought that it ought to be put on a statutory footing in the following words.

> "A person who is in a position to prevent an offence, because he is in control of property or for some other reason, is not to be taken to be an accessory merely because he fails to prevent an offence."[14]

If that were the law, Parliament would have to make special provision whenever it wished to make a person liable for not preventing an offence.

And would not that be a desirable state of affairs? In fact, Parliament already takes this responsibility in respect of certain offences, by creating the offences of "permitting" or "suffering" or "allowing" other offences, which we have already studied (§ 6.4). A person convicted of permitting, etc, does not become a party to the offence permitted: his liability is a distinct one.

The courts have left open the question whether the inclusion in legislation of an offence of permitting impliedly excludes the law as to accessoryship in relation to the permitter.[15] In

---

[12] *Tuck* v. *Robson* [1970] 1 WLR 741, 1 All ER 1171.

[13] Misuse of Drugs Act 1971 s.8. Curiously, the section does not extend to occupiers who permit their premises to be used for the injection of heroin, or for any other consumption of a controlled drug except the smoking of cannabis, cannabis resin or prepared opium.

[14] For a contrary view on policy see Lanham, *op. cit.* n. 4 above.

[15] *Carmichael & Sons (Worcester) Ltd.* v. *Cottle* [1971] RTR 11, Crim.LR 45; cp. *Crawford* v. *Haughton* [1972] 1 WLR 572, 1 All ER 535.

other words, is the only possible charge one of permitting, or can the permitter in a suitable case be charged also as accessory? The reasonable answer is that the permitting offences merely extend liability to people who are inactive, and do not exclude the application of the ordinary law of complicity to those who are active.

§ 15.8. PERFORMANCES WITH SPECTATORS

Few performances with spectators are illegal. The most likely instance of illegality is an obscene performance, which is primarily the responsibility of the producer and performers. The question arises whether members of the audience are liable as accessories if they knew the nature of the performance beforehand. This is not a case of mere omission, since the spectators would have knowingly come. Nor is it a case where the illegality would take place independently of the audience. There would be no spectacle if there were no spectators (whether the spectators pay for admission or not). It may therefore seem logical to hold that the spectators are accomplices, just as one who knowingly buys from an illegal seller is an accomplice in the sale (§ .4 n. 4). Evidence of acts of encouragement during the performance would not, on this view, be necessary for liability, since in the nature of the case the mere presence of the audience is not only an encouragement but a determining factor.

But this conclusion involves absurdities. A law that seems to require or at any rate to allow the police to charge hundreds or even thousands of people as spectators of an event, or as an audience at a seditious lecture, would be unworkable. Moreover, each individual member of the audience may quite reasonably feel that the show does not depend on him; if he does not attend, many others will, and it will still take place. Some members of the audience may attend disapprovingly, to satisfy themselves of the full heinousness of what is being done, or perhaps to get evidence for a prosecution. If attendance at a seditious lecture involves the audience, than buying a seditious publication would involve the purchaser. The conclusion is intolerable. So the only wise course for the courts is to rule that, as a matter of law, members of the audience are not accomplices by reason of being there, and that neither payment nor applause by them makes them accomplices.

The courts have not gone as far as this, but the law is not altogether clear. The position is said to be that a spectator does not become an accessory merely by being present with knowledge of what is proceeding[1]; but, as already noticed, the clarity of this rule is marred by judicial expressions of willingness to accept presence as "evidence" of encouragement.[2] In one case it was suggested that spectators of an illegal prize fight would become implicated if they applauded.[3] But the point awaits final determination; and it may be strongly doubted whether either

---

[1] *Coney* (1882) 8 QBD 534; *Clarkson* § .7 at n. 3.

[2] See § .7. In *Wilcox* v. *Jeffery* [1951] 1 All ER 464 there was evidence beyond that of mere attendance; see *The General Part*, 2nd edn 359.

[3] *Coney*, n. 1 above, at p. 557 ("actions intended to signify approval").

applause or laughter by a spectator ought to be taken as extending liability beyond those who put on the performance, however disgusting the affair may be to the right-minded citizen.

This is another example of a point that has already been emerging in this chapter, that the logic of accessoryship can be pressed too far. It is not a head of liability that should be applied blindly. Some curtailment is necessary if the law is to be kept within reasonable limits.[4]

§ 15.9. THE SCOPE OF THE CONTEMPLATED PURPOSE

A person charged as accessory is responsible only for crimes committed within his own purpose, or within the purpose of the perpetrator of which he has knowledge, and a question on this should always (in case of doubt) be left to the jury, whether the defendant has raised the point or not.[1] Something was said on the contemplated purpose in § .4, but further problems remain.

Granted that as a general rule the defendant charged as accessory must have known what the crook was crooking, so to speak, the facts of the case may show that he had only a misty idea of what was in the perpetrator's mind. To what extent does this afford him a defence?

For many years the courts said that the accessory must know the facts, or that what is done must be part of the common purpose. But the rule is now qualified: where a person assists (or incites) another in a criminal purpose, it is enough that that he knows that the crime in contemplation would be one of a certain range. He is then an accessory to whichever crime within the range was actually in the perpetrator's mind. This was established by the House of Lords in *Maxwell*.[2]

> Maxwell was told to drive a car to an inn. He was a member of a terrorist organisation and knew that he was to act as a guide to others who would follow him in another car and who would attack either the inn or the people inside or would make some other terrorist attack in the vicinity; and he knew that the following car would contain weapons. Apparently he did not know whether the attack would be by means of guns or by planting a bomb or by starting a fire or otherwise. The men in the following car placed a bomb in the inn. The House of Lords held that Maxwell was rightly convicted as accessory to an offence under the Explosive Substances Act 1883 of doing an act with intent to cause an explosion likely to endanger life or cause serious injury to property (section 3(*a*)), and to an offence of being in possession of a bomb with the same intent (section 3(*b*)).

It could hardly be said that Maxwell *intended* to cause an explosion, because he did not know for sure that that was the plan of the people he

---

[4] A technical reason for exempting spectators may sometimes be found by attaching a particular construction to the statute under which they are charged. Cp. § .15 at n. 14. But the question should also be dealt with by a suitable refinement of the law of complicity.

[1] *Lovesey* [1970] 1 QB 356E.
[2] [1978] 1 WLR 1350, 3 All ER 1140, 68 CAR 142.

was helping. For all he knew, the plan might have been to start a fire with a few cans of petrol. But it was enough, to convict him as accessory, that he knew that causing an explosion ranked among the possible plans of his confederates. Knowledge of the perpetrator's intent *or possible intent* is sufficient, without having the intent yourself. Similarly, on the charge of being an accessory to possession, knowledge of the possibility of the perpetrator's possession is sufficient.

The conviction seemed anomalous on its face because the prosecution had charged Maxwell as perpetrator, and their lordships pointed out the undesirability of doing this when the defendant was clearly an accessory.

Maxwell demonstrates that the so-called "common purpose" rule is not to be read narrowly. Maxwell was a very subordinate member of the gang and left it to his companions to decide which crime was to be committed. It is now clear that if D1 and D2 set out to rob, and D2 knows that D1 *may* be carrying a gun and *may* use it, D2 will an accomplice in an offence committed by D1 with the gun, if it is in the course of the robbery or of escaping afterwards. Again, if D2 lends cutting equipment to D1, and under cross-examination admits that he knew it was intended to be used for some dishonest acquisition of property, it is open to the jury to find that the range of acquisitive offences (theft, robbery, burglary, handling) came within his contemplation, even though he did not sit down and work them all out.[3]

If the foregoing reasoning is correct, it is a mistake to suppose that *Maxwell* extends liability to the accessory only when the accessory contemplated that a crime of some definite "type" would be committed. The majority opinions in the Lords are not limited in this way. All that they require is that the crime should be one of those in the defendant's contemplation. Of course, when the defendant does not know the precise crime it is likely that he will expect it to belong to some particular genus, e.g. "terrorist crime" or "profitable fraud." But not necessarily so: the range of crimes in his mind as possibilities may include an assortment resulting from his past experience of what the perpetrator is accustomed to do.

In these cases the accessory doesn't write a completely blank cheque. The crimes in his contemplation are supposed to be limited in some way. What if all that the alleged accessory knew was that shady work was afoot?

The answer is unclear.

> In *Scott*[4] the defendant opened a bank account in a bogus name on behalf of two men. She knew that something illegal was going on. In fact the men were illegally importing cannabis. It was held that the defendant was not a party to a conspiracy to import cannabis.

Presumably the court would have held that she was not an accomplice either; but the decision looks indulgent. Suppose that under cross-examination the defendant admitted that "something illegal" included the importation of drugs, as a purpose within the range of what her associates might do. It is difficult to see why she should not be inculpated.[5] If so, the

---

[3] *Maxwell* overrules *Bainbridge* § .4 n. 2 on this point.

[4] (1978) 68 CAR 164. *Contra*, *Thambiah* § .4 n. 1, where it was assumed that the defendant knew that "some profitable fraud" was projected, and this made her an accessory to forgery. She might have been held, more broadly, to have contemplated that some profitable non-violent illegality was in the air (e.g. smuggling cannabis); indeed, any profitable illegality might have been furthered by the help she gave.

[5] In *Patel* [1970] Crim.LR 274 it was held that the defendant's intention to assist another in his possession of a bag, whatever its contents might be, did not make him guilty as accessory to the possession of cannabis, which the bag in fact contained. Knowledge that the bag contained a controlled drug was necessary. It would seem that since *Maxwell*, if it is proved that the defendant intended to assist in the possession of any contents, legal or illegal, this would be sufficient for a conviction.

defendant should be liable as accessory without express admission (and should be liable for conspiracy too), if the jury can conclude from the evidence that the offence was one of the types of illegality that may fairly be taken as having been within the defendant's contemplation. If the associates had been planning to murder and rob, this might well be outside the range of illegality in the defendant's contemplation.[6]

Couldn't accessorial liability be extended also to a case where the offence committed is very similar to that contemplated? D2 supplies D1 with cutting tools thinking D1 means to use them to cut into a safe that has already been stolen by someone else. In fact they are used for another burglary. The two crimes are similar in that both involve dishonesty in relation to property. Shouldn't D2 be regarded as an accomplice?

If liability is extended by consideration of whether crime A is like crime B, we lack any firm limit to the rule. Polonius readily gave his assent to several successive propositions: that the same cloud was very like a camel, a weasel and a whale. Similarity is in the eye of the beholder.

The opinions delivered by three of the five lords in *Maxwell* (Edmund-Davies, Fraser and Scarman) are perfectly clear on this. All three agree that the question, and the only question, is the range of the defendant's contemplation.[7] All three referred with approval to the judgment of Lowry CJ in the court below, where he said:

> "The situation has something in common with that of two persons who agree to rob a bank on the understanding, either express or implied from conduct (such as the carrying of a loaded gun by one person with the knowledge of the other), that violence *may* be resorted to. The accomplice knows, not that the principal *will* shoot the cashier, but that he may do so; and, if the principal does shoot him, the accomplice will be guilty of murder. A different case is where the accomplice has only one offence A in contemplation and the principal commits offence B. Here the accomplice . . . is not guilty of aiding and abetting offence B. . . . The relevant crime must be within the contemplation of the accomplice and only exceptionally would evidence be found to support the allegation that the accomplice had given the principal a completely blank cheque."

Similarly Lord Fraser said of the defendant in the particular case:

> "The possible extent of his guilt was limited to the range of crimes any of which he must have known were to be expected that night. . . . If another member of the gang had committed some crime that the appellant had no reason to expect, such as perhaps throwing poison gas into the inn, the appellant would not have been guilty of using poison gas."

By "had no reason to expect" his lordship evidently meant "cannot be inferred to have expected."[8]

Unfortunately, the speeches of Viscount Dilhorne and Lord Hailsham are less precise.

---

[6] Ashworth in *Crime, Proof and Punishment*, ed. Tapper (London 1981) 66,70 suggests that even since *Maxwell* "a general criminal intent remains insufficient." No doubt a tribunal would be slow to find that the defendant assented in advance to absolutely every possible crime. But this only means that it is a question of evidence and common sense, not of fixed law. Cp. Lowry CJ, quoted below.

[7] Their lordships spoke sometimes of the defendant's contemplation, sometimes of his knowledge, but it is plain that no distinction was intended.

[8] It may be suggested that in the case of incitement, where the perpetrator's departure from the plan is merely in the manner of execution, the inciter may be liable if the perpetrator thought that he was carrying out the inciter's purpose. See later. This rider is inapplicable to accessoryship by helping if, as in *Maxwell*, the perpetrator is the dominating criminal and has no intention of trying to act within the alleged accessory's purpose. Even so, Lord Fraser's example of an act outside the purpose is unconvincing. Terrorism involves the commission of dreadful crimes, chosen for their dreadfulness, and murder by poison gas, although not usually undertaken by terrorists, is not outside their general purpose.

They need not be examined in detail, because if there is any conflict between them and the three majority lords, the latter are clearly the superior authority.

Maxwell knew that some crime was going to be committed, and was merely uncertain which it would be. The same principle must, however, apply where the defendant is uncertain whether the other person intends to commit a particular crime or intends a lawful act such as giving someone a warning.

A historical note will assist understanding of the previous case-law. The requirement of knowledge by the accessory was developed by the courts principally in the "common purpose" rule, it being said that the accessory is not responsible for an act going beyond the "common purpose." This way of putting the matter is doubly misleading.

1 It suggests that the accessory is liable for an act within the common purpose. This is correct if the act is fully within the common purpose, but an accessory is not liable for the use of unagreed means towards the common purpose, which means themselves amount to the crime charged. Two robbers agree that they will use slight force but will not use a weapon. If one of them uses a weapon in committing the robbery, both are liable for the *robbery*, but the one who did not use the weapon is not liable for inflicting injury even though, as it turned out, the infliction of the injury was the only way of successfully carrying out the robbery. A person is not liable as accessory merely because the crime serves the general aim.
2 It suggests that there must be a common purpose. In the typical case of two or more persons going out to rob there may be said to be a common purpose to rob. But when one rogue lends another a gun for the commission of a robbery, the lender not intending to take any other part or to share the proceeds, talk of common purpose is hardly apt. The lender may be indifferent to the question whether robbery is committed or not, or devoutly hope that it will not be, but he knows of the plan and that makes him an accessory.

For these reasons, and particularly since the decision in *Maxwell*, it is desirable to avoid the expression *common* purpose, and to speak instead of the contemplation *of the alleged accessory*.

The practical problems that arise relate to evidence. Wrongdoers are not likely to admit what their contemplation was; and indeed they may not have clearly envisaged what might be done. In practice, the tribunal of fact (whether jury or magistrates) is forced to draw common-sense inferences from the events proved. If two criminals both use force in committing a crime, the jury will readily infer, and be allowed to infer, that both had agreed to use this force, so that each will be responsible for the force used by the other. The same will apply if they both use force in trying to escape after the crime. But this is so only if the acts of force are roughly commensurate. If D2 uses mild force, and his companion D1 unexpectedly uses great force (as, by using a gun which D2 did not know him to be carrying), D1's conduct may be regarded as going beyond the inferred common purpose.[9]

If the evidence shows that D2 knew that D1 was carrying the weapon, the inference will be almost irresistible that the use of the weapon was contemplated by D2.[10] However, it is not a fixed rule of law that D2 must be convicted in these circumstances. If D2 can convince the jury (or convince them of the reasonable possibility) that, although he knew that D1 was carrying a gun, he thought that this was merely a matter of habit, or underworld prestige, or of defence against a rival gang, and did not know of D's intention to use it on this occasion against this victim, he will not be a party to such use.[11] There is merely a common sense inference that criminals who carry weapons do so for a purpose, and that an accomplice who knows that the weapon is carried also knows the purpose. The inference should not be drawn if the evidence excludes it.

---

[9] *Morris* [1966] 2 QB 110.
[10] See *Smith* [1963] 1 WLR 1200, 3 All ER 597.
[11] *Per curiam* in *Betty* (1963) 48 CAR 6. Cp. the *Three Soldiers'* case (1697), Foster's *Crown Law* 353.

The upshot seems to be, in this type of case, that D2 is liable for force used by D1 if D2 intended such force to be used or knew for certain that D1 would use such force in pursuance of his known purpose or would use it if the circumstances seemed to him to require it. D2 is not liable if he believed that D1 would not use such force or if the use of such force was specifically excluded by agreement between them (even though, in the latter case, D2 realised that D1, being an unreliable person, might possibly use it).

It is common practice for only one of a gang of robbers to carry a gun, the others being armed with coshes, pickhandles or ammonia. Suppose that the gun-carrier uses the weapon to kill or inflict harm. The others say that they thought that the gun would be used only to frighten. Assuming that the jury credit the defence, what is the position?

If the gunman used the gun intentionally, that would obviously be outside his purpose as known to his companions (the "common purpose" as it is usually known). The others would be guilty neither of murder nor of manslaughter. If the gunman accidentally shot and killed, when intending only to frighten, he would be liable for manslaughter, both negligent and constructive—the latter because using a loaded gun to frighten was an unlawful act (assault), and everyone would realise the risk of some harm resulting. As we shall see (§ .12 at n. 2), the law of constructive manslaughter applies to accessories as much as it does to the perpetrator, so if they knew that the gun was or might be loaded they will be accessories to manslaughter.

If the gunman, intending to frighten, accidentally caused injury, he is liable under section 47, apparently, since this section creates a degree of strict liability (§ 9.4), but not under section 20 which requires *mens rea* as to causing injury (§ 9.3). The same propositions apply to the other members of the gang. If the use of the gun to frighten was within the contemplated purpose, they are liable (presumably[12]) under section 47 but not section 20.

What if Donald tells Ronald to assault someone, and Ronald goes beyond his instructions and assaults the victim so seriously as to kill him. Ronald is convicted of murder. Donald is not an accessory to murder, but can he be convicted as accessory to assault, or manslaughter?

Yes as to assault. The fact that Ronald has not been convicted of assault is immaterial.[13]

The killing being outside Ronald's known purpose, Donald would not be guilty of manslaughter in respect of it. He has authorised only a non-lethal assault.[14] Whether or not this rule is strictly logical, it is merciful.

To recap very briefly, I understand that a person is liable as accessory for acts that are within the perpetrator's known purpose, and also for consequences of acts within the known purpose that are a matter of strict

---

[12] This on the assumption that the principle of *Creamer* extends to other unintended consequences for which there is strict liability. See § .12 at n.2.

[13] *Lord Mohun* (1692) Holt KB 479, 40 ER 1164.

[14] *Lovesey* [1970] 1 QB at 356F. The headnote to *Betty*, n. 11 above, is misleading, since the killing was there held to be within the common purpose. The killer's accomplice can be implicated in an accidental killing: *Creamer* § .12 n. 2.)

liability. Suppose the perpetrator commits the intended crime in a different way from that intended?

There is little direct English authority, though the question is discussed in the institutional works. The general answer undoubtedly is that the alleged accessory is not responsible for a deliberate change of plan by the perpetrator, but is for his accident or mistake in carrying out the plan.

I don't see why a deliberate change of plan should let the accessary out, if it is still the same crime as he incited or helped. Iago said: "Do it not with poison; strangle her in her bed," and Othello complied. Had Othello, ignoring Iago's advice, used poison to kill Desdemona, that would surely not have exempted Iago from liability as accessory.

The theory of the common law is that the alleged accessory is entitled to delimit the scope of his participation in an intended crime. That is the basis of the "contemplated purpose" rule. If the inciter or helper says: "You may overpower the night watchman and tie him up, but you must not use a weapon or do him serious injury," this means that he is not a party to anything intentionally done against his instructions. Similarly, to take a more horrific example, if the satanic inciter says: "I have insured my wife against a traffic accident, and I want you to see that she falls under a lorry this afternoon," he is on principle not guilty of murder if the assassin then uses a knife. But in your variant of the Othello story the jury would undoubtedly be encouraged to find that the purpose contemplated by Iago (or the purpose understood by Othello to be contemplated by Iago) was merely the killing of Desdemona, and that Iago's remark about the method was merely a matter of tactics which did not delimit the purpose.

It may be suggested, then, that the rule is that the inciter or helper is liable if (1) the crime committed was within his contemplation (putting aside the merely tactical details, as already noticed), or (2) the crime committed was of the same abstract kind as the one contemplated, *and* the perpetrator tried to carry out what he understood to be the alleged accessory's intention.

The second part of the rule may be illustrated as follows. Suppose that in the previous example the instigator did not make it clear that it was important for him that his wife should be killed in that particular way. The perpetrator therefore thought that the instigator merely wanted the victim killed, and thought that the mention of a faked traffic accident was only a suggestion as to the best means. In that case the instigator would presumably remain a party to a murder of the wife committed by some other method.[15]

On the question of other mistakes in carrying out the plan, the Law Commission Working Party expresses the rule as follows.

> "The accessory is liable notwithstanding that the principal makes a mistake as to the identity of the victim or of the property affected by

[15] For a discussion see Lanham in 96 LQR 96 121–123. *Robinson* 1968 (1) SA 666 appears to me to be rightly decided as a case where the perpetrator clearly travelled outside the accessory's contemplated purpose; but Lanham criticises the decision.

the offence, or a mistake as to the victim or property intended by the accessory to be affected."

This is right on principle, because the perpetrator is trying to carry out the offence that was within the accessory's contemplation. But, it may be suggested, the inciter will not be responsible if the perpetrator misunderstands his instructions to the extent of committing a different crime, such as murder instead of burglary.[16]

What about a case of transferred intention?

The Law Commission Working Party proposes a principle similar to that already stated for mistake.

> "The accessory is liable to the same extent as the principal where the intended offence takes effect on an unintended victim or property, unless the principal consciously allows the plan to miscarry."

The last words mean that if the perpetrator deliberately changes the victim, and so acts outside the inciter's contemplation, the inciter is not a party to that crime. So if the inciter gives the perpetrator a gun and tells him to murder the Prime Minister, and the perpetrator shoots his wife's lover instead, the inciter is not a party to this murder.

Why not? The inciter incited a murder, and a murder was committed with the weapon that he supplied.

The fact that you supply an accomplice with a gun with murderous intent does not involve you in every murder the accomplice chooses to commit with the weapon. The inciter does not become involved in a murder merely because he has incited murder in the abstract. He must have incited the particular murder, the factual situation—though he will be responsible for an accidental miscarriage of the plan, and probably for some degree of misunderstanding of the perpetrator, as before explained.

Does this mean that if you incite a burglary, you can get off by saying that they deliberately burgled some house other than the one you instructed?

In acquisitive crimes the judge might encourage the jury to find that the defendant was principally concerned to get money dishonestly, and that some change of plan to suit the circumstances or the opportunity was within his contemplation. Whether this inference can be drawn as a matter of common sense depends upon the facts. Alternatively, it may be suggested, the defendant is liable if the crime committed is the same in the abstract as the one contemplated, and the perpetrator believed that he was acting within the inciter's intention.[17]

---

[16] For another treatment see Lanham in 96 LQR 117–119.

[17] The general question is discussed by Lanham in 96 LQR 123–124. He puts the case of D2 ordering D1 to steal an ox (as a draught animal); D1 cannot find an ox, so he steals a horse. Lanham says that D2 "ought to be liable even though he did not authorise or command the theft of the horse." I would suggest that D2 is liable only if it is found as a fact that the theft of the horse, as a draught animal, was in the circumstances within the terms of his command, or was believed by D1 to be within those terms. No doubt this question will usually give the same result as Lanham's more simple-seeming (but analytically more dubious) question: was the crime the direct consequence of what was commanded etc.?

What if the perpetrator lets the plan miscarry without having intended that things should take the course they do?

That is a borderline case. There are two extreme situations. On the one hand, the perpetrator may deliberately change the plan, when the inciter (as already said) is not inculpated in the unauthorised crime. On the other hand, the perpetrator may muff it, when the inciter is liable as an accessory. The intermediate situation is where the perpetrator sees that the plan is miscarrying and allows it to do so. This is illustrated by the case of our old acquaintances, Saunders and Archer (§ 11.5).

> Archer, you remember, counselled Saunders to murder Mrs Saunders by giving her a poisoned apple, and Saunders allowed the apple to be eaten by his child instead. He did not have the courage to confess that he had planned to kill his wife, or the wit to make some excuse for taking the apple from the child. It was held on these facts that Archer was not guilty as an accessory to the murder of the child. He had counselled the murder of the wife, whereas Saunders had with full knowledge brought about the death of his child.

In order to understand the extent of the decision, let us imagine some slight changes of fact. (*a*) Suppose that Archer had counselled Saunders to murder his wife by shooting her, and that in attempting to carry out this proposal Saunders had accidentally shot his child instead. On these facts Archer would clearly have been guilty. The intention would have been transferred in law for both Saunders and Archer. (*b*) Now suppose the actual facts of the case except that Saunders was not present when his wife passed on the apple to the child. Here again, it seems, Archer would have been guilty. The apple would be like a bullet that by accident found its mark in the wrong person.

The point of difficulty about the actual facts of the case was that Saunders realised what was happening and consciously, deliberately, allowed his child to become the victim rather than his wife. This was taken to be the same as if Saunders had purposely changed his mind and decided to kill his child rather than his wife. It was a change of plan which meant that Saunders was no longer carrying out Archer's plan at all. Put in this way, the decision sounds reasonable, though it is near the line. The court might have held that the miscarriage of the plan was involuntary rather than intentional, since Saunders was trapped in a situation resulting from his criminal purpose. He could not (or thought he could not) save the child except by avowing his own guilt. Still, the point is sufficiently doubtful to justify leniency.[18]

§ 15.10. RECKLESSNESS AS TO CIRCUMSTANCES

Normally the accessory by incitement *intends* the offence to be committed,

---

[18] For a survey of conflicting theories and conflicting overseas decisions on transferred intention see Lanham in 96 LQR 110–117, 119–121. His discussion seems to confirm the wisdom of the rule suggested by the Working Party. At p. 121 he puts a case where D2, a terrorist leader, sends D1 to murder X, a public figure; X is not available so D1 murders Y, a colleague of X's. Lanham suggests that D2 is liable for this because the killing of Y is a direct result of his orders. It seems to me that this is too broad a test. The killing is not the direct result of D2's orders if D1 deliberately changed the plan. D2 may be held to be an accessory only if killing Y was (or was thought by D1 to be) within D2's plan (D2's principal object being to procure the murder of a public figure, and the particular victim not being material). Lanham then expresses the opinion that *Saunders and Archer* is on all fours with his hypothetical, but it is not. In the absence of evidence as to Archer's intention, there is no warrant for supposing that he would have regarded the change of victim as being within the advice he gave.

Saunders and Archer was decided in 1575, when the inchoate offence of incitement had not been developed. At the present day, a person like Archer could be convicted of that offence. (Notice that when the alleged perpetrator and accessory are indicted together, the perpetrator's name stands first.)

either in all events or if the circumstances so require. But it seems reasonable to say that he (and also the helper) can be implicated by recklessness, provided that the offence can be perpetrated recklessly and that the perpetrator acts within the contemplated purpose. Two examples may be suggested.

> D2 incites D1 to hit a night watchman over the head in order to render him unconscious. D1 does so and thereby inflicts grievous bodily harm on the watchman. D1 is liable for recklessly inflicting the harm, and D2 doubtless is too.
>
> D2 incites D1 to send a begging letter making a statement of fact that, as D2 knows, may or may not be true. If it is untrue and the victim sends money, both D1 and D2 are guilty of obtaining it by (reckless) deception.

These examples show that when the courts say, as they frequently do, that a person charged as accessory must know the facts, this is too narrow a statement of the law. In crimes where recklessness is sufficient for the perpetrator it is also sufficient for the accessory, provided that the perpetrator acts within the contemplated purpose.

We now have a decision bearing out this view of the law: *Carter* v. *Richardson*.[1]

> The supervising driver of a learner-driver whose blood-alcohol was above the limit (this being an offence of strict liability for the learner-driver) was held to have aided and abetted the offence because the supervisor "was aware that the principal consumed an excessive amount of alcohol or was reckless as to whether he had done so." The supervisor had not actively contributed to the offence, but in continuing to sit with the driver and thus legalising the act of driving he had implicated himself in it. (The supervisor had brought himself to the unfavourable attention of the police by claiming at first to have been the actual driver, in order to protect the learner-driver, and confessed the truth only after it was established that he himself was above the blood-alcohol limit. Would he have been charged if it had not been for this?)

Since the particular offence was one of strict liability for the perpetrator, it could *a fortiori* be committed recklessly by him. It is true that numerous authorities say that a person is not an accessory to an offence of strict liability unless he actually knows the facts (§ .12); but it seems that recklessness must now be accommodated within the rule.

§ 15.11. WHERE THE PERPETRATOR IS LIABLE FOR NEGLIGENCE

In offences of negligence, like manslaughter (on one view) or careless driving, a person will be liable as accessory if what the perpetrator did was

---

[1] [1974] RTR 314, Crim.LR 190.

within his contemplation and if he knew (or was reckless as to) the facts that made the conduct negligent.

> In *Salmon*,[1] several people went together to practise with a rifle which could be deadly at a mile. They fired at a target 100 yards away in a field; one of the shots killed a boy in a garden 400 yards away. It was held by the CCCR that all could be convicted of manslaughter by negligence, though it could not be proved who fired the fatal shot.

It appears that not one of the defendants realised the danger or knew of the presence of the boy within range; yet this possibility did not prevent the conviction of accessories. Presumably the explanation is that each defendant, regarded as an accessory, knew the facts that made the conduct negligent on the part of whoever was the perpetrator. They all knew that the shooting was taking place with a rifle and that people might be within range.

The same rule is applied to negligent races on the highway.

> Two persons agreed expressly or by mutual understanding to race their horses and carts on the highway. Both drove with gross negligence, and a pedestrian was killed by one of them (it was not known which). Both were held guilty of manslaughter, since each had encouraged the other and it did not matter who was the perpetrator.[2]

The point seems to have been that as regards each driver, looked upon as an accessory, what mattered was not his own negligence but the fact that he knew that his friend (regarded as the perpetrator) was driving as he was and knew all the circumstances that made the driving negligent. In addition to having this knowledge, each driver encouraged the other in the dangerous course of conduct, for the sake of having a race.

Contrast the following facts.

> D1, driving a car, passes D2. D2 angered by this, accelerates to pass D1; and so a kind of competition develops between the two drivers, and each drives at a negligent speed. A pedestrian is killed by one of the drivers, it is not known which. Only the driver who killed the pedestrian is guilty of manslaughter; and if his identity cannot be established, neither driver can be convicted of this crime. Here neither driver wished the other to drive at speed or intended to give him encouragement in the affair. Knowingly causing another person to do an act is not sufficient to constitute incitement to do it.[3]

§ 15.12. WHERE THE PERPETRATOR IS STRICTLY LIABLE

Where the offence is of strict liability for the perpetrator, this kind of

---

[1] (1880) LR 6 QBD 79. Cp. *The General Part*, 2nd edn § 122.

[2] *Swindall* (1846) 2 C & K 230, 175 ER 95.

[3] See *Mastin* (1834) 6 C & P 396, 172 ER 1292. But see the discussion of *Attorney-General's Reference*, above § .4 at n. 6.

liability does not extend to the accessory. The accessory is not liable without *mens rea*—a principle testified by an almost unbroken line of authority since *Callow* v. *Tillstone*.[1] This was what is sometimes known as a "strong" decision, meaning one of doubtful justice.

> Callow, a veterinary surgeon, gave a farmer a certificate that his meat was fit for human consumption. The farmer knew that the meat was unfit because the animal, a heifer, had died from eating yew. Callow knew that two other cattle that had been feeding with this heifer had died from eating yew, and the examination he made of the dead heifer was utterly perfunctory. The farmer sold the meat to a butcher, who exposed it for sale; the meat was then condemned as unfit. It was held that although the butcher was strictly liable for exposing unfit meat for sale, Callow could not be convicted as accessory since all that was found against him was negligence.

This means that in regulatory offences the doctrine of strict responsibility in respect of the circumstances of an offence applies only to the perpetrator. Accomplices require *mens rea.* The remarkable result in *Callow* v. *Tillstone* was that the shopkeeper, who was utterly without fault, could be convicted, while the negligent author of the offence could not be. However, it would seem that Callow could now be convicted on the basis of recklessness if the court were satisfied that he had no belief that the meat was fit (§ .10).

The law seems to me to be illogical. If an offence of recklessness is equally an offence of recklessness for the accessory, and an offence of negligence is equally ditto for the accessory, I don't see why an offence of strict liability should not be at least an offence of negligence for the accessory. In fact, I don't see why it shouldn't be an offence of strict liability for him.

I should be reluctant to see strict liability extended, but there would be much to be said for a rule that in offences of strict liability the accessory is liable for negligence. That, however, is not the law as it stands.

> One of the few cases holding that strict liability extends to accessories is *Creamer*.[2] The Court of Criminal Appeal there held that the only mental element necessary for constructive manslaughter is intending to commit a dangerous and unlawful act. Then, if death follows, it is manslaughter. The court held that a person could be convicted as accessory to the manslaughter if he knew of the dangerous and unlawful act (meaning, the facts making it dangerous and unlawful); it was not required that he, any more than the perpetrator, should foresee the death.

Reverting to *Callow* v. *Tillstone*, although the decision looks unjust on the particular facts, the principle can be defended in most cases on the ground that accessories generally have less

---

[1] (1900) 83 LT 411, 64 JP 823, 19 Cox 576. Cp. *Bowker* v. *Premier Drug Co.* [1928] 1 KB 217; *Ferguson* v. *Weaving* [1951] 1 KB 814; *Tinsley* [1963] Crim.LR 520; *Dial Contracts Ltd.* v. *Vickers* [1972] RTR 386; *Stanton & Sons Ltd.* v. *Webber* [1973] RTR 86.

[2] [1966] 1 QB 72. Cp. *Trinneer* [1970] SCR 638 (Can.). For a discussion see Lanham in 4 Crim.LJ (Aus.) 78. But note the effect of the "contemplated purpose" rule: § .9.

control over and knowledge of the situation than the perpetrator. In particular, it is generally the perpetrator (the factory owner or seller or other person carrying on a business directly affected by the law) who is expected to know what he may and may not do, and to take anxious precautions to comply.

This rationale would suggest that ignorance of the specialised law should be a defence to the person charged as accessory; yet it is not.[3] One would have thought that the same reasoning that gave the alleged accomplice a defence of ignorance of fact would have given him a defence of ignorance of law where the relevant law is highly specialised. Anyway, in *Callow* v. *Tillstone* the vet must have known the law, and was being paid in order to make sure that it was complied with; yet he was allowed the defence of ignorance of fact; so the legal position is indefensible on any view. Perhaps a reasonable rule would be to say that where the alleged accomplice himself carries on the specialised business or profession, or is so closely associated with it that he ought to know the relevant law, he is strictly liable in the same way as the perpetrator, but otherwise can set up a defence of ignorance of fact or law. Alternatively, the question could be left to be settled by the legislation in question.

Parliament has in fact accepted the responsibility in some instances, though it has not allowed a defence of ignorance of law nor distinguished between those who are and are not involved in the specialised activity. Modern statutes often include a provision extending strict liability to accessories, and do it in a wholesale way because they bring in everyone who contributes to bringing about the offence, whether he is carrying on a related business or profession or not.[4] Such a provision would now operate if the facts of *Callow* v. *Tillstone* occurred again.[5]

Suppose that the defendant is a company, as in National Coal Board v. Gamble. How can you speak of knowledge or recklessness in relation to a company?

A company is affected by the knowledge of its governing director or manager, but not by the knowledge of a subordinate employee (§ 44.2). It follows that a company can be accessory to an offence only if one of its directing officers has the requisite mental state.[6] That is why the conviction of the National Coal Board in *NCB* v. *Gamble* was wrong, whether the weighbridge clerk could rightly have been convicted or not.

§ 15.13. POLICE INFORMERS

Consider the case where a police informer pretends to help but really intends to frustrate the crime. He should not, in common sense, be an accessory, even though he gives what is technically an act of help, and even though in the event he fails to frustrate the crime. The Law Commission Working Party expressed this by proposing that a person should not be an accessory if he acted "with the purpose of preventing the commission of the offence or of nullifying its effects."[1]

Obviously you do not nullify an assault by helping in it and then having the assaulter

---

[3] § .2 at n. 14.
[4] See § 44.6.
[5] Food and Drugs Act 1955 s.113.
[6] See *John Henshall (Quarries) Ltd.* v. *Harvey* [1965] 2 QB 233.

[1] Cp. *Egginton* § 17 n. 1; Smith and Hogan, 4th edn 138–140. See, however, the doubtful position in conspiracy: § 18.3 *fin*.

arrested. When drinking after hours has taken place, the "effects" are not nullified by arresting the drinker. For the most part, therefore, the police and their informers would not be given a dispensation to engage in crime under the proposed rule, and they have no such general dispensation under the present law.[2] However, common sense suggests that the effect of theft may be nullified by allowing it to occur but having the guilty parties arrested immediately after so that the property is restored unharmed to its owner. In such circumstances the informer does not intend that the owner shall be permanently deprived of his property, which is what the law of theft aims against.[3] The Working Party's proposed rule (which the courts could implement as a matter of common law, if they wished) could allow police informers to abet (but not perpetrate) any acquisitive offence if they intended to see that the criminals were frustrated after committing the offence.

§ 15.14. WITHDRAWAL

A person who has incited a crime can still (in general) escape complicity in it if he expressly and clearly countermands the crime or withdraws his assent in due time before it is committed[1] (i.e. in time to enable the perpetrator to prevent its commission[2]); but he will remain liable for any previous incitement or conspiracy, as an inchoate offence.

There need not even be an express withdrawal of advice and consent, if the inciter has made his change of heart clear by conduct, as by quitting the gang.[3] Probably he can also avoid complicity by going to the police, or by giving timely warning to the intended victim.

The above rule applies only when the defendant has done no more than encourage or otherwise incite the commission of the crime, as by agreeing to take part in it. If he has acted positively to assist the crime, he must, it seems, do his best to prevent its commission, by warning the victim or by other means, short perhaps of going to the police.[4]

> Where a person who, having given information enabling a burglary to be committed, repented and tried to stop his companion going on with the project for two weeks before the companion committed the crime, this was held to be sufficient to let him out of liability for the crime[5] (though he would remain liable for incitement and conspiracy). But where one burglar gave a knife to his companion to use against anyone who might interrupt them, but on someone approaching, said: "Come on, let's go," suiting the action to the word, this was held to be

---

[2] See [1980] Crim.L.R. 130 nn. 7, 8.

[3] In *Macdaniel* (1755) Fost. at 121, 168 ER at 60, it was held that D was guilty as accessory to robbery when he arranged that the robber should be stimulated to commit the robbery, his object being to claim the reward for apprehending a highway robber. There was no evidence that D's object was to see that the property was returned to the victim. Even so, the apprehension of the robber would have meant that there was a good chance of the victim getting his property back, and it would seem that in such circumstances there was no theftous intent on D's part. The point was not argued.

[1] *Croft* [1944] KB 295; *Barnard* (1979) 70 CAR 28 (see note, [1980] Crim.LR 235). For a discussion of policy see Wasik in [1980] Crim.L.R. 785.

[2] See Lanham in 97 LQR 588–589, and the article generally.

[3] Foster, *Crown Law* 354.

[4] See Lanham in 97 LQR 579–585. Some American decisions suggest that a person who has given help must either withdraw the help or, if he cannot do that, must go to the police. But the American Law Institute's Model Penal Code s.206(6) requires only that the defendant "gives timely warning to the law enforcement authorities or otherwise makes proper effort to prevent the commission of the offence." Going to the police was not made a requirement in *Grundy*, next note.

[5] *Grundy* [1977] Crim.L.R. 543.

> insufficient to exempt him from complicity in a stabbing that his companion proceeded to inflict with the knife; and the Court of Appeal seemed to indicate that the defendant could on the facts have dissociated himself from the crime only by physically intervening to prevent the use of the knife.[6]

This restriction upon the right of withdrawal is an exception to the usual requirement that *mens rea* and *actus reus* must be contemporaneous. In effect the defendant is made liable for negligence in failing to prevent the crime.

If one of a band of criminals is arrested, does this prevent him from being responsible for what his companions afterwards do in pursuance of the common purpose?

He remains responsible if his arrest is unknown to the others.

> In *Johnson and Jones*[7] D1 and D2 entered a house with intent to steal; D2 was apprehended, without D1 becoming aware of the fact, and D1 afterwards stole an article in the house. The trial judge, Maule J, ruled that D2 could be convicted as accessory.

If the arrest is known to the others, it would seem that the arrest should be accounted an involuntary withdrawal from the plan, so that the party arrested is liable only to the extent that he would be liable on a voluntary withdrawal.

> If, for example, a number of criminals make forcible resistance to arrest, and one of them is arrested, and ceases resistance and encouragement to his companions, it seems that he will not ordinarily by implicated in an act of force subsequently committed by another of the gang.[8] The reason is that when he is seen to be arrested the encouragement he has given his companions by joining in their forcible resistance comes to an end. But if he has supplied a companion with a weapon to be used in resisting, the arrest will not end his liability for the use of the weapon, any more than in the case of voluntary withdrawal, unless perhaps he offers to try to persuade his companion not to use the weapon.

§ 15.15. LEGISLATIVE EXCLUSION

The law of complicity is very wide, but it is well known, and normally the legislature may fairly be presumed to intend it to apply to its new edicts.

Occasionally, however, the court may feel able to collect from the statute a legislative policy exempting the unnamed party from

---

[6] *Becerra* (1976) 62 CAR 212. See generally Lanham, 97 LQR 579–585; see this also on countermanding instructions to an innocent agent.

[7] (1841) C & M 218, 174 ER 479.

[8] *Jackson* (1673) Hale *PC* i 464. Lanham in 97 LQR 575–579 suggests that these authorities are not conclusive on accessoryship by inciting, and that there is no reason in policy why an involuntary withdrawal should excuse. But to deny the excuse would look harsh.

responsibility. An example is where legislation is designed for the protection of a certain class of persons, who are not directly struck at by it, and who by reason of nonage, poverty, social isolation or the like are deemed by the courts to be unable to protect themselves fully against exploitation. Such persons do not become accessories to an offence committed in respect of them by giving their consent to it.[1]

> The only clear instance in the reports is in respect of the crime of unlawful sexual intercourse with a girl under 16.[2] The statute is intended to protect young girls even against themselves. Therefore, the girl who consents to or instigates her own seduction is not an accessory to an offence committed by the man.[3]

The "victim" rule, as it may be called, applies only where the person who is in the vulnerable position is excluded from the class of perpetrators. If a person can be a perpetrator, then *a fortiori* he can be an accessory.

For example, even a youth under 16 can perpetrate a consensual indecent assault upon a female under 16.[4] He will therefore be an accessory if he incites such a female to commit an indecent assault upon him. Equally if the female is over 16.

A youth over 14[5] (even though he is under 16) can perpetrate buggery upon another or gross indecency with another male; he can therefore abet in acts of these kinds committed upon him.[6] Even girls under 16 can be convicted of consensual indecent assault upon boys under 16; they can be convicted as perpetrators, and therefore can be convicted as accessories.[7] No legislative intent to protect the youngster from the operation of the law can be perceived in these cases. However, prosecution practice is wiser than the drafting of the legislation.

The "victim" rule is only one example of the proposition that the courts may find that a person is excluded by implication from liability as accessory to a statutory offence. Others may be suggested.

> There is a long and well understood tradition in our law that prostitution is not an offence in itself. But the prostitute is hedged about by restrictions, so that it is quite difficult for her to continue her way of life within the law, and the law also directs itself against those who help her in her trade. For example, it is a statutory offence for the occupier of premises to permit them to be used for habitual prostitution.[8] Suppose that a man who has a woman lodger permits her to use her room for habitual prostitution. The man commits an offence under the statute, but it would be wrong to convict the woman as accessory to the offence, because that would run counter to the policy that can be seen to underlie all the legislation, of leaving

---

[1] See Hogan in [1962] Crim.LR 683; Williams in [1964] *ibid.* 686.

[2] *Tyrrell* [1894] 1 QB 710.

[3] The victim rule has been recognised by statute in connection with conspiracy. See § 18.9. For another possible instance of the rule see *Grace Rymer Investments* v. *Waite* [1958] Ch. at 845–846.

[4] § 10.3 n. 5.

[5] A youth under 14 cannot perpetrate buggery, any more than rape, and for the same spurious reason (§ 10.8 n. 16). Logically, he should be liables if he acts as the passive partner, the presumption of incapacity being irrelevant; but the courts hold otherwise. See Smith and Hogan, 4th edn 440.

[6] § 10.6.

[7] A girl under 16 can logically be convicted of indecent assault upon a youth under 16 in respect of acts done during sexual intercourse. It may be assumed that she would not be charged with this.

[8] SOA 1956 s.36.

untouched the prostitute who carries on her occupation in accordance with the rules restricting the ways in which she can do so.[9]

As another example, if a father has an incestuous relationship with his daughter under 16, the daughter does not commit incest: not as perpetrator, because the statute expressly excludes girls under 16, and not as accessory, because the exclusion of such girls as perpetrators implies their exclusion as accessories. The point arose in *Whitehouse*,[10] where the court reached the right result but gave the wrong reason. It was held that the girl could not be an accessory because she was the victim of the offence. This is wrong because incest is not an offence against the person. Its basis is either "moral" (incest is widely thought to be wrong in itself) or eugenic, not a matter of protecting the young—as is shown by the fact that it applies to intercourse between fathers and adult daughters and between adult brothers and sisters. It is true that a girl under 16 is omitted from the offence, whether committed with a father, brother, or any other male within the forbidden degrees; but this is probably because it was thought when the legislation was passed that most of the girls under 16 who participate in incest will have been sexually imposed upon, and therefore it would not be right to include any young girls in the law. So the proper reason for holding in *Whitehouse* that the girl was not within the law of incest was simply that it was the intention of the statute to exclude her.[11]

Can it not be said that in every case where Parliament penalises one party to a bilateral transaction, it must have intended to leave the other party free from liability? Yet you said earlier that the law is otherwise. For example, where a statute makes it an offence to sell something, the buyer is counted as an accessory. If Parliament meant that, it would surely have brought both of them within the prohibition.

---

[9] The point has not arisen above magisterial level. In *King* (1914) 10 CAR 117 the CCA held that a prostitute who gave her immoral earnings to a man was not an accessory to his offence of living on her immoral earnings, for the purpose of the "accomplice warning" in the law of evidence; but no reason was offered. In *Pickford, ibid.* 269, the rule was approved and the reason given was that the woman might have acted under compulsion. A Canadian county court judge again approved the rule but offered as the reason that the offence was for a *man* to live off a woman's immoral earnings; a woman could not be an accessory to the offence because she could not perpetrate it: *Williams* [1935] 2 DLR 696. The reason is clearly mistaken: an accessory need not have the qualification required for a perpetrator. The best justification for the rule in *King* is that the statute is intended, at least in part, to protect the prostitute from exploitation. But this is not the only reason for the statute: another is to prevent men from building up illicit fortunes by organising prostitution. This would suggest that the woman should be regarded as an accomplice. Duress could not be a defence in respect of a continuing course of conduct.

[10] [1977] QB 868. For the actual decision see § 19.5.

[11] For a similar reason, *Sockett* § 18.9 n. 1 appears to be wrongly decided. It was held in that case that a non-pregnant woman could be convicted as accessory to a man's attempt to abort her, although, because of the wording of the statute, she could not have been convicted of an attempt to abort herself. Smith and Hogan, 4th edn 138, support the decision with the comment: "A pregnant woman can be convicted of using an instrument on herself so it cannot be argued that this section was passed for the protection of *women* and it would be curious that Parliament should have intended to protect non-pregnant women from themselves, but not pregnant women" (who can be convicted of attempting to abort themselves). Why Parliament exempted non-pregnant women from liability for attempting to abort themselves is a matter of speculation, but it may have been because many women who mistakenly believed themselves to be pregnant attempted an abortion, and no good reason was seen for rendering them liable to prosecution. On the other hand the Parliament that passed the OAPA of 1861 evidently saw good reason for punishing the pregnant woman who operated on herself and also the professional abortionist who operated on any woman, pregnant or not. This was all that Parliament expressly said. It probably forgot about the law of complicity; but the rational view is that since Parliament exempted the non-pregnant women who acted for herself it would surely have intended to exempt her from complicity in an abortion if the matter had been brought to its attention.

This is quite an important point, on which the American and English courts have diverged. When a statute makes it an offence for one party to enter into a transaction, the English courts automatically convict the other party as accessory if he knew the facts. In the example you give, although the buyer is not within the definition of the offence as a perpetrator, there is no indication that buyers are in any sense a protected class (unless, of course, the legislation is clearly intended for the protection of buyers[12]). In the English opinion, therefore, such a statute does not show an intention to except buyers in the same way as some sexual offences except girls under 16. The American courts hold the opposite, and have the better reason. When the legislature has referred to a bilateral transaction and made it an offence in one party only, it is improper to extend the law to catch the other party under the doctrine of accessoryship, because the legislature, when it applied the offence to sellers, must have considered whether to bring buyers within the prohibition also, and its silence on this point is an indication of intention not to bring the buyer in.

> In consequence of the English rule, it has been held that a thief who disposes of the goods to a handler (receiver) can be convicted as accessory to the handling.[13] Normally, of course, a thief will be charged with theft; but if he is charged with handling, the prosecutor believing that he received the goods from a thief, and it transpires at the trial that he was himself the thief who sold to a handler, he can frequently be convicted under the indictment for handling.

The decision looks wrong. Handlers are subject to a higher maximum punishment than thieves. Since the legislature has distinguished between thieves and handlers, it is unsound to hold that a thief can be a handler by reason of accessoryship.

The furthest that the English courts have gone is to hold that complicity is to some extent excluded where the offence is defined in terms too narrow to involve some of those who (in a sense) take part in its commission. A statute makes it an offence to *keep* (meaning to manage) a betting house or brothel, or to *carry on* a prohibited business. On such wording the only people who can become accessories by helping are those who help to manage or carry on the business. For example, players at an unlawful game do not aid the occupier in using the premises for unlawful gaming, because "using" is held to mean "managing."[14] (If a buyer helps the seller in the act of selling, it is not easy to see why a person who is managed does not help the manager in the act of managing; but such is the law.)

The Law Commission Working Party has proposed that the American rule should be adopted in the projected code.

> "A person does not become an accessory to an offence if the offence

---

[12] An example might be the person who buys drugs for his own consumption from a trafficker. Although drug addicts can commit an offence of illegal possession, there would be no good reason for bringing them into the more serious offence of trafficking (Misuse of Drugs Act 1971 s.3) as accessory, since the statute against trafficking was obviously made for their protection.

[13] *Carter Patersons Ltd.* v. *Wessel* [1947] KB 849.

[14] *Jenks* v. *Turpin* (1884) 13 QBD 505; cp. Heydon in [1973] Crim.LR 276.

is so defined that his conduct in it is inevitably incidental to its commission and such conduct is not expressly penalised."

It seems right in such a case that the legislature should be required to state fully the persons who are to be liable.

§ 15.16. COMPLICITY AND LIMITATIONS ON THE CRIMINAL LAW

Traditionally, the liability of the alleged accessory depends on that of the perpetrator. The basis of the common law is that the accessory's liability is derivative from that of the perpetrator. The rule may seem like the most obvious common sense, for unless there is a perpetrator there cannot have been a crime, and "there will be no foundation on which accessory crime can rest" (Lord Denman CJ).[1] (Lord Denman did not speak with complete precision, because at common law there is no "accessory crime;" there is a single crime with several parties.)

The general rule is not merely a piece of pedantry. The law of complicity cannot turn non-crimes into crimes. It is not a crime for a man to desert his wife, so, obviously, it ought not to be a crime for another person to help him to desert his wife.

Yes, but that is a case where the act is not prohibited. Suppose that a person commits what may be called a criminal act but is not responsible, on account of lack of mens rea or some other personal excuse. Why should not an accessory be liable?

Here the courts are generally able to surmount the difficulty by a technique already mentioned: the physical actor is treated as a puppet, so that the guilty actor who activates him to do the mischief becomes responsible not as an accessory but as a perpetrator acting through an innocent agent.

The Law Commission Working Party formulated the following definition of an innocent agent.

> "A person acts through an innocent agent when he intentionally causes the external elements of the offence to be committed by (or partly by) a person who is himself innocent of the offence charged by reason of lack of a required fault element, or lack of capacity."

For instance, one can murder or wound through an innocent agent, such as a person who is irresponsibly insane. Not only common law but statutory offences can be committed by proxy, as the example just given of wounding shows. When Fagin sends Twist (aged under 10[2]) to steal handkerchieves, Fagin "appropriates" a handkerchief, within the meaning of the Theft Act, at the moment when Twist takes it. Fagin is the perpetrator, although absent, since a child under 10 cannot commit a crime. If Dodge gets Dupe to write a false document (or "instrument" as the law of forgery calls it), so that it would be a forgery if he wrote it himself, then if Dupe does not know of the falsity Dodge can be held responsible for "making" a forgery by the hand of Dupe.

---

[1] *Tyler* (1838) 8 C & P at 618, 173 ER at 644.

[2] If the child is 10 or over he may on the facts not be an innocent agent: see § 28.2.

It does not matter that it was the "innocent agent" who started the affair.[3] The innocent agent need not be instructed to commit the criminal act; it is enough that he is caused to commit it (as where he is told that he may, thus leading him to believe that the act is lawful).[4] Where a person manipulates an innocent agent in these ways it is the same as if he acted through a robot or an animal: in law the act is his.

We saw in § .9 that the perpetrator will often remain guilty of the crime even though his purpose takes effect by accident upon a different victim, or upon a mistaken victim, or in an unintended mode. This rule applies equally to acts through innocent agents.[5]

So the doctrine of innocent agency avoids any failure of justice that might otherwise occur as a result of the rule that there cannot be an accessory without a perpetrator?

It does so largely, but not entirely.

- The doctrine of innocent agency probably applies (as the Law Commission Working Party says) only when the perpetrator intended the offence to be committed, not when he was merely negligent.
- There is the further limitation that the doctrine can be used only when it is plausible to say that the defendant did the forbidden act in the forbidden circumstances. The Law Commission Working Party puts it thus.

> "A person is not guilty of committing an offence through an innocent agent when the law provides or implies that the offence can be committed only by one who complies with a particular description which does not apply to that person, or specifies the offence in terms implying personal conduct on the part of the offender."

An example of the first of these limitations (where the law specifies a particular description) is as follows.

> It is an offence for the holder of a justices' licence to sell liquor to a police officer knowing that he is on duty.[6] A person who orders a drink for such an officer, falsely telling the publican that the officer is not on duty, cannot be convicted of selling the drink through the innocent agency of the publican. He himself is not the holder of a justices' licence, and does not sell the drink; so he does not qualify to be a perpetrator.[7] The publican does not perpetrate the offence either, because he does not know the officer is on duty. So there is no offence to which the liar can be an accessory, at any rate if traditional principles are applied.

An example of the second limitation (where the law implies personal conduct) is *Thornton* v. *Mitchell*.[8]

---

[3] *Tyler* (1838) 8 C & P 616, 172 ER 643.

[4] *Clifford* (1845) 2 Car. & K 202, 175 ER 84.

[5] Illustrations are *Saunders and Archer*, § 11.5, and *Michael*, § 16.10. Michael intended to act through the nurse as innocent agent; in fact the nurse's child took over, but Michael was still responsible for the act of the child, since substantially her criminal purpose was carried out. (Incidentally, this again illustrates the point that an "innocent agent" need not be an agent in the sense of one having authority to act.) Saunders did not intend to act through an innocent agent, but his wife became one when she passed on the poisoned apple to the child. Saunders's intention was transferred as a matter of law from her to the child, for it was upon the child that his evil act took effect.

[6] Cp. *Sherras* v. *De Rutzen* [1895] 1 QB 918.

[7] That only the holder of the licence can be convicted as perpetrator in such cases is the foundation of the law of "delegation." See § 43.3.

[8] [1940] 1 All ER 339.

> A bus was being reversed, and the conductor in accordance with the usual custom assisted the driver by signalling that all was clear at the back. On this occasion the conductor negligently gave the all-clear signal when there was a pedestrian behind the bus; the driver backed and the pedestrian was injured. The driver was charged with driving without due care and attention, and the conductor was charged as abettor. The charge against the driver was dismissed, because he had reasonably relied on the signal given by the conductor, and so had not been careless. This meant that the conductor had to be acquitted also, because there could be no abettor to an offence that had not been committed.

Could the conductor have been convicted of negligently conducting?

There is no such offence. Most people who act negligently are safe from the criminal law. As we have seen, it is only in exceptional cases, as with the offence of careless driving, that negligence is punished. There is a general tort of negligence, but not a general crime of negligence.

Could the conductor have been convicted of driving carelessly through the innocent agency of the actual driver?

This argument was not considered by the court, but on principle it should fail. First, the conductor did not intend to commit an offence, and there is no example in the books of the doctrine of innocent agency being used for an unintentional offence. Perhaps this point is not conclusive, but the second is. The notion of driving, as used in the Road Traffic Act, cannot be extended to cover people who do not actually drive, because it would lead to absurdities. The driver of a vehicle must pass the driving test and have a driving licence. If the conductor of a bus, or a passenger in a car, were deemed to drive whenever he gave instructions to the driver, it would follow that such conductor or passenger would be required himself to take the test and hold a licence. This would be unreasonable. The word "drive" must be taken to have such a strong bodily connotation that only the actual driver can be the perpetrator of a driving offence.

The decision in *Thornton* v. *Mitchell* does not mark the end of the story. Two sex cases arose, in which the courts were determined to uphold a conviction, and to do this they invented new and remarkable doctrines. First there was the thoroughly nasty case of *Bourne*.[9]

> Bourne compelled his wife to commit bestiality with a dog. Bestiality is an offence (a species of buggery)[10], but the wife had the defence of duress, and she was not charged. Bourne was tried on his own for abetting her, and was convicted. On appeal the obvious objection was raised that Bourne could not abet an offence that was not committed—a point on which one would have thought that the authorities were completedly solid. The Court of Appeal, driven to desperation, invented a concept of *de facto* crime for the purpose of upholding the conviction. The court held that the wife committed the

---

[9] (1952) 36 CAR 125.

[10] See SOA 1956 s.12(1): "It is an offence for a person to commit buggery with . . . an animal."

> offence in contemplation of law even though she could not be punished for it.

It does not seem to have been contemplated that Bourne could be convicted as perpetrator of bestiality. There was an obvious reason. The definitions of sex crimes refer strongly to personal bodily behaviour. Only by a violent wrench of the English language could it be said that Bourne himself committed the act of bestiality.

Instead, it was assumed that there was an offence to which he could be an accessory. The wife's defence of duress, said Lord Goddard CJ, was simply a "prayer by her to be excused from punishment," so that she was guilty of the offence. This does not truly represent the effect of duress, which is not a mere matter of mitigation: success in the defence results in a verdict of not guilty, which would mean that the wife did not commit an offence on traditional principles. It is conceptually improper, according to the theory of the common law, to imagine some ghostly offence committed by the wife for the purpose of convicting the husband as accessory.[11]

In the second case, *Cogan*,[12] the Court of Appeal took the step of applying the doctrine of innocent agency to an act of sexual intercourse.

> A husband compelled his wife to have sexual intercourse with Cogan, who believed that the wife was consenting. Cogan having had his conviction of rape quashed on appeal, the question arose whether a conviction of the husband as aider and abettor could stand. The Court of Appeal held that it could, since the defendant was liable as perpetrator and the form of the conviction did not matter.

This decision saved the law from much public odium, but its legal basis is demonstrably unsound. Lawton LJ, delivering the judgment of the court, advanced two reasons. The first and chief one was that the husband could have been indicted as principal and "convictions should not be upset because of mere technicalities of pleading." To the argument that a husband could not rape his own wife the court replied that the reason for that rule was that the law presumes consent from the marriage ceremony, and that there was no such presumption on the facts of the present case.

Although this may sound like robust common sense, the fact remains that it was the first occasion on which a person was convicted of crime as perpetrator for doing something through an innocent agent when he could not have been convicted had he done it himself. Moreover, the court directed itself exclusively to the difficulty that the defendant was the husband, and did not consider the wholly distinct difficulty arising from the bodily connotation of rape.

The decision was rendered possible by the fact that the defendant happened to be a man. Rape can be perpetrated only by a man; the statute says so. If Parliament had entertained the extraordinary notion of raping by means of the genitals of another, it would not have limited the offence to males. As it is, the position is that if duress is applied by a man, he can be convicted of rape on facts like *Cogan*, whereas if the duress is applied by a woman it would need an even greater degree of hawkishness than that displayed by the court in *Cogan* to call her a constructive man. Yet it is highly illogical that a man can commit rape through an innocent agent when a woman cannot, because if the notion of innocent agency is held to be applicable, so that the bodily acts of the innocent agent are attributed to the instigator, the sex of the instigator (the fact that the instigator lacks the sex organ of the innocent agent) becomes irrelevant.

The second ground taken by the court, though apparently only by way of *obiter dictum* and

---

[11] This criticism of the decision was accepted by Lord Edmund-Davies in *Lynch* [1975] AC at 710, and in the same case in the court below by Lowry LCJ. However, there are circumstances where it is impossible to avoid the concept of an excused offence, as in the case of an attack by a lunatic. See § 23.1.

[12] [1976] QB 217; cp. note, [1975] Crim.LR 585, and Buxton in 125 NLJ 1133.

not as a final opinion, was that the husband was rightly convicted of procuring the offence (that is, as accessory) because the woman had been raped: "No one outside a court of law would say that she had not been." Speaking, as always, with every respect to the Queen's justice, this will not do at all. It uses popular or sociological language, on the question whether the fact of "rape" has occurred, instead of legal language, on the question whether the crime of rape has been committed. It is in effect the same doctrine as that in *Bourne*, that an offence that is excused for the "perpetrator" is still an offence in law, to which there can be an accessory. If this is the law, it is law newly minted by the courts.

So that unsettles that. How does one state the present law?

Whatever the technical deficiencies of *Bourne* and *Cogan*, these decisions undoubtedly reached a desirable result. The best way to put the new rule is to say that when a person commits what may be called a criminal act, for which he is not responsible because he lacks *mens rea* or other requisite fault element or has some other excuse, another person can be convicted as accessory if he is in fact responsible for the act (that is to say, would be legally responsible if the other had the requisite fault element and lacked any excuse).[13] This rule could be used to justify the conviction of the conductor in *Thornton* v. *Mitchell*. The difficulty with it is that the conviction registers a falsehood and defames the innocent "perpetrator:" the conductor is convicted of aiding and abetting careless driving by the driver, when the driver was not careless.

The only completely satisfactory solution of these problems is by legislation. What we need is a new offence specially devised to deal with the difficulty revealed by these cases.[14]

§ 15.17. UNDERCOVER MEN AS INNOCENT AGENTS

One other exception to the doctrine of innocent agency is based upon the notion of justice, and is similar to the rule already stated for accessories (§ .13). The Law Commission Working Party again speaks.

> "A person is not guilty of committing an offence through an innocent agent when the innocent agent acts with the purpose of preventing the commission of the offence or of nullifying its effects."

If D asks X to help him in committing a crime, and X assents purely for the purpose of procuring D's conviction, and obtains the consent of the intended victim, what X does is not attributed to D. Anything that D does will, of course, inculpate him; and he will be guilty of incitement (dealt with in Chapter 19); but it would be unjust to allow X in these

---

[13] Although the courts may now apply such a rule, it considerably alters the previous understanding of the law. For example, it would have secured a different outcome in *Kemp* [1964] 2 QB 341: the alleged perpetrator having been held on appeal to be not guilty for lack of *mens rea*, the conviction of an alleged accessory (who possessed *mens rea* and had engineered the whole affair) was quashed. The point was not argued, because it was thought too clear for argument. The rule assumed to be the law in *Kemp* is the foundation of the law of innocent agency (which was invented to get round it), and also of the liability of publicans for the acts of their delegates (a matter to be considered in § 43.3).

[14] See [1982] Crim.LR 737. See this article generally on the subject of excuses; also § 23.1 at n. 6.

circumstances to manufacture a consummated crime on the part of D by conduct of his own. The point is carried by the old case of *Egginton*.[1]

> Egginton tried to persuade the watchman of a building to help him to steal from it. The watchman informed his employer, who told him to pretend to co-operate. He opened the yard door for Egginton, and they went together through an open door into the building (the latter door had also, apparently, been opened by the watchman). It was held that Egginton could not be convicted of burglary because at common law (which required a "breaking" in a technical sense) there was no "breaking" of the building by Egginton. There would have been a "breaking" if Egginton had opened the door; but he could not be made responsible for the "breaking" by the watchman, when the watchman was intending only to incriminate him.

§ 15.18. THE SEMI-INNOCENT AGENT

There may be different degrees of *mens rea* between the instigator and the actor, and it is possible for the instigator to have the higher degree, or of course the lower degree.[1]

> D1 incites D2 to assault V, knowing that V has a weak heart and hoping he will die. D2 assaults V thinking that no more is intended, and V dies. Assuming that D2 is not guilty of murder, the question is whether D1 can nevertheless be convicted of committing murder through an innocent agent. In fact D2 is a semi-innocent agent.

Before 1973 it was thought to be clear that an instigator could be guilty of a crime of greater enormity than that intended by the person who physically did it. This rule is stated by the institutional writers,[2] and it follows logically from the doctrine of innocent agency. It means, for example, that while a person who kills under provocation is guilty only of manslaughter, another who assists the killing and who is not affected by the provocation can, on principle, be convicted of murder.

However, a complication was introduced into the law in *Richards*,[3] the case of 1973 before referred to.

> The defendant, Mrs Richards, told two accomplices to beat up her husband badly enough to put him in hospital for a month. She held a light at a window to indicate when her husband left the house, and the accomplices then attacked him, but only so as to infict a comparatively slight injury. The accomplices were convicted of unlawful wounding contrary to OAPA s.20, but Richards was convicted of wounding her

---

[1] (1801) East, *PC* ii 666. Cp. Fletcher in 89 HLR 496 n. 108.

[1] See as to the lower degree *The General Part*, 2nd edn 390 n. 1. Where a perpetrator goes outside the contemplated purpose and commits a murder, his companion is not guilty of manslaughter: § 15.9 at n. 14.

[2] Particularly East, *PC* i 350. The principle is enacted in respect of diminished responsibility by the Homicide Act 1957 s.2(4).

[3] [1974] QB 776, powerfully criticised in [1974] Crim.LR 96, in Smith and Hogan, 4th edn 132–134, and by Smith in *Reshaping the Criminal Law*, ed. Glazebrook (London 1978) 128–130.

> husband with intent to cause him grievous bodily harm contrary to section 18. On appeal Richards's conviction was reduced to unlawful wounding, on the ground that Richards, not being present, was not what would earlier have been described as an abettor, and could not by reason of incitement be convicted of a crime of higher degree than the persons who actually did it.

The decision introduces a needless technicality into the law.

- There is no reason for distinguishing between the accessory who is present and the accessory who is absent.
- Formerly the law did draw a distinction between a principal in the second degree (aider and abettor), who was present at the time of the crime, and the accessory before the fact, who was not. But the notion of presence was extended by the doctrine of constructive presence: one who helped at the time of the crime, even at a distance, was constructively present and was an abettor. The court was therefore mistaken in denying that Richards was an abettor.
- The Criminal Law Act 1967 applies the rules for misdemeanours, where all parties are principals at common law, to the former felonies; consequently, the foundation for the distinction between abettors and accessories has disappeared. The Act is not mentioned in the judgment.
- Above all, no mention is made in the judgment of the doctrine of innocent agency, which applied to felonies in the old law as much as to misdemeanours. If a person can act through a completely innocent agent, there is no reason why he should not act through a semi-innocent agent. It is wholly unreasonable that the partial guilt of the agent should operate as a defence to the instigator.

For all these reasons, the decision is unlikely to settle the law permanently.

§ 15.19. STATUTORY OFFENCES BY COMPANY OFFICERS

For company officers, the common law of accessoryship is supplemented by statutory provisions. Many statutes creating particular offences, especially those relating to trade, provide that a director or other officer of an incorporated company that is guilty of an offence under the Act shall be implicated in the offence if it was committed with his consent or connivance, or even merely facilitated by his negligence. Some of the older statutes go further and shift the burden of proof: they require the officer to prove that he did not know of the offence or connive in it, but this is no longer the practice in drafting.[1]

§ 15.20. ASSISTANCE AFTER THE CRIME

The law of complicity is, with one exception, confined to acts done before

[1] *The General Part*, 2nd ed. § 284.

or at the time of the crime in question. A person who assists a criminal after he has committed the crime to avoid apprehension or conviction does not become a party to the crime, though he may himself commit various offences in doing so.

The one exception relates to treason. Formerly, persons who helped felons to escape were "accessories after the fact." That law is now gone, but those who help traitors to escape are still "principals after the fact" to treason, since the reform of this antiquated branch of the law has not hitherto seemed sufficiently pressing to justify parliamentary time being spent on it. We will not spend our time on it either.

A person who tries to help his friend to evade justice may be guilty of perjury (if he lies when on oath), or of contempt of court, or of an offence under the Criminal Law Act 1967 section 4 of impeding the apprehension or prosecution of a person who has committed an arrestable offence. But the most general offences, which can be committed both before and after the crime in question, are those of obstructing the police and obstructing justice.[1]

Is it an offence to fail to tell the police when you know a crime has been committed?

Generally not. The exceptions are not very important.

(1) It is the offence of misprision of treason not to reveal treason (or, perhaps, contemplated treason). The principal forms of treason are "levying war against the King in his realm" and "being adherent to the King's enemies in his realm or elsewhere."[2]

(2) The Prevention of Terrorism (Temporary Provisions) Act 1976 section 11 makes it an offence to fail to give information about acts of terrorism, past or future.

(3) There is a very limited statutory offence of bargaining for an advantage in return for not giving information to the authorities about an arrestable offence.[3]

SUMMARY

A perpetrator (or principal) is one who, being within the criminal prohibition, offends against it with any necessary fault element. He may act himself or through an innocent agent or instrumentality, and he is also a perpetrator whenever he is responsible for the act of another. § .1

Accessories include the former principals in the second degree (who "aid and abet") and the former accessories before the fact (who "counsel and procure"). A person may be guilty as accessory although he cannot commit the crime as perpetrator, lacking some qualification. In law, accessories "commit" the offence, just as the perpetrator does. Considerable laxity is allowed in drawing the indictment or information; and where the perpetrator is unknown all can be charged as perpetrators, or (probably) all as accessories. Nevertheless, a known accessory should be charged as such. Ignorance of the criminal law is no defence even to accessories. § .2

---

[1] See Smith and Hogan, 4th edn. 722 ff.; Law Com. Working Paper No. 62.
[2] Smith and Hogan, 4th edn. 796 ff., 802; Law Com. Working Paper No. 72.
[3] CLA 1967 s.5(1).

Accessories may be defined at the present day as those who incite or help the offence. Incitement includes encouragement and authorisation, but probably there must be an element of particularity in the crime incited. Incitement of the whole world will probably not create complicity if someone carries out the crime. In the absence of co-operation, action will not be taken to be an encouragement merely because the actor knows that what he is doing will encourage another person to act illegally. § .3

Help may be given before or during the crime, and includes co-operation in a bilateral transaction. The perpetrator need not be aware of the help. But the facilitation of crime for the purpose of entrapment and without communication with the offender does not inculpate. § .4

Minor help is sufficient, and no defence of "ordinary business supply is recognised. § .5

But a person who merely delivers an instrument of crime to its owner (not having otherwise put himself out to assist the crime) is probably not an accessory; and an alleged accessory probably has a defence if he believed that he was compelled by the civil law to give his co-operation, or even if he was doubtful as to his position in the civil law but acted in accordance with what he regarded as his business or moral obligation. § .6

Subject to what has been said, a person who knowingly gives help in the commission of an offence is an accessory even though he does not wish to promote the criminality. But a person who merely facilitates an offence for the purpose of entrapment does not thereby become a party to it. § .4, .5

Generally, an omission to prevent crime does not create complicity. Even deliberate presence at the scene of the crime is not enough. In some situations a person who has the legal authority to forbid conduct (owner-passengers, supervisors of learner-drivers, employers) can be implicated in an offence if he fails to prevent it; at least, his failure to do so is "evidence" of encouragement. § .7

Although the law is not settled, the sensible view is that members of the audience do not become accomplices in an illegal performance merely by their presence, though it has been judicially said that they can become implicated by applauding. § .8

In offences requiring *mens rea*, an alleged accessory is not responsible for an offence that was outside his contemplation ("outside the common purpose," as the courts frequently say). In practice the offences in the accessory's contemplation will always be limited to some extent, but whether this is a legal restriction on liability is unclear. Where the perpetrator commits the crime in an unexpected way, or makes a mistake as to the victim or property aimed at, the accessory is probably liable if (1) the perpetrator nevertheless acts within his contemplation, or if (2) the perpetrator believes that he is acting within the plan suggested or accepted by the accessory, and the crime committed is of the same abstract kind as that contemplated by the accessory. The accessory is responsible also in cases of transferred intention unless the perpetrator consciously allows the plan to miscarry. § .9

Provided that the alleged accessory knows the perpetrator's intention, as described above, recklessness as to circumstances is sufficient to convict him where such recklessness is sufficient for the perpetrator. § .10

In offences of negligence a person can be liable as accessory if what the perpetrator does is within his contemplation and if he knows or is reckless as to the facts that make the conduct negligent. § .11

Strict liability does not extend to the accessory, who must know the facts or be reckless as to them. Exceptionally, the accessory can be liable for constructive manslaughter. Companies are affected by the knowledge of their directors and certain other controlling officers. § .12

An alleged accessory is probably not liable if he acted only to prevent the offence or to nullify its effects. § .13

He can also escape complicity by a clear and timely withdrawal, except that if he § .14

has given material assistance he must take steps to prevent the commission of the crime. How energetic those steps must be is not altogether clear. The arrest of a member of the gang is a kind of involuntary withdrawal by him, which is presumably governed by the same principles as a voluntary withdrawal. It can have no effect on liability unless it is known to the other accomplices.

A statute may exclude complicity expressly or by implication, but the only examples of implied exclusion so far recognised are (1) where the statute was passed for the protection of a class of persons of which the alleged accessory is a member, and (2) where the statute is so narrowly worded that the alleged accessory cannot be said to give help to what the perpetrator does. The courts do not see an implied exclusion in the fact that the statute names only one party to a bilateral transaction. § .15

The traditional rule is that there can be no accessory if there was no perpetrator. The practical effect of this can often be evaded by the doctrine of innocent agency, under which the person really to blame becomes the perpetrator. But innocent agency can probably be invoked only where the defendant intended the crime to be committed; also, it is inapplicable if only the innocent agent was qualified to commit the offence. The courts have now gone beyond the common law by holding that a person can be an accessory to bestiality committed by a person who has the excuse of duress (*Bourne*) and (*obiter*) to "rape" committed by a person who has the excuse of no *mens rea* (*Cogan*). These decisions were based upon a notion of *de facto* crime, and it is uncertain how far this extends. § .16

The doctrine of innocent agency is excluded if the innocent agent was acting for the purpose of obtaining the defendant's conviction. § .17

There may be a semi-innocent agent, but an anomalous qualification was imposed upon this rule in *Richards*. § .18

Liability (but not complicity) is extended by the creation of statutory offences of "permitting," and there are special offences for company officers. § .19

Assistance given after the crime, to escape justice, does not create complicity, except in treason; but other crimes may be committed. § .20

CHAPTER 16

CAUSATION

I only assisted natur', ma'am, as the doctor said to the boy's mother, arter he'd bled him to death.

Dickens, *The Pickwick Papers*.

§ 16.1. KILLING IN HOMICIDE

THE common law definition of murder, and similarly that of manslaughter, requires that the defendant should have "killed" his victim, and that the death should follow within a year and a day (§ 11.1).

A "killing" can take place by any means. There need be no direct physical act. If the victim asks his way on a dark night, and the defendant, intending to cause his death, directs him to a path that he knows will bring him to the cliff edge, and the victim suffers a fatal fall, this is clearly murder, though the defendant has done nothing more than utter words. So we may say that "killing" means conduct causing death in any way that the law regards as sufficient.[1] What these ways are has to be considered.

What of accelerating the victim's death?

This is a "killing" in law. Since we are all fated to die at some time, every instance of killing is an instance of accelerating death; and even if death is hastened by as little as five minutes it is still a criminal homicide. So it is no defence to a person who stabs another to death to show that the victim was already dangerously ill.[2] All the same, as we shall see, there are some cases where the courts will ignore minimal causation (§ .5).

Why require that the death must follow within a year and a day?

In origin the rule was perhaps dictated by the desire to limit difficult problems of causation.[3] The CLRC proposed the continuation of the rule on the ground that it would be wrong for a person to remain at risk of a charge of homicide for a long time.[4] He may have been convicted and sentenced for causing serious injury; if the victim then dies from the injury, it would be undesirable to have a fresh trial for murder.

Do problems of causation arise only in homicide cases?

These are the most important in practice, but a causal question is capable of arising in other offences, particularly those against the person

---

[1] It can even be unlawful homicide to cause a person to catch a disease of which he dies: *Castell* v. *Bambridge* (1730) 2 Strange 854, 93 ER 894.

[2] *Dyson* [1908] 2 KB 454; *Pankotai* [1961] Crim.LR 546.

[3] For the requirement see *Dyson*, last note; 1st edn 325 n. 4.

[4] 14th Report 17–18.

or property. For example, the offence under section 18 of the Offences against the Person Act is of *causing* grievous bodily harm. The wording of sections 20 and 47 is different: the one speaks of *inflicting* grievous bodily harm and the other of *occasioning* actual bodily harm, but these verbs, also, imply a requirement of causation.

Similarly, the offences under the Criminal Damage Act 1971 imply that the act of the defendant has caused the damage.

The notion of causation may also appear in general penal legislation, where the context may give the word a special meaning. "Causing" something to be done sometimes bears the narrow meaning of giving an order or direction to do it.[5]

§ 16.2. BUT-FOR CAUSATION

An important distinction must be taken. The question of causation, as it is generally used in the law, involves both a problem of causation *sine qua non*, and a problem of imputability.[1]

A convenient English equivalent of the term causation *sine qua non* is but-for causation (properly speaking, but-for . . . not causation). For a factor to be a but-for cause, one must be able to say that but for the occurrence of the antecedent factor the event would *not* have happened.

Surely the notion of but-for causation is ridiculously wide, because it takes us back to Adam and Eve. The criminal's mother is a but-for cause of his crimes, and so is his grandmother, and all his ancestors to infinity.

That is perfectly true, but two factors limit the judicial enquiry. First, one starts with the defendant who is charged; his mother does not come into it, much less Adam and Eve. Secondly, but-for causation is only half the story; the defendant who was the but-for cause of the harm is not responsible unless his conduct was also the *imputable* cause. We still have to deal with imputable causation.

Is the notion of but-for cause a useful one? Where the cause is a positive act, isn't it too obvious to be worth stating? If D shoots V and V drops down dead, surely you don't have to prove that the bullet entering V's heart caused him to die?

When but-for causation is obvious (as it usually is), it is not discussed. Certainly the answer to your last question is in the negative. But occasionally an issue of this kind may require expert assistance.

> D may administer poison to V, who may die shortly afterwards, yet an autopsy may reveal that V died not of the poison but of heart disease. There will then be medical evidence at D's trial to the effect that the poison did not cause the death, meaning that V would in any case have died at the time and in the way he did, and that the poison did not play any contributory part. If the jury believe this evidence, or, rather, if

[5] *Shave* v. *Rosner* [1954] 2 QB 113 (on the Construction and Use Regulations).

[1] For a short bibliography see 1st edn 326 n. 1.

they are not sure that it is untrue, they must acquit of murder—though D may, of course, be convicted of the attempt.

We may summarise, then, by saying that but-for causation is of legal interest only in the comparatively rare cases where, notwithstanding appearances, it is absent; that when it is alleged to be absent, this raises a question of fact for the jury, who may decide by ordinary experience but may have to be assisted by expert evidence; and that the burden is on the Crown to prove beyond reasonable doubt that the defendant's act (or omission) was a but-for cause.[2]

The last point occasions some difficulty in respect of expert evidence, because an expert may not be willing to commit himself to more than the statement that the result would "probably" not have happened as it did apart from the defendant's act or omission. Notwithstanding that the expert will not commit himself to more, the jury (somewhat strangely) are entitled to draw a sure inference of causation from the evidence.[3] Nevertheless, they should be reminded that they themselves must be sure; and the hesitation or reserve of the expert should surely be a factor leading the appeal court to scrutinise a conviction with care.

The courts assume in manslaughter cases like Stone (§ 12.3) that an omission can be a cause. But surely a non-event cannot be a but-for cause of an event.

Whatever the philosophical view may be, the courts certainly assume, and must assume, that an omission can be a cause (just as lack of oxygen or food is commonly regarded as a cause of death).[4] (However, a court can, and should, say that a reference to causation in a statute does not cover omissions, in the absence of express words or necessary implication: § 7.3 n. 10). That is not a rule of causation but a question of the legal import of words.

The application of the usual burden of proof to the issue of causation is of considerable importance in cases of omission, and sometimes gives the court the opportunity of arriving at a merciful conclusion.[5] On any charge involving causation by omission it behoves the defence to go into the evidence of causation most carefully.

What about two but-for causes contributed by different defendants? Doesn't your definition imply the paradox that if two persons independently cause an event, neither causes it?

To provide for this, an exception for cases of multiple causation has to be inserted into the definition. It is possible for two sufficient causes, C1 and C2, to be present together, so that E follows both, when usually it

---

[2] An example is *Dyos* [1979] Crim.LR 660.

[3] *Cato* [1976] 1 WLR 110, 1 All ER 260, 62 CAR 41; *Stone* [1977] 2 WLR at 173B.

[4] The idea that an omission cannot be a cause is made the foundation of an elaborate legal theory by George P Fletcher. See the summary of his views in [1979] Crim.LR 628.

[5] See *Morby* (1882) 15 Cox 35. Graham Hughes in 67 Yale LJ 627–631 criticises the rule on the ground that it affords too easy a let-out in cases of manslaughter by omission. But it accords with the ordinary principle as to the burden of proof resting on the prosecution; and if some morally guilty persons are acquitted as a result, this is because the law knows no general crime of negligence endangering life where death cannot be proved to have followed.

follows only one or the other. Both C1 and C2 are causes, even though in the particular situation one or other (as the case may be) was not necessary to be present. An example is where two fatal wounds are given independently at the same time. See more in § .9.

Suppose that D1's shot entered the lung and would have caused the victim's death in an hour, but D2's entered the heart and killed him instantaneously?

Then, of course, only D2 has killed him. D1 is guilty of an attempt.

The but-for cause is sometimes referred to as the factual cause, or the *de facto* cause, or the scientific cause. The important thing is to distinguish it from cause in another sense, the "imputable" (or "legal" or "effective" or "direct" or "proximate") cause, to which we now turn.

§ 16.3. IMPUTABLE CAUSATION

When causation is in issue, the defendant's act (or omission) must be shown to be not only a but-for cause but also an imputable or legal cause of the consequence. Imputable causes are some of the but-for causes. In other words, the defendant's act, being a but-for cause, must be sufficiently closely connected with the consequence to involve him in responsibility. The lawyer is interested in the causal parentage of events, not in their causal ancestry. The Model Penal Code expresses the principle by stating that a person is not criminally responsible for a result if it is "too remote and accidental in its occurrence to have a just bearing on the actor's liability or on the gravity of his offence."[1]

Several attempts have been made to find a suitable name for this second notion of cause. To call it the "direct" or "proximate" cause (as is often done) is misleading, because several stages may intervene between the so-called direct cause and the effect. D may send poisoned chocolates to V, who lives at the other side of the world; if V eats the chocolates and dies, the law will certainly regard D as responsible for the death, though his act was far removed in space and considerably removed in time from its effect. To call D's act the "effective" cause is unhelpful, because every cause must by definition be effective—if an act is not effective to produce a given result, it is not a cause of it.

Sometimes (looking at the situation backwards instead of forwards) imputable causation is stated in terms of "remoteness of consequence." To say that a particular consequence is "too remote" is only another way of saying that the defendant's act (or omission) is not an imputable cause.

Going back to the formulation in the Model Penal Code, the use of the word "just" indicates the true nature of the problem. When one has settled the question of but-for causation, the further test to be applied to the but-for cause in order to qualify it for legal recognition is not a test of causation but a moral reaction. The question is whether the result can fairly be said to be imputable to the defendant. Sometimes the question of fairness is settled by rules of law, sometimes it is left for impressionistic decision in the individual case. If the term "cause" must be used, it can best be distinguished in this meaning as the "imputable" or "responsible" or "blamable" cause, to indicate the value-judgment involved.

---

[1] POD s.2.03 (2)(*b*), (3)(*b*).

The word "imputable" is here chosen as best representing the idea. Whereas the but-for cause can generally be demonstrated scientifically,[2] no experiment can be devised to show that one of a number of concurring but-for causes is more substantial or important that another, or that one person who is involved in the causal chain is more blameworthy than another.[3]

What are the principles governing imputable causation?

Hitherto the judges have made little progress in establishing such principles. Generally, of course, no problem arises. Where causation is obvious, the judge may give no direction upon it, even in a homicide case, and even though the burden of proof of causation is supposed to rest on the prosecution. "In homicide cases," said Robert Goff LJ, "it is rarely necessary to give the jury any direction on causation as such."[4] Even when a direction is given, it is usually in very general terms, without so much as distinguishing between factual and legal causation. The judge will use one of the adjectives already mentioned, telling the jury that the defendant's act must have been the "efficient" or "direct" or "proximate" or "substantial" cause of the result, or something beyond a trivial cause, or that the result must not have been too "remote" Or he may tell them that in law the defendant's act need not be the sole cause, or even the main cause, of the result, it being enough that the act contributed "significantly" to that result.[5] This is good enough if the defendant's act was clearly an imputable cause, and it may be good enough in cases where no precise rule can be formulated. It is unsatisfactory in some of the cases to be discussed in this chapter, where the proper result may seem doubtful to the layman and a vague direction may produce discordant verdicts which could have been avoided if more specific guidance had been given.

The direction to the jury should distinguish, where necessary, between the two kinds of causation, and the jury should be informed with some precision of any rules of law that are involved. If the issue is one of but-for causation, it should be enough to ask the jury whether the defendant's act (or omission) was a cause of what happened, explaining that this means: would the event have happened in any case? There is no need to talk about "substantiality."[6] But if the issue is whether the alleged cause was an imputable cause, and if the proper view is that for some specific reason the alleged cause was not or may not have been an imputable cause in law, it should be a misdirection to instruct the jury no more fully than this.[7]

---

[2] But only when the relevant features of the situation can be reproduced as an experiment, so that the effect of removing the alleged but-for cause is revealed.

[3] Unless, of course, the experiment merely seeks to summarise people's opinion as to what act is blameworthy.

[4] *Per* Robert Goff LJ in *Pagett* (1983), The Times, February 4, [1983] Crim. LR 393.

[5] *Ibid.*

[6] In *Cato* [1976] 1 WLR 110, 1 All ER 260, 62 CAR 41, where the issue was one of but-for causation, the court said that the act had to be the substantial cause of death, or at any rate something more than "the mere *de minimis* contribution." I do not follow how a but-for cause can ever be insubstantial or minimal. Either the event would have happened without the alleged but-for cause, or it would not.

[7] In *Cato*, last note, a conviction was upheld although the judge had merely asked the jury whether the defendant's act caused, contributed to or accelerated the death, the court saying that "the jury knew perfectly well that he [the judge] was talking about something more than the mere *de minimis* contribution." If there had been any issue on imputable causation the direction should have been regarded as inadequate.

Similarly, if the proper legal view is that the defendant's act *was* a cause in law, the judge should be entitled to tell the jury so.

This was the practice during the 19th century. Courts would robustly tell the jury whether or not the defendant was responsible for the consequences on given facts. There are now indications that the judges will again do this, if the facts are sufficiently strong.

> In *Pagett*[8] the defendant was a gunman who shot at armed police, using a girl as a shield. The police returned his fire in self-defence, and accidentally killed the girl. Pagett, charged with the murder of the girl, was acquitted by the jury of murder but convicted of manslaughter,[9] and his appeal against conviction was dismissed.

The case will be discussed later as an application of the principles of causation. At present we are concerned with it only as an instance of the judge's function. On the question of causation the trial judge had directed the jury that it was for him to decide as a matter of law whether the defendant caused the death. On this the Court of Appeal commented: "No legitimate criticism can be made of the judge's direction. Strictly speaking it was for him to direct the jury on the applicable principles of law, leaving it for them to decide as a question of fact, on those applicable principles, whether the necessary causal link had been established. In practical terms that was precisely what the judge did."

The first of these sentences seems to deny criticism of the judge, while the second sentence seems to express some faint criticism. Perhaps the court means that it is best for the judge not to say frankly that the causation question is for him, but that all the same he may instruct the jury in such terms that where the facts are clear they have no causation issue to decide. There is no virtue in such hair-splitting.

The theoretical problem may be clarified if we distinguish between cases where there is and is not a relevant rule of law on the subject of imputable causation. If no satisfactory rule can be formulated, and it is a matter of "gut reaction," the proper verdict on the point being subject to legitimate doubt, the jury can be told that they must decide whether in fairness the result should be attributed to the defendant. (The direction is unnnecessary if it obviously is imputable to him.) If a rule can be formulated, which ought to govern all similar situations (which was the case in *Pagett*), the judge should be entitled to announce it firmly to the jury, and where necessary to exclude irrelevant evidence.

The last proposition is supported by another recent case, *Malcherek*,[10] where the control of the trial judge was emphasised.

> Malcherek stabbed his wife in the abdomen; her heart stopped in

---

[8] N. 4 above.

[9] The conviction was on the basis of constructive manslaughter, but obviously it could have been for reckless manslaughter. The CA made it plain that if the jury had convicted of murder, presumably on the doctrine of *Hyam*, the conviction would have been upheld.

[10] [1981] 1 WLR 690 (see §§ .10 n. 2, .13). Cp. the dictum in *Blaue*, referred to *ibid*. 696F and discussed in 1st edn 331.

hospital and she was put on a ventilator, but, her brain being irretrievably damaged, she was taken off. On a charge of murder the trial judge refused to leave the issue of causation to the jury, and D was convicted. On appeal the defence sought to introduce evidence to suggest that the doctor had switched the machine off prematurely, but the court refused to hear the evidence. In such circumstances, the court declared, where a doctor decides "that the patient is for practical purposes dead," and switches off, this does not in law prevent the assailant from being responsible.

Granted, then, that rules of imputable causation are rules of law, we must consider what these rules are. Subject to what is to be said in § .9 as to the new intervening act, no problem generally arises when the defendant has intentionally produced the consequence.[11] The chief difficulties relate to unintended consequences. It may be suggested that five rules are supported either by authority or by common sense:

— the rule that negligence must be relevant (§ .4);
— the minimal causation principle (§ .5);
— the ordinary hazard principle (§ .7);
— the reasonable foresight principle (§ .8); and
— the principle of the new intervening act (§ .9).

§ 16.4. CAUSATION AND NEGLIGENCE

Where negligence (or recklessness) is in issue, a limiting rule straddles the divide between but-for and imputable causation. The rule is that the negligence proved against the defendant must be negligence in a relevant respect. The case must be such that the accident would not have happened if he had not been negligent. In other words, the defendant is not liable for an event that is not causally connected with the feature of his conduct that was negligent. The rule has some applicaton to manslaughter and causing death by reckless driving.

An illustration in the reports is *Dalloway*.[1] The driver of a horse and cart let the reins lie loose on the horse's back. This was of course a negligent way of driving. A child ran across the road, and was knocked down and killed. Erle J directed the jury that if the driver by using the reins could have saved the child he was guilty of manslaughter, but that if they thought he could not have saved the child by pulling the reins they must acquit him.

In other words, the question was this. Assuming that the defendant had been driving carefully, holding the reins, would the death have occurred? A defendant is not guilty of causing a death by negligence if the victim ran out at a moment when no one—not even a person who had been behaving carefully throughout—could have pulled up.

---

[11] But see *Lewis* (1922), discussed in Chap. 34, where an intended consequence was held not to be caused in law.

[1] (1847) 2 Cox 273.

In *Dalloway* there was an element of but-for causation connecting the defendant's driving with the death of the child. Had Dalloway not been travelling in his vehicle at that time and that spot, his vehicle would not have hit the child. Moreover, he was negligent, perhaps grossly negligent. But it was also necessary to show (on a charge of manslaughter) that the death was causally connected with the negligent failure to hold the reins.

§ 16.5. THE DEFENCE OF MINIMAL CAUSATION

Of the assorted adjectives mentioned in § .3, "substantial" currently finds the greatest favour; and if this word is used in instructing the jury a conviction is pretty safe from being upset on appeal. However, the Court of Appeal regards it as being too favourable to the defendant.[1] The preferred direction is to tell the jury that they can convict the defendant if his conduct (for example, his reckless driving) was "a cause" of the death, being something more than a purely trivial cause (a *de minimis* contribution, as it is ungrammatically termed). The reference to "a cause" is presumably to but-for causation, while the reference to minimal contribution seems to express the idea that imputable causation is lacking. This direction at least gives the jury some pointer to the fact that they are entitled to use common sense (or moral instinct) on questions of causation.

It may have been a notion of minimal causation that was in the mind of Devlin J in *Adams*.[2] As we have seen (§ .1), the acceleration of death is supposed to be enough for criminal liability, so that the defendant is not normally allowed to say that the victim would in any event have died before long. But in *Adams* Devlin J directed the jury that when health cannot be restored a doctor "is still entitled to do all that is proper and necessary to relieve pain and suffering even if measures he takes may incidentally shorten life." The passage as a whole seems to imply the view that what the doctor does by way of approved medical practice is not a cause in law. It plays such a minor part in causing the death that it can be excluded from consideration. A more satisfactory reason would be the doctrine of necessity, at which Devlin J perhaps glanced in his use of the word "necessary."[3] But we may applaud his attitude without enquiring too closely into its legal basis.

§ 16.6. THE UNEXPECTED TWIST

Most problems of causation relate to what may be called the unexpected twist, which is to occupy the rest of this chapter. Subject to what is to be said later, an unexpected twist in the outcome of conduct does not

---

[1] *Hennigan* [1971] 3 All ER 133, 55 CAR 652, and cases there cited; *Malcherek* § .3 n. 10.

[2] See Williams, *The Sanctity of Life and the Criminal Law* (Eng. edn) 289; [1957] Crim.LR 365. Cp. §§ 12.8 at n. 10, 16.13.

[3] Other interpretations have been offered. Hart and Honoré, *Causation in the Law* 308–309, suggest that Devlin J might have rested his opinion on "absence of intent when the effect of the drug is not known;" but that would not let the doctor out if the effect is known, and the judge gave no indication that he regarded this as the decisive point. For another discussion see Beynon in [1982] Crim.LR 18.

necessarily put the end result outside the mental element, or mean that the conduct is not the imputable cause of the result.

> For example, D attacks V intending to stab him in the arm, but V jumps back, falls and cracks his head. Assuming that both the harm intended and that suffered are grievous bodily harm, there is no difficulty from the point of view either of *mens rea* or of causation in convicting D of causing grievous bodily harm with intent, under section 18 of the OAPA. The legal category is "grievous bodily harm," and it does not matter that the defendant intended one form and did another.[1]

Such facts are very similar to transferred intention, except that here the intention takes effect upon the person intended, and the only variation is in respect of the way in which it takes effect or in respect of the precise description of the injury. The unexpected twist principle does not supplant the primary requirement of a mental element for the particular crime. In a crime of intention, the ultimate result must be as intended by the defendant[2]; but the mode by which the intended result occurred need not have been intended.[3]

Where, as in the case of criminal damage, the offence is defined in broad terms so that it covers a great variety of causal nexus, the unexpected twist principle can have unwelcome results, particularly in making the defendant subject to conviction for doing much greater damage than he expected. The solution here would be to sentence on the basis of what was within the range of what the defendant must have foreseen.

A problem of justice can also arise where the defendant is still at an early stage in his effort to commit the crime when events are, so to speak, taken out of his hands. Professor Smith suggests that the defendant can be liable for the result if he had reached the stage of attempt, but otherwise not.[4] He puts two hypotheticals.

> D prepares a poisoned apple with the intention of giving it to his wife, V, to eat tomorrow. V finds the poisoned apple today, eats it and dies. Or D is cleaning his gun with the intention of shooting V tomorrow. The gun goes off accidentally and kills V.

It would obviously be too harsh to convict D of murder in the second case; his liability is for manslaughter. As to the first case, the answer may depend on the more detailed facts. If D put the poison by his wife's bedside, intending to administer it to her when she woke up, the jury should be allowed to find that he has launched himself sufficiently far on his ghastly plan to be guilty of an attempt, and therefore (according to Smith's suggestion) to be guilty of murder if the wife unexpectedly wakes up and drinks the poison herself. If on the other hand the poisoned drink is still in the kitchen, the result should probably be different. The question of attempt is further considered in § 17.5.

Whatever the theory may be, the law is not always applied with full rigour. On a charge of murder the trial judge may permit or encourage the jury to return a verdict of manslaughter. Or he may accept a plea to manslaughter, even when in strict law it is murder. The unexpected twist principle would probably meet with general acceptance in obvious cases. But the criminal law should, so far as possible, avoid saddling people with liability for results markedly different from what was intended or foreseen. So it is important not merely that the law should be applied with discretion but that we should find rules that satisfactorily

---

[1] A neat illustration from Papua and New Guinea is *Kipali-Ikarum* [1967–68] P & NGLR 119. It would probably be necessary that what happened should be reasonably foreseeable, as explained below; but this could easily be established on the facts given.

[2] Subject to the law of transferred intention.

[3] Another good example of the unexpected twist principle is *Michael* § .10 n. 1.

[4] [1983] Crim.LR 105.

state *what* twists in the outcome are to be regarded as beyond the range of responsibility ascribed to the defendant.

§ 16.7. THE ORDINARY HAZARD PRINCIPLE

This is a narrow principle and has not come before the English courts, but it seems obvious.

> D attacks V intending to stab him to death; V runs away, and in his fight is struck by lightning and dies. One would say that D is not guilty of murder, though he is guilty of attempted murder. Why is he not guilty of murder? Because it was not he that killed V, but the lightning? But if V had jumped over a cliff or into a river in an effort to escape, or to commit suicide in despair, or had accidentally fallen over the cliff or into the river in his flight, D would have been accountable for the death, and we should not have said that it was not D who killed V but the water or the hard ground. What is it that makes us feel that the lightning is different?

The most obvious answer is that being struck by lightning is an ordinary risk of life that people do not seek to avoid. One is no more subject to being struck by lightning when one is running away from an attacker than when one is taking a walk. The attacker has not substantially increased the victim's risk.

Another example of the ordinary hazard principle is where the victim of an attack dies in a traffic accident when he is being conveyed by ambulance to hospital, or dies as a result of a fever which sweeps through the hospital. Assuming that his death was not contributed to by his weak condition, the attacker is not guilty of it, because the effect of the attack was merely to place the victim in a geographical position where another agency produced his death. The attack did not substantially increase the risk of the fatal result, because anyone may die in a traffic accident or epidemic.[1] Of course, a reasonable man mulling over all the possible consequences of an attack might think of these possibilities; but they would not be possibilities rendered any more likely by the fact of the attack. Even if it could be shown that there was slightly more risk of dying of fever in hospital than elsewhere (perhaps because of the presence in hospital of resistant bacteria), this would probably be accounted too insignifcant to affect the decision.

Contrast the case where the victim died of hospital fever, but a contributory factor was the weakness caused by his injuries, so that he would not have died if it had not been for his weakness. Probably the attacker would then be guilty of criminal homicide (murder or manslaughter), for on these facts there is a *medical* (and not merely a fortuitous) connection between the wound and the death. It is like the case of a wound turning gangrenous and causing death, where the wounding is clearly the cause of death.

In the absence of English authority, the ordinary hazard principle is a matter of theoretical speculation. In most but not all applications it can be regarded as a particular application of a test of reasonable foresight, on which decided cases can be found.

---

[1] Cp. *Bush* v. *Commowealth* (1880) 78 Ky. 268, where the defendant was aquitted of unlawful homicide even though the disease was communicated to the victim by a surgeon operating on a bullet wound inflicted by the defendant. See Jerome Hall, *Studies in Jurisprudence and Criminal Theory* (New York 1959) 171.

§ 16.8. THE REASONABLE FORESIGHT PRINCIPLE

To say that a consequence, to be imputed to the defendant, must be within the risk that would be apprehended by a reasonable man is much wider than the ordinary hazard principle. Under the name of the "risk principle" it has been discussed by writers on the tort of negligence, and it also makes an appearance in the criminal case of *Roberts*.[1]

> Roberts was driving a girl from a party, and, according to the view of the facts that (in the opinion of the Court of Appeal) the jury must have taken, he pestered her with advances, held her coat and told her that he had beaten up girls who had refused him. She jumped out of the moving car and suffered injury. The chairman of Sessions directed the jury that on these facts Roberts would be guilty of an assault occasioning actual bodily harm under OAPA s.47. He was convicted, and the conviction was affirmed on appeal. The court said: "The test is: Was it [the injury] the natural result of what the alleged assailant said and did, in the sense that it was something that could reasonably have been foreseen as the consequence of what he was saying or doing?"[2]

In previous cases of similar type[3] the test laid down had generally been whether the victim acted reasonably in his endeavour to escape. *Roberts* widens the area of liability and also puts it on a more intelligible footing. Whether it is prudent for a woman to jump from a rapidly moving car to avoid rape is a question on which opinions may differ, but at any rate it is fully understandable, and the possibility of it could well have been foreseen by the attacker.

The reasonable foresight principle gives the jury the opportunity of exempting the defendant where what happened is particularly unusual and it would be unfair to hold him liable. But the intentional wrongdoer will rarely be advantaged by it. Although he has a theoretical opportunity of escaping a consequence brought about by the victim's unforeseeable reaction, a jury would probably be loth to describe an act done to escape as not reasonably foreseeable. Anyone who makes a serious or distressing attack on another should realise that the victim may try to escape, and in panic may try to escape in a very dangerous way. However the question of causation is in the last resort decided by the jury, and the jury may take a merciful view.[4]

> The facts of a New York case[5] would seem to illustrate conduct that is not reasonably foreseeable, but the court did not take this view. D gave a lift in his car to an 18-year-old girl: and during the journey offered the girl $1 to have sexual intercourse. The girl in panic jumped from the car, when it was moving at about 25 m.p.h., fractured her skull and died. D was convicted of manslaughter, though he had neither made an attack on the girl nor threatened her, the court holding that her effort to escape was a "natural consequence" of D's act. One may gravely doubt whether it was reasonably foreseeable,

---

[1] (1971) 56 CAR 95. Cp. *Mackie* [1973] Crim.LR 54 (Crown Court).

[2] For the interpretation of s.47 as being an offence of half *mens rea* see § 9.4. The CA did not say, though it surely was the fact, that the chairman was at fault in not leaving the question of foreseeability to the jury; but perhaps an argument based on this error would have been dismissed under the proviso.

[3] In particular, *Pitts* (1842) Car. & M 284, 174 ER 509. See also *Cartledge* v. *Allen* [1973] Crim.LR 530 (a very questionable decision on the facts as reported), which reverted to the formulation current before *Roberts*.

[4] As they did in *Pitts*, last note, where they acquitted the defendant of homicide notwithstanding the judge's direction.

[5] *People* v. *Goodman* (1943) 182 Misc. 585, 44 NYS 2d 715.

and in English law there would be the further difficulty of finding an initial act of gross negligence on D's part.

An event may be reasonably foreseeable as part of a generic risk, even though it is improbable in its details. This observation is illustrated by an old anonymous case, generally known as the harlot's case (1560)[6].

> "A harlot woman was delivered of a child. She laid it away, alive, in an orchard; and covered it with leaves. A kite struck at it with his claws. In consequence of being thus stricken, the child died very soon afterwards. She was arraigned of murder; and was executed. . . . For she had intended the child's death; and *voluntas reputatur pro facto*."

The last remark—that the will is taken for the deed—is not literally true; what should have been said was that since the woman intended to cause the child to die (of exposure), the fact that it died in a somewhat unexpected way was irrelevant. If the child had been killed by a vagrant she would not on principle have been guilty of murder, for, as we shall see, the intervention of a responsible actor would have made the death too remote a consequence of the infant's exposure.

Kites were common in 1560, and appointed themselves scavengers to the City of London. Now they are rare; but if the drama of the harlot's case were to be repeated, the baby being killed by one of these birds, the result would surely be the same. The harlot intended her baby to die as the result of withholding from it the human protection that an infant needs. This is the way in which the baby did die, and the unlikelihood of the particular mode of death (if it was unlikely) was immaterial. We may express the principle by saying that a risk is involved in the defendant's conduct, and an event is within the risk, if a reasonable person would have contemplated the event as part of the general risk involved in such conduct, whether as the major risk or as some subsidiary risk; *and it is immaterial that a subsidiary risk was so unlikely in itself that if it had stood alone the conduct would not have been negligent.*[7]

Another way of explaining the rule would be to say that although the test of risk is usually stated as one of reasonable foreseeability, in practice it is not a question whether the reasonable defendant, if asked beforehand what he foresees, would immediately respond in terms of what later happens. What happens may be only one out of an infinite number of possibilities, and yet it is regarded as foreseeable for legal purposes if it is the kind of thing that does happen without causing surprise. The question is one of the normality of what happens when looked at with hindsight rather than foresight. This is so, at least, in the law of tort, where the risk principle is relatively well developed.

Again, the victim need not be the specific victim that the reasonably foreseeing defendant would primarily have contemplated: it is enough that he belongs to the general class of persons who in a larger view would be within such reasonable contemplation. Indeed, if one thinks only of the particular victim (great-uncle George who has paid an unheralded visit from Australia) the likelihood of his appearance may be so small that if this were the only risk the conduct would not be accounted negligent at all. What characterises the conduct as negligent is, frequently, the likelihood that members of a class may be involved; and the class may be defined merely as those who in fact come into perilous proximity.

Doesn't the risk principle, as applied to crimes requiring intention, contradict that requirement?

The objection overlooks the fact that rules of causation cannot make the defendant guilty of a crime of intention unless he intended the event specified in the law (such as the death of a human being). All that the rules do is to settle the question of liability where the event occurs in an unexpected way. The foreseeability rule is a *limitation* upon the general principle relating to the unexpected twist.

---

[6] Crompton's *Justice* 24.

[7] For the concluding words I am indebted to Mr M M Lemberg, whose unpublished dissertation on Causation is in the Cambridge University Library.

How does the rule in manslaughter excluding the victim's special sensitivity from consideration square with the risk principle?

The special sensitivity rule is an exception from the risk principle, but it can be justified on special grounds.

These special grounds start from the observation that the risk principle does not operate to negative liability if the event happened precisely as the defendant intended. Suppose that he aimed at the victim with a rifle and all the experts would have said that the victim was out of range; but he hoped to hit the victim and by some freak did so. The defendant is clearly responsible for hitting the victim. Questions of foreseeable risk arise only when there is some slight shift from the events that the defendant intended.

All the authorities on the special sensitivity rule seem to relate to manslaughter, where there was no intention to kill; but it can hardly be doubted that the same rule applies to murder. If the defendant intended to cause death and actually did so, it is irrelevant that the injury he inflicted would not have caused a normal person to die. This is somewhat similar to the case just put of the victim being out of normal range of the weapon. However, it is not quite so straightforward. The defendant may have aimed to stab the victim through the heart, but only succeeded in cutting him slightly, but the victim was a haemophiliac and bled to death. There is here a shift in the intended chain of causation, though (perhaps it may be said) only a slight shift. At any rate, it is intelligible that a court should refuse to pay attention to the victim's parlous state of health, if the defendant has substantially achieved his purpose.

The special sensitivity rule does not or should not qualify a requirement of *mens rea* or fault for the particular offence. An attacker whose *mens rea* is limited to the infliction of slight injury cannot become guilty of murder if, owing to the victim's sensitivity, the slight injury becomes serious and leads to death. A person who is negligent as to causing slight injury should not be guilty of manslaughter if, owing to the special sensitivity of the victim, the slight injury proves to be fatal. Manslaughter should require negligence as to death, or at any rate as to grievous bodily harm.

The law of constructive manslaughter is anomalous, because if strictly applied it turns a minor assault into criminal homicide if the victim dies because of his peculiar physical condition. The interpretation of OAPA s.47 as creating an offence of half *mens rea* can also have the effect that a person may be convicted of an aggravated assault although he neither intended to inflict bodily harm nor was reckless or even negligent as to it, if bodily harm follows because of the victim's special sensitivity. But if the bodily harm follows only because of the victim's effort to escape, it is clear from *Roberts* that the attacker is not liable under this section unless what the victim did was reasonably foreseeable.

Does the risk principle apply to the doctrine of transferred intention?

Apparently not. No case decides that it does, and one suggests that it does not.[8] It may be thought that in *Gore* (§ 11.5 n. 1) the defendant could not reasonably have foreseen that the apothecary would be poisoned, yet her intention was transferred.

§ 16.9. NEW INTERVENING ACT

An extreme view of criminal responsibility might be that a man is under a duty to act in such a way that others are not led to cause harm, so that in some circumstances he would be responsible for harm that is directly caused by others, even though without his authorisation or

[8] *Latimer* (1886) 17 QBD 359.

encouragement. This does not represent the criminal law. The legal attitude is that a man is primarily responsible only for what he himself does or incites. The fact that his own wrongful conduct provided the background for some consequential wrong act by another, and that he should have foreseen this act, does not make him responsible for it.

Putting the rule in terms of causation, the new intervening act (*novus actus interveniens*) of a responsible actor, who has full knowledge of what he is doing, and is not subject to mistake or pressure, will normally operate to relieve the defendant of liability for a further consequence, because it makes the consequence "too remote." Underlying this rule there is, undoubtedly, a philosophical attitude. Moralists and lawyers regard the individual's will as the autonomous prime cause of his behaviour. What a person does (if he has reached adult years, is of sound mind and is not acting under mistake, intimidation or other similar pressure) is his own responsibility, and is not regarded as having been caused by other people. An intervening act of this kind, therefore, breaks the causal connection that would otherwise have been perceived between previous acts and the forbidden consequence. (An intervening wrongful omission does not break it.)

The rule can be rationalised in psychological terms by saying that the intervention of the responsible actor diverts our retributive wrath from the defendant, the previous actor, who may appear to be so much less culpable than the later actor, and this switching of retributive feeling is expressed in causal language. Sometimes, too, we may feel that making people responsible for the subsequent behaviour of others, merely because they foresaw or could have foreseen that behaviour, would be too great a restriction upon liberty. Yet another way of explaining the rule would be to say that part of the object of the criminal trial is to dramatise society's rejection of the deed, and this is adequately done by prosecuting the immediate author. There is no pressing necessity to regard more remote authors as responsible for the harm itself, though they may well be prosecuted for other offences, such as attempt, or in appropriate circumstances as accessories. It is important that the law should not saddle a man with liability for consequences that not only he but also the general public would blame on someone else.

To take a fanciful case, suppose that D1 prepares a poisoned drink, intending to offer it to V. D2, who has his own score to settle with V, and who has observed D1's preparations, offers the drink to V, who takes it and dies. D2 was not acting in collaboration with D1. D2 is guilty of murder and D1 is not. If the poison which D1 left for V to drink had been administered to him by someone who did not know it was poisoned, D1 would have been guilty of murder. As it is, D2's criminal intent insulates him from liability.[1]

As another example of the rule, a person who provokes another to kill without inciting him to do so does not become guilty of murder or manslaughter, even though he realised or should have realised what the effect of his conduct would be.[2] Similarly, unintentionally provoking another person to break the peace[3] or to drive recklessly[4] does not make the provoker criminally responsible.

A painter makes a habit of painting pastiches in the style of a famous artist. He sells them, saying that they are his own work but realising the strong probability that eventually some of them will be resold at inflated prices to people who believe that they are genuine. Even if one of them is made an instrument of fraud, it would be going too

---

[1] Cp. *People* v. *Elder* (1894) 100 Mich. 515, 59 NW 237. For a less obvious illustration see *Hilton* (1838) 2 Lewin 214, 168 ER 1132. The doctrine of remoteness has been used to mitigate some extreme applications of the law of constructive manslaughter: *Bennett* (1858) Bell 1, 169 ER 1143.

In view of the dearth of recent authority on *novus actus*, courts that are unpersuaded by arguments for it may look more kindly upon the somewhat cloudy statement of principle in by Lord Wright, quoted in *Smith* [1959] 2 QB 35, that causation is broken by "something unwarrantable, a new cause which disturbs the sequence of events, something which can be described as either unreasonable or extraneous or extrinsic." A *novus actus* fits this description nicely.

[2] Cp. *Dubois* (1959) 32 CR 187 (Quebec).

[3] *Beatty* v. *Gillbanks* § 15.4 n. 8.

[4] *Mastin* § 15.11 n.3.

far to say that the painter is a party to the fraud. Perhaps there should be a law against selling pastiches not clearly marked as such, but there is not.

The *novus actus* rule is of fundamental importance at common law, because it underlies the doctrine of accessoryship. If D2 incites D1 to kill V, and D1 complies, D2 has prompted (in ordinary speech, caused) D1 to perpetrate the crime, and is himself an accessory to the crime, but he has not in law caused V's death. Fletcher states the principle as follows.

> "Aiding the crime of a responsible, self-actuating perpetrator does not 'cause,' 'control' or 'determine' the latter's conduct. The accessory contributes to the crime, but the execution is not his doing."[5]

As we have seen, there are certain important differences between the liability of the accessory and that of the perpetrator. If it were not for the *novus actus* rule the successful inciter would be liable as a perpetrator, which would require the law of complicity to be rewritten.[6]

The point just made also shows that the *novus actus* principle is distinct from the requirement of reasonable foreseeability. If D2 pays an assassin D1 to kill V, of course he foresees that D1 will do the killing, so that the requirement of foreseeability is satisfied; but still D2 is not a perpetrator of the crime.

The *novus actus* rule does not prevent liability arising for joint negligence in concerted action, even though it is the act of only one of the parties that produces the evil result.[7] The law of complicity creates liability where the normal rule for causation would not.[8]

Although a *novus actus* rule is recognised in the law of tort, it differs from the criminal rule in that if A instigates B to commit a tort, both A and B are regarded as causing the result as joint tortfeasors. The law of tort does not distinguish between degrees of complicity as the criminal law does.

The *novus actus* principle is so potent that it can even rescue a defendant from strict liability.

> In *Impress (Worcester) Ltd.* v. *Rees*[9] the appellant company's fuel store leaked oil into the Severn, after an unknown person had tampered with the valve. Normally (it was assumed) the leak would have been an offence of strict liability,[10] but the Divisional Court held that the company was not liable, because the intervening act of the stranger was an "intervening cause of so powerful a nature that the conduct of the appellants was not a cause at all but was merely part of the surrounding circumstances."

The pollution of the river was, of course, factually caused in part by the circumstance that the company had accumulated fuel near the river. But this was merely the background of the matter; in law, the only operative cause was the act of the mischief-maker. The distinction is between something operating directly to produce the result and something operating only indirectly through the wrongful intervener.

The *novus actus* principle was expressly recognised, for the law of

---

[5] George P Fletcher, *Rethinking Criminal Law* (Boston 1978) 582.

[6] The *novus actus* rule is also capable of explaining the doctrine of innocent agency, for the act of an innocent agent is not a *novus actus*.

[7] As in *Salmon* § 15.11 n. 1, and *Reid* (1975) 62 CAR 109.

[8] Where, however, there is no concerted action but only concurrent acts of negligence, the one party is not liable for the results of the negligence of the other, even though his own negligence is equal to that of the other and he might have foreseen the evil result of the affair in which both were engaged. The point emerges sharply by comparing *Swindall* with *Mastin*; see § 15.11 nn. 2, 3.

[9] [1971] 2 All E.R. 357.

[10] It has since been established that an offence of "causing" another person to produce a forbidden result does not carry strict liability: § 42.4.

homicide, in *Pagett*.[11] It was held not to prevent liability attaching on the facts of the case, for the reason to be considered in the next section.

Difficult problems can sometimes arise. Suppose, for example, that D1 and D2 successively and independently wound V with murderous intent, and V dies from the loss of blood caused by both wounds together, when he would not have died from either alone. Beginning with D2, the later assailant, he is guilty of murder, since he must take his victim as he finds him—in this case, weakened and bleeding from the first wound.

As regards the liability of D1, the question is moot. On the one hand it may be argued that he is not guilty of murder if the wound he inflicted would not alone have caused the death, because he is not responsible for the subsequent act of a fresh agent. The argument the other way is that both causes are physically operating to bring about death. Does the *novus actus* doctrine insulate D1 from liability in respect of the death? (If D1 and D2 acted at the same time, though independently, both would clearly be responsible, since their acts would be concurrent causes: § .2).

My own opinion is that D1 in the hypothetical should not be held liable for the death. But we do not hear much of the *novus actus* doctrine from the courts nowadays, and it is likely to prove in practice to be a fragile shield for the defendant when the facts are horrific.

The concurrent causation rule is applied in cases of nuisance. Two musical bands together (or two pig-farmers together) may be a nuisance when one alone would not. Two cars parked opposite each other may render a narrow highway impassable when one alone would not. Each defendant is clearly liable if all started their activities at the same time. But it has been ruled that where one was first on the scene, and did not at that time commit an offence, the subsequent act of the other does not make him responsible for causing a nuisance or unreasonable obstruction as the case may be. The first has not caused the act of the second, and what the first did, if it stood alone, would not have been an offence. (This particular ruling may be doubted; the offence being a continuing one, questions of intervening act can hardly arise.)[12]

§ 16.10. THE NON-RESPONSIBLE INTERVENER

We have seen, in discussing the subject of complicity, that if D incites an innocent agent to commit a criminal act, and the innocent agent does so, D is regarded as perpetrating the crime. Put in terms of causation, the rule is that if D has done the last act that he intended to do (instructing the innocent agent), he causes the result notwithstanding that the immediate cause was the act of another (the innocent agent), if there was no subsequent criminal volition of another. This principle is wider than the simple doctrine of innocent agency, as *Michael*[1] shows.

> Michael, a single woman, had an illegitimate baby boy a few months old whom she boarded out with a foster-mother. Intending to murder the infant she bought a bottle of laudanum, told the foster-mother that it was medicine, and directed her to give the infant a teaspoonful every night. The woman gave none, but put the bottle on the mantelpiece,

---

[11] § .3 at n. 8.

[12] *Langham* v. *Crisp* [1975] Crim.LR 652 (Crown Court). For the practical difficulties see comment in 139 JPN 669.

For a fuller discussion of the doctrine of new intervening act see Hart and Honoré, *Causation in the Law* (Oxford 1959), and review in J. Hall, *op. cit.* 187 ff.; Fletcher, *op. cit.* 366–368.

[1] (1840) 9 C & P 356, 173 ER 867, 2 Mood. CC 120, 169 ER 48.

> where a few days later her own small boy, aged about 5, being left alone with the infant, took the bottle down and administered half its contents to the infant, who died. Michael was convicted of murder, and the conviction was affirmed by the Court for Crown Cases Reserved.

No clear reason was given by the court for holding Michael responsible, but we may rationalise as follows. Michael intended to poison her baby with laudanum administered by the hand of another, and this very thing happened. The fact that she intended the killing process to be spun out was immaterial. (The trial judge in directing the jury assumed that it was necessary for the prosecution to show that a single teaspoonful of the liquid—the dose directed by Michael—was enough to kill the baby; but nowadays this would be regarded as too lenient a direction. Even if the dose of a teaspoonful each night would have killed only by reason of having a cumulative effect, the variation whereby half the bottle was administered at once would have been immaterial.)

The more striking deviation from Michael's plan was the intervention of a different, and unforeseen, actor. The small boy was innocent, being under the age of criminal responsibility, and Michael was responsible for the result that he helped to bring about, even though he was not Michael's intended tool. Michael had done the last act that she intended to do, and there was no affront to the sense of justice in saying that the variation in the chain of causation was immaterial.

The negative rules we are now studying are cumulative in effect. It is not enough to show that there was no new intervening act of a responsible actor; it must also be shown that what happened was reasonably foreseeable. There was ample evidence in *Michael* that the latter rule was satisfied. The defendant had placed the poison in the room where the baby was, and had described it as medicine for the baby. (It seems very likely that the boy of 5 who had administered it to the baby had been told or otherwise had come to believe that it was the baby's medicine, though the jury were not asked to consider this point.) The fact that some other member of the foster-mother's family might do the actual administering of the medicine was clearly within the risk she created, though of course the question was one for the jury.

The innocent agent or non-responsible intervener may, of course, be the victim himself. This type of problem was discussed in §.6.

Two decisions mentioned previously provide further examples of the non-responsible intervener: *Malcherek*[2] and *Pagett*.[3] The judgment in the latter case proceeds on the basis that the police were acting in self-defence, but the more obvious justification was that they were entitled to kill if necessary in the course of trying to make an arrest or to prevent violent crime or the escape of a violent offender. On any view the police were acting under the pressure caused by the defendant, and so were not exercising the unfettered volition presupposed by the *novus actus* rule.

The court did not consider the question whether the police were justified in shooting when this involved such a large risk to the hostage. Self-defence would not justify the killing of a non-aggressor. The act of the police marksman was very possibly justifiable as the lesser evil, if there was a great probability that otherwise the criminal would shoot someone else. But

---

[2] *Malcherek* § 16.3 n. 10.

[3] *Pagett* § .3 at n. 8.

even if the police made the wrong choice in the dilemma forced on them by the defendant, that should not make their act a *novus actus*. If for example D tosses a fused bomb towards V1, and V1, in order to protect his property, throws it towards V2, who is killed when it explodes, V1's act was illegal (he had no right to imperil another in order to protect his own property), but, being done in defence and in the agony of the moment, need not be accounted a new intervening act. D in this hypothetical could probably be convicted of the murder of V2 by transferred intention.[4] The same principle underlies the "escape" cases, like *Roberts* (§ .8 n. 1).

§ 16.11. DEATH THROUGH FRIGHT OR SHOCK

Where a person is attacked he does not commonly die of fright or shock, but if he does, his death may perhaps be attributed to the attacker on the special sensitivity principle.[1]

A person cannot reasonably foresee that another will die of fright when the other is not himself in danger. The law of constructive manslaughter and transferred intention should not be pushed so far as to say that if D assaults V1 he becomes guilty of the manslaughter of V2, a mere spectator, who, remarkably, dies of fright or shock in witnessing what happens to V1.[2]

Fright is more likely to result in death when it causes the victim to make an effort to escape (as by jumping out of the window). We have seen that the attacker can be convicted of murder or manslaughter if the victim's act was reasonably foreseeable,[3] provided that there is the mental state or other fault on the part of the attacker necessary for the type of homicide or other crime with which he is charged. The interpretation of OAPA s.47 as an offence of half *mens rea* means that, provided that the flight reaction and consequent injury were foreseeable by a reasonable man, they need not have been foreseen by the defendant.[4] Similarly, he can be convicted of constructive manslaughter if death results.[5]

---

[4] Cp. the tort case of *Scott* v. *Shepherd* (1773) 2 W Bl. 892, 96 ER 525; see also *Madison* v. *State* (1955) 234 Ind. 517, 130 NE 2d 35.

[1] See *Towers* § 12.5 n. 9; *Dugal* (1878) 4 Que.LR 350. There are accounts of "voodoo deaths" resulting from fear: see correspondence in the BMJ in 1965.

[2] Query, therefore, the American case of *Re Heigho* (1910) 18 Idaho 566, 110 Pac. 1029, 32 LRA (N.S.) 877, where the defendant was convicted of manslaughter though the only person killed was an onlooker (mother-in-law of the person he assaulted) who died of fright. The medical opinion is that an ordinary person is not likely to suffer any permanent effects from shock unless he is himself involved: see Havard in 19 MLR 478. Technically, no doubt, a combination of the law of constructive manslaughter and transferred intention would support *Re Heigho*; but it would be open to a court to refuse to combine the two doctrines. In *Towers* (last note) the evidence showed that the attacker was negligent and even reckless towards the baby (since the girl when attacked might have dropped it), and the way in which the baby actually died could perhaps be regarded as a mere difference of mode; even so, the decision was severe.

[3] To the cases previously referred to add: *Hickman* (1831) 5 C & P 151, 172 E 917 (spurring horse to escape and being thrown); *Halliday* (1889) 61 LT (N.S.) 701, 54 JP 312; *Curley* (1909) 2 CAR 109; *Beech* (1912) 23 Cox 181, 7 CAR 197, 76 JP 287, 107 LT 461; *Bird*, 1952 SLT 446; *Daley* [1980] AC 237; D W Elliott in [1974] Crim.LR 15; overseas authorities in Norval Morris and Colin Howard, *Studies in Criminal Law* (Oxford 1964) 25–26, and 31 Mich.LRev. 672–673. Although some of these cases do not expressly state a test of reasonable foresight, this seems to be the practical result of all of them.

[4] See D W Elliott, *op. cit.* and above §§ 9.3, 4.

[5] *Daley* [1980] AC 237.

Authority from the Victorian era declares that a person who treats another unkindly is not liable if the other dies of grief.[6] The reason is not stated. It may be disbelief in the causation: in the words of W S Gilbert, "hearts do not break; they sting and ache, but do not die." That is so generally, but statistical investigation indicates that grief can contribute to death.[7] Perhaps this cannot be well enough proved in the particular case to be of interest to the criminal law. If it can be, the special sensitivity rule might possibly be invoked to make the grief-giver responsible for causing the death, assuming that other requisites of criminal liability are present.

On the *novus actus* principle, a person who by atrocious conduct provokes another to commit suicide is not guilty of murder or manslaughter,[8] unless the victim acted in fear of violence. American courts hold that if D tortures V and causes V to commit suicide as the only means of escape, D will be guilty at least of manslaughter.[9] And if D murderously wounds V, and V commits an act of suicide because he cannot stand the pain and hopelessness of his condition, the suicidal act merely accelerating his death by a short space, D will remain guilty of murder.[10] We need not stop to consider how far the same result would be reached in borderline situations.[11]

§ 16.12. CONTRIBUTORY NEGLIGENCE OF VICTIM

The principle is that the victim's contributory negligence is no answer to a charge of crime.[1] In other words, it is generally no defence that the victim laid himself open to the act, or was himself guilty of negligence bringing it about.

This rule can have strange results. Suppose there are two burglars engaged together in blowing a safe in a grossly negligent way. If one is killed the other is presumably guilty of manslaughter, even though the victim participated throughout in the act of negligence. It can be argued that there should be a defence of negligent joint enterprise, but the courts have not hitherto recognised it.

---

[6] *Murton* (1862) 3 F & F 492, 176 ER 221. Cp. East, *PC* i 225; "Treating him harshly or unkindly, by which he dies of fear or grief, is not such a killing as the law takes notice of." This is now wrong for fear, but need not he wrong for grief.

[7] Grief resulting from bereavement can occasionally be a factor in the cause of death: one study found that nearly five per cent. of widowers over 55 died within six months of the death of their wives, which was 40 per cent. above the normal death rate ([1969] 1 BMJ 740).

[8] *Sawyer* (1887) 106 Sess.Pap. 301.

[9] As in *Stephenson* v. *State* (1932) 205 Ind. 141, 179 NE 633; but query whether the facts were strong enough to sustain the conviction, seeing that the deceased had several opportunities to escape. See also 31 Mich.LRev. 669; Hart and Honoré, *op. cit.* 294.

[10] See *People* v. *Lewis* (1899) 124 Cal. 551, 57 P 470, 45 LRA 783; but the decision is open to criticism on the ground that the court left it open whether the suicide might not have been due to remorse or a desire to shield the defendant. The court said it would not have been homicide by D if the wounded condition of V was "merely the occasion upon which another cause intervened, not produced by the first wound, or related to it in other than a casual way" (as if the deceased had been run over on the way to hospital). It was also said that the case would have stood otherwise if the wound, though painful, had not been dangerous, and V had known it was not dangerous but had taken his life to escape pain. For critical discussions see J Hall, *Principles*, 2nd edn 265, and *Studies* 173, 178; Hart and Honoré, *op. cit.* 223. See also *State* v. *Angelina* (1913) 73 WVa.146, 80 SE 141; *Jones* v. *State* (1942) 220 Ind. 384, 43 NE 2d 1017.

[11] It has heen held in the civil law that where the defendant by negligence inflicts injury on a person resulting in an anxiety neurosis and depression, and such person in consequence commits suicide, the death is attributable to the negligence: *Pigney* v. *Pointer's Transport Services* [1957] 2 All ER 807. But query if the same principle applies in the criminal law.

[1] The rule is well settled; a modern instance is *Hennigan* [1971] 3 All ER 133, 55 CAR 652.

Occasionally the contributory fault of the victim may be so great that the defendant's act is held not to be the imputable cause of the harm. An illustration is the "exhaustion of danger" principle, where the risk created by the defendant is at an end before the victim commits the careless act.

> In *Waters* (1834),[2] the defendant Waters, being on board a ship, and V, who was in a boat alongside, disputed about payment for some goods, both being intoxicated. There was a conflict of evidence as to what subsequently happened, but according to one witness Waters, to get rid of V, pushed away the boat with his foot; V, reaching out to lay hold of a barge, to prevent his boat from drifting away, overbalanced, fell into the water, and was drowned. Park J ruled that even if this evidence were accepted it was not a case of manslaughter.

No reason was given for the ruling, but a reason can easily be framed. If V had fallen into the water immediately upon his boat being pushed, it might perhaps have amounted to manslaughter, supposing that Waters knew that V was unsteady on his feet and probably too drunk to swim. But this is not what happened. V remained safe in his boat, and the only effect of the push was to cause him inconvenience, in having the boat drift from the place where he wanted it to be. At that point the risk caused by Waters's act was exhausted.

What if the victim having received an injury foolishly refuses treatment, so that his condition becomes worse?

The rule excluding from consideration the contributory negligence of the victim leading to his first injury does not necessarily entail the conclusion that the attacker is liable for an aggravation of the injury brought about by the victim. This is a separate question. As a matter of justice, it might be thought that the attacker ought not generally to be liable for the result of the aggravation; but the cases go the other way.

First, it is clear law that if D inflicts a serious injury on V, and V refuses, however unreasonably, to receive medical treatment and so dies from the injury, D is responsible for the death. The latest decision is *Blaue*.[3]

> Blaue stabbed V, penetrating her lung. She was taken to hospital, but, being a Jehovah's Witness, refused to have a blood transfusion, and died. The transfusion would probably have saved her. The judge directed the jury that they would get some help from the cases to which counsel had referred in their speeches, and said that they might think they had little option but to reach the conclusion that the stab wound was the operative cause of death—or a substantial cause of death. The jury convicted of manslaughter by reason of diminished responsibility (the diminished responsibility, of course, having nothing to do with the question of causation), and the conviction was affirmed on appeal.

Although the case follows certain ancient authorities, preferring them to opinions expressed in "textbooks intended for students or as studies in jurisprudence," it fails to notice that all the cases dated from a time when medical science was in its infancy, and when operations performed without hygiene carried great danger to life. It was therefore open to the court for the benefit of the defendant to consider the question afresh, and there were several reasons for doing so.

We have seen that it was held in *Roberts*[4] that where the victim sustains injury in an attempt

---

[2] 6 C & P 328, 172 ER 1262.
[3] [1975] 1 WLR 1411, 3 All ER 446, 61 CAR 271.
[4] § .8 at n. 1.

to escape, the test of imputable causation is one of reasonable foresight. This is a useful test, and one might have hoped that it would be generalised, but the court refused to apply it to the case where the victim is seriously injured and declines medical assistance.

It had been held in the law of tort that the test of reasonable foresight applies to facts like those in *Blaue*, but the court was not impressed by the argument. It thought that on the undisputed evidence the stab wound inflicted by Blaue caused the death, and that the judge could have told the jury so. Of course it was a cause of the death, but V's refusal of treatment was an additional but-for cause. The court described the defendant's act as "the physical cause of death," and regarded that as conclusive. But in cases of multiple causation it is unconvincing to select one cause as "the" cause.

The best reason for the decision, though not one given in the judgment, is that Blaue would have been guilty of unlawful homicide if the victim had had no chance of obtaining medical assistance, and therefore (it may be said) should be equally guilty if the victim chose not to avail herself of such assistance. Still, there is a difference. The decision means that if the death penalty for murder were restored, the attacker might be hanged purely as a result of the unreasonable decision of the victim not to accept proferred medical help. The criminal law should avoid the appearance of harshness, and to make it more stringent than the civil law in the matter of causation is particularly surprising. Lawton LJ, speaking for the court, explained the difference between the criminal and civil law by saying that "the criminal law is concerned with the maintenance of law and order and the protection of the public generally." This overlooks that Blaue was in any event punishable severely for wounding with intent.[5]

Assuming that *Blaue* settles the law, there is doubtless one limitation upon the rule, namely, that it does not apply where the injury inflicted by the defendant was trifling.[6]

What if the victim is guilty of a positive act of foolishness aggravating his injury?

In general the aggravation will again be placed at the door of the defendant, at any rate if the victim's act was within the range of reasonable foresight.

> In *Wall* (1802)[7] the defendant, a colonial governor, sentenced a soldier to an illegal flogging of 800 lashes, from which flogging he died. There was some evidence that the deceased had drunk spirits after the flogging, which would not have helped him; but he was then, according to the evidence, in a dying state.[8] In directing the jury, Macdonald LCB said: "I apprehend there is no apology for a man if he puts another in so dangerous and so hazardous a situation by his treatment of him, that some degree of unskilfulness and mistaken treatment of himself may possibly accelerate the fatal catastrophe." Governor Wall was convicted of murder and executed. Here, the deceased evidently drank the spirits in order to gain some relief from the suffering caused to him by the flogging (alcohol was regularly used as an anaesthetic before the discovery of more effective drugs). The spirits were the ordinary army ration which was placed by the man's bedside each day[9]; and when he drank the spirits he was probably in no condition to exercise a proper judgment. These considerations make the case a somewhat special one, to be used with caution in stating the law.

---

[5] As always, trial courts may act more leniently than the CA lays down. In *Urquart*, Daily Telegraph, January 4, 5, 1979, a Jehovah's Witness injured in a road crash refused a blood transfusion and died; the evidence was that he would almost certainly have lived if he had accepted the transfusion. The jury (agreeing with the writers of students' text-books and works on jurisprudence!) acquitted the driver of causing death by dangerous driving but convicted him of dangerous driving.

[6] For the distinction in the old authorities between mortal and non-mortal wounds see [1957] Crim.LR 510–511.

[7] 28 St.Tr. 51 at 145.

[8] See the report at p. 158.

[9] Though a surgeon testified that it was against orders to allow spirits into the hospital, and that drinking liquor was dangerous for the deceased in his condition.

In another case, where the victim of an attack rode his horse afterwards, and so perhaps contributed to his own death by preventing healing, the attacker was still held guilty of manslaughter.[10]

These authorities show that where the victim took understandable measures to relieve his suffering, or went on with his ordinary life without fully realising the danger caused by the wound, his conduct does not necessarily sever the causal connection that the law sees between the wound and the death. But the cases do not decide that no supervening act of rashness by the deceased affects the responsibility of the defendant. If the victim's acts were not reasonably foreseeable, and particularly if the wound given were not in itself likely to cause death, and the victim by egregious folly introduced infection into it, a jury might well find, and be in effect required to find, that the defendant's act did not substantially contribute to the death.

A dictum in *Blaue* causes some difficulty. Casting around for reasons for its decision, the Court of Appeal prayed in aid the special sensitivity rule, that "those who use violence on other people must take their victims as they find them." The court said:

> "This in our judgment means the whole man, not just the physical man. It does not lie in the mouth of the assailant to say that his victim's religious beliefs which inhibited him from accepting certain kinds of treatment were unreasonable."

Probably the dictum was meant only to explain the actual decision; if applied more widely it would have sweeping results. D rapes V who commits suicide because she is neurotically inclined, or because she hopes to get D into more serious trouble by so doing. Or, D assaults V, cutting his finger; V could take medical advice or apply a proper dressing, but he stupidly binds up the wound with a filthy rag, falls ill, still refuses to accept medical assistance, and dies. Are V's neurosis or vengefulness or stupidity to be reckoned as part of the victim that D must "take"? It would be carrying the law of constructive manslaughter very far to regard these as cases of manslaughter.

In one respect the dictum is clearly contrary to authority. D assaults V in some minor way, which would not be very frightening to a normal person, but V inexplicably jumps out of the window (which is far above the ground) and dies. According to *Roberts* (§ .8) and previous cases D is not guilty of constructive manslaughter by reason of this unforeseeable reaction of the victim. But the dictum in *Blaue* would make him guilty.

The problem, like others in the theory of causation, would become much easier of solution if constructive manslaughter were abolished, because then it could often be disposed of by saying that the defendant who inflicted only a slight injury was not guilty of gross negligence as to the causing of death.

Similar questions can arise where the death is contributed to by the subsequent acts of third parties. The usual form of the problem relates to negligent (or other improper) medical treatment.

§ 16.13. IMPROPER MEDICAL TREATMENT

When a person has injured another, who dies, the courts are very chary of allowing the assailant to adduce evidence suggesting that the doctors were in some way at fault in their treatment of the victim, in order to escape liability himself for causing the death. The doctors are not on trial, and are not represented; and even if it is alleged that the medical treatment fell short of perfection, whether by act or omission, the court will now generally exclude evidence on the subject, on the ground that it could make no difference to the outcome. We have already seen one example of

---

[10] *Flynn* (1867) 16 WR 319 (Ir.). Cp. *Mubila*, 1956 (1) SA 31 (victim of serious wounding getting out of bed in hospital).

this in *Malcherek* (§ .3).[1] However, the court may perhaps be persuaded to admit evidence of gross medical negligence if the injury inflicted by the defendant was demonstrably not serious.[2]

SUMMARY

Questions of causation arise where a law expressly or impliedly requires that a given result be produced as an element of the offence, *e.g.* murder, manslaughter, the aggravated assaults under OAPA ss.18, 20 and 47, and criminal damage. In homicide cases the death must follow within a year and a day, but it is no defence that death was merely accelerated. § .1

For an act or omission to be a cause of an event it must cause the event in the sense that the event would not have occurred but for the act or omission. However, two sufficient causes may operate together, whether independently or complementarily. The necessity for proving but-for causation can be particularly important in cases of omission. § .2

In addition, the conduct in question must be an imputable cause of the event. Intended consequences are nearly always imputed; the problems relate to unintended consequences. Trial judges now generally elide the two kinds of causation by asking the jury whether, (e.g.) the defendant's conduct was a substantial cause, or something more than a purely trivial cause. Occasionally, however, the trial judge will be upheld in excluding an alleged cause as a matter of law. § .3

In cases of negligence it must be shown that the result was caused by the feature of the defendant's conduct that is accounted negligent. § .4

The jury may be instructed to ignore a purely trivial cause, without being guided as to what a trivial cause is. But the idea of trivial causation was perhaps in Devlin J's mind when he said that a doctor may relieve the pain of a dying patient even though his measures shorten life. § .5

A person's conduct may be regarded as an imputable cause of an event notwithstanding that the sequence of occurrences following his conduct was unexpected; and he may be held to intend an event notwithstanding that the event occurred in an unexpected way. But he is not responsible if what happened was too far from his initial fault to be justly regarded as his responsibility; and on this question the following rules have some support in authority or common sense. § .6

An event is not imputable to the defendant if it was the result of an ordinary hazard. § .7

Also, an event or chain of causation is not imputable to the defendant if he did not foresee it and if a reasonable person would not have contemplated the risk as part of the general risk involved in the conduct in question; but if the risk is one of a group of risks that were generically foreseeable, it does not matter that the particular risk was so unlikely that if it had stood alone the conduct would not have been negligent. An injury sustained in fleeing from an attack can be a foreseeable risk. The special sensitivity rule appears to be an exception from the risk principle. § .8

A wrongdoer is not liable for a *novus actus interveniens*, that is, for an evil caused by the interposition of some other responsible person who acts knowingly and § .9, .10

---

[1] Cp. *T J Smith* [1959] 2 QB 35; *Blaue* [1975] 1 WLR at 1415.

[2] In *Jordan* (1956) 40 CAR 152, where the medical treatment was accounted "palpably wrong," and the victim would not otherwise have died, this was held to sever the chain of causation. The decision was criticised as being medically mistaken, and is now judicially regarded with reserve as being "very exceptional:" *Malcherek* [1981] 1 WLR at 696D.

otherwise than under pressure caused by the defendant's act. A *novus actus* can exempt the defendant even in a case of strict liability.

The death of a victim may be attributed to the attacker even though it occurred directly through fright or shock, or through an attempt by the victim to escape where his act was reasonably foreseeable. § .11

The contributory negligence of the victim is not a defence in itself, but sometimes it is this negligence rather than the fault of the defendant that alone is regarded as causing the result, as where the "exhaustion of danger" principle applies. At least where the defendant has inflicted a serious injury on another, the victim's unreasonable failure to accept medical help does not make his consequential death too remote, and even the victim's negligent aggravation of his injury does not necessarily do so. § .12

Improper medical treatment preventing recovery will not make the death too remote if the wound inflicted by the defendant was the medical cause of death. There may be rare exceptions when the wound was slight and the medical negligence great. § .13

Chapter 17

ATTEMPT

The attempt and not the deed confounds us.
Macbeth II ii.

§ 17.1. INCHOATE OFFENCES

So long as a crime lies merely in the mind it is not punishable, because criminal thoughts often occur to people without any serious intention of putting them into execution.

Others, I am not the first,
Have willed more mischief than they durst.

The position is different when some step is taken to put the desire into effect. A man who starts on a criminal path but who is checked before he can accomplish his purpose may commit what is in itself an offence—conveniently called an inchoate offence. This may be defined as an offence committed by doing an act with the purpose of effecting some other offence (called the "substantive offence" or "consummated offence" or "completed offence").

Anciently the law was otherwise, no penalty being provided for those who did not accomplish their criminal object. At that time the criminal law was not clearly separated from the law of tort, which provided compensation only when some injury had actually been inflicted. "The idea of punishment is but slowly severed from that of reparation, and where no harm is done there is none to be repaired."[1] The change in the law was largely the work of the king's courts.[2] From the latter part of the 17th century onwards they developed the three inchoate crimes of attempt, conspiracy and incitement.[3]

§ 17.2. THE RANGE OF THE LAW OF ATTEMPT

The offence of attempt at common law was put into statutory form, with some amendments, by the Criminal Attempts Act 1981.[1] References in this chapter are to this Act, unless otherwise stated. Examples of punishable attempts are:

— attempting to obtain property by deception by posting a letter containing a false statement, though it never reaches the victim;

---

[1] Pollock and Maitland ii 509.

[2] F C Milsom, *Historical Foundations of the Common Law* (London 1969) 373 finds some traces of an earlier development in the local courts. Credit for the development has also been given to the Star Chamber (see Thomas G Barnes in [1977] Crim.LR 325–326), but the evidence is thin.

[3] See Thomas G. Barnes in [1977] Crim.L.R. 325–326.

[1] The Act implements, in the main, a report of the Law Commission. See generally Ian Dennis in [1980] Crim.LR 758, [1982] Crim.LR 5.

— attempted arson by soaking a building with petrol in order to set it on fire;
— attempted murder by trying to draw a pistol upon the victim.

Sometimes an attempt to commit one crime is at the same time another completed crime. If D passes a forged bank-note to V, with intent to defraud, hoping to be given change for it, he is guilty of attempting to obtain money from V by deception; but he is also guilty of the full offence of using a forgery.

Apart from a few statutory exceptions, of small importance,[2] an attempt may be to commit "any offence which, if it were completed, would be triable in England and Wales as an indictable offence" (section 1(4)).

> This means, for example, that even offences of unlawful possession can be attempted,[3] and so can offences that may be regarded from one point of view as being themselves "inchoate" (e.g. psychic assault).[4] The question of attempt to commit offences of omission will be briefly considered later (§ .5 at n. 1).

The most important restriction is that an attempt to commit a summary offence is not criminal unless some special statute so provides.

What about offences triable either way?

An attempt to commit such an offence is similarly triable either way.[5]

One difference between trial on indictment and summary trial may be noted. On a trial on indictment, if the jury acquit of the substantive offence they may, by statute, convict of an attempt to commit it, without any necessity for an express count for attempt in the indictment.[6] Unfortunately this is not possible in magistrates' courts, where, for some unfathomable reason, express charges are required.[7]

The inconvenience of this can be avoided if informations are laid both for the consummated offence and for the attempt, the two charges being tied together.[8] If the prosecution have forgotten to lay an information for the attempt, they may, on an acquittal of the completed offence, immediately lay an information for an attempt; but the witnesses must then be heard over again!

What if the court is sure that the defendant was up to no good, and was in fact attempting to commit some crime, but is not sure which?

He cannot be convicted of an attempt, because the prosecution can only charge an attempt to commit a particular crime.

In practice, obvious suspects can often be convicted of some offence. Burglary, for example, can be committed with one of a number of intents, and the prosecution need not

---

[2] S.1(4)(*c*) excludes conspiracy and offences under CLA 1967 s.4 (1) (assisting offenders) and 5 (1) (agreeing for a consideration not to disclose an arrestable offence).

[3] Such prosecutions are not infrequent, and have not been challenged on the point of law. See, e.g. *Foo* (1976) Current Sentencing Practice, ed. D A Thomas, 11020.

[4] See Dorcas White in [1980] Crim.LR 780.

[5] MCA 1980 Sched. 1 para. 34.

[6] CLA 1967 s.6(4).

[7] *Pender* v. *Smith* [1959] 2 QB 84.

[8] S. 4(2); the rule has now been generalised by judicial decision: § 7.8 at n. 2. The difficulty can also be got over by charging an attempt whenever the position is doubtful. If it turns out that the defendant completed the offence he can still be convicted of the attempt. Cp., for the Crown Court, CLA 1967 s.6(4); *Webley* v. *Buxton* [1977] QB 481.

prove which the defendant had (§ 38.3). Again, the defendant may be convicted of a possession offence like possessing a firearm or other offensive weapon, or of "going equipped" (§ 38.7), or interfering with a vehicle (§ 38.6). These offences either do not require proof of intent to commit some other crime or allow conviction where the defendant evidently had one of a specified range of intents but it may not be certain which.

Are attempts often prosecuted?

Notwithstanding the range of the offence, the police and other prosecuting authorities do not generally wish to add to their load by prosecuting attempts. The required intention is frequently hard to prove, and anyway the police may think that a warning is sufficient. If they make a charge, they may well prefer a charge of a specific offence like carrying a firearm. Nevertheless, attempts to commit serious crimes are prosecuted from time to time; and the law of attempt frequently supplies a justification for arresting a would-be offender (§ 22.2).

§ 17.3. THE PUNISHMENT OF ATTEMPT

On conviction of attempt the court may (with a few exceptions) impose any penalty that would be within its powers for the completed offence: section 4.[1] In practice, the punishment for an attempt will generally be less than for the consummated crime. If a man shoots at another, intending to kill him, and succeeds, he is sentenced for "life." If he misses, although he could receive a life sentence, in practice he will be treated much more leniently.[2] Often the attempter receives a discount of 50 per cent. or more.

Why should the law punish a mere attempt? The attempter thinks he will succeed. If all those who succeed are punished, then people will be sufficiently deterred even from making a bid. So couldn't the mere attempter be let off?

An attractive argument, but it simplifies too much.

Clearly, the police who find a man attempting a crime must be given power to foil him. Often they can do this only by detaining him, and detention normally presupposes the making of a charge. It therefore presupposes an offence.

This is by no means a strong reason in itself, but it is supported by another. We may feel it necessary to punish the unsuccessful attempter by way of particular deterrence. Otherwise, he might merely resolve to be more careful in future. To some extent, letting off the attempter would also

---

[1] Subs. (5) excepts the special penalties provided in SOA 1956 s.37 and Sched. 2. The mandatory sentence for murder does not apply to attempted murder.

[2] In the particular example the use of the firearm could still result in a substantial sentence. But in some other cases great indulgence is shown. In *Roy Jones*, The Times, March 3, 1976, a father who attempted to murder his two daughters after his wife had left him, by giving them drugged ice-cream, was given a jail sentence of 2 years, *suspended*. Examples of the more usual outcome are *Taylor* [1978] Crim.LR 236 and *Townsend* (1980) 144 JPN 12.

weaken general deterrence, which depends upon society's success in making things unpleasant for malefactors.[3]

These arguments are, I think, persuasive where the crime attempted is one of those distinctly betokening a criminal mentality. They are not so persuasive in respect of minor offences—which is one reason why summary offences are not made the subject of criminal attempt.

Then let me change my previous stance, because I am also vexed with the opposite doubt. If you punish attempts at all, surely leniency is irrational. Why not punish them like consummated crimes? Attempters are just as wicked, and often just as dangerous, as those who complete the crime—if the attempter doesn't repent and is just dished. The difference between murder and attempted murder may be due not to the skill or lack of it shown by the attacker in carrying out his purpose but to the skill or lack of it shown by a doctor treating the victim, or the speed with which the victim is transported to hospital.

One should be careful in propounding a view that would increase the level of punishment of serious crimes on apparently logical grounds. The prisons are chock-a-block, and no opportunity of mitigating sentence should be rejected unless it carries pronounced disadvantages.

Judges never say why the sentence should be reduced for failure. Probably the reason is that they think in retributive terms. We do not feel so angry with people who fail, and who in fact do no harm, as with people who suceed in their mischief. But if one thinks in terms not of simple vengeance but of ethical retribution, it seems hard at first sight to resist the argument that the attempter is morally just as guilty as the succeeder.

However, there are solid utilitarian reasons for comparative leniency in the case of attempters. Two may be mentioned in particular.

- The institution of punishment works best when the punishment is felt by those who receive it to be deserved. A person who actually does harm frequently feels a sense of guilt, and accepts punishment as being just. If no harm occurs he is unlikely to feel guilt, or at any rate as much guilt.[4]
- Even the utilitarian, who himself rejects retribution as a basis of punishment, may take it into account in the way just suggested and also as a statement of the attitude of the general public. In a democracy, the administration of the law must to some extent take note of public opinion. Where the act does not evoke alarm, punishment can be lenient without producing a general feeling that the courts are becoming soft; and severe punishment might be thought to be unjust. Now as to attempts, since many people take the crude retributive position, requiring punishment to balance the harm actually inflicted, a law that punished attempts as severely as consummated crimes would give the appearance of harshness; and the law would tend to lose public support.

The comparatively mild attitude of the courts towards attempts shows

---

[3] As always, the argument based on general deterrence is more comprehensive than one based on particular deterrence. D takes a shot at V, but misses because V is out of range. D may now go closer and kill V. But perhaps when D took the first shot he had only one bullet, and events may afterwards happen that make him give up his first purpose. It is not obvious that we are justified in punishing such an unsuccessful attempter on a speculation that he may try again in the future. But we are justified in punishing him under a general edict that no one must even *try* to commit a crime.

[4] We may "ask ourselves whether if we were punished the same for culpably causing harm and for having a 'close call,' we would regard ourselves as justly treated. My submission is that we should not." Fletcher, *Rethinking Criminal Law* 483.

the practical importance of the doctrine of transferred intention. If D shoots at V1 and hits V2, he can be convicted of attempting to wound V1 or actually wounding V2; but the punishment on the latter charge is likely to be considerably more severe than on the former. The lenient treatment of attempts depends upon the fact that the evil result has not occurred. Where it has, even though to a person or property that was not intended, general opinion would probably regard the law as inadequate if the case were treated as a mere attempt.[5]

§ 17.4. THE MENTAL ELEMENT AND IMPOSSIBILITY

Section 1(1) defines a criminal attempt.

> "If, with intent to commit an offence to which this section applies, a person does an act which is more than merely preparatory to the commission of the offence, he is guilty of attempting to commit the offence."

It was mentioned in § 7.7 that the Act abolishes the former rule that one cannot attempt the impossible. The Act deals with the matter in the following two further subsections of section 1.

> "(2) A person may be[1] guilty of attempting to commit an offence to which this section applies even though the facts are such that the commission of the offence is impossible.
> (3) In any case where—
> (*a*) apart from this subsection a person's intention would not be regarded as having amounted to an intent to commit an offence; but
> (*b*) if the facts of the case had been as he believed them to be, his intention would be so regarded,
> then, for the purposes of subsection (1) above, he shall be regarded as having had an intent to commit that offence."

This rather cumbrous provision boils down to the rule that in an attempt you take the facts as the defendant believed them to be. If, on the supposed facts, he would have been guilty of an attempt, then he is guilty of it.

So Bluebeard would be guilty of an attempt to murder if he gave his helpmate a glass of water to drink, believing it to be a dose of poison?

Yes.

---

[5] Ashworth is unimpressed by arguments like the above. He would punish cases of transferred intention as attempts, but would punish attempts as consummated crimes. So in relation to transferred intention his two proposals cancel out. See his contributions to *Reshaping the Criminal Law* and *Crime, Proof and Punishment*, and my reply in [1983] CLJ 86–88. For other arguments see 1st edn 370.

[1] This flaccid phrase might in itself be read as reaffirming the common law, which punished attempts that were impossible only in the means chosen, but not other impossible attempts. But it is stiffened by subs. (3), which uses the imperative "shall." Clearly, it was not the intention of the section merely to restate the common law, or to give the courts a discretion to continue to allow a defence of impossibility in some unspecified circumstances. "May be" must mean "shall be, if the other conditions of liability are satisfied."

Suppose he thinks he has actually committed a crime? He stabs a corpse thinking it is alive, and thinks he has killed it.

He is still guilty of an attempt.

Suppose it isn't a question of impossibility but of lack of an ingredient of the crime? A man receives goods mistakenly believing that they are stolen. Can he be convicted of attempting to receive stolen goods? One of the conditions required by law for the full crime is missing, namely stolen goods.

One cannot, perhaps, be absolutely certain that the courts will reach the same result in this type of case as in the previous ones, but they almost certainly will, and it was the intention of the Act that they should.[2]

Apply the plain words of subsection (3): if the goods were stolen, as the defendant believed them to be, he "shall be regarded as having had an intent to commit that offence." (The reason for the wording is that before the Act the judges had convinced themselves, by obviously fallacious reasoning, that the defendant did not intend to commit the offence.)

There is no analytical difference between your "question of impossibility" and your "lack of an ingredient of the crime." In the case of the supposed corpse, or an attempted theft from an empty pocket, which everyone will agree are cases of impossibility, one of the ingredients or conditions of the full crime is missing (a live human being who can be killed; property belonging to another), but obviously the intention of the Act is that an attempt can be committed. Similarly with your case of receiving stolen goods.

No problem arises in drafting a charge of attempting to receive stolen goods, because the charge may follow the words of the offence and say: "attempted to receive stolen goods, *believing* them to be stolen." It is true that this would involve a play upon words. In relation to charges of the completed offence, "believing" refers to near-certain and correct knowledge (§ 7.7). But in relation to a charge of attempting to handle goods that are in fact not stolen, we wish to make it bear the different meaning of positive but mistaken belief. The courts will probably refuse to attach any significance to this subtle change of meaning. It is simply a fortunate accident that the offence of handling is drafted in terms that prevent difficulty on a charge of attempting the impossible.

There may be a slight hitch with a charge of, say, attempting to possess articles in the mistaken belief that they were explosives, where the substantive charge is of knowingly possessing explosives (the substantive charge in this case not allowing the alternative of belief). If the charge of attempt said: "attempted to possess articles knowing them to be explosives," the charge would not be made out, on a strict interpretation, because you cannot know what is not so. If it said: "attempted to possess articles believing them to be explosives," the objection might be advanced that since there is no offence of possessing articles believing them to be explosives (as opposed to knowing them to be explosives) the charge would not state an attempt to commit an offence known to the law. It should be held, however, that in the case of an attempt the word "knowing" can properly be transposed into "believing," since it is a convention of our language that the word "know" cannot be applied to a mistaken belief.

Suppose a man thinks he is smuggling sugar into the country. There is a sugar shortage, and he thinks, mistakenly, that it is an offence to import sugar. Is that an attempt?

No, because the "offence" that he has in mind to commit does not exist as an offence. He is attempting an imaginary crime, not an impossible

---

[2] See Dennis in [1982] Crim.LR 10–11; Grubb in [1982] CLJ 26.

crime. In considering impossible attempts we are speaking only of mistakes of fact, not mistakes of law.

The rule about intention works both ways. It makes a person guilty of an attempt according to his intention, and it prevents him from being guilty of an attempt if he did not intend to commit an offence (that is to say, to commit the acts amounting to an offence—he need not know the law).

The requirement of intent (at least as to consequences) restates the common law. Its effect is powerfully shown by the rule for attempted murder. Murder can be committed by a person who intends only to do grievous bodily harm; but for attempted murder the prosecution must prove an attempt to kill: an intent to do grievous bodily harm is not enough.[3]

If a terrorist places a bomb by the front door of a Cabinet Minister, which does damage but fortunately does not kill anybody, could this be an attempt to murder?

If there were evidence that the terrorist hoped to kill, it would be. But if there were no evidence on the intent, and the inference from the evidence could be no more than that the terrorist was completely reckless as to killing, his particular object being to explode a bomb to create a sense of insecurity and to draw attention to his cause, then it would not be an attempt to murder. The terrorist could be dealt with for an offence in relation to explosives, under the Explosives Act 1883.

Isn't it rather narrow to insist upon intention? Can't one ever attempt recklessly?

Recklessness as to consequence is certainly not enough.

> It was held by the Court of Appeal in *Mohan*[4] that attempt at common law required intention in the true sense, and mere knowledge of the probability or high probability or likelihood of the consequence was not enough. The offence requires "proof of specific intent, a decision to bring about, in so far as it lies within the accused's power, the commission of the offence which it is alleged that the accused attempted to commit."[5] The court said that that there was nothing in *Hyam* (§ 11.4) to stand in the way of this conclusion. It can be taken for granted that the courts will interpret the Criminal Attempts Act in the same way.

The requirement of intention results in part from the ordinary meaning of the word "attempt." Suppose that D is throwing stones in the hope of breaking a window. He knows perfectly well that people are standing near and that he is in danger of hitting one of them instead. He is, therefore, reckless as to hitting a person; but we would not say that he is attempting to hit a person. His object is to break the window. Attempts go with objects, aims and purposes, not with collateral risks. The law of attempt

---

[3] § 11.3 n. 2.
[4] [1976] QB 1.
[5] *Mohan* at 10–11.

reflects common speech on this matter, or tries to do so. However, there is no reason why "oblique intention" should not be sufficient.[6]

If you attach importance to the ordinary meaning of "attempt," then surely recklessness as to circumstances (as distinct from consequences) should be enough. If a man tries to have sexual intercourse without knowing or caring whether the woman is consenting, and in fact she does not consent, everyone would say that he has attempted to rape her.

Yes. It was, indeed, held in *Pigg*[7], just before the Criminal Attempts Act came into force, that the man in such circumstances was guilty of an attempt at common law. In other words, one could attempt at common law if one was reckless as to the circumstances, provided that such recklessness was sufficient for the consummated offence, and that one intended to complete the criminal act (the sexual penetration in rape), and intended any necessary consequence (no consequence is necessary in rape). Whether this is still the position under the Act is not known.

Unfortunately, those responsible for the Criminal Attempts Act failed to incorporate in it the rule of the common law (as it is now settled to have been) or any other rule on this point. The Act for the first time made "impossible attempts" punishable, and the Government thought that it would be going too far to provide for the punishment of attempts that were both impossible and reckless. For example, suppose that a man tries to have sexual intercourse with a woman with her consent. Rape is out of the question on such facts. But suppose that although the woman consents, the man does not know it for sure, and is reckless as to whether she is consenting. If one can commit a reckless impossible attempt, such a man would be guilty of attempted rape!

Because of this type of problem (unlikely as such facts may appear), the Government decided that it had to choose between punishing reckless attempts and impossible attempts, and plumped for the latter.

Having made this election, however, it did not expressly rule out reckless attempts, because it supposed that it had excluded them by the requirement of intention for an attempt. As we have seen, however, there is no certainty that the courts will construe a requirement of intention as meaning that the actor must positively know the circumstances.[8] It seems very likely that the courts will regard the Act's requirement of intention for attempts as merely reaffirming the common law as stated in *Mohan*, and the courts did not regard the rule in *Mohan* as excluding liability for attempts that were reckless as to circumstances. The same rule will probably be applied to the construction of the Act, and it is in the public interest that it should be. It would mean that the decision in *Pigg* continues to apply under the Act. *Pigg* shows that, in the case of attempt, there is no inconsistency between requiring intention for the crime in general (as *Mohan* did at common law), that is to say intention as to the physical act and its required consequence, if any, and being satisfied with recklessness as to circumstances. If that is so, it must be the same where the requirement of intention is laid down by statute.[9]

Can't one attempt an offence of strict liability?

Yes if it is indictable, but the attempt requires intention, even though the

---

[6] See comment in [1975] Crim.LR 285–286; Dennis in [1980] Crim.LR 763. *Contra*, Enker in [1977] Am. Bar Foundation Research Jrnl 864–865. It may be said that oblique intention is included in the formula in *Mohan*; the defendant who foresees a consequence as certainly resulting from his act has taken a "decision" to bring it about (Grubb in [1982] CLJ 24).

[7] [1982] 1 WLR 762, 2 All ER 591, 74 CAR 352.

[8] § 6.7 *fin*.

[9] I have elaborated this in an article on reckless attempts in [1983] Crim. LR 365.

offence attempted does not. Whether recklessness as to circumstances is sufficient has just been discussed.

§ 17.5. THE ACT OF ATTEMPT

Section 1(1) (§ .4) defines an attempt as the doing of an act, and there should be no question, therefore, that an omission cannot be an attempt (whether to commit a crime of positive action or of omission). If the rule of law is not to be reduced to something like the game of croquet in *Alice in Wonderland*, where the mallets were flamingoes which wandered about during the game, a measure of fixity must be given to the basic legal terms; and for this reason the word "act" in a statute should not include an omission, in default of clear language on the subject. Unfortunately, it is never certain that the courts will adopt this interpretation in a given case.[1]

Once an intending criminal goes as far as to perform an act of attempt, his liability for that offence becomes fixed, whatever afterwards happens.

- It does not matter that the attempter subsequently gives up the attempt—for example, because he finds that someone is watching him,[2] or because he has a change of mind. (But if he changes his mind the court may possibly find that this indicates he never had a firm purpose.)[3]
- Nor does it matter that he goes on and completes the crime: his attempt does not "merge" in the crime.[4] Of course, if the police have evidence of a completed crime they will charge that. But if they charge an attempt, the defendant's impudent defence that he succeeded will not avail him. The same is true of the other inchoate crimes, incitement and conspiracy.

What does section 1(1) mean by saying that the act must be "more than merely preparatory to the commission of the offence"? If I lift my arm in order to strike someone on the head, I am preparing to strike him, but am also attempting to strike him, because when I bring my arm down I have struck him. It seems to me that every act done in order to commit the crime is preparation for committing it.

That is literally true. But "more than merely preparatory" has a special meaning for lawyers. It implies that one has to draw a line.

At common law the courts distinguished between acts that were merely preparatory to the offence, which could not be an attempt, and proximate

---

[1] It was the intention of the Government that crimes of omission should be attemptable (see Dennis in [1982] Crim.LR 7–8), but this was not written into the Act. In *Arthur* § 12.8 at n. 13, which arose before the Act, the judge allowed a charge of attempted murder by omission to go to the jury. Dr Arthur committed an "act" in prescribing nursing care only, meaning that for the time being the child was not to be fed. But if non-feeding is an omission, an order not to feed should surely be held to be an omission, not an act.

[2] *Taylor* (1859) 1 F & F 511, 175 ER 831.

[3] See Stuart in [1970] Crim.LR 519–541. Some foreign codes provide no punishment if the defendant desists; and the Model Penal Code allows a defence of repentance, under careful conditions.

[4] CLA 1967 s.6(4); *Webley* v. *Buxton* [1977] QB 481.

acts, which could.[5] In some degree the decision depended on what is politely called a visceral reaction. Occasionally the judges construed the notion of a proximate act so narrowly that obvious rascals who had gone very far towards committing the intended offence were acquitted. This was perhaps because the judges were inclined to think that no act could be "proximate" to the offence unless it was very near indeed (which is, indeed, the classical meaning of the word). The Criminal Attempts Act therefore discards the language of proximity while leaving the other half of the rule, or the other side of the coin (that the act must go beyond mere preparation), untouched.

The change has one obvious effect: it deprives us of convenient language. We no longer have a word for the act that goes beyond mere preparation, but must use the whole of that cumbrous phrase. Whether the change has any effect upon the law itself is at present unknown.

Surely there was some principle upon which the courts would generally hold that an act went beyond mere preparation?

Various ideas were mooted, by judges and commentators, but none of them gave much assistance, and one or two were positively misleading.[6]

Well, suppose the judge now wishes to give the jury a genuine instruction on the law, and not merely to lead them by the noses, what is he to say?

The best he can generally do is to tell the jury that the act must be "immediately and not merely remotely connected with the commission of the offence."[7] Having delivered himself of that advice he may perhaps be left with a feeling of inadequacy. However, the previous case-law throws up some more specific propositions for specific types of case, which the judge may at any rate "suggest" to the jury.

One such "suggestion" was, and is, obvious. If the defendant has done the last act that was needful for him to do to perpetrate the crime, he has inevitably passed beyond mere preparation.[8]

If, therefore, D incites X as an *innocent* agent to commit a crime, expecting that he will then commit it without further instructions, D can, on principle, be found guilty of an attempt to commit it (and will be the perpetrator if X does commit it).

If on the other hand D incites a guilty agent to commit a crime, D, although he is guilty of the special crime of incitement (Chapter 19), and although he will become an accessory if the incitee commits the crime, is not guilty of an attempt by reason of his incitement. Otherwise every incitement would be an attempt. The rule is confirmed by an express

---

[5] The law of attempt was developed by the courts in the later 1600s, at which time the rule was that any act manifesting a felonious intent was a misdemeanour. The law was not limited by any notion derived from the word "attempt." In time the law was both extended and restricted: it was extended to cases where the intent was to commit a misdemeanour, and it was restricted (by the decision in *Eagleton*, n. 8 below) to cases where there was a proximate act of attempt—which gives us the present law. See Glazebrook in 85 LQR 29–35, esp. at 33 n. 26. Having introduced the proximity test, the courts quite possibly became influenced by the language of attempt; but it would have been better if they had said that the limits of the law were to be settled by considerations of policy, not by pseudo-logical derivatives from the notion of attempt.

[6] On two of these suggestions see 1st edn 379–382.

[7] *Jones* v. *Brooks* (1968) 52 CAR at 616; *Stonehouse* [1978] AC at 68C.

[8] *Stonehouse* [1978] AC 55; cp. *Eagleton* (1855) Dears. 515, 169 ER 816.

provision in the Criminal Attempts Act.[9] In short, the law of attempt applies only to would-be perpetrators, not to would-be accessories. We shall return to this point later (§ .6).

What is "the last act that was needful for him to do to perpetrate the crime" depends in part on the law of causation, which may in turn depend in part on the law of attempt. The case has already been put of a man preparing poison to give his wife, when the wife unexpectedly drinks it without assistance, and dies (§ 16.6). It may be said that the man can be found guilty of murder on the "unexpected twist" principle, so that if he had been arrested immediately after preparing the poison he would have been guilty of an attempt on the last act principle. But against this it may be said that his act had not gone beyond mere preparation, so that he had not reached the stage of attempt, and from this it may be concluded that the man is not guilty of murder if the wife unexpectedly drinks the poison. It was suggested before that the solution should depend upon how close the man got towards administering the poison.

The law is evidently wider than this "last act" principle. An attempt can be committed where other acts remain to be done.

> A man draws a revolver from his pocket, intending to kill another, but his arm is seized before he can take aim. Clearly he is guilty of attempted murder; yet he has not reached the last intended act of pulling the trigger.[10]
>
> Similarly, it was held before the Act that when a man got into the driving seat of another's car he was guilty of an attempt to steal even though he had not yet started the engine or put the car in gear.[11]

It was even held that the first of a series of similar acts intended to result cumulatively in the crime could be a sufficient attempt. The principal case concerned a deep-dyed villain going incongruously by the name of White.[12]

> White put two grains of cyanide of potassium in his mother's nectar, intending to kill her. The dose was insufficient to kill, and the mother did not even drink the nectar, but, by coincidence, she died from natural causes a short time after. It was held that White was guilty of attempt to murder, whether he thought that the dose was sufficient to kill in itself, or whether he intended to kill by giving a series of doses having cumulative effect; and in the latter event it made no difference that in fact cyanide of potassium has no cumulative effect.

What acts were held not to be attempts?

In brief, the courts generally held that the defendant had to be on the brink of committing the crime. Reconnoitring, or looking for an opportunity to commit a crime, was never held to be sufficiently proximate.

The following illustrations have not been the subject of decisions, but pretty clearly would have been regarded before the Act as mere reconnoitring, not going beyond preparation.[13]

---

[9] S.1(4): "This section applies to any offence . . . other than . . . (*b*) aiding, abetting, counselling, procuring or suborning the commission of an offence." See J C Smith in *Crime, Proof and Punishment*, ed. Tapper (London 1981) 21–26.

[10] *Linneker* [1906] 2 KB 99.

[11] *Cook* (1964) 48 CAR 98. (Under the Theft Act 1968 it is quite possible that the full offence of theft is committed when the thief touches the car, or at any rate when he opens the car door: see the discussion of appropriation in Chapter 33. If so, the attempt comes at a still earlier time.) Opening a van door was held to be an attempt to steal an article inside: *Hussein* 67 CAR 131, [1967] Crim.LR 219. And a man who pushed his motor cycle towards the entrance to a public road, with intent to ride it, was held to attempt to ride it on the road: *Shaw* v. *Knill* [1974] RTR 142, [1973] Crim.LR 622.

[12] [1910] 2 KB 124.

[13] They were given in a police memorandum to the House of Commons Committee on the Criminal Attempts Bill, February 10, 1981, paras. 147–148, 163.

> A man is seen going along a row of terraced houses, pausing at each and appearing to examine them to see if they are secure; whenever anyone passes he conceals himself. He has convictions of burglary.
>
> In a busy market a youth successively follows a number of women whose purses can be seen at the top of their shopping bag or pram; he runs off when spoken to.
>
> A man drifts along a road and knocks on houses to see if anyone is at home. When challenged he fails to give a convincing explanation of his behaviour.

If two men behaved like this together they could, theoretically, be convicted of conspiracy to steal. But a conspiracy charge is not of much use to the police in small cases, because it is purely indictable.

Before the Act the police could charge a summary offence of "being a suspected person loitering with intent to commit an arrestable offence;" but this "sus" law came under attack because it was alleged to be used oppressively against the coloured population. So the offence was abolished by the Act. This piece of history makes it even less likely that the law of attempt will be extended to reconnoitring cases.

Another type of conduct that may safely be said not to amount to an attempt is the acquisition of information or materials for a proposed crime. Before the Act there was some authority for saying that acquiring materials for certain crimes was either an attempt or a special common law offence; but the Act (section 6(1)) expressly abolishes these special offences. Clearly the intention is that they shall not be punishable except under express statutory provisions. (There are, in fact, very wide provisions: see § 19.6.)

Even the lengthy pursuit of an unsuspecting victim was ruled in one case not to amount to an attempt; but the point has not come before the Court of Appeal.

> The case was *Komaroni*,[14] where the two defendants admitted that they had driven after a lorry at night with the intention of stealing from it when the driver should leave it unattended to get a meal. During the journey, when the lorry got stuck on an ice-bound hill, the defendants, abhorring violence, helped the driver to start it moving again. The driver, suspicious of his escort, drove on through the night without stopping. It was ruled by Streatfeild J that the defendants' conduct amounted to mere preparation.

Here the plotters were not merely looking for their victim; they had actually found him. What if the defendants were armed and intended to murder the driver when he stopped? Would it still have been held that they were not guilty of attempt until the moment when they had him in their gunsights? If so, the law of attempt is allowed very little operation.

The two defendants did not go without punishment, because they pleaded guilty to conspiracy; but the question of attempt retains practical importance in a case of this kind where there is only one attempter.

Somewhat inconsistently, there were cases holding that it could be an attempt to commit a consensual sexual offence (such as an offence of homosexuality, or unlawful sexual intercourse with a young girl) if the defendant enticed the other party to go to the place contemplated for the commission of the offence, provided that the defendant made known to

---

[14] (1953) 103 LJ 97.

such party what was intended.[15] The logical relevance of the qualification is obscure.

A farcical example of the restrictive approach to the law of attempts was *Robinson*.[16] It seems to show that to be guilty of an attempt the defendant must be on the brink of consummating the crime.

> The title role in the case was played by an impecunious jeweller. When the curtain rises, Robinson is discovered inside his shop with his legs and one hand tied. He is shouting "I am bound and gagged: open the door." A passing policeman hears the cries and blows his whistle. (How Robinson manages not merely to articulate but to make his words heard in the street outside when he is gagged we do not know, but I tell the tale as it is told in the Law Reports.) Reinforcements arrive; the officers burst into the shop and release Robinson, who explains that he has been robbed of the jewellery in his safe. The police with their quick intelligence look behind the safe, where they find the jewellery, which Robinson has of course insured against theft.

On these facts Robinson was convicted by a jury of attempting to obtain money from the insurers by false pretences (an offence now replaced by that of obtaining by deception). But the conviction was quashed by the Court of Criminal Appeal, which held that the police had moved too fast. They should have waited for Robinson to write to the company to claim the money. As it was, Robinson had merely prepared the background for the deception, and was not guilty of attempt.

But Robinson's intention in staging his tableau was clear.

An act does not become an attempt merely because the *mens rea* is obvious. Although the decision has been criticised,[17] it is by no means obviously wrong in terms of the traditional law of attempt. If Robinson bought a rope with which to truss himself up for the purpose of his intended fraud, that would obviously be merely preparatory. The court was not demonstrably in error in holding that staging the robbery was merely a preparatory act to making a claim on the insurers. Robinson's deceptive behaviour did, however, go further along the path of criminality than merely buying a rope.

Whatever the theoretical argument may be, the decision in *Robinson* puts the police "on the spot." As soon as Robinson realised that he was found out he desisted from the enterprise: there was no longer any point in claiming from the insurance company. But if the police had refrained from searching until after the fraudulent letter was written and posted, they might not have found the jewellery, because by that time Robinson might have hidden it better. Good police practice demands prompt action, but the law of attempt stultifies it. (A latter-day Robinson could, however, be convicted of the summary offence of making a false report wasting the time of the police.[18])

---

[15] *Gammon* 123 JP 410, [1959] Crim.LR 448; *The General Part*, 2nd edn 628 n. 26. It seems that even a solicitation by letter can be an attempt: *Honor* [1918] NZLR 510; *Cope* (1921) 16 CAR 77.

[16] [1915] 2 KB 342. Cp. *Comer* v. *Bloomfield*, 55 CAR 305, [1971] Crim.LR 230, where the cheat actually wrote to the insurers asking whether he could make a claim; again there was held to be no attempt. Contrast *Murray* [1982] 1 WLR 475, where the false information in fact reached the knowledge of some of the persons intended to be deceived. For other restrictive decisions see Stuart in [1970] Crim.LR 516.

[17] See in particular the reservation expressed by Lord Edmund-Davies in *Stonehouse* [1978] AC at 75.

[18] CLA 1967 s.5.

Another merry anecdote, equally infuriating for the police, is *Kyprianou* v. *Reynolds*.[19]

> Kyprianou approached drug pedlars and said, or perhaps hissed: "What you got tonight boys—hash or heroin? I got money upstairs." At this point Kyprianou observed for the first time that police officers were listening. It was held that he was not guilty of attempting to obtain cannabis or heroin, because he had, in the phrase used in the law of contract, merely issued an "invitation to treat." Presumably an offer to buy would have been an attempt.

A Working Party appointed by the Law Commission proposed that these problems should be resolved by enacting that an attempt is committed by taking a "substantial step" towards committing the crime. Both Robinson and Kyprianou (and also Komaroni) clearly took a substantial step. Instead of beginning with the crime, and looking backwards to see what was proximate, one would begin with the defendant's intention and look forwards to see what was a substantial step in pursuance of it. This would give the law of attempt a wider scope. The Working Party also proposed that the statute should contain illustrative examples, so that the legislature could make its own "case-law" on what is the essentially political matter of deciding when the law of attempt should begin to operate; these examples could show both what is an attempt and what is not. Unfortunately, as I think, the Commission rejected the advice of its Working Party and instead put forward its own anaemic recommendation which is now in the Act.[20] Since the new formula (devoid of illustrative examples) can mean everything or nothing, it appears to make the position worse confounded.

In a jury trial, who decides whether the act goes beyond mere preparation: judge or jury?

Section 4(3) enacts:

> "Where, in proceedings against a person for an offence under section 1 above, there is evidence sufficient in law to support a finding that he did an act falling within subsection (1) of that section, the question whether or not his act fell within that subsection is a question of fact."

This puts the common law, as declared (or rather changed) by the House of Lords in *Stonehouse*,[21] into statutory form. The effect is that:

1 The trial judge can rule as a matter of law that the act did not go beyond mere preparation; so he can withdraw the case from the jury.
2 If the judge thinks that the act can reasonably be regarded as having gone beyond mere preparation he should leave the question to the jury; but he may sum up, it was judicially said, "in such a way as to make it plain that he considers that the accused is guilty and should be convicted."[22] He may not rule as a matter of law that the act went beyond mere preparation, even though it plainly did. He must, in theory, leave the jury to ponder the question, telling them that the matter is for them; though if he fails to do so an appeal may be dismissed under the proviso.[23]

---

[19] [1969] Crim.LR 656. Cp. [1955] Crim.LR 66.
[20] For a discussion see 145 JPN 588.
[21] N. 8 above. The common law before that unfortunate decision, which treated proximity as a question of law, was incorporated in the Canadian Code (RSC 1970 C–34 as amended) s.24 (2).
[22] *Per* Lord Salmon in *Stonehouse* at p. 80B.
[23] As in *Stonehouse*, n. 8 above.

The rule is really rather silly. It means that the jury, who may be thoroughly mystified by the judge's direction, must be given the opportunity to return a perverse or stupid verdict of acquittal even though an attempt was quite clearly committed on the undisputed facts.

Stonehouse was cited to the Court of Appeal in *Pagett* (§ 16.3 at n. 8) in the hope of persuading the court that questions of imputable causation were entirely for the jury and should not be removed from the jury by the judge. The court responded with the ambiguous pronouncement that has already been studied; but the outcome was that the trial judge was upheld in telling the jury that in law the defendant's act was a cause of the death, assuming of course that the facts alleged by the prosecution were found. *Stonehouse*, said the court, "simply established in a particular context the well-established principle that it is the function of the judge to direct the jury on the applicable law and that he must not deprive the jury of their right to decide, on the law so stated to them, whether in fact the relevant offence had been committed." The difficulty of this dictum in relation to criminal attempts is that the only principle of law stated by Parliament is largely vacuous.

It seems to me that in Robinson the judges did not really leave the jury to decide whether an attempt was committed. They decided it for themselves, and overruled the jury's opinion.

Yes. Before the decision in *Stonehouse* the courts treated the question of proximity in attempt, quite rightly, as one of law—which was why the appellate court felt able to quash Robinson's conviction. Since *Stonehouse* and section 4(3), previous decisions like *Robinson* can be given legal force only by "reinterpreting" them, so that instead of being decisions that as a matter of law an attempt was not committed, they become decisions that as a matter of law there was no evidence for the jury that an attempt was committed. On its face the Act seems to leave a large scope to the jury to make their own decision; but it does not absolutely oblige the courts to change their former practice in ruling against liability. Quite possibly, trial judges will continue to withdraw the case from the jury if no attempt was committed according to the pre-Act decisions, leaving the jury to choose between convicting and acquitting only if the judge thinks that a conviction would be reasonable. It would be well if this course were followed, because if juries were allowed to give full play to their own hunches there might be great variation in the verdicts.

Are you suggesting that if facts like Robinson occurred again, the trial judge would be bound by that decision to rule that there was no case to answer and withdraw it from the jury?

Section 6(1) provides that "the offence of attempt at common law and any offence at common law of procuring materials for crime are hereby abolished for all purposes." Conceivably, these words may be construed as demolishing all decisions on attempt at common law, so that they lose their force under the Act. This would allow the judge in your question to ignore *Robinson*, which would, as regards that particular issue, be beneficial.

However, the point is by no means certain. If section 6(1) wipes the slate completely clean, then there is now no law on the question whether an act goes beyond mere preparation (or, in legal jargon, can be regarded by a reasonable jury as going beyond mere preparation), though of course the Court of Appeal may start building up a body of law again. But it would have been an inglorious reform if the Act merely abolished the old law without putting anything clear in its place.

The legal argument for saying that the Act has made no real difference is much stronger than the argument that it has. The Act does not seem to have been intended to make any real difference. Although it abandons the language of proximity, so that a judge who used this expression in directing the jury would probably be reproved on appeal, it does *not* enact that the proximity rule shall cease to be law. Common law attempts are turned into statutory attempts, but there is no indication that the criteria of what is meant by an attempt (as opposed to mere preparation) have changed.

The Act follows the recommendations of the Law Commission, which left out the reference to proximity because it did not like the word, not because it intended to enlarge the number of non-preparatory acts that would be punishable as attempts. The Commission said:

> "The literal meaning of 'proximate' is 'nearest, next before or after (in place, order, time, connection of thought, causation etc.).' Thus, were this term part of a statutory description of the *actus reus* of attempt, it would clearly be capable of being interpreted to exclude all but the 'final act;' this would not be in accordance with the policy outlined above."[24]

The Commission's fear is difficult to understand, since the notion of proximity was part of the common law, and if it had been put into statutory form the courts would have construed it in accordance with the decisions. The courts did *not* interpret proximity to refer only to the "final act."

However, the abandonment of the language of proximity appears to be only a matter of words. The Act preserves the rule that the act of attempt must go beyond mere preparation, which in the past was only another way of saying that it must be "proximate." If this interpretation is true, the "reform" effected by the Act in this part of the law is almost entirely vacuous. Pending a better drafted statute, that would be the best way to regard it.

§ 17.6. ATTEMPT AND ACCESSORIES

A person may be accessory to an attempt.[1]

Take for example the case where D incites X to commit a crime.

- D is guilty, at the moment of incitement, of incitement.[2] (And if, as would be usual, D and X act by arrangement together, both are guilty of conspiracy to commit the crime.)
- When X attempts to commit the crime, D becomes an accessory to the attempt.
- When the attempt succeeds, D becomes accessory to the crime.

D's liability as accessory at the second stage presupposes three things.

1 That an act of attempt was committed.
2 That the attempt was incited (or helped) by D.
3 That D intended the crime to be committed, or at any rate did not intend to frustrate it.

As to (1), if X has not reached the stage of attempt, D's incitement or effort to help does not make him a party to an attempt, because there is no attempt by the contemplated perpetrator yet.

To put the matter in a nutshell, the law is that one can be accessory to an attempt when there is an attempt, but one cannot attempt to commit a

[24] Law Com. No. 102 para. 2.48.

[1] J C Smith in *Crime, Proof and Punishment*, ed. Tapper (London 1981) 26–27.
[2] Incitement probably does not cover the mere supply of materials, etc. See § 19.1.

crime as accessory—one cannot attempt to abet. To attempt means to attempt to *perpetrate* a crime, not to attempt to *abet* it. If somebody does attempt to perpetrate the crime, then others can be guilty of abetting the attempt, but that is a different matter.

If a man can conspire to commit an offence as accessory, I don't see why he can't attempt to commit it as accessory.

The reason is that conspiracy as a crime is not limited by the beyond-preparation doctrine, as attempt is. It would be strange if a person could be guilty of attempting a crime as accessory when the intended perpetrator has not reached the stage of attempt. Suppose that X asks D for the loan of a knife, saying that he wants to kill V. D lends him the knife, but X does not use it or try to use it. X has not attempted to commit murder, and the same principle that exempts X from liability for attempt (namely, that the stage of attempt has not been reached) protects D also.[3]

Reverting to rule (3) above, this is important in respect of police informers. If such an informer has infiltrated a gang and helped them in attempting a crime, intending that they shall be frustrated by the arrival of the police, the informer is not an accessory to the attempt, any more than he will be accessory to the full crime if (contrary to his plan) it is carried out (§ 15.13). Just as the perpetrator of an attempt must intend to bring about the crime in view, and not merely go through the motions of an attempt, so must his helper.

It logically follows that if D2 hands D1 some liquid which he lyingly says is poison, and incites him to put it into V's coffee for the purpose (in D1's mind) of killing V, and D1 does so, D1 is guilty as perpetrator of an attempt to murder, but D2 is not an accessory.[4] The intention to murder was that of D2 alone. If D1 were accessory to the attempt, the police informer discussed in the previous paragraph would also be an accessory, which would be absurd. The difference between the police informer and the practical joker is that the informer is acting in the public interest while the joker is a mischief-maker, but this is only a difference in their motivation, not in their intention.

SUMMARY

Inchoate offences are committed when some step is taken to put a criminal intention into effect, which step is regarded as sufficiently serious to be punishable although the crime in view has not been accomplished. § .1

It is a statutory offence under the Criminal Attempts Act 1981 to attempt to commit any indictable offence, with small exceptions. The attempter may be sentenced to fine and imprisonment up to the maximum specified for the consummated crime. In practice a substantial discount is given. § .2

An attempt is judged according to the facts as the defendant believed them to be, so one can attempt the impossible. There must be an intention to commit the crime in question. At common law recklessness was sufficient in respect of circumstances (*Pigg*); whether this is still so under the Act is unclear. § .3

The act of attempt is defined as "an act which is more than merely preparatory to the commission of the offence." Whether the courts will stretch the meaning of "act" to include an omission is undecided. An act that goes beyond mere preparation, and so constitutes an attempt, was formerly called a proximate act; but the statute abandons this term. Under the Act, if the judge holds that there is § .5

[3] See Smith, *op.cit.* at 32–34, 36–39.

[4] Nor is he guilty of incitement: § 19.3.

evidence of such an act of attempt for the jury, he must then leave the jury to decide whether it went beyond mere preparation, however clear the case may be. The judge may, however, withdraw the case from the jury on the ground that there is no sufficient evidence. Before the Act the judges did this to such an extent that they only left the case to the jury if they themselves thought that the act, if proved, went beyond mere preparation. Whether the statute will now cause the judges to extend the idea of an attempt remains to be seen.

There can be an accessory to an attempt, but there cannot be an attempt to become an accessory. § .6

Chapter 18

CONSPIRACY

Open-ey'd Conspiracy
His time doth take.
The Tempest II. i.

§ 18.1. CONSPIRACY AND ITS OBJECTS

Conspiracy, the most complex of the inchoate offences at common law, may seem somewhat arbitrary. If the mere intention of one person to commit a crime is not criminal, why should the agreement of two people to do it make it criminal? The only possible reply is that the law (or, if you prefer, the Establishment) is fearful of numbers, and that the act of agreeing to offend is regarded as such a decisive step as to justify its own criminal sanction.[1]

At common law there could be a criminal conspiracy to commit various non-criminal acts, such as a tort, and even acts that were not legally wrong at all but were thought by the judges to be sufficiently improper to be repressed by the law of conspiracy. So, even where it was not legally wrong for one person to do the act, it could be a crime for two persons to agree to do it. After prolonged argument this doctrine was expunged from the law by the Criminal Law Act 1977, apart from two partial survivals which were intended to be temporary (see section 5).

1 Conspiracy to defraud at common law is preserved, while preparations are made to supersede it by statutory offences. The rules for statutory conspiracy under the Act do not apply. See more in § 31.5.

2 There are vague common law offences of conduct tending to corrupt public morals or outrage public decency. Such acts are probably punishable even when committed by individuals, in which case a conspiracy to do them is now a statutory conspiracy. However, should it be held that they are punishable only as conspiracies, they are excepted from the Act, so that such conspiracies remain governed by the common law; but again it is proposed to supersede these common law offences in due course by more specific statutory offences. Whether they will be superseded in this way, having regard to the limited powers of the Law Commission and the inanition that generally attends efforts at law reform, remains to be seen. In any case these matters lie outside the scope of the present work.

---

[1] Here, as generally in law, "sanction" means punishment. See further on the history and justification of (or reasons against) the law of conspiracy Sayre in 35 HLR 393; Ian Dennis in 93 LQR 39; and the radical, jaundiced, and somewhat flawed but interesting polemic by Robert Spicer, *Conspiracy* (London 1981).

§ 18.2. THE DEFINITION OF STATUTORY CONSPIRACY

Except as just stated, the common law of conspiracy has been superseded by the Criminal Law Act 1977. The rest of this chapter is concerned with conspiracies under the Act. For reasons of space, it does not, in general, deal with the common law, except where this is the same as statutory conspiracy.

Section 1(1) of the Act[1] provides the central definition of the new statutory offence.

> "If a person agrees with any other person or persons that a course of conduct shall be pursued which, if the agreement is carried out in accordance with their intentions, either
> (*a*) will necessarily amount to or involve the commission of any offence[2] or offences by one or more of the parties to the agreement, or
> (*b*) would do so but for the existence of facts which render the commission of the offence or any of the offences impossible,
> he is guilty of conspiracy to commit the offence or offences in question."

This definition substantially repeats the common law, except that:

- It is more restricted than the common law in requiring the object of the conspiracy to be criminal.
- It is wider than the common law in not requiring the object of the conspiracy to be possible.
- It creates doubts as to the mental element which did not exist at common law.

The conspiracy may be to commit a mere summary offence,[3] though in that case a prosecution requires the consent of the DPP.[4] Trial must be by jury, since the conspiracy charge is thought to raise too many difficulties of substance and procedure for magistrates to try. (A more solid reason is that conspiracy may lie so much in the mind and so little in the outward manifestation of illegality that the safeguard of jury trial is thought essential.)

An important result of the Criminal Law Act is that it gives the police power to arrest without warrant for statutory conspiracy, whenever the object of the conspiracy is to commit a crime punishable with at least 5 years' imprisonment.[5]

§ 18.3. THE AGREEMENT

Any agreement to commit the wrongful act, communicated to the other

---

[1] Act of 1977 as substituted by Criminal Attempts Act 1981 s.5 (1).

[2] Either an offence triable in England or murder (wherever triable): s.1 (4).

[3] Except a summary offence in contemplation or furtherance of a trade dispute: s.1(3).

[4] CLA 1977 s.4(1). If the summary offence can be prosecuted only with the consent of the Attorney General, a conspiracy charge requires his consent in place of the DPP's: s.4(2).

[5] This is because it fixes the punishment for conspiracy as a statutory matter and so makes conspiracies of the type referred to above "arrestable offences": see § 22.2. By a strange anomaly, a common law crime punishable at discretion is not an arrestable offence, but a conspiracy to commit it is, because the punishment for the conspiracy is fixed by CLA 1977 s.3(2) as imprisonment for life. For conspiracy to defraud see § 31.5.

party or parties,[1] constitutes a conspiracy.[2] The detailed means of carrying it out need not have been settled. The conspirators can be convicted even though the wrong plotted was to be committed only in the distant future, and though the plot immediately started to fall apart at the seams.[3] The act of conspiracy is itself regarded as a sufficient step in fulfilling the plan to be punishable.

Isn't there a danger that the law of conspiracy may be used to punish some nebulous agreement that the schemers might never have had the courage or ability to carry out?

Some prosecutorial discretion may be exercised in respect of vague conspiracies. But the only limitation upon the law is that there must be a concluded agreement to commit the wrong, not just the negotiation for such an agreement.[4] An agreement to commit the wrong on a condition, namely, if the opportunity shall arise, is sufficient.[5]

Does a man become a conspirator by knowingly supplying an article? A gang plan to commit a robbery. Needing a gun, they approach D, who, knowing of their purpose, supplies them with a weapon for a suitable consideration. The police have been on their tracks, and intervene before the robbery is committed. Is D guilty of conspiracy?

There is no English authority, but the answer would clearly seem to be no. If D initiated the plan, or were to participate in the spoils, he could be found to be a conspirator. If he agreed to provide a service for a fixed reward at the time of the crime, such as by driving the robbers to the bank, it would be reasonable to regard him as one of the plotters. But it would be going too far to say that a person has agreed that a crime shall be committed if he merely supplies the instrument of crime upon request.

Conspiracies are hatched in private. How can they be proved?

It is true that only rarely is it possible to establish a conspiracy by direct evidence. Usually, both the fact of the conspiracy and its objects have to be inferred from conduct.

A conspiracy charge can be embarrassing to the defence because of its vagueness, but this can be avoided if the prosecutor includes in the indictment particulars of the acts ("overt acts") alleged against each defendant sufficient to enable him to know as precisely as possible what is being alleged against him. Particulars are important when the conspiracy is inferred from conduct. If the conspiracy charge is left vague, as

---

[1] *Valerie Scott* (1978) 68 CAR 164.

[2] It might possibly be held, notwithstanding the statutory definition, that a conspirator must either encourage (or otherwise incite) the others or undertake (expressly or impliedly) to help. If A and B tell C that they have decided to commit a crime, and C indicates general approval without having any task assigned to him or inciting them, he could hardly be said to be a party to an agreement that the crime shall be committed. Of course, if C is to receive part of the proceeds that would be authorisation, and therefore incitement.

[3] And though defendant immdiately afterwards withdrew from the conspiracy. See Wasik in [1980] Crim.LR 788 n. 21.

[4] *Walker* [1962] Crim.LR 458; *Mills* [1963] Crim.LR 181; *O'Brien* (1974) 59 CAR 222.

[5] *King* [1966] Crim.LR 280.

unhappily it may be, each defendant will have to pick out the material allegations against him from the statements taken for the purposes of committal, which may be voluminous.

The overt acts in a conspiracy charge may be acts signifying agreement, acts preparatory to offences, or the offences themselves. Such acts are, of course, only evidence of the agreement.

So if three people conspire to steal, one, A, agreeing only to a non-violent theft while B and C secretly agree between themselves to use force, and in fact commit robbery with violence, the commission of this robbery by B and C does not make A guilty of conspiracy to rob.[6]

If a band of crooks have committed offences, can they be charged in the same indictment both with the offences and with conspiracy?

Yes.

And the jury can convict both of the main offences and of the conspiracy?

Yes. Conspiracy does not merge in the consummated crime.[7]

How do you settle the limits of a conspiracy? If terrorists foregather and plan to cause explosions in general, following this with more detailed plans to cause particular explosions, are these charged as one conspiracy or as many conspiracies?

The prosecution are not allowed to charge two conspiracies in one count. But they may charge a general conspiracy, and in support of that charge may adduce evidence of specific offences, such as (in the case instanced) an explosion in Manchester and one in London. These *could* have been charged as separate conspiracies,[8] but that does not affect the validity of the general count.[9]

However, if all that the prosecution can prove is that defendants D1 and D2 conspired in respect of the Manchester bomb, and that D3 and D4 conspired in respect of the London bomb, all four defendants cannot be convicted on the one count for the two conspiracies. A single count can charge only one offence, though the count may be against two defendants. The best that the prosecution can do if they have included only the general count is to ask for a conviction of, say, D3 and D4 on the general count, while accepting an acquittal of D1 and D2. Or conversely. This is a strange result, because it allows the prosecution in effect to choose which of the defendants are to be convicted, even though all have been shown to be guilty.[10]

Can conspirators adhere to the pact at different times?

Certainly. Conspirators may, for example, be enrolled in a chain—A

---

[6] See note in [1980] Crim.LR 236, commenting on *Barnard* (1979) 70 CAR 28, where there are misleading dicta on this point. The decision in *Barnard* is to be explained by the fact that A either had never conspired or had withdrawn from the conspiracy before it was carried out.

[7] In the event of such double conviction, there should be no more than a nominal sentence on the conspiracy count: *Stewart* [1982] 3 WLR 884.

[8] *Martin Coughlan* (1976) 63 CAR 33.

[9] *Greenfield* [1973] 1 WLR 1151, 3 All ER 1050.

[10] A general count for conspiracy will be struck out if the count itself and the statements in the committal proceedings show that there was no single conspiracy between the defendants but only a number of separate conspiracies: *per curiam* in *Greenfield* [1973] 1 WLR at 1156.

enrolling B, B enrolling C, and so on; and all will be members of a single conspiracy if they so intend, even though each member knows only the person who enrolled him and the person whom he enrols. Similarly, there may be a kind of umbrella-spoke enrolment,[11] a single person at the centre doing the enrolling and all the other members being unknown to each other by name, though they know that there are to be other members.

Provided that the mutual intent is present, therefore, persons may be members of a single conspiracy even though each is ignorant of the identity of many others. But if A intends to conspire solely with B, and C intends to conspire solely with B, there can be no common conspiracy involving A and C, since neither intends to conspire with any one but B. The two conspiracies involving different people cannot be charged in the same indictment. The fact that the two conspiracies have a common member, B, does not make them one conspiracy.

> As an example, suppose that an accountant proposes to each of a number of clients a particular means of defrauding the Revenue, and each client accepts the proposal. There is then a conspiracy between the accountant and each client separately, but not between the clients; and it makes no difference that the fraud is similar in all cases. Even if the clients know that others are committing the same fraud, that does not make them conspirators with each other. The purpose of the various parties must be not merely *similar* but *agreed*.[12]

What if a plain clothes police officer or his undercover agent, coming to know that some nefarious scheme is afoot, pretends to join it, in order to secure the conviction of the other parties. Is he guilty himself?

In the discussion of complicity it was suggested that a person should not be an accessory if he took part only with the purpose of preventing the commission of the offence or of nullifying its effects (§ 15.13). Unfortunately, no such limitation is incorporated into the rules for conspiracy in the Criminal Law Act. Literally, your police officer or informer comes within section 1(1), unless the courts let him out by holding that his mental reservation meant that he did not "really" agree. Presumably this view will be taken.

§ 18.4. CONSPIRACY IN RELATION TO OTHER INCHOATE CRIMES

By statute, a person cannot be convicted of incitement to conspire or attempt to conspire (whether to commit a statutory conspiracy or to defraud).[1] The reason given is that this would push liability too far back, to a stage where there is no agreement to commit the offence. The reason is highly questionable, and it would seem that all or almost all cases of incitement or attempt to conspire could be charged as incitement to commit the crime.[2]

---

[11] Usually called a "cartwheel" conspiracy—but it is a cartwheel without a rim. See *Ardalan* [1972] 1 WLR at 470.

[12] See *Griffiths* [1966] 1 QB 589. The court distinguished the earlier case of *Meyrick* (1929) 21 CAR 94 in a way that left it little application, and it would have been better to say that *Meyrick* was wrongly decided.

[1] CLA 1977 s.51(7) as amended; Criminal Attempts Act 1981 s.1(4)(*a*).

[2] That is to say, to commit it either as perpetrator or as accessory. See the fuller argument in § 19.4.

Intending accessories may be parties to a conspiracy. If D1, D2 and D3 conspire that D2 and D3 are to place a ladder against a building, so that D1 shall subsequently use the ladder to enter the building and steal, all three are guilty of conspiring to burgle (i.e. conspiring that a burglary shall be perpetrated by D1).[3]

Obviously, too, a conspiracy to incite a person to commit a crime, either as perpetrator or as accessory,[4] is criminal. Incitement being itself a crime, the conspiracy is to commit a crime.

§ 18.5. PROS AND CONS OF THE CONSPIRACY COUNT

Conspiracy charges are the bogey of the political Left, because of their use against people who take part in industrial and political disorder. But considerable changes have been made in the law, and at the present day these charges are neither so oppressive as their critics fear nor so efficacious as prosecutors seem to believe. The question mark that hangs over them is, in fact, whether they are worth while, having regard to the complexity they tend to add to the trial.

Although conspiracy is generally considered, and treated in the books, as an inchoate crime, in practice it is rarely prosecuted at the purely inchoate stage. Almost always some substantive crime has been committed in pursuance of it, for which all or most of the conspirators could be prosecuted as accomplices. As an inchoate crime, therefore, the law of conspiracy serves little social purpose.[1]

If a charge of conspiracy as an inchoate crime is of small use, isn't the same even more true of a charge of conspiracy when the crime has been committed? Why not charge the crime?

As was mentioned before, the prosecution can charge both. They gain two minor advantages in adding a conspiracy count to a charge for consummated crime.

1 In theory, and to some small extent in practice, adding the conspiracy count guards against the risk that the prosecution may fail to prove the consummated crime, while being able to prove the conspiracy. Difficulty might be caused if there were no conspiracy count. It would add to the costs, and might look like harassment, to indict members of a gang for conspiracy after they have been acquitted of the substantive crime. But in fact the problem rarely arises: that a crime was committed is generally quite clear, and the only question is whether the defendant was a party to an agreement to commit it. Alternatively, if the substantive crime

---

[3] This is now plain from the wording of the CLA (§ .2). Prof. Smith argues that the position is different if D1 is not a party to the conspiracy: a conspiracy by D2 and D3 to assist another (who is not a party) to commit a crime is not, in his view, criminal. See his reasoning in *Crime, Proof and Punishment*, ed. Tapper (London 1981) 35–36, 40–41.

[4] See § 19.4 on incitement to abet.

[1] Such advantage as there is in punishing inchoate conspiracies could be simply achieved if the law of attempt were shifted to a "substantial step" basis; the making of an agreement with another person to commit an indictable offence could then be declared to be a substantial step towards committing it.

cannot be proved (as in a fraud case), the conspiracy charge generally falls also.

2 At common law, conspiracy, like all other common law misdemeanours, was not subject to any maximum punishment. This rule was a target for the reformers, who argued that there was no reason why two people who committed a crime together should, by the addition of a conspiracy count, become liable to a higher sentence than the man who gave a solo performance. The Criminal Law Act acknowledges the justice of the criticism to some extent, since it provides that conspiracy is subject to the same maximum term of imprisonment as the completed offence.[2] But the old anomaly is allowed to remain in one respect: a conspiracy to commit a summary offence is punishable (on indictment, of course) by an unlimited fine, whereas if the summary offence were actually committed the fine that could be imposed by a magistrates' court would be limited by statute.

At common law, charges of conspiracy and incitement provided the prosecution with an unfair trump, since by charging these offences the prosecution freed themselves from a time-limit on prosecution[3] or the necessity for the consent of the Director of Public Prosecutions or other person.[4] For statutory conspiracy, these rules are now altered by the Criminal Law Act,[5] so that in these respects the advantages of adding a conspiracy charge disappear.

Conspiracy counts are sometimes said to help the jury to understand the "overall criminality" of what the defendants have done[6]; but it may be doubted whether they can do any more in this respect than could be done by the specific counts, including, if necessary, representative counts. Again, conspiracy charges are sometimes thought to allow the Crown to adduce evidence that would otherwise be inadmissible, but again this may be strongly doubted.[7]

Counterbalancing the two advantages for the prosecution in including a conspiracy count are two disadvantages.

1 If the evidence is that the offences were committed in concert and the jury convict of the offences but acquit of conspiracy, or *vice versa*, the conviction may be quashed for inconsistency with the acquittal.[8]

2 The addition of an unnecessary count increases the possibility of a mistake being made at the trial.

Quite apart from the above matters, there has long been an impression that the addition of a conspiracy count where the crimes in view are alleged to have been consummated is procedurally unfair to the defendants. Accordingly, the judge is required (by a practice direction[9]) to call upon

---

[2] CLA 1977 s.3. On conviction of conspiracy to murder, the judge has a discretion as to sentence. Where several crimes are committed, the sentences for these crimes (if they are not part of a single transaction) can be cumulative, but on a charge of conspiracy to commit them the maximum imprisonment is for the longest term applicable to any of the crimes contemplated, not for a cumulative term.

[3] *Simmonds* [1969] 1 QB 685.

[4] The rule still holds for incitement: § 19.2 n. 5.

[5] S.4(3), (4). The officer's consent must be specifically to a charge of conspiracy: *Pearce* (1980) 62 CAR 295. But one anomaly remains: since time runs from the commission of the offence, a conspiracy charge is not subject to a time limit attaching to the offence where the offence is not committed. And conviction of conspiracy does not enable the court to make a forfeiture order as for the completed crime: *Cuthbertson* [1981] AC 470.

[6] *Per* James LJ in *Jones* (1974) 59 CAR at 124.

[7] *The General Part* § 218.

[8] *Sweetland* (1958) 42 CAR 62. See the editorial criticism of *Dawes* [1978] Crim.LR 503.

[9] [1977] 1 WLR 537, 2 All ER 540.

the prosecution to justify the joinder, and if they fail to do so they will have to elect whether to proceed upon the substantive or the conspiracy counts. In any case, now that the conspiracy count no longer enables the prescribed maximum term of imprisonment to be disregarded, the attractiveness of the count to the prosecution largely disappears.

Whether there is any real unfairness in a conspiracy count, as such, that could not be rectified by the sensible conduct of the trial, may be questioned.[10] Obviously it is desirable to confine trials to a relatively small number of defendants (the chief offenders), and to a reasonably narrow class of acts, whether a conspiracy count is added or not; otherwise the jury may become confused.

A defect in the present procedure is that when the jury return a verdict of guilty they are not asked whether they find all the defendants to have participated in all the overt acts alleged against them. Judges appear to assume that the verdict means this, but obviously it may not do so, so that considerable injustice is possible. It may be that there is only one really serious overt act alleged (planting a bomb in a crowded store, which failed to go off), and if the jury are not satisfied that a particular defendant agreed to that the finding ought to be known.[11]

§ 18.6. THE CRIMINAL PURPOSE

It will be remembered that section 1(1) (§ .2) speaks of the purpose of the conspiracy as being to pursue "a course of conduct which, if the agreement is carried out in accordance with their intentions, either (*a*) will necessarily amount to or involve the commission of any offence or offences by one or more of the parties to the agreement . . ." or (*b*) would do so but for impossibility.

The meaning of "necessarily" has been the subject of speculation. The word is unfortunate, because it gives the impression, wrongly, that the only plans that can amount to a statutory conspiracy are those that are either absolutely infallible or absolutely impossible. In reality, many gradations can be found between these extremes, where the best laid schemes o' mice and men gang a-ley and yet are punishable in appropriate circumstances as conspiracies. The following hypothetical will illustrate the point.

> D1 and D2 agree to snipe at V from the roof of a building, hoping to kill him. They think that he is or may be within range, but in fact he is out of the range of the gun that they use. They are guilty of conspiracy to murder, it being immaterial that there are "facts [the positive fact that V is out of range, or the negative fact that V is not within range—it does not matter how one words it] which render the commission of the offence impossible." (The singular in statutes includes the plural, and the plural the singular, unless the contrary intention appears.[1])
>
> Although these facts are clearly covered under (*b*), they might be slightly different. It might be uncertain whether V was out of range or

[10] 128 NLJ 24.

[11] However, the judge in sentencing can always act on his own opinion of the culpability of the various defendants (subject to the restrictions stated in § 1.3).

[1] Interpretation Act 1978 s.6 (*c*).

> not, in which case it may be moot whether a conspiracy can be found under (*a*). Even if V was within range, it would not be certain that the assassins would hit him. They might shoot at him and miss. So (it may be argued) they will not "necessarily" kill him; so it is not a conspiracy within the section.

The argument has some attraction but of course the result would be absurd. The answer to it is that the "course of conduct" envisaged by the agreement means not only the physical acts of the conspirators but the intended result. In our hypothetical the intended "course of conduct" is not only shooting at V but killing him. When this "course of conduct" is "carried out in accordance with their intentions," it will necessarily be murder. (It is a mark of the defective wording of the Act, as it emerged from the parliamentary process, that such lengthy reasoning has to be set out in order to arrive at a common-sense conclusion. The defects in the wording were immediately pointed out by commentators,[2] yet no relevant changes were made—except on the impossibility issue—when the subsection, originally in the Criminal Law Act 1977, was replaced by a new version in the Criminal Attempts Act 1981.)

Doesn't your argument mean that the word "necessarily" is otiose?

Not necessarily! Donaldson LJ (as he then was) gave the following illustration of how it is capable of having a practical effect.[3]

> "A and B agree to drive from London to Edinburgh in a time which can be achieved without exceeding the speed limits, but only if the traffic which they encounter is exceptionally light. Their agreement will not necessarily involve the commission of any offence, even if it is carried out in accordance with their intentions. . . . Accordingly the agreement does not constitute the offence of statutory conspiracy."

Well, suppose that A and B agree to export aluminium. There is emergency legislation in force making such export an offence, but it is quite possible that the legislation will be repealed by the time the export is to take place. Would Donaldson LJ say that that is not a conspiracy?

The courts would probably distinguish a case where the parties gamble on a change in the law, as in your instance. And the courts would probably require a substantial possibility that the agreement may be carried out lawfully.

Then suppose that A and B agree to make a trespassory entry into a building in order to photocopy secret documents, and to shoot at anyone who attempts to impede them. They expect to be able to do the job without interference, but there is a substantial possibility that they will have to shoot. Isn't that a conspiracy to wound?

---

[2] Particularly Professor Smith in [1977] Crim.LR 598, 638.

[3] *Reed* [1982] Crim.LR 819.

One would have thought so,[4] but it is difficult to distinguish your hypothetical from that put by the Lord Justice. Perhaps one can say that the offence of wounding will be committed *in certain foreseen circumstances* if the agreement is carried out in accordance with their intentions. They have a conditional intent to shoot—an intent to shoot if they are interfered with.

But then, A and B in Donaldson LJ's example had a conditional intent to exceed speed limits—an intent to exceed them if the traffic should be heavy.

Yes, and the Lord Justice said that it is a conspiracy to agree to rob a bank "if when they arrive at the bank it seems safe to do so." That must be the law, since every conspiracy is dependent on its seeming to be safe to act at the time. The actual decision in the case before Donaldson LJ in the Court of Appeal was that it is a conspiracy to aid and abet suicide for the parties to agree to assist a person to commit suicide if upon investigation this seems the best course in the circumstances.

The line between conditional conspiracies that are criminal and those that are not seems to be too etherial and evanescent to be workable in the everyday world. Parliament would have done much better to have left the word "necessarily" out of the Act.

§ 18.7. THE MENTAL ELEMENT

The Act is again badly drafted on the mental element, making one undesirable change in the law and, for the rest, succeeding only in making obscure what was almost entirely plain before.

There is no reason why the mental element for conspiracy should differ from that for attempt, and probably it does not, except in respect of the one change in the law already mentioned. In other words, the mental element should basically be intention, with question marks added in respect of two possible extensions: foresight of certainty (§ 3.5) and recklessness as to circumstance. The Act removes the question mark as to recklessness by giving the wrong answer. Recklessness as to circumstances is now not enough for a conspiracy, if the plain words of the Act are accepted. This is because of section 1(2). The subsection is mind-twisting, and since not all readers will be interested in it the point is reduced to fine print.

Section 1(2):

> "Where liability for any offence may be incurred without knowledge on the part of the person committing it of any particular fact or circumstance necessary for the commission of the offence, a person shall nevertheless not be guilty of conspiracy to commit that offence by virtue of subs. (1) above unless he and at least one other party to the

---

[4] Cp., for a decision on a different part of the law, *Buckingham* § 19.6 n. 6.

agreement intend or know[1] that that fact[2] or circumstance shall or will exist at the time when the conduct constituting the offence is to take place."

In other words, where an offence can be committed without the perpetrator knowing of a required circumstance (e.g. where he is liable for recklessness as to the circumstance), there can be no conspiracy except between those who intend that the circumstance shall exist at the time of the offence or know that it will.

So if two people agree to try to get money by making a representation, which may or may not be true, and at that time are reckless about whether it will be true at the time when they obtain the money, and do not care whether it will be true or false, then, if the representation is untrue when they make it and get the money, they will be guilty of obtaining the money by reckless deception, but they are not guilty of conspiracy. It will be the same if one of the two knows that the representation is untrue; *both* must know that it is or will be untrue before there is any criminal conspiracy.

Section 1(2) was probably not drafted for the purpose of reaching this result, but it is the consequence of the wording.

If you are still with me you will be asking what the position is if the offence requires knowledge on the part of the perpetrator, so that the subsection does not apply. Take for example the offence of knowingly possessing explosives. D1 and D2 agree to receive a bag from X and to keep it for him. D1 knows that the bag will contain explosives. D2 knows that it may but is not by any means sure. Again D2 is not guilty of conspiracy. A man cannot attempt or conspire by recklessness to commit a crime requiring knowledge, because what he does in consequence of the attempt or conspiracy will not be the completed crime in question. This being so, D1 is probably not guilty of conspiracy either (§ .10).

Reverting to the hypothetical about making a representation, if the parties are found to have been "wilfully blind" to the possibility of untruth, they may be held to have known that the statement was untrue, but the doctrine of wilful blindness should not be used to extend a requirement of knowledge to cases of mere recklessness (§ 6.3).

It was said just now that the mental element required for conspiracy is basically one of intention, and to justify this conclusion the abominable subsection (1) must again be considered. Again those who prefer to pass over the detail can do so.

(1) *No liability where consequence unintended and not foreseen as certain.* On a superficial reading, section 1(1) of the Act may seem to impose liability for conspiracy on a person who did not intend the criminal consequence that he is charged as conspiring to bring about. It may seem to imply that if D1 and D2 agree on a course of conduct, D1 having a criminal intent and D2 not, both parties will be guilty of a criminal conspiracy if the agreement when carried out will involve D1 in liability for an offence—in other words, D1's guilt will bring in D2. An effort must obviously be made to avoid this result. Consider the following hypothetical.

D1 falsely tells D2 that V has asked D1 to burn down an old shed for him. D2 agrees to help, and together they take petrol to the site, where they are apprehended. D1 and D2 are charged with conspiracy to commit arson.

Here it is true to say, in some sense, that D2 has agreed that a course of conduct shall be pursued which, when carried out, will amount to the commission of the offence of arson (by D1); and from this the conclusion may perhaps be drawn that both parties are guilty of conspiracy to commit the offence. But this would be a misreading of the subsection, for two reasons.

First, arson involves burning a building without lawful excuse. D2 thought he had a lawful

---

[1] It would have been better if s.1(2) had been amended by the addition of the words "or believe," to provide for "impossibility" cases where the fact does not exist. You cannot know what is not so. Doubtless the court will hold that in impossibility cases the party "intends" the circumstance to exist, even though that word is not very apt.

[2] Presumably this word includes a negative fact. If conspirators agree to abduct a young girl, they intend or know that a negative fact (the absence of the parent's consent) shall "exist" (i.e. they intend or know that the corresponding positive fact shall not exist) at the time when they propose to do the act.

excuse. Therefore he has not *agreed* to a course of conduct involving an offence; he has agreed to a course of conduct, and the course of conduct will amount to an offence, but he has not agreed to one of the elements of the conduct that amount to the offence, because he did not know of this particular element among the facts of the case.

Secondly, the carrying out of the agreement "in accordance with their intentions" will not involve the commission of an offence, since D2's intention extended only to the burning of the shed with lawful excuse. What brings about the offence is not the mere burning of the shed but its burning without lawful excuse; D2 did not know of the absence of lawful excuse, and it was not part of his intention. In short, the word "intentions" in the subsection must be construed to refer to the common intention of the parties, and to include only items of unlawfulness known to both of them.

(2) *Recklessness as to consequence insufficient.*. The wording of section 1 is evidently intended to exclude this form of *mens rea* from statutory conspiracy, since a requirement of intention or knowledge is inconsistent with mere recklessness.[3]

The only qualification is this, that if "intention" is understood to include realisation of the high probability of the consequence, then this realisation will be sufficient for conspiracy under section 1(1). But it was pointed out in a previous discussion that the weight of authority is against this wide definition of intention,[4] which is in any case inconsistent with the plain meaning of section 1(1).

This makes a point of difference between conspiracy (and other inchoate offences as well) and accessoryship. We saw in § 15.10–11, that a person may be an accessory to an offence of *mens rea* or negligence if, in general, he has the same fault element in relation to the consequence as is required for the perpetrator. Conspiracy is different: recklessness or negligence as to the consequence are not enough, even though they are enough for the perpetrator.

> Consider again the facts of *Salmon* (§ 15.11). If D2 encourages D1 to fire a gun negligently, and D1 kills someone, D2 is accessory to manslaughter. But if D1 did not kill anyone, he and D2 could not be convicted of conspiring to commit manslaughter.

The reason for the distinction is that where the crime is completed the courts wish to avoid the difficulties of proof that would result from distinguishing too finely between the perpetrator and the accessories, so they hold that it is possible to encourage manslaughter by negligence; whereas if the crime remains inchoate the element of intention assumes prominence.[5]

(3) *Party not liable for conspiracy if he believed that the required circumstance would not exist at the time of the intended conduct.*. This conclusion follows *a fortiori* from our previous conclusion as to recklessness in relation to circumstances. If a person is not guilty of

---

[3] Professor Smith takes a wider view of the offence ([1977] Crim.LR 638–639), He seems to hold that if the consummated offence can be committed recklessly, then recklessness in relation to the consequence is sufficient *mens rea*, provided that the consequence would necessarily follow, granted the circumstances "intended or known" to the defendants. So if two parties agree to take a risk of inflicting serious injury on another, such that if death occurs they will be guilty of murder under the rule in *Hyam* (§ 11.4), and if in the circumstances "intended or known" to them death was necessarily involved, then this would be a conspiracy to murder, even though the parties did not know that death was necessarily involved. A practical case raising this problem is difficult to imagine, but the theoretical answer surely is that s.1(1) on its proper interpretation requires that the defendant must have *known* that the course of conduct agreed upon would necessarily (that is, inevitably, or at least practically inevitably) involve the commission of the consummated offence. To the philosophical determinist, speaking with hindsight, every course of conduct that has led in fact to *x* necessarily involved *x*, since in his view, everything that happens, necessarily happens; but this is evidently not the meaning of "necessarily" in the subsection. Liability for conspiracy is fixed at the time when the conspiracy is entered into, and does not depend upon what happens afterwards; so "necessarily" in the subsection must mean "necessarily in the expectation of someone"; and that someone, surely, is the defendant. The overriding purpose of s.1(1) is to make a person liable for conspiracy on the basis of his intention In any case, the parties would on the facts supposed be saved from liability for conspiracy by subs. (2); cp. Adrian Lynch in [1978] Crim.LR 207–209.

[4] § 3.4. Authority is decisively against it for the crime of attempt (§ 17.4), and there is no reason why conspiracy should be different.

[5] For an extended discussion see Orchard in [1974] Crim.LR 335.

conspiracy on account of recklessness as to circumstances, it follows that he is not liable if he believed that the required circumstance would not exist. But the subsection is not necessary to reach this conclusion in the case of crimes of intention. The reasoning here is similar to that under (1) above. Section 1(1) is not well drafted to deal with the question of knowledge of circumstances, but the right result can be achieved if the reference to the "intentions" of the parties is held to exclude liability where the party believed that the circumstances necessary to make the act a crime were not present. Subsection (2) makes it plain that a similar rule applies even though what is plotted will be an offence of recklessness, negligence or strict liability. Hence it is always a defence to a charge of statutory conspiracy to show that the defendant was under a misapprehension, such that if the facts had been as he supposed his conduct would not have been criminal.

As with accessories, a person charged with conspiracy need not know that what is agreed upon is a breach of the law, where ignorance of law would be no excuse in respect of the consummated crime.[6]

Does a person become a conspirator by agreeing to help in an illegal plan of which he knows no details?

It has already been mentioned that a negative answer was given in *Scott* (§ 15.9 at n. 4), but that case is perhaps not the last word on the subject.

§ 18.8. THE NECESSITY FOR TWO CONSPIRATORS

The rule that there must be at least two conspirators[1] has been used to reach the conclusion that husband and wife cannot conspire together, where there is no third party, because they are one person in law.[2] The reason is false, and the rule is of doubtful policy; but it is expressly preserved by the Criminal Law Act (s.2(2)(*a*)).

The provision in the Act emanated from the Law Commission Working Party, a majority of which defended the rule on the ground that it prevents the police from bringing improper pressure to bear on criminals. A man may be made to confess by threatening him that otherwise his wife will be charged with conspiracy with him. A weakness of this argument is that no steps have been taken to negate other ways in which the wife may become liable in crime. A wife may certainly be convicted as accessory to her husband's crime,[3] or presumably of inciting her husband to crime. And there may be a conviction of conspiracy between a husband, wife and third person. No sufficient reason can be found for singling out conspiracy as the one crime that husband and wife cannot commit together.

It may be known that the defendant has conspired with someone else, a shadowy figure whom the police never lay their hands on. Can the defendant nevertheless be convicted?

He may be indicted for conspiracy with a person unknown.

---

[6] This is clear from the wording of section 1 of the Act, following the common law.

[1] Cp. *McDonnell*, § 44.2 n. 4.

[2] See the scholarly judgment of Oliver J in *Midland Bank* v. *Green* [1979] Ch. at 510 ff., affd. [1982] 2 WLR 1.

[3] *Manning* (1849) 2 C & K at 904a, 175 ER 379; *Browning* v. *Floyd* [1946] KB 597; *The General Part*, 2nd edn § 123 n. 14; Richard Card in [1973] Crim.LR 679.

D1 weaves a plot with D2. They are found out, but D2 escapes. D1 is tried and convicted of conspiracy. Then D2 is caught and put on trial. Is the conviction of D1 admissible in evidence against him?

No. D2 is entitled to fight the issue of his own innocence, without being prejudiced by the conviction of D1.

What if D1 and D2 are tried together for conspiring together (without any other parties being named)? Can the jury convict D1 and acquit D2?

The common law was in a muddle on this, but the position is now clarified by the Criminal Law Act 1977.[4] The answer is that in a suitable case they can. For example, D1 may have confessed, and his confession is admissible against him but not against D2. However, if the evidence against the two defendants is substantially the same the judge should direct the jury that it would not be right for them to convict one of conspiracy and acquit the other. If there is any doubt as to the case against one they should acquit both.[5]

I don't understand why D1's confession that he conspired with D2 is not evidence against D2.

It is if the confession is made in the witness-box at the joint trial. But if it was made to the police it is hearsay evidence in respect of D2, though it is admissible against D1 as a confession. Even if D1 pleads guilty, this is not evidence against D2, because it is not a statement made on oath but only a statement of intention not to contest the charge.

But if D1 pleads guilty, so that there is no trial of the case against him, and then D2 gets off, D1 will have a sense of grievance.

If D2 is acquitted the judge may allow D1 to withdraw his plea and be tried, when it seems on the evidence that there might otherwise be a miscarriage of justice. But when the evidence explains the situation, D1's conviction will doubtless be allowed to stand.

These rules of procedure and evidence do not affect the proposition that on a charge of conspiracy against a particular person it must be proved that he and another person took part with the requisite guilty mind. See further, § .10.

§ 18.9. LIABILITY OF AN EXEMPT PARTY

The next question is whether a person can be liable for conspiracy to commit a crime that he cannot himself commit. He ought not to be, and generally he is not, but there are anomalous exceptions. The matters to be

---

[4] Section 5(8) and (9).

[5] *Longman* [1981] Crim.LR 38; cp. *Holmes* [1980] 1 WLR 1055, 2 All ER 458, and Boulter in 131 NLJ 637.

discussed in this and the next section are not of large importance, and readers who do not want this detail may pass them over.

First as to the general rule: where a person would not be liable for the consummated crime because he lacks the mental element, then he is also free from liability for conspiracy. See § .7. (Even if the consummated crime does not require a mental element, a person cannot be liable for conspiracy unless he knows the facts: see in particular s.1(2) of the Act, already discussed.)

Where a person cannot by law perpetrate a crime, owing to some special exemption, he can still, obviously, be guilty of conspiring to commit the crime if he can be an accessory to it. So if a husband, who cannot generally perpetrate a rape upon his wife, agrees with his friend to help the friend to rape the wife, the husband and the friend can be guilty of conspiring together. This was so at common law,[1] and it remains so under the wide words of section 1(1).

The anomalous cases are those arising from the wording of section 1(1), which makes D1 guilty of conspiracy if he agrees that D2 shall do what will for D2 be a crime, notwithstanding that D1 could not himself commit the crime, even as accessory. Provided that D1 has the requisite mental element, he becomes a conspirator.

> Take abduction as an example. We have seen that the parent or guardian of a child (e.g. the mother) cannot be guilty of the offence of taking the child from its parent or guardian (e.g. the father) (§ 9.12 at n. 6); and it may well be (though the point has not been decided) that the mother in the example is not guilty of abetting a third party (such as her brother) to abduct the child. But in such circumstances the mother, though not guilty of the substantive offence, appears to be made guilty of conspiracy by the Act. Her brother will commit the offence of child abduction (assuming that he knows that the mother has been deprived of her right to custody of the child, so that he has no claim of right).[2] Therefore, the case falls within section 1(1): the mother and her brother have agreed that something shall be done that will be an offence for her brother. The mother is not the victim of the offence; so she is guilty of conspiracy.[3]

Parliament doubtless did not intend this result, but it is the effect of amendments to the Law Commission's Bill made in the House of Lords at the insistence of the legal peers, who did not appreciate the consequences of what they were doing.

Special provision is made by the Act on one point. Suppose that a girl under 16, who cannot be a party to her own seduction, is charged with conspiring with her seducer. In this particular case she is exempted by reason of the fact that she is the victim of the intended offence: Criminal Law Act 1977 section 1(1):

> "A person shall not by virtue of section 1 above be guilty of conspiracy to commit any offence if he is an intended victim of that offence."

Although this provision meets the particular point, it is clumsy draftsmanship, because it is capable of being construed too widely, and yet, in one respect, is too narrow. However, problems are not likely to occur frequently.

The provision is too wide if it is construed to apply to anyone who is regarded as adversely affected by the offence. The word "victim" should be construed to mean a person who cannot perpetrate the offence, and who cannot be convicted as accessory to it because, being the

---

[1] In *Whitchurch* (1890) 24 QBD 420 a woman who (not being pregnant) could not have been convicted of perpetrating an abortion on herself was convicted of conspiring with another that that other should perpetrate the abortion on her. This can be explained by reference to the later case of *Sockett* (1908) CAR 101, 72 JP 428, 24 TLR 893, where it was held that such a woman could be accessory to her own abortion. Clearly, a person can conspire to commit an offence where he would he liable as accessory to the offence. It may be doubted, however, whether *Sockett* was correctly decided. The court might well have discovered a legislative intention to exempt the non-pregnant woman (cp. § 15.15 n. 11). Even so, she may now be convicted of conspiracy by reason of the unhappy wording of the CLA: see below.

[2] See *Duguid*, below § .10 at n. 4.

[3] To add to the anomaly, if the brother had a claim of right because he did not know that the mother had been deprived of legal custody of the child, the mother would not be guilty of conspiracy because s.1, while not requiring double liability for the consummated offence, requires double knowledge of the facts.

victim of the offence, he is assumed to fall outside its scope. Contrast the youth of 17 who, not being exempted from the homosexual offences, cannot be regarded as the "victim" of those offences as a matter of law, even though he may be regarded as the victim from the moral point of view. Since he can be convicted as perpetrator, it follows that he can be convicted as accessory; and therefore he should be liable for conspiring, and there is no reason why section 2(1) should apply.

In another respect the provision is too narrow. The rule that an intended victim of an offence is not an accessory to it is merely one instance of what should be regarded as a wider proposition, that a person is not an accessory to a statutory offence if it was evidently the intention of the legislature to exempt him. The Act fails to provide exemption from conspiracy on this wider ground, so the possibility arises of a person who cannot be convicted as accessory to an offence when committed yet being liable for conspiracy to commit it.

The case of *Whitehouse* has already been partly considered (§ 15.15 at n. 10). The court held that if a man defiles his daughter aged under 16, she cannot be convicted of incest—not as perpetrator, because the statute leaves her out of the wording of the offence, confining the offence to the father, and not as accessory, because she was the victim of the offence. No doubt a future court will accept this reason and hold, in consequence, that the girl is the "victim" of the offence within section 2(1) above, and so cannot be guilty of conspiring to commit it. But it has already been suggested that the court was wrong in applying the "victim" rule in *Whitehouse*, and should have put the exemption on the wider ground that the legislature showed an intention not to include the daughter in the offence. If the exemption is placed on this wider ground, and not on the "victim" rule, section 2(1) would not apply. Section 1(1) would make her liable, since she is party to an agreement for an offence to be committed by her father. There would be a considerable anomaly if the daughter were to be held not guilty as accessory to incest when it is committed, because of the obvious intention of the statute, and yet guilty of conspiracy to commit it because of the inept wording of the Criminal Law Act.

Although the problem can be avoided for incest if the court uncritically accepts the *ratio decidendi* of *Whitehouse*, there are other possible situations that cannot be dealt with in this way. The instance of abduction has already been given.

§ 18.10. AGREEMENT WITH EXEMPT PARTY

The previous discussion concerned the liability for conspiracy of an exempt party, where he entered into an agreement with one whom we may call a liable party. We must now consider the liability for conspiracy in these circumstances of the liable party. Granted that he will be liable for the consummated offence when it is committed, is he liable for conspiracy if his agreement to commit the crime is with an exempt party and no one else?

The Law Commission reached a clear and satisfactory decision on this question. In their view, the liable party should never in these circumstances be liable for conspiracy. His liability should be left to the law of incitement, attempt and complicity.[1] The Bill proposed by the Commission would have given effect to this proposal, but it was amended in the House of Lords in a way that makes it somewhat obscure. If you would like to have a summary of the resulting provision in tabloid form, it is that (1) the liable party is not liable for conspiracy if the other party (or all the other parties) lacked *mens rea*, but (2) is liable if the other party is exempted by reason

[1] Law Commission, *Report on Conspiracy and Criminal Law Reform* (Law Com. No. 76, 1976) paras. 1.50–1.58.

of some special rule of law, except in two cases: where the other party is either a small child or the victim.

(1) We will begin with cases where the exempt party is exempt because he lacked *mens rea*. It has already been argued that section 1 requires all parties to a criminal conspiracy to know the facts (note the words "their intentions" in section 1(1), and the additional provision in section 1(2)). If the other parties are not guilty of conspiracy because they did not know the facts, then the defendant is not guilty of conspiracy either.

An illustration would be where D1 engages D2, an innocent agent, to handle stolen goods. D2 is not guilty of conspiring to handle stolen goods, because he lacks the intention, so D1 is not guilty either, because section 1 (1) requires a joint intention. This construction of the Act is in accordance with the common law.[2]

A problem arises for the police and their informers. Suppose that Dl, wishing to steal V's furniture, is looking for an assistant. He ropes in D2, who unfortunately for him is a policeman. D2 pretends to agree, in order to frustrate the plan. Is D1 guilty of conspiracy?

It has already been suggested that D2 may perhaps be held not guilty of conspiracy because he does not really agree to the commission of the offence, but only pretends to agree.[3] If that is so, D1 is not guilty either. Section 1(1) does not apply, for the same reason as before: it requires two "intentions," and here there is only one. The fact that D2 thinks that D1 is agreeing with him does not matter. There is no conspiracy within the subsection. The exemption of D1 may not be sound policy or common sense, but the Act does not embrace him. If, however, D2 is held to be guilty, then of course D1 can be convicted of conspiracy with him.

(2) Next, the fiddling rules for cases where the exempt party is exempt by reason of some special rule of law. The effect of the Act, reversing the proposal of the Law Commission, is to make the liable party liable for conspiracy in these circumstances, with certain exceptions presently to be noted. The Act therefore preserves the effect of *Duguid*,[4] a case on abducting children.

It was held that Duguid could be convicted at common law of conspiring with a mother to abduct her child from its guardian; yet the mother herself could seemingly not have been convicted of conspiracy, since she was not within the scope of the consummated crime.[5]

We have already seen (§ .9) that owing to the incompetent wording of the Act the mother herself would now be liable for conspiracy, there being nothing in the Act to exempt her, notwithstanding that it was the intention of the Offences Against the Person Act to exempt her from liability for the consummated offence. So the problem under discussion would no longer present any difficulty in this particular case.

The Act establishes certain exceptions to the general principle. Section 2(2):

"A person shall not by virtue of section 1 above be guilty of conspiracy to commit any offence or offences if the only other person or persons with whom he agrees are (both initially and at all times during the currency of the agreement) persons of any one or more of the following descriptions, that is to say—
(*a*) his spouse;
(*b*) a person under the age of criminal responsibility; and
(*c*) an intended victim of that offence or of each of those offences."

Paragraph (*a*) has already been dealt with (§ .8). Paragraph (*b*) means that an agreement between an adult and a child under 10[6] cannot be a conspiracy. This is important chiefly for sexual offences. The child may solicit the adult to commit the offence, and the adult may agree; if matters remain at that stage, it would be harsh to hold the adult guilty. If on the other

---

[2] *Curr* [1968] 2 QB 944. See further § 19.5.
[3] § .3 fin.
[4] (1906) 70 JP 294, 75 LJKB 470.
[5] The last point was left open in *Duguid*; but see now *Austin* § 9.12 n. 6.
[6] See the definition in s.2(3). Where the child is aged 10–14, and is exempt from liability because he does not know the act to be wrong (see § 28.1), the adult can still be liable for conspiring with him.

hand the adult solicits the child, this can well be held to be an attempt on his part to commit the offence (§ 17.5 at n. 15). So there is no need to treat the case as one of conspiracy, and a solid argument against doing so.

Paragraph (*c*) has the same effect where a man agrees with a girl under 16 that they shall have sexual intercourse together. The girl will in law be regarded as the victim of the offence, even if she instigated it, and the man will escape a conspiracy charge. Similarly if a father agrees with his daughter upon an act of incest, the daughter (of whatever age) is apparently regarded as the victim, and the father is not liable for conspiracy.[7]

SUMMARY

Conspiracy as an inchoate crime was punished at common law, and conspiracy to § .1
defraud still remains governed by the common law. So do conspiracies to corrupt public morals or outrage public decency, in the unlikely event that these objects, when carried out, are not punishable for individuals. Other forms of conspiracy are now governed by the Criminal Law Act 1977 (as amended by the Criminal Attempts Act 1981), and are dealt with in the rest of the chapter.

Statutory conspiracy is defined in section 1 (1). It may be to commit any offence, § .2
with minor exceptions.

The indictment should give particulars of the overt acts relied upon to prove the § .3
conspiracy. Two conspiracies must not be charged in one count. A plain-clothes officer who pretends to take part in a conspiracy is probably not liable for this offence, because it can be held that he did not really agree to commit the crime in view, within section 1 (1).

An incitement or attempt to conspire is not punishable; but there can be a § .4
conspiracy to incite.

Conspirators are subject to the same maximum term of imprisonment as for the § .5
consummated crime. The fine, however, is at large. Conspiracy is subject to the same procedural restrictions as the substantive offence. A prosecutor who joins a conspiracy count to a count for the substantive offence must specially justify this if it is to be allowed.

Statutory conspiracy requires a purpose by the conspirators "that a course of § .6
conduct shall be pursued which, if the agreement is carried out in accordance with their intentions, either (*a*) will necessarily amount to or involve the commission of any offence by one or more of the parties to the agreement, or (*b*) would do so but for the existence of facts which render the commission of the offence impossible" (section 1 (1)). The word "necessarily" ought to have been omitted as unnecessary. Donaldson LJ suggested that a conspiracy that may be carried out lawfully is not criminal, since it does not necessarily involve an offence; if this is correct it seems to open a gap in the law.

"Course of conduct" presumably includes intended conequences, and § .7
consequences conditionally intended.

Although section 1 (1) is unclear, the mental element seems to be an intention to commit the offence in contemplation. Section 1 (2) states in effect that even when an offence does not require knowledge of a circumstance, conspiracy requires that the defendant and at least one other party should intend that the circumstance will exist or know that it does exist. This evidently excludes recklessness as to circumstances, and it does so even though the offence is of strict liabiltiy. The rule must be the same if the offence requires knowledge on the part of the perpetrator.

Husband and wife cannot conspire together, if no third party is involved. There § .8

---

[7] See *Whitehouse* § .9. For incitement see § 19.5.

may be a conspiracy with a person unknown. The acquittal of one alleged compirator need not involve the acquittal of the other, even though no third conspirator is alleged to have been involved, provided that the essentials of conspiracy are proved against the defendant.

Anomalously, a person can be guilty of conspiracy to commit a crime, under the wording of the CLA, even though he is an exempt party—i.e., he would not be liable in any degree for committing the crime. The only exceptions are (1) where the exemption is because he lacks the mental element and (2) where it is because he is the "victim," this word presumably meaning the person who is free from liability for the consummated crime because he is regarded as the victim of it. § .9

If A, a non-exempt party, conspires with B, an exempt party, then if B's exemption is for lack of the mental element, A is also free from liability for conspiracy, section 1 (1) postulating two "intentions." If B's exemption is under some special rule of law, A is liable for conspiracy, except in two cases: where B is exempt as being a child under 10, and where B is exempt as being the victim (see above). § .10

Chapter 19

INCITEMENT AND OTHER INCHOATE OFFENCES

When you've once said a thing, that fixes it, and you must take the consequences.
The Red Queen to Alice.

§ 19.1. THE MEANING OF INCITEMENT

The common law offence of incitement (or solicitation) is committed when one person "counsels, procures or commands" another to commit a crime, whether as perpetrator or as accessory, and whether or not the person incited does what he is urged to do. (If he does it, the inciter will of course be an accomplice and will normally be charged as such; but on a charge of incitement it is no defence to show that the crime was actually committed.) Any persuasion or encouragement (including a threat) is sufficient.

What about a cool suggestion, without attempt to persuade, the suggester having no interest in the matter one way or the other?

A suggestion may, of course, be persuasive in itself, particularly for those who, as Shakespeare put it, "take suggestion as a cat laps milk." But the authorities do not give a clear answer to your question. It cannot be said with certainty that the law of incitement applies to anything except deliberate persuasions or encouragements to crime.

In *Fitzmaurice*,[1] the defendant approached X and informed him of a proposed robbery, inviting his co-operation, for which he impliedly promised reward. Fitzmaurice's conviction of incitement was upheld on appeal, the court saying that the trial judge had "rightly focused the attention of the jury on the element of persuasion which it was necessary for the prosecution to prove." As an example of a case where this element would be lacking, the Court of Appeal instanced the case of a person whose role is "limited to informing certain named individuals that the planner of the enterprise would like to see them." He would not be guilty of incitement.

This indicates that something more than a mere suggestion is required. Whether this is so or not, it seems that persuading or attempting to persuade X to do something, knowing that this will induce X to commit an offence, is sufficient.

In *Invicta Plastics Ltd.* v. *Clare*,[2] the company advertised in a periodical a device that when installed in a car warned the driver that a police radar trap was operating. The company was convicted of inciting readers of the publication to use unlicensed apparatus for wireless telegraphy in contravention of the Wireless Telegraphy Act 1949.

Suppose a person facilitates a crime by supplying tools, materials or information, so that if the crime is committed he would be an accessory. If it is not committed, is he an inciter?

Apparently not, if he does not persuade or encourage the commission of the crime.[3]

---

[1] [1983] 2 WLR 227. Cp. *Hendrickson* [1977] Crim.LR 356.

[2] [1976] Crim.LR 131, The Times, December 3, 1975.

[3] This was submitted by counsel for the defence in *Fitzmaurice*, n. 1 above, and although the CA did not comment upon the submission specifically, the court's insistence upon the element of persuasion in an incitement was evidently an acceptance of it.

If the supplier is the person who initiated the idea, then he has obviously incited the crime; but if the would-be perpetrator goes to the supplier and asks for the supply, the fact of supply should not be regarded as an incitement, any more than it should be regarded as a conspiracy (§ 18.3). Nor is the supplier guilty of attempting to abet the crime, for the reason given before: the law does not know of a doctrine of attempted abetment. So the mere supplier of an instrument of crime does not commit any offence at common law if the crime is not committed. It is true that, by a somewhat anomalous extension of the law of complicity, he will become a party to the crime if it is committed, unless after supplying the instrument he makes quite strenuous attempts to prevent it being used (§ 15.14). But even if he makes no effort to prevent the crime, he escapes liability if it happens not to be committed, unless he happens to be guilty of some specific statutory offence,[4] or unless the would-be perpetrator attempts to commit the crime—in which case the supplier will be an accessory to the attempt. The analysis appears to be the same where a person upon request gives information helpful for the commission of a crime.

The incitement may be directed to persons generally, as it was in *Invicta Plastics* (above),[5] and it may, presumably, incite a general course of crime. If the person incited gives ear and assents to the plan proposed, he and the inciter become conspirators.

Can a person incite the commission of a crime upon himself?

Not if his consent negatives the crime. He cannot criminally incite someone to burgle his house, for instance. Yes, generally, in other cases (such as inciting another to kill him).

However, the rule that the protected victim of a crime cannot be a party to it (§ 15.15) must apply also to incitement. Such a person cannot be convicted of inciting the commission of a crime upon himself or herself. For the legislative policy is evidently the same, whether or not the offence incited is committed.

Can one incite the commission of an impossible crime, if one believes it to be possible?

No. At common law one could not attempt or conspire to do the impossible, unless the impossibility related solely to means and not to the end in view.[6] The rule has been changed by statute for attempt and conspiracy, but nothing has been enacted for incitement, and it was accordingly held in *Fitzmaurice*[7] that the impossibility rule still governs this crime.

The Law Commission, in recommending the change for attempt and conspiracy, refrained from making any recommendation for incitement, chiefly because the Commissiion was not ready to consider that offence in detail. However, the Commission did express the opinion that the courts might be able to declare that the law for incitement is in line with the new law for the other two offences, without statutory help.[8] The suggestion was received with some scepticism, and has now been falsified by the decision in *Fitzmaurice*. However, the court made it clear that nothing but the most complete impossibility would exclude liability. If the

---

[4] Such as supplying the means of abortion: § 13.8.
[5] Cp. *Most* (1881) 7 QBD 244.
[6] On the difficulty of the means-end distinction see *Harris* (1979) 69 CAR 122.
[7] N. 1 above.
[8] Law Com. No. 102, Part IV.

projected crime, though impossible at the time, might become possible before it was expected to be committed, the incitement would be an offence.

§ 19.2. THE PUNISHMENT OF INCITEMENT

Incitement is an unreformed common law misdemeanour, left studiously aside by the legislature, and so is punishable on indictment with imprisonment and fine at discretion.

Normally, in practice, the punishment would not be greater than for the consummated offence. But when the CLRC proposed that this limit on punishment should be made statutory for attempt (a proposal accepted by Parliament: § 17.3), a majority of the committee decided to refrain from proposing the same rule for incitement, on the ground that the inciter should sometimes be punished more severely than the perpetrator.

The argument to the contrary is the same as in the case of conspiracy: if Parliament has laid down a maximum punishment for the commission of the offence, the punishment ought not to be exceeded by the court merely because it is found that the part played by the defendant included an element of incitement.[1] Even though the inciter may sometimes be more blameworthy than the perpetrator, this is an element of aggravation that, like other possible elements of aggravation, was presumably considered by Parliament when fixing the maximum for the offence.

An incitement to commit an offence triable either way is triable similarly.[2] This is the same rule as for attempt. It will be remembered that the rule for conspiracy is otherwise, since conspiracy is purely indictable.

Can there be incitement to commit a summary offence?

In common sense, no. Incitement, a purely indictable offence, is not appropriate to summary offences. There is no sufficient reason why such a minor form of incitement should be punishable at all, let alone punishable on indictment. Yet it was held in *Curr*,[3] on doubtful grounds, depending largely on the construction of certain legislation, that an indictment would lie. Since then, the relevant legislation has changed, the question now depending on the construction of the Magistrates' Courts Act 1980 s.45(1), which provides that "any offence consisting in the incitement to commit a summary offence" shall be triable only summarily.[4] On its natural interpretation this subsection does not penalise incitement to a summary offence, but simply provides for the mode of trial when the law creates such an offence, which (it may be thought) it generally does not.

Do procedural provisions attaching to substantive crimes apply to incitement? For example, if there is a time-limit on prosecuting for the substantive crime, does this apply to incitement?

Apparently not. The judges failed to apply such procedural safeguards to conspiracy charges until statute intervened (§ 18.5). They failed to apply

[1] E.g. D1 incites D2 to help him (as accessory) in committing a crime, and D2 does so. D1 in his capacity as perpetrator cannot be given more than the maximum punishment for the crime. It seems remarkable to hold that as inciter he can be given a greater punishment.

[2] CLA 1977 Sched. 3 para. 35.

[3] [1968] 2 QB 944. See criticism in 138 JPN 548.

[4] When incitement is tried summarily, it is subject to the same maximum as the summary offence: CLA 1977 ss.28(1), 30(4).

a requirement of DPP's consent to a charge of incitement.[5] Since no statute applies these safeguards to charges of attempt and incitement, the conclusion is inevitable, though regrettable, that they will not be applied.

§ 19.3. THE MENTAL ELEMENT FOR INCITEMENT

The mental element required for incitement is probably an intention to bring about the crime, or (presumably) recklessness as to a circumstance included in the definition of the crime. This was held to be so for attempt in *Pigg* § 17.4, and there is no reason for not applying the same rule to incitement.

Why shouldn't it be enough if the defendant was reckless as to the consequence? The hated President of Mendacia is due to visit these shores, and D publishes an article urging refugees from Mendacia to see that he does not live to return. On D's trial for inciting to murder, he says that his object was to frighten the President from coming, though he realised that there was a risk that he might come and be shot in consequence of the article. Should such a defence be allowed?

Authority is lacking. Very likely it would be disallowed. The difficulty is that to admit the concept of reckless incitement would perhaps extend the offence too far.

What if the person charged with incitement knew that the offence could not be committed, and therefore did not intend it to be committed? Take your previous example where D incites X to burgle D's own house. Suppose X believes the house belongs to someone else. Is that incitement?

On principle no, because D does not intend the crime to be committed.

X will be guilty of attempting the crime if he tries to do it and if on the facts as he supposes them to be it would be a crime; but this is because he intends to commit the crime. D does not intend the crime to be committed, because he knows that in the circumstances it cannot be. That he intends X to go through the motions of an attempt is nothing to the purpose.[1] It is true that an argument could be advanced for making D guilty of inciting X's attempt, but it should be rejected. The inchoate crimes are punished because of their tendency to produce the substantive crimes which are the real mischief, and they should not be used against people who do not intend to produce this real mischief.

Another application of the same principle is as follows. We have seen (§ 15.13) that a person cannot be charged as accessory to a crime if he intended to frustrate it. The same rule applies to the inchoate offences of attempt, incitement and conspiracy. If the defendant positively believed that he would be able to foil the plot he cannot be guilty.[2] Suppose a police informer joins a gang who plan a crime, and, for the sake of appearances, he expresses

---

[5] *R* v.*Assistant Recorder of Kingston-upon-Hull, ex p. Morgan* [1969] 2 QB 58.

[1] *Contra*, Smith and Hogan, 4th edn 214 (ii).

[2] *Brown* (1899) 63 JP 790; *The General Part*, 2nd edn § 194. It was pointed out in § 18.3 *fin*. that some doubt has been created for conspiracy by the Act of 1977, but the statutory words are capable of being read as not affecting the previous law on the point.

approval and gives some measure of assistance, knowing that the police will intervene in time to prevent consummation. His companions may be guilty of conspiracy and, later, of attempt, but he himself will not be guilty of either; nor will he be guilty of inciting the attempt. If things go badly wrong from the police point of view and the crime is consummated before they can intervene, the informer will not be guilty as accessory to it.

§ 19.4. INCITEMENT, ATTEMPT AND ACCESSORIES

It seems probable, as was suggested before (§ 17.6) that the law draws a sharp distinction between incitement and attempt. A person who incites another to commit a crime is not guilty of attempting to commit it as an accessory.

Can a person be guilty of attempting to incite?

Apparently yes.

The charge was possible at common law,[1] but there is a subtle problem of interpretation of the Criminal Attempts Act 1981 s.1(4)(*b*). This excludes "aiding, abetting, counselling, procuring or suborning the commission of an offence" from the class of attemptable crimes. However, it seems to have been intended to exclude only acts of attempted accessoryship, *i.e.* acts charged as an attempt to become an accessory to a crime.[2] It does not, apparently, exclude a charge of attempting to commit the inchoate crime of incitement. When Parliament wishes to refer to incitement as an inchoate crime it uses that word, not the language of "aiding, abetting, counselling and procuring."[3]

Can there be an incitement to incite?

No reason why not.[4]

Can one abet an incitement, and incite abetment?

Certainly one can be an accessory to an incitement, as when D1 writes a letter to X inciting him to commit a crime and D2 knowingly delivers the missive for him. My own opinion is that one can also incite the abetment of crime, but there is an opinion the other way.

---

[1] *IR* v. *Chelmsford JJ, ex p. Amos* [1973] Crim.LR 437.

[2] Cp. J C Smith in *Crime, Proof and Punishment*, ed. Tapper, 32 on the ambiguity of the statutory words.

[3] See MCA 1980 Sched. 1 para. 35.

[4] It was ruled in *Bodin* [1979] Crim.LR 176 that a charge of inciting to incite was bad when it was worded as a charge of inciting another to commit the crime ultimately in view. The judge proceeded to express the opinion that it would have been bad even if properly worded; *sed quaere*. See the editorial note to the case; and cp. *Macdaniel* § 15.3 at n. 4. The point was not discussed in *Cromack* [1978] Crim.LR 217; see the editorial note.

Professor Smith in [1979] Crim.LR 178 finds an anomaly in the fact that although incitement to conspire has now been made non-criminal by Parliament (§ 18.4), there has been no statutory abolition of the crime of incitement to incite. "An incitement by A of B to commit an offence seems necessarily to amount to an incitement of B to conspire with A to commit the offence. Parliament has expressly declared that the latter is not to be an offence and it might be argued tht to charge the defendant with inciting to incite is to evade the declared will of Parliament." The premise is mistaken: a letter written by A to B inciting him to commit an offence is not a conspiracy between them to commit it if B does not reply, even though he afterwards acts in accordance with the incitement. So there is still a theoretical difference between incitement to incite and incitement to conspire; but it is true that the vast majority of the former incitements also amount to the latter. On the rest of Smith's argument, it seems to me that the reply is that Parliament could have abolished the offence of incitement to incite when it abolished incitement to conspire, but it refrained from doing so—the reason being that the Law Commission, which was pulling the strings, had decided to leave incitement alone for the time being.

There would be no point in charging an incitement to attempt, since this is necessarily an incitement to commit the crime in question: *Cromack*, above. The single case where the question of incitement to attempt raises a practical problem is where the inciter knows the attempt to be impossible, as to which see § .3.

The case under consideration is that of D3 inciting D2 to help D1 in the commission of a crime to be perpetrated by D1. D2 decides to do nothing. I see no reason of policy or logic impeding D3's conviction of incitement. Prof. Smith, however, offers an argument the other way.[5] Suppose that D3, knowing that D1 intends to commit burglary at a certain house, incites D2 to help D1 (without his knowledge) by leaving a ladder for him in the garden of the house. If D1 perpetrates the burglary with the aid of the ladder D2 and D3 are of course accessories to it. But if D1 does not perpetrate the burglary or attempt to do so, D2 is not an accessory to any crime, nor (for reasons given in § 17.6) an attempted accessory, and neither is D3. Nor, according to Professor Smith, is D3 guilty of inciting D2 to become accessory to burglary, because the act incited was not, in the result, a crime.

The weak step in this argument is the last. It is true that the act incited was not criminal in the events as they occurred; but it would have been criminal if the expected event (the burglary by D1) had occurred.

It may possibly be argued that even if Smith's contention is wrong as a matter of common law, liability for incitement to abet is now precluded by the statutory abolition of incitement to conspire (§ 18.4). But this argument, too, would in my opinion be unsound. (1) If D3 incites D1 to perpetrate a crime, D3 is guilty of incitement. (2) Equally where he incites D1 and D2 to perpetrate the crime jointly, even though this involves inciting them to conspire. (3) Equally where he incites D1 to commit it with the aid of D2, even though this too involves the creation of a conspiracy. (4) And equally, surely, where he incites D2 to help D1 (by arrangement) to commit the crime. To say that the last case is not a criminal incitement because one cannot incite to conspire logically involves the same conclusion for (2) and (3); so the argument is destructive not only of incitement to abet but of incitement to joint perpetration and incitement to perpetration with a helper. Incitement to conspire was abolished on the proposal of the Law Commission, which thought that this form of incitement put liability too far back; once it is realised that an incitement to conspire is in fact, in virtually every case, an incitement either to perpetrate or to abet, the fallacy of the Commission's reasoning becomes apparent.

§ 19.5. INCITEMENT OF A NON-CRIMINAL

There can certainly be liability for attempting, conspiring or inciting a person to commit a crime through an innocent agent, because perpetrating a crime through an innocent agent is regarded like any other perpetration of crime. If, therefore, D2 incites D1 to commit a crime through the innocent agency of X, D2 will be guilty of incitement in the usual way, and if X performs as intended D1 will be the perpetrator and D2 an accessory.

But D1's words of persuasion to X, the innocent agent, are not incitement in law, since incitement presupposes a guilty incitee. D1 will be guilty of attempting to commit the crime though an innocent agent if he has gone beyond mere preparation, as almost certainly he has.[1]

To expand the point, suppose that D gives X, an innocent agent, a letter to post; the letter makes a dishonest claim on an insurance company. If X does not post the letter, D can still, on principle, be convicted of attempting to obtain money from the company by deception, since he did everything necessary to be done by him to perpetrate the crime.

---

[5] *Crime, Proof and Punishment*, ed. Tapper, 29–32, 39–40.

[1] See § 17.5 n. 8, and the valuable note by J C Smith in [1977] Crim. LR 547–548. The opinion stated in the text assumes that *Hope* v. *Brown* [1954] 1 WLR 250, 1 All ER 330 will now be regarded as wrongly decided; see the criticism in [1955] Crim.LR 66.

But suppose that D has been "working on" the innocent agent, trying to get him to agree to do the act, and much remains to be done by D by way of preparation if the agent does agree to do it. The persuasion may not be sufficiently proximate to be an attempt, so it is important to know whether it can be incitement. The rule now settled is that it is not. One can only commit criminal incitement of a guilty agent, so to speak, not of an innocent one. If, for instance, a man tries to persuade another to commit the *actus reus* of a crime requiring *mens rea*, concealing from him the facts that make the act criminal, he is not guilty of incitement.[2] He would be guilty if the agent knew the facts, but by concealing the facts from the agent the plotter provides himself with a full defence to a charge of incitement.[3] Moreover, by concealing his defence from the prosecution until the trial is half way through he may avoid having a count for attempt added to the indictment.

The rule attracted public attention by reason of the decision in *Whitehouse*, the facts of which were partly given before.[4] Whitehouse was charged not only with conspiring with his daughter to commit incest but with inciting her to commit incest with him (it was not shown that incest was actually committed), and the Court of Appeal held that he was not liable on either count. Since the girl was exempt from committing incest, her father could not be guilty of inciting her to commit it, for "the crime of incitement consists of inciting another person to commit a crime."

Although this premise may sound common sense, it is in fact ambiguous. Why should not the crime of incitement include the incitement of an innocent agent to commit what will be a crime for the inciter? The point would not be of great importance if the act of incitement of an innocent party were held to amount to an attempt, and on principle it always should be, yet this possibility was apparently ruled out by the prosecuting authorities in *Whitehouse*. Even if many cases of inciting innocent agents can be charged as attempts, there is no reason why the crimes of attempt and incitement should not overlap in this respect.

The Criminal Law Act meets the specific situation in *Whitehouse* by creating a new offence for the case where a man incites his grand-daughter, daughter or sister, being under 16, to commit incest with him.[5] This is botching legislaton of an objectionable kind. If *Whitehouse* was regarded as unfortunately decided, the proper course was to reverse it in principle, not merely in the instance. The argument for punishing Whitehouse is no stronger than the argument for punishing a man who incites a child under 14 to an act of gross indecency with him; yet the latter remains unpunishable for the incitement as such.[6]

§ 19.6. OTHER INCHOATE OFFENCES

The inchoate offences we have been considering were developed at common law, but there are some statutory specimens.

Statutory offences relating to selling goods are now generally worded so as to include not only attempting to sell but also displaying for sale.

---

[2] *Curr* [1968] 2 QB 944.

[3] Smith and Hogan, 4th edn 215 point out that on principle the question is whether D *believed* that the person he was inciting had the requisite mental element. If he did, D should be guilty of incitement even though the agent was in fact innocent.

[4] § 18.9 *fin*. Since this decision and *Curr*, n. 2 above, the decision on this point in *Bourne* (1952) 36 CAR 125 is questionable. However, if the theory of *de facto* crime is accepted (§ 15.16), it can be argued that it is properly held to be a criminal incitement to incite such a crime. Carrying this point further, J C Smith in *Crime, Proof and Punishment*, ed. Tapper, 41–42 suggests that where D2 incites D1 to assist or incite X to do an act that is not a crime for X, if the circumstances will make D1 guilty as accessory to X's non-crime. D2 should be guilty of incitement upon uttering the words of incitement, and of committing the crime as accessory upon D1 doing as he is told. It should be noted, however, that no concept of *de facto* crime appears in *Whitehouse*, below.

[5] CLA 1977, s.51.

[6] The contrary was assumed in *Assistant Recorder of Kingston-upon-Hull* [1969] 2 QB 58, wrongly as it now appears.

Statutes create various offences of possessing prohibited articles, the object of which is frequently to prevent the articles being used for criminal purposes. Examples are the statutory offences of possessing explosives[1] or firearms,[2] having offensive weapons,[3] possessing implements for certain forgeries and counterfeiting,[4] and possessing anything with intent to commit an indictable offence against the person[5] or any damage to property.[6] Other offences of this kind will be listed in Chapter 38.

Some of these statutory offences may themselves be the subject of a common law attempt, so that the operation of the law is pushed still further back in the realm of what (from the point of view of the ultimate criminal intent) is mere preparation. For example, it is a statutory crime to supply or procure a thing for the purpose of abortion[7] and there may be an attempt at common law to commit this statutory offence of procuring.[8]

As was remarked before, the line between inchoate and substantive offences is not firm, for a number of crimes are defined in such a way as to include what the man in the street might regard as an attempt. This is so with assault, abortion, and blackmail. The full crime of burglary is committed as soon as the premises are trespassed upon with the requisite intent.[9]

SUMMARY

It is an offence at common law to incite the commission of an offence. Persuasion or encouragement is enough; supplying the tools etc. of crime is probably not enough in the absence of encouragement. Probably the rule at common law still holds that one cannot incite the impossible, unless the impossibility relates only to means. § .1

The offence is punishable at discretion. It was held in *Curr* that the incitement may be to commit a mere summary offence. Procedural safeguards for the completed offence do not apply to attempt and incitement. § .2

Generally, the inciter must intend the ulterior crime to be committed, so it should be a defence that he knew the crime could not be committed, or intended to frustrate it. § .3

Apparently there can be an attempt to incite, incitement to incite, abetment of incitement and incitement of abetment. § .4

The use of words of persuasion to an innocent agent is not an incitement, but can be an attempt. The rule creates difficulty on facts like those in *Whitehouse*. § .5

---

[1] Explosive Substances Act 1883 s.4(1).

[2] Firearms Act 1968. S.16 prohibits the possession of a firearm with intent to endanger life or to cause serious injury to property. S.17 makes the use of a firearm to resist arrest severely punishable. S.18 makes it an offence for a person to have with him a firearm (or imitation firearm) with criminal intent. See the extensive interpretation of this in *Houghton* [1982] Crim.LR 112, and the critical editorial note. S.19 prohibits the carrying of a loaded shot gun or loaded air weapon or of any other firearm whether loaded or not in a public place without lawful authority or reasonable excuse. S.20 covers trespass with a firearm without reasonable excuse; s.21, possession of firearms by persons previously convicted of crime; s.22, possession of firearms by persons under 17.

[3] § 9.9 at n. 8.

[4] Forgery and Counterfeiting Act 1981 s.17.

[5] OAPA 1861 s.64 as amended by Cr.LA 1967 Sched. 2.

[6] § 41.10. A conditional intent, namely to use the article if necessary, is sufficient: *Buckingham* [1977] Crim.LR 674.

[7] § 13.8.

[8] *People* v. *Thornton* [1952] Ir.R 91; *The General Part*, 2nd edn § 197 n. 8.

[9] See § 38.1.

There are various statutory forms of inchoate offences, particularly the offences of possessing anything with intent to commit an indictable offence against the person or any offence against property. § .6

Part Four

DEFENCES

We have seen that the dividing line between the constituent elements of an offence and defences is largely arbitrary, though it has some importance in relation to the drafting of charges, burdens of proof, evidential burdens, and (in respect of unreasonable mistakes) substantive law. (It is not even the same line for these various purposes.) The title of this Part must be taken merely as a convenient rubric, gathering together certain restrictions upon liability, common to more than one offence, that are suitable to be dealt with at this point. The restrictions may pertain either to what may be thought of as the definition of offences or to what may be thought of as defences.

Chapter 20

IGNORANCE OF LAW

God forbid that it should be imagined that an attorney, or a counsel, or even a judge is bound to know all the law.

Abbot CJ in 1825 (2 C & P 113)

§ 20.1. THE GENERAL RULE

Almost the only knowledge of law possessed by many people is that ignorance of it is no excuse (*ignorantia juris non excusat*). This maxim was originally formulated at a time when the list of crimes, broadly speaking, represented current morality (*mala in se*), but we now have many other crimes that are the result of administrative or social regulation (*mala prohibita*), which are equally governed by the maxim.

The rule is, then, that whereas ignorance of fact can excuse, to the extent that it negatives any necessary *mens rea* or fault, even reasonable ignorance of law generally does not.

What is the distinction between fact and law? Is a matter one of fact because it is left to the jury?

The distinction now under discussion does not fully correspond to that drawn in relation to the functions of judge and jury. The judge will often leave the jury to decide the application of ordinary words in statutes (§ 2.6). In that context, the meaning of the statutory words may be said to be one of fact, in the sense that it is a jury question. But in the present context it is one of law. The citizen must accurately forecast not only the way in which the judge will interpret a statute, so far as he regards it as his function to do so, but also the way in which the jury will, so far as the question is left to them. (We have already noticed the rule in connection with value-judgments required to be made by the law: § 6.11).

So, not only is the citizen expected to know the existence and precise terms of all penal legislation pertaining to him, however obscure its wording or chaotic its arrangement, but he is required at his peril to make a correct forecast of the way in which the court will resolve any ambiguity. A barrister may, after research in a law library, write an opinion saying that the provision cannot be interpreted with any certainty; yet every member of the public is required to have precognition of the way in which the court will apply it.

To add to the anomaly, a judge in interpreting a statute may use a vast range of materials outside the statute or statutory instrument itself. He may refer to decided cases on the same and other statutes; and an Act may be interpreted in the light of other Acts—even repealed Acts. So it is not enough for the anxious layman to consult the legislation currently in force; he needs a law library of a size that can be found in very few towns, and to which, when it exists, he may have no right of access. He also needs a legal training to understand the material when he has found it.

What is the reason for the rule? How can Joe Bloggs be expected to know the law, particularly if he has no money to pay a lawyer?

An excellent question, which is not at all easy to answer. A critic might say that it is because lawyers are insensitive to the plain man's difficulties; and there would be a lot in that. But the orthodox answers are two.

1 The difficulty of proving that the defendant knew the law.
2 The risk that such a defence would make it advantageous for people to refrain deliberately from acquiring knowledge of their legal duties.

These reasons may look persuasive at first sight, but they have not prevented certain other systems of law allowing a limited defence.[1] In particular, the German Supreme Court has, off its own bat, decided to allow a defence of unavoidable ignorance of law. The German citizen is, of course, expected to find out what his legal obligations are, and the fact that he disagrees with the legal norm is no defence; but even with these limitations the rule is a significant concession. Professor Fletcher comments:

> "In its scope and sophistication, in the self-confidence of judicial role conveyed, this opinion by the German Supreme Court has no equal in Anglo-American precedents on substantive criminal law."[2]

The general refusal of the English courts to allow a defence of reasonable mistake of law is one instance of their disinclination to allow new defences. In *Abbott*,[3] for example, Lord Salmon, delivering the opinion of the Judicial Committee, declared that their lordships had no power to invent a new defence to murder even if they approved of it (although what was in issue was actually not the creation of an entirely novel defence but only the question of its limits).

Why do the courts limit themselves in this way? Utilitarian theory and ordinary notions of justice would suggest that there should be nothing to prevent the courts inventing new defences where this is desirable, because it does not violate the maxim *Nulla poena sine lege*, as extending the ambit of crimes does.[4] The argument for allowing reasonable mistake of law as a defence is particularly strong where the law is unclear even to the lawyer, and even stronger where it appears to be clear but is retrospectively changed by the courts. Neither of the two objections (stated above) to allowing a defence of mistake of law justifies the courts in extending the penal law under pretence of applying it, and then punishing the person who is the occasion of the extension. The justification for judicial activism is twofold: that the courts must, as part of their function of applying the law, clear up its obscurities; and that the failure of Parliament to keep the law up to date means that this task must in large degree be performed by the courts. The argument would be more acceptable if the courts gave the protagonist in the leading case an absolute discharge.

> Take the facts of *Shaw*.[5] Shaw published a booklet called *The Ladies' Directory*, being a directory of prostitutes, with photographs of some of them in the nude, and indications in code of their sexual practices. Before publishing it, being disposed to keep within the law, he consulted the police to know whether it would be legal, and they refused to advise him. Apparently he did not go to the length of consulting a lawyer. Had he done so, he

---

[1] Cp. for Scandinavian law, Andenaes in *Essays in Criminal Science*, ed. Mueller (London 1961) 217, and, for German law, Ryu and Silving in 43 Revista Juridica de la Universidad de Puerto Rico 20, and Kadish and Kadish, *Discretion to Disobey* (Stanford, Calif. 1973) 164–167; Fletcher, *Rethinking Criminal Law* 736–758. For another comparative study see Vera Bolgár in 52 Iowa L Rev. 626.

[2] Fletcher, *op. cit.* 747.

[3] [1977] AC at 767.

[4] See [1978] Crim.LR 128. A reason sometimes advanced for not extending defences is the fear that people who had been convicted under the previous law would then be queueing up at the Home Office for pardons and compensation. This is bureaucratic rather than judicial reasoning, and the objection could be met by the court assuming power to declare that its decision in any particular case is not retrospective in respect of penalties already imposed.

[5] [1962] AC 220.

might well have been advised that there was no direct precedent for saying that the publication was unlawful; that, having regard to the advice of the Wolfenden Committee that prostitution should continue to be regarded as a permitted occupation, though subject to severe restrictions, a liberal-minded judge might well rule that the publication was lawful; but that a judge who looked at it in a moral light might equally well extend some offence or other to embrace it. In the result, Shaw was convicted of no fewer than three offences: publishing an obscene book (though it appears that the book was not sexually titillating as hard-core pornography is); being a male living on the earnings of prostitution (an offence designed to catch pimps; Shaw merely supplied the prostitutes with a commercial service on a contractual basis, and could not have been convicted of this offence if he had been a woman); and a vague common law offence of conduct intended to corrupt public morals. On this basis, Shaw was sentenced to 9 months' imprisonment.

A further point arises out of this one: the citizen generally has no ready means of obtaining an authoritative ruling from a governmental agency on the meaning of penal legislation which may affect him. He may have in mind some costly enterprise, with no certain and inexpensive way of knowing whether it will be stopped. Why should not a Department entrusted with the administration of the particular branch of law be empowered to give a decision on its meaning which, if in favour of the subject, and until successfully challenged in the courts, would protect him against criminal proceedings?[6]

Some slight movement can be detected on this matter. The civil courts will now hear an action for a declaration brought against the Attorney-General or a Government Department, the most important condition being that criminal proceedings must not already have been started.[7] The court has a discretion whether to hear the case, and it is unknown whether an action by someone whom the judges regard as unsavoury (such as a prostitute) would be allowed. If the outcome of the action is favourable to the citizen, this may persuade the authorities not to prosecute him; but, astonishingly, some judges have said that the favourable outcome will be no defence to him if he is charged.[8]

There are some exceptions to the rule that ignorance of the law is no defence, the following being the most important.

§ 20.2. MAKING THE LAW ACCESSIBLE

Although a statute takes effect without promulgation, there is authority for saying that it will not operate upon a continuous proceeding (such as making a voyage) until a reasonable time has been allowed for discontinuance; and unavoidable ignorance of the statute will be relevant in enquiring what is a reasonable time.[1]

Further rules apply to subordinate legislation. The more important legislative products of Government Departments (Government orders) are

---

[6] Legislation confers jurisdiction upon a Government agency to determine certain points, and the giving of an informal assurance to the citizen is a determination. See M A Fazal in [1972] Public Law 43.

[7] See particularly Woolf J in *Royal College of Nursing* v. *DHSS* [1981] 1 All ER 545. The case, which went to the House of Lords on the point of substance, shows the danger to the citizen that he will incur great costs if he seeks clarification of the law in this way, even if he is ultimately successful. For a full discussion see Feldman in [1981] Crim.LR 25.

[8] See Lords Denning and Roskill in the *Royal College of Nursing* case, last note. Brightman LJ in the CA, while giving an opinion on the specific question put to him, refused to provide detailed guidance on what precisely was required to make a medical abortion lawful, saying: "It is not the function of the court to decide how close to dangerous waters it is possible to sail without actually being shipwrecked" ([1981] 2 WLR at 288C). The effect is that citizens must refrain from doing not only what he statute clearly forbids but also what tight-lipped judges or future juries may conceivably hold that it forbids, a view that hardly seems consistent with ordinary notions of the rule of law.

[1] *Burns* v. *Nowell* (1880) 5 QBD at 454.

"statutory instruments," and in proceedings for an offence under a statutory instrument it is a statutory defence to prove that the instrument had not been issued by Her Majesty's Stationery Office, unless reasonable steps had been taken to bring its purport to the notice of those affected.[2]

This provision does not apply to sub-delegated legislation or to local authorities' bylaws, or even (presumably) to statutory instruments that are allowed to go out of print after being issued, though in these cases the common law may have something to say. Bailhache J held that no delegated legislation comes into force until it is published, so that ignorance due to non-publication is a defence.[3] Also, the Judicial Committee of the Privy Council has held that when a Government order is made *in respect of a particular person*, and no provision is made for acquainting him of it, he cannot be convicted of an offence under it committed at a time when he did not know that it had been made.[4] The opinion gives no indication that it is intended to apply where the order is in respect of a class of persons, or the public at large. But the courts may come to the view that any failure by the authorities to enable people to discover the relevant law can found a defence to a criminal charge, for example where a statute or statutory order is allowed to go out of print.[5]

These rules merely require legislation to be made available to the diligent enquirer. Government orders affecting a particular trade will generally reach those affected by being noticed in trade journals; and there will often have been prior consultation between the Government Department and representatives of the trade. But departmental draftsmen who are responsible for this legislation, with little effective control from Parliament, are not always alive to the importance of confining the duty to the smallest possible class of people and to those who are likely to come to know of it. Parliament itself is a sinner in this respect. When it was decided to impose an official specification for motor-cycle helmets, and to make noncompliance with regulations an offence, Parliament chose to word the offence as one committed by anyone who sells an infringing helmet—instead of confining the duty to the comparatively small number who manufacture or import such helmets.[6] Again, the Licensing Act makes it an offence for any person to consume liquor outside licensing hours. The law on the subject of licensing and permitted hours is intricate in the extreme, and it is absurd that the principal offence should be committed by members of the public, who rely upon the licensee for information as to what is permitted on the premises, while the licensee himself can be convicted only as an accessory.[7]

Government Departments sometimes bring new legislation to the public notice by advertisements. One of the most ambitious efforts to alleviate our ignorance is the Highway Code; but even this is wholly silent on many topics of road traffic law, and when a subject is touched upon the details are omitted.

The general rule is that *mens rea* may be present notwithstanding ignorance of law. If a defendant who knew the criminal law would have had *mens rea*, then one who does not know this law has *mens rea* also.

Exceptionally, ignorance of law is sometimes allowed to produce an absence of some particular form of *mens rea*. The insane, and children between 10 and 14, are exempt from liability if they did not know their act to be wrong (Chap. 28). Further exceptions or possible exceptions relate to superior orders, ignorance of the civil law, and the effect of particular statutory expressions.

---

[2] Statutory Instruments Act 1946 s.3(2).

[3] *Johnson* v. *Sargant & Sons* [1918] 1 K.B. 101. Cp. *Ross* [1945] 3 DLR 574, 84 CCC 107 (Can.); Model Penal Code s.2.04(3) (*a*).

[4] *Lim Chin Aik* [1963] AC 160.

[5] Ashworth in [1974] Crim.LR 654.

[6] Road Traffic Act 1972 s.33(2).

[7] Cp. *Timmis* v. *Millman* [1965] Crim.LR 107.

§ 20.3. OFFICIAL ORDERS AND ADVICE

Superior orders are not generally a defence to a charge of crime, but it has been suggested that a limited exception should be recognised for members of the armed forces. A soldier, sailor or airman is bound by military law to obey lawful commands without question; but he may not find it easy to decide on the spur of the moment whether a particular command is lawful or not. The *Manual of Military Law* adopts the harsh view that, whatever his dilemma, the serviceman has no defence to a criminal charge if the order is in fact unlawful.[1] On the other hand, the enlightened Model Penal Code of the American Law Institute allows a defence of unlawful military orders if the defendant did not know the order to be unlawful.[2]

> The authorities are sparse and in conflict. In the old case of *Thomas*[3] a naval sentinel who, being ordered to keep off all boats, fired at a boat and killed a man in it, was convicted of murder, notwithstanding that the jury found that he fired under a mistaken impression that it was his duty. A contrary view was taken by the Supreme Court of the Cape of Good Hope in *Smith*,[4] which is widely approved by commentators. The facts were that, during the South African War, a soldier was ordered by his officer to shoot a Boer civilian if he did not fetch a bridle, and obeyed the command by killing the Boer. He was acquitted of murder although the command was unlawful. Solomon J said: "If a soldier honestly believes he is doing his duty in obeying the commands of his superior, and if the orders are not so manifestly illegal that he must or ought to have known that they are unlawful, the private soldier would be protected by the orders of his superior officer."[5]

A serviceman may say that he obeys orders because they are orders; he does not enquire whether they are lawful or not. It may be proper, however, for a court to enquire whether it was reasonable for the defendant to obey the order, having regard to its gravity and apparent necessity, and to the consequences of disobedience to the defendant. In particular, the defence may be withheld where the act is a violation of the laws of war or would be regarded as an atrocity.[6]

There is a strong reason for viewing the serviceman sympathetically, because he is liable to severe punishment for disobeying orders. There is also an argument, though not so strong, for granting exemption to civilians on the ground of apparently reasonable civilian orders, as in the case of the police. Hitherto the argument has not met with favourable response from the courts.[7]

A related question concerns persons who follow official advice. Some authorities in the United States hold that a person is protected from

---

[1] See criticism by D B Nichols in [1976] Crim.LR 181; also S A de Smith, *Constitutional and Administrative Law*, 3rd edn 201–202; L C Green, *Superior Orders in National and International Law* (Leyden 1976).

[2] § 2.10.

[3] (1816) Russell, 12th edn i 87.

[4] (1900) 17 Cape of Good Hope SC Reports 561.

[5] In *Werner* [1947] (2) SA 828 it was held that *Smith* applied only to a soldier actually under the command of an officer who gave the order. Cp. *Kumalo* [1952] (1) SA at 387.

[6] See § 27.2 at n. 5.

[7] Lord Goddard CJ said in *Brannan* v. *Peek* [1948] 1 KB at 72 that the police have no right to commit offences to detect crime. That is undoubted, and indeed tautologous; but it does not preclude the possibility of allowing an excuse of reasonable reliance on superior orders. Nor does it necessarily deny that the intention of the policeman may negative a crime on his part.

prosecution if he makes a mistake of law resulting from an "official statement of the law."[8] But the courts interpret rather narrowly the class of people who can give an "official statement of the law;" it does not include unofficial advice from the police (except where a police officer asks for help in making an arrest, and thus impliedly represents that he is acting lawfully). There is much to be said in favour of the American rule, but it has been steadfastly rejected in the birthplace of the common law.[9] (A Delaware court has even held it to be a defence that the defendant used diligence to obtain professional legal advice and acted upon it,[10] but this opinion is exceptional in the United States; it carries obvious dangers, and has failed to find favour in England.[11]) English courts convict even when the defendant has been misled by official action into supposing that his conduct was lawful.[12] There is nothing in the books to suggest that a defence is allowed in such circumstances, so, of course, it cannot be allowed. Although the House of Lords theoretically can still take a more enlightened view in respect of official advice or misdirection, their lordships have never hinted that they will do so.

Sometimes express rules of law confer immunity for apparently lawful acts. In particular, a jailer or other officer who carries out an irregular sentence or order of a court is protected if the court had jurisdiction, and perhaps even if it had not.[13] The Control of Pollution Act 1974[14] marks a welcome departure in regulatory legislation in allowing a defence of misleading information "from persons who were in a position to provide the information," and also a defence of apparently lawful order from an employer.

§ 20.4. IGNORANCE OF THE CIVIL LAW

By far the most important limitation of the *ignorantia juris* rule is that it applies only to ignorance of the *criminal law*. Ignorance of the civil law can be a defence in offences requiring *mens rea*, because it can negative the *mens rea*.

In relation to offences against property, this proposition used to be expressed by saying that an offence was committed only by a person who acted "without a claim of right." Sometimes the defence of claim of right was rested on the fact that the statute had used the word "maliciously" or "unlawfully," which was thought to be of special significance[1]; but in fact

[8] Model Penal Code s.2.04(3)(*b*). See George Fletcher, *Rethinking Criminal Law* 755 ff.; Frank C Newman in 53 Col.LRev. 374; Kadish and Kadish, *op. cit.* 160–161 (but see *ibid.* 110 ff.). For Canada see Barton in 22 Crim.LQ 314. Cp. *Zemura* [1974] (1) SA 584 (Rhodesia).

[9] Cases under the Highways Act culminate in *Brook* v. *Ashton* [1974] Crim.LR 105. See also *Surrey CC* v. *Battersby* [1965] 2 QB 194; *Cooper* v. *Hall* [1968] 1 WLR 360,1 All ER 185 (parking offence); *Cohen (George) 600 Group Ltd.* v. *Hird* [1970] 1 WLR 1226, 2 All ER 650; *Bowsher* [1973] RTR 202, Crim.LR 373 (road traffic); *Arrowsmith* [1975] QB 678 (incitement to disaffection); *Jacey Ltd.* [1975] Crim.LR 409 (obscenity).

[10] *Long* v. *State* (1949) 44 Del. 262, 65 Atl, 2d 489.

[11] *Cooper* v. *Simmons* (1862) 7 H & N 707, 158 ER 654. See the powerful article on the whole subject by Peter Brett in 5 Melbourne Univ.LRev. 179.

[12] E.g. *Burgess* v. *West* [1982] Crim.LR 235 (misleading speed-limit signs).

[13] *The General Part*, 2nd edn § § 103 n. 1, 105 nn. 17–19; *Williams* v. *Williams* [1937] 2 All ER 559.

[14] S.3(4).

[1] See 2 Leg. Stud. 253, and *The General Part*, 2nd edn § § 108–109.

these words were not essential. At the present day a claim of right, in the sense of a mistaken belief that the civil law confers a legal right to do the act charged, may be said to be a defence to a charge of damaging property even when the statute has made no kind of reference to it.[2] In other words, in charges of crimes against property a mistake as to property rights is regarded as pertaining to civil law. There is a limit to the amount of law that the citizen can be expected to know, and the law of property falls beyond that limit. As we shall see in § 41.6, this rule is applied under the Criminal Damage Act. In relation to theft, since the Theft Act 1968 the language of "claim of right" has been abandoned and we speak instead of the offence being committed "dishonestly." A defence of honesty or claim of right is equally effective whether it rests on a mistake of fact (the defendant thought that the owner in handing over the thing had intended to give it to him), or on a mistake of the civil law (the defendant thought that he could seize possession as executor, but the will under which he acted was invalid).

Nor is this type of defence limited to offences against property.

> On a charge of bigamy, the defendant will not be heard to say that he did not know that bigamy was a crime, but it will be a defence that he (mistakenly but reasonably) thought that his first marriage was dissolved by divorce at the time of the bigamous ceremony, when as a matter of civil law the supposed divorce was invalid because it was pronounced by a court not having jurisdiction.[3] The law of divorce is not part of the criminal law, so a mistake as to it can be a defence.

In one respect the law of bigamy is anomalous. Ordinarily, when ignorance of the civil law negatives *mens rea*, it does not matter whether the ignorance is reasonable or not. But, owing to the peculiar development of the law of bigamy, the defence of mistake in that crime requires that the mistake should have been reasonable; and the same may be true for other statutory offences not incorporating an express requirement of *mens rea* (§ 6.7).

As another example of the width of the principle under discussion, it seems to be the general rule that a person does not become an accessory to an offence if he does only what he believes to be required by the civil law (§ 15.6).

What precisely is the difference between a mistake of the criminal law and of the civil law?

The word "precisely" asks for more than can be given. Obviously a mistake as to the law of tort, contract, trusts, property or family law relates to the civil law. On the other hand, offences against the person do not easily let in the defence, because they are regarded as being (for the most part) completely or exclusively defined by the criminal law itself. The law of private defence and arrest, for example, are exceptions from the

---

[2] For old authorities see *The General Part* § § 107 ff.

[3] Cp. *Gould* [1968] 2 QB 65. In that case the mistake was one of pure fact, but it seems clear that the decision would have been the same if it had related to the law of divorce.

criminal prohibition that are taken to be part of the criminal law.[4] The citizen is expected to know not only the law relating to the essentials of criminality but also the law relating to the main defences. They would appear in a well drafted criminal code. (Perhaps a more persuasive reason is the importance of protecting the body from harm; yet it may be gravely doubted whether a restriction of defences has any substantial effect in promoting bodily security.) Exceptionally a mistake as to the law of property can be a defence even to a charge of crime against the person. If a person mistakenly believes he is the owner of an article, and uses moderate force to obtain possession of it, he is entitled to be judged as if he were in truth the owner, at any rate if his mistake is reasonable.

Where the crime is one of strict liability, there will be no scope for a defence of claim of right. Since, for instance, a motorist is liable for driving without insurance even if he believed that he was insured, it is irrelevant whether his mistake was as to a pure matter of fact (the date when the policy expired) or as to the validity of the policy on some abstruse point of insurance law.

§ 20.5. THE EFFECT OF PARTICULAR STATUTORY EXPRESSIONS

In general, *mens rea* words do not let in a defence of ignorance of the criminal law. To take an obvious example, the offence of knowingly possessing explosives does not require knowledge of the statutory offence.

Some statutes creating offences stipulate that the act must be "without lawful excuse."[1] The phrase may be a useful reminder of the existence of general justifications and excuses, to those who are apt to forget them; but logically it should be unnecessary.[2] It is not read as exempting people from the duty to know and interpret all the relevant provisions, however obscure or complicated, of the statute under which they are charged.[3]

Ignorance of law is not in general a "reasonable excuse" within a statutory exemption. For instance:

> A statute empowered the police to require a driver to take a breath test in certain circumstances if he was driving or attempting to drive. The defendant, a driver, got out of his car and a policeman then required him to take a breath test. The defendant was word-perfect on the legislation, and declined to take the test on the ground that he was at that moment neither driving nor attempting to drive—which was, in the ordinary meaning of the words, the fact. He did not know that the courts had interpreted the statute in a common-sense way to include a driver who had only momentarily interrupted his driving. He was

---

[4] § 23.5 n. 7.

[1] E.g. threatening to kill (§ 9.9 n. 16) and threatening to commit criminal damage (§ 41.9).
[2] See § 6.10 at nn. 5–6.
[3] *Cambs. & Isle of Ely CC* v. *Rust* [1972] 2 QB 426.

convicted of the offence of failing without reasonable excuse to take the breath test, the trial judge having refused to leave the question of reasonable excuse to the jury; and the conviction was upheld on appeal.[4]

It is understandable that the courts should say that an unlawful refusal to comply with the directions of the police, on a layman's view of the law, when the law (to a lawyer) is quite clear, cannot constitute a reasonable excuse. One may hope, however, that decisions like this will not be taken as finally settling that no wrong opinion as to the law (including a wrong guess as to how the courts will decide a disputed point) can be reasonable.[5] A person who has mistakenly relied upon an official statement of the law should certainly be allowed a defence of reasonable excuse. Further, a misunderstanding of the law should be a reasonable excuse if the law is obscure even to a lawyer who applies himself diligently to its interpretation. As Maule J put it, in his inimitable way:

> "There may be such a thing as a doubtful point of law. If there were not, there would be no need of courts of appeal, the existence of which shows that judges may be ignorant of law."[6]

The word "wilfully" generates some problems. It has been mentioned that the courts construe it to mean "acting intentionally or recklessly without lawful excuse;"[7] and the same meaning is read into statutory malice.[8] Nevertheless, for the reasons already given, ignorance of law should not in general be read as a lawful excuse.

Cases on the statutory offence of wilfully obstructing the highway illustrate the point. Certain justifications for obstruction are recognised, such as reasonable temporary obstruction in the exercise of rights, and temporary obstruction under licence given under the authority of statute; but on a proper analysis these cases merely illustrate the meaning of "obstruction," and do not turn on the notion of wilfulness. Several cases show that a person's belief that the statutory offence contains an exception that it does not contain is no defence. If the defendant mistakenly believes, for example, that he has a right to hold a public meeting on the highway,[9] or to erect a bollard on the highway in order to protect his premises,[10] he will be convicted even of the offence of wilfulness, since these are mistakes as to the scope of the offence. However, the cases on the word "wilfully" are not entirely uniform, and there are instances of a person who has committed a public nuisance under a claim of right being acquitted.[11]

Some particular *mens rea* requirements in a statutory offence may indicate that the offence does not apply to those who mistake the law—even the law of which the statutory offence forms part. The courts have reached this conclusion in cases turning on the words "properly" and "qualified," both of which impliedly refer to the law.

In the first case, a statute (now repealed) made it an offence for any person to obtain a

---

[4] *Reid* [1973] 1 WLR 1283, 3 All ER 1020, 57 CAR 807. (The legislation has since been amended to cover those who have been driving.)

[5] See Ashworth in [1974] Crim.LR 660.

[6] *Martindale* v. *Falkner* (1846) 2 CB at 720, 135 ER at 1130.

[7] § 6.10 at n. 1.

[8] § 6.10 at n. 6.

[9] *Arrowsmith* v. *Jenkins* [1963] 2 QB 561.

[10] *Dixon* v. *Atfield* [1975] 1 WLR 1171. Cp. *Brandon* v. *Barnes* [1966] 1 WLR 1505, 3 All ER 296. See also *Wells* v. *Hardy* [1964] 2 QB 447 (for the present form of the offence in this case see Theft Act 1968 s.32 and Sched. 1 para. 2); *Brook* v. *Ashton* [1974] Crim.LR 105.

[11] *The General Part*, 2nd edn § 109.

family allowance "knowing that it was not properly receivable by him." It was held that a woman who received a family allowance on behalf of another person, in breach of the regulations but not knowing that she was doing anything wrong, had a defence. The offence was not committed unless the woman knew that her receipt of the money was improper under the regulations.[12]

The statute in the second case makes it an offence for a person to act as auditor of a company at a time when he knows that he is disqualified for appointment to that office. Another statutory provision states that an officer of a company is not qualified for appointment as auditor of that company. The defendant was a director (and therefore an officer) of a company, and acted as auditor for it, but he did not know the law and did not know that he was disqualified. A Divisional Court held that he was not guilty of the offence. Courts so often quibble by saying that regulatory offences are "not truly criminal" that it is refreshing to find the court on this occasion asserting roundly that it was a criminal offence, so that the word "knows" in the statute had to be read as meaning "knows."[13] (Apparently the word "knows" might have meant something other than "knows" in a non-criminal statute!) It is to be noticed that the notion of disqualification is itself entirely a matter of law; consequently, a contrary decision would have deprived the requirement of knowledge of almost all meaning.

The decisions on false statement and fraud are often indulgent, and need treatment on their own.

§ 20.6. FALSE STATEMENTS AND FRAUD

The word "false" in a penal statute is *prima facie* an *actus reus* word. When a statute prohibits the making of a "false" statement, the adjective is needed to express the fact that the making of a true statement is not forbidden. When the offence is of a serious kind the courts may treat the adjective as carrying also a *mens rea* implication, so that a person does not offend unless he knows his statement to be false; but in minor offences the presence of the word "false" need not prevent the statute from being construed as imposing strict liability.[1]

Assuming that "false" is read as a *mens rea* word, or that there are other indications in the statute that *mens rea* is required, will a person be liable if his statement is false because of his mistake of law? Many of our utterances that we may think of as simple statements of fact contain elements of law. For example, "I am the son of X (by adoption); I am married to Y; I have bought furniture; I have passed a driving test and have a driving licence." None of these statements would involve me in liability for a wilfully false statement if, unknown to me, they were false by reason of my mistake of law. This is obviously so if, as in these examples, the mistake relates to the civil law. Thus it has been held that a person who makes a statement in good faith but who misunderstands the civil law is not guilty of perjury,[2] or of a statutory offence of making a false statement,[3] or of forgery.[4] But where *mens rea* is required the judges occasionally go further than this, and, allow a defence of mistake relating to a statutory

---

[12] *Curr* [1968] 2 QB at 954–955. Cp. *The General Part*, 2nd edn § 109–110.
[13] *Secretary of State for Trade and Industry* v. *Hart* [1982] 1 WLR 481.

[1] § 42.2.
[2] *Crespigny* (1795) 1 Esp. 280, 170 ER 357.
[3] *Dadsworth* (1837) 8 C & P 218, 173 ER 467; *Ocean Accident and Guarantee Corpn.* v. *Cole* [1932] 2 KB 100.
[4] *Allday* (1837) 8 C & P 136, 173 ER 431.

scheme of which the penal clause forms part. The principle is, or should be, that where a statute penalises the making of a false statement, and expressly or impliedly confines the offence to statements that are wilfully or knowingly false, a mistake of law affecting the truth of the statement can be a defence.

An important example is *Wilson* v. *Inyang*.[5] This turned on a section of the Medical Act. To explain it, something should be known of the law relating to professional practice.

A few professions are protected by statutes which make it an offence for an unqualified person to engage in the profession. A prominent example is the profession of solicitor; another is the profession of veterinary surgeon. Only a qualified vet can operate on animals; only a qualified doctor or dentist can practise dentistry. With doctors who treat humans the position is different.[6] The establishment by statute of the profession of registered medical practitioners did not put an end to osteopaths (bone-setters), chiropodists, naturopaths, herbalists, faith-healers and others, who may be unkindly described as "quacks" (though they often perform useful services and are sometimes called in aid by doctors themselves). Such persons were allowed to continue to practise without any kind of qualification, the only penal rule being that they might not call themselves doctors or anything like it. An unregistered practitioner may even operate on a patient, though he runs great risk of being convicted of manslaughter if something goes wrong and the patient dies. The only medical treatments that are forbidden to laymen are in respect of venereal disease and abortion.

The rule against unqualified persons calling themselves doctors is in the Medical Act (now the Medical Act 1956 s.31, replacing earlier legislation in the same terms). This makes it a summary offence wilfully and falsely to take one of a number of medical titles, including that of physician, doctor of medicine, and surgeon. The settled interpretation of the section is that a person who is not registered under the Act must not appropriate one of the taboo words even though he adds some qualifying adjective. Thus in a case where the unqualified defendant argued that his use of the word "manipulative" before "surgeon" made his use of the term "surgeon" lawful because it told the public that he was not registered, the court drily remarked: "If the respondent is, as we must take him to be, sincere, there are many ways open to him of telling the public that he is not a surgeon other than the way of telling them that he is a surgeon."[7]

What, then, is the effect of the words "wilfully and falsely" in the section?

> In *Wilson* v. *Inyang*, Inyang was an African who had lived in England for two years and who had taken a correspondence course in "drugless therapy." He set up in practice and called himself a "naturopath physician, N.D., M.R.D.P." On a prosecution under the Act the magistrate took the view, in accordance with the authorities, that Inyang's use of the word "physician" (even though qualified by "naturopath") was not allowed under the section, but he held that Inyang could not be convicted because, on the facts, he honestly believed that he was entitled to use that expression. On appeal the Divisional Court (speaking through Lord Goddard CJ) affirmed the acquittal, saying that the question was not whether Inyang acted reasonably but whether he acted in good faith.
>
> In a case decided under the same section two years before, Lord Goddard had said that a mistake, to be a defence, must be based on reasonable grounds. But he now recanted and said that reasonableness was simply evidence of honesty, and not essential evidence. "A man may honestly believe that which no other man of common sense would believe. If he has acted without any reasonable ground, and has refrained from making any proper enquiry, that is generally very good evidence that he is not acting honestly. But it is only evidence. . . . In this case the magistrate . . . saw the defendant, heard his evidence, and formed an opinion as to his credibility and honesty. In view of his findings I do not think that the court can interfere."

This decision is an encouraging example of a shift of judicial opinion from an objective to a subjective test of criminal responsibility. It is a useful authority for the proposition that a requirement of wilfulness lets in a defence of mistake. However, the court did not advert to

---

5 [1951] 2 KB 799.

6 See [1977] 2 BMJ 839.

7 *Jutson* v. *Barrow* [1936] 1 KB at 245.

the problem of ignorance of law. Lord Goddard spoke as though the fact that *mens rea* was in issue automatically brought knowledge of law in issue, which is not always so. Inyang did not make any relevant mistake of fact. Even if he thought that the title he assumed was not misleading to the public, the offence did not require that the title should be misleading. If he had put up a brass plate saying "A B Inyang, physician and surgeon (not a registered medical practitioner)," this would hardly have been misleading but would pretty clearly have been unlawful, since the courts do not allow the use of taboo words even with explanation and qualification. Consequently, Inyang's mistake was purely as to the penal statute and its judicial interpretation.

Nevertheless, it is acceptable to say (and there were precedents for saying[8]) that the statutory offence in terms of "wilfully and falsely" taking a medical title was not committed, owing to the defendant's ignorance of law, even though the ignorance related to the very section under which the charge was made. A persuasive reason in support of the decision is that if it had been otherwise the statutory requirement of wilfulness would have had practically no effect. A person can hardly use the title of "physician" or "surgeon" without knowing that he is using it, and he can hardly make any mistake on the question whether he is registered under the Medical Act or not. However, *Wilson* v. *Inyang* should be regarded as resting on the word "falsely" (read as a *mens rea* word) and not on the word "wilfully" taken by itself.

Contrast the decision in *Roberts* v. *Duce*.[9]

> Roberts was granted legal aid on the basis of his declaration as to his "disposable income." He later received an educational grant (to buy books, etc.), and, naturally thinking that this was not "disposable income," did not notify the legal aid authority. It was held that the grant was disposable income within the Legal Aid and Advice Act, and Roberts was accordingly guilty of "wilfully" failing to notify it.

This accords with a number of cases on statutory wilfulness, but overlooks the fact that those cases were concerned with physical acts, not the utterance of words. It seems reasonable to say that any *mens rea* offence of false statement lets in a defence of mistake as to the law affecting the truth of the statement, even where the defendant has used an expression having a legal meaning without knowing that meaning, and the same should apply to the offence of failing to make a true statement. On this view, *Roberts* v. *Duce* was wrongly decided.

The rule just suggested for offences involving knowledge or wilfulness in relation to false statements is confined to the question of the truth of the statement. A person can be convicted of an offence of wilfully or knowingly making a false statement if he says what he knows is false, even though he wrongly believes that the falsity is on a matter with which the statutory requirement of truth is not concerned.

> D claimed sickness benefit and made a knowingly false statement that he has not worked during a certain period. However, he did not think that the false statement would affect the amount of benefit, and told the lie only because he did not want his employer to know that he had worked elsewhere. He was convicted of knowingly making a false statement for the purpose of claiming benefit.[10]

For reasons similar to those for making false statements, offences of fraud are regularly held to admit of a defence of mistake of law.[11] Whether these other offences admit of a general defence of good faith need not here be considered.

SUMMARY

In general, ignorance of the law is no excuse. This means that the citizen is §.1

---

[8] Particularly *Hunter* v. *Clare* [1899] 1 QB 635 and *Younghusband* v. *Luftig* [1949] 2 KB 354.
[9] [1974] Crim.LR 107.
[10] *Barrass* v. *Reeve* [1981] 1 WLR 408, [1980] 3 All ER 705.
[11] *The General Part*, 2nd edn § 113.

expected to forecast accurately the way in which the judge (and the jury, to the extent that the question is theirs) will interpret the law. However, the civil courts will hear an action for a declaration as to the law if criminal proceedings have not been started. Moreover, there are certain exceptions to the rule excluding mistakes of law from consideration, and the more important of these follow.

There is judicial authority for saying that a statute will not take effect upon a continuous proceeding until a reasonable time has been allowed for discontinuance; and ignorance of the statute will be relevant in enquiring what is a reasonable time. In proceedings under a statutory instrument it is a statutory defence that the instrument has not been issued, unless reasonable steps have been taken to bring its purport to the notice of those affected. Judges have shown a readiness to extend the defence of non-publication of delegated legislation. § .2

It is unsettled whether a member of the armed forces has the defence that he reasonably believed an order to be lawful. § .3

Ignorance of the civil law can be a defence if it negatives *mens rea*. This is frequently referred to as a defence of "claim of right." In theft it is represented by the requirement that theft be committed "dishonestly." On the other hand, the law of self-defence and arrest are taken to be part of the criminal law, and ignorance of their limits is no defence. § .4

Mens rea words in a statute (such as "wilfully") do not generally let in a defence of mistake of law. But if the statute requires knowledge or wilfulness in respect of a legal concept (as in the case of knowledge of impropriety, or knowledge of disqualification), this will let in the defence. Offences of doing something "without lawful excuse" apparently do not allow a defence of reasonable mistake of law. Offences of doing something "without reasonable excuse" have also been construed as excluding mistake of law, but it is still open to argument that where the defendant has made the fullest effort to ascertain the law he has a reasonable excuse for misunderstanding it. § .5

Where an offence of false statement expressly or impliedly requires the defendant to have known of the falsity of the statement, and where the truth of the statement involves a question of law, mistake of law ought to be allowed as a defence, and sometimes is. This is particularly so where the defendant has used words having a legal meaning without knowing that meaning. But the cases are not entirely uniform. Even in offences of false statement, a mistake as to the legal importance of the falsity is no defence. § .6

CHAPTER 21

INTOXICATION

Oh God; That men should put an enemy in their mouths, to steal away their brains.

Othello II. iii

§ 21.1. THE EFFECT OF INTOXICANTS

THE effect of alcohol on the brain is depressant from the beginning. Its apparently stimulating effect is due solely to the fact that it deadens the higher control centres (and progressively the other centres as well), so weakening or removing the inhibitions that normally keep us within the bounds of civilised behaviour. It also impairs perception, reasoning, and the ability to foresee consequences.

Alcohol is quite strongly associated with crimes of violence, but this does not necessarily mean that it is a causal factor.[1] Perhaps violent people tend to drink. We all know many people who drink a sociable glass; some perhaps even become inebriated, without being violent. However, case histories show that a few people, who are generally peaceable, for some idiosyncratic reason become highly violent and dangerous in their cups.

Alcohol is generally distinguished from drugs as a matter of speech, though scientifically speaking it is a drug. As regards the effect on *mens rea*, nearly all the cases concern alcohol, but other psychedelic drugs have come to present similar legal problems[2] which are answered on the same principles as those established for alcohol.[3] Cocaine, which is frequently injected with heroin, is an intense stimulant which in large doses causes acute paranoia. Stimulants (like amphetamines) and tranquillisers[4] and other sedatives (like the barbiturates) do not generally produce criminal behaviour (although theft and forgery are committed in order to obtain them). However, large overdoses can issue in violence, sometimes, apparently, as the result of producing a psychosis (insanity).

In the vast controversy surrounding cannabis (marihuana, hashish, pot), the evidence of any connection with criminality is almost entirely negative. Only occasionally, it seems, does its use precipitate a psychotic state.

The hallucinogens, including LSD, produce hallucinations, as their name implies; under their influence repressions and learned patterns of

---

[1] F H McClintock and others, *Crimes of Violence* (London 1963) 254, says that where crimes of violence arose from domestic disputes, etc. "some alcoholic drink had been recently consumed by about 20 per cent. of the offenders, but these data are of little value without some indication of the proportion of persons in these neighbourhoods who are habitually consuming alcohol during their leisure hours." Cp. *ibid*. 168, 232.

[2] See David Farrier, *Drugs and Intoxification* (London 1980).

[3] *Lipman* [1970] 1 QB at 156A.

[4] For a brief account of the medico-legal aspects of tranquillisers see Lader in 146 JPN 250.

behaviour are dissolved away. But again the connection with criminal behaviour is very slight. One writer comments:

> "There is a growing international literature of LSD disasters—a recent murder in America, a Swiss doctor who ecstatically jumped in a lake and nearly drowned, a Scandinavian woman who went out and stabbed her seducer. But alarming as these events are, it seems they happen rarely in comparison with the enormous number of licit and illicit LSD experiences in the western world."[5]

Although the consumption of alcohol is not generally an offence, we have certain offences of drunkenness.[6] The most important are:

— being found drunk in a public place;
— being drunk and disorderly in a public place;
— being drunk in a public place in possession of a loaded firearm[7];
— being found drunk in a public place in charge of a child under 7[8];
— being under the influence of drink or drugs when in (or having been in) charge of a motor vehicle in a public place (§ 14.6);
— having a blood-alcohol concentration above the prescribed limit when in (or having been in) charge of a motor vehicle in a public place (§ 14.6).

Legislation also strikes at the possession of what are compendiously described as "controlled drugs."[9] It has hitherto proved to be impossible to control access to glue and other solvents which are sniffed by juveniles; the practice has resulted in fatalities and occasionally in violence.[10]

§ 21.2. INTOXICATION AND RESPONSIBILITY

Intoxication presents problems in the theory of responsibility.

One who does a criminal deed when intoxicated may previously have led a blameless life. Drink (or a drug) perhaps had an unexpected effect on him, and the act may not reflect his real character. So it may look harsh to convict him of a crime, particularly of a very serious crime like murder. Moreover, the evidence of intoxication may satisfy the jury that he lacked the intention or other mental element normally required for the crime.

On the other hand, many offenders have imbibed before committing the criminal act, and this cannot be allowed as a general defence. By becoming intoxicated a man voluntarily impairs his own self-control and good judgment. He must be subjected to social control if there is a possibility that his mischievous conduct will be repeated.

---

[5] Peter Laurie, *Drugs* (Penguin Books 1967) 117. The other statements on drugs above are summaries of the conclusions of this author.

[6] See Stone, *Justices' Manual*, Index *s.v.* Drunkenness.

[7] For these three offences see Licensing Act 1872 s.12 as amended; there is also local legislation.

[8] Licensing Act 1902 s.1 as amended.

[9] Misuse of Drugs Act 1971 and Regulations thereunder.

[10] In *Waite* (1981), The Times, 13 October 145 JPN 677, a solvent abuser who slew his grandmother was convicted of murder, notwithstanding efforts to get a verdict of diminished responsibility. Proposals for legislative control of solvent abuse have not been thought practicable (146 JPN 588).

Why not treat the drunkard as insane?

Because the poisoning of the brain with alcohol or other drugs is a knowingly self-induced condition. Volition enters into it in a way that it does not into insanity. The threat of punishment may cause a person to moderate his intake of intoxicants, and it may cause even the intoxicated person to control himself. Some may be inclined to dispute this assumption; but obviously it would be inimical to the safety of all of us if the judges announced that anyone could gain exemption from the criminal law by getting drunk.

This distinction between intoxication and insanity is not entirely realistic: an addict is as much in the grip of his own failing as a psychotic. Alcoholic addiction causes brain damage. But courts do not draw the line as sharply as may appear. On the one hand, a person who successfully sets up a defence of insanity is not released: he goes to a psychiatric hospital for as long as he is thought to be a public danger. On the other hand, an alcoholic or drug addict who is convicted of crime need not be punished: the court may put him on probation for treatment,[1] if considerations of deterrence are not paramount and if treatment is available.

Most drunkards who commit serious crimes are sent to prison (and on conviction of murder the court has no option); whereas an irresponsibly insane person who sets up his insanity as a defence may have a "special verdict" (of insanity), in which case he will at least be safe from prison. If an insane person does not specifically set up an insanity defence even he may go to prison, as we shall see, though this outcome is now unlikely.

Isn't it possible to be both drunk and insane?

Drunkenness is not itself insanity, but drinking may result in what is thought of as insanity (for example, *delirium tremens*), or it may be symptomatic of insanity, or bring out latent insanity. The same is true for other drugs. Here the ordinary defence of insanity is open, within rules to be discussed in Chapter 28. If it succeeds there must be a special verdict, and the defendant goes to hospital.

From the social point of view an insanity verdict is not the preferred outcome. It is unlikely that either a special hospital or an NHS hospital would willingly accept an alcoholic as an in-patient for any length of time, if at all. Such methods of treatment as exist require the active desire of the patient for treatment, and the problem is one of motivation. The desirable solution is some legal mechanism by which the alcoholic or drug-addict can be held to be legally responsible, and therefore punishable—not by way of retribution, but in order to induce him to accept treatment or otherwise to discontinue his habit,[2] or in the last resort to contain him for some time for the protection of the public. What we have to consider is how this legal responsibility can be secured.

§ 21.3. INTOXICATION AND INTENTION

We have already seen that the House of Lords in *Caldwell* solved the

---

[1] With or without a condition of residence in a hostel. Given motivation, outpatient treatment for alcoholism with Antabuse under supervision can be successful. CJA 1972 s.34 enables the Home Secretary to set up medical treatment centres (commonly referred to as detoxification centres) for alcoholics against whom a criminal charge would otherwise have been preferred. Few have been opened; but there are some units under the NHS, as well as some drug rehabilitation centres for drug addicts.

[2] For illustrations of sentencing practice see *Willens* 142 JPN 652; *Heather* [1979] Crim.LR 672. Notable success has been claimed for supervised treatment with Antabuse for alcoholic addition: see Dr Colin Brewer in 283 BMJ 1466 and 29 Probation Jrnl, March 1, 1982.

problem of the intoxicated offender by creating a kind of constructive recklessness. If the courts had begun with this solution it is unlikely that they would have felt the need for any other. But before *Caldwell* they had hit on a different solution for intention, employing a totally unsound juristic construction which still remains to disfigure the law.

An explanation must start in the 1920s, when it was thought that the ordinary *mens rea* principles applied to the ascertainment of intention even when the defendant was drunk.

So drunks were let off these charges?

Not necessarily. The law was, and is, that evidence of intoxication is not a passport to an acquittal. The mere fact that a man was drunk when he committed a criminal act is not an excuse. Drink may have loosened his inhibitions, made him more irascible, caused him to do terrible things that he would not have done when sober; but on none of these accounts would it entitle him to be acquitted.

On the other hand, the courts recognised that evidence of intoxication could cause the jury to doubt whether the defendant intended to bring about the damage or injury that he did; and in this indirect way the evidence of intoxication could lead to an acquittal. Subject to what is to be said later, this is still the position.

Can the drunk get off even a charge of murder in this way?

Yes.[1]

But if the evidence of intoxication gets him off, then intoxication is a passport to an acquittal.

Whether the evidence of intoxication leads to an acquittal depends on the circumstances and on the view taken of them by the jury. An intoxicated person *can* decide to kill somebody. If he rushes at the victim and stabs him, the jury may come to the conclusion that he intended to kill. Suppose a man, having taken drink, in a fit of temper pushes his wife under a bus. The jury may be satisfied that he intended to kill her, and convict him of murder. Indeed, the fact that the man was intoxicated may make them more convinced that he lost his temper to such a fearful extent. But if the evidence seems to show that he only stumbled against his wife, the fact that he was intoxicated may fortify any doubt the jury may have had about his intention, and lead them to acquit him of murder (and also of wounding with intent).[2]

So the question is whether the evidence of intoxication negatives the capacity to form the required intent?

If you summed up to a jury in that way a conviction would be quashed

[1] *Beard* [1920] AC 479; *Sheehan*, [1975] 1 WLR 739, 2 All ER 960, 60 CAR 308.
[2] In which case the prosecution bear the usual burden of proof of intent: *Sheehan*, n. 1 above.

on appeal; but you would not be the first judge to step on that particular banana-skin. Such a direction puts the matter too unfavourably to the defendant. Of course, if he couldn't form the intent, he didn't; but the converse is not true. As I said, a person who is under the influence may have been quite capable of deciding to kill someone, but the evidence may indicate that he did not so decide. The simple question for the jury is: Are you sure that the defendant had the requisite state of mind? For this purpose it is relevant to consider the fact of intoxication.[3]

I don't want to come another tumble, but how sloshed must a man be before he gets off a charge of murder by giving evidence of intoxication?

Once more: it is not the simple fact of intoxication that puts the defendant in the clear, so we do not need a rule about the degree of intoxication that has to be regarded.

> A person who is charged with theft of an umbrella may give evidence that he is an absent-minded professor and did not think what he was doing, or that he was drunk; the evidence may help him to an acquittal, but what gets him off is not the fact that he is a professor, or was drunk, or both, but that the jury or magistrates are not sure that he intended to steal.

What if a person deliberately gets drunk for the sake of "Dutch courage" to commit murder or some other serious crime?

That is a special case. He can probably be convicted even though he was an "automaton" at the moment of acting.

A man decides to commit murder, and gets drunk in order to nerve himself to carry it out; in fact he gets so drunk that the jury feel unable to say that when he did the deed he had any idea what he was doing. To acquit him would obviously be too lenient. Indeed, the probability is that even in his drunken state he remembered the intent that he had formed when sober—because otherwise it would be difficult to explain his actions. However that may be, it is an intelligible rule that the defendant is to be held guilty of a crime of intention in such circumstances because his conduct must be regarded as a whole; and Lord Denning on one occasion expressed an opinion to this effect.[4] Suppose, to take an analogy, that a man sets a time-bomb to kill people, and is asleep when it goes off; obviously he is guilty of murder. Similarly, if he fuddles himself with drink in order to commit murder, he turns himself into a kind of human time-bomb.[5]

During the 1920s it was thought that this was the whole of the law on the subject of intoxication in relation to the mental element. But some judges were apprehensive that we were being too lenient to drunkards, and so they set about to change the law by introducing a distinction between what they called crimes of specific intent and crimes of basic intent. The old law continues to apply to crimes of specific intent, but in crimes of basic (or

---

[3] *Sheehan*, n. 1 above; *Purdage* [1975] Crim.LR 575; 1st edn 420.

[4] *Gallagher* [1963] AC at 382. The majority did not express concurrence in Lord Denning's view, because they decided the case on a different point. It had been argued that the defendant was iresponsibly insane, and the majority held that the question of insanity was to be judged by reference to the time of the act, not some earlier time when he took alcohol (because at that earlier time he might not have been insane, yet he might have been insane at the time of the act). Lord Denning's opinion, on the other hand, supposed that insanity was out of the case; on that assumption it was surely right.

[5] The *mens rea* antedates the *actus reus*, as in the situation considered in § 11.6 and § 12.7. See also § § 7.5, 15.14.

general) intent the jury will be instructed not to take evidence of voluntary intoxication into account in deciding the issue of intention. The seal of approval was placed on this development by the House of Lords in *Majewski*[6].

I gather from what you said before that murder is a crime of specific intent, where the old law still applies. What others are there?

The principal are wounding with intent,[7] criminal damage with intent to endanger life,[8] and theft.[9]

Although the defendant is acquitted of one of these serious crimes by reason of evidence of intoxication, there will generally be a fall-back offence for which, under the new dispensation established by the House of Lords, the prosecution can get him convicted, because it is an offence of basic intent which is not disproved by evidence of intoxication. For example, the drunken killer may be acquitted of murder; but he will be convicted of manslaughter (as he always could be). So broad is the law of manslaughter that it applies even when a person has killed another when in a state of minimal consciousness.

> In *Lipman*,[10] the defendant killed his bedmate when he was under the infuence of LSD (hallucinating that he was fighting snakes in the centre of the earth). He was convicted of constructive manslaughter because he had committed an unlawful act, and sentenced to 6 years' imprisonment.

The decision caused discomfort to commentators, but the House of Lords regarded it as authoritative in *Majewski*. It is clear from the latter case that Lipman's "unlawful act" was in attacking his female companion. This attack was an assault, his state of confused consciousness being the result of voluntary intoxication. One may have serious doubts, however, about the severity of the sentence.

Similarly, the drunkard (I call him a drunkard, but he may be equally incapacitated by (other) drugs, which are legally regarded in the same way as alcohol[11])—the drunkard may be acquitted of wounding with intent but may now be convicted of various lesser crimes because they are regarded as crimes of basic intent: assault, unlawful wounding, etc.,[12] or rape.[13]

---

6 [1977] AC 443. The name is anglicised in pronunciation as spelt.

7 *Pordage* [1975] Crim.LR 575, and *Majewski, passim.*

8 *Caldwell* § 5.3.

9 *Ruse* v. *Reed* [1949] 1 KB 377; *Kindon* (1957) 41 CAR 208; *Foote* [1964] Crim.LR 405. Nor could the drunken taker be convicted on the basis of recklessness, since theft cannot be committed recklessly. Offences involving an intent to deceive or defraud are also taken to be of specific intent: *Durante* [1972] 1 WLR 1612, 3 All ER 962.

10 [1970] 1 QB 152. The basis of the decision has been debated (see 1st edn 435–436), but it is now in line with *Caldwell*. Wein J in *Howell* [1974] 2 All ER at 810 suggested that it is a form of manslaughter standing on its own!

11 § 21.1 n. 3.

12 Also of assault occasioning actual bodily harm, or assault on a constable in the execution of his duty. See *Majewski*, n. 6 above. Cp. *Bolton* v. *Crawley* [1972] Crim.LR 222.

13 Rape is a crime of basic intent (*Woods* (1981) 74 CAR 312); anyway, voluntary intoxication is no defence because rape is also a crime of recklessness. Similarly with indecent assault: *Burns* (1973) 58 CAR 364.

He may be acquitted of criminal damage with intent to endanger life, but on certain lesser charges the evidence of intoxication will generally be of no help to him: criminal damage being reckless whether life will be endangered, or criminal damage simply, whether of the intentional or reckless variety.[14] These are crimes of basic intent.

The drunkard may be acquitted of theft, which involves an intent to deprive the owner permanently of the thing. So if he comes out of a pub after a merry evening and rides off on someone else's bicycle by mistake, the evidence of intoxication will help to get him off the charge of theft. Also of burglary when that involves an intent to steal. But he may (it is held) be convicted of taking a conveyance without the owner's consent (sometimes called the joyriding offence). This is supposed to be a crime of basic intent to which evidence of intoxication is irrelevant.[15] (But the opinion has to be qualified, as we shall see (§ .5 at n. 3).)

Suppose the thing the drunkard takes is not a vehicle but something else, like a watch.

In that event there is generally no lesser charge that can be used against him. However, even if the evidence of intoxication saves him from being convicted in respect of the original taking of the watch, he can be convicted of theft if he decided to keep it after he had sobered up.

If theft of a watch is a crime of specific intent, what is the corresponding crime of basic intent?

There is no crime of basic intent applicable in this case. A crime of specific intent means an act intentionally done with a certain specific (ulterior) intent. The act itself may or may not be a crime of basic intent. Consequently, one cannot always find a crime of basic intent underlying a crime of specific intent. When a conveyance is taken, we happen to have the joyriding offence (basic intent) underpinning the crime of theft (specific intent), but no lesser offence of basic intent generally applies to the taking of other objects. As another example of this, attempt is classified as a crime of specific intent,[16] but the act of attempt need not be an offence apart from the attempt. If the drunkard gets off the charge of attempt he will generally be safe from any other charge in respect of that incident.

Why ever do we have these terms "specific intent" and "basic intent"? I don't really see that the law makes sense.

The way in which we came to have these expressions, as a historical matter, is perfectly clear. They result from the desire on the part of the judges to change the law. I will tell you the story; it is of interest as a case-study in the way the judges see their own role, and the kind of

---

[14] For the proposition that intentional damage under the Criminal Damage Act 1971 s.1(1) is an offence of basic intent see *Jaggard* v. *Dickinson* [1981] QB 527; for recklessness see *Caldwell* n. 8 above.

[15] *MacPherson* [1973] RTR 157, Crim.LR 457; *Majewski* n. 6 above at 477D.

[16] *Majewski* at p. 483D. So intoxication must be taken into account on a charge of attempted rape, though it is not on a charge of rape itself! See Graham Parker in 55 Can.BR 701.

manipulation of the law that they consider proper; but otherwise it is purely historical, so it shall go into small print.

Before *Majewski* the leading case on the subject of intoxication was *Beard* (1920).[17] Lord Birkenhead, delivering in effect the judgment of the House of Lords, stated that evidence of intoxication could be taken into consideration in deciding whether the defendant had a "specific intent essential to constitute the crime." He did not explain what he meant by "specific," but we can say with some confidence that his judgment indicates that he had nothing very much in mind, and it is a great pity that he did not cross the word out of his speech before delivering it. That he attached no significance to the word is shown by the fact that immediately after the sentence in question he repeated it in essence but modified it by omitting the word "specific" and substituting the phrase "the intent necessary to constitute the crime.[18] Moreover, at the end of his speech he stated expressly that his remarks were meant to apply not only to crimes requiring a "specific intent" but also to crimes not requiring a "specific intent," "for," he said, "speaking generally (and apart from certain special offences), a person cannot be convicted of crime unless the *mens* was *rea*."[19] He could hardly have made it clearer that, whatever distinction he had in mind between specific intents and other intents, he (and therefore the House of Lords for whom he was speaking) meant his remarks to apply to all intents. That, indeed, was how his opinion was understood for many years.

But judges then conceived the fear that gullible juries would turn dangerous drunks loose upon the community (there is little or no evidence that they have done so). Since so many crimes were worded to require a mental element, and since nothing was to be expected from the Government and Parliament, which do not think it an important part of their function to settle legal difficulties, the judges silently came to the conclusion that the only remedy was the accustomed one of do-it-yourself. The technique was to take Lord Birkenhead's phrase "specific intent" and to assert that what he said applied *only* to crimes having that requirement (whatever meaning might be found for it, Lord Birkenhead having assigned none). In *Majewski* the law lords were pressed with the argument that Lord Birkenhead did not mean what he was now supposed to have meant, but they brushed aside the argument with the assertion that he could not have meant what he said.

We must now study the highly artificial distinction between specific and basic intent in greater depth.

§ 21.4. SPECIFIC AND BASIC INTENT

The rule in *Majewski* depends upon the assumption that an intelligible distinction can be made between specific and basic intent. But the law lords in that and other cases, while unanimous that there is such a distinction, and while agreeing on some of its applications, have failed to agree on a definition of the two intents. What can be said is that the definition that best fits the actual decisions, and the one representing the dominant judicial opinion, is the one we had before for what we then preferred to call "ulterior intent."[1] A specific intent is an intent going beyond the intent to

---

[17] Note 1 above.
[18] [1920] AC at 501–502.
[19] *Ibid.* at 504. I discussed this further in *The Mental Element in Crime* (Jerusalem and Oxford 1965) 40 ff., and in 1st edn 435.

[1] § 3.1.

do the act in question.[2] The bodily movement is willed or intentional, and it is done with some further intent specified in the offence. In murder (the judges appear to suppose), it is an act done with intent to cause death; in the crime of wounding or causing g.b.h. with intent, an act done with intent to cause g.b.h.; in burglary, trespass with certain unlawful intents, and so on.

How come that murder is a crime of specific intent? Surely the intent is "basic," as you have defined this word. The murderer intends to kill; he need have no intent beyond that. A motiveless murder is still murder. Similarly with the wounder.

I am glad that you have not allowed my glib explanation to pass unchallenged. It followed that given by the courts, but in common sense, as you say, murder and wounding with intent (or, at least, the commonest forms of the latter crime) involve only the so-called "basic" intent. In neither murder nor causing g.b.h. with intent to cause g.b.h. does the law specify any result that must be intended to follow from the attack.

The courts have not stated clearly how they conceive the intent as specific. Perhaps in the case of causing g.b.h. with intent to cause g.b.h. they do not realise that the words "with intent" are used in a somewhat unusual sense, or it does not suit their purpose to advert to this. The phrase "with intent" in the definition of a crime normally refers to an ulterior intent (e.g. in the crime of assault with intent to rob, or wounding with intent to resist arrest), but in the crime of causing g.b.h. with intent to cause g.b.h. no such ulterior intent is required. Causing g.b.h. with intent to cause it merely means intentionally causing g.b.h.

Another possible explanation depends on the fact pointed out before,[3] that while some verbs have consequences wrapped into them, some have not. When we talk of killing (or wounding) a person, we may conceptualise or verbalise the event in either of two ways. We may take killing (or wounding) to mean doing an act (striking etc.) that causes death (or a wound), where the act and its consequence are treated as two separate events; or we may have a composite notion of "doing an act of killing" (or "an act of wounding"), where the result is included in the notion of the act. The choice is only a question of words, but it is a choice with legal implications under the rule in *Majewski*. Traditionally, murder is thought of as a "killing," and that is how it is legally described. But, the judges' scheme being to have a rule that will let the drunkard off the graver charge only, they decide to think of murder for this particular purpose as 'an act done with intent to cause death (and succeeding in that purpose)" rather than as a self-contained act of "intentional killing." Similarly, they regard an intentional wounding as "doing an act with intent to cause a wound" rather than an act of "intentional wounding." This is one of many examples that could be given of judges making a meaningless distinction of language yield legal results.

It is not even true that murder is necessarily an intentional killing. Intentionally causing grievous bodily harm without intent to kill is murder if death results. Besides, if one can turn a crime into one of specific intent by saying that achieving a result by doing an act with intent to achieve it involves a specific intent, then I commit a crime of specific intent when I move my fist with intent to bring it into painful contact with your nose, and succeed in doing so, or when I put your car in motion as a result of having done something (started the engine,

---

[2] See Donaldson LJ in *Jaggard* v. *Dickinson* [1981] QB at 532H: "The distinction between a general or basic intent and a specific intent is that whereas the former extends only to the *actus reus*, a specific intent extends beyond it." By *actus reus* he evidently intended the physical act, regarding a specified consequence as not part of the act (though in another use of language it could be so regarded). For discordant views in the Lords see lst edn 429–430; Clarkson in 41 MLR 478.

[3] § 3.2.

etc.) with that purpose; yet neither of these crimes (assault, and taking a conveyance) involves a specific intent in law. Reasoning based on the idea of specific intent is phoney.

Further, the distinction accords only roughly with a social or moral classification of crimes. There is no social difference between stealing someone else's watch and deliberately smashing someone else's watch, but the first (theft) is regarded as a crime of specific intent while the second (criminal damage) is a crime of basic intent.

Another anomaly emerges when one compares criminal damage with wounding with intent. "Wounding with intent" under OAPA s.18 in most cases merely means intentionally wounding, and it is precisely analogous to intentionally damaging property. Now if a drunkard on the rampage swings an iron bar at a window and smashes it, the jury (or magistrates) can (subject to what is to be said later[4]) convict him under the rule in *Majewski* of intentionally damaging the window, the jury being instructed to disregard his intoxication when the offence is one of basic intent, as this offence is. But if he had wounded a man by doing essentially the same thing, his intoxication would have been taken into account on a charge under section 18 to help show that he did not intend to wound anyone, the crime under section 18 being one of specific intent.

There is no relevant difference between the two cases on the facts. The man broke the window, or he caused the window to be broken; he wounded the victim, or he caused the victim to be wounded. Why should the court's choice of words be such as to make the first crime one of basic intent and the second crime one of specific intent?

Do not think that what I am saying will be of the slightest use to you in legal practice. The judges will resolutely close their minds to any argument based on ordinary legal, linguistic or logical reasoning in this area of policy. It is not even profitable to cite the explicit language of an Act of Parliament. The decision in *Majewski* is a classical illustration of the truth that no authority can compel judges to arrive at a decision to which they are strongly averse. When counsel for Majewski used a logical argument in the House of Lords criticising the doctrine of specific intent, he was informed that "the common law of England is founded on common sense and experience rather than strict logic." Their lordships therefore approved the dichotomy of criminal intent notwithstanding that they had reached no agreement between themselves on its basis, and notwithstanding that no definition of the two intents explains the purported applications of the distinction made by the courts and approved in *Majewski*. So ours not to reason why; we must just respectfully receive the twin lists of crimes of specific and basic intent as handed down to us.

How do the courts get round section 8 of the Criminal Justice Act[5]?

Some of the lords who took part in the decision in *Majewski* resolved that problem by disregarding it. Lord Elwyn-Jones LC (with whom several other lords concurred) confronted the statute and attempted the perilous task of offering a reason for not applying it. His words were as follows.

> "In referring to 'all the evidence' [the section] meant all the *relevant* evidence. But if there is a substantive rule of law that in crimes of basic intent the fact of intoxication is irrelevant (and such I hold to be the substantive law), evidence with regard to it is quite irrelevant."[6]

If this is a reason, it is one of gossamer thinness. The interpretation reduces the section to impotence. It means that anything that would have been withheld from the jury's consideration before the section was passed can still be withheld from them because the judges declare it to be irrelevant.

---

[4] Text at n. 9 below.
[5] § 3.3.
[6] [1977] AC at 476A.

Evidence of intoxication is logically relevant to the issue of intention. No one can stop the judges saying that it is legally irrelevant, but that is a weasel phrase, if ever there was one. To say that intoxication is legally irrelevant is only to say that the courts are determined not to pay attention to it as a factor in evidence on the question of intention. But section 8 was passed to rule out artificial treatments of the notion of intention. The object of the section was to prevent the trial judge doing what the judge did in *DPP* v. *Smith*, namely telling the jury that as a matter of law they must ignore certain evidence on this issue. That is the very thing that the judges are again doing under cover of the doctrine of basic intent.

It is true that section 8 was not intended to affect the rules of the admissibility of evidence in general; it does not mean, for example, that the jury can have regard to hearsay evidence which the law treats as inadmissible on any issue. But the section, which is addressed to the courts and not to the ordinary citizen, surely means that judges must not invent rules to exclude evidence on the specific issue of intention, which is what they had been doing before the Act, and what since *Majewski* they have continued to do when evidence of intoxication is adduced.

It is true, too, that if the courts treat a particular crime as being of strict liability, intent is not in issue and evidence on that question would be logically irrelevant to the matters to be decided. But crimes of basic intent are not of strict liability. As their description indicates, they are crimes of intention.[7]

Can I switch to ask about crimes of basic intent? When a crime of this kind is charged, do the courts refuse to allow the defendant to adduce evidence of intoxication?

They allow the evidence to be given by either side. The prosecution may give it to show the background of the case, and even to support the contention that the defendant intentionally did the dreadful thing charged against him, because the drug had weakened his inhibitions.[8] The defendant is free to give it in the hope of persuading the jury that he was fuddled with drink and had no illegal intention. But the judge, applying *Majewski*, will direct the jury that the evidence cannot negative the "basic intent" required for the crime.

The appellate judgments are vague about the practical implications of the rule, but what it means, almost certainly, is no more than that the jury must disregard the evidence of intoxication in determining the defendant's intention. *They can and should have regard to any other evidence on the subject.* Therefore, the jury must decide how they would have viewed the case if they had not known that the defendant was intoxicated.[9]

> If (to take illustrations given before) a drunkard makes a fire on the floorboards or hits someone very hard over the head, and afterwards says that he intended no damage or injury, the tribunal of fact should have no difficulty in saying that they would have found that a sober person on like facts intended damage or injury, if only because he would have realised that damage or injury was inevitable; so they

---

[7] For example, the CA said in *Mowatt* that under OAPA s.20 the defendant must have "an awareness that his act may have the consequence of causing some physical harm to some other person." (See § 9.3 at n. 7.) Yet according to *Majewski* the jury are not allowed to consider evidence of voluntary intoxication as negativing this awareness. See more in 1st edn 426–427.

[8] See the Australian dicta quoted by Fairall in [1980] Crim.LJ 268.

[9] There is a subtle distinction, and instructing the jury upon it will add to their intellectual troubles. The prosecution are not called upon to establish that the intoxication did not cause the act, and the jury, consequently, are not called upon to find that the defendant would have done the act intentionally even if he had not been intoxicated. Where the act is "out of character" it may be obvious that the intoxication caused it, but that is no defence.

could dismiss the argument that the drunkard did not intend it. But if, in the case of a sober defendant, the evidence would be consistent with his not intending the result, then the tribunal should not find that an intoxicated person intended it (unless, conceivably, the fact of intoxication itself tips the balance and persuades the tribunal that the intoxicant had reduced the defendant's inhibitions). If the drunkard is not to be treated more leniently than the sobersides in the findings of fact, he is not to be treated more severely either.

This is expecting the jury to perform awful mental gymnastics.

It is, but there seems to be no other practical interpretation of the law, so long as the rule in *Majewski* prevails.

The alternative that comes to mind is for the trial judge to instruct the jury that, the defendant having given evidence of voluntary intoxication, they need not consider the question of intention, the crime now having become one of strict liability. The trouble is that this would raise a question as to the degree of intoxication required to bring the rule into operation—a trouble that you scented when you asked me that rather jocular question about getting "sloshed."[10] The law can hardly be that evidence (perhaps introduced by prosecution witnesses, or elicited from the defendant in cross-examination) that the defendant had consumed a couple of pints of beer turns what would otherwise have been an offence requiring *mens rea* into an offence of strict liability. It is only intoxication of a certain degree that could possibly do this. But how can one define the degree? This difficulty is so serious that we can safely take the view previously stated as being the correct one. Nevertheless, there are indications that the rule in *Majewski* is misunderstood by some judges and magistrates, who assume that when evidence of intoxication is given there is nothing to be decided on the issue of intention.

The type of problem that can arise may be illustrated by a hypothetical based on an incident that occurred in New Zealand. At a midnight party at which liquor has flowed, a number of young men are capering about dressed in grass haka skirts. They are in high spirits, and one of them, merely to add to the merriment, takes a flaring torch and sets his friend's skirt alight. The friend is seriously burnt. When charged with inflicting g.b.h. under OAPA s.20, the doer of the stupid act gives evidence that although he was rather tipsy he certainly thought that the fire would be immediately and easily put out, so that there was no risk; otherwise he would never have done such a thing.

Recall that the mental element under section 20 is intention or recklessness. On the argument previously advanced, if the prosecution rest their case on intention the jury are not absolved from deciding that issue because evidence of intoxication has been given. They must decide whether the evidence, putting aside the evidence of intoxication, shows that the defendant intended to do g.b.h., or leaves them in doubt on the subject; and in the above hypothetical they will probably have no difficulty in finding at least a doubt, so that they acquit on that charge.

If, as is likely, there is an alternative charge alleging recklessness, the jury must then decide whether the doer was reckless as to causing the harm. At first sight the prosecution may seem to have a cast-iron case on recklessness under the rule in *Caldwell*, but the defence is not devoid of possible arguments. It may be urged that the defendant was not subjectively reckless; that he was not *Caldwell* reckless apart from the special rule for intoxication because he believed his act to be safe, and that he was not reckless under the special rule in *Caldwell* for intoxication if the jury find that he might not have seen any risk even if he had not been intoxicated. Very likely the last question would be resolved against the stupid prankster, but anyway it is the question to be asked.

You said some time ago[11] that on a charge involving specific intent, such as

[10] § .3, text after n. 3.
[11] Text at n. 2 above.

murder or wounding (or causing g.b.h.) with intent, the defendant would be acquitted if the evidence was that owing to intoxication he accidentally lurched against someone, who fell under a bus. Do I gather that he could be convicted on those same facts of unlawful wounding or assault? He did not attack anybody.

The only member of the House of Lords to deal with this problem in *Majewski* was Lord Salmon, and he appears to have contemplated that the drunkard would not be liable for a "pure accident."[12] This seems reasonable at first sight. *Majewski* may be said to apply only to what may be called acts of aggression, where the defendant tried, in however confused a way, to interfere with the person or property of another. For (the argument may run) the rationale of the intoxication rule does not apply to acts of intoxicated clumsiness. However, the other lords in *Majewski* did not incorporate the limitation into their opinions.

The solution lies in the argument previously advanced, that even on a charge of a crime of basic intent the jury must have regard to all the evidence except the evidence of intoxication in determining the defendant's intention. If the evidence is that the defendant stumbled against someone who then fell under a bus, the defendant's explanation that he fell, from whatever cause, would readily be accepted as negativing intention in the absence of evidence of malign motive.

The rule in *Majewski* has been accepted by the Supreme Court of Canada.[13] But the High Court of Australia is more determined to preserve the intellectual integrity of its penal law; it rejected the decision of the House of Lords in *DPP* v. *Smith*, and now it has rejected *Majewski*.[14] (We have still to see whether it continues its independent line by rejecting the third case of the unhappy trio, *Caldwell*.)

The CLRC proposed in its report on offences against the person that the implausible device of specific intent should be abolished, intoxicated trouble-makers being judged honestly on the issue of intention but made automatically liable for crimes of recklessness.[15] It hardly needs to be said that this would be a very welcome simplification of the law. As we have seen, the House of Lords has implemented the second of the two recommendations by judicial fiat; but it has not attempted any clean-up in compliance with the first.

§ 21.5. INTOXICATION AND MISTAKE

The drunkard (or, of course, drug-taker) who does what may be called a criminal act (the *actus reus* of a crime) owing to a mistake of fact is the target of three rules of law. *Majewski* may make him constructively guilty of intending what he does; *Caldwell* may make him constructively reckless

---

[12] Lord Salmon said: "An assault committed accidentally [*sic*] is not a criminal offence. [But] a man who by voluntarily taking drink or drugs gets himself into an aggressive state in which he does not know what he is doing and then makes a vicious assault can hardly say with any plausibility that what he did was a pure accident which should render him immune from criminal liability." This implies that if the case is not one of assault (or, presumably, of intentional attack upon property) but of "pure accident" even an intoxicated person can escape liability. See further, 1st edn 424–425.

[13] *Leary* (1977) 33 CCC (2d) 473.

[14] *O'Connor* (1980) 29 ALR 449. See Fairall in [1980] 4 Crim.LJ (Aus.) 264.

[15] 14th Report, Cmnd 7844, para.267.

as to it; and the doctrine of *Albert* v. *Lavin* (§ 6.8), that a mistaken belief as to a matter of defence cannot be considered unless it is reasonable, may make him guilty of negligence even when the crime requires intention. Further complication is caused by statutory provisions relating to knowledge or belief. How is one to sort all this out?

The answer will make this the stodgiest chapter in the book, and readers who have no immediate concern with the problem of intoxication and mistake will probably find that it imparts more information than they wish to have. If you do not wish to involve yourself in it you will not find your understanding of the rest of the book impaired if you choose to pass it over.

Well, then, dear reader, if you are still here, it seems that a legal problem in this area can best be solved by asking three questions; and they must be asked in the following order.

First question: does the offence include a requirement of knowledge or belief that a fact exists?

If the offence requires proof of knowledge of a fact, evidence of intoxication can help to negative that knowledge. A beautifully fair, simple and rational rule, and would that the rest of the law on this subject were the same!

> For example, take the offence of handling stolen goods knowing them to be stolen. A man may buy goods at a low price from a suspicious-looking character in a public house, and when charged with handling stolen goods he may support his defence of innocence by saying that he was a bit light-headed and did not notice circumstances that otherwise he would have noticed. It has been judicially assumed that the defence is allowable.[1] Although handling is not a crime of specific intent, because the handler need have no intent beyond his present intent to handle, it is a crime with a specific requirement of knowledge, and the courts, very properly, do not feel able to exclude evidence of intoxication in adjudicating whether the statutory requirement of knowledge was present.

Awkwardly, the law is different if it refers not to knowledge but to intent (even though intention includes knowledge). Suppose, to take a hypothetical based on an actual incident, a man charged with assaulting a policeman gives evidence in his defence that after taking a drug he hallucinated and thought he was about to be attacked by a great black bear. The "bear" was the policeman. All the offences against the person presuppose action directed against a human being, and if the drug-taker's hallucination were treated in the same way as a sober mistake it would give immunity from conviction of a crime of intent. Now the law according to *Majewski* states that assault is a crime of basic intent and that evidence of voluntary intoxication cannot negative the intent. So our drug abuser would be convicted of assault—even of intentional (as opposed to merely

[1] *Durante* [1972] 1 WLR 1612, 3 All ER 962.

reckless) assault if the jury or magistrates think that they would have accounted the assault intentional had they not heard the evidence of drug-taking.

I don't see why there should be this distinction between the issue of knowledge (on which you say that evidence of intoxication can afford a defence, even in crimes of basic intent) and the issue of intention (where, on a charge of a crime of basic intent, such evidence is unlikely to exclude liability).

The distinction is illogical, but it does not seem to work too badly in the present instance. The decision in *Majewski* is motivated chiefly by a desire to secure the conviction of drunkards who act aggressively, and the main crimes of aggression are defined in terms of intention or recklessness, not of knowledge.

Some offences do not expressly require the prosecution to prove the defendant's knowledge that a fact was present but allow a defence of belief that the fact was absent, which (apart from the burden of proof) comes to very much the same thing. The effect of such a provision was before the court in *Jaggard* v. *Dickinson*,[2] a prosecution under the Criminal Damage Act s.1(1). The discussion of this case will become difficult, and the point is a finicking one; so if by this time your interest in the subject is on the wane I now give you a second opportunity to escape: you may skip the rest of the First Question and pass to the consideration of the Second Question.

The subsection just mentioned was explained before, in connection with *David Smith*, and you may like to re-read that discussion (§ 6.2 at n. 4) before proceeding.

> Ms Jaggard after a convivial evening in a tavern bethought herself of sleep. She seems to have been on very good terms with the owner of a certain house, because he (if it was a "he") had given her permission to use it as if it were her own. History does not record whether she was living in it, but we are told that that was the house to which she chose to repair for slumber. All the doors of the house she tried were locked, so she had to break a window to get in.
>
> As you may have guessed, from the lady's appearance in the law reports and this textbook, she had selected the wrong house.
>
> She was charged with criminal damage under section 1(1); evidence was given of her intoxication and consequent mistake; but the justices nevertheless convicted. They reasoned that this was a crime of basic intent (as it was), Jaggard's intoxication was voluntary (it was), and so *Majewski* told them to ignore evidence of intoxication on the issue of intent (it did). Full marks for the justices? No. Marvellous to relate, the conviction was reversed by the Divisional Court.

Under the definition of the offence in section 1(1) (which was given before in the discussion of *David Smith*), if it had stood alone, Jaggard's conviction would quite possibly have stood. The evidence of intoxication would have had to be ignored on the question of recklessness and also of intention (the crime being one of basic intent), and by closing their eyes to such evidence the justices might have been justified in finding that the defendant damaged the property of another without lawful excuse, both intentionally and recklessly. But the Act contained a further provision. Although the wording of the offence does not say in terms that the owner must not have consented to the act, or that the offender must have known that he had no right to damage the property, section 5(2)(*a*) covers a good deal of the ground by allowing a defence of belief in the existence of certain exempting facts. This provision, like the rest of the Act, was the work of the Law Commission, who were thorough-going subjectivists and wished to make sure that the issue of belief in right would be judged

[2] [1981] QB 527.

according to the defendant's real state of mind. The subsection accordingly provides in effect that the defendant has a defence if he believed that the owner (i) had consented or (ii) would have consented if he had known the circumstances. Jaggard's belief was that she was acting with the owner's consent (as she would have been, if it had been the right house). Section 5(3) provides, to make assurance doubly sure, that 'for the purposes of this section it is immaterial whether a belief is justified or not if it is honestly held.' The Divisional Court applied the section and allowed a defence according to its terms. In adjudicating whether Jaggard had the requisite belief one had to look at all the facts, including the evidence of intoxication.

It may seem difficult to fit this decision in with the other cases on intoxication. The courts ignore evidence of intoxication when a statute requires proof of intention for a crime of basic intent. Why are they suddenly so submissive to Parliament when the statute refers to knowledge or belief?

There is no clear-cut answer to this question. But when the judges honour the intention of Parliament on a *mens rea* issue, it would be surly to remind them of all the occasions when they have not done so and are not doing so. The decision is an occasion for rejoicing. Indeed, one wonders why the prosecution was ever brought. The damage Jaggard did was small, and the mistake she made was unlikely to be repeated. No sufficient social purpose would be served by convicting the drunkard who in very unusual circumstances damages property in the belief that he has a right to do so. He is civilly liable to the owner, and that is enough.

The decision in *Jaggard* can be technically, very technically, distinguished from *Majewski* by saying that the latter case applies only to statutory requirements of intention, and from *Caldwell* by saying that that applies only to statutory requirements of recklessness (whereas *Jaggard* involved an issue of knowledge). The Criminal Damage Act is not merely worded in terms of intention or recklessness; it also contains the specifically subjective provision in section 5(2). The court in *Jaggard* v. *Dickinson* felt that in view of the wording of section 5(2) it had reached the limit of possible disobedience to an Act of Parliament. (Not that it confessed that the courts ever do disobey Parliament, of course.) Donaldson LJ said that section 5(2) and (3) had to be applied so as to give a defence even to drunkards, because it was illegitimate to read the section as though it contained an exception for voluntary intoxicaton.

So much for the actual decision. Suppose the case had fallen within the other part of section 5(2)(*a*), because Jaggard, though not believing that the owner had consented, believed that the owner would have consented if he had known the circumstances? It seems that Jaggard's mistake would then have related to a matter of defence, so that normally (apart from section 5) it would be no defence unless it were reasonable; and presumably a belief brought about by intoxication would never be accounted reasonable, because a reasonable sober person would not have held it. (See under the Second Question, below.) Even so, it seems plain from the judgments in *Jaggard* v. *Dickinson* that the court would loyally have accepted section 5 according to its plain meaning, having regard to its explicit wording, and allowed the evidence of intoxication to be taken into account.

What, then, if the facts were slightly varied so as to fall outside section 5 altogether? Suppose that Jaggard had besottedly believed that the house was her own. She would then not have had any belief that the owner "consented." (You can hardly talk of your own consent to what you do to yourself.) So section 5(2) would not have applied according to its words; and probably the court would not have stretched the words to cover the case—even though in common sense the case would be on all fours with the situations mentioned in section 5, or, indeed, *a fortiori*. The court would probably decide to leave the case to fall under Question 3. This does not mean that the defendant would be convicted. On principle, she should still be acquitted, for reasons to be given later. And that is common sense, for if a drunkard is acquitted when he thinks that he is breaking into a friend's house with his permission, it would be strange indeed if he were convicted when his belief was that he was breaking into his own house.

The earlier case of *McPherson*,[3] which at first sight looks very similar in point of principle, was not cited in *Jaggard* v. *Dickinson*.

---

[3] [1973] RTR 157, Crim.LR 457. Cp. *Majewski* [1977] AC at 477D.

> *McPherson* held that the offence of taking a conveyance, being one of basic intent, did not permit evidence of intoxication to show that the defendant was incapable of forming any intent. The section of the Theft Act 1968 creating this offence contains a provision (section 12(6)) virtually identical with that in section 5(2)(*a*) of the Criminal Damage Act, saying that no offence is committed if a conveyance is taken in the belief that the taker has lawful authority or that he would have the owner's consent if the owner knew of the circumstances, but counsel for McPherson did not rely on this provision.

The two cases differ in one relevant respect. McPherson's defence was not one of belief in the owner's consent; it was one of complete absence of any mental state, and so did not fall within section 12(6) which requires the defendant's positive belief. So the case is properly distinguishable from *Jaggard* v. *Dickinson*. Evidently, if Jaggard's defence had been that she was too drunk to know what she was doing, she would have been convicted.

These subtleties are highly unsatisfactory, particularly because the outcome of the case may depend on the wording of legislation that was drafted without the problem of intoxication in mind.

Second question: does the issue relate to a definitional element or to a matter of defence?

After this long discussion I revert to the supposition that you have some problem case on intoxication, and I now suppose that your case does not concern a requirement of knowledge or belief. You are therefore driven to consider the difficult and obscure distinction between the definition of an offence and matters of defence (§ 6.8).

If the mistaken belief relates to the definition of the offence (such as a man's belief that the woman with whom he is performing the act of sex has consented; this belief was held in *Morgan* § 6.6 to relate to a definitional element), then you pass to Question 3.[4]

If the mistake relates to a matter of defence, then to be a defence it must be reasonable; so if due to intoxication it is disregarded, and that is the final answer. In the 19th century, in the happy days before the invention of basic intent and the rule against unreasonable mistakes, the drunkard who attacked in imaginary defence was let off a charge of assault and everything else except manslaughter and the special intoxication offences like being drunk and disorderly.[5] Now, in our more enlightened and tolerant age, he can be guilty even of a crime of specific intent.

> If, for example, a person kills another in the firm but drunken and mistaken belief that he has to act immediately in self-defence, he can (astonishing as it may appear) be convicted of murder. (Not that he would be likely to be; a verdict of manslaughter would be wangled somehow.)

Third question: is the offence one of specific or basis intent?

If no statute introduces an issue of knowledge or belief, and if the defendant sets up a mistaken belief as to a definitional element and not as to a matter of defence, you come to the *Majewski* question. Is the offence one of specific or basic intent?

The reasoning then trifurcates.

---

[4] In the "black bear" hallucination discussed previously, the mistake should be regarded as definitional, notwithstanding that it also relates to the necessity for self-defence.

[5] 1st edn 454 n. 15.

- If the offence you are considering is of specific intent, the evidence of intoxication will be taken into account on the issue of intention.
- If it is an offence of recklessness, *Caldwell* will apply, and will greatly limit the utility of evidence of intoxication.
- If it is an offence of basic intent (and, of course, the same offence may be both an offence of recklessness and one of basic intent), *Majewski* will apply, and will render evidence of intoxication legally irrelevant on the issue of intent.

If you wish to keep to the highroad you can end your reading of this section here. If you have previously wallowed with me in the complexities of *Jaggard* v. *Dickinson*, I have something more to add.

Go back to the hypothetical of a woman like Jaggard breaking into someone else's house when drunk, except that in this hypothetical her drunken belief is that it is her own house. She is not protected by section 5, so you passed to Question 2. Here you would have found that her mistake relates to a definitional fact (whether she is damaging "property belonging to another," as section 1(1) of the Criminal Damage Act specifies). This means that you did not go down the snake of unreasonable beliefs in Question 2, but went on to the present Question. *David Smith* shows that the mistake would be a complete defence for a sober person, on general *mens rea* principles. But it is an offence of basic intent; so a mistake due to intoxication is affected by *Majewski* (as regards intention), as well as by *Caldwell* (as regards recklessness).

We may consider more closely the question for the jury (or, of course, for magistrates) in the above hypothetical. It seems that the question for the jury on intention would be: Putting out of your minds the evidence on intoxication you have heard, would you, without that evidence, have found that beyond any reasonable doubt the defendant intended to damage the property of another, i.e. that he knew that this property belonged to another, and is not telling the truth when he now says that he believed it was his own? Asking this sort of question is extremely artificial, but it seems to be the one required by *Majewski*, read in the light of other principles of law.

There is no inevitability of a conviction on the issue. The defendant may give evidence that he mistook the house; the two houses (his own, and he one he broke into) may be close together and look much alike; the visibility may have been bad; the defendant has never been convicted of an offence of dishonesty or damage; he did not steal anything, and had no ascertainable motive for breaking into a neighbour's house, and so on. So the jury may well say (I think they would be bound to say) that they would have acquitted even if they had not heard the evidence of intoxication. They would believe the defendant when he said he mistook the house, even leaving aside the evidence of intoxication; or at least they would not disbelieve him.

On the issue of recklessness, the question for the jury under *Caldwell* is or should be: Are you sure that if the defendant (not some hypothetical reasonable person) had been sober he would not have made a mistake? (See § 5.3.) If you are sure, find him reckless; if not, acquit. So *Caldwell*, like *Majewski*, does not necessarily condemn the person who makes a mistake when intoxicated.

These points were not taken in *Jaggard* v. *Dickinson*, but they may be thought to show that the magistrates would have been wrong in convicting even if section 5 had not been included in the Act. The magistrates laboured under what seems to be a common misapprehension, that voluntary intoxication in the case of a crime of basic intent precludes any defence of lack of *mens rea*. In my opinion it is not so, or should not be so.

Apply the same two questions on a charge of rape where the defendant sets up a defence of belief in consent resulting from his intoxication. The jury would probably find it easy to reach the conclusions (i) that (on the issue of intention or knowledge) if they had not heard the evidence of intoxication they would have found that the defendant knew that the woman was not consenting, and (ii) that (on the issue of recklessness) if he had been sober he would have known of the risk (or of the fact) that she was not consenting. So the man would probably go down on both counts, of intention and recklessness.[6]

What if liability depends on negligence?

Offences of negligence require, at most, a basic intent, but some of them do not require that. The principle clearly is that the intoxicated defendant must comply with the same standard of care as the sober one.[7]

The almost intolerable fictions and complexities that beset problems of intoxication are a sufficient condemnation of the refinements that the courts have introduced into what could and should be straightforward law. The position would be immensely improved if the requirement of reasonableness for sober mistakes were abolished (as recommended by the CLRC), and also (again as recommended by the CLRC) the rule in *Majewski*. The drunkard would still be more than adequately catered for by crimes of recklessness coupled with the intoxication rule in *Caldwell* (the latter preferably put on a statutory footing and subjected to certain qualifications).

§ 21.6. INVOLUNTARY INTOXICATION

We have been speaking of "voluntary" ("self-induced") intoxication.[1] The law is different for involuntary intoxication, as where I think I am partaking of some innocent libation when in fact my companion has laced it with gin; or where I become unwittingly affected by medicine, not having been warned by my doctor.[2]

In crimes of specific intent the only question is one of *mens rea*. In crimes of basic intent, the House of Lords recognised in *Majewski* that involuntary intoxication negativing *mens rea* would be a defence, even though voluntary intoxication would not. The distinction between voluntary and involuntary intoxication depends upon whether the defendant knowingly took an intoxicating substance otherwise than under medical advice.[3]

---

[6] Lord Simon assumed in *Majewski* ([1977] AC at 477D–E) that a drunken belief of this kind would be automatically disqualified from consideration, but it is suggested that the question has to be examined as stated in the text above.

[7] See *Lipman* § .3 at n. 10, where, however, the decision was put on constructive manslaughter.

[1] The qualifiers must be read in a technical sense; neither is completely satisfactory. Intoxication may be the result of the defendant's own act and yet not be thought of as self-induced—namely, where the defendant did not know he was taking an intoxicant (see next note). Intoxication is voluntary for the present purpose even though the defendant did not mean to become intoxicated, if he knew he was taking an intoxicant.

[2] For an example of a drug taken under medical advice see *Quick*, § 29.2. The intoxication of an addict is not thought of as involuntary.

[3] A statutory definition was proposed by the Butler Committee on Mentally Abnormal Offenders, Cmnd 6244 of 1975, para. 18.56. In *Eatch* [1980] Crim.LR 650, where the defendant said that his intoxicating drink was, unknown to him, fortified with something more potent, the judge left it to the jury in general terms to decide whether the defendant's mistake was due to voluntary intoxication. A curious question arises where a drug is taken under medical advice but the patient disregards accompanying advice as to his regimen under the drug (as, that he should take regular meals after a dose of insulin). If he disobeys the instructions (not taking regular meals), a state of intoxication that results may be regarded as voluntary. See J C Smith in [1973] Crim.LR 436–437.

Isn't the distinction whether the defendant was at fault?

No: whether he knowingly took a drug that in sufficient quantity would be intoxicating. It seems that intoxication would be regarded as voluntary if the defendant knowingly took an intoxicating substance, even though it had an unexpectedly great effect upon him. He need not, apparently, have set out to become intoxicated.[4] The whole matter will be further examined in Chapter 29.

In crimes of negligence, an exemption for involuntary intoxication (or, rather, non-negligent intoxication) is obviously required by both logic and justice. Where a hopelessly drunk person does some fuddled act that is legally characterised as negligent, his real negligence consists in having incapacitated himself by drink. So, if he was not negligent in getting drunk, he should be excused.

SUMMARY

Drunkenness is not generally an offence unless it occurs in a public place or § .1
relates to the charge of a motor vehicle.

Intoxication is not in itself insanity, being a self-induced condition. It may, § .2
however, result in insanity.

In *Majewski* the House of Lords finally established the rule that although § .3
evidence of intoxication can negative *mens rea* in crimes of specific intent, it cannot do so in crimes of basic intent. The former class includes murder, wounding with intent, criminal damage with intent to endanger life, theft, offences involving an intent to deceive or defraud, and attempt. If a person deliberately gets drunk in order to commit a crime his prior intention may be coupled with his later act. Crimes of basic intent include various lesser offences against the person and property.

The theoretical basis of the distinction is extremely unsatisfactory, and it accords § .4
only roughly with a social or moral classification of crimes. When a crime of basic intent is charged, evidence of intoxication does not totally exclude the issue of intention, but intention must be judged solely on the other evidence. If, for example, the evidence is that the defendant caused injury by lurching into someone the tribunal may find that the injury was unintentional.

When evidence is given of a mistake caused by intoxication, three questions § .5
arise. (1) Does the offence include an element of knowledge or belief that a fact exists? If so, the court will generally give the defendant the full benefit of the requirement, interpreted subjectively. (2) Did the mistaken belief relate to a matter of defence? If so, it is no defence. (3) Other cases fall to be decided by applying the principles relating to crimes of specific intent, basic intent, and recklessness.

Evidence of involuntary intoxication is regarded as relevant even for crimes of § .6
basic intent. Intoxication is voluntary when the defendant knowingly took an intoxicating substance otherwise than under medical advice.

---

[4] But Lord Elwyn-Jones stated the law narrowly in *Majewski*. See J C Smith in 1 Ox.Jrnl.Leg. Stud.129.

Chapter 22

DISCIPLINE AND AUTHORITY

Second Watchman:	If we know him to be a thief, shall we not lay hands on him?
Dogberry [a constable]:	Truly, by your office, you may; but I think they that touch pitch will be defiled.

Much Ado About Nothing III. iii

§ 22.1. DISCIPLINE

PARENTS have the right to use reasonable disciplinary measures against their children, but what is reasonable will vary according to the spirit of the time. The right lasts up to an age that is not altogether clear but is perhaps 16 and is certainly no higher that 18.[1] School-teachers may also administer discipline in respect of matters pertaining to the school. This is frequently said to rest on implied delegation from parents, but there are difficulties. Perhaps anyone who has temporary supervision of children, including a bus conductor, may do what is reasonable to control them.[2]

Discipline includes the use of force to restrain the juvenile from misbehaving. At common law it includes corporal punishment. Such punishment can now, according to the circumstances, be regarded as a breach of the European Convention on Human Rights.[3] Although the Convention does not take direct effect in English law, it may well have an effect on the decision what discipline is reasonable. The general subject of parental and school discipline is treated in works on the law of tort and will not here be further considered.

Some disciplinary powers are given by legislation. This is so for discipline in prisons and the armed forces (though corporal punishment has been abolished). At common law the master even of a merchant vessel may take all reasonable means to preserve discipline by crew and passengers,[4] and the authority is now supplemented by statute for ships[5] and aircraft.[6] Of course, the master's discipline no longer means lashing or putting in irons; it involves no more than restraining passengers or crew who are endangering the vessel or those aboard, or who are seriously disrupting life aboard. Presumably, similar powers are possessed at common law by the

[1] It need hardly be said that husbands have no right to chastise or imprison their wives: *Reid* [1973] QB 299.

[2] See Eekelaar in 89 LQR 224.

[3] See the decision of the European Court of Human Rights in *Campbell and Cosans* (1982), discussed by Pogany in 132 NLJ 344.

[4] *The Lima* (1837) 3 Hag.Adm. 346, 166 ER 434; *Hook* v. *Cunard SS Co. Ltd.* [1953] 1 All ER 1021.

[5] Merchant Shipping Act 1970 s.79; § 36.4. See also, for offences by passengers, MSA 1894 s.287.

[6] Tokyo Convention Act 1967 s.3; Air Navigation Order, SI 1972 No. 129 art. 46 (cp. reg. 83 on penalty); § 36.4.

authorities of a psychiatric hospital. Quite apart from common law powers, the Mental Health Act 1959 s.141 (as amended) erects a statutory barrier to protect the staffs of psychiatric hospitals against prosecutions in respect of compulsorily detained patients: the consent of the DPP is needed, and bad faith or negligence must be proved.[7] The subject of discipline thus merges into that of public authority.

§ 22.2. PUBLIC AUTHORITY: POWERS OF ARREST

The powers of interference with persons and property possessed by public officials (and by private individuals on public grounds) are extremely numerous. The rest of this chapter is concerned only with the right to use force to prevent crime or effect an arrest. We begin with arrest, but with a prefatory remark.

The law of arrest has for centuries been an Augean stable, because of its neglect by the Home Office. New statutory powers of arrest are continually being added, but they vary vastly in their details and are obscure on many points. Despite the practical importance of the subject we can deal with it only in outline, because not only is it complicated but it is not wholly relevant to a book on the substantive criminal law. It comes within our purview for two reasons.

First, a *valid* arrest is a justification on the charge of an offence like assault and false imprisonment, which would otherwise be regarded as being committed against the person arrested. An *illegal* arrest, in contrast, is not, properly speaking, an arrest at all[1]; it can be called an "arrest" only when the word is used in invisible quotation marks. An illegal "arrest" is no more an arrest than an illegal "marriage" is a marriage. It is a false imprisonment, and frequently involves an assault.

Secondly, certain offences connected with the administration of justice involve proof that the defendant was resisting or escaping from arrest or other unlawful detention, or helping someone else to do so. These offences are escape, rescue, assault with intent to resist arrest, wounding with intent to resist lawful apprehension, and (where a question of arrest is involved) assaulting an officer in the execution of his duty.[2]

In these two ways the law governing the validity of an arrest enters into the substantive law. Nevertheless, it belongs primarily to criminal procedure. For this reason the following relatively brief statement of the law is reduced, for the most part, to the gabble of small print, and the

---

[7] The following were decided on the section before its amendment by MH(A)A 1982: *R* v. *Bracknell JJ, ex p. Griffiths* [1976] AC 314; *Carter* v. *Commr. of Police of the Metropolis* [1975] 1 WLR 507, 2 All ER 33; *Runighian* [1977] Crim.LR 361; *Kynaston* v. *Secretaries of State* (1981), The Times, February 19, discussed by Ash in 131 NLJ 297.

[1] See Clarke and Feldman in [1979] Crim.LR 702, [1980] *ibid.* 74.

[2] In these cases the burden of proving that the custody was lawful and also the evidential burden are on the prosecution: *Dillon* [1982] 1 All ER 1017; see note in [1982] Crim.LR 439.

reader is left to decide whether he wishes to include it within his present study.

An arrest may be on warrant or without a warrant.

The police have a general power to arrest on warrant. Warrants of arrest are obtained from magistrates, and there are certain rules limiting their issue.[3] In practice the police generally try to get along without warrants.

Powers of arrest without warrant (summary arrest) are bewildering in their variety. They are given not only by the common law and general Acts of Parliament (some operating in particular areas only[4]) but by local Acts of Parliament, many of which are not available in law libraries; and they are given both to the police and, less commonly, to persons holding particular positions and the public at large.

Since the requirements of a valid arrest vary from one statute to another, the law is a minefield for the arrester, and the police cannot be expected to have more than a rough knowledge of it. The arresting officer, acting under stress, often cannot verify his powers with reasonable precision; yet he is liable in damages if he exceeds them. Nor are the powers always adequate. We lack any *comprehensive* provision allowing an offender to be summarily arrested, even when he is caught in the act, even when he is obstructing the police in the execution of their duty,[5] and even when an arrest is necessary to establish the offender's identity.[6] Much wider powers will be given to the police if a proposed Police and Criminal Evidence Bill is passed, but there will still be many matters pertaining to the law of arrest that will remain in doubt.

Three powers of summary arrest may be picked out as being of some width.

(1) By an Act of 1851 anyone can arrest any person found committing an indictable offence in the night (that is to say, between sunset and sunrise).[7]

(2) By the Criminal Law Act 1967 s.2 as amended, everyone can arrest for what is inelegantly termed an "arrestable offence." This is defined as an offence for which the sentence is fixed by law (in effect, murder), or one that carries a sentence of imprisonment under any enactment for at least 5 years.

Note the words "under any enactment." Theft is an arrestable offence, because it carries a possible 10-year sentence under statute (even though the particular offender is afterwards discharged without punishment). But false imprisonment, libel, blasphemy and an attempt to pervert justice (which are offences at common law) are not arrestable, notwithstanding that they carry a theoretically possible life sentence, because this sentence is not specified in a statute. The reason for the limitation is that the common law offences have not been recently looked at by Parliament, and it was not thought wise to extend a comprehensive arrest provision to them.

---

[3] MCA 1980 s.1; D A Thomas in [1962] Crim.LR 520,597.

[4] E.g. the wide power given by the Metropolitan Police Act 1839 s.64, which allows the arrest of "loose, idle and disorderly persons" for any offence.

[5] *Wershof* v. *Comr of Police for the Metropolis* [1978] 3 All ER 540, 68 CAR 82. The point is frequently overlooked, both by the police and by lawyers.

[6] See 66 LQR 465. On powers of arrest in general see L H Leigh, *Police Powers in England and Wales* (London 1975); Thomas in [1966] Crim.LR 639; Williams, [1954] Crim. LR 6 and [1958] *ibid.* 73, 154. Brief and incomplete lists of statutory powers of arrest can be found in Moriarty, *Police Law*, or W J Williams, *Police Law*, Chap. 3.

[7] Prevention of Offences Act 1851 s.11. See 135 JPN 135.

An attempt to commit an arrestable offence is itself arrestable; so anyone can arrest for it.[8] So is a statutory conspiracy to commit an arrestable offence, and also a statutory conspiracy to commit a common law offence.[9]

An offence is not technically "arrestable" for legal purposes merely because it carries a special power of summary arrest under statute. There are many such special powers, but the only offences to which the name "arrestable" is given are (*a*) those just specified and (*b*) other offences declared by certain statutes to be "arrestable" even though they do not come within the definition of an arrestable offence. The meaning of an 'arrestable offence' is important because certain rules of law make use of this concept.

(3) Anyone can arrest at common law for a breach of the peace. "Breach of the peace" is a traditional legal expression and is a ground of arrrest, though it is not the name of an offence. All that a person need say when arresting on this ground is that he is arresting for a breach of the peace,[10] but the full rule as stated by the House of Lords is that

> "every citizen in whose presence a breach of the peace is being, or reasonably appears to be about to be, committed has the right to take reasonable steps to make the person who is breaking or threatening to break the peace refrain from doing so; and those reasonable steps in appropriate cases will include detaining him against his will."[11]

This is a minimum statement. Shortly before, in a different case, the Court of Appeal had stated the law more widely in four ways[12]:

- By allowing arrest for a breach of the peace already committed in the arrester's presence.[13] (The court did not add, as it should have done, that such arrest must be made immediately after the act.[14]); Nor did the court add, as it might have done, that reasonable suspicion would be enough—though it is unlikely that the arrester would make a mistake about what happens in his presence.)
- By allowing arrest not merely to make the offender stop his present offending but in order to bring him before the magistrates to punish him or have him bound over;
- by including any breach of the peace that is reasonably apprehended to take place in the immediate future, *whether in the presence of the person who intervenes or not*, and
- by giving a clear right to arrest without the restriction to "appropriate cases" made by the House of Lords (which their lordships left unexplained).

By this time you will be burning to know what a breach of the peace is. Is it a breach of the peace to give someone a push, or an uppercut under the chin? For many years the matter remained obscure; but the Court of Appeal in the case just referred to defined the expression as meaning, and as meaning only, "an act done . . . which either actually harms a person, or in his presence his property,[15] or is likely to cause such harm. . . ."[16] This definition includes an assault committed upon the arrester himself.[17] It does not cover swearing and making a loud noise as such; but making a disorderly noise can readily arouse a reasonable fear of a breach of the peace.[18]

---

[8] CLA 1967 s.2(1).

[9] CLA 1977 s.3; § § 18.2, 31.5. A common law conspiracy is not arrestable, since it is punishable at common law and not under an enactment. (Common law conspiracies have been mostly abolished.)

[10] *Howell* [1982] 1 QB at 427H.

[11] *Albert* v. *Lavin* [1981] 3 WLR 955. *Podger* [1979] Crim.LR 524 was wrongly decided: see [1982] 1 QB at 426C. For an example of detaining without arrest see *King* v. *Hodge* [1974] Crim.LR 424.

[12] *Howell* [1982] 1 QB, particularly at 426C.

[13] A person (such as a police officer) who comes late upon the scene may arrest with the authority of a person in whose presence the breach was committed: [1954] Crim.LR 584.

[14] Cp. *Wills* v. *Bowley* § 22.3 n. 4.

[15] Damaging property, even though only to a small extent, is anyway an arrestable offence:§ 41.1. It is strange that trivial damage is arrestable while an assault causing a serious affront is not.

[16] *Howell*, at p. 426G.

[17] But a person obviously ought not to arrest because he fears an assault on himself; an arrest is likely to precipitate the assault.

[18] On noise see *Hickman* v. *O'Dwyer* [1979] Crim.LR 309. See generally on breach of the peace 146 JPN 199, 217.

Independently of the common law, a police officer may of course arrest under a statutory power, such as the power to arrest for threatening etc. conduct under the Public Order Act 1936 s.5.[19] There is no power to arrest for obstructing the police.[20]

§ 22.3. ARREST ON REASONABLE BELIEF OR SUSPICION

Many powers of arrest are worded in terms of reasonable belief or reasonable suspicion or apprehension. The adjective "reasonable" is meant to give reassurance to the public that arrests will be made only on solid grounds, but in practice it is rare for either magistrates or the higher courts to find that a suspicion felt by the police was unreasonable. Claims that an arrest was made for reasonably apprehended breach of the peace are allowed by the courts so routinely that the inclusion of the word "reasonably" is generally functionless.[1]

It seems, though the matter is not clear, that:
- the wording in terms of "reasonable *belief*" theoretically requires the arrester to believe with the certainty required for a conviction, while
- a person who arrests on "reasonable *suspicion*" need not positively believe that the arrestee has committed an offence; it is enough that he reasonably believes that grounds exist for bringing him before a magistrate.[1]

What is perhaps not so obvious is that a person who is empowered to arrest when he reasonably suspects an offence must not only adduce evidence that there were reasonable grounds for suspecting; he must give evidence that he himself suspected.[2] Otherwise the arrest will be pronounced unlawful. What is even less obvious is that when the statute gives power to arrest if the arrester has "reasonable cause to suspect" the offence, it is still not enough that the arrester had such reasonable cause, if he does not say in court (the validity of the arrest being under enquiry) that he suspected.[3]

Even where the statute in terms gives a power of arrest only where an offence has been committed, the courts boldly interpret this as validating arrest on reasonable belief, although no offence has been committed. This is so, at least, if the power of arrest is given in terms of persons taken *in flagrante delicto*—i.e. where the offence was in process of being committed or had been committed immediately before the arrest.[4]

In laying down this rule the courts continue to luxuriate in complexity. The rule, while it confers a power of arrest upon the police, does not always clearly protect private persons making a "citizen's arrest", and where the offence was not committed the rule allows arrest

---

[19] For the offence see § 9.9 at n. 19; for the power to arrest see the Act s.7(3). The court in *Howell* (at p. 424A) expressed the tentative opinion that an arrest for a breach of the peace would cover an arrest under s.5, and this seems clearly right.

[20] § 9.8 n. 13. According to Austin in [1982] Curr.L Prob. 190 the police may express themselves as arresting for "obstruction," so that if challenged they can say that they meant obstruction of the highway (for which they can arrest). The proper answer to this ploy would be to hold that, being ambiguous, the communication is inadequate under the rule in *Christie* v. *Leachinsky* § 22.4 n. 5.

[1] For two examples see 146 JPN 217–218; *Ricketts* v. *Cox* § 9.7 n. 27. But see Bailey in [1982] Crim.LR 475–477. A complainant who wishes to challenge the reasonableness of police conduct stands his best chance of being upheld if he sues for damages; the question being purely financial, the courts are more likely to reach a conclusion favourable to him. Cp. *Reynolds* v. *Commissioner* [1982] Crim.LR 600, where the plaintiff was awarded £12,000 damages for one day's illegal detention.

[2] See Bailey and Birch in [1982] Crim.LR 549–551. A constable may act on information given him by others: *Siddiqui* v. *Swain* [1979] RTR 454.

[3] *Siddiqui* v. *Swain*, last note. It was further held, surely unreasonably, that the fact that the arrester was not cross-examined on the question of his belief makes no difference. See Bailey and Birch in [1982] Crim.LR 550–551.

[4] *Wills* v. *Bowley* [1982] 3 WLR 10. The rule applies even though the offence presented no danger to the public: *ibid*. See also note in [1982] Crim.LR 580.

only on reasonable belief that the offence *was* committed, not (a subtle, confusing and totally unnecessary distinction) reasonable suspicion that it may have been or even probably was committed.[5]

Some statutes expressly cover both arrest for an actual offence and arrest for a putative (reasonably suspected) offence. An important but again somewhat complex example is section 2 of the Criminal Law Act 1967 (the "arrestable offence" section mentioned before). The reason for the complexity here is unmeritorious: it is that the CLRC, which proposed the measure, was deeply suspicious of private arresters, particularly store detectives, and therefore wished to continue a rule previously invented by the judges, making the private arrester strictly liable for the correctness of his suspicions in one arbitrarily-defined situation. To this end, subsections (2)–(4) make separate provision for present and past offences. They run as follows.

> "(2) Any person may arrest without warrant anyone who is, or whom he, with reasonable cause, suspects to be, in the act of committing an arrestable offence.
> (3) Where an arrestable offence has been committed, any person may arrest without warrant anyone who is, or whom he, with reasonable cause, suspects to be, guilty of the offence.
> (4) Where a constable, with reasonable cause, suspects that an arrestable offence has been committed, he may arrest without warrant anyone whom he, with reasonable cause, suspects to be guilty of the offence.

These rules need careful study if their effect is to be understood. To begin with arrests by constables (an expression that includes prison officers), the rules mean that the arrest is valid if the constable reasonably suspects that the person arrested has committed the offence or is in the act of committing it.

If the arrest is by a private person (e.g. a store detective, a security guard, a steward at a public event, or a private vigilante), the law differs in an important respect. The private arrester cannot arrest for a past arrestable offence unless the offence in question was committed *by someone*, though not necessarily by the person arrested.

> If you, a private person, arrest on reasonable suspicion of a past theft, for example, you will be safe if the article in question was stolen by someone (even though not by the person you arrested). But if the article was lost by its owner and there was no theft you will be liable in damages to the person you have arrested.

Moral: do not arrest under this rule, but let the suspect depart unhindered. The responsibility for the failure of justice will rest not on you but on the legislature, in not giving you proper legal protection when arresting.

A rule like that in section 2, allowing arrest on reasonable but mistaken suspicion, applies only in respect of suspicion of matters of fact. If the arrester's mistake was one of law—if he believed that some act was an arrestable offence when it was not—he has no defence. His mistake as to the criminal law relating to justification is no more a defence than any other mistake of law. See § 23.5 n. 7.

The question may be asked why the arrester's belief or suspicion is required to be reasonable. Granted that one ought not to arrest on what one knows is merely a wild surmise, should not an arrest be valid if it is based on a belief (reasonable or otherwise) in facts that, if true, would show that an offence was committed or would otherwise afford a reasonable suspicion to justify an arrest?

Arrest on correct "hunch."

It may be strongly argued that if the statute allows an arrest where an offence is being or has been committed, then if the offence was in fact committed the arrest is lawful even though the arrester's suspicion was

---

[5] The rule does not clearly protect the private arrester unless the statute requires him to convey the arrestee forthwith before a justice: see the report at pp. 36E, 46H–47A. For the limitation to reasonable belief see the report at p. 47F.

unreasonable. It may be difficult for an arrester to forecast whether a court will subsequently regard his suspicion as reasonable; but the question ought not to be raised if the suspicion was in fact correct.

In addition to this practical argument there is an argument of policy and justice. The law in giving a power of arrest does so in order that offenders may, where necessary, be brought to justice. If this end has been secured, the arrester ought to be given qualified praise, and ought not to be penalised merely because he did not accurately know or believe the facts. What he did was objectively lawful.

There is some authority in support of this opinion, though also some the other way.[6] The point is, however, clear for section 2 of the Criminal Law Act: by expressly covering both actual criminality and reasonable suspicion of criminality the section obviously validates an arrest on unreasonable but correct suspicion. Otherwise the reference to actual criminality would be meaningless.

Duty to release when innocence established.

Where an arrest is allowed on reasonable suspicion, the arrester must, of course, release the suspect as soon as he realises that his suspicion was unfounded.[7]

The police frequently do not do this; they bring the suspect before the magistrates, even though they do not then press the case, because they believe that, whatever the law may say, by not confessing their fault they are safer from an action for false imprisonment.[8] The police may lawfully continue to hold the suspect on another charge, provided that they satisfy the requirements of the law of arrest. The initial arrest, if valid when made, is not invalidated by the fact that the police afterwards substitute a different charge.[9]

Arrest where no offence yet committed.

By the Criminal Law 1967 section 2(5):

> "A constable may arrest without warrant any person who is, or whom he, with reasonable cause, suspects to be, about to commit an arrestable offence."

When the police exercise this power it is not clear what they arrest for. Of course, if the suspect has reached the stage of attempt the police can arrest him for that. The question whether he has reached that stage need not be considered until the question of charging arises.[10]

Even if the suspect has not yet committed an attempt, the police may after arresting him find evidence that he was committing or had committed some other offence, such as "going

---

[6] See 2 Leg. Stud. 244–247. Cp. § § 7.7 at n. 3, 23.2 at n. 11.

[7] *Wiltshire* v. *Barrett* [1966] 1 QB 312.

[8] Another explanation was suggested, perhaps ironically, by C H Rolph in his cautionary tale *Mr Prone* (London 1977) 163: "He had been formally charged, they said—an irrevocable status in many a policeman's mind, a stigma from which a man may be cleansed only in a court of law. He was in the Wrong Book. You couldn't make a Refused Charge of him now."

[9] *Gelberg* v. *Miller* [1961] 1 WLR 153, 1 All ER 291. So an arrest may be made on a "holding charge" ([1954] Crim.LR 17), except that the police cannot continue to hold a person on a charge that they now realise is unfounded.

[10] Charging means the making of the formal charge in the police station; it is a matter of police practice and has no legal effect as a matter of substantive law.

equipped" (§ 38.7). They can charge such other offence, or simply warn the suspect and release him. The only other possibility is to bring the suspect before magistrates and have him bound over.[11] The suspect cannot be bound over unless he agrees; but if he does not agree he can be immediately sent to prison![12]

Section 2(5) does not apply to a citizen's arrest. Wisely, the law does not generally allow private people to arrest for feared offences in the future. But a private person can prevent crime under section 3 (§ .6), and can arrest (or at least temporarily detain) for a feared breach of the peace at common law.

The police have wider powers of early intervention under other legislation. They can arrest for attempting (or entering into a statutory conspiracy) to commit an arrestable offence, and under some special statutes for attempts to commit other offences. (But the fact that a statute empowers them to arrest for an offence does not in itself empower them to arrest for an attempt to commit it.[13]) They can arrest for various firearms offences,[14] for having offensive weapons in a public place,[15] and for the offence of being found on certain private premises for an unlawful purpose.[16] These and other provisions are in addition to the power to prevent crime to be considered in § .6.

§ 22.4. OTHER CONDITIONS OF A VALID ARREST

A constable or other person who proposes to make an arrest may merely announce the arrest to the suspect. He must use clear words: a polite request to the suspect to accompany him to the police station is insufficient. He must ensure that the arrestee understands that he is no longer a free man.[1]

If the suspect submits, he is taken to be under arrest. If he does not submit, there is no arrest until the arrester touches the suspect, telling him that he is under arrest. Thus if a suspect, on being told that he is under arrest, runs away, the policeman must pursue him and touch him before he is legally arrested.[2] The suspect's running away before arrest is no offence in itself. If he runs away after arrest he is guilty of an escape, and any who assist him are guilty of rescue. If, after being arrested, he simply refuses to accompany the officer, he is doubtless guilty of obstructing the officer in the execution of his duty.[3]

Where immediate action is required the arrester may, it seems, use immediate force to detain the suspect; the force is legally justified, but it would seem that the arrest is not complete until the arrester has made proper communication to the person arrested.[4]

The suspect must be informed at the time of arrest what essentially is alleged against him. This rule was established at common law in the

---

[11] This possibility was envisaged by the CLRC which recommended the measure: 7th Report para. 16.
[12] 16 MLR 425.
[13] [1955] Crim.LR 69.
[14] Firearms Act 1968 s.47
[15] Prevention of Crime Act 1953 s.1(3).
[16] § 38.5.

[1] *Inwood* [1973] 1 WLR 647, 2 All ER 645.
[2] See [1943] Crim.LR 12–14.
[3] For the offence see § 9.7.
[4] See Lanham in [1974] Crim.LR 294–296

celebrated case of *Christie* v. *Leachinsky*.[5] It requires the arrester to tell the suspect briefly the act for which the arrest is made (you killed X; you obtained goods from Y by deception), unless in the circumstances this is obvious to the suspect[6] or communicating with him is impracticable, as where the suspect fights or runs away.

Where the arrest is on warrant common sense suggests that the arrester should, in addition, state this fact. A statute requires that the warrant should, on the demand of the arrestee, be shown to him as soon as practicable; and obviously the suspect cannot claim to see the warrant if he has not been told that it exists. In one case the court, in an *obiter dictum*, said that a person is not entitled to know whether his arrest is on warrant or not, so long as he is told the act for which he is arrested[7]; but this cannot be right.

An arrest that is initially invalid can be subsequently (though not retrospectively) legalised—for example, by telling the arrestee the ground of the arrest when he arrives at the police station. The suspect is then lawfully arrested from that moment, but can still complain of his former illegal detention.[8]

The amount of force that may be used in the event of resistance to arrest is obscure; see § .6.

Various other problems relating to arrest have been omitted from this discussion, such as those relating to the right of entry upon premises to make an arrest,[9] the duty to bring the suspect before the magistrates, interrogation, search, fingerprinting, medical examination and identification procedures.

§ 22.5. DETENTION WITHOUT ARREST

The term "arrest" is generally used in connection with arrest for offences. In addition, the law gives certain powers to detain apart from offences or the suspicion of offences. For example, some mentally disordered persons may be removed to hospital[1]; a constable in uniform may stop drivers of

---

[5] [1947] AC 573. See also *John Lewis & Co.Ltd.* v. *Tims* [1952] AC 676; [1954] Crim.LR 16–17. An arrest is not invalidated merely because the arrester adds allegations that do not themselves justify the arrest (*Gelberg* v.*Miller* [1961] 1 WLR 753, 1 All ER 291), or mistakenly says that the arrest is on warrant (*Kulyncz* [1971] 1 QB 367). Since the officer who leaves out some fact that the court regards as essential will be guilty of false imprisonment, he is well advised to include as many charges as possible (valid or not) when he arrests. See also Bailey and Birch in [1982] Crim.LR 551–554.

[6] The "obvious ground of arrest" will lose its efficacy if the arrester states another ground which gives him no power to arrest: *Waters* v. *Bigmore* [1981] Crim.LR 408. So it is best for the arrester to be as vague and general in the communication he makes as is legally allowed, and he is well advised to avoid specifying the section of a statute that he thinks gives him authority.

[7] *Kulyncz*, n. 5 above, at 372C. The statutory rule is in MCA 1980 s.125(3); cp. Thomas in [1962] Crim.LR 527–531.

[8] *Kulyncz*, n. 5 above.

[9] For an indication of the complexity and obscurity of the law see note to *McLorie* v. *Oxford* [1982] Crim.LR 603; also Bailey and Birch in [1982] Crim.LR 554–557.

[1] Particularly under the Mental Health Act 1983 ss.135,136.

motor vehicles,[2] and an officer who has required a driver to supply a specimen under the excess alcohol provisions may detain him temporarily after he has provided the specimen[3]; and the police may detain people temporarily to search them for firearms[4] or illicit drugs[5] or (in the Metropolis[6] and some other areas) for property unlawfully obtained, where possession of these articles is reasonably suspected.[7]

It has been held that a statutory power to detain for search implies a power to detain for questioning without searching,[8] though presumably the questioning must be limited to the possession of objects for which there is power to search. Apart from this, and from powers of arrest, the common law recognises no power to detain except in certain situations of extreme necessity. The procedure laid down by statutes and by the judges for the exercise of the power of arrest would be set at naught if the police could achieve the same purpose by purporting to detain without arresting. In particular, as was remarked in the chapter on assault (§ 8.3), the police have no general power to detain suspects for questioning without arresting them (and even upon arrest their powers of interrogation are supposed to be limited). Illegal detention is a false imprisonment, and in practice would generally involve an assault; and the suspect's refusal to stay or to answer questions is not an obstruction of the police in the execution of their duty.[9] It is thought that this is still the law notwithstanding the disconcerting decisions on obstructing the police that have already been discussed.[10]

In practice, as we all know, the police do, illegally, detain people for questioning, because they feel that this is necessary in the public interest; and the judges turn a blind eye to the practice, for the same reason, unless the point is directly in issue before them. The trouble is that the practice thus winked at lacks necessary safeguards.

§ 22.6. FORCE TO PREVENT CRIME AND ARREST CRIMINALS

Force used in arrest and for the prevention of crime is legalised by the Criminal Law Act 1967 s.3, and this is almost the sole authority to be considered for the modern law.

> "(1) A person may use such force as is reasonable in the circumstances in the prevention of crime, or in effecting or assisting in

---

[2] RTA 1972 s.159, as amended by Transport Act 1981 s.26. The section does not state the purpose for which stopping is authorised. On stops for breath tests see § 14.6.

[3] RTA 1972 s.11 as substituted by Transport Act 1981.

[4] Firearms Act 1968 s.47.

[5] Misuse of Drugs Act 1971 s.23(2)(*a*).

[6] Metropolitan Police Act 1839 n. 66.

[7] See Leigh, *op. cit.* § .2 n. 6, Chap. 7. The rule in *Christie* v. *Leachinsky* (§ .4 n. 5) applies to these detentions: *Pedro* v. *Diss* [1981] 2 All ER 59, 72 CAR 193; *McBean* v. *Parker* [1983] Crim. LR 399; *Brazil* v. *Chief Constable of Surrey* The Times, April 8, 1983, [1983] Crim. LR 483.

[8] *Green* [1982] Crim.LR 604.

[9] See the authorities in § 8.3 n. 7, and for the offence see § 9.7 n. 13.

[10] § 9.7.

the lawful arrest of offenders or suspected offenders or of persons unlawfully at large.

(2) Subsection (1) above shall replace the rules of the common law on the question when force used for a purpose mentioned in the subsection is justified by that purpose."

Before the Act it was doubtful how far the police or private persons could use force to prevent minor offences.[1] The police now have unlimited powers under the section, subject to the requirement of reasonableness.[2]

In theory the section applies equally to private persons, but the ordinary citizen would be unwise to use force to prevent a motor cyclist from riding without protective headgear, for instance. He would run the risk of a finding that *no* force could "reasonably" be used to prevent such an offence. The section does not say that moderate (non-extreme) force can always be used when necessary to prevent a crime, so perhaps the citizen has to decide two questions: whether it is reasonable to use any force, and if so what force is reasonable.[3] But the section might perhaps be interpreted more widely. It does not say that force may be used *if* it is reasonable to prevent crime; it seems to assume that force may be used, declaring only that it must be reasonable (*scil.*, in amount). We await judicial determination of this.

Need it be apprehended that the crime will be committed immediately?

No.[4] But the force used must be immediately necessary. You may use force if it is immediately necessary to disarm a man who is running off to commit a crime elsewhere.[5]

Isn't this talk about reasonable force merely a disguise for the fact that there is no rule? Suppose someone is making off with my valuables, and I happen to have my shotgun handy. I want to know whether I can shoot. If the law simply tells me that I can do what is reasonable, that is pure waffle.

Your impeachment cannot be altogether contradicted. Section 3 gives no real guidance on the question when extreme force (involving the infliction of death or serious injury) may be used for the prevention of crime.

Before the Act there was authority for saying that anyone might kill to prevent a robbery,[6]

---

[1] The case law showed that the police could use force to prevent unlawful intimidation (*Tynan* v. *Chief Constable of Liverpool* [1965] 3 All ER 99), the obstruction of the highway (*Despard* v. *Wilcox* (1910) 74 JP 115, 22 Cox 258; *Tynan* v. *Chief Constable,* above; *Reed* v. *Wastie*, [1972] Crim.LR 221, The Times, February 10, 1972), and sedition (*Thomas* v. *Sawkins*, below at n. 22), and that anyone could prevent a felony or breach of the peace (*Timothy* v. *Simpson* (1835) 1 CM & R 757, 149 ER 1284).

[2] An illustration is *Reed* v. *Wastie*, last note; but although the decision was rested on s.3, the police had in fact power to arrest for the obstruction of the highway: see Highways Act 1959 s.121(2). Section 3 applies in respect of mere summary offences, and entitles the police to arrest if this is the only way of preventing the offence being committed or continued: *per* Lord Denning MR in *R* v. *Chief Constable of Devon and Cornwall* [1981] 3 WLR at 976E. (Lord Denning said "where the offender fails to give his name and address;" there is no specific authority for this qualification, but it should usually follow from the requirement of reasonableness.)

[3] The CLRC, in its 7th Report recommending the measure (Cmnd. 2659 of 1965 para. 23), said: "In the case of very trivial offences it would very likely be held that it would not be reasonable to use even the slightest force to prevent them."

[4] *Cousins* [1982] 2 WLR 621.

[5] *Farrell* v. *Sec. of State for Defence* [1980] 1 WLR at 179C–E.

[6] Hale, *PC* i 481.

"manifest theft,"[7] burglary,[8] arson,[9] rape,[10] or, in general, any "forcible and atrocious"[11] crime (whatever that meant). It would have been politically impossible in 1967 to get any such rules through Parliament; the best that could be done was to ask Parliament to approve a rule so vague that it is hardly a rule at all. So we are given only the test of reasonableness; and the old law is expressly abolished. On a charge of murder or manslaughter (to take examples), the jury are left to decide whether it was lawful to kill.

"Reasonableness" here gives a spurious unity to two questions:

1 Was the force used *necessary* , or believed to be necessary (or, rather, reasonably—there is no escaping the word—believed to be necessary) to prevent the offence? (Was there any other way of preventing it, according to the facts as they were reasonably believed to be, and—even if force had to be used—would a smaller degree of force have been sufficient?) This is a question of fact, apart from an incidental question of valuation in respect of the reasonableness of a mistaken belief.
2 Was the force *proportionate* to the evil to be avoided? This is a question of evaluation or social judgment.

We may call these the factual and evaluative questions respectively. They are much the same as the principle applied in relation to private defence, where further observations will be made upon them (Chap. 23).

On the factual question, suppose that the force used was not necessary in fact but the defendant mistakenly thought it was. Do you mean that if his belief in necessity was unreasonable he has no defence under the section?

If the courts were so disposed they could hold that the question of reasonableness is to be judged on the facts as the defendant believed them to be—in other words, that his belief need not be on reasonable grounds. On this construction, the question would be whether the force would be reasonable on the assumption that the defendant's belief was true. But, as we have seen (§ 6.8), the courts are now determined to require that a belief as to a matter of defence must be reasonable; and on one occasion the House of Lords assumed that this is how section 3 is to be interpreted. The defendant's conduct is not reasonable unless his belief was reasonable.

In *Attorney-General for Northern Ireland's Reference*,[12] a soldier in Northern Ireland shot and killed a suspected terrorist who had started to run away when challenged. The man turned out not to be a terrorist. For reasons that are hard to understand Parliament has not provided in any part of the United Kingdom that persons reasonably suspected of terrorism may when necessary be killed to prevent their escape; whether this is lawful is left to the courts to decide in their administration of section 3. The judge in Northern Ireland, sitting without a jury, acquitted the soldier of murder, one of the reasons

---

[7] See George P Fletcher, *Rethinking Criminal Law* 860–861.
[8] Hale, *PC* i 42; *Dennis* (1905) 69 JP 256; Leitch in 18 NILQ 322.
[9] Hale, *PC* i 488.
[10] Hale, *PC* i 486.
[11] Blackstone, *Commentaries* iv 180; but cp. *ibid*. 182.
[12] [1977] AC 105.

given being the somewhat surprising one that he had not intended to kill or seriously injure the deceased. On a reference to the House of Lords, their lordships, while expressing no disapproval of the judge's finding of fact, also discussed the legality of the shooting in terms of a legislative provision in Northern Ireland identical in terms with section 3. Lord Diplock, with whom several other members of the House concurred, assumed that the law was that if a person sets up a belief "the jury would have to decide whether any reasonable man on the material available to the accused could have shared that belief."[13] The test of reasonableness will probably be applied with particular indulgence to a person who has acted in good faith in the stress of the moment. Lord Diplock said: "The jury should remind themselves that the postulated balancing of risk against risk, harm against harm, by the reasonable man is not undertaken in the calm analytical atmosphere of the court-room after counsel with the benefit of hindsight have expounded at length the reasons for and against the kind and degree of force that was used by the accused; but in the brief second or two which the accused had to decide whether to shoot or not and under all the stresses to which he was exposed."[14]

It is the jury who make the evaluation, provided that there is sufficent evidence for the issue to go to the jury. To quote Lord Diplock again, the question for the jury is:

> "Are we satisfied that no reasonable man (*a*) with knowledge of such facts as were known to the accused or reasonably believed by him to exist (*b*) in the circumstances and time available to him for reflection (*c*) could be of opinion that the prevention of the risk of harm to which others[15] might be exposed if the suspect were allowed to escape justified exposing the suspect to the risk of harm to him that might result from the kind of force that the accused contemplated using."[16]

With the alleviations accepted by Lord Diplock there is probably little difference in practice, so far as the police and armed forces are concerned, between a defence of reasonable belief and a defence of belief, since an allegation of a wholly unreasonable belief would in any case be unlikely to be credited. However, a woolly word like "reasonable" is quite capable of a surreptitiously differential application, being adjudged indulgently for the forces of law and strictly for the private citizen. The CLRC has recommended an amendment of section 3 to permit a defence of belief simply (the evaluative question, however remaining objective).[17]

Another example of the evaluative question, somewhat more difficult than that presented in the Northern Ireland case, may be helpful.

> A group of strikers are trying to prevent me from driving along a stretch of highway leading to a factory. Assume that they are not exercising their statutory right of peaceful picketing. They form a line across the road. I am no match for them in a fight, but I can break the blockade by driving at them, with the risk of killing one of them. I do this, and run one of them down. Suppose that I am charged with manslaughter and set up a defence under section 3. On the question of fact, whether there was any other way in which I could enforce my right of passage, it may be argued that I should have driven slowly forward to give the strikers the chance to move away; but then they might have

---

[13] At p. 137H.
[14] At p. 138C.
[15] Presumably meaning "others than the suspect." The defendant would be entitled to count himself among those "others."
[16] *Ibid.* at p. 137F.
[17] 14th Report, Cmnd 7844, paras. 283, 287.

> clambered on the car, obstructed my vision and prevented me from proceeding. However this factual question is answered, the legal position obviously is that my right of passage along the highway is not sufficiently important to justify me in deliberately killing an obstructer or inflicting serious injury upon him. The legal point is so clear that the judge could probably direct the jury as a matter of law that they need not consider any defence under section 3.[18] The governing consideration is not the factual question but the evaluative one.

As the Report to the Criminal Code Bill of 1879 put it:

> "We take one great principle of the common law to be, that though it sanctions the defence of a man's person, liberty, and property against illegal violence, and permits the use of force to prevent crimes, to preserve the public peace, and to bring offenders to justice, yet all this is subject to the restriction that the force used is necessary; that is, that the mischief sought to be prevented could not be prevented by less violent means; and that the mischief done by, or which might reasonably be anticipated from the force used, is not disproportioned to the injury or mischief which it is intended to prevent."[19]

Apart from such generalities, little guidance is to be obtained from the authorities on what is reasonable to prevent crime. The only safe course for the citizen is not to use more than mild force. He may threaten more force than he may lawfully use.[20] He is not well advised to kill or inflict serious injury in defence of property or economic interests; the spirit of the time is against it. Don't "have a go;" let the criminal get on with it. This course may be pusillanimous and it may be contrary to the public interest, but the law does not provide the intervener with sufficient protection.[21]

Does the section allow the use of force against innocent third parties?

One can imagine a case where the use of mild force against an innocent third party would be adjudged reasonable and lawful. But injuring or endangering third parties would be unlikely to be held reasonable unless to avoid even greater danger to life, when the question in effect becomes one of necessity (§ 26.6).

Is it justifiable to commit a minor offence in order to frustrate a serious offender?

Section 3 will apply if the minor offence is one of using force. The section does not expressly authorise mild non-forcible measures to prevent crime.

Could the police be justified in using force to enter and remain on property in order to prevent crime?

Yes according to the general formula of the section, but difficulties loom up.

---

[18] In *Att.-Gen.'s Reference* [1977] AC at 137E, Lord Diplock said: "What amount of force is 'reasonable in the circumstances' for the purpose of preventing crime is, in my view, always a question for the jury in a jury trial, never a 'point of law' for the judge." His remark has been repeated by other judges, e.g. in *Cousins* [1982] QB at 530C. It is reminiscent of what Lord Diplock said in *Camplin* on provocation (§ 24.3 at n.4); but the two defences are legally different. On a defence of provocation, the evaluative question must now always be left to the jury, the former control of the judge being excluded by statute. On a defence of preventing crime the judge retains the control that he has over all defences other than provocation (see § 2.4 at nn. 7–10). S.3 of the CLA does not say, as s.3 of the Homicide Act 1957 does, that the question of reasonableness shall be left to be determined by the jury; it leaves the division of functions between judge and jury to the general law. Perhaps Lord Diplock was here speaking in relation to the Attorney-General's power to refer a point of law. It cannot be supposed that he was denying the power of the judge to withdraw the defence from the jury.

[19] C 2345 p. 11.

[20] *Cousins* [1982] QB at 625B.

[21] See generally Bennett and Rowe in 151 NLJ 991.

In the pre-Act case of *Thomas* v. *Sawkins*[22] the police entered a public meeting on private premises, reasonably believing that if they were not present seditious speeches would be made, and incitements to violence would occur. They were requested to leave, but used mild force in order to remain, and this was held to be justified as an exercise of the power of the police to prevent crime at common law.

One reason given for the decision was that the police had a right to be at the meeting because it was advertised as a public meeting and the police were members of the public; but this was obviously fallacious. Ordinary members of the public could have been requested to leave. Another reason was that since the police could use force to prevent crime, they could, *a fortiori*, enter premises to prevent crime. The decision was, of course, unpalatable to civil libertarians, and its authority remained doubtful before the Criminal Law Act; but that Act now seems to allow the use of force without restriction (save as to reasonableness), and therefore seems to allow force to be used to enter and remain on private property—whether a public meeting is taking place or not.

Some further support is given to this type of argument by a dictum in the Court of Appeal.

"If force is permissible, something less, for example, a threat, must also be permissible if it was reasonable in the circumstances."[23]

The *a fortiori* argument would suggest that if the police can fight their way in to private premises, then they can enter surreptitiously without force, if this is reasonably necessary to prevent crime; and that having entered they can, subject to the same restriction, blow open safes and copy private documents! But, as a judge once said, "an argument can be pressed to an absurdity, as a bubble may be blown until it bursts." It seems very unlikely that when Parliament passed the Act of 1967 it intended to allow the police to do a kind of "Watergate" for law-promoting reasons; or to sit in on a private meeting of an extreme political group, merely because the police reasonably feared that seditious statements would be made.

Suppose that an offence has been committed. What guidance does section 3 give in respect of the amount of force that can be used in making a lawful arrest for a crime that is not of great gravity?

The abstract principles are the same as those already considered, and, once more, they give little help. Before the Act there was authority for saying that even a sneak thief (if a felon) could be shot in order to prevent the theft or prevent his escape.[24] But this was never beyond doubt; and anyway section 3 abolishes the common law. Nowadays the citizen would be ill advised to use a gun against a fleeing thief, at any rate if the theft is a minor one.

In a case before magistrates, the defendant fired a shotgun at a man who, being surprised when attempting to break into his house, was running away; the intruder fell, and was discovered to be a notorious burglar whom the police had been seeking for 10 years, and who subsequently asked for 675 offences to be taken into consideration. The defendant was rewarded by being fined £5 for unlawful wounding.[25]

---

[22] [1935] 2 KB 249. See § 9.7 at n. 29.

[23] *Cousins* at p. 530B.

[24] *Dadson* (1850) 3 C & K 148, 175 ER 499, 2 Den. 35, 169 ER 407. *Contra, Murphy* (1839) 1 Craw. & Dix 20 (Ir.).

[25] 133 JPN 337, 547.

The doubt concerning the law affects the police and the armed forces. The subsection requires the force used to be reasonable, which seems to mean that the harassed officer has to decide not only whether he has power to act and whether the force he uses is necessary to stop the suspect in his tracks but in addition, and on the spur of the moment, a question of social values. In the past the police have been saved the difficulty of decision by the fact that they were unarmed; but nowadays if they are after armed men they are likely themselves to be armed. The officer can reckon to be safe in shooting an escaping murderer or escaping robber or other violent offender if he fears immediate danger from him to himself or others.[26] But the law is surprisingly unclear if he only fears possible danger in the future, or if he merely seeks to arrest for a past murder without fearing any danger from this offender for the future. Moreover, serious doubt remains whether it is reasonable for him (when he cannot otherwise effect an arrest) to shoot or otherwise use deadly force against someone who has not used or threatened force but is going off with the Crown Jewels, or the proceeds of a large bank robbery, or a Rolls Royce, or a Mini; or against one of the innumerable petty offenders that he has to deal with. How is he to draw the line? Would not the right rule be that the police are legally entitled to use all force necessary to arrest for an arrestable offence, or to prevent escape from such arrest, and to use necessary force short of the infliction of death or g.b.h. in respect of other offences? The way in which this power is exercised should be left to their own governance.[27]

The above discussion concerns the arrest of the fleeing offender. The subject of the resisting offender will be considered in § 23.4.

SUMMARY

§ .1 Parents, school-teachers and masters of vessels have certain disciplinary powers at common law. There are also statutory provisions for discipline in merchant ships, aircraft, prisons and the armed forces. Prosecutions against the staff of psychiatric hospitals in respect of compulsorily detained patients are subject to special restrictions.

§ .2, .3 Lawful arrest is a justification on a charge of various offences like assault, while the fact that a purported arrest is unlawful is a defence to a charge of resisting arrest etc. The text outlines some of the powers of arrest with and without warrant. An arrest will generally be valid notwithstanding the arrester's reasonable mistake of fact as to a ground of arrest, but not where the mistake was one of law (such as on the question whether the conduct intended was a crime).

§ .4 An arrest is effected by the use of words of arrest coupled with (1) touching the arrestee or (2) his submission to arrest. For the arrest to be lawful the arrester must state broadly the facts for which he is arresting (*Christie* v. *Leachinsky*), unless this is obvious or impracticable.

---

[26] See Lord Diplock's restricted statement quoted in § 23.2 n. 5.

[27] See further, 1st edn 443–444. An alternative rule would be that the police can use lethal force only if they reasonably fear that the person against whom they act will otherwise cause death or serious injury. This formula, which probably approximates to the present law in practice, would of course require the police to allow some very serious offenders (including some murderers and arsonists) to escape. See the provision in the Model Penal Code quoted by C P Walker in 43 MLR 594. In *Att.-Gen. for Northern Ireland's Refce* [1977] AC at 137D Lord Diplock said: "It has not been suggested that shooting to kill or seriously wound would be justified in attempting to effect the arrest . . . of a person who, though he was suspected of belonging to a proscribed organisation . . . was not also believed on reasonable grounds to be likely to commit actual crimes of violence if he succeeded in avoiding arrest." His lordship did not consider the possibility that all members of the Provisional IRA in Northern Ireland (the proscribed organisation he referred to) are guilty of complicity in the murders committed by that organisation, even though for reasons of policy they may not be charged as such.

There are various powers of detention without arrest, but except in the case of powers of search they give no power to detain for questioning without arresting. § .5

By the Criminal Law Act 1967 s.3(1), a person may use such force as is reasonable in the circumstances in preventing crime or in effecting or assisting in the arrest of offenders or suspected offenders. The test of reasonableness involves two questions: Was the force necessary (or reasonably believed to be necessary), and was it proportionate to the evil to be avoided? Both questions are left to the jury, provided that there is evidence sufficient to go to the jury on the defence. The jury should uphold the defence unless no reasonable man would have acted as the defendant did, given the circumstances and the time available to him for reflection (Lord Diplock). Section 3(1) fails to give guidance on many practical questions. § .6

CHAPTER 23

PRIVATE DEFENCE

Self-defence is the clearest of all laws: and for this reason—the lawyers didn't make it.

Douglas Jerrold

§ 23.1. THE SCOPE OF PRIVATE DEFENCE

JERROLD was not a lawyer, or he would have known that lawyers did create the right of self-defence, or at least restored it after taking it away. In early times, a homicide in self-defence or by misadventure "deserved but needed a pardon."[1] In the reign of Henry VIII such "excusable" homicides came to result in an acquittal. The limits of the right of self-defence are very much a matter of law, and, perhaps because lawyers did make it, the right is by no means free from doubt and difficulty. We may start with the generalisation that self-defence is, within limits, an excuse for any crime against the person or property.[2]

May one defend a stranger?

Some of the old books merely state a right to use force necessary to protect oneself and one's family, as though it does not extend to protecting strangers. Morally and rationally it ought to allow the defence of anybody. In our own times judges have evaded the issue by saying that, whether or not one can *defend* a stranger, one can prevent the commission of a crime against a stranger—which comes to much the same thing.[3] But other authorities, ancient and modern, take the sensible view that the right to defend others is not limited by family relationship.[4]

Because defence is not limited to self-defence, it is convenient to use "private defence" as a more general expression. Another useful term for force used in private defence is "protective force" (adopted in the Model Penal Code). Protective force can be used to ward off unlawful force, to prevent unlawful force, to avoid unlawful detention and to escape from such detention.

---

[1] Pollock and Maitland, 2nd edn ii 477 ff., 574.

[2] It applies not only to common law offences like affray (*Sharpe* [1957] 1 QB 552; cp. *Khan* [1963] Crim.LR 562; *Taylor* [1973] AC at 983) but to offences under statutes that make no provision for it and do not qualify the offence by the word "unlawfully": *Hanway* v. *Boultbee* (1830) 1 M & Rob. 15, 174 ER 6, 4 Car. & P 350, 172 ER 735; *Rose* (1847) 2 Cox 329. Cp. *Prince* (1875) 2 CCR at 178. So self-defence is available on a charge of assaulting a police officer in the execution of his duty: *Kenlin* v. *Gardiner* [1967] 2 QB 510; or resisting or obstructing the police: *Mahomed* [1938] AD 30 (S Africa); or threatening to kill: *Cousins* [1982] QB 526. In *Breau* (1959) 32 CR 13 (New Brunswick) it was held that a moose could be shot in self-defence notwithstanding that the statute did not mention this.

[3] *Duffy* [1967] 1 QB 63. In *Devlin* v. *Armstrong* [1971] NI at 35–36 it was specifically denied that the right of self-defence applied in respect of strangers; but that was the last of seven reasons for dismissing a hopeless appeal.

[4] *Walter* v. *Jones* (1634) 2 Rolle's Abridgement 526 (C) 3; East, *PC* i 289–292; *Tooley* (1709) 11 Mod. at 250, 88 ER at 1020; *Prince* (1875) 2 CCR at 178; *Spartels* [1953] VLR 194; *People* v. *Keatley* [1954] IR 12; *People* v. *Williams* (1965) 205 NE 2d 749; Russell, 12th edn i 680–681.

In the event of aggression, may one use protective force against someone who was not the aggressor? For example, could one take a hostage from the aggressor's family?

No. But self-defence may be exercised against one who may be called an innocent aggressor, like a lunatic. In other words, protective force may be used, and may be used only, against one who himself uses or is about to use (or is reasonably believed to be using or to be about to use) force that is unjustifiable in law, or who is (or is reasonably believed to be) guilty of false imprisonment. If any wider defence is allowed by law, it can only be under the doctrine of necessity.[5]

But if a raving lunatic attacks you and he doesn't know what he is doing he doesn't commit a crime; so how come you can defend yourself against him? Surely you can't defend yourself against a lawful act.

The lunatic has an excuse, on the ground of lack of *mens rea*; but his act of aggression is not authorised by law. It is not *justified*. This is one of the differences in law between a justification and an excuse.[6]

If two men fight, and one says he was acting in self defence, isn't there a formidable problem of proof?

Yes, and, in particular, a person who kills in what he conceives to be self-defence is subject to the serious risk that the emergency will not appear to the jury in the same light that it appeared to him.

When looking back at the incident, the fact likely to make the strongest impression is that a man has been killed; the transitory fear felt by the person prosecuted has left no memorial to compare with the tragic reality of the corpse. If there is a survivor of the incident on the other side, his account of what happened is likely to differ essentially from that of the defendant before the court. Even impartial spectators are unreliable witnesses to a sudden affray that is over in a few minutes or seconds. When the issue is one of self-defence, everything depends on which side was the aggressor, and the temporal order of events is therefore of high importance. But experiments indicate that this is difficult to establish by oral evidence. In particular, witnesses have been shown to have been unable to recall words with accuracy.[7] Hence arise two dangers in the administration of the law: unjust conviction, and unmerited acquittal after a concocted defence. Of the two risks, the former has to be taken the more seriously, and for this reason the law casts the burden of negativing the defence of self-defence upon the prosecution, only the evidential burden being rested on the defendant.[8] If the case is clearly one of self-defence the judge will not even allow the case to go to the jury.[9]

The position is easier if there is a past history that helps to establish who was at fault or what

---

[5] See Chap. 26.

[6] See [1982] Crim.LR and § 15.16 n. 14.

[7] Williams, *The Proof of Guilt*, 3rd edn Chap. 5.

[8] § 1.4. For the direction to the jury see *Abraham* [1973] 1 WLR 1270, 3 All ER 694, 57 CAR 799. It is not clear whether the judge must leave private defence to the jury if the evidence clearly indicates that the defendant went beyond the necessity of defence. For conflicting decisions see *Leary Walker* [1974] 1 WLR 1090; *Abraham*, above. It seems from *Leary Walker* that even if there is evidence of self-defence the judge need not leave the issue to the jury unless the defendant raised that defence. See, however, *Palmer* [1971] AC 814.

[9] § 2.4 n. 14. In *Ball* (1967) 131 JPN 723 an angry crowd besieged Ball's house, threw bricks through his windows and shouted threats. Ball appeared at his bedroom window and, after shouting due warning, fired a shotgun, wounding one of the rioters. Roskill J not only directed Ball's acquittal on a charge of wounding but bound over six prosecution witnesses to keep the peace. Cp. *Frankum* (1972) The Times, May 11.

a party may be expected to have believed. Evidence is admissible as to previous friction or threats to show which was the aggressor,[10] or what the actor feared from his assailant.[11] It seems that the evidence may even include the character and habits of the assailant.[12] Evidence may also be given of previous crimes in the neighbourhood, to help to support the actor's belief that another attack was imminent.[13]

§ 23.2. THE NECESSITY FOR DEFENCE

The defence of private defence resembles that of preventing crime in the twin requirements that the act must be immediately necessary (there must be no milder way of achieving the end) and proportional to the harm feared. Both questions, the factual and the evaluative, are frequently left to the jury as a single, unanalysed, question of reasonableness. This saves the trouble of sorting them out, but may lead to regrettable confusion.

> *Necessity*. A behaves aggressively towards B; B squares up to him and A makes to retreat, showing clearly that he has thought better of attacking. A blow given him by B cannot be justified, because the necessity for defence has passed.[1]
>
> *Proportionality*. A is about to slap B's face; B is a weakling who can avoid the slap only by using a gun. B is not justified in shooting, but must submit to being slapped.

On the necessity question, is a pre-emptive strike allowed?

It is sometimes thought that defence is allowed only against immediately threatened violence.[2] Clearly, force may not be used to meet a threat of violence in the future,[3] when there is still time for the person threatened to seek police protection. If he acts prematurely the judge may perhaps withdraw the defence from the jury, on the ground that there was no evidence of necessity when the defendant acted. But, as was said before in connection with the prevention of crime, there is a distinction between the immediacy of the necessity for acting and the immediacy of the threatened violence. The use of force may be immediately necessary to prevent an attack in the future. If, for example, there is a present hostile demonstration indicating that violence is about to be used, the defender[4] need not wait till his assailant comes within striking distance, or gets his

---

[10] *Humphreys* (1919) 14 CAR 85, 84 JP 48.
[11] *Griffin* (1871) 10 SRNSW 91 (Aus.); *Gunn* (1943) 7 JCr.L 28; *Muratovic* [1967] Qd.R at 29.
[12] *Griffin*, last note.
[13] *Viliborghi* v. *State* (1935) 45 Ariz. 275, 43 P (2d) 210.

[1] *Priestnall* v. *Cornish* [1979] Crim.LR 310.
[2] In *Devlin* v. *Armstrong* [1971] NI at 33, Lord MacDermott LCJ said that where the defence is against an expected attack, "the anticipated attack must be imminent", quoting *Chisam* (1963) 47 CAR at 134, which in turn quoted Lord Normand in *Owens,* 1946 SC(J) 119. The word "imminent" is also used in American statutory formulations. The CLRC thought there should be a firm rule that the feared attack must be imminent: 14th Report para. 286.
[3] *Mead* (1823) 1 Lew. 184, 168 ER 1006.
[4] The "defender" need not be the defendant; the question of the lawfulness of force in self-defence may arise if such force was used by the victim of the force used by the defendant, as on an issue of provocation. But I shall in general use "defendant" to mean the defender, because that is the more convenient word to use for the typical case where the defender is being prosecuted.

finger on the trigger.[5] Moreover, force may lawfully be *threatened* in advance of the immediate necessity for using it.[6] For these reasons it is best to regard the question of the immediacy of the threat as something that enters into the calculation of necessity, rather than as an independent rule.

The requirement of reasonableness is unhappy. Enough has been said in criticism of it,[7] and the CLRC has recommended that it should be expunged from the law.[8] In practice, as we have seen, the requirement may be construed indulgently to the defendant,[9] for, as Holmes J memorably said in the United States Supreme Court, "detached reflection cannot be demanded in the presence of an uplifted knife."[10] As we shall see in the next section, the requirement is now stated in such mitigated terms as to cast doubt on whether it still forms part of the law.

Can one act in self-defence by accident, so to speak? That is to say, without knowing that the other is himself about to attack you?

The question is unlikely to present itself in that form, but it may arise somewhat differently. Suppose that D acts, as he believes, in self-defence. He is prosecuted for the injury he inflicts, and it is argued for the prosecution that although he may have believed in the necessity for self-defence he had no reasonable grounds for the belief. However, the evidence shows that in fact he was under such a necessity, for reasons that he did not know at the time. This is the same problem as was mentioned in relation to arrest,[11] and the same answer should be given. If there is in fact a case for acting in self-defence, the investigation into the legality of the act should be foreclosed. The defendant's action is lawful irrespective of what the defendant believed or of the grounds of his belief.[12] The law would be oppressive if it said: It is true that you took this action because you felt it in your bones that you were in peril, and it is true that you were right, but you cannot now assign reasonable grounds for your belief, so you were only right by a fluke and will be convicted.

If a person is set upon, is he obliged to try to run away, if he can, instead of acting in self-defence?

The law now is that he is not under a duty to retreat as such, but he must

---

[5] In *Att.-Gen. for Northern Ireland's Reference* [1977] AC at 136D, Lord Diplock said: "The facts . . . are not capable in law of giving rise to a possible defence of "self-defence." The deceased was in fact, and appeared to the accused to be, unarmed. He . . . was running away." But later he said (at p. 138B): "There is material upon which a jury might take the view that the accused had reasonable grounds for apprehension of imminent danger to himself and other members of the patrol if the deceased were allowed to get away and join armed fellow-members of the Provisional IRA who might be lurking in the neighbourhood;" so he held that the defence of preventing crime could avail. Cp. § 22.6 at n. 5. Although the point is little more than theoretical, it is hard to see why private defence should be excluded. Cp. Beale in 3 Col.LRev. at 529.

[6] *Cousins* [1982] QB 526.

[7] § 6.8; 1st edn 451–455.

[8] 14th Report paras. 283, 287.

[9] § 22.6.

[10] *Brown* v. *United States* (1921) 256 US 335. In *Reed* v. *Wastie* [1972] Crim.LR 221,The Times, February 10, 1972, Lane J said: "One does not use jeweller's scales to measure reasonable force." See also *Palmer* [1971] AC at 832.

[11] Arrest on correct hunch, § 22.3 at n. 6.

[12] See 2 Leg. Stud. 249–252.

take any opportunity of disengaging himself. The Court of Appeal formulated the rule in the following terms.

> "It is not, as we understand it, the law that a person threatened must take to his heels and run in the dramatic way suggested by counsel for the appellant; but what is necessary is that he should demonstrate by his actions that he does not want to fight. He must demonstrate that he is prepared to temporise and disengage and perhaps to make some physical withdrawal; and that that is necessary as a feature of the justification of self-defence is true, in our opinion, whether the charge is a homicide charge or something less serious."[13]

The defender must, therefore, whenever possible, make a kind of symbolic retreat, or use words having a similar effect, in order to demonstrate that he is not the aggressor. If he makes a lusty defence, the aggressor may suddenly find that he himself has to act in defence; and there is an obvious danger that both parties may then conceive themselves as defenders. To avoid this, each party is required to make his stance clear to the other, whatever the origin of the affair may have been.

The importance of this rule becomes apparent when one considers the ordinary brawl. Group fights in public houses and elsewhere tend to escalate as friends of the original antagonists decide to join in. Youths take very seriously the need to show loyalty to their friends who become involved in fights.[14] Those who go immediately to the assistance of a defender are acting lawfully, so long as they keep to the limits of defence; but as more join in on each side it becomes more difficult, as a practical matter, to maintain the distinction between attack and defence, especially when the legal question is not how the fracas started but what each new entrant believes.

The fact that the defender must do what he can to indicate to his adversary that he is willing to discontinue the fight is sufficient to show that the rules of private defence and the prevention of crime are different. It is sometimes suggested that section 3 of the Act of 1967 (§ 22.6) has swallowed up the law of private defence, or else that its limitations have somehow superimposed themselves upon defence[15]; but there is no reason why this should be so. The two defences have always been distinct,[16] and nothing in section 3 indicates otherwise. When a person has two defences (private defence and public authority; private defence and provocation, etc.), he is allowed the benefit of whichever is the more favourable to him on the facts. It is true that section 3 (2) states that section 3 (1) replaces the previous rules of the common law in relation to the purpose of preventing crime and arresting offenders, but the "purpose" of private defence is different, and is not affected.

Where a combatant attempts to disengage himself, but is compelled to go on fighting in self-defence, his acts should on principle be lawful, even though he was originally the aggressor. So if he is at that stage compelled to kill in defence, he should not be guilty of murder or manslaughter. His liability should be for what he did originally.[17]

The proposition that a person when attacked is not bound to run away is a qualification upon the general rule that defence is limited to acts of necessity. Another qualification is that a person is entitled to reject an unlawful demand. If V says to D: "If you don't do as I tell you I will kill you," D is clearly entitled to refuse to obey the order and to resist any consequent attack upon him by V, even though he could have avoided the necessity of self-defence by complying with the order.

---

[13] *Julien* [1969] 1 WLR 839, 2 A11 ER 856. Cp. *McInnes* [1971] 1 WLR 1600, 3 All ER 295. See more in 1st edn 459–462.

[14] See D J West and D P Farrington, *The Delinquent Way of Life* (London 1977) 96–97.

[15] E.g. Smith and Hogan, 4th edn 325.

[16] For differences between the two defences see 1st edn 455.

[17] For the considerations of policy in not removing a justification on account of prior misconduct see Robinson in 82 Col.L.Rev. 217 n. 67. *Contra*, Ashworth in [1975] CLJ 300–301. Cp. § 26.2 n. 3.

§ 23.3. THE PROPORTIONALITY RULE

In the example of the proportionality rule given at the beginning of § .2, the use of the gun may be "necessary" to avoid the apprehended evil of being slapped, but it is disproportionate to that evil, and therefore unlawful. "For every assault it is not reasonable a man should be banged with a cudgel" (Holt CJ).[1] The proportionality rule is based on the view that there are some insults and hurts that one must suffer rather than use extreme force, if the choice is between suffering the hurt and using the extreme force. The rule involves a community standard of reasonableness, and is left to the consideration of the jury.[2] It can bear hardly on the defender, but much depends on the way in which judges and juries administer it; and that, again, may depend on whether they happen to empathise with the frightened defender or with his injured (or dead) assailant. If the defendant's reaction was disproportionate, the attack he feared or was resisting will go only in mitigation.

The previous examples of the proportionality rule are too trivial to be helpful. The real-life problem arises where a person is fiercely attacked by a bully whom he can resist only by the use of a lethal weapon. It is now so common for brutal men to kick their opponent about the head after he has been felled to the ground that anyone who is attacked may reasonably dread this possibility.

In order to give proper width to the right of self-defence an Australian court stated the law negatively: "Would a reasonable person in the defendant's situation have regarded what he did as out of all proportion to the danger to be guarded against?"[3] A somewhat different approach to the problem was adopted by the Court of Appeal in *Shannon*,[4] basing itself on the following dictum of Lord Morris:

> "A person defending himself cannot weigh to a nicety the exact measure of his necessary defensive action. If a jury thought that in a moment of unexpected anguish a person attacked had only done what he honestly and instinctively thought was necessary that would be most potent evidence that only reasonable defensive action had been taken."

Approving this statement, the Court of Appeal quashed a conviction because the trial judge had not conveyed the point to the jury and had not directed them broadly in Lord Morris's words. The real issue, the court thought, was: "Was this stabbing within the conception of necessary self-defence judged by the standards of common sense, bearing in mind the position of the defendant at the moment of stabbing, or was it a case of angry retaliation or pure aggression on his part?" In future, an instruction to the jury in these terms will evidently be necessary in many cases of self-defence.

---

[1] *Cockcroft* v. *Smith* (1705) 2 Salk. 642, 91 ER 541.
[2] Subject to the usual rule that there must be evidence for the jury: § 22.6 n. 18. And see § 6.11.
[3] *Rainey* [1970] VR 650. Cp. the remarks of Lord Diplock, § 22.6 at n. 13.
[4] *Shannon* (1980) 71 CAR 192.

The facts of *Shannon* were that the deceased, a heavily built man who had convictions for violence, had been making threats against Shannon for having (as he believed) "grassed" him. Shannon, who had no history of violence or aggression, must have been living in fear of an attack for some time. When the attack came he fought back, the fight (though evidently largely one-sided) being described by a bystander as "pretty frightening." Shannon's evidence was that he was being held very tightly by the neck and was being dragged down and "kneed;" he feared that if he fell while in the grip of his attacker he would have "got beat up by his feet." He lashed out with a scissors and inflicted a fatal blow. On the issue of self-defence the judge left the case to the jury with the bald question: Did the defendant use more force than was necessary in the circumstances?" On this the jury, surprisingly, returned a conviction of manslaughter. The conviction was quashed, as already said, for inadequate direction to the jury; but the Court of Appeal expressed no other criticism of the verdict. We are left with the impression that if in a similar case the judge reads out Lord Morris's dictum to the jury, who nevertheless convict, the conviction will stand.

On the dictum, it is not easy to see how "what the defendant thought" could be evidence of what it was reasonable for him to do. The usual opinion is that the question what is reasonable, in the multifarious applications of that word, is for the unaided vote of the jury, and is not a matter for "evidence" in the ordinary way. It looks very much as though the dictum is a way of escaping from the test of reasonableness without acknowledging the fact. This conclusion is strengthened by the above-quoted remark of the Court of Appeal, which (epitomising a lengthy statement of Lord Morris) distinguishes sharply between "necessary self-defence" on the one hand and "angry retaliation or pure aggression" on the other. The dichotomy allows no place in between for unnecessary but putative self-defence. All putative self-defence, it seems, falls into the category of "necessary self-defence." In this part of the judgment, the idea that the defendant's belief is merely evidence of reasonableness has suddenly vanished; indeed, the very word "reasonable" is dropped. It seems, therefore, that the decision makes a radical change in the law. At least where the defender fears death or serious injury, there is no proportionality rule any longer; and a good thing too—in view of the jury's verdict in *Shannon*. German law, it seems, gets on without a proportionality rule,[5] and so could we, where the facts are similar to those in *Shannon*. The reasoning in the decision is fudged, but that is the price one pays for a beneficial change in the law.

Suppose Shannon had used his scissors upon a mugger; would the view of the court have been the same?

If the thief were trying to drag his bag from him, and the victim of the robbery stabbed the thief merely in order to avoid losing his property, the authorities give no indication of the legal position. All that one can clearly do by way of defence against robbery is to give the robber blows and *threaten* him with a weapon.[6] For some reason that is not clear, the courts occasionally seem to regard the scandal of the killing of a robber (or of a person who is feared to be a robber) as of greater moment than the safety of the robber's victim in respect of his person and property.[7] Possibly, if the matter were fully argued, the court would apply the same rule as in *Shannon*, but one does not know. The jury's verdict in *Shannon* is a standing warning to all defenders of the legal danger of killing an adversary, even in self-defence.

---

[5] See George Fletcher, *Rethinking Criminal Law* 871 ff. It does not follow from *Shannon* that we could get on without a proportionality rule where the defence is against a non-violent invasion of property rights.

[6] *Cousins* [1982] QB at 530D shows that one can threaten force even when one cannot lawfully use it. The decision departs from earlier cases: [1957] Crim.LR 221–3.

[7] In *O'Shea* (1978) 142 JPN 472 a man who feared he was about to be set upon by a gang of youths was sent to prison for 4 years for accidentally killing one of them in the course of defensive action; and the CA affirmed the sentence.

To what extent can one carry weapons by way of defence? Could I carry a hefty spanner to use if I am attacked on the street at night?

Not legally. It is, you will remember, an either way offence under the Prevention of Crimes Act 1953 section 1 for a person to have "with him" an offensive weapon in a public place without reasonable excuse.[8] Offensive weapons are (1) those that are offensive *per se*,[9] and (2) those that are capable of an innocent use (your spanner) but are carried for the purpose of causing injury to the person. It does not matter that the injury contemplated will be defensive.

But you said that reasonable excuse is a defence. Why isn't self-defence a reasonable excuse?

We are not allowed to make a habit of carrying a weapon for defence, because every weapon could be used for that purpose, and the excuse could be used by thugs as well as by honest men. The defence of reasonable excuse is available, but is given a restricted interpretation; it might justify a man in carrying a weapon after being attacked within the last day or two, or perhaps for a little longer; but even the fact that he has been mugged does not give him an indefinite licence to carry a weapon. There must be "an imminent particular threat affecting the particular circumstances in which the weapon was carried."[10] The question of reasonable excuse is one for the jury or magistrates, but the magistrates, at least, will be expected to guide themselves by the above principle stated by the higher courts.

By the way, if you carried the spanner without any intention to strike anyone with it, but only to frighten off an attack, it would not be an "offensive weapon," not being offensivc *per se* and not being carried for the purpose of causing injury.[11] And if you did not intend to strike anyone with the spanner when you carried it, but used it on the spur of the moment when attacked, it would still not be an "offensive weapon" and you would still not be guilty of having it with you for an offensive purpose.[12]

Again, you would not commit an offence under the Act of 1953 if you used a spanner that you snatched from an assailant in order to strike him, or one that you happened to see when you were being attacked, for the same reason as before—it would not be an "offensive weapon" and you would not "have it with you."[13] These two escape-routes from the Act (depending on an understanding of what is an offensive weapon and when the user had it "with him") are quite distinct from the question of what is a reasonable excuse.

---

[8] See § 9.9 at n. 8.

[9] "In themselves." Examples are flick knives (*Gibson* v. *Wales* [1983] Crim.LR 113) and coshes (*Grieve* v. *Macleod* [1967] Crim.LR 424).

[10] *Evans* v. *Hughes* [1972] 1 WLR 1452 at 1455G, 3 All ER 412, 56 CAR 813. Cp. *Taylor* v. *Mucklow* [1973] Crim.LR 750; *Pittard* v. *Mahoney* [1977] *ibid.* 169; *Giles* [1976] *ibid.* 253. It was even held in the peculiar circumstances existing in Northern Ireland that a person could have a firearm "for a lawful object" within the Explosive Substances Act 1883 s.4 (1) if he had it only for self-defence: *Fegan* [1972] NI 80.

[11] *Rapier* (1980) 70 CAR 17, [1980] Crim.LR 48.

[12] *Humphreys* [1977] Crim.LR 225.

[13] *Bates* v. *Bulman* [1979] 1 WLR 1190, 68 CAR 21; see note, [1979] Crim.LR 532.

Are guns in the same position?

Most guns are offensive weapons within the Prevention of Crimes Act, and, in addition, the private possession of firearms is strictly controlled under the Firearms Act 1968 and other Acts. Even if you have a licence from the police to possess a firearm, carrying the weapon is an offence under section 19 of the Act, except that the courts will allow the statutory defence of "reasonable excuse," which is construed in the same way as in the Prevention of Crimes Act. The fact that you were acting under this general permission does not allow you to shoot. When you can do so depends on the law of private defence.

If I were carrying a gun or spanner illegally I might be punished for it, but all the same I would use the weapon if I were being murderously attacked.

On principle you would be within your rights in doing so. The fact that your possession of the weapon is punishable under statute is no more relevant to a charge of assault or manslaughter than would be the fact that you have stolen it.

Such is the logic of the matter,[14] but there is no indication that the courts accept it. In *Shannon* a question was made at the trial whether or not the defendant was carrying the scissors when he was attacked, and the trial judge did not warn the jury that the question was irrelevant; nor did the Court of Appeal suggest that the judge should have done so. When the defendant has armed himself against attack, and particularly when he has armed himself illegally, this is quite likely to be a circumstance of prejudice against him; he will not be looked upon so benignly as the defendant who possessed himself of a weapon in the stress of the moment.[15]

The older authorities try to clarify the law of private defence by declaring that extreme force (otherwise called "deadly force," that is, force involving the intentional or reckless infliction of death or serious injury) may be used to avoid extreme harm, but not otherwise. "Extreme harm" included death or serious injury but might also include other serious harms like rape.[16] The modern authorities, however, leave the rule of "reasonable relationship" at large, at least in the case of defence of the person.[17]

This abandonment of the relative precision of the old law seems unfortunate, for reasons already sufficiently stated in connection with section 3 of the Criminal Law Act. If the proportionality rule survives the decision in *Shannon*, would it not at least be desirable, for the sake of protecting defendants from the vagaries not only of juries but (one must add) of judges, and from gusts of public opinion, that certain fixed rules should be laid down beforehand as to the occasions on which extreme force can be used for self-preservation? The list need not be exhaustive, for the rule could be that extreme but necessary force can be used in specified cases (*a*), (*b*), etc., "and in all other cases where such force would not be regarded

---

[14] Cp. 1st edn 444 n. 26.

[15] I call this a matter of prejudice, as I think it is. *Contra*, Ashworth in [1975] CLJ 298–299. In *Shannon*, n. 4 above, there seems to have been considerable discussion at the trial whether the scissors used by Shannon as a weapon were being carried by him at the time of the attack, and no instruction appears to have been given to the jury on how they were to view the question.

[16] See A V Dicey, *Introduction to the Study of the Law of the Constitution*, 8th ed App. IV (not reprinted in later editions).

[17] For invasions of property rights see § .6.

by any reasonable person as disproportionate to the threat."[18] Such a rule would have protected Shannon from an unjust conviction better than the rule stated by the Court of Appeal.

§ 23.4. FORCE IN ARRESTING A RESISTING SUSPECT

When force is used to arrest, a distinction must be drawn between the resisting and the fleeing suspect—fleeing, that is, without violent resistance. Where the suspect flees, the officer's justification for the use of force rests exclusively on section 3(1) (§ 22.6). Where the suspect forcibly resists lawful arrest, Hale lays it down as clear law that the officer may in the last resort use fatal force, irrespective of the crime for which he is arresting.[1] This legal result is achieved by combining the law of arrest with the right of self-defence. An officer who is endeavouring to effect an arrest is not obliged to give back, but may press forward against resistance, meeting the resistance with self-defence according to the usual rules, except that he is clearly under no duty to retreat. As the struggle gains in ferocity, and the offender is obliged to use more and more extreme measures against the officer if he is to avoid being disabled, the point is reached at which the officer comes to fear that he will himself suffer death or grave harm unless he retreats or uses extreme violence, and in such circumstances he may use that violence. The fact that section 3 and the right of defence act together in this way shows that the right of defence remains separate from section 3.

Where the offender is armed with a lethal weapon, the fatal point in the struggle may be reached quickly, the legal analysis of the situation being in no way affected. Nor is the legal position any different in theory where both parties are armed with firearms. In such circumstances the officer must, for his own protection, shoot first if the other shows any sign of reaching for his gun. If the suspect is being beseiged and is armed, the police are frank that when they decide to shoot, they shoot to kill.[2] Presumably the law allows this, even though the result is that the police bring back not the suspect but a corpse. Their duty is not merely to arrest but, if they cannot arrest a dangerous offender, to prevent him from continuing at liberty. However, we have no explicit authority on the

---

[18] The CLRC (with one dissentient) declined to propose any such rules. Professor Smith explains the committee's decision on the ground that cases arise on which there will be differences of opinion on whether the defensive force was justified (1 Leg. Stud. 127), but that is the very reason why I think there should be fixed rules. Cp. Ashworth in [1977] Crim.LR 99.

[1] *PC* i 481, 494, ii 117–118. Cp. Co. *Inst.* iii 56; Hawkins i c. 28 ss.17–19; Foster 270–271; Blackstone, *Commentaries* iv 179; East, PC i 307; Stephen, *HCL* i 193; *Mackalley's* case (1611) 9 Co.Rep. 61b, 65b, 77 ER 824, 828; *Simmonds* (1965) 9 WIR 95 (Jamaica).

[2] In 1979 the deputy chief constable of Essex said in evidence at an inquest that there could be no question of shooting to wound an armed man in a siege. "When the officer pulls the trigger he must know that he's going to take a life. A policy of shooting to wing or wound is extremely dangerous" (Daily Telegraph, May 22, 1979). Cp., for the view of American courts, Warner in 21 Can.BRev at 207. If the officer is entitled to act when the other is armed, he is, of course, entitled to act merely on the reasonable belief that the other is armed.

question since the Act of 1967; and the police have to recognise that public opinion is sensitive on the use of guns by the police.

These rules apply whether the suspect is presenting his face to the officer or is engaged in a "running fight," firing perhaps from the rear of a car. American authorities apply them where an arrest is validly made by a private person,[3] and on principle this is clearly right.

Since the right to kill a resisting criminal depends upon the law of self-defence combined with the rule that an arrester need not attempt to withdraw, it applies to all manner of lawful arrests and not merely to arrest for serious crimes. If a desperado, wanted on any ground, barricades himself with arms in a house he may be deliberately shot if that is the only way to quell his dangerous resistance. Under section 18 of the Offences against the Person Act it is a crime to wound to resist arrest (§ 9.1), and, where this crime is committed or attempted, an additional ground is furnished for shooting the resisting criminal, even when his original crime was not of a character to justify the use of fatal force in arrest apart from resistance. The arrester, as soon as the weapon is used against him, may ignore the original charge and proceed to use force on the basis that he is arresting for the crime of attempting to wound to resist arrest.

§ 23.5. DEFENCE AGAINST THE POLICE

The right of self-defence avails against the police, so the citizen is permitted (in theory) to use reasonable force against an officer to avoid being illegally arrested. He is not guilty of assaulting the officer in the execution of his duty for two separate reasons: the officer is not acting in the execution of his duty, and there is no assault.

The French have a doctrine of *rebellion*, according to which it is unlawful to resist a police officer even though he is acting illegally: the citizen must submit, and seek his remedy afterwards in the courts. But in Britain the normal right of self-defence exists, even where the only purpose of the defendant is to avoid being arrested or detained,[1] and even where the police believe themselves to be acting in the execution of their duty, if in fact they are acting illegally.[2] Whether our rule is politic, or fair to the police, may be questioned[3]; but in

---

[3] *State* v. *Towne* (1916) 180 Ia. 339, 160 NW 10.

[1] *Mabel* (1840) 9 C & P 474, 173 ER 918; *Kenlin* v. *Gardiner* [1967] 2 QB 510.

[2] See [1954] Crim.LR 8–11; *Townley* v. *Rushworth,* 62 LGR 95, The Times, December 5, 1963; *Kenlin* v. *Gardiner,* last note. "If in fact they are acting illegally" includes cases where the courts invent a new rule *ex post facto*, making the conduct of the police illegal when there was no direct authority for saying so before. See Austin in [1982] Curr.LProb. 189. Conversely, the courts suddenly invent new powers for the police, making resistance to them illegal when there was no previous authority in point.

[3] The Model Penal Code, POD s.3.04(2)(*a*), provides that "the use of force is not justifiable under this section to resist an arrest which the actor knows is being made by a peace officer, although the arrest is unlawful." The Comment to the Tentative Draft says: "There ought not to be a privilege to employ force against a public officer who, to the actor's knowledge, is attempting only to arrest him and subject him to the process of law." See to the same effect the Uniform Arrest Act s.5, and discussion in Kadish and Kadish, *Discretion to Disobey* (Stanford, Calif. 1973) 108–109, 158–159. Legislation in the USA meets the situation in a variety of ways. For an argument in favour of the rule at common law see Paul G Chevigny in 78 Yale LJ 1128. In his view, resistance to outrageously wrong arrest is perfectly natural, and the defendant should not be penalised for it. Even granting this, the difficulty is that one can hardly distinguish as a matter of rule between an outrageously wrong arrest and one that is wrong only for breach of some technical rule or limitation. Practical difficulties with the right to resist will be mentioned presently.

practice, because the law relating to police power is so obscure, it gives people very little freedom to defy the police with safety.

Can you use force against the police after being arrested, to prevent them taking liberties with you that they oughtn't?

Yes. Persons in custody have been upheld by the courts in forcibly resisting the taking of fingerprints outside statutory powers,[4] and the removal of a woman's brassiere without adequate cause.[5]

How much force may you use against the police?

The practical answer, as regards the attitude of some courts, is: "only force that is so mild as to be ineffective."

In the bra case, the defendant, resisting having the garment taken, scratched the policewoman's hand and kicked her knee. The Divisional Court, while allowing her appeal against conviction of assaulting the officer in the execution of her duty, said, obiter, that she was guilty of a common assault on the officer because she (the defendant) had used more force than was necessary. This opinion was particularly strange because in fact the force used had been unavailing: the bra had been removed. Apparently the only lawful force, in the view of the court, was something less than that required to make the police desist from what they wanted to do.

Such pronouncements on the question of necessity stultify the right of self-defence, and so are too absurd to be accepted with patience; but the issue of proportionality is difficult. A strongly-built man who tries to resist an illegal arrest by a single officer will very likely not succeed unless he inflicts some injury on the officer; and if he does, a judge might suggest to the jury that the infliction of injury on one who is known to be a police officer would be disproportionate to the evil involved in an illegal but temporary deprivation of liberty.[6] Possibly the judge might even withdraw the defence from the jury, for reasons similar to those already discussed in relation to the prevention of crime. An attempt by the police merely to take an impression of fingerprints or to remove a bra might be regarded as justifying an even smaller degree of force in resisting. There is, therefore, a head-on clash between the idea that the citizen can use force to prevent illegal action against him by the police and the proportionality rule. In view of the obscurity of the law and the fact that the courts are understandably reluctant to allow people to fight the police, the practical advice to everybody is not to do so. The resister is likely to get the worse of it, one way or the other.

Can you resist arrest on the ground that you are innocent, if you are innocent?

Not necessarily. Most powers of arrest are worded or interpreted in

---

[4] *Yvonne Jones* [1978] 3 All ER 1098, 67 CAR 166.

[5] *Lindley* v. *Rutter*, The Times, August 1, 1980. The police apparently acted under their own rule, designed to prevent suicides.

[6] See the authorities discussed by L H Leigh in 30 MLR 341–342.

terms of reasonable suspicion. If the officer reasonably suspects someone, the arrest is not made invalid by the suspect's innocence.

What if you resist arrest, believing the arrest to be unlawful when in fact it is lawful?

Ignorance of the criminal law is no excuse, and for this purpose the law of arrest (as well as the law of self-defence) is regarded as part of the criminal law,[7] for obvious reasons of policy. Hence a person who violently resists a lawful arrest believing it to be unlawful but not mistaking any fact can be convicted—even of the serious offence under OAPA 1861 s.18.

This rule, which is inevitable, makes nonsense of the supposition that the right to resist an illegal arrest by the police is a valuable safeguard of liberty. So great is the complexity of the law that no wise person would resist arrest, even if he suspects it to be illegal, because he cannot be sufficiently sure of his opinion. The safest ground for resistance is that the officer has not stated the reason for arrest, under the rule in *Christie* v. *Leachinsky*.[8]

But you may use force against a man if you reasonably think he is a thug, although in fact he is a police officer who is properly trying to arrest you under a statutory power?

Yes. Even if the plain-clothes officer tries to establish his status, the suspect may lawfully defend himself by force if he reasonably believes that the officer's claim to official status is a pretence.[9] On such facts, each party is lawfully permitted to use force against the other.

This means that, as said before,[10] the offence of assault upon a constable in the exercise of his duty is one of full *mens rea* in respect of the assault element. To this extent the defendant's ignorance of the officer's status can avail him.

Suppose the arrest is lawful but the police officer uses unreasonable force. May the arrestee defend himself against the unreasonable force?

In theory yes, to avoid being hurt.

I say "in theory" because where there is a conflict of evidence between a policeman and a citizen the officer tends to be believed. If therefore the defendant says that he was submitting to arrest but the officer aimed a blow at him, and that he only hit the officer to avoid being hit himself, while the officer denies the blow and says that the defendant was resisting arrest, the officer is likely to be believed in a magistrates' court, which does not wish to brand him as a liar. There is more chance of acquittal on a trial by jury.

If your friend has been arrested, may you wade in to rescue him provided you believe on reasonable grounds that the arrest is unlawful?

Consider this chain of reasoning.

1 Protective force may be used both against unlawful injury and against unlawful detention.
2 It may be used on the facts as they reasonably appear to be.
3 It may be used to protect third persons, at any rate one's son.

---

[7] *Bentley* (1850) 4 Cox 406; *Agnew* v. *Jobson* (1877) 13 Cox 625; Stephen J in *Tolson* (1889) 23 QBD at 188; *Gelberg* v. *Miller* [1961] 1 WLR 153, 1 All ER 291; cp. *Reid* [1973] 1 WLR at 1289; *Barrett* (1980) 72 CAR 212 (mistake as to the validity of court process); *Hills* v. *Ellis* § 3.2 n. 8; Zuckerman in 88 LQR 256; ALI Model Penal Code, POD s.3.09(1); *The General Part*, 2nd edn 336–340.

[8] § 22.4.

[9] *Kenlin* v. *Gardiner* [1967] 2 QB at 519–520.

[10] § 9.7.

4 It may be used against the police.
Therefore protective force may be used by a person if on the facts as he reasonably believes them to be this is necessary to prevent the unlawful detention of his son by the police.

All the premises in this argument are amply supported by authority, and the conclusion follows inexorably from them. But the Court of Appeal in *Fennell*[11] fractured two of the links leading to the conclusion, and so enabled itself to dodge the conclusion. The case is probably of small importance, and its chief interest is in showing how some judges will go to considerable lengths to evade the operation of settled legal principles for pragmatic reasons.

> Fennell's son had been arrested for taking part at 11.15 p.m. in a street fight which it took the police some time to stop. Fennell, protesting a belief in his son's innocence, told one of the officers that he would hit him unless his son was released. As the officer did not respond Fennell hit him on the jaw. Fennell was prosecuted for assault on the police constable, and it was argued in his defence that if he genuinely believed on reasonable grounds that the restraint of his son was unlawful he was justified in using reasonable force to free him. The proposition of law was rejected by the trial judge and on appeal; and Fennell was convicted.

Understandably, the judges did not relish the idea that a father could rescue his son from the police, but the problem was to escape from the precedents. The Court of Appeal improvised a solution by drawing a distinction within proposition 1, between injury and detention, for which there was no previous authority, and by curtailing proposition 2 so as to make the offence of assaulting a constable one of strict liability in a respect for which there was again no previous authority. Widgery LJ:

> "It was accepted in the court below that if the arrest had been, in fact, unlawful the appellant would have been justified in using reasonable force to secure the release of his son. This proposition has not been argued before us and we will assume, without deciding it, that it is correct. . . . Where a person honestly and reasonably believes that he or his child is in imminent danger of injury it would be unjust if he were deprived of the right to use reasonable force by way of defence merely because he had made some genuine mistake of fact. On the other hand if the child is in police custody and not in imminent danger of injury there is no urgency of the kind which requires an immediate decision and a father who forcibly releases the child does so at his peril."

Therefore, since the detention of the son was lawful, the defendant's belief (even if reasonable) that the facts of the case made it unlawful was no defence.

As was said before, the earlier authorities held that the offence of assaulting a constable was not entirely of strict liability, but required *mens rea* in respect of the requirement of an assault. We are now told that it is of strict liability even in respect of the assault, if the defendant was acting against the police to free another person. But the court would apparently still allow a person to use force against the police to secure *his own* freedom from illegal detention, and it would certainly allow a father to use force against the police to prevent them from illegally *injuring* his child. In short, the exception made by this decision from the previous rules is directed exclusively to the facts of the particular case.

The problem that vexed the court could have been settled, without departing from the authorities, by a different line of reasoning. The argument that Fennell honestly and reasonably believed that the arrest was unlawful and therefore was justified in using force contained an ambiguity.

- If it meant that Fennell did not know the law of arrest, that was his look-out. We are all supposed to know the law of arrest, or at least cannot take any advantage from not knowing it.

---

[11] [1971] 1 QB 428.

- If it meant that Fennell believed in facts that made the arrest unlawful, we must consider what those facts were. The police had a right to arrest on various grounds:
  - at common law for a breach of the peace committed in their presence;
  - under the Prevention of Offences Act 1851 s.11 for an indictable offence committed in the night (Fennell's son was presumably suspected of affray, which is an indictable offence);
  - for assault occasioning actual bodily harm (if the police suspected him of that); this was punishable with 5 years' imprisonment and therefore was an arrestable offence.[12]

  The first and third of these grounds of arrest certainly cover cases of reasonable even if mistaken suspicion, and the second probably does too.[13] From this the conclusion follows that to justify the attempted rescue it was necessary that Fennell should have believed either that the officer did not suspect his son or that there were no facts that could give the officer reasonable grounds for suspicion. For Fennell to say: "I know my son was innocent" would, even if correct in fact, not exclude the possibility that the arrest was lawful. Now it is virtually impossible to credit a defence that the defendant knew or believed that the officer did not know or believe any fact that would create a reasonable suspicion against his son. The evidence in the case fell far short of establishing such a remarkable frame of mind on the part of Fennell. The appeal could have been dismissed on that ground.

It might be good policy to enact that no one is entitled to use force for the purpose of rescuing another from the custody of the police who act in the belief that they are within the law. But at present we have no such legislation, and on principle there is a right to rescue if the arrest is in fact unlawful. It is anomalous, therefore, to deny the operation of the usual *mens rea* principle in these circumstances. Nor is there any need to deny it, because it cannot advantage a would-be rescuer like Fennell.

§ 23.6. DEFENCE OF LAND AGAINST TRESPASSERS

A man is entitled to use necessary and moderate force in defence of property.[1] Hence he may use this degree of force to prevent trespass or to eject trespassers, to re-enter upon land (subject to what is to be said in § .8), and to defend and recapture chattels (§ .9). For all these purposes the force used must not only be the minimum necessary (or reasonably believed to be necessary) to achieve the object but also (according to the older authorities) be moderate—that is, must fall short of the intentional or reckless infliction of death or grievous bodily harm.[2] Exceptionally, death may be inflicted in defence of the dwelling-house (§ .7), and perhaps in effecting an arrest or preventing crime (as already discussed).

It is not certain that the old restriction to moderate force still survives. As we have seen, the courts have apparently abandoned the distinction between moderate and extreme force in relation to defending the person. Perhaps the rule now is the same for the defence of property as for the defence of the person, that the jury are left to decide generally whether the force was necessary and "reasonable," i.e. proportionate. But, on

---

[12] § 22.2.
[13] See § 22.2, .3; [1958] Crim.LR 73.

[1] Including trespassers on a vehicle, like a ship: *Canadian Pacific Rly* v. *Gaud* [1949] 2 KB 239.
[2] The well-known case on the limitation is *Moir* (1830), Russell on *Crime*, 12th edn i. 441. See also *Wild* (1837) 2 Lew. 214, 168 ER 1132; *Taylor* v. *Mucklow* [1973] Crim.LR 750.

principle, the judge retains the power to withdraw the defence from the jury if it is not supported by evidence on which a reasonable jury could act, and the exercise of this power may enable him to continue to give effect to the old distinction. In the absence of express decision it will here be assumed that the old restriction to moderate force survives.

Must the owner ask the trespasser to leave before forcibly ushering him out?

The requirement of minimum force generally means that the trespasser must be asked to leave (or to desist from an attempted entry), and a reasonable time allowed for compliance, before force is used against him, for otherwise it is not clear that force is necessary. That the occupier must first require the trespasser to leave or desist is not an inflexible rule of law (though it is often said to be[3]): if the trespasser is evidently determined to use force to enter, moderate force may be used to expel him without any words being uttered.

What if the trespasser fights back?

The occupier (or person acting under his authority) may go on using moderate force. It is not clear whether he can escalate to extreme force for his own safety, if he can avoid the necessity by allowing the trespasser to remain.

What if the man was not a trespasser but the occupier thought he was?

The law of trespass and title to land is regarded as belonging to the civil law, not the criminal law, and a mistake as to it can be a defence. So, if the occupier reasonably believes that the person ejected is a trespasser, he commits no offence.

On the other hand if the occupier mistakenly believes that he is entitled to shoot the trespasser he does commit an offence in shooting, because the limits of the power to eject trespassers are part of the criminal law. These limits would be stated in a well-drawn penal code.

Can the occupier of property who is pestered by a trespasser ask a policeman to help him?

Traditionally, the police do not generally assist in the eviction of trespassers, looking upon this as a civil matter. Sometimes, however, they do so: they may eject trouble-makers from a football ground, acting on behalf of the management. This saves them time: if they arrested the offenders, they would have to go to the station with them.

The general practice of inactivity by the police may change as a result of remarks made in the Court of Appeal. The court pointed out the danger of a breach of the peace (i.e. of a fight) if ordinary citizens try to run trespassers out themselves, even if the trespassers are demonstrators who announce their intention not to use violence but only to make nuisances of themselves; and the court therefore encouraged the police to help.[4] This was spoken in a case concerning interference with statutory undertakers, but there is no reason why the position should not be the same for ordinary landowners and householders.

---

[3] See, e.g. Lanham in [1966] Crim.LR 372.

[4] *R* v. *Chief Constable of Devon and Cornwall* [1981] 3 WLR 967; see particularly Lawton LJ on p. 977G–H.

According to the old authorities, when a policeman ejects trespassers as the agent of the occupier he acts in a private capacity, not in the execution of his duty. But Lawton LJ on one occasion said that he did not regard these old cases as still being good law; and in any case a court would now readily find that a constable who ejected trespassers at the request of the occupier or his agent would be entitled to do so as preventing a possible breach of the peace,[5] in which case a trespasser who resists, even though merely by being inert, would be guilty of obstructing him in the exercise of his duty.

Could a student evict a trespasser from his college or hostel room, or from his room in lodgings?

Primarily, the right of defence of property is given to the occupier (possessor). It seems, however, that even a licensee of the land (like the student in your question) can eject trespassing strangers,[6] though he cannot eject the occupier or someone permitted to be there by the occupier.[7]

Where actual damage to property is apprehended, it is possible that even a stranger might defend it on the owner's behalf against a wrong-doer. As we shall see,[8] the Criminal Damage Act allows anyone to damage property in defence of the property of another (killing a marauding dog in defence of a neighbour's sheep), and there is no good reason why the use of force against a human being should not be allowable on the same ground.

Since we are in the area of judge-made law, the judges can go on making up new rules. It has been held that where a statutory body has the legal right to enter land for a specified purpose, it can use the force reasonably necessary to remove demonstrators who try to obstruct its operations.[9]

Can a trespasser be detained until he gives his name and address?

The law relating to the duty to give name and address is in a highly defective condition,[10] and the answer to your question is in the negative. Trespass is not generally a crime, and the landowner's remedy is supposed to be to sue for damages in tort; but the law does not enable him to find out who the trespasser is.

> This proposition was overlooked in *Bow*.[11] A gamekeeper found Bow and other men on a private estate in the early hours armed with air rifles. Reasonably suspecting them of poaching, he blocked their escape with his Land Rover, driving it across the lane. (The report does not specify, but presumably this lane was a private road on the estate.) Bow got into the Land Rover, released the hand-brake and cruised down the lane to a spot where he could pull off the lane. He and his companions then made off in their own car. Bow was convicted of taking a conveyance under the Theft Act s.12(1), and the conviction was affirmed on appeal, the court holding that it was immaterial that Bow's purpose was to remove an obstruction to his own exit.

This is a disappointingly simple-minded manner of interpreting penal legislation, which one would have hoped that the courts had outgrown. The statute was not passed to prevent people

---

[5] *Coffin* v. *Smith* (1980) 71 CAR 221. Cp. *R* v. *Chief Constable*, last note. Query, however, the assumption made by the CA in the latter case that the forcible eviction of passive resisters would be likely to cause a breach of the peace. The lawful use of force to evict a trespasser would surely not be a breach of the peace, and there was no evidence to justify the general fears of the court that the passive resisters might themselves use force. For a rare example of a Divisional Court finding that a constable who forcibly moved a person did not reasonably fear a breach of the peace, and therefore was acting outside his duty, see *Hickman* v. *O'Dwyer* [1979] Crim.LR 309.

[6] *Hall* v. *Davis* (1825) 2 C & P 33, 172 ER 16; cp. *Tao* [1977] QB 141.

[7] *Dean* v. *Hogg* (1834) 10 Bing. 345, 131 ER 937. One joint occupier cannot eject another, even if he is making a nuisance of himself; but see the dictum in *Holmes* v. *Bagge* (1853) 1 E & B 782, 118 ER 629.

[8] § 41.6.

[9] *R* v. *Chief Constable of Devon and Cornwall* [1981] 3 WLR at 975E, 977F, 982G.

[10] See 66 LQR 465.

[11] [1977] RTR 6. See criticisms in 126 NLJ 1177, [1977] Crim.LR 176.

removing cars that were obstructing, and it was a sharp interpretation to say that Bow committed a "taking" in this case. Moreover, there was the question of implied exceptions from the offence. All such legislation should be read, *prima facie*, as subject to the general law allowing excuses or justifications, and it is not good enough to affirm a conviction merely by saying, as the court did, that "motive is immaterial." If the motive is to do a lawful act, it can be material. The gamekeeper might have arrested the men under the Game Acts,[12] and his obstruction of the lane would then have been lawful as part of the arrest; but he did not say that he was making an arrest. That being so, one would have thought that he had no right in law to prevent them from making an exit by driving out. Perhaps Bow should have asked the gamekeeper to move the Land Rover before doing so himself, but since the gamekeeper was evidently determined not to do so, Bow's failure to make the request should not have been sufficient to convict him of the offence. His moving of the vehicle should have been justified by necessity.[13] Putting aside mere matters of prejudice, the case was a simple one in which A drives his car to a spot and leaves it there for the sole purpose of blocking B's exit. To be told that B commits an offence in moving it in order to get out is astonishing. Even if the court failed to find any justification for Bow's act, there was the question of excuse: the statute explicitly makes belief in lawful authority a defence.[14]

Can one set up static deterrents like man-traps?

The former practice of setting spring guns or man-traps to injure trespassers is specifically prohibited by statute, unless they be set in a dwelling-house between sunset and sunrise.[15] The general answer, therefore, is that man-traps are unlawful. Even traps not mentioned in the statute are unlawful. If, for example, a shopkeeper rigs up a device to electrocute intruders, and someone is killed by it, this is manslaughter.[16]

But what about the exception? Is it lawful to set a man-trap in a dwelling-house at night?

The section does not positively authorise the setting of infernal machines in a dwelling-house at night, but merely says that nothing in the section shall make such an act unlawful. It is still possibly open to argument that one who sets such a machine in a dwelling-house at night, with the result that an intruder is killed, is guilty of manslaughter, or, if the intruder is grievously injured, is guilty of the crime of wounding with intent under section 18, since he hoped and intended that the intruder would be so injured. Oddly, there would be more difficulty in convicting of malicious wounding under section 20, or of an assault occasioning actual bodily harm under section 47, because it may be argued that the injury is caused "indirectly" but it is likely that an injury caused by an infernal machine would be held to involve an assault,[17] and that anyway it is sufficiently "direct" to come within the rule in *Wilson* (§ 9.5). Unlawfully giving someone an electric shock is the offence of administering a noxious thing,[18] so an electrocution device could result in liability on that score.

---

[12] Provided that they had refused to give name and address: Game Act 1831 s.31.

[13] See § 26.6.

[14] See Chap. 32, and the dictum of Lord Denning cited in § .10.

[15] OAPA 1861 s.31. Since the section says "spring gun, mantrap or other engine," it has been held that a device for electrocuting trespassers is not included! See *Munks* [1964] 1 QB 304. The decision overlooks the wide traditional meaning of "engine"; see OED, *s.v.*

[16] In *Pratt* The Times, October 9, 1976, the defendant pleaded guilty to manslaughter on such facts and received a suspended sentence.

[17] § 8.3.

[18] § 9.10 at n. 13.

This is an area where the law is quite capable of clashing with public opinion. There would be little public sympathy for a landowner who is punished when he sets horrible traps for small-time poachers. But what if a person who has been plagued by repeated burglaries booby-traps his premises with an explosive device and gives full notice of it? (In France, where one thief was killed and his companion lost an eye as a result of such a device, set in such circumstances, a petition bearing 6000 signatures was organised to protest against the property-owner being prosecuted.[19])

What about revolving spikes and guard dogs?

The rule at common law can probably be said to be that things like spikes or broken glass on walls are lawful as devices to deter trespassers if they are not likely to cause serious injury and if the device is visible in ordinary daylight and its use is otherwise reasonable in the circumstances. Revolving spikes might quite possibly be held to be unreasonable; they may perhaps be held to be reasonable to prevent burglaries but perhaps not simple trespass. Keeping an ordinary kind of dog for defence of property is time-hallowed,[20] but it would not be lawful to train the dog to be unreasonably solicitous of your interests (gripping an intruder by the throat). The owner of the dog would become guilty of one of the usual crimes (such as manslaughter) on the principles relevant to them. In addition, there are special statutory provisions for keeping guard dogs under full control.[21] (Guard dogs in private homes or on agricultural land are exempt.)

§ 23.7. DEFENCE OF THE DWELLING

The law has always looked with special indulgence on a man who is defending his dwelling against those who would unlawfully evict him. When necessary, he may even go so far as to take life, for "the house of every one is to him as his castle and fortress."[1] This ancient rule was reaffirmed by the Court of Criminal Appeal in *Hussey* (1924),[2] when, remarkably, it was assumed to give a tenant the right to shoot a lessor (his landlady) who had given him a notice to quit that happened to be invalid. The landlady evidently thought that the notice was valid, and so (as the tenant must have known) thought she had a legal right to enter the premises and evict the tenant. Hussey did not fear death or injury; he simply faced eviction. It seems extraordinary that the right to shoot should have been extended to these circumstances.[3] The decision in *Hussey* has been criticised, but if the doctrine of precedent retains any force it represents the present law.

---

[19] The Times, April 27, 1978.

[20] The Animals Act 1971 s.5(3)(*b*) is a tort statute recognising the right to keep a dog in reasonable circumstances for protection against trespassers. See *Cummings* v. *Grainger* [1976] QB 397.

[21] Guard Dogs Act 1975 s.1. Cp. *Hobson* v. *Gledhill* [1978] 1 WLR 215.

[1] This proverbial remark is in *Semayne's* case (1604) 5 Co.Rep. at 91b, 77 ER at 195. Cp. 78 LQR 259. The rule as stated in the text above is not laid down in that case, but it goes back to Bracton f. 144b; cp. Hale, *PC* i 486.

[2] 18 CAR 160.

[3] See, for a contrary view of the law, Hawkins, *PC* i Chap. 28 s.23.

The condition is important: we have observed several instances of modern courts rewriting the law to suit their own opinions, and no one would be well advised to act on the assumption that *Hussey* would now be followed. Support for altering the ancient law might be found in the European Convention on Human Rights, which, after establishing the "right to life," provides, in article 2(2)(*a*), that there is a right to kill in defence only if the defence is that of "any person from unlawful violence." It seems probable, however, that this saving clause was meant to cover the person who is resisting violence or apprehended violence in an attack on his property.

In any case, the law is likely to be changed when the subject of private defence is put into statutory form. Nowadays it is virtually unknown for anyone to be evicted from a dwelling-house except by some one who thinks he has some sort of right to do so, and public policy pretty clearly indicates that the occupier should have no right to use extreme force against such an evicter even though the eviction is illegal. Abolition of the right to shoot to avoid eviction would not affect the right to shoot by an occupier who fears that the attacker will inflict death or serious injury on him.

The more difficult legislative question is whether there should be a right to shoot to avoid unlawful eviction by one who is known, or believed, not to be acting under a claim of right. The problem rarely arises in practice, if only because of the difficulty of getting a gun licence. Still, some people have guns; and if a man may shoot to prevent a burglary, as almost certainly he may,[4] it would seem to follow *a fortiori* that he can shoot to avoid being turned out of his house. A man, said Cardozo J, "is under no duty to take to the fields and the highways, a fugitive from his own home."[5]

The rule in *Hussey* does not apply where the defence is against a trespasser who does not seek to evict the inhabitants. But where an occupier is faced (especially at night) with an unknown intruder who may inflict injury on himself or his family, he will very readily be understood to have feared injury, and will be likely to be thought justified in resisting with any necessary force, even to the extent of using a lethal weapon.[6] However, no more than moderate force may be used against a gate-crasher at a party, say. The mere fact that the trespass is in a dwelling-house does not justify the infliction of extreme harm.[7]

§ 23.8. RE-ENTRY UPON LAND

The general principle stated at the beginning of § .6 applied at common law in favour of an owner exercising a right of re-entry on land (including buildings). It is, however, qualified by the Criminal Law Act 1977, which extends the offence of violence for securing entry[1] to cover even those who

---

[4] In 1972 Cusack J directed the acquittal of a householder who fatally stabbed a drunkard who was endeavouring to break in at night: *Frankum*, The Times, May 11.

[5] *People* v. *Tomlins* (1914) 213 NY 240, 107 NE 496.

[6] See David Lanham in [1966] Crim.LR 369–370. See, however, *Boyer* (1981) 145 JPN 220. The defendant was associating with a divorced woman; one evening the woman's former husband broke into his house, demanding to see her; the defendant shot and killed him, saying in court that he feared that he or the woman would be subjected to violence. Convicted of manslaughter, he was sentenced to 5 years' imprisonment. In this case the identity of the intruder was known; also, the defendant had not uttered a warning. Private defence was therefore ruled out, but, even so, it was a remarkably severe sentence

[7] [1966] Crim.LR at 371.

[1] For this offence see § 41.12.

have a right to the possession of premises.[2] The owner of a factory is therefore forbidden to use violence to eject work-men who are engaged in a sit-in. The offence does not extend to those who have a right of entry not based on an interest in or right to possession or occupation of the premises (so it does not affect rights of entry possessed by the police), nor to the displaced *residential* occupier of the premises.[3] This means that a person who has been wrongfully evicted from his dwelling (that is, from any house, flat, room, caravan etc. in which he was living) can still exercise his right of re-entry to the same extent as at common law; but a landlord cannot use violence to expel his tenant at the end of the tenancy, even though the landlord wishes to live in the house himself.[4]

The upshot is that the displaced residential occupier and those acting on his behalf can use necessary and reasonable (moderate?) force to effect a re-entry.[5] The right probably exists even though the wrongful possessor is known to be acting under a claim of right.[6] But he in his turn is probably entitled to defend the possession to which he believes himself entitled[7]; so blows may be exchanged without either party being criminally liable for them.

§ 23.9. THE PROTECTION OF MOVABLES

Necessary and reasonable (moderate?) force may be used to prevent unlawful damage to movables (chattels), or to prevent their dispossession.[1] The requirement of moderation would certainly be stressed if the attacker is known to be acting honestly (under a claim of right). If the attacker is a would-be robber, extreme force may be used under section 3[2] if it is reasonable in the circumstances. We have already sufficiently noticed the inadequacy of this formulation as a guide to conduct (§ 22.6).

In *Blades* v. *Higgs*,[3] the House of Lords accepted the unseemly proposition that an owner of goods may use force to recover them from a wrongful possessor, even though that possessor was a shopkeeper who had paid for the goods. The Canadian Code[4] adopts the more civilised principle that force in recaption may be used only against one who took by way of

---

[2] CLA 1977 s.6(2).

[3] *Ibid.* s.6(3); see the explanation of this term in s.12. For the difficulties, see A T H Smith in [1977] Crim.LR 146–167. See also, as to protected intending occupiers, § 46.12.

[4] The use of force by a landlord without a court order is also an offence under the Protection from Eviction Act 1977 s.1; cp. *Davidson-Acres* [1980] Crim. LR 50. It seems that an owner who forcibly enters property in breach of the CLA or the Rent Act could be charged with an offence against the person instead of an offence under those Acts, notwithstanding *Hemmings* v. *Stoke Poges Golf Club Ltd.* [1920] 1 KB 720, the Acts having impliedly abrogated the common law right of forcible entry; but the point is not absolutely clear, at any rate for the CLA.

[5] *McPhail* v. *Persons Unknown* [1973] Ch. at 456.

[6] On the analogy of *Hussey*, § .7 n. 2, and *Blades* v. *Higgs*, § .9 n. 3.

[7] *The General Part*, 2nd edn § 115 at n. 20.

[1] *Green* v. *Goddard* (1704) 2 Salk. 641, 91 ER 540; *Russell* v. *State* (1929) 219 Ala. 567, 122 So. 683.

[2] CLA 1977 s.6(2).

[3] (1865) 11 HLC 621, 11 ER 621; see criticism in Pollock, *Torts*, 15th edn 293 n. 81.

[4] S.38(1) (RSC 1970 Chap. C–34).

trespass; the *bona fide* purchaser (or *mala fide donee*, for that matter) must be sued if he is to be made to give up the goods.

§ 23.10. ABATEMENT OF NUISANCE

Another form of self-help is abatement of nuisance, as where a member of the public removes an obstruction in the highway. The right extends even to a private nuisance, where there is an obstruction to a private right of way.[1] Presumably there is a right to use moderate force to get past a person who is deliberately obstructing a highway or other way.[2] Lord Denning MR put the law even more widely:

> "Every person who is prevented from carrying out his lawful pursuits is entitled to use self-help, so as to prevent unlawful obstruction."[3]

This proposition goes beyond the decisions, but it is a useful principle that might well be developed. In any case the law of abatement of nuisance can perhaps be supplemented by the doctrine of necessity, which is discussed in § 26.8.

SUMMARY

In general, private defence is an excuse for any crime against the person or property. It probably applies to the defence even of a stranger, and may be used not only against culpable but against innocent aggressors. § .1

In general, defence is allowed only when it is immediately necessary against threatened violence. A person who acts under a mistaken belief in the need for defence is protected, except that the courts hold that the mistake must be reasonable. The best that can be said of this qualification is that it is construed leniently, at least in favour of the forces of order. On principle, it should be enough that the force used was in fact necessary for defence, even though the actor did not know this; but the law is not clear. There is no duty to retreat, as such, but even a defender must wherever possible make plain his desire to withdraw from the combat. The right of private defence is not lost by reason of the defender's having refused to comply with unlawful commands. § .2

The force used in defence must be not only necessary for the purpose of avoiding the attack but also reasonable, i.e. proportionate to the harm threatened; the rule is best stated in the negative form that the force must not be such that a reasonable man would have regarded it as being out of all proportion to the danger. The question of proportionality is for the jury. A person may lawfully threaten more force than he would be allowed to use. § .3

The carrying of firearms and other offensive weapons is generally forbidden, but (1) a thing is not an "offensive weapon" if it is not offensive *per se* and is carried only to frighten; (2) a person does not "have it with him" if he merely snatches it up in the emergency of defence, and (3) there is the defence of "reasonable excuse" where the defendant acted reasonably under an "imminent particular threat affecting the particular circumstances in which the weapon was carried."

---

[1] A public nuisance is a crime as well as (in some cases) a tort, whereas a private nuisance is only a tort except where it is made a specific statutory offence.

[2] Cp. *Beatty* v. *Gillbanks* § 15.4 at n. 8.

[3] *R* v. *Chief Constable of Devon and Cornwall* [1982] QB at 470G.

An arrester need not give back, and the right of self-defence may entitle him in the last resort to kill a resisting criminal when he could not lawfully kill a fleeing criminal. § .4

The right of defence avails against the police if they act illegally, but the defender cannot take benefit from a mistake as to the law of arrest or self-defence. It was held in *Fennell* that a person who rescues another from police detention does so at his peril of the detention being lawful, and cannot set up a mistake of fact. § .5

The occupier of premises may use necessary and reasonable force to defend them against a trespasser, or one reasonably thought to be a trespasser; and it seems that even a licensee (such as a lodger) can eject trespassing strangers. It is a statutory offence to set spring guns or man-traps, except in a dwelling-house between sunset and sunrise. It has not been decided whether the exception operates to confer an exemption from the ordinary law of offences against the person. Such defences as spikes and dogs are lawful if reasonable. Guard dogs must, by statute, be kept under full control, except in private houses or on agricultural land. § .6

The traditional rule is that even death may be inflicted in defence of the possession of a dwelling; and in *Hussey* this was applied even where the aggressor was acting, and was known to be acting, under a claim of right. § .7

A displaced occupier who uses violence to re-enter upon premises commits an offence under the Criminal Law Act 1977, apart from the displaced *residential* (or intending residential) occupier, who is given exemption. The latter may, therefore, use necessary and reasonable force to re-enter. § .8

Necessary and reasonable force may also be used to prevent unlawful damage to chattels, or to prevent their dispossession. According to *Blades* v. *Higgs*, it may be used even against a person who is known to claim the right to retain the goods, if the claim is invalid. § .9

Another form of lawful self-help is in respect of abatement of nuisance. § .10

CHAPTER 24

PROVOCATION

"Now we are even," quoth Steven, when he gave his wife six blows to one.
Jonathan Swift, *Journal to Stella*

§ 24.1. SCOPE OF THE DEFENCE

HALF the intentional killings of adult males are in a rage or a quarrel, and another 14 per cent. in jealousy or revenge.[1] The two emotions involved are anger and fear. Anger is the domain of the law of provocation, fear that of the law of private defence—though fear is also capable of amounting to provocation.

For crimes in general, provocation is matter of mitigation, to be considered by the judge in his discretion after conviction. There are no limiting rules. (Even a person who takes umbrage and assaults someone when under the influence of alcohol may receive some consideration on account of provocation.)

Murder is an exception. Provocation is a legal defence, but not one that necessarily allows the defendant to go free. If the jury accept the defence they are directed to return a verdict of manslaughter (which, as usual, is regarded as an included offence on a charge of murder). This is the form known as voluntary manslaughter, because the defendant intended to kill or otherwise had the mental element for murder. The judge has the usual wide range of discretion for manslaughter.

The life sentence is now never given for a provoked killing, even though it is theoretically possible. The Court of Appeal insists that if the jury have accepted a defence of provocation, or if the defendant to a murder charge has been allowed to plead guilty to manslaughter, the judge must accept the view of the facts implicit in the conviction, notwithstanding that he himself thinks there was no sufficient provocation. He must give a discount—generally a substantial discount—on what would have been the term served for murder.[2] With rare exceptions the sentence is now no longer than 7 years. Subject to this limit, sentences vary from excessive severity to extreme and sometimes unwise leniency, though with most, of course, in the middle range. Usually the sentence is for 5 or 3 years, but a person who kills in circumstances arousing particular sympathy may

[1] Evelyn Gibson, *Homicide in England and Wales 1967–1971* (Home Office Research Studies, 31) Table 16.

[2] *Jama* (1968) 52 CAR 498. Cp. *Paget* [1968] Crim.LR 397; *Wells* [1978] Crim.LR 570.

receive a suspended sentence,[3] probation,[4] or even a conditional discharge.[5] The witness to the harrowing history of the matter is, of course, the defendant; the other party, who might have given conflicting evidence, has been silenced. As much depends on the judge as on the circumstances: a judge who thinks in terms of the provocation received will sentence on the shorter side, while one who thinks in terms of protecting "the sanctity of life" will be more severe.[6]

Is provocation a defence when the defendant actually intended to kill?

It has sometimes been thought not. But the law is now clear that the answer is yes.[7]

If the defendant was obviously provoked, and severely provoked at that, will the prosecution ever reduce the charge to manslaughter off their own bat?

The practice is that magistrates do not commit, and the prosecution do not indict, for voluntary manslaughter. The indictment is for murder, the jury being left to convict of manslaughter if they think fit.[8] Occasionally, however, magistrates take the merciful course of committing for trial on the manslaughter charge only.[9] The defendant when charged with murder may offer a plea of guilty to manslaughter, and if this is accepted there will of course be no trial. The Crown often accepts a plea to voluntary manslaughter when the case does not fall within the rules for provocation to be studied in the following pages.[10]

Why do we need this law of provocation in murder? If we allowed the judge to have a discretion in sentencing for murders, would there then be any point in having a defence of provocation?

It is sometimes said that even then the judge would derive help from the verdict of the jury. In other crimes provocation can reduce punishmment, but only in murder does it regularly have a dramatic effect. So the jury relieve the judge of some responsibility.

Yes, but you say that on a verdict of voluntary manslaughter the judge may in practice give anything from about 7 years to a discharge. So the verdict of the jury does not really afford him much assistance. The punishment he actually metes out must depend on his own view of the facts as given in evidence. So I still don't see the point of taking the verdict of the jury. Why not let the judge decide on provocation for himself?

---

3 *Walsh*, The Times, July 5, 1974 (striking down drunken father for insulting his wife); *Westwood*, The Times, July 23, 1974 (wife stabbing husband who was having an affair); *Wright*, The Times, October 14, 1975 (husband killing unfaithful and grossly humiliating wife). A particularly surprising example is reported in The Times, November 21, 1973: a woman after a quarrel with her landlord beat him to death with his cricket bat. Her plea of guilty to manslaughter on the ground of provocation was accepted, and the judge, thus set free to decide the sentence, gave the woman a *suspended* sentence of 15 months' imprisonment.

4 *Ratcliffe*, The Times, May 13, 1980 (wife killing callous husband).

5 *Robertson*, The Times, May 22, 1975 (wife killing drunken, violent and depraved husband).

6 For a detailed study see A J Ashworth in [1975] Crim.LR 553, and on the virtual 7-year limit see *Donachie* [1983] Crim.LR 200.

7 *Martindale* [1966] 1 WLR 1564, 3 All ER 305.

8 But if there is any doubt about the mental element the prosecution may charge involuntary manslaughter, if only in order to shorten the proceedings: Wasik in [1982] Crim.LR 32.

9 A rare example is *Symondson* (1896) 60 JP 645.

10 Wasik, *op.cit.* 32–33.

I have given you the orthodox answers. My own answer would be two-fold. First, the conviction of manslaughter instead of murder explains to the public the leniency of the sentence. It avoids the headline: "Murderer gets suspended sentence."

Secondly, the defence of provocation resulting in a conviction of manslaughter serves the same function as other "included offences": it allows the jury to participate to a limited extent in sentencing. For most crimes they are expected to trust the judge to give the right sentence, but for a crime as serious as intentional homicide, where there are circumstances that appeal strongly to the sense of sympathy, it would impose a strain on the jury if they were not allowed to express a finding of mitigation.

But provocation is not the only point that may appeal strongly to the sense of sympathy. If it is a question of sympathy, why not allow a defence in all cases of murder (reducing it to manslaughter) where the jury think there are strong grounds of mitigation?

A partial answer is that the law does allow the defence of diminished responsibility in murder, which has the same effect as the defence of provocation. Diminished responsibility is supposed to be confined to circumstances of mental abnormality, but, as we shall see in Chapter 30, it is in practice stretched to cover some other circumstances calling strongly for compassion, such as mercy-killing.

It is true, however, that we have no general defence of mitigating circumstances in murder. There would be much to be said for allowing the jury a general discretion to return a verdict of murder with mitigating circumstances, if it were not for the fact that this would enable terrorists when put on trial to protract the proceedings with evidence of their supposed grievances. Mitigating circumstances can of course be taken into account by the parole board in deciding when to recommend parole.

You say that provocation is a defence to murder. In that case, isn't it also a defence to attempted murder?

The short answer to your question is that it has not yet called for consideration by the Court of Appeal.

The long answer is that the point is puzzling because logic gives conflicting answers.

The logic of the legal rules is this: if the crime intended had been committed it would not have been murder, so failure cannot amount to attempted murder. A man can attempt a crime only if he would be guilty of the crime if he succeeded. Logically, the case should be one of attempted manslaughter, and there is no reason why there should not be a conviction of this, though the point has never been brought before the courts.

Ah, but there is an opposing logic. This rests not on the legal rules but on the reasons for them. Provocation is allowed as a defence in murder (it is said) only because murder carries a fixed sentence.[11] Attempted murder does not carry a fixed sentence, so that the provocation may be allowed for in the punishment. There is no more reason for having a defence of

[11] This is the general opinion: *sed quaere*. See the previous discussion.

provocation to attempted murder than to any other crime not carrying a fixed sentence. Therefore, the killer in the case under discussion is guilty of attempted murder.

A possible answer to the latter argument is that not only murder but also attempted murder is so serious a crime that it is right that the existence of the provocation should be registered in the verdict, reducing the crime to attempted manslaughter. (Or, of course, if the defendant wounded the other party he could be convicted of the wounding.)

Formerly, the law was clear that the case was not one of attempted murder,[12] but in recent years trial judges have assumed the contrary, the older authorities not having been brought to their attention.[13] As said before, the question has not been decided at appellate level; but the CLRC has recommended the legislative reinstatement of the old rule.[14]

Isn't provocation just a form of revenge?

Killing in provocation is indeed a kind of killing in revenge, but we refrain from calling it that. The term "revenge" is used for retaliatory action that is planned and cold-blooded. Provocation refers to action in the heat of the moment, or action that is the product of desperation in intolerable circumstances.

Provocation as a defence to murder, unlike provocation as mitigation in other offences, has inevitably attained a degree of legal definition. The basic rules are simple, at any rate as a matter of words. It has been laid down that the judge should ask the jury two questions (and he is advised to ask them in this order[15]):

"1 Did the defendant as the result of provocation lose his self-control? If the answer is "No, he certainly didn't," then there is no provocation and you should convict of murder. But the burden of proving absence of provocation is on the prosecution, so if your answer is "Yes, he may have," then the defendant is over the first hurdle.

2 The question then is: "Was the provocation enough to make a reasonable man do as the defendant did?' "[16]

These two questions are sometimes labelled the subjective and the objective, the subjective relating to the defendant's loss of self-control, and the objective being an evaluation in terms of the hypothetical reasonable man. But in fact, as will be shown, the so-called subjective question traditionally involves a non-subjective element: the recency of the provocation. It would be better to call the two questions "factual" and "evaluative" respectively.

---

[12] *Thompson* (1825) 1 Mood. 80, 168 ER 1193; *Bourne* (1831) 5 C & P 120, 172 ER 903; *Beeson* (1835) 7 C & P 142, 173 ER 63; *Thomas* (1833) *ibid.* 817, 356; *Hagan* (1837) 8 C & P 167, 173 ER 445. The cases were decided on the special offence of wounding with intent to murder, which is now merged in the general crime of attempt to murder (OAPA 1861 s. 15 having been repealed by CLA 1967 Sched. 3). For conflicting overseas cases and a general discussion see Peter English in [1973] Crim.LR 727.

[13] *Bruzas* [1972] Crim.LR 367; *Campbell* (1977) 38 CCC (2d) 6 (Can.). In *Peck*, The Times, December 5, 1975, a man who stabbed his wife after he had caught her in her nightdress with his friend was convicted of attempted murder and sentenced to 12 years' imprisonment. It is very doubtful, on the authorities, whether the conviction was right, the question of provocation presumably not having been left to the jury. In any case, 12 years would be out of line with normal sentencing practice on conviction of manslaughter by reason of provocation. It is anomalous if the judges regard a killing more indulgently than an attempt to kill. See also *Jack* (1970) 17 CRNS 38 (Br.Col.).

[14] See [1980] Crim.LR 538.

[15] *Brown* [1972] 2 QB 229.

[16] In *Brown*, last note, the judge had framed the question numbered 2 above as: "*May* the [deceased's] acts have been of such a character as would have caused a reasonable person to lose his self-control and to react as the prisoner did?"—as though a burden of proof lay on the Crown. But in *Phillips* [1969] 2 AC at 137 the Privy Council rightly held that this question was one not of fact but of the jury's opinion; it involved a normative judgment. There could be no question of burden of proof. See also *Ives* [1970] 1 QB 208.(For another, but unlikely, interpretation of the word "may" see § 24.4 at n. 3.)

§ 24.2. THE FACTUAL QUESTION

The defendant bears an evidential burden in respect of provocation,[1] subject to a provision in the Homicide Act to be studied later. Therefore the judge can withdraw the defence from the jury if there is no reasonable evidence to support the defence on the factual question (loss of self-control). Nevertheless, judges now rarely withdraw the issue from the jury on the factual question, though the judge has sometimes told the jury that the evidence of provocation is extremely thin, or even that he himself cannot see any such evidence.

The factual question is sometimes expressed in purportedly psychological terms. Did the circumstances take the defendant over his threshold of tolerance? Could he prevent himself from acting as he did? Or—the favourite question—did he lose his self-control?

These seem to be useless or misleading formulations. By hypothesis the defendant passed his limit of tolerance, because he killed. To ask whether a person could prevent himself from doing something conjures up the absurd notion that he is two people, one trying to act and the other trying to stop him. Talk about losing self-control is acceptable as a way of speaking of an act done in the heat of anger, but it means no more than that. The angry man who kills in the heat of his anger has presumably lost his self-control; the angry man who does not kill (when he would rather like to) has to that extent kept his self-control; what does the test of self-control add to the test of killing in anger? And what is the point of saying that killing in the heat of anger involves loss of self-control? One who kills in a rage does what he wants to do in those circumstances, just as much as the calculating robber does. There is a difference in his emotional state, in motivation, and in the degree of reflection, but that is not well expressed by speaking of self-control. (Indeed, the killer may have evinced some retention of self-control and yet have the defence of provocation: he may have killed with one calculated thrust of a knife, when if he had gone completely berserk he might have delivered 20 wounds.[2]) So although judges sometimes instruct juries as if the question "Did he lose his self-control?" is self-explanatory, it would be better if more informative words were used. The jury may, for example, be told that the defendant must have acted in "heat of blood," in an "ungovernable passion" causing a "dethronement of reason," a ' 'temporary suspension of judgment"—the authorities are full of such language, though it would be clearer (and carry the same meaning) to say that he must have acted freshly after the provocation when in a great temper.

Soberly stated, there are two propositions.

(1) The defendant must have killed because he was provoked, not merely because provocation existed. There must be a causal relationship between the provocation and the killing. So if the defendant sought the provocation in order to kill his opponent the killing will not be mitigated.[3] Except in such circumstances the requirement of causal relationship hardly limits the defence, because where there is provocation followed immediately by a killing the causal relationship will be readily inferred unless there is evidence of premeditation.

---

[1] *Lee Chun-Chuen* [1963] AC 220; *Ibrams*, n. 12 below.

[2] See *Ashworth* in [1976] CLJ 306.

[3] East, *PC* i 239, citing *Mason* (1756) Fost. 132, 168 ER 66; cp. *Mawgridge* (1707) East, *PC* i 243, J Kel. 119, 84 ER 1107, Holt KB 484, 90 ER 1167; *Lynch* (1832) 5 C & P 324, 172 ER 995; *per* Coleridge J in *Kirkham* (1837) 8 C & P 115, 173 ER 422; *Selten* (1871) 11 Cox 674.

Such as evidence that he was carrying the weapon about with him?

A man who carries a weapon with which he kills will be in danger of failing in the defence of provocation *if* the jury think that the provocation was a mere pretext for the use of the weapon. But there is no rule excluding the defence merely because the defendant had the weapon on him. Even though he was carrying the fatal weapon, the defence of provocation is capable of succeeding if he had no intention of using the weapon before the provocation was offered.[4]

(2) The law attempts to distinguish between a killing in cold anger, when there is a deliberate decision to kill after weighing up the pros and cons, and an impulsive killing in hot blood where there is no weighing up at all. In practice the distinction generally depends upon the immediacy of the defendant's response to the provoking event. The provoking event must be sufficiently recent for the defendant to be passionately affected by it at the moment of killing.[5]

Where provocation has been given and cooling time has elapsed, smaller incidents may reopen the provocation than would be sufficient to constitute provocation if there had been no previous incident. The old provocation, like an old wound, may be reopened by a new affront, which need not in itself be sufficient to constitute provocation; and a person who kills when smarting under the fresh attack will be entitled to be judged on the whole background of his act.[6]

The immediacy (or "heat of the moment") principle was emphasised in a direction to a jury by Devlin J (as he then was) in *Duffy*,[7] which has been much admired and often read to juries by later judges.

> "Provocation is some act,[8] or series of acts, done by the dead man[9] to the accused which would cause in any reasonable person,[10] and actually causes[11] in the accused, a sudden and temporary loss of self-control, rendering the accused so subject to passion as to make him or her for the moment not master of his mind. . . . Circumstances which merely predispose to a violent act are not enough. Severe nervous exasperation or a long course of conduct causing suffering and anxiety are not by themselves sufficient to constitute provocation in law. . . . What matters is whether this girl had the time to say: "Whatever I have suffered, whatever I have endured, I know that Thou shalt not kill." Similarly, circumstances which induce a desire for revenge, or a sudden passion of anger, are not enough. Indeed, circumstances which induce a desire for revenge are inconsistent with provocation, since the conscious formulation of a desire for revenge means that a person has had time to think, to reflect, and that would negative a sudden temporary loss of self-control which is of the essence of provocation."

---

[4] *Fantle*, below § .3 n. 2; cp. *Hopkins* (1866) 31 JP 105, 10 Cox 229; *Lett* (1963) 6 West Indian Reports 92. The fact that the defendant was carrying the weapon may actually be to his advantage on the issue of cooling time.

[5] East, *PC* i 238, 251. For authorities on cooling time and the psychological basis of the rule see 1st edn 481–483.

[6] Thus it was ruled in *McCarthy* [1954] 2 QB 105 that where an indecent assault was followed by an invitation to sodomy, the words were capable of reviving or continuing the provocation, though at that time they would not have been sufficient in themselves (direction of trial judge not disapproved by CCA). Cp. the note on *Prince* [1941] 3 All ER 37, 28 CAR 60, in 28 CAR at 140; *Hopper* [1915] 1 KB 431; *Parker* [1964] AC 1369; *Finley*, The Times, November 24, 1964 (provocation by adultery revived by the adulterer's grinning at defendant); *Peter Davies*, § .3 n. 8; *Wells* [1978] Crim.LR 570; Ashworth in [1975] Crim.LR 557 and [1983] *ibid.* 125. But there are some contrary authorities: see Wasik in [1982] Crim.LR 31.

[7] [1949] 1 All ER 932.

[8] Reference should now be made also to words: see later.

[9] But it may now be another person: § .3 at n. 9.

[10] It would be better to say "which might cause a reasonable person:" § .4.

[11] It would be more accurate to say "may have actually caused:" § .1 at n. 15.

It may be questioned whether the direction does not state the law too restrictively. It fails to tell the jury that affronts over a long period of time inducing the desire for revenge do not preclude the defence of provocation, if immediately before the last affront the defendant did not intend to kill. Nor does it tell the jury that the last affront may be comparatively trivial, merely the last straw that makes the worm turn, so to speak. Later cases at trial level show greater readiness to recognise the effect of cumulative provocation. But the Court of Appeal still insists that a defence of provocation, even in cases of long-standing provocation or emotional stress, needs a finding of something that can be called provocation immediately before the killing.[12] So if the defendant is to hope for leniency on this, it must be at the hands of the trial judge.

The "immediacy" principle makes sense when the provocation is an assault, but immediacy doesn't seem very important when the provocation is a spouse's infidelity, which may be a long-standing grievance becoming worse for being brooded over. It's irrational to think of "simmering down" when jealousy and anger have been built up over the years. "To be wroth with one we love doth work like madness in the brain."

You have a point. Certainly if one looks at the practice of trial courts and the verdicts of juries one sees a slight movement of opinion in favour of relaxing the immediacy rule. The types of case in which this is sometimes done in practice (without admitting it) are those of great stress resulting from physical cruelty by a spouse or parent, where the defendant did not find it possible to distance himself (or, more commonly, herself) from the persecutor. There is also some indication of the same tendency in cases of prolonged marital infidelity.

However, as said before, the requirement of immediacy still applies at appellate level, and the CLRC has recommended its continuance.[13] It would be difficult to abolish (except as regards a killing within the family) without extending provocation to cover revenge-killing. Where the provocation is not immediate leniency depends on the judge accepting a plea to manslaughter, or the jury indulgently finding a verdict of manslaughter. If the judge instructs the jury on the immediacy principle in traditional terms and the jury therefore reject the defence, or if the judge withdraws the provocation issue from the jury on the ground that such provocation as there was was not recent, the result will be a conviction of murder, and the Court of Appeal has shown no sign of readiness to intervene. Even if the conviction is of manslaughter, there is very wide disparity of sentencing in these cases, ranging from virtual let-off (which is open to the objection of dangerously diluting deterrence) to a prison sentence of several years (even in cases where the defendant had endured years of misery at the hands of the person he killed). So the outcome is very much a lottery.

Two examples may be given of the vagaries of sentencing. According to the newspaper report in one case, a woman's plea of guilty to manslaughter of her husband by reason of provocation was accepted where she had told the police that her husband was accustomed to force her to have sexual intercourse with him by burning her on the breast and arm with a lighted cigarette. She borrowed a carving knife from a friend and six days later stabbed her husband to death with it. Sentence: probation.[14] The court does not seem to have considered the danger that if such sentences were frequent the carving knife might become accepted as offering a cleaner and speedier break with the past than the divorce court.

In the other case, two sisters, together with their mother, had to deal with a brutal and drunken father. When he was in one of his violent rages they floored him by hitting him over

---

[12] *Ibrams* (1982) 74 CAR 154.
[13] 14th Report para. 84.
[14] The Times, May 13, 1980.

the head, and the sisters resolved that if he was again violent towards them after coming round they would kill him. He attacked them again, and one of them stabbed him to death. In strict law this could have been held to be murder, because of the deliberate planning; but the jury returned a verdict of manslaughter. The elder sister, aged 21, was sent to prison for 3 years, upheld on appeal.[15] Certainly a prison sentence was justified, but there was severe provocation in fact, and the length of the sentence has evoked doubts.

The time is overdue for the Court of Appeal to extend the defence of provocation in family killings, but at the same time to give guidance in sentencing so as to achieve a better compromise between sympathy and deterrence.

The immediacy rule can always be by-passed, even if the trial judge wishes to enforce it, if the defendant can get medical evidence bringing him within the law of diminished responsibility.

§ 24.3. THE EVALUATIVE QUESTION

The evaluative question refers to the supposed conduct of the reasonable man, meaning by that a reasonable man/woman[1]/youngster of the defendant's age. The governing enactment is section 3 of the Homicide Act 1957:

> "Where on a charge of murder there is evidence on which the jury can find that the person charged was provoked (whether by things done or by things said or by both together) to lose his self-control, the question whether the provocation was enough to make a reasonable man do as he did shall be left to be determined by the jury; and in determining that question the jury shall take into account everything both done and said according to the effect which, in their opinion, it would have on a reasonable man."

In addition to the evaluative question there were formerly rules at common law limiting what would be regarded as provocation. In particular, words were generally incapable of being provocation.

Partly because of this, and partly because of a series of restrictive decisions in the House of Lords on the evaluative question, it came to be thought that the law of provocation was too narrow. The remedy hit upon was curious. Instead of rethinking the law, Parliament decided to increase the function of the jury at the expense of the judge; hence the wording of section 3. Its effect is threefold.

(1) It prevents the judge from withdrawing the defence of provocation from the jury on the ground that there is no evidence on which a jury can find that a reasonable man would have acted as the defendant did. The jury alone decide that question, and they decide it according to their opinion.

---

[15] *Maw* (1980); see 130 NLJ 1163. See also the study of sentencing practice by Wasik in [1982] Crim.LR 29.

[1] See § .4.

(2) As a corollary of the first point, the section prevents the judge from telling the jury in positive terms how a reasonable man would behave. He cannot direct the jury as a matter of law that a reasonable man would not have behaved like that, for it would be stultifying to leave a defence to the jury and at the same time direct them that they cannot entertain it. That would amount in effect to not leaving the defence to them. There would be no harm in suggesting how a reasonable man might be expected to act, but certainly a judge could no longer lay it down to the jury, as judges did before the Act, that "fists might be answered with fists but not with a deadly weapon."

(3) By the casual parenthesis the section establishes that words can be provocation. This change in the law applies both in respect of informative words (such as a confession of adultery, made either by the adulterous spouse or by the interloper[2]) and in respect of insults. It makes a large extension of the defence of provocation, which had previously been confined to severe blows and the "ocular demonstration" of adultery.

The section continues the test of the reasonable man, yet it seems strange to suppose that the reasonable man would ever kill as the result of a merely verbal insult. Did we not as children incant the lines: "Sticks and stones may break my bones but words will never hurt me"? Although it would always be open to a jury to reject a defence based on insults, the question must be left to them.

Is the reasonable man who is the test of provocation supposed to have the defendant's blemishes? The most hurtful insults are those that remind one about one's own defects.

Yes: the reasonable man is supposed to have the defendant's physical defects. Before the Act the House of Lords had held that even hurtfully true insults were no palliation of a killing. It was to alleviate the law on this point that section 3 was passed.

> In the case just mentioned, an impotent youth visited a prostitute to try to establish his own virility; he failed in the proof, and she taunted him, whereupon he killed her; on a charge of murder, the judge directed the jury in terms of what the reasonable or ordinary person would have done, and appeals against conviction of murder were dismissed.[3] If the case arose again the judge would have to direct the jury to consider whether a reasonable impotent youth might have reacted in that way.

But the abolition of the rule about words is only the tip of the iceberg. It seems that the section has abolished any and every restriction that may have existed on the acts that are capable of being provocation. Section 3, said Lord Diplock in *Camplin*,[4]

> "abolishes all previous rules of law as to what can or cannot amount to provocation. . . . The judge is entitled, if he thinks it helpful, to

---

[2] As in *Fantle* [1958] Crim.LR 782, [1959] *ibid*. 584.
[3] *Bedder* [1954] 1 WLR 1119, 2 All ER 801, 38 CAR 133.
[4] [1978] AC at 716C,G.

suggest considerations which may influence the jury in forming their own opinion as to whether the test is satisfied; but he should make it clear that these are not instructions which they are required to follow; it is for them and no one else to decide what weight, if any, ought to be given to them."

Similarly Lord Morris[5]:

"All questions are for the jury. . . . The courts are no longer entitled to tell juries that a reasonable man has certain stated and defined features."

Even before the Act it was clear that an attack by the deceased on a third person could be provocation to the defendant.[6] But it was not clear whether the seduction of the defendant's daughter, for example, could be a provocation to him, or an extremely offensive trespass (slashing off the heads of his prize tulips), or cruelty to animals. Since the Homicide Act there can hardly be any doubt that every act[7] of annoyance must be left to the jury if there is some evidence that the defendant was in fact angry and committed the act of violence immediately after the provocation.

This conclusion is borne out by *Peter Davies.*[8] Before the Act, it had been held that adultery by the defendant's wife did not mitigate his killing of their child: provocation had to come from the victim.[9] This disregarded the psychological phenomenon of "displacement." However, in *Peter Davies* it was held that provocation can come from a source other than the victim, and the change in the law was specifically derived from the wording of section 3.

The facts were that Davies lived happily with his wife until they met X, who conducted a campaign of seduction of the wife. She left Davies, who was in a state of extreme jealousy and resentment. Davies made various threats against the lives of his wife and X, and on the occasion in question he went, armed with a shotgun, to the library where his wife worked and saw her coming down the steps to greet her lover. Thereupon he shot and killed her. A conviction of murder was upheld on appeal, notwithstanding that the judge had directed the jury to consider only the act of the deceased wife and not the act of X in walking towards her. This, said the court, was a technical misdirection (X's act could be provocation for the killing of the wife), but the misdirection could not have produced a miscarriage of justice because the jury could not have considered the act of the wife except in its relation to the act of X. The wife was going to meet X, and it was this fact, rather than X's act, that was the provocation relied upon by the defence.

---

[5] *Ibid.* at 720D.

[6] *Mawgridge* (1707) J Kel. 119, 84 ER 1107.

[7] It must be an act ("everything both done and said" in s. 3). It was held in Malawi that belief that the deceased was a witch was merely a belief in a state of affairs, and the state of affairs did not amount to a provoking event: *Lufazema* (1967) 4 African LR, Mal. 355. This decision was under the Penal Code which required provocation to be "sudden," and it was apparently recognised that a person's sudden belief that he has discovered an *act* of witchcraft may be a provoking event.

[8] [1975] Q.B. 691. See A T H Smith in [1975] CLJ 188. Cp. *Twine* [1967] Crim.LR 710; [1974] ASCL 64].

[9] Except that it has long been recognised that in cases of transferred intention provocation is transferred with the intention: *Porritt* [1961] 1 WLR 1372, 3 All ER 463, 45 CAR 348.

We do not, of course, know why the jury rejected the defence: perhaps they did not think it would ever be reasonable for a jealous husband to kill his wife; or perhaps they saw premeditation in Davies's carrying of the gun; or perhaps they thought that the substantial provocation was too stale (the spouses had been living apart for three months). Technically it could be revived by slight new provocation; but if the mere sight of the faithless wife meeting her lover were regarded as sufficient at any time to revive the provocation, there would be no limit to the time at which the jilted husband could kill, within the limits of the defence.

Trifles light as air are to the jealous confirmations strong as proofs of holy writ.

Davies did not need confirmation of the association between his wife and her seducer.

Would the sight of the wife walking down the library steps *without* the presence of her lover have been something "done" within the meaning of section 3 as a possible provoking event that would have had to be left to the jury? The answer must surely be no. To say that the mere sight of one who had formerly given provocation walking down steps is a provoking event would wholly abrogate the rule of law that the killing must immediately follow the provoking event. In *Peter Davies,* the issue of provocation was properly left to the jury because the wife was actually meeting her lover.[10]

The wife's act of walking down the steps was lawful. Does the decision mean that a lawful act can be provocation?

Before the Homicide Act it was hardly possible for a lawful act to be provocation. Adultery could be provocation, but, though not a crime, it was illegal in some way, being a matrimonial offence. There was a rule of long standing that lawful blows could not be provocation[11]; *a fortiori* lawful acts not involving blows. (The only relaxation before the Act was that one judge was prepared to say that infidelity by a mistress could be provocation, even though the mistress was under no legal tie.[12])

The exclusion of lawful blows was justifiable on grounds of policy, for otherwise the deliberate killing of a police officer who was compelled to use force to make an arrest or in self defence could have been mitigated on account of provocation—unless the defence were excluded under the test of a reasonable man.

The Homicide Act, in allowing insults as provocation, inevitably alters the position, because an insult uttered in private is neither a crime nor even a tort. Section 3 contains no restriction to unlawful acts, and the courts

---

[10] The trial judge left the case to the jury on the footing that they could review the whole course of conduct of the wife. The CA inexplicably said that this was "too generous a direction." Surely it was well established that a new provoking act can revive the old, in which case the jury must consider the old with the new.

[11] *Mawgridge* (1707) J Kel. 119, 84 ER 1107; *Bourne* (1831) 5 C & P 120, 172 ER 903; *Sees,* The Times, April 21, 1961,231 LTJo. 246.

[12] *Larkin* (1943) 29 CAR 18 (giving facts not contained in [1943] KB 174).

seem to be ready to allow any provocative conduct to be taken into consideration, even though that conduct was itself provoked by the defendant.[13] Consequently, there is no longer any reason why the defence should not be available (if the jury uphold it) to the jilted lover who kills the object of his affections or her new lover, or the man who kills his irritating neighbour, or the parent who kills a constantly crying baby. Even the rule about lawful blows seems to survive only as a consideration that the jury can take into account when applying the test of reasonableness.

> For example: D attacks V, V responds in self-defence, and D then kills V. At his trial for murder D gives evidence that he did not originally intend to kill Y but was angered by his blows. It seems that the judge should, strictly, since the Homicide Act leave a defence of provocation to the jury, even though V's acts were lawful.

So if the Minister for Education and Science addresses a students' meeting, and a student, taking umbrage because the Minister says that he will not consider raising grants, shoots him dead, this could be provocation?

Presumably, though I hasten to add that the jury would be unlikely to allow it to be the act of a reasonable man.

And if a bank clerk refuses to hand the keys of the strong room to a robber, and the robber shoots him, this also could be provocation for the killing?

I can only repeat that, so far as it appears, the judge would have to leave the evaluative question to the jury. He might withdraw the defence on the factual question, because the evidence that the robber carried a gun showed premeditation. Conceivably, too, if the court were pushed to it, it might be held that such circumstances are outside the notion of provocation. Provocation traditionally means a wrongful act,[14] even though the notion of wrongfulness is extended to include infidelity by a spouse, and, now, insults. So it might possibly be held that even since the Homicide Act the judge can imperatively direct the jury that a completely lawful act cannot be provocation.[15] The argument for a direction of this kind is particularly strong where the alleged provocation is an act done in obedience to public legal duty, such as the act of a police officer in arresting. If the judge can direct the jury that such a case does not constitute provocation in law, then he can on such facts tell the jury that

---

[13] As in *Whitfield* (1976) 63 CAR 39, where the defendant by pestering his estranged wife at her place of work caused her to insult him. Yet in *Edwards* [1973] AC 648, the Privy Council on appeal from Hong Kong held that a blackmailer whose victim attacked him could not rely on the predictable results of his own conduct as constituting provocation in relation to his retaliatory killing of the victim. According to this, if the victim reacted by blows with the fist, this would not be provocation (though if he went to extreme lengths, as by using a knife, this could be). Cp. *Leung Ping-Fat* (1973) 3 HKLJ 342. This restriction of the defence is highly doubtful as a matter of common law (cp. *Squire* (1975) 31 CRNS at 326–327 (Ont.)), and in any case is irreconcilable with s. 3; a provision like s. 3 was in force in Hong Kong under the Homicide Ordinance, and it is remarkable that the Privy Council made no reference to it. See A J Ashworth in [1973] Crim.LR 483 and note in [1972] Crim.LR 783.

[14] See Ashworth in [1976] CLJ 307.

[15] The Privy Council in *Palmer* [1971] AC at 825, on appeal from Jamaica, even doubted whether an illegal arrest could now be provocation, although the old cases held that it could. But the doubt was plainly wrong. In England the issue would have to he left to the jury under the Homicide Act.

he is withdrawing the issue of provocation from them. But such a restriction of the legal meaning of provocation would qualify what was said in *Camplin*, and would in effect be a reintroduction of legal rules on the evaluative question. It would be better to honour the intention of Parliament, so long as section 3 remains law, by leaving the jury to make the evaluation. If in the circumstances you have imagined the jury scandalously accept that the bank clerk's act was provocative, Parliament will have to reword the law in a more sensible way.[16]

What if the judge refuses to leave the issue of provocation to the jury when he should, or misdirects them on it, so that they return a verdict of murder?

The Court of Appeal will quash the conviction of murder and substitute one of manslaughter, with such sentence as it thinks appropriate for that. It will not apply the proviso.[17]

And what if the judge gives an impeccable direction but the jury perversely refuse to mitigate the killing?

The conviction will apparently stand.

At one time the judges would robustly upset what they considered to be a perverse verdict.[18] But practice has changed, and a verdict of the jury rejecting the defence of provocation seems to be regarded as final.[19] There is nothing in section 3 to compel this attitude, which is hard to explain. The non-interventionist policy of the Court of Appeal adds to the danger of divergent verdicts in an area where the law is unhelpful.

One type of case where discordance is perhaps particularly likely is that of killing in jealousy. An Australian judge said that he would be sorry to think in this day and age that homicide following a confession of adultery necessarily justifies a manslaughter verdict[20]; and it is probable that a verdict embodying this view and convicting of murder would be upheld, when another jury applying traditional attitudes might convict of manslaughter.

§ 24.4. DIFFICULTIES WITH THE REASONABLE MAN TEST

The introduction of the reasonable man into the law of provocation is strange. Elsewhere the "reasonable man" test is used to indicate a standard of care required by law. The reasonable man is careful, moral, prudent, calculating, law-abiding. How absurd, then, to imagine that he is capable of losing all control of himself and committing a crime punishable with imprisonment for life!

To say that the "ordinary" man will commit this crime is hardly less inapt. The reason why provoked homicide is punished is to deter people from committing the offence, and it is a

---

[16] See the excellent draft by Macaulay for the Indian Penal Code, reprinted in [1978] Crim.LR 526. Cp. NZ Crimes Act 1961 s. 169 (5). The CLRC proposed to settle many questions by the repeal of section 3 coupled with improvements in the law, but, regrettably, refrained from proposing a specific rule relating to lawful official acts. See 14th Report paras. 81–88; [1980] Crim.LR 537.

[17] See § .7 at n. 4. *Whitfield* (1976) 63 CAR 39 leaves open the possibility of the proviso being applied on unspecified occasions. *Peter Davies*, above n. 9, was exceptional because the misdirection was held to be irrelevant. See generally § 2.7.

[18] *Ayes* (1810) Russ. & R 167, 168 ER 741.

[19] In *Hodges*, The Times, March 20, 1962, the CCA affirmed a conviction of murder while saying that "there was ample evidence to go to the jury to suggest that the appellant was labouring under intense provocation."

[20] *Per* Herron CJ in *Stone* [1965] NSWR at 899.

curious (and erroneous) forecast of failure for the law to assume that, notwithstanding the possibility of heavy punishment, an ordinary person will commit it.

Killing upon provocation is very unusual. This is particularly true of killing in jealousy, which is a long established instance of provocation. In 1980, adultery was alleged in 48,879 petitions for divorce[1]; and doubtless many spouses discovered this conduct without taking divorce proceedings, and many others took proceedings without giving adultery as a ground. We lack figures of voluntary killings for adultery, but, in comparison with the instances of adultery, they must be insignificant. To say that the ordinary man or woman kills for adultery is a grotesque untruth, and has been so for centuries.

Perhaps the provocation must be great enough to make the ordinary man wobble.

A hard test to apply. We might be more realistic if instead of speaking of all reasonable men or any reasonable man (as Devlin J did in *Duffy*[2]) we spoke of *a* reasonable man (as section 3 does). Alternatively or additionally, it might be better, instead of asking what the (or a) reasonable man *would* do, for the judge to ask the jury to consider what the (or a) reasonable man *may* do.[3] Not all reasonable men kill their wives discovered in adultery, but one reasonable man in a few hundred thousand may do so. It is nevertheless an odd conception of the reasonable man. Besides, since no one supposes that the law's reasonable man exists, there is no sense in putting a statistical probability on his occurrence.

So we just shunt the question off to the jury. What on earth are the poor things to go on?

Perhaps they do not trouble with it, and simply ask themselves whether the defendant was badly provoked. Or perhaps they try to imagine whether they would have done it themselves. Gross variation of judgment is possible, because people's capacity for sympathetic self-identification with others (empathy) varies.

Take again the question of sexual jealousy. Many jurors will say to themselves with complete truth and conviction that they would never kill their spouses for unfaithfulness; yet they are allowed by legal tradition to say that the reasonable person will, or at least may. To empathise successfully they have to imagine not merely that they have been given up by their loved one but that they were as jealous and distraught as the defendant was. Whether they find provocation or not may depend on their success in making the effort of imagination. Again, how successful is the average juror likely to be in imagining his own behaviour if he were deserted by a homosexual partner? He can hardly think of himself with a homosexual partner in the first place.

The Criminal Law Revision Committee has proposed that the test should be reworded so that provocation is a defence to murder if, on the facts as they appeared to the defendant, it can reasonably be regarded as a sufficient ground[4] for the loss of self-control leading the

---

[1] Judicial Statistics 1980 p. 68.

[2] § 24.2 n. 7.

[3] There were variations of wording on these points in *Camplin*. Their lordships appeared to see no difference between asking what effect the provocation *would* have on a reasonable man (the formulation in s. 3) and what effect it *could* or *might* have. See [1978] AC at 716C, D, 718F, 719B, E, G, 720D, 721D, 722A. The proper word, surely, is "might" or "may."

[4] The word "ground" was carefully chosen. The committee did not want to say "excuse," because that might lead the jury to think the excuse had to be a complete exculpation. "Reason" would be out of place for an act that was by hypothesis unreasonable. "Ground of mitigation in respect of the loss of self-control" might be clearest.

defendant to react against the victim with murderous intent.[5] The rewording would not solve the problem for the jury, but the committee thought it might express the question in slightly clearer words. It is a logical improvement to make the word "reasonably" refer to the jury's reasoning faculty instead of attaching to what the defendant did.

You said before that the reasonable man is supposed to be afflicted by the defendant's physical imperfections if the question is how he is to be imagined as reacting to an insult.[6] Does the law always allow the jury to invest the reasonable man with the defendant's characteristics?

The answer is not simple. The leading case on the provocation defence is now *Camplin*, where Lord Diplock, speaking with the concurrence of the other Lords on this particular point, explained it in the following terms.

> "In my opinion a proper direction to a jury on the question left to their exclusive determination by section 3 of the Act of 1957[7] would be on the following lines. The judge should state what the question is using the very terms of the section. He should then explain to them that the reasonable man referred to in the question is a person having the power of self-control to be expected of an ordinary person of the sex and age of the accused, but in other respects sharing such of the accused's characteristics as they think would affect the gravity of the provocation to him; and that the question is not merely whether such a person would in like circumstances be provoked to lose his self-control but also whether he would react to the provocation as the accused did."[8]

Elsewhere in his opinion Lord Diplock made it clear that the "ordinary man" into whom the reasonable man is thus turned is not to be discovered by observation. He is "possessed of such powers of self-control as everyone is entitled to expect that his fellow-citizens will exercise in society as it is today."[9] A value-judgment is involved, and it is made by the jury. No evidence is allowed to be given on how reasonable men behave, or even on "how a pregnant woman or a 15-year-old boy or a hunchback would, exercising reasonable self-control, react in the circumstances."[10]

That factual evidence is impossible on how *reasonable* people behave is obvious, since such evidence would be question-begging. (The scientific witness cannot select his exemplars of behaviour without first having decided that they are reasonable men.) The passage, as worded, does not conclude the question whether evidence is admissible to show how pregnant women etc. *do* behave, but Lord Diplock probably meant to say that it is not admissible; and other authorities suggest the same conclusion.[11]

I think I am now quite lost. To start with, I don't understand why Lord Diplock's "age and sex" should come into it. We are talking about a standard, aren't we? Surely we expect youths and women to restrain themselves from killing just as much as adult males. In fact the female of the

---

[5] 14th Report paras. 81–82.

[6] § 24.3 at nn. 3–4.

[7] § 24.3.

[8] [1978] AC at 718E.

[9] *Ibid.* at 685A, 717A. Lord Morris regarded the reasonable man as a "mythical person" (p. 719H), evidently meaning an imaginary person.

[10] *Ibid.* at 716E, 727F.

[11] For the exclusion of psychiatric evidence on the behaviour of the ordinary man see Samuels in [1981] Crim.LR 764–765.

species is less dangerous than the male, but the point should have no legal relevance.

Your words come like a breath of fresh air. The legal relevance of age was decided in *Camplin*, and the decision perhaps resulted in part from the analogy of the law of negligence, where age is taken into account. But the analogy is imperfect. Negligence is considerably concerned with questions of judgment and experience, which depend on age; whereas provocation is concerned with self-control, which, in the basic matter of not killing, should be acquired contemporaneously with the acquisition of the physical power to kill. However, it is humane to say that the jury can take youth into account; whether it is logical or not, the rule works in the direction of leniency.

Sex should be completely irrelevant. Lord Diplock spoke as if there were or might be some sex difference in respect of the power of self-control in the abstract. That proposition, if seriously advanced, would operate to the disadvantage of the gentle sex. It must be so much easier to restrain oneself from violence if one has oestrogen in one's blood instead of androgen; so a woman who gives way to an impulse to violence must be more blameworthy than a man! This would be a paradoxical result of introducing a reference to sex here. In fact no one would want to pursue such a line of reasoning.

Lord Diplock's reference to pregnant women did not imply that any special legal considerations were involved in pregnancy; in fact he said the opposite. It has not been suggested that pregnant women as a class are unduly prone to violence. Pregnancy is simply one of the facts of existence that may sometimes lead to tragedy. A woman may be depressed by her pregnancy, and may perhaps kill her former lover who rejects her; but that is merely an instance of the circumstances that drive people to great anger. The jury may have to consider any one of an infinite number of such circumstances. (That a male juror may have to imagine himself pregnant may sound strange, but it is no harder for him to imagine himself a pregnant woman who has been jilted than it is for a female juror to imagine herself a youth who has been taunted for impotence by a prostitute.)

Well, then, with age and sex cleared out of the way as being very largely red herrings (though I appreciate that they must now be mentioned to the jury—as though jurors hadn't got enough to bother them already), what about Lord Diplock's "characteristics"? Was he merely referring to a characteristic that may give sting to a jibe?

To some extent at least he certainly had that in mind. It is not only a question of jibes. In one case the court accepted that knocking away a man's crutch could be provocation, taking account of the fact that the man was one-legged.[12] His disability was his very sore spot. All the pain and inconvenience suffered from it in the past were concentrated into rage when an attack was directed against the thing that did something to

[12] *Raney* (1942) 29 CAR 14.

alleviate the disability and was at the same time its symbol. Sex may itself be a characteristic from this point of view, as where (to take an illustration given by Lord Simon in *Camplin*) a woman is taunted as a whore.[13]

Beyond that we are left in some darkness. Although Lord Diplock did not expressly answer the question whether his "characteristics" can be matters that do not bear on the particular provocation, it may be thought that the answer can be spelt out from what he said. If the characteristics do not relate to the provocation they must, one would suppose, relate to the defendant's ability to control his reaction to it; but the implication of the model direction is that the defendant's general ability to control himself is to be regarded as independent of his 'characteristics." Although the defendant has only one leg, he can (or should be able) to control his temper as well as the next man; but his handicap may determine the circumstances that infuriate him. Which leads to the conclusion that the "characteristic" must relate to the provocation. If this is so, *Camplin* does not affect the proposition that a defendant who fails to show normal self-control is not entitled to a manslaughter verdict merely because he had an artificial leg, was impotent, was under stress, had been sleeping badly, had had a row with his wife, or, in short, was irritable either by nature or on any other account. "Characteristics" therefore do not include matters that bear simply on the general capacity for self-control.

The conclusion, if correct, casts doubt on *Raven*,[14] where the Recorder of London, purporting to apply *Camplin*, ruled that a man whose physical age was 22 but whose mental age was only 9 years was to be judged by reference to "a reasonable man who has lived the same type of life as the defendant for 22 years but who has the mental age of the defendant." This means that the reasonable man must in these circumstances be assumed to be mentally deficient! The ruling may perhaps be justified as an extension to "mental age" of the *Camplin* rule for ordinary age. At the same time, it must be said that the concept of "mental age" is only a convenient expression for performance in an intelligence test, and is not normally regarded either in law or in psychology as a substitute for actual age. The ruling was a merciful concession to people who are very mentally retarded; that is all.

Further difficulty is caused by a dictum of Lord Simon in *Camplin*. Seeking some reason for introducing a reference to the reasonable woman, he suggested that it would "presumably" be relevant to provocation that a female defendant was menstruating or in the menopause when provoked.[15] The fact that a woman is menstruating or about to do so does not relate to a particular provocation (or is most unlikely to do so). It may affect her "capacity for self-control," because it makes her irritable; but that is generally regarded as being governed by an objective test, which does not vary as between women who are menstruating and those who are not; and the same applies to the menopause (which of course may affect men as well). To hold that evidence may be given to show that the defendant was in some way particularly liable to be provoked because of his own make-up and not for any reason

---

[13] [1978] AC at 724E. Cp. Lord Morris at 721E.
[14] [1982] Crim.LR 51.
[15] See n. 13.

connected with the particular provocation would considerably change the law, for the rule in the past has always been that the peculiar irritability or sensitivity or excitability of the defendant does not affect the evaluative test; and this, indeed, was recognised in *Camplin* itself.[16] It is the whole purpose of the evaluative question. "We boil at different degrees," said Emerson; but the law has a notion of normal boiling point. For these reasons the dicta about menstruation and the menopause must be regarded as mistaken.

What if the defendant was drunk? Is his drunkenness a "characteristic" which is attributed to the reasonable man as modifying the usual standard, or do you ignore it and expect the defendant to have the self-control of a sober person?

The latter. The courts have for many years refused to look indulgently on intoxicated people whose condition has made them unusually irritable and unrestrained. This was reaffirmed by the Court of Appeal after *Camplin* in *Newell*.[17] The Court of Appeal there held that intoxication is not a "characteristic" within the rule in *Camplin*, and therefore must be disregarded; further, that even if it is a "characteristic," the characteristic must be connected with the provocation if it is to be considered, which intoxication normally is not.

In sober people the emotional impulse released by anger is under the control, to a certain extent, of the higher brain centres, and it is just these centres that are depressed by alcohol. Hence a drunken person may be provoked to an aggressive reaction by a stimulus that would cause only slight irritation to a sober person.[18] Why the drunkard must be excluded from the defence is not clear; perhaps the exclusion is based on moralistic grounds, or grounds of justice (a sober defendant would have a grievance if a lower standard of behaviour were permitted for drunkards), or on the fear that murderers would make a point of becoming intoxicated before the deed.[19]

Will the outcome of the case ever vary on account of the defendant's race or culture?

Not because the defendant's race makes him more sensitive or excitable than the ordinary inhabitant of this country. All the lords in *Camplin* impliedly, and Lord Simon expressly, ignored questions of race and culture in constructing the concept of the reasonable man. On the other hand all of their lordships agreed that race was relevant on questions of insult. Lord Diplock:

> "To taunt a person because of his race, his physical infirmities or some shameful incident in his past may well be considered by the jury to be more offensive to the person addressed, however equable his temperament, if the facts on which the taunt is founded are true than it would be if they were not."[20]

---

[16] At p. 716E. Cp. *per* Viscount Simon LC in *Mancini* [1942] AC at 9; *Kwaku Mensah* [1946] AC at 93; *Holmes* [1946] AC at 599.

[17] (1980) 71 CAR 331. See A T H Smith in 44 MLR 567. The Appellate Committee refused leave to appeal to the House of Lords. Cp. *McCarthy* [1954] 2 QB 105; *Gallagher* [1963] AC at 380–381; cp. 17 MLR 457.

[18] See Ward in 2 Jrnl. Forensic Medicine (S Af.) 165–166.

[19] Before 1954 it was not at all clear that no consideration would be given to the drunkard. See 1st edn 484 n.4. Although the defendant's intoxication does not relax the evaluative requirement, evidence of it is admissible on the question whether he in fact lost his self-control: *Tennant* (1975) 31 CRNS 1 (Ont.); *Squire* (1975) 31 CRNS 314 (Ont.).

[20] [1978] AC at 717C. Cp. Lord Morris, p. 721C, and Lord Simon, p. 726C.

Can the jury take account of the defendant's culture as making him more susceptible to a particular kind of affront, if it is not directed against his culture as such? Suppose that in a particular culture it is a point of deeply-ingrained honour to react strongly against a particular type of insult.

The point was not dealt with in *Camplin*. On one occasion, an Italian in England who was provoked to homicidal frenzy by a remark directed against his lady friend was judged by English standards, neglecting the fact that this type of insult is regarded far more seriously in Mediterranean countries than in Britain.[21] But this was before *Camplin*, and the decision might now be otherwise. The Italian in England may receive favourable consideration not because, as an Italian, he is particularly excitable, but because some insults are more grievous to him than they would be to an Englishman. It must be confessed, however, that the distinction is fine. Moreover, it may be said that making any concession on the ground of culture may be socially divisive, and may, in addition, land the courts in having to view sympathetically some ferocious "subculture" to which a youthful delinquent belongs.[22]

Suppose that the defendant believed that something provoking had happened, when it had not. Does the reasonable man test mean that the defendant has no defence of provocation unless his mistake was reasonable?

The reasonable man test does not necessitate saying that the defendant's mistake must be reasonable. It would be perfectly possible to apply the test to the facts as the defendant believed them to be (reasonably or not).[23] What the evaluative test is concerned to exclude is unusual deficiency of self-control, not the making of an error of observation, or of inference on a point of fact. And the CLRC has (as we have seen) recommended that this should be the law. But the present determination of the courts not to recognise mistakes relating to defences unless they are reasonable probably means that the law is now otherwise.

The point has chief practical importance in connection with intoxication, for a person under the influence of drink or drugs is particularly prone to mistake the intention of another.[24] The courts have in the past been ready to allow the drunkard a defence of mistaken provocation, with no restriction as to reasonableness.[25] They have recently become more severe on intoxicated mistakes; but it may still be argued that since it is only a question of palliating the offence, intoxication can be given in evidence on the question of putative provocation, even though it is not one of Lord Diplock's "characteristics" in relation to the power of self-control.

---

[21] *Semini* [1949] 1 KB 405.

[22] See further, on variant cultures and provocation, 1st edn 490–493.

[23] Thus in *Manchuk* [1938] SCR 18 (Can.), a mistaken belief was allowed as creating a case of provocation although it seems to have been wholly unreasonable: see the fuller facts in [1938] SCR at 351. see also Model Penal Code, POD s.210.3.

[24] An extraordinary instance is that of Booth the actor (the brother of Lincoln's assassin), who on one occasion, when he was playing Macbeth under the influence of liquor, refused to be killed, and chased Macduff murderously through the stalls.

[25] *Letenock* (1917) 12 CAR 221. Cp. *Raney* (1942) 29 CAR 14; *Wardrope* [1960] Crim.LR 770, 24 JCrL 178; also [1954] Crim.LR 753.

A mistake may be the result of an insane delusion, as in paranoia, in which case the law of insanity can apply.[26] Medical men now recognise that the *crime passionelle* is sometimes the result of intense worry and depression reaching the psychotic state of morbid jealousy, when the jealousy may be based on beliefs that are without foundation.[27]

§ 24.5. THE RULE OF REASONABLE RELATIONSHIP

The reasonable man test applies not only to the fact of killing but also to the mode of killing. There are two fights: in one the victor finishes off his opponent by stabbing him neatly through the heart when he is lying on the ground; in the other he stamps on his face. Assuming that the previous events provided provocation for the killing, so that the first victor gets a verdict of manslaughter, the jury may convict the second of murder, because he adopted an "unreasonable" mode of killing.

Before the 1940s, any serious assault was provocation for a killing, and the law did not examine the mode of killing. Where there was a serious assault, a killing was mitigated even though it was accomplished in a horrific way.[1] The law was simply, in the words of Hannen J: "It must not be a light provocation; it must be a grave provocation; and undoubtedly a blow is regarded by the law as such grave provocation."[2] The question was not the vileness of what the defendant did but the limits of the law of murder.

A change of judicial opinion seems to have occurred with the judgments of the House of Lords in *Mancini* (1942)[3] and *Holmes* (1946),[4] where their lordships stated a requirement of "reasonable relationship" between the provocation and the response—the response apparently being taken to include not merely the fact of killing but the *mode* in which the killing was effected.

The rule was criticised by commentators on the ground that it was inconsistent with the foundation of the defence of provocation, namely that the defendant has lost his self-control. If a man has lost his self-control to the extent of killing in a frenzy of rage it may seem inconsistent to require him to have kept his self-control to the extent of being able to discriminate in the measures he uses.

The Homicide Act is ambiguous, but it can be read as affirming a rule of reasonable relationship relating to the mode of killing (what we may call a modal reasonable relationship rule). Section 3 states the question as being "whether the provocation was enough to make a reasonable man do *as he did*"—perhaps meaning, kill in the way the defendant did, not "kill in one way or other, it does not matter what." On the other hand, "as he did" might be interpreted to refer to killing in the abstract, rather than to the mode of killing.

However this may be, certain dicta in *Camplin* reaffirm a modal rule. It will be remembered that in his model direction to the jury in that case Lord Diplock included the words:

---

[26] See Chap. 28. Jealous delusions are a conspicuous symptom of alcoholic paranoia.

[27] See R N Mowat, *Morbid Jealousy and Murder* (London 1965); Shepherd in 107 Jrnl. of Mental Science 687. See also Jeffrey A Gray, *The Psychology of Fear and Stress* (London 1971).

[1] *Ayes* (1810) Russ. & R 167, 168 ER 741.

[2] *Selten* (1871) 11 Cox 674.

[3] [1942] AC at 9.

[4] [1946] AC at 599.

> "The question is not merely whether such a person [i.e. the reasonable man] would in like circumstances be provoked to lose his self-control but also whether he would react to the provocation as the accused did."[5]

This does not rub the point in, and the jury might not fully understand its significance (they might, conceivably, interpret the words "react as the accused did" to refer merely to the fact of killing). But that is only a matter of expression: a judge who spelt out the modal rule for the jury in clearer language would evidently be upheld. Happily, the CLRC has recommended the abolition of the rule.[6]

§ 24.6. PROVOCATION AND MENTAL DISORDER

Provocation is traditionally a defence for "normal" people. Abnormal people can shelter under it, but only on the same conditions as apply to normal ones. If they want their abnormality to be taken into account they must raise a defence appropriate to them—insanity or diminished responsibility.

The introduction of the latter defence by section 2 of the Homicide Act (see Chap. 30) has greatly alleviated the responsibility for murder of those who have some degree of mental disorder. The defence can include even a difficulty in controlling one's actions, provided that it is due to an abnormality of mind.[1]

The courts allow the defendant to raise the defences of provocation and diminished responsibility together, and either of them, if successful, will result in a manslaughter verdict. The judge may ask the jury, for the purpose of sentence, whether they put their verdict on the one ground or the other[2]; but the jury may put it on both grounds.[3]

Strictly, the defence of provocation ought not to succeed in such circumstances unless the jury think that, notwithstanding the evidence of diminished responsibility, a reasonable man would have done as the defendant did. In other words, the evidence of diminished responsibility should not in logic assist the verdict of provocation. No doubt in practice it tends to do so.[4] Success in the combined defence of provocation and

---

[5] [1978] AC at 718E. Cp. his words at 717A, and his interpretation of *Mancini* at p. 714H; also Lord Morris at 720E ("It is for the jury to consider all that the accused did"). Somewhat strangely, Lord Diplock stated that *Mancini* and *Holmes* (as well as *Bedder*) "ought no longer to be treated as an authority for the law of provocation;" but presumably all that he meant (in relation to the reasonable relationship rule) is that this is not a rule to be applied by the judge (which, since the Homicide Act, is obvious). The rule is still, it seems, a rule on which the judge can and should direct the jury. For a further discussion of the whole question see 1st edn 493–495.

[6] 14th Report para. 86.

[1] *Byrne* [1960] 2 QB 396.

[2] As in *McPherson*, The Times, June 18, 1963; cp. § 30.2.

[3] As in *Holford*, The Times, March 29, 30, 1963; the case did not go on appeal. In *McPherson*, last note, the CCA held that the jury could have put their verdict on both grounds.

[4] Cp. *Brown* (1971), discussed by Ashworth in [1975] Crim.LR 560, where, upon a defence of provocation, medical evidence was allowed that the defendant was "prone to diminished responsibility when under severe stress." A defence of diminished responsibility can also take account of provocation, even outside the strict rules of provocation: § 30.3.

diminished responsibility has an advantage for the defendant in respect of sentence: it may well result in a more lenient outcome than a defence of provocation alone[5]; and it is virtually free from the risk of a life sentence that attends a defence of diminished responsibility by itself.[6]

§ 24.7. EXCESSIVE DEFENCE

A person in a panic may go far beyond what is necessary for his own safety. Suppose he over-reacts to an attack by killing his adversary when this is not justified by the law of self-defence. On principle he is still entitled to the provocation defence, reducing his guilt to manslaughter. A person who reacts to a blow often does so in mixed fear and anger, and there would be no sense in trying to confine the provocation defence strictly to action in anger. Both fear and anger release hormones that prepare the body for violent action, and both tend to result in violence.

> There's no philosophy but sees
> That rage and fear are one disease;
> Though that may burn, and this may freeze,
> They're both alike the ague.[1]

That excessive action in self-defence can reduce murder to manslaughter has been recognised by overseas courts, and in *McInnes*[2] Edmund Davies LJ conceded, what was obvious, that "the facts upon which the plea of self-defence is unsuccessfully sought to be based may nevertheless . . . go to show that [the defendant] acted under provocation." Long before the Homicide Act it had been established that an apprehended attack can constitute provocation, even though the defendant has not sustained a blow.[3] From this it seems to follow that in every case in which the defendant believes that he has to defend himself against a serious attack, but for some reason oversteps the limits of self-defence (because the attack he fears is not sufficiently serious to justify killing in self-defence, or

---

[5] Contrast the outcome of the two cases noted in [1977] Crim.LR 232 (though no certain conclusion can be drawn, if only because they were decided by different judges). Conversely, when diminished responsibility is set up an element of provocation may reduce the sentence below that which might have been thought appropriate if the evidence of diminished responsibility had stood alone. See *Whyburd* (1979) 143 JPN 492.

[6] § 30.2. The CLRC recommended that the jury should be allowed to take account of both provocation and any disability, physical or mental; and the judge should be left to decide whether to ask the jury to signify on what basis they are returning their verdict (14th Report para. 83). The committee did not specify that the disability must come within the rules for diminished responsibility, but it intended that the rule excluding cases of voluntary intoxication should continue (para. 86). There is some conflict between the recommendations, seeing that a person can by becoming intoxicated disable himself from exercising normal self-control.

[1] Coleridge, *Biographia Literaria*, Chap. 2.

[2] [1971] 1 WLR 1600, 3 All ER 295.

[3] *Kessal* (1824) 1 C & P 437, 171 ER 1263; *Greening* (1913) 9 CAR at 106; *Letenock* (1917) 12 CAR 221; *Semini* [1949] 1 KB at 409; *Cornyn*, The Times, March 4, 1964; East, *PC* i 243. Evidence may be given of past attacks by the deceased to show the nature of the attack that is feared: *Hopkins* (1866) 31 JP 105, 10 Cox 229.

because it is held that he is unreasonable in fearing an attack, or in fearing an attack of that degree of seriousness, or in not realising that he has some other escape) the circumstances can still amount to provocation.

Need the judge direct the jury on provocation if the defendant has not raised the defence?

Defending counsel are well aware of the truth of Aldous Huxley's adage that several excuses are always less convincing than one. If the defendant says that he did not strike a blow, it would be fatal to the credibility of the defence if it were to be said, in the alternative, that if the defendant struck a blow it was provoked. So the general principle is that on a charge of murder, if the evidence suggests the possibility of provocation, the judge must instruct the jury on that issue even though the defence have not raised it, and even though it is in conflict with the defendant's own testimony. If he fails to do so and the jury convict of murder, the conviction cannot be upheld if there is any evidence on which a verdict of manslaughter could have been given. In such circumstances the Court of Appeal will substitute a conviction of manslaughter[4]; and it will do this even though on a proper direction a conviction of murder would have been upheld. Strangely, there are cases where this general principle has not been accepted, for reasons that are difficult to follow.[5]

There is much to be said for the automatic rule recognised in varying degrees in other jurisdictions (and also hinted at in some of the older authorities in England[6]) that whenever the defendant directs himself to using force in private defence but exceeds the limits allowed for private defence he is entitled to a verdict of manslaughter rather than murder.

The rule is supported by certain passages in the old writers,[7] and was accepted by Macaulay and the other Commissioners for the Indian Penal Code,[8] and by the Criminal Law Commissioners of 1833.[9] In consequence, it passed into a number of overseas codes.[10] It has been accepted in the Republic of Ireland[11] and by the High Court of Australia[12] as a

---

[4] *Mancini* [1942] AC 1; *Kwaku Mensah* [1946] AC 88; *Porritt* [1961] 1 WLR 1372, 3 All ER 463, 45 CAR 348; *Lee Chun-Chuen* [1963] AC 220; *Robinson* [1965] Crim.LR 491; *Rolle* [1965] 1 WLR 1341,3 All ER 582; *Palmer* [1971] A.C. at 823; cp. *Cobbett* (1940) 28 CAR 11; *McLean* [1947] 1 DLR 844; *Bonnick* [1978] Crim.LR 246. The rule was accepted in *Peter Davies* [1975] QB at 701, subject to the qualification that "where the judge has been guilty of a misdirection, which was itself inspired by the action of defence counsel, it may be exceedingly difficult for anyone seeking to upset the conviction to say that a miscarriage of justice has occurred." Presumably this qualification will not apply when it is clear that defence counsel could not raise the defence of provocation without weakening the force of some other defence. Cp. *Squire* (1975) 31 CRNS at 322 (Ont.). See, on the whole subject of "defences in double harness," Gooderson in *Reshaping the Criminal Law*, ed. Glazebrook (London 1978) 138 ff.

[5] *Palmer* [1971] AC 814 (PC); *McInnes* [1971] 1 WLR 1600, 3 All ER 295. See 1st edn 499.

[6] See Peter Smith in [1972] Crim.LR 524.

[7] Foster, *Crown Law* 277; East, *PC* i 243.

[8] Macaulay, *Works* (London 1866) vii 505.

[9] Fourth Report 271 art. 40.

[10] See, e.g. the Penal Code of the Bahamas s. 345, cited in *Rolle* [1965] 1 WLR 1341, 3 All ER 582, and the Nigerian Penal Code s. 222 (2), identical with the Indian Penal Code s. 300 (2), commented upon in 122 NLJ 867.

[11] *People* v. *Dwyer* [1972] IR 416; see Glazebrook in [1975] CLJ 14.

[12] *Howe* (1958) 100 CLR 448; cp. *Yugovic* [1971] VR 816. See Norval Morris and Colin Howard, *Studies in Criminal Law* (Oxford 1964) Chap. 4. For the USA see Perkins in 36 JCr.L & Cr. 426; 36 Ky.LJ 443. In Canada the rule was rejected on the ground that an act done for self-defence is calculated and is therefore not provoked: *Faid* (1983) 2 CCC (3d) 513; but query this reasoning. For Scotland see *McCluskey* v. *HM Advocate*, 1955 SLT 215; Gordon in [1972] Crim.LR 660. To bring the doctrine into play, the defendant must have been acting by way of present defence, not merely to forestall future attacks: *Yambiwato* [1967–8] P & NGLR 222.

statement of the common law; and in Victoria a killing is also held to be mitigated if it is the result of excessive force used in arresting a criminal, or even in defending property.[13] "If the occasion warrants action in self-defence or for the prevention of felony or the apprehension of the felon but the person taking action acts beyond the necessity of the occasion and kills the offender the crime is manslaughter—not murder" (Lowe J). As the Indian Code Commissioners pointed out, when the use of moderate force is completely lawful, it is too extreme to regard the actor as a murderer on account of an excess of force. It may be said that he is less culpable than the killer who acts on provocation in anger, because the defender has the right to use some force and it may be hard for him to form a cool judgment as to when to stop. The principle should apply equally to killing in cases of attempts to prevent crime[14] or of necessity or duress, where the fatal force is not totally excused in the circumstances but should nevertheless be mitigated. However, our courts have been extraordinarily resistant to attempts to procure the recognition of the rule in modern English law, and the Judicial Committee of the Privy Council has expressly rejected it.[15]

As the law now stands, therefore, defence counsel who sets up self-defence in answer to a murder charge should always consider carefully whether to rest his defence in the alternative on provocation.

SUMMARY

Provocation is a defence to a charge of murder, but if successful requires a conviction of manslaughter, informally called voluntary manslaughter. This sets the judge free in sentencing. According to the older authorities, provocation is also a defence to a charge of attempted murder; and the defendant should then logically be convicted of attempted manslaughter, or on appropriate facts of wounding with intent to do g.b.h. Recent decisions, arrived at in ignorance of these authorities, assume that provocation is no defence to a charge of attempted murder. The prosecution do not indict for voluntary manslaughter, but it is an included offence on a charge of murder. § .1

There are two main questions for the jury. First, the factual question, usually worded as: "Did the defendant as the result of provocation lose his self-control?" What this somewhat metaphysical formula really means is, first, that the defendant must have killed by reason of the provocation, and, secondly, that the killing must have occurred while the defendant was in the heat of anger when the provoking event was still recent. A comparatively trivial affront may revive stale provocations. The evidential (not the persuasive) burden is on the defence. The judge may therefore withdraw the defence from the jury if it is not supported by reasonable evidence on the factual question. § .2

The second main question for the jury is evaluative: "Was the provocation enough to make a reasonable man/woman/youngster do as the defendant did?"

The Homicide Act 1957 s. 3 bears on this in three ways.

1 It prevents the judge from withdrawing the evaluative question from the jury.
2 It prevents the judge from instructing the jury in imperative terms how a reasonable man would behave.
3 It not only extends the notion of provocation to provocative words, but has

---

[13] *McKay* [1957] VR 560. See Norval Morris in 2 Sydney L.Rev. 414.

[14] The question was raised in *Att.-Gen. for Northern Ireland's Reference* [1977] AC 105, but the majority of the House of Lords refused to pronounce upon it. Only Viscount Dilhorne held (at p. 148F) that if a person intentionally killed in self-defence or to prevent crime, the force used being excessive, the verdict must be murder or nothing; a manslaughter verdict, he thought, was out of the question, because that would be "to make entirely new law." Lords Diplock and Simon merely said that the question did not arise; they did not dismiss the possibility of the defence out of hand (pp. 139D, 152A).

[15] *Palmer* [1971] AC 814.

apparently abolished every restriction that may have existed on the acts that are capable of being provocation. So, for example, provocation can come from a source other than the victim (*Peter Davies*). Seemingly, too, lawful acts can now be provocation, though it does not follow that the jury will accept them as such.

A verdict rejecting the defence of provocation seems to be regarded as final. § .3

The reasonable man test is paradoxical, and gives little guidance to the jury. It § .4
would be an improvement to ask not what a reasonable man *would* do but what he *might* do. According to the House of Lords in *Camplin*, "the reasonable man is a person having the power of self-control to be expected of an ordinary person of the age and sex of the accused, but in other respects sharing such of the accused's characteristics as they [the jury] think would affect the gravity of te provocation to him." By "characteristics" appears to be meant those relevant to the provocation (e.g. impotence or race where the provocation concerned those facts), not merely factors (such as unusual irritability) going to general self-control. So in *Newell* the CA held that intoxication was not a "characteristic" and did not reduce the capacity for control required of the defendant.

According to *Camplin* the question for the jury "is not merely whether such a § .5
person [the reasonable man] would in like circumstances be provoked to lose his self-control but also whether he would react to the provocation as the accused did." This means that not only must the act of killing be "reasonable" but the mode of killing must be as well.

Although mental disorder is supposed to be irrelevant to provocation, a § .6
defendant is allowed to raise the defence of diminished responsibility in double harness with provocation, and the jury may give a joint verdict on both.

An act of aggression that does not justify the defendant in killing in self-defence § .7
can be sufficient provocation to mitigate the killing. Also, the judge must direct the jury on provocation when the evidence raises the issue even though the defendant has not raised it. However, the latter proposition is sometimes not accepted. The overseas rule is greatly preferable, that on a defence of self-defence the judge should direct the jury that an act that oversteps the limits of self-defence can still in appropriate circumstances mitigate the killing.

CHAPTER 25

CONSENT AND ENTRAPMENT

For when success a lover's toil attends,
Few ask, if force or fraud attained his ends.
Alexander Pope, *The Rape of the Lock*

FEW, perhaps, but among them are likely to be police, prosecutors, judges and juries.

§ 25.1. THE IMPORTANCE OF CONSENT

To begin at the beginning: the notion of consent enters into a discussion of offences both on the negative and on the positive side.

1 Negatively: things may not be done to a person without his consent, merely on the ground that they are done for his benefit. This protects us from busybodies who think they know what is good for us better than we do ourselves. The exceptions to the principle (in relation to sane adults) are narrow, and the most important of them will be indicated in the next chapter.

2 Positively: anything may be done to a person[1] if he consents to it, whether it is for his benefit or not. Just as we can decide what we do not want done to us, so we can decide what we do. Again the principle is not without exceptions.

Examples of the second (positive) principle: a person impliedly consents to being tackled when he plays rugger, to being punched when he boxes, and to having his tooth extracted when he visits the dentist. These consents prevent the act from being an assault. Similarly, a passenger's consent to travel by a conveyance means that there is no false imprisonment; and a human "guinea-pig" who voluntarily takes a noxious drug for the purpose of medical research is not the victim of a crime of poisoning.

The details of the defence are judge made. As we have seen (§ 2.4), the burden of negativing consent rests on the prosecution. The defendant probably does not carry even an evidential burden,[2] though the evidence of assault, or rape, or other offence against the person, given by the prosecution will normally be sufficient to discharge their evidential burden of non-consent and to take the case to the jury. Evidence of the use of force, or the threat of force, or the use of certain serious frauds upon him, to prevent him from making opposition, is sufficient to negative consent without asking the complainant in the witness box whether he consented.

Can consent be retrospective? What if the victim of a crime, not having consented beforehand, now wishes to hush the matter up?

The law does not allow him to do so. If the police think that the victim

---

[1] Or in respect of his property. The present chapter is chiefly concerned with consent to what would otherwise be an offence against the person. Consent in relation to property is more specifically considered in the chapters on property offences.

[2] In *Morgan* [1976] AC at206E Lord Hailsham said that in rape "there is no burden at the outset on the accused to raise the issue of consent."

has been intimidated they may bring the offender to court. On the other hand, if they think that no good purpose would now be served by prosecuting they may hold their hand.

§ 25.2. THE MANIFESTATION AND VITIATION OF CONSENT

Consent is hard to define. To consent to do something, and to wish or want to do it, are not the same. I may consent to visit my great-uncle George, when I decidedly "do not want" to go. I go, complainingly, because he wants to see me, because I am told I must go by someone I do not want to offend, because I feel I ought to go, because I have some faint hope of benefiting myself from the visit, and so on. As I keep telling you, I do *not* want to go, but I consent to go. Everyone who goes, consents to go, unless he is shanghaied or goes at pistol point or is tricked by being told that he is going somewhere else. I think that every reader will recognise this as a statement of the way in which we use the word "consent;" yet I have not succeeded in giving a positive content to the word.

Since offences against the person and property generally require *mens rea*, the prosecution must show not merely that the complainant did not consent but that the defendant *knew* that the complainant was not or might not be consenting.[1] ("Might not be" to provide for recklessness.)

Problems rarely arise if consent is expressly given. As to implied consent, the defendant is entitled to infer the complainant's consent if all the following circumstances are present.

1 The complainant knows that the act is being or is proposed to be done in respect of his body (or property) by the defendant who is present before him. The requirement of knowledge on the part of the complainant follows from the very meaning of "consent." "Consent" means consent *to* something. One cannot consent *in vacuo*. But whether the details of what is done must be known—ah! that is the question. We shall revert to it in § .5.

2 The complainant has the ability to signify refusal of consent. This condition and the previous one mean that an unconscious person cannot consent (unless a question arises as to his previous consent continuing to be valid after he fell unconscious). The present condition means in addition that a person who, though aware of what is happening, is paralysed or overpowered does not consent.

3 The complainant fails to signify his refusal. Refusal of consent may be signified either symbolically (by words or gestures) or by physical resistance. Words withholding consent (or even token resistance to a sexual overture) may be belied by absence of strong resistance where such resistance is possible and is to be expected if consent is withheld.

As an illustration: if a patient in hospital is told by a doctor that he is to have a certain operation, and does not signify dissent but allows

[1] See the discussion of *Morgan* in § 6.6.

himself to be wheeled to the operating theatre, he would normally be taken to consent; and the fact that he is very doubtful in his mind about agreeing to the operation is irrelevant.[2] Similarly, a woman who submits to intercourse that she finds disagreeable, when she could decline it, consents to it; how little she likes it is of no legal interest. It does not matter in these cases whether we say that the complainant actually consented as a matter of law or that the defendant was entitled to suppose that he or she was consenting.

There are three classes of case in which though consent may appear to have been given it will be deprived of its legal effect.

1 Where certain circumstances detract from the effectiveness of choice. Rules of law decree that an apparent consent is "vitiated" if it is produced by mistake or fear of certain kinds. (The two forms of vitiation reflect rules 1 and 2 above. Mistake can prevent such consent as was given from being relevant to what was actually done, and coercion producing fear prevents the victim from signifying refusal.)
2 Where the complainant is one of certain classes of person who are deprived by law of the "capacity" (ability) to consent, because of the likelihood that such persons by reason of disability cannot choose in the normal way. The people so disabled are certain juveniles and certain mentally disordered persons.
3 Where rules of public policy deprive us all of the legal ability to consent to certain acts that are regarded as immoral or socially injurious.

Although the name "public policy" is given only to the third situation, an element of public policy enters into the first two. All three bristle with philosophical as well as legal problems. A discussion of them will occupy the rest of the chapter. We begin with the rules (so far as they can be stated) on the vitiation of consent, starting with fear. They are so uncertain in many respects that they afford much opportunity to the activist judge to extend the empire of the penal law.

§ 25.3. THE VITIATION OF CONSENT BY FEAR

Many decisions that we take in life are the result of choosing between evils. We opt for one course, which we dislike, because the alternative is more objectionable still. This unpleasantness of choice does not, in ordinary language, destroy the reality of the choice or the existence of consent.

However, there are extreme cases where fear resulting from threats will nullify consent in law. It would not commend itself to public opinion to say that a man who has obtained sexual intercourse by threatening a woman with a knife is not a rapist. The line between using force to overcome a woman and using a serious threat to prevent her from offering resistance is too fine to be the basis of a legal distinction.

It is a purely verbal question whether the second case should be regarded

---

[2] Cp. *O'Brien* v. *Cunard SS Co.* (1891) 154 Mass. 272, 28 NE 266.

as one in which the woman consents under compulsion or as one in which she does not truly *consent* but simply gives *submission, acquiescence* or *complaisance*. However one expresses it, there is no effective consent in law.

The threat need not be of extreme violence.[1] Common sense suggests that a person who submits to an act only because he believes that otherwise he will be overpowered and have it done to him anyway does not consent in law, even though the force necessary to overpower him will be small and non-injurious.[2]

> Suppose that the police illegally require a suspect to make an impression of his finger-prints. (Illegally, because they have not obtained an order of the magistrates, as they should.) If an officer presses the suspect's fingers on to the sheet, the suspect co-operating by placing his fingers in place in the sheet, this can be regarded as an assault, because the suspect believes that if he resists force will be used. The doctrine of vitiation of consent enables the law to be invoked against the officer.

Probably the threat need not be of force to the complainant: a threat in respect of, say, the complainant's children is sufficient. It may be implied from conduct: an intruder in a house who orders the female occupier to submit to sexual intercourse would not need to back his command with an express threat. It may be implied from past conduct: the woman may know from unhappy experience that it is useless to resist.[3] It may be implied from numbers, as in a "gang bang."[4] And if a man takes advantage of a state of fear induced in the victim by another, it will be the same as if he had induced it himself.

In the last of these situations the requirement of a threat by the defendant vanishes, and the truth is that no threat is necessary. What matters is not the threat but the woman's belief as to what will happen if she does not acquiesce. If she submits to sexual intercourse from fear of force, and the man knows this, her consent is vitiated and the man has the requisite *mens rea* for rape, even though he did nothing to cause the fear.

Where the threat does not relate to the use of force, the traditional and proper view is that the obtaining of sexual intercourse by means of the threat is not rape.

Isn't that too narrow a view of the law? Oughtn't the rule to be that a woman's mere submission to sexual intercourse is not enough to establish her consent if there was some constraint operating on her mind?

One reason for having a narrow rule is that threats vary greatly in their malignancy, the least serious amounting to little more than the offer of an improper bargain. Rape is such a serious crime, and regularly attracts such

---

[1] Distinguish duress as a defence, which probably needs a threat of serious injury. See Chap. 27.
[2] See *Hallett* (1841) 9 C & P 748, 173 ER 1036; *Day* (1841) *ibid.* 722, 1026.
[3] *Jones*, (1861) 4 LT(NS) 154.
[4] *Hallett*, n. 2 above. Cp. *Hogdon* [1962] Crim.LR 563 (taking a conveyance).

severe sentences, that it is important that it should apply only to the gravest cases. Moreover, any temptation to which the courts might otherwise be subjected, to extend the law to cover objectionable people, has been removed by the enactment of a statutory offence of obtaining sexual intercourse by threats (§ .4). This is the proper charge to use when the threat does not relate to the use of force.

The opinion I have just offered as to the proper rule is supported by all the authorities except the single recent case of *Olugboja*,[5] which goes much further. In this case your "constraint" idea was accepted by the trial judge, and not emphatically rejected by the Court of Appeal. Ologbuja's conduct was so unscrupulous and overbearing that if we had a crime of obtaining sexual intercourse by gross sexual imposition (otherwise than by rape) he would rank as a prime candidate for conviction. He might even have been convicted of rape, without any commentator voicing criticism, if the female complainant had given evidence that she feared the use of force and if the direction to the jury had been in conventional terms. But apparently the female complainant was not asked the vital question: Why did you take off your trousers? And the conviction of rape was procured and justified on grounds so woolly that we now seem no longer to have any firm bounds to the crime.

The facts cannot be shortly summarised without the risk of creating an unfair impression. The complainant was a girl of 16; the parties had started together on a social basis; and the sexual intercourse was admitted. The evidence creating difficulty for the prosecution in obtaining a conviction of rape on normal principles was that the complainant removed her own trousers on being directed by Olugboja to do so; that Olugboja uttered no threat of violence, and the complainant apparently did not say at the trial that she feared the use of force; that she did not resist the sexual penetration, though she struggled when she thought that after penetration Olugboja was going to ejaculate inside her, and he accordingly withdrew; and that after Olugboja had taken her home she complained to her mother, the police and a doctor about the conduct of Olugboja's companion (who had raped her shortly before), but not about Olugboja (who, she even said, had not touched her, though that was evidently false).

The trial judge introduced an innovation in his direction to the jury by making "constraint" a ground for vitiating consent. "You will . . . decide whether or not there were any constraints operating on her will, so that you are satisfied that in taking her trousers down, and letting him have sexual intercourse with her, she was not, in fact, consenting to it." Apparently the judge did not spell out to the jury what "constraints" he had in mind, but presumably they were that the complainant and her girl friend had been tricked by the two defendants into allowing themselves to be driven to the bungalow where the events occurred; that she was dependent on the defendant or his companion to drive her home again; that she had reason to believe that she was not going to be driven home immediately; and that she had just seen Olugboja's companion dragging her friend into a bedroom to rape her.

Dunn LJ, delivering the judgment of the Court of Appeal said:

> "We do not think that the issue of consent should be left to the jury without some further direction. . . . They should be directed that consent, or the absence of it, is to be given its ordinary meaning and if need be, by way of example, that there is a difference between

[5] [1981] 3 WLR 585, 3 All ER 443.

> consent and submission; every consent involves a submission, but it by no means follows that a mere submission involves consent.[6] . . . In the less common type of case where intercourse takes place after threats not involving violence or the fear of it, . . . [the jury] should be directed to concentrate on the state of mind of the victim immediately before the act of sexual intercourse, having regard to all the relevant circumstances; and in particular the events leading up to the act and her reaction to them showing the impact on her mind. . . . The dividing line in such circumstances between real consent on the one hand and mere submission on the other may not be easy to draw. Where it is to be drawn in a given case is for the jury to decide. . . . Looked at in this way we find no misdirection by the judge in this case. We think it would have been better not to use the word "constraint" in explaining the offence, but whenever he used it the judge linked it with the word 'fear,'[7] so that in the context the word seems to us to be unexceptional [*sic*]."

These remarks are disturbing, because they suggest that the judge can direct the jury with great laxity, uttering a series of platitudes without giving them any real guidance. The court assumes that fear can vitiate consent in rape even though it is not fear of violence (or, presumably, of force short of violence); and yet the court makes no effort to specify the sort of fear or threat that has this effect. A threat in the wide sense is simply a statement by A that he will act in some way that B will not like if B acts in some other specified way; and the jury are apparently left as a kind of sovereign legislature to decide what statements of this kind in a sexual case will make A a rapist. Moreover, the court seems to think that consent is a state of mind which the jury can distinguish factually from "submission" without any criteria enabling a line to be drawn. The judgment astonishingly misunderstands the authorities it cites on this question.[8]

If the complainant did not fear force, there was apparently no direct evidence before the court as to what she did fear. If she submitted herself to the defendant because she thought it would be the quickest way of getting home, was he properly convicted of rape?

But the statutory definition of rape[9] is that it is unlawful sexual intercourse without consent. Surely the question must be left to the jury in general to

---

[6] It is pointed out in the note in [1981] Crim.LR 717 that both parts of this statement are wrong. A consent eagerly given between equal partners does not involve a submission (which implies giving in to a dominant will), and a mere submission does involve consent if there are no vitiating factors. Many a wife (or cohabitee) has submitted to the attentions of a man with whom she is bored, because for one reason or another she does not care to reject them; and in so doing she consents to the contact. The court quoted one of a series of cases in the earlier 19th century holding that a youngster who is sexually interfered with by an adult (particularly by one who is in some authority over him) does not "consent" but only "submits;" this mode of reasoning became unnecessary when legislation created sexual offences by adults that did not require proof of non-consent; and the special doctrine of submission was not extended to complaisances by adults. See § .13 at nn. 8, 9.

[7] He did not. Even when the judge added a reference to fear, he stated this as an alternative to constraint; and he does not seem to have suggested what the complainant's fear might have been.

[8] The court quoted the Heilbron Group and the CLRC for the proposition that consent may be vitiated by intimidation other than threats of force; but in fact the two reports did not say or intend anything of the kind.

[9] § 6.6 at n. 11.

decide whether the threat, of whatever kind it was, was such as to negative any real consent.

That was the reasoning on which the court proceeded. But it overlooks the history of the law on this subject, as well as the philosophical difficulty of defining consent.

The old writers defined rape as involving an act against the woman's will by force, fear or fraud,[10] but in fact the cases went no further than to allow the "will" or consent to be vitiated by one kind of fear (namely, of force) and one kind of fraud (namely, as to the nature of the act). The change from "will" to "consent" took place in the 19th century, so that the Act of 1976 (§ 6.6) was purely declaratory. The change was made simply to make it plain that sexual intercourse with an unconscious woman (where she had no "will" either way) could be rape. It was certainly not the intention to set the jury free to decide in general whether or not there was a "real" consent.

Speaking of interferences with the person generally, and not merely of rape, pressure to consent may take the form of various persuasions—the appeal to the conscience of the complainant to permit medical experimentation upon him, the invocation by the experimenter of his scientific authority, the threat by a man to give up his association with a woman if she does not consent to sexual intercourse, the offer of a bribe. Inducements of these kinds may sometimes be regarded as morally improper, or as fit for prosecution as the statutory offence of threats, without reaching the conclusion that they are such as to negative consent in law. *A fortiori* where the threat is a proper one. Employers, for example, have no power to search employees on suspicion of theft without their consent, but they may search an employee with his consent, the employee realising that if he refuses consent the employer is likely to call the police. It would be absurd to regard the consent as thereby vitiated.

The point remains that consent must be voluntarily given. So it must be a question of fact in each case whether it was.

Yes, in a sense; but everything depends on what you are looking for to establish or negative voluntariness. There is no positive test of the voluntariness of consent, only a negative test. Consent is voluntary when it is not given as the result of certain pressures. Questions of policy are involved in deciding what pressures are sufficient to nullify consent, and guidance must be given by rules of law.

The paradox of the voluntary-involuntary distinction is that it is the positive-looking member of the pair (voluntary) that carries the negative meaning (here, no relevant threat or fear), and the negative-looking word (involuntary) that has positive force. We shall see that the same is true in the law of duress (where the distinction is equally useless as a guide to reasoning); and the words play the same trick in the law of evidence, where they are used in connection with confessions. A confession is "voluntary," and therefore admissible in evidence, if it is not "involuntary," the latter signifying "the result of promises, threats or oppression by a person in authority." In all three contexts "voluntary" has no meaning except as the negation of certain factors.

Among the threats other than of force that may possibly vitiate consent, the strongest

---

[10] See *Lang* (1975) 62 CAR 50.

candidates are threats of imprisonment or of prosecution (whether on good grounds or maliciously).

In a South African case[11] a threat of malicious prosecution for an imprisonable offence by a policeman was held to vitiate a woman's consent to sexual intercourse, so that the officer could be guilty of rape. But in England a judge directed the acquittal of a policeman on a charge of rape founded on an allegation of such a threat.[12] The point is not of great moment for sexual intercourse, because in any case a charge could be brought of the statutory offence of threats to obtain sexual intercourse. It is more important for indecent assault. On one occasion a probationary constable who found a youth committing some misdemeanour gave him the option of going to court or a flogging; the youth chose the flogging and was hit on his bare buttocks. As a result, the constable was charged at the Crown Court with this and other indecent assaults. The age of the youth is not stated in the brief report, and in any case the matter was not argued because the constable pleaded guilty on all counts.[13]

Reverting to the vitiation of consent in rape, if a threat of imprisonment is to be accepted as sufficient it must, surely, be a threat of something more than temporary restraint. Even if in *Olugboja* there was an implied threat to keep the complainant in the bungalow for the night if she did not yield herself,[14] that should not have been accounted a sufficiently serious threat to make the threatener guilty of so serious a crime as rape. Even on that view of the facts, the case should not have been treated as anything more than the statutory offence of threats[15].

Before the upheaval in the law created by the decision in *Olugboja* one could at least have been reasonably certain that economic pressure is insufficient. "My poverty, but not my will, consents" is a distinction hitherto unknown to the law. (Were it recognised, anyone without an independent income who took a job on the factory floor or at a desk would be able to bring proceedings for false imprisonment; for in performing his job he is psychologically chained to one place.) Again, what courts of equity call undue influence has always been thought to be insufficient; and a man who compels a woman to submit to his unwelcome attentions by threats of exposing her past life has never been imagined to be guilty of assault or rape. Even consent given under protest, and in tears, is still consent.

In the civil case of *Latter* v. *Braddell*,[16] it was held that no assault was committed when a mistress required her maid to be medically examined to see if she were pregnant. The maid submitted to the examination, under tearful protest, and her action against the mistress for assault failed. Perhaps there was economic coercion and perhaps there was undue influence, but neither vitiates consent in the law of tort. It must be said, however, that even *Latter* v. *Braddell* was one of the cases lumped together by the court in *Olugboja* as those where a criminal jury could find lack of consent on an "appropriate direction." This contemplates that a jury in a criminal case can ignore general principles established in the civil law, even in relation to so serious a crime as rape.

In the first edition of this book the decision in the Rhodesian case of *McCoy*[17] was characterised as wrong, but no firm opinion on any of these topics can now be entertained. It was an extreme case of what is now known as sexual harassment, the abuse of economic power in the work-place.

An air hostess broke a regulation of the company, and McCoy, the manager, offered her a caning as an alternative to being disciplined by being grounded, which would have meant loss of pay. She accepted, and the caning was administered in humiliating

[11] *State* v. *Volschenk*, 1968 (2) PH, H 283 (D). I am indebted for this reference to an unpublished paper by Dr. A J Ashworth.

[12] *Kirby*, The Times, December 19, 1961.

[13] 136 JPN 264.

[14] On the question of false imprisonment see § 9.11 at n. 5.

[15] See § .4.

[16] (1881) 50 LJQB 166, 448.

[17] [1953] 2 SA 4, 15 EED 992.

circumstances. McCoy was convicted of assault, one of the reasons given being that the woman had not freely consented.

There is certainly a case for saying that this conduct should be reached by the criminal law. One way of looking at it would be to say that McCoy was in breach of his duty to his employer, the company, in turning to his own advantage the authority given him. In fact he could in England have been charged under the Prevention of Corruption Act 1906, for having corruptly obtained a consideration (namely, a sexual complaisance) as an inducement for showing favour in relation to his employer's affairs.[18] A better way of dealing with the malpractice would be a statute forbidding employers and their agents to abuse their economic power by imposing certain socially undesirable penalties or substitutes for penalties (particularly sexual submissions) upon employees. Since we lack any specific statute on the subject,[19] if a case of gross abuse of power by an employer or his manager comes before the court the judges are very likely to express their disapproval by manipulating the doctrine of consent. But, reverting to the case of *McCoy*, if one looks at the matter from the point of view of the particular woman employee involved in the case, it may be said that she exercised the choice that McCoy gave her in the way that suited her own interest. Assuming that in the regular course McCoy would have ordered the woman to be grounded, and that this would have been the proper action on his part, what happened was that he offered to be bribed by her, in a non-pecuniary way, not to do his duty. She herself thought the humiliation and pain of the caning preferable to the official penalty, and she was benefited by being given the option. McCoy's real offence was one of abusing his position; behaviour like his needs to be punished on public grounds, but should not be punished as an assault. The decision cannot be reconciled with the principles of the crime of assault, because, in the first place, the harm done appears to have been insufficient to negative consent on account of the seriousness of the injury,[20] and, in the second place, economic pressure should be regarded as insufficient to negative consent. The court said that "the complainant's consent was not real in that she did not give it freely and voluntarily," but this is the fallacy already considered, of supposing that one can make deductions from the notion of voluntariness without considering its technical legal meaning.

Suppose that the manager had offered the woman sexual intercourse as an alternative to being grounded, and that she had accepted. If her consent were regarded as being nullified, the manager would be guilty of rape, which would be absurd. To carry the point further: suppose it was the woman who took the initiative in offering to participate in a sexual act, in return for the manager's changing his intention to ground her. Here the initiative in the act of bribery would come from the woman, but her state of mind would be exactly the same as before: one of accepting the sexual act in order to buy off the discipline that could lawfully be imposed. Could it possibly be said that her consent was not "real" and should be ignored?[21]

We come back, then, to the proposition that the best policy is to limit rape to acts done by force or under the threat of force (which is its ordinary meaning). But the court in *Olugboja* thought that even on a charge of rape all such cases could be left to the jury with what it vaguely called "an appropriate direction." This is one more manifestation of the deplorable tendency of the criminal courts to leave important question of legal policy to the jury.

---

[18] See Chap. 40.

[19] Except the Truck Act 1896 s. 1 in respect of fines.

[20] The English decision in *Donovan* is open to the same objection: see § 25.18 at n. 8.

[21] If economic pressure were accepted as negativing consent, the question would arise whether the degree of pressure must be balanced against the degree of harm to which consent is obtained. It may be argued that a threat to dismiss a woman employee vitiates her consent to being beaten but not to sexual intercourse, on the assumption that her reluctance to be beaten is stronger than her reluctance to submit to intercourse. But of course this assumption would only be true for some women, and might depend on such factors as the degree of pain expected in the proposed beating. A rule of this kind would be unworkable. By hypothesis the woman has submitted to the unwelcome act, and by hypothesis has done so under the threat in question; so she has indicated her own view that the threat implied an evil worse than the submission. It seems, then, that the only practicable rule is in terms of the kind of threat made, irrespective of the magnitude of the evil to which the complainant is caused to submit. (Whether a person is able in law to give consent to certain serious harms is an independent question to he discussed later.)

A special problem arises where a prisoner or patient in a psychiatric hospital is offered an operation in order to hasten his release. A sex offender may be offered castration, or a mentally subnormal woman may be offered sterilization. The reason for the first may be that it offers the only hope of making the offender sufficiently safe to be released; the reason for the second may be a fear that the patient will become pregnant, and that if she has a child, or another child, she may be unable to cope. (The question whether these operations will in fact produce the expected advantage or are necessary to avoid evil is not here considered.) Some say that the inmate's consent can never be "real" and "uncoerced" in these circumstances,[22] which implies that the operation must always be unlawful unless it can be justified by necessity (a highly dubious ground of validation if one starts from the premise that consent has been given under coercion). Yet there may be cases where an operation is genuinely likely to accelerate release. It must be realised that if the fact of institutionalisation vitiates consent, this is true even for minor procedures like inserting a contraceptive device in the womb. The only sensible solution is to say that the consent is not the less "free" because of the coercion inherent in the situation. The control of improper practices must be left to the ethics of the medical profession, or, if need be, to express legislation.[23]

§ 25.4. COITION OBTAINED BY THREATS: SEXUAL OFFENCES ACT S. 2 (1)

The statutory offence supplementing the law of rape has already been mentioned. By section 2 (1) of the Sexual Offences Act 1956:

> "It is an offence for a person to procure a woman, by threats or intimidation, to have unlawful[1] sexual intercourse in any part of the world."

The punishment is 2 years' imprisonment. This provision in the 1956 Act was taken from earlier legislation that was aimed primarily against the "white slave traffic"—the traffic in girls who arc by one means or another led into a life of prostitution—but it is not limited to prostitution.

Since the offence under section 2 (1) is incomplete until intercourse has taken place[2] it seems at first sight to add little to the ordinary crime of rape.[3] But:

1 Whereas rape is punishable by the English courts only if committed in England, the crime under section 2 (1) is punishable in England wherever the intercourse may take place, provided that the threats or intimidation took place in England.

2 The more important difference between the offence under section 2 (1) and rape is in respect of the threats. "Threats or intimidation" are not defined, and they are taken to include more than the threats that

---

[22] See D. W. Meyers, *The Human Body and the Law* (Edinburgh 1970) 39, 43.

[23] See Goldstein in 84 Yale LJ 697–698.

[1] It will be remembered that this word means sexual intercourse outside marriage; so the husband is exempted as in rape: *Chapman* [1959] 1 Q.B. 100.

[2] *Mackenzie* (1910) 75 JP 159. However, a man who unsuccessfully threatens could presumably be convicted of an attempt.

[3] A minor difference from rape is that in this offence the perpetrator is the threatener (be he man or woman, and whether, if a man, he is the person who commits the act of intercourse or not: *Williams* (1898) 62 JP 310).

traditionally vitiate consent at common law. "Intimidation" presumably means an implied threat. But there must be some limit, and it would seem reasonable to say that, if the threat is not of a kind to vitiate consent, it must be a threat of such a nature as is likely to overcome resistance by an ordinary woman, and must not be merely a threat to withhold a benefit from her.[4]

It cannot be imagined that an offence is committed if a man, faced with a rebellious mistress, tells her that unless cohabitation is resumed she shall not have a mink coat, or will be turned out of her flat. A proposal to withhold a benefit that the defendant is not bound to give cannot reasonably be described as a threat for the purpose of the section. The question is not, or should not be, how important it is for the woman to receive the benefit. The mistress's flat may be her only home, but that is not a reason for saying that the man's threat to evict her is a threat within the meaning of the section. The man is entitled to leave the woman, to whom he is not married, and it would be wrong and impolitic to say that if he expostulates with her, pointing out that the inevitable consequence of her present conduct will be the rupture of their relations, the result, if he succeeds in changing her attitude and sexual intercourse is resumed, is that he commits an offence.[5]

These considerations may have been overlooked in two cases in which a city councillor and a housing officer were convicted of attempting to commit the offence under s. 2 (1) by offering a young wife a council house in return for sexual intercourse. Full details are not reported, and no appeals were taken[6]; but it would seem that any threat there was in the situation did not fall within the restricted definition just suggested. If the man merely offered to help the woman to jump the housing queue, the convictions were surely improper. If he threatened to make a bad report on her to the housing committee, that could well be regarded as a threat within the subsection. In any case, the defendants committed offences under the Prevention of Corruption Acts.[7]

While section 2 (1) provides a useful supplement to the law of rape, no similar statutory provision supplements the law of indecent assault. Threatening to cause a woman economic loss or social injury if she does not submit to fellatio (oral sex) is no offence, unless the court regards her consent to the act as vitiated. What is lacking in our law is an adequately worded and sanctioned offence of threatening language and behaviour, irrespective of whether the threat is carried out.

§ 25.5. THE VITIATION OF CONSENT BY MISTAKE

It is often said that consent is vitiated by fraud, but the point is not limited to fraud. Fraud can induce the complainant to make some mistake of fact,

---

[4] Cp. Hogan in *Reshaping the Criminal Law* ed. Glazebrook (London 1978) 182 at n. 23. Query whether an implied threat not to drive the complainant home that night unless she submitted (as might perhaps have been found in *Olugboja*: § .3) could have been regarded as sufficient. Borderline cases are always possible, but there is danger in adopting too wide an interpretation of the statute.

[5] Even a threat to deprive the woman of something she has a right to expect should not necessarily be sufficient (a threat by her debtor not to pay the £100 he owes her).

[6] *Auckland,* The Times, July 26, 1967; Young, The Times, February 15, 1969 (though here the nature of the charge is not mentioned).

[7] See Chap. 40.

but it is also possible for the complainant to make a *spontaneous* mistake, which raises the same legal problem. To what extent does the complainant's mistake as to what is happening nullify or preclude his or her consent?

Consider the case where a man makes a false statement to a woman in order to obtain her consent to sexual intercourse. If he represents himself as being rich when in fact he is poor, few would argue that her consent is "vitiated," so that the man is guilty of rape or assault. The traditional rule for both these offences is that they are acts done without consent. When, if ever, is fraud so serious that it can be said to destroy any "real" consent?

The answer is given by the previous observation that consent always means consent to something. If you consent to A, you do not for that reason consent to B. It may be said that in rape, the issue is the woman's consent to sexual intercourse with this man. If she does not know that the act is one of sexual intercourse, or if she is mistaken as to the identity of the man, then she does not consent, but *otherwise she does*. One must have regard to the decencies of language, and it cannot properly be asserted that the woman does not consent where she merely mistakes some attribute of the man (that he has career prospects, that he has been vasectomised, that he intends to marry her, that he is free from venereal disease). If the man is guilty of fraud in these matters he can be punished for the statutory offence of obtaining sexual intercourse by fraud (§ .7). There is, therefore, no need to inflate the grave offence of rape to make it cover sexual deceits in general.

The law was settled in this sense in *Clarence*, which has already been discussed in connection with OAPA section 20.[1]

> It will be remembered that the facts were that Clarence, knowing that he was suffering from venereal disease, had intercourse with his wife, and thus communicated the disease to her. In holding that Clarence was not guilty under section 20, because there was no assault, the Court for Crown Cases Reserved took the view that the wife's consent to the contact was not vitiated by Clarence's nondisclosure of his condition; and Stephen J expressly held that the rules for both rape and assault were the same. He stated the law thus: "The only sorts of fraud which so far destroy the effect of a woman's consent as to convert a connection consented to in fact into rape are frauds as to the nature of the act itself, or as to the identity of the person who does the act. I should myself prefer to say that consent in such cases does not exist at all, because the act consented to is not the act done."

Suppose that on facts like *Clarence* the man is not the woman's husband and is charged with rape. It would be ludicrous to classify the act as rape merely because the man did not tell the woman that he was diseased. The same moral offence would be committed by a woman who knowingly transmits disease to a man; but a woman cannot commit rape. Clearly, the rape charge would merely be a device for punishing a totally different

[1] § 9.5.

wrong. Again, the legal question of transmitting disease can arise if disease is transmitted otherwise than by intercourse. It would be most unsatisfactory to make the issue of criminal liability turn on the question whether the communication happened to be by physical contact that was otherwise unobjectionable.[2]

Stephen J's rule does something to nail down the doctrine of vitiation of consent. If it be granted, it must necessarily govern spontaneous mistake as well as mistake produced by fraud; indeed, there was no fraud in *Clarence*.[3] The point was made by the High Court of Australia.

> "In considering whether an apparent consent is unreal it is the mistake or misapprehension that makes it so. It is not the fraud producing the mistake which is material so much as the mistake itself."[4]

We now consider in more detail the two kinds of fundamental mistake recognised by Stephen J.

§ 25.6. MISTAKE AS TO THE NATURE OF THE ACT

An example of a mistake as to the nature of the act is the unlikely case of *Flattery*.[1]

> Flattery induced a woman to submit to intercourse by pretending to perform a surgical operation. Although the report is not altogether clear, it may be taken that the woman did not know the physical nature of the act. Flattery was convicted of rape.

Here the woman submitted to the act and made no protest. She did not scream and shout for help, but accepted what was happening, and perhaps found the supposed surgery unexpectedly pleasant. There is a great factual difference between the violently resisting or terrified woman in the ordinary case of rape and the woman who happily submits because she has been deceived. In the latter case any mental discomfort she feels is only in retrospect when she discovers the truth, though of course she may suffer the physical consequence of being pregnant or infected with VD. Still, it is not unreasonable to say, where the error is as fundamental as this, that one of the essential elements of consent is lacking.

On the other hand, the decision of the Court of Criminal Appeal in *Williams*[2] is clearly wrong.

> Williams was a singing master who persuaded a female pupil to submit

---

[2] It was suggested in *Clarence* that the defendant might have been liable for administering a noxious thing, on the assumption that disease germs were noxious things. If this application of the poisoning offence is justified, consent would clearly be no defence, because the wife did not consent to being given the disease. However, the poisoning offence has not in fact been charged in a case of communicating disease.

[3] On the undesirability of finding constructive frauds see §§ 34.2, .9.

[4] *Papadimitropoulos* (1957) 98 CLR at 260.

[1] (1877) 2 QBD 410. The defendant's conduct in this case also amounted to indecent assault: *Case* (1850) 1 Den. 580, 169 ER 381, 4 Cox 220.

[2] [1923] 1 KB 340.

to intercourse under the pretence that it was treatment for breathing. His conviction of rape was affirmed.

The conviction accorded with principle if the woman knew nothing about sex and thought that what her instructor was doing was merely an exercise to improve her lungs. If on the other hand she knew the facts of life and was willing to be persuaded that one of the benefits of the act of sex was an improvement in breathing, then she did not mistake the nature of the act, even though in her innocence she may not have realised that the man's motives had nothing to do with singing. Since the court did not enquire into the question, the decision must be regarded as unsound. This is borne out by the judgment of the High Court of Australia already referred to, given after a full review of the authorities.

> "Rape is carnal knowledge of a woman without her consent; carnal knowledge is the physical fact of penetration; it is the consent to that which is in question; such a consent demands a perception as to what is about to take place, as to the identity of the man and the character of what he is doing. But once the consent is comprehending and actual the inducing causes cannot destroy its reality."[3]

§ 25.7. COITION OBTAINED BY FRAUD: S.3(1)

We must again pause to consider an offence similar to rape.

Section 3 (1) of the Sexual Offences Act is a provision analogous to that already given for the procurement of intercourse by threats, and again was in origin passed to combat the "white slave traffic."

> "It is an offence for a person to procure a woman, by false pretences or false representations, to have unlawful sexual intercourse in any part of the world."

Here again the statutory crime overlaps rape. The false pretences may be by words or conduct, and they are not limited to pretences as to the nature of the act or the identity of the actor. This is the offence that ought to have been charged in *Williams*. The trouble, as so often happens, was that the prosecutor charged the wrong offence, and the court felt obliged to come to his rescue.

Clarence was not charged with this crime (under the statute then in force), but if he had been, and if he had not been married, he might perhaps have been convicted, on the theory that an offer of sexual intercourse carries an implied representation of freedom from communicable disease. But the better view is that it is improper to carry implication to these lengths; an omission to disclose facts, however important, is not in itself fraud.[1] Even downright lies should not invariably be regarded as falling within the subsection. It can hardly be supposed that any boastful lie told by a man (even if told expressly) makes him guilty of the offence if the lie procures the woman's consent to intercourse. How many men have

---

[3] *Papadimitropoulos* (1957) 98 CLR 249. Cp. *K* 1966 (1) SA 311 (S Rhodesia).

[1] See § .5 n. 3; Lynch in [1978] Crim.LR 612 n. 3; but cp. *ibid.* 619 n. 21.

caused a woman to yield by deceitfully saying "I love you"? There is a strong argument for saying that the subsection does not extend to a false pretence as to the deceiver's state of mind.[2]

Although prosecutions are rare, the subsection has been used against men who obtained sexual favours from women under a false promise of marriage, concealing the fact that they were already married.[3] In these cases there was an implied false pretence as to a fact (that the defendant was unmarried), not merely as to his intention to marry the woman.

§ 25.8. QUESTIONABLE DECISIONS OUTSIDE THE LAW OF RAPE

While the question as to the "nature of the act" is moderately precise in relation to sexual intercourse, it becomes cloudy if the charge is of abduction or indecent assault and the argument relates to the defendant's motives. Here the courts have been preoccupied less with the decencies of language than with the desire to stamp out indecencies of behaviour. When the judges are determined to put down bad men, inadequacies in other parts of the law tend to result in distortions of the law of consent.

An illustration is *Hopkins*,[1] which arose under the abduction provision now in section 20 of the Sexual Offences Act 1956. The offence is committed where a girl is abducted from her parent "against his will," which must mean "without his consent."

> Hopkins obtained the consent of the mother of a girl of 10 to take her away, on the false pretence that he was taking her into the service of a lady. He was convicted of abduction. The trial judge, Gurney B, stated that he would reserve the point for the consideration of the CCCR, but afterwards did not do so because Hopkins was convicted of attempting to have sexual intercourse with the girl, and was sentenced only for that.

Here the fraud was not as to the identity of the actor, and it could not well be said to be as to the nature of the act prohibited by the statute, which was taking the girl away. The offence as it stands may be too narrowly drawn if it does not cover takings by fraud. Nevertheless, in ordinary language a taking by fraud is not a taking against the will of the parent.

---

[2] It was held in interpreting the former offence of obtaining property by false pretences that for the purpose of the Larceny Act the defendant's state of mind was not a "fact" capable of being the subject of a false pretence: *Dent* [1955] 2 QB 590. (This was changed by express statutory provision for the present law of obtaining property by deception: see § 34.1.) *Dent* may still govern the interpretation of the words "false *pretences*" in s. 3 (1), but a court that wished to do so could evade the argument by holding that a "false *representation*" can be as to a state of mind. Still, it is hard to imagine that a declaration of love, or a promise of marriage, was intended to be covered, at any rate if the intercourse takes place in the United Kingdom. The conduct primarily struck at by the section was the inducement of women to go abroad on a statement that they would have employment as actresses, dancers and so on, when in fact they were meant to become prostitutes. To lure a woman abroad for a base purpose on a false promise of marriage might also be thought deserving of punishment. The trouble is that the statute is not limited to luring the woman to go abroad.

[3] One instance is cited by Hogan in *Reshaping the Criminal Law*, ed. Glazebrook 183; another is *Booth*, The Times, October 29, 1977.

[1] (1842) 1 Car. & M 254, 174 ER 495. Cp. *Cox* [1969] 4 CCC 321 (Ont.).

Gurney B referred to certain old authorities to the effect that a person who borrowed an article by fraud took it without the consent of the owner and so was guilty of larceny (which required the taking to be without consent). But in devising this doctrine the judges took great liberties with words, their object being to extend the law of larceny. The old law of larceny has been abolished, and it would be wrong to extend the same fiction of lack of consent to other offences.

As has already been said, to the extent that fraud vitiates consent the same result should logically follow from spontaneous mistake, not procured by fraud. We have seen that this is because consent requires a certain amount of knowledge of the facts, and the requisite knowledge may be absent either because of mistake induced by fraud or because of mistake spontaneously arising but known to the defendant. It follows that if section 20 applies to all cases of fraud, it also applies to all cases where the parent is under some spontaneous mistake as to the taking of his daughter, the mistake being known to the abductor. It would be widening the words of the section even further than in *Hopkins* to say that it extends to spontaneous mistakes by the parent (known to the defendant) as to any matter affecting the giving of his consent.

The CLRC has proposed that the existing offences of child-stealing and abduction of girls under 16 should be replaced by an offence of abducting a child under 14 without the parent's consent or by a deception upon him.[2] If this proposal is implemented it will dispense with the need for fictitious vitiations of consent.

Another decision which is open to much the same objection is *Rosinski*.[3]

> Rosinski for his own lewd purposes undressed a woman and rubbed her with some liquid, causing her to believe that this was necessary for therapy. It is not clear from the reports whether he also pretended to have a medical qualification, but when the case was decided many unqualified persons purported to perform cures. Rosinski was convicted of assault, and the conviction was upheld by the CCCR.

No reasons were given. Stephen J, it will be remembered, said that the rule for the vitiation of consent applies as much to indecent assault as to rape.[4] For indecent assault, as for rape, the fraud must be as to the nature of the act or the identity of the actor. By a stretch, the woman's mistake induced by Rosinski may be said to have related to the nature of the act. She thought it was a medical treatment, whereas Rosinski's purpose was carnal. On the other hand, her mistake did not relate to any of the objective facts, but only to what was in the defendant's mind.[5]

The foundation of the doctrine of mistake in relation to consent is the truism that a person who consents to A does not thereby consent to B. A man who consents to having his appendix out does not consent to having his *vas deferens* cut when he is unconscious (and even if he were conscious he would not know what the surgeon was doing). Stephen J therefore explained the doctrine of vitiation of consent by saying that "the act consented to is not the act done" (§ .5). But the complainant in *Rosinski* knew exactly what act was done. She knew that Rosinski was rubbing a liquid on her body. To say that she did not consent, if that denial

---

[2] 14th Report para. 240.

[3] (1824) 1 Lewin 11, 1 Mood. 19, 168 ER 941, 1168. Cp. *Case* (1850) 4 Cox 220; *Commonwealth* v. *Gregory* (1938) 132 Pa.Super. 507, 1 Atl. 2d 501; *Maurantonio* [1968] 2 CCC 115, 65 DLR 2d 674, 2 CRNS 375 (Ont.).

[4] § .5.

[5] Presumably, if the defendant acted from a mixed motive, partly proper and partly improper, the "reality" of the complainant's consent could not be denied. In *Bolduc* (1967) 63 DLR 2d 82, the Supreme Court of Canada held that consent to a genuine medical examination was not vitiated by the fact that, unknown to the patient, a man accompanying the doctor was not medically qualified.

is rested on "the nature of the act," is to make that notion distinctly metaphysical. When the true objection to what the defendant has done is that he was fraudulent and has invaded the victim's privacy, his conduct is turned into an assault by the pretence that consent is lacking.

The courts are tempted into this species of judicial fraud by the fact that otherwise the deceiver will go scot-free. There is no offence of obtaining a sexual or other bodily submission by fraud, other than a submission to sexual intercourse. Unless we have such a statutory offence, and unless the judges are prepared to use it in place of fictitious assaults, we are unlikely to be able to make an honest woman of what Pollock used to call "our Lady the Common Law." Unhappily, the defect will remain in the law even if the reforms now proposed by the CLRC are enacted, since the committee shied away from considering the general subject of consent, and did not propose any offences to replace the weirder extensions of the doctrine of vitiation of consent.

But if the law embarks on deciding what is "the nature of the act," isn't it reasonable to make a distinction between medical and sexual acts? If, in the case of copulation, the courts ask whether the victim of the deceit was aware that it was a sexual, as opposed to medical, act, why should not the same question be asked where some other sort of bodily contact is in issue?

It seems to me that the courts should not permit themselves to classify acts in an infinite variety of ways for the purpose of affirming or denying consent. Stephen's rule as to "the nature of the act" was intended to limit the doctrine of vitiation of consent, not to permit the courts to expand it by inventing new notional classes of acts. Is there to be a legal distinction not only between medical and sexual acts but between cosmetic and sexual acts? Between medical-experimental and sexual acts? Between therapeutic/diagnostic and experimental acts?[6] Between safe medical experiments and risky ones?[7] What if the experimenter says he is testing the safety of a therapeutic ointment, when he is really testing the safety of a cosmetic?

I do not think, by the way, that *Flattery* establishes a distinction between medical and sexual acts. The woman who was deceived by Flattery presumably did not know that his penis was entering her body; she was therefore unaware of what was happening. Had she merely misunderstood Flattery's purpose in copulating with her it should not have been either rape or assault.

§ 25.9. MISTAKE AS TO THE IDENTITY OF THE ACTOR

At common law false personation did not turn an act of sexual intercourse into rape, though it was an assault (an odd distinction). A woman who yielded believing that the man was her husband gave consent to the act and so was not regarded as being raped.[1] The rule was reaffirmed by the Court

---

[6] See Skegg in 15 Med.Sci.Law 125; § .11 at n. 5.
[7] See Skegg, *op.cit.* 126–127.

[1] This despite the traditional definition of rape, stemming from the institutional writers, that the offence can be committed "by force, fear or fraud." The decisions rejecting false personation (and therefore, *a fortiori*, all other kinds of fraud, except fraud as to the nature of the act, as founding a charge of rape) refute the last item in the definition.

for Crown Cases Reserved in 1868.[2] It was strictly logical. If a man slips into bed with a woman pretending to be her husband, and has intercourse with her, the woman happily accepts the intercourse as she would if it were in fact her husband. It does not look at all like rape, which was originally based upon the notion of force and still normally involves force. However, the lack of legal provision for such an escapade was naturally liable to cause a public outcry. The law of obtaining sex by fraud could not be used against the man where, as in the case just mentioned, he did not make any representation as to his identity but merely relied on a spontaneous mistake by the woman. Parliament therefore intervened by including a provision in an Act of 1885, now represented by the Sexual Offences Act 1956 s. 1 (2).

> "A man who induces a married woman to have sexual intercourse with him by impersonating her husband commits rape."

Presumably he "impersonates" the husband merely by acting like a husband in a case where he knows that the woman is mistaken.

The Act does not apply to the impersonation of a woman's lover. Presumably the Parliament of 1885 thought that women who took lovers were not worthy of any special protection against imposters; and the Act of 1956 was merely consolidating.

Stephen J, as we have seen, rejected the common law rule, or thought it had ceased to apply. In saying that fraud as to the identity of the actor vitiated consent,[3] he assumed that the common law was superseded by the statute, without noticing the limited way in which Parliament expressed itself. It is true that the Act of 1885 (unlike the Sexual Offences Act) was worded in declaratory form, as though it were merely stating a particular instance of the existing law. This fact, together with Stephen J's prestige, may induce the courts to accept his opinion and say that mistake as to the identity of the actor vitiates consent, whether there is fraud or not and whether the mistake relates to the husband or not.[4] Nevertheless, the only English decisions on the point go the other way. The declaratory wording of the Act of 1885 is not conclusive, because Parliament uses declaratory language when it does not wish its enactment to be used as an argument for saying that the law was different previously, or would be different if it were not for the enactment. In other words, the Act is not meant to prejudice other questions. Even if Parliament firmly believes that the Act it is passing is unnecessary (which it could not have believed in 1885, since the statute ran counter to the latest decision of the CCCR), its mistaken belief cannot establish the fact. As Lord Radcliffe said, "the beliefs or assumptions of those who frame Acts of Parliament cannot make the law."[5]

Notwithstanding such legal arguments, the present tendency of the courts

---

[2] *Burrow* LR 1 CCR 156.
[3] (1888) 22 QBD at 43–44.
[4] See *Papadimitropoulos* (1957) 98 CLR at 260 (Aus.).
[5] *IR Commissioners* v. *Dowdall, O'Mahoney & Co. Ltd.* [1952] AC at 426.

to extend rather than to restrict the criminal law is so pronounced that Stephen's principle will probably be accepted as a minimum statement of the vitiation of consent. In that event, rape will be committed by a man who impersonates a lover. (Whether Stephen's principle will be accepted as a *limiting* statement, as Stephen intended it to be, is a different matter.)

Does section 1 (2) apply where the woman has been deceived into committing bigamy? In other words where she believed that the man in her bed was her husband because (although she knew who he was) she wrongly thought she was married to him?

Obviously not. The subsection applies only in respect of a married woman, and only to a case of impersonation—not to a mistake by the woman as to the validity of her marriage. Her mistaken belief that the man has been married to her is a mistake as to his legal attribute, not as to his identity.

In de Maupassant's Boule de Suife there is a saucy tale of a man who masquerades as a woman and acts as a lady's maid, bathing his mistress. Is he guilty of indecent assault if the bathing involved touching his mistress indecently?

On principle no. The mistress's mistake as to the sex of her "maid" is a mistake as to attribute, not as to identity, and so does not vitiate her consent even if a mistake as to identity does so.

I should have thought that the sex of a person is so important that it should go to identity.

My own view is that the law would become undesirably imprecise if a mistake as to some characteristic of a person, even so important a characteristic as sex, were regarded as a mistake of identity.

The distinction between identity and attributes is drawn by the civil courts. A mistake of identity occurs only where the person under the mistake confuses two real people, X and Y, by supposing that X is Y. It is not a mistake of identity when you think that a man is a woman, unless you think that he is some specific woman; or that you believe an unqualified person to be a qualified doctor, unless you believe him to be some other real person who is a doctor. That, at any rate, is the meaning of a mistake of identity in the law of contract,[6] and there is no reason why this concept should be any different in the criminal law.

Then what offence has the man committed?

None. There is no general crime of fraud in English law. Obtaining property by deception is a crime (Chap. 34); so is obtaining sexual intercourse by false pretences, as we have just seen; and there is a crime of conspiracy to defraud (Chap. 31). But we have no crime of procuring

---

[6] See.23 Can.BRev. 271, 380.

submission to a bodily interference by fraud. We should have, but we haven't.

Suppose that a man who is a doctor of theology induces a woman to submit to an intimate examination by falsely pretending that he is a doctor of medicine. Surely that is an indecent assault?

Liability follows *a fortiori* from *Rosinski*,[7] if that is correctly decided. Yet fraud as to having a medical qualification is fraud as to an attribute, not as to identity, even if fraud as to the identity of the actor vitiates consent.[8]

The point can be made clearer if we imagine a case where a doctor examines a woman patient unnecessarily, merely because he obtains carnal sensations in doing so. It is difficult to believe that the woman's consent would be regarded as vitiated. If this opinion is well founded, it should make no difference that the person making the examination misrepresented his qualifications as well as his motive, for these misrepresentations do not go to the nature of the act or the identity of the actor. Since the decision in *Rosinski* antedates *Clarence*, and the reasons that moved the CCCR are not reported, it should now be reconsidered.

Do you mean to say that a gentleman from the East with a bogus medical degree who undertakes a serious surgical operation and makes a hash of it is not guilty of an aggravated assault?

He ought to be guilty of an offence in a rational system of law, but the offence should be one of fraud. In practice, no doubt, the court would convince itself that he is guilty of an aggravated assault, *Clarence* notwithstanding.

The strain in these cases comes from trying to make offences of force cover offences of fraud. As was said before, the only satisfactory solution is one that now requires legislation. What we need is a broad doctrine of consent coupled with a statutory offence of taking advantage of specified mistakes resulting in the giving of consent to a bodily interference. Also, falsely claiming a medical qualification should carry a higher penalty than it now does.[9]

§ 25.10. DRUGS AND CONSENT

There is no special rule on the subject of drink, (other) drugs, and consent. A surgical consent form signed when the patient is under such heavy sedation that he is unable to understand the form would obviously be

---

[7] Above § .8 at n. 3.

[8] Cp. *Wellard* [1978] 1 WLR 921, 3 All ER 161, 67 CAR 364, where the defendant, pretending to be police officer, required a girl to accompany him. The jury found that the girl felt compelled to do so, and convicted the defendant of kidnapping, the verdict being upheld on appeal. There was no discussion of vitiation of consent. It may be tempting to suppose that the girl's consent was vitiated by fraud. But, for reasons stated above, it causes fewer problems to regard her consent as vitiated by duress, the threat of force being implied.

[9] It is an offence under the Medical Act 1956 s. 31 wilfully to pretend to be a registered medical practitioner, but the penalty is only a fine.

worthless. If a man, in order to cause a woman to succumb to his wishes, stupifies her by drugs so that she does not know what is happening or is physically unable to make resistance, then of course she does not consent, so the man can be guilty of rape.[1] There is also a superfluous statutory offence covering the situation.[2]

Alcohol is a kind of drug. What about the man who makes an attempt on a lady's virtue by plying her with unsuitable liquors?

If the effect is to overcome the woman, in the way just stated, the man will if successful in his endeavour be guilty of rape. But the usual effect of alcohol is merely to reduce self-control, so that a woman who would not normally submit to sexual intercourse may offer no resistance to it. She may know what is happening, and be physically able to express dissent, but have her normal inhibitions removed by alcohol.[3] In such circumstances there is consent to the sexual act.[4] Whether the man would be guilty of administering a noxious thing under the OAPA was discussed in § 9.10.

What has just been said is subject, as always, to judicial vagaries.

> In a New Zealand case,[5] a driver was suspected by the police of being under the influence of drink. He stoutly maintained that he was sober, and, to prove it, rolled up his sleeve for the doctor to take a blood sample. The test revealed a blood alcohol level of 170 mg. per 100 ml., and the man then succeeded in obtaining damages against the doctor on the argument that he was too drunk to be capable of consenting to the assault!

§ 25.11. "INFORMED CONSENT" AND OPERATIONS

The limits of the legal notion of consent are of great importance to doctors as a matter of civil law, but a criminal prosecution of a doctor, on the ground that he has not fully informed his patient of the nature or effects of an operation, is unlikely.

Suppose that a patient assents to an operation, but does not realise that it will render him impotent. Does he "consent"? Even if he is held not to, the surgeon will not be liable for a criminal assault if he believed that the patient consented. But sometimes the surgeon may be constrained to admit that he knew that his patient did not realise the possibility of a certain side-effect of the operation. There would obviously be great danger for surgeons if patients could prosecute or sue in respect of all the side-effects that were unknown to them.

American courts have developed a doctrine called "informed consent": a consent not based upon proper understanding of the relevant facts is no consent. Although the proposition may be accepted to a certain extent, great caution is needed in its application.

It may be that as a matter of civil law a surgeon is under a duty of care and a contractual duty to give the patient reasonable information about a proposed operation.[1] Whether that

---

[1] See *Lang* (1975) 62 CAR 50.
[2] Sexual Offences Act 1956 s. 4.
[3] An illustration of a "tranquillizer" having this effect is given in [1956] 2 BMJ 1116.
[4] *Lang*, n. 1 above.
[5] (1966) unreported, discussed by P D G Skegg in 36 MLR 371.

[1] See Skegg in 15 Med.Sci.Law 127ff.

is so or not, it ought not to be accepted as representing the criminal law. There is nothing to prevent a patient putting himself generally into the hands of the surgeon, without enquiring too specifically what is to be done; in other words, he can consent generally to such surgery as is thought necessary.[2] Even if his consent is to a particular operation, the operation does not become a criminal assault just because the surgeon omits to give him information as to its effects.

Supposing (against the above argument) that some disclosure were required from the surgeon, it would be wrong to expect him to catalogue the possible adverse effects and to give his patient a full balance-sheet of the pros and cons of the operation. A patient who asks for medical advice inevitably puts himself in the hands of his doctor. The patient is often in a highly emotional state and may be frightened out of his wits if the surgeon offers him a recital of past medical disasters.[3] It is the doctor who has to take the difficult medical decision, not the patient. A doctor should not be criminally liable even if he unduly minimises the risks of a therapeutic procedure.[4]

A doctor who engages in medical experiments with human beings may have his conduct more severely scrutinised than one who acts for the purpose of therapy. There is here no obvious need for not alarming the patient.[5] As a matter of good practice, the doctor should make the fullest disclosure. At the same time, it would seem to be wrong to use the criminal law to control the amount of disclosure required. Such legal control as is needed can, surely, be provided by the civil law.

While our courts are likely to treat doctors with great consideration, and while on principle there is no difference between the doctrine of consent in relation to doctors and to unqualified practitioners, human justice does not always follow the rules of logic. Judges are likely to react against unqualified people who indulge in doubtful practices against the bodies of others, and the doctrine of consent is sufficiently malleable to enable convictions to be upheld.

> In *Burrell* v. *Harmer*[6] a tattooist tattooed two boys aged 12 and 13, causing their arms to become inflamed and painful. The magistrates convicted him of an assault occasioning actual bodily harm, rejecting his defence that the boys consented, on the ground that they did not understand the nature of the act; and the conviction was upheld on appeal.

These boys did not expect the painful result. But it is difficult to see how the doctrine of consent can rationally distinguish between a surgeon and a tattooist, and equally hard to imagine that the court's attitude would have been the same if a surgeon and orthodox surgery had been involved. The judges were, of course, actuated by a desire to protect boys from tattooists, and to do that they were prepared to bend the notion of consent. It would have been better to leave the problem to Parliament; and in fact Parliament acted two years later by making the tattooing of minors (persons under 18) a specific offence.[7] As we shall see, later developments

---

[2] Skegg, *op. cit.* 127, 129.

[3] Anyone doubting this should read the amusing piece by William P Irvin reprinted in Katz, Goldstein and Dershowitz, *Psychoanalysis, Psychiatry and Law* (New York 1967) 716.

[4] Cp. Skegg, *op. cit.* 131.

[5] See Bernard M Dickens in 24 Univ. of Tor. LJ 381. On the line between therapy and experimentation see Dickens in 113 Can.Med.Assn.Jrnl. 635. Cp. § .8 at nn. 6, 7.

[6] [1967] Crim.LR 169.

[7] Tattooing of Minors Act 1969, applied in NI by S R & O 1979 No. 926. On the rationale, see Hogan in *Reshaping the Criminal Law*, ed. Glazebrook 180 n. 20.

in the doctrine of consent may have made tattooing illegal even for adults (§ .19).

§ 25.12. MENTAL DISORDER

A woman may be so subnormal in intelligence, or so mentally ill, that she cannot consent to sexual intercourse; but the Supreme Court of Victoria rightly allowed this possibility very limited scope. That a mentally retarded woman readily gives way to "animal instincts" is not to the purpose.[1] The Australian court said that for a woman to lack capacity to consent to intercourse:

> "it must be proved that she has not sufficient knowledge or understanding to comprehend
> (*a*) that what is proposed to be done is the physical fact of penetration of her body by the male organ or, if that is not proved,
> (*b*) that the act of penetration proposed is one of sexual connection as distinct from an act of a totally different character."[2]

This was a low requirement of understanding, but there are two reasons for making the requirement low. First, this is necessary to prevent men who have intercourse with willing but sexually innocent girls from being convicted of rape. Secondly, it is necessary in order not to forbid sexual expression to women of low intelligence. Every offence has the effect of diminishing the liberty of the defendant, but when a person is convicted on account of a consensual activity the practical result is to restrict not only his liberty but that of the person with whom he acts.

However, statute has stepped in: it is a specific offence for a man to have sexual intercourse with a woman who is a defective, that is to say who suffers from 'an arrested or incomplete development of mind which includes severe impairment of intelligence and social functioning."[3] This restricted offence implies a legislative decision not to forbid sexual activity with women who, though impaired, are not severely impaired, subject of course to the requirement of consent.

The section makes special provision for the defendant's mistake. It provides, in subsection (2):

> "A man is not guilty of an offence under this section . . . if he does not know and has no reason to suspect her to be a defective".

The concluding words ("and has no reason to suspect") are an impractical limitation upon the defence, because the diagnosis of the degree of mental defect mentioned in the section

---

[1] *Fletcher* (1886) LR 1 CCR 39.

[2] *Morgan* (1970] VR 337. The rule would be more clearly expressed in positive terms: the woman must both know the physical facts and know that the connection is sexual; failing either knowledge, she does not consent in law. This formulation is greatly superior to the English pronouncements of the 19th century. See *Fletcher*, n. 1 above; *Pressy* (1867) 10 Cox 635; *Barratt* (1873) LR 2 CCR 81. Even so, (*b*) may be doubted: see § .6.

[3] Sexual Offences Act 1956 ss. 7, 45, as amended by the MH(A)A 1982 s.65 (1) and Sched. 3 para. 29.

requires an expert. No ordinary man, who does not know what diagnosis has been made, is likely to be able to tell the difference between an impaired and a severely impaired woman, at any rate in quite a broad band of marginal cases—even if he knew the statutory definition of the degree of mental impairment required. To look for *mens rea* or an unreasonable failure to spot the girl's handicap when a man in a cinema finds a complaisant girl next to him and has intercourse with her, she being in fact severely impaired,[4] is an impossible undertaking.

The procurement of a defective woman (as above defined) to have unlawful sexual intercourse is an offence under the Sexual Offences Act s. 9, and the occupier of premises where the act is done is brought in by section 27. Also, such a woman cannot consent to an indecent assault; nor can a defective man.[5]

Doubts are now being felt about the wisdom and justice of these provisions. Doctors who work in hospitals for the mentally impaired take the view that even severely impaired people have the right to express their sexuality and to enjoy tender and close relationships. Mentally impaired men and women sometimes marry each other, and together achieve a greater degree of independence than either could do unaided.[6]

Patients certainly need protection from sexual interference by those who have the care of them, but this is provided by the Mental Health Act 1959,[7] which forbids unlawful sexual intercourse by a male member of staff in a hospital or psychiatric nursing home with any female patient (whether mentally disordered or not).

Both mentally impaired and mentally ill people can consent to therapeutic procedures, and operations are regularly performed upon them. The consent of an impaired patient is easily obtained, but that fact does not rob the consent of its validity. Mentally ill persons should have the right both to give consent to therapeutic procedures and to withhold such consent, unless there are extremely good reasons against this. As Professor Goldstein wrote, when criticising certain American decisions, "a finding of incompetence which deprives [the patient] of authority to decide for himself constitutes the ultimate disregard of his human dignity."[8] The doctor will obtain the consent of the nearest relative as a matter of good practice; but there is no reason to suppose that the relative has a right of veto over an operation judged necessary for the patient's health, if the patient himself consents. The patient should be held to consent if he knows that therapy is proposed (such customary details being communicated as he is capable of grasping) and does not object. The question of operations without the patient's consent is discussed briefy in § 26.8.

A doctor would be unsafe in operating non-therapeutically upon a mentally disordered person (as by way of medical experiment), even with the patient's purported consent. Nor can parents of a minor patient who is mentally disordered give effective consent to an operation that is not for the benefit of the patient.[9]

§ 25.13. MINORS

The law relating to consent by and on behalf of minors is not altogether clear, but a measure of certainty is given to it by the Family Law Reform Act 1969 s. 8.

> "(1) The consent of a minor who has attained the age of 16 years to any surgical, medical or dental treatment which, in the absence of

[4] In *Hudson* [1966] 1 QB 448 the court gave an indulgent interpretation to "has reason to suspect."
[5] Sexual Offences Act 1956 ss. 14 (4), 15 (3), as amended by MHA 1959.
[6] See M and A Craft, *Sex and the Mentally Handicapped* (London 1978). The CLRC *Working Paper on Sexual Offences*(1980) paras. 92–107 provisionally proposes that section 7 should be replaced by a civil procedure enabling a non-molestation order to be made in any particular case that requires it.
[7] S. 128 (1) (*a*).
[8] 84 Yale LJ 691.
[9] This seems plain from *Re D (A Minor)* [1976] 2 WLR 279. Cp. *Re B (A Minor)* § 12.8 at n. 14.

consent, would constitute a trespass to his person, shall be as effective as it would be if he were of full age; and where a minor has by virtue of this section given an effective consent to any treatment it shall not be necessary to obtain any consent for it from his parent or guardian.
(2) 'Surgical, medical or dental treatment' includes any procedure undertaken for the purpose of diagnosis, and this section applies to any procedure (including, in particular, the administration of an anaesthetic) which is ancillary to that treatment as it applies to that treatment.
(3) Nothing in this section shall be construed as making ineffective any consent which would have been effective if this section had not been enacted."

The particular purpose of the section is to clarify the law for the reassurance of doctors. It is limited to "treatment," which would cover not only (as it says) diagnostic but also preventive procedures. Independently of the section, a youngster over 16 can presumably give consent to a blood donation, organ transplant or medical experiment, even if they are not "treatment" (which may perhaps be regarded as an open question).[1] In any case he can do so at 18, which is the age of majority.[2]

Suppose an adolescent over 16 refuses consent to an operation: can his parent nevertheless give it?

The section is silent, but the reasonable implication is that when the youngster has attained 16 only he can consent to medical treatment.[3]

Can an under-16 consent?

In general, persons under 16 can consent to bodily contacts, and therefore (according to the better view) can consent to therapy.[4] Further, a girl of (say) 15 who knows the facts of life can give a consent to sexual intercourse that will prevent the act being rape by the man, though of course he commits a statutory offence not depending on lack of consent. Hence the under-16's power to give consent is not limited to acts done for his or her benefit. In one case the consent of a 13-year-old boy to be tattooed was held by a recorder to bar the criminal conviction of the tattooer[5]; but, as has already been mentioned,[6] the tattooing of persons under 18 was subsequently made an offence. These analogies indicate that a girl under 16 can consent to an abortion without the concurrence of her parents. Similarly, Woolf J held, in an action for a declaration, that a girl

---

[1] In 1977 a question was asked in Parliament concerning a boy of 16 who consented to the removal of a kidney for transplant: *Parl. Deb.*, H of C, vol. 924 col. *486*. The minister replied that in such circumstances legal advice should be sought!

[2] Family Law Reform Act 1969 s. 1.

[3] David Foulkes suggests in 120 NLJ 194–195 that if the doctor refrains from asking a minor of 16 or 17 for his consent, the consent of the parent may be valid instead; *sed quaere*. Theoretically, the youngster can be overridden in his refusal of consent if he is made a ward of court, as he can be up to the age of 18; but it seems unlikely that the judge would exercise this power, unless possibly the treatment is necessary to save life.

[4] Therapy can also be justified under the doctrine of necessity, independently of consent: § 26.8.

[5] *Dilks* (1964) 4 Med.Sci.Law 209. Cp. *Sutton* § 10.4 at n. 7.

[6] § .11 n. 7.

under 16 could give a valid consent to medical treatment (including the provision of birth control facilities).[7]

Although the above is the theory of the law, the predisposition of the courts to manipulate the law of consent to secure the conviction of suitable persons has again to be reckoned with. Before the statutory offences of sexual intercourse with and indecent assault upon young girls were established in their present form, the judges readily held that what was called a "submission" (an apparent consent) by a young girl (even as old as 13) to a sexual act was to be disregarded, by assuming on almost no evidence that she either did not fully realise the nature of the act or merely submitted in fear of the man.[8] The same view was taken when young boys were sexually interfered with.[9] The statutory law now reduces the need for a strained interpretation of the doctrine of consent, and the question remains chiefly important in non-sexual cases. Here again, as we have seen, the court twisted the doctrine of consent in relation to the tattooing in *Burrell* v. *Harmer*.[10] If in that case the tattooing had not caused inflammation there would have been no ground for impugning the "reality" of the boys' consent. However, the child may be so young as to make it unreal to say that he understands what is proposed and can consent. The determining age is sometimes referred to as "the age of discretion."

A particularly thorny problem is presented by the search for a kidney from the family of a patient needing a transplant. The survival rate is greatest from donors who are close blood relatives, particularly identical twins. But much unhappiness may be caused within the family when the question of offering a transplant arises, and most surgeons will perform transplants from living donors only if persuaded that the donor will feel deprived if he is not allowed to help his dearly beloved relative.[11] On the other hand, the giving of a successful transplant is often a cause of great satisfaction to the donor, while failure to offer it may bring about self-reproach. The problem should be regarded as one of medical ethics, not a matter for legal control, provided that the youngster has reached the age of discretion and consents. His consent to surrender an organ should be valid.[12]

If an under-16 consents, can the parent veto it?

Where a child under 16 gives what from his point of view is a valid consent to some interference with his body, it would seem on principle that the fact that the parent forbids the interference does not make it illegal.

Obviously, a father who forbade his young daughter to engage in sexual intercourse would not thereby make the intercourse rape on the part of the man, for rape requires non-consent by the sexual partner; non-consent of the parents is irrelevant. For the same reason it would seem that there can be no assault on the child when the child gives a valid consent so far as he is concerned. This means that a parent could not forbid a doctor to perform an abortion on his daughter with her consent, or to fit her with an intrauterine contraceptive device.[13] The decision of Woolf J, already quoted, supports this. In any case, as will be seen later,[14] the view now

---

[7] *Gillick* v. *West Norfolk AHA*, The Times, July 27, 1983. Cp. 46 Med.Leg.Jrnl 26.

[8] *Nichol* (1807) R & R 130, 168 ER 720; *Day* (1841) 9 C & P 748.

[9] *Lock* (1872) LR 2 CCR 10. Although the question left to the jury was cloudy in the extreme, if the jury found consent, even in the case of young persons, this was of course conclusive in favour of the defendant: *Martin* (1839) 9 C & P 213, 173 ER 807; *Read* (1849) 3 Cox 266.

[10] Above § .11 n. 6.

[11] [1971] BMJ 202; cp. [1971] 4 BMJ 229.

[12] For opinions *contra* see Foulkes, *op. cit.* 195.

[13] See n. 7 above. The latter question is discussed in the Report of the (Lane) Committee on the Working of the Abortion Act, Cmnd. 5579 of 1974, paras. 243–245, a majority of members taking the view that the doctor would be justified in exceptional cases. Cp. Dickens in 13 Osgoode Hall LJ 556.

[14] § 26.8.

taken is that the parent cannot forbid a life-saving operation. The judge said, according to the newspaper report that whether a child was capable of giving the necessary consent would depend on the child's maturity and understanding and the nature of the consent required.

If an under-16 can consent at common law when of the age of discretion, what is the point of the provision in the Family Law Reform Act for the over-16s?

It seems that the section does nothing that would not be so without it, but it gives a measure of reassurance to doctors.

Can a parent give consent on behalf of his child under 16?

Parents certainly have some authority to give consent for under-16s, but the limits are doubtful. A father could obviously not legalise the rape of his daughter.

To begin with therapeutic procedures; it is accepted that a parent[15] can consent on the child's behalf when the child is too young to consent, being too young to understand what is proposed to be done. When the child is above the ill-defined "age of discretion," the ideal is to have the concurrent consent of parent and child. The position is unclear if the child, being old enough to consent, withholds consent; and a doctor would be unlikely to take any action in such circumstances except perhaps to save the child's life or to avert serious injury. The view taken by the Medical Defence Union, upon legal advice, is that a parent cannot insist on his daughter undergoing an abortion even if it is medically recommended; "a girl old enough to become pregnant is likely to be regarded by the courts as having a right to be consulted before any decision is made to terminate her pregnancy."[16]

Another problematical area relates to non-therapeutic procedures. Sir Roger Ormrod said: "It is doubtful whether parents can or should authorise any form of non-therapeutic intervention which might adversely affect the child;"[17] but there may be differences of opinion on what will adversely affect the child. When it is desired to have a judicial ruling on a particular proposal, this can be done by having the child made a ward of court. Many circuit judges are empowered to act in wardship proceedings, and a decision can generally be obtained in urgent cases almost immediately. Any person having a proper interest in the child can apply, a may the child himself by his next friend. The court acts in what it judges to be the best interests of the child. This procedure is preferable to having a care order made by magistrates in favour of the local authority, for the purpose of overruling the parents, which is a practice of doubtful legality. However, the intervention of the judge is not essential, and many decisions will be taken by the parents and children themselves.

Non-medical circumcision of male infants is practised by Jews and Muslims, and some hospitals will take over the religious rite on the ground that it is better that it should be done hygienically than otherwise. (One medical school of thought regards circumcision as beneficial to health and sexual relationships, but the question is controversial.) It is inconceivable that any judge would hold this immemorial usage to be illegal. Much less confidence can be felt about the sexual mutilation involved in clitoridectomy, a practice widespread in Africa where it is regarded as a status symbol. In 1975 a Nigerian woman who incised the cheeks of her two sons, aged 9 and 14, with their consent and approval at a family ceremony, found herself in the Central Criminal Court and was convicted under section 47 of the OAPA. She was given an absolute discharge, but the judge uttered a warning against

---

[15] By the Guardianship Act 1973 s. 1 (1) both mother and father have the same authority in relation to the upbringing of a minor; if they disagree, either of them may apply to the court to settle the matter.

[16] Medical Defence Union, *Annual Report 1972*, p. 27. Cp. Eekelaar in 89 LQR 225. Lord Denning, speaking of the under-16s, said that "the child's views are never decisive" (*B* (*B R*) v. *B* (*J*) [1968] P at 473); *sed quaere*.

[17] 46 Med.-Leg.Jrnl 25.

any repetition of the offence by the natives of Nigeria "or any other part of Africa."[18] The prosecution attracted adverse comment in the Press. In a similar case at Kingston upon Thames in 1978 the jury acquitted the parents of "malicious wounding," apparently with the approval of the judge.[19] (It does not appear whether the technical meaning of "malicious" had been explained to the jury). Somewhat inconsistently, vocal opinion was strongly against the mother who wished to have her handicapped daughter of 11 sterilised, notwithstanding that the mother was motivated by concern for the girl.[20] In the United States the question has been litigated whether parents can authorise the removal from a twin of a paired organ (a kidney) for transplant to the other twin, the donor twin being of the age of discretion and giving his consent; the attitude of the courts was favourable, on evidence that the donor twin would be psychologically affected if he were not allowed to save the life of his sibling.[21] Presumably a parent can consent to medical experiments on his child that cause only minor discomfort (such as a finger-prick to obtain a drop of capillary blood).[22]

This is all very messy. Notwithstanding the many doubts that have been expressed, the reasonable view is that a parent can authorise anything to be done to the child that is (or that the parent believes to be) not against his interest, and even something against his interest if it is compensated by sufficient advantage to others and is not seriously detrimental to the child—though probably not, in either case, if the child is old enough to understand what is involved and is either left uninformed or withholds assent, and certainly not if the operation involves the unjustifiable infliction of grievous bodily harm (whatever that may be held to be) without compensatiing advantage to the child.[23]

If the parents of a child who is below the age of discretion refuse to allow an operation for their child when this is for his benefit, can the doctors go ahead and do it?

This will be considered in § 26.8.

§ 25.14. CONSENT AND PUBLIC POLICY

The relation between criminal law and morality has been much discussed. It usually comes down to the question whether society, through the law, has any right to interfere with solitary conduct, or conduct between consenting adults, that does not affect any third person. The rest of this chapter will consider the question in some limited contexts. We shall be concerned not with problems of law and law reform in relation to specifically sexual crimes, such as homosexual offences, still less with questions of public policy relating to the control of drugs, gambling, and suchlike, but only with the extent to which consent is vitiated on grounds of public policy in crimes like murder, manslaughter and assault.

The two sides that line up on the issue are one aspect of the schism between the philosophy of libertarianism and that of authoritarianism.

---

[18] *Adesanya*, The Times, July 16, 17, 1974.

[19] 142 JPN 526.

[20] *Re D (A Minor)* § .12 n. 9.

[21] See P D G Skegg in 36 MLR at 377–379; and see this valuable article generally on consent by minors.

[22] See Dickens in 43 Med.-Leg.Jrnl. 166; Ross G Mitchell in [1964] 1 BMJ 721.

[23] The pronouncement of Lord Lane in *Attorney-General's Reference (No. 6 of 1980)* would, if accepted, impose a more severe limitation. See § .18.

Libertarians support the individual's claim to autonomy. Everyone prizes the right to live his own life, not to be made to conform to important decisions made on his behalf by others. This principle yields the two postulates stated in § .1—that, in general, (1) nothing must be done to a person without his consent and (2) anything can be done to him with his consent. (In this chapter we are chiefly concerned with the second of these postulates.) Our own courts have not formulated the principle categorically, but it was neatly expressed by an American judge. "Anglo-American law," declared Schroeder J "starts with the premise of thorough going self-determination."[1]

For English law this is a large overstatement. Cases like *Stone*[2] and *Wilkinson*[3] show that our courts are unstable in their allegiance to the principle, and often seem to be more interested in inventing exceptions to it than in giving effect to it. In other words they frequently prefer the opposing philosophy, that of authoritarianism or paternalism, which again has two postulates. The one relevant to this chapter is that nothing must be done to a man, even with his consent, if it is to his disadvantage or is otherwise regarded as antisocial. (The other, to be considered in the next chapter, is that anything can be done to a man, even without his consent, if this is necessary for his own or the public good, as seen by the legislature or the courts).

The leading philosophical exponents of the libertarian view were the individualists of the 19th century, led by J S Mill, who contended[4] that the law could properly be used against the individual only to prevent him from harming others. Its most celebrated affirmation in the present century was by the Wolfenden Committee on Homosexuality and Prostitution,[5] though neither they nor Mill considered the principle in the context of the consensual infliction of harm.

Authoritarians are concerned with what they see as social or metaphysical harms as well as the more obvious and indisputable harms perceived by the libertarians. The best-known statement of moral authoritarianism in the present context is by Lord Devlin. In his view, the consent of a person against whom force is used is no excuse to the person who uses the force, if the basic common morality of society is infringed.[6]

It is true that consent is sometimes regarded as nullified on grounds of public policy. But it is going too far to say that the mere infringement of "basic common morality" nullifies consent. If that were so, fornication would involve an assault (at least by the man), or would have done so when it was more discountenanced by opinion than it is now. So would mutual masturbation by males. The extent of the doctrine of public policy requires careful consideration, which we must now give it. We commence with the most extreme alteration of personal condition known to mankind: death.

---

[1] *Natanson* v. *Kline* (1960) 350 P 2d 1093 at 1104.

[2] § 12.3 n. 3.

[3] § 12.4 n. 5.

[4] On *Liberty* (1859). There are many reprints.

[5] Cmnd. 247 of 1957.

[6] *The Enforcement of Morals* (London 1959) 8, reprinted as Chap. 1 of the same author's *The Enforcement of Morals* (London 1965). For discussions see H L A Hart, *Law, Liberty and Morality* (London 1963); Graham Hughes in *Essays in Legal Philosophy*, ed. R S Summers (Oxford 1968) 183; [1966] Crim.LR 132; J Glover, *Causing Death and Saving Lives* (Harmondsworth 1977) Chap. 5.

§ 25.15. ABETTING SUICIDE

The response of the Christian religion and consequently the common law to the human tragedy of suicide was to condemn it. Suicide was regarded as a crime, and this had a number of consequences.

The superstitious horror of suicide in European culture has partly pagan origins. The notion of suicide as a sin is not biblical; it was invented by St. Augustine of Hippo, and he intimates pretty clearly what his reason was. Some Christians were choosing to end their lives immediately after baptism, in the belief that this was the only sure way of avoiding sin and proceeding to heaven. To prevent this decimation of believers, Augustine taught that suicide was itself a sin greater than any that was likely to be committed by remaining alive. So English law stigmatised suicide as a felony; the *felo de se's* property was forfeited, leaving his family impoverished; and his body was denied Christian burial. Even when these unfeeling practices were given up, suicide remained legally equivalent to self-murder for a number of purposes, including, to some extent, the law of attempt.[1]

The law was changed by the Suicide Act 1961, which enacts that "the rule of law whereby it is a crime for a person to commit suicide is hereby abrogated." One result is that it is no longer a crime to attempt suicide; also, there is now no question of transferred intention in these cases. If D shoots at his own head with intent to commit suicide, but misses and kills V, this is not now murder of V as it used to be, though D is likely to be convicted of manslaughter on the ground of gross negligence.

The Act of 1961 does not altogether efface the religious prohibition of suicide from the law, because it expressly continues to impose a considerable measure of responsibility upon persons other than the suicide or would-be suicide. At common law, one who incited or assisted another to do away with himself was guilty as of inciting or abetting a crime, as a deduction from the supposed guilt of the deceased. This way of looking at the matter is no longer possible, but the Suicide Act in effect continues the old law by making it a statutory crime to aid, abet, counsel or procure[2] a suicide or attempted suicide. We may call it "abetting suicide" for short. The offence carries the very severe penalty of 14 years' imprisonment, to provide for those who induce the suicide of others for some nefarious purpose of their own; but the wording is not limited to cases of bad intention. The law of attempt applies, so even when no suicide or attempted suicide takes place there can be liability for an attempt to commit the statutory offence of abetment.[3]

---

[1] See Williams, *The Sanctity of Life and the Criminal Law* (London 1968) Chap. 7; N St John-Stevas, *Life, Death and the Law* (London 1961) Chap. 6; Koessler in 107 Missouri LRev. 143; Cmnd. 1187 of 1960.

Legal rules have never prevented a high rate of suicide. There were 3,689 deaths officially recorded as due to suicide or self-inflicted injuries in 1975 (OPCS Monitor, *Deaths by Cause*, September 1, 1976), but the actual number was estimated to be some 50 per cent. higher.

[2] To procure is to produce by endeavour; so the word covers the provision of help to one who himself wishes to commit suicide: *Reed* [1982] Crim.LR 819.

[3] *McShane* (1978) CAR 97. The result is to extend liability much beyond that which existed at common law for inciting suicide; see Ash in 132 NLJ 180. On liability for publishing literature explaining methods of suicide see § 15.4 n. 11.

Lanham in [1980] Crim.LR 215 advances the argument that it can be murder to instigate another's suicide, but this has not been regarded as English law for more than a century. The reason is that the person who commits suicide, if he is of sound mind and under no relevant mistake, is in law the sole author of his death (cp. § 16.9), so that the liability of another person at common law can only be accessorial.

Do you abet someone's suicide by deciding not to prevent it?

Presumably not, since a bare omission is not included in abetment as a form of complicity in crime.[4] A person who fails to prevent a voluntary death by starvation or by the rejection of medical assistance may be in peril of being convicted of manslaughter, but he can only be convicted by the disregard of an important legal principle (§ 12.4).

In practice the law of abetting suicide is generally lightly applied; on average there are only one or two prosecutions a year, and the outcome is almost invariably a let-off (suspended sentence, probation or bind-over).[5] The question of principle is: if one person can lawfully commit suicide, why should it be an offence for another to help him?

Can I offer an explanation? It is because we still think suicide immoral. We no longer punish attempted suicide, because punishment is not likely to deter, and because it can only aggravate the depression of the person who has attempted suicide, and make it more likely that he will repeat the attempt. These reasons do not prevent helpers from being punished.

Yes, but why should the law deny the terminally ill patient the right to obtain the help of others to control the time and manner of his dying? There is a case for punishing those who assist suicide by young people (who may go through a temporarily difficult phase, and whose suicide is a cruel blow to parents), or who *persuade* others to commit suicide, or use fraud, or assist the act for selfish reasons. But is it sensible or humane that doctors, or even relatives, should be inhibited from providing a person who is dying in pain or distress with the passport to oblivion that he seeks?[6]

§ 25.16. CONSENT-KILLING AND DEATH PACTS

A person cannot consent to his own death. The rule is not based upon utilitarian considerations even though these may sometimes buttress it. It

---

[4] See § 15.7. The exception relating to those who have a right to control the situation can hardly apply cases of suicide. On the ethics of preventing suicide see J Glover, *op.cit.* Chap. 13.

[5] Thus a man who had helped his wife to commit suicide having been "goaded and cajoled" by her for 30 years to do so was put on probation, the judge saying that he should not have found himself in a criminal court: The Times, May 15, 1980. In an altogether exceptional case in 1977, a daughter who tried to get her wealthy mother to kill herself, in order to inherit from her, was sentenced to 2 years' imprisonment: *McShane*, last note. In 1975 a spinster of 55 was prosecuted for aiding her sister, aged 73, to commit suicide by leaving sleeping tablets within her reach; this was the sister's third, and successful, suicide attempt. The jury acquitted (The Times, July 22), but the defendant must have been subjected to anxiety for the period of more than three months after her first appearance before the magistrates. In 1978 Derek Humphry's *Jean's Way* attracted much attention and sympathy; the author described how he had procured and handed to his wife a powerful dose of drugs in order that she might put an end to her life, as she had long planned; she was suffering from terminal cancer. No prosecution was brought.

[6] Some doctors help their patients surreptitiously. A favoured means in the past was the "Brompton mixture," consisting of morphia, codeine, alcohol and syrup. This was administered medically to relieve suffering; but when the doctor judged that the dying was unduly protracted he might leave a large bottle of the mixture by the bedside, warning the patient on no account to take all at once or he would surely die.

A majority of the CLRC recommended that assisting a person who has already decided to kill himself should remain within the offence because it would not be easy for juries to distinguish this case from one of positive persuasion (14th Report, para. 135). But, as a note in 131 NLJ 1123 remarks, "the difficulties of trial by jury would not seem a sufficient reason for retaining the substantive law in an unsatisfactory state."

is a theocratic survival in our predominantly secular law; and religious ("transcendental") arguments are still its main support.

What is the difference between killing a person with his consent and assisting his suicide?

The first is generally murder, while the second is the statutory offence just considered. The distinction between them is the distinction between perpetrators and accessories. If a doctor, to speed his dying patient's passing, injects poison with the patient's consent, this will be murder; but if the doctor places the poison by the patient's side, and the patient takes it, this will be suicide in the patient and the doctor's guilt will be of the abetment offence under the Suicide Act (not abetment in murder). Although this is the theoretical distinction, a case of consent-killing is occasionally reduced to one of assisting suicide.[1]

The distinction may be thought to have no moral relevance, since the doctor assists the patient's death in both cases. But one or two points may be made. If V asks D to help him to die, D may reasonably say: "I do not approve of what you propose, and will not do the job for you. But you are entitled to act on your own responsibility; and since you are ill and cannot obtain the means of suicide yourself, I do not mind supplying them to you." Besides this, the fact that the patient takes the poison with his own hand helps to allay fears that perhaps he did not really consent. Suicide is more clearly an act of self-determination than consent to be killed, and requires greater strength of purpose.[2]

The question may again be asked whether there is any social value in denying the doctor's right to help his patient in this way in terminal cases. Several unsuccessful attempts have been made to change the law, but they have foundered because of the united opposition of the churches and of the medical profession itself. Doctors fear that if they were given the legal power to terminate their patient's lives, although with consent, they would lose the confidence of their patients.[3]

---

[1] E.g. *Robey* (1971) 1 CAR (S) 127.

[2] On the ethics of the matter see Glover, *op.cit.* 183–184.

[3] The third Bill introduced by Lady Wootton in the House of Lords on behalf of the Voluntary Euthanasia Society in 1975 provided that "an incurable patient who causes his own death by overdosing or other intentional action shall be deemed to have died by misadventure." This would allow recovery on a policy of life insurance, and a physician who knowingly provided the overdose would not be guilty of assisting suicide. The Bill was rejected.

The German code establishes a compromise offence of killing on request, punishable with 5 years' imprisonment (Fletcher, *Rethinking Criminal Law* 332). The CLRC in its Working Paper on OAP tentatively proposed an offence of mercy-killing punishable with 2 years' imprisonment, but this modest suggestion for an alleviation of the law (which would not have gone so far in leniency as the present practice of the courts) met with immense opposition from Christian bodies and societies, and the committee became fearful that continuing it would imperil the larger reform. So the proposal disappeared without trace in the final Report.

There is now a large literature on the legalisation of voluntary death. My own views and suggestions will be found in my book *The Sanctity of Life and the Criminal Law,* Chap. 8, and in 63 Proc.Roy.Soc.Med. 663 and 41 Medico-Legal Journal 14 (reprinted in part in *Beneficent Euthanasia*, ed. M Kohl (Buffalo, NY 1975) 145). The opposing views were debated by Kamisar and myself in 42 Minn.LRev. 969; 43 *ibid.* 1 (reprinted in part in *Euthanasia and the Right to Death*, ed. A B Downing (London 1969) 85, in *Social Ethics*, ed. Mappes and Zembaty (New York 1977) 44, in *Contemporary Issues in Bioethics*, ed. Tom L Beauchamp and LeRoy Walters (Encino, Calif. 1978) 308, in *Ethical Issues in Death and Dying*, ed. Beauchamp and Perlin (Englewood Cliffs, NJ 1978) 2201, and in *Applying Ethics*, ed. Vincent Barry (Belmont, Calif. 1981) 239. See also J Glover, *op.cit.* Chaps. 3,14. A full presentation of the case against is *Your Death Warrant?* ed. J Gould and Lord Craigmyle (London 1971).

The Archbishop of Canterbury, Dr. Coggan, in his Stevens Memorial Lecture, quoted writings against the legalisation of euthanasia and said: "The warnings given in these books seem to me to be so weighty as to make the case very strong indeed for leaving the issues much as they now are in the hands of doctors" (70 Proc.Roy.Soc.Med. 80). The lawyer must, however, comment that at present the law does not leave the issue in the hands of doctors; it treats euthanasia as murder.

The only alleviation of the traditional attitude is that according to a ruling of Devlin J, as we have seen,[4] a doctor is entitled to administer drugs in order to overcome pain, even though the result may be to shorten life. Devlin J based his conclusion on the doctrine of causation, which is unconvincing because it obscures the value-judgment involved. However, the practical effect of the judge's direction is welcome. It could well be supported on other grounds by saying that the administration of pain-killing drugs in these circumstances is justified by necessity. When, in the last stages of illness, a certain amount of drug is administered in order to deaden pain, it may lawfully be administered even though the physician knows that it will also accelerate the patient's death.[5] But he may not deliberately choose an amount of the drug that is not necessary to relieve pain and that is designed solely to kill.

Humanitarian feeling is allowed to prevail in respect of the duty to make positive exertions to prolong life in terminal illnesses. A doctor could not successfully be charged with murder, manslaughter or abetting suicide merely because, in the terminal stages of disease, he does not take exceptional measures to prolong a doomed existence, whether at the patient's request or not. This could be put on the ground that he has not actively shortened life, and that his decision not to intervene is justifiable in the circumstances. It would also seem that no question of suicide is involved in a patient's decision not to struggle further for existence.[6]

What is the position if two lovers make a suicide pact with each other, and one survives?

Two forms of death pact (suicide pact) must be distinguished: the killing-suicide pact and the double-suicide pact.

The killing-suicide pact is an agreement between A and B that A shall first kill B and then commit suicide. If A performs the first part and then fails to complete the bargain, his responsibility is reduced from murder (as at common law) to manslaughter by the Homicide Act 1957.[7]

The double-suicide pact, where each party agrees to kill himself, is in legal analysis a case of mutual abetment of suicide. The responsibility of the survivor therefore rests on the Suicide Act (for abetting suicide), not on the Homicide Act (for killing).

How exactly is the line drawn between the two kinds of death pact?

The answer is again given by a simple application of the law of complicity. It depends on who does the act of killing. If a husband and wife agree to commit suicide, and together they seal their garage and sit inside, one of them starting the car engine, then if, say, the husband survives and the wife dies the husband's guilt will depend on who started the car. If he

---

[4] § 16.5.

[5] For ecclesiastical opinions in support see the Bishop of Exeter's sermon printed in [1960] 2 BMJ 128, and Pope Pius XII's remarks reported in The Times, September 18, 1958. Dr. Coggan, in his Stevens Memorial Lecture, approved the following statement of Chancellor E Garth Moore: "It would seem reasonably certain that the giving of a pain-killing drug to a patient *in extremis* can he justified, not only by the theologian's law of double effect, but also by the common law doctrine of necessity, even where one of the effects of the drug is the probable shortening of the patient's life. This is because the evil averted, namely the agony of the patient, is greater than the evil performed, namely an act leading to the probable shortening of his life" (70 Proc.Roy.Soc.Med. 76).

[6] See § 26.7 n. 4.

[7] S. 4. The burden of proving the existence of the pact is placed upon the defendant, and it must be shown that he himself had the settled intention of dying at the time when he killed his companion in pursuance of the pact. The words "killing himself or" in s. 4 (1) are repealed by the Suicide Act. Although the statute does not expressly make a suicide pact a defence to a charge of attempted murder, it should logically be a defence. See the analogous point discussed in § 24.1 at nn. 11–14.

did, he will be guilty at common law of murdering his wife, though since it was a suicide pact his guilt will be reduced to manslaughter under the Homicide Act. If the wife started the car it will be suicide by her, and the husband will be guilty under the Suicide Act of abetting suicide.

But it may be a pure accident which of them started the car and which of them survived.

No doubt, but the distinction between the perpetrator and the accessory necessitates the enquiry.

There is little practical difference between the two statutes, but the proper statute must be referred to in the indictment.[8]

It hardly needs to be said that a suicide pact requires an agreement. If, for example, a husband tells his wife that he is going to commit suicide by taking tablets, and his wife says that in that case she is going to join him, then if both take tablets (neither helping or encouraging the other) and one survives the survivor cannot, on those facts alone, be convicted. It is merely a case of two concurrent decisions to commit suicide, each of which is lawful.

§ 25.17. FIGHTS AND GAMES

Killing in a duel is murder, consent not being recognised as a defence to this charge.[1] The judges have set their faces even against fisticuffs (whether as public spectacles, or in anger, or as a way of settling a dispute), and hold that the consent of the combatants is again, in general, no defence. The present law rests on *Attorney-General's Reference (No. 6 of 1980)*,[2] where it was held that the combatants are guilty of assault (or of an aggravated assault) if they intended to inflict actual bodily harm or were reckless as to it.

Although most fights have always been discountenanced, the scope of the prohibition has been variously stated, and the objection to consensual fights has been put on different grounds at different times. Sometimes it was the likelihood of serious injury to the combatants, sometimes the risk of public disorder, sometimes the fact that public fights encouraged idleness and indulgence in betting.[3] The Court of Appeal has now put the law on a definite and comprehensive footing. The court held that a fight is unlawful even though it takes place in private, with fists only; even though there is no question of any wider breach

---

[8] The difference of penalty—life as against 14 years—is only theoretical. In practice the charge under the Homicide Act arises only on a prosecution for murder, which will be undertaken by the DPP. The consent of the DPP is expressly required for a charge under the Suicide Act. This should be a safeguard against callous prosecution, but instances of these have occurred. In 1977 a recently married young couple who were desperately unhappy about money and housing made a suicide pact: the wife stopped breathing after taking barbiturates, and was resuscitated. When she had recovered she was charged with abetting her husband's suicide, and was placed on probation (*Sperring*, The Times, May 18, 1977). Perhaps the DPP's office has learnt the lesson: in 1980 the Director recommended no prosecution where a woman of 61 survived a suicide pact with her husband (The Times, December 19).

For an account of the poignant circumstances in which death pacts are carried out see John Cohen in (1973) 2 Medikon 17. It is hard to see what point there is in retaining the legal provision.

[1] *Rice* (1803) 3 East 581, 102 ER 719.

[2] [1981] QB 715.

[3] See 1st edn 534–537.

of the peace; even though there is no question of grievous bodily harm; and even though it is a consensual fight engaged in as a means of settling a quarrel—if, in any of these cases, actual bodily harm is intended or caused[4]; and the court clearly contemplated that a bleeding nose and bruises to the face would be "actual bodily harm." In such circumstances each party is guilty of an assault upon the other, the consent to fight being rendered ineffective in law as a matter of public policy.

This wide doctrine of vitiation of consent on grounds of policy is a judicial invention for putting the law of assault to a purpose for which it was not intended. It turns an offence designed for the prevention of aggression into one that gives a judge and jury discretion to punish people for what they deem to be improper. Since this was an Attorney-General's reference and no defendant was before the court, the court did not find it necessary to pretend that it was merely stating the existing law. The precedents directly in point were of a low order of authority, while other cases indicated that the law was narrower. The only relevant English case cited in the judgment was a nineteenth century decision on prize fights; such fights involved a considerable risk of death or grievous bodily harm and presented a much more serious social problem than a fist fight between two disputing teenagers (which was the occasion of the particular reference).

The attitude of the court was that it could nullify a person's consent in any case where the public interest did not require that consent should be a defence, and, in the opinion of the court, it "is not in the public interest that people should try to cause, or should cause, each other actual bodily harm for no good reason."

These are wide words, but if the decision is read as being confined to the subject of unregulated fights the policy is understandable. Such fights involve the appreciable possibility of causing more injury than the combatants intend or contemplate. They tend to occasion apprehension among members of the public and can spread into wider disorder; and the police in putting them down may themselves be injured. Moreover, when the giving and accepting of challenges to fight are socially allowable, the acceptance of a challenge is apt to be forced on a man as a matter of "honour." It is true that the courts had, by reviving the law of affray, provided themselves with a powerful weapon for dealing with major public disorder; but by now extending the law of assault they enabled magistrates' courts to be used to suppress minor fights.

Then what about boxing and other bouts by way of sport?

Lord Lane CJ, after the sentence just quoted, added:

> "Nothing which we have said is intended to cast doubt upon the accepted legality of properly conducted games and sports, lawful chastisement or correction, reasonable surgical interference, dangerous exhibitions, etc. These apparent exceptions can be justified as involving the exercise of a legal right, in the case of chastisement or correction, or as needed in the public interest, in the other cases."

Apart from chastisement or correction, the legality of the items in this list will normally depend upon consent, which is allowed to operate in these cases.[5] Although the list is presented as a statement of matters to which the court's outlawing of bodily injury will not extend, there is the disturbing thought that in fact the list may operate to extend that pronouncement. Were it not for the list of "apparent exceptions" the decision might have been regarded as confined to injuries inflicted in fights. But the "apparent

---

[4] The court said "intended and/or caused," presumably meaning that the parties must either intend such harm or be reckless as to it. See [1981] Crim.LR 554.

[5] On the question of acts done outside the rules of a game see 1st edn 537 § 21; *Billinghurst* [1978] Crim.LR 553.

exceptions" seem to imply that the judges have empowered themselves to declare that the occasioning of any injury, even by consent, is unlawful except to the extent that they are prepared to accept "apparent exceptions" in the public interest; and "in the public interest" simply means that the judges approve of the activity. Traditionally they approve of boxing; presumably this is "needed in the public interest." (Why is it needed? Is not the point rather that there is no public interest against it?—though serious doubts are now felt on the subject of head injuries in this sport.) According to the dictum, the courts are even prepared to countenance "dangerous exhibitions." No qualification about reasonableness appears here, but it would be unwise to rely on the omission; a judge could always defeat the argument by pointing out that Lord Lane was merely endorsing the "accepted legality" of such exhibitions, and did not say how far the "accepted legality" went. But why are dangerous exhibitions needed in the public interest?

Lord Lane expressly reserved the right of judges (with the assistance, of course, of juries) to pronounce upon what are and what are not "properly conducted games and sports," and even upon what are and what are not "reasonable surgical interferences." Does this mean that the propriety of medical operations performed by members of a highly responsible profession with the full consent of the patient are subject to the scrutiny of judge and jury?

There may be some looseness in the drafting of Lord Lane's list; but what seems to emerge is that in the matter of bodily injuries, widely interpreted, three judges sitting in the Court of Appeal have now legislated judicial paternalism to the full extent. Although the court mentioned that it had heard "interesting legal and philosophical debate," no echo of any philosophy is heard in the judgment. The court did not utter a word in support of the idea that people have the right to do what they like with their own bodies, so long as they do not harm others.

§ 25.18. DESIRED INJURIES

There is no direct authority for saying that a person commits a crime in injuring himself, even seriously. This cannot be an assault, which presupposes an offender and a victim.[1] Nor would it be right for the courts to invent a crime of self-injury as a matter of common law. An ancient crime of maim (mayhem) still exists; but there is no recorded instance of such a charge being brought for an injury inflicted by a man on himself. Now that it is no crime for a man to kill himself, or to attempt to do so, it would be somewhat illogical to punish him for inflicting upon himself a

[1] There is a theoretical problem on OAPA 1861 s. 18 (§ 9.1), which, unlike s. 20 and the poisoning sections, does not say "any *other* person." But it is hard to imagine that self-injury would be held to be both unlawful and "malicious," and anyway no prosecutor has yet charged under s. 18 for such an act.

lesser degree of injury, particularly if this is in the course of an attempt to destroy himself.

Self-injury is not infrequent, particularly in prisons. Mentally disturbed people, particularly young people and particularly girls, practise various kinds of self-abuse and self-mutilation, from sticking pins in their own legs, arms and eyes[2] to wrist-slashing and overdoses of drugs. Some are given to swallowing objects, so that they have to receive continual operative treatment. The propensity is medically called Munchausen's syndrome. Prosecutions are unknown.

If it is accepted that self-mutilation is not a crime, the conclusion should follow that those who incite it or help it are not guilty either, provided that they do not inflict the injury. The inciter should not be guilty of "causing" grievous bodily harm under section 18, because the subsequent voluntary act of the self-maimer severs the chain of imputable causation.[3] The inciter or helper is not guilty as accessory, because there is no crime, not even the ghostly crime involved in the doctrine of *Bourne* (§ 15.16). To argue otherwise involves asserting that section 2 of the Suicide Act, making it an offence to abet suicide (.15), was unnecessary.[4] There is no statutory provision for abetment of self-maim as there is with suicide. However, if the self-maim is an attempted suicide, abetting it comes within the statute.

The position is different when the injury is inflicted by another. The weight of 19th century authority favoured the view that it was unlawful to inflict on another an injury amounting to a maim or endangering life.[5] (A maim was an injury that rendered a man less able to fight in defence of himself and his country.[6]) At the present day there is no doubt that the judges would extend the rule at least to the infliction of any serious and permanent injury, whether a maim or not. One justification is that the injured person is more likely to become a charge upon the public—in modern terms, is more likely than others to be in need of supplementary benefit.

And in need of treatment under the National Health Service.

That is true, but it is an insidious argument. It is true, because in making a utilitarian calculation one cannot neglect the strain on the health service. According to one estimate, tobacco smokers cost the NHS £2m a week; and that is certainly an argument for attempting to restrain smoking, if only by making cigarettes expensive. The burden placed on brain surgeons by the serious head injuries sustained in motor cycle accidents was one reason why the wearing of crash helmets was made compulsory. But the argument is insidious because if pressed to any length it would require all hazardous expeditions and performances to be made illegal. Even the objection to people making themselves a charge on the public could be pressed so far as to stop us from engaging in dangerous sports. These are considerations that, in extreme cases, may be judged by the legislature decisive reasons for interfering in particular activities. In the absence of legislation, they do not support judicial action to interfere with consensual conduct.

---

[2] Some drug addicts stick needles into their own eyes and blind themselves in order to get rid of terrifying hallucinations. See [1972] 2 BMJ 766.

[3] § 16.9.

[4] See the parallel reasoning in § 20.

[5] See 1st edn 238 ff.

[6] Hawkins, *PC* i Chap. 44; Coke, *Institutes* i 288a; Stephen, *Digest*, 4th edn 148–159; Skegg in 16 Med.Sci.Law 264.

The best reason for the law is that if there were no legal intervention, mentally disturbed people might prevail upon others to do them irreparable injury. It is hard to imagine any normal person consenting to be seriously and permanently injured, except for some adequate medical or social reason—in which case the injury should be lawful.

Doesn't the decision in Attorney-General's Reference now tighten the law further?

It can be read as vitiating consent to any bodily injury, unless justified. But in this application the decision would be contrary to at least one decision, admittedly of low authority, but expressing the law as it was then understood: *Dilks*,[7] where a recorder held that the consent even of a 13-year old boy to be tattooed barred the criminal conviction of the tattooer. Parliament subsequently made it a special offence to tattoo minors, but did not alter the law of consent to assault and did not forbid the tattooing of adults. It would be farcical if a burly middle-aged seaman who paid for being tattooed were regarded as having been criminally assaulted by the tattooer. If the tattooing were done without consent it would certainly be bodily harm; but the consent prevents it from being an assault. Similarly, it is impossible to believe that a Jewish rabbi commits an assault on an infant whom he ritually circumcises. There may be nothing against the public interest in the practice of circumcision, but what Lord Lane required was that something should positively justify such "harms" in the public interest. Is there a general public interest in this country in maintaining Jewish religious practices—as opposed to allowing them to be maintained? His lordship was primarily concerned with the question of fighting, which was subject to the special considerations before stated; his wider remarks were obiter.

There was, indeed, one decision in support of Lord Lane's view, which he cited, namely *Donovan*.[8] This concerned sadism (the association of the sexual impulse with cruelty).[9]

> Donovan privately caned a girl of 17, for the purpose of gratifying his sexual tastes. On being charged with common assault and indecent assault he offered evidence that the girl had consented. The evidence of consent seems, from the summary of it given in the judgment, to have been cogent; yet the jury convicted, perhaps because they disapproved of Donovan and his ways. They found in effect that the girl had not consented. The verdict was quashed on appeal for misdirection, but the Court of Criminal Appeal took occasion to go into the general question whether the girl's consent, if established, would be a defence in law. The view expressed was that "if the blows struck were likely or intended to do bodily harm to the prosecutrix," her consent would be no defence. "For this purpose we think that 'bodily harm' has its ordinary meaning and includes any hurt or injury

---

[7] § .13 n. 5.

[8] [1934] 2 KB 498. An argument in support of the decision is advanced by Fletcher, *Rethinking Criminal Law* 770–771.

[9] For an extended study of sado-masochism and consent see Leigh in 39 MLR 130.

calculated to interfere with the health or comfort of the prosecutor. Such hurt or injury need not be permanent, but must, no doubt, be more than merely transient or trifling."

In laying down this wide rule (which was entirely obiter) the court was perhaps influenced, like the jury, by its aversion to the defendant's conduct. It exercised the prerogative of discriminating between activities of which it approved and those of which it disapproved. Swift J said: "Nothing could be more absurd or repellent to the ordinary intelligence than to regard his conduct as comparable with that of a participant in one of those 'manly diversions.' " Although the criminal law had directed itself against homosexual deviations, it had not specifically provided for heterosexual sadism. By ruling that the consent of the victim was no defence in respect of "bodily harm," including even an interference with comfort, the court in effect proposed to extend the operation of the law of assault to cover a sexual quirk.

The reasoning in the judgment commenced as follows:

> "If an act is unlawful in the sense of being in itself a criminal act, it is plain that it cannot be rendered lawful because the person to whose detriment it is done consents to it. No person can license another to commit a crime. So far as the criminal law is concerned, therefore, where the act charged is in itself unlawful, it can never be necessary to prove absence of consent on the part of the person wronged in order to obtain the conviction of the wrongdoer. There are, however, many acts in themselves harmless and lawful which become unlawful only if they are done without the consent of the person affected."

This passage is open to the obvious objection that it is a tautology. The first three sentences say merely that if an act is a crime irrespective of consent, then consent is no defence, while the last says that if the act is a crime only when done without consent, then consent is a defence. Such premises do not assist in the determination of the case.

The court proceeded to say that "as a general rule, although it is a rule to which there are well-established exceptions, it is an unlawful act to beat another person with such a degree of violence that the infliction of bodily harm is a probable consequence." For this proposition no authority was offered. If it is correct, the legality of professional boxing matches, where the object is to knock the opponent senseless, would be put in doubt. The proposition is true where the victim does not consent, and also for injury inflicted in unregulated fights, but whether it is true for a sexual beating with consent needed consideration. In any case, there is no reason to suppose from the facts stated that bodily harm in any realistic sense was likely.

The court in *Attorney-General's Reference* accepted the criticism of *Donovan* that the reasoning was tautologous, but said nothing further in opposition to it. Moreover, the court's general statement of principle was evidently meant to approve the decision. The Court of Appeal, like the Court of Criminal Appeal in *Donovan*, started from the premise that all infliction of bodily harm is unlawful unless it is for the public benefit; if this proposition is accepted, and since no one argues that a sadistic beating is for the public benefit, such a beating must be unlawful. But the proposition is open to the criticism that it attaches no value to the individual's autonomy. The proper question should be not whether a consensual beating is required by the public interest but whether there is anything against it.

Legal intervention is most likely where, as in *Donovan*, the conduct in question is regarded as immoral. The very few examples of prosecutions in

England for risks knowingly run belong to this area. Two others come to mind.

> In *Pike*,[10] the defendant procured his mistress to be anaesthetised[11] with her consent, his object being to gratify his sexual perversion of copulating with an unconscious woman. The anaesthetic was a wholly improper and dangerous one, and caused her death. The deceased woman was as much in possession of the facts as Pike was, but Pike was convicted of manslaughter. A defence of consent to run risk, or of negligent joint enterprise, was not even argued; and no doubt it would have been rejected if it had been.
>
> Similarly, in *Cato*[12] it was the deceased who prepared the syringe and took responsibility for the propriety of the dose; yet the defendant who administered it was convicted both of manslaughter and of administering a noxious thing under OAPA 1861 s. 23. On the latter charge, the Court of Appeal said that the substance was noxious "having regard to the potentialities of heroin." The forbidden consequence specified in section 23 is the endangering of life or the infliction of grievous bodily harm, and Cato did not intend to do either. The jury found that he knew that the injection was "likely to do some harm," but there was no evidence to support even that limited finding. The court merely accepted an obviously perverse verdict without enquiring into it.

The court in the latter case specifically considered the defence of consent only in connection with manslaughter, and it dealt with it in an extremely curious way. The decision was that the trial judge was justified in telling the jury that consent was no defence. But the court added:

> "Of course in a perfect world the judge, when faced with this question, would have dealt with both aspects of the matter in contrast. He would have said 'It is not a defence in the sense that merely by proving Farmer's permission the matter is at an end; but when you come to consider the questions of gross negligence or recklessness of course you must take it into account.' Whether he would have gone further we very much doubt. If a persistent juror had said 'Well, what do you mean by 'take into account?' What have we got to do?,' it may very well be that the judge would be stumped at that point and really could not do any more than say "You must take it into account." Lawyers understand what it means, but jurors very often do not, and although I have taken more time to discuss this point than perhaps it really requires, we have come to the conclusion that there is not here any matter which gives us cause to think that the conviction may be unsafe or unsatisfactory."

If the law really contains a rule that the judge would be "stumped" to explain to the jury, it is high time that it were changed. The same applies to rules that do no more than tell juries to "take things into account."

At the time when *Pike* and *Cato* were decided it was generally thought that consent was vitiated only in respect of death or grievous bodily harm. Since *Attorney-General's Reference* it seems also to be vitiated in respect of slight harm. The jury's finding in *Cato* that the defendant knew that the injection was likely to do some harm was, under Lord Lane's doctrine, sufficient to make Cato guilty of an assault even though no more than slight harm had occurred. The CLRC, it will be remembered, took the view that the injection of one drug addict by another should not be brought within

---

[10] [1961] Crim.LR 114, 547.
[11] For a more specific account see § .20 at n. 3.
[12] § 9.10 at n. 15.

the poisoning offence, but should be dealt with, if at all, by statute.[13] But under Lord Lane's doctrine the prosecution now have an additional line of attack without needing legislation: the injecting addict can, according to this, be prosecuted for assault. The common law is a hydra-headed monster!

Lord Lane's doctrine, if accepted, also has an interesting effect upon the rule in *Clarence*.[14] This is because the doctrine of vitiation of consent does not appear to require that the person upon whom "force" is used should know of the danger of harm. If the person using the force intends or is reckless as to harm, and if such harm is caused, the inflicter is presumably guilty of an assault even though the recipient of the force was in a state of ignorance as to the danger. It follows that Clarence, knowing that he was likely to infect his wife, was guilty of an assault upon her (a husband can be guilty of an assault upon his wife, even if it consists in an act of copulation[15]), because the wife's consent to the contact was vitiated on the ground of public policy.[16] The point is another illustration of how far Lord Lane's dictum takes us (if it is accepted) from the traditional idea of an assault.

It may be strongly doubted whether the very rare show trial for consensual immoral acts serves any social purpose. Moreover, a law is objectionable if, while general in its terms, it is used only against those who engage by mutual consent in deviant activity. The result is to give full rein to the prejudices of prosecutors, judges and juries.

If a person consents to be injured, and if inflicting such injury is an assault (e.g. because it amounts to g.b.h.), is he an accessory to the offence of inflicting the injury upon himself?

There is no authority.[17] If the view is accepted that a person ought not to be criminally liable for self-injury, it should follow that for the same reason he should not be liable as accessory if he consents to be injured.[18] There is a certain justification for the law directing itself against the other person who inflicts an injury amounting to g.b.h., but not against a person who is so abnormal that he seeks it.[19]

§ 25.19. SURGERY

The previous discussion has shown that the validity of consent to harm is a grey area in the law. It is sufficiently uncertain to have given rise to the

---

[13] § 9.10 at n. 16.
[14] § 9.5.
[15] § 10.8 at n. 13.
[16] Adrian Lynch in [1978] Crim.LR makes this point for cases where the person who suffers the contact knows of the risk of infection, but says that the argument does not hold if, as in *Clarence*, such person is unaware of the risk. But this, as Lynch perceives, would be an extraordinary distinction. Liability in the latter case should follow *a fortiori* from liability in the former. The vitiation of the victim's consent depends not upon the victim's knowledge but upon the assaulter's. Cato was condemned because he was found to have known of the risk; whether his companion knew of it was immaterial.
[17] The old case of *Wright* (1603), which is distinguishable, was discussed in 1st edn 539–540.
[18] See § 15.15.
[19] See Fletcher, *op.cit.*.

opinion[1] that the judges have a commission to pronounce upon the legality of all forms of surgery; and certainly the pronouncement in *Attorney-General's Reference*,[2] conferring the benediction of the judges on "reasonable surgical interference," seems to confirm that opinion. In practice, of course, the courts would find in favour of such "interference," if the question ever arose, almost as a matter of routine.

There have been doubts about sterilisation "of convenience," i.e. as a form of birth control.[3] However, medical practice came to accept the operation after counsel advised the BMA that it might be performed without fear of legal repercussions.[4] For some time there was less certainty about castration, which, unlike sterilisation, is a de-sexing operation. It may occasionally be recommended as the only way of obtaining relief from abnormalities in the sexual urge, and in these cases the judges would certainly regard it as lawful. Moreover, the so-called sex-change operation has come to be accepted as lawful.[5] A change from male to pseudo-female sex organs involves castration: the penis and testicles are removed and a pseudo-vagina constructed from the scrotum. Now castration was regarded as a maim at common law, because it was thought to reduce the will to fight. Yet the male-"female" sex-change is performed openly by reputable surgeons. If the issue were raised, the operation could be supported as conducive to the patient's mental health; and Ormrod J accepted its legality on this ground.[6] Again, no one has ever doubted the legality of the operation of prefrontal leucotomy, which, by severing the frontal lobes of the brain, changes the personality of the patient in certain cases of mental illness. Therapy also gives moral support to some cosmetic surgery, but not all. The justification for padding bosoms, chiselling noses, and restoring hymens lost in pre-marital encounters, is that the patient is pleased and may be socially or maritally advantaged, rather than that the operation is a psychiatric necessity.

A more serious interference with the body is in taking an organ for transplant, such as a kidney. Nevertheless, no serious legal doubts have been expressed about such operations upon adult donors, where a paired organ is surrendered for the benefit of another.[7]

It may be questioned whether the criminal law has any acceptable place in controlling operations performed by qualified practitioners upon adults of sound mind with their consent, whether for reasons of therapy, charity or experiment. Controls exercised by the medical profession itself should be accepted as sufficient. If any particularly serious problems arise they should be left for the consideration of Parliament. In a civil case relating to an operation changing a male to a pseudo-female, Ormrod J said:

> "There is obviously room for differences of opinion on the ethical aspects of such operations but, if they are undertaken for genuine therapeutic purposes, it is a matter for the decision of the patient and the doctors concerned in his case. The passing of section 1 of the Sexual Offences Act 1967[8] seems to have removed any legal objections which there might have been to such procedures."[9]

---

[1] See, e.g. D W Meyers, The Human Body and the Law (Edinburgh 1970), *passim*.

[2] § .17.

[3] Williams, *The Sanctity of Life and the Criminal Law* (London 1958) Chap. 3; Meyers, *op. cit.* Chap. 1; Bartholomew in 2 Melbourne Univ.LRev. 77, 397.

[4] [1960] 2 BMJ 1510, 1516. The opinion was reaffirmed by counsel advising the Medical Defence Union: [1966] 1 BMJ 1597. Cp. Skegg in [1974] Crim.LR 694 n. 8.

[5] For earlier doubts see Meyers, *op. cit.* Chap. 3.

[6] See below at n. 9.

[7] See Dworkin in 33 M.L.R. 353; Skegg in [1974] Crim.LR 33,698.

[8] Which in general legalised adult homosexual practices.

[9] *Corbett* v. *C* [1971] P at 99.

There is no reason why the same view should not be taken for all medical procedures, assuming that the patient has capacity to consent. The law would still play a part in determining legal capacity in the case of the young and the mentally abnormal.

If this is so, the only threat presented by the law in respect of operations on the body is to those who are not medically qualified. The examples of tattooers and rabbis have already been given. It is impossible to believe that either is guilty of an assault.

§ 25.20. DANGEROUS FEATS

The foregoing discussion has concentrated on cases where hurt is intentionally inflicted. We now turn to those where the "victim" knowingly assumes the risk of being hurt (or killed). The only purpose of the defendant is to do something that, as he knows, involves the risk of hurt to another, the other consenting to run the risk.

The law relating to dangerous feats and performances, such as the climbing of vertical surfaces and brief defiances of the law of gravity on the flying trapeze or hang-glider, is obscure. Certainly no crime is committed if the whole affair is reasonable; but can one go further and say that the law does not interfere even if it is reckoned unreasonable? Granted the power of the courts to nullify consent to hurts intentionally inflicted, it does not follow that the general criminal law dictates what dangers may be lawfully encountered in behaviour that is not only unaggressive but not intended to harm.

One way of settling many problems is by pointing out that there is not, and never has been, any crime of self-manslaughter. Suicide has always meant intentional suicide[1]: in effect (though not in legal theory) self-murder. For no purpose is it a crime for a person to kill himself negligently.[2] Anyone who incites or helps him cannot be guilty of manslaughter as a perpetrator, because he is not the perpetrator; and he cannot be guilty as accessory, because of the absence of the crime.

This point was overlooked in *Pike*.[3]

> Pike anaesthetised his mistress with her consent, or incited her to administer the anaesthetic to herself—the evidence did not make it clear which. His object was to gratify his sexual perversion of copulating with an unconscious woman. The anaesthetic was a wholly improper and dangerous one, and caused her death. The trial judge, Hilbery J, directed the jury that, given the requisite *mens rea*, the defendant could be convicted of manslaughter whether he administered the anaesthetic himself or provided it for the deceased woman to take.

The court did not focus on the self-manslaughter point, and the ruling is clearly contrary to principle. Since the case might have amounted to accidental self-killing, rather than to a killing by Pike, he should have been acquitted.

---

[1] *R* v. *City of London Coroner, ex p. Barber* [1975] 1 WLR 1310.
[2] *The General Part*, 2nd edn § 131 pp. 393–394.
[3] [1961] Crim.LR 114, 547.

It is true that, according to *Bourne* and *Cogan*,[4] a person may be accessory to a non-existent crime, or may commit the *actus reus* through an innocent agent. But even if these decisions are given their fullest width, they do not apply here. Suppose for the sake of argument that the two cases decide that where an alleged perpetrator has a personal defence, an alleged accessory not having that defence can be held liable. The difficulty is not that the mistress has a personal defence. There is no *actus reus*. Since the Suicide Act, even intentional self-killing is a perfectly lawful activity; and negligent self-killing always was lawful. It took an express provision in the Suicide Act to make the abetment of suicide a crime, and there is no statute making the abetment of negligent self-killing a crime. The decisions in *Bourne* and *Cogan* should not be taken as making a man guilty as accessory in these circumstances.

Nor does the doctrine of innocent agency affect the question. It could not be argued that Pike killed his mistress with her own hand, because the doctrine of innocent agency has not been extended to negligent acts. Besides, it is not proper to use the doctrine where the alleged agent is innocent because the act is perfectly lawful. The doctrine applies only where the act would be unlawful for the agent, but for the lack of fault by the agent or some personal defence that he (or she) has.

Apart from these technical arguments, it would be unfortunate if the accessory to *de facto* self-manslaughter could be convicted, because it would mean that people who help mountaineers and others to fit out foolhardy expeditions might be convicted of manslaughter if a member of the party dies. There has never been any such prosecution, and it would be undesirable to have a rule of law making the prosecution possible.

The foregoing reasoning helps the defendant only when he does not do the act that kills. If he does, he must find his defence along some other line. One solution would be to seize upon the only fully liberal phrase in the judgment in *Attorney-General's Reference*,[5] permitting "dangerous exhibitions." It has already been noticed that the liberality may be illusory, because of Lord Lane's reference to "accepted legality". But if dangerous exhibitions are truly allowed, then dangerous feats not intended as exhibitions must presumably be allowed as well. In other words, "assumption of risk" must be a defence to a manslaughter charge in these cases. Alternatively, it is always possible for the court to regard the value of the activity, taken in conjunction with the voluntariness of participation, as excluding a finding of negligence.

The proper rule would be that the common law has no application to feats of skill or endurance. There have always been people who have taken a pleasure in such things; and few would count the preservation of life as the worthiest way of living. "Surely," said R L S, "the love of living is stronger in an Alpine climber roping over a peril, or a hunter riding merrily at a stiff fence, than in a creature who lives upon a diet and walks a measured distance in the interest of his constitution." Activities like these are valued not only because they present difficulties to be overcome but often, paradoxically, because of the danger. Motorcycle racing is a conspicuous example. It attracts participants and spectators precisely because of the risks—even though the organisers take great pains to minimise them. The same is true of those who climb down dark holes, or who make free-fall parachute descents.[6] Some psychiatrists see therapeutic value in exhilarating hazards for people suffering from neurotic ills. The soundest policy for the criminal courts would be to dissociate themselves from these questions, by holding that the consent of a person to run the risk of death, otherwise than in

---

[4] § 15.16.

[5] § .17.

[6] The Minister of Aviation refused to make the use of barometric safety devices compulsory in such descents, and he gave as his reason that part of the attraction of parachuting, as with mountaineering, was the calculated flirtation with death. *Parl.Deb.*, H of C, vol. 678 col. 6.

combats, is a defence to a charge of manslaughter. Unless the law abrogates control over this area, the courts will be faced with the invidious task of deciding between risks that people may and may not legitimately run in respect of their own bodies.

The proposition should be accepted not only for open-air sports but for cinema "stuntmen" and circus entertainers. Risks are taken every day in these performances, and sometimes accidents happen, but the police rightly take no notice.

A rare example of a prosecution is the New Zealand case of *McLeod*.[7] McLeod was an expert marksman who, in the course of a performance of his skill, invited a member of the audience to hold a cigarette in his mouth which was to act as a target. The invitation was accepted, and McLeod aimed at the cigarette ash with the object of knocking it away. No injury would have occurred but for the fact that the voluntary assistant moved his head just before the defendant fired, which caused the bullet to enter his cheek. It was held by the Court of Appeal, on the construction of a section of the New Zealand Code, that if the assistant had died it would have been manslaughter, since "a lethal weapon was used and in risky circumstances." It may be doubted whether the fact that a potentially lethal weapon was used was itself sufficient to carry the decision, for it was not used with the intention of causing injury. Moreover, if some element of risk in the performance was enough to make it illegal at common law, many other exhibitions and feats of endurance would come under the same condemnation.

That dangerous performances should not be controlled by the operation of the common law of manslaughter seems to be supported by the fact that Parliament has itself made a notably limited entry into the field. The Children and Young Persons Act 1933 ss. 22–24 contains prohibitions in respect of dangerous performances by persons under 16; and the Hypnotism Act 1952 allows the local authority, or other body that licenses places of public entertainment, to regulate exhibitions of hypnotism; the latter Act provides that hypnotism must not be demonstrated on a person under 21.[8]

We may end this discussion by observing that Parliament has not entirely excluded consensual and self-directed negligence from penal restraint. The Health and Safety at Work etc. Act 1974 imposes a duty on employees to take care even for themselves. It has long been accepted that employees may properly be made liable, at least in theory, for not using safety precautions like goggles: factory workers are subject to a great temptation not to use them when they are uncomfortable or hinder earnings, so paternalistic considerations are allowed to prevail—even though prosecutions of employees may be very rare. Enforcement is by inspectors who primarily use persuasion. It is different when an effort is made to impose safety precautions on the general public, because here enforcement is necessarily by the police, who are not well utilised on matters not relating to public order. However, after heated debate Parliament made the wearing of crash helmets compulsory for motor cyclists,[9] and the wearing of seat belts compulsory in the front seats of vehicles.[10] Strain upon the National Health Service is not in general a reason for proscribing dangerous activities, but when the safety precaution is simple and casualties are high the medical argument can outweigh that based on personal liberty.

§ 25.21. ENTRAPMENT

The courts of the United States have created a defence of entrapment where an offence to which the actor was not "predisposed" has been actively instigated by the police or by an undercover agent on their behalf.[1]

---

[7] [1915] 34 NZLR 430.

[8] The Hypnotism Act was "panic legislation" by private member's Bill resulting from an incident in which stage hypnotism performed upon a girl of 19 had ill effects. There is not much sense in saying that a girl of 16 can swing on a circus trapeze but not undergo stage hypnotism, See Nigel Walker in 11 Howard Journal 215.

[9] Road Traffic Act 1972 s. 32.

[10] Transport Act 1981 s. 27.

[1] The basis of the defence is controverted. See George Fletcher, *Rethinking Criminal Law* 541–544.

English courts reject the defence.[2] Whether this is the right attitude is a matter of opinion, but a workable rule would be somewhat difficult to draft and administer.[3]

Of course, entrapment can be a matter of mitigation where the offender was not the prime mover in the scheme and might have refrained from committing any offence if he had not been tempted. Entrapment is not even mitigation if undercover agents merely pretend that they are in the market to buy things like drugs or obscene publications, and do not use extraordinary persuasion in order to overcome reluctance. The courts recognise that consensual offences (such as in the realm of sex, drink, drugs and gambling) generally cannot be detected without some testing of suspects, and criminal organisations frequently have to be infiltrated by police spies who must necessarily show enthusiasm for the undertaking.

Judges have sometimes spoken strongly against the police using *agents provocateurs,* in the sense of people who cause offences to be committed.[4] One principle that has been distinctly laid down is that where an informer has been employed in such a way as to affect "the quality of the offence," this fact must be disclosed at the trial.[5] However, when a police officer gives evidence that he acted "on information received," the defendant cannot cross-examine him to ascertain the identity of his informant; so if the defendant alleges that he was unfairly tricked and the police deny it, he may have considerable difficulty in proving his contention.

SUMMARY

In general, anything may be done to a person (or in respect of his property) if he consents to it. § .1

The burden of proving non-consent rests on the prosecution. Since offences against the person and property require *mens rea*, the prosecution must prove that the defendant knew that the complainant was not or might not be consenting. § .2

Consent that appears to be given may be deprived of its effect in certain ways. Consent is vitiated by the fear that force will be applied to the complainant or anyone else; and a threat of force may be implied from the circumstances. According to *Olugboja* the jury can be directed in general terms to decide whether there was "real consent" or "mere submission" on the part of the woman, without entering into the question of threats; *sed quaere*. Even before this decision it was doubtful what, if any, threats other than of force vitiated consent. Economic pressure or undue influence was not enough. On principle, even a threat of dismissal from employment should not be enough. § .3

However, the crime of rape is supplemented by a section making it an offence to procure a woman, by threats or intimidation, to have USI in any part of the world. The section is held to cover threats other than of force, but the courts have not considered whether any limitation is to be placed on the meaning of the word for this purpose. No similar section supplements the law of assault. § .4

Consent can be vitated by mistake, whether resulting from fraud or not. Stephen § .5

---

[2] See *Sang* [1980] AC 402, and Heydon in [1980] Crim.LR 129. Also, in general, the Canadian courts: *Bonnar* (1975) 34 CRNS 182 (Nova Scotia). A judge has no discretion to exclude evidence obtained in this way: *Sang*, above. The Law Commission, after a full study, decided not to propose that the defence should be created by statute: *Criminal Law: Report on Defences of General Application* (Law Com. No. 83), Part V.

[3] See Heydon in [1973] CLJ 268; K J M Smith in [1975] Crim.LR 12; Ashworth in [1978] *ibid.* 137; Barlow in 41 MLR 266.

[4] Responsive to this opinion, the DPP may abandon charges that appear to have been induced by an *agent provocateur.* In 1976, drug charges against 27 people were dropped when the activities of one Cornelius Buckley, as police informer, were discovered.

[5] *Birtles* [1969] 1 WLR 1047, 2 All ER 1131, 53 CAR 469.

J said that vitiating fraud in the case of rape must be as to the nature of the act or the identity of the actor; and this would extend to mistakes of these two kinds not resulting from fraud (if known to the defendant), and, presumably, to crimes other than rape.

The first part of Stephen J's proposition means that, in rape, the woman's consent is vitiated if she does not know that the defendant's penis is entering her body. Some pronouncements are disposed to extend the doctrine of vitiation more widely. § .6

But here again rape is supplemented by a section making it an offence to procure a woman, by false pretences or false representations, to have USI in any part of the world. Once more, the courts have not considered whether any limitation is to be placed by construction on the very wide words of the statute; and again it does not apply to assault. § .7

It has been held that a girl is abducted from her parent without his consent if consent is obtained by a false statement that she is being taken into employment; and a woman who allowed a man to rub her body, having been defrauded into believing that this was therapeutic, was held not to consent to the act as an indecent assault; but these decisions are questionable extensions of the doctrine of vitiation of consent. § .8

Although Stephen J said that mistake as to the identity of the actor vitiates consent, the law is in doubt. At common law, impersonation of a woman's husband did not turn USI into rape, but by statute (now SOA s. 1 (2)) it is declared to be rape. Whether impersonating a woman's lover would now have the same effect independently of the statute has not been decided. Mistake as to the defendant's medical qualification should not on principle vitiate consent, being merely mistake as to an attribute, but legislation is needed. § .9

There is no special rule for drugs and consent, though the SOA provides an unnecessary offence on the subject. § .10

On one occasion it was held that a boy's ignorance that tattooing would cause his arm to become painful destroyed his consent to the act; but the decision may be questioned. In particular, it would be unfortunate if a doctrine of "informed consent" were used against surgeons as a matter of criminal law. The tattooing of minors is now a statutory offence. § .11

It is an offence to have USI with a woman who suffers from an arrested or incomplete development of mind which includes severe impairment of intelligence and social functioning; and no such person can consent to an indecent assault. There is no reason to doubt that a mentally disordered person can give a valid consent to a therapeutic procedure if he knows that therapy is proposed (such customary details being communicated as he is capable of grasping) and does not object. § .12

By statute, a person can consent to therapy at the age of 16. But this is a minimum provision, and the common law of consent is wider. Probably a parent cannot consent on behalf of his child of that age, and perhaps cannot consent on behalf of a child who has reached the earlier "age of discretion," if the child himself does not consent; but the parent can consent to a therapeutic procedure on behalf of his child under the age of discretion. There is a doubt as to non-therapeutic procedures. § .13

Consent may be disregarded on grounds of public policy. § .14

Suicide was legalised by the Suicide Act 1961, but abetting suicide was made a statutory offence at the same time. There can be an attempt to commit the offence. Presumably it is not an abetment to fail to prevent suicide. § .15

Killing by consent is murder, except that Devlin J ruled that the administration of drugs to relieve pain in hopeless cases is not in law a cause of death. If a killing-suicide pact is entered into, and the killer survives, his guilt is reduced to manslaughter by the Homicide Act 1957. The survivor of a double-suicide pact is guilty of abetting suicide. § .16

It was held in *Attorney-General's Reference* (1980) that those who take part in a fight are guilty of assault if they intend to inflict actual bodily harm or are reckless as to it. The court said that it "is not in the public interest that people should try to cause, or should cause, each other actual bodily harm for no good reason;" but the court did not intend "to cast doubt upon the accepted legality of properly conducted games and sports, lawful chastisement or correction, reasonable surgical interference, dangerous exhibitions, etc. These apparent exceptions can be justified as involving the exercise of a legal right, in the case of chastisement or correction, or as needed in the public interest, in the other cases." § .17

It would seem that a person does not commit a crime in injuring himself, and it should follow that those who incite or help the infliction of the injury are not liable either, provided they do not inflict it themselves. But dicta in *Attorney-General's Reference* supports the controversial dictum in *Donovan* that a person cannot effectively consent to suffer any (even trivial) actual bodily harm at the hands of a sadist, who is therefore liable for assault in inflicting it. The former dictum appears to apply to all injuries that the courts regard as not justified in the public interest. But neither of these pronouncements can be taken to settle the point definitively. § .18

It seems probable that the courts will not investigate the merits of a particular surgical operation, though the doctrine of *Attorney-General's Reference* may be used against unqualified people who do not purport to give treatment, such as tattooists. § .19

The law relating to dangerous feats is again obscure. Since there is no crime of self-manslaughter, those who help a person to do a dangerous act as a result of which he dies are presumably guilty of no offence. Prosecutions are not brought against those who, in the course of a dangerous feat, themselves do an act that causes the death of another. Dangerous performances by persons under 16 are controlled by statute. There are also examples of paternalism in legislation. § .20

No defence of entrapment is recognised. § .21

Chapter 26

NECESSITY

In all human institutions, a smaller evil is allowed to procure a greater good.
Oliver Goldsmith, *The Vicar of Wakefield*

The fact that the defendant broke the letter of the law in mitigating circumstances may be a ground for reducing or cancelling punishment, but is not generally a defence in the sense that it prevents conviction. Although from the human point of view we may understand the strength of a temptation to which the defendant was subjected, still we say that he did wrong, and we express the opinion by registering a conviction, even though this is followed by giving the defendant an absolute discharge or other virtual let-off. But there are certain situations, necessity, duress and self-defence among them, where (at least in some circumstances) the defendant is entitled to be acquitted, and not merely to be treated leniently in the matter of punishment.

§ 26.1. THE THEORY OF NECESSITY

The word "necessity," as we customarily use it, has a special meaning. A particular act is never necessary in the sense that there is literally no option. Some choice is always present, even though one of the alternatives is to meet one's own death. Necessity in legal contexts involves the judgment that the evil of obeying the letter of the law is socially greater in the particular circumstances than the evil of breaking it. In other words, the law has to be broken to achieve a greater good.

But good can never come out of evil.

If I give an instance where good comes out of what seems to have been evil, are you then going to say that the apparent evil was not really evil? For, if so, I can obviously never defeat your proposition; but the proposition will then be uninformative, because tautologous.

Certainly we should be very cautious about inflicting an admitted evil in the hope that good will come. Generally it would not be justifiable to do so. The doctrine of necessity concerns cases in which it is justified.

Surely necessity can never justify a breach of law?

As we shall see, the defence of necessity is controversial. Judges are suspicious of it because they fear that it may be subversive. But if the validity of the defence is acknowledged, then it is only the letter of the law, or the apparent law, that is broken under necessity. If necessity is a legal justification, then the law itself is not truly broken.

It is said that good motive is no defence. How does necessity differ from this?

One who acts from necessity acts from a kind of good motive. Good motive falling outside the doctrine of necessity is not a defence to a criminal charge,[1] though it may be a ground for reducing punishment.

But does our law really recognise the defence?

There are two views.

- The first is that necessity is not a general defence, but is recognised within the definitions of some particular offences.[2] A few statutes painstakingly provide for the defence, at least in part, as when the Protection of Animals Act 1911[3] penalises the infliction of "unnecessary" suffering, or when the Control of Pollution Act 1974[4] allows a defence that the acts were done "in an emergency in order to avoid danger to the public," or when the Road Traffic Act 1974 s. 7 (1) provides that vehicles may be parked on verges and footways if this is necessary to save life or for other similar purposes. But Parliament is not generally so imaginative. The more usual position is that the statute is silent about emergencies, but may incorporate wide words that could give the courts an excuse for reading in the defence of necessity. For example, if negligence or unreasonableness or even recklessness is in issue, necessity can be taken into account. (A man charged with careless driving says that he had to cross over to the wrong side of the road to avoid a collision.) It seems even to be allowed that the fact that a person is driving in an emergency is a factor to be weighed in deciding whether his driving was without due care.[5] Criminal damage requires that the damage be caused without lawful excuse; so if there is a rail accident and a passenger breaks into an unoccupied house in order to telephone for help, it may be contended that his damage to the door is not an offence because it has lawful excuse. Or if the aforesaid passenger seizes a motor bicycle in order to go for help, his consumption of the petrol would be held not to be dishonest, and therefore not to be theft, dishonesty being part of the definition of theft. If a statute prohibits something being done "wilfully," the courts hold that this word implies that the conduct is unlawful only if done "without lawful excuse."[6] The weakness in arguments built upon this last phrase is that it is (very reasonably) held not to let in defences not otherwise recognised by law.[7] Conversely, it can be argued with much force that a word like "unlawfully" should not be required in order to ensure that ordinary legal excuses are implied in the definition of the offence.[8] A more generous statutory phrase is

---

[1] *Chandler* [1964] AC 763.

[2] In support of this opinion see P R Glazebrook in [1972A] CLJ 87. In *Lynch* [1975] AC at 691F Lord Simon declared that the defence of necessity "has been decisively rejected in the criminal law generally," but this was dissenting and obiter, and in support he mentioned only *Dudley* (§ .3) and theft by the starving (§ .5), and neither illustration is conclusive, as will be shown.

[3] S. 1. Contrast the Conservation of Wild Creatures and Wild Plants Act 1975 s. 1, which restricts the killing of protected creatures even when they are damaging property.

[4] S. 3 (4) (*d*). Cp. for heavy lorries the Heavy Commercial Vehicles (Controls and Regulation) Act 1973 s. 2 (1); also the Prevention of Oil Pollution Act 1971 s. 5 (1).

[5] See *Wood* v. *Richards* 65 CAR 300, [1977] RTR 201, Crim.LR 295. But see *Jones* § 27.3 n. 10.

[6] *Rice* v. *Connolly* [1966] 2 QB at 419.

[7] *Tegerdine* [1983] Crim.LR 163; and see n. 14 below.

[8] See Exshaw in [1959] Crim.LR 503.

"without reasonable excuse," which plainly admits of excuses not otherwise recognised by law.[9]

- The alternative view is that necessity or lesser evil is a general defence in the criminal law, like nonage, insanity, self-defence and duress.[10] Such a defence is recognised in the statutory law of a number of countries, including the State of New York, West and East Germany, the largest of the Soviet Union republics,[11] and as a matter of common law in Canada.[12] In English common law it has been recognised in multifarious cases, and has been supported by a number of writers including Stephen.[13] There is little logic in saying that necessity can excuse where the offence happens to have the word "unlawfully" or some such expression in the definition but not where there are no words upon which the defence can be hung; for it must often be an accident of drafting whether a word like "unlawfully" is put in or not. Moreover, to say that necessity can come in as a "lawful excuse" under statute presupposes that it is recognised by law as an excuse.[14] If it is, there is no reason why its availability should depend upon the statutory phrase.

The old books contain a plethora of maxims justifying necessity as a defence.[15] The specific instances commonly given were pulling down houses to prevent the spread of fire, and entering upon land to dig trenches and bulwarks against the enemy. It was also recognised that prisoners could lawfully leave a prison in case of fire, even though prison-breach was a crime under a statute that made no mention of the defence of necessity. The prisoner, as the judges forcibly expressed it, "is not to be hanged because he would not stay to be burnt." Wills J on one occasion said that "a municipal regulation may be broken to save life or put out a fire,"[16] and it may be supposed that his mention of municipal regulations and fires was by way of illustration only, to save going into details. In a storm at sea, the cargo may be jettisoned for the safety of the passengers.[17] There is a right to land on the shore (even where it would otherwise be a trespass) in cases of peril or necessity,[18] and travellers who find the highway (including a footpath) "foundrous" may proceed on the adjoining land. In modern

---

[9] See R I E Card in [1969] Crim.LR 359, 415.

[10] I have written in favour of this view in 6 Current Legal Problems 216 and in *The General Part*, 2nd edn Chap. 17. See also, on the whole subject, Law Commission, *Published Working Paper No. 55* (HMSO 1974), and further references there given.

[11] See Kadish and Kadish, *Discretion to Disobey* (Stanford, Calif. 1973) 120–121, 150–151. Fletcher, *Rethinking Criminal Law* 774 says that in the present century it has become standard for revised criminal codes to recognise the defence.

[12] See Leigh in [1978] Crim.LR 151. Also by the Supreme Court of Victoria: *Loughnan* [1981] VR 443.

[13] *Digest of Criminal Law* (London 1877) 19.

[14] Cp. the rule that "without lawful excuse" does not let in a defence of ignorance of the criminal law, since the law does not recognise such a general defence: § 20.5 n. 6. *Dixon* v. *Atfield* [1975] 1 WLR 1171, 3 All ER 265, indicates an exception that proves the rule: the law allows reasonable temporary obstructions to a highway, but not unauthorised permanent obstructions: the latter, therefore, unlike the former, cannot come within the phrase "lawful excuse" in the Highways Act 1959 s. 121 (1).

[15] 6 Current Legal Problems 216.

[16] *Tolson* (1889) 23 QBD at 172.

[17] So held in a case reported by Coke: *Mouse's* case (1608) 12 Co.Rep. 63, 77 ER 1341.

[18] Halsbury's *Laws of England*, 3rd edn xxxix 564.

times it has been held justifiable to burn a strip of heather to prevent a fire from spreading.[19]

Of all the possible instances of necessity, the saving of life is of course the strongest. Devlin J said, in a civil case:

> "The safety of human lives belongs to a different scale of values from the safety of property. The two are beyond comparison and the necessity for saving life has at all times been considered a proper ground for inflicting such damage as may be necessary upon another's property."[20]

There are other authorities of more recent date supporting the defence, including dicta in the House of Lords,[21] but also some that favour a one-eyed approach, disclaiming any power in the judges to assess values lying outside the letter of the law. Even the modern authorities giving qualified support to the defence generally do so by way of *obiter dictum* only. We may notice here, as elsewhere, that the enthusiasm of the courts in developing criminal liability is but imperfectly matched by their readiness to recognise proper defences.

Is a defence of necessity really required, when the court can in a proper case give an absolute discharge?

An absolute discharge vindicates the defendant to a considerable extent, and although it follows what is technically a conviction, the conviction is eliminated for most purposes.[22] Still, this is not a completely satisfactory solution from the defendant's point of view.

- The court cannot give a discharge where the conviction is of murder. Here the only possibility is a pardon, and on this the remarks of Lord Morris in *Lynch*[23] are worth quoting.

  > "It is most undesirable that cases should arise in which a just conclusion will only be attained by the prerogative of pardon. I would regret it if on an application of legal principles such cases could arise. Such principles and such approach as will prevent them from arising would seem to be more soundly based."
- If the defendant is regarded as having acted rightly, even the technical conviction seems obnoxious.
- A professional man like a doctor wishes to comply with the law in his practice (partly, but not entirely, because of the fear of disciplinary proceedings). It is the conviction, not a fine, that he particularly wants to avoid. And many non-professional people feel the same way.
- When the court gives an absolute discharge it cannot award costs against the prosecution, as it can in case of acquittal. So the defendant may be badly out of pocket.

---

[19] *Cope* v. *Sharpe* [1912] 1 KB 496. Yet see *Workman* v. *Cowper*, § 41.6 n. 1.
[20] *Southport Corporation* v. *Esso Petroleum Co. Ltd.* [1956] AC at 228.
[21] See §§ .4, 27.4 n. 2.
[22] Powers of Criminal Courts Act 1973 s. 13.
[23] [1975] AC at 672E.

- The court has a discretion whether to give a discharge or not, and there may be no certainty that it will do this. Some judges are powerfully influenced by the fact that, in their view, the law has been broken. And the possibility of being punished may be a disincentive to act in a way that is socially desirable.

At this stage in the discussion it will have become obvious that the defence of necessity involves fundamental questions as to the morality of conduct. The notion of necessity easily earns a bad name because it is invoked equally by despots and by rebels.

> So spake the Fiend, and with necessity,
> The tyrant's plea, excus'd his devilish deeds.

Little as we may relish abuses of the doctrine, from the autocrat's *raison d'État* to the Marxist-Leninist advocacy of violent revolution against democratic governments, necessity has been accepted by overseas courts as a justification for governmental action after the collapse of lawful authority.[24] Still, in the ordinary working of the criminal law necessity cannot be allowed as an excuse for the wholesale disregard of rules. Rules are meant to supersede individual judgment, where individual judgment has been found by experience to be unreliable. Necessity can be recognised only where the application of the rules would be disastrous, and in a genuine emergency, so specific in character that the acceptance of the defence does not imperil the general rule. On multifarious occasions it would be highly convenient and quite safe to violate the traffic law, as by judicious excess of speed limits or careful crossing of the lights against the red. The private necessity of getting to an important appointment cannot be recognised, because to recognise it would destroy the rule and impair the important purposes that the rule subserves.

§ 26.2. THE WORKING PARTY'S FORMULATION

After considering these and other matters the Law Commission Working Party on Codification[1] recommended the recognition of a necessity defence in the following terms.

> "It should be available where the defendant himself believes that his conduct is necessary[2] to avoid some greater harm than that which he faces.
>
> The harm to be avoided must, judged objectively, be found to be out of all proportion to that actually caused by the defendant's conduct.
>
> The harm to be avoided . . . may . . . be directed against himself or his property or against the person or property of another."

---

[24] S A de Smith, *Constitutional Law*, 3rd edn (London 1977) 68.

[1] Law Commission, *Published Working Paper No. 55* p. 38. Cp. [1978] Crim.LR 136.

[2] The requirement of necessity implies, of course, that there must be (or be thought to be) no alternative and less socially expensive way of avoiding the harm (Fletcher). Fletcher also stipulates that the harm avoided must be immediate: see his defence of this position in his *Rethinking Criminal Law* 795.

At the same time, the Working Party proposed two limits to the defence.

"The defence should not apply where the defendant has put himself into a position where he must commit one offence in order to avoid another." "For example, legislation prohibits driving onto the shoulder of a motorway: suppose that D negligently runs out of petrol and drives onto the shoulder in order to avoid obstruction of the motorway. . . . The provision permits D to be prosecuted for driving onto the shoulder. . . ."[3]

"The defence should not be available where the greater harm, which the defendant alleges he was seeking to avoid by committing the offence with which he is charged, consists of the doing by some other person of an act which that person was legally entitled to do."

The second limitation was aimed largely against political "demonstrations," as by invading the pitch when a cricket match is in progress. A third limitation might well have been stated: that the defence should not avail if a legislative decision to exclude the justification plainly appears.[4]

These recommendations of the Working Party were eventually rejected by the Law Commission itself, which thought the difficulties in the way of recognising a general defence of necessity so great that the defence should be specifically negatived by statute.[5] But the Commission did not consider all the consequences of its proposal, particularly in relation to medical operations (§ .7).

The main difficulty felt by the Commission appears to have been in respect of certain "human rights." The doctrine of necessity is an expression of the philosophy of utilitarianism; but utilitarianism does not exercise undisputed sway over our minds. Many people give allegiance to a notion of human rights or fundamental values; and sometimes, at least, these interests do not merely enter into the utilitarian calculus but supersede it. As an example, a doctor could not take blood from an unwilling patient in order to save the life of another patient, even though the blood-group is a rare one and the blood can be obtained in no other way.[6] This particular conclusion can perhaps be reconciled with utilitarian theory by saying that if we are to have a scheme of compulsory blood donation it must be done by a proper statutory arrangement, not left to the

---

[3] Cp. *Oakley-Moore* v. *Robinson* [1982] RTR 74, where a driver who parked his car within the prohibited approach limits to a pelican crossing because he had run out of petrol was not allowed to rely on the defence in the regulations that he had been prevented from proceeding by circumstances beyond his control. This, however, was a case not of necessity but of impossibility. Fletcher, *op.cit.* 796–797 criticises the limitation of the defence that the defendant must not have brought about the risk that he invokes to justify his conduct (which is to some extent the situation that the Working Party had in mind). The objections that he makes to the rule are not entirely convincing, and having regard to the prevalent resistance to recognising the defence it would be wise for a court or legislature to incorporate the rule. For the same problem in relation to private defence see § 23.2 at n. 17.

[4] Fletcher, *op.cit.* 793–4.

[5] Law Commission, *Criminal Law: Report of Defences of General Application* (Law Com. No. 83, 1977) Part IV. For criticisms see Huxley in [1978] Crim.LR 141; Williams, *ibid.* 128. Cross's criticism was the most concise: "I feel bound to say that the Law Commission has achieved the apotheosis of absurdity by recommending that our proposed criminal code should provide for a defence of duress while excluding any general defence of necessity:" 28 U of Tor.LJ 377.

[6] The point is made by Glazebrook in [1972A] CLJ 99.

arbitrary decision of individual doctors. It is also pointed out that the recognition of important values does not entirely exclude a defence of necessity, for, first, these values can be given special weight in estimating the balance of interests, and, secondly, their existence does not affect the determination of cases where they do not appear.[7] In any event, the theoretical difficulty is no greater than in the law of tort, where the defence of necessity is relatively well established. In order to make the position clear, it may be desirable for a penal code to make certain express provisions for the supremacy of human rights, at least in relation to the individual right of self-determination (to be discussed in §§ 10 and 11). The main problem presented by human rights is in respect of the right to life, to which we now turn.

§ 26.3. NECESSITY AS A REASON FOR KILLING

Some of the instances of necessity given in § .1 may seem acceptable because they involve clear social preferences. In particular, every one agrees nowadays that property rights are subject to the social interest; we no longer believe in the sacred right of property. But many of us do believe in the sanctity of life—the "natural right" of every man to his own life—and consequently believe that killing is absolutely wrong. This is an area, therefore, in which the defence of necessity, if allowed at all, is given very narrow scope.

But one can kill in self-defence. Isn't that just an example of necessity?

No. Private defence overlaps necessity, but the two are not the same.

- Unlike necessity, private defence involves no balancing of values. Not only can a person kill by way of defence, but he can kill any number of aggressors to protect himself alone.
- On the other hand, private defence operates only against aggressors (voluntary or involuntary). With rare exceptions the aggressors are wrongdoers, while the persons against whom action is taken by necessity may not be aggresssors or wrongdoers.

As we have seen,[1] the decision in *Bourne* can be regarded as an example of the defence of necessity, though it was a case not of homicide but of feticide. The decision has perhaps ceased to be important in England in abortion cases, since they are now governed by the Abortion Act which seems to supersede the common law defence.[2] At the same time, the decision remains an excellent example of the basis of the doctrine of necessity.[3]

---

[7] See Paul A Robinson in 82 Col.LRev. 215 n. 62.

[1] § 13.4 at n. 13.

[2] S. 5 (2) of the Act provides that anything done to procure a miscarriage is unlawfully done unless authorised by s. 1.

[3] For the *Morgentaler* cases, where *Bourne* was followed in Canada, see Leigh in [1978] Crim.LR 151; Dickens in 14 Osgoode Hall LJ 229.

Might this defence apply where a parent has killed his grossly malformed infant?

Doubtless not. It may of course be argued that the value of such an infant's life, even to himself, is minimal or negative, and that if parents are obliged to rear him they may be disabled from having another and normal child. But it is not a case for applying the doctrine of necessity as usually understood. The child when born, unlike the fetus, is regarded as having absolute rights. Besides, there is no emergency. It is said that malformed neonates are from time to time discreetly disposed of in maternity hospitals; but we must wait for public opinion to crystallise before the law can provide for it.[4] (The question of letting a malformed infant die is of course different.)

The usual view is that necessity is no defence to a charge of murder. This, if accepted, is a non-utilitarian doctrine; but in case of a serious emergency is it wholly acceptable? If you are roped to a climber who has fallen, and neither of you can rectify the situation, it may not be very glorious on your part to cut the rope, but is it wrong? Is it not socially desirable that one life, at least, should be saved?[5] Again, if you are flying an aircraft and the engine dies on you, it would not be wrong, but would be praiseworthy, to choose to come down in a street (where you can see you will kill or injure a few pedestrians) rather than in a crowded sports stadium.

But in the case of cutting the rope you are only freeing yourself from someone who is, however involuntarily, dragging you to your death. And in the case of the aircraft you do not want to kill anyone; you simply minimise the slaughter that you are bound to do one way or the other. The question is whether you could deliberately kill someone for calculating reasons.

We do regard the right to life as almost a supreme value, and it is very unlikely that anyone would be held to be justified in killing for any purpose except the saving of other life, or perhaps the saving of great pain or distress. Our revulsion against a deliberate killing is so strong that we are loth to consider utilitarian reasons for it.

But a compelling case of justification of this kind is the action of a ship's captain in a wreck. He can determine who are to enter the first lifeboat; he can forbid overcrowding; and it makes no difference that those who are not allowed to enter the lifeboat will inevitably perish with the ship. The captain, in choosing who are to live, is not guilty of killing those who remain. He would not be guilty even though he kept some of the passengers back from the boat at revolver-point, and he would not be guilty even though he had to fire the revolver.

---

[4] On the moral and policy question see *Infanticide and the Value of Life*, ed. Marvin Kohl (New York 1978).

[5] Smith and Hogan, 4th edn 274 make the interesting suggestion that in some cases the cutting of the rope may be justified on the ground of minimal causation. Cp. Devlin J's ruling in *Adams* § 16.5. But the slightest acceleration of death is normally regarded as sufficient for criminal homicide. The persuasive element in such cases, surely, is that of necessity.

Here the captain or commander is exercising authority, and in any event he is defending others from what is in fact dangerous aggression. That does not support a general defence of necessity.

The fact that the case involves an exercise of authority does not mean that it cannot be regarded as an instance of necessity. Moreover, a case of necessity need not be a case of aggression in the ordinary sense.

Suppose that the boat was overcrowded from the start, so that some of those in it must be sacrificed if the boat is to be saved from capsizing. This situation arose in the American case of *United States* v. *Holmes* (1842).[6]

> Holmes was a member of the crew of a boat after a shipwreck who had, under the orders of the mate, thrown out 16 male passengers. The grand jury having refused to indict him for murder, he was charged with manslaughter.
>
> The judge directed the jury that Holmes's act was illegal, but only for two specific reasons: (1) such sailors as were not necessary for navigation ought to have been sacrificed before the passengers, and (2) the choice of these sailors, and of any passengers who had to be thrown out with them, should have been determined by lot, there being plenty of time to do so. Holmes was convicted of manslaughter and sentenced to 6 months' imprisonment.

The first ruling now looks odd in our less class-conscious society,[7] and even the second is open to some doubt on the facts of the case. The drawing of lots may commend itself to the devout as an appeal to Providence. A secular justification would be that, if a dreadful choice of victim has to be made, and everyone realises it has to be made, the drawing of lots is the fairest and most civilised method. But when it is a question of an overloaded boat, it may be sensible to decide that the weightiest members of the party shall go first—there would hardly be justification for throwing two slim members overboard to save one bulky member! The appeal of the lottery is that it prevents purely personal consideratiom entering into the choice; but there are other ways of excluding personal considerations. If a sailor is detailed to lighten the boat by so many souls, and simply pitches out those who first come to hand, the selection of victims is just as haphazard as if determined by lot. This may be both a kinder and a more practicable way of performing the operation than by going through the agonizing process of drawing lots. However this may be, the decision in *United States* v. *Holmes* does recognise that, in extreme emergency, and subject to reasonable conditions, a deliberate killing can be justified by the necessity of saving lives. If the choice is between doing nothing, when the whole boat will founder, and throwing out half the people, with the chance of saving the rest, it is useless for the law to continue its usual prohibition of murder.

The only English decision on this type of case is *Dudley* (1884).[8]

> The crew of the yacht *Mignonette* were cast away in a storm, and were compelled to put into an open boat: in this boat they had no water and little provisions. On the twentieth day, having had nothing to eat for eight days, and being 1,000 miles from land, two of the crew (named Dudley and Stephens) agreed that the cabin-boy should be killed with a knife in order that they might feed upon his body; and one of them carried out the plan. On the fourth day after that they were rescued by a passing vessel, in the lowest state of prostration. The two men were charged with murder, but the jury refused to take the responsibility of convicting in such tragic circumstances. They found a special verdict in which they declared that "if the men had not fed upon the body of the boy they would probably not have survived to be

---

[6] 26 Fed.Cas. 360, No. 15383.

[7] Sailors are regarded as owing a special duty to protect passengers, but that duty hardly means that a sailor is a special subject of sacrifice where no activities are called for on his part and he is adversely affecting the passenger merely by his existence.

[8] 14 QBD 273.

so picked up and rescued, but would within the four days have died of famine; that the boy, being in a much weaker condition, was likely to have died before them; that at the time of the act there was no sail in sight, nor any reasonable prospect of relief; . . . that assuming any necessity to kill any one, there was no greater necessity for killing the boy than any of the other three men; but whether, upon the whole matter, the prisoners were and are guilty of murder, the jury are ignorant, and refer to the Court." The question was considered by a Divisional Court of five judges, who held that the act was murder.

So the men were supposed to lie down and die?

Theoretically yes, but their sentence of death for murder was commuted by the Crown to one of 6 months' imprisonment. So one could say that they were allowed to survive at a bargain price.

Most of the judgment is unconvincing, but ultimately, perhaps, it depended on the view taken by the court of the particular facts.[9] The court might conceivably have allowed the defence if it had been persuaded that the act was really necessary at the time when it was done (though it may be added that the court's refusal to accept that this was the case was highly questionable). Even if the case decides that the justification of necessity can never apply to the taking of life, it does not follow that necessity cannot be a defence for lesser departures from the ordinary law.

To bring out the stark question in *Dudley*, let us suppose that the boat was equipped with an experimental radio transmitter, although radio-telephony was not in general use. The crew were able to make contact with Whitehall, which arranged for a ship to go to the rescue, but it could not arrive for seven days. The boat was lying off the trade routes, so it was unlikely that any other vessel would effect a rescue. The crew had reached such a stage of exhaustion that very soon none of them would be able to wield a knife. In these circumstances they asked to speak to the Home Secretary. They put the question to him: should they all accept death, or may they draw lots, kill the one with the unlucky number, and live on his body? In this way all but one will be saved. What should the Home Secretary reply? What would you reply, if you were Home Secretary?

Although *Dudley* concerned the relative force of necessity and the right to life, the facts were very special. It was a case of a number of persons involved in a common disaster all of whom were likely to die in a matter of days or hours if no action were taken to save some of them. The victim was alive, but his prospect of remaining alive for more than a short time was minimal, so that his "right to life" was of very small value. These considerations suggest that the defence of necessity might have been accepted without imperilling the general supremacy of the right to life.

If it had been accepted that Dudley and Stephens had a right to kill the cabin boy, wouldn't it follow that the cabin boy had no right to act in self-defence?

Your suggested conclusion does not follow. It would be possible for the law to refrain from intervening either way. The killing of the cabin boy might be justified as a matter of necessity, while defensive action by the cabin boy might be excused by reason of "compulsion of circumstances," an arguable defence to be noticed later.[10]

---

[9] For a full examination see Williams in 8 Cambrian LRev 94; Fletcher, *Rethinking Criminal Law* 823–827.

[10] See § 27.4 and [1982] Crim.LR 740. A situation in which each of two contending parties is justified or excused (for different reasons) in using force against the other is not unknown in the law: cp. § 23.5 at n. 9.

You say that necessity is a matter of the lesser evil. Assuming that it may justify killing one to save two or more, could it ever justify killing one to save one other?

Only where necessity overlaps self-defence, which is as much as to say no. A person can certainly be killed by a person who is threatened by an aggressor. If V is a culpable aggressor against D1, he can be killed by D1 in self-defence, or by D2 in defence of D1. Even if V is a lunatic who is not criminally responsible, he can be killed in private defence.

Another example of a case that can be analysed as one of private defence is as follows. A shipwrecked man is clinging in the sea to a plank that is only big enough to support one. Another tries to join him on the plank, but the man in possession beats the assailant off, and the latter is drowned. This may look like a situation of necessity, but the act can be adequately justified as one of private defence, the assailant's attack being technically wrongful.

Suppose the assailant had shaken off the man who was first in possession of the plank, and that the latter had drowned?

Lord Chancellor Bacon discussed this case in a literary work,[11] and thought that the assailant's act would be justified by necessity. This seems hard to support, on the doctrine of necessity as now understood, for that doctrine applies only where the value preserved is greater than the value destroyed in breaking the letter of the law. Where it is merely a case of life for life, the doctrine of necessity must generally be silent, because the two lives must be accounted equal in the eye of the law and there is nothing to choose between them. Necessity cannot justify here, but circumstances may go so strongly in alleviation that the defendant is pardoned or his sentence greatly shortened. (An alternative solution, for which indeed Bacon's hypothetical may be cited in support, would be to recognise an excuse of compulsion of circumstances, as before mentioned.)

May not necessity sometimes justify action even if it is a case of one for one, where the two people you are weighing against each other are not really equal? I know you said this is an unlikely solution for the malformed infant. But could not a doctor take an organ from a dying patient to transplant to a patient who can be saved?

No: and although that answer is obvious, a thoroughgoing utilitarian who supported it would be hard pressed to justify his position. Few people are wholly consistent utilitarians, because, as was said before, our thinking is tinged with notions of human rights and moral absolutes. Transplants are taken from fresh cadavers, or (in the case of paired organs) from living volunteers, not from unwilling donors.[12]

---

[11] *Maxims* (1630).

[12] Setting aside the special problem where a patient who has suffered "brain death" and is on a ventilator has his organ removed for transplantation while his heart is still beating under the action of the ventilator. This involves the problem of the time of "death." See § 12.8.

§ 26.4. NECESSITY AND STARVATION

According to the institutional writers, the poor (even if starving) are not allowed to take the law into their own hands.[1] The law does not recognise a necessity to eat. A face-saving reason formerly advanced for the rule was that sufficient provision was made for the poor in this country by charity and State aid. The reason has attained greater reality in modern times, though for one reason or another people may still be utterly destitute. If someone steals as the only way to relieve hunger he will be convicted, but will certainly receive a discharge, with the assistance of the probation officer to obtain the social security payment to which he is entitled, and quite possibly a gift from the poor box to tide him over.

It was no doubt with this position in mind that Edmund Davies LJ (as he then was) said on one occasion[2] that although necessity "may in certain cases afford a defence . . . [in] an urgent situation of imminent peril," it is not a defence to murder or theft. Both exceptions are too absolutely stated. There can be no reasonable doubt that necessity would be a defence where hunger arises in an extraordinary situation from physical and not economic causes, as where a group of miners are trapped underground and have to consume the rations of their comrades who have escaped or are dead. In any case, such conduct would not be theft because it would not be dishonest, as theft requires. The miners would be entitled to assume the consent of those who owned the food.

Another dire conflict between extreme need and the maintenance of public order arises in relation to housing. In the case just mentioned, the Court of Appeal held that necessity does not justify the homeless in "squatting" in unoccupied buildings. The court gave a certain support to the defence of necessity, while not applying it to the facts of the case.

§ 26.5. NECESSITY AND DRIVING OFFENCES

The law makes a certain provision for emergencies in driving. Firemen, the police and ambulances are expressly exempted from speed limits,[1] and the regulations allow them to treat the red light signal merely as a "Give Way" sign if observance of the signal "would be likely to hinder the use of that vehicle for the purposes for which it is being used on that occasion."[2]

The question is how far the court will allow drivers in general to disobey traffic rules under the doctrine of necessity. There is very little indication that they will. At about the same time as the "squatting" case just mentioned, and before the aforesaid regulations had been made, a

---

[1] See Glazebrook, *op. cit.* 115–117.
[2] *Southwark LBC* v. *Williams* [1971] Ch. at 745. Cp. Lord Denning at 743–744.

[1] Road Traffic Regulation Act 1967 s. 79.
[2] Traffic Signs Regulations and General Directions, SI 1975 No. 1536 reg. 34 (1) (*b*).

differently constituted Court of Appeal denied (obiter) that necessity could justify the driver of a fire-engine in crossing against the lights, even to save life.[3] This was understandable, since the question of a fire-engine crossing against the lights is not one of unforeseen emergency but of proper practice on the part of the fire service; if an exemption were thought proper, it was to be expected that the legislature would make it—as it afterwards did.

More questionable was a decision that where a man woke up intoxicated in a car, to find it coasting downhill, and steered it to a grass verge to avoid a possible collision, he was guilty of driving it while under the influence of drink.[4] Since the defence of necessity was, surprisingly, not raised, the case is no authority on this question; but in fact a clearer occasion for the recognition of the defence could hardly be imagined. A driver who has too much to drink and who goes to sleep in his car before driving off again can be convicted of being under the influence of drink when "in charge" of his car. But if (as in the case just mentioned) it is a passenger who is drunk and asleep in the car, and if he wakes up to find that the vehicle is running downhill, and all that he does is to bring it to a safe stop, what is wrong in his conduct? What do we expect him to do: remain passive while a fatal accident takes place?

The regulations do not provide specially for doctors in respect of driving offences. In practice, when they are on an urgent call and cause no danger, doctors are unlikely to be prosecuted for a technical offence. If convicted they will probably receive an absolute discharge, and the circumstances will be seen as a "special reason" for not disqualifying them in a case otherwise requiring disqualification.[5]

Drivers who drive with excessive blood-alcohol do not escape conviction by giving evidence of the necessity of their errand, but it is conceded in theory that a situation of sufficient urgency can be a "special reason" for not disqualifying. Hitherto the courts seem not to have accepted that a special reason existed on the facts.[6] It may be contended that the proper approach would be to say that public safety generally prevails over private exigencies, but that if the risk is sufficiently small (as if the defendant is only slightly above the permitted blood-alcohol level) and the social need sufficiently great, necessity can be a defence.

It will be seen that the decisions give little support for necessity as a defence in driving cases where the law has been broken in the letter (as opposed to charges of negligent driving[7]). However, there is one driving case in which the court recognised the doctrine of necessity without intending to do so, the reason being the paradoxical one that the court was intent on supporting not an acquittal but a conviction. The case was *Johnson* v. *Phillips*.[8]

Johnson stopped his car behind an ambulance in a narrow one-way

---

[3] *Buckoke* v. *GLC* [1971] Ch. at 668.

[4] *Kitson* (1955) 39 CAR 66. See Glazebrook in [1972A] CLJ at 95–96.

[5] See [1962] 1 BMJ 412; [1971] 1 BMJ 513; *Taylor* v. *Rajan* [1974] QB 424. A story of a Manchester GP told in the Daily Telegraph indicates that doctors are not exempt from pressure by the police. "Finding himself being waved down as he exceeded the speed limit on his way to an urgent call, he drove firmly past the police car, brandishing a stethoscope to indicate his mission. The police rapidly overtook him again, brandishing a pair of handcuffs to indicate theirs."

[6] See *Fraser* v. *Barton* [1974] RTR 304, Crim.LR 188; *Evans* v. *Bray* [1977] RTR 24, [1976] Crim.LR 45.

[7] As to which see above § .1 n. 5.

[8] [1976] 1 WLR 65.

street. A police officer asked him to reverse to the next street because he was obstructing the removal of injured persons and other ambulances were expected. Johnson refused, and was convicted of obstructing the officer in the execution of his duty. The conviction was affirmed on appeal, the court pointing out that it was the officer's duty to protect life and property, and the manoeuvre required was not dangerous, even though it involved a breach of the letter of the law.

If Johnson had executed the manoeuvre on his own initiative, and some stupid person had prosecuted him, Johnson would very probably have been convicted, though given an absolute discharge, since convictions are routine in traffic cases. But, the case having been decided, the conclusion would seem to be compulsory that Johnson would have had a good defence had he complied with the order and reversed in the wrong direction along the street.[9] It would seem to follow, also, that in a sufficient emergency he might have done this without a policeman to tell him to do the obvious. We are surely not members of a nanny State in which we cannot even help an ambulance without being told to do so by a policeman. The case may perhaps convince the courts that even a traffic regulation absolute in its terms may properly and lawfully be disregarded if this involves virtually no risk, and the social gain is sufficiently large.

§ 26.6. THE ENFORCEMENT OF LAW AND RIGHTS

One of the most celebrated pronouncements in our law repudiates the doctrine of necessity as a means of enlarging the powers of the Executive.

> "And with respect to the argument of State necessity, or a distinction that has been aimed at between State offences and others, the common law does not understand that kind of reasoning, nor do our books take notice of any such distinctions."[1]

All that this means, however, is that the courts are not supposed to extend governmental powers merely by reference to the necessities of government. If the Government wants powers, it must obtain them from Parliament; and when it has obtained them, it must keep within them, not stretch them under the plea of necessity. The principle is not regarded as impeding the grant of powers at common law for certain recognised purposes, such as the preservation of the peace and the saving of life. In *Humphries* v. *Connor*,[2] for instance, it was held that a constable may commit what would otherwise be an assault upon an innocent person in order to remove a provocative emblem he is wearing if that is the only way

---

[9] Ursula Ross in [1977] Crim.LR 190 suggests that Johnson might not have had a defence of necessity "since he would presumably have lacked the requisite belief that his action was necessary." But necessity being a justification and not merely an excuse, the defendant should not on principle be required to show that he knew of the necessity. See 2 Leg. Stud. 243–252 and [1982] Crim.LR 741.

[1] Lord Camden in *Entick* v. *Carrington* (1765) 19 St. Tr. 1029.

[2] (1864) 17 Ir.CLR 1. But the police cannot take a person into protective custody: *Connors* v. *Pearson* [1921] 2 IR 51. See further, § 9.7 at nn. 20 ff.

of preserving the peace.[3] At the present day action of this kind may be justified under section 3 of the Act of 1967[4]; but when *Humphries* v. *Connor* was decided it was a matter of common law. Similarly the police may, for the saving of life, reverse the traffic flow.[5] But they have no authority to commit offences in order to obtain evidence, and still less is such authority given to an unofficial "stooge" or decoy used by the police.[6]

Of course the officer or informer may escape conviction in particular circumstances for lack of *mens rea*: for example, for lack of intention in theft or burglary. He is not guilty of attempt or conspiracy or as accessory if he intended to frustrate the commission of the full offence.[7] His mere pretence at being a conspirator will probably not make him an accessory to the crime when it is committed, if his pretence was not causally connected with the crime. If, however, he went beyond mere concurrence and incited or helped the commission of the crime, without intending to frustrate it, he would be in breach of the law, notwithstanding that his intention was only to expose the others, and the doctrine of necessity would not be taken as a reason for the extension of police powers.

There is no indication in the authorities that private persons can break the letter of the law in order to prevent serious crimes. The provision in the Criminal Law Act 1967 s. 3[8] probably does not justify the commission of offences in general,[9] but in extreme circumstances the docrine of necessity should do so. For example, to prevent a burglary (or to arrest the burglars) it might be justifiable to drive an uninsured car to inform the police.

If I find someone's car occupying my parking space, or if he has left his car blocking my exit from the car park, can I, by way of defence of my interests, break his window in order to move his car?

As to the first part of your question, probably yes: you are ejecting a trespassing object.[10] As to the second part, a person who is unlawfully imprisoned can obviously break out, even though the property of innocent third parties is damaged in the process. But the courts have been unsympathetic to claims to preserve mobility where no false imprisonment was involved. Reference may again be made to *Bow*,[11] where the relevance of the defence of necessity was overlooked. Magistrates have convicted motorists who, when their exits were blocked on private premises, damaged other cars or the jammed exit barrier of a car park in order to get free. The value of personal mobility is recognised in law in the defence of abatement of public nuisance, which justifies the removal of an obstruction to the highway. There is no reason why the law should not equally allow the removal of unjustifiable obstructions to egress from private premises, where this is reasonable in the circumstances; and the German courts have in fact allowed it as an example of private defence.[12]

---

[3] On the meaning of breach of the peace see § 22.2 at n. 15–18.
[4] § 22.6.
[5] *Johnson* v. *Phillips* § .5 n. 8.
[6] *Smith* [1960] 2 QB 423. Cp. Heydon in [1973] CLJ 268. It is true that the police are unlikely to bring charges against their own number or their informers; but the theoretical liability can have the paradoxical result that the offender is regarded as an accomplice of the real culprits whom he is trying to bring to justice, so that his evidence against them needs the "accomplice warning."
[7] § 15.13.
[8] See § 22.6.
[9] § 22.6 at nn. 20–21.
[10] A Twickenham solicitor who did this had his conviction of criminal damage set aside by the Crown Court: Middlesex Chronicle, August 20, 1982.
[11] § 23.6 at n. 11.
[12] Fletcher, *Rethinking Criminal Law* 864.

(Wherever possible, of course, the help of the police should be invoked before taking drastic action, and an unreasonable failure to do this would bar the defence.)

§ 26.7. OPERATIONS UPON SANE ADULTS

Since necessity involves an evaluation, the right of self-determination is one of the values taken into account. Accordingly, the general principle of law is that a person cannot be medically treated without his consent. The point is more likely to concern legal practitioners in the civil courts than in the criminal, since it is highly improbable that a prosecution would be brought against a doctor who has transgressed in good faith in the interest of his patient. But to doctors themselves the matter appears in reverse: whereas a civil action can be settled out of court, and the doctor will be defended and the damages paid by his defence society, the remotest fear of a criminal prosecution is of grave concern to him. The criminal law, therefore, is almost entirely self-operative upon doctors, without any need for actual enforcement.

One who is suffering from an infectious disease may be carried off to hospital under the order of a magistrate[1]; this is for the protection of the public, not particularly for his benefit, and it does not mean that anything may be done to him in hospital, beyond keeping him in bed in the usual way.

There is an unqualified rule that if an adult patient of sound mind utters any words forbidding an operation the doctor's hands are tied. People are not bound to accept even the unanimous opinion of doctors.[2] Partly this is because medicine is not an exact science. Notwithstanding every advance, cases still occur where operations are performed mistakenly and disastrously. (Surgeons are notoriously reluctant to submit to the scalpel themselves.) But the more important reason is the general agreement that this area of personal liberty must be preserved. There is no overwhelming public interest in compelling people to submit to the cure of non-infectious complaints. Members of the religious sect known as Jehovah's Witnesses think blood transfusions wrong, and will not accept them even when they know that they will otherwise die; and doctors respect their wishes, as they must.[3]

Theoretically, any dying patient has the right to refuse further treatment even though his only object is to make an end of his own sufferings.[4] In practice, such requests are from time to time ignored, for various reasons: the doctor's training biases him towards treatment, and

---

[1] Public Health Act 1936 s. 169.

[2] The proposition is universally agreed, even though English judicial authority for it is fragmentary, Lord Devlin supported it extra-judicially in his *Samples of Law Making* (London 1962) 91—which is powerful authority, seeing that he is a leading exponent of moral authoritarianism. See also Ian Kennedy in [1976] Crim.LR 217–218.

[3] An instance of a Witness being left to die in hospital was reported in The Times, April 6, 1967; the coroner's inquest returned a verdict of accidental death. But on one occasion, after much hesitation, a witness was given a transfusion when unconscious although this was known to be against his wish and that of his relatives: Pulse, December 2, 1972. Cp. *Erickson* v. *Dilgard* (1962) 44 Misc. 2d 27, 252 NYS 2d 705; Louisell in *Ethics in Medical Progress*, ed. G E W Wolstenholme and Maeve O'Connor (London 1966) 82–83; 83 Yale LJ 1648.

[4] A Florida court accordingly held that a 73-year-old man who was kept alive only on a respirator was entitled to demand to be removed from the respirator in order to die: *Pearlmutter* v. *Florida Medical Center* (1978), noted in 129 NLJ 77. In 1982 a New York judge ruled that a man blinded and without legs as a result of diabetes had the right to be sent home from hospital to die: The Times, October 2.

imbues him with the idea that he knows what is best for the patient; he fears criticism if he allows the patient to die; and the dying patient is often old, in great pain or under sedation, so it is easy to argue that his expressed desire to die may not express his "real" wish.[5] It is temptingly easy to subject a seriously ill patient to a kind of "Catch 22:" either he is of sound mind, in which case he will obviously want to live, or he is not, in which case other people must take the decision for him. The defender of the patient's autonomy will of course dismiss such arguments. To disregard the expressed wish of a dying patient on the ground that he cannot really mean what he says is to substitute paternalism for self-determination. It should be beyond doubt that a doctor who does anything to his patient without consent is guilty of an assault.[6] No question can arise of abetting suicide, first because it would seem that inaction by the patient cannot be a suicide in law, and secondly because, since the law gives the doctor no authority to act against his patient's wishes, his failure to do so is not the breach of any duty by him and cannot be an abetment.[7]

What if the patient's consent cannot be asked for? A man is found injured and unconscious; he is rushed to hospital, where he is operated upon to save his life.

Although English authority is lacking, the operation is clearly lawful. This was stated by an eminent United States judge, Cardozo J.

> "Every human being of adult years and sound mind has a right to determine what shall be done with his own body. . . . This is true except in cases of emergency where the patient is unconscious and where it is necessary to operate before consent can be obtained."[8]

We have here a kind of hybrid between the defences of necessity and consent. It is not an ordinary case of consent, because consent is not in fact given; so from that point of view the justification must be one of necessity. On the other hand, the justification would clearly not avail if the surgeon ascertained, before the patient fell unconscious, that the patient withheld his consent. So it is not a case where social necessity overrides a refusal of consent. American writers have called the defence, with more punch than accuracy, "future consent."[9] The surgeon is entitled in the circumstances to suppose that what he does will be ratified by a grateful patient, having nothing to cause him to believe the contrary; and he will be protected in law even though the patient turns out to be ungrateful. His defence must, to repeat, be grounded on necessity; the only distinctive feature is that the defence is curtailed when it conficts with the patient's express exercise of his right of self-determination.

It would be an illegitimate application of the doctrine of future consent to subject a depressed and protesting patient to a brain operation on the ground that the operation will change the patient's personality and he will then be pleased he had it. That is a bootstrap argument, and ought to be rejected. The general question of operations on the mentally disordered will be briefy considered in the next section.

Sometimes, in the course of an operation, a surgeon sees a need for some other operation. He is generally protected in performing this by the consent form signed by the patient, which authorises such further or alternative operative measures as may be found to be necessary. But sometimes a consent form has not been offered to the patient, as when a maternity

---

[5] See the admirable discussion by Ian Kennedy in [1976] Crim.LR 217.
[6] This notwithstanding the flaccid direction in *Smith* § 12.4 at n. 6.
[7] See Kennedy, *op. cit.* 226 ff.; Zellick in [1976] Public Law 179; § 25.15.
[8] *Schloendorff* v. *Society of the New York Hospital* (1914) 211 NYR 125, 105 NE 92.
[9] The expression was coined by Wexler in 57 Minn.LRev. 289, 334.

patient is under anaesthetic when it is discovered that delivery by caesarean section is necessary. In such circumstances the Medical Defence Union encourages its members to do what is required,[10] the justification being either implied consent or necessity. The surgeon would of course be ill advised to perform an unexpected operation having serious consequences if there is no great urgency for it.[11]

§ 26.8. PERSONS UNDER DISABILITY

Persons under disability lack the full right to self-determination, so that various things may be done to them without their consent, either under the authority of explicit rules of law or generally because of the necessity of the case. For example, as we saw in § 25.13, a parent may to some extent give consent on behalf of his young child. When he sends his child to hospital, he does not thereby surrender to the doctor in charge his parental right to decide what is good for the child[1]; the doctor must, at least in the first place, seek the parent's consent for an operation to the same extent as he would seek the consent of an adult patient.

But what if it is a question of saving the life of the child? Must the doctor watch the child's life ebb away if the child can't give consent and the doctor can't get the parent's consent to act?

If the parent cannot be consulted, the doctrine of future consent (§ .7) may be applied: the doctor is entitled to believe that what he does will be ratified by the parent. Although the question has not come before the courts, there can hardly be any doubt that this will be the answer.

The difficulty arises where the parent is consulted and wishes his child to be allowed to die. This problem has been encountered with Jehovah's Witnesses who refuse to let a child have a blood transfusion. Here it is generally agreed that the turning-point is reached: the doctor can refuse to allow the parent's wishes to prevail over the child's "right to life." However, the theoretical basis on which the hospital doctor is allowed to act is in doubt. Much the clearest ground is the doctrine of necessity.[2] If the doctor wants specific legal protection he can have the child made a ward of court and ask for the judge's authority to proceed.[3] But this is not necessary.

The above states what the doctor *may* do. Whether he is legally required to do so is another matter. On principle, if the child is of the age of discretion and rejects a transfusion, it should not be given him. If the child is below the age of discretion the doctor may still think it right

---

[10] *MDU Annual Report* 1967 p. 12. Cp. *Barnett* v. *Bachrach* (1943) 34 A 2d 626; *Marshall* v. *Curry* [1933] 3 DLR 260; Skegg in (1974) 90 LQR 512.

[11] In 1969 a woman who was sterilised without her consent during a caesarean delivery recovered damages, even though the operation was performed because having more children might be dangerous to her health or life: [1969] 1 BMJ 456.

[1] Cp. *Rogers* v. *Exeter and Mid Devon Hospitals Management Committee* [1974] CLY 850.

[2] See [1978] Crim.LR 132–134.

[3] See § 25.13 at n. 17.

to comply with the parents' wishes, but he would be well advised to obtain the ruling of a judge.[4]

When can mentally disordered people be taken to hospital without their consent?

Those who come within a statutory definition may be taken to hospital on the certificate of two doctors (exceptionally, one doctor), either for their own protection or for that of the public.[5] This is commonly called "civil commitment" (as opposed to "criminal commitment" resulting from a prosecution, which is to be studied in Chap. 28). The technical name for it, however, is "admission" to hospital, not commitment, a word that is thought to be too stigmatic.

If a constable finds a person who appears to him to be mentally disordered in a public place, he may take him off for medical examination under the Mental Health Act 1983 section 136. Or, if a doctor comes to the conclusion that a person is mentally disordered he may certify for his emergency admission to hospital for assessment under section 2 . The Act does not empower the doctor to enter premises or to examine the patient by force, but once the certificate has been given and other procedures have been complied with the patient may be taken to hospital. There are also powers to remove people from their homes when they have reached the "last stage of all," or are otherwise unable to cope.

An old or mentally disordered person may be unable to look after himself properly in his house, and may be living in squalor. Wide powers are available to move him compulsorily to hospital. One is given by the Mental Health Act. When a person is believed to be suffering from mental disorder and is being ill-treated or neglected, or, being unable to care for himself, is living alone, a magistrate may issue a warrant authorising a constable to enter the premises and remove such person to a "place of safety;" he may then be medically examined and, if thought fit, civilly committed.[6] Equally draconic powers are given by the National Assistance Act 1948 s. 47 (as amended). Under the latter Act the medical and judicial safeguards are minimal.

The uprooting of old people under these powers, though sometimes unavoidable, has often been resorted to too readily. It has been called "slow euthanasia," because the old people when moved, though well looked after physically, generally suffer from apathy and dejection, often amounting to intense grief. A quarter of them die within three months of admission; yet some of these were physically healthy when admitted. For others, death is long drawn out and miserable.[7] Although in extreme cases an old bod's right of self-determination has to be overridden, it is far better to arrange for insanitary conditions to be cleaned up, and domiciliary and health services provided, and to put up with the mess and uncertainty that remains, than to move anyone forcibly from his home if this can be avoided.

When a person has been moved to hospital or an institution in this way, can he be compulsorily treated?

The powers just described to remove people from their homes do not

---

[4] Ormrod LJ, in the discussion following his lecture, said that although the interests of the child are paramount these "may include the anticipated response of the parents." In other words, it is not right to save the child's life if he will then be rejected by his parents. See 46 Med.-Leg.Jrnl 31. This may well be important not only in case of religious belief but for malformed children.

[5] Under the Mental Health Act 1983 Pt. I.

[6] MHA 1983 s. 135.

[7] A A Baker in [1976] 2 BMJ 571; Alison J Norman, *Rights and Risk* (Nat. Corpn for the Care of Old People 1980).

carry powers of compulsory treatment. But the Mental Health Act 1983, Part IV, gives certain powers of compulsory medical treatment for mental disorder, hammered out after long debate. This does not apply to informal patients, only detained patients.[8]

Treatment may be given under the direction of the responsible medical officer (RMO) without the patient's consent and without special safeguards except in three cases.

1 Psychosurgery (operations for destroying brain tissue or its functioning), and such other operations as may be specified by regulations, require not only the opinion of the RMO but both the consent of the patient and a concurring opinion from three assessors (a psychiatrist and two lay persons), who confirm that the patient is capable of giving his consent.

2 Treatments specified in regulations (which are almost certain to include electro-convulsive therapy (ECT)) require either the consent of the patient or a second opinion (from an independent psychiatrist after consulting two non-doctors who are members of the patient's therapeutic team).

3 Drugs (such as tranquillisers for psychotic patients and anti-depressant drugs for those with depressive illnesses) can be given without the patient's consent or legal requirements for the first three months, in order that the patient's condition can be stabilised. After that medication has the same requirements as in 2 above—either the patient's consent or a second opinion. There is an overriding right to give treatment in certain situations of urgency without complying with these requirements (s. 62).

Does the rule against interfering with people mean that a person can never be forcibly prevented from committing suicide?

One study showed that of 100 *successful* suicides no fewer than 93 of those concerned seemed on the evidence to have been mentally ill, generally on account of a depressive condition.[9] It seems reasonable to say that if a person is found attempting to commit suicide and nothing is known about his state of mind, the attempt is evidence of mental disorder. Anyone is entitled at common law to apprehend a person who is mentally disordered and who is a danger to himself or others, the purpose of the apprehension, of course, being to get him to a doctor.

Unfortunately, a limitation of this rule is that the person so detained must actually be mentally disordered, so if the person attempting suicide turns out to be *compos mentis* it seems that the detention is unlawful, and constitutes at least the tort of assault and false imprisonment.[10] Even so, taking the instruments of suicide away from him might be justified under the doctrine of necessity, since this doctrine, unlike the law relating to arrest and detention, always allows a person to act on the facts as they reasonably appear to him to be.[11] The powers given by the Mental Health Acts may, of course, be invoked.

While cases may occur in which hospitalisation would clearly be justified, particularly in the case of young people, the fact remains that the law does not provide for anyone being kept alive without his consent. Formerly, suicide was regarded as a felony; so interfering with a

---

[8] See Gostin in 132 NLJ 1199.

[9] See 125 Br.Jrnl.Psychiatry 355.

[10] See Lanham in [1974] Crim.LR 516.

[11] The word "reasonably" is inserted because of the decisions that putative defences require reasonableness. But this was not always so: in *Bourne* § 13.4 at n. 13 the doctor was said to be protected if he acted in good faith. The rule is embodied in the Abortion Act. Specifically on the subject of preventing suicide see *Meyer* v. *Supreme Lodge KP* (1904) 70 NE 111 (New York) (administering antidote to would-be suicide lawful). A Canadian court held that a would-be suicide who forcibly resists an attempt by a police officer to stop him can be convicted of assaulting the officer in the execution of his duty: *Dietrich* (1978) 39 CCC (2d) 361.

would-be suicide could be justified as the prevention of felony; but now, by the Suicide Act 1961, suicide is legal. If a patient has a perfectly sound reason for desiring not to "keep right on to the end of the road" (as if he is suffering from a fatal and painful disease), a doctor has no warrant to interfere with him. Some would say that even a mentally ill patient should be allowed to drink the hemlock; and that is a reasonable view if medication has failed to make the patient change his mind. Indeed, the Samaritans (who do noble work in trying to help people so that they do not commit suicide), if they are called to someone who has committed a suicidal act and who wishes to die, do not attempt to save his life, but simply hold his hand while he is dying, taking the view that they have no right or duty to interfere. But these considerations do not mean that people who have intervened in good faith in an emergency have much to fear from the law. Even if the law does not technically validate what they do, they would almost certainly, if prosecuted, be given an absolute discharge.

Can a hunger-striking prisoner be forcibly fed?

This horrible practice was upheld in *Leigh* v. *Gladstone*,[12] an action brought by a suffragette (who had been forcibly fed in prison) against the Home Secretary.

> Lord Alverstone CJ directed the jury that prison officers were entitled to force-feed a prisoner. There was not, and is not, anything in the Prison Rules that could fairly be read as justifying this. The Chief Justice enabled himself to reach his conclusion by a notable paralogism. He said that "it was the duty, both under the rules and apart from the rules, of the officials to preserve the health and lives of the prisoners, who were in the custody of the Crown."

This proposition ignored the essential facts of the case. It is the general duty of prison officers to take care for the lives of prisoners; but is it their duty to preserve life by force against the prisoner's wish? The latter does not follow from the former. To take an analogy: a hospital doctor must take care for his patients, but he is not under a duty and is not at liberty to preserve their lives against their wishes.

In 1974 a Government pronouncement was widely thought to have marked the abandonment of the practice, except where the prisoner's capacity for rational judgment was impaired by illness. However, the statement did not in fact affect the discretion given to the medical officer to do as he wished,[13] and some prisoners have since then been forcibly fed—usually on the ground that they are mentally disordered. Some may think that if a person is facing a long stay in prison it is perfectly rational for him to prefer to fade out.[14]

§ 26.9. JUDGE AND JURY

Where a statute allows "reasonable excuse" as a defence, the judges are disposed to place strict limits upon it. Magistrates are virtually directed by the Divisional Court whether they can or cannot allow the excuse in the particular case. Judges are directed by the Court of Appeal not to leave the defence to the jury except in circumstances that seem right to the Court of

---

[12] (1909) 26 TLR 139.
[13] See the full study by Graham Zellick in [1976] Public Law 153.
[14] Zellick in 127 NLJ 928.

Appeal.[1] So "reasonable excuse," although it is a defence for breaking the letter of the law, is itself a matter of law.

The position should be the same for the defence of necessity, assuming that that defence is recognised as a general one at common law. When a judge rules on particular facts that necessity is *not* a defence, he is deciding the question of values, namely that the importance of obeying the letter of the law is supreme on those facts. It may be thought that the positive decision, that necessity is an allowable defence in the particular case, should also belong to the judge, assuming that the jury find the facts necessary to support it. Necessity is essentially a normative doctrine; it curtails legal rules. The evaluation should be by the judge both because uniformity of decision is important and also because the judge is better qualified to pronounce on traditional values. In *Bourne*[2] it was clearly the judge who laid down the new rule for therapeutic abortions; all that he left the jury to decide was whether the doctor had acted in good faith for the purpose specified by the judge as constituting a valid defence.

If it is accepted that the evaluation of necessity is for the judge, this makes a point of difference from other doctrines, like negligence in careless driving and dishonesty in theft, which, as said before, may operate very like the defence of necessity. These matters are for the jury, subject however to a certain control by the judge.

Some of the authorities supporting the defence show that although the evidential burden of raising it rests on the defendant, the persuasive burden of negativing it rests on the prosecution.[3]

§ 26.10. IMPOSSIBILITY

Little discussion of a defence of impossibility is to be found in the books. In so far as the courts allow it, this is generally done under other rubrics, such as the mental element, negligence or duress. But in two types of case impossibility should be a defence independently of any other.

1 In offences of omission, if the act to which the law obliges cannot be performed, and the defendant was not at fault in bringing about the impossibility, he should not be held liable for the failure. In other words, sheer impossibility should be an excuse for not performing a positive obligation. It is no use the law's butting its head against a brick wall.

   Sometimes, by no means always, the courts accept this. An affirmative example is an old case holding that a person is not liable for not repairing a road if the road has been washed away by the sea.[1] But the more common case of impossibility by failure of subject-matter is that of failing to produce a piece of paper that one is expected to have; and here

---

[1] See authorities in § 2.4 n. 14.
[2] § 13.4 at n. 13.
[3] See *Bourne* [1939] 1 KB at 691; *Trim* [1943] VLR 109 (Aus.).

[1] See *The General Part*, 2nd edn 747 n. 1. See also § 7.3 n. 17.

the courts show no indulgence. A person who has borrowed a car and who does not produce a test certificate to the police as required is not allowed the defence that no certificate exists, even though its nonexistence was not his fault.[2] This is in accordance with the general practice of the courts for regulatory offences, where absence of fault does not excuse.[3] Of course, the difficulty of ensuring that one has a test certificate is not comparable with the difficulty of replacing a road over land eroded by the sea. The problem presented by offences of strict liability is to be considered in Chapter 42.

2 Certain cases of inconsistent duties can be regarded as impossibility of full performance, because both duties cannot be discharged. In the example previously given of an air pilot whose engine fails,[4] he is under a duty not to kill people on the street and also not to kill people in the sports stadium; and he best reconciles the conflicting demands of the law by killing the smaller number of people in the street. It is impossible for him to fulfil both duties.[5]

§ 26.11. MINIMAL VIOLATIONS

English law is popularly supposed not to concern itself with trifles. But those who have this belief are likely to be disabused of it if they come to court.

If the words of a statute have clearly been offended against, an infraction will generally be found although the defendant meant no harm, or only minimal harm.[1] In particular, the courts will strictly enforce rules that are accurately quantified.

> A driver who exceeds the speed limit by one mile an hour would be liable to conviction, but in practice the police do not prosecute for small excesses.[2] The alcohol limits for drivers have been strictly applied, an excess of as little as one mg. in 100 ml. of urine leading to conviction,[3] but in calculating the excess the justices are (very questionably) allowed to make a deduction to allow for a margin of error in the laboratory test.[4]

The court in one case[5] expressed the view that the police should not prosecute when the excess of alcohol is truly minimal, but the indulgence would be against the public interest. There is a distinction from speeding offences: if a speed limit were enforced rigorously, no

---

[2] This appears from *Davey* v. *Towle* [1973] RTR 328. *Stockdale* v. *Coulson* [1974] 3 All ER 154 is a somewhat indulgent exception, probably dependent upon the wording of the statute. Contrast with the latter case *Pilgram* v. *Dean* [1974] 1 WLR 601, 2 All ER 751, where a statute made two such offences cumulative. See Bennun in 128 NLJ 1123.

[3] Cp. *Strowger* v. *John* [1974] RTR 124, where however the question of liability for interference by a stranger was left open.

[4] § .3, text after n. 5.

[5] Cp. Fletcher, *Rethinking Criminal Law* 852–855.

[1] This would explain the decision in *Wells* v. *Hardy*, § 20.5 at n. 10.

[2] For the variation of police practice in this respect, see Elliott and Street, *Road Accidents* (Harmondsworth 968) 34.

[3] *McGarry* v. *Chief Constable of Bedfordshire*, The Times, May 18, 1982.

[4] *Walker* v. *Hodgins* (1983) The Times, March 1. The BMA leaflet on the subject states that most people with 40 mg. alcohol in 100 ml. blood are incapable of driving safely; the statutory figure of double this limit was evidently meant to allow a generous margin of error. To allow an extra 6 mg., as this decision permits the justices to do, is evidently not in accordance with the legislative purpose.

[5] *Delaroy-Hall* v. *Tadman* [1969] 2 QB 208. See also, as to excise licences, *Nattrass* v. *Gibson* [1968] CLY 3464.

driver could safely drive at the limit (speedometers are imperfect, and anyway one cannot watch the dial the whole time), so that traffic in a 30 m.p.h. area would be slowed to a maximum of say 25 m.p.h., which is unlikely to be what Parliament intended. In contrast, nothing but good would result if no one consumed alcohol before driving. The figure of 80 mg. allowed is a concession to a pernicious practice, and the concession having been made it ought not to be extended by police discretion, which is likely to continue ingrained social attitudes. Drinking drivers do not go by scientific measurements, and they presumably know that unless they keep well within the permitted maximum they are at risk.[6]

It might be thought that what is law for the defendant is law for the prosecutor, but on at least one occasion this was not so.

> A "restricted road" for the purpose of the 30 m.p.h. speed limit means a road having a system of street lighting by means of lamps placed not more than 200 yards apart.[6] A driver, being charged with speeding, carefully measured the distances and found that, of the four street lamps on the stretch in question, two were 200 yards 18 inches apart. But the court robbed him of his triumph by holding that the excess was too small to be material.[7]

When Parliament laid down the maximum distance between street lamps it presumably allowed a comfortable margin beyond the usual distance, in order to allow for local conditions and mistakes in measurement. The distance having been specified, it was surely not for the courts to alter it, particularly when they make a practice of reading the law strictly against the defendant.[8]

The usual, and proper, rule applied by the courts is that if traffic signs, etc, do not conform strictly to the statutory conditions they are inoperative. So when a driver crossed double white lines in apparent breach of a statute, but those double lines improperly had an intermittent white line painted between them, he lived to offend another day.[9]

When the offence is not numerically quantified, and the application of a word involves questions of the little less and the little more, the courts have more leeway to disregard trifles, but they generally do not choose to do so. They rarely adopt the maxim *De minimis non curat lex* in words, and almost as rarely apply it in practice.

> A few positive examples *de minimis* may be harvested. Where a driver unintentionally immobilised another car for a very short time, and the car was easily restarted, magistrates were held to be entitled to find that no "accident" had occurred.[10] And where a moneylender was under an obligation to make a memorandum of a loan, it was held that clerical errors would not necessarily invalidate it.[11] Any obstruction of

---

[6] The danger of allowing the police to nullify the law by discretion is vividly shown by prosecution practices for the offence of driving while disqualified. This should invariably be regarded as a serious offence to be adjudicated by the courts, yet in some police districts warnings are frequently given instead of prosecuting. See Elliott and Street, *Road Accidents* (Harmondsworth 1968) 124. Road Traffic Regulation Act 1967 s. 72.

[7] *Briere* v. *Hailstone* [1969] Crim.LR 36.

[8] The court expressly proceeded on the *de minimis* principle. There were two posts erected within the regulation distance, but the court rightly did not base its judgment on that fact, for two lamps could hardly he held to constitute a "system of street lighting."

Sometimes the court may excuse some defect in the prosecution case by having regard to the purpose of the law. In *Sharples* v. *Blackmore* [1973] RTR 249, Crim.LR 248, the back of a speed-limit sign was painted black instead of the regulation grey. It was held that the requirement was directory, not mandatory (in effect, had no legal force), because the operative part of the sign was the front. Although the result may look like common sense, more particularly because the sign was back-to-back with a derestriction sign, so that the shade in which the back was painted was invisible anyway, it may be questioned whether the court should take to itself the authority to decide what part of a legal specification of a sign is to he taken as essential and what not, when the regulation itself does not distinguish.

[9] *Davies* v. *Heatley* [1971] RTR 145, Crim.LR 244.

[10] *Morris* [1972] 1 WLR at 231, 1 All ER at 387.

[11] *London & Harrogate Securities Ltd.* v. *Pitts* [1976] 1 WLR 264, 2 All ER 184; on appeal [1976] 1 WLR 1063, 3 All ER 809.

a highway, even of the smallest degree, is said to be a public nuisance; but at the same time it is allowed that an obstruction may be so trifling (particularly, though not only, when it is temporary) that it does not "in law" amount to an obstruction.[12] In effect, though not avowedly, these cases accept the *de minimis* principle.

A physical assault is defined as the application of force, however slight, and this enables the courts to administer due punishment to the rascal who steals a kiss.[13] There are obvious reasons for understanding the word "force" in this technical sense; normally, a slight touching would be dismissed from consideration as an ordinary social contact.[14]

The most striking rejection of the *de minimis* maxim is in relation to the unlawful possession of controlled drugs (drugs of abuse). The statute is held to apply to the smallest quantity of the drug. "If the scale do turn but in the estimation of a hair, thou diest."

This was a decision of the House of Lords. Previously, the Court of Appeal had arrived at the sensible principle that there was no offence in possessing minute quantities of a forbidden drug, if they were too small to be usable. But the Lords took a right about turn in *Boyesen.*[15] The possession of 5 mg. of cannabis resin (the normal range for a reefer cigarette being 50–100 mg.) was held to be a sufficient quantity to be unlawfully possessed. Lord Scarman, speaking for the House, said:

> "The possession of any quantity which is visible, tangible, measurable and capable of manipulation is a serious matter to be prohibited if the law is to be effective against trafficking in dangerous drugs and their misuse."

Lord Scarman conceded that the quantity must be sufficient to amount as a matter of common sense to "something." Therefore, microscopic traces of a drug in the defendant's pockets, pipe or hypodermic syringe would not be sufficient. He also recognised that quantity can be relevant to the issue of knowledge; if the amount is very small the prosecution may be unable to prove that the defendant knew he had anything.

The decisions assembled above are not entirely satisfactory. They fail to organise any coherent principle, and in the drugs case, *Boyesen*, the Lords seem to have lost their usual sense of fairness. The argument they accepted, that the Misuse of Drugs Act cannot be confined to the possession of drugs in "usable" quantities because that word does not appear in the Act, is unconvincing. The words "capable of manipulation" do not appear either, though Lord Scarman was apparently prepared to accept them as a limitation of the offence. If their lordships' decision appears reasonable, it is because a person who possesses residual traces of a drug has probably possessed a larger quantity in the past. But on that basis the proper course would be to convict the defendant of having possessed the drug in the past.[16] Such a conviction is all that is required for the proper enforcement of the law, and it is one

---

[12] The attitude of the courts seems to have become stricter than formerly. See *Almeroth* v. *Chivers & Sons* [1941] 3 All ER 53, and other cases in Pratt and Mackensie's *Highways*, 21st edn 113.

[13] § 8.1 at n. 6.

[14] § 8.3. There is less justification for the decision that "actual bodily harm" means "bodily harm, however slight" (§ 9.2 n. 2), since that repeals the word "actual."

[15] [1982] 2 WLR 882.

[16] The possession of traces may be evidence of an offence of possession having been committed previously. It is sometimes objected that on such a charge the court would have to weigh the possibility that the defendant came into possession of the container when it was in its present condition, i.e. virtually empty; and also of the possibility that when the defendant came into possession of the full container he immediately emptied out the contents because he did not wish to have them. However, these would seem to be fanciful speculations in the absence of evidence, and the tribunal of fact would normally be justified in inferring the prior possession of the larger quantity. *Contra, Carver* [1978] QB at 478B.

to which no one could possibly object. In contrast, a person who is convicted of possessing drugs when he only has an unusably small amount in his possession may understandably feel that he is the victim of legal pedantry or chicanery, since an unusually small amount (if there is no question of the amount being saved up to be accumulated) is not within the mischief aimed against by the Act. At any rate, as a matter of general principle the rule stated in the Model Penal Code is surely right, that an act that is so trivial as to be outside the harm or evil sought to be prevented and punished by the offence is outside its range.[17]

SUMMARY

Necessity involves a judgment that the letter of the law may justifiably be broken to achieve a greater good. According to one view, it is a defence only when the statute creating the offence allows for it. According to another, it is a general defence, though subject to limiting rules. § .1, .2

The decision in *Bourne*, on therapeutic abortion, can be regarded as having been based on necessity, but it is now superseded by the Abortion Act. The usual view, based on *Dudley,* is that the defence does not avail to a charge of murder; but hypothetical cases can be put in which it should, provided that the act results in a net saving of life. § .3

Necessity should justify theft of food where the hunger arises in extraordinary circumstances from physical causes, but there is no authority directly in point. The defence does not justify the homeless in "squatting," the necessity here being only economic. Nor, apart from legislation, has it been recognised as a defence in driving cases, though in some extreme circumstances considerations of justice suggest that it should be. On one occasion the doctrine was used to justify the *conviction* of a driver of obstructing the police § .5

The police are not allowed to disobey the ordinary law in order to obtain evidence. And hitherto the doctrine has not been thought to justify a driver in damaging property to free a blocked car, though the point has not arisen before the superior courts. § .6

It is generally conceded that a certain defence, which can hardly be anything other than necessity, is allowable in respect of medical operations, though here again the authorities are scanty. In respect of operations upon sane adults, the defence avails only when the patient's consent cannot be asked for, and the doctor does not know that the patient withholds consent ("future consent"). § .7

A doctor is probably justified in operating on a child without the consent of the parent in case of necessity, though the child, when of the age of discretion, should be allowed the adult's right of self-determination. There are statutory powers of dealing with mentally disordered and incapable people. In practice, whatever the theoretical ground may be, it is doubtless lawful to prevent a suicide, though how long the prevention may be persisted in is an open question. It has been ruled that hunger-striking prisoners can be forcibly fed, but the reasoning behind the pronouncement is suspect. § .8

On the assumption that necessity is a defence, the judge should be regarded as having authority to rule on the application of the defence to particular circumstances. § .9

The cases on impossibility fail to yield any principle of importance. In general the issue is settled by reference to other principles. § .10

When a statute quantifies a rule in numerical terms, the courts will generally enforce it strictly against the defendant. But the *de minimis* maxim may be given § .11

[17] S. 2.12 (POD). The principle should not apply to rules stated in terms of numerical quantities.

some application where words of customary imprecision are used in defining the *actus reus*; here the courts may not regard (or juries may not be encouraged to regard) minimal events as falling within them. The decision of the Lords on the possession of controlled drugs is an exception.

Chapter 27

DURESS AND COERCION

> In the calm of the court-room measures of fortitude or of heroic behaviour are surely not to be demanded when they could not in moments for decision reasonably have been expected even of the resolute and the well disposed.
>
> Lord Morris of Borth-y-Gest [1975] AC at 670

§ 27.1. DURESS AS A DEFENCE

A man may be "compelled" by a threat to do something to which he is strongly averse. Happily, the law on this subject is not shrouded in quite the same doubt as the defence of necessity. Subject to certain rules, a threat that is sufficiently grave to be accounted "duress"[1] can operate as a defence. This was established by the House of Lords in *DPP for Northern Ireland* v. *Lynch*, following earlier authorities.[2] It is equally well settled that the burden of negativing the defence, once raised, rests on the Crown, though an evidential burden rests on the defendant.[3] The Law Commission has proposed that these rules should be cast in statutory form, and that the defendant should be required to give advance notice of the defence to the prosecution.[4]

For practical reasons duress is confined to threats of death or serious personal injury. Widgery LJ expressed the law thus:

> "It is clearly established that duress provides a defence in all offences including perjury (except possibly treason or murder as a principal) if the will of the accused has been overborne by threats of death or serious personal injury so that the commission of the alleged offence was no longer the voluntary act of the accused."[5]

So the idea is that duress makes the act involuntary?

When Widgery LJ spoke of the will being overborne, he used figurative language. A person who is acting under duress makes a decision to give way to the duress. The view taken by the majority of the House of Lords in *Lynch* was that duress is a defence on its own, and does not negative either the doing of the act charged or the *mens rea*.[6] This is plainly right.

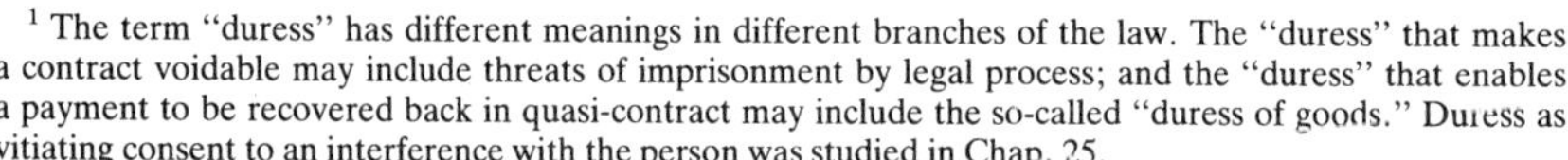

[1] The term "duress" has different meanings in different branches of the law. The "duress" that makes a contract voidable may include threats of imprisonment by legal process; and the "duress" that enables a payment to be recovered back in quasi-contract may include the so-called "duress of goods." Duress as vitiating consent to an interference with the person was studied in Chap. 25.

[2] [1975] AC 653. See K J M Smith in 38 MLR 566.

[3] *Bone* [1968] 1 WLR 983, 2 All ER 644. For an Australian example of the withdrawal of the defence from the jury see [1968] Crim.LR 596.

[4] *Criminal Law: Report on Defences of General Application* (Law Com. No. 83) Pt. II. The proposal for notice is criticised by A T H Smith in [1978] Crim.LR 127.

[5] *Hudson* [1971] 2 QB 202 at 206.

[6] See Ian Dennis in 96 LQR 220-228; *Hurley* [1967] VR 526; *Fitzpatrick* [1977] NI 20, and note by Rowe in 42 MLR 102. For this reason, it seems that *Steane* [1947] KB 997 should have been decided on duress, not on the absence of intent. See *The General Part*, 2nd edn § 18, and the comments on *Steane* in the NI Court of Criminal Appeal in *Lynch* [1975] NI at 49F–H.

If D1 seizes D2's hand and by direct force makes D2 pull the trigger of a revolver which kills V, we would certainly say that the killing was done by D1 and not by D2. But if D2 is caused by threats to shoot V, it is proper to say that D2 has killed him, though perhaps under duress. Aristotle suggested, as one reason for classifying such an act as voluntary, that "an individual may resist the threat and suffer the evil rather than do what he thinks to be wrong; he will then be praised, and his resistance will show that it was not inevitable that a person should submit to the threat."[7] We may add that the notion that the act is involuntary would automatically make duress a defence to all charges of crime, whereas the courts treat the question whether exceptions should be made as one of policy. Moreover, it is a question of policy what should be counted as duress.

The Law Commission, in an important Report,[8] put forward two propositions.

1 Certain very terrible threats should excuse from all crimes.
2 Less terrible threats should be matter of mitigation only. If the crime is a minor one the mitigation may result in an absolute discharge, but that is in the discretion of the judge.

As to what threats should fall within proposition 1, the Law Commission adopted the rule stated by Widgery LJ, that duress must amount to a threat of death or serious injury, with the modification that the injury threatened may be physical or mental, and may be to the defendant or to another; also, what matters is not what threat was intended but what threat the defendant believed (*not* "reasonably believed") to exist. (Under the present law, however, the belief must be reasonable.) The Commission slipped in the qualification that the threat must be such that in all the circumstances of the case the defendant could not reasonably have been expected to resist it.

May there not be serious threats other than those mentioned by Widgery LJ and the Law Commission? What about a threat to destroy a man's dwelling? Or to cause him to lose his job? Or a blackmailing threat to his character?

Many of us are subject to pressures, external and internal, to cause harm to others. The law is by definition a system of counter-pressure, its aim being to influence individuals to make acceptable social decisions. This counter-pressure cannot be lifted merely because the individual finds strong personal reasons for acting contrary to the law. Constraint is a defence only when it is of so immediate and pressing a character that it seems to be futile or unconscionably harsh to maintain the prohibition. As a practical matter, the threats you mention must be left to general mitigation, though the threat to burn a man's dwelling could afford him a defence for some minor transgression under the doctrine of necessity. I

[7] *Nicomachean Ethics* Book 3, Chap. 1.
[8] N.4 above.

think, however, that a threat to torture should be added to the Widgery list as a case of duress, since a person may find torture unendurable even though it does not involve physical injury.

You agree that if the threat is not of death or serious injury (or perhaps torture) the question has to be left to the judge as a mattery of mitigation. Why not do so in all cases? Why let the jury come into the picture when the threat is of some particular kind?

Voices are still raised to say this. But the question whether a person ought to be punishable in such cases is one of general policy, resting upon an assessment of what the criminal law is capable of effecting and what it is right that it should try to do; and the matter ought not to be left to the shifting sands of discretion.

For good measure, three other reasons may be advanced for allowing duress as a defence, and not simply as a matter of mitigation.

1 Allowing a specific defence means that the evidence is brought out fully before the jury. It is a criticism of our trial system that when evidence is admissible only in mitigation, so that it is no concern of the jury, it is not considered and probed with the same thoroughness as evidence going to liability.[9]
2 There is a special argument for murder. If duress were not allowed as a defence the judge would have to pass a life sentence.
3 A last argument is perhaps the most decisive. In a case of overwhelming duress, no punishment can in justice be imposed on the unhappy victim of the duress. The moral rigorist may assert that there must nevertheless be a conviction, to maintain the supremacy of the higher morality. But, as Rupert Cross remarked, "an absolute discharge or an instant release under the prerogative of mercy are strange methods of enforcing absolute moral prohibitions."[10]

Certain distinctions between the defences of duress, necessity and private defence are perhaps worth stating.

Private defence does not excuse one for acting against an innocent third party, as duress does. And private defence can justify the defence of property, while duress in respect of property is not a defence to a criminal charge.

There is a closer kinship between duress and necessity. Many cases of duress could be resolved as cases of necessity, by a balancing of values. If a gunman threatens to shoot my wife immediately if I do not give him the keys of my employer's safe, and I yield to the threat, I could justify as choosing the lesser evil if that defence is allowed; in any case I have the defence of duress.

But, first, we have seen that doubts exist about the lesser evil doctrine, particularly in relation to murder, while the law of duress is much clearer. Secondly, duress need not suppose a choice of the lesser evil. A person who assists in a killing under the fear of death has the defence of duress, whereas necessity, regarded as an application of utilitarian ethics, could not justify in a case of one for one. Thirdly, in necessity the balancing of evil against evil is left at large, and this often presents hard problems. It is both possible and desirable to achieve greater precision with the defence of duress.

The idea of duress as involving a choice of evils has had some influence on legal thought; in particular, it underlies some (not all) of the remarks made in *Lynch*.[11] But the arguments the other way are now generally preferred. The defence of duress (specially defined) is not a justification of the crime (as necessity is or should be), but an excuse. The defence is allowed

---

[9] Cp. Lord Edmund-Davies in *Lynch* at p. 707E.
[10] 28 U of Tor.LJ 376.
[11] For a discussion see 1st edn 579–580.

not because it achieves the greater good or lesser evil but because the exceptional circumstances make it unlikely that the law can effectively continue its prohibition, and make punishment for doing the act seem harsh or unjust.[12]

§ 27.2. CRIMES EXCEPTED FROM THE DEFENCE

It will be remembered that Widgery LJ mooted two exceptions from the defence: treason, and murder as principal.

Prosecutions for treason are virtually confined to the circumstances of war. Perhaps in war even the private citizen is expected to cast himself in a heroic mould. But remarks made in *Lynch*,[1] as well as the weight of earlier authority, are in favour of allowing the defence of duress to a charge of treason.

As for murder, the decision in *Lynch* was that duress can be a defence to a person charged as accessory to murder (even though he is what used to be called a principal in the second degree, helping at the time of the crime). This decision is now undoubtedly the law. It would be unreasonable to exclude the defence of duress to an accessory on a charge of murder where the accessory has done something quite trivial, like handing over a gun. For there can be no advantage to anyone in refusing to hand over a gun if you can be shot and the gun taken from your dead body.

That is a highly tendentious example. What the defendant did may not be trivial. Do you say that if a terrorist threatens Droop to injure him seriously if he does not make a telephone call that will lure an unsuspecting victim to his death, and Droop complies, Droop is not and ought not to be guilty of murder?

We would admire Droop if he rejected the proposal and accepted the injury. The doctrine of necessity would hardly excuse such a deed as is proposed to him, because the injury to Droop is not demonstrably a greater evil than the death of the victim. But if Droop lacks the moral fibre to resist the threat, it seems pointless to punish him. (And if you still despise Droop, consider that the threat may be not to injure him but to torture him, and not only him but his wife and children.)

Consider a terrorist organisation with a single boss and an iron discipline. Every member carries out orders, knowing that if he refuses he will be shot or kneecapped. If you allow duress as a defence, only the boss can be punished.

There is much overseas authority for saying that the defence is not open

---

[12] The point is well developed by Cross in 28 U of Tor.LJ 369. See also Fletcher, *Rethinking Criminal Law* 829–833.

[1] [1975] AC at 672F, 680E, 701E, 708C.

to people who have voluntarily become members of an illegal organisation. This restriction was accepted by the CCA in Northern Ireland as a matter of law,[2] and the House of Lords refused leave to appeal from the decision.[3] So we can be sure that it forms part of English law.[4]

What would you say if the defendant has helped to plant a bomb that kills scores of people? Is he to be permitted to save his own skin in that way? In the Nuremberg trials those who took part in the mass extermination of Jews were not allowed to defend themselves by saying that they themselves feared that they would be executed if they disobeyed orders.

The point you make about the Nuremberg trials is powerful, but the problem of atrocities committed by soldiers and others who are under orders has special features. If members of the armed forces are allowed defences of duress and superior orders, responsibility is confined to a very few people at the top. Perhaps, for overwhelming social reasons, these defences have to be withheld from members of the armed forces (or others subject to discipline) in respect of acts of killing or torturing that are clearly contrary to civilised standards of behaviour. In practice, because of the numbers of people involved, it would be only those with appreciable authority who would be prosecuted. But whatever solution is found need not govern ordinary cases involving civilians.[5]

Your question about the bomb raises difficult issues of morality and social policy. There is an argument for saying that we should nourish the hope, however faint, that the threat of punishment may be enough to tip the balance of decision by those who have only doubtfully sufficient fortitude to undergo martyrdom for the sake of moral principle. But even if duress were not allowed as a defence in your hypothetical, the circumstances would go so strongly in mitigation of punishment that the defendant would probably serve only a comparatively short sentence, which in itself would probably (if he knew of it beforehand) be insufficient to avail against the threat. There is also the question whether the conviction and punishment in what may be highly unusual circumstances are likely to be known later on to other people who are similarly placed. (Lawyers exaggerate the extent to which decisions of the courts are known to and remembered by the populace.)

You said that the decision in Lynch was about accessories to murder. Is the perpetrator of murder ever allowed the defence of duress?

Shortly after *Lynch*, the Judicial Committee of the Privy Council, sitting on appeal from Trinidad and Tobago, held, in *Abbott* v. *The Queen*,[6] that

---

[2] *Fitzpatrick* [1977] NI 20. It was further held that the defendant could not revive the defence of duress for his own benefit by trying to leave the organisation.

[3] The Times, November 23, 1976.

[4] The Law Commission proposed that the restriction should operate only when the defendant knew he might he called upon to commit a serious offence (*op. cit.* above § .1 n. 4). On the limits of the restriction see further Rowe in 42 MLR 102.

[5] See Dennis in 96 LQR 215–216.

[6] [1977] AC 755. See Beaumont in 40 MLR 67.

the defence is not open at common law to a person charged as perpetrator of murder. (The membership of the Judicial Committee is largely the same as that of the Appellate Committee of the House of Lords, but the law lords who decided *Abbott* were not quite the same as those who sat in *Lynch*. While they accepted *Lynch* as a binding statement of the law, the majority in *Abbott* were less favourably disposed to the defence than the majority in *Lynch*—though *Lynch* itself contains various remarks suggesting the distinction between perpetrators and others.) Decisions of the Judicial Committee are treated with great respect by United Kingdom courts (as the House of Lords is), but are not binding upon them. It is therefore possible, though unlikely, that an English court might refuse to follow *Abbott*.

But surely a distinction between the perpetrator and the accessory is indefensible. There may be no moral difference between them.

That is true. Compare the person who is forced to drive a bomber to a crowded pub and someone who is forced to carry the bomb into the pub and leave it there.[7] The former is an accessory, the latter the perpetrator; but on facts like these the legal distinction is too fine to be morally or psychologically relevant. For this and other reasons the Law Commission proposed that *Abbott* should be rejected and that the defence of duress should be extended by statute to all crimes.

In *Lynch*, Lord Morris suggested a reason for the distinction: the accessory, under terrible threat, may temporise by helping in the plan while hoping that something will intervene to save the victim, whereas a perpetrator knows that he is doing the immediate killing. But this distinction does not quite fit. A perpetrator who sets a bomb because he is under duress may hope that it will not go off, or that someone will find it in time, while an accessory who helps in the killing of a victim then and there has no hope that anyone will intervene.

Something depends on how the line between perpetrators and others is drawn. In *Abbott*, the defendant held the victim (a girl) while a hired assassin attempted to stab her to death; however, she was still alive when the defendant and others joined in burying her. The Judicial Committee said: "The facts make it obvious that the appellant was a principal in the first degree in that he took an active and indeed a leading part in the killing."[8] But this has never been the test of a principal in the first degree. An accessory may take "a leading part in the killing" by devising the plan and supervising its execution; this does not make him a perpetrator.[9] On traditional principles, what made Abbott a perpetrator was not the fact that he held the victim while she was stabbed but only the fact that he took an immediate joint part in her final despatch by burying her alive (even though at that time she was mortally wounded). Morally, the former conduct was worse than the latter, because the latter conduct, though very cruel, merely accelerated the girl's death by a short time.

The absurdity of the distinction was adverted to by the Court of Appeal in *Graham*,[10] a case of murder so cold-blooded and brutal that it makes the demand for the restoration of capital punishment understandable. Graham set about helping to throttle his wife by pulling the plug at one end of an electric flex, which was around her neck, while his companion in iniquity

---

[7] Cp. J C Smith in [1976] Crim.LR 564.

[8] [1977] AC at 762B. Cp. p. 767G, saying that the principle of *Lynch* does not extend to "a man who takes part in the actual killing." Whether this sentence accords with traditional principle depends upon what is meant by "the actual killing." Cp. [1976] Crim.LR 564.

[9] See §§ 15.1, 16.9. Cp. Dennis in 97 LQR 209–211.

[10] [1982] 1 WLR 294, 1 All ER 801, 74 CAR 231.

pulled the other end. The wife was killed, but Graham said that in fact he did not take an effective part because the plug came off in his hand when he began to pull it. If that was so, his guilt was only that of an accessory (abettor) by being present and encouraging, not that of perpetrator. The court commented that the jury would be puzzled to be told that Graham's guilt depended on whether the plug did come off in his hand.

But the decision in the case presents its own problems. The trial judge left the defence of duress to the jury without asking them to find whether the defendant was the perpetrator of the murder. In effect he decided not to follow *Abbott* (as technically he was not obliged to do, for the reason before given). Those who think *Abbott* an unfortunate decision would regard this as in itself a commendable line to take. The objection to the judge's ruling is a different one, that there was no evidence of duress. The evidence was merely that Graham's companion was sometimes given to violence. The report gives no indication that a threat was made to Graham, and Graham took an active part in arranging that his wife should be murdered. Obviously it cannot found a defence of duress to show merely that the defendant voluntarily associated with a man of whom he was rather afraid, and took part with him in planning and executing a crime. A defence of duress requires a threat, express or implied, not merely general evidence of fear. Remarkably, counsel for the Crown conceded that it was open to the defendant to raise the defence; equally remarkably, the trial judge accepted this opinion without question, and left the defence to the jury; more remarkably still, the Court of Appeal did not voice even the mildest criticism of the judge's pusillanimity. The court did indeed "doubt" whether counsel for the Crown were right to concede that the question of duress arose; "the words and deeds of King relied on by the defence were far short of those needed to raise a threat of the requisite gravity." But the court went on to say that the Crown having made the concession, the judge was right to leave the question of duress to the jury in the way he did. The puzzle is why the Court of Appeal thought he was right to leave it to them at all. Judges are not bound to accept concessions made by counsel in a criminal case.

Probably the judge left the issue to the jury because he thought they could be relied upon to reject the defence (as they did); and he deemed it safer to leave the question to the jury than to run any risk of having a conviction quashed on appeal. This is simply one more instance of the debilitating effect upon the administration of justice of the Court of Appeal's inability to direct a new trial. If it were known that the Court of Appeal could do this, instead of freeing criminals on technicalities, there would be fewer feeble directions to the jury and fewer unmeritorious appeals. In *Graham*, however, the judge should have been able to satisfy himself that there was no risk in withholding the defence from the jury.

Revolted by a blood-chilling murder, and because the facts were so unfavourable to the defence of duress, the Court of Appeal cudgelled its brains to find ways of debilitating the defence as a matter of law. It expressly left open four questions, thus hinting that in the view of the court they were all possibilities.

> (1) "Whether, in murder, duress, if available, excuses a defendant from criminal liability altogether or only reduces his offence to manslaughter[11];
> (2) whether in murder a fear of physical injury (rather than death) can ever amount to duress;
> (3) to what extent fear of death or injury to persons other than the defendant may be relied upon;
> (4) whether a fear of false imprisonment can be relied upon."

There was nothing on the facts to raise questions 2 and 3, or, it seems, 4; so it can only be surmised that the court was recording for the benefit of future courts all the possible ways in which bits and pieces might be chipped out of the defence. If the courts cannot administer the law properly, a defence like that of duress is bound to raise anxiety. But there was no occasion

[11] The Court of Appeal, in *Graham*, left open the question whether a person acquitted of murder on the ground of duress could still be convicted of manslaughter. It may be taken that the question is not open for abettors. If it had been regarded as a legal possibility, the House of Lords would presumably have substituted a conviction of manslaughter in *Lynch*, but it did not do so; nor did the majority even consider doing so. Their lordships' opinions clearly imported that duress, if available as a defence, is a complete defence. Lord Simon, indeed, suggested that duress should reduce murder to manslaughter, but his was a dissenting speech. The suggestion was approved by Lord Salmon (of the majority) in *Abbott*, so it might be adopted for perpetrators of a killing. See Dennis in 96 LQR 213.

for concern on the facts of *Graham*, because, as the Court of Appeal said, the defence should not have been allowed to come into issue.

Reverting to *Abbott*, the distinction resulting from that decision and *Lynch* does not apply to a charge of attempted murder. It has never been suggested that the defence of duress is denied to the attempted perpetrator of murder. Yet the punishment of attempt is at discretion, while that of murder is fixed by law, so that, on grounds of justice, a defence to the charge of murder is much more important for the person accused of murder than for one accused of attempt to murder. Again, a person who inflicts grievous bodily harm on another can set up a defence of duress; it seems strange that if the victim happens to die, and the charge is murder, the defence should be ousted.[12]

§ 27.3. OTHER LIMITS ON THE DEFENCE OF DURESS

If a person when threatened is able to make resistance or to flee from the wrongdoer, he must of course do so rather than give way to the duress.[1] The facts must be such that there was no way (known to the defendant) of avoiding the threat without committing the infraction or one of greater gravity. If on the uncontradicted evidence the defendant could have made his escape, then, on principle, there is no evidence of duress for the consideration of the jury—though the trial judge may think it safer to leave this question to the jury, while directing them upon it.

Before the surprisingly indulgent decision in *Hudson* it was thought that the defence was not open if the defendant could seek police protection, whether or not the police were able to defend him effectively. Otherwise, a terrorist could confer standing immunity on any timorous citizen for doing terrible deeds.[2]

> In *Hudson*,[3] two girls, aged 19 and 17, committed perjury when giving evidence at a criminal trial, because (they said) of threats of injury made before the trial and the presence in court during it of one of those who had uttered the threats. They were indicted for perjury. The trial judge declined to leave the defence of duress to the jury, on the ground that the girls were in a court of law when they committed the offence, and protection was readily available for them if they had asked for it. They were convicted. The Court of Appeal, however, took the view that the defence ought to have been left to the jury, and the conviction was quashed.[4]

---

[12] Cp. Dennis in 96 LQR 218.

[1] See *Lynch* [1975] AC at 679D.

[2] In *Lynch*, at p. 706A, Lord Edmund-Davies quoted the opinion of the court below that the threat need not be "immediate" if it overbore the will of the defendant at the material time. It seems better to say, with the Law Commission, that it need not be immediate if the defendant had no real opportunity of seeking official protection. A threat of future injury should generally be ruled out for this reason. Cp. Lord Morris at p. 675F, Lord Simon at p. 686B.

[3] [1971] 2 QB 202.

[4] *Contra, Taonis* [1974] Crim.LR 322, where the CA assumed that the traditional restriction was valid, though the appeal before them was only against sentence.

The decision seems to have owed more to the judges' innate chivalry than to a steely-hearted consideration of what public policy required. The girls could have sought police protection immediately after giving evidence; and although they might have thought, with good reason, that the police would not be able to shield them indefinitely, yet that consideration should not be sufficient to support the defence. The Law Commission proposed that duress should not be allowed as a defence if the defendant had an opportunity to seek official protection. This proposal, if accepted, would overrule *Hudson*.

An even graver question arises if a member of the defendant's family is kidnapped and if the defendant is threatened that the victim will be killed or seriously injured if he does not commit some criminal act. The defendant goes to the police, but obviously the police cannot prevent the carrying out of the threat, so the defendant does as the thug tells him. The Law Commission proposed that the defence should again be excluded, by means of a provision that

> "the fact that any official protection which might have been available in the circumstances would or might not have been effective to prevent the harm threatened is immaterial."

This is a severe rule, but it is required by public policy. Otherwise the possibility arises of a man being free in society, programmed to commit a list of heinous crimes without legal sanction because a relative of his has been kidnapped. The recognition of such a rule might even increase kidnappings, and it would probably increase the readiness of the person threatened to comply with the demands.[5]

Suppose that the defendant was very cowardly. Someone with more backbone and intelligence might have seen that the threat was probably only bluff, and might have called the bluff. Is the defendant still allowed the defence?

The defence will be allowed only to those who showed reasonable firmness.

The Law Commission, it will be recalled, accepted an "objective" limitation upon the defence: the threat must be such that the defendant could not reasonably be expected to resist. In *Graham*[6] the Court of Appeal agreed with the limitation; the court left open the question whether a threat of serious physical injury could amount to duress on a charge of murder, and held that even a threat of death was insufficient unless an objective test was satisfied. The court phrased the proper direction to the jury as follows.

> "(1) Was the defendant, or may he have been, impelled to act as he did because, as a result of what he reasonably believed King had said or done, he had good cause to fear

---

[5] A somewhat similar question is capable of arising among people who believe in witchcraft. If X threatens D to kill him by spiritual powers if D does not commit a specific criminal act, and D, having had an opportunity to go to the police, commits the act because of the threat, has he the defence of duress? See *Salaca* [1967] NZLR 421 and note, 31 MLR 84. Obviously the police, according to D's belief, are as helpless as he is; but it seems essential to maintain the principle that he must rely on them.

[6] [1982] 1 WLR at 300G.

that if he did not so act King would kill him or (if this is to be added) cause him serious physical injury? (2) If so, have the prosecution made the jury sure that a sober person of reasonable firmness, sharing the characteristics of the defendant, would not have responded to whatever he reasonably believed King said or did by taking part in the killing? The fact that a defendant's will to resist has been eroded by the voluntary consumption of drink or drugs or both is not relevant to this test."

The direction accepts the test of a person of reasonable firmness (qualifying this by postulating that he is a person "sharing the characteristics of the defendant;" it is impossible to reconcile this wholesale importation of personal characteristics into a supposedly objective test[7]). Whether an objective limitation upon the defence in these terms is necessary or desirable may be doubted. It spoils such precision as the rule for duress would otherwise have. Also, it puts great strain on the notion of reasonableness. Normally, in law, this word implies a value-judgment. Surely, the jury are not to be asked whether it was *moral* for the defendant to give way to the threat; that would be a hard question to answer, and to ask it would largely renounce the decision of the House of Lords in point of policy to allow duress as a defence. There would be the same objection if the jury were asked to consider whether it is *politic* to allow the defence in the circumstances—whether allowing the defence might lead to an increase of terrorism. Policy questions were decided in *Lynch*, and there is nothing left under this head for the consideration of the jury.

Perhaps the Court of Appeal's direction is intended to relate to the degree of risk of the threat being carried out, as it would be estimated by a man of reasonable firmness. But if this is the meaning of the model instruction to the jury it could have been more clearly expressed.[8]

The direction does not explicitly require a threat, but presumably the circumstances envisaged are those in which there would be at least an implied threat.[9] (In view of the absence of evidence of a threat in *Graham* it is surprising that the Court of Appeal did not require the jury to be expressly directed on the point.) The requirement of reasonable firmness would usually mean that the person who thinks he is being threatened by implication must if possible put his fears to the test by trying to temporise, arguing with the person making the demand if this can be done with safety. He will then discover whether or not he is under threat.

Need the villain have instructed the defendant to commit the offence? Suppose the defendant, in fear of the villain, simply committed the offence in his endeavour to get away?

On principle, the offence must be one expressly or impliedly ordered by the villain, the order being backed up by his threat. (Or the defendant must have believed that.)

An illustration of this limit upon the defence is the extraordinary case of *Jones*.[10] Two plain-clothes officers went to investigate Jones, who was sitting in his parked car, at 1.20 a.m. Thinking that they were thugs Jones drove through the built-up area at up to 50 m.p.h., going through traffic lights at the red, and ending up outside a police station where he dashed inside for "safety." He was convicted of dangerous driving and did not appeal. He did not have the defence of duress,

---

[7] The phrase is evidently an echo of Lord Diplock's opinion in *Camplin*, the provocation case (§ 24.4 at n. 8). But Lord Diplock put in an objective criterion ("having the power of self-control to be expected of an ordinary person") of which there is no analogue in the model direction in *Graham*.

[8] Cp. A T H Smith in [1978] Crim.LR 123–125.

[9] Previous authorities assumed that there must be a threat, express or implied. No express threat was uttered in *Lynch*, but the person who gave the order was a ruthless gunman, and the manner of his instructions indicated that he would tolerate no disobedience. Cp. [1975] AC at 679B, C. There was therefore evidence from which a threat could be implied; but it was a totally different case from *Graham*, where evidence of a threat or even of an instruction appears to have been completely lacking.

[10] (1963) The Times, December 18.

because he had not been ordered to drive dangerously, and did not think he had been. He did not have the defence of self-defence, since that defence is presumably available only in respect of acts done against an aggressor, or one thought to be an aggressor. Dangerous driving affected the public at large. But (1) at that time of night there would have been little danger to the public—surely much less than the danger feared by the defendant for himself; so why was it not a case of necessity? (2) The charge would now be for careless driving or reckless driving, both of which involve an evaluation of the defendant's conduct in all the circumstances. Might it not be held that his conduct was reasonable on the facts as he believed them to be?[11]

§ 27.4. COMPULSION OF CIRCUMSTANCES

If the reason for allowing the defence of duress is the unlikelihood that the law's threats will be effective on a person who is wrongfully threatened with death or serious injury, the same reason should support a defence where the duress arises not from human threat but from pressure of circumstances. This is another way of looking at some (by no means all) cases of necessity, and it should be a valid argument even if the courts reject a general defence of necessity. The defence has been named compulsion of circumstances.[1] It would operate not theoretically as a justification (as necessity is) but as an excuse, similar to the excuse of duress; and this may make it more palatable to some people on facts like those in *Dudley*, where the moralist may be unwilling to accord a justification but will accord an excuse. Our courts have not so far had to consider the argument, and they can be expected to view it with extreme reserve, as they do with all proposals to extend defences. Nevertheless, the analogy with duress may be persuasive.[2]

Instances of the suggested defence are the following.

- In *Jones* the defendant was in the same state of fear as if he had been ordered by a thug at gunpoint to drive at that speed. So why should the law distinguish between traditional cases of duress and such a case of compulsion of circumstances?
- Suppose that in the *Mignonette's* boat there was an armed man who threatened to shoot Dudley if he did not hold the cabin boy down while his throat was cut. On the authority of *Lynch* Dudley should have the defence of duress if he complied with the demand. The

---

[11] See § 26.1 at n. 5.

[1] See generally George P Fletcher in 47 SCalif.LRev. 1269, and in his *Rethinking Criminal Law* 818–829, 834–835.

[2] In *Lynch* [1975] AC 653, which accepted duress as a defence to a charge of abetting murder, Lord Wilberforce (of the majority) and Lords Simon and Kilbrandon (dissenting) agreed that duress is generally a defence and that necessity is a defence resting on the same principle; Lord Simon in particular said (at p. 692G) that duress is "merely an application of the doctrine of 'necessity' ", quoting my *General Part*. I formerly held this view, and have since repented of it; I now think that the two doctrines rest on different foundations. All the same, they are closely similar in practical effect; and if the three lords had spoken of "compulsion of circumstances" instead of "necessity" the analogy would be even closer.

Incidentally, it is useful to have this support for the defence of necessity from the three lords. If it comes to be held that necessity, like duress (§ 27.2), is no defence to the perpetrator of murder but is to an accessory, it would follow that, as between Dudley and his companion Stephens, the one who wielded the knife would have had no defence while the one who did not would have. The objections to such a distinction are obvious, and they are just as powerful in relation to duress.

reason why he is allowed the defence is that he cannot be expected to resist. Then why should he not be allowed a defence if his fear arises from the circumstances in which he finds himself?

- Even if a defence is rejected in the case just put, it might be allowed where a threatening emergency arises affecting the victim equally with his killer, and a fair criterion is used to enable one to survive when this has to be at the expense of the other (as where lots are drawn).
- Cases of involuntary "aggression" may be treated in the same way. The notion of an involuntary aggressor would include the mountaineer whose weight is dragging another to his death (where the rope may be cut), and other instances where it is the existence of the victim that is specifically creating the danger to the person who kills him. This might be extended to cover Bacon's suppositional case about the plank.[3]
- The same might possibly apply in a variant of the plank case, where a swimmer dislodges the swimmer who is in possession of the plank. If is not a case of necessity (since there is an equality of evil), or of defence; but an excuse might be allowed, on the principle *sauve qui peut*, because legal regulation seems hopeless.[4]

It will be seen that other defences may fail to apply to cases like the foregoing, and yet they fall in some degree under similar principles to those of established defences. The examples are distinguished from general cases of necessity in that they involve fear of death or serious injury, and do not necessarily involve a choice of the lesser evil from the public point of view. They are distinguished from duress in that the fear is not caused by an illegal threat.

The argument for recognising an excuse holds even where the defendant has chosen what is on utilitarian theory the greater evil. Consider the following hypotheticals.

> D, driving along a narrow road with a sheer drop on one side, suddenly finds two drunkards fallen senseless in front of him. (1) By his side is a terrorist, fleeing from the police; he forces D at gunpoint to drive over the two drunks. D has the defence of duress, at any rate if he only injures the men. (2) But suppose there is no terrorist, and no duress, but D's brakes fail, and he is faced with the choice of either running down and killing the two drunks or himself plunging to his death over the cliff. D chooses to stay on the road.[5]

Necessity could not possibly justify in case (2), if utilitarian principles are applied, since it is a case of two-for-one. Nor is it a case of duress, unless that concept is extended to compulsion of circumstances. Yet the argument for such an excuse is in all relevant respects the same as for the excuse of duress.

§ 27.5. OTHER FORMS OF COMPULSION

There is a defence of coercion, akin to but distinct from duress, which is open only to married women who act under coercion from their husbands and in their husband's presence; it does not extend to treason or murder.[1] Details have not been clarified by the courts because the defence is rarely raised; but a circuit judge recently left it to the jury in general terms, explaining that it included "moral coercion," the only condition being that the wife must prove that her "will was overborne" so that she was "forced unwillingly to participate."[2] The Law Commission has recommended the abolition of the defence.[3]

---

[3] § 26.3 at n. 11.
[4] See Cross in 3 Univ. of Tas.LRev. 8.
[5] The problem is posed by Kadish, Schulhofer and Paulsen, *Criminal Law and its Processes,* 4th edn 798.

[1] See *The General Part*, 2nd edn § 248; *Lynch* [1975] AC at 694D. 713A.
[2] *Richman* [1982] Crim.LR 507.
[3] Arguments in favour of continuing the defence are advanced by Pace in [1979] Crim.LR 82.

The question whether the control exercised by a hypnotist can be a defence to the patient has not come before our courts.[4]

SUMMARY

Duress is accepted as an excuse; and, as usual, the evidential burden rests on the defendant. The preferable view is that duress in this connection is limited to threats of death or serious injury or (possibly) torture, whether to the defendant or to a third party (or the defendant must reasonably believe in the existence of such a threat). § .1

Treason is not an exception. The defence is open even to a person who abets murder (*Lynch*, HL). But according to the Judicial Committee in *Abbott*, duress is no defence to a person charged as "principal in the first degree" to murder; and the Board attached an untraditionally wide meaning to this phrase, including within it even an assistant who "took an active part in the killing." In *Graham* the CA did not disapprove of the judge's having left the defence to the jury where the defendant was a perpetrator of the killing, but the court suggested a number of qualifications that may possibly be imposed upon it hereafter. The defence is not open to those who have voluntarily become members of an illegal organisation. § .2

The defence presupposes that the defendant could not escape. The usual view is that a person threatened must seek police protection if possible, though *Hudson* is an indulgent decision the other way. Further, the defence is allowed only if the defendant showed reasonable firmness (*Graham*). § .3

It is argued that the courts should accept an excuse of compulsion of circumstances, analogous to duress. § .4

The wife's defence of coercion by her husband who is present at the time is still available, though rarely raised; it includes "moral coercion." § .5

[4] For brief discussions see *The General Part*, 2nd edn § 250; James Marshall in 52 Virginia LRev. 1267–1269.

CHAPTER 28

CRIMINAL CAPACITY

> The misery of the insane more thoroughly excites our pity than any other suffering to which humanity is subject; but it is necessary that the madness should be acknowledged to be madness before the pity can be felt.
>
> Trollope, *He Knew he was Right*

§ 28.1. STATE IMMUNITIES

CERTAIN persons are exempted from the operation of the criminal law, or from its effects, on the ground of official status: foreign visiting sovereigns, foreign diplomats, and members of foreign armed forces (apart from special arrangements by statute).

A rule of construction of statutes declares that they do not bind the Crown in the absence of express words or necessary implication, and this sometimes has the result of exempting officers of the Crown from the operation of penal statutes when such officers are acting on behalf of the Crown. Apart from this rule, officers of the Crown are fully subject to the criminal law in their private capacity (that is to say, they are liable to pay any fine themselves, unless the Crown does so *ex gratia*). The Crown itself cannot be prosecuted, for that would be *Regina* v. *Reginam,* which is thought to be impossible (it is not, of course); and the same rule applies in favour of Government Departments and other Crown agencies. On the other hand, some public bodies are not regarded as emanations of the Crown.

The immunity of the Crown is an indefensible exception from the rule of law. It means, for example, that Government Departments and certain other public bodies are generally not bound by public welfare legislation. Thus hospitals and some places of education are regarded as being exempt from the Health and Safety at Work Act. However, the Road Traffic Act 1972 is an exception, because it expressly binds the Crown in respect of many of its provisions. The problem of enforcement is solved by an interesting device: if proceedings are brought in relation to a vehicle in the public services of the Crown, the appropriate Department nominates someone as the person who causes or permits the vehicle to be on the road, and who can be treated in the proceedings as though he were the employer.[1] (Of course, the Crown will pay any fine, etc, imposed upon him.) In one case where a Department nominated the senior civil servant in overall control of thousands of vehicles operated by the Department as the statutory whipping-boy, a Divisional Court questioned the propriety of a procedure that could result in a single person undeservedly collecting a phenomenal number of road traffic convictions; and the court suggested that the Departments might instead nominate the fictitious defendant John Doe.[2]

These matters are discussed more fully in larger or more specialised

---

[1] S. 188 (8), (9). See [1981] Crim. LR 416.
[2] *Barnett* v. *French* [1981] 1 WLR 848. For some technical hitches see 145 JPN 190.

works, including works on constitutional and international law, and need not concern us further.

§ 28.2. CHILDHOOD

No one under 10 (the tenth birthday) is criminally responsible.[1]

The authorities have a choice between bringing criminal and civil proceedings. Youngsters of any age up to 17 can be brought before the juvenile court in civil proceedings as being in need of care. (The juvenile court is a specially constituted magistrates' court.) The proceedings can be brought by the local authority, a constable or authorised person (in effect an officer of the National Society for the Prevention of Cruelty to Children), if he is satisfied that one of a number of conditions is fulfilled. One of the conditions (generally known as "the offence condition") is that the child or young person[2] is guilty of an offence (excluding homicide) and that he is in need of care and control which he is unlikely to receive unless the court makes an order.[3] But care proceedings are rarely used with respect to the offence condition, it being thought preferable to charge the youngster criminally if he is of the age of criminal responsibility. Care proceedings are not supposed to be punitive, but the child and his parents are likely to see them as that if they are brought specifically in respect of an offence; so it is best that for offences the ordinary criminal procedure should be used.

Criminal proceedings against children and young persons can generally be brought only in the juvenile court, but a juvenile is triable in the adult court for homicide, or where he is a young person and the offence charged is of certain grave kinds, or where he is charged jointly with an adult.[4] Before prosecuting, the police must inform the local authority, which is then under a responsibility to make investigations and provide the court with a "social enquiry report" in respect of the juvenile, unless they are of opinion that it is unnecessary to do so (i.e. in trivial cases).

A number of police forces, including the Metropolitan Police, have established Juvenile Bureaux, a centralised system for obtaining information about juvenile offenders and deciding how best to deal with them. The bureau will usually obtain a report on the juvenile from the local authority social service department, the probation service and the educational welfare service; and a bureau officer may visit the home. The senior police officer will then decide whether to prosecute, or to administer a caution, or to take no action. Before a caution may be administered the police have to be satisfied that they have sufficient evidence to justify a prosecution, the victim and the juvenile's parents must agree to the matter being dealt with by way of caution, and the juvenile must admit the offence. The caution is administered formally by a senior officer in uniform.

What is the magic of the age of 10? Why not 12, or 14, or 16?

The age at common law was 7. It was raised to 10 in 1933, and general opinion is now against raising it further.[5]

Of course any age must be arbitrary. The governing considerations are pragmatic. At what age does one wish to be able to administer legal

---

[1] Children and Young Persons Act 1933 s. 50, as amended by CYPA 1963 s. 16.

[2] In statutory language, a "child" is a person up to 14, "a young person" one who is between 14 and 17 (these figures, as always, indicating birthdays). The two groups together are sometimes referred to in statutes as "juveniles." For sentencing purposes there are also "young adults" (17–21).

[3] CYPA 1969 s. 1 (2) (*f*).

[4] CYPA 1969 s. 6 as amended; CLA 1977 s. 34. See Richman in 143 JPN 130.

[5] CYPA 1969 s. 4 makes it (generally) 14, but that provision has not been brought into force owing to a change of policy since the Act was passed.

punishment to a juvenile? Even if it is only to be a fine, or sending him to an attendance centre or detention centre, still if the outcome is to be punitive in intent this implies that the offender must be legally responsible. Precocious children get to know the age of criminal responsibility and are quite apt to say to a policeman: "You can't touch me. I'm under 10." Even if punitive sanctions are intended to be used only for particularly bad offenders, they still imply that criminal responsibility must be attributed to offenders of that age. (It is true that punishment could be meted out in nominally civil proceedings, or by way of school discipline under legal auspices. But the abandonment of criminal procedure would carry some danger of either injustice or ineffectiveness or both.)

Although children are criminally responsible from the age of 10, those under 14 receive the benefit of an archaic rule of the common law that a child in this age-group cannot be convicted, however uncontrollable he is, unless he knew that what he was doing was wrong—which seems to mean either legally wrong or morally wrong.[6]

Juvenile courts generally manage to pay little respect to the rule, but it is forced upon their attention from time to time by pronouncements of the judges. A particulaly regrettable feature is that the courts have failed to place an evidential burden on the defence to show lack of "mischievous discretion" as it is called.[7] So the defending advocate can submit no case on the basis that the prosecution, forbidden to cross-examine the child at a stage when he has not yet elected to give evidence, have adduced no evidence on the subject.

The rule is also perverse in the discrimination it makes between children from good homes and bad. The child from a good home who does mischief on an isolated occasion is readily found to have known better, and therefore to be criminally responsible (though in his case, with anxious parents, the intervention of the law may be unnecessary), whereas the child from a thoroughly bad home with neglectful parents, lacking knowledge of ordinary moral notions, who most needs the curb of the law, in default of any other, gets the full benefit of the presumption. Once he is convicted, the child's conviction can be given in evidence against him to prove mischievous discretion (at least if the conviction is on a matter broadly similar to that with which he is now charged)[8]; but to give it in evidence is objectionable on the ground that it puts evidence before the magistrates that is prejudicial if they have to resolve, as a disputed issue, whether the child did the act attributed to him.

The rule is a survival from a time when children were treated punitively by the courts, and is long overdue for abolition. Nowadays, courts in dealing with children and young persons are enjoined by statute to "have regard to the welfare of the child or young person,"[9] but this does not say that such welfare is the *only* consideration. The courts look, or ought to look, to the protection of society, but an effort is made to eliminate punitive aspects, except, sometimes, in relation to particular deterrence.

A great deal of law limits the use of adult punishments for juvenile offenders and provides special forms of disposal for them.[10] In order to limit the size of this book questions of sentencing are in general being excluded. Consequently, nothing further need be said here on juveniles.

---

[6] [1954] Crim.LR 493.

[7] See *JBH and JH (Minors)* v. *O'Connell* [1981] Crim.LR 632, and critical commentary there and in 145 JPN 571.

[8] *R* v. *B* [1979] 1 WLR 1185, 3 All ER 460. See Fisher in 130 NLJ 752.

[9] CYPA 1933 s. 44 (1) as amended.

[10] See Cross and Ashworth, *The English Sentencing System*, 3rd edn, read with the amendments in CJA 1982 Part I.

Childhood and mental disorder raise problems of responsibility, and we must consider further what we mean by this term.

§ 28.3. RESPONSIBILITY AND MENTAL DISORDER

"Responsible" is used in different meanings. An employer giving a reference to an employee may say that he is a "responsible person," meaning that he is of good character, efficient in work, and so on. Obviously that is not the meaning of "responsibility" in the criminal law. The worse a person's character is (that is to say, the more irresponsible he is), the more firmly he must be held "responsible" in the sense of "accountable."

We are speaking, therefore, of responsibility in the sense of moral or legal accountability. A person is *morally* responsible if he can justly be blamed and perhaps punished when he does wrong. We do not regard a dog as responsible, or a babe in arms, or a gibbering lunatic. On much the same principle they are not regarded as *legally* responsible, i.e. legally liable to punishment through the agency of the courts.

Society has two alternative ways of dealing with mischief-makers. Normally we regard them as responsible, which means that they can be left free in society, subject to punishment when they misbehave, the punishment being designed either to correct the offender for the future or to serve as a warning to others, or both. But there are those (young children, and the very severely mentally ill or retarded) whom we think it would be useless or wrong to treat in this way. Although they are not responsible, the fact that they are not subject to punishment through the courts does not mean that they are left without social control. Undisciplined small children can be made subject to a care order, and mentally disordered people can be put into hospital. For adults, legal non-responsibility is far from being an enviable state. Occasionally it may be more desirable than being punished, but often it is not.

How is it determined whether a mentally disordered person is responsible in law?

I will start by telling you how it cannot be determined. A frequent misunderstanding is that a psychiatrist is able, merely by examining a man and applying psychiatric or psychological principles, to decide whether he was legally responsible when he did a particular deed. The enquiry cannot be made in these terms, since responsibility (in the absence of further definition) is not a scientific or objective fact. Only when the law has supplied factual criteria of responsibility can the psychiatrist's report assist in deciding the question of legal responsibility.

A further general observation is that the question of responsibility can be dodged, or deprived of much of its significance, by blurring the responsible/non-responsible distinction. This is now what the law largely does. Offenders (i.e. legally responsible wrongdoers) can generally be treated by a court as if they were non-responsible: they can be sent to hospital, or simply discharged, instead of being punished. Conversely, people who could claim non-responsibility may be punished if (as may quite understandably happen) they do not choose to rely upon their immunity. These matters must occupy us in more detail.

The subject of mental disorder as it appears to the lawyer is closely connected with admission to a mental hospital, the current euphemism for which is "psychiatric hospital." There are two kinds of such hospital: psychiatric hospitals (or general hospitals with psychiatric wings) operating under the National Health Service (NHS), and "special hospitals" (secure hospitals) under the Department of Health and Social Security (DHSS).[1] The relevant legislation is chiefly the Mental Health Act 1983.[2]

The police may decide not to charge a minor offender who is mentally disturbed, and may permit him to return to his relatives or to enter hospital voluntarily ("informally"). Or a person may in some cases (e.g. if he is mentally ill) be compulsorily admitted to hospital on medical certificate without court proceedings (civil commitment[3]), whether he has committed an offence or not.[4]

The commitment (or, in legal terms, admission) to hospital may be "for assessment," under a comparatively simple procedure, or "for treatment." The latter requires two medical certificates, which (in the case of mentally ill patients) must certify that the admission is necessary for the health or safety of the patient or for the protection of other persons.[5]

So much for hospitalisation outside the criminal process. In addition, certain procedures apply specifically to persons suspected of criminal acts.

- If a person is charged with an offence and remanded in custody (i.e. to prison) before trial or sentence, he may be transferred to hospital by administrative direction.[6]
- If he is put on trial he may be found by a jury to be unfit to stand trial ("unfit to plead," "insane on arraignment"), in which case he must be sent to such hospital as the Home Secretary directs.[7]
- If he is tried, he may succeed on an insanity defence, when again the court must send him to hospital.
- If the defence is not set up, or is rejected by the jury or magistrates, the defendant can still (in many cases) be sent to hospital by the judge or magistrates.
- Or, if sent to prison, he can be administratively transferred to hospital, but this will not in practice be done unless the mental disorder is "frank" and the defendant is obviously an unsuitable person to be kept in prison.

---

[1] Confusingly, the Department of Health and Social *Security* is presided over by the Secretary of State for Social Services.

[2] See Gostin in 132 NLJ 1151.

[3] An informal and unofficial term.

[4] MHA 1983 Pt. II.

[5] MHA 1983 s. 3.

[6] MHA s. 48.

[7] Criminal Procedure (Insanity) Act 1964 ss. 4, 5 (1) (*c*) and Sched. 1. A deaf and dumb person who cannot communicate can also be found to be unfit to stand trial.

Of all these various possibilities, only the insanity defence raises a question of responsibility in the technical legal sense. To discuss it, we must consider the kinds of mental disorder.

§ 28.4. WHEN MENTAL DISORDER IS A DEFENCE

"Mental disorder" is the widest possible expression for disorder of mind: it is much too wide to be recognised as a complete defence to a charge of crime. The definition in the Mental Health Act 1983 s. 1 (2) is as follows.

> "In this Act 'mental disorder' means mental illness, arrested or incomplete development of mind, psychopathic disorder and any other disorder or disability of mind."

The concluding words are so wide that they cover a mere neurosis, such as claustrophobia (fear of confined spaces). If a claustrophobic on Dartmoor punches someone on the nose, his malady is no reason for letting him off a charge.

It would not be causally connected with the assault. But suppose the claustrophobic panicked when he was in a car, and struck out?

Even then he would not have a defence, though the medical evidence would no doubt induce the court to treat him leniently.

But surely insanity is a defence?

The general principle of English law may sound strange: even those mentally disordered people who may be called insane can be held responsible. Insanity *per se* is not a defence.

What if the man was completely off his head and did not know what he was doing?

In that case he would lack the mental element necessary for the crime.

The law still rests on the answers given by the House of Lords in *McNaghten's* case (1843).[1] The facts that gave rise to this famous pronouncement are now only of historical interest, but may be mentioned briefly.

> One Daniel McNaghten shot Sir Robert Peel's secretary, perhaps thinking that it was Peel himself. McNaghten, who suffered from what today would be called paranoia, was actuated by the morbid delusion that he was being persecuted by "Tories." He was acquitted on the ground of insanity, being committed to hospital in the usual way; but the supposed leniency of the verdict caused a public outcry. The law of insanity was debated in the House of Lords, and their lordships decided to require the judges to advise them on the relevant legal

[1] 10 Cl. & F 200, 8 ER 718. The spelling of the defendant's name varies. For convenience I have adopted one of the two versions used in the Law Reports, though it is probably wrong. See generally *Daniel McNaughton: His Trial and its Aftermath*, ed. D J West and A Walker (London 1977).

principles. This is an ancient right of the House of Lords, no longer exercised; and it is subject to some theoretical difficulty, because technically the answers given by the judges, divorced from a consideration of any particular case, are not binding as a precedent. The joint answer given by fourteen judges as a result of the *McNaghten* case has, however, been so frequently followed and approved that it must be taken as authoritative, at any rate for the most part.

The answer reads, in its essential portion, as follows. (I have inserted the lettering and numbering.)

> "The jurors ought to be told in all cases that every man is to be presumed to be sane, and to possess a sufficient degree of reason to be responsible for his crimes, until the contrary be proved to their satisfaction; and that to establish a defence on the ground of insanity, it must be clearly proved that, (A) at the time of the committing of the act, the party accused was labouring under such a defect of reason, from disease of the mind, (B) as not to know (1) the nature and quality of the act he was doing, or, if he did know it, (2) that he did not know he was doing what was wrong."
>
> The judges added (3) that if the defendant "labours under [a] partial delusion only, and is not in other respects insane, we think he must be considered in the same situation as to responsibility as if the facts with respect to which the delusion exists were real."

The judges' explanation was as follows.

> "For example, if under the influence of his delusion he supposes another man to be in the act of attempting to take away his life, and he kills that man, as he supposes, in self-defence, he would be exempt from punishment. If his delusion was that the deceased had inflicted a serious injury to his character and fortune, and he killed him in revenge for such supposed injury, he would be liable to punishment."[2]

This answer lays down a double test for exemption. (A) The defendant must have been suffering from "a defect of reason, from disease of the mind." (B) If he was, there are two or perhaps three further questions for the jury.

1 Is it the case that, in consequence of this defect of reason, the defendant did not know the nature and quality of his act?
2 If he did, did he not know it was wrong?
3 Was he under a delusion?—if that question can ever arise, having regard to question 1.

Although the *McNaghten* rules save the defendant from criminal liability, they do not, of course, protect him from being sent to hospital. In fact, as we shall see, if he succeeds in the defence he *must* be sent to hospital.

What is "a defect of reason, from disease of the mind"?

"Disease of the mind" is no longer in medical use, though doctors

---

[2] 10 Cl. & F at 211, 8 ER at 723. Daniel McNaghten was acquitted by the jury, before the formulation of the rules now associated with his name; but under those rules he should have been convicted.

(psychiatrists) are still prepared to humour the lawyers by saying in court that a particular person suffers or does not suffer from it. The current medical phrases are mental illness and (a wider expression) mental disorder. But these do not precisely indicate the meaning of "disease of the mind."

The judges in *McNaghten* appear to have used the phrase convertibly with "insanity," but this is an equally baffling expression. Lawyers used to believe that insanity was a medical term, yet psychiatrists have long declared that they do not know what it means, and assert that it can only be a legal concept, which in fact it is. Insanity is a social judgment founded upon, but not precisely representing, a medical diagnosis.

A *rough* medical translation is "psychosis," meaning the more serious kinds of mental illness, generally involving hallucinations or delusions.[3] Examples of psychoses are schizophrenia, manic-depressive psychosis and cerebral[4] arteriosclerosis. A deep depression is psychotic if it involves an irrationally bleak prophecy of future prospects. There is a classification of mental disorders, accepted as authoritative, in *Glossary of Mental Disorders and Guide to their Classifcation,* published by the World Health Organization (1974).

All this makes the practical legal position very confused. Some judges still imagine that "disease of the mind" is a concept to be applied or not applied by the jury merely on the say-so of a medical witness. Some medical witnesses still imagine that they are perfectly free to exercise their own idiosyncratic judgment on whether or not to apply the label in the particular case. They may say to themselves: "this man is mentally ill, or brain damaged, therefore he has what these legal chaps still call a disease of the mind." The conclusion does not necessarily represent the legal position. I am conscious that these remarks do not give a helpful answer to your enquiry, but we shall return to it in the next chapter.

As said before, the three *McNaghten* questions are principally concerned with *mens rea. McNaghten* was decided at a time when this doctrine was still cloudy. Looking back, we can see that the judges' answers amount to little more than an assertion that the defendant cannot be convicted without the necessary mental element. Question 1, "Did he know the nature and quality of his act?" means "Did he know what he was doing?" (Did he know that he was killing someone; did he know that he was sticking a knife into someone; did he know he was burning someone's house down?) This is a *mens rea* question.

Suppose that the defendant attacked someone in the insane belief that he was acting in self-defence. He knew he was hitting the victim on the head. Would he be said to have known the nature and quality of his act?

If an insanity defence is raised in such a case it may be held that since the defendant did not apprehend all the circumstances relevant to liability for the crime, he has the defence under question 1. But if the judge is in any doubt as to the law he can instruct the jury under question 3, the delusion question, and this clearly lets the defendant out. Had the facts been as he supposed, it would not have been a crime.

What is the difference between a delusion and a mistake?

The psychotic patient with a delusion persists in his false belief despite evidence to the contrary which an ordinary person of that age, religious belief and culture would accept.

---

[3] A hallucination is a disturbed perception—the patient hears "voices" or sees apparitions. A delusion is a belief resulting from disturbed thinking, such as the paranoia suffered by McNaghten.

[4] Pronounced "*ser*ebral."

It can be a difficult distinction. The psychiatrist may have to assess (for example) whether the defendant was labouring under an insane delusion that his brother was trying to kill him, or a stupid suspicion to the same effect. The answer may depend on the degree of absurdity of the belief, the tenacity with which it was held in the face of the evidence, etc. In practice a delusion is not a single false belief, but spreads out into abnormal beliefs over a segment of life.

In sum, the *McNaghten* rules can be read as saying little more than that insanity may negative *mens rea*. However, they are not well framed to express this. In particular, question 3 (whether the defendant laboured under a partial delusion) is misleading. It suggests that although the defendant may not be liable in full degree he may be liable in some lesser degree. Normally, at least, this is not so. If his delusion was as to some ingredient legally necessary for the crime, he cannot be convicted.

The only one of the *McNaghten* rules not going to *mens rea* as that is now understood is question 2, relating to knowledge of wrong. This is held to mean knowledge of *legal* wrong.[5] Unless very benevolently interpreted it adds almost nothing to the other questions. The reason for saying this is that in practice insanity is never set up in the Crown Court except on charges of the gravest crimes; and a person would have to be very deranged not to know that killing or stabbing a person or burning a house is illegal: so deranged that the jury would probably refuse to find that he knew what he was doing.

The judges' opinion puts the burden of proving mental disorder having the specified consequences upon the defendant, but the proposition that the defence must be "clearly" proved is no longer accepted. All that is required is the usual degree of proof required of a defendant when the burden is on him—proof on the balance of probability.[6]

When mental disorder negatives the mental element required for the crime, it knocks away the case for the prosecution. Since the burden rests on the prosecution to prove the mental element, surely it should be for the prosecution to negative a McNaghten defence, not for the defendant to prove it.

That would be the logical view.[7] It is not the present law, but the CLRC proposed that it should be enacted as law.[8] Their recommendation has been repeated by the Butler Committee on Mentally Abnormal Offenders.[9]

§ 28.5. THE SPECIAL VERDICT

Where insanity negatives the mental element necessary for the crime, it might seem that the defendant would be entitled to an ordinary acquittal. Not so. The verdict returned by the jury is one of "not guilty by reason of insanity,"[1] known more succinctly as the special verdict.[2] It finds that the

[5] *Windle* [1952] 2 QB 826.
[6] *Sodeman* [1916] 2 All ER 1138.
[7] It was accepted as law in *Pantelic* (1973) 1 ACTR at 5, 21 FLR at 257 (Aus.).
[8] 11th Report, Cmnd. 4991 of 1972 para. 140.
[9] Cmnd. 6244 of 1975 para. 18.39.

[1] Criminal Procedure (Insanity) Act 1964 s. 1.
[2] Distinguish the other sense of this expression: where the jury find the facts and leave the decision to the judge, as in *Dudley*, § 26.3.

defendant did the act[3] (otherwise the verdict would be a plain not guilty), but fell within the *McNaghten* rules. Since a homicidal maniac cannot be automatically set at large, the law since 1800 has been that the judge must order the defendant to be detained. This is known as mandatory commitment. Formerly he was detained at the "pleasure" of the Sovereign (acting on the advice of the Home Secretary); now he is explicitly subjected to the discretion of the Home Secretary. The terms of the order are that the defendant be admitted to a hospital specified by the Home Secretary,[4] where he will remain until the Home Secretary otherwise directs. Detention is frequently in a special hospital (Broadmoor, Rampton or Moss Side), but may be in a local psychiatric hospital.

Although the verdict of insanity is one of acquittal, an appeal against it is now given by statute.[5] The right of appeal is not likely to be exercised except in the rare cases where the defendant fought in the alternative for an acquittal or a special verdict.[6]

One thing puzzles me. If the McNaghten rules amount to little more than a denial of mens rea, why can't the defendant say: 'I am not setting up a defence of insanity. I am denying mens rea, with the aid of medical evidence, and although I may be a bit wonky upstairs I want an ordinary acquittal, not your poisoned gift of an insanity verdict"?

It depends upon what you mean by "wonky upstairs." If the mental disorder was a temporary affliction, you are right in suggesting that the defendant may sometimes get a clean acquittal; this is under the doctrine of automatism to be discussed in the next chapter. But if the defendant was insane it is different. The law now accepted is that if defending counsel adduces evidence that the defendant's mind was disordered at the time of the deed, for the purpose of negativing *mens rea*, counsel for the Crown may show that the particular abnormality from which the defendant was suffering amounted to insanity in law, in order to prevent him from being set at large.

The point was overlooked in *Charlson*.[7]

> Charlson suddenly hit his son over the head with a mallet, for no obvious reason. He was a devoted father, and all he could say about his act was that he remembered doing something dreadful to his son. A number of charges were brought, including attempted murder and unlawful wounding, and the defence set up was "automatism" and not insanity. Evidence was given by the prison doctor to the effect that though Charlson was not suffering from a disease of the mind, and was sane, he might be suffering from a

[3] This must be understood to mean "went through the motions alleged against him." In *Sullivan* § 29.2 n. 9 the CA said that if the defendant did not know what he was doing, in no legal sense could his physical movements be said to be his acts; nevertheless, the court recognised that the insanity defence would be available, and assumed that there would be a special verdict—not noticing that the special verdict must find that the relevant "act" was committed. The only possible explanation is that the Act of 1964, like the legislation that it replaced, used the word "act" in a sense that was "no legal sense."

[4] *Ibid*. s. 5 (1), as amended. At one time the person so detained was called a "criminal lunatic"; later the kinder expression "pleasure patient" was used (since detention was during the King's pleasure). The Act of 1964 discontinues the reference to the Sovereign's pleasure.

[5] Criminal Appeal Act 1968 s. 12.

[6] As where the defendant argued that, although he was insane, the injury he inflicted was necessary in self-defence. The CA may, if it allows the appeal in such circumstances, order the defendant to be admitted to hospital for assessment, with or without treatment: CAA 1968 s. 14 (2), as amended. Another instance is where the defendant set up a defence of diminished responsibility which was countered by evidence of insanity on the part of the prosecution: see Chap. 29.

[7] [1955] 1 WLR 317, 1 All ER 859.

cerebral tumour which could be the cause of impulsive acts of violence over which he would have no control. Barry J directed the jury that only the defendant could raise the question of insanity, which he had not done, and that they could not convict him unless they were satisfied that he knew what he was doing at the material time. On this, the jury returned a verdict of "not guilty," and Charlson was discharged.

The direction by the learned judge was seriously defective.

1 The medical evidence does not seem to have gone far enough to establish loss of awareness, and the usual view is that a mere tendency to explosive outbursts does not negative intention, however sympathetically the judge may view it when he comes to considering the disposal of the defendant.

2 It is not for a medical witness to decide conclusively what amounts to legal insanity. The fact that a particular doctor chooses to restrict the term "disease of the mind" to functional mental disorder is no reason why the law should exclude from the concept of insanity cases of physical pathology. The general medical opinion, as expressed in the *Glossary of Mental Disorders,* is that a psychosis may be either functional or organic—and doctors hope that in the end an organic basis will be found for all the psychoses.

3 A defendant who gives evidence of what he describes as non-insane automatism should be regarded as putting his sanity in issue whether he wishes to do so or not, so as to make it possible for the prosecution to give evidence of insanity, or to argue that the evidence of the defendant himself shows insanity.

The proper outcome of *Charlson* would have been either (*a*) a conviction, for reason 1 above, with a sentence allowing the unfortunate man to enter hospital for an operation on the tumour, if that was the recommended remedy, and otherwise a psychiatric hospital order, or (*b*) a verdict of insanity, for reasons 2 and 3 above, with persuasion directed to the Home Secretary (if any were needed) to permit the same course as in (*a*) above.

The ruling of Devlin J (now Lord Devlin) in *Kemp*[8] is now generally accepted as expressing the true view of the law.

Kemp inflicted an injury on his wife at a time when he was suffering from arterio-sclerosis, and, according to all the medical witnesses, did not know what he was doing. This disease sometimes diminishes the flow of blood to the brain, and so causes the patient to perform acts of violence during a state of impaired consciousness. The defence did not contend that the disease amounted to insanity, but attempted to get the best of both worlds by arguing that it negatived *mens rea* while not requiring a special verdict. Devlin J ignored the differing linguistic preferences of the medical witnesses who had been called before him, and ruled that on the medical evidence arterio-sclerosis could amount to a disease of the mind within the *McNaghten* rules. His ruling is evidently a departure from the view in *Kemp*.

In *Bratty*,[9] Lord Denning considered these two rulings, and expressed a preference for the view of Devlin J.

You said that insanity defences are rare in the Crown Court. Do I gather that the reason is that defendants prefer to be convicted rather than to be detained in hospital at the sweet will of the Home Secretary?

That is one reason. The Home Secretary is naturally cautious in allowing the discharge of people who did dreadful violence while insane. Of course, if a person is charged with murder and chooses to allow himself to be convicted, he will have a mandatory sentence of life imprisonment, which

[8] [1957] 1 QB 399. Cp. *Holmes* [1960] WAR 122 (Aus.); *Pantelic* (1973) 1 ACTR 1, 21 FLR 253 (Aus.).

[9] [1963] AC at 411–412; cp. *Shields* [1967] VR 706 (Aus.). The opinion is combated by Berthan Macaulay in [1963] Crim.LR 817; cp. [1964] *ibid*. 243.

will again be at the what you term the sweet will of the Home Secretary. But what the mentally disordered defendant can now do is to set up a defence of diminished responsibility instead of insanity; we shall see the advantage of this defence in Chapter 30.

There are two subsidiary reasons for the neglect of the *McNaghten* defence. As has been seen, the insanity defence, unless indulgently interpreted, is extremely narrow. In only a tiny proportion of cases can it be said that the defendant attacked someone or set fire to a building but, by reason of mental illness, did not know what he was doing or that it was illegal. Again, some defendants dislike the stigma of a finding of insanity more than they dislike a criminal conviction. They would rather be thought bad than mad. Nor is it only a question of stigma. Some people who have sampled both prison and psychiatric hospital assert a preference for prison. The company and conditions are better. Not all would make this choice, but, as will be shown, offenders who prefer hospital can often get there without setting up an insanity defence.

These somewhat complex considerations show that even the abolition of mandatory commitment would not necessarily increase the number of insanity defences very considerably. But if it were replaced by giving the judge discretion to make a hospital order, this would be much palatable to the defendant because he would then have a legal right (enforceable by application to the Mental Health Review Tribunal) to be discharged from hospital in certain circumstances (§ .6.). Moreover, the abolition of mandatory commitment might be accompanied by an extension of the insanity defence, as proposed by the Butler Committee (§ .9).

If it is all so complicated, and if the defendant is mad, how can the defendant calculate the pros and cons of an insanity defence?

We are presupposing that at the time of the trial he knows what is going on. If there is doubt about this, a jury will be empanelled to decide whether the defendant is fit to stand trial.

Does the defendant really decide, or is it his counsel?

Counsel leaves the choice to his client, but advises him—in forthright terms, if necessary—on the likely consequences of setting up the insanity defence.[10]

You give reasons why the defendant usually prefers not to raise the insanity issue. Can't the prosecution raise it?

Not before conviction, apart from certain exceptions.[11]

It is tempting and indeed common to speak of a defendant "pleading" insanity, but this expression is not strictly accurate. Generally, as was observed previously, the defences to a criminal charge are not formally recorded or reduced to a written pleading. All that the defendant has to do is to intimate his defence, supporting it either by cross-examination of the witnesses for the Crown or by adducing evidence himself. This is true for mental disorder. If the prosecution have evidence that the defendant was or is suffering from mental disorder (generally because of a report by the prison medical officer), they will pass this evidence to the defence before the trial, to be used or not as the defence wish.[12]

The main reason for the rule leaving the initiative with the defence is that if the defendant

---

[10] The issue of insanity may come in under a plea of not guilty. The defendant cannot plead mental disorder in order to avoid the strain of the trial. He cannot plead "not guilty by reason of insanity," in the hope of having the plea accepted by the prosecution. It is hard to see why not. Provided that the defendant has legal advice, it would often be a kindness to him to enable him to avoid trial.

[11] §§ 29.1 at nn. 12–13, 30.1 at n. 2.

[12] *Stanley Smith* [1979] 1 WLR at 1450.

denies that he did the act it would be prejudicial to him to allow evidence to be given by the prosecution that he was mentally disordered, because that might lead the jury too readily to assume that he did it. The vast majority of mentally disordered (even psychotic) people are not dangerous to others.[13]

The effect is, then, that the criminal law can't be used to put a nut case into hospital if he prefers to be punished on tariff principles?

That is a misunderstanding. Although the prosecution cannot adduce evidence of the defendant's mental disorder before conviction, unless he raises the issue of responsibility, both the prosecution and the defence can offer such evidence after conviction. Once the defendant has been convicted prosecuting counsel has the right and duty to put before the court (Crown Court or magistrates) any medical reports he has that may justify a psychiatric disposal; or the court may obtain its own report (§ .6. n. 1). A hospital order may then be made without the defendant's consent, or a psychiatric probation order (PPO) may be made with his consent. But even if a hospital order is made, the patient has legal safeguards for getting out as soon as nothing more can be done for him (§ .6); these safeguards do not apply on a special verdict.

The great range of discretion allowed to a judge after conviction compares strikingly with his entire lack of discretion after an insanity verdict. Mandatory commitment distorts the law and legal practice, and there is an unanswerable case for allowing the judge a discretion not to send the defendant to hospital on a special verdict when this is unnecessary (just as he has a discretion on conviction of any crime except murder). The CLRC recommended this,[14] but the recommendation was rejected by the Home Office, which obtained the concurrence of the Chief Justice of the time in its own opinion that the liberalisation of the law would be too dangerous. The question was again considered by the Butler Committee on Mentally Abnormal Offenders; by this time the higher judiciary had changed its mind, and supported liberalisation, which was, therefore, again recommended by the Butler Committee.[15] But no committee reports could induce the Home Office to withdraw its opposition to any change. Ministers listen primarily to their civil service advisers, not to outside advisers, however expert or highly placed.

Is there a form of special verdict for magistrates' courts?

No; and mandatory commitment does not apply to magistrates. A person who is tried summarily can set up mental disorder in order to negative *mens rea* and the court may give him an ordinary acquittal. Alternatively, the magistrates may find that he did the act (or made the omission) and, without recording a conviction, make a hospital order.[16]

---

[13] The rule leaving the initiative with the defence is clear on the English authorities, apart from certain exceptions (n. 11 above). For Australian decisions creating doubts see Colin Howard in [1967] Crim.LR 402–403, [1968] *ibid.* 590–591. On the policy issue see Ashworth in [1979] Crim.LR 482–483.

[14] Cmnd. 2149 of 1963 para. 34.

[15] Cmnd. 6244 of 1975 para. 18.42.

[16] MHA 1983 s. 37 (3). The offence must be punishable by the magistrates with imprisonment. Justices may use this power where it is uncertain whether the defendant is fit to stand trial: *R* v. *Lincoln (Kesteven) Magistrates' Court, ex p. O'Connor* [1983] 1 WLR 335. See Wasik in 147 JPN 211.

This is a discretionary power, and one rarely used; the magistrates generally prefer to discharge the defendant, perhaps arranging for him to be examined with a view to being civilly committed to hospital.[17] Because of the wide discretion of magistrates as to disposal, in contrast to the rigorous rule in the Crown Court, defences based on mental disorder are much more frequent on summary trial than on trial on indictment.

§ 28.6. THE HOSPITAL ORDER

The court can make a hospital order on conviction of any crime except murder,[1] provided that it is punishable with imprisonment. There must be medical evidence that the offender is suffering from mental illness or one of certain other mental disorders, and a hospital must be found that will consent to receive the offender as a patient. The hospital may again be a special hospital or an NHS hospital.

What is meant by mental illness?

There is no legal definition of the term, and psychiatrists do not completely agree upon its meaning. Some classify neurosis as a mental illness, others call neurosis a personality disorder. But the doctors do not merely certify mental illness. When the hospital order is made on the ground of mental illness, two doctors must certify that the offender is suffering from a mental illness "of a nature or degree which makes it appropriate for him to be detained in a hospital for medical treatment."

Typical bureaucratic jargon. "Appropriate," indeed! They don't promise to do anything for the patient, or even say that they can.

That is so. But the implication is that the certifying doctors hope to be able to improve the offender by treatment.

So this is the practical solution of the *McNaghten* problem: almost everyone is held responsible, and the only question is whether he is treatable.

A hospital order is not inevitable. If the defendant is seen to be pretty harmless (perhaps because he is aged, or his disorder has been brought under control since the event charged, or his offence was not serious) he may simply be released on probation (usually with a condition of mental treatment, whether as an out-patient or less usually as an in-patient),[2] or even given an absolute discharge. On the other hand, if the mental disorder is not severe he

---

[17] A police officer may take him to hospital under MHA 1983 s. 136.

[1] MHA 1983 s. 37 (1). When a person kills with "diminished responsibility" a conviction of murder can be avoided by convicting of manslaughter instead. See Chapter 30. To assist the court in making its decision about a hospital order, a defendant may be remanded on bail or in custody or to hospital for a medical report, or it may make an interim hospital order to enable the hospital to determine whether the defendant is likely to benefit from treatment. As an alternative to a hospital order, the court may make a guardianship order, the guardian being given the power to require the patient to reside at a specified place and to attend for medical treatment or for training: s. 40 (2) and Pt. II.

[2] Powers of Criminal Courts Act 1973 s. 3.

may be sent to prison (even though prison is not the right place for him), especially because no hospital will take him[3] and he must be kept in secure custody, or because his offence is too serious for him just to be turned loose.

You said that the main question for a hospital order is whether the offender is treatable. But before making the order doesn't the judge have to decide whether the defendant was responsible for his actions?

The abstract question of responsibility rarely enters in. Usually, if the court has medical evidence that the defendant is treatable and should go to hospital, and if a hospital is prepared to take him, the judge will be glad to make a hospital order instead of adding one more inmate to the prisons. Hence the virtual demise of the issue of responsibility.

But hospital orders are made because the chap is round the bend at the time of sentence, whereas McNaghten relates to his condition at the time of the act.

True. If the evidence is that the offender was disordered at the time of the act but has recovered since, a hospital order cannot be made, but the judge may of course release him on probation, or give him an absolute discharge.

Does the present law give the disturbed offender sufficient protection? I can see that the judge will make a hospital order if he is of opinion that this is the most suitable method of disposing of the case. But the judge may think that the most suitable method of disposing of the case is to send the offender to prison. So what protection has a mentally ill offender against a severe judge?

He can appeal from a sentence of imprisonment and ask to have a hospital order substituted.[4] But in practice, if a hospital order can be made and seems to be necessary the judge will almost always make it.

"Almost always"? If the offender is mentally ill, surely it should be "always." A man ought not to be punished for being ill.

It does not follow that the offence was the result of the illness. And sometimes the necessity to keep the offender from doing it again is an overriding consideration.

The choice between prison and hospital is often not straightforward, either from the point of view of the community or even from that of the offender.

- As regards incapacitation, a mentally disordered person may be detained in a special hospital in conditions that protect the public to the same extent as if he were in prison. Since he may be kept in hospital for longer than he would have been kept in prison on tariff principles, the protection to the public may be even greater. But there is great pressure on the special hospitals, which cannot always take patients who are not in the highest degree dangerous. Moreover, the patient's disorder and objectionable conduct may not be sufficiently serious to justify his prolonged detention on medical grounds. Doctors object to being "jailers in white coats," and NHS hospitals in particular will let out a patient as

---

[3] NHS hospitals are not keen on taking offender-patients, because such patients may be disruptive, because the staff dislike having them, and because hospitals lack secure accommodation. The Butler Committee recommended the creation of secure psychiatric units (as other committees had done before), but little has been achieved. See 146 JPN 228.

[4] See *Morris* [1961] 2 QB 237; *Cox* [1968] 1 WLR 308.

soon as they feel they can do nothing further for him. So the judge may feel obliged to send the offender to prison.

- Then there is the question of deterrence. In some forms of mental illness the best hope of preventing a recurrence of the objectionable conduct will lie in treating the illness rather than punishing the offender. However, mental illness cannot always be cured even if it can be alleviated. Many people suffering from schizophrenia are at large in the community and manage to maintain themselves in employment. They may be helped by drugs but cannot be permanently cured. There is no point in keeping them in hospital unless their behaviour is too objectionable to allow them to continue at liberty. If such a person commits some minor offence (a petty theft for example), it may be better from every point of view to treat him as responsible and to give him some minor punishment in the ordinary way, or to put him on probation, rather than to subject him to the serious loss of liberty that may be involved in commitment to hospital. It is good social policy to try to convey even to mentally or socially handicapped people that good behaviour is expected of them, and that they are accountable for what they do—unless a therapeutic approach offers either a better promise of improving their conduct or a humane alternative to a severe and profitless prison sentence.

Suppose a hospital order is made and after a time the doctors feel they can't improve their patient. Does the patient stay inside, or is he let loose?

All patients compulsorily detained under civil commitment or hospital order are entitled to an annual medical review. The legal position now depends on the Act of 1983, which greatly relaxes the control over detained patients.

After six months of detention (and again in every subsequent year), the responsible medical officer (RMO) must, to justify further detention, certify that (in the case of mental illness) treatment is likely to alleviate, or prevent a deterioration of, the patient's condition, or that if the patient is discharged he is unlikely to be able to care for himself. Nor is the matter left entirely to the RMO. Six months after the court order an application may be made to the Mental Health Review Tribunal (MHRT) for the patient's discharge. The tribunal has a general discretion to discharge the patient, and if discharge is refused the application may be renewed every year. (The same rule applies to civilly committed patients.) In considering the question of discharge the tribunal will apply the criteria applicable to the RMO's certificate. It is true, of course, that the tribunal will be considerably influenced by reports from the hospital doctors, but the patient can offer his own evidence, medical and other.

But that means that a dangerous offender may be set free just because he is untreatable and yet able to fry sausages for himself.

That is a risk the judge must take into account when deciding whether to make the hospital order in the first place. But he can, if he thinks it necessary to protect the public from *serious* harm, add what is called a restriction order.[5] This gives some extra control over the patient, but not to anything like the extent that a *McNaghten* committal does.

---

[5] MHA 1983 s. 41. The restriction order may be for a defined period or indefinite: *Haynes* [1982] Crim.LR 245. Magistrates cannot make a restriction order themselves, but on conviction of an either way offence they may commit the defendant for sentence to the Crown Court (under certain general provisions to this effect), and the Crown Court may make the restricted hospital order. See *Gardiner* [1967] 1 All ER 895.

The patient subject to a restriction order has the same right to an annual medical review as other detained patients, and the MHRT has much the same powers of review. The tribunal *must* direct the discharge of the patient if satisfied that he is not suffering from one of specified forms of mental disorder (including mental illness) of a nature or degree which makes it appropriate for him to be detained in hospital for medical treatment *or* that such treatment is not necessary for the health or safety of the patient or for the protection of other persons. The special feature of the restriction order is that if discharge is ordered it is conditional, i.e. subject to such conditions as the tribunal or (later) the Home Secretary imposes, unless the tribunal decides to make the discharge absolute. In other words, the restriction order does not impose a restriction upon the discharge of the patient, but only a possible restriction upon him after discharge. So a restriction order is not nearly as bad as a newspaper headline may make it appear.

Before 1982 the restriction order had a much more fierce effect; the patient could not be discharged at all without the consent of the Home Secretary. The change in the law was made in obedience to a decision of the European Court of Human Rights indicating that mental patients cannot be detained at the discretion of the Executive. But no change has been made in the law relating to mandatory commitment after an insanity verdict. It is, to use the vernacular, haywire that the Home Secretary cannot keep a grip on a lunatic *convicted* of homicide and sent to hospital, but can keep a grip on a lunatic *acquitted* of homicide on an insanity defence and sent to hospital.

§ 28.7. THE KINDS OF MENTAL DISORDER

Among the kinds of mental disorder catalogued by the Mental Health Act (§ .4) are "mental illness,"[1] "arrested or incomplete development of mind," and "psychopathic disorder." "Arrested or incomplete development of mind" refers to the condition of those formerly called defective or feeble-minded or subnormal persons—our language is littered with abandoned expressions for mental disorder, the search being constantly made for some words that will express the same thing more kindly. The Mental Health Act 1983 now subdivides arrested or incomplete development of mind into mental impairment and severe mental impairment.[2]

The two concepts are defined as follows. (I have italicised the words in which the definitions differ.) Section 1 (2):

> " '*Severe* mental impairment' means a state of arrested or incomplete development of mind which includes *severe* impairment of intelligence and social functioning and is associated with abnormally aggressive or seriously irresponsible conduct on the part of the person concerned. 'Mental impairment' means a state of arrested or incomplete development of mind *(not amounting to severe mental impairment)* which includes *significant* impairment of intelligence and social functioning and is associated with abnormally aggressive or seriously irresponsible conduct on the part of the person concerned."

A severely mentally impaired person can be civilly committed to hospital (like mentally ill

[1] See § .6, text after n. 1.
[2] Doctors also speak informally of "mental handicap" or of the "intellectually retarded patient."

persons) if treatment seems possible, and may be kept there so long as he continues to need treatment or cannot care for himself.[3] A mentally impaired (or severely mentally impaired) person can be made subject to a hospital order like one who is mentally ill, if two medical practitioners certify that treatment is likely to alleviate or prevent a deterioration of the condition.[4]

The question whether these unfortunates come within *McNaghten* will be discussed in the next section.

What is psychopathic disorder?

This expression (otherwise called psychopathy[5] for short) means a personality disorder involving antisocial attitudes (for which reason the term "antisocial personality disorder" is often preferred). The *aggressive* psychopath is prone to outbusts of violence; the *inadequate* psychopath is one who commits petty offences time after time because he cannot function adequately in society. Section 1 (2) of the Mental Health Act 1983 makes an effort to give precision to the concept.

> "In this Act "psychopathic disorder" means a persistent disorder or disability of mind (whether or not including significant impairment of intelligence) which results in abnormally aggressive or seriously irresponsible conduct on the part of the person concerned."

Section 1 (3) goes on to declare that a person is not to be regarded as mentally disordered by reason only of promiscuity or other immoral conduct, sexual deviancy, or dependence on alcohol or drugs.

Although the Act treats psychopathy as though it were an established form of mental disorder, for which patients may be civilly committed,[6] it is controversial whether there is any such psychiatric entity that can be regarded as "resulting in" bad conduct. Barbara Wootton's argument that psychopaths are identified merely from their objectionable behaviour, and that they are merely an intractable class of serious criminals,[7] has gained increasing support. The term can be regarded as a declaration of interest in the subject of habitual criminality by the medical profession.

Can a psychopath set up a McNaghten defence?

Psychopathy is not an affliction that prevents the patient from knowing what he is doing, or that it is wrong.

One cannot be completely dogmatic on the legal position. Much may depend on the opinions or choice of language of the medical witnesses in the particular case. Suppose that the defence are able to produce a psychiatrist to say that the defendant when in his explosive outburst did not know what he was doing?[8] Should it ever happen that the jury are led to find that a psychopath did not know what he was doing owing to his complete loss of self-control,

---

[3] MHA 1983 s. 20 (4).
[4] MHA 1983 s. 37 (2).
[5] Accent on second syllable.
[6] MHA 1983 s. 3 (2).
[7] Wootton, *Crime and Penal Policy* (London 1978) 230 ff.
[8] In *Att.-Gen. (N.I.)* v. *Gallagher* [1963] AC 349 the medical evidence was that the defendant was or might be an aggressive psychopath, and one medical witness expressed a doubt whether the defendant knew what he was doing, or whether it was wrong, but refused to go beyond this expression of doubt; the other witnesses were prepared to say in effect that the doubt was unfounded.

it would be important for the judge to take the view that psychopathy is a disease of the mind, for only in that event would a special verdict be possible—the alternative would be an ordinary acquittal, which would leave the defendant free to have his explosive outburst again.[9] It seems unlikely, however, that a jury will ever take an indulgent view of psychopathy, if the Crown is armed with orthodox medical evidence on the meaning of this expression.

The problem of psychopathy has vexed some philosophers, because it may seem that a psychopath cannot help his condition, and so should not be responsible.

The typical aggressive psychopath has apparently uncontrollable episodes of violence, is entirely self-centred and has no guilt feelings. This behaviour is consistent with brain damage, or with genetic defects, or with disturbed upbringing. Some studies have shown that 40 per cent. of psychopaths suffered parental deprivation in childhood, as against only five per cent. of controls. Now a person is not responsible for having brain damage, or for having a particular chromosome formation, or for having been parted from his mother when a child. It can plausibly be said, therefore, that the psychopath is not to blame for his conduct.

At the same time, several arguments can be advanced for saying that the psychopath is properly held responsible, and even punishable. Psychopaths are discovered *merely* by noticing that they are persistent offenders, or persistent offenders of a particular type (though they may suffer from other forms of mental disorder besides their psychopathy). Even medical men can be found to agree that "nothing is gained by trying to draw a distinction between psychopathic and chronic offenders."[10] There would, therefore, be a serious problem of justice if psychopaths, meaning habitual offenders, were regarded as exempt from the criminal law. As Lady Wootton pointed out, were such a claim conceded it would not be long before occasional offenders had to be accorded the same exemption, for their wickedness is surely less than that of the chronic offenders.[11]

Anyway, we have in general no other method of dealing with psychopaths who behave intolerably than by custody, which means prison. On the whole psychopaths have proved to be as intractable to the attentions of the doctors as they have been to the agents of the law; but sporadic efforts continue to treat them (in hospitals and prisons) by behaviour conditioning or "conversational therapy" or "relationship therapy." Most, therefore, go to ordinary prisons, from which a few are transferred to Grendon psychiatric prison, where they talk their problems out. Many improve after the age of 30, and more after 40; and one may hope that a few short sentences of imprisonment or other punishment may hasten the psychopath's ability to control himself. If there is to be any prospect of keeping him in society, he must be retained within the sanctions of the criminal law. Moreover, even psychiatrists and psychologists who claim some success in treating the condition have expressed the opinion that the psychopath's acceptance of treatment may come more readily after a spell in prison as punishment than before.

Can the judge make a hospital order for a psychopath?

Yes,[12] but few NHS hospitals will accept psychopathic offenders. Moreover, the judge may himself be wary of taking this course. For reasons explained in the last section, doctors cannot retain patients in hospital merely by way of preventive detention after treatment has failed, or is producing no further results; yet a psychopath who is untreatable may

[9] In *Gallagher*, last note, the lords expressed different views. Lords Tucker and Denning seemed to accept that psychopathy was a "disease of the mind," but Lord Goddard denied it. However this may be, a patient who is regarded as a psychopath by one doctor may he diagnosed as mentally ill by another, and, there being no legal definition of mental illness, the second diagnosis may be accepted by a court. See *W* v. *L* [1974] QB 711.

[10] P D Scott in [1960] 1 BMJ 1642.

[11] The Listener, September 24, 1959. See also address in [1963] 2 BMJ 197, and her *Crime and the Criminal Law*, 2nd edn (London 1981) Chap. 3.

[12] Two medical practitioners must certify that treatment is likely to alleviate or prevent deterioration in the offender's condition.

still need detention in the public interest. The Butler Committee has recommended that adult psychopaths should in general be taken out of the scope of hospital orders and that further efforts should be made to treat them in prison. Penal establishments can operate a strictly disciplined regime based on rewards and punishments, which would hardly be accepted in a mental hospital. The Home Office and DHSS between them seem to have dug a grave for the more important recommendations of the Report, but if it is ever implemented a psychopathic prisoner could still be transferred to a hospital that is willing to take him on.[13]

§ 28.8. MCNAGHTEN, NEGLIGENCE AND RECKLESSNESS

On its face, the first *McNaghten* question is concerned with the defendant's knowledge (which means, also, his intention); but the topics of recklessness and negligence also need to be considered.

Whether *McNaghten* applies to crimes of negligence remains uncertain; it has not been tested in the courts, because no lunatic having an adviser in his senses would set up an insanity defence to a charge of negligence.

A more substantial problem arises for recklessness, particularly because there may be the possibility of bypassing McNaghten and obtaining an ordinary acquittal. Suppose a man is charged with arson, and says that he did not realise that the small fire he lawfully made would spread to other people's property, or that he did not realise that life would be endangered; and suppose that to support this defence he offers evidence that he has a low IQ. If the defence is credited (or not discredited), what should be the outcome?

Before *Caldwell* the courts on three occasions recognised that evidence of mental illness (schizophrenia) or mental "backwardness" or "limited intelligence" could be given to enable the defendant to win an outright acquittal on a charge involving recklessness. This was when the fully subjective theory of recklessness prevailed, and was a consequence of the Court of Appeal's loyal acceptance of section 8 of the Criminal Justice Act.[1]

The position since *Caldwell* is unclear. The effect of that decision depends upon the answer to the question previously discussed,[2] whether the word "obvious" used by Lord Diplock is to be read as meaning "obvious to a reasonable man" (which our defendant is not) or "obvious to the defendant" (if he had thought). Lord Diplock used the word in both senses, and evidently did not think the problem through, but the

---

[13] See further, on psychopaths Ashworth and Shapland in [1980] Crim.LR 628.

[1] *Hudson* [1966] 1 QB at 455; *Wallett* [1968] 2 QB 367; and especially *Stephenson* [1979] QB 695. Before the CJA, in *Ward* [1956] 1 QB 351, the CCA had upheld a murder conviction on a direction to the jury that was capable of being understood as imposing an objective test of recklessness for a person of poor intelligence.

[2] § 5.5 (2).

interpretation most consistent with his general theme is the second. On this interpretation, the defendants in the cases just mentioned would still be acquitted if the jury find it reasonably possible, in the light of the medical evidence, that even if the defendant had stopped to think he would not have seen the risk.[3] However, their lordships' refusal to give leave to appeal in *Elliott* v. *C* (§ 5.5 at n. 3) indicates a rejection of the interpretation.

Certain arguments reinforce the opinion that the objective rule for recklessness in *Caldwell* should not be regarded as affecting the mentally disordered. One is the emphasis placed by Lord Diplock upon blameworthiness and moral turpitude as the foundation of his opinion.[4] But the more powerful argument is based on the intoxication rule. The rule stated by Lord Diplock (and therefore by the House of Lords) for intoxicated defendants was what was previously called a conditionally subjective one; the question for the jury is whether this defendant would have seen the risk if he had been sober.[5] If mentally disordered people are subjected to a totally objective test, the best advice to them, if they wish to avoid all legal risk, would be to live in a permanent alcoholic haze, for then if they do any mischief they will be adjudged on the conditionally subjective test for drunks in general. But of course it is incredible that the law should be more lenient for those who intoxicate themselves than for those who suffer from a genetic disadvantage. It follows that the conditionally subjective test applied to drunkards should apply also to the mentally disordered.

The confusion in Lord Diplock's opinion on this point has an obvious explanation. His lordship seized on the provision in the Model Penal Code because it was the only respectable authority he could find for his intoxication rule[6]; and he disregarded the fact that the MPC proceeded in general on a subjective view of recklessness. The intoxication rule was expressed in the MPC to be an exception, and was therefore stated in the conditionally subjective form. (The jury are to imagine that the defendant was not intoxicated, and then apply the usual subjective test.) Lord Diplock suppressed the subjective provisions of the code but accepted the intoxication rule verbatim, perhaps without realising that the particular wording made sense only against the background of a subjective theory.

But surely if a person gives evidence that he is mentally disordered and therefore did not see a risk that anyone else would have seen in what he did, he did not know the nature and quality of his act and should have an insanity verdict?

This point has not been argued, but it seems to be maintainable. It involves holding that the "nature and quality" of the act include its foreseeable consequences, and that is not too broad an interpretation of the word "quality." This given, there would be no theoretical difficulty in bringing in schizophrenics who take insane risks, and the same rule should apply to the mentally impaired. If the defendant is so low in intelligence that it can seriously be argued that he set fire to a house, for instance, without realising that this involved danger to those sleeping inside, and if

---

[3] See especially *Stephenson*, n. 1 above, where the CA pointed out that a schizophrenic cannot be found to have closed his mind to the obvious if his illness "might have prevented the idea of danger entering [his] mind at all." Cp. Syrota in [1981] Crim.LR 659. But it must be confessed that, as Griew has pointed out ([1981] Crim.LR 748) Lord Diplock looked upon *Stephenson* with no favour, and intended to overrule it, at least in respect of some of the things said in it.

[4] § 5.5 at n. 7.

[5] § 5.3.

[6] He could also cite *Majewski*, but that case was primarily concerned with the question of "basic intent." It did not clearly apply to statutes expressly requiring recklessness as to a consequence, as did the statute before the court in *Caldwell*.

evidence of the mental impairment is given, then on principle he should not be entitled to an ordinary acquittal but at best should have an insanity verdict. (And if he merely gives evidence that he did not realise the danger, the Crown should on principle be allowed to give evidence of his mental impairment amounting to insanity in order to ensure that he does not obtain a complete acquittal: § 29.2). Although mental impairment is not insanity in the ordinary use of language, there is authority for saying that it can amount to insanity in law.

In McNaghten's time even doctors spoke of "insanity" as including imbecility,[7] and there are later legal approvals of this usage, though the matter has not been finally decided.[8] Sometimes, however, evidence has been given on behalf of the defendant that he was of inferior intelligence, for the purpose of showing that he did not intend or foresee a result of his conduct that the jury might otherwise have inferred that he intended or foresaw; and the evidence was not taken to require an insanity verdict as opposed to an ordinary acquittal.

Since the new classification of mental impairment in the Mental Health Act, the obvious solution would be to say that severe mental impairment qualifies for a special verdict, while mental impairment *simpliciter* does not stand in the way of an ordinary conviction or acquittal.[9] An impaired person may, because he is stupid, accidentally set fire to a house, but if it is an accident it is unlikely to be repeated and the defendant can safely be given an ordinary acquittal. Or he may attack someone and, because he is stupid, not realise that he is inflicting as much injury as he does, but although in consequence he is acquitted of wounding with intent, he is likely to be convicted of unlawful wounding, and then he can (if thought necessary) be punished for that, or alternatively sent to hospital, or in a suitable case put on probation. On the whole, therefore, the public interest does not seem to require that every mentally impaired person who does harm should be accounted irresponsible under *McNaghten*. That would be a very severe rule, because of the consequences of an insanity verdict.

§ 28.9. LEGISLATIVE PROPOSALS

The humane use of hospital orders and other non-punitive disposals does not provide a complete answer to the demand that the test of mental incapacity to commit a crime should be modernised. At one time there was a movement to exempt people who suffered from "insane impulse" or "irresistible impulse." Although this has been incorporated in the statute law of several common law countries, the argument that it should excuse from responsibility has never been accepted in our law,[1] largely because it is thought that the irresistible impulse is unprovable.

In the United States, the notion was espoused in the Model Penal Code, but with a certain change of language. To avoid giving the impression that the irresistible drive must be impulsive or of sudden occurrence, the Code speaks instead of "capacity to conform to the law."

"A person is not responsible for criminal conduct if at the time of such conduct as a result

---

[7] Nigel Walker, *Crime and Insanity in England* (Edinburgh 1968) i 116.

[8] To the references in *The General Part*, 2nd edn § 147, add Morris and Howard, *Studies in Criminal Law* (Oxford 1964) 39–42. See also the Butler Report, Cmnd. 6244 para. 18.25.

[9] See n. 1 above. In *Kemp* [1957] 1 QB 399 Devlin J (as he then was) said that "brutish stupidity" was not a disease of the mind. This opinion is not inconsistent with saying that *severe* mental impairment is a disease of the mind.

[1] Except as reinforcing a *McNaghten* defence: *Att.-Gen.* v. *Brown* [1960] 1 All ER 734.

of mental disease or defect he lacks substantial capacity either to appreciate the criminality of his conduct or to conform his conduct to the requirements of the law."

This provision has been adopted into the law of several of the United States, and a version of it is accepted in Northern Ireland.[2]

A fatal objection to the practicality of the solution is the impossibility of drawing a line between an impulse that is irresistible and one that is merely unresisted. Take two schizophrenics, A and B, whose clinical symptoms appear to be the same. Both are involved with their friends in arguments that cause them to go into towering rages, but whereas A stabs to death his opponent in the argument, B does not. If A is prosecuted for murder, a psychiatrist may be ready to testify that by reason of his disease he was deprived of capacity to conform to the law, as is indeed shown by the fact that he did not conform to it. B, not having stabbed, does not appear before the court, so we do not hear psychiatric evidence about him; but presumably our psychiatrist would say that he had the capacity to conform to the law, as is shown by the fact that he conformed. All that we ever observe is that individuals conform or fail to conform. For practical purposes, therefore, a judgment that the defendant by reason of mental disease *lacked the capacity* to conform to the law does not differ in any way from a judgment that he suffered from a mental disease and by reason of that disease *did not* conform to the law.

An observation by Barbara Wootton may be added.

"Nor is there any better foundation for the layman's tendency to imagine that temptations which he himself has never experienced should be more powerful than those that he has, merely because they strike him as either pointless or exceptionally revolting. How can it be proved that the temptation persistently to steal bicycles and only bicycles, or to cut off girls' hair, is harder to resist than the temptation to fiddle one's expenses in the public service, or to draw supplementary benefit to which one is not entitled? The former category of offences is certainly abnormal in a statistical sense in that they are relatively unusual; but both categories alike are well-established patterns of behaviour."[3]

But surely it is quite obvious that conformity is much harder for some people than for others. Drug addicts find it more difficult to obey the law against drugs than other people do. You can make a common-sense judgment that a particular mental sufferer was unable to conform to the law.

About the only offender of whom one can say that he could in no circumstances act otherwise than as he did is the patient suffering from mania, who cannot be restrained except by being held down. Your drug addict would be unlikely to use his syringe while he was being covered by a revolver, with orders to desist. For the most part, difficulty in conforming to the law is a question of degree. It is not a usable test of legal responsibility.

The above remarks do not mean that it is impossible to improve the law. The Butler Committee on Mentally Abnormal Offenders proposed that in place of *McNaghten* the jury should return a special verdict where at the time of the act the defendant was suffering from severe mental illness (to be defined by statute) or what is now called severe mental impairment.[4] Mandatory commitment would disappear.

---

[2] Criminal Justice Act (Northern Ireland) 1967 ss. 1, 3 ("mental abnormality which prevents him from controlling his own conduct").

[3] *Crime and Penal Policy* 229.

[4] Cmnd. 6244 para. 18.26. See Nigel Walker in [1981] Crim.LR 596–597, and Susanne Dell in [1983] Crim.LR 431.

SUMMARY

The immunities of the Crown, and immunities granted under international law, are not fully discussed in this work. § .1

Criminal responsibility starts at the age of 10. Between 10 and 14, the prosecution are supposed to prove not only the matters ordinarily required but also that the juvenile knew his act to be wrong, legally or morally. The requirement, when insisted on, creates serious difficulties. § .2

Responsibility in its technical sense means moral or legal accountability. Legal responsibility depends upon legal criteria, not just upon psychological pronouncements. However, the importance of the concept in relation to mental disorder is greatly reduced by various rules. § .3

A person may enter a psychiatric hospital voluntarily, or upon civil commitment, or in connection with criminal proceedings. Examples of the latter are where the defendant is found unfit to stand trial, or is the subject of an order made as a result of the trial.

Mental disorder is widely defined in the Mental Health Act 1983 s. 1 (2); it means "mental illness, arrested or incomplete development of mind, psychopathic disorder, and any other disorder or disability of mind." It is not in itself a legal defence. Legal irresponsibility depends upon *McNaghten*. A. The defendant must have been suffering from "a defect of reason, from disease of the mind." B. If he was, there are the following further questions for the jury. 1. Is it the case that, in consequence of this defect of reason, the defendant did not know the nature and quality of his act? 2. If he did, did he not know it was wrong? 3. Was he under a delusion? (if that can ever arise, having regard to question 1). These questions pertain to *mens rea*, except that question B2 refers to knowledge of legal wrong, which is not normally a *mens rea* requirement. The burden of proof of the insanity defence is, anomalously, placed on the defendant, but he need only establish it on the balance of probability. "Disease of the mind," otherwise called insanity, is a legal concept, though one involving a social judgment; it is not precisely the same as the medical concept of psychosis. § .4

Success in the insanity defence in the Crown Court leads to a special verdict, "not guilty by reason of insanity." It finds that the defendant did the act but fell within the *McNaghten* rules; and the judge must thereupon commit the defendant to a hospital to be named by the Home Secretary, to remain until such time as the Home Secretary directs otherwise. If the defendant gives evidence of a disordered mental state in the hope of denying *mens rea* without being accounted insane, the prosecution may contend that the mental disorder amounted to a "disease of the mind" requiring a special verdict. So great is the desire of defendants to avoid mandatory commitment that the insanity defence is now rare (and, in general, only the defendant can introduce it); rather than raise this defence the defendant may plead guilty (to a lesser offence, if possible). This inflexibility does not extend to magistrates' courts, where there is no special finding and no mandatory commitment. § .5

If the defendant is convicted of an imprisonable offence and there is medical evidence that he is then suffering from certain forms of mental disorder, including mental illness, the court may make a hospital order, provided that a bed can be found. The court will almost always make this order when there is hope of effective treatment and when the other conditions are satisfied. When a person is detained under a hospital order the Mental Health Review Tribunal will order his discharge if no further treatment is required or if the patient can care for himself. A judge of the Crown Court may combine the hospital order with a restriction order; in theory this does not impede the patient's discharge, but only enables conditions to be imposed on his discharge. § .6

"Arrested or incomplete development of mind" means "severe mental impairment" and "mental impairment." Those severely mentally impaired can be § .7

committed to hospital civilly, and such people, as well as those who are mentally impaired *simpliciter*, may be committed under a hospital order. "Pyschopathic disorder" means a personality disorder involving antisocial attitudes; it is defined by MHA s. 1 (2) as "a persistent disorder or disability of mind (whether or not including significant impairment of intelligence) which results in abnormally aggressive or seriously irresponsible conduct;" but it does not cover "promiscuity or other immoral conduct, sexual deviancy, or dependence on alcohol or drugs." Psychopaths can be civilly committed to hospital, and also sent there under a hospital order; but few NHS hopitals will accept them, and serious offenders generally have to go to prison. Psychopathy is not generally regarded as negativing the kind of cognitive capacity that founds a *McNaghten* defence.

A *McNaghten* defence is highly unlikely on a charge of negligence. On a charge § .8
involving recklessness, there is a strong argument for saying that the defendant must be acquitted if the jury are not satisfied that the defendant himself (with any mental disabilities he may have) would have realised the risk if he had stopped to think. Hitherto it has been supposed that the acquittal must be a clean one; but it may be held that where the disability is one of serious mental impairment, or is otherwise insanity in law, there should be a special verdict.

CHAPTER 29

AUTOMATISM

> To define true madness,
> What is't but to be nothing else but mad?
>
> *Hamlet* II. ii

§ 29.1. AUTOMATISM: SLEEPWALKING AND CONCUSSION

IT was said in the last chapter that lawyers formerly tended to assume that insanity is a medical concept upon which doctors can pronounce, while doctors reject the use of the term for any purpose except the humouring of lawyers. As things have developed, judges have been forced to attach their own meaning to "insanity," because this expression (or its equivalent "disease of the mind") denotes the distinction between the kind of acquittal called the special verdict, which consigns the defendant to hospital, and the ordinary acquittal whereby he walks out of court a free man.

For example, the law obviously distinguishes between a sane mistake (or ordinary forgetfulness) as to a relevant fact and an insane delusion. In neither case does the defendant "know the nature and quality of his act," but in the former he gets a clean acquittal, if the offence requires *mens rea*, while in the latter there must be a special verdict.

> An illustration of the former is *Clarke*,[1] where a woman was charged with theft from a supermarket. Her defence was that she had taken the goods in a state of absent-mindedness resulting from depression. She was convicted, but the conviction was quashed on appeal.

Depression can amount to a psychosis, but a court would naturally be reluctant to say that simple forgetfulness, even if resulting from psychotic depression, manifests a "defect of reason from disease of the mind" within *McNaghten*.

The most prominent instances of mental disorder negativing *mens rea* yet not amounting to insanity are those that are sometimes called "involuntary acts" but now more frequently go by the name of automatism, or, more fully, non-insane automatism.

Does automatism mean that the behaviour is virtually mindless?

Yes in medical usage, but the legal meaning has developed far beyond that. The term "automatism" is used medically only in connection with epilepsy, and in its proper medical sense it is rare even in that disease. Although attacks of *grand mal* and even *petit mal* very occasionally result in violence, this is usually not because the sufferer is a complete automaton

---

[1] [1972] 1 All ER 219.

but because of confusion or delusion or a rage response.[2] On the lips of lawyers, however, "automatism" has come to express any abnormal state of consciousness (whether confusion, delusion or dissociation) that is regarded as incompatible with the existence of *mens rea*, while not amounting to insanity.[3] It is sometimes called "altered" or "clouded" consciousness; perhaps "impaired consciousness" is the best name, but the orthodox one can be used if we bear in mind that it does not mean what it says.[4]

What do we mean by consciousness? A bee perceives the symbolic dances of other bees, and is genetically programmed to make the appropriate response by following the direction indicated; but we have no warrant to describe a bee as being "conscious" in any sense relevant to human activity. Consciousness, for man, means not simple perception, the awareness of the here-and-now, but the ability, at least in limited degree, to remember the past and foresee the future, so as to make informed choices. On principle, therefore, a disease or other event seriously impairing consciousness in this sense exempts from liability. Putting aside two or three ill-considered decisions, the great weight of authority shows that a person whose consciousness is badly impaired can have the defence of automatism even though he is still able to co-ordinate movements, as in driving a car (§ .5). Whether the exemption is a special verdict (a *McNaghten* exemption) or an ordinary acquittal is a matter we shall have to consider.

Automatism is sometimes regarded as being incompatible not only with the mental element in crime but with the notion of an act. If it were a matter of pure theory this could be characterised as an unnecessary refinement,[5] but the "act" doctrine has the advantage of making automatism a defence to a charge of an offence of strict liability requiring an act.[6]

Which side bears the burden of proof?

Although the "black-out" defence is legally recognised, it is a defence too easily feigned to be accepted without severe scrutiny. So the courts have laid down that the evidential burden in respect of the issue of non-insane automatism rests upon the defendant,[7] and, moreover, that medical evidence must (where appropriate) be given in its support before the judge is bound to leave this issue to the jury.[8] If there is sufficient evidence

---

[2] John Gunn and George Fenton in [1971] 1 The Lancet 1173.

[3] Lord Kilmuir in *Bratty* [1963] AC at 401 accepted the definition of automatism "as connoting the state of a person who, though capable of action, is not conscious of what he is doing. . . . It is a defence because the mind does not go with what is being done."

[4] Because automatism is a legal concept, a psychiatrist should be asked to testify to the mental condition as psychiatrically recognised, not to "automatism." It is for the judge to make the translation (subject to what is to be said in .2 at nn. 6–8). In most of the conditions referred to legally as automatism the psychiatrist would speak of an altered state of consciousness.

[5] See § 28.5 n. 3.

[6] See *per* Lord Denning in *Bratty* [1963] AC at 409; and cp. *ibid.* at 407 (Lord Kilmuir), 415 (Lord Morris); *per* Lord Edmund-Davies in *Majewski* [1977] AC at 491G. Cp. § .5, and § 42.1 n. 1.

[7] *Hill* v. *Baxter* [1958] 1 QB 277; *Bratty* [1963] AC at 405. "Loss of memory afterwards is never a defence in itself, so long as he was conscious at the time:" *per* Lord Denning in *Bratty* at p. 409.

[8] The courts have sometimes waived the requirement of medical evidence for concussion: *Budd,* § .6 n. 2; *Connolly* (1965) 52 MPR 11 (Nova Scotia); *Scott* [1966] VR 277 (Vict.). But in *Stripp* (1978) 69 CAR 318 the absence of clear medical evidence in support proved fatal. The question was whether the defendant's behaviour was due to concussion or to intoxication; he gave evidence of possible concussion, but the doctors were unable to testify that he had been concussed; and it was held that the defence of automatism should not have been left to the jury. Medical evidence must be given if the defendant says only that he had a black-out: *per* Lord Denning in *Bratty* [1963] AC at 413–414; *Cook* v. *Atchison* (1968] Crim.LR 266. Cp. *Dervish*, The Times, November 10, 1967, [1968] Crim.LR 37; *Tsigos* [1964–65] NSWR 1607; *The General Part,* 2nd edn § 289; Mackay in [1980] Crim.LR 351–353; § 14.2 n. 13. In *Stanley Smith* [1979] 1 WLR 1445, 3 All ER 605, 69 CAR 378 the trial judge did not insist upon medical evidence to support a sleepwalking defence, as he might have done; but the prosecution gave such evidence in rebuttal.

(whether coming from the defendant or from the Crown[9]) to pass this "initial hurdle"—to "lay a foundation" for the defence, as the judges sometimes say—the jury will be directed that the persuasive burden of proving the mental element rests on the prosecution.[10] Strangely, the defendant is not required to testify.

It will be seen that, apart from the outcome of the case, there are two minor differences between *McNaghten* and the doctrine of non-insane automatism.

- *McNaghten* includes the "knowledge of wrong" test, which does not apply to automatism. This is a trivial point.
- The burden of proof is different. Under *McNaghten* it rests on the defence. Here again the distinction is trivial in practice, as well as being absurd, and a potential headache for the jury.

If the defendant adduces evidence of what he calls non-insane automatism, can the prosecution reply with evidence of insanity?

Since *Kemp*[11] the prosecution can certainly adduce medical evidence as to the effect of the evidence given by the defendant. It seems clear that the prosecution may also, in such circumstances, adduce evidence of insanity in reply to evidence of non-insane automatism, since the defence of non-insane automatism puts sanity in issue.

Lord Denning in *Bratty* seems to have taken the view that the rule is not limited to the issue of automatism: whenever the defence put the defendant's state of mind in issue, the prosecution can show that his state of mind amounted to insanity.[12] The rule, if accepted, would apply where the defendant gives evidence that he was so drunk as not to know what he was doing: the prosecution should be able to reply with evidence to show that the drunkenness had induced insanity (such as *delirium tremens*, or alcoholic paranoia). Similarly, if the defendant gives evidence that he made a mistake of fact (for example, in fancying that he was being attacked), the prosecution should be allowed to show that this was not a sane mistake but an insane delusion.

It is true that Lord Denning's wider rule would make a considerable inroad into the general proposition that only the defendant can introduce the issue of insanity. But the purpose of that rule, presumably, is to protect the defendant from prejudice if his defence is that he did not do the act. In cases of the type now being considered no prejudice would be caused to the defendant on the issue of guilt by allowing the evidence to be introduced, because by hypothesis he confesses that he did the act (otherwise, a defence that he lacked the mental state would be in practice impossible), and it is wrong that if the defendant's mental state is in issue the court should be misled by one-sided evidence of it.

Smith and Hogan[13] express the opinion that "it is unlikely that D's 'state of mind' will be regarded as in issue [for the purpose of Lord Denning's rule] where he relies on a mere mistake of fact (even one induced by drunkenness), for 'state' of mind in this sense is put in issue in every case requiring *mens rea* by a mere plea of not guilty." This reasoning may be questioned. The rule referred to in the concluding words about the guilty plea is traditional, but is misleadingly worded. Its only effect is that questions of *mens rea* (and *actus reus*) cannot

---

[9] *Bratty* [1963] AC at 406; *Hatenave-Tete* [1965–66] P & NGLR 336; *Clarke* (1973) 16 CCC (2d) 310 (Nova Scotia).

[10] This was accepted in *Bratty* [1963] AC 386.

[11] § 28.5 n. 8. 1.

[12] [1963] AC at 411–412. The Butler Committee proposed that the rule should be enacted: Cmnd 6244 para. 18.48.

[13] 4th edn 177.

be excluded from the trial as not having been specially pleaded. The rule does not affect the evidential burdens, and therefore does not mean that a plea of not guilty puts the mental element *actively* in issue as a matter that has to be left to the jury. The evidential burden on the mental element is generally on the prosecution, and when not on the prosecution it rests on the defence. Until the evidential burden is discharged by giving appropriate evidence there is no issue on the mental element on which the jury can properly be asked to find. Conversely, automatism is not actively in issue unless the defence give evidence upon it. On these matters, importance attaches not to the pleading but to the evidence that has been given. If the defence have given evidence of automatism, mistake or intoxication, for the purpose of negativing an inference as to a mental element that would otherwise arise from the prosecution evidence, no legal principle prevents the prosecution from giving evidence to show that the alleged automatism, mistake or intoxication manifests some form of mental disorder. Consequently, there is no reason why "state of mind" in Lord Denning's principle should be confined to an abnormal state of mind.

Have any rules of law been settled on what amounts to non-insane automatism?

Certain kinds are well recognised in practice. Two clear instances, which have been accepted by the courts without any reservation, are sleepwalking and concussion. To these we may add involuntary intoxication.

Sleep-walking. It has happened from time to time that a person has killed or wounded another with whom he is asleep in bed, or while walking in his sleep or immediately upon rousing from sleep and while still in a state of semi-consciousness. Such a person has always been acquitted of murder or wounding,[14] but there is no need to base the acquittal upon the absence of an "act." Clearly the defendant has killed or wounded; it would be a perversion of language to say otherwise; but he is acquitted for lack of a mental element. Some degree of normality of consciousness is essential for the legal notions of intention, recklessness and knowledge.

The position is not altogether simple, because the acts of a sleep-walker are in a sense purposive. The sleep-walker does not always proceed as the cartoonists imagine him, with eyes tightly closed and arms outstretched. His eyes may be open and he may appear to be in perfect control. He will open a door and turn a corner, walk downstairs, open a drawer, take out a carving-knife, and return to the bedroom where his wife is asleep. But after waking up he will not remember his deed (except sometimes as a dream). Although his acts have a certain purpose (indeed, he may have an understandable reason for killing his wife), it is the purpose of a dream-state. He is not acting with his normal conscious mind.

The commonest precipitant of sleep-walking or other behaviour during

---

[14] *Bratty* [1963] AC at 403, 409; *Carpenter* (1976) The Times, October 14; Nigel Walker, *Crime and Insanity in England* (Edinburgh 1968) i 167–172; Sanford J Fox in 63 Col.LRev. 653; Mackay in [1980] Crim.LR 351 n. 7; Fairall in 5 Cr.LJ 341–343 (Can.). Cp. § .3 n. 3. In *Boshears* (1961), Sunday Pictorial February 19, an American airman who strangled a girl while asleep was acquitted of murder although he had consumed vodka. In *Hughes* (1978), The Times, May 3rd, the Crown offered no evidence against a woman who had risen in the night to fetch a knife "to peel potatoes," evidently while still asleep, and then stabbed her husband with it. It was afterwards reported that the couple continued to sleep together, but the husband now locked the bedroom door and put the key in a wardrobe with a combination lock, only he knowing the combination (Sunday Times, May 7th). See also Podolski in 1 Med.Sci.L 260; Leslie Watkins, *The Sleepwalk Killers* (London 1976), collecting gory instances and including some legal trials.

sleep or semi-sleep is dissociation (§ .4), but it is also attributed to hypoglycaemia (§ .3) and nocturnal epilepsy (§ .2). Sometimes dissociation results from brain disease, but more normally it is a hysterical symptom. The dissociated sleep-walker may act out a subconscious desire, but is not aware of it; and subconscious desire does not engage criminal responsibility. (There is, of course, a danger of the defence being feigned, but many instances are self-evidently genuine; the sleep-walker is horror-struck when he wakes and discovers what he has done, and may commit suicide or lose his reason in remorse.[15])

Although sleep-walkers have always received an absolute acquittal for what they do, no social inconvenience has hitherto resulted. There seems to be no recorded instance of a sleep-walker doing injury a further time after being acquitted. However, since the decision in *Sullivan*, to be discussed in the next section, it seems very likely that sleepwalkers will in future find themselves saddled with an insanity verdict.

Concussion. This is temporary damage to the brain resulting from a blow, and may produce a confusional state. It is accepted as justifying an ordinary acquittal.[16]

Involuntary intoxication was discussed in § 21.6. If "intoxication" is taken in a wide sense the phrase can cover various types of involuntary poisoning impairing consciousness, as where a driver is almost overcome by exhaust fumes but continues in his confused state to try to control the car.[17] Again an ordinary acquittal follows.

§ 29.2. EPILEPSY

Epilepsy is an affliction of at least ·5 per cent. of the population. Although it is certainly a disease of the brain, it is not classified as a psychosis, and sufferers are rarely dangerous to others even during an attack. Epilepsy does not predispose to criminal conduct in the usual sense, but it can cause accidents or near-accidents if not controlled by drugs.[1] A driver will be incapacitated nt only by a grand mal attack (the epileptic fit in thę usual sense) but by petit mal epilepsy in which his mind simply fails to function for a few seconds. Also, the sufferer may in rare instances perform complicated acts in a somnambulist condition (the psychomotor attack), and these may unintentionally cause injury. Although most patients can be helped by drugs to lead a normal life, a few severely brain-damaged patients must be kept in hospital, particularly if this is necessary to prevent them from taking alcohol. A very few psychotic epileptics have to live in Broadmoor.

---

[15] A classification of causes will be found in Mangalore N Pai, *Searchlight on Sleep Disorders* (London 1969) 126 ff.

[16] *Bratty* [1963] AC at 403; *Quick* [1973] QB 910 at 918, 920–922; above n. 8; Fairall in 5 Cr.LJ 340 (Can.); § .5. See also n. 8 above on medical evidence.

[17] See Fairall in 5 Cr.LJ 344 (Aus.); below § .5. Cp. n. 8 above on medical evidence.

[1] See James A Lewis (Director of the Seizure Clinic at the University of Colorado Medical Center) in 232 Jrnl.Am.Med.Assn. 1165.

There is considerable danger of a miscarriage of justice if the sufferer is unaware of what happened and of his affliction. Therefore, a defence to a charge of shoplifting that "I had a blackout" or "something came over me" ought not to be scornfully rejected without a medical examination precluding the possibility of brain abnormality, unless of course the evidence is convincing that the defendant was acting purposefully—and even this evidence may be misleading.

The question whether epilepsy is to be regarded as a "disease of the mind" depends on the meaning of that term. Literally, it is, but something more than the literal meaning should be required for legal purposes. What that something more is was stated by Lord Denning in a much-quoted passage. He said:

> "It seems to me that any mental disorder which has manifested itself in violence and is prone to recur is a disease of the mind. At any rate it is the sort of disease for which a person should be detained in hospital rather than be given an unqualified acquittal."[2]

A criticism of this is that Lord Denning referred only to the danger of violence, when he should, for completeness, have included the danger of damage to property. Further, the statement is inadequate as a definition of "disease of the mind" unless it is accompanied by the converse proposition that for legal purposes a disease of the mind is an affliction that is likely to manifest itself again in a dangerous way. In other words: future danger, disease of the mind; no future danger, no disease of the mind.[3] This converse or negative side of Lord Denning's definition is necessary to prevent mandatory commitment having too wide an application, though whether the courts will recognise it is still in doubt.

Formerly, epilepsy was automatically treated as a kind of insanity, future danger or not. In one case a woman, having an epileptic seizure while filling a kettle to put it on the fire, put the kettle on the oven and her child on the fire. This was a pure mishap, which might happen to any of the thousands of epileptics who lead an almost normal life in society; yet the unfortunate woman was immured in Broadmoor, away from her husband and friends—a tragic reproach to the law of mandatory commitment and the incompetence of the Home Office of the day.[4]

This would not happen now. At worst the woman would be committed for a short time to a local hospital, though whether any commitment to hospital at all would make medical sense may be doubted. However kind the outcome of the case may be, it is hard to appreciate the purpose of prosecuting in such circumstances.

More recently, the courts have accepted on a number of occasions that when the injury inflicted by the sufferer from an ordinary epileptic fit is the merest accident, and there is no reason to suppose that he presents a continuing source of danger, a verdict of automatism is appropriate. A

---

[2] [1963] AC 386 at 412.

[3] This negative proposition was rejected by the Supreme Court of Canada in *Rabey*; see § .4.

[4] W C Sullivan, *Crime and Insanity* (London 1924) Chap. 9. Cp. *Perry* (1919) 14 CAR at 51.

psychiatric hospital would not accept such a patient under a hospital order, except perhaps briefly for assessment, since he would not be regarded as in need of in-patient treatment; and there would be no social purpose in an insanity verdict on such facts. In driving cases, particularly, epilepsy is now regularly regarded as being distinct from insanity (§ .5). In *Quick*,[5] the Court of Appeal accepted overseas authorities to the effect that an epileptic seizure can be regarded as producing non-insane automatism.

However, we also have powerful authority the other way.

> In *Bratty*, the House of Lords held that the medical evidence in the case pointed to the defendant's alleged state of psychomotor epilepsy at the time when he killed a young girl as being a disease of the mind within the *McNaghten* rules. It was in this case that Lord Denning proposed the test of insanity quoted above.

There may appear at first sight to be a conflict between *Bratty* and the authorities previously quoted, but the reconciliation is that the statements holding that epileptic attacks did not amount to insanity were made in cases where the injury inflicted was accidental and unlikely to be repeated, whereas in *Bratty* the court thought that the defendant might present a continuing danger. In most cases of epilepsy where injury is caused the act is obviously non-purposive, whereas Bratty's act, however confused his state of mind, looked purposive—he took off a girl's stocking and strangled her with it.[6] The decision in *Sullivan*, which is to be noticed presently, may perhaps be explained on the same ground as *Bratty*.

If the question is one of the defendant's dangerousness, who decides it, judge or jury?

McNaghten seemed to suppose that the question of sanity or insanity was for the jury. This is certainly so on the question whether the defendant knew what he was doing, etc.; but in *Kemp* Devlin J held that the question whether the evidence showed insanity as opposed to non-insane automatism was one of law for the judge, and Lord Denning approved his view.[7] It has also been approved by the Supreme Court of Canada. Ritchie J said:

> "The general rule is that it is for the judge as a question of law to decide what constitutes a "disease of the mind," but that the question of whether or not the facts in a given case disclose the existence of such a disease is a question to be determined by the trier of fact."[8]

A dictum in *Quick* may seem to go the other way and to say that the question is for the jury,[9] but probably this was intended to refer only to the

[5] [1973] QB at 922, approving *Cottle* [1958] NZLR 999 and *Cooper* v. *McKenna* [1960] Qd.R 406. For other authorities treating epileptic seizures as instances of non-insane automatism see *Charlson* [1955] 1 WLR at 320; *Hill* v. *Baxter* [1958] 1 QB at 283, 287; *Holmes* [1960] WAR at 125 (Aus.); *Sell* (1962) 106 SJ 355. *Contra, Johnson* (1975) 28 CCC (2d) 305 (New Brunswick). See also Fairall in 5 Cr.LJ 337–340 (Aus.).

[6] The point is made by J C Smith in [1983] Crim.LR 258.

[7] § 28.5 at n. 9. So also *Hartridge* (1966) 48 CR 389 (Sask.).

[8] *Rabey* (1980) 15 CR (3rd) 225.

[9] [1973] QB at 923.

factual question stated by Ritchie J. The jury are a most unsuitable body to decide the legal question. In *Sullivan*[10] the House of Lords treated the question as being one of law.

Can the defendant find out, before he sets up a defence of epilepsy, whether his case is going to be treated as one of insanity or not?

In the past judges have agreed to give a preliminary ruling. This procedure was used in *Quick* and *Sullivan*.

> Sullivan was charged with assault occasioning a.b.h. He attacked a friend and kicked him about the head and body while he was recovering from a minor seizure caused by petit mal epilepsy. The medical evidence was that it is extremely rare for a sufferer from petit mal to act violently during an epileptic seizure; that such violence is unpredictable; and that the sufferer would not be conscious of what he did. The defence sought the judge's ruling that this evidence showed only non-insane automatism, but the judge ruled against the submission, holding that the evidence would indicate a disease of the mind. So the defendant, to avoid mandatory commitment, asked to change his plea to guilty. This was accepted by the judge (although it was clear to all concerned that Sullivan had lacked the intent necessary for the crime). Since the defendant had been put in charge of the jury the judge directed the jury to convict, and put the defendant on a PPO.
>
> On appeal the Court of Appeal and House of Lords affirmed the judge's ruling on the insanity point. Lord Diplock (with whom the other lords concurred) expressed the opinion that a "disease of the mind" for legal purposes might manifest itself only for a short time and might be either organic (as in epilepsy) or functional. He left open the question whether the procedure adopted after the judge's ruling was legal and proper.[11]
>
> This decision is of great concern to sufferers from epilepsy, and is capable of having wider implications. Lord Diplock made one concession: he intimated that he did not exclude the possibility of non-insane automatism where temporary impairment resulted from some external factor such as a blow on the head causing concussion or the administration of an anaesthetic for therapeutic purposes. Nevertheless, the *ratio decidendi* is capable of fixing an insanity verdict on epileptic sufferers who inflict harm in what is clearly an accident, like the unfortunate Broadmoor patient mentioned before. Possibly the decision in *Sullivan* may be distinguished from this case on the ground that the evidence showed an attack by Sullivan, whereas the woman who put her baby on the fire did not intend to attack the baby. But even that distinction would not, it appears, exclude an insanity verdict where the defendant has stabbed another person to death when sleepwalking. If so, the decision is retrogressive. It will greatly extend the operation of mandatory commitment, undoing the efforts of earlier courts to reach a humane and sensible outcome in these cases. Lord Diplock did not mention Lord Denning's test. If, as seems likely, the next step to be taken by the House of Lords will be to disapprove the procedure accepted by the trial judge in *Sullivan*,

[10] [1983] 3 WLR 123.
[11] The CA, however, had approved the course taken by the judge.

> the only way in which the epileptic or sleepwalker can avoid being needlessly committed to hospital will be by pleading guilty in the first instance (either to the offence charged or, in the case of murder, to manslaughter with diminished responsibility), offering evidence of his malady in mitigation. Perhaps the House of Lords will find a way of preventing even this strategy.

This development should clinch the argument (if clinching is needed) against mandatory commitment. The CLRC recommended in 1963 that the judge should be given a discretion as to disposal,[12] but the recommendation was rejected by the Home Office, which obtained the concurrence of the Chief Justice of the time in its own opinion that the liberalisation of the law would be too dangerous. The question was again considered by the Butler Committee on Mentally Abnormal Offenders; by this time the higher judiciary had changed its mind, and supported liberalisation, which was, therefore, again recommended by the Butler Committee in 1975.[13] But no committee reports could induce the Home Office to withdraw its opposition to any change. Ministers listen primarily to their civil service advisers, not to outside advisers, even though the outside advice has been sought by the Ministers themselves.

§ 29.3. HYPOGLYCAEMIA

Hypoglycaemia,[1] a deficiency of blood-sugar, can both impair the consciousness and induce an aggressive outburst. It may come about as the result of fasting followed by the consumption of alcohol,[2] or when a diabetic takes an overdose of insulin or subjects himself to unusual fatigue or lack of food. Deficiency of insulin produces the opposite condition, hyperglycaemia, excess of blood-sugar, which can also be caused by alcohol.[3] This can have somewhat similar symptoms.

Hypoglycaemia has come before the courts several times and is clearly held to be capable of producing a state of non-insane automatism. In *Quick*[4]:

> The defendant, charged with assault, was a diabetic who had taken insulin, as prescribed, on the morning of the assault, and had drunk a quantity of spirits and eaten little food thereafter. He contended that at the time of the assault he was in a state of automatism due to hypoglycaemia, but the trial judge intimated that this would be taken as an insanity defence, so Quick changed his plea to guilty. The conviction was reversed on the ground that if Quick's condition produced automatism it would not amount to insanity.

While the readiness of the Court of Appeal to concede the defence of non-insane automatism in principle is welcome, it by no means follows that the defence would have been accepted by the jury on a proper direction. The immediate and main effect of hypoglycaemia seems to be to induce aggression; only in its later course would the condition induce a semi-

---

[12] Cmnd 2149, para. 34.
[13] Cmnd 6244, para. 18.42.

[1] Pronounced "hypoglykeemia."
[2] [1968] 1 BMJ 463; and see next note.
[3] Gerald B Phillips and Henry F Safrit in 217 Jrnl.Am.Med.Assn. 1513.
[4] [1973] QB 910.

conscious state.[5] This was the effect of the medical evidence before the court of trial, and it would seem to suggest that there was at least a stage in which Quick was guilty of an assault while in possession of his senses, even though he was rendered aggressive by the fall in his blood sugar. A bodily condition inducing aggression is not in itself a defence to a criminal charge, but a matter to be considered in sentencing.

Lawton LJ reinforced his decision that automatism produced by hypoglycaemia was not a disease of the mind by proposing a new principle. He accepted Lord Denning's proposition (§ 29.2 at n. 2) as stating the general rule, but grafted an exception upon it. The Lord Justice thought that if Lord Denning's statement stood unqualified, then Quick was setting up a defence of insanity, and to avoid that unhappy conclusion an exception had to be imposed upon the rule.[6]

> "Common sense is affronted by the prospect of a diabetic being sent to . . . hospital, when in most cases the disordered mental condition can be rectified by pushing a lump of sugar into the patient's mouth. . . . A malfunctioning of the mind of transitory effect caused by the application to the body of some external factor such as violence, drugs, including anaesthetics, alcohol and hypnotic influences[7] cannot fairly be said to be due to disease."

This "external factor" doctrine has been approved in Canada,[8] and now by the House of Lords in *Sullivan* (§ .2); but it presents difficulties. On what ground did Lawton LJ think that Quick came within Lord Denning's proposition? If a diabetic falls into a hypoglycaemic state through an accidental overdose of insulin, there is no great reason to think that the mental disorder, the hypoglycaemic state, will recur; and even if there is such reason, there may be little reason to suppose that the state will again issue in violence. In that event the condition should not be accounted a disease of the mind within Lord Denning's rule. If Quick was not deemed to be mad under Lord Denning's rule, and if he was not mad in the ordinary meaning of the word, the external factor doctrine was not needed to save him from the imputation of madness. On the whole, it would be much better if the courts kept to Lord Denning's plain rule; the external factor doctrine adds nothing of value to it.[9]

The external factor doctrine is also open to the objection that it creates arbitrary distinctions. If a diabetic suffers a hypoglycaemic episode merely because he has not eaten enough, any injury he inflicts must result in an

---

[5] See Podolsky in 45 JCr.L, Cr. & PS 675; John N Cumings (ed.), *Biochemical Aspects of Neurological Disorder* (Oxford 1959), Chap. 14, and other references in 63 Col.LRev. 647 n. 14. The difficulty of a diagnosis of hypoglycaemia is aggravated by the fact that as many as 42 per cent. of normal people have glucose values below 50mg/100ml after meals without showing symptoms.

[6] [1973] QB at 922E.

[7] It is by no means clear that a criminal act committed under hypnotism would not involve liability; all that Lawton LJ says is that it is not a disease of the mind. On hypnotism see references in Robinson, 82 Col.LRev. 225 n. 93, 228 n. 103; Fairall in 5 Cr.LJ 347–348 (Aus.).

[8] In *Rabey* (1980) 15 CR (3rd) 225, Dickson J (dissenting) stated the rule in *Quick* and described it as "accepted legal doctrine." The majority also accepted it, but gave it a questionable application. See § .4.

[9] Notwithstanding the support that Dickson J seemed to give to *Quick* (see last note), he quoted the above remark in the 1st edn of this book with approval, and added: "This view finds ample support in the legal literature" (references given). See also the support given to Lord Denning's rule by the Butler Committee, Cmnd 6244 para. 18.25.

insanity verdict according to this doctrine, since no external factor is involved. If on the other hand the diabetic produced his state of automatism by taking insulin, or by a combination of fasting and consuming alcohol, this would be accounted non-insane automatism.[10] There is nothing to be said for drawing the line in this way.

§ 29.4. DISSOCIATION

Dissociative states (whether or not occurring during sleep) are medically classified as hysterical neuroses, in the absence of organic brain disease. The extreme form is the "split personality" of the type of Jekyll and Hyde; but some doctors doubt the genuineness of this form in the very few cases where it has been alleged to occur. The accepted description of dissociation is given in the *Glossary of Mental Disorders*.

> "The most prominent feature is a narrowing of the field of consciousness that seems to serve an unconscious purpose; it is commonly accompanied or followed by selective amnesia. There may be dramatic but essentially superficial changes of personality sometimes taking the form of a fugue (wandering state). Behaviour may mimic psychosis, or rather the patient's idea of psychosis."

This definition is well salted with suspicion; and the scepticism with which the defence is naturally regarded is one reason for the problem it presents in a criminal trial. Hysterical dissociation is difficult to diagnose with certainty because the psychiatrist can only accept the patient's word, apart from considering what the patient now avers in relation to his general conduct at the time.

Whether dissociation is accepted as negativing criminal liability depends upon the circumstances and the strength of the psychiatric evidence.

> Where the defendant, having caused a collision, drove dangerously in order to evade the police, making a clean get-away so that they were not able to arrest him till some time later, the trial judge took a strong line by withholding a defence of hysterical fugue from the jury, and was upheld by the Court of Appeal, notwithstanding psychiatric evidence that the defendant's subconscious mind took over so that he would not have appreciated what he was doing.[1]

The case was unpropitious for the recognition of the defence. One finds it hard to believe that a man who was obviously trying to evade the police did not know what he was doing; in fact the psychiatrist called by the defence, who talked about the defendant's subconscious mind taking over, admitted his belief that the defendant knew he was driving away from the accident, and intended not to allow the police to stop him. So the psychiatrist's evidence was self-contradictory. Nevertheless, the court's judgment is itself unsatisfactory. The court excluded the defence on the ground that the defendant's mind "was working to some extent. The driving was purposeful driving, which was to get away from the scene of the accident." This remark is true, but, because it is unaccompanied by further explanation, it fails to carry complete conviction. In sleepwalking cases (which are often diagnosed as states of

---

[10] See §§ .6, .7.

[1] *Isitt* [1978] RTR 211, 67 CAR 44. Cp. Fairall in 5 Cr.LJ 344–345 (Aus.).

dissociation) the sleeper's mind is working "to some extent" (as a dreamer's is), and his acts may be purposive. An example is where he dives out of the bedroom window, evidently under the impression that he is diving into a pool. The difference is that for the window-diver there is no pool, whereas the driver in the present case was in fact successfully shaking off the police. Because we all dream, and because the fact of sleepwalking is well authenticated, a defence of sleepwalking can be intrinsically probable, while the driver's defence of dissociation during his waking hours, when he has a strong motive for lying, is intrinsically improbable; but is not the question of probability for the jury?

> In a case at sessions,[2] a woman charged with shoplifting was acquitted on psychiatric evidence that for two hours her memory had gone completely blank while "part of her personality took command." The doctor added: "As long as there is a split in her personality there is a likelihood that this will happen again"; but his remark did not induce the court to treat the case as one of insanity.

This is the kind of case in which everyone in court is ready to co-operate to ensure an acquittal. The defendant is probably a respectable lady; what she did was uncharacteristic, and no motive can be seen for her to steal. Professor Bluglass expresses the psychiatrist's problem in the following words:

> "The exact state of mind at the time of the act, weeks or months ago, is usually impossible to determine. The psychiatrist well knows that such a lady is not a criminal; respectable, middle-aged ladies rarely embark upon a life of crime. The consequences of conviction are sometimes severe. . . . The pressures upon the psychiatrist to express his understanding of her behaviour in terms acceptable to the court are heavy. The psychiatrist must establish doubt relating to the ability to form the necessary intent to steal."[3]

In the only English case where a defence of dissociation was raised to a charge of murder, the defence was taken to involve not an issue of criminal guilt in general but only an issue of diminished responsibility.[4] The case did not go on appeal, and the question of total exemption from responsibility was not considered.

These instances show that a psychiatrist's diagnosis of dissociation is likely to be differently received according to the circumstances. Take the charge of shoplifting. It is easy to accept that sometimes, perhaps through depression or anxiety, a person may be unable to concentrate on what he is doing, and so may load supermarket goods into the wrong basket, and even wander into the street, without intent to steal; there is no need to call his conduct a dissociative state in order to decide that it does not amount to theft. When a sleepwalker causes injury the hypothesis that he is acting out a dream is strongly supported by evidence of the nature of this condition; the sleepwalker is out of touch with reality, except the bizarre and distorted reality of a dream, and he is brought back to reality only by waking him up.[5] But where a person who is fully awake flees from the police, or attacks another in jealousy or anger, a defence of dissociation is hard to credit, however many experts are called to give evidence in support of it. How strange, the layman may say, and how very convenient for the defendant, that this alleged state of dissociation descended on him at the

---

[2] The Times, February 21, 1970.

[3] Robert Bluglass, *Psychiatry, The Law and the Offender* (ISTD 1980) 8.

[4] *Eeles*, § 30.3 at n. 11.

[5] By the way, the common belief that it is dangerous to wake up a sleepwalker is mistaken. On the contrary, it is dangerous not to do so, because the sleepwalker may harm himself.

very moment when he had reason for evading the police, or when he was face to face with a person whom he had a strong motive for attacking. The more down-to-earth explanation of the defendant's "narrowing of the field of consciousness" is that it resulted merely from an overwhelming passion which led him to pay no attention to ordinary moral or prudential considerations; this is not inconsistent with the supposition that he was perfectly aware of what he was doing, psychiatric evidence to the contrary notwithstanding.

Although the definition of dissociation speaks of a narrowed field of consciousness, the fact is that we often narrow our field of consciousness (that is, the field of our attention) without being thought to be in a state of dissociation. A family occupying a house next to a railway line may be unmindful of the noise and vibration of a passing express, while their visitor is overwhelmed by the racket. When we are concentrating on one particular matter we may be oblivious of other things that are happening. Moreover, consciousness varies with bodily states.

> "When tired, bored, or slightly poisoned by alcohol, we are suffering from a partial loss of consciousness. From the excited state of great efficiency under stress, through normal work-a-day moods, to states of dullness, coma and stupor, there is a continuous series of states where consciousness is less and less active. . . . Only in deep sleep is the cortex inactive, as judged by the electroencephalograph."[6]

Experience in Canada and Australia[7] shows the danger for the administration of justice of psychiatric evidence of dissociation. Their courts have had to adjudicate upon a spate of defences of dissociation where the defendant had killed or caused injury (or in one case raped a child of 5) in circumstances that would normally be thought of as provocation or extreme mental stress, and not as raising any doubt as to legal responsibility. These courts have come to accept that the defence can bar a conviction. In Canada the language of a "psychological blow" has gained currency; evidence of such a blow can support a psychiatric hypothesis of dissociation which must be left to the jury as negativing the necessary intent. But the principle is not limited to cases of "psychological blow:" the British Columbia Court of Appeal accepted the possibility of a state of dissociation arising merely from anxiety after the defendant's wife left him.[8]

However, the Supreme Court of Canada has now declared that success in the defence should normally lead to an insanity verdict: *Rabey*.[9] The reasoning was closely similar to that subsequently adopted by the House of Lords in *Sullivan* (§ .2).

> Rabey discovered a letter written by the girl of whom he was enamoured, indicating that she had no regard for him. Reading this letter did not immediately induce any alteration in his consciousness, but the next day, on meeting her, and after a short conversation with her, he struck her with a geological specimen and attempted to strangle her. A psychiatrist called for the defence gave it as his opinion that at the crucial moment Rabey was in a state of dissociation, and the jury acquitted him of charges of wounding and attempted murder. It was held that the verdict should be one of not guilty on the ground of insanity (this resulting, in Canada as in Britain, in committal to hospital at the discretion of the executive).

The reasoning of the majority of the Supreme Court, like that of Lord Diplock in *Sullivan*, accepted the "external factor" doctrine of *Quick*, but for a very different purpose. Lawton LJ had enunciated the doctrine as a limitation upon Lord Denning's test. The Lord Justice

---

[6] Cobb, *Foundations of Neuropsychiatry* (1958) 117–118, quoted by Don Stuart, *Canadian Criminal Law* (Toronto 1982) 78.

[7] On the Australian cases see Fairall in 5 Cr.LJ (Aus.) 345–347.

[8] *MacLeod* (1980) 52 CCC (2d) 193.

[9] (1980) 15 CR (3d) 225. See the powerful dissenting judgment by Dickson J, and the survey of the whole problem by Mackay in [1980] Crim.LR 350. In support of the decision see Kenneth Campbell in 23 Cr.LQ 342 (Can.) See also Fairall, *op.cit.* 136, 335.

stated who were *not* to be held to be suffering from disease of the mind, and did not suggest that the converse of his principle was an infallible pointer to those who *were* so suffering. To say that the presence of an external cause of mental trouble saves a man from the imputation of madness, as was held in *Quick*, does not imply that the absence of an external cause necessarily means that he is mad. The Supreme Court, however, (adopting the judgment of Martin J in the court below) took Lawton LJ's principle as working both ways, as declaring what is insanity as well as what is not.

> "Any malfunctioning of the mind or mental disorder having its source primarily in some subjective condition or weakness internal to the accused (whether fully understood or not) may be a 'disease of the mind'. . . . The ordinary stresses and disappointments of life which are the common lot of mankind do not constitute an external cause constituting an explanation for a malfunctioning of the mind which takes it out of the category of a 'disease of the mind.' "

In other words, the Supreme Court held that a person who is in a state of dissociation has at that time a disease of the mind even though there is no likelihood of a recurrence, if the dissociation is caused by one of the ordinary stresses of life. (The court said "may be" a disease of the mind, but in the context of dissociation this evidently meant "is" a disease of the mind.) The court therefore rejected the negative version of Lord Denning's statement which was suggested before.[10]

One can see a certain argument of policy supporting the decision in *Rabey*. The idea that a case that would otherwise be regarded as one of provocation or emotional upset should result in total non-responsibility and an ordinary acquittal because of the rather dubious diagnosis of a psychiatrist is unattractive to the lawyer. Since, on *mens rea* principles, the defence cannot be excluded from the consideration of the jury, a way of reducing its possible popularity among people charged with serious crimes is to hold that success in it will subject the defendant to mandatory commitment.

But the court did not say that it was using mandatory hospital commitment as a means of inducing defendants not to set up a defence of dissociation; indeed, it emphasised its expectation that a defendant found not guilty on account of insanity would be discharged from hospital if he were found not dangerous and required no further treatment. This would obviously be the right course, and in cases of alleged dissociation would largely nullify any deterrent effect of the order.

The rule is unsatisfactory on principle, because, first, to regard a dissociated person as suffering from a "disease of the mind" is to attach a highly artificial meaning to that phrase. As the minority judgment pointed out, Rabey

> "exhibited no pathological symptoms indicative of a previously existing, or ongoing, psychiatric disorder. On medical evidence accepted by the trial judge, the prospect of a recurrence of dissociation is extremely remote. There was no finding that the appellant suffered from psychosis, neurosis or personality disorder. He does not have an organic disease of the brain. This was an isolated event. The appellant has already spent several weeks in a mental institution undergoing psychiatric, neurological and psychological assessment, the result of which did not indicate a need for treatment."

Secondly, the principle that the court invented by propounding the converse of the rule in *Quick* has an unhappy effect on the law of automatism in relation to epilepsy and sleepwalking. As said before, hysterical dissociation is one of the main causes believed to account for sleepwalking, yet the case-law of all common law jurisdictions shows that prosecutions for acts done while sleep-walking must result in an ordinary acquittal. It is difficult to explain the courts' difference of attitude towards dissociated states occurring during sleep and those alleged to occur while the subject is awake, apart from the fact that the judges find the former more readily credible.

Thirdly, the judgment of the majority of the Supreme Court seemed to involve itself in an unhappy distinction between the effect of external events upon "normal" and "abnormal"

---

[10] § .2 at n. 3. On the conflicting medical evidence in the case see Allen Bartholomew in [1981] Crim.LR 68.

people.[11] To attribute Rabey's conduct to his "psychological or emotional makeup" rather than to an "external cause" (Rabey's discovery that the victim, his girl friend, did not love him) involved an assumption about Rabey's psychological vulnerability about which there was little evidence apart from the circumstances of the deed itself. Besides, a finding that the event was caused by Rabey's special vulnerability does not explain why he should be committed to hospital, if the evidence is that no repetition of such an attack is to be expected.

The courts should eschew any effort to discourage the defence of dissociation by interpreting it as evidence of insanity, or by withholding psychiatric evidence from the jury. The defence, if supported by medical evidence, should be adjudicated upon by the triers of fact, and if successful should result in an ordinary acquittal. But what is urgently needed is that the psychiatrist who deposes to dissociation in improbable circumstances should be subjected to skilled and deeply sceptical cross-examination, and that the Crown should, where possible, call counter-evidence. One procedural change required in the law (apart from a reconsideration of the whole issue of mental disorder in relation to criminal conduct[12]) is a provision requiring the defence to give advance notice of the issue of automatism or of any other psychiatric or psychological evidence on the mental element.[13] At present, the defence of automatism can be sprung upon the prosecution, which may not be armed with the evidence to meet it.

§ 29.5. AUTOMATISM IN NEGLIGENT DRIVING

In the days when there was an offence of dangerous driving and when it was held to be a matter of strict liability, the courts alleviated the law by saying that if a person while driving fell unconscious at the wheel, or continued to make bodily movements in a state of automatism, he was no longer "driving," and could be acquitted. Examples were where the driver was stunned by a blow,[1] had a heart attack, or had an attack of *petit mal* epilepsy (not knowing that he was subject to this).[2] The doctrine was even extended to cases of people who drove in their sleep (i.e. while "sleepwalking").[3] The same exemption was accorded where the charge was of careless driving, though here no very refined reasoning was

---

[11] The court considered a case where the state of dissociation arose from the shock of being attacked, or being involved in a serious accident, or seeing one's loved one attacked; no final opinion was expressed, but it seems that the court would have accepted a defence of non-insane automatism in such circumstances, because such events might affect the normal person. For a criticism see Mackay in [1980] Crim.LR 358 n. 48, 359; he points out the difficulty or impossibility of saying that in *Quick* the hypoglycaemic episode was not primarily internal to the defendant.

[12] The Butler Committee proposed a new arrangement which would greatly improve the law. There should be a new verdict of "not guilty on evidence of mental disorder," to replace the present special verdict, which would give the court certain discretionary powers, but exclusion would be made of transient states not related to other forms of mental disorder, and arising solely as a consequence of (*a*) the administration or non-administration of drugs or (*b*) physical injury; evidence falling within this exception could lead to an absolute acquittal, as now. The proposal would have the effect of ending talk of "disease of the mind" and applying a form of special verdict to a successful defence of sleepwalking, epilepsy or dissociation, but the effect would not be nearly so draconic in such cases as the present special verdict. See Cmnd 6244 of 1975, para. 18.23.

[13] For this proposal of the Butler Committee see the Report, para. 18.49.

[1] *Per* Lord Goddard CJ in *Hill* v. *Baxter* [1958] 1 KB at 282–283; *Carter* [1959] VR 105; cases in § .1 n. 8.

[2] *Lewendon*, The Times, December 14, 15, 16, 1961, [1962] 1 BMJ 196. Cp. *Hill* v. *Baxter*, last note, at p. 283; *Spurge* [1961] 2 QB at 210.

[3] Magistrates accepted this defence in a case reported in The Times, March 3, 1967. The defendant, who was given to sleepwalking and who adduced confirmatory medical evidence, got out of bed in the middle of the night, took out his motor cycle and crashed into a car, finally waking up in hospital. He was acquitted of driving without due care, without insurance, and without an excise licence.

required, because the evidence clearly showed that there had been no carelessness.

While this application of the doctrine of automatism is generally approved because it avoids injustice, the law is really absurd from start to finish. First, it is wrong that any driving offence (apart from "ticket" offences) should be construed as carrying strict liability; they should be regarded as offences of negligence. Reckless and careless driving being offences of fault, the doctrine of automatism is no longer needed for them; but it continues to be needed for the many other driving offences that continue to be construed as carrying strict liability. Secondly, it is often pedantic (or would be pedantic, if it were not for the praiseworthy motive) for the courts to say that a person driving in a state of clouded consciousness is not "driving." What else is he doing? It would be verbally acceptable to say that a person who has slumped unconscious over the wheel is no longer driving, if the only effect he has on the motion of the car is that the weight of his foot is still depressing the accelerator.[4] But in the ordinary use of language a man who rides a motor-cycle in his sleep is riding it, just as a seal that rides a motor-cycle at a circus rides it; he may not be functioning at a high cognitive level, but his brain is sufficiently active to enable him to make the complicated physical movements required.

We shall return to this point presently, when we come to driving offences of strict liability. For the moment it is enough to say, that, on a charge of careless driving, the defendant's conduct must be compared with that of the reasonable man; for this purpose one has to assume that the reasonable man is suddenly seized with the same bodily affliction as the defendant; and on that assumption the defendant's conduct does not diverge from that of his ideal exemplar.

But there may be evidence of fault: for example, where a driver goes on driving knowing that he may drop off to sleep any minute.

In that event the cases recognise that there can be liability. The driver is not guilty of reckless or careless driving by reason of what he does when asleep; but all the same he can be convicted of careless driving if he falls asleep at the wheel, on the theory that he was guilty of the offence not at the moment when the crash occurred but at the prior moment when he should have realised that he was sleepy and should have stopped driving.[5] Similarly, a driver may be convicted if he drives knowing that he is subject to an epileptic attack or a diabetic coma[6]; in theory he is guilty of careless (or even reckless) driving even when he is driving perfectly well and nothing untoward occurs.[7]

---

[4] On one occasion it was held that a totally unconscious driver was "driving": *Purvis* v. *Hogg* [1969] Crim.LR 380. But that was under the blood alcohol legislation. See the critical comment in the Crim.LR.

[5] *Kay* v. *Butterworth* (1945) 173 LT 191, 110 JP 75, 61 TLR 452; *Henderson* v. *Jones* (1955) 119 JP 305. Cp. *Sibbles* [1959] Crim.LR 660; *Budd,* § .6 n. 2; [1967] Crim.LR 196–197. Yet it was held, illogically, that if a person drove when he was under the influence of drink to such an extent as to be incapable of having control of the vehicle, but did not do anything dangerous, he could not he convicted of dangerous driving: *Ward* [1954] Crim.LR 940; presumably the same would now he held for careless driving. There is an obvious inconsistency. The sleepy driver is not driving with an an appearance of danger when he is awake; yet he can be convicted of driving carelessly at that time. See note, [1961] Crim.LR 626; Samuels in 124 NLJ 1061.

Although the drowsy driver is supposed to stop, the courts look upon him with an unsympathetic eye if he stops on the hard shoulder of a motorway in order to sleep. They convict him of an offence of stopping unless he had no reason to suppose that he would be sleepy when he joined the motorway: *Higgins* v. *Bernard* [1972] 1 WLR 455, 1 All ER 1037; cp. [1967] Crim.LR 196 n. 22; [1972] *ibid.* 243; 131 JPN 20. This attitude hardly promotes public safety.

[6] In *Moses* v. *Winder* [1980] Crim.LR 232 a driver who fell into a diabetic coma was convicted of careless driving, but the reason given was that he had forewarning and did not take adequate steps. Presumably he would also have been convicted if he knew that a coma would befall him without warning.

[7] *Spurge* [1961] 2 QB at 210.

It is rare for a driver to fall fast asleep at the wheel, but momentary loss of consciousness may occur, and is now a recognised phenomenon under the name of "microsleep."[8] A sleep-deprived person can lose consciousness for a few seconds, when the eyes remain open but the mechanisms that keep the body alert are momentarily switched off; and he will not afterwards know what happened. If he is driving he may be involved in a "mystery accident." A defence based on this hypothesis is unlikely to succeed, because in the absence of evidence it would be accounted a "fanciful doubt" and dismissed from consideration.[9] Presumably the only concrete evidence that could be adduced (apart from expert evidence as to the possibility of the condition) would be evidence that the defendant was deprived of sleep; but then his driving in that condition could be found to be negligent for that reason.

What if a person who is at the wheel but is in a state of automatism fails to give way at a Give Way sign?

It was held in *Hill* v. *Baxter*[10] that not conforming to a traffic sign is an offence of strict liability, but that automatism can exculpate. The defence failed on the facts because the defendant had not given sufficient evidence to raise it.

What if the driver was at fault in losing consciousness just before he came to the traffic sign?

In *Hill* v. *Baxter*, Lord Goddard CJ declared that the evidence was compatible with the driver's having fallen asleep at the wheel, which could not be a defence. The last part of this statement may frequently be true for a charge of careless driving, when the carelessness can be backdated to the driving while awake. But as regards the failure to conform to the traffc sign, there is an obvious difficulty. When the defendant failed to conform to the sign, he was asleep and not "driving." At the earlier time when he was awake, he did not fail to conform to the sign in question because he had not then reached it. The problem is part of the general question whether automatism induced by the defendant's own fault is a defence: see the next section. The problem can be avoided in traffic cases by charging the defendant with careless driving instead of with the offence of strict liability. He can be convicted of the offence if he drove while feeling sleepy; the question of automatism does not then arise.

How far gone must the driver be, not to be accounted "driving"?

Of course this question cannot be answered in the abstract, but the weight of authority holds that if the defendant was driving in what is medically accepted as a state of severely impaired consciousness, then he is not "driving" in contemplation of law.[11] This proposition accords with other cases on automatism, such as the sleepwalking cases where the defendant has stabbed or killed; that he has literally wounded or killed is

---

[8] The defence was set up in 1974 (The Times, December 3), but no outcome is reported.

[9] Cp. *Oakes* v. *Foster* [1961] Crim.LR 628; *Richards* v. *Gardner* [1974] *ibid.* 119; § 14.2.

[10] [1958] 1 QB 277.

[11] Above nn. 1–3; Mackay in 96 LQR 503; [1967] Crim.LR 199 ff. The tort case upon which Mackay comments is complicated by the tendency to look upon this branch of the law as a form of social insurance. See Grace Smith in 130 NLJ 1111. In criminal law the simple question should be whether the defendant, having regard to the disability that overcame him, was negligent.

undeniable, but the law regards the *actus reus* as missing because of the volitional element incorporated in that notion.[12]

Some decisions are out of line.

In *Watmore* v. *Jenkins*[13] it was held that a diabetic driver who, without fault, fell into a hypoglycaemic state when driving, continuing in his car for five miles until he crashed into a parked vehicle, was still "driving" and was guilty of dangerous driving. There was not "such a complete destruction of voluntary control as could constitute in law automatism." The similar decision on driving in an alleged state of dissociation has already been noticed.[14] However reasonable these decisions may appear as interpretations of the ordinary meaning of "driving," they reach an unjust result and do not accord with other authorities. The offence of dangerous driving being abolished, the question could arise today only in relation to offences of strict liability like failure to conform to traffic signs.

Could a driver get off a charge of driving when unfit through drink, on the ground that he is so besotted that he is not in law driving?

This is perhaps possible. But the proper view is that on a charge of driving when unfit, the word "driving" must, by force of the context, be taken to include the control of a vehicle when in a state of impaired consciousness by reason of voluntary intoxication.[15] Driving offences are of basic intent, so that voluntary intoxication is no excuse (§ .6). In any case, such a person could be convicted of being in charge of the vehicle when unfit to drive through drink or drugs.[16] A person who is in charge of a car continues in charge even when he falls asleep, and therefore continues in charge if he falls into a drunken stupor.

If a person is acquitted of a driving offence on a defence of automatism, can't the court do anything to stop him driving, if he is mentally or physically unfit?

A court that tries a driving case is required to inform the Home Secretary if it appears that the defendant may be suffering from a dangerous disease or disability.[17] This applies to all disabilities, such as defective eyesight, as well as afflictions like epilepsy and alcoholism.[18] The licensing authority can then have the disability investigated, and if necessary the driver's licence can be withdrawn. There are special conditions for the issue of licences to epileptics.[19]

§ 29.6. AUTOMATISM AND INTOXICATION

The previous discussion leads on to a wider question. How far is the

[12] § .1 n. 6.

[13] [1962] 2 QB 572. See [1967] Crim.LR 201–204.

[14] *Isitt* § 29.4 n. 1.

[15] A dictum in *Bullen* v. *Keay* [1974] RTR 559 may be read as suggesting that one who drives erratically when in a coma caused by drink or drugs is not guilty of driving while unfit; but this cannot be right. Cp. [1974] Crim.LR 372; Fairall in 4 Crim.LJ (Aus.) 270–272). It would make nonsense of the offence of driving while unfit if extreme unfitness negatived the "driving." The implication from *Majewski* clearly is that incapacity of any kind produced by drink or drugs voluntarily taken does not exclude liability. See also above n. 5.

[16] Subject to the defence provided by RTA 1972 s. 5 (3) that there was no likelihood of his driving while unfit.

[17] Road Traffic Act 1972 s. 92.

[18] 144 JPN 521.

[19] Motor Vehicles (Driving Licences) Regulations 1976 reg. 22. See *Secretary of State for Transport* v. *Adams* [1982] RTR 369.

defence of automatism displaced by evidence that the condition was produced wholly or in part by the defendant's voluntary intoxication?

As was suggested at the end of the last section, the answer must be governed principally by *Majewski*.[1] If the crime is of specific intent, automatism is a defence in the usual way. If it is of basic intent, voluntary intoxication producing the automatism is fatal to the defence (whether the automatism is regarded as negativing the intent or the act).

Putting this in another way, it may be said that in crimes of basic intent *Majewski* rides rough-shod over all doctrines of *mens rea* and *actus reus*. The evidence of voluntary intoxication and its consequential muddled state of mind are to be ignored in deciding whether the defendant intended the result in question. This interpretation of the law is essential, because the law would be even more confused than it now is if the courts distinguished between "ordinary" voluntary intoxication and such intoxication resulting in automatism. Intoxication resulting in a confusional state is both intoxication and automatism, and is governed by *Majewski*. The operation of the rule is illustrated by *Lipman* (§ 21.3 at n. 10).

The only problem is where the state of automatism is produced by a combination of intoxication and another cause. Surprising as it may seem, it is now well settled that such circumstances are to be judged as cases of automatism without applying the rule in *Majewski*. In other words, the intoxication can be a defence even in crimes of basic intent. *Majewski* operates only where the confusional state is produced by voluntary intoxication alone. The intervention in substantial degree of any other causal factor means that the confusional state can be found to be inconsistent with, and therefore to negative, the required mental element.

The combination of factors just referred to may occur in different ways.

1 Voluntary intoxication may bring about some factor or event that itself wholly produces the state of automatism. A drunkard staggers and falls, hitting his head; he then inflicts some injury without knowing what he is doing. The medical evidence is that the defendant was concussed, and that his confusional state was, medically speaking, due entirely to the concussion, the defendant's intoxication being merely a historical cause of the concussion. Here the usual defence of automatism will avail.[2] The rule would be obvious if the concussion were not causally connected with the intoxication, but it is applied also where (as in this example) the concussion is produced as a result of the defendant's intoxicated state.

2 As in case 1, except that the medical evidence is that the defendant's confusional state was the result both of voluntary intoxication and (in substantial degree) of another cause. For example, the evidence may be that it was immediately caused by the combination of concussion and voluntary intoxication. Here again it is held that automatism is a defence.[3]

What will create a flutter in the dovecotes will be a case in which evidence of alcoholic intake is combined with evidence from a friendly psychiatrist that when the defendant imbibed he was in a highly emotional state, the result being to produce dissociation which would not have occurred without the presence of both factors!

---

[1] § 21.3. Cp. *Stripp* (1978) 69 CAR 318.

[2] *Budd* (1961) The Times, November 8, [1962] Crim.LR 49; *Stripp*, last note (*obiter dictum* disapproving the judge's direction printed in 69 CAR 319–320). The short report of the former case is not altogether clear, but it seems that the blow causing the concussion was received in a car collision in which the defendant was one of the drivers, and he seems to have been intoxicated at the time. Cp. *Keogh* [1964] VR 400 (Vict.).

[3] *Stripp*, n. 1 above; cp. *Burns* (1973) 58 CAR 364; and see the discussion of the Canadian cases by Mackay in [1982] Crim.LR 150–151.

3 As in case 2, but the second factor is the taking of a drug which potentiates the intoxicant and increases its effect. If the drug was taken for the purpose of increasing intoxication, the case is obviously governed by *Majewski* (indeed, Majewski himself had produced his condition by taking drugs as well as drink). On the other hand, if the drug was taken for some other purpose, as for a stomach upset, the defendant not realising the effect it would have, and if the intoxicant would not have produced the state of automatism by itself, the defence of automatism is available.[4] This is only another way of saying that the intoxication is not regarded as voluntary, and therefore is not covered by *Majewski*. The rule was expressed by the Butler Committee, with the subsequent approval of the CLRC, in the following words.

> "Voluntary intoxication" means intoxication resulting from the intentional taking of drink or a drug knowing that it is capable in sufficient quantity of having an intoxicating effect; provided that intoxication is not voluntary if it results in part from a fact unknown to the defendant that increases his sensitivity to the drink or drug. The concluding words would provide a defence to a person who suffers from hypoglycaemia, for example, who does not know that in that condition the ingestion of a small amount of alcohol can produce a state of altered consciousness, as well as to a person who has been prescribed a drug on medical grounds without warning of the effect it may produce."[5]

4 As in case 2, except that the second factor is a "disease of the mind." A person who is prone to psychotic outbursts triggers such an outburst by drinking. As a matter of common sense it would seem that the verdict on such facts should be one of insanity. One case holds that a verdict of non-insane automatism would be permissible,[6] but the decision has been rightly criticised by Smith and Hogan.[7] A verdict of insanity should be the correct one even if the outburst was triggered by taking drugs for a medicinal purpose, if there is sufficient likelihood of repetition.

§ 29.7. OTHER SELF-INDUCED AUTOMATISM

Turning to factors other than intoxicants, the present law is that no such factors showing fault on the defendant's part prevent him from setting up a defence of automatism, unless the defendant was subjectively reckless. The rule is simple to state, but a consideration of the authorities bearing on it will take the rest of the section.

No case before 1973 suggested that a defence of automatism is excluded because the condition was produced by the defendant's fault, other than voluntary intoxication. That other factors were then regarded as irrelevant is a fair inference from some of the cases on concurrent causation mentioned in the last section; for if automatism is a defence even when it results from some fault-factor (e.g. concussion caused by intoxication) plus continuing intoxication (itself a fault-factor), then one would suppose that the same rule must apply where the disorder of consciousness is created by a single fault-factor other than intoxication.

However, in *Quick*,[1] the Court of Appeal embarked on an ill-considered legislative venture. Speaking through Lawton LJ, the court proposed (obiter) a new rule, one of policy but conjured out of the authorities by carrying selection to extreme lengths. The court took the unusual course of founding the rule not on legislation or a judicial decision but on a mere submission of counsel in an earlier case.[2] The submission was as follows.

> "Automatism is a defence to a charge of dangerous driving provided that a person takes reasonable steps to prevent himself from acting involuntarily in a manner dangerous to

---

[4] *Burns*, last note. See Mackay, *op.cit.* 151–152.
[5] Butler Committee Report, Cmnd 6244, para. 18.56.
[6] *Burns*, n. 4 above.
[7] Smith and Hogan, 4th edn 166.

[1] For the facts see § .3 at n. 4.
[2] *Watmore* v. *Jenkins* (1962] 2 QB at 580.

> the public. It must be caused by some factor which he could not reasonably foresee and not by a self-induced incapacity."

This submission was expressed to be confined to dangerous driving, in which connection, even if valid at the time, it has lost its importance because of the abolition of the offence. In any case, the submission indicates a misapprehension as to the law relating to automatism in driving offences. When, for example, a driver proceeds along Church Lane in a sleepy condition, and falls asleep at the wheel just before entering High Street, where he is involved in an accident, he cannot be convicted of careless[3] driving in High Street, because in contemplation of law he did not "drive" in High Street, and it makes no difference that his involuntary accident in High Street was the result of his own previous fault. He can, indeed, be convicted of careless driving, but this must be laid as having taken place in Church Lane, when the driver was undoubtedly "driving."[4] It will be seen that the law relating to driving offences provides no support for the proposition that self-induced automatism is no defence, but rather the contrary.

On the frail basis of counsel's argument, together with a judicial decision of limited relevance, the Court of Appeal purported to lay down a general rule.

> "A self-induced incapacity will not excuse, see *R.* v. *Lipman*, nor will one which could have been reasonably foreseen as a result of either doing or omitting to do something, as, for example, taking alcohol against medical advice after using certain prescribed drugs, or failing to have regular meals while taking insulin."[5]

Quick himself seems to have come within this rule, because he was taking insulin and had eaten very little. It looks, therefore, as though his incapacity was self-induced. However, his conviction on plea was quashed because the judge had wrongly ruled that in the circumstances a defence of automatism would amount to an insanity defence. The Court of Appeal expressed the opinion that had the matter been left to the jury, the jury might properly have convicted the defendant on account of his fault in not eating, or alternatively in not taking a lump of sugar if he felt the attack coming on.

The dictum was clearly wrong, and *Lipman* was not an authority for it. On the court's rule, Lipman should have been convicted of murder, whereas he was only convicted of manslaughter, a crime of negligence. Extended argument on the point is no longer needed, because the Court of Appeal has now changed its collective mind. The dictum in *Quick* was disapproved in *Bailey*,[6] where the facts were similar to those in *Quick*.

It was held in *Bailey*, first, that the fact that automatism was self-induced could not make the defendant guilty of a crime of specific intent; so such evidence could not support a conviction under OAPA section 18.

Secondly, the court pointed out that even for crimes of basic intent the rule relating to self-induced incapacity applies only in respect of intoxication.[7] It does not apply, for instance, to a diabetic who fails to take

---

[3] The offence of dangerous driving having been abolished, the point can now arise only for careless, or possibly reckless, driving.

[4] Cp. *Budd* § .6 n. 2, where the notice of intended prosecution for dangerous driving specified "High Street, Northfleet," and the prosecution were confined to evidence of dangerous driving in that street (when the defendant was acting involuntarily), and could not give evidence of dangerous driving at an earlier stage in his journey. The result was that the prosecution failed. However, if the defendant had fallen into a drunken stupor, he could very probably have been convicted of driving when unfit in High Street, since the law of voluntary intoxication must override the defence of automatism: § .5 at n. 14.

[5] This proposition, as worded, failed to express the court's evident intention. The court cannot have meant that an incapacity that is self-induced but without fault is no excuse. Presumably, "self-induced" means "self-induced with fault," in which case all the words after "*Lipman*" could have been omitted. Cp. Mackay in [1982] Crim.LR 148–149.

[6] [1983] Crim.LR 760.

[7] The decision on this point accords with earlier authority. Before *Quick*, it had been assumed that mindlessness produced by voluntary intoxication was governed by its own rules, not by the general law of automatism. See Lord Denning in *Bratty* [1963] AC at 414. Cp. *Hartridge* (1966) 48 CR at 408, 410 (Sask.); *Pearson* [1966] NZLJ 539.

food after insulin. The rule in *Majewski* was invented with sole reference to the problem of voluntary intoxication, when the judges were prepared to uphold convictions in defiance of the plain wording of Acts of Parliament. It would be regrettable if an indefinite range of fault-factors were now to be given the same effect as intoxication, and the decision in *Bailey* fortunately excludes this possibility.

The decision in *Bailey* is supported by the earlier case of *Stripp*,[8] where the Court of Appeal expressed the opinion that automatism can be a defence if:

- it was caused by concussion, even though the concussion might have been produced by an accident that was due to the taking of alcohol; and it can also be a defence if:
- it was caused partly by the concussion aforesaid and partly by the continuing effect of alcoholic intake. "If it was a question of two causes operating, we venture to think that the prosecution would not be able to discharge the burden of proof," i.e. of the mental element.

If concussion caused by voluntary intoxication can found a defence of automatism, it follows that, in general, all other fault-factors can found the defence. Recklessness apart, the single exception is voluntary intoxication directly operating in isolation from other factors to negative a basic intent or the *actus reus*.

The court in *Bailey* did not altogether rule out criminal liability for injuries inflicted in a confusional state resulting from hypoglycaemia. A person can, it was held, be liable for recklessness causing the commission of a crime of basic intent if he knew what would happen if he did not take food after his insulin and if there were no circumstances excusing his failure to take food. This is another instance of the mental element antedating and not being concurrent with the physical act causing the injury. The court made it clear that it was not speaking of the fictitious recklessness attributed to drunkards in *Majewski* and *Caldwell*, but meant real recklessness: knowledge by the defendant that in failing to take precautions against a loss of consciousness he was endangering others.

SUMMARY

In order to escape from mandatory commitment, the courts allow that some forms of mental disorder can negative *mens rea* without resulting in an insanity verdict. Most instances fall under the doctrine of (non-insane) automatism, whereby a person who by reason of impaired consciousness lacks the mental state necessary for the crime charged can be acquitted in the ordinary way, his condition not being regarded as a disease of the mind. The evidential burden rests on the defendant, who must generally support the defence with medical evidence. It seems clear that the prosecution can reply with evidence of insanity (and according to Lord Denning it can do this in all cases where the defendant puts his state of mind in issue). The main instances of automatism according to authorities before 1983 are sleepwalking, concussion, involuntary intoxication, some cases of epilepsy, hypoglycaemia, and dissociative states. § .1

Accidental injury inflicted during an epileptic fit has usually been treated as automatism, but if the defendant is regarded as dangerous it is treated as insanity and leads to a special verdict (unless the defendant pleads guilty). The distinction was expressed by Lord Denning in the generalisation that "any mental disorder § .2

[8] § .6 n. 1.

which has manifested itself in violence and is prone to recur is a disease of the mind." It was formerly thought that the converse was also true: that no mental disorder is a disease of the mind unless it is likely to manifest itself in a dangerous way. However, the decision of the Lords in *Sullivan* (1983) seem to deny this. It states that an epileptic attack causing a defect of cognition is to be attributed to a disease of the mind; and any such malfunctioning shows a disease of the mind even if it is of short duration and even if it does not show an organic defeat. This vastly extends the legal notion of a disease of the mind. The only exception recognised in *Sullivan* is where temporary impairment results from an external factor. It may be noticed, however, that *Sullivan* concerned an act of aggression, not, it seems, a complete cognitive failure.

Automatism resulting from hypoglycaemia was recognised as a defence in *Quick*, § .3
Lawton LJ inventing the "external factor" doctrine which was afterwards approved in *Sullivan*. If Quick was in an automatic state, this was because he had taken insulin, which was an "external factor"; consequently, he was not to be regarded as insane. But it is irrational that he should be accounted insane if his hypoglycaemic condition resulted simply from his not having eaten enough, without taking insulin.

Dissociation is a form of automatism looked upon with considerable suspicion; § .4
whether it is allowed depends very much on the facts and the strength of the medical evidence. The decision of the Canadian Supreme Court that it can only result in an insanity verdict was an unhappy expedient, but it seems from *Sullivan* that English courts will now take the same view.

Automatism can negative an allegation of driving, but the doctrine has no special § .5
utility on a charge of careless or reckless driving, where it is enough to say that the fault element is lacking. However, the fault element may be found in driving at an earlier stage when the defendant knew or (in the case of carelessness) should have known of his potential disabiiity. On a charge of a driving offence of strict liability, such as failing to observe a traffic sign, the doctrine of automatism must be utilised to give exemption; and here it is logically difficult to qualify the doctrine by reference to prior negligence. According to the weight of authority, a driver may be in a state of automatism even though he is controlling the vehicle.

The decision in *Majewski* implies that automatism is no defence to a crime of § .6
basic intent if it is produced by voluntary intoxication. But in cases of concurrent causation, where intoxication combines with some other factor to produce automatism, the latter defence avails.

According to the decisions in *Stripp* and *Bailey*, automatism is a defence even § .7
though it is self-induced, unless (1) the crime is one of basic intent and the confusional state was caused solely by voluntary intoxication, as said above, or (2) the defendant was reckless that the incapacity would result from his act or omission—i.e. he realised that he would become dangerous to others if he did not take steps, and unreasonably failed to take those steps (e.g. by taking food after insulin).

CHAPTER 30

DIMINISHED RESPONSIBILITY

Many a man is mad in certain instances, and goes through life without having it perceived.

Samuel Johnson

§ 30.1. DIMINISHED RESPONSIBILITY: THE NATURE OF THE DEFENCE

EXCEPT in cases of murder the judge has a discretion in sentencing that enables him to deal sensibly with the mentally disordered. For murder, legislation is needed. The Government, having seen insuperable difficulties in a proposal of the Royal Commission on Capital Punishment to extend the insanity exemption, decided instead to extend the discretion of the judge by allowing a defence of "diminished responsibility." Section 2 (1) of the Homicide Act 1957 reads in part as follows.

> "Where a person kills or is a party to the killing of another, he shall not be convicted of murder if he was suffering from such abnormality of mind (whether arising from a condition of arrested or retarded development of mind or any inherent causes or induced by disease or injury) as substantially impaired his mental responsibility for his acts and omissions in doing or being a party to the killing."

The essence of the matter is that the defence has two elements:

1 abnormality of mind, arising from:
- arrested development or
- inherent causes or
- disease or injury, and

2 resulting substantial impairment of mental responsibility.

The general notion of diminished responsibility (as it is called in the margin of the section) was borrowed from Scotland, where it had been developed as judge-made law; and section 2 of the Homicide Act has in turn been adopted in some other parts of the common law world. If the defence is established (and the burden of proving it on a balance of probability rests on the defendant[1]), the jury convict of manslaughter, which means that the judge has the usual wide range of discretion as to disposal.

Can the defence be set up in a case really falling within the insanity defence?

Yes. But, by statute, the prosecution can reply with evidence of

[1] Homicide Act s. 2 (2); *Dunbar* [1958] 1 QB 36. The persuasive burden resting on the defence implies an evidential burden as well, and the judge will not leave the defence to the jury in the absence of medical evidence: *Dix* (1981) 74 CAR 306.

insanity,[2] and if the jury accept that it is really a *McNaghten* situation they will return a special verdict accordingly.[3]

Has the defence worked well in practice?

Although section 2 (1) may be said in a sense to have "worked" (indeed, it has had highly beneficial results), it has meant that psychiatrists have been put under pressure to testify in terms that go beyond their professional competence. This has not led them to express much open discontent. When their sympathies are engaged they will adapt themselves to any legal formula.[4] But the fact is that section 2 (1), with its requirement that the defendant's abnormality of mind should have substantially impaired his mental responsibility, is as embarrassing a formula for a scientifically-minded witness as could be devised.

- "Mental responsibility" is an ill-chosen expression, since responsibility is a legal or ethical notion, not in itself a clinical fact relating to the defendant. One can intelligibly speak of "legal responsibility" (liability to conviction) or of "moral responsibility" (liability to moral censure). But the draftsman avoided the words "moral responsibility," because he did not want to bring moral questions into the criminal law. And it would make no sense to talk about substantial impairment of legal responsibility, because legal responsibility in the sense of liability to conviction either exists or does not. (It is true that section 2, when it operates, downgrades the responsibility from murder to manslaughter. But this downgrading cannot be used as a criterion for operating the section: that would be begging the question.)
- The difficulty is compounded by the use of the word "substantial." Even if there were a scientific test of impairment, the question of substantial impairment is one of subjective estimation, not of medical science. The intention of the Act was that the jury should decide the substantiality of the impairment, but they are unfitted to do this without help, and doctors are prepared to testify on it.[5]

Shouldn't DR be accounted automatism?

Permit me to say that your question shows a certain confusion. If the defendant's mental disorder amounts to automatism, he receives a plain acquittal and there is no need for a defence of "diminished" (as it is sometimes abbreviated in informal speech). To amount to automatism, the disorder must negative *mens rea*. If the disorder does not negative *mens rea*, and if the charge is murder, the defendant (assuming that he has no other defence) must be convicted of something. The advantage of the defence of diminished is that it reduces the conviction from one of murder to one of manslaughter.

---

[2] Criminal Procedure (Insanity) Act 1964 s. 6. This is the converse of the rule stated in n. 6 below.

[3] If the jury reject the defence and convict of murder, the CA may take a different view and substitute a conviction of manslaughter: *Spratt* [1980] 1 WLR 554, 71 CAR 125.

[4] Indeed, it has been said that s. 2 (1) suits psychiatric witnesses better than the insanity defence (Nigel Walker, *Crime and Insanity in England* (Edinburgh 1968) i 160), presumably because it is vaguer. Some of the problems presented to psychiatrists by the defence are discussed by Neustatter in 101 Medico-Legal Jrnl 92–101.

[5] See *Lloyd* [1967] 1 QB 175. The evidence taken as a whole can justify the jury in rejecting uncontradicted medical evidence for the defence: *Walton* [1978] AC 788; *Kiszko* (1979) 68 CAR 62. If there is nothing to cast doubt on the doctors' evidence the judge is justified in telling the jury that they are bound to accept it, at least on the question of abnormality of mind; probably, however, he should tell them that they can make up their own minds on the question of substantial impairment of responsibility. See M D Cohen in 131 NLJ 667.

Yes, but why shouldn't it be provided that diminished is a complete defence?

That is out of the question. "Diminished" has been held to cover such forms of disorder as morbid jealousy, reactive depression, and psychopathy, as we shall see. Where the defendant has committed the forbidden act with the forbidden state of mind, it would be against public policy to exempt him from responsibility and therefore from all forms of social control.

Do the prosecution ever charge manslaughter by reason of diminished, or do they always charge murder?

The latter. The issue arises only if the defendant introduces it or sets up a *McNaghten* defence.[6]

In practice the defence of diminished cannot be set up, for obvious reasons, if the defendant denies that he committed the act. So if the denial is disbelieved the conviction will be of murder, notwithstanding that evidence of diminished could have been given. This is an unhappy situation for the defendant, who can give no evidence in mitigation after a murder conviction. It is another argument against the mandatory sentence in murder.[7]

When a person is charged with murder, can he plead guilty to manslaughter on the ground of diminished?

He is allowed to do so, though the usual qualification applies that the defendant cannot insist upon pleading to the lesser offence. His plea needs to be accepted by the prosecution, who then ask for the leave of the court. The prosecution doctors almost always support the defence, and the plea is generally accepted.[8]

§ 30.2. SENTENCING FOR DIMINISHED RESPONSIBILITY

The defence of "diminished" has the superficial attraction of offering an escape from the mad-bad dichotomy. It enables (so it may be thought) a transition to be made from complete responsibility to complete irresponsibility. Those who are completely normal are completely responsible; those who are so insane as to come within the *McNaghten* rules are irresponsible; those who are on the borderline of such extreme insanity have diminished responsibility.

There is a danger in such reasoning. The law appears to imply that

---

[6] Where there is a defence of insanity, the prosecution can show that the case is in reality one of diminished responsibility: Criminal Procedure (Insanity) Act 1964 s. 6.

There is no good reason why the charge should always be one of murder. Generally, it is true, it must be of murder because medical evidence is not available at the committal proceedings; but if the necessary evidence becomes available in time the committal should be for manslaughter, except in the unlikely event of the defence resisting the evidence. The Butler Committee recommended this course (Cmnd 6244, para. 19.19), but the DPP has apparently taken no notice of the recommendation.

[7] See Susanne Dell in [1982] Crim.LR 809. If the defence is not advanced at the trial, the CA may refuse to hear medical evidence on the subject, particularly if the medical reports do not clearly support the defence. See *Melville* [1976] 1 WLR 181, 1 All ER 395. See also *Williams* [1965] Crim.LR 609.

[8] Dell, *op.cit.* last note.

dangerous killers may be entitled, on account of their supposed mental disorder, to receive a comparatively light sentence, and thus may be turned loose on the community after a very few years in confinement.

This was in fact the line taken by some judges in the first cases that arose under the Act. But presently the absurdity came to be recognised, and the general practice arose of sentencing dangerous offenders convicted under section 2 to imprisonment for life. The paradoxical result was that a person who "won" on a defence of "diminished" was often sentenced in the same way as if he had lost on that defence and been convicted of murder.

When the first Mental Health Act came into force in 1959 it was realised that the new powers would be particularly appropriate to cases under section 2 of the Homicide Act. In *Morris*[1] the Court of Criminal Appeal laid it down as a general principle that "in the ordinary case where punishment as such is not intended, and where the sole object of the sentence is that a man should receive mental treatment and be at large again as soon as he can safely be discharged, a proper exercise of the discretion [resulting from a finding of diminished responsibility] demands that steps should be taken to exercise the powers" of that Act, that is, to make a hospital order.

Do the courts still send people to prison who have succeeded in the defence?

Imprisonment remains quite a common outcome, being imposed in about a third of cases of diminished responsibility. Most offenders, however, receive hospital orders, and some are dealt with non-custodially (e.g. by a PPO).[2]

The rule in *Morris* was expressed to apply only "in the ordinary case where punishment as such is not intended." The court added, though without explanation, that even where there was substantial impairment of responsibility the offender might still "have some responsibility for the act he has done, for which he must be punished." This may suggest that the offender is, say, one-third responsible and so should receive one-third the normal sentence. But in fact the courts often send these offenders to prison for life, if they are sent to prison at all.[3] The absurdity of reconciling this practice with the notion of substantially diminished responsibility needs no emphasis, though the indeterminate sentence is necessary if the judge is unable to assess the danger that will be presented by the offender in future.

The frequency of prison sentences for "diminished" has not operated to reduce what may be called the popularity of the defence. Instead, the defence under section 2 (1) has almost completely ousted the issue of insanity.[4]

---

[1] [1961] 2 QB 237.

[2] *Criminal Statistics, England and Wales, 1981.*

[3] In 1981 there were 75 cases of diminished; 35 of the offenders received hospital orders and 14 sentences of life imprisonment; 12 received fixed terms of imprisonment (up to 10 years). Before the decision in *Partridge*, n. 6 below, a fixed term sentence was supposed to be given only in exceptional circumstances, as in *Fulker* [1972] Crim.LR 579, where there was provocation and the defendant had recovered from the so-called mental disorder by the time of the trial. Occasionally the trial judge gives a relatively short fixed term although the degree of danger presented by the offender cannot be assessed, and the CA is then powerless to substitute a life sentence on appeal: *Stofile* [1969] Crim.LR 325. It may however substitute a hospital order: *Bennett* [1968] 1 WLR 988, 2 All ER 753. The trial judge himself, after sentencing the offender to a short fixed term, may think better of it and bring the offender back (within one month) and make a hospital order indefinite in time.

[4] Evelyn Gibson and S Klein, *Murder* (HMSO) 1961 9, 40.

So the upshot of the tale is that, with our national genius for compromise, we have solved the problem of distinguishing legal irresponsibility from responsibility by making almost everyone responsible but entrusting the judge with a wide discretion which is generally exercised on pragmatic grounds. If there are the requisite medical recommendations the judge will normally make a hospital order.[5] If for one reason or another the offender has to be sent to prison and is regarded as dangerous, the sentence will normally (and should) be for "life." However, the latter practice is now threatened by an extraordinary decision of the Court of Appeal which seems to revert to a purely retributive or tariff approach to the sentencing of dangerous offenders who obtain a verdict of diminished.[6]

The following are the chief reasons why the offender may go to prison.

- No hospital will take him, or the judge thinks the offender can only be entrusted to a special hospital and no special hospital will take him.
- The doctor cannot hold out any substantial hope of improving the offender's behaviour, and it is plain that if the proposed treatment proves to be ineffective the offender will soon be discharged from hospital and will be a menace or source of serious loss to the community. As was pointed out in § 28.6, no hospital (not even a special hospital) can keep a patient under a hospital order merely because he is thought to be dangerous, if nothing further can be done for him. Even so, the judge will often chance a hospital order, on the argument that it offers a better hope of improving the offender's conduct than a prison sentence would do. But sometimes the judge may feel that, since medical science offers no assurance, he must pin his faith on old-fashioned incapacitation and deterrence.
- The defendant disputes the medical evidence and prefers prison.
- The defence of diminished was combined with one of provocation, and was really a way of escaping from a limitation on the law of provocation.[7]

Isn't the problem that we lack any institution for people who are so mentally affected that we feel it unjust to send them to an ordinary penal institution as though they were normal, and yet who are not certainly treatable and must be confined indefinitely in the public interest?

That may well be so. The special hospitals like Broadmoor formerly fulfilled this role, but the hospital order no longer gives assurance that the offender will be kept under control for as long as the public interest may demand.

Although we have swept the problem of responsibility under the carpet, its continued existence is shown by the case of Sutcliffe, the multiple murderer (the "Yorkshire Ripper") (1981).[8] All the doctors (including the prison medical officers) concurred in the view that he suffered from paranoid schizophrenia and would be properly convicted of manslaughter on the ground of diminished responsibility. The prosecution were therefore agreeable that he should plead to manslaughter. This course, while making no difference to the sentence, would have saved the expense of a trial and spared the feelings of relatives who would otherwise have to hear the horrible details of how their loved ones died. But the judge rightly refused to accept the plea; Sutcliffe was tried for murder, the psychiatrists were subjected to gruelling cross-examination, and the jury convicted of murder. Leave to appeal was refused by the Court of Appeal.

The jury's verdict can technically be justified on the ground that although Sutcliffe satisfied the medical criteria for the defence, his responsibility (having regard, perhaps, to the gravity and persistence of his crimes, and his cunning in avoiding detection—showing that he was not entirely beyond the restraint of the law) was nevertheless not "substantially" diminished. But

---

[5] *Cox* [1968] 1 WLR 308, 1 All ER 386.

[6] *Partridge* [1982] Crim.LR 320. In *Norman* (1982) 146 JPN 147 the CA not only seemed to say that a fixed sentence could be given on the basis of the defendant's degree of "responsibility," but accepted that 7 years was "the top end of the scale"!

[7] See § 24.6.

[8] For the case in the CA see The Times, May 26 1982.

this is only a form of words, which means little when we have no clear idea of the "responsibility" we are talking about. The reality is that the jury thought Sutcliffe should go to prison for an indeterminate time. Everyone would agree that, however Sutcliffe's mental state may be categorised, such a man must be detained for the indefinite future. The only certain way of achieving this is a sentence of life imprisonment.

It seems strange that the law of diminished adds yet another form of manslaughter. Doesn't it make things difficult for the judge in sentencing to have so many different variants of this crime? How does he know which sort the jury have found?

You are right in suspecting the existence of a problem. We have manslaughter by gross negligence, constructive manslaughter, provocation-killing and diminished responsibility—all in theory punishable with imprisonment for life. But provocation-killing by itself never[9] attracts a life sentence, while killing with diminished may well do so. In practice, if there is evidence to support both defences the judge will not give a life sentence.[10]

The general answer to your question is that the judge may question the foreman as to the basis of the verdict, for the purpose of sentence.[11] He is not obliged to do so,[12] but if he does he must accept the opinion as to the facts reported by the foreman.

Would it be a solution to the problem presented by Sutcliffe's case if we merged murder and manslaughter in a single offence of unlawful killing?

This proposal has attracted many people.[13] But it would leave the judge with even less assistance from the jury's verdict than he has now. And the jury would be deprived of the right to decide the most important issue in most homicide cases.

The importance of the defence of diminished responsibility has been greatly reduced by the abolition of capital punishment. Although the defence is still relatively common, no information is available on whether it is of advantage to defendants. Sometimes it may only mean a longer period of detention for the offender than would otherwise have been his fate, because it puts on record his mental instability and so makes the Parole Board particularly cautious in recommending release. But the recent decision of the Court of Appeal mentioned before now offers dangerous psychopaths a real hope of returning to their old ways without too long an interruption.

A drawback of this solution of the problem of responsibility results from the rule that a person who is guilty of murder or manslaughter cannot claim a share in his victim's estate under his will or on his intestacy, or a social insurance benefit depending on the death (e.g. widow's benefit), whereas an irresponsibly insane killer can do so. The rule can cause hardship to a person who kills when mentally disordered but not being *McNaghten* mad; and

---

[9] Well, hardly ever. See the aberrant and harsh decision and sentence in *Cascoe* [1970] 2 All ER 833.

[10] See § 24.6.

[11] *Matheson* [1958] 1 WLR 474, 2 All ER 87, 42 CAR 145; *per* Diplock LJ in *Warner* [1967] 1 WLR at 1213–1214; *Lamb* [1967] 2 QB at 984. The decision *contra* in *Larkin* [1943] KB 174 is now disregarded. A verdict is valid although the jury fail to pronounce upon a particular fact as the judge requests: *Devizes Corpn* v. *Clark* (1835) 3 Ad. & E 506, 111 ER 506.

[12] Subject to any guidance given by the verdict or plea, the judge sentences on his own view of the facts: § 2.6 at n. 6. For making a hospital order, all that he needs is the appropriate medical evidence.

[13] See 131 NLJ 613.

although the court is now empowered to grant relief from the forfeiture of rights, there is no certainty that it will do so.[14] The killer meets similar difficulty if he seeks to enforce an insurance policy on the victim's life, and here the court has not even been given a discretion to allow him to claim.

§ 30.3. SCOPE OF THE DEFENCE OF "DIMINISHED"

The words in brackets in section 2 (1) (§ .1) confine the defence to mental abnormality "arising from a condition of arrested or retarded development of mind"—that is, mental impairment or severe impairment—"or any inherent causes or induced by disease or injury." The object of the words in brackets was to exclude such emotions as rage, jealousy and hate. Although these emotions do not constitute diminished responsibility in themselves, they can trigger off the "inherent causes." Indeed, the courts are now so indulgent towards this defence that they accept medical evidence saying little more than that the defendant was severely affected by provocative events, in effect disregarding the bracketed words in this respect, and making the defence overlap (and, indeed, extend) that of provocation when it has the blessing of a doctor.[1]

The bracketed words also exclude drunkenness or the influence of drugs; and here the courts generally insist more strictly upon the limitation. If there is evidence of intoxication and, in addition, evidence of a pathological condition, the jury are supposed to be directed to consider the latter evidence alone, without reference to the intoxication[2]; but trial judges do not always adhere to this.

The courts have extended the defence even to cases of psychopathy and irresistible impulse.[3] However, the judge by his disposal can usually deprive the defendant of any undesirable benefit from the manslaughter verdict, unless the Court of Appeal interferes in the inexplicable way that sometimes happens. A dangerous psychopath is likely to go to prison, "diminished responsibility" notwithstanding.[4]

The notion that ability to conform to the law can be measured is particularly puzzling. The position seems to be that if the doctors say that

---

[14] Forfeiture Act 1982 (see Kenny in 132 NLJ 897). On the common law rule see *Re Giles* [1972] Ch. 544; Earnshaw and Price in 37 MLR 481.

[1] As in *Coles* (1980) 144 JPN 528. Coles had slept on his wrath before killing his wife, so that he was presumably outside the defence of provocation. Cp.*Knowles* (1979), Daily Telegraph, January 25; a wife waited till her brutal husband was asleep and then killed him; her plea of diminished was accepted.

[2] *Fenton* (1975) 61 CAR 261. The court said that "cases may arise hereafter where the accused proves such a craving for drink or drugs as to produce in itself an abnormality of mind;" but the statute requires that the abnormality should arise from "inherent causes." In *Terry* [1961] 2 QB at 320 the defence was left to the jury because the defendant was an unstable personality, although the doctors testified that but for the drugs taken by him the killing would not have occurred (see at p. 321).

[3] *Matheson* [1958] 1 WLR 474, 2 All ER 87, 42 CAR 145; *Byrne* [1960] 2 QB 396; *Rose* (1961) 45 CAR 102; *Jennion* [1962] 1 WLR 317, 1 All ER 689, 46 CAR 212. Some medical men regard psychopathy as due predominantly to defective upbringing, which is not an "inherent" cause, but even then it can be regarded as "arrested or retarded development of mind" (in the sense of what was formerly termed "moral imbecility"). Pre-menstrual tension can also found a defence of diminished and serve as a ground of mitigation; see *Sandie Smith* [1982] Crim.LR 531; Susan Edwards in 146 JPN 476; cp. *ibid.* 583, 796.

[4] E.g. *Harvey* [1971] Crim.LR 402.

the defendant was *unable* to conform to the law, for one of the reasons stated in the section, this necessarily implies "substantial" impairment of so-called "mental responsibility."[5] If he has substantial difficulty in conforming to the law (whatever that may mean), he also comes within the section.[6] Lord Parker CJ recognised some of the problems.

> "The step between 'he did not resist his impulse' and 'he could not resist his impulse' . . . is incapable of scientific proof. *A fortiori* there is no scientific measurement of the degree of difficulty which an abnormal person finds in controlling his impulses. These problems, which in the present state of medical knowledge are scientifically insoluble, the jury can only approach in a broad common-sense way."[7]

Barbara Wootton's comment on this was:

> "Apart from admiration of the optimism which expects common sense to make good the deficiencies of science, it is only necessary to add that the problem would seem to be insoluble, not merely in the present, but indeed in any, state of medical knowledge. . . . Neither medical nor any other science can ever hope to prove whether a man who does not resist his impulses does not do so because he cannot or because he will not."[8]

Isn't it possible that the killer suffered from abnormality of mind etc. at the time of the killing, and so can plead diminished, and yet is not mentally ill etc. (within the terms of the MHA s. 60), so that a hospital order cannot be made?

Certainly. The defence has been successfully raised on thin grounds in cases evoking sympathy although there were clearly no reasons for a hospital order. Mental abnormality can be discovered in a "reactive depression"—in effect a perfectly natural (though severe) depresssion caused by extreme adversity.[9] Another diagnosis is of morbid jealousy, which is classified as a psychosis. The sentence may be anything from about 3 years in jail down to a virtual let-off, depending on the circumstances and the judge. A defence of diminished, supported by benevolent psychiatrists, is a safe course for the defendant if he is clearly not a public danger.

> A woman of 67 stabbed her aged husband to death in a fit of jealousy (based on mistaken grounds) and then tried to kill herself; her plea of guilty to manslaughter with diminished was accepted and she was given probation with a condition of a year's residence in hospital.[10] (Although a year in hospital may sound a depressing prospect, she would be an informal patient and could be discharged, or discharge herself, at any time—except that she would be at a slight risk of being brought back to court for breach of the condition of her probation.)
>
> A man who had been tormented for years by his neighbours (the

---

[5] See *Byrne*, n. 3 above.
[6] *Simcox* [1964] Crim.LR 402.
[7] *Byrne* [1960] 2 QB at 404.
[8] *Crime and the Criminal Law*, 2nd edn (London 1981) 77–78.
[9] Examples are *Pachy*, The Guardian, November 14, 1961; *Bathurst* [1968] 2 QB 99.
[10] *Miller* (1972), The Times, May 16.

worst neighbours you can possibly imagine, who suffered from mental trouble) went berserk and shot dead the family of three; psychiatrists, bless them, stated that he acted in a state of hysterical dissociation, and the jury returned a verdict of diminished responsibility. With his triple source of irritation cleanly removed the defendant's mental condition had improved wonderfully, and the judge felt able to give him the comparatively lenient sentence of 3 years' imprisonment.[11]

In another case a man who stabbed his wife to death with a carving knife obtained a verdict of diminished by reason of his physical condition (diabetes, which presumably produced a hypoglycaemic episode), and, since he had been "driven to distraction by matrimonial problems," the judge simply put him on probation.[12] Another man did not even have to suffer the inconvenience of probation; he strangled his wife in jealousy, and was given a suspended sentence.[13]

A "slave son" of 21 shot and killed his father and mother. He had been ill-treated by them all his life: horsewhipped, overworked without wages, and made to sleep in a dog-kennel. The jury returned a verdict of manslaughter on the ground of provocation and diminished responsibility, and the judge passed a suspended sentence with supervision order.[14]

Clemency could not be so readily exercised if the offence were characterised by the jury as murder. What is important about the doctrine of diminished responsibility is not only that it gives the judge a discretion in sentencing but that it enables him to exercise that discretion leniently, by removing the emotive reference to murder.

Commenting upon the artificiality of the defence in such cases, Lady Wootton wrote:

> "When homicide has resulted from such common human motives as sexual jealousy or the desire to escape from pecuniary embarrassment, it is hard not to believe that juries were moved more by the familiarity than by the abnormality of the offender's mental processes."

A particular curiosity in the diagnosis of reactive depression is that, although it can undoubtedly amount to a psychosis, it is hard to characterise as due predominantly to "inherent causes." (An *endogenous* depression is due to inherent causes.) Similarly, hysterical dissociation is a neurotic reaction to stress. There is of course a personal factor, but so there always is in human conduct, which is never completely uniform and predictable.

In short, the defence of diminished is interpreted in accordance with the morality of the case rather than as an application of psychiatric concepts. Where sympathy is evoked, as Lady Wootton observes, it "seems to be dissolving into what is virtually the equivalent of a mitigating circumstance."[15] But the complaisance of some doctor is still required to give legal admissibility to the defence.

One may question whether leniency has not sometimes gone too far; but there can be no doubt of the beneficial effect of the defence in mercy-killing cases. Here it is invariably accepted by the jury on the flimsiest medical evidence, and thankfully used by the judge as a reason for leniency. While the outcome of these cases is now humane, it is achieved, as Dr Bluglass wryly observes, only because we

> "continue to rely upon psychiatrists interpreting what is, often, a rational act in terms of

---

[11] *Eeles* (1972), The Times, November 22. On the argument advanced in Chapter 24 a defence of provocation would also have had to be left to the jury in such circumstances.

[12] *Nicholls* (1974), The Times, October 5.

[13] *Asher* (1981), The Times, June 9.

[14] *Ireland* (1983), The Times, March 26.

[15] *Crime and the Criminal Law*, 2nd edn (London 1981) 76.

mental abnormality, referring in justification to the stress, anxiety or even depression associated with the pain and helplessness of watching a relative die."[16]

In a case of 1965 a father who killed his mongol infant was put on a PPO.[17] In 1971, a man who placed his severely handicapped son in the River Stour and watched him float away received the same clemency.[18] Evidence had been given that the boy functioned at the level of a baby and had a short life expectancy. The judge told the defendant that he would be required to "undergo treatment as a doctor may prescribe for the next few weeks or so," and he added: "I hope that in the passage of time you will be able to forget about this matter." Similar solutions have been found where the mercy-killing was of an old person dying in pain.[19]

Although the judges are to be warmly congratulated for humanity in mercy-killing cases, the invocation of the psychiatrist and the probation officer could not have been regarded as necessary for any of the purposes for which those persons are normally used. It was merely an attempt by the judge to render workable a law that is grossly out of accord with present thought, and to maintain, as is required by his office, an appearance of official disapproval towards an act that most people nowadays would regard as a normal reaction to an impossible situation.

§ 30.4. INFANTICIDE

A forerunner of the general defence of diminished responsibility was the special rule for infanticide, which is still in force.

At common law, infanticide by the mother was murder, but there were generally circumstances of mitigation which prompted a widespread desire for change in the law. In the days of capital punishment it was highly distasteful to pass a death sentence that everyone in court—apart perhaps from the unfortunate woman herself—knew would not be carried out. Consequently, a special statute was passed.

The present law rests on the Infanticide Act 1938[1]:

> "Where a woman by any wilful act or omission causes the death of her child under the age of 12 months, but the balance of her mind was disturbed by reason of her not having fully recovered from the effect of giving birth to the child or by reason of the effect of lactation consequent upon the birth of the child, then . . . she shall be guilty of . . . infanticide."

Infanticide is punishable like manslaughter, so the judge has a complete discretion as to sentence. From 1976 to 1981, for example, the outcome was always a hospital order or probation order; occasionally in other years the woman has simply been given a discharge.

The prosecution will normally charge infanticide and not murder if the evidence of mental unbalance is available to them in time for the committal proceedings; and the DPP will exert

---

[16] *Psychiatry, the Law and the Offender* (ISTD 1980) 10–11.
[17] *Gray*, 129 JPN 819.
[18] *Price*, The Times, December 22.
[19] As in *Keith Jones* (1979), The Times, December 4. See generally Leng in 132 NLJ 76; [1980] Crim.LR 517.

[1] Replacing with amendments an Act of 1922.

himself to obtain such evidence if it is obtainable. If murder is charged, the woman may be allowed to plead guilty to infanticide (in which case there is no trial and no medical evidence), or if the case goes to the jury they may find her guilty only of infanticide.

Although "puerperal psychosis" appears in the books, and depression after childbirth is common, women now rarely kill their babies from this cause. The reason is that at the first sign of mental trouble the baby is removed from its mother. A study of cases where married women had killed their children found no particular association with the period following childbirth.[2] As for the reference in the statute to lactation, there is no evidence that this is associated with mental disturbance. The association is a legal fiction, designed to extend the lesser offence to the full year after childbirth. In reality, the operative factors in child-killing are often the stress of having to care for the infant, who may be unwanted or difficult, and personality problems (in short, the "battered baby" syndrome); these stresses affect the father as well as the mother, and are not confined to a year after the birth.

The Infanticide Act is the result of the sympathetic feelings of the judges and others, but it also reinforces them. When a woman does away with her infant everyone assumes, on slight evidence, that she was mentally unbalanced by reason of the consequences of childbirth.[3] But if the woman botches the killing and merely injures the child the Act does not apply; she will be charged with attempted murder or wounding with intent, and is quite likely to go to prison. Or if a mother kills both her newborn baby and an older child the Act does not save her from a charge of murder in respect of the older child, notwithstanding that any mental disturbance from which she suffered would have affected both killings. Of course, she can set up a defence of diminished responsibility in respect of the older child.

SUMMARY

The Homicide Act 1957 s. 2 introduced a new defence of diminished responsibility to a charge of murder, reducing the crime to manslaughter, the burden of proof (on a balance of probability) resting on the defendant. There must be medical evidence to raise the issue. The judge may accept the defendant's plea to manslaughter on the basis of diminished responsibility. § .1

The defence has almost completely ousted the defence of insanity. Most offenders receive hospital orders, but about a third go to prison (mostly on a life sentence), and some are dealt with non-custodially. When the jury return a verdict of manslaughter, the judge may, for the purpose of sentence, question the foreman as to the basis of the verdict. § .2

The defence is not open if the mental abnormality was not the result of inherent causes or disease or injury; so intoxication is excluded. But psychopathy and irresistible impulse have been held to be included if the mental expert is willing to testify that the abnormality has an inherent cause. Evidence of a reactive depression, morbid jealousy, hysterical dissociation or hypoglycaemic episode is particularly likely to result in a lenient disposal if the facts arouse sympathy. Cases of mercy-killing now regularly result in some mild form of disposal, such as probation, or a hospital order which is not expected to last for long. § .3

The Infanticide Act 1938 provides that where a woman kills her child under the § .4

[2] D J West, *Murder followed by Suicide* (London 1965) 147.

[3] The ready acceptance of parliamentary diagnosis was travestied by an examination candidate who wrote: "The shock of childbirth may produce an effect that no man can tell, and may cause lactation."

age of one year and the balance of her mind is disturbed by the birth or lactation, she is guilty of infanticide, punishable like manslaughter. The offence is unnecessary since the introduction of the general defence of diminished responsibility, the only real difference between the two being that the prosecution charge infanticide where possible, instead of murder, and so save the woman some distress.

Part Five

THE PROTECTION OF PROPERTY

CHAPTER 31

TYPES OF PROPERTY OFFENCES

> We come now to the principal object of law—the care of security. That inestimable good, the distinctive index of civilization, is entirely the work of law. Without law there is no security; and, consequently, no abundance, and not even a certainty of subsistence; and the only equality which can exist in such a state of things is an equality of misery.
>
> Jeremy Bentham, *Theory of Legislation*

§ 31.1. THE MAIN OFFENCES

OFFENCES in respect of property may be divided in various ways. Most are acquisitive offences (the main offences of dishonesty), but there are also offences of damage or destruction which are non-acquisitive. Offences of dishonesty do not necessarily relate to property (one may, for example, commit perjury in the hope of avoiding going to prison), but the great majority of them do.

Some offences of dishonesty concentrate on the interest invaded, while others focus on the defendant's conduct. To illustrate the first group, it can be an offence:

- to appropriate a person's property dishonestly;
- to cause him to execute a valuable security by deception;
- to get him to provide services by deception;

and so on. Under such legislation, no offence (apart from an inchoate offence like attempt) is committed if the rogue does not succeed in appropriating the property, getting the valuable security executed, and so on.

The second group strike at certain dishonest *behaviour*, whether or not it produces the desired result. No one must:

- concoct a fraudulent plan in company with another; or
- forge a document in order to cause prejudice to someone; or
- make a false account; or
- tell lies of various specified kinds; or
- dishonestly suppress certain documents.

Although the latter type of drafting may be limited as to the means used, it is almost unlimited as to the dishonest end in view.

The present chapter will sketch the two main examples of the first group of offences, theft and obtaining property by deception, and then consider the most important example of the second group, conspiracy to defraud. Further attention will be paid to theft and deception in later chapters; but the present book does not seek to give more than an outline of this part of the criminal law. More detailed studies of the main offences are contained in Griew's *The Theft Acts 1968 and 1978* (4th edn, cited here as "Griew") and J C Smith's *The Law of Theft* (4th edn, cited here as "Smith").

§ 31.2. THEFT: THE HISTORY

The common law got itself into a tangle over theft, or larceny as it was called. Basically, this crime was confined to the *taking* of a *thing* from the possession of another without his consent. It did not cover misappropriation by a *possessor* of the thing (he could not take what he already possessed), and it did not (at least in its original form) cover the theft of a *notional balance of account*.

However, the proposition that possessors could not steal was eroded by subtle rules. For example, a servant (employee) was said not to possess his master's article, although he held it in his hands. He only had custody of it; his master retained possession; so a dishonest appropriation by the servant was a "taking" from his master's possession and therefore larceny. The artificiality of the rule was shown by the fact that if a wrong-doer stole the thing from the servant, the servant was regarded as being in possession. The indictment could "lay the property" in the servant. So the servant was both in possession and not in possession: not in possession if the question were whether he stole from the master, and in possession if the question were whether a stranger stole from him. The object of these two contradictory rules was simply to procure the conviction of wrongdoers; but the practical necessity for the law to contort itself in this way showed that the premise from which it proceeded was socially inadequate.

Even heroic judicial action was found not to be enough to cure the defects of the common law. Sundry statutory offences had to be created—obtaining by false pretences, embezzlement, larceny by a bailee, fraudulent conversion, obtaining credit by fraud, false accounting, and a number of summary offences.

The Theft Act 1968 recasts the law, largely as a result of recommendations made by the CLRC.[1] (All references to sections in this and the next eight chapters are to this Act, unless the contrary is expressed or clearly implied.) The Act abandons the latinate term "larceny"[2] in favour of the Old English "theft," and it makes it clear that we can use "steal" as the verb. Theft is no longer confined to the taking of specific corporeal things. The Act sweeps away all the offences specifically mentioned in the last paragraph and replaces them by a series of simpler offences, chief among which is theft. Theft rolls up what was larceny, embezzlement and fraudulent conversion in the old law, while offences of deception replace obtaining by false pretences and obtaining credit by fraud.

---

[1] The Act has been copied, with most of its warts, in certain other common law countries. For Northern Ireland see the Theft Act 1969.

[2] The word "larcenous" was formerly in use as the adjective from "larceny." There is no accepted adjective from "theft," but the word "theftous" will here be used.

One effect of the new definition of theft is to abolish the rule that possessors cannot steal. Therefore, there is little necessity nowadays to assert pedantically that an employee only has custody of his employer's goods and not possession. The object of this proposition in the old law was to enable the employee to be convicted. Since it is no longer needed for that purpose we might well admit that he has possession. But the old ways of speaking are likely to persist, and occasions may still arise (though no longer in relation to theft) where the lawyer may think it important to assert that the employer who entrusts an article to an employee does not part with possession of it.

§ 31.3. THE DEFINITION OF THEFT

The new offence of theft created by the Act was intended to be as free from technicality as human ingenuity could devise. Things have not worked out like that. Troublesome questions of interpretation have arisen. Still, it is true that almost everyone whom common sense would regard as a thief is now a thief in law. If the Act departs from common sense, that is chiefly because it brings within the notion of theft some forms of dishonesty that some people might prefer to call by other names (breach of trust or deception). If the Act is sometimes hard to apply, that is chiefly because it has to operate against the background of the law of property, which is itself complicated.

Theft is defined in section 1 (1).

> "A person is guilty of theft if he dishonestly appropriates property belonging to another with the intention of permanently depriving the other of it; and "thief" and 'steal' shall be construed accordingly."

Does that mean that you can't steal from a possessor who is not the owner, such as a hirer or borrower?

A thief can be charged with stealing either from the owner or from the possessor, as the prosecutor pleases. Ever since earliest times the law has to some extent muddled up the notions of possession and ownership, because it traditionally regards the possessor as being the owner, the proprietor, as against third parties, unless such third parties have a better right to possess than he has. In other words, the law protects the possessor against wrongdoers as though the possessor were the owner. This is expressed in section 5 (1).

> "Property shall be regarded as belonging to any person having possession or control of it, or having in it any proprietary right or interest (not being an equitable interest arising only from an agreement to transfer or grant an interest)."

The effect of the subsection is that the prosecutor when drawing the indictment may "lay the property" either in the owner or in a bare possessor.

Can the property be laid in an owner who has never been in possession?

Yes. If A sells goods to B, so that the property (ownership, title) passes to B, and the goods are stolen before being delivered to B, the property may be laid either in A (who is now only the possessor) or in B (the owner who has not yet taken possession).

It may be noticed here that the word "property" has two meanings. Sometimes it refers to physical property (furniture etc.), while sometimes it means property rights—ownership, the right of property. If I say that "the property in this furniture is in me," I mean that the ownership is in me—that I am the owner. (The double use of the term "property," as meaning both physical things and ownership, was the basis of a witticism of G K Chesterton's: "Thieves respect property; they merely wish the property to become their property that they more perfectly respect it." What thieves do not respect is the right of ownership.)

Suppose A lends £5 to B, and while B is walking away with it a bandit steals it from him. Is this a theft of the debt by the bandit?

No, not of the debt, because the lender continues to be owed the money by the borrower. The thief has simply stolen *money* from the borrower. The thief has not stolen anything from the lender, because the money became the borrower's when it was "lent" to him.

Legally there is a difference between the loan of a chattel and the loan of money. If I ask you for the "loan" of a bicycle, and you comply, you will remain the owner of the bicycle, and I shall obtain only possession; in law I shall be a bailee. But if I ask you for a "loan" of money, and you comply, I shall obtain the ownership of the notes and coins that you hand to me. This is because you do not expect me to return the money *in specie* (as lawyers say); you merely have a right in *personam* against me for the repayment of an equivalent sum.[1] The borrower of money is a debtor and the lender is a creditor.

But surely a creditor can get the loan back from the debtor?

He can bring an action and get judgment for payment of the money. But the creditor cannot just walk into the debtor's house and make off with money in the drawer, or with the TV set, in repayment of the loan. The creditor does not own any property of the debtor's. If a judgment remains unsatisfied he can apply to have a bailiff of the court levy execution on the debtor's property, selling his furniture if necessary to satisfy the judgment. In the case of the loan of the bicycle, on the other hand, the lender still owns the bicycle.

What was that bit in section 5 (1) about an equitable interest?

Do not trouble about the bracketed words in the subsection at the moment. Suffice it here to say that property ordinarily exists at law; that is, it was recognised by the old courts of common law. This is legal property, or property without complications. But property can also exist in equity behind a trust; this was the invention of the former Court of Chancery. In other words, the legal title to property may be vested in

---

[1] Of course, if I "borrow" a pound note for performing a party trick, I am a bailee of the note, because the specific note is supposed to be given back.

trustees, who hold it on trust for a beneficiary; the beneficiary is the owner in equity, and may be said to have the equitable title. (The above is a simplified account of the position, but it is good enough for our purposes.) Either the trustee or the beneficiary may be named in the indictment as the person to whom the property "belongs;" no question will be raised.

What if the indictment lays the property in the wrong person?

Happily, the mistake is usually harmless. Provided that there has clearly been a theft from someone, it does not matter that the indictment names the wrong owner, unless the circumstances are very unusual and mentioning the wrong owner has misled the defendant in his defence. Normally the trial court can, upon application, give leave to amend the indictment or information, and even if no amendment is made a conviction to correct a mistake as to ownership a conviction will be upheld on appeal. The comforting rule for prosecutors is that the ownership of the property is an "immaterial averment."[2]

What is an appropriation?

This was chosen as a wider term than the "taking" previously required for theft. In order to make the meaning clearer, section 3 (1) provides that "any assumption by a person of the rights of an owner amounts to an appropriation."

I am glad you think that makes it clearer. It's far from being clear to me. Does it mean that the thief assumes that the owner has rights?

No. The thief assumes to himself, i.e. grabs for himself, so far as he can, what would otherwise have been the rights of the owner.

But theft does not alter the ownership. The owner still has all his rights. So how can the thief have assumed them?

The section must refer to the thief taking for himself some of the advantages to which the owner is entitled, such as possession of the thing. In short, "appropriation" means the *usurpation* of rights.

A word as to sentencing. The maximum sentence for theft under the Act is 10 years' imprisonment,[3] but this is meant only for cases of the utmost seriousness, and the ordinary offender, particularly the first offender, can expect lenient treatment. Theft is triable either way, and the vast majority of charges are tried summarily. In the following pages we shall frequently speak of the jury as the triers of fact, but wherever the context so admits this expression is intended to include the magistrates on summary trial.

§ 31.4. OBTAINING BY DECEPTION

The offence of obtaining money or other property by deception can be prosecuted by the police (or, of course, the DPP) under section 15 (1) of

---

[2] *Etim* v. *Hatfield* [1975] Crim.LR 234. Cp. A T H Smith in 126 NLJ 243.
[3] S. 7.

the Theft Act (replacing the former law of obtaining by false pretences). The subsection reads as follows.

> "A person who by any deception dishonestly obtains property belonging to another, with the intention of permanently depriving the other of it, shall on conviction on indictment be liable to imprisonment for a term not exceeding 10 years."

Like theft, the offence is triable either way. The indictment (or information) will state the offence as "obtaining property by deception, contrary to section 15 (1) of the Theft Act 1968;" then it will give particulars showing the nature of the deception and what property was obtained and from whom. Minor trading frauds are generally dealt with not under this section but by a Town Hall official known as the trading standards officer (sometimes called the consumer protection officer), bringing a charge under the Trade Descriptions Act 1968, or, in the case of a sale of unfit food, by an environmental health officer bringing a charge under the Food and Drugs Act 1955. There is other legislation for the protection of consumers which need not be detailed.

Some elements are common to theft and the offence of obtaining under section 15 (1). Both require a dealing with property belonging to another, and both require dishonesty and an intention to deprive the other permanently. Both are punishable in the same way. But "property" for theft does not cover all interests in land, whereas it does for the deception offence; and whereas theft requires an appropriation, the deception offence requires an obtaining.

Subsection (4) offers assistance on the meaning of deception.

> "For purposes of this section 'deception' means any deception (whether deliberate or reckless) by words or conduct as to fact or as to law, including a deception as to the present intentions of the person using the deception or any other person."

What it says is that "deception" means "deception. . . . " How very true. But couldn't Parliament have been a bit more forthcoming?

The offence before the Theft Act was called obtaining by false pretences, and everything that was a false pretence will pretty clearly be deception under the Act; but the notion of deception may be wider than that of false pretences. Deception may be defined as words or (other) act producing a mistaken belief, accompanied by the necessary mental element on the part of the deceiver. (A somewhat similar notion is found in the law of tort, where it is called deceit, and in the law of contract, where it is generally called fraud; but these concepts are not quite the same as deception in the criminal law.)

Does one have to keep to the absolutely rigid truth? All sorts of petty humbugs are used in business matters. Assuming a false name, for instance. Do they fall foul of section 15 (1)?

You may be thinking of "puffery," which is discussed later. As to names, English law is free and easy. "Lord" George Sanger ran a circus under a title of nobility that he simply assumed. A man can give himself a new name or go under a business or professional name if he wishes, and nearly all women change their names. Section 15 (1) is not infringed because there is no dishonesty. But if it can be shown that a name was assumed in order to get a fraudulent benefit, there can be an obtaining by deception. An example is where a person of bad character assumes another name in order to get credit.

Subsection (4) says "by words or conduct." How can one weave the tangled web without using words?

Cases on the law of contract and tort as well as on the criminal law illustrate how a false representation may be implied from conduct. A person who dons a uniform (like an undergraduate gown in days when students wore such dress[1]) impliedly represents that he belongs to the organisation that gives him the social right to wear it. So if he gets goods on credit on the strength of the uniform he can be guilty of obtaining property by deception.[2] Again, it has been held by the civil courts that a farmer who sends a cow to market impliedly represents that it is not diseased, and is fit to rub shoulders with other cows;[3] but whether such a representation should be implied in criminal matters is debatable.

What if a person uses deception to get the hire of a car?

This does not come under section 15, because the fraudster does not intend to deprive permanently; but there is a statutory offence of obtaining services by deception, which will be studied in due course (§ 34.11). There is also an offence of "making off without having paid" (§ 40.1). We shall return to the discussion of section 15 in Chapter 34.

§ 31.5. CONSPIRACY TO DEFRAUD

Conspiracy to defraud is one of the open-ended forms of conspiracy that have survived all attack. The particular reason for paying attention to it at this point is that it is a general stop-gap offence. Even when conduct does not fall within any of the substantive offences of dishonesty, one may have to consider whether it may not still be caught in the net of conspiracy to defraud.

The offence is doubly remarkable. First, in the width given to the notion of fraud. In ordinary speech this word generally denotes a deception—a false representation or trick working on the victim's mind, or sometimes a misappropriation of trust property by a trustee. But the judges, intent on catching crooks, and mindless of the niceties of language, held that the

---

[1] *Barnard* (1837)7 C & P 784, 173 ER 342.

[2] The wearing of certain uniforms is also a specific offence, e.g. a police uniform (Police Act 1964 s. 52 (1) as amended).

[3] *Bodger* v. *Nicholls* (1873) 28 LT 441. *Ward* v. *Hobbs* (1878) 4 App. Cas. 13 seems to depend entirely on the exclusion clause.

surreptitious or forcible taking of property without deception was also a defrauding at common law; so a robber, a burglar, and a pickpocket defrauded their victims.[1] We shall see that this point is still important where the taking is for a limited time, so that it is not theft. Even where the conspirators have a state of mind that would in ordinary language be called fraudulent, there may be no deception of the sort required by the Theft Act, and yet they may be guilty of conspiracy to defraud. We shall return to this point in the chapter on obtaining property by deception (Chap. 34).

Secondly, the ends that the conspirators have in view may be of the most varied character. The object need not be to commit a crime, but may be to commit one of certain kinds of tort, or even certain moral wrongs that are not torts. It need not be to make a profit, but may be merely to inflict a loss.[2] It need not involve dishonesty in respect of property, but may be a dishonest endeavour to obtain certain acts or forbearances, such as to obtain a Government licence or permission.[3]

The major limiting factor in all forms of conspiracy to defraud is the necessity to prove dishonesty. A summing up is defective if it tells the jury that an intent to act to the prejudice of another's right *is* an intent to defraud. Such an intent suffices for the offence only if it is dishonest, and this must be emphasised to the jury.[4]

I remember that a conspiracy to defraud remains a crime at common law, and cannot be charged as a statutory conspiracy (§ 18.1). Is the difference between the two kinds of conspiracy important?

The rules do not differ markedly, apart from the fact that a statutory conspiracy must be to commit an offence, not just some wrong in general. Otherwise, the chief difference is that a conspiracy at common law (and therefore a conspiracy to defraud) is not an arrestable offence[5] while a statutory conspiracy can be.[6] And there is the procedural point that a statutory conspiracy must be charged under the Criminal Law Act 1977, while a conspiracy to defraud is charged as being contrary to the common law.

Then take, say, a conspiracy to obtain property by deception. Is that a statutory conspiracy to violate the Theft Act section 15 (1), or is it a common law conspiracy to defraud? Or both?

This point has caused some trouble, owing to the defective drafting of the Criminal Law Act. The answer, as settled by the Court of Appeal, is

---

1 See *per* Viscount Dilhorne in *Scott* [1975] AC at 837–838.

2 *Ibid.* at 838–839.

3 See generally 1st edn 638–641.

4 *Landy* [1981] 1 WLR 355 at 365–366. On the meaning of dishonesty in this context see § 32.5. The court said that conduct such as acting to the prejudice of another's right is only possible *evidence* of defrauding (p. 366C). But if all the kinds of defrauding are only evidence of defrauding, what is defrauding? The answer, it seems, is that defrauding means dishonest conduct, and acting to the prejudice of another's right is one of the forms of conduct that juries may regard as dishonest.

5 *Spicer* [1970] Crim.LR 695.

6 That is to say, will be arrestable if the offence aimed at will be arrestable (as theft, for example, is). See § 18.2 n. 5.

that the conspiracy *can* and (at least generally) *should* be charged as a statutory conspiracy to commit the specific offence (or offences).[7]

Whether it *may* still be charged as a conspiracy to defraud is not certain.[8] In a clear case, where there is no doubt that the conspiracy, if it existed, was to commit a statutory offence, it should be charged as a statutory conspiracy. Charges of conspiracy to defraud should be reserved for cases where at least part of the objects of the conspiracy were fraudulent objects that did not amount to any specific crimes.

The problem of interpretation arises because section 5 (2) of the CLA says: "section 1 above shall not apply in any case where the agreement in question amounts to a conspiracy to defraud at common law." Does this mean "amounts *and amounts only to* a conspiracy to defraud at common law" (i.e. is to do something fraudulent that is not in itself a crime)? Or does it mean "amounts to *anything that could have been charged as* a conspiracy to defraud at common law" (including conspiracies to commit crimes like theft)? The latter interpretation would mean that a conspiracy to steal simply *could not* be charged in those terms any longer; it could not be charged as a statutory conspiracy, and would be left to the unreformed common law of conspiracies to defraud. To everyone's relief the Court of Appeal has, at least in effect, attached the former meaning to the words. So prosecutors can still charge a conspiracy to steal as a conspiracy to steal, as they always could, and are not forced to charge it as a conspiracy to defraud, which would be absurd. Whether it can still be charged as a conspiracy to defraud remains an open question. Anyway, a conspiracy to steal, since it can be charged as a statutory conspiracy, is an arrestable offence.

Does a charge of conspiracy to defraud give proper notice to the defendant of what is alleged against him?

The indictment should contain particulars of the fraud alleged, sufficient to identify it with reasonable precision[9]; and if particulars are lacking they may be ordered.

Although the law has attained a certain degree of precision, it is open to objection on two grounds.

1 There is no reason for making liability depend upon the act being done by two people. If it is objectionable for two, it is objectionable for one. If it is unobjectionable for one it should be unobjectionable for two.
2 The notion of defrauding is inherently vague. In itself it is merely a label for what the courts regard as dishonest. The law should be more certain than this. It should specify more exactly what is and is not allowed.

But the definitions of both theft and obtaining by deception include a requirement of dishonesty. If you object to the requirement in conspiracy to defraud, you must object to it in these other crimes also.

Your first statement is correct, but your conclusion does not follow. In

---

[7] *Duncalf* [1979] 1 WLR 918, 2 All ER 1116.
[8] See the discusson of *Duncalf* in 1st edn Suppt p. 21.
[9] See *Landy*, n. 4 above.

theft and obtaining by deception, dishonesty is merely a limit on liability. As a philosopher would say, it is a necessary but not a sufficient condition. For theft you must appropriate property belonging to another, etc.; for obtaining you must obtain property by deception, etc. The requirement of dishonesty is an extra. In the case of conspiracy to defraud there appears to be no other requirement, apart from the agreement. Anything that the jury labels (and is allowed to label) as dishonest becomes punishable as the object of a conspiracy to defraud. This is too vague a test to serve as the foundation of criminal liability.

For the above two reasons, the Law Commission are engaged on drafting a series of specific offences to be put into statutory form, after which the crime of conspiracy to defraud will, we hope (and the Home Office willing) be abolished.[10]

SUMMARY

§ .2 The Theft Act 1968 s. 1 introduces a new definition of theft, replacing the former requirement of taking by one of appropriation. This means that a possessor can steal the property. Employees can still steal, as they always could, and for some purposes it will continue to be important to say that the employee has simply custody of money and goods entrusted to him by his employer, not possession.

§ .3 By section 1 (1), "a person is guilty of theft if he dishonestly appropriates property belonging to another with the intention of permanently depriving the other of it." Property is regarded as belonging to any person having possession or control of it, or any proprietary right in it; the latter includes an equitable right. Details matter little, because the ownership of property is an immaterial averment. It is declared that "any assumption of the rights of an owner amounts to an appropriation;" this refers to a usurpation of rights.

§ .4 Section 15 (1) of the Act makes it an offence where "a person by any deception dishonestly obtains property belonging to another, with the intention of permanently depriving the other of it." " 'Deception' means any deception (whether deliberate or reckless) by words or conduct as to fact or as to law, including a deception as to the present intentions of any person."

§ .5 Conspiracy to defraud, which is purely indictable, remains as at common law. It is a wide offence because, notwithstanding its name, it does not require a fraud in the usual sense. The object may be to commit a crime, a tort, or even a moral wrong pure and simple. The prosecution must, however, prove dishonesty. A conspiracy to commit a specific offence can and (at least generally) should be charged as a statutory conspiracy.

---

[10] Law Commission, Working Paper No. 56; Buxton in 38 MLR 339.

CHAPTER 32

THEFT: THE MENTAL ELEMENT

> Of the contrivances which mankind has devised to lift himself from savagery there are few to compare with the habit of assent, not to a factitious common will, but to the law as it is. We need not go so far as Hobbes, though we should do well to remember the bitter experience which made him so docile. Yet we can say with him that the state of nature is "short, brutish and nasty," and that it chiefly differs from civilised society in that the will of each is by habit and training tuned to accept some public, fixed and ascertainable standard of reference by which conduct can be judged and to which in the main it will conform.
>
> O W Holmes J, *The Spirit of Liberty*

THE general definition of theft in the Theft Act section 1 (1) was given in § 31.3. We may extract from this definition, amplified by further explanations in other sections and by judicial interpretation, a series of rules. The first two relate to the mental element, and are studied in this chapter.

1 At the time of appropriation the thief must intend to deprive another person permanently of his property (§§ .1–.4).
2 The appropriation must be dishonest (§ .5).

The phrase formerly used to describe the mental element in stealing was *animus furandi*. For the sake of speaking English (even though rather peculiar English) we shall speak of it as theftous intent. Its two elements are the intent to deprive the owner permanently, and dishonesty.

The two elements are independent. One may *dishonestly* appropriate property intending to deprive the owner temporarily ("borrowing" his lawn-mower when the taker knows that the owner does not wish him to do so). That is not theft. Or one may honestly appropriate goods intending to deprive the owner permanently of them. That is not theft either. (A diner at a restaurant intends to deprive the proprietor permanently of the food consumed, but he is not guilty of theft if he intends to pay for it, because he is honest. If, after consuming the meal, he declares that it was a culinary disaster and that he is not going to pay, he is still not guilty of theft, whatever his civil obligation may be. He will be guilty of the offence of "making off without paying" if his complaint was only a dishonest excuse for not paying: see Chap. 40.)

§ 32.1. THE INTENT TO DEPRIVE

Theft requires an intention to deprive the owner; it is not concerned with any intention the thief may have to benefit himself.

But surely the thief doesn't want to deprive the owner for the hell of it, so to speak. He wants to get the property himself. Depriving the owner is incidental. So why doesn't the Act say that the thief must intend to get the property himself?

Exceptionally, the thief may simply want to deprive the owner—as where a postman, who has been too lazy to deliver letters, destroys them. He wants to destroy the evidence against himself, and for that purpose wants to deprive the owner of them. Even when the thief wants to acquire the property, this involves depriving the owner—and he intends this deprivation, because he knows it is an inseparable part of what he wants.

Could it be theft to deprive a person recklessly?

It was not theft at common law, and would not be theft under the Act except to the extent that section 6 applies (see § .3). The hole in the law is plugged to some extent by conspiracy to defraud, which is committed by a conspiracy to subject another person to a financial risk that he would not have wished to run if he had known the facts.

A remarkable example concerns company directors. They are in a peculiar position, since they are in charge of the property of the company and yet are not, technically, trustees for the shareholders. Although they may commit specific offences of dishonesty in relation to the company property, no statute declares that they commit a criminal offence in making use of the property in a rash way. Yet in *Sinclair*,[1] where directors took a risk by handing over the whole of the company's assets without security, they were held in the circumstances to be guilty of a conspiracy to defraud the company, its shareholders and creditors. The Court of Appeal said:

> "To cheat and defraud is to act with deliberate dishonesty to the prejudice of another person's proprietary right. In the context of this case the alleged conspiracy to cheat and defraud is an agreement by a director of a company and others dishonestly to take a risk with the assets of the company by using them in a manner which was known not to be in the best interests of the company and to be prejudicial to the minority shareholders."

The case shows that an intention to take a risk with someone else's property, or to cause him by fraud to take such a risk, for purposes of one's own, is capable of founding a charge of conspiracy to defraud. The essence of the offence is not causing a loss (because it does not matter whether loss is caused or not); it lies in subjecting another person to an unwanted pecuniary risk. The conspirators knowingly take this risk on the victim's behalf.

§ 32.2. PERMANENT DEPRIVATION

The traditional notion of theft involves an intent to deprive the owner permanently, not just to make a temporary use of his property. A man is not guilty of theft in "borrowing" a neighbour's lawn-mower for the day while the neighbour is out, even if that is reckoned as dishonest. The same requirement appears in the offence of obtaining property by deception.

Is the law the same if a shop assistant "borrows" money from his employer's till, intending to replace it when his ship comes in?

Unlike the taker of the mower he intends to deprive his employer of those particular coins or notes permanently, even if he has every prospect of replacing them in a short time. So he can be guilty of theft.[1]

---

[1] [1968] 1 WLR 1246, 3 All ER 241,52 CAR 618. Cp. *Allsop* (1977) 64 CAR 29, discussed by Smith in [1977] Crim.LR 642; *Landy* [1981] 1 WLR 355.

[1] See *Halstead* v. *Patel*, Chap. 33 § 17 *ad* n. 7; *McCall* (1971) 55 CAR 175; *Duru* [1974] 1 WLR 2, [1973] 3 All ER 715.

But isn't that a very technical view? One pound note is as good as another. Nobody feels deprived if the pound in his pocket is changed into two 50p pieces.

Lawyers express the point by describing money as "fungible." A fungible is any property that is regarded as equivalent to other property of the same kind (corn, cement, petrol, postage stamps).[2] In ordinary life, and for nearly all legal purposes, money is treated as a fund rather than as a number of pieces of metal or paper. But in the present context there is a valid social reason for insisting that the actual money borrowed is not intended to be returned. The opposite view would let off any filcher of money who hoped one day to be able to restore it. True, a woman who takes another woman's pearl necklace to wear at a party is not guilty of theft if she intends to restore it, notwithstanding that she may lose it and so not be able to restore it. That is bad enough, but it would be worse if the same rule were extended to the high-handed "borrowing" of money with intent to spend it.

However, there are circumstances where a person who takes money intending to return an equivalent sum will not be guilty of theft, not because he does not intend to deprive the owner permanently (he does) but because he is not dishonest. When an appropriation is and is not dishonest will be considered presently.

Isn't there a danger of thieves getting off by saying that they intended to give the thing back?

Sometimes yes. If a person makes off with a book from a library, or a picture from an art gallery, his defence that he intended to return it might have sufficient credibility to save him from conviction of theft, even though grave suspicion remains.

But a more serious difficulty is presented by people who take up an article to see if it is worth stealing. The crook may, for example, take a lady's handbag, peer inside and finger the contents, returning the handbag when he finds only lipstick etc. in it. It was held in *Easom*[3] that such a person cannot be convicted of theft (even though his general criminal intent is obvious), because his conduct shows that, as things turned out, he did not intend to steal what was actually in the bag.

Could he be guilty of attempted theft?

Yes since the Criminal Attempts Act 1981.[4]

Before the Act, *Easom* decided that the taker could not be convicted of an attempt since he lacked a present intent to steal. The Court of Appeal restated this opinion in a later case where Lord Scarman made a remark of which he must have repented afterwards (because it

---

[2] Although it is customary to instance these goods as fungibles, there is in reality no legal list. As Professor Goode says, "whether assets are fungibles depends not on their physical characteristics but upon the nature of the obligation owed with respect to them" (92 LQR 383). When a person orders a new Maestro, all Maestros of the specified model are fungibles for the purpose of the contract; but if the contract were to buy a particular Maestro it would not be a fungible.

[3] [1971] 2 QB 315.

[4] See § 17.4.

led to what came to be known as "the thieves' charter"), that "it cannot be said that one who has it in mind to steal only if what he finds is worth stealing has a present intention to steal."[5]

The decision in *Easom* was right at the time, not because the defendant did not intend to steal but because the law then was that one could not attempt the impossible. One could not attempt to steal something that was not there. Easom did not intend to steal the things that were in the handbag (a notebook, tissues, cosmetics and a pen, if you are curious to know), as was proved by the fact that he put them all back. But he did intend to steal anything of value that might be there. Following widespread criticism of the absurdity of the law, the Court of Appeal silently determined to repudiate its own decisions, and even decisions of the House of Lords. Their lordships said that in similar circumstances to those in *Easom* the crook could be convicted of attempting to steal "some or all of the contents of a handbag." This was laid down, even before the Criminal Attempts Act, in two burglary cases before the Court of Appeal in which Lord Scarman's dictum was in effect acknowledged to be wrong. The court said:

> "If the jury . . . are satisfied that at the moment of stealing he intended to steal anything in the building . . . the fact that there was nothing in the building worth his while to steal seems to us to be immaterial. He nevertheless had an intent to steal."[6] Similarly, the court said that on a charge of attempting to steal from a receptacle where nothing of value was there, the thief can be convicted of attempting to steal "some or all of the contents of the pocket/bureau" (or whatever it might be).[7]

These dicta were irreconcilable with the authorities on the impossibility rule when they were uttered, but have become undoubted law since the Act of 1981.[8] Indeed, since that Act the prosecution should not be limited to the formula suggested by the Court of Appeal. If it is known what the thief hoped to find, he should be convictable of attempting to steal that.[9] If he thought the handbag contained the Kohinoor diamond, or a revolver, or a microfilm of secret defence information (which MI6 had cleverly led him to believe was there), he is, on principle, guilty of attempting to steal it. It is right that his criminal record should show that he attempted to steal a revolver etc., not that he attempted to steal lipstick. No importance attaches to the fact that the article in question was not there, or even that no such article existed, since we have now got rid of the "impossibility" rule in attempt.

On the last proposition, a possible snag that may occur to you relates to the wording of the indictment. If the indictment said: "attempted to steal a diamond known as the Kohinoor, the property of Mabel Bloggs" (the owner of the handbag), the answer might be made that, as everyone knows, the Kohinoor is one of the Crown jewels, and not the property of Mabel Bloggs or anyone other than the Queen. Although an argument of this type has not been specifically considered since the passing of the Criminal Attempts Act, it is clearly bad on principle. For one thing, averments of ownership in an indictment are immaterial. A more substantial and important answer to the objection is that by the Criminal Attempts Act a person is deemed to intend, and therefore to attempt, what it would be his intention to do if the facts had been as he believed them to be (thus ponderously enacting the ordinary meaning of the English language).[10] If the crook thought that Mabel Bloggs had the diamond in her bag, he committed an attempt to steal that diamond from her. The rules of pleading

---

[5] *Husseyn* (1978) 67 CAR 131.

[6] *Walkington* [1979] 1 WLR 1169, 2 All ER 716.

[7] *Re Attorney-General's Reference* [1979] 3 WLR 577, 3 All ER 143. A similar rule was applied before the Criminal Attempts Act to attempted theft in the poorly reasoned case of *Bayley* [1980] Crim.LR 503. See the criticism by J C Smith in 1 Leg.Stud. 122–123.

[8] However, one of the points decided in *Easom* is still the law. If in a case like *Easom* the defendant is charged with stealing the contents of the handbag (which on inspection he found he did not want), he cannot even today be convicted of attempting to steal such contents (under a statute allowing conviction of an attempt on a charge of the substantive crime). If he did not steal the unwanted contents, he did not attempt to steal them either. So held in *Easom*, which is still good law on this point. Easom could nowadays be convicted of attempting to steal, but there must be an express count for the attempt, and it must be so worded that it can be read as relating not to the objects actually in the container but the objects that the defendant hoped to find.

[9] See [1983] CLJ 94–95.

[10] See the Act, s. 1 (3) (§ 17.4).

must subordinate themselves to this legislative declaration, so that a charge of attempting to do something must always be read as a charge of attempting to do what it was in the defendant's mind to do, never mind the actual facts.

§ 32.3. CONSTRUCTIVE INTENT TO DEPRIVE PERMANENTLY

In order to widen the scope of theft, section 6 adopts the device of deeming certain intents to be an intent to deprive the owner permanently. If you enjoy verbal puzzles, subsection (1) of this section may amuse you. If, on the other hand, you believe that the object of penal legislation is to give clear guidance to the citizen, judges, magistrates' clerks, advocates and legal advisers, its wilful opacity will lower your spirits.[1]

> "A person appropriating property belonging to another without meaning the other permanently to lose the thing itself is nevertheless to be regarded as having the intention of permanently depriving the other of it if his intention is to treat the thing as his own to dispose of regardless of the other's rights; and a borrowing or lending of it may amount to so treating it if, but only if, the borrowing or lending is for a period and in circumstances making it equivalent to an outright taking or disposal."

Unriddle me that.

It is gobbledygook, but careful thought will extract some sense from it. The subsection has two limbs, divided by a semicolon, the second limb providing a partial definition of the word "treat" in the first limb. The second limb, within its limits, is overriding (because of the words "if and only if"). We may therefore restate the subsection (beginning with the second limb) as follows.

An appropriator is to be regarded as intending to deprive the owner permanently of the thing if his intention is:

1 to borrow the thing from the owner, provided that the borrowing will be for a period and in circumstances making it equivalent to an outright taking[2]; or

2 to lend the thing to a third person, provided that the lending will be for a period and in circumstances making it equivalent to an outright disposal; or

3 to treat the thing as his to dispose of (otherwise than by borrowing or lending as above) regardless of the owner's rights,—

even though in each of these cases the thief did not mean the owner to lose the thing itself.

As regards proposition 1, what did our illustrious legislature mean by "borrowing"? Does it mean a real borrowing or a dishonest "swiping"?

In the context, "borrowing" must signify an unauthorised

---

[1] Do not blame the CLRC for this section. It was inserted by the Government when the Bill was before the Commons.

[2] The Act says "is to be regarded" in the first limb and "may amount to so treating it" in the second limb. The reason for using "may" instead of "will" does not appear.

"borrowing"—a temporary taking for use (a shockingly inappropriate meaning to attach to the expression in an Act of Parliament). Further, in the context of the whole subsection "borrowing" must be understood to mean a taking for temporary use, or for some other purpose involving temporary retention, not amounting to a disposal.[3] If the taking is with a view to disposing of the thing it comes within proposition 3, not within proposition 1.

The operation of the subsection may be considered in the following contexts.

(1) In interpreting the law of larceny the courts applied what may be called a "ransom" principle.

> Suppose that D, noticing V's briefcase standing in a hotel lobby, took it off and then wrote to tell V that he could have it back if he paid a ransom. That was held to be theft. But if D took the suitcase as before and then returned it to V saying that he had found it, and hoping for a reward, this was not theft, because D intended V to have the article back in any event.[4]

There is no reason why these propositions should not apply also under the Theft Act, as a matter of interpretation of the words "with the intention of permanently depriving the other of it." In the first of the pair of examples the owner is to be deprived permanently unless he pays up, and that can be regarded as an intent to deprive permanently without the assistance of section 6 (1).

Whether it also comes within the subsection is by no means obvious. If D's taking of the briefcase was with intent to "borrow" within the meaning of the subsection (under proposition 1 above), it was theftous within the subsection only if D intended to borrow the briefcase for a period *and* in circumstances making it equivalent to an outright taking. These words are apt for a case where D takes the article intending to keep it for a long time, or for an appreciable part of its useful life; but in the case we are supposing the taking and holding to ransom may have been a brief affair. It may be thought to fall better within proposition 3: D intended to treat the thing as his own to dispose of. The trouble is that we do not know that D did intend to dispose of it; he may have intended to keep it, if the attempt to get a ransom did not come off. The most sensible conclusion is that there is really no need to resort to the subsection at all in this case.

Another example of the ransom principle is where D misappropriates a cheque drawn by V. D intends to cash the cheque, and V will get it back after it has been cashed.[5] Although V gets it back, he has to "buy" it, so to speak, by honouring it. So D's taking of the cheque is theft, both as a matter of general interpretation and, more specifically, as an application of section 6 (1) since D intended to treat the thing as his own to dispose of (by cashing it).

---

[3] I am indebted for the suggested interpretation to Griew 2–74 n. 26.

[4] [1981] Crim.LR 136–137.

[5] In *Duru* [1974] 1 WLR 2, [1973] 3 All ER 715, the CA made heavy weather of the point: see below at n. 10. Cp. *Wakeman* v. *Farrar* [1974] Crim.LR 136; *Kohn* (1979) 69 CAR 395.

I don't see the problem here. Surely, when you steal a cheque you steal money.

The cheque is not money, even though for some legal purposes it is regarded as equivalent to money. If the owner, discovering the loss of the cheque, stops payment of it, the thief will get no money from the bank, but he is still guilty of theft of the cheque as a piece of paper,[6] for the reason just given. If the thief cashes the cheque, he can be charged with theft of the cash, as we shall see.[7]

Cheques are more likely to be obtained by deception than to be stolen, and section 15 (the deception section) incorporates section 6 for the purpose of this offence. The same intent is therefore required for both crimes.

As yet another example of the "ransom" type of case, it would clearly be theft to appropriate a railway ticket dishonestly from the Railways Board, even though the Board will get it back on the completion of the journey.[8] (Similarly where a ticket is obtained by deception.) One cannot steal a railway journey, or the right to make it, but one can steal a document evidencing the right. If the case is regarded as coming under proposition 1, it can well be held that the taking was equivalent to an outright taking because the taker got the full use of the ticket. After he had finished with it, it had no value.

When someone steals a railway ticket in order to use it dishonestly, what he really gets is the ride.

It may be true that what the thief really wants is the ride. But he may be arrested before he gets the ride; or he may take the ticket in order to sell it to someone else. In any case he is guilty of stealing the ticket.

The other half of the common law rule, that it was not theft to take an article intending to give it back without conditions (even though the taker hoped to make a profit by the taking) is not, in general, touched by section 6.[9] This is a defect in the law, which results from the unfortunate perpetuation in the Act of the common law requirement of an intent to deprive *permanently*.

(2) The second example of a section 6 (1) "borrowing" as "equivalent to

---

[6] *Kohn*, last note.

[7] § 33.11, where there is also a discussion of theft of the cheque as a thing in action.

[8] For authority before the Act, see *Beecham* (1851) 5 Cox 181; cp. *Boulton* (1849) 1 Den. 508, 169 ER 349; *Kilham* (1870) LR 1 CCR 261.

[9] The ruling of the recorder in *Johnstone* [1982] Crim.LR 454,607 appears to have been intended to give effect to this principle, but it may be questioned on the facts. D, a drayman, delivered bottles of drinks to an honest retailer, collecting empties for credit in respect of the deposits paid. He dishonestly did not record some of these empties, and delivered these to a dishonest retailer, having conspired with the latter that he should claim the deposits on them and share the money with D. It was ruled that D was not guilty of theft of the empties; he intended them to go back to his employer, and so was not treating them as his own to dispose of. But when he received the empties from the honest retailer, the employer became liable to credit the deposits to the honest retailer; D's delivery of the empties was a wrongful disposal of them, and the employer would have got them back from the dishonest retailer only on crediting him with the amount of the deposits, to which he was not entitled. On a reasonable view, therefore, D could have been regarded as coming within s. 6, and in any case he could have been convicted by reason of the ransom principle at common law. It was not a case where the employer was expected to pay the dishonest retailer only as a matter of grace.

an outright taking" is where a thing is dishonestly taken to be restored in a substantially different state. Here the appropriation is capable of being theft.

In *Duru*,[10] the defendant was charged with obtaining a cheque by deception, contrary to section 15 (1). This offence, like theft, requires the intention of permanently depriving the other of the thing (see § 31.4). The cheque after being obtained had been paid into a bank account and collected on behalf of Duru. It was held that although the cheque would be returned to the drawer (the payer) after it had been honoured and cancelled, at that point "it ceases to be, in its substance, the same thing as it was before"; so the offence was committed. The decision was based primarily upon an interpretation of the phrase "with the intention of permanently depriving the other of it," without the aid of section 6 (1); but the court added that it would have been prepared to reach the same result by applying the subsection.

The cheque form as a piece of paper was obviously the same before and after it was paid in and collected, apart from the cancellation mark stamped upon it. It is not the physical substance that dramatically changes but the legal effect. A cheque that can be sued on turns into one that can no longer be sued on, because it has been discharged. The court's exercise in metaphysics was unnecessary, for the decision could have been rested simply on the ransom principle. Other cases can be put, however, in which the ransom principle would not apply but a "changed state" principle would. For example, D takes V's horse and kills it, restoring the carcase to V (as he intended to do all along).[11] This could be held to be theft under section (1) of the Act without the aid of section 6 (1) (since what the owner gets back is not a horse but a carcase); alternatively, it can be regarded as theft because D intended "to treat the thing as his own to dispose of" (proposition 1 above). He "disposed of" the horse by killing it.

(3) Professor J C Smith has another idea. He suggests that taking an article to use for a time or to lend for a time is equivalent to an outright taking (within proposition 1 above) if the intention is to keep it till all the "virtue" has gone out of it.[12] This suggested rule overlaps the last; *Duru* might have been decided the same way by applying it.

The law relating to misappropriation of a cheque may become clearer if one contrasts it with the position where a building society account book is misappropriated. D takes V's book intending to make a dishonest withdrawal by forging V's signature, and then to return the book surreptitiously to V. Does D commit any offence? Not until he forges the signature or attempts to obtain money by the deception. He does not commit theft when he takes the book, because V's account will not be affected by his intended fraudulent act, done without V's authority. The building society book will retain all the "virtue" it possessed previously.

Suppose a student tiptoes into the Professor's room before the examination, takes the examination paper, copies it out, and is discovered when he is returning it. As a result, the paper has to be reset. Would that be an

---

[10] [1974] 1 WLR 2, [1973] 3 All ER 715. Cp., for the old law, Spencer in [1977] Crim.LR 654 nn. 4, 5.
[11] The illustration is given in Smith para. 128.
[12] Smith paras. 128–130.

example of the property losing its value under Smith's interpretation of the subsection?

Smith thinks so.[13] In one case where these facts occurred the student was acquitted of theft, but the point under section 6 (1) was not argued.[14]

Why couldn't it be said that the student has stolen the confidential ideas in the paper?

Secrets are not property. They are neither material things nor legal rights.

Industrial and trade secrets are often immensely valuable, are legitimately bought and sold, and for some purposes are regarded as property. Civil courts will award an injunction or damages in respect of a breach of confidence or a breach of contract relating to confidential information of commercial value.[15] Nevertheless, such information has not yet attained the status of property for the purpose of theft.[16] An employee who in breach of contract communicates his employer's secret know-how to a third party does not deprive the employer of the information.

No, but he deprives him of the secret. The result may be to drain the secret of practically all its commercial value.

That is so, of course. But the traditional lawyer will feel that to speak of a secret as though it were a thing is too metaphysical.

The difficulty with secrets relates not only to the intent to deprive permanently but to the question of appropriation. Granted that you can in a sense deprive a person of a secret by blurting out the secret, do you "appropriate" the secret by blurting it out? If it is a commercial secret you may in a sense appropriate part of its *value* by making yourself a joint possessor of the secret, but appropriating the value of the secret is not quite the same as appropriating the secret. Smith's "value" rule, even if it becomes judicially endorsed, as one hopes it will be, relates only to the intent to deprive. It does not assert that appropriating value without appropriating property is theft. No problem of appropriation arises with the student who takes the examination paper into his possession; he appropriates the physical paper, if only for a short time. If he merely managed to read the questions when they were lying on the Professor's desk, the argument that he has not appropriated any property would be an insuperable obstacle to his conviction of theft.

These considerations show that the definition of theft does not well fit cases of industrial espionage. There is a very strong case for extending the criminal law to the protection of trade secrets and other valuable confidential information (such as the scenario of a play) deliberately obtained by industrial espionage or knowingly in breach of confidence, but the way to achieve this is somehow to goad Parliament into action on the subject.

Suppose a person takes a thing and drains off some but not all of its virtue before returning it. He might take a new garment and wear it so that it now has only used-garment value.

In order to avoid difficult questions of degree, Smith suggests that the

---

[13] [1979] Crim.LR 119.

[14] *Oxford* v. *Moss* (1979) 68 CAR 183.

[15] See, e.g. *Fraser* v. *Thames Television Ltd* (1982), The Times, October 23.

[16] For discussions see Tettenborn in 1 The Company Lawyer 267 and in 129 NLJ 967–968, 130 NLJ 406–407; Tapper, *Computer Law* (New York 1978) Chap. 4.

word "virtue" in his proposed rule must mean "all virtue." If the taker intends to restore the thing with a little virtue left in it, the taking is not theft. On this rule, your hypothetical taker of the garment would not be guilty of theft. Nor would it be theft to take a copyright document, photograph it, return it, and sell copies of it. The original would retain some value—unless the taker had so flooded the market that the product was no longer economically saleable. The alternative would be to speak in terms of "substantially" all the value being gone, and such a rule would certainly give a more realistic scope to the law of theft.

(4) Section 6 (1) may apply where a person dishonestly takes a bicycle or a car to travel for a distance and then abandons it. An appropriation with intent to abandon can be held to come within proposition 3; the taker, by abandoning the thing, "treats it as his own to dispose of." At common law, if there was a possibility of the owner getting the thing back the taker did not commit larceny (because he did not intend to deprive the owner permanently, but was only reckless as to permanent deprivation),[17] but it apparently becomes theft under section 6 (1). If this is a correct view, the *mens rea* of theft now covers recklessness. It is to be noted that the theft is committed when the thing is abandoned, irrespective of whether the owner afterwards recovers it.

The same applies if the bailee of the vehicle (a borrower or hirer) wrongfully abandons it. Although he may have "borrowed" within the second limb, the charge against him is based not on the borrowing but on the subsequent abandonment—the disposal, and so it is be judged according to the first limb.

The position is doubtful where a person wrongfully takes an article and sells it to someone, making sure that the owner is informed where his article is so that he can get it back. If the owner is given this information, he can recover his property without having to pay for it. All the same, Smith is of opinion that the taker can be regarded as guilty of theft because he appropriated the article intending to treat it as his own to dispose of.[18] But this overlooks the words "regardless of the other's rights." The taker partly disregarded the owner's rights in taking his property, but he was not totally regardless of them, since he enabled the owner to get the property back without making any payment (except possible expenses of recovery). In substance, what he intended was a temporary deprivation, though he took the article as an instrument of fraud against a third party. If the case is within section 6, why did Parliament use the words "regardless of the owner's rights"? It is to be noticed that in a similar case where the disposal is by way of pawn Parliament thought it desirable to include an express provision making the act theft (section 6 (2)).

These are about the only instances of the application of the provision for "borrowing" in the second limb of section 6 (1) that have hitherto been suggested.

It might seem reasonable at first sight to say that a case like *Easom*[19] furnishes another example of a dishonest "borrowing" that should be regarded as equivalent to an outright taking. D takes up an article belonging to another, intending to steal it if he decides upon examination that it is worth stealing. Then he satisfies himself that it is not, and relinquishes it. Since D has possessed himself of the article and it will be only by his own good grace that he gives it back, it is very near to being an outright taking. But it is hard to say that the taker intended to "borrow' the article for a period and in circumstances making it equivalent to an

---

[17] See [1981] Crim.LR 134–135.

[18] Smith para. 120. Cp. Griew para. 2–74 illustration (iii).

[19] § .2 at n. 3.

outright taking (merely taking up the article to look at it does not fall well within these words), or yet that he intended to treat the thing as his own to dispose of (he has not yet reached a final intention in the matter). Anyway, the court in *Easom* refused to apply section 6 (1) to the case, and we must now regard it as beyond argument that theft is not committed.

This concludes the discussion of "borrowing" in the subsection, and we turn to the expression "lending." It is difficult to think of likely examples of a case where D appropriates V's article intending to lend it to X in such circumstances that the lending is equivalent to an outright disposal, but this would certainly be the case if the lending were for practically all the useful life of the article, or resulted in a substantial change in it.

In view of the grave difficulties of interpretation presented by section 6, a trial judge would be well advised not to introduce it to the jury unless he reaches the conclusion that it will assist them,[20] and even then (it may be suggested) the question he leaves to the jury should not be worded in terms of the generalities of the subsection but should reflect those generalities as applied to the alleged facts. For example, the question might be; "Did the defendant take the article, intending that the owner should have it back only on making a payment? If so, you would be justified as a matter of law in finding that he intended to deprive the owner permanently of his article, because the taking of the article with that intention is equivalent to an outright taking."

We shall study the intent to deprive further in relation to appropriations by an owner (§ 33.8).

Deficiencies in the law of theft are partly made good by various offences of temporary taking, to which we now turn.

§ 32.4. OFFENCES OF TEMPORARY DEPRIVATION

A conspiracy to take property temporarily in order to make an unlawful profit from it can be charged as a conspiracy to defraud.[1]

> An extreme example is one of the cases arising out of what has come to be called "pirate selling." A number of rail stewards pleaded guilty to charges of conspiracy to defraud the Railways Board by washing out used disposable coffee cups and using them to sell their own coffee to passengers, pocketing the proceeds.[2] Since there was no trial, the points of law involved were not considered.

The charge might be based on any of three conceivable grounds. First, the fact that the stewards were making a surreptitious profit out of their employer's property. This would be a doubtful argument in respect of the disposable coffee cups, since it might be held that they were sold to the passengers who bought drinks, and so ceased to be owned by the Railways Board. The defendants made improper use of the rolling stock to sell their own drinks, but they were being lawfully carried and did not take the rolling stock from the possession of the Board even temporarily. Secondly, the stewards committed a dishonest breach of contract; but wide as is the law of conspiracy to defraud, it surely does not cover *any* combination to commit a dishonest breach of contract (e.g. employees playing cards in the employer's time, or conducting their own profitable business in the employer's time). Thirdly, the stewards may be said to have intended to defraud the rail passengers; but the Board was evidently more

---

[20] Cp. *Warner* (1970) 55 CAR 93, where the trial judge caused nothing but trouble by unnecessarily injecting the subsection into his direction to the jury.

[1] *Scott* [1975] AC 819; § 33.3.

[2] The Times, April 22, 23, 1977.

concerned about the fraud upon itself than about the fraud on its passengers. On the whole, therefore, it seems that the most straightforward basis for the conviction of conspiracy to defraud was the fact that the stewards used the employer's rolling stock to conduct a private business, taking customers from the employer.[3] This is an illustration of how the notion of conspiracy to defraud can constantly sprout new heads.

Remember, however, that a conspiracy to defraud is not triable summarily, and a prosecutor is unlikely to encumber the Crown Court with a minor charge. The "pirate selling" was so charged because it was becoming a widespread fraud.

Other offences of temporary taking are statutory. Two in particular may be mentioned.[4]

Art galleries are given special protection against people who surreptitiously "borrow" their exhibits. Section 11 makes it an offence (not theft) to remove articles from places where the public are allowed entry to view (as, a museum or art gallery).[5] The section applies only where the public are allowed to "view" a building or a (non-commercial) collection housed in it, and the section is confined to articles "displayed" (or kept for display) to the public. A public library does not naturally fall within these terms, unless the book is taken from a show-case in the library. Also, a person who "borrows" the church candlesticks for a party cannot be convicted under the section.[6]

The most important statutory offence of temporary deprivation is that of taking conveyances (i.e. vehicles). This is frequently called the joyriding offence, because it is committed by juvenile offenders for whom the car is an otherwise unobtainable status symbol. But the offence is also committed as ancillary to theft; the thief makes off with a car in order to commit other thefts, abandoning it afterwards. Taking and abandoning someone else's car is theft by virtue of section 6, on the argument previously advanced,[7] though for some reason no charge of this nature is reported to have been brought. (Perhaps prosecutors have been daunted by the prospect of having to rely on section 6.) Also, the driving of a vehicle will almost inevitably involve theft of the fuel and unlawful abstraction of electricity from the battery (see later), notwithstanding an intent to return the thing itself. But a prosecution for such trivial aspects of the offence would look unduly technical; so Parliament has created a special offence. Previous legislation is superseded by section 12 of the Theft Act,[8] the key provision being in subsection (1).

> "A person shall be guilty of an offence if, without having the consent of the owner or other lawful authority, he takes any conveyance for his own or another's use or, knowing that any conveyance has been taken

[3] The defendants were doubtless guilty of theft of the proceeds of the fraud, provided that they could be found to be dishonest in respect of the proceeds; see § 33.10. See also, for obtaining by deception, § 34.9 at n. 6.

[4] For others see [1981] Crim.LR 130–131.

[5] See *Durkin* [1973] QB 786.

[6] *Barr* [1978] Crim.LR 244.

[7] § .3 at n. 17.

[8] For some technical details see Wilkinson, *Road Traffic Offences*, 11th edn 329 ff, and for a sociological study see Howard J Parker in New Society, January 3, 1974. See also the offence of vehicle interference: § 38.7.

without such authority, drives it or allows himself to be carried in or on it."

The offence is triable either way, and is deemed to be an arrestable offence. Conveyances include boats and aeroplanes; bicycles are covered by a subsection of their own. As for the mental element, there must (according to the words of subsection (1)) be a purpose to use the conveyance,[9] and in addition subsection (6) provides a defence of claim of right.[10]

"A person does not commit an offence under this section by anything done in the belief that he has lawful authority to do it or that he would have the owner's consent if the owner knew of his doing it and the circumstances of it."

The offence is committed primarily by the taker of the vehicle, but subsection (1) brings in his passenger.[11] (It is an offence by other legislation to get or hold on to a moving vehicle unlawfully for the purpose of being carried or drawn.[12])

The courts have cut down the wording of the section in one way but remarkably extended it in another. The *actus reus* specified for the main offence is a taking; and this has been held, very sensibly, to require the conveyance to be moved,[13] since that is the ordinary meaning of the word in this context. A moving is not necessarily a taking, but there can be no taking without a moving. The specified *actus reus* requires the taking to be "for his own or another's use," but the judges have apparently decided to ignore these words. At any rate, it was held in *Bow*[14] that even moving a car to get it out of the way can be an offence under the section.

The specious argument accepted by the court was that taking a conveyance for use means using it as a conveyance; driving off the conveyance to move it is using it as a conveyance; driving off a conveyance for any purpose is therefore an offence. But a "conveyance" means in effect a vehicle (the wider word was employed only in order to bring in sea and air conveyances, which might not be thought of as vehicles). "Using a conveyance as a conveyance" means not simply driving it but "using a vehicle as a means of transport for people or freight." A person who moves a vehicle to get it out of the way does not use it as a means of transport, and therefore does not use the vehicle as a conveyance. Moreover, to say that the offence is one of taking vehicles for use as conveyances is too narrow; taking off another's motor cycle in a van in order to dismantle the engine to see how it works should be regarded as within the section; it is certainly within the words of the section. The court, recognising an immediate danger in its own interpretation, said that pushing an obstructing vehicle out of the way for a yard or two would not be using it as a conveyance. Why only "a yard or two"? Bow had coasted downhill with the obstructing vehicle for 200 yards; but

---

[9] See Stephen White in [1980] Crim.LR 609.

[10] It is immaterial that the user is illegal: *Clotworthy* [1981] RTR 477.

[11] The law may be that if the passenger discovers in the middle of the ride that the vehicle is being illegally used, he must, generally at least, request to be let out: *Boldizsar* v. *Knight* [1980] Crim.LR 653. But see *Diggin* (1980) 72 CAR 204 at 207, where the CA cast a healthy doubt on the proposition.

[12] Road Traffic Act 1972 s. 30. Yet it is not an offence to stow away on a vehicle while it is at rest, for the purpose of being carried.

[13] *Bogacki* [1973] QB 832; *Miller* [1976] Crim.LR 147; *Diggin* n. 11 above. For the way in which the misinterpretation came about see White, *op.cit.* n. 9 above.

[14] *Bow* [1977] RTR 6. But see *Shimmell* v. *Fisher* [1951] 2 All ER 672, where Lord Goddard CJ said *obiter* that the statute "is not meant to deal with the case where a person is moving a vehicle simply for his convenience, because, for example, it is blocking his doorway."

probably he did this to avoid leaving it where it would obstruct the way. It is difficult to avoid the suspicion what really brought about the decision to uphold Bow's conviction was that he was not a householder removing an obstruction to his entrance but a suspected poacher attempting to get away from a gamekeeper. It has already been suggested that a taking of this kind, even if *prima facie* an offence under the section, may very well be justified by necessity or the abatement of nuisance.[15]

It is only right to add to the above criticism of the decision in *Bow* that the phrase in the Act "for his own or another's use" needs legislative reconsideration. If the words are given the effect that ought to be attached to them, they mean that the removal of a car out of spite, so as to cause the owner inconvenience, does not come within the offence. On the other hand, the facts of *Bow* show that the simple removal of these words from the section would also be unsatisfactory.

Provided that the taker moves the conveyance, and provided that the conveyance can be got into by a person who can then control it (see subs. (7) (*a*)), it is not necessary that the taker should get into it. So a person who makes off with someone's inflatable boat in his own car is guilty of taking a conveyance![16] Something on wheels that cannot be controlled by a person sitting inside or on it (a perambulator or supermarket trolley) is not a conveyance.

The taking must be without the owner's consent. Where the owner consents to a particular journey being made, the borrower will commit an offence under section 12 if he makes a different journey. So if an employee properly drives home in the firm's car but then improperly uses it to visit a public house, he is held to "take a conveyance" within the meaning of the section. The distinction is between a wholly unauthorised journey and a mere deviation from the authorised route, which would not be an offence even though made for the employee's own purposes.[17]

What if the borrower uses fraud to obtain the conveyance?

The mere fact that a person obtains the use of a conveyance by fraud does not negative the consent of the owner.[18] The owner consents, even though he was deceived into consenting. But this proposition does not apply to fraud as to the journey to be made.

> Suppose that a man gets the loan of a car to drive to Bristol, falsely saying that he wants to visit his grandmother; he does not commit the offence if he in fact drives to Bristol, even though his purpose was exclusively to visit his girl friend. But if he drives to York, then he is guilty because that journey is not consented to. The essence of the offence is the use on a different route from that to which consent was given.

In view of the complexity and anomalies introduced into the law by the concept of permanent deprivation, there is a strong argument for eliminating this element from the definition of theft.[19]

§ 32.5. DISHONESTY

Even if the defendant appropriated property belonging to another with the

---

[15] See the discussion of *Bow* in § 23.6 at n. 11.

[16] *Pearce* [1973] Crim.LR 321.

[17] *McKnight* v. *Davies* [1974] Crim.LR 62. Cp. *Phipps* [1970] RTR 209, 54 CAR 300 (borrower), and § 43.5 at n. 7.

[18] *Peart* [1970] 2 QB 672 can still he taken as authoritative on this point, but in the light of the cases in the last note it is plain that it would no longer be followed on its facts. A hiring procured by fraud can be an offence under the Theft Act 1978; see § 34.11.

[19] See [1981] Crim.LR 129.

intention of keeping it, he will still not be guilty of theft if he did not appropriate it dishonestly. (It will have been noticed that the offence of obtaining property by deception under section 15 (1) also requires dishonesty.)

The notion of dishonesty in theft fulfils a double function.

1 It expresses the ordinary *mens rea* principle applied to theft. The defendant must know that he is appropriating "property belonging to another," or (perhaps) be reckless in this regard.

Not only a mistake of fact but a mistake as to the civil law can negative dishonesty. If you take someone else's umbrella believing it is yours you are not guilty of theft for two reasons: you were not dishonest, and even if the requirement of dishonesty had not been inserted in the subsection the courts would undoubtedly hold that you lacked the mental element for theft.

2 The requirement of dishonesty also provides a special defence of morality.

A historical note. It may seem strange that a moral concept should be introduced into the law of theft. The explanation goes back to the Larceny Act 1916, which put the common law into statutory form and incorporated into the definition of larceny the requirement that it should be done "fraudulently and without a claim of right made in good faith."

A claim of right was a belief by the defendant that he owned the article or otherwise had the legal right to take it. Such a belief would negative *mens rea*, and so was a defence on ordinary principles. There was, therefore, no objection to the *concept* of claim of right, but the *name* was slightly misleading for a jury, who had to be made to understand that the question was not whether the defendant had an actual right to the property but whether he believed he had a right.

The second requirement, that the act be done fraudulently, was open to more serious objection, as being both vague and inapt. Inapt, because one would not ordinarily speak of a robber who makes a brusque demand as acting fraudulently. Vague, because no one knew what "fraudulently" meant in the context of larceny. In general it was not held to add anything to the meaning of "without a claim of right."

The CLRC thought that the single word "dishonestly" (copied from the Model Penal Code) made a clearer substitute for both parts of the old phrase. Obviously a pickpocket acts dishonestly, while one who takes property believing it to be his own does not.

The notion of dishonesty is partly (but only partly) defined in section 2. Section 2 (1):

> "A person's appropriation of property belonging to another is not to be regarded as dishonest—
> (*a*) if he appropriates the property in the belief that he has in law the right to deprive the other of it, on behalf of himself or of a third person; or
> (*b*) if he appropriates the property in the belief that he would have the other's consent if the other knew of the appropriation and the circumstances of it; or
> (*c*) (except where the property came to him as trustee or personal representative) if he appropriates the property in the belief that the person to whom the property belongs cannot be discovered by taking reasonable steps."

In each of these three cases the judge must instruct the jury that the defendant is to be acquitted if he satisfies or may satisfy the specified condition.

Paragraph (*a*) means that a mistake as to the civil law can negative dishonesty.[1] (Not, of course, a mistake as to the criminal law: it is no excuse for a defendant that he did not know of the existence of the basic law of theft, but there is no hardship in that: one can hardly imagine anyone—apart from the most pitiable cases in psychiatric hospitals—who does not know that theft is regarded as wrong.) The paragraph covers not only a mistaken belief that one owns the property but also a mistaken belief that one is otherwise entitled to it—e.g. that one has contracted to buy it and is entitled to take it under the contract. Even a belief that one owns the property is no defence if one also knows that one is not entitled to possess it—as in a case where the owner surreptitiously takes the article back from an unpaid repairer who has a right to retain it until he is paid.

The burden of proving dishonesty rests on the prosecution. If the defendant used a subterfuge, that is very strong evidence of dishonesty, but it is not conclusive. Honesty is most easily found when the act was done openly. Unreasonableness of a belief is not fatal to a defence of honesty,[2] but is of course some evidence that it was not genuinely held.

Suppose a man is owed money. Since the debtor refuses to pay, the creditor takes his wallet from him at the point of a knife, extracts the amount owing and returns the rest. Would that be theft?

No, because the taking is not dishonest. The rule has long been settled (and has been reaffirmed since the Theft Act) that such behaviour is not theft, the defendant having a claim of right. And because it is not theft it is not robbery either, since robbery presupposes a theft.[3] The judge must not ask the jury whether the defendant believed he had a right to use a knife to get the property, because that is not the question. The question of honesty relates to the defendant's belief in his right to the property, not to his belief in his right to use the particular means to get it.[4] One can be an honest ruffian.

But the creditor has no right to the specific notes and coins that happen to be in the debtor's pocket. He merely has a right to be paid.

That is true. Lawyers distinguish between an obligation and a proprietary right, between a *ius in personam* and a *ius in rem*. The layman may not realise this; if he is kept out of his money by a debtor who has a stuffed wallet, he may see nothing illegal in helping himself. If so, he acts honestly. Paragraph (*a*) restates this position because it is not limited to a belief as to ownership. What matters is the defendant's belief in his right to appropriate the property.

Suppose the defendant is a lawyer, who knew the difference between obligation and property, and who nevertheless used high-handed methods to exact due payment.

He does not come within the words of paragraph (*a*), because he lacked the required belief that what he did was legal. Nevertheless he may be

---

[1] It may be noted that, independently of the question of honesty, magistrates' courts have no jurisdiction to try a case where a question of title to land is involved. But it would seem that if the question is the defendant's belief in his title to land, they may try it: see note to *Eagling* v. *Wheatley* [1977] Crim.LR 165.

[2] *Lewis* § 34.10 n. 7.

[3] *Robinson* [1977] Crim.LR 173.

[4] Similarly, it is not burglary for a person to break into premises to take a thing to which he believes himself to be entitled: *Knight* (1782) East *PC* 510.

found to have been honest if he believed that he acted morally. That is a question for the jury.

Reverting to the honest ruffian: a forcible taker, though not guilty of theft or robbery, is guilty of assault,[5] and may be guilty of blackmail.

Paragraph (*c*) above is intended chiefly to cover finding, particularly finding on the highway (an expression that includes streets and public squares).[6]

Section 2 (2) provides:

> "A person's appropriation of property belonging to another may be dishonest notwithstanding that he is willing to pay for the property."

This wholly useless provision does not say that the appropriation will be dishonest, only that it may be, which means that it may or may not be. The subsection leaves us no wiser.

Does the judge exercise any control over the jury in deciding whether the appropriation was dishonest?

Precious little. How much, will take a little time to explain.

It might be thought, as a deduction from general principles of law, that the defendant would bear an evidential burden in respect of a defence of honesty (just as he does in respect of private defence), and that the judge would be able to withdraw the issue from the jury if there is no "evidence that can properly be passed to the jury for their consideration."[7] When the CLRC proposed the use of the term "dishonestly" in defining theft it certainly did not contemplate that the jury would be left in complete freedom to uphold a defence that the defendant was carrying out a "Robin Hood" policy of robbing the rich to provide for the poor; or a policy of stealing from his employer on the ground that his services were so valuable that he was morally entitled to higher wages; or a policy of stealing from persons of some selected class (capitalists, bookmakers, or people of a particular race) who in his opinion should be made to pay money. Although a judge can never force a jury to convict, it was to be expected that he would strictly enjoin them that no possibility of honesty fell to be considered on such facts. However, things have developed in a way that seems to deprive the judge of almost all control, even the verbal control of giving a firm instruction to the jury on matters like those just listed.

The rot commenced with the decision of the Court of Appeal in *Feely*,[8] where it was held, applying the general rule in *Cozens* v. *Brutus*,[9] that "dishonestly" is an ordinary word which must be left to the jury to interpret, the court assuming that the jury will apply it according to "the current standards of ordinary decent people."

> The case concerned the manager of a betting shop who took £30 from the till for his own purposes. This was contrary to his instructions, but he had a right of set-off for this amount in respect of money owed him by his employer, so he did not put his employer financially at risk. His conviction of theft was quashed because the trial judge had removed the issue of dishonesty from the jury.

---

[5] *Skivington* [1968] 1 QB 166; cp. *Boden* (1844) 1 C & K 395, 174 ER 863. These cases show that ignorance of the civil law is no defence in respect of offences against the person. Cp. § 20.4 n. 4.

[6] The paragraph is defectively worded: see 1st edn 664–666.

[7] The phrase used by Lord Morris: see § 2.4 at n. 8.

[8] [1973] QB 530.

[9] § 2.6.

The judge was wrong not to allow the jury to acquit on the dishonesty issue. Indeed, if the jury after a proper direction had convicted on such facts, the conviction should have been assailable on appeal as being unsafe or unsatisfactory. But the judgment of the Court of Appeal gave rise to foreboding, not because of the actual decision for the particular defendant but because of the rule stated by the court that honesty is entirely a question for the jury, applying their own assessment of decent current standards.

The practice of leaving the whole matter to the jury might be workable if our society were culturally homogeneous, with known and shared values, as it once very largely was. But the object of the law of theft is to protect property rights; and disrespect for these rights is now widespread. Since the jury are chosen at random, we have no reason to suppose that they will be any more honest and "decent" in their standards than the average person; indeed, it is not impossible that they will fail to achieve unanimity or near-unanimity except upon a standard lower than the average.

Evidence of the poor level of self-discipline now prevailing abounds—and this without taking any account of tax defaults. Observers agree upon a very large scale of theft: not merely shoplifting and fare bilking but stealing from employers by employees and an assortment of frauds perpetrated upon customers by employees. Great numbers of employed people of all classes believe, or affect to believe, that systematic dishonesty of various kinds is a "perk." It is tolerated by many employers, provided that it does not exceed some ill-defined limit; and some employers even encourage fiddles when they are at the expense of customers, since this is a way of increasing employees' remuneration without cost to the employers. For the employee, illicit remuneration has the advantage of being untaxed. Fiddling also brings non-material rewards: it is a pleasant departure from routine, a game of chance against the risk of detection, all the better since the consequences of detection are now rarely serious. So highly do some workers value the practice that a change in the system of work threatening to interfere with it, or an attempt by employers to prosecute offenders, is met by strikes. Notable examples were the strike at Heathrow Airport when baggage loaders were arrested for pilferage in 1973, and the strike of warehousemen at Ipswich docks when the police enquired into the theft of goods in 1974. Strikes have also followed dismissals for pilfering. It was reported in 1982 that 2000 bus drivers had been cautioned for pocketing fares. London bus drivers and Tube ticket collectors stole more than £30m of fares in one year; and London Transport was prevented by union resistance from making collectors account honestly for excess fares.[10] If ordinary people in steady employment develop these lax notions about the right of property, it seems from the judgment in *Feely* that the law of theft is to be automatically adjusted to suit. So the law ceases to provide Holmes's "standard of reference by which conduct can be judged."

The danger presented by *Feely* of encouraging a decline in standards is partly offset by the fact that minor charges of pilfering are likely to come before magistrates rather than juries, and magistrates may be better able to resist the decline than jurors. Also, whereas there is no appeal from acquittal by a jury, magistrates are kept on rein by the Divisional Court; this gives the opportunity for the development of rules of law on the subject of honesty, binding on magistrates.[11]

But in addition to the sociological objections to *Feely* there is the philosophical objection that it mistakes the meaning of honesty. Honesty, as the concept was used in the Theft Act, was not intended to refer to current standards of behaviour, in such a way that a dishonest society becomes honest by definition. Honesty means at least three things, all of them largely independent of prevailing mores:

1 Respect for property rights.
2 Refraining from deception, at any rate where this would cause loss to another.

---

[10] See Jason Ditton, *Part-Time Crime* (London 1977); Stuart Henry, *The Hidden Economy* (London 1978); Outer Circle Policy Unit, *Policing the Hidden Economy* (London 1978); Gerald Mars, *Some Implications of Fiddling at Work* and *Cheats at Work* (London 1982); Stuart Henry (ed.), *Can I Have it in Cash?* (London 1981).

[11] See, e.g. *Halstead* v. *Patel* § 34.10.

3 Keeping a promise, at any rate where the promisee has supplied consideration for the promise or will suffer loss if it is not kept.[12]

The most important of these meanings for the law of theft is the first. Respect for property rights is not inconsistent with the invasion of property rights in specific cases for good reason (as in situations of necessity), but it is inconsistent with the appropriation of other people's property for personal advantage. The judge should therefore be able to rule that evidence of depredations approved by the opinions of the depredators is not evidence to support a defence of honesty.

Relying entirely on jury standards, without firm direction by the judge, was bad enough; but some decisions after *Feely* made matters far worse by asking the jury to apply not even their own standard but that of the defendant himself whose behaviour was under scrutiny: did the defendant believe that what he did was honest? In *Boggeln* v. *Williams*[13]:

> Boggeln was charged with dishonestly using electricity, an offence (akin to theft) provided for in section 13 of the Act.[14] He had failed to pay his electricity bill, and was disconnected. He then told an Electricity Board employee that he intended to reconnect the supply, which he did. Convicted by the magistrates, Boggeln successfully appealed to the Crown Court, which found as a fact that he was not dishonest, even though he knew that the Board did not consent to his use of the electricity, since he intended to pay for it and genuinely believed that he would be able to do so. On further appeal by case stated to the Divisional Court the acquittal was upheld, two members of the court attaching great importance to Boggeln's belief in his own honesty.

If one asks whether Boggeln respected property rights, the answer is not clear-cut. He did not respect them, because he knew for a fact that the Board did not consent to his use of its property, and there were no circumstances entitling him to disregard that fact. But he did, in a sense, respect them, because he intended to pay and thought that the Board would not in fact be disadvantaged. The objection to the decision is not in respect of the outcome (though it certainly attaches an indulgent meaning to the notion of honesty) but to the judges' supposition that the defendant was entitled as a matter of law to set his own standards.

The danger of this attitude was shown in *Gilks*,[15] where a bookmaker paid money by mistake to a punter, and the latter accepted the money although he knew he was not entitled to it. The punter, charged with theft, said in the witness-box that in his view bookmakers were fair game. The deputy chairman gravely left this defence to the jury, asking them whether in their opinion the defendant thought he was acting honestly. The jury very sensibly rejected the defence, and the conviction was upheld on appeal; but the Court of Appeal did not question the propriety of leaving the defence to the jury, or the terms in which the judge had done so.

Subjectivism of this degree gives subjectivism a bad name. The subjective approach to criminal liability, properly understood, looks to the

---

[12] For a fuller discussion see 1st edn 670–671.

[13] [1978] 1 WLR 873, 2 All ER 1061.

[14] § 33.2 at n.10.

[15] [1972] 1 WLR 1341,3 All ER 280; 56 CAR 734.

defendant's intention and to the facts as he believed them to be, not to his system of values (§ 6.11). Gilks merely profited by the book-maker's mistake; but what if a person charged with robbing or burgling a bookmaker says that in his opinion bookmakers are fair game for robbers and burglars? Again, can the defendant go quit by avowing a belief that it is all right to "rip off" banks, insurance companies, multinationals, and anyone who is regarded as "filthy rich"?

The extreme extension of the honesty defence to pure subjectivism has now been slightly, but only slightly, curtailed by a case that one can only with difficulty refrain from turning into an expletive: *Ghosh*.[16] Here the Court of Appeal failed to renounce the doctrine of *Feely*, and did not wholly reject (but only modified) the notion in *Gilks* that the defendant's views on honesty are important. The new rule established by the court incorporates a double test of dishonesty, stated by Lord Lane CJ in the following words.

> "A jury must first of all decide whether according to the ordinary standards of decent and honest people what was done was dishonest. If it was not dishonest by those standards, that is the end of the matter and the prosecution fails.
>
> If it was dishonest by those standards, then the jury must consider whether the defendant himself must have realised that what he was doing was by those standards dishonest."

If the answer to the second question is no, the prosecution again fails; otherwise it succeeds on that issue.

The decision has one other importance: Lord Lane took the opportunity of affirming that the test of dishonesty is the same for conspiracy to defraud as for theft—a matter that had previously fallen into doubt.

Lord Lane may have conceived his judgment as a rescue operation, but, if so, it is a rescue that still leaves the heroine in considerable peril. The second question stated in the decision presents an even greater threat to the standard of honesty than the first. If the defendant stoutly maintains that he considered his act was honest, and that to his certain knowledge his friends (all of whom are decent chaps) would agree with him ("Everyone I know regards bookmakers as fair game;" "We were taught this fiddle by the foreman, and my mates would say I was a fool if I didn't use it;" "We all think it's OK to pad the expense account, to make up for the working time for which the boss doesn't pay us;" "Everyone whips paint and so on in this job; it's regarded as a fair perk"), the jury may be unable to agree upon a finding that in fact the defendant knew the opposite. This difficulty may beset even magistrates, who may be quite clear in their own minds what dishonesty is, but gravely hampered in applying the right standard when they are directed by the Court of Appeal to make enquiry into the defendant's idiosyncratic opinions.

Perhaps the only comfort to be derived from *Ghosh* is that the rule making honesty depend on what the defendant thinks about honesty must, surely, involve the placing of an evidential burden on the defendant. Otherwise the prosecution's position becomes impossible. So it should be acknowledged that the trial judge has the power to withdraw the issue of honesty from the jury if on no possible view of the evidence can it be taken to raise a doubt as to dishonesty. He might, for example, rule that the defendant's evidence of a widespread fiddle among his workmates is no evidence of the honesty of the practice fit for the consideration of the jury; nor is it evidence of the defendant's belief in honesty, because it is simply directed

---

[16] [1982] QB 1053.

to the wrong question. Honesty, even in the sense of customary morality, refers to the opinions of ordinary decent people, not just to the opinions who are subjected to the same temptations as the defendant and who succumb to them. Moreover, even if the judge has withheld the issue of dishonesty from the jury with technical impropriety, this should not be fatal if the evidence of dishonesty is overwhelming.[17]

One thing bothers me. I can see that there can be an honest appropriation, but the definition of obtaining property by deception also requires dishonesty. How can there be an honest liar?

There are such things as spotlessly white lies. (A policeman deceives a desperate villain into surrendering his gun.) But apart from this, the requirement of dishonesty goes to the *obtaining*, that is to say to depriving the defendant of his property. It enables the jury to find that although the defendant was dishonest in the sense that he told a lie, he was not dishonest in the obtaining of the property, because he either was entitled to the property or thought he was. The Report of the CLRC (upon which the Act was founded) put the point in this way.

> "Owing to the words 'dishonestly obtains' a person who uses deception in order to obtain property to which he believes himself entitled will not be guilty; for though the deception may be dishonest, the obtaining is not."

The wording of the section means that it is a misdirection for the judge to tell the jury to consider whether the defendant believed he had a right to obtain the property *by deception*. The words "by deception" must be omitted.[18] Even a lawyer who knows the general law is not guilty under section 15 if he obtains by deception property to which he believes he is entitled.

If this were the only point on which dishonesty was important under section 15, and on the assumption that "entitled" means "legally entitled," the requirement of proving dishonesty would not be a serious restriction of the offence. But as the word is now interpreted the same range of problems may be introduced under section 15 as under section 1. A man may admit that he obtained money by deception but get off a charge under section 15 by saying that he had so arranged things that he did not think that the person deceived would be disadvantaged.[19]

Section 2 of the Act, giving a partial definition of dishonesty in relation to theft, is not applied to the offence under section 15, though a jury would be most unlikely to construe the latter offence more rigorously because they lack the assistance of section 2.

A majority of the Supreme Court of Victoria in *Salvo*.[20] has resoundingly rejected the rule in *Feely*. In a forthright judgment, Fullagar J (construing the similar provisions of the Victorian statute) shot down the English Court of Appeal's notion that the uninstructed juror would know the meaning of dishonesty as it appeared in the Act (and particularly as it

---

[17] See 1st edn 673–674 and the discussion of *Potger* below § 34.10. In *Lewis* § 34.10 n. 7, where the judge had misdirected the jury on honesty, the CA applied the proviso.

[18] *Salvo* [1980] VR 401.

[19] In *Greenstein* [1975] 1 WLR 1353,[1976] 1 All ER 1, the jury rejected a defence of honesty, but there is nothing in the decision to prevent the same argument being raised in another case.

[20] n. 18 above.

appeared in the section corresponding to our section 15). He rejected the "moral obloquy" test for the reason that it bases criminal liability upon shifting sands; and he held that the word "dishonestly" is to be understood to express an absence of a belief in legal (as opposed to moral) right to deprive the other of the property. In other words, he construed dishonesty as bearing the meaning formerly carried by the phrase "without a claim of right." In his opinion, it is the duty of the judge in each case to indicate to the jury by reference to the facts what is required to constitute dishonesty in this sense.

Alas, Fullagar J's fusillade, splendid though it is, is not logically so effective as it may appear on first reading. In particular, a technical objection to his interpretation of "dishonestly" is that in effect the interpretation accepts section 2 (1) (*a*) of the English Act (which is taken over into the Victorian Act) as expressing the full meaning of the word for the purpose of the Act. Thus, subject to the extension of that meaning made by paragraphs (*b*) and (*c*), the interpretation makes section 2 exhaustive of the meaning of the word, whereas the section shows that it is not meant to be exhaustive. This objection does not, however, destroy the force of Fullagar J's criticism of the English practice of leaving the issue of dishonesty at large to an uninstructed jury.

The best solution, it may be suggested, would be legislation that in effect restores the former concept of conduct without a claim of right, in place of the concept of dishonesty, a claim of right being defined as in section 2 (1) (with some amendments). This would be a legislative acceptance of what Fullagar J thinks the law should be. Professor Elliott suggests an addition in order to alleviate the law: it should be provided that to amount to theft an appropriation must be "detrimental to the interests of the other in a significant practical way;" and similarly for the obtaining under section 15.[21] However, such a provision would presumably leave it open to the defendant to say that he *believed* that his appropriation was of this kind, and this may cause trouble—an employee can always believe that his small defalcations do not affect his employer in a significant practical way. It seems, therefore, to be better to go back to the unqualified rule of the common law. Moreover, section 2 (2) should be rewritten to establish that dishonesty is never negatived merely by an intention to pay or repay for the property or money taken. The defendant would, however, have a defence where paragraph (*b*) of subsection (1) applies.

One always has a sense of hopelessness in proposing legislation in Britain, so the possibility of judicial reform is to be considered. The meaning of dishonesty has not yet come before the House of Lords. When it does, there is some possibility that a bombardment of the House based on *Salvo* will have an effect. What must be found is a definition of dishonesty (outside the specific situations mentioned in section 2) that will not depend exclusively on general opinion, and one that will nevertheless go beyond the rules in section 2. I would suggest that the definition should be that dishonesty involves a disregard for rights of property. Professor Smith's suggestion, however, is that a judicial definition of dishonesty might be achieved by using substantially Professor Elliott's formula: a person appropriates dishonestly "where he knows that it will or may be detrimental to the interests of the other in a significant practical way."[22] We can at least be certain that almost any definition making the position independent of current social attitudes would be better than the rule in *Ghosh*.

SUMMARY

Under the Theft Act 1968, the mental element required for theft is twofold. §.1
First, at the time of appropriation the thief must intend to deprive another person permanently of his property. In general, subjecting another person dishonestly to a financial risk, whereby he loses property, is not theft, but a conspiracy to do this can be a conspiracy to defraud.

[21] [1982] Crim.LR 395.
[22] [1982] Crim.LR 609.

When a person's money is physically taken and spent, he loses it permanently. So a "borrowing" of money without the owner's consent can be theft, notwithstanding an intent to repay it, for the same money is not returned. A person who takes up a bag etc. to see what is inside, returning it when he finds nothing valuable, is not guilty of theft (*Easom*), though he can be convicted of attempted theft of the property he hoped to find. § .2

Section 6 widens the scope of the law of theft. Subsection (1) may be analysed into three propositions. An appropriator is to be regarded as intending to deprive the owner permanently of the thing if his intention is (*a*) to "borrow" (without authority) the thing from the owner, provided that the borrowing will be for a period and in circumstances making it equivalent to an outright taking; or (*b*) to lend the thing to a third person, provided that the lending will be equivalent to an outright disposal; or (*c*) to treat the thing as his own to dispose of (otherwise than by "borrowing" or lending as above) regardless of the owner's rights. More specifically: § .3

1 A dishonest taking without consent is theft if the owner is to have his article back only on making or procuring a payment in money or kind, or upon providing or procuring a service. Examples are the taking of a cheque or railway ticket. This "ransom" principle (as it may be called) was recognised at common law as an interpretation of the "intent to deprive the owner permanently," and it can also be regarded as an applicaton of (*a*) or (*c*) above.
2 It is also theft if the thing is to be restored in a substantially different state.
3 It has been suggested that theft is also committed if the thing is to be restored only after its virtue has departed from it.
4 It is probably theft under (*c*) to take a vehicle, drive it for a distance and then abandon it, subjecting the owner to the risk of non-recovery; but the point has not arisen under section 6.

A plot by two people to take an article temporarily can be charged as a conspiracy to defraud. In addition, there are two statutory offences: taking articles on public display, in certain circumstances, and taking a conveyance for use without the consent of the owner or other lawful authority (or, knowing that it has been so taken, driving it or allowing oneself to be carried in or on it). There is a defence of claim of right. It has been held that the conveyance must be moved; but the decision in *Bow* virtually repeals the reference to "use." The owner's consent must be as to the journey that is made; subject to this, the defence of consent generally avails although the consent was obtained by fraud. § .4

The second mental element required for theft is dishonesty. Section 2 (1) instances three cases of honesty: belief in legal right to deprive the other; belief that the other would consent if he knew; and belief that the owner cannot be discovered by taking reasonable steps. *Feely* decided that the general question of dishonesty is to be decided by the jury according to "the current standards of ordinary decent people;" if the appropriation was honest by those standards, it is not theft. But *Ghosh* adds a second proposition: if the appropriation was dishonest by those standards, it is still not theft if the defendant did not know it was dishonest by those standards. The requirement of dishonesty applies not only under s. 1 to theft but under s. 15 to obtaining by deception, and in the latter offence the requirement goes to the obtaining, not to the deception. It follows that a claim of right to the property can be a defence to the charge of obtaining by deception. § .5

Chapter 33

THEFT: THE ACTUS REUS

Property and law are born and must die together.

Jeremy Bentham, *Principles of a Civil Code*

The *actus reus* of theft may be discussed under five propositions.

1 There must be property (§§ .1–.3).
2 The property must belong to another (§§ .4–.11).
3 The thief must appropriate the property (§ .12).
4 It is immaterial that the owner is induced by fraud or threats to consent to parting with the title to the property; but
5 in other cases it is doubtful how far theft can be committed if the act of appropriation is lawful. (Chap. 3).

Further details of the matters discussed in this and the following chapters will be found in the more specialised treatises, and also in the first edition of this work.

1. There must be Property

§ 33.1. PROPERTY AND THEFT

That there must be property is an independent requirement of the law of theft. My small son "belongs" to me, and is in my possession or control; but he is not stealable under the law of theft because he is not property. An employee who plays poker during working hours may be said to be dishonest with his employer's time, but he does not steal because time is not property. It is impossible to filch from another his good name, except by poetic licence, because a good name is not property. The notion of property, therefore, is a key concept in the law of theft. It is a notion of the civil law, so the ambit of the law of theft depends directly upon the civil law.

The property alleged to have been stolen is stated in the indictment, but only in a general way. The following is an example.

Statement of Offence

Theft, contrary to section 1 of the Theft Act 1968.

Particulars of Offence

AB on the day of stole 600 T shirts belonging to CD.

Almost every prosecution starts as an information before magistrates, which is in somewhat similar form to the indictment (except that there are no counts in an information, which must not charge more than one offence). Theft is triable either way, so if the defendant consents he can be tried summarily on the information instead of being "sent for trial."

In the above example, don't you need a count for each separate T shirt?

Where many articles are stolen together, or over a period of time in a continuous course of conduct, so that separate thefts cannot be identified, the theft of all may be charged in one count. If the thefts occur in different places (even if only in different departments of a department store, on the same occasion) it is safer to charge them in separate counts.

Suppose it can only be proved that 300 T shirts were stolen?

The defendant can be convicted under the indictment (or information) of stealing the part of the property charged that he is proved to have stolen. There is no need to amend the charge.

Suppose the prosecutor had a larger stock of T shirts, from which he alleges that 600 were stolen. Is any difficulty caused by the fact that the 600 had no marks to distinguish them from the rest?

The general statement that 600 were stolen is sufficient. Even the date of the alleged offence need not be precisely stated. The prosecution can charge that various items, or a general balance of items, were stolen between stated dates.

Suppose the prosecution is against the manager of the shop who is 600 T shirts down on his stock. He has given evasive explanations of the shortage and is obviously dishonest. Is he charged with stealing the shirts or the proceeds?

It would be safest to charge him with stealing the money. In practice, the jury or magistrates would be strongly inclined to assume that the manager had sold the shirts in the shop, at the prices he was supposed to sell them at, and to convict him of dipping into the till, since the great probability is that that is what he did.

Couldn't one just charge the defendant with theft, without mentioning the property?

The court upon the defendant's application would require such an indictment (or information) to be amended to state the property. It need not state the serial numbers of the currency notes or the brands of the shirts, but it must state in general what is alleged to have been stolen.

What is covered by the term "property"?

"Property" is defined for the purpose of theft in section 4 (1).

> " 'Property' includes money and all other property, real or personal, including things in action and other intangible property."

What is the difference between real and personal property?

"Real property" (otherwise called "realty") means freehold land. "Personal property" (otherwise called "personalty") means all other property, including leasehold land, movables ("chattels"), and money.

Can one steal a thing of no value?

At common law the thing had to have some value, but the rule was so interpreted that it had practically no effect, except in wholly artificial applications. Anyway it is not repeated in the Theft Act. One may steal, for example, a commercially worthless piece of paper, because there are many pieces of paper that people want to keep, even though they have no market value. If the thing were derisively worthless, like a used matchstick, the prosecution could not establish dishonesty.

Can one steal a corpse, or a bit of the human body like hair?

The traditional rule is that there is no property in a corpse, which was accordingly regarded as not larcenable (unless labour had been expended on it, as by reducing it to an anatomical skeleton). Presumably the same rule applies to theft. However, there is a plethora of offences relating to corpses at common law and under statute, and for the purpose of this book it is enough to say that almost any wrongful disposal of or interference with human remains is an offence.

A miscreant who wrongfully cuts off a damsel's tresses would be charged with an offence against the person. If he dishonestly takes the tresses after someone else has cut them off, it would presumably be an ordinary case of theft, since a person must be regarded as owning parts of his body after they have been severed.

§ 33.2. CORPOREAL PROPERTY

The title of this section is the general name for tangible property, whether land or chattels.

The common law declared, with superficial logic, that there could be no larceny of land. That a man could not steal the sitfast acres was obvious, in days when stealing involved a taking and carrying away. But the courts (with a view, it is said, to restricting capital punishment) went further, and held that parts of the land (gravel, growing timber, buildings) could not be stolen even by being severed and carried off.

The basic rule that there can be no theft of land survives the sweep of the new broom. The Book of Deuteronomy pronounces a curse on the man who dishonestly shifts his neighbour's landmark; but the framers of the Theft Act decided not to take a cue from this, even though dishonest practices are not unknown when new housing estates are being laid out. The worst curse laid upon the boundary-mover by English law is to make him liable for a civil trespass. After occupying his ill-gotten strip for 12 years he will even get title to it as a "squatter."

The restriction upon the scope of theft is effected by section 4 (2) of the Act, but some important qualifications are imposed upon it. Omitting some of the rigmarole, it runs as follows.

> "A person cannot steal land, or things forming part of land and severed from it by him or by his directions, except in the following cases:
>
> (*a*) when he is a trustee, and he appropriates the land by dealing with it in breach of the confidence reposed in him; or

(*b*) when he is not in possession of the land and appropriates anything forming part of the land by severing it; or

(*c*) when, being in possession under a tenancy, he appropriates any fixture."

The law's benevolence to squatters is meant to assist in settling disputed claims, particularly in respect of boundaries, which are often hazy on title deeds. It makes for easy decision to say that the occupier who has mown or seeded the boundary strip for 12 years shall be entitled to it. Would it not be anomalous (the argument runs) if a squatter, notwithstanding that he has obtained title to land, could be charged with theft of it?

But the argument is defective. There is no reason why the squatter should not be subject to the law of theft before he gets title by lapse of time. When he does get title, he could be given a retrospective defence. In effect there would be a 12-year time limit on prosecution.

This solution not having been adopted, the Theft Act has the unhappy result of perpetuating in the criminal law the archaic distinction between land and chattels. A squatter can be convicted of theft of chattels that he finds on the land, though not of part of the land itself, or of buildings on it.

To illustrate the refinements of the law, the following are chattels; a mobile caravan, windfall apples, and a heap of dung. All these are personal property, which the squatter (or anyone else) takes on peril of being convicted of theft.

The following are "part of the realty"; a caravan fixed on brick piers, a farm gate, growing apples, and dung spread on the land; these things the squatter cannot steal.[1] All the same, taking away a building like a fixed caravan would be criminal because it would amount to criminal damage.

Is it theft to take wild flowers and plants?

The answer is given by section 4 (3). Picking wild mushrooms, flowers, fruit or foliage is theft only if the taking is for reward or for sale or other commercial purpose. But the taker is guilty of criminal damage if he visibly damages the rest of the plant (as if he clumsily tears off branches).

The modern interest in conservation has resulted in a statute making it an offence, in general, to *uproot* any wild plant without reasonable excuse.[2] This does not apply to the mere picking of flowers, but some rare specimens that are threatened with extinction are forbidden to be picked.[3] Beware, therefore, of plucking a posy consisting of such listed plants as ghost orchid, alpine sow-thistle and oblong woodsia. Some bylaws in public parks and nature reserves make it an offence to pick anything.[4]

What about poaching?

For tens of thousands of years man was a hunter, and even after the rise of agriculture the chase remained a passion of the nobility, as poaching was of the peasantry. Notwithstanding the desire of the privileged classes to

---

[1] Sir E Parry, *My Own Way* 250 relates an Irish case that furnishes an apt commentary upon these distinctions. The question was whether dung was real property. A lawyer made an admirable argument to show that it was. The farmer was called upon to reply and said: "I'm puzzled indeed by all these strange words. But the lawyer says, fair play to him, that cows is personal property, and the hay they eat is personal property, and I ask your Honour, as one man to another, how, baiting miracles, personal property can go on eating personal property and evacuating "—he used a homelier verb"—real property—well, your Honour, it's beyond my understanding."

[2] Conservation of Wild Creatures and Wild Plants Act 1975 s. 4 as amended.

[3] *Ibid.* s. 5 as amended. This section, unlike s. 4, applies to the landowner as well as to other persons.

[4] See in particular National Parks and Access to countryside Act 1949 s. 20; unfortunately the Nature Conservancy cannot under this Act forbid the landowner himself to plough up rare species, though for some very rare species he is subject to the Act of 1975, above n. 2.

preserve their game, the law of larceny was not applied because wild animals were not regarded as property. The provision in the Theft Act starts with what appears to be a bold rejection of this rule, but speedily relapses into orthodoxy. Section 4 (4):

> "Wild creatures, tamed or untamed, shall be regarded as property; but a person cannot steal a wild creature not tamed nor ordinarily kept in captivity, or the carcass of any such creature, unless either it has been reduced into possession by or on behalf of another person and possession of it has not since been lost or abandoned, or another person is in course of reducing it into possession."

This means that the poacher does not steal, though he commits an offence under antiquated legislation known as the Game Acts and Poaching Acts.[5]

Although the judges held that animals were not property when in the wild state, they withheld the benefit of this rule from poachers who were so unsporting as to go off with a creature that someone else had shot. As soon as the animal falls dead it is regarded, by the occult operation of the law, as falling into the possession and ownership either of the shooter (if he has not abandoned the chase) or, failing him, of the landowner.[6] An unlawful taking of the carcass by another will therefore be theft.

Poaching legislation is intended to protect the person having the sporting rights. Other legislation, having the different object of conserving endangered species of wild animal, makes it an offence to kill etc. certain protected species.[7] It is also an offence to possess such animals, live or dead, for sale.[8] The Protection of Birds Act 1954 is intended to give wide protection to wild birds, their nests and eggs, but the monetary penalties are barely adequate. (Even as increased in 1977,[9] the maximum penalty in respect of most birds is only £50, going up to £500 for some species; but a rare osprey egg, for example, or a peregrine falcon can be sold for a much greater sum.)

Can you steal things that come out of tubes—gas, electricity and water?
Domestic gas is personal property, so a householder who fraudulently bypasses the meter to burn gas for nothing commits theft of the gas. He is entitled to use the gas only if it goes through the meter in the proper way.

Electricity is not scientifically regarded as a physical thing, like gas, but is a form of energy. A cyclist who holds on to the back of a lorry appropriates energy but does not commit theft; so appropriating electricity is not regarded as theft either.[10] (The cyclist commits the summary offence already noticed.[11]) To solve the problem of classifying electricity, its dishonest use, waste or diversion achieves the dignity of a special offence, under section 13 of the Act. (The name used in the marginal note is "abstracting of electricity"; this is not very apt, since the electricity when

---

[5] Some is modern, such as the Salmon and Freshwater Fisheries Act 1975, as amended. Deer-slaying is big-time crime, and the penalty for it under the Deer Acts 1963 and 1980 is very modest. See also the legislation preserved in Theft Act 1968 Sched. 1.

[6] See, as to the landowner, *Blades* v. *Higgs* (1865) 11 HLC 621, 11 ER 1474.

[7] Conservation of Wild Creatures and Wild Plants Act 1975 ss. 1, 3.

[8] *Ibid.* s. 2 as amended.

[9] CLA Sched. 6.

[10] Hence an entry to make dishonest use of electricity is not burglary: *Low* v. *Blease* [1975] Crim.LR 513.

[11] § 32.4 at n. 12.

unlawfully used returns to the power station, though at a reduced voltage; it is true, however, that power is abstracted.)

Could a thief be charged under the section (do you call it an electric charge?) for pressing the starting-button of someone else's car?

Magistrates have convicted for this under section 13 (or under the corresponding provision in the Larceny Act which is superseded by section 13). Other convictions involving minimal abstractions of electricity are: when a trespasser in a house telephoned to Australia, or when a hoaxer in a kiosk put through a free call (999) for the fire brigade, or dialled 100 and addressed obscenities to the operator (magistrates have regularly assumed that the free 100 call is lawfully usable only for the purposes contemplated by British Telecom), or when a "phone phreak" by illicit electronic means made a long-distance call without a charge being registered. Some of these convictions are of doubtful legality (particularly on the issue of dishonesty), but they have not come before a higher court.

Some misuses of electricity could be prosecuted in other ways. There is an offence of using a telephone with intent to avoid payment under the British Telecommunications Act 1981 s. 48. (The section does not confer a power of summary arrest; this is a reason why the police prefer to arrest on your electric charge, which is arrestable.) Another summary offence is the making of a grossly offensive, indecent, menacing or false and annoying telephone call: section 49 of the same Act (replacing earlier legislation). Bomb hoaxers commit their own special offence under the Criminal Law Act 1977 s. 51; this is triable either way and can carry a prison sentence. These hoaxers are a menace not only for the disruption they cause but because emergency services speeding to the scene of the alarm create a public risk. Hoaxing the police into wasting their time is generally an offence under the Criminal Law Act s. 5 (2); this too can carry a prison sentence, but does not extend its protection to the ambulance service. False alarms of fire are punishable under the Fire Services Act 1947 s. 31 as amended. Repeated hoaxes are indictable as a public nuisance.[12]

Water in a pipe or other container is the subject of property, though a prosecution for drawing water from a tap is highly unlikely. When water is standing on land in a pond, lake or reservoir it is regarded as land, and is no more the subject of theft than is land in general.

Percolating water is ownerless, *res nullius*, so that (apart from statutory regulations about to be mentioned) any landowner may abstract as much as he pleases. When the water is flowing in a defined channel (as a stream or river) the rights of the riparian owner to abstract it are limited, but if he exceeds his rights s. 4 (2)[13] probably saves him from a charge of theft, even though his appropriation is a tort to the lower riparian owners. Subject to certain exceptions, it is an offence to abstract water from any source in a river authority area without a licence from the authority.[14]

§ 33.3. INCORPOREAL PROPERTY

Section 4 (1) (set out in § .1) mentions "things in action and other intangible property" as the subject of theft.

[12] So ruled in *Norbury* [1978] Crim.LR 435.
[13] Set out at the beginning of this section.
[14] Water Resources Act 1963 s. 23.

"Things in action" (also archaically called "choses[1] in action") are rights that can be enforced only by bringing an action and not by taking possession; they are property rights to the extent that they can be bought and sold. The most obvious thing in action is the creditor's right to payment of a debt. Shares, patents, copyrights, and trade marks have also been called things in action, but Parliament has taken away that name from patents (which, however, remain intangible property, otherwise called incorporeal property.[2])

Should I entangle with the police if I pirated a pop music cassette?

Infringing a patent, copyright or trade mark is not theft. However, your pirating, or any other infringement of copyright, is a summary offence.

The pecuniary penalty in the criminal courts for the infringement itself is low[3] (though it becomes unlimited if a conspiracy to commit the statutory offence is proved). A prison sentence of two years may be imposed in the case of musical or dramatic recordings.[4]

If the infringer operated with a companion (as would be inevitable if the business were conducted on any scale), all could be roped in for conspiracy to defraud, punishable with imprisonment for life.People who make a dishonest profit from the property of another can be punished in this way even though there is in law no appropriation of that property with intent to deprive the owner permanently. An illustration is *Scott.*[5]

> The case turned on a large-scale conspiracy to bribe cinema employees to hand over films that were being shown; the films were copied in breach of copyright and then returned, the pirated copies being distributed commercially. This amounted to breach of copyright and the offence of corruption of the employees, but it was not theft of the copyrights, and no deception was involved. The House of Lords held that a charge of conspiracy to defraud the owners of the copyrights would lie.

The infringer is also liable in damages, which can take away all his profit[6]; and an injunction may be granted against him to prevent him from continuing his offences.[7]

Strangely, infringing a patent or trade mark is not even the most lowly offence.[8] Conceivably, the infringer can be convicted of theft of the illicit proceeds of infringing articles—but no one has yet advanced this argument in court.[9] Of course the aggrieved owner has civil remedies.

If none of these infringements is theft, why does the Act say that things in action are property for the purpose of theft?

Theoretically there can be theft of these rights, but only when the whole

---

[1] Pronounced "shozes."

[2] Patents Act 1977 s. 30 (1).

[3] The maximum per "transaction" under the Copyright Act 1956 s.21 as amended by CJA 1982 is £200.

[4] 2 years under the Dramatic and Musical Performers' Protection Act 1958 s. 1 as amended by Performer's Protection Act 1972. For breach of copyright in general the maximum under s. 21 is 2 months' imprisonment on second conviction.

[5] [1975] AC 819. The punishment is not limited to the statutory penalty for breach of copyright, because conspiracy to defraud, unlike the statutory offences, requires proof of dishonesty: see Lord Wilberforce in *Rank Film Ltd* v. *Video Information Centre* [1982] AC 380 at 441C, G–H.

[6] A particular advantage of the civil action over the criminal prosecution is that the defendant has no privilege against self-incrimination and may be compelled to answer questions, particularly as to his suppliers and customers. See Supreme Court Act 1981 s. 72; *Universal City Studios Inc.* v. *Hubbard* (1983) The Times, February 1.

[7] But no civil remedy is available to the performers of music etc. in respect of a recorded performance, since this is not a matter of copyright and the only proceeding allowed by statute is criminal; see *RCA Corpn* v. *Polland* [1982] 3 WLR 1007, 3 All ER 771, and Mitchell in 133 NLJ 527.

[8] Apart from the possibility of an offence under the Trade Descriptions Act.

[9] On the argument that the wrongdoer became a constructive trustee of the receipts on sale of the infringing articles. See § 31.16.

patent, copyright or trade mark is appropriated, as in the highly unlikely event of a trustee of a patent wrongfully selling it for his own benefit.[10]

You said before that trade secrets are not property,[11] but that there can be a conspiracy to defraud in dishonestly infringing a copyright. Wouldn't a conspiracy to discover a trade secret be a conspiracy to infringe copyright?

Copyright exists in documents and other things in permanent form, not in oral statements or other information not reduced to writing. Bribing an employee to reveal a valuable secret process would be the offence of corruption.[12] Whether the use of deception to get the information from an employee would be a conspiracy to defraud, if practised by two people, is doubtful; it can only be said that the law is very obscure.[13]

Two other points may be made. If an employee unlawfully extracts information from a computer he can be charged with dishonestly using electricity under section 13 unless he is authorised to use the computer. An employee who improperly makes a profit from his employer's secrets may be guilty of theft of the proceeds.[14] The manufacture or use of radio "bugs" without the sanction of the Post Office is a summary offence as an infringement of their monopoly, but of course the penalty is piffling.[15]

It is absurd and disgraceful that we should still be making do without any legislation specifically designed to discourage this modern form of commercial piracy. Abstracting or divulging an official secret is an offence under the Official Secrets Act 1911 sections 1 and 2; but Leviathan is not much concerned to protect the secret and immensely valuable know-how of its subjects.

You mentioned debts as things in action. Do you steal a debt if you get a loan of money by deception?

The proper charge would be obtaining the money by deception.

Then how can you steal a debt as a thing in action?

The notion of theft of a debt presupposes that the debt is in existence before the theft, which is why contracting a debt by fraud is not theft of the debt. However, a creditor is regarded as having property in the debt, as a thing in action. He can transfer (assign) his property, the debt, to a third party. So a rogue who persuades a creditor by fraudulent means to assign book-debts to him would be guilty of obtaining the debts by deception, or, it seems, of stealing them.[16] A much more likely instance of this kind of theft occurs in relation to cheques, and will be considered in due course.[17]

---

[10] Possibly it is theft for a person to purport to sell another's thing in action (or other property) without any title to do so. See § .12.

[11] § .3 at n. 16.

[12] § 40.3.

[13] See 1st edn 639–640, 688–689.

[14] § .10.

[15] Wireless Telegraphy Acts 1949 to 1967; see the Act of 1949 s. 14 as amended, and the Act of 1967 s. 7 (1), (6). In 1973 a man who made these devices was fined £30 (The Times, July 6th).

[16] See Chap. 35.

[17] § .11.

I have registered the fact that a thing in action is not stolen unless it is wrongfully disposed of or acquired. What about shares? Does a person steal shares when he burgles a house and purloins share certificates?

The share certificates are stolen as pieces of paper, which can always be stolen[18]—the punishment of course taking account of their commercial value. The thief could be charged with stealing "shares," but strictly speaking he has stolen share certificates. On the other hand, if trustees of shares sell them for their own profit they steal the shares, because they deprive the equitable owner of the shares which are things in action.

2. The Property must belong to Another

§ 33.4. THE PROTECTION OF OWNERSHIP

Since theft can only be of property belonging to another, one cannot steal from a person who according to the civil law is neither the owner nor the possessor of the property. Some examples:

> V lends D money. Subsequently, D dishonestly decides not to repay the loan. Since the property in the money passed to D when it was lent to him, he is not guilty of theft (or any other offence) in respect of what is now his own money.
>
> D consumes a meal in V's restaurant. The property in the food necessarily passes to him when he consumes it. Subsequently, he dishonestly decides not to pay the bill, and slips out when the waiter is not looking. He is not guilty of theft, but is guilty of the statutory offence of making off without having paid: § 40.1.
>
> A driver fills up with petrol. Nothing is said between the driver and the assistant as to the passing of property, but the intention must have been that the property in the petrol passed when the petrol entered the tank of the car. This is because the owner of the filling station does not contemplate the possibility of siphoning out the petrol if he is not paid. So if, when the assistant's back is turned, the driver suddenly conceives a dishonest intention and drives off without paying, he does not commit theft of the petrol—it is now his petrol.[1] He is guilty of making off without having paid.

But suppose it was a self-service station and no assistant was looking on when D filled up. Would the property in the petrol still pass to D?

Yes. The installation of the self-service pump is an offer to drivers to help themselves. The driver accepts the offer, and thus creates a contract with the filling station proprietor. The property in the petrol passes to him under this contract.

Suppose the diner and the driver intended not to pay when they consumed the meal or took the petrol.

Then they are guilty of obtaining the goods by deception as to their

---

[18] Cp. *Duru* [1974] 1 WLR at 8D, [1973] 3 All ER at 720D.

[1] See as to the restaurant *Corcoran* v. *Whent* [1977] Crim.LR 52, and as to the petrol, *Edwards* v. *Ddin* [1976] 1 WLR 942, 3 All ER 705. (In *McHugh* (1976) 64 CAR 92 the CA affirmed a conviction of theft under the proviso while conceding that the defendant was not guilty of it!) Another instance of the same principle is *Stuart* (1982) The Times, December 14.

intention to repay—assuming, in the case of the driver, that he was seen filling up (see § 34.1). Whether they can, in the alternative, be convicted of theft in these circumstances is postponed for consideration to Chapter 35.

The above instances (summarising the effect of decided cases) show that a person who agrees to buy goods cannot be guilty of theft by reason of anything he does with the goods after the ownership and possession have passed to him. He can commit theft if either ownership or possession has not passed. (The problem presented by the passing of a voidable title is still to be considered, as also is the fiction of ownership in another established by secton 5 (4); see Chapter 35.)

The possession of a thing is transferred in various ways, but chiefly by physical delivery. The ownership of a thing is also transferred in various ways, but chiefly by sale, or by a delivery made with the intention of passing ownership. A gift, for example, is generally made by delivery (though it can be made in other ways, as by deed).

The legal property (ownership) in goods can pass without the possession of the goods being transferred. As already mentioned, it can pass by sale. By the Sale of Goods Act 1979 s. 17 the property in specific or ascertained goods passes under a contract of sale when it is intended to pass. Certain rules are set out in section 18 for establishing the intention of the parties unless a different intention appears. Rule 1 of section 18 is as follows.

> "Where there is an unconditional contract for the sale of specific goods in a deliverable state the property in the goods passes to the buyer when the contract is made, and it is immaterial whether the time of payment or the time of delivery, or both, be postponed."

So if I choose a TV set in a shop, and the seller promises to deliver it tomorrow and to bill me for it in due course, then if he dishonestly sells it to someone else (because supplies have run short and he can now get a better price) he commits theft from me. The set became my property under the contract, and it remains my property though it is still in his shop.

The Sale of Goods Act provides a precise terminology for expressing these situations. Before the property passes in goods contracted to be sold, the contract of sale is called an "agreement to sell." The instant that the mystic property passes the agreement to sell becomes a " sale."[2] In the instance just given of the TV set the contract of sale was a "sale" from the start; there was no point of time at which it was a mere "agreement to sell."

Suppose I give a neighbour money to buy a certain used car for me, and he buys the car but immediately afterwards succumbs to the temptation of selling it again for his own dishonest purposes. Does he steal the car from me?

Yes. An agent is to be thought of as a kind of conduit pipe, transmitting property rights and obligations from his principal to a third party, and back from the third party to the principal. So your neighbour would steal the car from you. When he bought the car the property (ownership) passed directly from the seller to you as undisclosed principal in the transaction.[3]

Conversely with an authorised *sale* by an agent: if the owner of a shop instals an assistant behind the counter, and a customer buys and pays for

[2] Sale of Goods Act 1979 s. 2.

[3] Whether the ownership passes at law or only in equity is disputed. But even if it passes only in equity, that is enough to make the dishonest agent guilty of theft.

an article, the money becomes the employer's money as soon as it is handed over; so if the assistant pockets it he steals from his employer.[4]

Suppose a customer in a shop chooses a camera and says he will take it away with him. The salesman has packed it up and written out the bill, and is expecting to be paid, when the customer runs out with the camera and disappears. Is that theft by the customer, or is it just another case of "making off without paying"?

In an ordinary shop transaction like this the court would have no difficulty in finding (under s. 17 of the Sale of Goods Act) that the shopkeeper did not intend the property (ownership) to pass until payment had been made or credit expressly given.[5] The camera is still the property of the shopkeeper, and the customer has stolen it from him.

If an enterprising tradesman sends me pornographic books without my consent, in the hope that I will pay for them, can I put them on the fire?

You would be an "involuntary bailee"—an odd name, since you would not be a bailee at all. A true bailee (a borrower, hirer, repairer etc.) has agreed to receive temporary possession of the thing from the owner. You would technically be subject to the law of theft; but if you simply dispose of an embarrassing object, and are frank about it, you are unlikely to be thought dishonest.[6]

I should like to ask a question about finders. The dishonesty section (section 2) says that a person is not generally dishonest if he believes that the owner cannot be found by taking reasonable steps. Suppose a finder says to himself: "I know how the owner can probably be found, but I think he must have abandoned this thing, so I will keep it."

If he believes that he is not dishonest. But of course the jury may refuse to credit that he really thought it. Their opinion may be determined by the value of the article. An owner, when he loses an article of some value, does not abandon it merely by giving up the search and giving up hope of ever finding it again. It is still his, and nearly everyone would realise the fact.

---

[4] Technically he could be charged, instead, with theft from the customer, though in practice this would not be done. The assistant (assuming that the customer knows he is an assistant, and does not suppose him to be the owner of the shop) impliedly represents to the customer that he is acting on behalf of his employer in receiving the money; if he then means to keep it for himself, he obtains it from the customer by deception, and therefore by theft. The reasoning underlying this argument will be developed in Chap. 35.

[5] Verdicts to this effect have been regularly upheld in criminal cases. See *Slowly* (1873) 12 Cox 269; *Edmundson* (1912) 8 CAR 107. In *Martin* v. *Puttick* [1968] 2 QB 82 it was held to make no difference that the goods were wrapped and handed to the customer. In *Stephens* (1910) 4 CAR 52 the rule was applied even where the shopkeeper allowed the defendant's confederate go off with the goods, the defendant then refusing to pay for them. See also *Lacis* v. *Cashmarts* [1969] 2 QB 400. (In *Davies* v. *Leighton* (1978) 68 CAR 4 the court suggested that the position might possibly be different if the salesman were a manager; *sed quaere*.) Oddly, the civil courts have not been so definite about the proposition in the text: see Heaton in [1973] Crim.LR 741–742.

[6] The Unsolicited Goods and Services Act 1971 s. 1 gives the recipient of such goods the right to keep them after a specified time (6 months, or 30 days if he has served notice on the sender to take the goods back); so technically he is not supposed to destroy them before that. The section does not apply where goods are sent to a trader. S. 2 of the Act makes it an offence to demand payment for unsolicited goods. Sending unsolicited goods is not an offence in itself, except in relation to books on sexual techniques (s. 4). See generally Palmer in 128 NLJ 763.

There are rules of the civil law governing the rights or non-rights of finders of things on other people's land which can affect the law of theft, but the details may be left to the books on tort and property. One rule may, however, be mentioned: a trespasser on property has no right to anything he finds there. Failing any other claimant, the possessor of the land is entitled.[7]

Certain statutory offences are committed if a person who finds an article in a public conveyance or a taxi fails to hand it in. Also if a person finds a stray dog and keeps it without taking it to the police.[8] "Scheduled" ancient monuments (including archaeological sites) are given some protection in that it is a summary offence to interfere with them.[9]

Suppose a "dip" is seen to steal something from a woman's handbag, but the woman was immediately lost in the crowd and cannot be traced. How is the indictment worded?

It lays the property in a person unknown.[10]

The fact that the name or even the identity of the owner is unknown is never a bar to a charge of theft. However, the facts must make it clear that *someone* has been the victim of theft, even though we may not be certain who that someone is. Although the theft may be established by circumstantial evidence, circumstances of mere suspicion are not enough. The offence must, as always, be proved beyond reasonable doubt.

An example of suspicion being so strong as to amount to proof is the diverting tale of Noon at midnight.[11]

> A police constable saw Noon at 12.30 a.m. carrying a bundle which he suspiciously moved to the other arm when he observed the constable. When asked what he was carrying, Noon showed a cushion wrapped in a man's raincoat, saying that they were his mother's. The constable pointed out that the raincoat was a man's, to which Noon replied; "So what, why can't my mother wear a man's rain-coat?" At that moment two tea towels fell from under Noon's coat. One of them bore a price tag. When asked where he got them from he replied; "You've just found them on the floor." These evasive replies were held to constitute a case to answer, and a conviction of larceny from a person unknown was upheld.

There was very considerable suspicion in that case, amounting to reasonable certainty of a theft. If it had not been so strong an inference the prosecution would have failed.

Local legislation in a few cities and counties creates a remarkable summary offence of unlawful possession. This is committed by anyone who is found conveying goods that are reasonably suspected to have been stolen or unlawfully obtained, if he fails to give a satisfactory account to the magistrate of how he came by them. This legislation forces the defendant into the witness-box, and his unsatisfactory answers on cross-examination will enable him to be convicted of the summary offence.[12]

Can one spouse steal from the other?

Yes.

---

[7] *Hibbert* v. *McKiernan* [1948] 2 KB 142.

[8] By the Dogs (Amendment) Act 1928 the finder must either return the dog to the owner or take it to the police station; if he does the latter he may remove it on condition that he keeps it for not less than a month. The police may destroy a stray dog under certain conditions (Dogs Act 1906 s. 3).

[9] On finding generally see 1st edn 697–701.

[10] Indictment Rules 1971 r. 8; *Hibbert* v.*McKiernan*, n. 7 above.

[11] *Noon* v. *Smith* [1964] 1 WLR 1450, 3 All ER 895. Cp. *Burton* (1854) Dears. 282, 169 ER 728; *Joiner* (1910) 4 CAR 64, 26 TLR 265, 74 JP 200; *Fuschillo* [1940] 2 All ER 489, 27 CAR 193 (receiving).

[12] See *Sargent* v. *West* [1964] Crim.LR 412. For a criticism of the legislation see [1960] Crim.LR 598.

Formerly the law of theft did not apply between spouses, but the Theft Act (s. 30 (1)) now makes no exception for husband and wife. However, it would obviously be unwise to use the criminal law for petty misappropriations of household articles by spouses. Spouses often contribute to a common fund, and it may not be clear what is whose; and a wife who runs the home may feel morally entitled to things that legally belong to the husband. Often it would be hard to prove dishonesty. As a safeguard, therefore, the consent of the Director of Public Prosecutions is generally required in these cases.[13]

§ 33.5. THE PROTECTION OF POSSESSION

It was shown in § 31.3 that the law protects not only owners but bare possessors. Even a person who has temporary control of a thing, like a secretary in respect of her typewriter, is regarded for the purpose of an indictment as having "property" in it. It is the employer who in law has not only ownership but possession of the typewriter; the employee merely has "custody" or "control," but this custody is equivalent to ownership as against wrongdoers. On a charge of theft, the property may be laid in either the employer or the employee.

Can someone possess a thing without knowing of its existence?

Yes, for the purpose of the law of theft.[1] The possessor of an old bureau possesses valuables in a secret drawer even though they are unknown to him. He has also the rights of an owner against third parties. So if an intruder or repairer finds the valuables, and dishonestly keeps them, he will be guilty of stealing from the owner of the bureau.

If the owner of the bureau sells it, he is taken not to intend to sell the unknown contents[2] so he is still entitled to these contents as against the buyer. Of course the seller would be subject to the same rule; he would be required to surrender the articles to the person who sold the bureau to *him*, if that person can be found, and so back to the person who originally hid the articles; but difficulties of proof would often prevent ownership being traced back so far. The buyer of a bureau who keeps an article he finds in it could not generally be convicted of theft, since he could so easily say that he thought he had a right to it. But if he had taken legal advice, for example, and been told that it was not his, he could probably be convicted.

If a person has a coin-operated gas meter, and dishonestly takes out of the meter the coins he has himself put into it, is he guilty of theft of the coins or of the gas?

Of the coins. If the meter was provided by the Gas Board, he steals from the Board. As soon as a coin is inserted into the meter, it becomes the property of the supply board, because that was the intention of the parties

---

[13] See s. 30 (4) as amended, and *Withers* [1975] Crim.LR 647.

[1] Cp. *Woodman* [1974] QB 754. But a person cannot be charged with an offence of possession if he does not know of the existence of the thing: see § 42.6.

[2] *Merry* v. *Green* (1841) 7 M & W 623, 151 ER 916. Cp. *Thomas* v. *Greenslade*, The Times, November 6, 1954, [1954] CLYB 3421; *Moffatt* v. *Kazana* [1969] 2 QB 152 (purchaser of house finding secret hoard; held, vendor entitled). For the rights of the lessor and lessee of land see *Elwes* v. *Brigg Gas Co.* (1886) 33 Ch.D 562.

to the agreement.[3] In much the same way, a person who takes coins from a telephone kiosk steals from British Telecom; the kiosk is owned and possessed by British Telecom, and those who use it know that in putting coins into the box they are transferring the money to the British Telecom.

A similar rule (it may be called the container rule) applies where an employee who is not in a shop receives something from a stranger. It may sometimes be doubtful whether he has received it in his capacity of employee or privately, so if he acts dishonestly the question may arise whether he steals from the employer or from the stranger. The question is readily answered if the employee put the thing into his employer's container before appropriating it; here it is well established that by putting it into the employer's container (which in law was in the employer's possession, the employee himself having only custody) he constructively put it into the possession of his employer, and at the same time it became the property of his employer.

> In *Williams* v. *Phillips*,[4] a dustman who had agreed with his employer, the Corporation, that the profits of gleaning from refuse ("totting") should be shared between the Corporation and its dustmen, put refuse from household bins into the Corporation dustcart and then dishonestly appropriated it from the cart. He was convicted of larceny from the Corporation, the possession of the refuse having passed from the householder to the Corporation when it was put into the Corporation cart.[5]

Suppose the dustman had appropriated the article direct from the householder's dustbin.

The court then has to decide what the householder's intention was; to abandon his garbage, not caring who took it away, or to make a gift of it to, and only to, the Corporation. It is really construing intention out of thin air, since the householder probably never thought about the matter; but the court will undoubtedly say that his intention was that his refuse should be taken only by the Corporation, or according to its direction. So, if the dustman acted dishonestly, it would be theft from the householder.[6]

§ 33.6. TRUSTEES AND COMPANY DIRECTORS

As we have seen, even the trustee of property (who is its legal owner) can steal it if he dishonestly appropriates it with the intention of defeating the equitable interests of the beneficiaries. Although he is the legal owner of the property, he is not the beneficial owner—the owner in equity. In the

---

[3] *Martin* v. *Marsh* [1955] Crim.LR 781. But see [1956] Crim.LR 74 as to "pass meters."

[4] (1957) 41 CAR 5.

[5] Cp. *Reed* (1854) Dears. 257, 169 ER 717: *Mallison* (1902) 66 JP 503, 20 Cox 204.

[6] See the judgment in *Williams* v. *Phillips*, above n. 4. It is also a summary offence to "sort over" refuse: Public Health Act 1936 s. 76 as amended. The reason for the prohibition is the danger to public health in salvaging filthy and often verminous objects; nevertheless, dustmen continue to regard totting as a "perk." See also Control of Pollution Act 1974 s. 20.

ordinary case, therefore, the trustee will be guilty of theft on the general principle of section 5 (1).[1] Sometimes, as in the case of charitable trusts, there is no owner in equity, and a special provision is needed to bring the case within the net. Section 5 (2)

> "Where property is subject to a trust, the persons to whom it belongs shall be regarded as including any person having a right to enforce the trust, and an intention to defeat the trust shall be regarded accordingly as an intention to deprive of the property any person having that right."

If trust property is stolen by a third party, the indictment may lay the property either in the trustee (the legal owner) or in the beneficiary (the owner in equity). If it is stolen by the trustee, the indictment will lay the property in the beneficiary or other person having the right to enforce the trust (the Attorney-General in the case of charitable trusts).

We have seen that failure to pay a debt or to perform a contract—even a dishonest failure—is not in itself theft. The victim must (in general) have some property right (*ius in rem*), that has been infringed, not just a right against a particular person (*ius in personam*). However, equity blurs the line between property and contract. A person whom the common law looks upon as a mere debtor may in equity be a constructive trustee of money, and the difference for the law of theft is vital. If D is the constructive trustee of a fund for V, then if D dishonestly appropriates the fund he is guilty of theft. We shall return to this in § .10.

It will be remembered that section 5 (1) excepts from proprietary interests "an equitable interest arising only from an agreement to transfer or grant an interest." These words "disapply" (to use convenient jargon) the rule of the civil law that when a person contracts to sell land, the purchaser is regarded as having an equitable interest in the land from the moment of the contract, even though the legal conveyance has not been made.[2] The owner (vendor) becomes a kind of trustee for him, but the subsection provides that this trust is to be ignored for the purpose of the law of theft. The reason is that if the owner wrongfully conveys the land to some other person, what he does is in substance a breach of his contract to sell the land to the first purchaser, and it was not thought right that the first purchaser should be protected by the law of theft.[3]

Can company directors steal from their own limited company?

Yes, but not, it seems, by dealing with the company's property in a way that they are authorised to do.

As we have seen, a person who registers a limited company creates a new legal person. A business man may "turn himself and his wife" into a private limited company, transferring part of his assets to that company. The man and his wife may both be directors, but if they dip into the till without proper authority given by the Board of Directors they may in suitable circumstances be convicted of theft from the company. (If a businessman merely goes into partnership with his wife, he and she together could not have stolen their own property, even

---

[1] § 31.3.

[2] The rule depends on the fact that the remedy of specific performance is available to enforce the contract, and it therefore applies also to contracts to sell shares, and even (it seems) to contracts to sell goods if they are of special value, not ordinary market commodities. See Smith 33.

[3] Yet, as was mentioned before, a person who sells an ordinary chattel, passing the legal title to it, and who then dishonestly sells it to someone else, does commit theft. He is unlikely to be prosecuted.

though what they did was meant to defraud their creditors. The possibility of stealing from a limited company arises only because the company is itself a legal person.)

Contrast with dipping into the till a case where the directors pass a resolution to sell off the company's assets below value to favoured relatives in order to defraud shareholders or creditors. The directors are not, it seems, guilty of theft in carrying out the resolution, since the property is transferred with the authority of the owner, the company.[4] As said before, directors are not trustees for the shareholders. However, the courts see no difficulty in convicting directors of conspiracy to defraud.[5]

Many unincorporated organisations have to do without legal personalities: most clubs, societies and associations, and even registered trade unions and friendly societies. The property of these organisations is put in the names of trustees, and if a trustee misappropriates the property he commits theft.

§ 33.7. THEFT AND SUBSEQUENT POSSESSORS

When an article is stolen and passed from hand to hand, each fresh possessor is capable of stealing it—subject to certain principles of the law of property, and to the overriding section 3 (2) of the Theft Act.

> "Where property or a right or interest in property is or purports to be transferred for value to a person acting in good faith, no later assumption by him of rights which he believed himself to be acquiring shall, by reason of any defect in the transferor's title, amount to theft of the property."

The reason for this provision was that Parliament agreed with the CLRC in thinking that it would be too harsh to make an innocent purchaser guilty of theft merely because, after discovering the defect in his title, he could not bring himself to give up what he had bought.

For those who are interested, the main provisions of the law are as follows. They may be stated as a number of hypotheticals.

1 D1 makes off with V's thing, say his car from a car park, and disposes of it to D2. D1 is guilty of theft and gets no title to the thing; consequently, he passes no title to D2, even though D2 buys it from him in good faith, the maxim being *Nemo dat quod non habet*[1]—a person cannot give something that he has not got.

(*a*) If D2 knows the facts when he receives the car, he is guilty of theft by this act of appropriation,[2] as well as of handling stolen goods (Chap. 39).

(*b*) If D2 does not know the facts when he receives the car, he can still become guilty of theft on account of what he does after coming to know the facts, unless he gave value for the car to D1. If he gave value for the car in good faith (that is, not knowing of the theft), then section 3 (2) protects him from a charge of theft in retaining it.[3]

2 D1 obtains V's thing by deception. This is an offence under section 15 (1), and it is also theft, at least sometimes (Chap. 35). If V, by reason of the deception, intends to pass the property in the car to D1, D1 will get the property, though his title will be voidable for

---

[4] See *Pearlberg* [1982] Crim.LR 829 (Crown Court). See, however, § 35.3 at n. 3.
[5] See *Sinclair* § 32.1 at n. 1.

[1] "Nemo" may be anglicised in pronunciation as "neemo."
[2] *Stapylton* v. *O'Callaghan* [1973] 2 All ER 782.
[3] Neither is he guilty of handling. See § 39.4.

fraud.[4] This means that he will become the owner until V avoids (rescinds) the transaction, according to certain rules.

(*a*) If D1 then sells the thing to D2, who knows that the thing has been dishonestly come by, D2 gets only the title that D1 had—a voidable title. All the same, D2 does not commit theft in buying from D1, because he does not dishonestly appropriate the property of another. The property belongs to D1 at the moment of sale, and D2 is not dishonest in relation to D1. V no longer owns the thing; he has a right to avoid the transaction with D1, but a right to avoid is not ownership. D2's only offence is one of handling stolen goods (though this is in theory a more serious offence than theft itself).

(*b*) If D1 *gives* the thing to D2, who takes it without knowing the facts, D2 commits no offence.[5]

In cases (*a*) and (*b*), even if V then avoids his transaction with D1, this will not make D2 a thief retrospectively. However, D2 must, on coming to know of V's rescission, return the thing to him; otherwise he will then commit an appropriation that is capable of being theftous.

(*c*) If D1 *sells* the thing to D2, who takes it without knowing the facts, D2 obtains a completely valid title, as a *bona fide* purchaser. This is because the owner's rather fragile right to avoid his transfer to the cheat D1 comes to an end as soon as third party rights supervene. D2 will commit no offence even if he holds on to the thing after coming to know the facts, because the property no longer "belongs to another."

The last hypothetical, 2 (*c*), is an exception from the *Nemo dat* rule. There are various other exceptions, two being specially noteworthy.

1 If a trustee in breach of trust sells the trust property (thus committing theft, if he acts dishonestly) to a person who takes without notice of the breach of trust, the latter obtains a good title.

2 If money is stolen, the coins and notes initially continue to belong to the victim of the theft. But if the thief spends the money, the recipient taking it in good faith, the recipient gets a good title to the money (because money is "negotiable").[6]

It follows that if the buyer from the trustee in the first case, or the person who received the money in good faith, giving value for it, in the second case, subsequently comes to know of the tainted origin of what he has got, he will still be safe from a charge of theft or of handling. His protection rests not upon section 3 (2) but upon the fact that when he decides to hold on to the property after discovering the truth it is not property belonging to another. It is his property, and he is entitled to keep it.

§ 33.8. THEFT BY AN OWNER

An owner of goods can himself steal them. He may, for example, steal them from a co-owner—though in the case of co-ownership of chattels difficulty may arise in deciding what acts of use by one owner can be said to be dishonest against the other.[1]

It used to be held that larceny could be committed by an owner from a possessor who was not an owner but had an interest in the goods, such as

---

[4] There is an exception if D1 induced V to sell him the article by means of a fraud that created a fundamental mistake. This will make the contract of sale completely void (legally non-existent), and D1 will get no title to the thing, just as in case 1. This complexity is left for discussion to books on the law of contract.

[5] Even if D2 subsequently comes to know the facts, he will not become guilty of handling by reason of retaining the thing on his own behalf. See § 39.4.

[6] Both of these are known as the bona fide purchaser, colloquially (though not forensically) as the b.f.p. His full title is the bona fide purchaser for value without notice.

[1] See *Bonner* [1970] 1 WLR 838, 2 All ER 97n.

a pawnbroker (pledgee)[2]; and the same rule follows from section 5 (1) of the Theft Act.[3] The rule means that an owner can steal his own goods from an unpaid seller. Consider again the hypothetical concerning the TV set.[4] Even if the contract of sale in that case had expressly provided that the property should pass immediately, the seller would still have a seller's lien (right to retain the goods until the price is paid).[5] If the price is not paid the seller can (after giving notice) resell the goods, deducting what is owed to him from the price obtained, and suing the buyer for any deficit.[6] It will be seen that the seller's lien is a substantial interest, and a dishonest taking by the buyer in order to evade the lien would be theft, notwithstanding that the buyer is technically the owner.

I must now ask you to consider one of the most extraordinary cases decided under the Theft Act, *Turner (No. 2)*.[7] To understand the case one must know that when an article is handed to a repairer for repair, the repairer has the right to retain the article until he is paid his charges. This is the repairer's lien. The owner cannot say: "Give me my property back, and I will pay your bill some other time." The rule applies, for example, to a motor mechanic who repairs a car.

You don't mean to tell me that if I have my car repaired when I am on a journey, and cannot immediately pay the bill because it is a much larger repair than I expected, the repairer can refuse to give me back the car until I pay?

Probably the repairer would be reasonable and accept a cheque, but he would not be obliged to do so. (Your sensible course would have been to obtain an estimate in advance, not to be exceeded without your permission.)

What if the owner disputes the amount of the repair bill?

He must tender what he thinks is really owing. If he is right in his assessment of the sum properly due, and the tender is refused, he can safely go off with his car if he can get hold of it, or he can sue for damages for the illegal detention.

And if he doesn't tender enough?

He is not supposed to go off with his article—though if he does not know about liens he would not commit theft in doing so, because he would believe that he has in law the right to deprive the repairer of the car.[8]

To go on with *Turner (No. 2)*, the facts were as follows.

> Turner left his car at a garage for repair, and surreptitiously took it away when the repair was completed, without paying the bill. The facts abundantly showed dishonest intent. He was convicted of

---

[2] *Rose* v. *Matt* [1951] 1 KB 810.
[3] For the subsection see § 31.3.
[4] § .4 at n. 2.
[5] A lien (pronounced "lee-en" or "leen") is a kind of charge upon goods somewhat similar to a mortgage. The goods are a security for a debt, the lienee being the creditor.
[6] Sale of Goods Act 1979 s. 48.
[7] [1971] 1 WLR 901, 2 All ER 441.
[8] S. 2(1) (*a*): see § 32.5.

stealing the car from the repairer, notwithstanding that the judge had directed the jury that they were not concerned with any question of lien.

In fact the garage proprietor had the repairer's lien. It was because the repairer had a protected right to possession that Turner clearly acted wrongly in going off with the car, even though it was his own car. If the judge had directed the jury in terms of the lien, therefore, Turner would certainly have been guilty of theft on the authorities, assuming that he knew of the lien. However, the judge told the jury that they need pay no attention to any question of lien.

Why did the judge ignore the lien?

Judges are strongly inclined to exclude questions of civil law wherever they can from the law of theft.[9] The effort cannot be wholly successful, since the Act requires the appropriation to be of "property belonging to another," which, as we have plentifully seen, imports the civil rules of property (and their problems) into the criminal law. Where the judges have excluded the civil rules, the result has been to introduce confusion, uncertainty and anomalies into the criminal law.

The judge in effect directed the jury to assume that the owner of property could commit theft from his bailee at will. We must therefore suppose, against the fact, that the repairer of Turner's car had expressly agreed not to exercise a lien. In that case the repairer was a bailee at will. If the owner was entitled to repossess himself whenever he wished, how could his act possibly be a crime? Yet not only was he convicted but the Court of Appeal affirmed the conviction.

The court assumed that the only questions were: was the repairer in possession, and did the owner take the car from his possession with subjective dishonesty? If so, it is theft. Nothing else matters. This means that theft can be committed without an *actus reus* in the sense in which that term is generally used for consummated crimes. It is hard to believe that the decision represents the law.

The decision is open to the following objections.

- On the assumption that the repairer was a bailee at will, the bailment could be determined (ended) immediately, by the owner requesting the return of the car. The bailee, therefore, had no substantial interest in the property: no right to keep it, as against the owner, for any appreciable time. In these circumstances it is extraordinarily technical to say that Turner intended to *deprive* the bailee permanently of the thing. The bailee had no sufficient interest to make the statement substantially true. The bailee was not deprived, because he had no interest of which he was deprived. It is perfectly lawful for the owner to demand the thing back from his bailee at will; and even if the owner neglects the formality of demand, still the bailee is not, except in the most technical sense, deprived of anything to which he has a right as against the owner.
- If the bailment was at will, Turner was hardly guilty of *dishonesty* in respect of the bailee's property-right in going off with his car. He would probably believe, within section 2 (1), that he had a right to deprive the other of it. Technically he might be wrong, since he ought to give notice to determine the bailment, the bailee then being bound to return the thing immediately. But a layman would be unlikely to know this, and even a lawyer might not.

[9] See Chap. 35.

Turner's dishonesty in trying to get out of paying his bill ought not to make him guilty of theft, if he were not dishonest in respect of proprietary rights (including the right of a possessor.who has a charge upon the thing).

- If the bailment was at will, Turner did not intend to *appropriate* the car in any save the most technical sense. It was already his, and in substance he alone had the right to possession of it.
- Lastly, a person should not be held guilty of theft if *he has the right to do what he does*. This can be brought out more vividly by supposing the following case.

> D, a collector of coins, takes a fistful of coins from the pocket of a fellow numismatist, intending to steal them. When he examines them he finds that they are his own coins, previously stolen from him. In the civil law, D would have been justified in retaking his property if he had known it was his property; and the fact that he did not know it was his property cannot make his act illegal. Justifications (as opposed to excuses) for doing things exist whether you know of them or not. If D's act was not illegal, it cannot, in common sense, be theft.

We shall come back in Chapter 35 to the proposition that an appropriation that is perfectly lawful cannot generally amount to theft.

It seems possible that if the objections to the decision were argued in a later case, if the point arose again, *Turner* would not be followed.[10] Certainly that decision did not prevent a circuit judge from going the other way in *Meredith*.[11] Admittedly this is an authority lower in the judicial hierarchy than *Turner*, but much better bottomed in good sense.

> Meredith left his car in a road and it was towed away by the police under statutory powers. The statute then in force gave the police no right to retain the car when the owner came to collect it,[12] though the owner was liable to pay a charge if his vehicle had caused an obstruction, unless he preferred to face a prosecution for obstruction. Meredith went to the police station to collect his car, but the station was crowded and so he simply drove his car away from the yard. A circuit judge ruled that he could not be convicted of stealing the car from the police, because the police had no right to retain the car. Yet the police were undoubtedly in possession of it, and on a literal reading of *Turner* Meredith should have been convicted, at any rate if what he did was thought to be "dishonest."

Even if *Turner* is overruled, it may perhaps be held to be theft for an owner dishonestly to take his article back from a hirer. But the point is a difficult one, and has not been decided.[13]

§ 33.9. PROPERTY TO BE DEALT WITH IN A PARTICULAR WAY

Section 5 (3) states a rule that is often quite difficult to apply.

"Where a person receives property from or on account of another,

---

[10] J R Spencer in [1982] Crim.LR 270 points to the decision as exhibiting a frequent failing of appellate courts. On an appeal against conviction by an unmeritorious defendant who can point to a substantial misdirection, the Court of Appeal prefers to hold that there has been no misdirection than to quash the conviction.

[11] [1973] Crim.LR 253.

[12] The law has since been changed, the police and local authorities being now empowered to retain custody of removed vehicles until charges are paid. See Road Traffic Act 1974 s. 19.

[13] See 1st edn 705–706.

> and is under an obligation to the other to retain and deal with that property or its proceeds in a particular way, the property or proceeds shall be regarded (as against him) as belonging to the other."

What does the subsection mean by an "obligation"? Is it a legal or a moral obligation?

Parliament is not in the habit of legislating about moral obligations as such; and that Parliament should do so without making its meaning plain is inconceivable. "Obligation," then, should mean a legal obligation, an obligation under the civil law; and there is authority for this view.[1] It is for the judge to interpret the civil law and state it to the jury, and for the jury to find any relevant facts.

The subsection is a compendious statement of a principle underlying a number of rules of the law of property. Where a person receives property from or on account of another, and is under an obligation to the other to retain and deal with (it would have been better if the subsection had said "to retain *or* deal with") that property or its proceeds in a particular way, the property or proceeds generally *do* belong to that other, either at law or in equity. If the recipient dishonestly appropriates the property he commits theft of property "belonging to another," the other having a "proprietary right or interest" within section 5 (1).[2] To this extent, section 5 (3) is superfluous. (Whether the effect of the subsection extends beyond the civil law of property need not be considered here.)

Unpicking the subsection, it will be seen to provide for two cases: where property is received *from* another, and where it is received *on account of* another. In the first case, where V transfers a chattel or money to D for a particular purpose, V will as a general principle be regarded as retaining either the legal or, at least, the equitable ownership; and both forms of ownership are protected by the law of theft.

> An example would be where V gives D, a jobbing painter, £100 to buy paint for some work that V wants him to do. The jury (or magistrates) must decide whether the understanding was that the painter should spend that money (or other money representing it: see later) on the paint, or whether the understanding was that the money was a general advance to D, which he could spend as he liked (as a contribution to a holiday on the Costa Brava if he wished), buying the paint perhaps later on with money that he had not yet earned. If the jury find that the former was the understanding, and convict the painter of theft on the ground that he has dishonestly misappropriated the money, the conviction will be upheld on appeal.

That was an example of money received from another, the recipient being under an obligation to the payer to deal with the money in a

[1] The decision to the contrary in *Hayes* (1976) 64 CAR 82, which was criticised in 1st edn 710–711, is irreconcilable with the subsequent pronouncement in *Mainwaring* (1982) 74 CAR 99 at 107; the latter case correctly states the law, and was applied by a circuit judge in *Cording* [1983] Crim.LR 175.

I need hardly say that I intend the phrase "legal obligation" in the text to include an equitable obligation. The words "law" and "legal" refer to the whole of the law, including equity, unless the context makes it clear that a contrast between the common law and equity is intended. In the latter case the word "law" may refer only to the common law, and similarly with "legal."

[2] For the subsection see § 31.3.

particular way. The second type of case envisaged in the subsection involves three parties, money or other property being received by D from X on account of V.

> The buyer of a house (X) pays a deposit to the estate agent, D, who receives it in a fiduciary capacity on behalf of his principal, the seller (V). If D dishonestly misappropriates it the jury can convict him of theft from V. He has received money on account of V, and is under an obligation to V to deal with the money in a particular way, namely for the benefit of V.

The legal position in the case of the estate agent is clarified by the Estate Agents Act 1979 section 13 (1), which declares that when an estate agent receives money he holds it on trust. A person may, of course, receive money on trust quite apart from any Act of Parliament, if such is the intention of the parties.

Contrast with the estate agent the position of a travel agent who receives money from clients by way of payment in advance for tickets. The reasonable construction here may be that the travel agent is entitled to treat the money as an ordinary business receipt, being merely under a contractual obligation to buy the tickets for the client. In that case it cannot be said that the travel agent is under an obligation to retain and deal with *that* property in a particular way.[3]

Section 5 (3) refers in one breath to "property or its proceeds," as though the two were virtually the same. This reflects certain rules of the civil law. Both the common law and equity allow property to be "followed" into its proceeds (the exchange product).

> Take again the hypothetical of the jobbing painter. If the understanding was that he was to spend the specific money on paint, and if he does so, the paint he buys will belong to his employer, being the "proceeds" of the money he was given. If he buys a coat for his wife instead of paint, the coat will belong to his employer: it does not matter that the exchange was wrongful.
>
> If the painter does not need the paint immediately, there is nothing wrong in his paying the money into his bank account, provided that he keeps the account in credit to that amount, and that he eventually draws "the money" (i.e. a similar sum of money) out again to buy the paint.

Rules of law and equity govern the "following" or "tracing" of funds into and out of bank accounts, which need not be considered in this introductory account of the law of theft. Nor will space allow a discussion of the many legal and practical problems that are capable of arising.[4];

§ 33.10. MAKING PROFITS WITH ANOTHER'S PROPERTY

A question of theft can arise where it is the law rather than the intention

---

[3] See *Hall* [1973] QB 126.

[4] For a fuller discussion see, in addition to the standard treatises, 1st edn 709–720.

of the payer or other transferor that establishes the right of V to receive the money or other property. Section 5 (3) does not state whether it is meant to apply to this case—whether property is received "on account of another" when the person handing over the property had no notion that the recipient would be required by law to hold it on account of another—but it clearly does; and this was held before the Act under legislation similarly worded.[1]

A limitation upon the scope of the phrase "on account of another," established under the old law, will probably not operate as a restriction of the Theft Act.

> It was formerly held that if an employee improperly used his employer's property to make money (as, by letting out his tractor), and kept the proceeds, he did not commit embezzlement of the proceeds, because he did not receive the proceeds "on account of" his employer within the meaning of the embezzlement statute (now repealed). The proceeds were his, even though he was liable to his employer in damages in contract and tort. The employer's action for damages against his employee, for breach of contract or in tort, is an action *in personam*, not an action to recover property in the defendant's hands that belongs to the plaintiff. No doubt, the damages would be such as to wipe out the employee's profit; nevertheless the money he earned never was the employer's as a matter of law.[2]

As has just been suggested, the decision should be different when similar facts arise under the Theft Act. Even if the old case is held to be determinative of the meaning of the words "on account of another" in section 5 (3), that subsection plainly does not cover all contingencies. We must always remember section 5 (1), which explains that it is theft to steal from a person having "any proprietary right or interest." Now although on the facts we are considering courts of law regarded the employee's illicit earnings as his, courts of equity (that is to say, the courts in the exercise of their equitable jurisdiction, which all courts have) have developed a wide doctrine of constructive trust, meaning a trust not created expressly but imposed by equity as a matter of justice. A person who occupies a fiduciary position (such as an employee) and who derives a profit from the unauthorised use of property belonging to the person to whom he owes the fiduciary obligation becomes a constructive trustee of the proceeds. The court would allow him fair remuneration for the work he has done (if outside his contract of employment with the owner) and for materials he has supplied in order to earn the profit, but the balance belongs in equity to the owner of the property.[3] The dishonest appropriation of this balance must, on principle, amount to theft.

Thc point has arisen in cases of so-called "pirate selling."[4] The rail

---

[1] *Grubb* [1915] 2 KB 683.

[2] *Cullum* (1873) LR 2 CCR 28. Recollect that an employee who wrongfully uses the employer's "conveyance" can sometimes he convicted of taking a conveyance without authority, under the Theft Act s. 12. See § 32.4. There is also the possibility of the employee being convicted of corruption: see § 40.

[3] See Goode in 92 LQR 534–535.

[4] For this see §§ 32.4, 34. For an extended discussion see A T H Smith in [1977] Crim.LR 395.

steward who uses his own materials to make coffee and sandwiches which he sells to customers is not guilty of theft of his employer's time, nor of theft of the customers, nor of theft of the use of the kitchen equipment, because there are no such crimes; but on principle there can be theft of the proceeds, to the extent that they belong in equity to the employer. A rail steward on one occasion pleaded guilty to this charge at the Central Criminal Court,[5] so the legal issues went without argument. The argument in favour of liability would have been that since the steward used the railway rolling stock and its equipment for the purpose of making a profit, he was a constructive trustee of the proceeds for his employer, and in not accounting for them he appropriated them.

But the Railways Board did not know that this profit had been earned.

That does not matter. A person can own property although he does not know it.

The practical difficulty in these cases lies in establishing dishonesty. The employee is not to be expected to know the rules of equity, and he may well believe that the money he has earned with the employer's property is his own, especially if he has contributed his own property, labour or skill. The employee's knowledge that he has committed a civil wrong against the employer is not equivalent to knowledge that he is wrongfully appropriating the employer's property, or that he is under an obligation to deal with the earnings for the employer's benefit. Even if the employee betrays a feeling of guilt, as by lying about the matter, that can be attributed to his knowledge of having committed a civil wrong, not to his knowledge that he has committed theft. So, unless the employee had legal advice before misappropriating the proceeds, he might succeed in a defence that he was not dishonest.[6] An intention to commit a breach of contract is not necessarily theftous dishonesty.

But is that proposition sound? The employee when prosecuted and cross-examined says: "I knew that what I did was not really honest and that I wasn't supposed to do it. I knew that if I was found out I could get into some kind of legal trouble. But I did the boss no harm, and I certainly had no notion that the money I made belonged to him." Surely he should be accounted dishonest. He made no effort to find out the legal position. He concealed what he had done because he knew that if the truth came out he would probably have to disgorge. Never mind that he did not know the difference between a debt and a trust. Very few laymen do. You make the law of theft unworkable, in its application to fiduciary relationships, if you make it depend on knowledge of the distinction.

There is something to be said for your view. The objection to it is that,

---

[5] The Times, April 26, 1977. Previously, magistrates had dismissed a similar charge: The Times, February 17, 1977.

[6] An employer like the Railways Board who is faced with persistent dishonesty of this type may of course improve his chances in a prosecution by circulating his employees advising them of the civil and criminal law. But in any case the person guilty of pirate selling can be convicted of obtaining money by deception, or of "going equipped" (§ 34.9 at n. 6).

as said before, theft must be of property belonging to another, and if the defendant did not realise that the proceeds belonged to another (or that he was under the obligation specified in subsection (3)) he lacked the *mens rea* for the crime. A breach of contract as such is not generally a crime. If the defendant believes that he is only committing a breach of contract, he lacks criminal intent. In practice, a charge of theft probably could not properly succeed unless the employer has warned the employee of the position, either before the misdemeanour or when the illicit proceeds are in the employee's hands.

Another possible illustration of a constructive trust is where an agent is conducting a negotiation for his principal, and the other party gives the agent a bribe. The obvious course for a prosecutor is to charge the agent with corruption;[7] charging theft presents difficulties. The better view of the civil law is that the agent becomes a constructive trustee of the bribe, and therefore, given dishonesty, can steal it. But a criminal court appears to have rejected this argument.[8] It would in any case be necessary for the prosecution to show that the employee knew that he was bound to render the bribe *in specie* to his employer, which might be difficult.

Yet another illustration relates to trade secrets. It was said in § .3 that a trade secret is not property for the law of theft. But a person who unlawfully uses a trade secret may sometimes be regarded as a constructive trustee of the profits, and in that case he may, other conditions being satisfied, be guilty of the theft of the profits.

§ 33.11. STEALING CHEQUES

When a cheque is stolen, three possible forms of theft may be committed: of the cheque as a piece of paper, of a thing in action, and of the proceeeds of the cheque. An illustration of successful charges under the first two heads is *Kohn*.[1]

> Kohn was a company director who made out company cheques to third parties for his own benefit. He was convicted of theft of the cheques as pieces of paper, this theft occurring when he sent each cheque to the payee; it made no difference whether the bank account was in credit or not. He was also convicted of theft of a thing in action, namely the debt owed by the bank to the company in respect of the bank account.[2]
>
> Conviction of the latter type of theft depended upon evidence that the account was in credit or that the cheque was within the agreed

---

[7] § 40.3.

[8] *Powell* v. *MacRae* [1977] Crim.LR 571. A turnstile attendant accepted £2 to let a man without a ticket into a match. Held that the money was a bribe and not the property of the stadium, so a conviction of theft was quashed. This view accords with the civil case of *Lister* v. *Stubbs* (1890) 45 Ch.D 1, where it was held that the agent became an equitable debtor to his principal for the amount of the bribe, but did not hold the bribe on trust for the principal. But the decision is difficult to reconcile with *Reading* v. *Att.-Gen.* [1951] AC 507, and is contrary to the view generally taken as to the doctrine of constructive trust: see Goode in 92 LQR 535–536.

[1] (1979) 69 CAR 95.

[2] Cp. *Duru* §32.3 at n. 10.

overdraft facility; and the theft took place only when the bank honoured the cheque.

The analysis on the second point appears to be that the bank owes a debt to its customer; this debt, the thing in action, is *pro tanto* extinguished when the bank honours the cheque, and the extinguishment is regarded as an appropriation. Alternatively, the defendant can be held to appropriate part of the account through the act of the payee in cashing or obtaining a credit in respect of the cheque.

What about theft of a cheque by a pickpocket or burglar?

Once more the thief can be charged with stealing the cheque as a piece of paper (of the value of £x[3]) from the drawer (the person who has the bank account) or other person from whose possession the thing was taken. On conviction the thief can be punished according to circumstances, and if he has cashed the cheque that is of course an important circumstance.

Alternatively, if he has cashed the cheque (whether at a bank or by obtaining cash for it from someone else) he can be convicted either of stealing the cash or of obtaining it by deception.

3. The Thief must Appropriate the Property

§ 33.12. APPROPRIATION BY A NON-POSSESSOR

We saw in § 31.2 that the idea of theft at common law was that of the taking of a thing out of the possession of another without his consent. This was socially inadequate in two main ways.

- It was confined to the theft of physical things; so if someone dishonestly effected a transfer from my bank account to his own, he did not commit theft. You could not steal an intangible like the bank's debt to its customer because you could not "take" it.
- The prohibition of taking did not affect people who were already in possession of the thing, as borrowers, hirers etc.; they could not "take" what they already possessed, so they could not steal it—even though they made off with it. Or so lawyers reasoned. The law of larceny was extended piecemeal to cover such situations, but it was a thing of fiction and patchwork.

When the CLRC embarked on its ambitious recasting of the law it needed a new word to express the basic *actus reus* of the new idea of theft. The law of tort had a concept called "converting the property to one's own use," but the committee thought that the word "conversion" would not be readily intelligible to the jury (it might cause them to think that the property had to be changed into something else); so the committee chose instead the word "appropriation" to express the same idea.

An appropriation may come about either by a wrongful taking or in other ways. The essence of an appropriation in the ordinary sense is that it involves taking control of property in a way showing an intention to deprive the owner. The definition in the *Shorter Oxford English Dictionary*, approved by the Court of Appeal in *David Morris*,[1] is "to take for one's own or to oneself." Putting this in another way, it is an act having

---

[3] Though the cheque is a piece of paper, its value in law is that of the obligation that it embodies. See Goode in 92 LQR 377 n. 69.

[1] [1983] 2 WLR 768.

the practical (though not necessarily legal) effect of giving someone else's property the character of being yours. We may call this the ordinary or dictionary meaning of the term. In this sense, it would obviously be an appropriation to eat another's food wrongfully, or ride off on his bicycle, or deliver his bicycle to another person, or spend his money, with intent in each case to deprive him of his property.

You mean of course that these are all acts done without the consent of the owner.

I wish I were allowed to mean that, but alas no. The Theft Act does not specify that the owner must not consent (as the former Larceny Act did). If I ask to borrow your bike and ride off with it secretly intending to sell it, I appropriate it when I first take it, even though I take it with your consent.

It was held under the old law that although larceny was a taking without the owner's consent, this meant "without the owner's full and free consent." Some imperfect consents by the owner, marred by fraud or mistake, were not held to stand in the way of a conviction of larceny. In the last example, if a false pretence were used to get permission to borrow the bike, the borrower intending to steal it, he was guilty of theft the moment he borrowed the bike; the law pretended that the owner had not consented to his having it at all. In order to avoid any fiction the CLRC decided to leave out the question of the owner's consent from the main definition of theft.

You say that it is an appropriation to ride off on a person's bicycle with intent to deprive him of it. When exactly does the appropriation take place? When the thief begins to ride?

At latest then: perhaps when the thief merely lays hands on the bicycle. The CLRC was conscious that the concept of appropriation might cause problems in marginal cases like this, and therefore decided to give the expression a more specific meaning in addition to its general dictionary meaning. We have already had part of section 3 (1); it runs in full as follows.

> "Any assumption by a person of the rights of an owner amounts to an appropriation, and this includes, where he has come by the property (innocently or not) without stealing it, any later assumption of a right to it by keeping or dealing with it as owner."

We may call this the extended sense of appropriation. We thus have (as the Court of Appeal recognised in *Morris*) the dictionary sense of appropriation, and, in addition, the extended sense. It was said before (§ 31.3) that the "assumption" of rights in the subsection must mean a usurpation of rights; so the definition must mean that an appropriation includes doing anything in relation to the property that only the owner can lawfully do or authorise.[2] It has been held that even the assumption of a single right is enough.

---

[2] And even an owner can commit theftous appropriation where his rights are limited in some way. See §§ .6, .8.

The leading authority on the meaning of section 3 (1) is now *Morris* (above), where the defendant took articles from the shelves of a self-service store and attached to them price labels that he had removed from cheaper articles. At the check-out he was asked for and paid the lower prices. Then he was arrested.

Morris appropriated the articles in the dictionary sense, one might suppose, when he freed them from the owner's control by going off with them after passing the check-out point. But Lord Lane CJ, speaking for the Court of Appeal, expressed the opinion that there would be an appropriation in the extended sense at an earlier point of time: either when the customer dishonestly removed the articles from the shelves intending to steal them, or when he switched the price labels. The removal of an article from the shelf was an appropriation (moving the article being one of the rights of ownership), and the switching of the labels (whether it happened before or after the removal from the shelf) was evidence that the appropriation (the removal) was dishonest. If the jury were not satisfied that at the time of the removal from the shelf Morris's intention was dishonest, the second part of section 3 (1) came into operation: Morris had come by the property without stealing it, and the later switching of the labels was a dealing with the article as owner, and so was an appropriation.

But when Morris switched the labels he did not intend to deprive the owner starting from now. He was only preparing to deprive him later on, when he passed the check-out point.

Your argument was apparently not presented to the court; but presumably a court faced with it would say that the intention may relate to the future. The thief need not intend his appropriation in the extended sense to be the act that deprives the owner; it is enough that the act is part of what he intends to do to deprive the owner. When Morris misbehaved at the supermarket shelves he intended to deprive the owner, even though he was not to get possession (and so actually deprive the owner) till later, when he had passed the check-out point.

The supermarket consented to people taking things from shelves, so surely that could not be an appropriation even in the extended sense. OK: we have to say that assuming the rights of an owner is an appropriation. But when Morris took down the articles from the shelves, he was acting with the implied consent of the owner, and so was not assuming the rights of an owner; he merely handled the thing in the way the owner allowed him to do. That was in no way a derogation from the owner's rights.

Your reaction is common sense, but unfortunately not the law as at present settled by *Morris*. (The decision is under appeal to the Lords.)

The Court of Appeal could have distinguished. As was shown before, an appropriation in the dictionary sense may be an act done with the consent of the owner (who may not realise that he is being deprived of the thing). This, however, assumes that the defendant intends to deprive the owner *now*, by this act of appropriation. In contrast, an appropriation in the extended sense need not involve an intent to deprive the owner at this moment, but it does involve usurping the rights of an owner, which means doing something with the property to which the owner has not in any sense consented. As you say, if the defendant is acting with the owner's authority he does not usurp the owner's rights.

For this reason, it seems to me that *Morris* misinterprets section 3 (1). Starting from the undoubted premise that the dictionary meaning of appropriation, or at any rate what the law understands by the dictionary meaning, does not contain an element about the lack of the owner's consent, the court proceeded to infer that section 3 (1) does not contain this element either. But the conclusion does not follow. It is more consonant with the sense of section 3 (1) to require an absence of consent for its operation. And this produces a result that accords with common sense, which the decision in *Morris* does not. It is against common sense to say that an act done with the owner's authority is an assumption (or usurpation) of his rights. When Morris was standing at the shelves he did not appropriate the articles in the dictionary sense, because he intended to go through the cash point with them, hoodwinking the cashier into accepting the lower price; he had not at that time freed them from the owner's control. And he did not appropriate the articles in the extended sense, because he did not assume the rights of an owner merely by taking the articles from the shelves within the permission given to him and the rest of the public.

Why didn't the court say that changing the labels was the appropriation?

I do not know. Had it done so, no problem would have arisen. The owner did not consent to the labels being changed.

The court acted against the advice of the commentators,[3] and it overruled or disapproved a number of decisions that had been taking a more sensible line by holding that there was no appropriation under section 3 (1) until the defendant began to act outside the owner's permission. The reason why the court decided the case as it did was that it thought that it was bound by the decision of the House of Lords in *Alan Lawrence*[4]; but that case was distinguishable as one in which the appropriation was of the dictionary type. These matters will be considered more fully in Chapter 35.

Do you mean that a man who has merely taken something down from the shelf of a supermarket and has done absolutely nothing wrong can be convicted of theft merely because the beaks subsequently come to the conclusion that he was evidently a shifty character and intended to steal?

Incredible as it may appear, yes. The court in *Morris* recognised that this was the consequence of the way in which it was choosing to decide the case; and the law, as you imply, is thoroughly bad, even though in *Morris* itself the dishonest intent was abundantly proved by the switching of the labels. It is hard to understand why the Court of Appeal regarded the harmless taking down of an article from the shelf as an appropriation within section 3 (1), when the court was so careful to avoid saying that the utterly wrongful switching of the labels before taking the article from the shelf was one.

I gather that the effect of Morris is that the thief's act can be an appropriation although it is only a step towards depriving the owner; and

---

[3] See, e.g. A T H Smith in [1981] Crim.LR 586–588.

[4] [1972] AC 626.

also that the step can appear innocent on its face (to a person who does not know of the thief's secret intention). Suppose that an employee receives money from a customer, and does not give the customer a receipt because he secretly intends not to account for the money to his employer. Does he, by reason of his secret intent, commit theft the moment he receives the money from the customer?

That is the way the cases are going, and it comes close to dispensing altogether with the *actus reus* that is supposed to be required for a consummated crime. Consider *Monoghan*.[5]

> A cashier in a supermarket took money from a customer in payment for goods and put it in the till but did not ring it up (so there was no record of it). She dishonestly intended to take it out and keep it, but she was arrested before doing this. One would have thought that the forces of law had pounced too soon; but the Court of Appeal upheld a conviction of theft on the ground that Monaghan was guilty of this offence when she put the money into the till.

Assuming for the sake of argument that there was no other money in the till (an unlikely contingency), it is difficult to see how, on any view of the law, putting the money in was an appropriation. Monaghan did not appropriate the money in the dictionary meaning of the word; she did not, at that stage, keep it for herself. Nor was it an appropriation within section 3 (1), because Monaghan did not by putting the money into the firm's till assume the rights of an owner.

It may be said in reply that the decision can be supported on the ground that Monaghan was not authorised to put a customer's money into the till except on condition that she rang it up. But that would be a strange way to look at the employer's intention. He would surely rather have the money put into the till, even though with an irregularity, than not put in at all. Anyway, the money belonged to the firm, and the till was the proper place for Monaghan to put it. The fact that she failed to ring it up would have grounded a charge of false accounting,[6] but ought not rationally to have made her guilty of theft at that moment. The courts now say that a person can be guilty of theft in doing what he is entitled and even supposed to do; but it is a thoroughly dangerous and unprincipled rule. It makes theft depend not on anything wrongful that the defendant does but merely on what goes on in his mind. Monaghan supplied evidence of her dishonest intention, but evidence of criminal intent should not be sufficient for conviction of a consummated crime without proof of some objective illegality. Failing to ring up the till could not reasonably be regarded as an appropriation of the money, and neither could the fact of putting the money into the till.

The decision presents even greater difficulties if one makes the realistic supposition that there was other money in the till. Monaghan's intention in that case was not to remove the particular notes and coins received from the customer but any notes and coins amounting to that value. On that view, the prosecution had to face a second, and (one would have thought) equally insurmountable difficulty, relating to proof of intent. Monaghan was then not guilty of theft of the particular notes and coins that she put into the till, because not only did she not take them but she did not necessarily intend to take them. They were merely part of a fund of money from which she intended to steal in future. Nor could the argument for the prosecution be helped by saying that Monaghan was guilty of theft of an unidentifiable part of the money in the till. There was no appropriation of an unidentifiable part.

---

[5] [1979] Crim.LR 673.
[6] § 40.4.

We shall return to the subject of appropriations with consent in § 35.3.

Suppose a would-be thief moves the article very slightly?

It was held even before the Act that where a pickpocket lifted a man's wallet to the edge of his pocket, and was then detected, he had committed larceny by "taking and carrying away,"[7] and there can be no doubt that the slightest movement of the thing with criminal intent could still be theft.[8]

What about just touching? Suppose a would-be thief puts his hand on the door-handle of my parked car, dishonestly intending to drive it away and steal it. At that moment the constabulary arrive. Has he appropriated the car?

The Court of Appeal in *Morris* fought shy of saying that switching price labels without removing the articles was an appropriation. But, on principle, any unlawful touching of the object should be an appropriation within section 3 (1).

The object of the formula was to give as much precision as possible to the moment of theft; and holding that the first unlawful touching is theft would certainly achieve this precision. If a pickpocket or mugger puts his hand on my wallet in my pocket, his act would in all probability be regarded as a completed theft. However, theft by touching the door handle of a car is not an offence that the police are likely to charge, unless there is something more than touching. They would charge, if anything, the summary offence of vehicle interference (§ 38.6). Charging theft, or even attempted theft, would look too heavy-handed; and it might be hard to prove whether the defendant intended to steal the vehicle or only something inside it. Besides, charging the summary offence stops him from opting to go for trial.

A further word of caution: what is here said about appropriation presupposes that the defendant is not a trustee or bailee or other person who is permitted to deal with property belonging to another. Whether lawful acts, acts within the scope of the defendant's authority, can be a theftous appropriation will be considered in Chapter 35.

Is it an appropriation to prevent the owner getting at his property?

Statistically, the odds are in favour of an affirmative answer, because the courts have not yet decided that any act is *not* an appropriation. It generally seems as though they will affirm that anything is. They are not going to let a rascal off because of the technicalities of appropriation. The few cases deciding against an appropriation on the facts then before the court have been overruled or disapproved.

At the same time, one can strongly argue that it should not be an appropriation for a non-possessor to impede the owner's access to his property, even if his object is to deprive the owner permanently. For instance, it should not be theft to lie to the owner as to where his property is, if the property is neither in the defendant's possession nor in the possession of someone whom the defendant wishes to help to steal it. Again, if an owner is trying to sell his property it should not be theft for the defendant to tell the prospective purchaser, falsely, that the owner

---

[7] *Taylor* [1911] 1 KB 674.

[8] Held in *Corcoran* v. *Anderton* [1980] Crim.LR 385 that it is the full offence of theft (and therefore robbery) for a robber to drag a woman's handbag from her grasp. Probably the offence is committed as soon as the robber touches the bag.

does not own the property.[9] The notion of appropriation should be held to apply only to an act in relation to the property, not just to speaking about the property.[10] Even where a non-possessor puts a physical impediment in the way of the owner's getting at the property, this looks more like an attempted appropriation than an actual one. Certainly the defendant does not "deal with it as owner" within section 3 (1). He merely prevents the owner dealing with it.

Whether these acts would amount to an appropriation if the defendant is in possession of the property of another will be considered in the next section.

What about offering to sell the property? A cheat offers to sell me V's car which V has parked in the street. V reappears and the cheat is arrested, the car not having been touched. Is the cheat guilty of theft?

It seems that the courts will answer this question in the affirmative—though they oughtn't.

> In *Pitham*,[11] X had a friend—well, an acquaintance—in prison, whose house was left uninhabited in consequence. X perceived that this offered him a good opportunity to make cash at the unfortunate prisoner's expense by selling his furniture. So he went to the prisoner's house in the company of Pitham, showed Pitham some of the furniture and invited him to buy what he wanted. Pitham accordingly returned to the house with an appropriate conveyance and took off some of the furniture (knowing full well that it was being stolen). He was charged with theft and handling stolen goods.

One would have thought that the proper verdict on these facts would have been that Pitham was guilty of theft (and X also guilty as an accessory by instigating him). But the jury acquitted Pitham of theft and convicted him of handling stolen goods. Now, the rule is that a person cannot be convicted of handling if he merely dealt with the goods "in the course of the stealing."[12] Therefore, in order to uphold Pitham's conviction of handling the Court of Appeal had to find that the theft was over and done with before Pitham removed the goods. So this was what the court did. It held that the theftous appropriation took place when X made an offer of the goods (or invited Pitham to treat for them; it is not clear which X was regarded as having done). This act was an appropriation by X because it amounted to assuming the rights of the owner.

The incident is an example of how the law is shaped by the misdirections of trial judges, the misunderstandings of juries, and the extreme reluctance of the Court of Appeal to upset convictions based on a wrong charge. Would the court's decision have been the same if X and Pitham had been

---

[9] In *Oakley* v. *Lyster* [1931] 1 KB 148, where the defendant falsely denied the plaintiff's title to goods, the tort of conversion was held to be committed; but there the defendant was in possession of the goods. The Torts (Interference with Goods) Act 1977 s. 11 (3) now provides that a denial of title is not of itself conversion. Cp. Winfield and Jolowicz, *The Law of Tort*, 11th ed. 454.

[10] But see *Pitham*, below.

[11] (1976) 65 CAR 45.

[12] See § 39.2 at n. 8.

convicted, instead, as accomplices in theft, and if both had appealed against the convictions? Pitham was hardly an accomplice to X's offer, so on this supposition the Court of Appeal could have upheld the convictions only by saying that Pitham committed theft by removing the furniture, X being guilty as accessory. And that, for a certainty, is what the court would have done. An argument by X that he was not an accessory to Pitham's theft because he had himself already stolen the goods by offering them to Pitham, and that one cannot steal the same goods twice by successive acts of appropriation, would have been rejected. The correct rule of law would then have emerged, namely that a mere offer by a non-owner to sell goods is not an appropriation. Instead, because the conviction could not be upheld unless the court affirmed the opposite, and incorrect, rule, this is what it did.[13]

Appellate judges will always be subject to an irresistible impulse to lay down wrong law in cases like this, so long as their powers in the event of a misdirection are so limited. It is absurd that when the line between thieving and receiving depends upon what is "in the course of the stealing," the fact that the jury decide wrongly between the two lets the culprit off.

You are too severe upon the court in Pitham. It seems to me that the court was incontrovertibly right in holding that offering to sell goods is one of the rights of an owner.

Permit me to say, on the contrary, that this is just the sort of specious argument that courts will so readily accept when it serves to maintain the conviction of an offender, although they would probably have seen the fallacy if the argument were less convenient. Let me put to you an extreme case, or more extreme case. This will often be found a good way to proceed. " 'I took an extreme case,' was Alice's tearful reply. 'My excellent preceptress always used to say, When in doubt, take an extreme case. And I was in doubt.' " Suppose that the Duke of Omnium's butler proposes to the first parlourmaid that they should seek a new and more rewarding life together in Canada. "I have found the key to his Grace's safe," he says; "so I will take off a tidy amount of cash and jewellery. You can take as much of his Grace's silver as you can get." Somebody has been listening, and the butler is arrested. Is he already guilty of stealing the Duke's silver? The butler has given his permission for the silver to be taken, and since only the Duke (acting personally or through his authorised agent) can lawfully permit the silver to be taken, the butler has assumed the rights of an owner. But of course a conclusion that he has already stolen the silver would be preposterous.

To approach more closely to the facts of *Pitham*: suppose that Pitham had been innocent. He was in fact a guilty offeree, but what if he had believed that X was the householder and was lawfully entitled to the furniture, when in fact X was only the lodger? X would be guilty of attempting to obtain money from the offeree by deception; and if the offeree accepted the

---

[13] See on the last point the dry remark of J C Smith quoted by Koffman in [1982] Crim.LR 337, and the latter's own comment at the foot of that page.

offer and took the furniture X would be guilty of theft through an innocent agent. But to say that X would be guilty of theft merely by making the offer is jurisprudentially preposterous. How could X's offer, made in respect of something not in his possession, not operating to transfer the ownership of the thing and not followed by a taking of possession, intelligibly be called an appropriation?

The fallacy in the court's reasoning lies in the ambiguity of the word "right." This comprises at least three different notions: rights in the strict sense (correlative to duties), liberties and powers.[14] An owner has a *liberty* to handle his property, to possess it and transfer possession, to destroy it, and so on; and he has a *right* against other people that they shall not do these things without his consent. If they do, they commit a tort as a civil wrong and (on principle) an appropriation for the purpose of theft. (Not to mention the appropriations they commit, according to the House of Lords, when they do these things *with* the owner's consent.) The owner also has a *power* to transfer the ownership in his thing by giving it away, selling it etc. (A legal power is an ability to alter legal rights.) But whereas the owner has a right against others that they shall not deliver his thing to a third person (because that involves a physical interference with it, which is a tort), he has no general right in the strict sense that they shall not contract to sell it, or to purport to pass ownership in it. He does not need such a right, because other people generally do him no harm in offering his goods for sale, and *cannot* pass ownership in them except by his authority. Their purported exercise of the power is not an infringement of the rights of an owner; it is merely an unsuccessful and wholly nugatory effort to usurp one of the powers of the owner.[15] The purported offer of sale by X was, so far as the rights of the owner were concerned, so much wind. A stranger who thus uses empty words of sale does not commit a tort against the owner, unless he causes possession of the thing to be taken[16]; and there is no reason why he should be convicted of stealing it.

Of course it is an appropriation for a person to pass title to the goods of another without his authority, under one of the exceptions to the rule *Nemo dat quod non habet.*[17] This injures the owner and is a violation of his right.

Is it an appropriation for a person to buy a thing after using deception to persuade the seller to sell it?

This topic, and various other problems of appropriation, will be discussed in Chapter 35.

I suppose it would be theft if a postman wrongfully opens a letter, and then flushes it down a lavatory to conceal what he has done?

Certainly. Section 1 (2) provides:

> "It is immaterial whether the appropriation is made with a view to gain, or is made for the thief's own benefit."

Whether destroying a thing without taking possession of it is theft is doubtful. It is not an appropriation in the ordinary meaning of that word: a bomber does not appropriate the

---

[14] The classical exposition of these distinctions is Hohfeld, *Fundamental Legal Conceptions* (New Haven, Conn. 1923).

[15] See, however, *Rogers* v. *Arnott* § .13 n. 4.

[16] *Consolidated Co.* v. *Curtis* [1892] 1 QB at 498. Some other commentators, to whom I am obliged for their notice of my remarks, do not agree with my opinion. Two of these are Koffman and Griew. The former, in [1982] Crim.LR 334, objects that "the facility to sell goods is clearly one of the perquisites of ownership." I have offered an answer to this in the text above. Griew 34 objects (1) to my argument that there was no conversion of the goods by X, on the ground that this ties theft too closely to the technicalities of the civil law of conversion, and (2) to my argument that X committed no wrong against the owner in respect of the furniture, on the ground that X's act can be regarded as wrongful because it is theft. These two objections, taken together, seem to me to assert a nebulous wrongness while denying any possibility of proving or disproving it. To say that X's act was wrongful as theft begs the question; apart from the law of theft, how can it be proved that his act was wrongful or not wrongful except by referring to the civil law?

[17] This is settled to amount to the tort of conversion.

property he bombs. However, section 3 (1) is peremptory; any act falling within it is, we are told, an appropriation; and destroying property is certainly one of the rights of the owner of the property. In practice there would be no point in testing the scope of the law of theft; the sensible charge for destruction without taking is one of criminal damage.

Is it theft to set free someone's budgerigar?

It is probably an act of criminal damage or destruction,[18] but there is no reason why it should not, instead, be charged as theft. Here section 3 (1) is valuable; setting the bird free is one of the rights of an owner. It should also be theft to let gas escape without authority, or to let someone's tyres down (unless the jury or magistrates refuse to regard the act as dishonest, which, in the case of releasing air, they may well do). Here again a charge of criminal damage is a possible alternative.

§ 33.13. APPROPRIATION BY A POSSESSOR

It seems that if a person receives possession of the property of another with intent to steal, this is an appropriation.[1] If he receives the property in good faith the theft is committed at the first subsequent dishonest and wrongful appropriation. It would be an appropriation if the hitherto innocent possessor wrongfully contracts to sell the article and delivers it, or gives it away, or destroys it. It would also be an appropriation to hide someone else's article with the object of keeping it; or for a possessor to tell the owner that it has been lost; or for a possessor to refuse to return it to the owner, or to deny his title to the property, which is only another way of informing him that he is not going to get it back. These are all modes of committing the tort of conversion (now subsumed under wrongful interference with goods), and they are acts that can further an intention to steal. They can all be regarded as appropriations in the dictionary sense, and they are also appropriations in the extended sense of section 3 (1), which applies where a person who has come by the property without stealing it makes "any later assumption of a right to it by keeping or dealing with it as owner." Even using the thing should be enough if the bailee's right to keep it is at an end.

Suppose the hire-purchaser of an article dishonestly sells it? Is this merely a breach of contract to keep the article in his possession, or is it theft?

Assuming *mens rea*, it is theft. A hire-purchaser is a hirer, a bailee; he does not become the owner till he makes all the payments that are due. In the usual contract of hire-purchase of a car, the car dealer sells the car to a finance company for cash, and the finance company lets the car to the hire-purchaser. This is done by documents signed by the hire-purchaser in the car dealer's office.

So the answer is that if the hire-purchaser knows the law, and if he

---

[18] Chap. 41.

[1] At any rate if he takes without the owner's consent or by fraud. See Chap. 35.

delivers the article to the person to whom he has wrongfully sold it, he is guilty of theft from the finance company, the owner of the car.

And if he does not deliver it?

If a bailee has contracted to sell the bailed article and did not intend to deliver it, but was only defrauding the third party and intended to restore the article to its owner, he could not be guilty of theft because he would not intend to deprive the owner permanently.[2] But if he was to receive payment from the third party only upon delivering the article, it would be easy to prove the intent to deprive. In that case, he would be guilty of theft on the authority of *Pitham*[3] (if "authority" is not too strong a word to use for a case that is so unsatisfactory in its reasoning).[4]

Even if *Pitham* is held to be wrong, the bailee in your hypothetical might perhaps be convicted of theft by reason of the second part of section 3 (1); he has "come by" the article and has thereafter (it may be argued) assumed the right to it by dealing with it as owner. However, one may still question whether a mere offer to sell, or even an actual sale that is ineffective to pass title and is not accompanied by delivery, can properly be called a "dealing" within the subsection. The bailee's act looks much more like an inchoate offence: an attempt to obtain money from the purchaser by deception, or (if the purchaser knows the facts) a conspiracy with the purchaser to defraud or to steal, or an attempt to steal. As was said before,[5] a non-owner who offers the article for sale is not even guilty of a tort; he is not regarded as having converted the thing to his own use, because he has passed neither possession nor property.

Can it be an appropriation for a possessor merely to retain an article, intending not to return it?

This is undecided. The question can arise (1) in the case of a bailee, if he retains the article beyond the period of the bailment, or otherwise after his rights have come to an end, and (2) in the case of other persons who initially took possession in good faith, if they retain the article after coming to realise who the owner is. Presumably the courts will say that the intention of section 3 (1)[6] is to turn the wrongful "keeping as owner" into theft.[7]

This statutory phrase does not settle the problem of duty. If a person consciously and by a positive act acquires possession of the property of another, and if his right to retain it comes to an end, it can be said that he is under a duty to return it, and that the *actus reus* of theft is committed when a reasonable time has elapsed for him to return it without his having done so. The question is more difficult if he did not acquire possession of the property of another consciously and by a positive act. For example, someone may send me through the post a valuable document to which I am not entitled and (when I open the package) know I am not

---

[2] The bailee cannot be said to intend to "treat the thing as his own to dispose of regardless of the [owner's] rights" within the first limb of s. 6 (1) (§ 32.3), because he does not actually dispose of the article (he does not pass either ownership or even possession of it), and he does not intend to dispose of it; he intends only to pretend to dispose of it. J C Smith, apparently with the approval of D W Elliott (*Reshaping the Criminal Law*, ed. Glazebrook (London 1978) 289–290) holds that s. 6 (1) supplies the *mens rea*, *sed quaere*. S. 6 (1) says nothing about *mens rea*.

[3] § .12 n. 11.

[4] But there was a pre-Act case to the same effect for offers by bailees: *Rogers* v. *Arnott* [1960] 2 QB 244.

[5] § .12 n. 15.

[6] § .12.

[7] See the fuller discussion in 1st edn 733–734.

entitled. If I put it on the mantelpiece and trouble myself no further, do I commit theft? Am I under a positive duty to bestir myself if I have done nothing to put myself under an obligation to do so? The authorities do not say, but the answer should be in the negative.

It seems from *Morris* (discussed in the last section) that a bailee commits theft simply by forming a dishonest intent, when he has not begun to act outside the terms of the bailment.

One can exercise the rights of an owner many times in succession with the same stolen object. Does one steal it every time?

The general answer is no. The Act assumes that appropriation is one event—consider, for example, section 3 (1), which makes keeping or dealing with a thing as owner a theftous appropriation only if the possessor has not already stolen the thing.[8]

In common sense a thief does not steal the thing afresh every time he uses it; and the only firm rule, therefore, is that the first theftous appropriation is the last—for that particular thief. (Friends of his who borrow the thing can commit a new theft for themselves.) But a thief ought not to be able to use this rule purely as a technicality for his own advantage, arguing that he has been charged with the wrong act of appropriation—"no, I did not steal it on Tuesday; I stole it on Monday." It would seem reasonable to say that the precise act of appropriation is an immaterial averment (like ownership), where nothing turns on it. Sometimes, for example, it is doubtful whether a person steals (1) by dishonestly coming into possession of property or (2) only later, by doing something wrong with the property; on a charge of stealing by doing the wrong act in (2), it ought not generally to be a defence that the defendant had already stolen by obtaining the property.

When a purely technical point is raised on appropriation, the judge may think it wise to have the indictment amended; but this ought not to be essential except where the guilt of the defendant or someone else depends upon whether the theftous appropriation was one act or another.

In the type of case last mentioned, where the time of appropriation is material to guilt, problems may arise. Readers will already have gathered the way in which appellate courts are likely to deal with them. They will define appropriation in the particular case in such a way as to affirm the conviction of a dishonest person. That is not a rule of law, but a proposition about how the courts are likely to act in fact.

The precise time of a theft marks the dividing line between being an accessory to the theft and being a handler of stolen goods. To be an accessory to crime involves doing an act before the crime is completed; one cannot be an accessory by an act done afterwards. To be a handler of stolen goods, in contrast, one must handle them "otherwise than in the course of the stealing."[9] The object of this phrase is to prevent the actual thief and his helpers being convicted of handling by dealing with the goods that they have just stolen; so the phrase should rationally be read as meaning "after the stealing." But what is likely to happen in practice may be illustrated by hypotheticals.

Case A. Suppose that burglars enter an unoccupied house and load its valuable contents into a van. They then call up an associate (who has not hitherto been in the plot) and ask

---

[8] On the general question see Smith para. 48; Griew § 2–45; Koffman in [1982] Crim.LR 338–339; [1978] Crim.LR 69; corrective note on *Anderton* v. *Wish* (72 CAR 23) in [1980] Crim.LR 657 and 145 JPN 423. Even if successive acts closely related in time can each be regarded as an appropriation, it is clear on principle that there should not be multiple convictions; see Griew in [1979] Crim.LR 292. On charging thefts together when they are committed on more than one occasion see Archbold, 41st edn 1–61.

[9] Section 22 (1); see § 39.1.

him to come to drive the van to a hide-out and store the loot. This is done. If the associate is convicted of handling, an appellate court is likely to uphold the conviction, rightly, on the ground that the appropriation was completed before he arrived, so that his act was done otherwise than in the course of the stealing—even though the act was commenced at the scene of the theft and shortly after the theft.[10]

Case B. The same facts as before, but the associate is convicted as an accessory to the theft. The appellate court is again likely to affirm the conviction, this time on the ground that the appropriation was not completed at the time of the defendant's intervention.[11] The commentators will be left to puzzle how the decision is to be reconciled with that in Case A. In order to defend itself against a charge of inconsistency, the court may fudge the issue by saying[12] that "the question of whether, when and by whom there has been an appropriation of property has always to be determined by the jury having regard to the circumstances of the case."

The question of the time of appropriation is also important on a charge of robbery, which requires force or threats to be used "immediately before or at the time of" stealing.[13] These words in the statute were intended to exempt from a charge of robbery a thief who used force after the theft, even if he used it immediately afterwards. But if a thief uses force on his victim immediately after the theft, perhaps to prevent him from raising the alarm, and if he is convicted of robbery, the Court of Appeal will affirm the conviction on the ground that the time of stealing has a certain spread: *Hale*.[14] This decision can then be cited in other cases[15] as a useful precedent for saying that theft continues after the act of appropriation has been completed; and the puzzlement of the commentators as to what is meant by an appropriation will be deepened.

We are unlikely to attain a rational rule as to the time of the theft so long as the courts act in this unprincipled manner. One can sympathise with their desire not to let guilty people escape on technicalities, but this could be done more satisfactorily, and without legislation, if the appellate court dismissed an appeal (on the ground that no miscarriage of justice has actually occurred) where the only thing wrong about a conviction is that it is technically for the wrong crime. This would attain the same result as the present practice, but would not warp the theory of the law to the same extent. Preferably, the appellate court should be empowered by legislation, or even by an assumption of power at common law, to substitute a conviction of the crime that was committed in fact, when such substitution occasions no injustice; and legislation might permit it even when the jury have acquitted of the crime of which they should have convicted.

SUMMARY

Theft is of property. Probably a person owns parts of his body as soon as they are severed. A corpse is generally not property, but interference with corpses can be one of a number of offences. § .1

Land and its parts cannot be stolen except (1) by way of breach of trust, or (2) by a non-possessor who severs part of it, or (3) by a tenant who appropriates a fixture. "Parts of the land" include growing things and fixtures; also water in a § .2

---

[10] *Pitham* § 39.2.

[11] Cp. the dictum in *Hale* quoted with approval in *Gregory* (1981) The Times, December 1, [1982] Crim.LR 229.

[12] As in *Gregory*, last note.

[13] s.8 (1); see § 36.1.

[14] § 36.1

[15] As it was in *Gregory*, n. 11 above.

pond. Picking wild mushrooms, flowers, fruit or foliage is not theft unless done for reward or for a commercial purpose. A wild creature (or its carcass) cannot be stolen unless (1) it is tamed or ordinarily kept in captivity, or (2) another person has reduced it into possession or is in the course of so doing. The dishonest use, waste or diversion of electricity is an offence under section 13.

Property includes things in action and other intangible property. It therefore includes copyrights, patents and trade marks, but mere infringement is not an appropriation. Infringing copyright is a statutory offence and can also be a conspiracy to defraud. Similarly, although a debt is a thing in action, non-payment of the debt is not an appropriation of it. In effect, things in action can be stolen only by being wrongfully assigned, though documents evidencing them can be stolen as valuable pieces of paper. Trade and industrial secrets are not property for the purpose of theft, but they may be given a measure of protection by charging industrial espionage as one of a number of offences that are not specifically concerned with that activity. § .3

The property must belong to another. Therefore, once a person has obtained ownership and possession, he cannot (in general) commit theft of that property. Conversely, once an owner has passed the ownership in his thing to another he can commit theft of it even though it remains in his possession. Ownership may pass through an agent. In an ordinary shop transaction, the property in goods does not pass until payment is made or credit given, and if the buyer runs off with the goods he commits theft. The loser of an article does not abandon the ownership merely because he abandons the search. The charge may lay the property in a person unknown. § .4

There can be theft from a bailee or employee. Generally speaking, an article put into another person's container which is in his possession falls into his possession also, so that if the article is dishonestly taken this can be theft from him. § .5

Where trustees steal the trust property, the theft is from the persons entitled to enforce the trust. Trusts include constructive trusts. Company directors are not trustees for the shareholders; they can steal from the company, but not, it seems, by dealing with the company's property in a way that they are authorised to do. § .6

The general principle is that a non-owner cannot pass title (*nemo dat quod non habet*). So if D1 steals from V, and sells or gives the thing to D2, who takes it knowing the facts, D2 commits theft of V's property as well as D1. In practice, however, D2 would usually be charged with handling rather than with theft. If D2 gave value for the thing in good faith, his subsequent discovery that the thing was stolen will not make him guilty of theft in respect of anything he does with the thing: section 3 (2). § .7

An owner may steal from a co-owner, or from a possessor who has a charge over the property, such as a lien. Difficulty caused by the *ratio decidendi* in *Turner* (*No.* 2). § .8

By section 5 (3), theft can be committed by a person who "receives property from or on account of another, and is under an obligation to the other to retain and deal with that property or its proceeds in a particular way." This summarises rules of the civil law, but may go beyond them. Where the subsection applies, theft can be committed either of the original property or of its proceeds, meaning property into which it has been converted (the exchange product). § .9

Under the old law, it was not a crime to make and retain a profit by wrongfully using the property of another. But such a profit is the subject of a constructive trust, and on principle the appropriation of it can be theft, except that it may be hard to establish dishonesty in relation to this property. § .10

When a cheque is stolen, this is theft of a piece of paper as a thing of value; when the thief is credited with the cheque, he steals a thing in action; if he cashes the cheque, he can be convicted of stealing a thing in action or of stealing the proceeds as representing the cheque. § .11

An appropriation in the ordinary or dictionary sense involves taking control of § .12

property in a way showing an intention to deprive the owner. Such an act of appropriation may or may not be with the consent of the owner. In addition, the extended definition of appropriation in s. 3 (1) means that the assumption (usurpation) of even a single right of the owner is an appropriation: CA in *Morris*. In this case it was held that a supermarket customer who removes an article from a shelf appropriates it, and it makes no difference that the act is done with the consent of the owner; *sed quaere* whether this is a correct interpretation of the subsection. The second part of the subsection declares that appropriation "includes, where he has come by the property (innocently or not) without stealing it, any later assumption of a right to it by keeping or dealing with it as owner;" therefore, if the customer acquired the dishonest intent only after taking the article from the shelf, he would be guilty of theft in keeping or dealing with it as owner, e.g. in switching price labels. Probably, the mere unlawful touching of an article, if accompanied by the requisite intents, would be an appropriation under the subsection. It was held in *Pitham* that a non-possessor who offers to sell another's property appropriates it; *sed quaere*, because his act does not affect the owner until he delivers the article to the buyer.

In general, if a person receives possession of the property of another with intent to steal, this is an appropriation; if he receives the property in good faith the theft is committed at the first subsequent dishonest and wrongful appropriation. An example would be refusing to give the thing back on demand. Another example would be denying the owner's title. A bailee or other non-owner who sells an article will probably be held guilty of theft if he sells it, even though he does not deliver it or pass title, though this is questionable on principle. Apparently a bailee commits an appropriation by merely retaining the article after his right to keep it has come to an end. A theftous appropriation can take place only once, and is not continuous during the time that the thief is in possession; but the courts may give it a certain extension in time. § .13

CHAPTER 34

OBTAINING BY DECEPTION

O, slings and arrows—arrows all too broad,
My gamble failed, and then they called it fraud.
"J P C," *Poetic Justice*

THE offence of obtaining property by deception has already been outlined (§ 31.4). Its requirements may be sorted out as follows.

1 There must be a deception (§§ .1–.5).
2 The deception must be deliberate or reckless (§ .6).
3 There must be property belonging to another (§ .7).
4 The defendant must obtain the property (§ .8).
5 The obtaining must be by the deception (§ .9).
6 The obtaining must be dishonest, and be accompanied by an intention to deprive the owner permanently (§ .10).

The chapter will conclude with a discussion of obtaining services by deception (§ .11).

§ 34.1. (1) THERE MUST BE A DECEPTION: DECEPTION AS TO INTENTION AND BELIEF

Most, if not all, deceptions result from false representations, express or implied. Whether a representation is made by conduct is a question of fact for the jury, but whether a representation *can* be inferred from the defendant's conduct is a question of law for the judge.[1]

Before the Theft Act the courts refused to recognise a false pretence as to a person's intention, or other state of mind, as being sufficient for the crime. Now, however, section 15 (4) (quoted in § 31.4) brings in deception (express or implied) as to intention. Although the section does not say so, this must apply to deceptive promises.

> Consider again the jobbing painter who gets money to buy paint. He says to one of his employers: "I'll paint your railings tomorrow; will you let me have £50 towards the paint?" The employer gives him the money. If the painter did not intend to do the work and obtained the money by this falsity he is guilty of an offence under section 15 (1). He has falsely represented his own state of mind. This being so, it seems obvious that the same result must follow if instead of a statement of intention there is what is in terms a promise. Suppose the conversation between the employer and the jobbing painter runs like this.
> Employer: "I want my railings painted. Can you promise to do them for me tomorrow?"
> Painter: "Yes, but I shall need £50 to get the paint."

[1] *Per* Viscount Dilhorne in *Charles* [1977] AC at 186D–187B.

Clearly, the effect is the same as before. In other words, *every promise is an implied representation that the promisor intends to keep his promise,* because a promise makes no sense unless the promisor intends to perform it.

This rule makes a certain breach in the traditional principle that the criminal law should not be used to enforce contracts. But it applies only when the defendant has obtained property, or committed some other deception offence, such as obtaining services (§ .11) or an overdraft (§ 40.2) by deception. And it applies only when the defendant at the time of the obtaining did not intend to perform his part.

Is it the same where there is no express promise? Micawber orders a meal in a restaurant, or buys petrol at a filling station, and departs without paying.

These are cash transactions, and the customer impliedly represents that he is in a position to pay cash and intends to do so.[2] Lord Reid said;

> "Where a . . . customer orders a meal in a restaurant, he must be held to make an implied representation that he can and will pay for it before he leaves."[3]

This applies to all transactions in which immediate payment is customarily expected. If a diner in a restaurant, having consumed a meal, confesses that he has no cash with which to pay, and does not offer a plausible explanation of mistake or forgetfulness, this will be strong evidence that when he consumed the meal he did not intend to pay for it.

Similarly, dishonest intent may be evidenced by immediately-following conduct. If a diner leaves the restaurant hurriedly without paying, this subsequent conduct is evidence of his prior dishonest intention when he entered into the transaction.[4] (But if he had the money to pay, the police will very likely not prosecute, because they will consider that the defendant would probably be acquitted on giving evidence of forgetfulness.)

These hypotheticals of the diner and the driver exemplify legal principles, but in the particular instances the charge would now be of making off without having paid (§ 40.1) rather than of obtaining by deception.

What about a credit transaction? Two racketeers set up in business and at first pay the bills they incur to wholesalers. Then they run up a lot of large bills all at once, auction their stock and fade away. Will the police be on their tracks?

Lawyers call this a "long firm fraud," for some arcane reason.[5] The ordinary man knows the phenomenon as the fly-by-night firm. The practice is to charge a single conspiracy to defraud, or, where a company is involved, the offence of fraudulent trading,[6] giving particulars of A, B, C, etc. who have been defrauded. But there is no reason why the defendants should not be indicted for obtaining goods by deception from A, B and C contrary to section 15 (1) (in separate counts). You put each victim into the

---

[2] Nowadays, payment by cheque backed by a cheque card would be sufficient, or payment by credit card if there is a sign up acccepting that kind of credit card.

[3] *Ray* v. *Sempers* [1974] AC at 379. Cp. *Nordeng* (1975) 62 CAR at 126, where the CA said: "That the bill be paid at (or before) the end of his stay is a representation made by the conduct of a traveller who books in at an hotel." (Strictly speaking, the court should have said: "That he intends to pay the bill" etc.).

[4] Cp. *Aston* [1970] 1 WLR 1584, 3 All ER 1045, 55 CAR 48.

[5] See Michael Levi, *The Phantom Capitalists* (London 1981) 12; and see this work generally.

[6] § 40.7.

box and ask him: "Why did you supply these goods to these men on credit?" Answer: "Because I thought they were an honest firm." The mere ordering of the goods is an implied representation of honesty.

Although prosecutors seem to prefer a charge of conspiracy to defraud to a charge under section 15 in big cases, charges under section 15 have succeeded where people have dishonestly ordered goods from a mail order catalog with no intention of paying.[7]

Does every firm guarantee its own solvency? Take a bank or travel agency that is financially ailing. A travel agent has lost a lot of money this season, and his debts exceed his assets. It is possible that if he continues to trade things may improve and all will be well. But it is also possible that they will get worse, in which case, when he takes a customer's advance payment on a holiday tour, he may not be able to provide the tour nor to refund the cash. Faced with this dilemma, perhaps the very scrupulous agent would put up the shutters. But then his customers will certainly lose some of their money, whereas if he says nothing and goes on trading there is a chance that everyone will be happy.

You have put your finger on a difficult problem. In one case a judge ruled that the directors of a bank that failed could be charged with conspiracy to defraud when they took cash from customers knowing that they were insolvent.[8] The learned judge confined his opinion to bankers, who trade with other people's money, and said that the rule did not extend to ordinary traders. But on another occasion, when it was proved that the defendant traded through a company knowing that he was hopelessly insolvent, he was convicted of fraudulent trading.[9] On principle, a person who is guilty of conspiracy to defraud or of fraudulent trading in these circumstances is equally guilty of obtaining by deception. The difficulty relates to marginal cases, as in your question. If a firm is only marginally insolvent and there is hope of business picking up it would be harsh to say that fraud is established merely because the doors are not at once closed. Probably it is a question of degree: if the firm is hopelessly insolvent it will be possible to find deception and a dishonest obtaining.

Could a man be punished under section 15 (1) for a deception to relieve people of their money by offering them a get-rich-quick scheme involving illegality, when in fact he had no intention of operating the scheme?

Certainly. The illegality of what the cheat promises is no defence to a charge of obtaining by deception. An example in the reports is where a woman obtained advance payments for promised prostitution, having no intention of supplying the expected service.[10]

Can there be a deception as to a future fact? A hotel proprietor accepts my cash for reserving a room in his new wing for August, saying that he fully

---

[7] See the unreported case noticed by Lawson in 145 JPN 533.
[8] *Parker* (1916) 25 Cox 145.
[9] *Inman* [1967] 1 QB 140. For the offence see § 40.11.
[10] *Caslin* [1961] 1 WLR 59, 1 All ER 246, 45 CAR 47.

expects the wing to be completed by then. In fact he knows that the prospects are slim, and the wing is not completed.

Section 15 (4) refers to deception "as to fact." Literally this could cover a future fact, but there is something incongruous in the notion of a deception as to the future.

A more acceptable line of reasoning presents itself. Although section 15 (4) refers only to deceptions as to intention, there can scarcely be any doubt, nowadays, that the criminal law extends to any deception as to a state of mind, including belief (as the civil law has long done). "The state of a man's mind," said Bowen LJ in a civil case "is as much a fact as the state of his digestion."[11] So the proper way to word the charge against the hotel proprietor would make it a deception as to his belief that the future fact (the completion of the wing) will come about. Still, there is no profit in pedantry, and a charge worded in terms of a deception as to the future should usually be read as relating to the defendant's state of mind.[12] Alternatively, a deception that in terms refers to the future may be understood to mean that the existing facts are such that the future facts will occur.[13]

§ 34.2. SILENCE AND DECEPTION

Where there is no active deception and no representation can be implied, the general rule is that mere silence cannot amount to deception. This is a historic principle not only of the criminal but of the civil law. Various civil remedies are available independently of fraud, but silence constitutes neither fraud nor deception. Deception means telling a lie, not simply failing to reveal the truth.

> Consider a case where a customer in a shop sees an article bearing a price-tag so low that he knows there has been a mistake. He asks for the article and buys it at the marked price. Obviously, by buying it he does not impliedly represent that no mistake has been made as to the price, nor even that he knows of no mistake as to the price. Nor has he done anything positive to induce the seller's mistake. So he is not guilty of obtaining the article by deception.

The distinction between mere silence and deception is the foundation of this part of the law, and the courts ought to maintain it strictly, even when they are tempted to depart from it to convict a rogue. If there are to be any "constructive deceptions," or any duties of candour imposed by the criminal law, this should be done expressly by legislation stating when disclosure is required.[1]

---

[11] *Edgington* v. *Fitzmaurice* (1885) 29 Ch.D at 483.

[12] The argument is supported by *British Airways Board* v. *Taylor* [1976] 1 WLR 13, 1 All ER 65 on the Trade Descriptions Act. On the philosophical question see Alan R White in 90 LQR 15.

[13] *Charles* [1977] AC at 191B. See generally J C Smith in [1977] Crim.LR 616–617.

[1] See A T H Smith in [1982] Crim.LR 729–731.

Suppose the buyer in your hypothetical admits he knew that if the assistant had realised the mistake he would not have parted with the article at that price.

It would make no difference to a charge under section 15 (1). The customer is still not a deceiver.

The position would also be the same if the customer tendered the article to the assistant or cashier. The tendering of the article bearing the mistaken price marking is not a deception by the customer.[2] In essence it is merely a failure by the customer to disclose his knowledge of the seller's mistake.

The line between silence and deception is more difficult to draw than may at first appear, particularly because the silence rule does not apply if a false representation can be genuinely implied, as in the instances given in a previous chapter.[3]

Is there an implied representation of title to sell? An art dealer finds, after he has acquired a valuable painting, that it is stolen property. He sells it to an innocent purchaser without telling him that it is stolen, and later the purchaser has to give it back to the true owner. Has the art dealer obtained the price from the purchaser by deception?

The criminal courts hold that it is open to the jury to imply a representation by the seller that he is able to pass the title that as a matter of law he purports to pass.[4]

"As a matter of law." But when the ordinary person buys a picture in a shop, what is in his mind is that he is going to take it home with him. He doesn't think of some unknown person coming on the scene and claiming it. So how has he been deceived? What was the false belief he had when he bought the picture?

I surmise that the answer the courts would give, assuming that they require an actual false belief, is that the buyer contracts for ownership, not merely temporary possession. Even if he is not a lawyer and does not think in terms of ownership, he believes he is going to have the right to enjoy the picture "for ever," which means that there is no other claimant who can lawfully dispossess him. That is his false belief.

The implied representation as to title is exceptional. A seller is not taken to make implied representations as to the quality or fitness of the article he sells. The civil law implies terms in the contract on these matters, but does not make breach of them a fraud, any more than the criminal law makes

---

[2] *Per curiam* in *Kaur* v. *Chief Constable of Hampshire* [1981] 1 WLR 578 at 583D, 2 All ER 430, 72 CAR 359. For a further discussion with conflicting opinions see [1981] Crim.LR 677; [1982] *ibid.* 64 (J C Smith and Williams); A T S Smith in [1982] *ibid.* 729.

[3] § 31.4.

[4] *Re Pinter* (1891) 17 Cox 497; *Edwards* [1978] Crim.LR 49. The application of the rule made in the latter case seems wrong; it was held that when the squatter in a house (who paid the rates) let some rooms to V, he could, on principle, be convicted of obtaining the rent from V by deception. The valid argument for the defence (rejected by the CA) was that a squatter as a possessor can create a tenancy of the premises which is valid as between him and the lessee. Cp. J C Smith's note to the case. Moreover, the facts made the inference almost irresistible that V knew he was dealing with a squatter, in which case there was in any case no deception.

them a deception. If a prosecution were brought under section 15 (1) merely on the ground that an article sold was unfit, to the knowledge of the seller, the judge should, on principle, withdraw the case from the jury. A false representation is not to be implied merely because the buyer will be unpleasantly surprised when he discovers the truth. There may, however, be special circumstances in the case indicating that the seller did represent the article to be of a certain type or condition or to have a particular suitability.

Suppose I am buying a used car and ask the seller whether all the gadgets are working. He replies: "The reserve tank is not operating," craftily failing to mention that the door locks, the automatic windows and the windscreen wipers are not working either.

The jury or magistrates may find deception if, as here, the defendant uttered a misleading half-truth. Blackburn J once said, in a civil case:

> "I think that it must in every case depend upon the nature of the transaction, whether the fact not disclosed is such that it is impliedly represented not to exist; and that must generally be a question of fact proper for a jury."[5]

A man's silence may also be a tacit acceptance of a proposition put to him during negotiation.

Suppose a man trades in his car with 80,000 miles on the milometer, and it mysteriously sheds half that mileage before the car is resold by the dealer.

This practice is so common that those interested in the sale of used cars have felt it to need a name: "clocking." Such nefarious trading tricks are normally prosecuted by trading standards officers under the Trade Descriptions Act 1968.[6] Section 1 (1) provides:

> "Any person who, in the course of a trade or business,—
> (*a*) applies a false trade description to any goods; or
> (*b*) supplies or offers to supply any goods to which a false trade description is applied;
> shall, subject to the provisions of this Act, be guilty of an offence."

The offence is normally tried summarily, but it can be punished with a 2-year jail sentence on indictment (and many clockers are sent to prison). The Act contains elaborate definitions of what is meant by "applies," "false" and "trade description," and a rich case-law has built up. Other sections create other offences of false statements for business purposes. The offences are primarily of strict liability, but certain defences of mistake, accident, etc. are allowed; these are touched upon in Chapter 44.

Reverting to the milometer (odometer) frauds, the Trade Descriptions Act does not apply to private sales, so the private seller who stoops to

---

[5] *Lee* v. *Jones* (1864) 17 CBNS at 506, 144 ER at 204.

[6] See *Hammerton Cars Ltd* (1976) 63 CAR 234; Samuels in 133 NLJ 238. For the procedural difficulties see Newsome in 143 JPN 605–606; Lawson in 145 JPN 515.

clocking is convicted under section 15 (1). The milometer represents that the car has done the mileage shown and no more, unless the buyer is otherwise informed. Theoretically the dishonest dealer could be charged under section 15 (1) as well, but for some reason a charge of conspiracy to defraud appears to be preferred in serious cases to one under section 15 (1).

As we shall see in the next chapter, the courts have sometimes construed the law of theft so widely that a person who acquires money or other property by dishonestly failing to disclose something may possibly be guilty of theft even though the nondisclosure does not affect the validity of the transaction and he obtains a perfectly valid title to the money or other property. However, these facts have not arisen, and when the general question is more fully considered the courts will perhaps introduce some limitation into the law of theft.

Although it is common sense that a deceptive misrepresentation can be implied from conduct (as in the case of the townsman wearing an undergraduate gown mentioned before[7]), the permission given to juries and magistrates to imply a representation puts them on a slide that can easily end in the punishment of mere nondisclosure, in the absence of tight control by the judges; and unhappily that control is sometimes lacking. To find a representation truly implied by words or conduct is one thing; to "find" a fictitious representation, purely because the defendant is a scoundrel, is quite another. Two decisions of the House of Lords provide striking examples: *Charles*[8] and *Lambie*.[9] The rules they establish are simple: that a person who uses a cheque card or credit card impliedly represents to the person who gives credit that he, the card-holder, is acting within the terms of his contract with the bank, notwithstanding that the person who gives the credit is not interested in this question. That the rule is politic cannot be denied, since it enables fraudulent persons to be convicted; but whether they should be convicted by this interpretation of the law is another matter, since it involves stretching the notion of implied representation beyond breaking-point.

Charles concerned cheque cards. As all the world knows (or at any rate all the world who reads the back of bank cheque cards), the bank promises the recipient of a cheque that the bank will honour the cheque provided that it complies with certain conditions expressed on the cheque card. The recipient of a cheque written in accordance with the conditions is not concerned with the state of the drawer's bank account, which is a matter solely between the drawer and the bank. It might be thought, therefore, that the drawer of a cheque that is valid under the terms of the cheque card cannot in so doing be guilty of deceiving the person who gives the credit. But the House of Lords determined otherwise.

> Charles wrote a series of cheques on the strength of his cheque card, knowing that the total greatly exceeded the overdraft he was allowed. The manager of a club to whom the cheques were given in payment for gaming chips was ignorant of this excess, and made no enquiry since he did not regard the matter as concerning the club (as, financially, it did not). Charles was convicted of obtaining an overdraft (resulting from the bank's honouring of his cheques) by the deception impliedly addressed to the gambling club.[10] It was a case of obtaining the benefit (the overdraft) from A by means of a deception addressed to B. (Charles was not charged with an offence under section 15 (1) of

---

[7] § 31.4.
[8] [1977] AC 177.
[9] [1982] AC 449.
[10] For the offence see § 40.2.

obtaining gaming chips from the club by the same deception, but on the court's reasoning he would clearly have been guilty of that as well.) The conviction was reluctantly upheld by the Court of Appeal, which intimated that it would have found against an implied deception if the authorities had not hindered this course. The House of Lords again upheld the conviction, but without the reservations and doubts.

The deception found by the House of Lords was based on an implied representation supposed to have been made by Charles that he was acting within the rules laid down by the bank for the use of cheque cards, that is to say that he was within his credit limit. Lord Diplock said that the card-holder

> "by exhibiting to the payee a cheque card . . . represents to the payee that he has actual authority from the bank to make a contract with the payee on the bank's behalf that it will honour the cheque on presentment for payment."

If an implication of this kind were the only way to give commercial efficacy to the transaction, of course it should be made; but it is not the only way. The cheque card with its terms on the back is a general offer made directly by the bank to people who accept cheques on the strength of the card. The card-holder is a bearer of the offer, but need no more be regarded as the bank's agent to contract than was the newspaper that carried the celebrated advertisement by the Carlisle and Cumberland Banking Co., or the newsagent who sold the copy of the newspaper to Mrs Bragg, an agent for the Banking Co.[11] The position in *Charles* would have been the same if Charles's bank had written directly to the payee of each cheque in the terms of its offer on the cheque card. And even if the card-holder was the bank's agent to contract on its behalf, his agency (his power to bind the bank towards the payee) did not incorporate the limitations expressed in the contract between him and the bank. The bank bound itself to the payee irrespective of the card-holder's observance of its rules.

In all previous cases where representations had been implied, they concerned matters of importance to the alleged representee. Here the representation was of no importance to the club as payee of the cheques. It is remarkable to imply a representation by the card-holder that he was not acting in breach of his contract with a third party (the bank), when it was immaterial to the alleged representee whether he was so acting or not. In such circumstances, the supposed implied representation is merely a verbal device for giving an appearance of propriety to a conviction of obtaining by deception.

It is sometimes thought that the decision in *Charles* was justified by the fact that the club manager gave evidence (1) to the effect that had he known of the irregularity in Charles's use of his cheque card, he would not have accepted the cheques. But he also said (2) that if there was a cheque card he would take no account of the state of the card-holder's account with his bank, because "it is the bank who takes the risk." The first of these statements shows that if there was an implied representation by Charles, then the manager was influenced by it to accept his cheques; but it does not itself establish that there was such a representation. The rule that the benefit must be obtained by reason of the deception (§ .9) is a necessary condition of the deception offence, but it is not a sufficient condition. Another condition is that there must be a deception. The mere fact that a person will be surprised and disconcerted when he discovers a particular fact, and that he would have acted otherwise if he had known the fact in time, does not establish a deception; for if it did, every deliberate and material non-disclosure would constitute a deception.

The third case, *Lambie*, concerned not a cheque card but a credit card, and the decision is open to much the same criticism as *Charles*. The main difference between the two types of card is that with the credit card the bank makes its own standing contracts in advance with the particular suppliers who are willing to accept its credit card. The question whether the abuse of credit card facilities involved any criminal offence had long been discussed in Whitehall, but no one had done anything about it.

> When, therefore, Miss Lambie went on a little spending spree in a Mothercare shop, using a Barclaycard beyond her credit limit, someone selected her as a sacrificial lamb to get the law clarified by the soothsayers. Notwithstanding Lambie's transgression of the bank's rules, no harm could befall Mothercare, who could still claim from the bank under

---

[11] *Carlisle and Cumberland Banking Co.* v. *Bragg* [1911] 1 KB 489.

their contract with the bank. The departmental manager of Mothercare who dealt with the matter acted properly under the credit card contract and had no notice that Lambie was not entitled to use her card. In the result, Lambie was convicted of the offence of evading a debt by deception. (The provision under which she was convicted is now repealed, but the important legal question would have been the same if she had been charged with obtaining the goods from the shop by deception, and in this respect the decision still governs.[12])

On appeal the Court of Appeal, showing admirable impartiality, intellectual rigour, fidelity to the law, and self-restraint, quashed the conviction. In the opinion of the court, Lambie gave no implied representation to the shop as to her right to use the card. The shop was not interested in this question, being protected by its contract with the bank. The Oxford shop assistant who sold goods on credit to the townsman wearing the undergraduate gown certainly thought that he was an undergraduate; but the Mothercare manager did not suppose that Lambie was within Lambie's credit limit, because she was not concerned with the question. Indeed, she confirmed this in evidence. "I would not worry about what went on between the customer and Barclaycard."

Alas, the decision of the Court of Appeal was reversed by the House of Lords, which restored the conviction.

The reason given by their lordships followed the lines laid down in *Charles*. In the opinion of the House Lambie impliedly represented that she had authority from the bank to make a contract (as agent for the bank) with the shop, the contract in question being not Lambie's purchase of goods but a collateral contract involving a promise by the bank to the shop to honour the Barclaycard.

This way of looking at the matter involved even greater difficulty than in *Charles*. In the credit card transaction there was already in existence a contract between the bank and Mothercare, a contract in the conclusion of which Lambie had played no part. The fact that the contract operated only when a card-holder made a purchase did not make the card-holder an agent of the bank to negotiate its liability. The supposition of an agency on Lambie's part was, therefore, superfluous and unwarranted. Credit card agreements are drawn up with meticulous care by commercial lawyers, and nowhere do these agreements suggest that the card-holder acts as an agent in any capacity for the bank when he or she uses the card. From the point of view of the law of contract full efficacy can be given to the credit card arrangement without implying any such agency. The *only* purpose, it appears, of this implied agency asserted by the House of Lords is to convict the dishonest card-holder of deception. In no other respect is the card-holder an agent of the bank. No agency need be implied in order to create a relationship between the bank and the shop, because that relationship is already established in the contract between the bank and the shop. The reason why the bank is liable to the shop is not because the card-holder has contracted on its behalf, but because the bank has directly contracted with the shop.[13]

Finally, if it must be taken that Lambie represented to the shop that the bank would under existing arrangements pay the shop, her representation was true. The bank would and did pay the shop. The criticism of Lambie was not that she defrauded the shop but that she defrauded the bank; but it is a strong thing to say that a person who deals with A impliedly represents to A that he is not defrauding B, A having no pecuniary interest in the question whether this fraud is committed or not.

§ 34.3. DECEPTION OTHERWISE THAN BY REPRESENTATION

Properly considered, the notion of an implied representation should not give a large extension to liability for deception. But the question arises whether there may not be a deception without any false representation, either express or implied. A card-sharper keeps an ace up his sleeve, or a

---

[12] Lord Roskill, delivering the opinion of the House of Lords, supposed that the question before them would have been straightforward if the proceedings against Lambie had been under section 15 (1) ([1982] AC at 456F). In fact it would have made no difference, since the question of deception is the same for both offences.

[13] See the devastating criticism of the case on this point by Francis Bennion in 131 NLJ 1041. Also § .9.

gambler throws with loaded dice. Does he get his winnings by deception? One would think so; yet it is artificial to say that a player impliedly represents that he does not keep aces up his sleeve or has not got loaded dice. Again, bookmakers may "fix" a race by bribing the jockey riding the favourite not to win, or may dope his horse. With more subtle guile, a racehorse owner may enter an inferior runner, bet heavily on him, and then secretly switch him for a much faster horse. Or he may dope the favourite to improve the chances of his own animal. It would impose an impossible strain upon the theory of representation to find implied representations in cases of this kind.

These particular malpractices could be dealt with as offences under the Gaming Act 1845 section 17, which is a comprehensive provision covering all deceitful practices in relation to wagering on "any game, sport, pastime or exercise." Where two or more persons are involved they are charged as conspiracies to defraud. But the general question is capable of arising outside the limits of these offences.

A historical note may help the argument. Formerly, the law of obtaining by false pretences presupposed a representation, at least in theory. But there was also an offence of being a common cheat (not necessarily involving a representation), which was almost entirely abolished by the Theft Act. And there was a form of larceny known as larceny by a trick which again covered trickery even when there was no representation (as where the victim was bamboozled into buying a purse thinking it was full of coins, when it was in fact empty); this also is abolished, with the rest of larceny, by the Act. In their place we have the offence under section 15 (1); and it is to be noticed that all that this requires is a deception. It does not say that the deception must take the form of a representation, express or implied. In recommending the measure the CLRC said;

> "The word 'deception' seems to us (as to the framers of the American Law Institute's Model Penal Code) to have the advantage of directing attention to the effect that the offender deliberately produced on the mind of the person deceived, whereas 'false pretence' makes one think of what exactly the offender did in order to deceive. 'Deception' seems also more apt in relation to deception by conduct."[1]

So far the effect of the change has not been specifically considered by the courts, and its importance has received insufficient attention from commentators. It is clear that the intention of the Act was that deception should mean any false belief implanted by the defendant in the victim's mind; and if this is so it should make no difference whether it was produced by means of a false statement or by what may generically be called a trick—provided, in either case, that the defendant committed a positive act of deception and was not guilty merely of a failure to inform. In the above examples the deception is the trick the player or gambler uses. It is not a mere omission, but a positive act of deception. If a man paints a sparrow to look like a canary and sells it as a canary, the deception is the painted sparrow; it does not matter that the seller never mentioned the word 'canary,' and we need not imagine an implied false representation that the bird is as it appears to be.

As another example, take again the question of wrong price-labels. If the customer himself

---

[1] 8th Report, Cmnd. 2977 of 1966, para. 87.

changes or alters the label, then that, coupled with the tendering of the article or the offer to purchase, is regarded as an act of deception[2]; yet it would be very forced to find a representation by the customer that he has not altered the label. His liability for deception is best rested on his deceptive act in relation to the goods.

The rule would also be sauce for the seller. If a seller takes active steps to hide a defect in an article he is selling, it has long been accepted that this "industrious concealment") can amount to fraud,[3] provided that the other party is misled.[4] But it is not easily regarded as fraud in the form of a false representation; it is fraud in the form of a trick.

The two forms of deception naturally take the names of deception by representation and deception by a trick, and in any revision of the law it would be well if these two forms were spelt out. Although this particular extension of the law seems to be socially desirable and semantically acceptable, it would be objectionably wide if the courts do not accompany it with insistence that there must be a positive act of trickery by the defendant. It should not be enough that he makes use of the opportunity provided by the misdeed of another. If a customer in a supermarket sees a small boy changing price labels, and he then takes advantage of this by himself buying the article at what he knows is less than its proper price, he should not be convicted of obtaining the article by deception, because he has not practised a deception, either himself or through an accomplice.

It may be at first sight tempting to argue some articles are so misleading that they cannot knowingly be sold without fraud, unless their deceptive nature is confessed: a letter falsely purporting to be written by Shelley, for example. The same argument may be used in respect of the switched price-labels. But the use of the forged letter can be prosecuted as using a false instrument,[5] and there is a danger of over-extending the idea of deception if it is applied to the use of false articles where the falsity is not the act of the defendant or his accomplice.[6] To maintain the principle that nondisclosure is not deception unless Parliament so provides, the courts should refrain from establishing a special department of deception for things deceptive in themselves.

§ 34.4. OBTAINING BY MEANS OF DUD CHEQUES

It was settled in the old case of *Hazelton*[1] that when a person draws a cheque he can be taken as impliedly representing that the cheque is a valid order for the payment of the amount stated.[2]

When *Hazelton* was decided there could be no representation as to intention, so the implied representation had to be worded in this way to

---

[2] *Per curiam* in *Morris* § 33.12 n. 4.

[3] As in the hilarious Irish case of *Gill* v. *McDowell* [1903] 2 IR 463, where the defendant sent to market a bullock, a heifer, and a hermaphrodite, dexterously revolving them so that the buyer thought they were all one-sexed (though he was unable to say in court whether he thought he was buying two bullocks and a heifer or two heifers and a bullock, so great was his confusion by that time).

[4] See *Cottee* v. *Douglas Seaton* (*Used Cars*) *Ltd.* [1972] 1 WLR 1408, 3 All ER 750, a case on the Trade Descriptions Act. In the civil case of *Horsfall* v. *Thomas* (1862) 1 H & C 90, 158 ER 813, the purchaser had no remedy because he did not examine the article and so was not misled by the seller's industrious concealment of a defect.

[5] § 40.6.

[6] This was another ground of decision in *Gill* v. *MacDowell,* n. 3 above: the hermaphrodite was itself a "living lie" ([1903] 2 IR at 469). *Sed quaere.*

[1] (1874) LR 2 CCR 184.

[2] Two other representions were stated: that the drawer has an account at the bank, and authority to draw on the account. The first of these is comprised in the representation that the cheque is a valid order. The second is erroneous. If the jury were directed that the drawer of a cheque represents that he has the bank's authority to draw the cheque, and that they have to decide whether the defendant in giving the cheque had that authority, it would logically be a misdirection, whatever *Hazelton* may say, because the answer is bound to be adverse to the defendant. No drawer of a cheque ever has the bank's authority to draw it. See Lord Diplock in *Charles* [1977] AC at 182E; Viscount Dilhorne, *ibid.* at 185F–186B; Lord Edmund-Davies at 190H–191C.

make it look like a representation of external fact. Since the Theft Act it is permissible to imply a general representation that the drawer intends and expects the cheque to be paid, and this is now the rational way to direct the jury.

What is the difference? If the cheque is a valid order, it will be paid.

Not necessarily. The drawer may secretly intend to stop payment or to empty his bank account after giving the cheque. The cheque is a valid order when drawn, but the drawer does not intend it to operate. Or he may give a cheque that he purposely omits to sign, hoping that the recipient will not notice; here the supposed cheque is not one at all, and so perhaps does not raise the *Hazelton* implication. In each of these cases the drawer will be guilty of deception under the general representation stated above.

In the respects just stated the *Hazelton* representation is too narrow; but sometimes it is too wide, or at any rate misleading. The cheque as presented may be an invalid order (no funds in the account and no overdraft arrangement), so that the giving of it may seem to be a breach of the *Hazelton* representation. But suppose that the drawer believes from his previous dealings with his bank that the bank will in fact allow him sufficient overdraft to honour the cheque; or suppose that he intends to pay in before the cheque is presented, or believes that a third party will pay in, so that it will be met.[3] In these circumstances the implied representation that he intends and expects the cheque to be met is true; and anyway the drawer cannot be guilty of obtaining by deception, because he is not dishonest.

In short, as Lord Reid put it, the law now is that:

> "If nothing is said to the contrary, the law implies that the giver of a cheque represents that it will be honoured"[4]

—meaning, that he represents his intention and expectation to be that it will be honoured.

These arguments suggest that the *Hazelton* representation is a misleading statement of the law and should be dropped.

The persistence of former ideas is shown by a case[5] where the question arose whether the deception offence could be committed where the defendant drew a postdated cheque on his bank. Held that it could, but the reason offered was that the giving of the cheque implied a representation that the state of facts at the date of its giving were such that it would be met on or after the date written on it. This reason is unconvincing and misses the mark. A person who gives a postdated cheque promises to meet the cheque on presentation after the stated date, but he does not warrant that he has already made arrangements for it to be met by the bank. The true reason why the cheat can be guilty under section 15 (1) notwithstanding that the cheque is postdated is the same as the reason why cheats in general are liable on dud cheques, postdated or not, namely that he does not intend to meet the cheque.

The obtaining of a cheque by deception is considered in § .7.

§ 34.5. THE FALSITY

For the deception offence to be committed, the representation must be

---

[3] That this intention prevents there being any deception was recognised in *Charles* [1977] AC at 185C, and in the court below: [1976] 1 WLR at 254G, quoting Phillimore LJ.

[4] *Turner* [1974] AC at 367. See also *Charles* [1977] AC at 182C, 186A, 191B.

[5] *Gilmartin* [1983] 2 WLR 547.

false. If it happens by accident to be true, the cheat is not guilty under section 15 (1).[1] He is guilty of an attempt to obtain by deception, and, strangely, may be guilty of theft (Chapter 35).

What about ambiguous statements?

If the utterer, like the witches in Macbeth, "palters in a double sense," intending his words to be understood in their untrue signification, it is deception.

Can't a person tell a lie if it is only a little one? A man may, to oil the wheels of a hire-purchase deal, exaggerate his weekly wage by half, or say he owns a house when he is only the tenant. Is that a crime?

In theory the law requires absolute honesty; but the police are unlikely to prosecute trivial deceptions. The examples you give are not trivial.

But surely it's all right to use a touch of blarney?

Subsection (4) implies that the deception must be as to fact or law, and there have been indulgent decisions of both the criminal and the civil courts to the effect that mere "puffery" (nebulous commendation) does not amount to a deception of fact.[2]

> Advertisers constantly suggest that a particular product will increase sexual attractiveness; they know that most people don't believe this, but some may. The law cannot take a strict view of statements that any ordinary person would realise are fanciful. Even the Trade Descriptions Act, which quite generally prohibits false trade descriptions, has been held not to be offended against by a statement that particular goods were "extra value."[3]

Although such misrepresentations of opinion are not noticed by the law, this is so only when the statement is too frothy or too obviously fanciful to be nailed down as a deception. The courts are now more ready than they formerly were to hold:

— that a statement can be one of fact even though couched in extravagant and emotive language, and

— that a person who expresses an opinion on a *particular* matter impliedly states that he does hold that opinion, so that if it is clear that he could not have held it, it will be deception.

As an example of "poetic" language being read as a statement of fact: where an unroadworthy car of pleasing appearance was described as a "beautiful car," this was held to be a false trade description because it was likely to be taken as intended to refer to the running of the car and not only to its appearance.[4]

---

[1] *Deller* (1952) 36 CAR 184.

[2] See Spencer Bower, *Actionable Misrepresentation,* 3rd edn 65–68. See this work generally on fraudulent misrepresentation.

[3] *Cadbury Ltd.* v. *Halliday* [1975] 1 WLR 649, 2 All ER 226. See, however, *Jeff* (1966) 51 CAR 28, where it was held that a representation that roof repairs had been done *and that £35 was a reasonable charge* was wholly a statement of fact, apparently because the sum indicated the extent of the repairs claimed to have heen done. *Sed quaere.*

[4] *Robertson* v. *Dicicco* [1972] Crim.LR 592, RTR 431.

Would section 15 bite where a buyer pretends that he won't give more (when he would if he had to), or a seller falsely pretends that he won't sell for less?
There is no authority, but presumably the courts would adopt the same common-sense attitude that they do in the puffery cases.

§ 34.6. (2) THE DECEPTION MUST BE DELIBERATE OR RECKLESS

This requirement is slipped into section 15 (4).[1] The deceiver must either have intended the deceit or have been reckless as to it. In cases of false representation, which are the commonest forms of deception, he must either have known that his representation was untrue or have made the representation recklessly, without knowing whether it was true or false. The word "reckless" is construed to bear a subjective meaning, so that negligence is insufficient.

That the notion of deceiving requires a mental element and is inapplicable to negligent misstatements was settled even for civil cases by the decision of the House of Lords in *Derry* v. *Peek*.[2] The point was best expressed by Lord Herschell. He conceded that a statement made recklessly, without caring whether it be true or false, forms sufficient foundation for an action in tort for deceit. But, he said,

> "to make a statement careless whether it be true or false, and therefore without any real belief in its truth, appears to me essentially different from making, through want of care, a false statement, which is nevertheless honestly believed to be true."

Such verbal confusion as may be caused by this form of statement arises from the double meaning of "careless"—knowing of the risk and running it nevertheless (recklessness) and not attaining the proper standard of care (negligence).

Lord Herschell's statement was accepted by the criminal courts in relation to the deception offence before *Caldwell*.[3] Although Lord Diplock did not address himself specifically to the question of deception in his opinion in *Caldwell*, it is reasonably clear that his opinion does not depart from the rule in *Derry* v. *Peek* for the deception offence. This is because his lordship's remarks left untouched the person who (as it was put previously[4]) positively believes that a circumstance (here, the fact falsifying his statement) does not exist. It would be remarkable if the law were otherwise, because it would mean that the criminal law of deception is more severe than the tort of deceit. Even if *Caldwell* theoretically overrides *Derry* v. *Peek* in criminal cases, two considerations make it unlikely that there will be any change in practice.

First, for a reason similar to that already advanced for rape,[5] it is probably impossible for a person who makes a statement to make it not thinking whether it is true or false. Either he consciously does not know whether it is true or false, in which case he is subjectively reckless within *Derry* v. *Peek*, or he positively knows it to be false or positively believes it to be true. There is no practical possibility of having a blank mind on the issue.

Secondly, even if it were possible to be negligently deceptive as a matter of law, the offence

---

[1] Set out in § 31.4.

[2] (1889) 14 App.Cas. 337 at 361.

[3] *Staines* (1974) 60 CAR 160. Cp. *Williams Bros. DSS Ltd* v. *Cloote* (1944) 60 TLR 270. Unfortunately, recklessness has not always been interpreted in a subjective sense in regulatory offences. See 1st edn 71–72, and particularly *MFI Warehouses Ltd* v. *Nattrass* [1973] 1 WLR 307, 1 All ER 762, for the strange interpretation of this word in the Trade Descriptions Act.

[4] § 6.6, text at nn. 3–4.

[5] § 6.6 at n. 12.

under section 15 (1) is not committed in the absence of proof of dishonesty as to the obtaining; and such proof would hardly be possible where there is merely negligence in making the false representation.[6]

As was intimated before, shady traders are normally charged under the Trade Descriptions Act, which saves the prosecution the trouble of proving knowledge or recklessness.

Suppose a cheat posts a letter containing what he knows may be an untruth, with intent to obtain money on the strength of it. Is he guilty of an attempted obtaining under section 15 (1)?

This is recklessness as to circumstances, and the legal problem was discussed in § 17.4.

Suppose that D made a statement to V which he mistakenly believed to be true when he made it. Afterwards he came to know of its untruth before obtaining property from V on the strength of it, and did nothing to reveal the true position to V.

On the authorities as they stand the question of D's liability is an open one; but the courts are quite likely to hold him liable under section 15 (1).

The legal question is whether D's representation can be regarded as continuing until it is acted upon.[7] To put the point in general terms, the acceptance of a doctrine of continuing representation would meet the situation where there is a material change of circumstances between the making of the representation and its being acted upon. The question may arise in either of two ways.

1 One, which you envisage, is where the representor mistakenly believed that his representation was true at the time when he made it, but subsequently learnt of its untruth, before accepting the property offered to him on the strength of the representation.
2 The other type of case is where the representation was in fact true when made, but subsequently the representor discovered that it had become untrue, before he received the property.

In the first of these cases the criminal act precedes (or appears to precede) the criminal state of mind. In the second case, in addition, one of the external elements of the offence (the falsity of the representation) is missing at the time when the representation is (first) made.

The difficulty of convicting under section 15 (1) may be overcome in both cases by finding that the defendant impliedly made a representation by continuing or renewed conduct of some sort. For the purpose of deciding whether such an implication can be made it is convenient to distinguish two types of case: where D co-operated in receiving the property after coming to know the truth (we may call this, for short,

---

[6] Cp. *Lewis* [1976] Crim.LR 383, where the rule that reasonableness was not in issue was derived not from the concept of recklesness but from that of dishonesty. However, it must be borne in mind that the dishonesty required for the offence in s. 15 (1) relates to the obtaining, not to the question whether the representation was true or false.

[7] A loose use of the phrase "continuing representation" may be noticed, but it has no bearing on the present discussion. The courts sometimes say that a fraudulent representation "continues" until it is acted upon, when all that they mean is that the victim may act upon the representation after a lapse of time.

bilateral obtaining), and where he was merely sent it by V and passively received it (unilateral obtaining).

In bilateral obtaining D (for example) goes to V to receive the property at his hands. Here the probability is strong that the jury would be encouraged to find an implied representation by D at the time of the obtaining, reaffirming his previous representation. Since at that time he knew the truth, he would be guilty of obtaining by deception.

The leading case is *Ray* v. *Sempers,*[8] which turned on evading a debt by deception, a statutory offence that has since been superseded by other offences with different wording.[9]

> A student, Ray, entered a restaurant and ordered a meal with honest intent. After consuming it he decided to "bilk" the restaurant. He remained at the table for ten minutes till the waiter disappeared, then fled. The House of Lords held by a majority that he had evaded the debt by deception, the deception consisting in sitting at the table till the waiter turned his back. While Ray was sitting at the table the waiter assumed he was honest and did not press for payment or call the police; this assumption was false, was deliberately caused by Ray, and was a deception.

The actual decision has been greatly reduced in importance by the change in the law already mentioned. In relation to a charge under section 15 (1) it would of course be found that a diner makes a new representation of honesty with each order. If he gives his whole order before the meal, and begins the meal honestly but decides not to pay after drinking the soup and before getting to the roast, the court would be very likely to hold that he impliedly represents his continuing honest intention on the acceptance of each dish.

In the second type of case, unilateral obtaining, D makes a representation to obtain property, discovers its falsity afterwards, does nothing, and accepts the property from the postman or other carrier when it is delivered to him. Here a representation cannot be implied when D accepts delivery (since he is not then in immediate communication with V, and it is impossible for an implied representation to come to the knowledge of V); and the stark question is whether D's representation is deemed to continue as a matter of law. In *Ray* v. *Sempers* three lords out of five were against a fiction of continuing representation as a matter of law, and the decision of the majority affirming the conviction was based on the fact that the parties were face to face.[10] On the other hand, there are civil cases upholding a doctrine of continuous representation, and a line between bilateral and unilateral obtaining is a somewhat unsatisfactory basis of distinguishing between criminal liability *vel non*.

Supposing that the fiction of continuing representation is not recognised for the purpose of section 15 (1), it may still be held that the representor

---

[8] [1974] AC 370.
[9] § 40.1.
[10] See 1st edn 759–760.

who accepts the property after coming to know of the falsity of his representation is guilty of theft. The way in which the law of theft supplements deception will be considered in the next chapter.

34.7. (3) THERE MUST BE PROPERTY BELONGING TO ANOTHER

For the most part, the deception offence is similar to theft in respect of the property involved. The definition of "property" is generally the same. And one can obtain by deception from a possessor, just as one can steal from a possessor.

The only difference is that whereas land cannot generally be stolen, this exception is not stated for the deception offence. Consequently, it is an offence under section 15 (l) to obtain a conveyance of the fee simple in (ownership of) land by deception, or to obtain the possession of land by deception if there is an intent to deprive the owner permanently.

A doubt arises in regard to leases obtained by deception. Can it be said that this is not an offence of obtaining *land* (or possession of land) by deception, because the deceiver intends that the land shall be restored at the end of the lease (even though it be in a hundred or a thousand years' time)? Or, on the contrary, is it to be said that this in an offence of obtaining the *lease* by deception, since the lease is an estate in land which the deceiver intends to get outright, even though the land is to go back at the end of it? The point has not been judicially considered in this country.[1] It is another example of the artificial questions that are apt to arise on the meaning of the intent to deprive the owner permanently. The sensible course for the prosecutor is to charge an offence of obtaining an act (the execution of the lease) by deception under the Act of 1978 (§ .11).

Obtaining a contract is not obtaining property. A debt is a thing in action, and therefore property, but this does not mean that the use of deception to obtain a contract under which money will be owed is an offence under section 15 (l). It will amount to the consummated offence only when the money is received. Debts as such come within section 15 (l) only if there is a pre-existing debt that is obtained—that is, where deception is used to persuade a creditor to assign a debt to the cheat.[2]

> D writes a letter to a friend making false statements in order to persuade his friend to lend him money. If the friend responds by sending D a cheque, this is a valuable piece of paper which is clearly property under the section. But the friend may go to the bank and fill in a credit transfer slip which has the effect of transferring "a sum of money" from his bank account to D's account. What is transferred to D is neither a piece of paper nor a physical sum but a notional sum. What D receives is the transfer of a thing in action—an assignment of part of the bank's debt to the friend so that the bank owes it to D.[3] This debt is property, and the offence can be charged under section 15 (1) as an obtaining of property, namely a credit in the bank account. In the same way, the obtaining of a cheque can be charged as an obtaining of a thing in action when the cheque is credited.[4] Or the deception may be charged as deception to obtain the execution of a valuable security.[5]

---

[1] The CA of Hong Kong took the first view in 1981; see the discussion by J C Smith in [1981] Crim.LR 498, making the additional point that the leasehold interest did not exist before the defendant obtained it.

[2] Cp. the similar point on theft: § 33.3.

[3] The assignment is voidable by the assignor on account of the fraud, but it operates as an assignment before it is avoided.

[4] Cp. § 33.11.

[5] § 40.8.

§ 34.8. (4) THE DEFENDANT MUST OBTAIN THE PROPERTY

The aim of section 15 (1) is to punish deceptions made to obtain property (ownership, possession or control); it does not touch deceptions that are known to cause a loss to the victim without resulting in some obtaining of property by the defendant or another.

> A man makes various applications for unit trusts, taking them up when they afterwards show a profit but breaking his contract to take them when they show a loss. He commits no offence under section 15 (1).[1] His dishonesty is solely in relation to the performance of a contract. (However, if two people work such a scheme in combination, instead of doing it separately, they are quite possibly guilty of a conspiracy to defraud.)

If the defendant has obtained property, the offence can be committed even though the obtaining caused no loss to the other party. The other party may, for example, have been insured against loss by fraud. Or he may be guaranteed against loss when he accepts a credit card or a cheque backed by a cheque card.[2]

The offence is committed if the defendant obtains ownership; but he need not do so. It is sufficient if he obtains possession or control (s. 15 (2)).

Triangular situations are covered: the deception may be of one person while the property belongs to another.

> A common situation is where a customer in a supermarket deceives the cashier and so obtains the supermarket's property. The customer is guilty of obtaining the supermarket's property by deception.

Under section 15 (2) it is sufficient if another person is enable to obtain the property. Putting the two rules together, we see that an offence of deception under section 15 (1) as extended by section 15 (2) may involve four people, namely where D defrauds A in such a way that B transfers property to C.

Section 15 (2) applies the offence where D uses deception to enable another person to *retain* property belonging to another that he has already obtained. It is not clear why this situation is provided for, while no such provision is made for the case where D uses deception to enable *himself* to retain goods. However, D in the latter case will generally be guilty of theft. He will also, it seems, be guilty of obtaining by deception if, being in possession of someone else's goods, he uses deception to obtain the ownership.

§ 34.9. (5) THE OBTAINING MUST BE BY THE DECEPTION

The little word "by" in section 15 (1) carries a weight of meaning. It is held that even if there has been a deception, and property has been obtained, the defendant is not guilty under the subsection unless there was a causal nexus between the deception and the obtaining.

The rule means that the deception must affect the victim's behaviour. Lord Roskill said in *Lambie*[1]: "the Crown must always prove its case and

---

[1] So ruled in *Reinhart* (1976) The Times, Sept. 23. It would probably be an offence under s.20 (2) (§ 40.8).

[2] See *Lambie* § .2 at n. 9, and § .9.

[1] *Lambie* [1982] AC at 461D.

one element which will always be required to be proved is the effect of the dishonest representation upon the mind of the person to whom it is made."

Does that mean that if a man tells a cock-and-bull story to get another to send him money, and the other "rumbles" him but sends money for the pleasure of getting him convicted, a charge of obtaining money by deception will fail?

Yes[2]; but the cheat is guilty of an attempt to obtain by deception. It is conceivable, as we shall see in § 35.4, that he may even be guilty of theft by receiving the money dishonestly; but there is a strong argument the other way.

Does the requirement of a causal nexus mean that the victim must always give evidence that he relied on the truth of the representation?

It is desirable that he should be asked the question in evidence, but this is not essential if "it is patent that there was only one reason which anybody could suggest for the person alleged to have been defrauded parting with his money, and that is the false pretence."[3]

Must it be found as a fact that the victim believed the statement to be true?

That would be too narrow a rule. The victim may be doubtful about the truth of the representation, but he may give the representor the benefit of the doubt. It can still be held that the victim relied on the statement.

If on the other hand the person to whom the statement was made testifies in court that although he believed the statement he was not actuated by it, and would have parted with the property even if the false statement had not been made, no offence under section 15 (1) is made out. Counsel for the defence should always cross-examine the alleged victim of the offence to try to get him to make an admission of this sort, if the facts suggest that such an admission may be forthcoming.[4] The victim may, for example, admit that when he bought the article from the defendant he was so anxious to have it that he did not care whether a statement made by the defendant about the article was true or false.

Reverting to Lambie,[5] I have been asking myself the question whether the victim must have thought of the possibility of the representation being false. The Mothercare manager probably did not consider that Lambie might be beyond her credit limit. As the manager said, it did not concern her whether she was or wasn't. If the manager did not consider it, can one say that Lambie's assumed false representation affected the manager's state of mind?

The cases do not discuss your problem, but the answer probably is that the victim need not have adverted to the question whether the representation was true or false—provided that, as already said, there is evidence that the victim would not have parted with the property if he had known the truth. (This supposes, of course, that there is a false representation.)

---

[2] *Mills* (1857) 7 Cox 263, 1 Dears. & Bell 205, 169 ER 978, a decision under the pre-Act law. Cp.*Hensler* (1870) 11 Cox 570.

[3] *Per* Humphreys J, quoted with approval by Lord Roskill in *Lambie* [1982] AC at 461C.

[4] See, e.g. *Royle* [1971] 1 WLR at 1771; *Edwards* [1978] Crim.LR 49.

[5] § .2 n. 9.

Lord Roskill, in the statement quoted at the beginning, said that the false representation must have an effect on the victim's mind; but, as you suggest, this may be difficult to discern if the victim paid no attention to the question whether the representation was true or not. For this reason it may be better to say that the false representation must have an effect on the victim's *behaviour*. The governing consideration presumably is how the victim would have behaved if he had known the truth. If, had he known the truth, he would not have given up the property, it follows that the false representation affected, if not the victim's mind, at least his behaviour.

But the Mothercare manager said that she would not worry about what went on between the customer and Barclaycard. Yet Lambie was convicted of evading a debt by deception. How then was it proved that Lambie's assumed representation affected the manager's behaviour?

Your question points to another criticism of the decision.

Lord Roskill, who in effect delivered the judgment of the House of Lords, dealt with the matter in this way.

> "If she [Miss Rounding, the departmental manager of Mothercare] had been asked whether, had she known the respondent was acting dishonestly and, in truth, had no authority whatever from the bank to use the credit card in this way, she (Miss Rounding) would have completed the transaction, only one answer is possible—no. Had an affirmative answer been given to this question, Miss Rounding would, of course, have become a participant in furtherance of the respondent's fraud and a conspirator with her to defraud both Mothercare and the bank."

The last sentence is mistakenly phrased. Miss Rounding's affirmative answer to a hypothetical question in court would not have made her guilty of conspiracy to defraud the bank or anyone else, though it may be true that her actual supply of the goods with knowledge of Lambie's fraud would have done so. Even the last proposition is not certain. A conspiracy to defraud requires proof of the defendant's dishonesty, and if the shop's agreement with the bank exempted it from any responsibility in respect of the customer's credit standing with the bank, it would, one would have thought, be impossible to prove dishonesty on the part of the manager in standing on the literal terms of the agreement. In any case, the question is not what Miss Rounding should have done but what she would have done. Whatever the strict legal position was, Miss Rounding might in fact have taken the view that even her actual knowledge that Lambie was exceeding her credit limit would be of no concern to her. She was not asked about it when she gave evidence. Lord Roskill said that Miss Rounding could not be expected to remember the particular transaction in detail, but no feat of memory was called for. Miss Rounding could have been asked the hypothetical question how she would have acted if she had known the facts; and she was not asked it. It was not a case of her not remembering the facts. In the absence of evidence on the point, there was a real possibility that Miss Rounding might have acted in the same way whether she knew the truth or not, and it should therefore have been held that the causal connection between the deception and the evasion of the debt was not made out.

The conclusion upon this aspect of the decision in *Lambie* is that it proceeded upon a particular (and highly questionable) view of the facts, and neither purported to, nor does, affect the established rule that the deception must operate upon the victim's mind or otherwise affect his behaviour.

The question whether a fraud affects the mind has arisen also in cases of "pirate selling."

Doukas[6] was another case of "pirate selling." A waiter was found carrying to his place

[6] [1978] 1 WLR 372. Cp. *Rashid* [1977] 1 WLR 298, 2 All ER 237, 64 CAR 201, where there was a misdirection.

> of employment wine that he intended to sell to his employer's customers under the pretence that it belonged to the employer. He was convicted of going equipped to cheat,[7] that is to say to obtain money by deception; and the conviction was upheld on appeal. The Court of Appeal scouted the notion that the customers might not have cared who supplied the wine they were consuming, the probability being that they would have objected to taking part in a "fiddle." (Even if Doukas had thought that some customers might not object if they were told the truth, he was reckless as to whether they would have objected or not.)

This decision was on the particular offence of "going equipped." If Doukas had been charged with obtaining money from the customers by deception, it should have been necessary to put a customer into the witness-box to say that he would not have bought the wine if he had known the facts. This evidence would have been enough for conviction, since Doukas was clearly reckless on the matter.

The requirement of causation inevitably involves problems on indirect causation. To some extent, the offence of obtaining by deception covers an obtaining that is not the direct result of the deception. As we have seen, the offence is committed if D deceives V1 with the dishonest purpose that property shall be obtained (by himself or another) from V2, the scheme succeeding in this respect.

Suppose a person gets a job by falsely stating his qualifications. Could he be convicted of getting his pay by deception?

The only judicial authority directly in point is *Lewis.*[8] This is a case of low authority (it was only a trial at assizes), but it has had significant results.

> The facts were that a woman obtained a post as a schoolmistress through a forged teacher's certificate. It was ruled that she had not obtained her *salary* by false pretences; the salary was paid in return for her services.

Yet Lewis would not have got the job, and consequently her salary, if it had not been for the pretence. Her object in making the pretence was to get the salary. Assuming, as is likely, that the employer would not have made her any payment of salary if the lie had not been operating on his mind, there was certainly a factual causal connection between the lie and the obtaining of salary. Why should it not be a causal connection in law?

Whatever the answer may be, the point has become largely theoretical because in the unlikely event of a charge being made it would now be for the specific offence of obtaining a pecuniary advantage by deception (§ 40.2). But the relevant part of this provision is confined to deception to obtain an "office or employment" (or an increase of pay), and it is not clear that deception to obtain a building contract, say, is covered. So in that respect the doubt created by *Lewis* as to the ambit of section 15 (1) remains a practical issue.

Isn't the point that the employer who is deceived into giving a job gets something for his money, namely the services of the employee? And the employer of the building contractor gets the building.

Well, suppose that a man peddles Christmas cards saying that all the

---

[7] For this offence see § 38.6.

[8] (1922) Somerset Assizes, Russell on *Crime*, 12th edn ii 1186 n.

profits go to charity. Would you hold that he is not guilty of obtaining money by deception, notwithstanding that he had no intention of giving the profits to charity, merely because he does in fact supply the cards? Again, suppose a man obtains a local authority mortgage by falsely pretending to be a first time buyer. His false representation does not go to his ability to repay, or to any other financial matter, but should he not be convicted? The proper principle is that where deception is used to obtain a loan of money or to sell goods, the offence is committed notwithstanding that the representation does not affect the commercial return that the victim is getting. In *Potger*[9]:

> a doorstep seller of magazines overcame sales resistance by falsely saying that he was a student and was taking part in a competition. He was convicted of obtaining property (subscriptions for the magazines) by deception, and the conviction was upheld on appeal.

No argument was advanced that there was no obtaining by deception because it was Potger's intention that the householders would receive the magazines.[10] They might have got the magazines, but they would not have entered into the contract but for the prior deception. Consequently, there was an obtaining by deception.[11]

This decision was clearly right. The deception used by Potger was not of a particularly serious character; but it would be unsatisfactory if the law of deception could not reach the aforementioned fraudulent seller of Christmas cards. Yet the Christmas card swindle could not be punished without adopting a principle fundamentally inconsistent with that in *Lewis. Potger* shows that deception can be committed even though the victim obtains economic value for his money, and, since *Lewis* denies that, and is of inferior authority, it must be wrongly decided.

Notwithstanding the logical objections to it, *Lewis* has been taken to settle the law in respect of remuneration for services, and the same principle has been extended to betting cases.

> In *Clucas*[12] it was held that a false representation made in order to induce a bookmaker to accept a bet did not found a charge of obtaining the winnings by false pretences (under the old law): the bookmaker had paid out the winnings because the punter won. On the other hand, cases on false statements made to secure entry to a race have been decided against the cheat; here the cheat who won the race

---

[9] (1970) 55 CAR 42.

[10] It seems that the magazines were not in fact supplied because Potger was arrested before he gave the orders to his firm. But the court said that "there is no suggestion that the magazines in question would not have been worth the money once the order had been given and they had been delivered in due course; which this court assumes would have happened."

[11] A similar decision was reached after argument in the High Court of Australia: *Balcombe* v. *Desimoni* [1972] ALR 513.

[12] [1949] 2 KB 226.

and received a prize was convicted of obtaining the prize by false pretences.[13]

The specific facts of *Clucas*, as of *Lewis*, can now be charged as an obtaining of a pecuniary advantage by deception (§ 40.3). Also, Clucas was later convicted of an offence of fraud in wagering under the Gaming Act 1845 s. 17.[14] Where two persons conspire to do as Lewis and Clucas did,they can be charged with conspiracy to defraud.

Can you deceive a machine—for example, by putting a false token into a parking meter?

The whole law of deception is geared to the deception of humans, and it would radically alter the concept if the courts extended it to the "deception" of machinery or electronic gadgets. Happily, the courts have not so far shown a disposition to take this step.[15] Very possibly we need a new offence of falsely manipulating computers and other machines, but it should be done by legislation. Obtaining goods from a vending machine by dishonest means can be charged as theft, and your car park deceiver might be convicted of theft of the ticket if the machine produces one. Alternatively, he might be convicted of making off without having paid (§ 40.1). Interference with road parking meters is a statutory offence.[16]

§ 34.10. (6) THE OBTAINING MUST BE DISHONEST, AND BE ACCOMPANIED BY AN INTENTION TO DEPRIVE THE OWNER PERMANENTLY

The requirement of an intention to deprive permanently has been sufficiently discussed in relation to theft. It means that a person who obtains the hire of a car by deception, intending to return the car at the end of the hiring, cannot be convicted under section 15 (1), though, as we shall see in § .11, he can generally be convicted of obtaining services by deception.

It has already been pointed out[1] that, to come within the subsection, the deception must be deliberate or reckless. Superimposed upon this is the requirement of dishonesty in obtaining the property. This has already been partly considered,[2] but a few points remain.

---

[13] *Button* [1900] 2 QB 597; *Lambassi* [1927] VLR 349 (Victoria). In the latter case the cheat obtained no advantage from his deception other than the opportunity of competing.

§ .3. See *Clucas* and *O'Rourke* [1959] 1 WLR 244, 1 All ER 438, following *Leon* [1945] KB 136. Both cases have been criticised on the ground that the doctrine of causal connection should be applied under the Gaming Act (see Law Commission, *Working Paper No.* 56, p. 16); but I do not follow the criticism. Even if it has some force in relation to the earlier part of the section (relating to "fraud in playing at" a game), it does not apply to the later part quoted in § .3.

S. 17 of the Gaming Act is restricted in its terms and would not apply, say, to a bet on an election. For decisions upon it, see Halsbury's *Statutes,* 3rd edn 14 : 528.

[14] § .3.

[15] See the dicta in *Davies* v. *Flackett* [1973] RTR 8, [1972] Crim.LR 708; Lamming in 122 NLJ 627; J C Smith in 69 LSG 576; Samuels in 146 JPN 173. Cp. *Cooper* [1979] Crim.LR 42. L H Leigh suggests in 38 MLR 321 that "deception of a machine" can be a deception of the "programmer," but the answer is that the deception does not reach his mind.

[16] Road Traffic Regulation Act 1967 ss. 31 (3), 42 (4).

[1] § .6.

[2] § 32.5 at n. 17.

The defendant's intention to pay for the property obtained by deception, and indeed his actual payment for it, do not necessarily negative dishonesty. Where, for example, a person obtains goods on a dud cheque, intending to pay for them later and knowing that he will be able to do so, it would be quite wrong if he were regarded as honest. Perhaps, since cases like *Ghosh*,[3] the question would have to be left to the jury, but it would be far better if the courts held that on such facts there is no evidence on which a reasonable jury can find honesty.

Where the victim was moved to enter into the transaction in whole or in part by non-economic considerations, the fact that the deceiver intended to render him the full economic advantage will not negative dishonesty.

> This is again illustrated by *Potger,*[4] the case of the fraudulent salesman of magazines. During the summing up the recorder failed to direct the jury on the necessity for dishonesty, and assumed that every deliberate falsehood involved dishonesty under section 15 (1). An appeal against conviction was dismissed, but only by an application of "the proviso."

In justifying this course, the court said that there were cases of deception (of which this was one) that could not have been made otherwise than dishonestly. This was a slip; it ignored the point already made, that the question is not the dishonesty of the deception but the dishonesty of the obtaining. The court's misunderstanding vitiates its consequential suggestion that a false statement is necessarily dishonest if made deliberately, but not if it was made recklessly. In fact an obtaining may or may not be dishonest irrespective of the question whether the deception was intentional or reckless.

Apart from certain special considerations to be mentioned in a moment, it would have been better to dismiss the appeal on the ground that an evidential burden of honesty rested on the defendant, and that he had adduced no facts to discharge the burden. Alternatively, the proviso might have been invoked not for the reason given but on the ground that even though an evaluative fact was not left to the jury, this is not fatal to a conviction if no reasonable jury, properly instructed, could have found in favour of the defendant. Both these methods of saving the situation were discussed previously in connection with dishonesty in theft.[5]

Two other remarks may be made about the case. (1) Part of Potger's defence was that such lies were commonly told by fellow-salesmen. Conceivably, this might have been regarded as sufficient evidence of honesty to take the issue to the jury. On the other hand, it is obviously no evidence of honesty that other rascals are operating in the same way as the defendant; what is needed is evidence that the defendant was or believed himself to be honest according to "the current standards of ordinary decent people." The practices of self-interested persons like the defendant himself can hardly suffice. (2) Although the jury must have found that the victim would not have entered into the contract if it had not been for the deception, the report does not state what evidence there was to support this conclusion. It could not be sustained unless the victim said in evidence, and was believed in saying, that he would not have contracted if it had not been for the deception.

Another example of the general proposition stated before, that an intention to make economic recompense need not negative dishonesty, is the type of case where a waiter (or rail steward) dishonestly sells his own food or drink to his employer's customers, pocketing the proceeds. It is not certain in advance whether a particular customer would object to the fraud if he came to know of it, but the waiter intends to conceal the facts and may be held to be

---

[3] § 32.5 at n. 15.
[4] § .9 at n. 9.
[5] § 32.5 at n. 16.

reckless whether the customer would object or not. He can therefore be found to be dishonest.[6]

Again, a person who by deception obtains an advance of money to which he knows he is not entitled can be convicted under section 15 (1) even though he intends to repay.

> In *Halstead* v. *Patel,*[7] the holder of a Post Office Giro account (Patel) drew a cheque on it in return for cash received at the Post Office counter, knowing that the account was not in funds and that he was not allowed to draw on it. It was held that if Patel had intended to put funds into the account before the cheque was presented, this intention might negative dishonesty; but since his intention was to get the money and on]y later to repay by paying into the account, he was guilty of obtaining by deception, notwithstanding that he would have had no difficulty later on in putting the account into credit.

The case illustrates the fact that an intention to make delayed recompense may not negative dishonesty, where immediate recompense (in this case, by putting a credit into the account) is required.

But you said that the dishonesty of the representation does not matter if the obtaining was honest.[8] Patel was honest in respect of the obtaining, because he intended to repay.

What the CLRC understood by its own legislative proposal was that if the obtaining is under a claim of right, the dishonesty of the deception does not matter. Patel had no claim of right. He knew that he was breaking the rules.

It isn't a question of claim of right. It's a question of honesty.

Yes: the CLRC did not expect the new word to be interpreted so much more laxly than the old phrase.

Halstead v. *Patel* came before magistrates, who must do as they are told by a Divisional Court; and that court was clear that Patel acted dishonestly. A Divisional Court would doubtless take the same view at the present day.[9] If on the other hand the case had come before a jury, the jury would presumably have been given free rein. Before the Theft Act the law was clear that an intention to repay money improperly taken did not generally give a claim of right. Persons were convicted of obtaining property by false pretences when they had obtained advances by deliberately overstating the value of their business, notwithstanding that they genuinely believed that

---

[6] See *Doukas,* § 34.9 n. 6. On a prosecution of the waiter under s. 15 (1) it would be wise to get the customer to give evidence that he would not have parted with his money had he not believed that the article supplied belonged to the employer. See § .9.

[7] [1972] 1 WLR 661, 2 A11 ER 147, 56 CAR 334. The court required the defendant's belief that he could meet the cheque to be "based on reasonable grounds," but this was corrected in *Lewis* (1975) 62 CAR 206. Reasonableness has nothing to do with dishonesty, except to the usual extent that absence of reasonable grounds is evidence of non-belief.

[8] § 32.5 at n. 17.

[9] This prognostication is supported by the fact that *Halstead* v. *Patel* was cited by the court in *Feely* with approval.

the investors would not lose their money[10]; and this is socially right. Developments since the Theft Act, however, show that juries will be allowed to loosen the law.

§ 34.11. OBTAINING SERVICES BY DECEPTION

Two particular deficiencies in section 15 (obtaining property by deception) are that it does not cover obtaining the hiring of property, or the supply of services, by deception. Therefore, it fails to provide, or to provide adequately, for the various instances of what is popularly called "bilking;" bilking a restaurant, a hotel, the railway, a taxi-driver, a car-hire firm and so on. (In the first two cases, the restaurant and the hotel, there is an obtaining of food, but prosecutors naturally feel that this does not express the real offence.) After some legislative vicissitudes bilking is now covered by the Theft Act 1978 section 1.[1]

> "(1) A person who by any deception dishonestly obtains services from another shall be guilty of an offence.
>
> It is an obtaining of services where the other is induced to confer a benefit by doing some act, or causing or permitting some act to be done, on the understanding that the benefit has been or will be paid for."

The offence, like that under section 15 (1), is triable either way.[2] Some elements of the two offences are similar: the deception[3]; the dishonesty; and the causal connection between the deception and the obtaining. The requirement of deception means that if a person sneaks into a cinema through the exit door, in order to view a film without paying, he commits no offence.[4]

I don't understand the reference to services. Is the offence about obtaining services, or not?

The word "services" is used only as a popular summary of the offence; it is legally superfluous since it does not control the operation of the section. The offence might better have been called "obtaining an act by deception." One does not have to enquire whether the act is "services" in the ordinary meaning of the term, and, conversely, an act is not covered merely because it amounts to services in the ordinary meaning.

The wide definition of "services" means that the offence covers the obtaining of an article or premises for temporary use by way of hiring or tenancy. The offence, unlike that under section 15 (1), does not require an intent to deprive the owner permanently of anything.

---

[10] *Hamilton* (1845) 1 Cox 244, *Carpenter* (1911) 22 Cox 618.

[1] For Northern Ireland see Theft (NI) Order, SI 1978 No. 1407.
[2] But the maximum punishment is 5 years.
[3] s. 5 (1) defines this in the same way as in section 15 of the Theft Act 1968.
[4] See J R Spencer in [1979] Crim.LR 26 n. 11.

Suppose a man hires a car. He pays the hiring charge, but, having no driving licence, shows a licence belonging to someone else. Any offence?

What you are asking is whether the deception must relate to the promise of payment. Section 1 is aimed against deception in general, not just pecuniary deceptions. The reference to payment in subsection (2) is made part of the definition of services, not of deception. Consequently, D in your question offends against the section.

The following are further illustrations showing that the defendant need not act for financial gain.

D hires a hall saying that it is for a Church of England group; actually he intends it for a meeting of the National Front.
D signs into a hotel during an epidemic, falsely denying that he has been in contact with the disease.
D jumps the queue for a council house by lying about his needs.

In all these cases an offence is committed, provided that the jury or magistrates find dishonesty.

But can the defendant be found to have been dishonest, if he has made payment in full?

No reason why not. The defendant was dishonest in getting services by a lie. If the Act had intended to confine deceptions to those relating to the other's prospect of being paid, it would have said so. All that the section requires is that the transaction should have been a commercial one.

Is it "services" to let a room without service? Does a theatre or museum provide services?

Yes, for the purpose of the Act. "Services" in subsection (1) is simply a joker word, standing only for the notion defined in subsection (2). It is narrower than the usual meaning of "services" because it does not cover gratuitous services. It is wider because it covers much conduct that would not ordinarily be described as performing a service. If the definition in subsection (2) were to be construed as confined to services in the ordinary meaning of the term, there would hardly have been any need for the subsection.

When a guest books into a hotel and his name is entered by the clerk accordingly, the guest obtains services under the definition in subsection (2), namely the act of writing his name in the book. This is a benefit, because the room is now booked for the guest; and it makes no difference that the guest is arrested the moment afterwards, and taken off to reside in a police cell. He has, in the eye of the law, obtained the services. (There is no significance in the fact that the section speaks of services in the plural; a single act is clearly covered.[5])

The "services" under subsection (2) are a benefit conferred in any of three ways.

1 *By the doing of some act.* The obvious examples are where a repairer repairs a customer's shoes and where a taxi carries a passenger. But the courts will probably find a benefit whenever a desired act has been done, as in the previous example of booking into a hotel.

---

[5] Why it was thought necessary to use the plural has not been stated. The judge will have to explain to the jury, if a charge is brought under both ss. 1 and 3 (see as to the latter § 40.1), that although s. 1 uses "services" and s. 3 uses "service," they both cover the singular and the plural.

Another example would be the hiring of a car. The important "service" here is permitting the car to be driven away; but giving the cheat the keys of the car, or even entering his name in the book as the hirer (thus creating a contract of hiring), would doubtless be a service with the peculiar meaning of the Act.

Further removed from the ordinary notion of "services," but still within the definition, would be the case where a thief pays a stolen cheque into his own bank account (perhaps forging an endorsement). He can be convicted under section 1 (1), since in crediting the thief's account the bank does an act, and the thief obtains a benefit because he can draw on the account if his deception is not discovered.

Even non-contractual acts (acts not intended to be part of the making or performance of a contract) can be brought within section 1.

> Suppose that D, a debtor, offers his creditor payment of the debt in cash, and writes out a receipt, which the creditor signs. D then goes off with the receipt and without paying. He has obtained the benefit of an act by deception, and is within the 1978 Act, but, since it is his own paper, he has not offended against section 15 (1) of the 1968 Act.

2 *By causing some act to be done*. This makes it plain that the act previously referred to need not be done by the person deceived. D by deception induces V to cause V's employee to do an act for D; V's employee may not know of the deception, but the case is within the statute.

3 *By permitting some act to be done*, as when a lodging-house keeper permits a new tenant to take up occupation, or a theatre or museum permits a person to enter.

What about conferring a benefit by omitting to do something?

The section does not apply.[6] A debtor who by deception persuades his creditor not to press for payment, promising to pay an extra sum by way of interest in consideration of being allowed time to pay, does not offend against section 1, though, as we shall see, he will in one particular case offend against section 2 (1) (*b*) (§ 40.1).

I now don't see why the section introduced the notion of benefit. Wouldn't the effect have been the same if it had simply referred to the victim doing an act, etc., without mentioning the question of benefit?

It seems that the requirement of benefit has little practical effect, because in almost every case where the victim has been induced to do an act etc. the defendant (or someone else, because it need not be the defendant) will be seen to have obtained a benefit. But some instances can be put in which it would presumably be held that a benefit has not been obtained, because the act in question is purely preparatory.

The benefit need not be of an ordinary commercial or transferable kind. A man who obtains the services of a prostitute by deception undoubtedly commits an offence under the Act.

But not if he obtains the consent of a non-prostitute by deception?

Quite. The Act limited itself to paid services because legislation designed primarily for the protection of property and transactions should not cover offences against the person.

The final words of subsection (2) require an understanding on the part of the victim that the benefit he conferred "has been or will be paid for." "Paid for" implies a payment in money or its legal equivalent (e.g. payment by cheque or credit card). A promise to transfer property other

---

[6] See Syrota in 42 MLR at 302–303.

than money (so-called "payment in kind") is not a promise of payment for legal purposes.

If no question of payment enters into the transaction, it cannot constitute an offence under section 1.

> D, a newspaper reporter, poses as a visitor in order to gain entrance to a hospital to interview a nurse. He is not guilty under the section.
> Nor is a person guilty under the section if he deceives a civil servant into giving a Government licence (like an export licence when that is required), if no payment is expected. If the licence is in writing, the offence can be charged as deception under section 15 (1) to obtain the licence as a piece of paper. When there is a plot involving two people they can be charged with conspiracy to deceive a public officer in relation to his exercise of legal authority. But a single person who gets by deception an oral Government licence for which no payment is to be made commits no offence, except where a statute creates a specific offence of fraud or false statement.[7]

On the other hand, the payment need not be due under an enforceable contract (recall the hypothetical of deceiving a prostitute).[8] Again, the subsection does not require that the payment should be made, or expected to be made, by the defendant. If a cheat books in at a hotel saying that his company will pay, this can come within the Act.

There is no reason why the supposed payment should be specifically for the particular service, if it is for matters included in the service. So the provision would cover the case where a cheat obtains entry to club premises, or the services of the AA or RAC, by falsely pretending to be a paid-up member.

The victim's understanding that the services have been paid for will generally be a mistaken understanding. However, these final words in the subsection are not limited to cases of mistaken belief as to payment. They also embrace cases where the victim rightly knows that he has been paid, if the deception is as to some matter other than payment. If the service is provided on the understanding that it has been or will be paid for, the fact that it has been paid for is immaterial. This may not at first be obvious on reading the section, but it is the clear meaning of the words. The reference to payment, let us repeat, was introduced only in order to give the offence a property or economic connotation, not for the purpose of confining it to financial frauds.

SUMMARY

The Theft Act s. 15 (4) brings in deceptions as to intention, and presumably as to belief as well. A buyer who intends not to pay for what he gets may be found to have deceived the seller as to his state of mind, whether the transaction was intended to be for cash or on credit. The illegality of what the defendant promises is no defence. A deception as to future facts may be punished either because it involves a deception as to intention or because future facts involve present facts. § .1

Mere silence is not enough, but a false representation may be implied from conduct, with the familiar division of functions between judge and jury. The jury may find an implied representation as to title. The jury may find that a person who presents a cheque card or credit card impliedly represents that he is not exceeding his credit limit with the bank, notwithstanding that the representee has no financial interest in the question. § .2

---

[7] Among specific offences may be mentioned abuse of parking facilities for disabled people by using orange badges under false pretences (Disabled Persons Act 1981 s. 2), and escaping the consequences of endorsable offences by deception (Transport Act 1981 s. 21).

[8] See Syrota in 42 MLR at 303–304.

Since the Theft Act there is no need to find a false representation as the basis of deception, because a trick aimed to deceive should have the same effect; but the point has not come before the courts. § .3

The drawer of a cheque makes (or can be found to make) two representations: that the cheque is a valid order for the payment of the amount, and that he intends it to be honoured, but only the second of these is necessary to give efficacy to the law. § .4

The representation must be false, but mere puffery does not amount to a deception of fact. § .5

The deception must be deliberate or reckless, and recklessness (either in theory or as a matter of practice) must mean subjective recklessness. If a person makes a statement that he then believes to be true, and afterwards (before obtaining property on the strength of it) either the statement becomes untrue or he discovers for the first time that it was untrue, and yet receives the property without taking an opportunity of correcting his statement, he will probably be held guilty under s. 15 (1), on the basis that the representation was continuing. § .6

The offence must relate to the property of another, and "property" for this purpose includes land. § .7

The defendant must obtain the property (whether ownership, possession or control), or he must enable a third person to do so. It is sufficient that he enables a third person to retain property, but not that he enables himself to retain it. § .8

The obtaining must be by the deception. This means that the deception must affect the victim's mind or behaviour in causing him to yield the property. The victim should give evidence of this, but the evidence is not essential if it is the only reason for his conduct that can be suggested. He need not have believed the statement to be true, but must not have known that it was false. He need not, it seems, have considered the question whether it was true or false. The prevailing view is that deception to obtain a contract does not mean that remuneration under the contract is obtained by deception (*Lewis*). But this is not altogether easy to reconcile with *Potger*. On principle there can be no deception of a machine. § .9

The obtaining must be dishonest, and must be accompanied by an intention to deprive the owner permanently. But the defendant's intention to pay for what he gets does not necessarily negative dishonesty. § .10

The Theft Act 1978 s. 1 supplements the Act of 1968 by creating an either-way offence of dishonestly obtaining services by deception. "Services" is exhaustively defined in subs. (2): "It is an obtaining of services where the other is induced to confer a benefit by doing some act, or causing or permitting some act to be done, on the understanding that the benefit has been or will be paid for." The deception may be of any kind; it need not refer to the promise of payment. The courts will probably find a benefit whenever a desired act has been done, so that the requirement of benefit is almost functionless, though some preparatory acts would be excluded. "Paid for" means a payment in money or its legal equivalent, not a "payment in kind." The fact that the service has in fact been paid for is immaterial. § .12

Chapter 35

THEFT AND ILLEGALITY

> They look upon fraud as a greater crime than theft, and therefore seldom fail to punish it with death: for, they allege, that care and vigilance, with a very common understanding, may preserve a man's goods from thieves; but honesty hath no fence against superior cunning; and since it is necessary that there should be a perpetual intercourse of buying and selling, and dealing upon credit; where fraud is permitted and connived at, or hath no law to punish it, the honest dealer is always undone, and the knave gets the advantage.
>
> Jonathan Swift, *Gulliver's Travels*

THE earlier discussion of the law of theft left to one side its grittiest complexities. These concern the common area covered by theft and obtaining by deception, and the differences between the two offences. They also bear on the fundamental question whether the act of theft need be one that is illegal apart from the Theft Act.[1]

In this chapter we shall be concerned with two main types of case. (1) Where D obtains ownership in the goods before his dishonest act of appropriation. (2) Where D obtains ownership contemporaneously with the appropriation. In (1) (to be considered for the most part in § .1) D generally cannot be guilty of theft; in (2) (to be considered in most of the rest of the chapter) he can be.

§ 35.1. WHERE D OBTAINS OWNERSHIP BEFORE THE APPROPRIATION

To state more exactly a rule already propounded in § 33.4, there can be no act of theft *under the general provision in section 1 (1)*[2] by a person who has obtained property (ownership) before the alleged act of appropriation. This follows from the rule that theft must be of "property belonging to another."

> Suppose that V sells an antique piece to D, and immediately afterwards finds that he made a great mistake because it was worth vastly more than he thought. He goes at once to D and tells him of the mistake, but D refuses to give the thing back. D is not dishonest, because he is entitled to keep to his bargain; but in any case the jury are not allowed to convict him of theft merely because they think (rightly or wrongly) that a decent person would have given the thing back. It now belongs to D, so he cannot steal it.

It is the same where D obtains only a voidable title. A voidable title is one that can be avoided at the option of the other party; but still it is title

---

[1] For a fuller discussion see [1977] Crim.LR 127, 205, 327.

[2] That is to say, apart from s. 5 (4); see § .7.

(ownership, property) until the former owner's option to avoid is exercised.

> D buys a valuable piece of machinery from V, V allowing him credit on D's assurance that he has a Government contract under which he is about to receive a large advance, so that he will be able to settle the account within a month. D spoke in good faith, but it transpires that he was misinformed and the Government contract has not been completed. The contract between V and D for the sale of the machinery is voidable by V on account of D's innocent misrepresentation, but it is not void for mistake. Consequently, a voidable title passes to D under the contract, and D cannot steal the article under the general provision in section 1 (1), in failing to restore it after he discovers the truth and before V has avoided the contract, even if he is regarded as acting dishonestly, because the machinery is his. The civil law no longer regards it as belonging to V, even though V can get it back if he validly avoids the contract.

When a person has sold goods under a voidable contract and validly avoids the contract, the property revests in him. So if the buyer thereafter dishonestly appropriates the goods (as, by selling them knowing that the contract has been avoided, and that he ought to give the goods back), his act can be theft.

Whereas a voidable title can pass under a voidable contract, no title at all passes under a void contract. The law of contract governs the question when there is only an apparent contract which is void, and when there is a true but voidable contract; this cannot be studied in detail here.

§ 35.2. OBTAINING OWNERSHIP BY FRAUD OR THREATS

Proposition 4 at the beginning of Chapter 33 ran:

4. It is Immaterial that the Owner is Induced by Fraud or threats to Consent to Parting with the Title to the Property

Swift, in the passage at the head of this chapter, conceived of theft as a crime of stealth or force. But the position in his day was that larceny was a graver crime than obtaining by false pretences; so the judges, always ready to tighten the law, created a certain overlap between the two crimes, with the result that a fraud case could sometimes be punished as larceny. This overlap is, perhaps unfortunately, continued and even extended by the Theft Act. A person who acquires a thing by fraud steals it, provided that the other requirements of theft are satisfied, even though he obtains a voidable title to the thing. So much, at least, appears to have been decided by the House of Lords in *Alan Lawrence*,[1] though the reasoning of the opinion occasions considerable difficulty.

---

[1] [1972] AC 626.

> An Italian student (Occhi by name) who had just arrived at Victoria station asked Lawrence, a taxi-driver, to take him to the Italian Centre. Lawrence said that the journey was very far and very expensive. In fact the correct fare was about 10*s*.6*d*. The student got into the taxi and proferred £1; Lawrence accepted this but then took from the student's open purse a further £6, the student making no protest. Lawrence was convicted of theft of "the approximate sum of £6," and this was affirmed on appeal by the Court of Appeal and House of Lords.

Two opinions are possible as to the overlap between theft and obtaining by deception, and as to the effect of the decision in *Lawrence* in relation to that overlap.

Both opinions agree that theft and obtaining by deception (let us call it "deception" for short) are committed if a person dishonestly obtains possession (but not ownership) of money or some article by deception, intending to keep it. Either offence can be charged, or both offences can be charged and a conviction obtained of one of them.[2]

It may be interjected here that even when the two offences overlap in this way, it is highly desirable as a matter of practice that prosecuting counsel should charge under section 15 (1) rather than for theft. For one thing, the deception charge gives the defendant better information of what is alleged against him, since the particulars will state the alleged deception (which they will not do on a charge of theft). The point is especially important in magistrates' courts, where the defendant may have no advance notice of what is the case against him apart from what is stated in the information. Moreover, charging deception enables the judge to give a crisper direction to the jury as to the elements that they are to look for. The mysteries of appropriation are removed from the case.

The difference of opinion arises if a cheat obtains ownership by deception. If a cheat deceives another into (say) selling him an article, the victim intending to pass the ownership in the thing, the cheat gets title, even though the fraud[3] means that it is only a voidable title. He can be charged with deception, but according to one opinion (which may be called the restricted theft opinion) not theft. He is not guilty of theft because he has got ownership. According to the other opinion (the unrestricted theft opinion) the prosecution once more have the option of charging him with theft, even though he has got ownership. It will be seen that the unrestricted theft opinion makes theft completely cover the ground of deception (except in certain minor respects, the chief being that deception but generally not theft applies to the acquisition of land).

Of the two opinions, the restricted theft opinion (which is advanced by Professor J C Smith[4]) is far preferable in point of policy, but the opinion is difficult (I think impossible) to derive from the words of the Act. It was, therefore, rejected by the House of Lords in *Lawrence*, but perhaps only by way of *obiter dictum*; and in any case Smith would say that the argument

---

[2] If both theft and obtaining by deception are charged, the conviction should be of one only. The decision in *Hircock* (1978) 67 CAR 278 allows double conviction, but it is contrary to principle and has been strongly criticised. See Griew in [1979] Crim.LR 292.

[3] See the debate between Smith and myself in [1981] Crim.LR 666, 679.

[4] The criminal law now uses the word "deception," but the law of contract uses "fraud," which is therefore the proper expression if one is speaking of the contract becoming voidable.

in favour of the opinion was not presented to the lords in its most effective form.

The argument for the defence was that since Lawrence had obtained the ownership of the student's money (whether ownership unalloyed or voidable for fraud), the money did not "belong to another;" it belonged to Lawrence, so he could not steal it. Viscount Dilhorne, speaking for the Appellate Committee, produced a powerful reply.

> "The new offence of obtaining property by deception created by section 15 (1) of the Theft Act also contains the words 'belonging to another.' 'A person who by any deception dishonestly obtains property belonging to another, with the intention of permanently depriving the other of it' commits that offence. 'Belonging to another' in section 1 (1) and in section 15 (1) in my view signifies no more than that, at the time of the appropriation or the obtaining, the property belonged to another . . . The short answer to this contention on behalf of the appellant is that the money in the wallet which he appropriated belonged to another, to Mr. Occhi"

This is a convincing argument so far as it goes, but Smith sidesteps it by making a different point. He says that the question depends not on the words quoted by Viscount Dilhorne but upon the meaning of appropriation. In Smith's opinion, one does not appropriate another person's property if one gets the entire proprietary interest in the thing.

But there is no greater appropriation of the property of another than getting the entire proprietary interest in it. If merely taking possession of another person's property is an appropriation (as you say everyone agrees), then getting both possession and ownership is a fortiori an appropriation.

I think that Smith would answer that the very meaning of appropriation is that one takes to oneself a thing that not only belongs to another at the moment of taking but continues to belong to another. The moment the thing ceases to belong to another, and becomes the property of the taker, the taker can no longer appropriate it, because thereafter he holds it as owner. So Smith says.

But in discussing appropriation you expressed the opinion that it is an appropriation to pass the victim's title to a third party without the victim's authority, and you cited the analogy of conversion in the law of tort.[5] If so, it must be an appropriation to get the victim's title yourself. Smith's argument, if it were valid, would mean that there is no appropriation in either case.

Yes. We have not yet finished this discussion, but must now return to examine the facts of *Lawrence* more closely. The transaction between Lawrence and the student needs legal analysis. Two interpretations are possible.

The first is that it was a straight case of obtaining by deception, the

---

[5] § 33.12 n. 17.

courts holding that Lawrence could be convicted of theft instead of the deception offence.

The deception was clear. Lawrence told a lie in saying that the journey was very far when he knew it was not. He also impliedy represented that the fare he was demanding and taking was the tariff fare for the journey. Throughout the Western world taxi fares in towns are governed by law, or otherwise by fixed scales of charges; they are not customarily matters of free bargaining on each occasion. (In London they are governed by law.) The student was obviously deceived into supposing that he was paying the regular price for the journey (he confirmed this in evidence). On the opinion now being stated, the property in the notes passed to Lawrence when he took them, since the student was willing that it should pass (believing that this money represented the correct fare). Lawrence, however, got only a voidable title to the money, because of his fraud. He was convicted of theft, though he coud have been convicted of obtaining by deception; and this implies acceptance of the unrestricted theft theory, according to which the two offences are concurrent in this respect. The interpretation is supported by the fact that Viscount Dilhorne thought it important to stress that the new definition of theft, unlike the old, does not require the act of theft to be committed without the owner's consent.

The alternative interpretation of the facts would deny that the actual decision in *Lawrence* supports the unrestricted theft theory. On this view, the student did not give any consent whatever to the taking of the excess fare, and therefore did not give Lawrence any title to the excess—not even a voidable one. It follows that there is nothing remarkable in the fact that Lawrence was convicted of theft. This interpretation is supported (1) by the statement in the lords' opinion that it had not been established that the defrauded student consented to the taxi driver acquiring his money, and (2) by the doubt expressed in the opinion whether the property in the money had passed to Lawrence.

I can't understand the doubt. The student allowed Lawrence to help himself from his open purse, and then accepted the ride in the cab. So he must have consented, and the property in his money must have passed.

Smith thinks that a different conclusion can be reached, and he argues the point in this way. The student impliedly authorised Lawrence to help himself from the purse to the extent of the proper fare, but no further. When Lawrence picked out (and appropriated) £6, he committed theft, because that was more than the proper fare (he had already more than received the proper fare when he was given the £1). It is true that the student then consented to Lawrence's retaining the money, but at that stage theft had already been committed. So the theft was a simple taking of money without consent.

I don't think Lawrence did appropriate the notes when he picked them out. He took them out provisionally, by way of demonstrating the amount he wanted. If the student had objected Lawrence would have given them back,

and would have either gone off or done some haggling. Lawrence did not regard the matter as finalised, and did not appropriate the notes, until the student accepted the situation and allowed Lawrence to drive him. It was then that the theftous appropriation took place, and it took place with the student's implied consent, even though the consent was given under a mistake as to what the proper fare was. The (voidable) ownership in the money passed to Lawrence, and it was at the same time theft.

Your analysis seems to me to be correct, but the important subject of enquiry is what the House of Lords held. For some reason their lordships were not convinced that the student had consented to the £6 being taken, but they failed to explain the ground of their doubt. They cannot possibly have supposed that Lawrence took the money like a pickpocket or robber, so Smith's theory (legally defective though I think it is) seems to be the only possible explanation of what was in their minds.

Well, then, their lordships were not convinced that property passed; but they held that even if it did pass Lawrence could be convicted of theft, because, since the property did not belong to him when he appropriated it, he appropriated the property of another. That is what they said, after all. So the decision still remains authority for the wider view of theft, and all the arguments to the contrary go for naught!

You have articulated the opinion of the lords better than they did themselves. I agree with you, but still wish to demonstrate the mischievous consequences of interpreting the law of theft too widely. If the lords were sufficiently persuaded of the mischief, they might be induced to say that *Lawrence*, though rightly decided on its facts, can be supported only on narrower grounds than were advanced in that case.

Since the student was plainly deceived, why wasn't Lawrence convicted of obtaining by deception?

It would have been better if he had been charged with that offence. But prosecuting counsel presumably thought he could avoid the bother and possible risk of proving an implied representation, by going straight for a conviction of theft. If he foresaw trouble in charging deception his apprehension was confirmed by another strange remark in Viscount Dilhorne's opinion.

> "If the appellant had been charged under section 15 (1), he would, I suspect, have contended that there was no deception, that he had simply appropriated the money and that he ought to have been charged [with theft] under section 1 (1). In my view, he was rightly charged under that section."

His lordship did not say that he would agree with the argument he imagined being advanced, and it would be completely unconvincing. For the reasons we have already had, I find it impossible to imagine that if Lawrence had been charged with the deception offence the charge would have failed.

However, the mischief of the decision begins to appear when one considers the implication of Viscount Dilhorne's dictum just quoted. It appears to mean that whether or not the facts show a deception, the defendant can be charged with theft. Now a deception charge under section 15 (1) requires the prosecution to prove (1) a deception and (2) dishonesty in the obtaining. If the prosecution can charge theft as a short cut, they will only have to prove dishonesty, and will not have to prove that the defendant deceived, or that the deception produced the obtaining. For example, in the cheque card case, *Charles*,[6] the House of Lords could only with great difficulty (and dubious propriety) find a deception. But on the literal interpretation of section 1 (1), where goods have been dishonestly obtained by a cheque card the prosecution could charge theft, and need not strain itself to prove a deception. Again, take a case where the defendant has sold goods and has not disclosed facts that an honest person would have disclosed. The traditional principle is that nondisclosure is not deception. Is the defendant nevertheless guilty of theft of the buyer's money? It would be highly unsatisfactory if the criminal law were expanded in this way, merely on the basis of the vague notion of dishonesty. On that view of the law, prosecutors might stop charging deception offences except in rare cases for special reasons, and almost every charge would be of theft.

I will now produce my own nostrum. The position would be saved if the courts could be induced to read into section 1 (1) an implied requirement of unlawfulness. Appropriating a person's property without his consent is unlawful; so is appropriating it with consent obtained (and "vitiated") by fraud or duress. The actual design in *Lawrence* is therefore correct. But I would suggest that some unlawfulness must be shown; and that is why there should be no conviction of theft in the hypothetical about nondisclosure. The money is not obtained unlawfully. This suggestion is not inconsistent with the decision in *Lawrence*, because the lords in that case must have been convinced that the taking was either without the student's consent or with consent induced by fraud, and either way it was unlawful.

By "unlawful" I mean unlawful by the civil law as a matter of property rights. The fact that the appropriation may amount to some minor criminal offence should not make it theft. Suppose that a London cab driver says to a prospective passenger: "Forget about fare tariffs. I am not going to take you unless you pay me £6." The passenger thereupon consents and pays up. Well, it is a dirty night, growing late, and no other cab is available. There is no deception, but a jury might say that it was dishonest of the cab driver to take advantage of the passenger's weak bargaining position; so the cabby might be convicted of theft on a wide view of the law. But it would be wrong to make a conviction of theft depend on such considerations; and the fact that the excessive fare is in breach of the cab fare tariff should not be regarded as turning the cabby's shabby conduct into the much more serious offence of theft.

Your suggestion may not be inconsistent with Lawrence, but it is with section 1 (1), which does not require unlawfulness.

There are certain ways in which I think that the requirement can

---

[6] § 34.2 at n. 8.

properly be implied, even though section 1 (1) does not express it. We shall return to this in due course.

Consider the £1 note that the student handed to Lawrence at the start of the transaction. Presumably the student was not certain whether he might obtain change from it or not, but he intended to pass the ownership in the £1 to Lawrence, subject to the question of change. Does it not follow that the £1 note became the property of Lawrence, so that he could not steal it?

The student intended to receive change if any was due, and change was due. It is not unreasonable to construe his intention to pass the property as subject to an implied condition, which condition was not fulfilled, so that the property did not pass. It is like the newsvendor who (in the old days when people could be trusted) left a pile of newspapers and a tin to receive the money. He impliedly consented to the taking of a newspaper if, but only if, the proper sum was placed in the tin. The student consented to Lawrence keeping the note if, but only if, the proper change was given. There were several decisions under the old law of larceny holding that a fraudster who did not give the expected change was guilty of larceny of the note. So Lawrence could have been properly convicted of theft of the part of the value of the £1 note representing the change that he ought to have given.

Suppose property is obtained not by fraud but by threats?

There is no doubt that property obtained by duress is theft, and two reasons may be advanced, quite apart from the over-wide doctrine of *Lawrence*. The first is that duress may totally nullify an apparent consent, and prevent property passing, not merely make it voidable. However, the law on the point is not altogether certain. Secondly, it is necessary to hold that an appropriation under duress is theft, in order to make sense of the offence of robbery, which presupposes a theft (Chap. 36).

§ 35.3. THE ARGUMENT FOR A REQUIREMENT OF UNLAWFULNESS

5. In Other Cases it is Doubtful how far Theft can be Committed if the Act of Appropriation is Lawful

An alarming possibility emerging from *Lawrence* briefly presented itself in the last section, namely that a person who obtains another's property dishonestly and with intent to deprive him permanently may be accounted guilty of theft without the necessity for proof of any other element. If true, this could mean that a person who obtains a perfectly valid title to property can be guilty of theft of it by reason of some dishonesty in the transaction that gives him the title; so the rule would give the prospect of a chasm between the civil law (which would regard the contract and resulting title as valid and enforceable) and the criminal law (which would regard the transaction as tainted with criminality). The rest of the chapter will be devoted to an examination of the problem.

We have seen that this situation has already materialised when a person commits an appropriation in the extended sense of section 3 (1), "any assumption of the rights of an owner." A customer in a supermarket takes down an article from the shelf. The article remains the property of the supermarket, and the act done in relation to it is lawful (in the civil law) because the owner consents to it; moreover, the doer does not intend the act to deprive the owner immediately; yet it is regarded as a theftous appropriation. This is thoroughly anomalous, and it has already been suggested (§ 33.12) that the courts have gone wrong on the point. When the CLRC very unwisely voted to omit from section 1 (1) both a requirement of unlawfulness and a requirement of absence of owner's consent, I do not think it contemplated that, as a result, the courts would use the flabby notion of dishonesty as a substitute for firm rules on the definition of theft.

The further distressing possibility now to be considered is that the courts may declare an act to be an appropriation although it not only is lawful but actually transfers title to the defendant—either a fully valid title or a voidable one.

To make dishonesty almost the sole requirement for theft would put a weight upon the notion of dishonesty that it was not meant to bear. The reference to dishonesty was intended as a restriction upon liability for what might *prima facie* look like theft. The CLRC proposed it as better conveying the meaning of the previous phrase "without a claim of right." Dishonesty was not thought of as the sole element saving people from conviction of theft in ordinary transactions like buying a bunch of bananas. To create an offence in which the *actus reus* is virtually nothing more than a dishonest act would offend against what the Americans call the principle of due notice of a criminal prohibition; it is too vague to be an adequate guide to conduct. As a restriction on liability for an act that is *ex facie* wrong the notion of dishonesty may be acceptable (though even there we have perceived trouble with it); but it is inadequate as a means of describing the forbidden act.

Problems are unlikely to arise on a sale of bananas, but they might on a sale of an *objet d'art*.

> Suppose that D buys an old sketch in an antique shop, for which he pays £5. He has made a special study of Leonardo, and knows that the sketch is his work; he also knows that it is worth tens of thousands of pounds. The dealer, of course, doesn't. D goes off proudly with the sketch.

It is inconceivable that on a charge of theft the jury would be left to decide whether they thought D was honest or not. No doubt they would find him honest, but they should not be left to make the decision. D is, in law, entitled to make a profit from his special knowledge. That is part of the fun in rummaging in antique shops and second-hand bookshops. D's contract to buy the sketch was valid, and D obtained a fully valid title. If the dealer refused to deliver the sketch, D could sue him in order to get it. It would be preposterous if on receipt of it D could be convicted of theft. And it would be almost as preposterous if the civil courts, taking notice of the Theft Act, decided that the law of contract is now to be modified by importing into it a vague injunction against dishonesty.

Although section 1 (1) does not make the absence of the owner's consent an element of theft, it cannot be imagined that an act done with the owner's full authority is theft. Suppose that V asks D to sell a horse for him. D sells the horse in accordance with his instructions, secretly intending to pocket the proceeds. Is D guilty of theft of the horse by selling it? (Assume that he is arrested before he even gets possession of the sale price.) Literally he assumes the rights of an owner (he assumes them because he has been allowed to exercise them), and he has a dishonest mind; but he cannot, surely, be guilty of theft when what he does is lawful. In effect this was the ruling of a circuit judge in a case[1] where directors of companies, acting (it seems) under the authority of resolutions that they themselves passed at meetings of the boards of directors, transferred part of the companies' bank accounts to their own private use. It was ruled that there was no case to answer on a charge of theft. The directors had authority[2] from the companies (which owned the accounts) to do what they did, and so their acts could not be theft. (The directors were the only shareholders, but the result should have been the same if there had been other shareholders, since it is the company, not the shareholders, that owns its property.) A different legal result could be achieved by finding that the directors in not acting for the benefit of the company were acting beyond their powers, *ultra vires*, and it is not easy to see why this conclusion was not reached by the judge.[3]

There are several ways of amending the Theft Act to make te legal position clearer, but the best hope for judicial correction of the law would be that already suggested: to imply a requirement of unlawfulness for theft.

One way in which this could be achieved would be for the courts to hold that dishonesty implies unlawfulness. Something like this appears to have been in the mind of the Court of Appeal in *Lawrence*.

> "Of course, where there is true consent by the owner of property to the appropriation of it by another, a charge of theft under section 1 (1) must fail. This is not, however, because the words "without consent" have to be implied in the new definition of theft. It is simply because, if there is such true consent, the essential element of dishonesty is not established. If, however, the apparent consent is brought about by dishonesty, there is nothing in the words of section 1 (1) . . . to make such apparent consent relevant as providing a defence."[4]

This passage is not very helpful as worded, but it would become helpful if the word "dishonesty" in the last sentence were changed to "deception" or "fraud." Consent brought about by an act of dishonesty can be valid, but consent brought about by fraud is defective. The question for the jury in the Leonardo hypothetical should be not whether the buyer was guilty of dishonesty but whether he was guilty of fraud; and on the facts stated there would be no evidence of fraud for the jury. If there was no fraud, and if therefore there was "true consent" on the part of the seller, then it would

---

[1] *Pearlberg* [1982] Crim.LR 829.

[2] Smith para. 31, while saying that there can be theft of property taken with the full *consent* of the owner (as in the entrapment situation, discussed in § .4), is of opinion that there cannot be theft if the act is done with the owner's *authority*. I regret I cannot see the distinction.

[3] See the powerful argument by G. R. Sullivan in [1983] Crim.LR 512.

[4] [1970] 3 WLR at 1107B.

follow, as the court said, that "the essential element of dishonesty is not established."

The Court of Appeal's dictum creates a concept of what may be called objective honesty, depending not upon the defendant's state of mind but upon the legal position. If the defendant obtained property from a person who gave "true consent," this presumably means that he gets a valid title to the property. Acting lawfully under the civil law, and getting a valid title, he is objectively honest; and it makes no difference that he may not have realised that he got a valid title and may have been subjectively dishonest.

Unfortunately, this notion of objective honesty was not applied in *Gilks*, to which brief reference has already been made.[5]

> This was the case in which a bookmaker made a payment by mistake. Gilks received a payment as though he had backed "Fighting Taffy," when in fact, as he knew, he had won a much smaller sum on "Fighting Scot." Gilks realised the mistake just before receiving the payment or at the moment when he was paid, but pocketed the money.
>
> When he was charged with theft, one submission made on his behalf was that the property in the money passed to him notwithstanding the bookmaker's mistake. This was rejected by the Court of Appeal, which held that no property passed. But there remained a further point. Even if the property in the money did not pass to Gilks, he was (it was contended) under no legal obligation to return it. By statute, wagering agreements are void, the attitude of the law being that they are too frivolous to take up the time of the courts. It had already been held that in consequence of this statute a bookmaker cannot sue in quasi-contract to recover back a payment that he has mistakenly made.[6] The Court of Appeal agreed that Gilks was under no legal obligation to return the money, but held nevertheless that he was rightly convicted of theft, on the literal reading of section 1 (1).

This is against the theory of objective honesty advanced above. When Gilks received the payment, he presumably did not realise that it was excessive until it was in his hand. At that moment (the court held) the civil law entitled him to keep it. If that were the case, then, in so far as his detention of the money was an appropriation of it, it was a lawful appropriation. The point does not really seem to have been made by his counsel, and anyway the Court of Appeal did not deal with it. The court passed to consider the question of dishonesty, holding that there was no evidence that Gilks believed he had a legal right to keep the money. That was so; but was his position made worse by the fact?

Whatever else is unclear about the notion of dishonesty, it is beyond doubt that a man cannot be dishonest if he knows or believes he has a legal right to act as he does. Immoral, perhaps, but not dishonest. This rule is expressly stated in section 2 (1) (*a*).[7] Suppose that Gilks had known the law, so that when he counted the money and realised the bookmaker's mistake he had said; "You have paid me too much, but I happen to know that by law you cannot sue me to recover back the excess, and I intend to stand on my legal rights and keep it." Similar letters are written by solicitors on behalf of clients every day, the function of lawyers being to advise and assist on law, not on morality. It is obvious that if these had been the facts Gilks could not conceivably have been regarded as dishonest, and the deputy chairman accepted this view of the law.[8] Can it make any difference that Gilks did not know the law? One does not become a criminal merely by believing that one is a criminal, where the act is lawful.

It is true that the law of attempt sometimes makes criminals out of evil-minded persons whose outward acts are lawful. But in these instances the defendant is trying to do something that will be a crime if he succeeds according to his intention and belief; he may therefore be called a dangerous person. In a case like *Gilks* the defendant is not trying to do anything beyond or other than what he does, and what he does is permitted by law.

---

[5] § 32.5 at n.15.
[6] *Morgan* v. *Ashcroft* [1938] 1 KB 49.
[7] § 32.5 at n. 1.
[8] [1972] 1 WLR at 1346B–C, 3 All ER at 284a.

To sum up, one way of achieving the desirable result, without the aid of fresh legislation, would be by interpreting the word "dishonestly" in a double sense. It should be taken to refer not only to the defendant's moral dishonesty but also to the actual legal position (legal dishonesty). A person acts honestly if what he does is perfectly legal and if he is not even obliged to make restitution in quasi-contract; and it makes no difference that he may think he is acting dishonestly. If this view had been accepted, Gilks would have been acquitted.

A case before *Gilks* in which the criminal court refused to acknowledge the relevance of the civil law to the law of theft was *Bonner,*[9] where it was said, obiter, that a partner could be guilty of stealing the joint partnership property by an act that was not a tort to his co-partner. The law of tort relating to the rights of co-owners was, and is, in a curiously unsatisfactory state,[10] so that it is in a way understandable that the criminal court should wish to cut away from its limitations. Nevertheless, it seems objectionable to say that an act that is lawful under the general law can be dishonest for the purpose of the law of theft.

Whether or not the foregoing argument on the double meaning of dishonesty is accepted, the courts could reach much the same result as a matter of statutory interpretation by applying the "golden rule" of construction, in order to avoid absurdity,[11] and in order to give a reasonable construction to the Theft Act as a whole. This could be done by reading section 1 (1) as being concerned exclusively with unlawful acts. Arguments in support are that it would be unreasonable to construe the subsection so widely as to render section 15 (1) almost nugatory and to produce a conflict between the criminal and civil law.

But when you seek to imply "unlawfully" into the subsection, aren't you really trying to put in the words "without the consent of the owner"? The House of Lords in Lawrence emphasised that those words are not there.

The word "unlawfully" would do some of the work of the missing phrase, but not all. It would also have some effects that the missing words would not have.

A person acts *lawfully* with regard to another's property if he has the full consent of the owner. In general, he acts *unlawfully* if he lacks the consent of the owner or if he uses fraud or duress to obtain consent.

It is true, as you say, that the House of Lords emphasised that theft does not require the absence of the owner's consent, but that was in a case in which either the owner (the Italian student) did not consent or his consent was obtained by fraud. It was not a case of the owner giving full consent. If the owner gives full consent to an act, that act ought not to be accounted theft, the reason being that the act is lawful.

The defendant's act of appropriation will be lawful if he obtains full title to the property, but it will also be lawful although the defendant gets no title, if his act is done with the owner's full consent. In *Morris,*[12] the case of the switched labels, the defendant had the owner's full consent to take articles from the shelves. It was not, of course, a consent to appropriate the articles before paying for them, but it was consent to the act of taking them from the shelves, which made the act of taking them (though not of switching the labels) lawful. Acceptance of the rule for which I am contending would therefore entail a reversal of the *ratio decidendi* of *Morris*; and this would be salutary.

As already said, such an interpretation of the law need not affect the result of *Lawrence*

---

[9] [1970] 1 WLR 838, 2 All ER 97n.

[10] It has been slightly improved by the Torts (Interference with Goods) Act 1977 s. 10.

[11] See 1st edn 770.

[12] § 33.12.

on its actual facts; the acquisition of a title that is voidable for fraud, or indeed duress, should continue to be capable of being theft. However, the question remains whether a person who gets a title that is voidable on other grounds may be guilty of theft. This will be considered in § .5.

To sum up the argument of this section, the courts could hold, first, that when a person obtains an indefeasible title to property, the means by which he does so are not to be accounted dishonest even though they may be frowned upon, because any other rule would unsettle the established principles of property law. This rule would entail disapproving the decision in *Gilks*, where the point was not considered.

Secondly, the House of Lords could hold that, to avoid absurdity, section 1 (1) is to be read as confined to unlawful acts (including fraud and duress); but it seems that the Court of Appeal has now, by its decision in *Morris*, precluded itself from taking this line.

§ 35.4. ENTRAPMENT AND CONSENT

Before the Theft Act, when larceny was defined as being done without the consent of the owner, the courts developed a sensible distinction between consent and facilitation.

If the owner, V, in order to catch a thief, puts out some marked money, or leaves a door or drawer unlocked, and lies in wait, he facilitates the theft but does not consent to it: his attitude is merely one of trying to find who is the thief, or to get evidence that a particular suspect is the thief. Similarly if the owner tells his employee E to put out marked money. In such cases if the thief takes the bait he is guilty of theft.

But suppose that D incites E to join with him in stealing from V; E tells V of the approach that has been made to him, and V instructs him to pretend to co-operate with D; E then *hands over the owner's property to D*, pretending that he has stolen it from V. In these circumstances V was formerly taken to consent to the taking, which therefore was not larceny.[1]

Various writers assume that the Act of 1968 has changed this by omitting the requirement of lack of owner's consent, and some of them welcome the conclusion that the thief can now be convicted of theft and not merely of an inchoate crime. For my part I think that such a conviction would be against principle, because D's act in receiving the money thrust into his hands on the owner's instructions is lawful, even though he imagines it to be unlawful. Unlawfulness does not follow merely from belief in unlawfulness, except in the case of inchoate crimes. Here D's crime was in inciting E to steal, or of attempting to corrupt E; he is not guilty of a consummated crime of theft.

If the Theft Act has changed the law, it would be not only contrary to principle but, in some circumstances, unjust. This is so if it was V who engineered the whole affair. Either from malice or because he wished to put the honesty of D to an extreme test, V got his employee E tothrust money into D's hands, pretending that he had stolen it from V. D

---

[1] *Turvey* [1946] 2 All ER 60, 31 CAR 154. See *The General Part*, 2nd edn 771 ff.

succumbs to temptation and accepts the money. If this makes D guilty of theft, although he in fact had V's consent to what he did, the law would be harsh, particularly because it does not recognise a defence of entrapment.

The right result can be reached under the Act by the means already suggested. It can be held that D's appropriation of the money is lawful, and therefore is not theft, though if he made any efforts to get the money they can still be charged as inchoate crimes.

A somewhat similar case is *Mills*,[2] where it was held that if the victim of an attempted deception sees through the deception but nevertheless parts with his money, the cheat cannot be convicted of obtaining by deception (though he can be convicted of an attempt to obtain). A literal argument based on section 1 (1) would result in the conclusion that the cheat is guilty of theft, since he is dishonest and appropriates property belonging to another. This illustrates the fact that the literal argument, since it does not require a causal connection between the dishonesty and acquiring an opportunity to appropriate property, would in effect abolish the causal nexus required in deception cases. The solution is the same as before: D, though guilty of an attempt, appropriates the money lawfully, since it was sent to him with that object.

§ 35.5. PROPERTY OBTAINED BY TRANSFEROR'S MISTAKE

We saw in § .3 that since *Lawrence* it must be accepted that the acquisition of a voidable title to property by fraud can be theft; and the same rule must apply to acquisitions by duress, assuming that this makes the title voidable (*a fortiori* if no title passes). So far as the authority of *Lawrence* goes, there is no need to extend the law any further. A person who obtains a title that is voidable on other grounds should not on so doing be liable to be convicted of theft, since these other grounds are for the most part too divorced from the idea of dishonesty, and the civil law is too fluid, to make a rule of this kind desirable. For example, contracts and titles are voidable for innocent misrepresentation and undue influence by the transferee, and for intoxication and certain spontaneous mistakes by the transferor. These vitiating factors sometimes make the contract void, in which case no title to property passes and the transferee can commit theft; but sometimes they only make the contract voidable. The desirable rule is that in the latter cases theft can be committed (fraud and duress aside) only by the operation of section 5 (4) (to be considered presently), or where an appropriation is made dishonestly after the contract has been avoided. Not long ago it seemed that the Court of Appeal might be prepared to take this position; but the indications are now the other way. The following discussion will concentrate on voidability for mistake.

Whether a mistake on the part of the transferor of property affects the passing of the property depends on the circumstances.

First, it may have no effect on the contract or on the passing of the property, as in the hypothetical of the Leonardo sketch in § .2.

Secondly, it may make the contract void and prevent any property

[2] § 34. 9 n. 2.

passing, as where V despatches goods to D by way of sale, believing that D is E. This mistake as to the identity of the parties, if known to D, will generally prevent D from obtaining title to the property, and if he dishonestly appropriates the property he commits theft.

Thirdly, intermediate cases are possible in which V's mistake is not so fundamental as to make the contract void, but still is sufficiently substantial to make it voidable. We need not enquire what these cases are, since that is a matter for the law of contract; but a single illustration may be given. A customer in a shop buys and pays for goods, knowing that the price charged, through a mistake, is less than the seller had planned. The buyer probably obtains title to the goods, but only a voidable title.[1] Is he guilty of theft in taking them off? The question arose in *Kaur* v. *Chief Constable of Hampshire*.[2]

> Kaur selected a pair of shoes from the £6.99 rack in a shop. One shoe had a price label for £4.99 and the other for £6.99. She took them to the cashier without concealing either price label, and when asked for the lower price duly paid it. Then she was arrested on leaving the shop. The Divisional Court held that she was not guilty of theft, notwithstanding a finding of fact by the justices that Kaur knew that £4.99 was not the correct price.

How did she know it wasn't?

Presumably because all the other shoes of the same kind were marked at £6.99.

All the same, it was a pretty trivial matter. I don't understand how Kaur came to be prosecuted. She was not dishonest. When there is some muddle or doubt about a price at a supermarket, the cashier or supervisor will normally give the customer the benefit of it. Kaur did not do anything dishonest to cause the double labelling.

Apparently Kaur was arrested because she was suspected of having switched the labels. Prosecutors sometimes proceed with a charge when they know that their case has become shaky, because they are afraid that otherwise the person arrested will sue for false imprisonment; but it is an entirely wrong course. There is no reason why the fact that they proceed with the charge should protect them from an action if the charge fails.

The argument on appeal assumed that Kaur was dishonest, and turned on the question of law only.

Everyone who is at all dishonest is adept at rationalising or condoning his dishonesty. Kaur was 75 per cent. honest, because she did not tamper with the price labels or endeavour to conceal them. A *perfectly* honest person like you, or anyway me, would have pointed out the

---

[1] A distinction must be drawn between two cases. One is where the seller, by a slip of the tongue or of the price label, asks less than he meant to ask; if the buyer knows of the mistake there is no contract, because of the absence of consensus. The other case is where the seller knows the price that he is asking but was led to ask it through a mistake; there is a consensus on the terms of the contract, but if the buyer knew of the mistake the contract is voidable by the seller. *Contra*, Professor J C Smith, who thinks (against the opinion of the court in *Kaur*) that there is no contract in either case. See [1981] Crim.LR 674–676, 680–681, [1982] *ibid*. 65–66.

[2] [1981] 1 WLR 578. See [1981] Crim.LR 666 (Williams), 677 (J C Smith), [1982] *ibid*. 64 (Williams, Smith), 391 (Hart).

discrepancy of labels to the cashier and said that the shoes came from the £6.99 rack. It is true, however, that vast multitudes of shoppers fall short of such a standard of honesty. They are quite willing to profit by a mistake made by a large corporation if it does not involve telling a lie. Moreover, there is no great social need to extend the law of theft to these cases of marginal honesty. As Lord Lane said, in delivering judgment, "the court should be astute not to find theft where it would be straining thc language and where an ordinary person would not regard the act to be theft."

Nevertheless the magistrates, who convicted Kaur, must have found her to be dishonest, perhaps because the issue of honesty was not contested before them. Nor was it contested on appeal. Honesty is a question of fact, and if the defendant had desired to appeal on that issue she should have taken the case to the Crown Court, which can consider points of both fact and law. This appeal was to the Divisional Court, which means that it was on a question of law only. It turned on the ownership of the shoes.

In the opinion of the court, the contract of sale was not void for the cashier's mistake, which was not fundamental; so property passed to Kaur under the contract. Her obtaining of ownership in this way was not theft. "She certainly assumed the rights of an owner when, having paid, she took the shoes from the cashier in order to go home," but this again was not theft, presumably because it was not an appropriation of property belonging to another. The contract was not voidable for fraud, since there was none; if it was voidable for the seller's mistake (a point that was left open[3]), "it had certainly not been avoided when the time came for the defendant to pick up the shoes and go."[4]

How can Kaur be reconciled with Lawrence?

Lord Lane said:

> "Happily in this case we are not concerned with the difficulties raised by the decision in *Lawrence*, because here the ownership of the goods had passed on payment, and the appropriation was at a later stage, when the shoes were put in the bag and carried away by the defendant."[5]

This fastens on the fact that Lawrence either (on one view) obtained no rights in respect of the money he took, or (on another view) obtained possession as well as ownership of the money at the same moment. (The moment was either when he took the money from the student's wallet with his tacit consent, or when, the money having been taken without the student's consent, the student subsequently ratified the taking.) At the moment (or immediately before the moment) when he dishonestly appropriated the money it belonged to the student, so the appropriation was theft. Kaur, on the other hand, obtained ownership by her purchase at the cash desk *before* she took possession of the goods; when she did so take possession of them (thereby appropriating them), they were her goods so she could not be guilty of theft.

Why wasn't it an appropriation for Kaur to obtain ownership of the goods by paying for them at the cash desk, even though she did not immediately

---

[3] But it surely was voidable. See n. 1 above.

[4] [1981] 1 WLR at p. 583G. If it had been so avoided, Kaur would have been deprived of the ownership, and could then have committed theft by walking out with the shoes.

[5] At p. 583 H.

get possession of them? At that moment the goods belonged to the supermarket, and Kaur surely appropriated them by getting the ownership of them.

The court did not explain why not. Kaur obtained either a completely valid title or a title that was voidable on account of the cashier's mistake (the court left open which); but even a voidable title is title, and it may be argued that a person who gets it "assumes the rights of an owner," even though he does not get possession until later. This line of reasoning, based on the literal words of sections 1 and 3 (and assuming that a requirement of unlawfulness is not read into section 1) would suggest that Kaur committed theft.

A supporting argument against the decision in *Kaur* as it stands is that the reasoning of the court on the time-split would apply equally to a case of fraud, and in that application it would be impossible to accept. A supermarket shopper picks up an article that bears no price marking, but he knows the price is £6. He hands it to the cashier telling her that the price is £4; the cashier accepts this price and puts it in the till. A voidable title now passes to the shopper. He takes up the article and goes off. On the reasoning of *Kaur* he is not guilty of theft (though he is guilty of obtaining by deception); whereas if he had kept his hand on the article the whole time, so that he obtained possession instantaneously with the payment of the price and the passing of the property, he would have been guilty of theft under *Lawrence*. Such an unconvincing distinction would be of no credit to the law. Nor would it be creditable even if the distinction were more pronounced. D buys a TV on credit from V, having falsely represented his means. He is to call to take delivery the next day, and does so. Here the acquisition of ownership by D substantially precedes that of possession, and on the principle of *Kaur* D is not guilty of theft, though if he had taken the article at the moment when he bought it he would have been guilty. Even on these facts there is no sense in the distinction. The only rational view is that D committed theft by fraudulently getting the ownership. So the decision in *Kaur* must be wrong on the time-split point.

However, *Kaur* can be explained and distinguished from *Lawrence* in one way, although it was not the way relied upon by the court. Lawrence's obtaining of the money was unlawful because he was guilty of deception (or, on an alternative interpretation of the facts, it was unlawful because the student did not consent), whereas Kaur had the cashier's consent and (as the Divisional Court expressly held) used no deception and committed no illegality in receiving the shoes. Even if her title to the shoes was voidable by reason of the cashier's mistake, it has already been suggested that a person who dishonestly obtains a voidable title to property should not necessarily be regarded as committing theft. If the defect in title does not arise from the use of unlawful means (fraud or threats of force), then obtaining the title is a lawful act and so (on the thesis here presented) cannot, on a rational view, be theft. The actual decision in *Kaur* accords with this principle, and is to be welcomed.

Unfortunately, that is not the end of the tale. The Court of Appeal has stopped up the foregoing line of argument. By the time he subsequently came to pronounce judgment in *Morris*,[6] Lord Lane had repented of his judgment in *Kaur*. He now said that *Kaur* could be supported only on the ground that the defendant was not dishonest. That, of course, was not the

[6] § 33.12.

subject of Kaur's appeal, and was not the basis of the judgment of the Divisional Court. Lord Lane's own wise remark in *Kaur* that "the court should be astute not to find theft where it would be straining the language" had ceased to seem convincing to him.

Apparently Lord Lane changed his mind because he had come to think that one can appropriate an article by an act done with the owner's consent. The proposition is true in itself, but does not mean that all appropriations with the owner's consent are theftous. What the Court of Appeal should have held in *Morris* was that an act done with the owner's consent can be an appropriation if and only if (1) there is an appropriation in the ordinary meaning of the expression and (2) the owner's consent is procured by fraud or duress. An act done with consent is not an appropriation if the defendant's act is an appropriation only by reason of section 3 (1) or if the consent is vitiated by some factor not involving illegality, as was the case in *Kaur*. Kaur, therefore, was rightly held not guilty of theft, because her appropriation of the property was not unlawful. Alas, we are precluded by the decision in *Morris* from saying that this is now the law. It seems that the courts, short at least of the House of Lords, are now committed to saying that anything that can conceivably be called an appropriation within the terms of the Act is an appropriation, owner's consent or no, unless the alleged appropriation is the obtaining of a completely valid title to the property in question.

A further rule relating to mistake will be considered in § .7.[7]

§ 35.6 LIMITATION OF AN AGENT'S AUTHORITY

Analogous to cases of fundamental mistake are those where property fails to pass because an agent acts outside his authority.

> A cashier in a supermarket dishonestly charges a friend less than the proper price for goods. The friend, if he knows of the fraud, will be guilty of stealing the goods.[1]

There are other instances of a limitation of the agent's authority preventing property from passing, but they will not be considered here.

§ 35.7. WHERE THERE IS AN OBLIGATION TO MAKE RESTORATION

Some of the general propositions in this chapter are modified by section 5 (4).

---

[7] For other problems on mistake see 1st edn 775–776, 778 ff.

[1] *Pilgram* v. *Rice-Smith* [1977] 1 WLR 671, 2 All ER 658, 65 CAR 142. Contrast *Kaur* § .5 at n. 2, where the cashier reasonably supposed that the price she saw on one of the labels was correct.

"Where a person gets property by another's mistake, and is under an obligation to make restoration (in whole or in part) of the property or its proceeds or of the value thereof, then to the extent of that obligation the property or proceeds shall be regarded (as against him) as belonging to the person entitled to restoration, and an intention not to make restoration shall be regarded accordingly as an intention to deprive that person of the property or proceeds."

When is a person who gets property by mistake "under an obligation to make restoration of the property or its proceeds or the value thereof"?

The obligation may be to pay money as a matter of quasi-contract or by reason of an equitable obligation, or it may, presumably, be a liability in tort, such as a liability to restore property or to pay damages for a tortious conversion, or liability for the tort of deceit. All these are matters of civil law into which we need not enter in depth.

Although section 5 (4) is useful in avoiding questions of civil law that might otherwise cause difficulty, it is somewhat anomalous because it can operate to make a person guilty of stealing his own property, or rather the value of his own property.

The most important type of quasi-contractual liability is the liability to repay money received under a mistake of fact on the part of the payer. A "mistake of fact" for this purpose includes a mistake as to whether the money is legally due.[1] The payee is, in terms of the subsection, under a legal obligation to make restoration (by repaying an equivalent sum), and if he dishonestly decides not to do so he can be guilty of theft.

For example: a wages clerk makes a mistake when preparing the pay packets, and an employee, in consequence, finds too much money in his packet. If the employee dishonestly decides to say nothing about it, he is guilty of theft of the excess payment under section 5 (4), and it makes no difference whether the clerk's mistake was in putting the wrong name on the pay packet (mistake of identity of recipient), or in putting a £10 note into the packet in mistake for a £1 note (mistake of identity of the thing), or in putting ten £10 notes into the packet in mistake for nine (mistake as to quantity of the thing). Indeed, the rule applies even though the clerk knew exactly what he was putting into the pay packet and merely mistook the number of hours that the employee had worked that week (mistake as to a motivating fact). Again, the rule applies whether the employee realised the mistake as soon as he received the pay packet, or whether he discovered it only after he had got home.

But that raises the old problem of dishonesty. Many an employee who finds his pay packet unexpectedly stuffed with notes merely regards it as a windfall. Nor would his wife think of saying anything if she found herself undercharged at a supermarket. "They" have had their whack on sundry other occasions, and have doubtless made mistakes to our detriment. Now

[1] See Goff and Jones, *The Law of Restitution* , 2nd edn Chaps. 3, 4. The authors suggest with much force that the rule should be held to apply to transfers made under a mistake of law, unless the payer makes the payment with full knowledge of the facts in settlement of an honest claim.

it is "their" turn to suffer. I haven't done anything to cause the mistake, have I?

The employee can readily be found to have known that he was or might be under a legal obligation to restore the excess sum to his employer, and the question for the jury will be whether he knew that his decision not to honour the obligation was out of accord with "the current standards of ordinary decent people."[2]

So the conviction of Alan Lawrence could have been justified under section 5 (4)?

Yes, and it is surprising that the subsection was not referred to in the opinions in the House of Lords. Lawrence was under an obligation to restore money received from the student because of the student's mistake as to the customary fare.[3]

Why wasn't section 5 (4) invoked in Kaur? Wasn't Kaur under an obligation to make restoration?

No—not until the seller avoided the contract on account of the cashier's mistake known to the buyer.[4] The difference between *Kaur* and *Lawrence* is that the one concerned chattels, the other money. The action in quasi-contract for money paid under a mistake of fact (which arises immediately money is paid by mistake) applies only for the payment of money, not for the delivery or redelivery of goods. When a voidable title has passed in respect of goods, they are not due back until the contract is avoided. When it is properly avoided the property revests automatically, and any dishonest appropriation then made will be theft without the need for section 5 (4).

> The possibly unequal working of the law as between money and chattels may be illustrated. (1) A sells goods to B; having consulted the wrong invoice he charges less than he should have charged, and B knows this. If B goes off with the goods he is not, if *Kaur* is still good law (now a very doubtful assumption), guilty of theft unless he is asked for the return of the goods and then dishonestly appropriates them. (2) A sells goods to B; by mistake B pays more than the price, and A knows this. A is guilty of theft of the money the moment he dishonestly accepts it, by reason of section 5 (4).

It follows that the word "property" in the subsection was a mistake on the part of the draftsman. It should have been "money," because that is the only form of property in respect of which the subsection has any practical operation.[5]

Is a moral obligation to make restoration an "obligation" within section 5 (4)?

No. That was decided in *Gilks*.[6] Gilks was convicted on a literal reading

---

[2] See *Ghosh* § 32.5 at n. 16.

[3] § .5 at n. 1.

[4] Even an avoidance by the seller would not impose a retrospective obligation on the buyer to make restoration for the purpose of section 5 (4). The buyer is liable for theft only if he appropriates the property after the avoidance of the contract.

[5] [1981] Crim.LR 676.

[6] [1972] 1 WLR at 1345D, 3 All ER at 283d. See above § .3 at n. 5.

of section 1 (1), not by applying section 5 (4). The court expressly held that section 5 (4) did not assist the prosecution, notwithstanding that Gilks was under a moral obligation to make repayment.

If an excessive sum is transferred by mistake, the transferee being entitled to part of the sum, he cannot be convicted of stealing the part he was entitled to?

Of course not; and it does not matter that he was given, say, a £5 note when he was entitled to £1. If he dishonestly keeps the note he is guilty of theft of £4, the notional sum to which he is not entitled. In *Lawrence*, it will be remembered, the taxi-driver was convicted of stealing "the approximate sum of £6," although he had received £7—he was given credit for the proper fare that he could have charged.

SUMMARY

There can be no theft under the general rule of s. 1 (1) where a person obtains § .1
ownership before the alleged act of appropriation. This is true even if he obtains only voidable ownership; but an act of dishonest appropriation after the title has been avoided can be theft.

Although the effect of the decision of the House of Lords in *Lawrence* is § .2
disputed, it seems to be that where the defendant is guilty of fraud not only an obtaining of possession but an obtaining of voidable title can be charged as theft if the case falls literally within section 1 (1) (as it almost always will). It may however be argued, at least before the House of Lords, that theft presupposes an unlawful appropriation, so that the law of theft applies only where a voidable title is obtained by fraud or duress, not where it is obtained in other ways.

The implication of a requirement of unlawfulness may be supported on a theory § .3
of objective dishonesty (an act that is lawful under the general law cannot be dishonest) or in order to prevent absurdity and to maintain established legal distinctions. It seems, however, that only the House of Lords can now make the implication, except that the Court of Appeal may hold that where a person obtains an indefeasible title to property, the means by which he does so are not to be accounted dishonest.

If a requirement of unlawfulness is implied, the old distinction between the § .4
facilitation of theft and an act of entrapment which does not result in theft (because the person entrapped acts with the consent of the owner and therefore lawfully, even though he does not know it) still applies.

It was held in *Kaur* that where a person obtains title to goods (whether the title § .5
is valid or voidable), he does not commit theft by the mere acquisition of the title (without possession) nor by subsequently taking delivery of the goods; but Lord Lane has indicated that he now thinks this decision wrong. One may suggest that a good reason for the decision would have been that Kaur did not commit theft, whether or not her acquisition of title was contemporaneous with taking delivery, because she was not guilty of fraud or duress, so that her act was not unlawful. Nevertheless, it seems that since the decision in *Morris*, so long as that stands, there can be an appropriation even with the owner has consented to transfer the property if the consent is tainted by mistake so as to make the transfer voidable (or, of course, void).

Property may fail to pass because an agent acts outside his authority, in which § .6
case the recipient can commit theft.

Where money is paid by mistake, the recipient being under an obligation to repay it, the money is deemed to belong to the payer (s. 5 (4)), so that the recipient can commit theft. § .7

CHAPTER 36

ROBBERY AND SIMILAR OFFENCES

There be land-rats and water-rats, land-thieves and water-thieves,—I mean, pirates.

The Merchant of Venice I iii

§ 36.1. ROBBERY

THE non-lawyer speaks of "robbing a bank" by driving a tunnel into the strong-room; but this is not legal usage. In law, robbery implies force or the threat of it. It is a form of aggravated theft, not triable summarily. Section 8 of the Theft Act provides a new definition.

> "(1) A person is guilty of robbery if he steals, and immediately before or at the time of doing so, and in order to do so, he uses force on any person or puts or seeks to put any person in fear of being then and there subject to force.
> "(2) A person guilty of robbery, or of an assault with intent to rob, shall on conviction on indictment be liable to imprisonment for life."

The definition is still largely free from judicial gloss, so that its legal meaning is to be gathered chiefly from a careful study of its terms; though a knowledge of some of the problems raised by the old case-law (when the definition of the offence was somewhat different) is a help.

In effect, subsection (1) means that the theft must be accompanied by force or the threat of force. The force used may be minimal.

> In *Dawson*[1] the defendant with two others surrounded V; one of them "nudged" him so that he lost his balance, and while he was thus unbalanced another stole his wallet. A conviction of robbery was sustained on appeal. The judge had left it to the jury to decide whether "force" had been used within section 8 (1), and this was held to be a proper course, since "force" is a word in ordinary use which juries understand. The judge had told the jury that the force had to be substantial, but the Court of Appeal left it open whether he was right to apply an adjective to the word of the Act.

The outcome of the case is clearly right; force used in order to cause the victim to lose his balance is evidently within the Act; and the use of the word "substantial" would be an unwarranted gloss. At the same time, it is regrettable that the Court of Appeal did not give further guidance on the meaning of the word. The proper approach, it may be suggested, is to say that force of any degree is, with one exception, sufficient for robbery. So it should be sufficient if force is used:

---

[1] (1976) 64 CAR 170. Cp. *Hale* (1978) 68 CAR 415, [1979] Crim.LR 596.

1 to prevent or overcome conscious resistance (a tug-of-war with the owner, or applying a chloroform pad to the owner's nose), or
2 to sever an article attached to the owner (breaking a watch-chain), or
3 in such a way as to cause injury (tearing an ear-ring from the lobe of the ear).

In each of these instances the force can reasonably be held to be within the section. But—and this is the exception—the force must be something more than the slight exertion of strength used by a "dip" to lift the victim's wallet by stealth from his pocket. Similarly, gentle force used to snatch an article by stealth or surprise should not be enough; otherwise robbery would include all theft from the person, which was obviously not the intention of the Act. Twitching a handbag from a woman caught unawares should not be robbery, but tugging it away when she offers resistance should be. There are no post-Act decisions on these questions.[2]

The force need not be used on the person stolen from; it is robbery to use force on a signalman in order to steal from a train.

The threat of force may be implied from conduct; so where several people surround the victim in such a way as to make resistance hazardous, if not vain, and steal from him, this amounts to robbery.

The threat must be to use force on the present occasion, not a threat to use it in the future by way of reprisal for failing now to submit to the proposed theft. But a threat of present force will readily be held to continue to operate on the victim's mind although the theft is not committed until some time afterwards.[3]

The force threatened must be "on any person"; a threat to damage property is insufficient for this crime (though sufficient for blackmail). And the threat must be of force to be applied to the recipient of the threat; so, oddly, it is not robbery to steal from a man by threatening to injure his baby if he resists, where the baby is not put in fear; but such conduct is again punishable as blackmail.

Subsection (1) says: "puts or seeks to put any person in fear." Suppose the defendant put the victim in fear without meaning to do so, and then took advantage of the fear to steal from him?

The subsection requires that the putting in fear must be "in order to steal." If the defendant did not intend to steal when he accidentally put the victim in fear, he is not guilty of robbery.[4]

The subsection says that the force or threat must be "immediately before or at the time of" stealing. When is the time of the stealing?

Theoretically, the stealing is complete upon the appropriation being

---

[2] In *Batchelor* [1977] Crim.LR 111 a man who snatched a bag from a woman pleaded guilty to robbery. It is surprising that the plea was offered and accepted on such facts. Cp. *Davis* (1980) 144 JPN 707.

[3] See note, [1981] Crim.LR 645. In the case there noted, the judge omitted "immediately before" in his direction to the jury, apparently on the ground that the original threat was being impliedly continued until the time of the theft.

[4] Cp. *Bruce* [1975] 1 WLR 1252, 3 All ER 277.

made—whenever that is.[5] Using force to escape with the loot after committing a theft is not sufficient for robbery, (*a*) because this is used after the theft and (*b*) because it is used in order to escape and not "in order to" steal. The previous legislation included force or threat made immediately after the theft; these words were purposely omitted from the Theft Act. However, in *Hale*[6] the jury were allowed to find that an appropriation continued for some undefined time after the taking. This interpretation takes away the force of the limiting words, demonstrating that there are some changes in the law that Parliament is helpless to make.

§ 36.2. ASSAULT WITH INTENT TO ROB

On a rational view of the law of attempt, every assault with intent to rob is an attempted robbery, and there is no need for a special provision. But before the Criminal Attempts Act it was feared that on some facts an assault might be held to be merely preparatory to a robbery; so the Theft Act provides this special form of aggravated assault.

Upon a charge of robbery there may be a conviction of theft (since robbery is aggravated theft), or of attempted theft; but there cannot be a conviction of assault with intent to rob, which needs a special count. Situations are conceivable in which there is a robbery without assault, as where a thief pulls an article from its owner who tries to prevent him from doing so. The pulling should be sufficient force for robbery, but it is not an assault,[1] unless of course there is an implied threat of a physical assault.

Two offences similar to robbery but outside the Theft Act may be briefly considered.

§ 36.3. PIRACY

English law recognises two forms of piracy, which may be distinguished as piracy *jure gentium* and municipal piracy respectively.

The first is recognisced both by English law and by international law (*jus gentium* as it used to be called). The importance of the latter fact is that this form of piracy is justiciable (triable) by the courts of all countries, irrespective of the place where it occurs. The definition of this form at common law and under old legislation has been superseded by the Tokyo Convention Act 1967 s. 4, which embodies part of the Geneva Convention of 1958. Piracy under the Act of 1967 means illegal violence, detention or depredation, committed by the crew or passengers of a private ship or private aircraft (or by the mutinying crew of a government ship or aircraft)—

(*a*) on the high seas, against *another* ship or aircraft or persons or property on board, or

---

[5] [1978] Crim.LR 69.
[6] N. 1 above.

[1] *Sherriff* [1969] Crim.LR 260.

(*b*) against a ship, aircraft, persons or property in a place outside the jurisdiction of any State (e.g. the south pole).

This definition does not cover violence used on the occasion of a mutiny or hijack on or over States or the high seas. But there are parts of the ancient definition of piracy that appear not to be superseded by the Tokyo Convention Act, which, therefore, continue to operate as part of English municipal law (though, since it is not piracy *jure gentium,* only where the act takes place within the ordinary jurisdiction of our courts, e.g. on a British ship). These depend upon certain old statutes, chiefly the Piracy Act 1698, s. 8, which covers revolt of the crew of a ship against their own master.

Piracy is generally punishable with imprisonment for life, but piracy accompanied by an assault with intent to murder, or an act endangering life, is theoretically (only theoretically) punishable by death.[1]

An offence of incitement to mutiny is created by the Incitement to Mutiny Act 1797 s. 1, and there are also various disciplinary offences applicable to merchant seamen.[2]

§ 36.4. HIJACKING

It will be seen that hijacking does not normally fall within the definition of piracy, but its emergence as an offence of international dimensions has caused it to be governed by international treaty. Legislation now in the Aviation Act 1982 s.1 gives effect to this treaty by creating an offence called "hijacking" in the marginal note. (If we are to suffer a neologism it might as well have been called "skyjacking," since it is confined to the hijacking of aircraft in flight.) In general, the offence is triable by our courts wherever it was committed.

The same act creates various offences of damaging or endangering aircraft, again triable by our courts wherever the act is committed. They include (s. 4) an offence of unlawful possession in an aircraft or aerodrome of such articles as firearms, imitation firearms, and other offensive weapons. There are many ancillary provisions.

SUMMARY

Robbery is aggravated theft, now defined in the Theft Act. The theft must be committed by force or threat of force. Force of any degree is enough, except that in common sense it should be something more than the slight "force" necessary merely to take the property from an unresisting owner. The threat of force must § .1

[1] Piracy Act 1837 s. 2.
[2] Merchant Shipping Act 1970 ss. 27–28, 30, as amended; there are also regulations under the MSA 1979.

be of force against the person, not against property; and it must be of force against the person threatened (who is "put in fear of being then and there subject to force"). According to the section the force or threat must be immediately before or at the time of stealing, i.e. the appropriation; but the courts give it a more extended spread than these words would suggest.

Assault with intent to rob is an aggravated assault. Pulling a thing from its § .2
resisting owner is robbery but not an assault.

Piracy *jure gentium* is now defined in the Tokyo Convention Act 1967. The chief § .3
form is a private attack on another ship or aircraft on or over the high seas. Revolt of the crew of a ship against their own master is a crime by English law (again called piracy): Piracy Act 1698.

Hijacking aircraft in flight is punishable, wherever committed, under the § .4
Aviation Security Act 1982. There are other statutory offences of endangering ships and aircraft.

CHAPTER 37

BLACKMAIL

"I can't believe *that*!" said Alice. "Can't you?" the Queen said in a pitying tone. "Try again: draw a long breath, and shut your eyes." Alice laughed."There's no use trying," she said: "one *can't* believe impossible things." "I dare say you haven't had much practice," said the Queen. "When I was your age, I always did it for half-an-hour a day. Why, sometimes I've believed as many as six impossible things before breakfast."

Lewis Carroll, *Alice Through the Looking-Glass*

§ 37.1. THE DEFINITION OF BLACKMAIL

THE crime of blackmail was formerly of great complexity. A revised and simplified form appears in section 21 of the Theft Act.

> "(1) A person is guilty of blackmail, if, with a view to gain for himself or another or with intent to cause loss to another, he makes any unwarranted demand with menaces; and for this purpose a demand with menaces is unwarranted unless the person making it does so in the belief—
> (*a*) that he has reasonable grounds for making the demand; and
> (*b*) that the use of the menaces is a proper means of reinforcing the demand.
>
> (2) The nature of the act or omission demanded is immaterial, and it is also immaterial whether the menaces relate to action to be taken by the person making the demand.
>
> (3) A person guilty of blackmail shall on conviction on indictment be liable to imprisonment for a term not exceeding 14 years."

How does this crime differ from robbery?

1 The threat in robbery is made to get property, whereas a blackmailing demand under the section has the wider purpose of making any gain or causing a loss. The purpose may be, for example, to get a job.

2 The full offence of blackmail is committed as soon as the demand is made; nothing need have been handed over (whereas theftous appropriation is essential for the crime of robbery).

3 Blackmail requires menaces; robbery requires the threat of force (or actual force); in practice the threat of force will almost always be a menace.

Getting property from someone by threatening immediate force against him is both robbery and blackmail, though it would invariably be charged as robbery.

Getting property by the actual use of force without threats (striking the victim without giving him a chance of surrendering) is robbery but not blackmail, which needs a menace.

Menaces other than threats of immediate force against a person who is put in fear can be blackmail but cannot ripen into robbery. Examples are;

— a threat by a "protection racketeer" to blow up a building;

— a threat to kill a third party who does not know of the threat;
— a threat to get the victim dismissed from his job; and
— a threat to make known discreditable facts about the victim.

Taking a hostage and extorting a ransom would generally be prosecuted as blackmail, kidnapping or false imprisonment, but if the hostage knows what is happening and so is put in fear it would also be robbery.

Blackmail is often severely punished by the courts (sometimes with unnecessary severity), because of the distress that it causes[1] and the ease with which a victim by the use of such threats may be made to part with large sums of money. Where the blackmailing threat is to reveal discreditable facts about the victim, judges generally allow the victim to give evidence in court under the name of "X."

§ 37.2. THE ECONOMIC MENTAL ELEMENT

It will be noticed that there are two mental elements.

The first, which we may call the economic mental element, is that the menacer must intend to make a gain or cause a loss.

The second is expressed in the Act by saying that the demand must be unwarranted; but the Act immediately makes it clear that what is warranted or unwarranted is subjective to the defendant. The question relates not to the objective nature of the demand but to the defendant's state of mind about his demand. For want of a better name I propose to call it the unscrupulous mental element, a scrupulous defendant being required to believe both (*a*) and (*b*) of subsection (1). It is considered in § .4.

The intent must be to obtain a gain or cause a loss—expressions that are defined in section 34 (l) to extend only to "gain or loss in money or other property." The object of this formula is to exclude a demand for sexual intercourse, for example. Such a demand does not fall within the notion of an offence in respect of property (with which alone the Theft Act is concerned). The requirement of an economic mental element means that many kinds of discreditable pressures are not an offence under the Theft Act or at all. Examples of threats where there is or may be no economic motive are threats to accuse of discreditable conduct made:

— to get the victim's consent to marry his daughter; or
— to compel the victim to use his influence to procure an honorific but unremunerated appointment for the blackmailer; or
— to get custody of the blackmailer's child when he is not entitled to the custody; or
— to dissuade the victim from prosecuting the blackmailer for some offence, or from reporting on the offence to the police[1]; or;

---

[1] E.g. in *Cossington* [1973] Crim.LR 319 a blackmailer who obtained £20 from homosexuals was sentenced to 7 years.

[1] But this would be an attempt to obstruct justice.

— to induce the victim not to reveal past discreditable conduct by the blackmailer; or
— to induce the victim to introduce the blackmailer to high society, or to nominate him for membership of an exclusive club.

Even an attempt to make a civil servant disclose military or political secrets by threatening to reveal that he is a homosexual would not be blackmail, though it would be an incitement to commit an offence under the Official Secrets Acts.

But in some of these cases the threatener may have hoped to make a gain eventually. Being introduced to high society, or getting an honorific appointment, might be turned to advantage.

The courts have not had to consider whether a hope of indirect economic advantage, not directly derived from the advantage that is immeditaly sought, is sufficient for the crime of blackmail. It may be held that general hope of advantage as a result of an improvement in the threatener's social, business or professional position is insufficient because it is too unquantifiable. But the more likely attitude of the judges would be to leave the jury to decide whether in all the circumstances a substantial part of the threatener's intention was to make a monetary gain.

If V is suing D for a debt or damages, could it be blackmail for D to use menaces to V to make him discontinue the action?

By section 34 (2) (*a*), " 'gain' includes a gain by keeping what one has." So the case is covered.

If a person demands payment of money that is due to him, is his intent to obtain a gain?

Again yes.[2] A bird in the hand, etc. But the creditor who makes such a demand will not be guilty of blackmail unless he has the unscrupulous mental element. We are leaving this matter over at present. (In practice the charge against the creditor who uses high-handed methods of debt collection is likely to be the special offence of harassment of debtors, which has already been mentioned,[3] and there are other offences of more limited ambit, as well as licensing controls over debt-collecting agencies which can be particularly effective.[4]) In the unusual case where a person is convicted of a blackmailing threat to compel the payment of money actually due, the courts sometimes take a very lenient line.[5]

§ 37.3. THE DEMAND WITH MENACES

Section 21 requires a demand[1] with menaces. Normally the making of the

---

[2] *Parkes* [1973] Crim.LR 358.
[3] § 9.9 at n. 27.
[4] See Lawson in 132 NLJ 287.
[5] E.g. in *Helal* (1980) 145 JPN 135.

[1] The demand is made where a blackmailing letter is posted: *Treacy* [1971] AC 537.

demand will be clear, but it may be difficult to establish if dressed up as a reciprocal contract. In particular, an announced intention to write one's memoirs may violate the spirit but not the letter of the section.

> The most notorious instance of such moral blackmail was that by Harriette Wilson, a courtesan of the early 1800s. Finding that her charms alone could no longer sustain her in her style of life, she conceived the idea of writing an account of her many lovers, charging an honorarium for each name left out.[2] If adroitly executed, such a plan might well escape the law of blackmail. A man who, having heard of the projected book, took the initiative of offering money to have his own contribution to the author's life passed by, could hardly claim that he had received a demand. However, there would be a strong likelihood of a court finding an implied demand if this is at all possible on the facts. Harriette went so far as to publish her memoirs by instalments, which increased the pressure on her victims.

It is hard to see any difference of meaning between a blackmailing "menace" and an ordinary "threat,"[3] except that the more intensive word "menace" enables the court to ignore very trivial threats. (By a curiosity of language menaces are commonly spoken of in the plural, but of course one menace is enough.)

Is it blackmail to threaten evil to someone other than the person threatened?

The threat is still "menaces" within the section.

Need the menace frighten the victim?

The menace will still be such although, owing to facts unknown to the blackmailer, it makes no impression on the person to whom it is addressed.[4] The fact that the blackmailer thinks he has or may have produced an effective menace is enough.

The court that decided this point also formulated an ordinary-man test of menace, saying that it must be "of such a nature and extent that the mind of an ordinary person of normal stability and courage might be influenced or made apprehensive so as to accede unwillingly to the demand."

> The advantage of this rule to the defendant is illustrated by the cautionary tale of the student who, organising a University rag, sent letters to local shopkeepers telling them that they could avoid "inconvenience" on rag day if they paid up to £5 each into the rag fund. He found himself in the dock, charged with blackmail, no less. Luckily he was acquitted on the direction of the judge, who took the view that the threat was not a menace because it was not likely to affect the mind of an ordinary person.[5]

Although the ordinary person test may have a certain utility, it also raises problems. (1) Whether an ordinary person would accede unwillingly to the demand depends not only on the terror of the threat but on the enormity of the demand. A millionaire, threatened with exposure for some youthful indiscretion, might prefer to pay up on a demand for £50, but the ordinary millionaire of normal stability and courage would probably balk at paying a million pounds. It can hardiy be the law that what would otherwise be a blackmailing demand ceases to be so because of its enormity. So the rule must be that a threat that would intimidate an ordinary person to accede to a small demand is a menace even if the demand is an immense

---

[2] One of the victims was Lord Brougham LC. See Kenneth Bourne ed., *The Blackmailing of the Chancellor* (London 1975).

[3] Cp. Lord Wright in *Thorne* v. *Motor Trade Assn.* (1937] AC at 817.

[4] *Clear* [1968] 1 QB 670.

[5] *Harry* [1974] Crim.LR 32; see the valuable commentary on this case. But a blackmailer cannot get off merely by using the language of request: *Robinson* (1796) 2 Leach at 766, 168 ER at 483.

one. (2) A blackmailer who plays upon the fears of a person *whom he knows* to be particularly sensitive or timorous can hardly defend himseif on the score of such sensitivity or timidity.[6]

On the whole, it may be thought that the ordinary person test creates more difficulties than it solves. The question should be left in the simple words of the Act: have menaces been used? The acquittal of the student can be explained on the ground that he was not apparently threatening anything more than good-natured horse-play.

Can a threat not to do something that it is one's duty to do be a blackmailing menace?

Obviously it can be. A threat not to feed someone whom the blackmailer has kidnapped would undoubtedly be sufficient, the blackmailer being under the usual duty to feed helpless persons in his charge.[7]

Then would it be blackmail for a debtor to shake his creditor down for a 50 per cent. discount by saying that otherwise he will not pay any part of the debt?

The debtor may believe that he ought not reasonably be asked to pay the full debt, in which case he could argue at his trial that he lacked the unscrupulous mental element. The difficulty arises if the debtor acknowledges that the debt was justly owing, and that he was acting unscrupulously.

It seems obvious that some means of excluding the situation from the section must be found. The solution would be to say that the particular threat is not a "menace." It has always been common enough for debtors who are in difficulties to attempt to obtain an agreed reduction in their debts, and a threat not to pay a debt could not be called a "menace" in the ordinary meaning of that word.

Who decides whether the threat is a menace?

The jury; but judges exercise the usual control.[8] In the case just put, if the judge left the case to the jury and the jury found that the threat to withhold payment of the debt was a menace, the Court of Appeal might perhaps quash a conviction, but the point is by no means clear.

Can a threat to bring a civil action be a menace?

The question is of practical importance only if there is evidence that the threatener did not believe that he had a just cause of action. If he believed he had a just claim, he lacked the unscrupulous mental element. If he did not believe it, and therefore was unscrupulous (because of para. (*a*)), then a threat of a civil action might well be found by the jury to be a menace, at any rate if the proceedings threatened would involve allegations against the defendant of discreditable conduct—for example, if it were a threatened action for a sexual assault. Not only the claimant but his

---

[6] It was held in *Lawrence* [1971] Crim.LR 645 that a conviction is not open to attack merely because the judge has not defined the word "menaces" for the jury; but the evidence made it clear that there was a threat of physical attack. The court added that in exceptional cases where because of special knowledge in special circumstances what would be a menace to an ordinary person was not a menace to the person to whom it was addressed, or *vice versa,* it was no doubt necessary to spell out the meaning of the word.

[7] § 12.3.

[8] See *Harry,* n. 5 above.

solicitor who lent himself to the false claim could be charged with blackmail.

§ 37.4. THE UNSCRUPULOUS MENTAL ELEMENT

We now pass to the more difficult of the two mental elements specified in the section. The Crown must disprove one or other of the two beliefs mentioned in the section, satisfying the jury either;

(*a*) that the defendant did not believe that he had reasonable grounds for making the demand, or

(*b*) that the defendant did not believe that the use of the menaces was a proper means of reinforcing the demand.[1]

Suppose that the threatener knew he had no legal right to the property demanded; could he still be found to have believed that he had reasonable grounds for making the demand, thus lacking the unscrupulous element under (a)?

Certainly. He may have won money on a wager, which is void by statute but generally regarded as binding in honour. So if a bookmaker has not paid out winnings, the aggrieved punters may well threaten to have him posted at Tattersalls,[2] because this is a recognised sanction against defaulting bookmakers.

A man's mistress or "unwedded wife" may claim against him money he has promised her, though she has taken legal advice and knows she cannot in law recover money promised on what the law regards as an immoral consideration. In cases of this kind it is fully understandable that the threatener believed he (or she) had reasonable grounds for making the demand, and therefore lacked the unscrupulous mental element under (*a*), even though he (or she) knew that it was not a legally enforceable demand.

Could the mistress threaten to expose the man to his wife if he does not pay money?

The question is for the jury. They may quite well find, at least in some circumstances, that the lady has skirted the law of blackmail.

In the debate on the Theft Bill when it was before the House of Lords, Lord Stow Hill criticised the blackmail section as follows.

> "I instance the case of a lady who supposes that she is in an interesting condition as the result of her association with a gentleman who is married. She has asked him to make provision for the expected arrival in this world of a new child, and he has refused. He is well off and she thinks, no doubt rightly, that his conduct is indescribably evil and selfish. She passionately thinks it, and so she goes to him and says, 'Look here, if you don't make an adequate settlement on this child I will tell your wife, I will tell your employers; I will write letters to the Press; I will do everything I can to make you make

---

[1] An evidential burden doubtless rests on the defendant. See *Harvey* (1980) 72 CAR 139 at 142; D J Lamming in [1974] Crim.LR 33.

[2] Cp. *Burden* v. *Harris* [1937] 4 All ER 559. A horse owner may be reported to the Jockey Club: *Bubb* v. *Yelverton* (1870) LR 9 Eq. 471.

a settlement on the child.' Does she, in these circumstances, commit the crime of blackmail?

"In order to test the matter a little further, and possibly to make the example a little more difficult, may I assume this: that she is a lady who feels that this unfortunate infant is going to be born into the world, through no fault of his, labouring under the stigma of being an illegitimate child. What would be a reasonable settlement in the case of an infant born in lawful wedlock into a family is not sufficient in his case; it must be a much more generous settlement. She might say: "You must give three-quarters of your wealth in order to make a settlement on this unhappy child which is going through life with this disadvantage." The amount she has in mind might be such that ordinary people would think it a wholly unreasonable request. But if the jury are to ask themselves, what does she think about it, what is her belief, however unreasonable it may be, however it might beggar the family of the married man, ought they not to come to the conclusion that she is not guilty; that she has the belief that she has (*a*) reasonable ground for making the demand, and (*b*) that the use of menaces is a proper means of reinforcing the demand? . . .

"May I put yet one more ingredient? Supposing it be the case that, contrary to her suspicions, she is not in the condition that I have described. She is in exactly the same condition, without knowing it, as she was before she met this man who is married. What then? A lady who has no anxieties of the sort that I have described, nevertheless believes that she has, and insists upon £1 million being settled. Where are we? Is that blackmail or is it not?"[3]

These questions received no reply. Nor has the point arisen in any reported case since the Act. It is true, however, that the lady would have a fair chance of being acquitted. Indeed, it was the intention of the Act to remove this type of claim, in general, from the scope of blackmail. In one case before 1968, a poorly educated girl who wrote to a man of position that if he did not pay her money for an alleged indecent assault she would "summons" him and "let the town knowed about your going on" was convicted of blackmail,[4] but this occasioned some adverse comment. The girl could lawfully have instructed a solicitor to write the man a letter saying that unless he paid so much damages for assault an action for damages would be brought for the assault; and the man would well understand that the real point of the threat to sue in such circumstances would be the threat of publicity. So the girl was really punished for not making her claim through the usual professional channel. Since the Theft Act she could not be convicted if she believed that she had been assaulted and that her threat was a proper one. Of course, if it could be shown that she had not been assaulted, her claim to believe that she had been would almost certainly be discredited.

There are further arguments in favour of keeping the law of blackmail to a narrow compass. We are accustomed to a considerable measure of anarchy in the harsh economic world. Under present arrangements, concurred in by all, trade unions are entitled to hold not only employers but the general public to ransom. Perhaps a powerful trade organisation or trade union threatens a small retailer or industrialist to put him on a "stop list" unless he pays a so-called "fine" or agrees to conform to rules designed to benefit the organisation. The leader of a trade union of public employees threatens to call a strike which will deprive the public of its water supply, fire service, electricity, sewage disposal, hospitals or schools unless his members have their pay substantially increased. A trade union sets up a "kangaroo court" to fine its members who have refused to take part in a strike, with the threat that if they do not pay the fines the union will procure their dismissal from their jobs. Although some control has been imposed on some of these forms of behaviour, so far society has been unable to deal effectively with most of them. Monopolistic practices by employers can to some extent be curbed under the legislation specifically directed against monopolies. But the attempts of both Labour and Conservative governments to impose curbs on trade unions have generally been defeated by the superior economic and political power of the unions. In this state of affairs, it would hardly be wise to extend the law of blackmail to economic pressures, except perhaps in extreme circumstances.

Take worse cases than those. The threatener says at his trial that he believed he had reasonable grounds because he was a poor man while the person he

---

[3] *Parl.Deb.*, H of L, vol. 289 cols. 248–249 (February 15, 1968).
[4] *Dymond* [1920] 2 KB 260.

threatened was a property tycoon who had made money in unconscionable ways. Or because the person threatened was a Jew and the funds were needed to re-establish Palestinians in their homeland. Or because funds were needed to finance an insurrection against "imperialism." He may put his case with burning passion. Some people have warped minds and appear genuinely to believe complete absurdities. Since the Act words the unscrupulous mental element in purely subjective terms, doesn't it mean that every blackmailer who acquires the White Queen's ability must be let off?

There is force in your criticism of the Act. If section 21 were now being enacted I think that some restriction would be imposed on the subjective test. At least, the statute would create a class of menaces that are absolutely forbidden, such as a threat to injure.[5]

However, the section need not be read as stating a rule of pure subjectivism. The question under (*b*) is whether the defendant believed that his menaces were "proper," and "proper" was intended by the CLRC to mean, and can be read as meaning, "proper in the minds of people generally." On this view the question is whether the defendant believed that people generally would approve (or not disapprove) of his conduct. The test accords with the model direction on dishonesty stated by the Court of Appeal in *Ghosh*.[6] In *Harvey*,[7] the Court of Appeal not only appeared to accept this interpretation of section 21 but in one respect went further.

> The defendants had made threats to kill, maim and rape; and the judge had directed the jury as a matter of law that threats to commit such serious criminal offences could not be a proper means of reinforcing a demand—not even though the demand was for payment of money that was thought to be morally due. On appeal against conviction the court said that the question whether the defendants believed that the injuries they threatened to inflict would be lawful should technically have been left to the jury; but since the threats were to do acts that any sane man knew were against the laws of every civilised country, the court applied the proviso and affirmed the conviction.

The decision is clearly correct, and seems in effect to extend to blackmail the rule in *Ghosh*, even though the court does not say so in terms. But the court went beyond the facts of the case before it, and (it may be strongly argued) went too far, when it said that if the defendant knows that the act he threatens is "unlawful," this is enough to show that he knows that his menace is not "proper" within the meaning of paragraph (*b*).

> " 'Proper' is plainly a word of wide meaning, certainly wider than (for example) 'lawful.' But the greater includes the less and no act which was not believed to be lawful could be believed to be proper within the meaning of the subsection."

---

[5] A threat to murder is an independent offence: § 9.9 at n. 16.

[6] § 32.5 at n. 16.

[7] N. 1 above.

The logic is defective. What the court evidently means is that "proper" is a word of narrower denotation than "lawful" (though it says the opposite). But when the argument is rewritten to make it logical, it remains unconvincing because the major premise is unconvincing. Even a judge would probably find himself forced to admit in some circumstances that an act is proper although unlawful, and public opinion would concede the point more readily than a judge. It is one thing to say that people generally would certainly frown on threats to kill and rape, another to say that they would certainly frown on a threat by a trade union leader to procure breaches of contract, or to organise a trespass upon factory premises; and it would be going even further to say that public opinion on such matters is so clear that the defendant, whoever he is, must have known of it. The Act makes the defendant's belief a jury question, not a matter to be settled by a misplaced reliance on logic.

Suppose, to take another example, that the defendant has threatened to continue to make harassing telephone calls to the debtor (a minor criminal offence) if the debt is not paid. A defence of belief in propriety must be left to the jury, and the judge's failure to do so should not constitute a case for the application of the proviso. In any case, the possibility of the proviso being applied on appeal does not displace the rule that the trial judge should *always* leave the question of the defendant's belief in propriety to the jury.

Although a modification of subjectivism in terms of what the defendant believed society would think proper solves some problems, it does not get over the difficulty of determining who constitute the "society" whose opinions (as judged by the defendant) are decisive. A political gangster may realise that people generally would disapprove of him but rest secure in the knowledge that he receives the approval of members of his own subculture. Whatever other people may think, he and his friends hold it to be perfectly all right to wring money out of rich companies by holding their executives to ransom, or out of airline companies to secure the safe return of their aircraft, and so on. To counter these claims by asserting the supremacy of the general culture over the subculture would be to write into the Act a test that is not there, though the courts will probably feel driven to do so if the question arises.[8]

A factor of prime importance in a blackmail case will frequently be the secrecy or the openness of the transaction. A man who thinks he is acting properly in making a threat will not try to conceal his identity, and demand that money should be left in used pound notes at a telephone kiosk. Again, it is in practice impossible for a defendant both to argue that he did not utter the menaces and that if he did they were justified. So, if he chooses merely to deny the menaces, and the jury find against him and the menaces were *prima facie* improper, the judge need not direct the jury on the unscrupulous mental element.

§ 37.5. EXTORTION

It is an offence at common law for a public officer to take, by colour of his office, any money or thing that is not due to him.[1] Presumably he must know that it is not due. Prosecutions are now unknown, but if a case arose it would be simpler to charge this offence than blackmail.

---

[8] In 1967, during a strike by lorry drivers, some pickets exacted "contributions to strike funds" from firms not parties to the dispute as a condition of letting their lorries through. Their action was repudiated by their trade union, and presumably the pickets knew that their behaviour would not be approved by general opinion; but no prosecutions were brought.

[1] Russell, 12th edn i 370.

SUMMARY

Under the Theft Act, the offence of blackmail is committed as soon as a § .1
blackmailing demand is made.

The defendant must intend to make a property gain or cause a property loss. § .2
Making a gain includes keeping what one has, and also getting a payment that one is entitled to.

The demand must be with menaces. A trivial threat may be held not to come § .3
within this word. It is not clear whether a threat by a debtor to withhold payment unless the debt is reduced would be capable of being a menace, but it should not be. A threat to bring an action may well be found to be a menace, if the other conditions of the crime are satisfied.

The demand must be unwarranted, the burden of proof of this resting, as usual, § .4
on the prosecution, though an evidential burden probably rests on the defence. The Act declares that a demand with menaces is unwarranted unless the defendant believes (*a*) that he has reasonable grounds for making the demand, and (*b*) that the use of the menaces is a proper means of reinforcing the demand. A person can have reasonable grounds for making a demand although he knows that the property demanded is not legally due to him. A person who knows that his behaviour will be generally condemned will be regarded as unwarranted in making the demand with menaces: *Harvey*.

It is the offence of extortion at common law for a public officer to take, by colour § .5
of his office, any money or thing that is not due to him.

Chapter 38

BURGLARY AND PREPARATORY OFFENCES

> With increasing well-being, all people become aware, sooner or later, that they have something to protect.
>
> J K Galbraith, *The Affluent Society*

§ 38.1. THE DEFINITION OF BURGLARY

Certain statutory offences of a preparatory kind are contained in the Theft Act and other legislation. We shall include burglary in this list, because part of the definition of burglary makes it a preparatory offence, even though most burglars go beyond preparation and actually commit an offence in the building.

The common law crime of burglary was extremely technical, and the Theft Act makes a fresh start. Section 9 runs as follows

> "(1) A person is guilty of burglary if—
> (*a*) he enters any building or part of a building as a trespasser and with intent to commit any such offence as is mentioned in subs. (2) below; or
> (*b*) having entered any building or part of a building as a trespasser he steals or attempts to steal anything in the building or that part of it or inflicts or attempts to inflict on any person therein any grievous bodily harm.
>
> (2) The offences referred to in subs. (1) (*a*) above are offences of stealing[1] anything in the building or part of a building in question, of inflicting on any person therein any grievous bodily harm or raping any woman therein, and of doing unlawful damage to the building or anything therein.
>
> (3) References in subss. (1) and (2) above to a building shall apply also to an inhabited vehicle or vessel, and shall apply to any such vehicle or vessel at times when the person having a habitation in it is not there as well as at times when he is.
>
> (4) A person guilty of burglary shall on conviction on indictment be liable to imprisonment for a term not exceeding 14 years."

Section 10 creates an offence of aggravated burglary, punishable with imprisonment for life, if the burglar has with him at the time of the burglary[2] any firearm or imitation firearm, any weapon of offence, or any explosive.

Whereas most offences under the Theft Act are triable either way, the more serious ones are purely indictable: robbery, assault with intent to rob, blackmail, and some forms of burglary. The precise rule for burglary

[1] This does not cover the offence of dishonestly using electricity: *Low* v. *Blease* [1975] Crim.LR 513. Nor the offence of taking a conveyance.

[2] See *Francis* [1982] Crim.LR 363.

is somewhat complicated, and it is enough to say that ordinary burglary simply for the purpose of theft is triable either way, whereas burglary involving violence is generally triable only on indictment.[3] Burglary of a dwelling-house (whether anyone is there at the time or not) is rightly regarded as much more serious than simple theft of an equivalent amount; even magistrates will frequently send the burglar to prison.

§ 38.2. ENTRY TO A BUILDING

Burglary requires an *entry* as a trespasser. It is not burglary to *remain* in a building as a trespasser with burglarious intent.[1] Even an actual theft in the building by a person who has become a trespasser will not constitute burglary if the thief was not a trespasser when he entered.

Is it an entry to get only part of your torso across the threshold?

Yes at common law. Even putting a finger through a window with intent to steal was sufficient.[2] The authorities at common law do not seem to have been considered in *Collins,*[3] where the Court of Appeal required a "substantial entry." It may be that this case does not finally decide the point. The merit of the common law was that it provided a clear rule. How much of the body must be over the threshold to constitute a "substantial entry"? It is not against common sense to say that an entry with a small part of the body can constitute burglary.[4]

Another problem concerns the use of instruments. If one person standing at his bedroom window shoots at another person in a room across the street, this is a trespass (because of the entry of the bullet) but it would be absurd to call it burglary. In common sense, the marksman does not enter as a trespasser. It is true that there was an entry in the old law of burglary, but the courts now have the opportunity to consider these questions afresh, and it would seem reasonable to require an entry by at least a part of the body.[5]

Does the doctrine of innocent agency apply to burglary under the Theft Act?

At common law one could enter through an innocent agent, e.g. through a small child (under the age of responsibility) who was put into the premises to steal.[6] There is little social need for this construction of the offence, since few people would feel alarmed by the entry of a small child: the case of entry by a child could be adjudged as simply theft or attempted

---

[3] For the precise rule see CLA 1977 Sched. 3 para. 28.

[1] But if found in the building the unwelcome entrant may be guilty under the Vagrancy Act: § .5.
[2] *Davis* (1823) Russ. & R 499, 168 ER 917.
[3] [1973] QB 100. See § .4 at n. 5.
[4] See Smith 169.
[5] *Contra,* Griew 76.
[6] See Griew 75.

theft by the adult. However, the courts will probably continue the old rule if the question arises.

Could an entry into an uninhabited building be burglary?

Yes. Buildings need not be habitations, so shops, offices, warehouses and churches are included. At common law burglary could only be in a dwelling-house, but this limitation has been removed. The expression "building" probably includes also small fixed structures like summer-houses and outhouses.[7]

It was not wished to extend the law to thefts from movables like a car or railway carriage. On the other hand, mobile homes needed to be included, and they are therefore expressly included provided that they are inhabited.

Is a cabin cruiser within the law of burglary when it is moored and unoccupied during the winter?

The courts will probably say that if it is inhabited for part of the year by a person who, when he leaves, intends to resume habitation, it is within the law of burglary for the whole year. See subsection (3).

So a person who steals from a motor caravan in a car park is a burglar even though the owner is not on holiday and is using the van for shopping?

It seems so, odd though that may be.

§ 38.3. THE INTENT

The intent required for burglary is clearly set out in section 9 (see § .1). A curiosity of the wording may be noticed. Whereas a person who trespassorily enters a building with intent to commit rape or damage is a burglar, one who enters without burglarious intent but who actually commits rape or damage after entry is not. On the other hand a trespasser in a building who actually steals or inflicts grievous bodily harm[1] or attempts to do so is a burglar even though he did not enter with that intent.

So, just to ram the point home, we may sort out six types of burglary.

1 Entry as a trespasser with intent to steal.[2]
2 Entry as a trespasser with intent to inflict g.b.h.
3 Entry as a trespasser with intent to rape.
4 Entry as a trespasser with intent to do unlawful damage.
5 Stealing or attempting to steal after entry as a trespasser.
6 Inflicting or attempting to inflict g.b.h. after entry as a trespasser.

Most people think of burglars as a specialised class of thieves. Isn't it strange to bring in other intents?

These other intents rarely arise, but the law of burglary has never been confined to cases where the intent is to steal. The historical justification for

---

[7] A "prefab" without foundations can be a building: *Leathley* [1979] Crim. LR 314.

[1] This expression refers to an offence under OAPA s. 20: *Jenkins* [1983] Crim.LR 386.
[2] As in the case of an attempt, it is sufficient that the intruder was prospecting for something that he might think worth stealing: *Walkington* [1979] 1 WLR 1169, 2 All ER 716, 68 CAR 427.

the special offence is the alarm that a criminal invasion of a dwelling-house causes. The alarm of the inhabitants would not be diminished by knowing that the intruders have come to maim or rape rather than to steal.

Can you take it for granted that the intruder has entered with one of the specified intents?

Certainly not. But of course the jury may infer criminal intent if it is the only reasonable explanation of suspicious behaviour.

Suppose Bill Sykes has entered a girls' school at night. Probably he intended to commit rape, but just possibly he intended to steal. Can he be convicted of burglary, without proving which?

Yes.

Where there is a doubt as to the intent, the different intents may be charged in the alternative in the same count.[3] Then the jury can convict even though they cannot decide between the intents alleged, if they are sure that the defendant had one of them. In this respect the charge of burglary is more favourable to the prosecution than a charge of attempt, where a single intent must be specified, since attempts to commit different crimes are themselves different crimes.[4]

I can see that this gives burglary the edge over attempt from the prosecutor's point of view. But on the whole I don't see that there was sufficient reason to preserve burglary in the Theft Act.

It is true that if the crime of burglary were abolished, this need not make any appreciable difference to the enforcement of the criminal law. But trespassory entry into premises is such a distinctive feature of aggravation of crime that it is beneficial to have it recorded in the type of conviction. The Court of Appeal has emphasised that burglary of dwelling-houses is so serious an offence that even adolescents engaging in it should expect to lose their liberty,[5] which they might not do for theft without this aggravating feature.

There was an additional reason for the crime of burglary before 1981, when the law of attempt was traditionally so circumscribed that one could not be sure that the courts would hold every burglarious entry to be a sufficient act of attempt to commit the crime in view, as going beyond "mere preparation." Perhaps since the Criminal Attempts Act they will; but we still do not know for sure.

There is also the point made just now, that the burglary charge saves the prosecution from having to prove the precise intent. And it means that one can apply the law of attempt to burglary itself: attempting to enter the premises can be attempted burglary.

§ 38.4. THE TRESPASS

Trespass in the law of tort includes any presence on property without legal

---

[3] § 6.10 at n. 11.
[4] See *Jones* v. *Brooks* (1968) 52 CAR 614.
[5] *Smith and Woollard* (1978) 67 CAR 211.

right—that is to say, otherwise than with the consent of the possessor (occupier) or by authority of law. This is also its meaning in the present context.

On a prosecution for burglary, must the occupier of the building produce his title deeds?

Trespass is a wrong to possession, not to ownership. It is enough for evidence to be given that someone other than the defendant was in possession and that the defendant was wrongfully in the building.

Need the defendant know that he is trespassing?

The Act on its face seems to impose objective liability in respect of the fact of trespass. But the courts imply a requirement of *mens rea*. The defendant must either know he is a trespasser or be reckless as to this.[1]

> So a man who enters a caravan with intent to steal would commit burglary unless he believes that the caravan is not inhabited within the meaning of the Act. Such a belief is unlikely, because if the intruder knows that it is or may be a private family caravan, he must realise that there is a possibility of the family having lived in it and coming to live in it again if they are not living in it at the moment.

When must the mental element exist?

At the time of the *actus reus*. We must therefore draw a distinction.

- If a man is charged with entering a building with intent to steal etc., he must have the full mental element at the time of entry, and therefore must know when he enters that he has or may have no right to enter.
- If he is charged with stealing in a building having entered as a trespasser (see s. 9 (1) (*b*)), it is enough that he knows he has no right to be there when he steals. If, therefore, a man enters the wrong house by mistake for one that he has a right to enter, discovers his mistake and steals in the house, he is guilty of burglary, notwithstanding that he did not know that he was trespassing when he entered.

Suppose a customer in a shop slips into the cashier's office and helps himself from the till?

He is gulty of burglary in entering a part of the building as a trespasser and stealing therein. He knows he has no right to be in the office. In this type of case, it is enough that the intruder has the burglarious intent when he enters the "part" of the building; he need not have had it when he first entered the building.[2]

---

[1] *Collins*, below at n. 5.

[2] It seems that a "part of a building" must be in some way physically marked off. Part of a shop marked off by counters on three sides, to which area the public are not admitted, comes within the notion: *Walkington* [1979] 1 WLR 1169, 2 All ER 716, 68 CAR 427. The court said that if there were a single table in the middle of a shop to which the public were not intended to have access, it would be difficult for any jury to find properly that it was "part of a building" for this technical purpose. (Would they be allowed to find it improperly?) There must be some restriction on the notion of "part of a building," otherwise the rule requiring intent at the time of entry would lose its force. It would seem, however, that a notice excluding the public say from one end of a room would make that end "part of a building."

What if the owner assists the thief's entry in order to trap him?

If it is merely a question of leaving the street door unlocked, this is not consent to an entry, even though it is done to catch a thief. But the owner may do more. If D tries to bribe V's employee to let him in, and the employee, having informed V, on V's instructions lets D in, the authorities at common law were conflicting on whether burglary was committed.[3] On principle, it is not. An occupier who with full knowledge of the facts lets another into his premises can hardly be heard to say that the other is a trespasser against him. Besides, the alarm caused by a criminal intruder in a building (which is the main concern of the law of burglary) hardly arises if the intruder has been let in knowing his criminal intention. D is, however, guilty of theft if he appropriates something inside.

Suppose a man knocks at the door of a house occupied by an old lady living alone; she lets him enter, and he then asks her for money, which she gives to him. Could this be burglary?

Yes if the jury find that she was intimidated and the man knew it. The intimidation would vitiate her apparent consent to his entry and he would be a trespasser. He need not know the law of trespass; it is enough that he knows that the person who lets him in is (or may be) intimidated.

Then does the grisly doctrine of vitiation of consent by fraud rear itself again?

In the law of burglary the discussion has taken a different turn, which we are presently to come to.

Can a member of the family be a trespasser, or is he one of the occupiers?

In civil law, occupation (possession) is a technical concept. The father of the family is the occupier if he is the owner or tenant of the house. Similarly the mother if she is. But other people may be there by the occupier's implied licence: the spouse and children, of course (who may be there even by authority of law so long as the occupier is bound to maintain them and they have no other home), guests, lodgers, and domestic employees.

Some or all of these people also have the occupier's implied authority to invite (licence) others to enter.

A thief sees a little boy of 5 playing at the open door of a house. He says: "Can I come in, sonny?" The little boy assents, so the thief goes in and steals something. Is this burglary?

Presumably the jury would be encouraged to find that a child of that age had no authority to invite a man to enter, and that the thief could not have believed that he had.

---

[3] *Egginton* (1801) East *PC* ii 666; Leach 913, 168 ER 555 (not burglary where the employee opened the door on V's order: § 15.17 at n. 1); *Johnson* (1841) C & M 218, 174 ER 479 (employee opened door on instructions of police; not burglary); *Chandler* [1913] 1 K.B. 125 (burglary where employee supplied D with a key); *The General Part,* 2nd edn §§ 254, 255.

Suppose the son of the family came home one day intending to steal from his father? Or brought in a boon companion who did so?

There are two decided cases bearing on these questions, and since they appear to be partly in opposition they cannot both state the right rule.[4] The first case, *Collins*,[5] defies the law's gravity.

> Collins was a young man who, intending to commit rape, stripped off his clothes and climbed a ladder by moonlight to the open lattice window of the bedroom in which the daughter of the house (aged 18) was asleep. She awoke, and became aware that the form poised at the window was that of a blond naked male in a state of visible lust. Immediately coming to the conclusion that he was her regular boy-friend, she opened her arms to him. Collins, though doubtless surprised at this friendly reception, took advantage of it. Later, putting on the light and discovering her error, the girl slapped him on the face, bit him, and retired to the bathroom. The next day Collins was charged not with rape or attempted rape, as he might have expected, but with burglary, of which offence he was in due course convicted. It was held on appeal that he was not guilty unless he knew at the time of entering that he was not invited by the girl to enter, or was reckless as to the fact. Since the jury had not been directed on this issue, a conviction of burglary was quashed.

The daughter of the family is not the occupier, and the young woman's mother, who appears to have been the occupier, would doubtless have objected to the defendant's entry. But the court said;

> "The point was raised that, the complainant [the girl] not being the tenant or occupier of the dwelling house and her mother being apparently in occupation, this girl herself could not in any event have extended an effective invitation to enter. . . . Whatever be the position in the law of tort, to regard such a proposition as acceptable in the criminal law would be unthinkable."

This seems to mean, and it is surely right, that an adult (or even younger) member of the family has a general implied authority to invite friends to the house, so as to prevent those friends being trespassers as a matter of criminal law, unless the parent withdraws that authority in respect of a particular person. If the authority is not withdrawn, it does not matter that the parent would be highly displeased by the presence of the friend.

The practical result of this view is supported by the *mens rea* doctrine. People are hazy about the law. When a member of the family invites his friend to the house, the friend naturally believes that he enters lawfully.

Surely the daughter of the family cannot licence her boy-friend to come in to steal?

It is a reasonable restriction of the general principle to say that a person who is a member of the occupier's family or who has a licence from the

---

[4] Griew 74 records two or three possible distinctions between the cases, but without enthusiasm.

[5] [1973] 1 QB 100.

occupier cannot sublicence the entry of another person for a known burglarious purpose. In *Collins*, however, the young woman did not know of Collins's initial intention to rape.

Where was Collins when he received the girl's invitation?

Collins was perched on the window sill, but whether on the outside sill or on the interior sill was not clear. The court first expressed the opinion that "that seemingly narrow point was of crucial importance," but later in the judgment said that:

> "unless the jury were entirely satisfied that the defendant made an effective and substantial entry into the bedroom without the complainant doing or saying anything to cause him to believe that she was consenting to his entering it, he ought not to be convicted."

We have already discussed the court's requirement that the entry should be substantial.[6] It is not clear what force the adjective "effective" is intended to have beyond that of the word "substantial."

Assume that (as the court held) the daughter was empowered to licence the young man's entry. Assume, too, that she purported to give him this licence before he entered the house. What effect did her mistake as to his identity have? Did Collins know that the girl believed him to be her boy-friend?

The court said:

> "If she in fact appeared to be welcoming him, the Crown do not suggest that he should have realised or even suspected that she was so behaving because, despite the moonlight, she thought he was someone else."

This may be thought to imply that the girl's mistake as to Collins's identity vitiated her consent to his entry, so that he was a trespasser, and that if he had known of the mistake he would have had *mens rea* as to the trespass. But the court did not decide the point. Since Collins did not know of the girl's mistake, and was not reckless as to it, the question of the legal effect of her mistake of identity did not arise.[7]

An important point must now be made. In addition to mistaking Collins's identity, the girl mistook his intention. There is no reason to suppose that when Collins found that the girl was inviting him into her bed he had given up his intention to use force *if necessary* to have her sexually. The attitude of mind of every rapist is that he will use force if necessary, and that was Collins's intention. Collins therefore entered as a would-be rapist, but this fact did not mean that he was a trespasser when he entered the room. A person who has a licence in fact to enter does not become a trespasser by reason of his criminal intent. Nor does a person who believes

---

6 § .2 at n. 3.

7 On the question whether mistake of identity vitiates consent, see § 25.9. In the law of contract a mistake of identity generally does not vitiate consent if the imposter is present. The person under the mistake is taken to intend to deal with the person actually present before him.

himself to have a licence to enter have the *mens rea* for trespass by reason of his criminal intent. This point was not expressly made by the court, but it is implicit in the decision.

The second of the two cases concerned two defendants memorably named Jones and Smith.[8]

> Smith's father had had two television sets stolen, and reported this to the police. The sets were then found in the joint possession of Smith Jnr (who apparently lived on his own) and his friend Jones. The precious pair had entered Smith Snr's house in the small hours and stolen the sets. On the police ascertaining the facts they were prosecuted for burglary. At the trial Smith Snr gave evidence to the effect that he had given his son unrestricted permission to enter the house, and that his son "would not be a trespasser in the house at any time." Nevertheless, the conviction of both defendants of burglary was affirmed.

There is no difficulty in this decision in relation to Jones's entry. For the reason already given, it could well be held that Smith Jnr had no authority to admit Jones for the purpose of thievery. The problem arises from the view taken by the court that Smith Jnr also was a trespasser. In common sense, a son cannot be a trespasser in his father's house unless the father expressly limits his right to enter. Even if the father had not given the evidence he did, there would surely be a strong presumption that a son, whatever his intentions, is a licensee in the house. The father's evidence should have put the point beyond doubt.

There is, however, one ground on which Smith's conviction could properly have been affirmed. Granted that Jones was a trespasser, and therefore a burglar, Smith was guilty as accessory in letting him in. Unfortunately, the Court of Appeal did not consider this simple way of upholding the conviction. Instead, the decision was rested on the fact, or assumed fact, that both defendants were trespassers in the civil law. The court said;

> "The decision in *R* v. *Collins* added to the concept of trespass as a civil wrong only the mental element of *mens rea*, which is essential to the criminal offence."

It may be doubted whether this attaches sufficient weight to the dictum in *Collins,* already quoted, relating to the consent given by the daughter of the family, which appears to regard the question of trespass as being possibly different in the civil and criminal law. If the plain man were asked whether on the facts of *Jones and Smith* the son was a trespasser, he would surely have replied that although the son acted wrongfully in respect of the TV sets, he was not a trespasser in the house.

The Court of Appeal laid down the following principle as the foundation of its decision.

> "A person is a trespasser for the purpose of s. 9 (1) (*b*) of the Theft Act 1969 if he enters premises of another knowing that he is entering

[8] [1976] 1 WLR 672, 3 All ER 54, 63 CAR 47.

> in excess of the permission that has been given to him, or being reckless whether he is entering in excess of the permission that has been given to him to enter. Provided the facts are known to the accused which enable him to realise that he is acting in excess of the permission given or that he is acting recklessly as to whether he exceeds that permission, then that is sufficient for the jury to decide that he is in fact a trespasser."

The trouble with judge-made law is that courts sometimes lay down a wide rule which serves their immediate purpose, without noticing the undesirable consequences that the rule may have in other applications. Entering "in excess of the permission that has been given to him" is a somewhat vague phrase, but what it evidently means is entering for a purpose not covered by the permission. In effect the decision implies (in contradiction of *Collins*) that a person who enters another's building with burglarious intent is always a trespasser at the moment of entry. If such a wide proposition is accepted, the consequence is that burglary is committed by various persons who may appear on the surface to be licensees; a customer in a shop, a house guest, and a butler, who steal in the building having entered for that purpose, notwithstanding that apart from their intention they would be lawfully there. It may even be burglary for a person to enter a telephone kiosk (which he is normally permitted to enter) to steal the contents of the coin box. A great extension is thus given to the crime.

There are strong reasons for saying that this is not a correct view of the law. It makes the crime of burglary unnecessarily wide; it is founded on a misunderstanding of the previous authorities; and it is inconsistent with the rationale of section 9.

The following are the detailed arguments against the dictum.

- The rationale of burglary as a special offence is, to repeat, the danger and alarm caused by the presence of a criminally-minded intruder in a building. This is unlikely to arise when the intruder has been permitted to enter—which is why the Act does not make it burglary for one who has been permitted to enter to commit one of the specified crimes after outstaying his welcome. The notion of consent or permission to enter should therefore be understood in its purely factual sense. Of course the commission of a crime may cause alarm, but the alarm is not increased by the fact that the judges describe the offender as a trespasser, when he has been permitted to enter in fact.
- The Act follows the recommendations of the CLRC, and there is no hint in the committee's Report that it contemplated this extension of the offence.[9] The committee's purpose was to simplify the law of burglary but not to deprive it entirely of an element of objective illegality. For this reason the offence was to require a trespassory entry. What reception would the committee's Report have had if it had proposed that an ordinary shoplifter would be guilty of burglary if he was found to have intended to steal when he entered the shop? The dictum in *Jones and Smith* removes the objective requirement, because it makes the burglarious intent determinative of the legality of the entry. In the great majority of cases where *de facto* licensees steal, it fuses the two requirements of burglarious intent and trespassory entry into a single requirement, namely the burglarious intent. It is thus contrary to the clear intention of section 9.
- The construction of the Act offered in *Jones and Smith* is inconsistent not only with the separate requirement of trespass but with the separate requirement of entry as a trespasser.

---

[9] See Cmnd. 2977 of 1966, para. 35.

As we have seen, a person who, having entered a building lawfully, remains in it unlawfully and in order to steal is not for that reason a burglar. This implies that the object of the section is to strike at intruding strangers. If a person is lawfully on the spot, he does not become a burglar by remaining unlawfully. If *Jones and Smith* is right, the section covers many people who are known to the occupier, who are known to him to be present, and who have to all appearances his permission to enter. This seems to deprive the statute's insistence that the defendant must *enter* as a trespasser of most of its practical effect.

- The decision runs counter to *Collins,* where it must have been held, as we have seen, that the defendant was not a trespasser although, since he intended to commit rape if necessary, he knew that his intention was "in excess of the permission." The court in *Jones and Smith* evidently did not realise this aspect of *Collins.* If *Jones and Smith* is right, Collins's conviction of burglary should have been upheld.
- The authorities in the law of tort do not establish that a secret intent can turn a licensee into a trespasser. They show that in the civil law, *acting* outside the implied condition of the licence can do so. A person who is *prima facie* licenced to enter is not a trespasser when he enters, even though he intends to act outside the terms of the licence. When he does so act, he becomes a trespasser in the civil law, but he did not enter as a trespasser. Therefore he cannot be guilty of burglary either under para. (*a*) or under para. (*b*), both of which require entry as a trespasser.
- The tort cases were motivated largely by a desire to prevent licensees from recovering damages for injury received when they were acting unlawfully on the premises. This has no bearing on the criminal law. In the criminal law, the notion of trespass should be given a broad, common-sense interpretation in the defendant's favour.
- It was held in an immigration case that fraud in procuring leave to enter the country makes the leave voidable but not void,[10] and the same principle should apply in respect of burglary. Moreover, fraud presupposes (1) a fraudulent act (not a mere nondisclosure of criminal intent) and (2) an effect of the fraud on the mind of the person who consents. To "imply" a representation by the defendant that he has no illegal intent would be a pure fiction—though one to which the courts are now, sadly, disposed.

  The court incorporated the mental element into its proposition of law (see the quotation above). But it may be questioned whether the jury acted reasonably in finding that Smith Jnr knew that he was or might be entering in excess of the permission given to him. If Smith Jnr were asked such a question, he might readily agree that he was stealing the television sets, but not that he was a trespasser in his father's house or had entered in excess of the permission given to him. His father did not mind his entry to the house as such. No doubt he would have objected to the TV set being taken, but the ordinary person would probably regard a question framed in terms of trespass to the house as an extraordinary legalism and an irrelevance.
- The rule in *Jones and Smith* occasions particular difficulty if part of what the defendant does is clearly within the licence. A shoplifter enters a shop to make a purchase in the liquor department (which has tight security) and to steal anything else in the rest of the shop that he can. The butler enters the house in order to butle, and also later in the day to go off with the spoons. Is he a trespasser or not?

The main conclusions to be drawn from the two cases are as follows.

1 It seems from *Jones and Smith* that a person who is normally licenced to enter premises is not licenced to enter them to steal from the occupier. Conceivably this rule, which has wide implications and is open to various legal objections, may not be followed, since the actual decision can be explained on the narrower ground next following.

2 Even if a person is licenced by the occupier to be on premises himself,

[10] *R.* v. *Home Secretary, ex p. Khawaja* [1983] 2 WLR 321, 1 All E.R. 765; the decision in the CA was affirmed on this point in the HL, Lord Bridge saying that leave to enter obtained by deception is not a nullity.

he cannot authorise another person to enter for a burglarious purpose of which he knows—or, very possibly, for the purpose of committing any crime against the occupier of which he knows. The thief who enters and steals will be a burglar, and the licensee who lets him in for the purpose of theft will be an accessory to the burglary.

3 Subject to rule 2 above, some persons licenced by the occupier can sublicence others to enter, and this is particularly so for members of the occupier's family, who can in general licence friends to enter, however unwelcome their presence may be to the occupier, unless the occupier expressly withdraws the authority. This is the result of *Collins*. The point is important only in very exceptional circumstances.

Suppose a man enters a museum as a member of the public. He hides in the lavatory until after closing time, then emerges and steals a gold statuette.

On the view of the law here put forward, the man's entry to the museum should not be accounted burglary, though this would involve the court in preferring *Collins* to *Jones and Smith*. For the same reason his entry to the lavatory is not burglary; he is licenced to enter the lavatory. Equally, when he emerges from it and enters the public rooms, it would be excessively technical to discover a burglary. In penal matters the judges should, in Bacon's words, "beware of hard constructions and strained inferences." Substantially, the thief has simply remained in the building, which is not sufficient.

Suppose he hid in the broom cupboard?

He would be a trespasser in that "part of the building," namely the broom cupboard, but it is not burglary because he does not intend to steal in "that part of it" (see s. 9(2)).

Suppose he has gone down to the nether regions to steal, where the public never had access?

That would be burglary, just as much as if the man had stolen in the private basement during opening hours.

§ 38.5. BEING FOUND ON PRIVATE PREMISES

Supplementing the law of theft and burglary is an offence in section 4 of the Vagrancy Act 1824 which is worded as a breach of the "Eleventh Commandment": thou shalt not be found out—or, rather, thou shalt not be found out *at the time*. The offence is committed only when a person is "found" on certain private premises "for any unlawful purpose." Although this and the other offences in section 4 are triable only summarily,[1] they

[1] Punishment, 3 months. If the offender has already been convicted of any offence under s. 4, he may be committed to the Crown Court as an "incorrigible rogue," and there sentenced to be imprisoned for one year (ss. 5, 10). The law on this and other aspects of the offence is archaic, particularly since the Crown Court cannot pass a suspended sentence or make a probation order. For legislative proposals see the Report of the Home Office Working Party on Vagrancy and Street Offences, 1976; the proposals in an earlier Working Paper were critically discussed by L H Leigh in [1975] Crim.LR 384–388.

have particular importance in that anyone may arrest a person who is found offending.[2] The minutiae of the offence are as follows.

The place. The defendant must be found "in or upon any dwelling-house, warehouse, coach-house, stable, or outhouse, or in any inclosed yard, garden, or area." There are many decisions on the meaning of these words, not all of which need here be considered; it will be sufficient to summarise some of the main points.

The words "in or upon" include persons found on the roof of one of the specified buildings.

A "dwelling-house" probably means a house or flat in which somebody habitually sleeps as his home, though he may be sleeping elsewhere at the time in question.

A "warehouse" probably includes a part of a shop used for the storage of goods and not open to the public,[3] but not the part of the shop that is open to the public.[4] It does not include a building where goods are kept temporarily while something is done to them (e.g. mail being sorted).[5]

Whether a "coach-house" now includes a garage is undecided. An "outhouse" must be closely connected with a house (and, it seems, must be physically connected with it, as by a wall); a building in a field is not an outhouse.[6]

Then as to the words "inclosed yard, garden or area," they do not include a very large area, even though enclosed, but do cover an area of the size usually described as a yard, within the precincts of a building like a house or an inn, and enclosed to a substantial degree (even though some permanent openings are left for access).[7] The words do not cover a tract of ground merely because it is called a "yard," as in "railway yard," "shipyard" and "vineyard."[8]

The meaning of "found." A suspect is "found" when he is perceived by the senses. A police officer who (being outside a house) hears the offender inside finds him there, even though the offender then makes an escape and is arrested outside. It seems that a person is not found in a building if he is merely seen emerging (through the door or otherwise).[9] It seems, too, that the offence is not committed unless the suspect is trespassing in the place.

The purpose. The suspect must be on the premises for an "unlawful purpose," which means any criminal purpose. The police can arrest and charge the offender even though it is not clear what precise mischief he was up to. If they get evidence of a particular unlawful purpose they may subsequently charge him with a more specific offence, such as burglary or attempt to steal.

The intent may be to commit a crime in the future.[10] But "unlawful purpose" does not include a purpose that is merely immoral or a matter of civil wrong; therefore it does not include the voyeur (Peeping Tom).[11]

The distinctions from attempt. (1) Entering premises, though an offence under section 4, may be held to be "mere preparation" and so not an attempt. This is particularly likely if the entry is into a yard and the intent is to steal in the building. (2) It may not be clear what crime the defendant intended; this would preclude a charge of attempt.

§ 38.6. VEHICLE INTERFERENCE AND TAMPERING

Suppose that a person without authority tries the handle of a parked car.

---

[2] S.6.
[3] *Hill* (1843) 2 M & Rob. 458, 174 LR 348.
[4] This was a "place of public resort" within the "suspected person" provision formerly contained in the Vagrancy Act but now repealed.
[5] *Holloran* v. *Haughton* [1976] Crim.LR 270.
[6] *Borley* (1844) 8 JP 263; Russell, 12th edn 1342–1343.
[7] *Goodhew* v. *Morton* [1962] 1 WLR 210, 2 All ER 771.
[8] *Quatromini* v. *Peck* [1972] 1 WLR 1318, 3 All ER 521.
[9] [1955] Crim.LR 72–73.
[10] *Re Joy* (1853) 22 LTJo. 80.
[11] *Hayes* v. *Stevenson* (1860) 3 LT 296.

If, upon being arrested, he confesses that he intended to steal the car, or to steal the contents, or to take a conveyance for use, he can be convicted of attempting to commit the relevant offence.[1] If it is clear that he intended to commit one of those offences but not clear which, he cannot be convicted of an attempt. To provide for these circumstances the Criminal Attempts Act 1981 section 9 creates a summary offence of vehicle interference.[2] Because it is only a summary offence it gives no right of trial and cannot be the subject of an attempt. But the offence is imprisonable, and a constable may arrest without warrant anyone who is or whom he with reasonable cause suspects to be guilty of it.

It must be proved that the defendant intended to commit one of the three offences above mentioned, but the prosecution need not prove which. If the defendant says that he only wanted to go to sleep in the car, or to look at the controls because he is interested in cars, and if this raises a reasonable doubt in the minds of the magistrates, he must be acquitted even though he clearly interfered with the vehicle.

Could the police give in evidence, to prove intent, that the defendant had previously been convicted of offences of dishonesty?

Strange as it may seem, the answer is no.

The Act does not define the concept of "interfering with a motor vehicle or trailer." The only reported case is a decision of the Crown Court on appeal from magistrates, where it was held that the conduct of two persons moving from one parked car to another, putting a hand on the door handle and looking inside, did not constitute interference, in the absence of evidence that they had opened the car doors or applied pressure to the door handles.[3] An editorial note to the case by J C Smith points out the leniency of the decision to the point of impracticability; the prosecution could not be expected to give evidence that the defendants had applied pressure to the door handles. That that was what they were doing was a reasonable inference from the evidence, in the absence of evidence to the contrary.

In addition to this offence there is a summary offence under the Road Traffic Act 1972.[4]

> "If, while a motor vehicle is on a road or parking place provided by a local authority, a person otherwise than with lawful authority or reasonable excuse gets on to the vehicle or tampers with the brake or other part of its mechanism," he commits an offence.

The draftsman of this provision cannot have heard of the *ejusdem generis* rule. In common sense the provision should be held to apply to all parts of the mechanism, the reference to the brake being superfluous; nevertheless, it may possibly be held to apply only to mechanisms like the brake, whatever they may be thought to be.[5] The police do not care to argue that tampering with the door of a car is tampering with the mechanism, and the

---

[1] *Jones* v. *Brooks* (1968) 52 CAR 614.
[2] See Dennis in [1982] Crim.LR 14–15.
[3] *Reynolds* v. *Metropolitan Police* [1982] Crim.LR 831.
[4] S. 29. Cp. § 41.2 at n. 7.
[5] See 7 The Conveyancer (NS) 128.

offence gives no power of arrest. On the other hand, it is useful where the tampering was malicious, done for the purpose of endangering persons or property or for an unknown purpose.

§ 38.7. GOING EQUIPPED FOR STEALING ETC.

Section 25 (1) of the Theft Act creates an important preparatory offence, triable either way, which is given the above title in the marginal note.

> "A person shall be guilty of an offence if, when not at his place of abode, he has with him[1] any article for use in the course of or in connection with any burglary, theft or cheat."

The offence is punishable on indictment with 3 years' imprisonment (subs. (2)),[2] which is more severe than the 2 years allowable for the offence of having offensive weapons.[3] Anyone can arrest on reasonable suspicion of the offence (subs. (4)).

What is a cheat?

Both "theft" and "cheat" are specially defined by subsection (5).

> "For purposes of this section an offence under section 12 (1) of this Act of taking a conveyance shall be treated as theft, and "cheat" means[4] an offence under section 15 of this Act."

So the possession of a bunch of car keys can be an offence although the prosecution.cannot prove whether the defendant's intention was to steal a car or only to make off with it temporarily. On the other hand, the subsection does not cover the possession of explosives for the purpose of salmon fishing, since poaching is not theft.

The prosecution need not establish the particular burglary, theft or deception that was intended.[5] Since the last three nouns in subsection (l) refer to the defendant's intention, it seems that an offence can be charged with all three words in the alternative,[6] so the prosecution would not even have to prove whether the particular offence intended was a burglary, a theft or an obtaining by deception, if it was clearly one of the three.

It will be seen that the offence is very widely defined. Although primarily aimed against the carrying of burglarious tools, it applies also to the possession of a large variety of other objects with the requisite intent, such

---

[1] These words include things in the defendant's parked car: cp. *Doukas* [1978] 1 WLR 372, 1 All ER 1061, 60 CAR 228.

[2] If the defendant intended to make off with a motor vehicle, the offence under s. 25 (1) carries endorsement of the defendant's driving licence and possible disqualification: RTA 1972 s. 93 (2) and (7).

[3] Prevention of Crime Act 1953 s. 1 (1).

[4] This is an exhaustive definition of "cheat," so it is not an offence to have an article intended for some cheating that is not an offence under s. 15. The trial judge made a mistake on this in *Rashid* [1977] 1 WLR 298, 2 All ER 237, 64 CAR 201.

[5] *Ellames* [1974] 1 WLR at 1397H, 3 All ER at 136c, 60 CAR at 13 (obiter). The court added that the prosecution need not prove that the defendant intended to use the thing himself.

[6] § 6.10 at n. 11.

as a car intended for use in a robbery, a pair of gloves to avoid leaving finger-prints, and an Old Etonian tie worn by a cheat. The offence is valuable because it makes professional burglars wary of carrying articles like jemmies and duplicate keys; they try to work with non-incriminating articles, which are generally less effective for their purposes.

This last point does not wholly justify the statutory provision, because it covers articles that are not incriminating in themselves as well as those that are. For example, a cheat who has with him any article that he proposes to sell by means of deceptive sales-talk is guilty of the offence.[7] Even a shopping bag in which a shoplifter intends to put his loot would be covered. J C Smith suggests that the test is whether the article is one that the defendant would not have had with him but for the contemplated offence[8]; but it may be doubted whether even this restriction is inherent in the subsection. If a shopper carries a bag partly to carry articles that he is going to buy (because it is not practicable to steal them) and partly to conceal articles that he is going to steal, the bag would still seem to fall within the offence. (The trousers that the shopper is wearing would not fall within the offence, not because he would be wearing them anyway but because he does not intend to use them for the offence. If he intends to secrete stolen articles in his trousers pockets, the trousers would literally fall within it! In this respect the name given to the offence by the marginal note—"Going equipped for stealing, etc."—is misleading. Marginal notes have no direct legislative effect, and it is doubtful how far they may be used as aids to construction.[9] But perhaps trousers could be excluded on the ground of avoiding absurdity.)

Even if Professor Smith's suggestion is accepted, the law still goes very far in making conviction depend upon little more than proof of the intent. There are obvious risks of miscarriages of justice; so the court should be careful to scrutinise the evidence. A criminal who carries an article that is not incriminating in itself is likely to "get away with it" if, upon being questioned by the police, he can offer some plausible reason for carrying it.[10]

Can a person who commits theft with an instrument be charged both with the theft and, under the subsection, with having the instrument?

Yes, if there is the appropriate evidence. But there would be little point in it. And the mere fact that the defendant is found to have committed the theft with the instrument is not enough for a conviction under section 25 (1), because that subsection (it has been held) looks to an intended future use, not to possession of an article that has been used.[11]

But if a person is found in possession of an article that he has just used to commit theft, he must previously have had it with him for the purpose of committing theft.

The Court of Appeal did not consider that point in the case just cited, presumably because it had not been argued. But presumably the prosecution would have to establish something more than momentary possession. If a person picks up a brick intending to use it to smash a shop window in order to steal the things inside, this would hardly be enough to

---

[7] *Mandry* [1973] 1 WLR 1232, 3 All ER 996, 58 CAR 27. Cp. *Doukas* § 34.9 at n. 6.

[8] Smith 187.

[9] *Schildkamp* [1971] AC 1.

[10] The Act provides, in subs. (3), that if the article is "made or adapted" for criminal use, this is evidence that the defendant had it with him for the forbidden purpose. The provision simply places the evidential burden on the defendant and does not affect the prosecution's persuasive burden. A trial judge would be ill advised to rely on it unless the defendant submits that there is no case for him to answer; and even then the judge should use it only for the purpose of rejecting the submission and not for the purpose of directing the jury in terms of a presumption. See § 2.3. See the criticism of subs. (3) in Griew 194–195.

[11] *Ellames* [1974] 1 WLR 1391, 3 All ER 130, 60 CAR 7.

establish an offence under the subsection. Nor would an offence be committed if an article, carried innocently, is used on the spur of the moment for an offence. "Has with him" would be construed to require something more continuous in the way of possession. The opinion is supported by the judicial interpretation of the similar phrase in the legislation against offensive weapons.[12]

Presumably "in connection with" is wider than "in the course of"?

Yes; so much so that the latter phrase seems unnecessary. The Court of Appeal said on one occasion[13]:

> "It is easy to think of cases where an article could be intended for use 'in connection with' though not 'in the course of' a burglary, etc., e.g. articles intended to be used while doing preparatory acts or while escaping after a crime."

Wide as the subsection is, the courts do not apply it to what may be called remote preparation for an offence.

> So it was held that where the defendant was in possession of a driving licence belonging to another person, intending to use it to obtain a job as a driver and subsequently to steal from his employer, his possession was too remote from the intended theft to come within the subsection.[14]

If a man is walking along the street when the police arrest him for having a burglarious implement with him, would it be a defence for him to show that he did not intend to use the implement that day, but only the next day or next week?

No. If he intended to use it, it does not matter when.[15]

Then if he takes it home with him, intending to have a good night's sleep before committing the burglary, why can't he be guilty of the offence of possessing the implement in his house?

The offence was not applied to the "place of abode" because it was thought that this would be an undue invasion of privacy. For example, such a provision might cause an over-zealous police force to "turn over" the houses of known criminals on a regular basis, which would look like persecution.[16] Only the home is exempted, not the place of work.

The offence under the Explosive Substances Act 1883 s. 4 of possessing explosives for an unlawful object is not limited in this way, and may be committed by possessing explosives in the home.[17] But the Act is used only

---

[12] See *Ohlson* v. *Hylton* [1975] 1 WLR 724, 2 All ER 490; *Giles* [1976] Crim.LR 253.

[13] *Ellames* [1974] 1 WLR at 1397F, 3 All ER at 136a, 60 CAR at 13.

[14] *Mansfield* [1975] Crim.LR 101.

[15] A decision to the contrary of a deputy recorder (135 JPN 281) is clearly wrong.

[16] It was held in *Bundy* [1977] 1 WLR 914, 2 All ER 382, that "place of abode" means a fixed place, so although a car can be a place of abode if it is in one spot and the defendant sleeps there, it is not his place of abode while he has it out on the road.

[17] Moreover, the limitation does not appear in the legislation penalising the possession of firearms and things possessed with intent to commit an indictable offence against the person or criminal damage: for references see § 19.6. Cp. *Kelt* [1977] 1 WLR 1365, 3 All ER 1099, Crim.LR 556.

for the prosecution of those who intend to commit large explosions, as for political objects. It is not the practice to make a charge in respect of small amounts of explosive held for the purpose of blowing safes.

Dart and Dash plan a robbery. They are to meet in Dart's house. Dash duly appears, equipped with his stocking-mask. Dart pockets his own mask, and they are about to leave the house when the police appear and they are arrested. Does the subsection mean that Dash is guilty of the offence but not Dart?

Dart is not guilty as perpetrator, since he is at his place of abode; but he is guilty as accessory to Dash's offence if (1) he knew that Dash had the mask with him for the forbidden purpose and (2) he intended to assist in the execution of the purpose; both these requisites are satisfied on the facts supposed.

SUMMARY

The Theft Act redefines the ancient crime of burglary. It establishes two forms, § .1
simple and aggravated. The following discussion is of the simple form. It may be committed (*a*) by entry with intent at the time of entry to commit theft, to inflict g.b.h., to rape, or to do criminal damage; alternatively, it may be committed (*b*) by stealing or attempting to steal, or inflicting or attempting to inflict g.b.h., after entry.

The entry must be as a trespasser into any building or an inhabited house or § .2
vessel. Remaining as a trespasser is not sufficient. At common law there was an entry if part of the body crossed the boundary, but *Collins* may have introduced a test of substantiality. Whether the use of an instrument or innocent agent to cross the threshold can be burglary under the Act is undecided; it could at common law.

The various intents in burglary may be charged in a single count in the § .3
alternative.

The defendant must be a trespasser, and must either know this or be reckless as § .4
to it (*Collins*). The mental element must exist at the time of entry under (*a*) above or at the time of stealing or inflicting g.b.h. or attempting to do so under (*b*). A part of a building counts as a separate building. On principle, the occupier's consent to entry given to trap the defendant should preclude trespass. The occupier may expressly or impliedly licence others to enter, and also to grant sub-licences. It seems from *Jones and Smith* that a licence does not extend to an entry with burglarious intent; but such a rule is inconsistent with the decision in *Collins* on this point, and the latter is greatly to be preferred. The conviction in *Jones and Smith* could have been better upheld by saying that a licensee cannot authorise another to enter for a burglarious purpose of which he knows, and if the licensee does so he is an accessory to the burglary. Subject to the latter rule, members of the occupier's family can in general licence friends to enter unless the occupier expressly withdraws this authority.

By the Vagrancy Act 1824 s. 4 it is a summary offence for a person to be found § .5
on certain private premises for any unlawful (meaning criminal) purpose.

The Criminal Attempts Act 1981 creates a summary offence of vehicle § .6
interference; the defendant can be convicted if he intended to steal the car or its contents or to take a conveyance for use; it need not be proved which. The Road Traffic Act offence of getting on a vehicle or tampering with the mechanism is still

useful to deal with freeloaders and persons who maliciously tamper with vehicle mechanisms.

The Theft Act makes it an either way offence for a person, when not at his place §.7
of abode, to have with him any article for use in the course of or in connection with any burglary, theft or cheat. "Theft" is defined to include taking a conveyance, and "cheat" to mean obtaining property by deception. It will probably be held, by analogy with decisions on having offensive weapons, that the offence is not committed if an article is suddenly acquired or used for one of the specified offences without prior intent. Nor does the offence apply to articles carried by way of remote preparation for an offence.

CHAPTER 39

HANDLING STOLEN GOODS

Cui prodest scelus,
Is fecit.
Seneca, *Medea*

§ 39.1. THE FORMS OF HANDLING

IN the war against theft the police can call certain ancillary provisions to their aid, such as the Scrap Metal Dealers Act 1964 which requires such dealers to be registered and regulates the manner in which they may carry on their trade. The most general weapon is the law relating to "handlers" of stolen goods.

Formerly, the offence of handling was called "receiving" stolen goods. The Theft Act widened it and gave it the wider name, so that now the offence covers not only the traditional receiver but a person who may be called a dealer in stolen goods (in a very wide sense of the expression). The definition in section 22 (1) is a draftsman's omelette.

> "A person handles stolen goods if (otherwise than in the course of the stealing) knowing or believing them to be stolen goods he dishonestly receives the goods, or dishonestly undertakes or assists in their retention, removal, disposal or realisation by or for the benefit of another person, or if he arranges to do so."

The offence is punishable with 14 years' imprisonment, in other words more severely than theft.

So handling is a graver offence than theft?

Yes and no. Minor handlings are treated as lesser offences than theft.

The reason why handling can be punished more severely than theft is because there have been notorious cases in the past where a professional receiver (like Jonathan Wilde) has been the centre of a great web of crime. (At the present day the most active professional "fences" are those who dismantle stolen cars in order to sell the parts; without their activities far fewer cars would be stolen.)

But all is not as it seems.

In the first place, sentences on handlers rarely exceed 7 years.[1] It does not look as though the increased punishment allowable for handling is needed. And if it is said that the extra dose is required for very large-scale handling, what about large-scale theft? This cannot be punished with more than 10 years' imprisonment unless burglary or robbery is involved. Why should there be any difference from handling?

In the second place, a conviction of handling is generally regarded as a *lesser* conviction

[1] D A Thomas, *Principles of Sentencing*, 2nd edn 168.

than one of theft, and attracts a lighter sentence. The usual handler is a man of easy morals who succumbs to the temptation of buying something cheap, knowing it has been dishonestly acquired; he did not bring about the theft and is not, in the words of one commentator, "a facility whose existence is a reasssuring part of the background against which thievery operates."[2] For these reasons he can expect to be sentenced more leniently than the thief himself. So a defendant who is charged with both theft and handling strives to get a conviction of handling (if he must be convicted) rather than one of theft.[3] He often offers a plea of guilty to handling on condition that the theft charge is dropped; and the jury, if given the choice between the two charges, often choose to convict of handling if they view the offence indulgently. Logically, however, it should almost never be possible for a dishonest handler to avoid a conviction of theft of what he handles, because a handler is, by reason of the handling, a thief as well.

Since the rest of this chapter will be spent in unpicking section 22 (1), begin by reading it carefully two or three times. It will be seen that the prosecution must prove three things.

1 That the defendant handled the goods.
2 That they were stolen.
3 That at the time when the defendant handled the goods, (a) he was acting dishonestly and (b) he knew or believed they were stolen.

As regards the first element, there are two main forms of handling:

(a) *receiving* (where the defendant comes into possession of the goods), and
(b) a group of nouns referring to various forms of dealing with the goods (where the defendant need not come into possession).

Arranging to receive or deal with the goods is also the full offence, not simply an inchoate offence.

But doesn't the handler have to touch the goods?

No. The person known in the underworld as a "placer" may simply talk on the telephone. He is guilty of handling if he "undertakes the realisation" of the goods, as by finding a buyer for them.

The subsection was drafted with the clear intention that it should create only one offence, capable of being committed in numerous different ways. But the courts, regarding this as undesirable, wish it to be treated as creating what are for most purposes two offences.

> "The first is . . . receiving. . . . The second is a new offence . . . and can be committed in any of the various ways indicated by the words from 'undertakes' to the end of the subsection. It follows that the new offence may and should be charged in a single count embodying in the particulars as much of the relevant language of the subsection, including alternatives, as may be appropropriate."[4]

In this statement Lord Bridge was summarising, while slightly

---

[2] D W Elliott in *Reshaping the Criminal Law*, ed. Glazebrook (London 1978) 294.

[3] This is particularly so if there has been, for example, a post office "snatch" totalling thousands of pounds, and D is found in possession of a mere £20 worth of the stolen postal orders. He will be anxious to say that he only handled this amount and was not a party to the theft as a whole.

Handling is triable either way, and most handlers are relatively happy to be dealt with summarily if given the chance.

[4] *Bloxham* [1983] AC at 113C.

misunderstanding,[5] a rule previously developed in the Court of Appeal. We will give the first offence (or variety of the offence) the name of *handling by receiving*. The second is conveniently called, for short, *handling by dealing*.[6]

The reason offered by the Court of Appeal for having two counts was that they give the defendant better information than a single count, but it is difficult to see how. A more convincing reason would be that breaking the numerous alternatives into two major questions clarifies the task of the jury and the jury's findings. Also, since the traditional receiver is likely to get a heavier sentence than one who gives minor assistance, it is helpful for the verdict of the jury to distinguish between them. However, the legal distinction between receiving and dealing imperfectly reflects the amount of help that may be given. A placer, who simply acts as an agent for sale, may be a big-time professional criminal, while a receiver may be someone who buys a watch cheaply in a pub, or even a girl who is given a stolen watch by her thieving boy-friend. The judge in sentencing must take account of all the facts of the case, including his knowledge of the defendant's previous convictions.

§ 39.2. HANDLING BY RECEIVING

Handling by receiving is committed by taking possession or control of the stolen goods.[1] The typical case is where the thief sells the goods to a professional receiver.[2]

Sometimes the receiver's possession or control is jointly with the thief or another person. Authorities under the pre-Act law establish that a person may receive by authorising his agent to receive, or by having goods delivered to his premises.

The thief's wife is not guilty of handling merely because she is willing for goods to be kept and used in the matrimonial home and thinks it nice to have these things.[3] But if she receives

---

[5] Lord Bridge said there are two offences. Previously, the CA had said simply that the single offence in subs. (1) should be charged in two counts (an unorthodox procedure); but the rule was only advisory, and an information charging "handling" *simpliciter* was not bad for duplicity. See Griew 189. Now Lord Bridge, *obiter*, says it is two offences. Notwithstanding that his lordship was speaking on behalf of the House of Lords, he must be regarded as being wrong. There is only one offence on the wording of the statute; the Court of Appeal has decided that there is only one offence; and Lord Bridge did not refer to the precedents or purport to overrule them. Of course, prosecutors would be well advised to treat the subsection as creating two offences. But if an indictment or information charges Lord Bridge's two "offences" as a single offence, the charge should assuredly be regarded as valid.

It is a pity that the courts have not gone further in splitting up the subsection *de facto*. The statement that handling by dealing should be charged in a single count is an inconvenient rule when the prosecution desire to charge both handling by undertaking and handling by assisting (see § 38.1,2). These two forms of handling would be much better put in separate counts.

[6] I am indebted to Professor Griew for suggesting this name, and my gratitude is not diminished by the fact that he himself finds it unnecessary to have it!

[1] The offence apparently does not continue over separate receivings, so each receiving must generally go into a separate count. However, suppose that the police have found an "Aladdin's Cave" of stolen property in the possession of the defendant, received over a considerable period of time, and they cannot identify the various receivings. In that case, it seems, all the receivings can go into one count. See *Smythe* (1980) 72 CAR at 13; Griew 190.

[2] In *Deakin* [1972] 1 WLR 1618, 3 All ER 803, 56 CAR 801, the buyer, instead of being charged with receiving, was charged with undertaking the realisation of the goods, under the later part of the subsection; and his conviction on this charge was upheld on appeal. The decision is obviously wrong, because it is the seller, not the buyer, who undertakes the realisation of the goods. (The seller was not guilty of undertaking the realisation because he did not sell for the benefit of another, so the buyer could not be brought in as an accessory to his sale.) The decision manifests the usual tendency of the Court of Appeal to uphold convictions of the wrong offence rather than let the fish out of the net.

[3] See *Kanwar* [1982] 1 WLR 845, 2 All ER 528, 75 CAR 87. Although this was decided on retaining, the same rule doubtless applies to receiving.

large sums of stolen money from the thief she can be convicted of handling by receiving,[4] and she can sometimes be convicted of assisting her husband to retain the goods (see next section).

The concluding words of the subsection, "or if he arranges to do so," appear to apply to all the preceding words, not merely to the words after "undertakes." If this is the correct reading, a person who arranges to receive stolen goods is guilty of handling as soon as he makes the arrangement.

You said that the receiver is also a thief. Doesn't that make an awful mix-up?

The handler by receiving is almost always a thief.[5] (And so is the handler by dealing.[6]) The handling is a fresh theft, distinct from the original theft that made the goods "stolen goods." The handler is guilty of handling, because his act is "otherwise than in the course of the stealing" that made the goods stolen goods; and he is guilty of theft, by reason of his own act of dishonest appropriation.[7] But it is not customary to charge a clear handler with theft, because the charge of handling better represents what he has done.

Take the converse question. Isn't the thief a receiver in getting the goods?

Generally not, because he gets the goods "in the course of the stealing" (see section 22 (1)), quoted in § .1). The goods must be stolen *before* the act of handling.

Suppose two crooks break into a factory and fill a sack with assorted items. After leaving they divide up the contents. Are they guilty of receiving from each other when they divide it up?

No, because the sack and its contents are already in their joint possession. The goods are stolen, and they know it—because they were the thieves; but there is no receiving at that stage.

However, this answer is largely theoretical. For reasons already given, your two crooks are unlikely to protest that they are thieves if they are being tried for handling; they prefer to be convicted of the handling, if anything. What may happen is that if they are convicted of handling they may appeal on the ground that there is no evidence that the goods were stolen when they received the goods. We shall return to this problem in a moment.

Can a thief be a handler of the same goods?

Yes, by an act done after the theft.

> If a master criminal who has got other people to carry out the actual theft subsequently handles the goods (as by receiving them), he may well be charged with the handling, even though he is an accessory to the theft, for here the handling is the more serious offence. His handling is not "in the course of the stealing" but distinctly subsequent to it.

---

[4] *Dadd* [1974] Crim.LR 439.

[5] *Stapylton* v. *O'Callaghan* [1973] 2 All ER 782; *Dolan* (1976) 62 CAR 36; *Sainthouse* [1980] Crim. LR 506.

[6] See Griew 188.

[7] This point appears to have been thoroughly misunderstood in *Gregory* [1982] Crim.LR 229; see the editorial note.

How long does "the course of the stealing" last? It seems a vague phrase.

In practice it means "after the theft,"[8] and it would have been better if the Act had said that. This is shown by *Pitham*,[9] where the Court of Appeal rightly reduced "the course of stealing" to something approaching a Euclidean point.

If the court was right in *Pitham* in saying that X committed theft when he offered the goods to Pitham (a big "if"), then it was perfectly right in saying that Pitham's acceptance and removal of the goods was a receiving. (The report does not make it clear whether Pitham removed the goods immediately on being made the offer or only on a return visit some time after, but there is no reason why the point should make any difference.)

Of course, if Pitham had been an abettor in the actual commission of the theft by X, it could not possibly have been held that he was guilty of handling.

Suppose a man is found in possession of stolen articles. Is he charged with theft or with handling?

A clear thief should be charged as such; so should a clear handler, because these are generally the most straightforward charges. If there is no evidence how the man came by the stuff the usual practice is to charge him with both offences, leaving the jury (or magistrates) to convict of whichever they think more likely. The judge is not over-tender to the defendant in this situation, and will generally skate over the question of the burden of proving whether it is the one or the other.

But how can he? The jury cannot convict the man of theft unless they are sure he stole, and they cannot convict him of handling unless they are sure that he obtained the goods "otherwise than in the course of the stealing". Unless they can decide between these two offences beyond reasonable doubt, they ought not to convict of either.

The courts have not pointed at all clearly to the solution of this problem, but a solution is available. The judge should direct the jury that they can convict of theft if they are satisfied that the defendant has dishonestly appropriated the property of another, whether he was the original thief or has since stolen it when he dishonestly came into possession of property previously stolen by another. The indictment should be worded so as to give sufficient latitude to the jury as to the time of the theft.

On one occasion when the defendant was charged only with handling and not with theft (a piece of folly on the part of the prosecutor, since the evidence left it uncertain which offence the defendant had committed) the Court of Appeal came to the prosecutor's assistance by holding that if there is no evidence that the defendant stole the property, the question of theft need not be left to the jury, who may than happily be allowed to convict of handling.[10] In effect the court put an evidential burden on the unfortunate defendant to raise the issue of his own guilt of theft, which obviously he would not want to do. This was a decision of

[8] Nothing turns on the distinction between "stealing" and "theft," because they mean the same: see s.1 (1). Smith 419 suggests that the reference in s. 22 (1) to "the course of stealing" shows that appropriation is a continuing, not an instantaneous, act. But this does not follow. It would possible to hold that appropriation is instantaneous, but that the "course" of the theft must be given a rather smudged meaning for the particular purpose of section 22. In practice, it seems, the courts do not take this view; at any rate for the purpose of upholding a conviction, they hold that the course of stealing, like appropriation, is theoretically instantaneous. See *Pitham* in text following.

[9] See § 33.12 at n. 11, and further discussion in § 33.13 at nn. 9, 10. Cp. Griew 187.

[10] *Griffiths* (1974) 60 CAR 14; see A T H Smith in [1977] Crim. LR 520.

expediency, that is to say the expediency of upholding the conviction of a man who had dishonestly got hold of two church candlesticks. But it was legally wrong; and it was not needed as a solution of the general problem. In case of doubt, the prosecution should charge both offences, or else should charge theft only.[11]

If handlers can be charged as thieves, what is the point of the handling offence?

There are four answers to your question, none of them utterly conclusive.

(1) Perhaps the best answer is that when a person has handled stolen goods a charge of handling is easier for the jury to understand than a charge of stealing.

(2) Handling is in theory punishable more severely; but, as we have seen, it is in practice generally treated more leniently. It therefore offers opportunities for plea-bargaining.

(3) Not all handlers are thieves. The law of handling is extended to goods obtained by fraud or blackmail, even when they would not for other purposes be regarded as being stolen (section 24 (4)). Here the handler is not necessarily guilty of theft. If (as will usually be the case) the blackmailer or cheat obtains a voidable title to the goods, a person who subsequently handles them will not be guilty of stealing them from the original owner, because the original owner is no longer the owner at the time of the act in question. Such a person can, however, be convicted of handling.

A person who arranges to handle is a handler, though he is not guilty of theft but of a conspiracy to steal or a conspiracy to defraud. The point also applies to handlers by dealing. Although some of these commit theft, it is not certain that all do.

(4) If a person is charged with handling and not with theft, the prosecution may be assisted in proving the mental element by giving evidence of the defendant's previous convictions or similar conduct on other occasions, subject to certain conditions (section 27 (3).[12]

This is not generally allowed on a charge of theft, or on a charge of both handling and theft. In order to get the benefit of the provision the prosecution may be tempted to charge handling when they really should charge theft; and the court should be astute to prevent this (instead of being astute to help the prosecutor, as it was in the case of the candlesticks).

Normally, thieves, accessories and handlers[13] are tried together, and technically different charges are regarded as being alternative.

§ 39.3. HANDLING BY DEALING: RETENTION

What we are calling handling by dealing turns on the four forbidden acts of retention, removal, disposal and realisation of the goods.

Like the other elements of handling by dealing (undertaking or assisting; arranging) these acts can be charged in the alternative. So a person can be charged with undertaking to retain, assisting to retain, arranging to undertake or arranging to assist the retention; and so with removing, disposing of and realising, through all the permutations.

Why isn't the person who furthers the thief's plans in these respects punishable as an accesssory to the theft?

Because theft is not a continuing offence; the appropriation is over by the time the handler comes on the scene. (I assume that the defendant did not help the thief by dealing with the goods "in the course of the stealing;"

---

[11] Even charging both offences can lead to trouble, if the jury are divided between them. See McConville in 143 JPN 287. The best course would be for the judge to direct the jury that if in doubt between the two offences they should convict of theft.

[12] See Griew 184–186.

[13] For the joint trial or handlers and thieves, see Theft Act s. 27 (1), (2).

if he did, he is not a handler but an accessory to the theft. Also, if he agreed with the thief beforehand that he would handle the goods, he is both an accessory to the theft by encouraging it and, when he later deals with the stolen goods, a handler.)

Is there any common idea underlying the four prohibitions? What is the subsection really aiming at?

The forms of handling by dealing are evidently intended to cover acts enabling the thief (or some other person implicated in his dishonesty) to *retain* (remain in possession of) his ill-gotten gains or to *dispose* of them. For the moment we will assume that "removal" and "disposal" are roughly comprised under the word "disposal."

It may be convenient to say at once what handling by dealing is intended to leave out. It is not intended to punish the thief for *using* the loot: he can be dealt with for that as a thief, and need not be made a handler as well. Nor does the subsection make his friends or employees guilty of handling if they share in the use.[1]

As an example, one does not handle stolen goods merely by allowing oneself to be driven in a stolen car, or by driving it on the general business of the thief.[2] Although handling includes the "removal" of goods, this does not mean that driving a stolen car, which is merely using it in the manner for which it is designed, is to be regarded as removing it. It should not be so regarded unless the driving is for the purpose of disposing of a stolen car, or of other stolen goods, or more safely retaining them. In any case, the act of driving could not be a handling if the driver was acting for his own purposes and not in order to benefit or assist another.[3]

The two forbidden acts, then, are the retention and/or disposal of stolen goods. These can each be committed in either of two modes: by *undertaking* and by *assisting in* their doing. "Undertaking" the act in question here means doing it.

The point may be briefly expanded. We saw in discussing manslaughter by omission that this word is ambiguous in some contexts. In ordinary speech, undertaking *to* do something is a promise to do it, while undertaking *something* generally means doing it. ("He undertook to journey to Rome" = he promised to go. "He undertook a journey to Rome" = he went.) In section 22 (1) the undertaking is of a noun, and is naturally read as the act of retention, etc. What the statute evidently means by the word "undertakes" is that handling can be committed by a person who retains, removes, disposes of or realises goods for the benefit of another.

In support of this opinion, it may be said that there would be little point in reading 'undertakes" as though it meant "promises," because an agreement for the retention etc. would be more naturally and explicitly charged as an *arrangement* to retain etc. under the concluding limb of the subsection. The word "undertakes" is evidently put in not to carry the meaning of a promise but simply to tie up grammatically with "assists." The draftsman would have done better to have avoided the ambiguity by rewriting the subsection.[4]

What is the statute getting at when it says "by or for the benefit of another person"?

Fortunately we now have the authority of Lord Bridge telling us what it

---

[1] *Sanders* [1982] Crim.LR 695.

[2] *Kanwar* [1982] 1 WLR at 847C.

[3] *Sloggett* [1972] 1 QB 430. But driving or being driven in a stolen car could be charged under s. 12 (§ 29.9). Probably it is not theft, since the person who drives the car for a temporary purpose does not intend for his own part to deprive the owner permanently.

[4] Cp. CLRC, 8th Report, para.128.

means. The word "undertakes" goes with "for the benefit of another person" and the word "assists" goes with "by . . . another person." Lord Bridge:

> "The offence can be committed in relation to any one of these [four] activities in one or other of two ways. First, the offender may himself undertake the activity for the benefit of another person. Secondly, the activity may be by another person and the offender may assist him."[5]

Spelling this out again in the words of the subsection, the handler may

1 *undertake* the retention or disposal of the goods (two words that we are using to cover all four activities)—i.e. he may retain or dispose of the goods—*for the benefit of another*, or he may

2 *assist another* in retaining or disposing of the goods.

With all these preliminaries over, we narrow our attention to the question of retaining stolen goods or assisting in their retention.

The CLRC, which proposed the offence in its present form, explained its rationale as follows (italics supplied).

> "We are in favour of extending the scope of the offence [from the receiving of stolen property] to certain other kinds of meddling with stolen property. *This is because the object should be to combat theft by making it more difficult and less profitable to dispose of stolen property.* Since thieves may be helped not only by buying the property but in other ways such as facilitating its disposal, it seems right that the offence should extend to these kinds of assistance."

The House of Lords quoted this passage in *Bloxham*[6] as a means of resolving any ambiguity that might be found in the subsection. Their lordships held that they were entitled to look at the committee's Report on which the Act was based in order to ascertain what was the mischief that the subsection intended to cure, and they discovered from the Report that there was no mischief calling for legislative intervention on the particular point with which they were concerned. The Report was, therefore, a useful aid to the interpretation of the Act.

The committee talks about the thief's disposal of the goods. I don't see what "retention" of the goods has to do with disposal. It's the opposite.

The word "retention" does not appear in the committee's statement of policy; but it may be said that what section 22 (1) does is to pick out certain particularly important activities by the thief after committing the theft, or by other persons in relation to the stolen goods, in which it is an offence to assist. The retention of the goods is one of them.

Who is the "another" that the subsection talks about?

Anyone other than the person who is charged with handling.

But if the defendant can retain the stolen goods for his own benefit, why can't he retain them for the benefit of his maiden aunt?

Although the subsection does not say so, what it is really aimed against

---

[5] *Bloxham* [1983] AC at 113G. This interpretation of the subsection had previously been carefully worked out by the commentators. The draftsman obscured his meaning by rolling the various alternatives into a complex sentence, and, worse still, by getting the two halves of his variations mixed up: he should have said "for the benefit of or by another person as the case may be."

[6] [1983] AC at 115C.

is retaining (or disposing of) the goods for the benefit of the thief (or of another handler), or helping the thief (or a handler) to retain (or dispose of) them. The draftsman did not want to make the thief himself guilty of handling by reason of his retention of the goods. If a person knowingly retains stolen goods for his own benefit, he can be charged with theft. The subsection states this limitation rather obscurely, by requiring that the defendant was not acting for himself. If, for example, he agreed to warehouse stolen goods, or if he let a garage to the thief, or to the thief's father (or his own maiden aunt, if you like), knowing that the garage was intended to house stolen goods, he is a handler.[7]

Underworld characters aren't generally altruistic. The chap who garages the goods for the thief is being rewarded for it, so he is acting for his own benefit.

Nevertheless, he is also acting for the benefit of the thief. We shall return to this point in § .4.

A more unexpected illustration of the offence than those just given is *Kanwar*.[8]

> A woman whose house contained (as she knew) goods stolen by her husband lied to the police in the hope of protecting her husband and retaining the goods. The Court of Appeal said that she committed no offence by having the stolen goods in the house (presumably it was her husband who was the owner or tenant of the house),[9] or in failing to disclose their presence to the police[10]; but her lies led to her conviction of handling by assisting her husband to retain the goods. This although the police knew she was lying and were not put off, since the court read the word "assist", with doubtful propriety, to include a person who did not assist but made an ineffectual effort to assist. This is not the only instance of the courts construing a word in an extended sense to include an attempt.

It looks unrealistic to say that Mrs Kanwar handled the stolen goods in talking to the police, though perhaps that is the result of giving a conglomeration of offences a conglomerate name. A more apt charge would have been under section 4 (1) of the Criminal Law Act 1967 (§ 15.20); but that charge would have required the consent of the DPP, and he would probably not have consented to the prosecution of a wife for attempting to shield her husband. Whether it was proper to use the Theft Act offence for the purpose of evading the restriction on prosecution in the Criminal Law Act is a matter that the court did not consider, since our judges do not regard it as part of their duty to control the exercise by prosecutors of their discretion in prosecuting. It almost never occurs to them to strike out a charge as being an abuse of the process of the court, as this one surely was.

Need there be mens rea at the beginning of the retaining? Suppose D agrees to warehouse goods for T, a thief, and after receiving them finds that they were stolen. He continues to keep them for T. Is he guilty of handling?

The subsection distinguishes between "receiving" (which may be for the defendant's own benefit) and "retaining for the benefit of another." The

---

[7] A difficult question may arise where a bailee dishonestly decides to keep the bailed article which is being warehoused for him. The point of time at which the bailee steals may be hard to fix (§ 33.13 at n. 6), and the point of time at which the warehouseman acts "otherwise than in the course of the stealing" will be similarly vague.

[8] [1982] 1 WLR 845, 2 All ER 528, 75 CAR 87; see note in [1982] Crim. LR 533.

[9] Had the house been in her name her conviction would very likely have been upheld. In *Brown* [1970] 1 QB 105 it was held that an occupier who expressly or impliedly allows another to place stolen goods on his property assists in their retention.

[10] See *Brown*, last note.

distinction relates to the time when the mental element is required. "Receiving" is once-for-all, but "retention" is a continuous affair.[11]

1 Handling by receiving (for oneself or another) requires that the defendant had the mental element at the time of receiving.[12] A person who receives goods innocently for his own benefit and dishonestly decides to keep them when he discovers they are stolen goods is not guilty of handling, because the *mens rea* comes after the *actus reus* is completed. (However, he can be convicted of theft, subject to the protection given to the buyer of goods by section 3 (2) of the Theft Act: § 33.7).

2 Handling by retention for the benefit of another is committed as soon as the mental element arises, even though it arises after the commencement of the retention. This is because retaining is a continuing act (and similarly assisting another person to retain the goods can be a continuing act). Guilty knowledge acquired while the act is continuing, i.e. during the retention, can incriminate. Therefore, D in your hypothetical would not be charged with handling by receiving; he would be charged with handling by retention of the goods for the benefit of T, and could be convicted of that offence.[13] D's only safe course, when he comes to know that the goods were stolen, is to inform the police, or at least to wash his hands of the affair by dumping them somewhere and informing the police of their whereabouts.

§ 39.4. HANDLING BY DEALING: DISPOSAL

Putting aside retention, we may say that the second part of the subsection is aimed against disposal of the goods, together with removal for the purpose of disposal.[1] (The word "realisation" was unnecessary, since every realisation of goods is a disposal of them.)

---

[11] It has been objected to this that the offençe is one of *undertaking* to retain, and that an undertaking is not a continuous transaction. The objection interprets an undertaking as a promise to retain, which I think is incorrect. For reasons given before, undertaking must be understood to refer to the act of retaining; and this act is performed continuously during the retention.

[12] *Alt* (1972) 56 CAR 457; Grainge [1974] 1 WLR 619, 1 All ER 928; *Smythe* (1980) 72 CAR 8 at 13. See also *Figures* [1976] Crim. LR 744, a ruling by a recorder which indicates that handling by receiving does not continue while the goods continue to be retained.

[13] *Brown*, n. 9 above; *Pitchley* (1973) § 39.5 at n. 8 (where the conviction was of assisting to retain but should have been of undertaking to retain; the actual decision is in any case open to question for a reason to be stated later). *Semble contra*, Smith para. 416 n.4. Discussing *Pitchley*, he says that Pitchley was not dishonest when he undertook the retention of the money, and seems to imply a doubt whether Pitchley's subsequent knowledge could make him guilty of handling. He asks whether "retaining" is an offence, *quasi dicere non*. If undertaking to retain means retaining, as I conceive, then retaining is an offence; the offence is not committed only at its inception but is a continuing offence, so that a subsequently-acquired knowlege makes it criminal.

[1] Griew 180 takes disposal to include destruction. Doubtless the courts will so construe it, since they construe any conceivable ambiguity in a criminal statute against an immoral defendant. But the legal argument to the contrary in the present instance is strong. In legal usage, a disposal of property practically always refers to an alienation of it. In the context of s. 22 (1), where it is associated with the words "receives" and "realisation," this is evidently what was intended. If Parliament meant to turn criminal damage into an offence of handling it could and should have said so in plain terms and unambiguously, not relied upon an unusual secondary meaning of the word "disposal."

The subsection therefore operates against "placers," those who help the thief to find a buyer for the goods, and also against those who help to transport the goods for sale, as by unloading them from (or, presumably, loading them on) a lorry.

One who agrees to supply oxygen cutting-equipment to open a stolen safe, to enable the contents to be spent or otherwise disposed of, becomes guilty of handling, because he arranges to assist in the realisation of the loot. But if the object was only to enable the thief to get at and use the contents (such as important documents that he wanted to keep), it should not be held to be handling, because then the person supplying the equipment is not assisting a disposal or retention but only an enjoyment.

As we have seen, handling by dealing (whether the dealing is by way of retention or of disposal) may take either of two forms: undertaking (do-it-yourself) or assisting. The undertaking or assisting must be "by or for the benefit of another person." This is a condensed way of saying that it must be by another person or for the benefit of another person. The limitation placed upon the offence by these words may be illustrated.

Suppose, to take the example of the safe already given, the thief had cut into the safe himself, to get at the money inside. In that case the opening of the safe would not be an offence under the subsection: the thief would not be doing the act for the benefit of another, and would not be assisting the doing of the act by another.

The idea underlying the subsection, though far from clearly expressed, is that there should be a distinction between handling by receiving (the first part of the subsection) and handling by dealing (the second part).

- The thief himself should be convictable of receiving if (for example) he were the master-mind behind the theft (§ .2). He falls within the words of the subsection, because it covers the person who receives for his own benefit, provided that the receiving was after the theft. This supposes that he was not in possession by reason of the theft, but received the goods from one of the other thieves afterwards.
- But the thief is not intended to be convictable of handling by dealing, because that would virtually efface the distinction between theft and handling. Every thief "handles" the goods (in a sense), unless he is arrested the moment after the theft. Accordingly, the intention of the subsection is that handling by dealing can only be undertaken for the benefit of another. In short, you receive for yourself (or for another), but can deal only for another.

This is the key to the understanding of the subsection. The handler may help a thief by undertaking the retention or disposal of the goods on his behalf. This is "undertaking for the benefit of another person." (Or the "other person" may be a receiver or other handler.) Alternatively, the handler may help the thief (or receiver) not by undertaking the job himself but by assisting the thief (or receiver or other handler) in doing the job. This is "assisting their retention, disposal etc. by another person." Unfortunately, the draftsman made two mistakes. First, he talked vaguely about "another person," when he should have said "the thief or (where the charge is not against the thief) another handler of the stolen goods." And instead of saying "for the benefit of" he should have used the more precise expression "on behalf of."[2] One can only hope that the courts will perceive the sensible intention behind the lax drafting.

Suppose the thief sells the stolen goods to a buyer who knows they are stolen. Is the thief guilty of handling by undertaking the disposal for the benefit of another, namely the buyer?

No. The point was established by *Bloxham*.[3]

> Bloxham bought a stolen car, not knowing that it was stolen. When he discovered the truth he resold it at a low price to a man who was prepared to take it without documents. Bloxham could not be prosecuted for theft, because he was protected by section 3 (2) of the Theft Act (§ 33.7), so the prosecutor cunningly charged him instead with handling by undertaking the disposal of stolen goods for the benefit of another. His conviction of this offence was upheld by the Court of Appeal, which refused leave to appeal to the House of Lords; but the House itself gave leave, and quashed the conviction.

There were strong reasons of policy for this decision. The effect of section 3 (2) is clearly to protect the person who initially came into possession of stolen goods in good faith from a charge of theft in selling them, and it would destroy the practical effect of this exemption if the same act were held to amount to handling. Besides, the decision of the Court of Appeal would have created a rule applicable equally to sales by thieves, even to sales by thieves to innocent buyers, whereas the CLRC's policy statement (which the House of Lords quoted) referred only to those who *help* thieves in the disposal. Since thieves who steal goods generally do so with the intention of selling them, the decision would have made all such thieves guilty of handling when they sold—which was certainly not the intention of section 22 (1).

But in addition to these reasons of policy there were arguments against the conviction based on the wording of the subsection. A man who sells an article does not assist the buyer to dispose of it, since the buyer does not dispose of it.[4] Further, such a seller in the ordinary way does not dispose of it for the benefit of another; he sells it for his own benefit, not for the benefit of the buyer.

But there is a benefit to the buyer in the transaction. Otherwise he wouldn't have bought the article, would he?

Yes: the sale benefits the seller, and the purchase benefits the buyer, but they are different benefits. The seller gets the benefit of the buyer's money and the buyer gets the benefit of the article bought. The point remains that one party does not act for the benefit of the other within the meaning of the subsection.

---

[2] I was a member of the CLRC when it considered the draft of this subsection, and therefore bear my share of responsibility for its defects. The draftsman was a very able parliamentary counsel, and we thought we considered his work carefully. Little did we realise what an ugly duckling we were fostering!

[3] [1983] AC 109. The credit for putting the law back on course on this point should go to J R Spencer; it is inconceivable that the lords' decision was not strongly influenced by his trenchant article in [1982] Crim. LR 682, but their lordships ungraciously gave it no acknowledgment.

[4] See *per* Lord Bridge, [1983] AC at 114A.

What about oblique intention?

This is a situation where one cannot apply that concept, and it is because of cases of this kind that I suggested in § 3.5 that intention should not be taken to include oblique intention if this does not serve the purposes of the law. The difficulty would have been avoided in the present instance if the subsection had said "on behalf of" another person. Bloxham obviously did not sell on behalf of the buyer.

Nevertheless, the doctrine of oblique intent must apply to some extent to charges of handling. Suppose that a man assists a thief to dispose of the goods because he wants to earn a reward from the thief. Obviously he will be held to have intended to assist. The intention is either a direct intention (the man wants to help, in order to earn his reward) or, at least, an oblique intention (he wants to earn his reward, but knows that in doing so he is assisting). Either way he is guilty of the offence.[5]

Could I put a problem for the sake of having a brief recap? Suppose a student buys a book from a fellow student. He pays for it in good faith, but later discovers that the seller is a thief who habitually steals from the local booksellers. What is his position?

He is not guilty of handling, even if he keeps the book, because he did not know it was stolen when he received it, and he does not retain it for the benefit of another. Nor is he guilty of theft in retaining the book: section 3 (2).

Would the student be guilty of handling if he sold the book or gave it away?

Bloxham shows that he would not perpetrate handling by selling the book, and section 3(2) again protects him from a charge of theft.

The student's position if he gives the book away is more parlous. He would be in danger of conviction of handling, absurd as that may sound, because it might be argued that the gift is entirely for the benefit of another. So also if he lent the book, or sold it and asked the buyer to pay the price to a charity or other gratuitous recipient. In each of these hypotheticals the student would literally have disposed of the book for the benefit of another. However, a court might be persuaded to find that such cases are outside the intendment of the Act. They fall outside the CLRC's policy statement, since they are not cases of helping the thief to dispose of the goods. They are not cases of helping a thief at all.

These problems again indicate defects in the draftsmanship of the subsection. One therapy would be to read "for the benefit of another" in a restrictive sense as meaning "on behalf of another," as already suggested. Alternatively or additionally, drastic surgery might be performed upon the meaning of the phrase "another person." We may hope, though perhaps without much confidence, that the courts would find that such cases as those just instanced fall outside any rational understanding of the intention of the subsection. The words "any person" should be taken as confined to the thief and (where the defendant is someone other than the thief) any person guilty of handling the stolen goods. It would be particularly absurd if a person who is not otherwise guilty of handling when he retains another's property becomes guilty of that offence merely because he allows a completely innocent person (his

---

[5] The proposition in *Kanwar* that the assistance must be given "for the purpose of enabling the goods to be retained" (p. 847D) need not be read as entirely excluding oblique intention. In *Chandler*, § 3.2 at n.1, the HL in effect included oblique intention within the notion of "purpose."

grandmother, perhaps) to use it, or uses it for the benefit of such person (driving his grandmother to church in a stolen car).[6]

The House of Lords could have settled these problems in *Bloxham* (they had all been ventilated in the literature), but it chose to confine its decision to the narrow facts of the case before it.

There are other perils for your unlucky student. Suppose he sells the book not to an innocent buyer[7] but to a buyer who knew the book was stolen. The buyer would be guilty of handling by receiving, and the student would, it seems, technically be guilty as accessory.[8] (He may even be accessory to theft by the buyer.)

Fortunately, such charges appear to be unknown in present practice, and would look like an attempt to strain the law. Even a thief should not be convicted of being an accessory to handling if he sells the stolen goods. The thief does not commit handling by the act of stealing, and it would be anomalous if the fact that he agrees to sell the goods were treated as making him a handler. (The problem would be solved if, as was before suggested, the law were changed to avoid implicating a party in a bilateral transaction which is forbidden only for the other party: § 15.15).

§ 39.5. STOLEN GOODS

The Act speaks of "stolen goods," but the definition section makes goods include money, and also other property like things in action (s. 34 (2) (*b*)). So a person who changes the thief's "hot" money for safe money can be guilty of handling by receiving.

The goods must be stolen. One consequence of this rule is that if a small child (under 10) brings home a bicycle that he has illegitimately "found," his parents who keep it are not guilty of receiving stolen goods, because the child is too young to be capable in law of stealing.[1] However,the parents may of course become guilty of theft (as perpetrators).

The goods must already be "stolen" when the defendant handles them. He must "know or believe them to be stolen goods," not goods that are intended to be stolen. This point is easily overlooked in the case of handling by making an arrangement. A person who arranges to receive or deal with goods that are to be stolen subsequently is not guilty of handling stolen goods, though he is guilty of conspiring to handle.

The fact that the goods were stolen may, of course, be found on the basis of circumstantial

---

[6] See Spencer in [1981] Crim. LR 685. The decision in *Bloxham*, n. 3 above, may be cited as giving some encouragement to the argument against a wide interpretation of the offence, though the particular point was not there considered. The argument is also reinforced by the policy implications of s. 3 (2), to which the House attached importance in *Bloxham*. According to the literal words of the handling section the friend of a b.f.p. who subsequently helps him to remove or sell the goods, knowing the facts, would be guilty of handling, but this was obviously not in the mind of Parliament.

[7] In which case the student would be guilty of obtaining money from the buyer by an implied deception as to his own title to sell, unless he believed that he had obtained a good title by buying in good faith.

[8] *Carter Paterson Ltd* v. *Wessel* [1947] KB 849. See criticism in § 15.15 at n. 13. In *Bloxham*, n. 3 above at p. 115A, Lord Bridge introduced a little healthy doubt into the position by saying that it was "conceivably" so.

[1] *Walters* v. *Lunt* [1951] 2 All ER 645, 35 CAR 94.

evidence, including the very low price at which they were sold to the defendant.[2] Nevertheless, several rules of law have the practical effect of hampering the prosecution in proving this issue. For example, an statement made by the thief (otherwise than on oath at the trial of the handler) is not admissible in evidence against the handler, on account of the hearsay rule.[3] Also, the fact that the defendant thought the goods were stolen does not generally prove that they were.

Goods constructively stolen

The notion of "stolen goods" is extended by the Act in three ways.

First, as already said, the notion is made to cover goods obtained by blackmail, or by deception contrary to section 15 (1) (s. 24 (4)).[4] Secondly, the offence is extended to cover the handling in England of goods criminally acquired abroad (s. 24 (1) as amended).[5]

The third and most important extension is that "stolen goods" are defined to include (in general) the proceeds of the originally-stolen goods. In other words, the doctrine of following, which applies in connection with theft (§ 33.9), applies also to handling to a certain extent. There is a complicated provision in the Act (s. 24 (2)) the main aim of which is to prevent the thief effectively "laundering" stolen property by exchanging it for other property. The subsection provides that a disposal of stolen goods *by a thief or (guilty) handler* causes the proceeds also (when in the hands of the thief or guilty handler) to be "stolen." Instead of eliminating the stolen property the disposal generally doubles it, much as the Hydra of Greek legend responded to having its head cut off by immediately sprouting two more.

There is, however, an important difference between the goods originally stolen and and goods received in exchange which are regarded as constructively stolen by the Act (let us call them the derivatively stolen goods). So long as the original owner has a right to recover the goods originally stolen, those goods remain stolen goods; so do goods received in exchange for them by a guilty possessor (thief or handler). But goods received in exchange for any of the foregoing goods by an innocent possessor are not "stolen." In other words, the Hydra effect does not occur where the proceeds of the originally stolen goods or of derivatively stolen goods are received by a person who does not know the facts.

Some examples may clarify this. The Hydra effect (the doubling of the quantity of stolen goods) is seen if the thief of a wad of notes trades them with his underworld associate for other notes. The original notes remain "stolen," and the notes received in exchange become tainted in the same way.

The Hydra effect does not occur if the thief spends the notes (whether the originally-stolen or the substituted notes) with a seller who receives them in good faith. The latter, being a *bona fide* purchaser of the notes, obtains a good title to them (this being a special rule of the law of property for currency and negotiable instruments), so they cease to be stolen; but what the thief receives from him in return has that quality impressed on it.

The Hydra effect is seen at its most terrifying when the theft is of goods in the usual sense

---

[2] *Overington* [1978] Crim. LR 692; *Hulbert* (1979) 69 CAR 243; *Mcdonald* 70 CAR 288,[1980] Crim. LR 242.

[3] See generally on the question of proof 1st edn 829-830; David Stone in 129 NLJ 1018; *Korniak* [1983] Crim.LR 109.

[4] Goods obtained by deception contrary to the Theft Act 1978 s. 1 (§ 34.11) are not declared to be "stolen." If, say, D obtains the hire of a car by deception, he can be convicted of obtaining services by deception, but the car will not be stolen goods for the purpose of the offence of handling. Nor does the offence of handling cover goods obtained by a conspiracy to defraud, unless of course the facts are such as to come within the definition of theft or under s. 15 (1).

[5] See *Figures* [1976] Crim.LR 744 and note thereto.

of the term (not money). If the thief of a car sells it, the proceeds in his hands are "stolen goods;" so if the thief hands these proceeds to his wife (who knows the facts), his wife can be convicted of handling the proceeds.[6] If Mrs Thief spends the money on a deep-freeze, anybody who knowingly helps her to buy it is guilty of handling in helping her to dispose of the "stolen" money; and the deep-freeze will also be "stolen goods." The car is still stolen goods; consequently, if the person who bought the car from the thief knew it was stolen when he bought it, he is guilty of handling by receiving. And so the chain of guilt can go on, all of it depending on the original theft.

When "stolen goods" come into the hands of a person who does not know they are stolen, then if such person changes the stolen goods for something else while still in that state of ignorance, the property he receives in exchange is not "stolen," but the goods he first received and now gives in exchange continue in the state of being stolen. So stolen "goods" in the narrow sense, unlike stolen money, can almost never be sanitised by being disposed of. (This is because the *Nemo dat* rule applies to goods in the narrow sense but not to money). If, for example, a Constable painting is stolen from an art gallery, and passes through the hands of several innocent buyers, it nevertheless remains the property of the art gallery and remains "stolen goods;" so if a dealer recognises it and yet dishonestly buys it, he will be guilty of handling stolen property by receiving. The fact that the dealer buys from an innocent buyer makes no difference.

In suitable circumstances a fund may be traced into and through a bank account. Suppose that X obtains a cheque by deception. The cheque as a piece of paper is "stolen goods." X pays it into his bank account, thus converting it into a thing in action (X's right against his bank). X then draws on the account in favour of D, who takes X's cheque, knowing that it represents the "stolen" asset, in whole or in part. D pays the cheque into his own bank account. If the fund received by D (by way of credit to his account) can be proved to represent the "stolen" fund, he can be convicted of receiving the relevant part of the fund as "stolen goods." *When* the fund drawn out can be taken to represent the fund paid in is a difficult and somewhat obscure question which will not here be considered.[7]

Remember that if an innocent recipient of stolen goods sells them, the proceeds in his hands are not stolen in the eye of the criminal law. This point was overlooked in *Pitchley*.[8]

> Pitchley's son stole some money and gave it to Pitchley for safe keeping; according to Pitchley he did not at that time know that the money was stolen. He put it in his bank account, and the next day came to know that it was stolen. He then did nothing because he did not wish to report his son to the police and did not think of returning the money to its owner. Pitchley's conviction of handling the money by assisting to retain it was upheld by the Court of Appeal.

It will be observed that the money originally stolen was converted by Pitchley into a thing in action (the debt owing by the bank to him). This thing in action was property, and therefore goods within the meaning of the section. Nevertheless, the case was wrongly decided because, by paying the money into his bank account, Pitchley innocently turned currency into a thing in action, which was not the same property as that stolen. Section 24 (2) states that the proceeds of stolen goods are stolen goods in the hands of a thief or guilty receiver, but Pitchley was neither; it follows that he could not be guilty of handling the thing in action as stolen goods. The

---

[6] See *Dadd* [1974] Crim. LR 439. This was a mistress, who is perhaps more in peril of conviction than a wife, but the same principle should apply to both.

[7] See *Att.-Gen.'s Refce (No. 4 of 1979)* [1981] 1 WLR 667, 1 All ER 1193, 71 CAR 341; for other commentaries see note in [1981] Crim. LR 51; Griew 174.

[8] (1973) 57 CAR 30. See § . 3 n. 12; Griew 179 n.44.

point was missed by counsel and the court. Probably, however, Pitchley could have been convicted of theft of the chose in action by "keeping as owner." See section 3 (1), reproduced in § 31.3.

When goods cease to be stolen

Goods cease to be "stolen" if they return to the possession of the owner or the police. The rule is stated in section 24 (3);

> "But no goods shall be regarded as having continued to be stolen goods after they have been restored to the person from whom they were stolen or to other lawful possession or custody."[9]

This rule is important if the owner of stolen goods or a police officer arrests the thief, takes the stolen goods from him, and then, hearing that a "fence" is about to arrive to collect the goods, sets a trap by concealing from the fence that things have taken an unexpected turn. The fence may take the goods, but if the court holds that the goods had then lost their character of stolen goods he will not be guilty of handling. Exceptionally, since an arrangement to handle is a handling, he can be convicted of handling the goods if it can be proved that his arrangement to receive them was made after they were stolen. In any case he can be convicted of attempting to handle, and this would be a perfectly proper case for using the law of attempt. (If the goods had never been stolen it might look over-sharp to charge an attempt, even though such a charge would be legally possible.)

Although the general rule stated in section 24 (3) is undoubted, a police officer who comes across stolen goods and who thinks that a receiver is about to appear may evade the operation of the subsection by refraining from taking the goods and simply standing by to await developments. If he does not take the goods into his custody, a receiver who comes to carry off the goods can be convicted of handling them. It is for the jury to decide whether the officer intended to take charge of the goods or whether he intended merely to interrogate the suspect when he appeared and to seize the goods (and the suspect) only if his answers were unsatisfactory.[10] Obviously, this is a nebulous question, but the judge may encourage the jury in any doubtful situation to find that the goods are still "stolen."

§ 39.6. THE MENTAL ELEMENT

Traditionally, the offence of receiving stolen goods requires knowledge that the goods are stolen. Negligence, or even recklessness, is insufficient.

But why isn't recklessness enough?

Because that would be an undue restraint upon commerce.

The offence of handling applies to all conceivable articles, which cannot be identified as being stolen merely by examining the articles themselves. It is important not to incriminate

[9] The subsection goes on to say; "or after that person and any other person claiming through him have otherwise ceased as regards those goods to have any right to restitution in respect of the theft." An example relating to money was given in the text. As another example, suppose that X induces V to sell him goods by deception, X thus obtaining a voidable title. V, after discovering the deception, decides nevertheless to affirm the contract, which he does. The goods now cease to be stolen, and D may safely buy them from X, even though he knows the facts.

[10] See 1st edn 832; *Streeter* (1980) CAR 113.

honest dealers who make no enquiry whether the goods they are buying are stolen because they have no sufficient reason to think that they are. People must be free to buy unless they positively know that the goods are stolen. The public interest in free trade is greater than the public interest in attempting to close every possibility of stolen goods being sold.

Section 22 (1) allows what appears at first sight to be an alternative to knowledge; the defendant must have known or *believed* the goods to be stolen.[1] The Criminal Law Revision Committee proposed this alternative in order to cover a case where a man buys goods at a ridiculously low price from an unknown seller and deliberately asks no questions.[2] The aim was evidently to cover "wilful blindness," which in law is supposed to come within the notion of "knowledge"; but there is much doubt what precisely wilful blindness means. The preferable view is that it extends the notion of knowledge to the case where the defendant, while lacking explicit information, is virtually certain in his own mind that the fact exists (§ 4.11). This is also conveyed by the word ' believes," from which it follows that the reference to belief was an unnecessary (and therefore misleading) addition to the section.[3]

Suppose a person acquires goods knowing that they are stolen but intending to return them to the owner?

Then he does not act "dishonestly." Apart from this point, it seems that the word has no useful function in relation to handling, but it may have other practical effects all the same. If a handler argues that he was not dishonest in knowingly buying a stolen article in a pub, because everybody does it, his defence would presumably have to be left to the jury, who might sympathise.

It is even possible for an intermediary to arrange with the owner to get his goods back for him for reward, by paying the thief for them, without committing the offence of handling.[4] But it is a statutory offence for the owner or anyone else to *advertise* a reward for the return of stolen goods with no questions asked, or stating that money paid for the purchase of the goods will be repaid.[5] The offence is not committed by making a private arrangement to the same effect.

SUMMARY

Handling stolen goods under section 22 (1) of the Theft Act is regarded in §.1

[1] He need not know the contents of a package, if he knows they are stolen: *McCullum* (1973) 57 CAR 645. Even a mistake as to the type of articles in the package would be no defence, being immaterial. It would be equally immaterial if the defendant thought that the goods had been "snatched" when actually they had been obtained by deception.

[2] Cmnd. 2977, para. 64. See § 7.7.

[3] Griew 181–182 offers a somewhat different opinion. For the difficulties experienced in summing up see 1st edn 833; *Albert Smith* (1976) 64 CAR 217; *Ismail* [1977] Crim. LR 557; *Reader* (1978) 66 CAR 33; *Pethick* [1980] Crim. LR 242; *Bellenie ibid. 437*; *Lincoln ibid.* 575; Beaumont in 142 JPN 528–529.

The prosecution may be assisted in proving the mental element by s. 27 (3), which allows previous convictions and similar facts to be given in evidence subject to certain conditions. See Griew 184–185. See also § 2.3 on the evidential burden. The doctrine of "recent possession" (§ 2.3 at n. 1) includes charges of handling by dealing: *Ball* [1983] 1 WLR 801.

[4] *Higgins* [1972] Crim. LR 213.

[5] Theft Act 1968 s. 23.

practice (though not in strict law) as two offences, which may be called handling by receiving (with which may be included arranging to receive) and handling by dealing (or arranging to deal). Although handling can receive a longer sentence than theft, in practice it is usually regarded as a lesser offence.

Handling by receiving means obtaining possession or control of the stolen goods. § .2
The handler's dishonest receipt of possession will almost always amount to an act of theft on his part. On the other hand the thief does not commit handling by receiving unless he does so "otherwise than in the course of stealing." The effect of *Pitham* seems to be that a receipt by an accessory to the theft or by a stranger is a handling by him even though it takes place a second after the theft, which is regarded as an instantaneous point of time. In case of doubt a person should be charged as a thief rather than as a handler, though he may be charged with both offences, leaving the jury or magistrates to decide between them.

Handling by dealing is suggested as an unofficial name of convenience for the § .3
offence stated in the second part of the subsection. It is committed where the defendant "undertakes or assists in their retention, removal, disposal or realisation by or for the benefit of another person, or if he arranges so to do;" once again he must act "otherwise than in the course of the stealing." The CLRC, which proposed the offence, stated its rationale as being that of helping the thief to dispose of the property (cp. the words "removal, disposal or realisation"); and the HL cited this part of the committee's Report as an aid to the interpretation of the subsection in *Bloxham*. Helping the thief to retain the property (as by lending him the use of storage space, or telling lies to the police in the hope of persuading them that the goods are not stolen) is also included, but not assisting the thief to enjoy the stolen property. The words "undertakes their retention" etc. refer to actually retaining the goods, not to a mere promise to retain; consequently, undertaking is an act that continues over a period of time. If goods are innocently received from a thief, and the recipient subsequently discovers that they are stolen goods, and yet dishonestly retains them for the benefit of the thief, he can be convicted of handling by undertaking their retention, though not of handling by receiving them. A person who undertakes the retention etc. of stolen goods does not commit the offence if he acts for himself (*Bloxham*).

The other types of handling by dealing may be referred to as handling by dispo- § .4
sal. Examples of handling in relation to disposal are where a man transports the goods for the purpose of sale or finds a purchaser for them, or arranges to try to do so. If a thief sells the stolen goods to a buyer who knows they are stolen, he is not guilty of handling by undertaking the disposal of the goods for the benefit of the buyer, since he sells it for his own benefit: *Bloxham*.

Handling is of goods, but this term is defined to include money and things in § .5
action. The notion of "stolen" goods is extended to cover goods obtained by blackmail or deception contrary to section 15 (1), and also to cover the handling in England or Wales of goods criminally acquired abroad. A disposition of stolen goods by a thief or (guilty) handler causes the proceeds also (when in his hands)to be "stolen." Goods cease to be "stolen" if they return to the possession of the owner or the police, but the courts readily allow juries to find that this has not happened. (§ .5)

The defendant must handle the goods knowing or believing that they are stolen. § .6
The reference to belief is presumably a reminder of the rule that knowledge is established if the defendant was practically certain that the goods were stolen. Additionally, he must have acted dishonestly.

CHAPTER 40

MISCELLANEOUS FRAUDS

Satan always finds somebody for idle hands to do.

O Henry, *A Midsummer Masquerade*

THE offences of obtaining property or services by deception, studied in Chapter 34, leave various diddles unprovided for, or insufficiently provided for.

§ 40.1. FRAUDULENT DEBTORS

A person may contract a debt honestly but afterwards behave dishonestly towards his creditor. Here the law steps warily, lest the mere failure to pay the debt becomes an offence. We have slowly been getting rid of imprisonment for debt in the civil law, and do not want to do anything in the criminal law that may bring it back. The police, too, are far from anxious to take on the role of debt-collectors. So a debtor who finds his liabilities too burdensome may fold his tent, like the Arabs, and as silently steal away. He may hide from his creditors, or go abroad, or otherwise stall on his debts, without (in general) infringing the criminal law.

In general. But infringement takes place in three main types of case: in the offence of "making off without having paid," in the use of deception to evade payment, and in fraudulent transfers of property and Bankruptcy Act offences.

(1) Making off without having paid

With the enactment of section 3 of the Theft Act 1978 a new technical term entered the law—"making off." The section creates an either way offence to deal with debtors who do their tent-folding at a filling station or restaurant or other place where they are expected to pay on the spot. As usual, I set out the section with the omission of distracting words.

"(1) A person who, knowing that payment on the spot for any goods supplied or service done is required or expected from him, dishonestly makes off without having paid as required or expected and with intent to avoid payment of the amount due shall be guilty of an offence.

(2) 'Payment on the spot' includes payment at the time of collecting goods on which work has been done or in respect of which services have been provided.

(3) Subsection (1) above shall not apply where the supply of the goods or the doing of the service is contrary to law, or where the service done is such that payment is not legally enforceable.[1]

---

[1] On debts by minors see Rowlands in 145 JPN 410.

(4) Any person may arrest without warrant anyone who is, or whom he, with reasonable cause, suspects to be committing or attempting to commit an offence under this section."[2]

The advantage of the provision is that it enables a conviction to be obtained even when no proof is available that the defendant had a dishonest intent when he ordered the article or service, or when he obtained it.

So the motorist who "makes off" with a tankful of petrol, and the diner who slips out of the restaurant and melts in the crowd after the meal, can be convicted, even though some credence is given to his story that he did not form the fraudulent intent until the petrol was in his tank or the meal in his stomach. The provision also covers hotel and taxi cheats, and freeloaders on public transport.

But can you say that goods are "supplied" at a self-service filling station?

An acute question. The answer is probably yes, because the customer presses a button which alerts the supervising clerk before the customer fills up. On the other hand the surreptitious thief in a supermarket is probably not "supplied."[3] He just takes.

What if a restaurant customer, having been served, creeps off but intends to pay later?

There seems to be a theoretical loophole in the offence as drafted, created by the words "and with intent to avoid payment of the amount due." They seem to say that even if the debtor does dishonestly make off without having paid as required or expected, still he is not guilty if he can say with some plausibility that he intended to pay later.[4] However, the words may possibly be read as meaning "with intent to avoid payment as required or expected," i.e. on the spot.

What if a diner is caught just outside the restaurant, trying to make his getaway?

The jury must be asked to consider what was the ambit of the "spot" where payment was supposed to be made. Presumably the offence is committed as soon as the defendant has quitted the restaurant, filling station etc. If he is only making for the restaurant door, that should on principle be only an attempt.[5]

Suppose the diner explains to the desk clerk that he is going to his car to get his wallet, or gives a cheque without a cheque card; he never comes back, and the cheque is not honoured.

In both your hypotheticals the debtor obtains his creditor's consent to

---

[2] The duration of the power of arrest is unclear. Until the debtor has made off no offence is committed; when he has made off the offence is complete and is no longer "being committed"! The courts will presumably hold that the offence is continuous while the debtor is making off and before he arrives at some more or less permanent stopping place. See *Drameh* [1983] Crim.LR 322. (The defendant in that case was guilty of an offence under s.2(1)(*b*) below, and could have been arrested for that.)

[3] A T H Smith in [1981] Crim.LR 590.

[4] The interpretation is rejected by Spencer in [1979] Crim.LR 37–38; Syrota in 42 MLR 307–308; Smith para. 249.

[5] See *Brooks* [1983] Crim.LR 188.

leave, but the consent is procured by deception. The section does not give a clear answer, and the commentators disagree between themselves.[6]

Against liability it may be said that the notion of "making off" does not naturally apply to a departure with the creditor's consent. Why does the Act use this colourful expression if it simply means "leaves"? And there is no need (some say) for the section to be interpreted extensively, since the debtor in your hypotheticals is guilty of an offence of evading the debt under section 2 (1) (*b*), to be discussed under (2) below.

On the last point, however, the evasion provision requires the prosecution to prove that the debtor intended never to pay, so that it is of limited use to the prosecution. That section 3 is properly applicable to these facts, and that the prosecution are not forced to rely only on section 2, may be realised when the reason for the wording of section 2 is understood. The offence of evading debts under section 2 was formulated leniently to let off the impecunious debtor who tries to put the creditor off by spinning a hard luck tale, or the tenant's wife who, finding the rent collector at the door and knowing that her husband is short of cash, falsely tells the collector that her husband is out, or the man who, having bought goods or obtained services on credit, and then finding that he lacks the means to pay, pacifies the creditor for the time being by giving him a dud cheque. The same leniency was not intended to be given to the person who knows before he contracts the debt that he will not be given credit because payment will be required on the spot. If such a person, after obtaining the goods or service, announces that he has no cash and that the supplier has to take an unbacked cheque, the supplier has an unenviable choice. He can refuse the cheque, wait till the debtor makes an exit, and immediately arrest him for making off. If he wants to avoid that unpleasantness and so reluctantly agrees to take the cheque (since he has no other option), and if the cheque is not met, there is no reason of substance why the offence of making off should not be regarded as committed.

Would a tenant who flits without paying his rent be guilty under section 3?

No. There is a difference in meaning between the "services" of section 1 and the "service" of section 3 (the making off section). Section 3 does not incorporate the special definition of "services" in section 1 (2) (§ 32.11), and there would be no warrant for reading it in. "Service" in section 3 is evidently intended to bear its ordinary meaning, whatever that is. The tenant of an unfurnished flat or house who bilks his landlord of the rent has not obtained a service, and anyway there is no requirement in an ordinary lease that the rent be paid on the spot.

In addition to the general provision in section 3, certain kinds of "bilking" are summary offences under special statutes. Examples are avoiding payment of bus, rail and taxi fares. These offences are useful because they enable the police to make sure that the defendant has to accept summary trial.

(2) Evading debts by deception

Except in the bilking cases just discussed, a debtor who simply removes himself from his creditor's reach is safe from the police. But if, silly man, he tells his creditor a lie to relieve the presssure, he will frequently commit a serious offence. This is under the Theft Act 1978 section 2 (1), which creates three offences of using deception to impede the creditor in

[6] For opinions against liability see the decision of a circuit judge in *Hammond* [1982] Crim.LR 611; Syrota, *op.cit.* 307–308; Bennion in [1983] Crim.LR 205.

exercising his civil remedies. In general the offences may be said to penalise the evading of (or attempting to evade) a debt by deception, but the Act does not speak of evading; instead it uses a variety of other expressions, and each of the three offences is limited in different ways. Readers who want the law in a nutshell may be satisfied to know that the broad effect of the section is to make it an offence to deceive the creditor into agreeing to waive the debt, or part of it; but it is not an offence to deceive the creditor into agreeing to wait for payment, unless the debtor intended never to pay.

Isn't the last rule excessively kind to the debtor? He has been deceitful; doesn't that show that he was trying to wriggle out of paying?

The courts held, in interpreting the pre-Act offence of evading debts, that the offence was committed by a debtor who gave the creditor a dud cheque in order to stave him off. But giving a creditor a dud cheque does him minimal damage. In a few days' time he will know that the cheque has not been honoured, and that may set him on the debtor with increased determination. Also, the cheque is now evidence of the debt and may save the creditor difficulties of proof. So there is no social necessity for regarding the giving of a dud cheque by a debtor as punishable, if the debtor is not seeking to evade the debt altogether and if it is not a payment-on-the-spot situation. This and the other reasons given before explain the wording of the present Act.

Here are the details of section 2 (1). I reproduce it with the omission of some parts that do not affect the main drift.

> "Where a person by any deception—
> (*a*) dishonestly secures the remission of the whole or part of any existing liability to make payment; or
> (*b*) with intent to make permanent default on any existing liability to make a payment, dishonestly induces the creditor to wait for payment or to forgo payment; or
> (*c*) dishonestly obtains any exemption from or abatement of liability to make a payment;
> he shall be guilty of an offence."

Paragraph (*a*) covers the use of deception to get the creditor to agree to waive the debt. Success in such a deception is likely to be rare. Creditors are not usually so generous as to waive debts, whether they have been deceived or not. The offence is completed only when the creditor agrees to the remission.

Since, according to the better view, one cannot deceive a machine, a charge under section 2 should not lie in respect of the fraudulent manipulation of a machine, as by putting a worthless disc into a parking meter in a car park. However, this could probably be charged as "making off;" and interference with a parking meter on the highway is a statutory offence.[7]

In (*b*) the creditor need not have agreed to anything; it is enough that he is induced as a matter of fact to wait for payment. The debtor may, to fend off the creditor, falsely say (for example) that he is out of funds, or is expecting a remittance; or he may give the creditor a dud cheque.

It was noticed under (1) above that this offence may be charged where payment was expected on the spot and the debtor uses deception to get the creditor's consent to leave—as

---

[7] Road Traffic Regulation Act 1967 s.42 (4).

where a man having taken a taxi says that he is going into the house to get cash, and then disappears by the back door.

The offence is committed only if it can be proved that the debtor intended never to pay. For example, it may be shown that the debtor used the time gained to hide his property, or (as in the taxi case) to do the Arabian disappearing trick. It is not clear whether the debtor's confession that he intended never to pay would be enough to convict him if all that he has at present planned that his deception will do is to make the creditor hold his hand. Anyway, merely giving a dud cheque or making up a tale about an expected remittance from his rich aunt is not enough for conviction, because it does not establish an intention never to pay.

A creditor is induced to "forgo" payment when he is induced not merely to wait a while but to give up dunning the debtor altogether. Examples are where the debtor by telling lies persuades the creditor that there never has been a debt or that the debt has been paid.[8] Presumably the offence will be committed on facts like those in *Charles* or *Lambie* (§ 34.2 at nn. 8, 9), though only by dint of the highly artificial reasoning favoured by the House of Lords. Apart from these banking cases the commonest example of (*b*) will be inducing the creditor to wait for payment.

Paragraph (*c*) overlaps the previous two paragraphs and has little independent utility. Like paragraph (*a*) it requires the agreement of the creditor to give the exemption or abatement. "Abatement" appears to be a mere synonym for the "remission" of paragraph (*a*) (such duplication of meaning is a dreadful sin in drafting). "Exemption" appears to refer to the grant of exemption (in whole or in part) from a liability that would otherwise arise in future, which because of the exemption never arises. The case is unlikely, but an illustration would be where a person obtains a ride on public transport by making improper use of a free pass issued to employees (such a person does not obtain services by deception, because there is no understanding that the benefit has been or will be paid for). The "exemption" provision has also been applied, by a stretch, to a case where a person, in order to evade payment for a rail journey he had made, "flashed" an inapplicable season ticket[9]; but such facts would have been better charged under (*b*). It may be noticed that any agreement by the creditor to remit the liability or to forgo payment or to grant an exemption from or abatement of liability will not be binding on the creditor if the agreement has been obtained by deception.

There are certain supplementary provisions in section 2, and the section presents many fine points of interpretation which need not be gone into here. The three offences are triable either way, and render the culprit liable to the draconian maximum of 5 years' imprisonment. Except perhaps where payment on the spot is required, no sensible debtor who knew the law would commit any of them, since they are unlikely to give him an advantage that he could not gain in safer ways—e.g. by making small payments off his debt combined with general protestations of being hard up.

(3) Fraudulent transfers of property and bankruptcy offences

A debtor who has not otherwise offended can still break the law if he salts his property away by transferring it to a third person (such as his wife), or, upon being sued, conceals or removes his property, with intent to defraud his creditors.[10] Presumably a transfer of property before embarking on a risky transaction would not be an offence if made at a time when the transferor owes no debts, but the law cannot be regarded as clear—particularly when there is the offence of conspiracy to defraud lurking behind the statutory offences.

More rigorous provisions apply to debtors who have become or are about to become bankrupt. A bankrupt is required to co-operate fully in

---

[8] *Holt* [1981] 1 WLR 1000, 2 All ER 854, 73 CAR 96, Crim.LR 499.

[9] *Sibartie* [1983] Crim.LR 470.

[10] Debtors Act 1869 s.13(2),(3); Bankruptcy Act 1914 s.156(2),(3), as amended by Bankruptcy (Amendment) Act 1926 s.6. The concealment or removal or property is punishable only if committed since or within two months before the date of any unsatisfied judgment against the debtor.

the bankruptcy proceedings, and may be punished for various acts of unhelpfulness; he is also liable for fraudulent acts committed up to 12 months before the presentation of the bankruptcy petition.[11]

Other offences by bankrupts may be briefly mentioned. To dispose of property obtained on credit is an offence if the debtor becomes bankrupt within 12 months, unless the disposal was in the ordinary course of trade or the debtor proves that he had no intent to defraud.[12] A bankrupt can also be punished if, being engaged in trade or business, he has materially contributed to the insolvency by gambling, or by rash and hazardous speculations unconnected with his trade or business.[13] Prosecutions for these offences are rare, but instances occur of prosecutions of an undischarged bankrupt for the offence of obtaining credit by fraud,[14] or of getting goods or services on credit (to the extent of £50) without informing the creditor that he is an undischarged bankrupt.[15]

§ 40.2. OVERDRAFTS; INSURANCE; ANNUITIES

The Theft Act 1968 section 16 creates miscellaneous offences under the name of obtaining pecuniary advantage by deception. The name (printed in the marginal note to the Act) is misleading, for on reading the section one discovers that pecuniary advantage is neither necessary nor sufficient for an offence. The section is limited to the very specific types of case specified in subsection (2); so dismiss the subject of pecuniary advantage from your mind, except for the purpose of drawing up a charge. Subsection 2 (*a*) has been repealed and replaced by provisions already studied. What remains, therefore, is as follows.

> "(1) A person who by any deception dishonestly obtains for himself or another any pecuniary advantage shall on conviction on indictment be liable to imprisonment for a term not exceeding 5 years.
>
> (2) The cases in which a pecuniary advantage within the meaning of this section is to be regarded as obtained for a person are cases where—
>
> (*b*) he is allowed to borrow by way of overdraft, or to take out any policy of insurance or annuity contract, or obtains an improvement of the terms on which he is allowed to do so; or
>
> (*c*) he is given the opportunity to earn remuneration or greater remuneration in an office or employment, or to win money by betting.
>
> (3) For purposes of this section 'deception' has the same meaning as in section 15 of this Act."

Subsection (2) (*b*) covers deception against certain financial firms. It

---

[11] BA 1914 s.154. Similar provisions in relation to the winding up of companies are contained in the Companies Act 1948 ss.328–330 as amended.

[12] BA 1914 s.154 para. (15).

[13] *Ibid.* s.157.

[14] *Ibid.* s.156(*a*).

[15] *Ibid.* s.155 as amended by Insolvency Act 1976 s.1; *Peters* (1886) 16 QBD 636; *Hayat* [1976] Crim.LR 508; *Miller* [1976] Crim.LR 562. This was held to be an offence of strict liability in *Duke of Leinster* [1924] 1 KB 311; *Salter* [1968] 2 QB 793. An undischarged bankrupt also commits an offence if he trades in another name.

operates as soon as an insurance, annuity contract or overdraft agreement[1] is obtained by deception, and does not require that any property should have been obtained.

As we have seen, the overdraft offence is committed even where the deception is made to a third party.[2]

The overdraft provision does not apply to bank credits (unless the courts construe an overdraft to include a bank credit, which would be out of accordance with commercial understanding but in line with the courts' methods of interpreting offences). In a bank credit the bank agrees to make a loan to the customer and credits his account accordingly; the account then stands in credit, even while the bank credit is being drawn upon, whereas an overdraft arrangement would show it as being overdrawn, though permissibly so. If a cheat obtains a bank credit by deception the proper charge is of obtaining services by deception (§ .34.11), since the bank is induced to confer a benefit by doing an act. (Indeed, obtaining an overdraft by deception could now be charged as an obtaining of services.)

Again, the overdraft provision does not apply to credit cards. In view of the decision in *Lambie*,[3] abuses of this facility can be prosecuted, presumably, under the Act of 1978 section 2 (1) (*c*) (§ .1 (2)), or as an obtaining of property or services by deception.

§ 40.3. REMUNERATED EMPLOYMENT AND WINNINGS

Subsection 2 (*c*) (§ .2) may be briefly dismissed. It covers situations like those in *Lewis* and *Clucas*,[1] where section 15 apparently cannot be used because there is supposed to be no causal nexus between deception and obtaining.[2] Authority is lacking on whether the paragraph applies to independent contractors.

§ 40.4. CORRUPTION

Corruption ("fixing" in the modern idiom) is sternly discountenanced both by the common law and by statute. Some forms of it—such as bribery in elections—relate to public law and are not our principal concern. Corruption for private ends is now governed chiefly by the Prevention of Corruption Act 1906 as amended. Section 1 (1) creates two[1] either way offences, defined as follows (omitting inessential words).

---

[1] It was ruled, remarkably, in *Watkins* [1976] 1 All ER 578 that obtaining the bank's agreement to an overdraft is not a mere attempt to get the overdraft; the full offence is immediately completed even though no overdraft is obtained; and this although the Act says "is allowed to borrow by way of overdraft." Equally remarkable was the decision in *Waites* [1982] Crim.LR 369 that a person who has no overdraft agreement is "allowed" by the bank to borrow by way of overdraft when he abuses his cheque card and so in effect forces an overdraft on the protesting bank.

[2] *Charles* § 34.2 at n. 8.

[3] § 34.2 at n. 9.

[1] § 34.9.

[2] A prosecution cannot be brought for a nondisclosure permitted by the Rehabilitation of Offenders Act 1974; but the limitations of this Act are sometimes overlooked. See 139 JPN 463.

[1] A third offence is mentioned in § .6.

"(1) If any agent corruptly obtains, or agrees to accept or attempts to obtain, for himself or for any other person, any gift or consideration, or

(2) if any person corruptly gives or agrees to give or offers any gift or consideration to any agent,—

as an inducement or reward for doing or forbearing to do, or for having done or forborne to do,[2] any act in relation to his principal's affairs,[3] or for showing or forbearing to show favour or disfavour to any person in relation to his principal's affairs. . . . "

Section 1 (2):

"The expression 'agent' includes any person employed by or acting for another; and the expression 'principal' includes an employer."

Section 1 (3):

"A person serving under the Crown or under any corporation or any municipal, borough, county or district council, is an agent within the meaning of this Act."

What about a venal county councillor? Is he an "agent"?

No, but the Public Bodies Corrupt Practices Act 1889, which overlaps the Act of 1906, establishes the similar offence of corruption of a member, officer or servant of a public body,[4] where the object of the bribe is that he should do or forbear to do anything in respect of any matter in which the public body is concerned. The Act enables the court on convicting to impose various disqualifications and forfeitures.

The defendant may say that he only made or received an innocent gift as a matter of friendship, but there is a rebuttable presumption, for the purpose of both the above Acts, that the consideration was given and received corruptly if it was given *by* a person holding or seeking to obtain a contract for public purposes *to* a public employee.[4]

Generally the only problem is one of proof. The Act strikes at every kind of backhander, kickback, baksheesh, rake-off, palm-grease, graft, sweetener, slush-money, or whatever it may be called, in relation to the affairs of the employer or public body. "Consideration" in subsection (1) of the 1906 Act evidently means any benefit to the agent; so it is capable of covering a sexual submission.

If I have a new car on order from a motor agent, and give him a few hundred pounds extra by way of pourboire to get higher in the queue, is that an offence?

A so-called motor agent is not an agent; he is a dealer. Paying the dealer

---

[2] Both this Act and the Act of 1889 (below) apply to a payment made for a past favour without prior agreement: *Andrews-Weatherfoil Ltd.* [1972] 1 WLR 118, 1 All ER 65, 56 CAR 31.

[3] These words are probably wide enough to cover any abuse of office by the agent, e.g. a policeman's extortion of money in consideration of not planting evidence. See *Att.-Gen. of Hong Kong* v. *Ip Chiu* [1980] AC 663. It is obviously no defence that the act also related to the affairs of some other principal: *Morgan* v. *DPP* [1970] Crim.LR 696.

[4] Prevention of Corruption Act 1916 s. 2. See § 2.5 at n. 3.

himself would be no offence, but making a secret payment to the dealer's manager may well lead to a conviction.

What if a dustman refuses to make an extra collection for a householder without receiving a little something for his pains?

If the householder offers the money, a charge is unlikely to be brought, whatever the legal position may be. If the dustman exacts the money, he can well be convicted.[5]

Suppose the householder and the dustman are put on trial together. The householder is acquitted because he did not know that the dustman was acting improperly, and so did not give the money corruptly. Does this mean that the dustman, who knew he was acting against orders, must be acquitted?

Corruption can be one-sided.[6]

What does "corruptly" mean?

An obvious example of a non-corrupt payment to an agent would be one made with the principal's approval. Also, certain gifts are regarded with general indulgence, such as tips to waiters, gifts on or about Boxing Day, and plying your customer's representative with food and drink. Problems may arise in distinguishing between a corrupt gift and a harmless courtesy such as a business lunch. The question of corruption must be decided by reference to the size of the gift, its customary nature, its openness, and other such factors. A gift of appreciable value not required by the obvious necessities of the situation should be accounted corrupt. It remains to be seen whether the judges will attempt to lay down reasonable principles on this subject or will leave the question at large to the jury, with the risk that standards may be lowered in consequence. Honest donors and recipients are given some protection by the fact that the charge requires the consent of the Attorney-General or Solicitor-General.[7]

However, apart from cases of the type just instanced it seems that the word "corruptly" is allowed little meaning by the courts. As a general restricton on the offence it was virtually repealed by the decision of the Court of Appeal in *Smith*.[8]

> Smith was intent on seeking out corruption in public places, and he therefore arranged for money to be offered to a mayor as an inducement to use his mayoral influence. Smith was himself charged, and his defence was that his only intention was to "expose" the mayor. The trial judge in effect withdrew this defence from the jury, who returned a verdict of guilty; and Smith received a sentence of 12 months' imprisonment. The conviction was upheld on appeal, the

---

[5] Charges were brought on such facts, and convictions obtained (after notorious scandals) in 1975: see The Times, December 10. The persons making the payments were virtually the subject of blackmail by the dustmen, and were not prosecuted.

[6] *Andrews-Weatherfoil Ltd.*, above n. 2; cp. *Millray Window Cleaning Co. Ltd.* [1962] Crim.LR 99.

[7] Act of 1906 s.2. For the reversal of the burden of proof in certain cases see § 2.5 at n. 3; *Braithwaite* [1983] 1 WLR 385.

[8] [1960] 2 QB 423.

Court of Appeal holding that Smith's motive was no defence. Smith had "corruptly" offered a gift to a member of a public body to do something in which the public body was concerned; it was enough for the offence that the offer was made deliberately and with the intention that the offeree should enter into a corrupt bargain.

Perhaps Smith's unofficial effort at the entrapment of elected officers was unwise. Conceivably it was immoral (though everyone who takes an interest in these matters is aware that outbreaks of corruption occur from time to time in local government areas, and it may be next to impossible for citizens who know something of what is going on to bring it to the light of day). But in any case it was a travesty of justice to use the law of corruption as a stick to beat the back of an anti-corruption campaigner. Smith's offer of money, if his account was believed (and the jury were not asked to consider whether it was or might be true) was not corrupt on his part. He did not intend the mayor to profit from the transaction, and presumably he did not intend to obtain any advantage from it himself. The court characterised the proposed bargain as "corrupt," but it would have been corrupt on the mayor's side, not on Smith's. Corruption, as we have seen, can be one-sided. The wording of the legislation clearly requires the characteristic of corruption to be found in the defendant's conduct, not necessarily in that of the other party. In support of its decision the court incanted the rule about motive being immaterial; but the requirement of a corrupt intent clearly made it material. The court said that Smith's intention was to corrupt the mayor, but in fact his intention, according to his defence, was to see if the mayor was open to corruption—Smith had no intention that the mayor should in fact be benefited. So the reasons offered by the court are wrong in every respect. Moreover, the decision has the unfortunate effect that a police detective now acts unlawfully in offering a bribe in order to obtain evidence even where it is known that bribes are routinely offered and accepted.[9]

Is the Act of 1889 exhaustive? Does it cover MPs for example?

Parliament did not go out of its way to bring its own members within the net; and, perhaps because the law is not quite explicit, MPs have hitherto escaped prosecution. But the view that they fall outside the offence is highly questionable.

The Prevention of Corruption Act 1916 defines "public body" to include "public authorities of all descriptions,"[10] and it would be astonishing if Parliament were held not to be a public authority of any description.

Quite apart from this legislation, there is a wide-ranging offence at common law of misbehaviour in a public office,[11] which covers bribery as one of its manifestations. (We are here trespassing upon the field of public law, but the line between private and public matters

---

[9] The decision in *Smith* has at least the virtue of apparently discrediting the rulings at first instance in *Lindley* [1957] Crim.LR 321 and *Calland* [1967] Crim.LR 236, which read the word "corruptly" as over-leniently as the court in *Smith* read it over-severely. See 1st edn 849–850.

[10] See the definition in the Prevention of Corruption Act 1916 s. 4 (2). A public utility is a public body for this purpose: *Manners* (1976) 64 CAR 143. Presumably a trading company supported by public funds, like British Leyland, is not a public body.

[11] *Llewellyn-Jones* [1968] 1 QB 429.

cannot be rigidly maintained.) The High Court of Australia has arrived at the salutary conclusion, after a review of the English authorities, that the common law offence can be committed even by Members of Parliament.[12] The fact that the offence remains unregulated by statute may be of some importance in political matters, since prosecutions for it, unlike the statutory offences, cannot be stifled at once by the Law Officers of the Crown.[13]

A limitation upon the offence under the Act of 1889 is that it is committed only where a consideration is obtained or bargained for. Most people would say that a member of a legislature or an administrator acts corruptly if he uses his office to do a favour for a friend (e.g. to get him a profitable contract), yet he commits no offence (except conceivably as a matter of common law). It makes no difference that he hopes for a return favour in the future (such as an MP's hope of a big contribution to party funds). Again, a mayor who has his driveway paved by city workmen without rewarding them commits no offence in respect of the appropriation of their time, though he can be convicted of theft of the materials provided.

Is the policeman with an itching palm subject to the criminal law, or only to police discipline?

In law the policeman is an independent public officer, not a servant of the Crown or of the authority that appoints him[14]—however unrealistic this view may be. But the Act of 1906 section 1 (3) (reproduced above) provides that a person "serving under the Crown" is an agent within the meaning of the Act. It has been held that a registrar appointed under statute comes within the definition in section 1 (3) even though he is not a servant of the Crown, since he performs a function of the Crown.[15] This may look like splitting hairs, but the decision is authoritative; and it clearly applies to the police, the preservation of the peace being a much clearer function of the Crown than keeping a register of births, deaths and marriages.[16] In addition to the law of blackmail, and the common law offence of misbehaviour in public office, there are offences in relation to the administration of justice; so the corrupt policeman is adequately catered for.

§ 40.5. FALSE ACCOUNTING

False accounting depends now on the Theft Act 1968 s. 17. It is a wide

---

[12] *Boston* (1923) 33 CLR 386 (conspiracy). Allegations of corruption by British MPs were made in The Observer, October 17, 1976; it was said that the DPP had submitted papers to the Attorney-General, Mr. Silkin, who "has had to conclude that MPs cannot be prosecuted because of a bizarre loophole in the law." A Select Committee of the House of Commons (HC 490 of 1977) absolved certain members of corruption, but found that some of them had fallen below the standard to be expected of them; the committee repeated the *canard* that corruption in Members was a matter for the House alone; "what may not be the subject of actions in the courts is a Member's conduct in Parliament." After a debate on this Report the House divided almost exclusively upon party lines, thus demonstrating its unfitness to pass upon the conduct of its Members. Apart from the Bill of Rights 1688 article 9, which protects the freedom of "proceedings" in Parliament, there is no vestige of authority for supposing that a criminal act committed in the House is outside the jurisdiction of the courts, or that Acts of Parliament do not apply to Members in what they do in their official capacity. See Zellick in [1979] Public Law 31, [1981] *ibid.* 287.

[13] The DPP may take over a prosecution in order to stifle it, but would then have to operate in the light of day.

[14] *Fisher* v. *Oldham Corpn* [1930] 2 KB 364 and other authorities considered in *Barrett* [1976] 1 WLR 946, 3 All ER 895.

[14] *Barrett*, last note.

[16] Two policemen, Cuthbert and Golden, were convicted of taking bribes in 1982 (The Times, July 21), the recorder commenting on the inadequacy of the maximum prison sentence (2 years, which remains unchanged notwithstanding that a royal commission in 1976 recommended an increase to 7 years). Cp. *McGovern* [1981] Crim.LR 269.

ranging offence even as drafted, and the Court of Appeal has made it wider still by cutting away an implicit restriction. Although called "false accounting" in the marginal note, the interpretation given to the offence makes it extend well beyond its name.

The offence is committed by certain acts in relation to "any account or record or document made or required for any accounting purpose." We may call this "an accounting record" for short. An accounting record includes, for example, a taximeter,[1] a gas-meter, a computer, and the entries in a diary of distances travelled for the purpose of an account.

What acts in relation to an accounting record are wrongful?

The section forbids three classes of act.

1 Falsifying the record (either in making it or afterwards), for example, by "padding" an expense account, or omitting a sum received that ought to have been included.[2]

2 After any record (even an honest one) comes into existence, destroying, defacing or concealing it.

3 Making use of an accounting record in furnishing information, knowing that it is *or may be* deceptive in a material particular.

Is the offence confined to written lies?

It is confined to acts relating to documents or similar records in permanent form. But if, to take an example, an employee orally gives his employer false information as to the expense he has incurred, for the purpose of its being entered in the employer's accounts, the employee has "entered" the false item through the innocent agency of the employer. And oral lies based on a deceptive record come under 3 above.

What is the mental element?

The act must be done "dishonestly, with a view to gain for himself or another or with intent to cause loss to another." There is also the special requirement of knowledge under 3 above.

Is the offence limited to employees?

No. It may be committed by anyone: any debtor or creditor, for instance. In particular, it may be committed by the honorary treasurer of

---

[1] *Solomons* [1909] 2 KB 980. Cp. *Edwards* v. *Toombs* [1983] Crim.LR 43

[2] As in *Edwards* v. *Toombs*, last note. The employee must know that it is his duty to include the item in his account, otherwise he is not dishonest in relation to the rendering of the written account. (One must distinguish between a duty to account as a duty to pay money and a duty to account as a duty to render a true accounting document.) In *Keatley* [1980] Crim.LR 505 a Crown Court judge ruled that the offence was not committed where an employee omitted from his account secret profits dishonestly made with his employer's property, since he was (in the judge's opinion) not under a duty to account for these profits. The ruling on the latter point may be questioned (§ 33.10 at n. 3), but it is perhaps possible to hold that an employee is not in breach of his accounting (documentary) duty in failing to include in his account profits that he holds for his employer not as the profits of his regular employment but as constructive trustee. In any case, the employee's dishonesty in making the secret profit does not necessarily involve dishonesty in not including the item in his regular account.

a members' club, or by a self-employed person in compiling an account for his customer or for his tax return. Moreover;

1 It strikes at preparatory acts. There need not, it seems, be any communication of the falsity to the intended victim; so the provision covers the falsification of computerised accounts by an employee.

2 The offence extends to the falsification of any document required for an accounting purpose, and the purpose of the maker of the document need not be primarily to cause an account to be made. It is enough that he knows that an account will result from the making of the document. So an employee who makes a false written claim to have made a journey, in order to obtain a cash refund of the fictitious expenses, is guilty of the offence, because he knows that when the employer has made the refund he will enter it in his accounts.

3 The falsity in the document need not be one that was intended to be incorporated into the account. The resulting account may be perfectly correct.

> The third point follows from the decision in *Att.-Gen.'s Reference, No.1 of 1980.*[3] The Reference was based upon a case where D advised householders to give false particulars on personal loan proposal forms addressed to a finance company to enable the householders to borrow money to pay for domestic appliances. The Court of Appeal decided that D was guilty of falsifying documents (the proposal forms) required for an accounting purpose, since when acted upon by the company they would result in a loan and therefore in an account. The documents were in fact received by the company and resulted in the loans being given, but the effect of the decision is that a householder who writes a lie on the form will be guilty as soon as he puts pen to paper. At that stage there would not be a sufficiently proximate act to make him guilty of attempting to obtain a loan by deception. It will be observed that when the loan is made the company's account showing the loan will be perfectly correct, since the loan is in fact made and is valid until avoided by the company for fraud.

Almost everything that a firm does becomes ultimately reflected in an account, so that the decision, taken at its largest, means that practically every document intended to deceive the firm and having a financial implication comes within the offence. This unduly inflates the offence and is not a fair reading of the section. The reason why the proposal form in the case before the court was "required" by the company was not primarily "for an accounting purpose." It was required in order to enable the company to decide whether to make a loan; until it had so decided, no question of an account would arise. Having decided to make the loan the company would make an account; but to take this remoter result into consideration goes beyond the intention of the section.

The section in its plain meaning refers to the falsification of accounts; it is extended to the falsification of documents required for the purpose of an account, but the implication is that the falsification of the document is such that it will make the account false. That this was the intention of the section is borne out by the fact that subsection (2) defines falsification as including the making of an entry that is false in a *material* particular; and "material" obviously

---

[3] [1981] 1 WLR 34. Cp. *Mallett* [1978] 1 WLR 820.

means "relevant to the accuracy of the account." The judges read "material" as including the meaning of "relevant to the decision of the firm whether to make a loan;"[4] but the statute is not about making loans; it is about making accounts.

4 The section also strikes at false accounts produced after the event, as where an employee who has been on the fiddle makes up false documentation in the hope of avoiding detection. Section 34 (2) (*a*) defines "gain" to includes keeping what one has, and "loss" (in this case the victim's loss) to include not getting what one might get. The section can therefore be used to strike at some cases of evading debts by deception. A point to notice is that it is not an offence under the section to falsify an account as a way of covering one's tracks if the object is to save oneself from prosecution: only if the object is to save oneself from having to disgorge ill-gotten gains. But almost invariably a person who has falsified an account to avoid prosecution would also have intended to avoid making restitution.

If the prosecution say that the books have been cooked as a cover-up, why don't they charge the theft that is being covered up?

If the allegation is that money has been stolen, that is normally the proper charge. But the defendant may argue that the money was taken or lost honestly, and that the accounting record was dishonestly concocted only in order to avoid a civil liability to repay the money. The offence of false accounting is still committed, even though there has been no other crime.[5]

Thus the advantage of adding a count for false accounting to a count for theft is that if the jury cannot agree that the defendant's appropriation of property was dishonest they may still convict of false accounting; and the defendant may be ready to plead to false accounting as a less grave offence while resisting a charge of theft.

Arising out of this, it will be seen that the word "dishonestly" in relation to false accounting includes the meaning of "lyingly"—knowing that the account is false or making it recklessly without belief in its truth. In theft, on the other hand, it refers chiefly to dishonesty in relation to property rights.

Offences of the same kind in respect of company accounts are created by the Companies Act 1967 s. 113.

The Revenue, holding that the penalties provided by these Acts are occasionally inadequate, supplement them by charging the offence of cheating. This existed at common law, but has now been abolished except in relation to revenue offences.[6] The Revenue authorities prize it because it is punishable at discretion.

§ 40.6. FALSE DOCUMENTS TO MISLEAD PRINCIPALS

An offence of peculiar scope, somewhat similar to false accounting, is

[4] The courts do not require evidence to be given that the document did influence the judgment of the lender; it is sufficient that the jury find without evidence that the document was false "in an important matter" (which is not, of course, what the statute says): *Mallett* [1978] 1 WLR at 823A.
[5] See *Eden* (1971) 55 CAR 193, and note in [1971] Crim.LR 417.
[6] Theft Act 1968 s. 32 (1) (*a*).

contained in section 1 (1) of the Prevention of Corruption Act 1906. It is defined thus:

> "If any person knowingly gives to any agent, or if any agent knowingly uses with intent to deceive his principal, any receipt, account, or other document in respect of which the principal is interested, and which contains any statement which is false or erroneous or defective in any material particular, and which to his knowledge is intended to mislead the principal. . . . "

The word "agent" bears the same meaning as in the rest of the Act of 1906 (see s. 1 (2), quoted in § .5).

The provision is little used and seems to be little known among prosecutors, but it has considerable potential. It means, for example, that a housing officer commits an offence if he knowingly includes misstatements in documents in order to deceive the Council in the allocation of houses, even though he receives no consideration for the favour he shows.[1] The agent need not intend to cause his principal to act; it is enough that he intends to conceal from his principal what is going on. Further, a third party commits the offence if he gives a false document to the agent in order to mislead the principal, even though the agent takes it innocently.[2] It is anomalous that the issue of liability should depend on whether the document is given to the agent or directly to the principal.

Two other offences in the Theft Act are of small practical importance because they are rarely charged.

§ 40.7. SUPPRESSION OF DOCUMENTS

The dishonest destruction or suppression of certain documents is an offence under section 20 (1) of the Theft Act 1968. The documents are;

- valuable securities (see § .8 for definition);
- wills; and
- government documents.

There must be an intent to make a gain or cause a loss.[1] Except where the document is only temporarily concealed, a person guilty under this section will almost inevitably be guilty of stealing or damaging the document, so the subsection has only limited value.

§ 40.8. DECEPTION IN RELATION TO VALUABLE SECURITIES

It is an offence under the Theft Act s. 20 (2) dishonestly and by deception to procure the making, alteration or destruction of a valuable security (or of a paper intended to become a valuable security). There must be an

---

[1] *Payne* [1965] Crim.LR 543.
[2] *Sage* v. *Eicholz* [1919] 2 KB 171.

[1] See Theft Act s.34(2)(*a*).

intent to make a gain or cause a loss.[1] A valuable security is very widely defined as a document relating to property rights or authorising the payment of money; the commonest example is a cheque. Apparently the expression does not include a will before the testator dies.[2]

§ 40.9. FORGERY AND COUNTERFEITING

The crime of forgery was invented by the judges, but now rests on the Forgery and Counterfeiting Act 1981. Unattributed references to sections in the following discussion will be to this Act.

Forgery is triable either way, and is punishable on indictment with the severe maximum of 10 years' imprisonment. It is defined in section 1.

> "A person is guilty of forgery if he makes a false instrument, with the intention that he or another shall use it to induce somebody to accept it as genuine, and by reason of so accepting it to do or not to do some act to his own or any other person's prejudice."

There is a twin offence of *using* a forged instrument, punishable in the same way as forgery (s. 3).

> "It is an offence for a person to use an instrument which is, and which he knows or believes to be, false, with the intention of inducing somebody to accept it as genuine, and by reason of so accepting it to do or not to do some act to his own or any other person's prejudice.

Do we need these offences? Couldn't forgery be dealt with as a kind of deception?

Nearly all forgery cases could be prosecuted as obtaining property or services by deception, or as an attempt to do so, or as the common law offence of manufacturing false evidence; and it is, therefore, distinctly doubtful whether we need a specific offence, except in certain special cases.

The most obvious special case relates to currency notes. A person who is found to have counterfeited thousands of currency notes could probably not be convicted of attempting to obtain money by deception, because he would probably not be held to have gone beyond "mere preparation;" so if it were not an offence to reproduce and possess such notes he could sell them to other members of the underworld and the police could do nothing about it.

But can't you make a copy of a currency note even as a picture?

Restrain your artistic talents in this direction. So important is it to prevent the copying of currency notes (and coins) that it is a special offence

---

[1] See Theft Act s.34(2)(*a*).
[2] Wills are expressly included in subs. (1) but noticeably not in subs. (2).

"to make a counterfeit of a currency note or of a protected coin without lawful authority or excuse" (s. 14 (2)); the only intention required is the intention to make the counterfeit,[1] i.e. something that resembles a currency note or protected coin to such an extent that it is reasonably capable of passing for one (s. 28 (1)). There are various ancillary offences to offences of counterfeiting, of which nothing need be said here.

In addition to the counterfeiting offences it is an offence by section 5 for a person knowingly to have certain false instruments in his custody or control; these include false share certificates, cheques, cheque cards, credit cards, and certain documents issued by public authorities (including postage stamps); also what may be called machines of forgery (any machine, instrument or material specially designed or adapted for making false instruments). A magistrate may issue a warrant authorising search for these machines of forgery, and also for false instruments (documents etc.) intended to be used in contravention of the Act (s. 7); similarly as regards counterfeits (s. 24).

If one puts aside the counterfeiting of money, as adequately provided for on its own (and the Act expressly excludes it from the crime of forgery), and also the offences in relation to the special documents just listed, the case for having a residuary crime of forgery becomes slim. The best that can be said for it is that it strikes at what would otherwise be mere preparation for criminality. A less compelling reason is that a conviction of attempted deception would not be thought to register the gravity of the offence of forging, say, a will; certainly the courts sentence for forgery more severely than they do for attempted deception, and more severely than they do for most cases of deception itself—though this, no doubt, is partly the result of having a specific offence of forgery with a high maximum sentence.

The various requirements in section 1 may be enumerated as follows. Forgery is—

1 making
2 a false
3 instrument
4 with the intention that he or another shall use it to induce somebody to accept it as genuine, and by reason of so accepting it to do or not to do some act to his own or any other person's prejudice.

The definition of "using" is similar, with the substitution of "use" for "makes" and with a further explication of the mental element.

(1) The making or using

The offence of forgery is complete when the instrument is "made," although it is never published or used. Forgery may be of part of an instrument, the rest being genuine (s. 9 (2)).

> So if D obtains V's autograph in his album, and then tears out the page and writes an IOU above the signature, he has obviously made a forgery, even though the signature is authentic. Conversely, if D finds a cheque that has been made payable to X, and forges an endorsement by X in order to receive payment under the cheque, he commits forgery: the body of the cheque is not forged, but the signature is, so that the instrument is again false in part.

The notion of making a forgery is taken from the common law and earlier legislation, and it is clear that one can "make" through an innocent agent. The Act provides (s. 9 (2)) that making includes altering; so the offence may be committed by erasing part of an instrument.

---

[1] *Heron* § 3.1 n. 4.

The Act does not define "using," but the term was clearly meant to be very wide. Showing a forged document to someone with the requisite intent would certainly be "using" it.

The offence of using presupposes that the instrument is forged in the strict sense, that is, that someone has committed the crime of making the document as a forgery.

> If John Jones picks up on the street a letter authorising a certain payment to be made to "John Jones," and if he then fraudulently asserts that he is the John Jones referred to, for the purpose of claiming the money, he is not guilty of "making" a forgery, and is not guilty of using one either, for the letter is not a forgery. If however he signs a receipt on the letter *this* will be a forgery.[2] The artificiality of the law is obvious.

Is it forgery to make a photostat copy of a forged document?

The Act provides special offences of making or using a copy of a false instrument, with *mens rea* (ss. 2, 4). A wise prosecutor would not ask the court to answer the difficult question you ask[3]; he would charge one of these special copying offences.

(2) The falsity

The meaning of falsity is exhaustively defined in section 9 (1)), which may be reproduced in compressed form as follows.

An instrument is false if it purports to have been—

- made (in its form or terms) by a person who did not in fact make it in that form or those terms; or
- made (in its form or terms) on the authority of a person who did not in fact authorise its making in that form or those terms; or
- altered by or on the authority of a person who did not in fact alter it or authorise its alteration in that respect; or
- made or altered on a date on which, or at a place at which, it was not in fact made or altered; or
- made or altered by an existing person but he did not in fact exist.

The word "terms" in the first two items means, for example, that forgery can be committed by altering the serial number on an instrument.

A cheque purports to have been made by or on the authority of the signer (drawer). So if a person who has been given a signed blank cheque fills it in for a sum larger than he was authorised to, he makes a forgery. The cheque, as filled in, was not authorised by the person who signed it.

Suppose I receive a cheque where the drawer has forgotten to fill in the date, or the amount in words. Can I safely fill in the missing particulars?

If you act honestly the court would say that you had the implied authority of the drawer.[4]

Suppose D writes to V ordering goods and fraudulently saying that he is doing so on behalf of X. In fact X has not authorised him. Surely that is not a forgery? It is simply a letter containing a lie.

It was not a forgery at common law, where the rule was that to be a

---

[2] *Hudson* (1943) 29 CAR 65.
[3] See 1st edn 876.
[4] See Bills of Exchange Act 1882 s.20.

forgery the document must not merely tell a lie but tell a lie about itself, i.e. about itself as a document. Most of the instances of falsity given in the Act are of "telling a lie about itself," but this is not so in the type of case you mention. Nevertheless, the Act seems to make it forgery.[5]

Can one commit forgery by signing one's own name? William Jones, deceased, had a son called John Jones, now also deceased; and the defendant John Jones writes and signs in his own name a letter claiming William Jones's estate, hoping that the executors will believe that William Jones's son is still alive and that he (the defendant) is that son.

The document, taken in conjunction with the circumstances, tells a lie about its own authorship, even though John Jones has signed his own name. So it is technically a forgery.[6] But the sensible thing to do (as with the example you thought up previously) would be to charge an attempted or actual obtaining by deception, not forgery. Although forgery is defined in wide terms for simplicity, there are acts coming within the definition that do not look like forgery and are best prosecuted in other ways.

The false date: surely it is not forgery to post-date a cheque?

By custom the date on a cheque is simply the date from which the cheque is to be valid; it is not necessarily the date on which it was drawn. Post-dating a cheque is a recognised mode of putting off the day of reckoning. Probably the maker of the cheque is not guilty of forgery even though he fraudulently hoped that the payee would send him goods not noticing the post-dating. (On principle, however, he would then be guilty of obtaining by deception, since the cheque is a fraudulent trick if it is intended to deceive in this way.)[7]

The most difficult type of falsity is the last: instruments in the name of a non-existent person. Such person may not exist either because he is dead or because he is a figment of the imagination.

That it should be forgery to concoct the will of a dead man in order to claim his estate is acceptable to common sense, though there is no great need to extend the offence in this way, since the case is adequately covered by the law of deception.

Extending the offence to forgery in the name of a fictitious person is capable of raising great philosophical (and therefore legal) problems, and it is regrettable that the Act perpetuates it. If our legislators had been wise they would not have made this extension; if prosecutors are wise, they will not use it; and if examiners are wise, they will not ask questions about it. The extension was made by the courts at a time when we had no offence of obtaining by false pretences, but was continued after the enactment of that offence, when it had become unnecessary. According to the case-law before the Act of 1981, which the courts will certainly continue to apply if prosecutors continue to request them to do so, it can, in general, be a forgery to sign any instrument in an assumed name, given the mental element.[8]

Suppose a man when booking in to a hotel signs a purely fanciful name and address in the register, because he means to slip out in the morning without

---

[5] See 1st edn 860–861 for a fuller discussion.
[6] See 1st edn 866.
[7] For a further discussion of false dating see 1st edn 862–863.
[8] See, e.g. *Gambling* [1975] QB 207; and cp. *Butler* (1954) 38 CAR 57; *Hassard* [1970] 1 WLR 1109.

paying his bill and does not wish to be traced. He is guilty of attempting to obtain goods or services by deception, on the implied representation that he has given the correct particulars; but surely he has not turned the hotel register into a forgery.

That particular entry is a forgery, in the beady eyes of the law.[9]

There are, however, certain qualifications. In general, English law shares Juliet's opinion about the emptiness of names, and allows a person to go by any name he pleases. Accordingly, it has been held that signing a "false" name can be forgery only when the name has been assumed as part of the general deception with which the forgery is connected.[10] If the defendant had been known by the assumed name before the present deception, he is safe from a forgery charge, even though in previously using the name he was engaged on some fraud, and in now using it he has some new dishonest intent, such as not to pay a debt.[11] Whether the victim of the present deception knew that the defendant had been using the name previously is immaterial; the fact is that the name has now become "his name," or one of his names, by usage. The paradoxical result is that if a man habitually uses the name "John Brown" to cheat hotels, he is (it seems) safe from a charge of forgery. But the point does not matter, because he can be charged with obtaining by deception if he did not intend to pay.

Another type of case where an assumed name is not that of a non-existent person seems to be where the cheat is known to his victim under his true name.[12] Presumably the reason is that the use of the assumed name does not affect the victim's conduct.

The greatest difficulty is where a cheat claims in the instrument in question that he has an attribute that he does not possess, such as that he is the son of X or the spouse of Y, where X has no son or Y has no spouse, or has a son or spouse who is not the cheat. Does the instrument purport to be made by a person who did not in fact make it, or by a person who does not in fact exist, or on the other hand does it purport to be made by the defendant with a false claim of the attribute in question? There are cases bearing on this, but we will not go into them.[13]

(3) The instrument

Clearly, it is not forgery to imitate a string of pearls, even though with fraudulent intent. The common law spoke of forging a "document." The

---

[9] Independently of any ulterior criminal intent, it is an offence for any person over 16 (even a British subject) when staying at a hotel or lodging house to fail to inform the keeper on arrival of his full name and nationality; the offence is punishable by a heavy fine and imprisonment (Immigration (Hotel Records) Order 1972, art. 4). This is very largely unenforced, but nothing in theory stops it being fired at a celebrity who is travelling incognito to escape the journalists, or an unmarried couple who wish to hide their guilty passion. It is a particularly bad example of the blunderbuss language that civil servants are allowed to get away with when they draft legislation.

[10] As in *Hassard* [1970] 1 WLR 1109, 2 All ER 647, 54 CAR 295.

[11] *Bontien* (1813) Russ. & Ry. 260, 168 ER 791; *Hadjimitsis* [1964] Crim.LR 128.

[12] See *Martin* (1879) 5 QBD 34, discussed in 1st edn 871.

[13] See 1st edn 866–871.

Act of 1981 prefers the rather recondite term "instrument," but defines it in such a way as to make documents its main component. Section 8 (1):

> . . . " 'Instrument' means—
> (*a*) any document, whether of a formal or informal character;
> (*b*) any stamp issued or sold by the Post Office;
> (*c*) any Inland Revenue stamp; and
> (*d*) any disc, tape, sound track or other device on or in which information is recorded or stored."

This definition still leaves us without a definition of a document. The term cannot include every writing. If any writing were a document, an imitation piece of Wedgewood china would be a false document by reason of the word "Wedgewood" on the underside. The Court for Crown Cases Reserved held in *Closs*[14] that a faked signature on a painting did not constitute a document, and again in *John Smith*[15] that printed wrappers used for baking-powder were not documents. It may, therefore, be suggested that to be a document, and therefore an instrument, the writing etc. must be made for the purpose of creating or establishing or transferring or modifying or terminating a right.[16]

The law of forgery is supplemented by other legislation penalising false imitations, such as the protection given to hallmarks by the Hallmarking Act 1973. Even false documents are made the subject of special offences of falsity by some statutes, independently of the law of forgery, the object being to clarify the law on particular points, or to make the case triable only summarily, or to punish deceitful conduct not amounting to forgery. An example is the offence of using a driving licence with intent to deceive;[17] this is committed by using someone else's genuine licence.

(4) The intent

For the offence of using a forged instrument the Act specifies that the offender must know or believe the instrument to be false. This is not stated for forgery, but is clearly implied. ("Or believe' presumably refers to wilful blindness.)

Both forgery and using a forged instrument require "the intention that he or another shall use it to induce somebody to accept it as genuine, and by reason of so accepting it to do or not to do some act to his own or any other person's prejudice." Section 10 defines "prejudice." "An act or omission is to a person's prejudice if, and only if it—

(*a*) will result—

(i) in his temporary or permanent loss[18] of property; or

in his being deprived of an opportunity to earn remuneration or greater remuneration; or

---

[14] (1857) Dears. & Bell 460, 169 ER 1082.
[15] (1858) Dears. & Bell 566, 169 ER 1122.
[16] See 1st edn 874; Smith and Hogan, 4th edn 626–629.
[17] RTA 1972 s.169.
[18] "Loss" includes not getting what one might get: s.10(5).

(ii) in his being deprived of an opportunity to gain a financial advantage otherwise than by way of remuneration; or

(*b*) will result in someone being given an opportunity—

(i) to earn remuneration or greater remuneration from him; or

(ii) to gain a financial advantage from him otherwise than by way of remuneration; or

(*c*) will be the result of his having accepted a false instrument as genuine, or a copy of a false instrument as a copy of a genuine one, in connection with his performance of any duty."

This definition makes the offence somewhat wider than the deception offence under the Theft Act 1968 ss. 15 and 16 in that the temporary obtaining of property is sufficient (e.g. the hiring of a car).[19] On the other hand, the general offence of obtaining services under the Theft Act 1978 s. 1 is not brought at one remove into the definition of forgery.

Special provision is made for "deceiving a machine." Forgery is committed by making a false instrument that will cause a machine to respond to it, and the (human) act or omission induced by the response of the machine is treated as as an act or omission to the person's prejudice.[20] This covers the use of bank cards giving automated pay-outs, but not a blank metal disk meant for insertion in vending machines, because that is not a document and therefore is not an instrument.

The fact that forgery comes down in the end to little more than a preparatory act of deception raises again the question whether there is any need for the offence. As a member of the former Working Party whose proposals the Law Commission threw to the winds when it drafted the Criminal Attempts Act, I take a morose pleasure in pointing out that had the Commission accepted our advice and procured the enactment of an offence of attempt in terms of taking a substantial step (the preparation or acting of a falsehood being declared to amount to taking a substantial step towards an offence of fraud or deception),[21] virtually all practical need for a crime of forging documents generally would have disappeared.

§ 40.10. FALSE STATEMENTS UNDER STATUTE

Statutes requiring information to be supplied usually penalise false statements, on oath or otherwise. These offences are not necessarily linked to the obtaining of an economic advantage. Some are contained in the Perjury Act 1911 (as amended), and the Law Commission has listed 58 other offences of this kind created since then.[1] Examples are false statements made to obtain social security benefits[2] or legal aid,[3] and false

---

[19] Also, there is no express requirement of dishonesty for forgery as there is for obtaining by deception. But this difference seems to be more apparent than real. If a person makes a false instrument to get property to which he has an actual right, he has no intent to cause loss for the purpose of the crime of forgery, and if that is so the same must be true when he mistakenly believes that he is entitled to the property. Cp. s. 10 (2) on false instruments made to obtain the performance of duty.

[20] s.10(3),(4).

[21] Law Com. Working Paper No. 50 p. 58.

[1] Law Commission, *Working Paper No. 33,* Appendix.

[2] Supplementary Benefits Act 1976 s. 21, as substituted by Social Security (MP) Act 1977 s. 14 (5). For the mental element see *Moore* v. *Branton* [1974] Crim.LT 439.

[3] CJA 1967 s.90 (1)

statements made in connection with the issue of licences and certificates. Some statutes even make it an offence to allow another to use deceptive documents. The making of false tax returns is covered by Part X of the Taxes Management Act 1970.

Two particular advantages, to the prosecution, of some of this legislation, as compared with section 15 of the Theft Act, is, first, that it saves the officials of a large government department from having to be called to prove that they were influenced by the false statement (when it may be hard to trace the officials who in fact dealt with the matter).[4] Secondly, these statutes frequently create summary offences, and so avoid the risk of a Crown Court trial. Even so, a tidy legal system would surely replace the present fragmentary offences by a general summary offence of making a false declaration in any statement required for any purpose by or under any statute.

§ 40.11. COMPANIES AND INVESTMENT

While the ordinary practitioner in the criminal courts is chiefly concerned with tricksters of the minor sort, a considerable body of law is provided to control the smooth-tongued wizards of the investment market, whose frauds, when they occur, tend to be on the mammoth scale.

The Companies Act 1948 (as amended) contains many provisions for the protection of shareholders and creditors of a company. In particular, it imposes criminal liability for misstatements in a prospectus (s. 44) or statement in lieu (s. 48 (5)). This is supplemented by a provision in the Theft Act (s. 19) making it an offence for the officer of a company or unincorporated association (such as a club) to make a false written statement with intent to deceive members or creditors. The latter section covers, for example, false statements in a company's annual report and accounts, and also false statements in prospectuses for shares. But false statements in prospectuses are more likely to be charged under the Companies Act 1948 s. 44, because under that section the offence is punishable even if only committed negligently.

The Prevention of Fraud (Investments) Act 1958 is designed to deal with "share-pushing," and protects, in particular, the unit trust investor. It provides for the licensing of dealers in securities, and contains wide provisions (s. 13) penalising the fraudulent inducement of persons to invest money (not necessarily in shares; for example, the Act has been used to punish tricksters who advertise an "infallible system" in the casinos).[1] However, the Act has not prevented large-scale malpractices, and is overdue for revision.

The Protection of Depositors Act 1963 (as amended) and the Banking

---

[4] See 143 JPN 167.

[1] The offence is drafted in extremely wide terms, covering dishonest concealments, and false statements and deceptive forecasts made intentionally or recklessly, "dishonestly or otherwise"—which appears to imply that recklessness means gross negligence.

Act 1979 s. 38 penalise fraudulent inducements to invest on deposit, and contain sundry ancillary and administrative provisions. The policy holder is protected by the Insurance Companies Act 1974, s. 62 of which penalises misleading statements inducing persons to enter into contracts of insurance.

In administering these provisions the Company Fraud Department of Scotland Yard keeps in touch with the Department of Trade and Industry, the Stock Exchange and various institutions in the City, and so tries to deal with large frauds before any money has been parted with.

Reverting to the Companies Act, section 332 (3) of the Act of 1948 (as amended by the Act of 1981 s. 96) creates an offence known as fraudulent trading. Every person who is knowingly a party to the business of the company being carried on "for any fraudulent purpose"[2] is guilty of an offence punishable with 2 years' imprisonment. The subsection is doubly anomalous:

1 it does not extend to partnerships or individual traders;
2 in theory it is totally unlimited as to the types of fraud, though in practice it probably adds nothing to the rest of the criminal law.

The chief importance of the subsection is in relation not to the breadth but to the muscle of the law. When a company has aroused the suspicions of the police, the Department of Trade and Industry can send one of its accountants to examine the company's accounts[3]; no such power is possessed in respect of partnerships or individuals, except in ordinary bankruptcy proceedings. In practice the department works in co-operation with the police, and may be able to supply them with the evidence needed for a prosecution for various offences.[4] Nevertheless, fraudsters often operate too quickly for the police to be able to secure the co-operation of the department.

Do you mean that the police could not inspect the books of a partnership?

If they have enough evidence for an arrest, they could arrest the partners at their place of business and carry off any incriminating documents then.[5] If they arrested the partners in their houses they could not lawfully search the business premises for evidence of offences.[6]

§ 40.12. CONSUMER PROTECTION

Mention has already been made of the Trade Descriptions Act 1968,[1]

---

[2] One fraudulent act is enough: *Re Gerald Cooper Chemicals Ltd.* (1977) The Times, November 23. Dishonesty must be established: *Cox* [1983] Crim.LR 167.

[3] Companies Act 1967 ss.109, 110; Protection of Depositors Act 1963 ss.18, 19. It is an offence to provide false information: CA 1967 s.114. Application may also be made to the court for an inspection order; but see Levi, *The Phantom Capitalists* (London 1981) 182–183, 298. Officers of a company that is wound up can be punished if they have not kept proper books of account: Companies Act 1976 s.12.

[4] The DTI can petition for a winding up in the public interest: Companies Act 1967 s.35(1); Protection of Depositors Act 1963 s.16.

[5] *Elias* v. *Pasmore* [1934] 2 KB 164.

[6] But a magistrate may issue a warrant to search for stolen goods: Theft Act 1968 s.26.

[1] As extended by TDA 1972.

which (among other things) creates various offences of false statement and description in relation to goods and services, not restricted to cases of fraud. This is supplemented by the Fair Trading Act 1973, which establishes the office of Director General of Fair Trading and enables him to smell out any "consumer trade practice" that operates to the detriment of consumers. The Director may refer the practice to a body called the Consumer Protection Advisory Committee, which may recommend to the Secretary of State for Trade and Industry that an order be made dealing with the matter; and the Secretary may then by statutory instrument give effect to the recommendation. Penalties may be imposed for contravention of the order.[2] The Director may also bring before the Restrictive Practices Court any businessman who is violating the criminal law, or is in breach of contract or other civil duty, in a way detrimental to consumers, and the court may order him to desist.[3] There is much other legislation for the protection of consumers, including the Weights and Measures Acts 1963–1979, the Consumer Credit Act 1974, the Unsolicited Goods and Services Act 1971 s. 3 (bogus directories), and (for food) the Food and Drugs Act 1955.

This account of the statutory control of trading frauds, long as it is, still takes no account of the control of specific activities such as mock auctions and auction "rings,"[4] and pretended clairvoyants.[5]

SUMMARY

Fraudulent debtors may commit a number of offences. (1) The Theft Act 1978 s. 3 creates an either-way offence where a person, knowing that payment on the spot is required or expected from him for any goods supplied or service done, dishonestly makes off without having paid as required or expected and with intent to avoid payment of the amount due. It is not clear whether the offence is committed when the debtor by fraud obtains the creditor's consent to leave, but the better view is that it is. Certain offences of "bilking" are also punishable summarily under special statutes. (2) Section 2 of the same Act creates three offences of deception to impede the creditor in exercising his civil remedies. (*a*) Deception to get the creditor to agree to waive the debt. (*b*) Deception to get the creditor to give up asking for payment, for the present or permanently, but only where the debtor intends never to pay. Paragraph (*c*) in addition covers deception to obtain an exemption from liability that would otherwise arise in the future. (3) There are various offences of the fraudulent transfer of property, and bankruptcy offences. § .1

The Theft Act 1968 s. 16 (2) (*b*) covers certain cases of obtaining a so-called pecuniary advantage by deception. These are to obtain an overdraft [agreement], an insurance, or an annuity contract. The provision has been held to cover the fraudulent use of bank cheque cards: *Charles*. (Obtaining a bank credit by deception would be an obtaining of services under the Theft Act 1978.) § .2

Subsection (2) (*c*) covers deceptions to obtain remunerated employment or to place a bet. § .3

The Prevention of Corruption Act 1906 as amended strikes at those who corruptly give consideration to an agent for doing or having done anything in § .4

---

[2] All in Pts.I and II of the Act.

[3] See Pt.III.

[4] See 1st edn 856.

[5] See 1st edn 857.

relation to his principal's affairs; and the agent is also brought in. Agreements and attempts are included. The CA in *Smith* appears to have held that a gift can be corrupt although there is no intention to corrupt; *sed quaere*. The Public Bodies Corrupt Practices Act 1889 creates a similar offence of corruption of members of a public body. In addition, there is a wide offence at common law of misbehaviour in a public office.

False accounting under the Theft Act s. 17 covers certain dishonest acts in relation to "any account or record or document made or required for any accounting purpose." The acts are (1) falsifying the record or (2) destroying or concealing it or (3) making use of the accounting record in furnishing information, knowing that it is or may be deceptive in a material particular. The act must be done "dishonestly, with a view to gain for himself or another or with intent to cause loss to another." The offence is widely defined or interpreted in four ways: it strikes at preparatory acts, since the false account need not be communicated; the purpose of the maker of the document need not be primarily to cause an account to be made; the falsity in the document need not be one that was intended to be incorporated into the account; and the offence is committed by falsifying accounts as a cover-up (since "gain" is defined to include keeping what one has). These rules give a great width to the offence, the most remarkable extension being that the offence can be committed although the account is perfectly correct (*Attorney-General's Reference*). There are similar offences for company accounts, and the Revenue can charge cheating at common law. § .5

The Prevention of Corruption Act 1906 includes a wide offence of giving to an agent a document containing a false statement intended to mislead the principal; and the offence is also committed by the agent who uses the document to deceive his principal. § .6

The dishonest suppression of certain documents (valuable securities, wills and government documents) is an offence under the Theft Act 1968 s. 20 (1), which covers even temporary suppressions. § .7

It is an offence under s. 20 (2) to use deception to procure the making, alteration or destruction of a valuable securities (the latter defined to include any document relating to property rights). § .8

The Forgery and Counterfeiting Act 1981 defines forgery as making a false instrument with the intention that he or another shall use it to induce somebody to accept it as genuine, and by reason of so accepting it to do or not to do some act to his own or any other person's prejudice. There is a similar offence of using a false instrument. Counterfeiting currency notes and protected coins is an offence of basic intent, and there are auxiliary offences; also, it is an offence to possess certain instruments including false share certificates, cheque cards, credit cards, certain documents issued by public authorities, and machines of forgery. Returning to the offence of forgery, "making" includes altering an instrument. There are special offences of making or using a copy of a forged instrument. An instrument is "false" if it falsely purports to have been made or altered by or on the authority of a person, or at a particular date or place, or by an existing person who did not in fact exist. The last rule means that it can be forgery to use an invented name. "Instrument" is defined as any of the following: a document, a device on which information is recorded, a UK postage stamp, and an Inland Revenue stamp. The fact that an article carries writing is not held necessarily to make it a document. As regards the intent, an act is to a person's prejudice only if it would result or has resulted in loss of property, or would give or has given a remunerated office, or would be or was the result of a person's having accepted a false instrument as genuine, in performing his duty. § .9

Various statutes create offences of false statement. § .10

Among many offences relating to companies, investment and consumer protection, mention may be made of the Companies Act 1948 s. 332 (3), creating the offence of fraudulent trading. § .11

CHAPTER 41

DAMAGE AND TRESPASS

A ridiculously oversimplified misreading of history manages to present all human progress in terms of a battle between freedom, which is assumed to be good, and prohibition, which is assumed to be bad. In fact, of course, civilisation owes quite as much to those who limit freedom as to those who expand it. Stopping people doing things, that was the first necessity, with freedom only coming as a secondary luxury.

Peregrine Worsthorne

§ 41.1. CRIMINAL DAMAGE

THE offence of criminal damage (formerly called "malicious damage") now rests on the Criminal Damage Act 1971,[1] and section references in the first part of the chapter will be to this Act unless otherwise expressed. There are three main offences and two ancillary offences. The three main offences may be called, for short, (1) simple damage, (2) dangerous damage, and (3) arson. The two subsidiary offences are (1) threats and (2) custody with intent.

All are punishable with a maximum of imprisonment for 10 years (the same as theft), except arson and dangerous damage, which are punishable on indictment with imprisonment for life. All are triable either way,[2] except that;

- simple and dangerous damage (not including arson) are (with one exception[3]) triable only summarily if the damage done is minor (that is, not exceeding £200), unless the offence charged is "one of two or more offences . . . which appear to the court to constitute or form part of a series of two or more offences of the same or a similar character."[4]
- other cases of dangerous damage (and arson when it complies with the definition of dangerous damage) are triable only on indictment.

In fact the vast majority of cases of vandalism are disposed of summarily. Even arson can be, if the arsonist is not reckless in endangering life.

Simple damage is defined in section 1(1).

---

[1] Extended (in substance) to Northern Ireland by the Criminal Damage (Northern Ireland) Order SI 1977 No. 426.

[2] MCA 1980 Sch.1 para.29. If the Crown does not wish magistrates to try the case it can sometimes prevent this by charging an affray.

[3] The exception referred to is anomalous and questionable: a count for damage not above £200 may be added to an indictment after committal for another offence if there is no charge of criminal damage before the magistrates: *Considine* (1980) 70 CAR 239, discussed in 144 JPN 536.

[4] MCA 1980 s.22(7). The offence is technically "triable either way" for collateral purposes (e.g. the award of costs). CLA 1967 s.2(1) as amended by CLA 1977 Sch.12 ensures that the offence remains "arrestable." See also MCA 1980 s.33.

S.22(7) works horribly. (1) It is absurd that dangerous damage is included. If D damages V's car brakes, or meddles with the electrical wiring in V's house, in order to endanger and frighten V, the fact that the damage is minor ought not to prevent committal for trial, because the gravamen of the charge is the danger, not the damage. The anomaly is all the greater because a charge of minor arson can be sent to the Crown Court, and so can a charge of threat or of custody with intent, although the threat or intent is to do damage of less than £200 and although no danger to life is involved. (The prosecution may sometimes evade the

> "A person who without lawful excuse destroys or damages any property belonging to another intending to destroy or damage any such property or being reckless as to whether any such property would be destroyed or damaged shall be guilty of an offence."

§ 41.2. THE DAMAGE

Although the Act carefully says "destroys or damages," every case of destroying must be one of damaging.[1]

Actual damage is required, and the court may refuse to find damage where minimal damage has been caused without direct intent—as where a few men play football in a grass field used for grazing.[2] But quite small provable damage is sufficient.[3]

Could that ubiquitous offender, Bill Stickers, be prosecuted under the Act?

For acts done without authority he is usually charged under local Acts or bylaws[4]; but on principle he could be charged with criminal damage. Dirt has been jocularly defined as matter in the wrong place, and affixing matter in an unwanted place is capable of being regarded as damage. Other examples would be: spreading jam on someone's car-seat, putting sugar in his petrol, and defacing his walls with aerosol paint.[5]

> The law on the subject of minor damage was cast into some doubt by the decision of a Crown Court on appeal from magistrates in *"A" (a Juvenile)*.[6] The defendant had been convicted of criminal damage for spitting on the back of a police sergeant's uniform which he was

---

restriction in s.22 by charging an attempt to inflict a.b.h. or g.b.h.) Further, whereas magistrates trying a case of damage above £200 (with no danger to anyone) can sentence the offender to six months; and whereas dangerous damage of above £200 can earn a life sentence, for under-£200 damage (even though dangerous) the maximum is three months. (2) Where the value is doubtful the magistrates can apprise the defendant of their reduced sentencing powers on summary trial as a bait to induce him to accept summary trial—an unpleasant transaction. See 142 JPN 339, 446. (3) Equally unpleasant is the procedure whereby on an over-£200 charge where the defendant elects for trial, the prosecution can trump his ace by offering no evidence and then charging minor damage on the same facts: *R* v. *Canterbury JJ, ex p. Klisiak* [1982] QB 398. (4) The legislation creates an arbitrary distinction between charges of damage and destruction: see 143 JPN 254, 369, 383. (5) The interpretation of the exception for offences in series has caused much difficulty. The Act should have confined the minor-damage exception to cases where the minor damage is charged alone or in conjunction with other summary offences. As it stands, the courts are required to fragment connected charges, some going for trial and some being tried summarily although the factual background is the same. See 145 JPN 199. (6) Where D1 and D2 are jointly charged with minor damage and D2 is also charged with other offences in series, D2 may elect for trial but D1 has to be tried summarily. See 145 JPN 195.

[1] But the distinction can be important in respect of jurisdiction and compensation. See § .1 n. 4 (4).

[2] Cp. *Eley* v. *Lytle* (1885) 50 JP 308, 2 TLR 44, decided under the previous legislation.

[3] For the old law, see e.g. *Foster* (1852) 6 Cox 25.

[4] Marking or billposting on a wall etc. in London is an offence under the Metropolitan Police Act 1839 s.54(10). Prosecutions may also be brought under the Town and Country Planning (Control of Advertisements) Regulations 1969 to 1975.

[5] Cp. *Roper* v. *Knott* [1898] 1 QB 868 (damaging milk by adding water); *King* v. *Lees* (1948) 65 TLR 21, 47 LGR 42 (urinating in taxi-cab). But it seems that unlawfully daubing a wall would not be damage if it is regarded as an amelioration: *Fancy* [1980] Crim.LR 171 (Crown Court). In 1981 workmen who painted property out of spite were sent to prison: The Times, November 3.

[6] [1978] Crim.LR 689.

wearing. The conviction was set aside on the ground that the spittle could readily have been wiped off with a damp cloth, and the raincoat was not rendered "inoperative." Spitting upon a satin dress, on the other hand, could be damage if removing the spittle left a mark.

The case is not of high authority, and seems to be a lenient application of the law. On the occasion in question the officer's raincoat was already covered with similar spittle, and if the one youth before the court who spat upon it was not guilty of damage, neither were any of the others; yet collectively they had made it necessary to wash the coat (and during the period of washing it would be what the court called "inoperative").

Displacing the parts of a machine in order to render it temporarily useless amounts to damaging it even though the parts are not damaged.[7] Similarly, it should be damage to separate a fixture from a building.[8] Enabling someone's pet animal to escape would doubtless be a constructive destruction of it! Releasing breeding mink from their cages, whereby their value was reduced although they were recovered and were not physically damaged, was held to cause damage by the Supreme Court of the Republic of Ireland.[9] Letting the air out of someone's tyres would best be dealt with as the offence of tampering with a vehicle,[10] but it should also be accounted damage and, theoretically, theft of the air.

Would it be damage if a dissatisfied employee sabotaged the business by instructing its computer to wipe clean the company's computer programmes and files?

Your example shows that the notion of damage must include any deleterious change in the condition of property.

§ 41.3. PROPERTY

The definition of property for the purpose of criminal damage in section 10 (1) broadly follows that in the Theft Act 1968, but there are two main divergencies.

1 There can generally be no theft of land or a building as such, but criminal damage can be committed to land or a building.
2 Taking wild mushrooms and the flowers, fruit or foliage of "a plant growing wild" can be theft if the taking is for a commercial purpose. But wilfully squashing the mushrooms, or damaging the foliage etc. of such a plant, is not criminal damage whatever the purpose. The test of commercial purpose is not incorporated in the Criminal Damage Act, because it is hardly apposite.

Felling someone else's tree can be criminal damage, because a tree is presumably not a plant, and anyway the felling is not merely damage to foliage etc. Burning gorse bushes could be criminal damage for the second reason, unless, perhaps, burning the gorse is regarded as

[7] This was held under the former Malicious Damage Act: *Fisher* (1872) LR 1 CCR 7; cp. *Tacey* (1821) Russ. & Ry. 452, 168 ER 893.

[8] Where a metal sheet is removed from a house without damaging the sheet, the charge should be of damage to the house (the aggregate entity), not to the sheet. See *Woolcock* [1977] Crim.LR 104, 161. Magistrates have held that squatters who take off a Yale lock and replace it with one of their own do not commit criminal damage (The Times, August 22, 1975), but the matter has not been tested in a higher court.

[9] *Rexi Irish Mink Ltd.* v. *Dublin CC* [1972] IR 123.

[10] Road Traffic Act 1972 s. 29 (§ 38.6 at n. 4).

an amelioration[1]. The exclusion of "foliage" presumably allows one to take a small branch of foliage from a shrub without being guilty of criminal damage (query if from a tree).; but it would not extend to damaging the whole of a shrub. Taking the whole plant would be criminal damage to the land, and it would also be theft of the plant, even though not for a commercial purpose.

Questions may arise on what is meant by "growing wild." A shrub is not "growing wild" if it has been planted; but what if, though self-sown, it has been fertilised or pruned? On principle the prosecution would have to show that the defendant knew the plant was cultivated or was reckless as to this.

§ 41.4. BELONGING TO ANOTHER

Subsection (1) is confined to "property belonging to another"[1]; so it does not penalise the antisocial destruction of one's own property. However, this can sometimes be an offence under subsection (2), to be dealt with presently.

Formerly, setting fire to one's own house as a step towards defrauding the insurance company was arson; this is not so under the Act of 1971,[2] though it can be an offence under subsection (2),[3] or alternatively attempted obtaining by deception, in appropriate circumstances.

Can a person be guilty of criminal damage to property in his own possession?

Yes if he does not own it. A tenant who sets fire to the house would be guilty; so would a person who first drives off someone else's car and then deliberately damages it.

Will a landlord commit an offence if he sets fire to his tenant's house?

The Act provides that the custody of another person is equivalent to ownership,[4] so that the landlord would be guilty of criminal damage.

There are certain statutory offences of damaging or destroying property even though it may be one's own and in one's own possession—cutting down a tree that is the subject of a Tree Preservation Order, demolishing a listed building,[5] and catching and

---

[1] Cp. *Fancy* § .2 n. 5.

[1] Nevertheless, an allegation that a particular person owns the property is, as in theft, an immaterial averment: *Pike* v. *Morrison* [1981] Crim.LR 492.

[2] *Denton* [1981] 1 WLR 1446, [1982] 1 All ER 65, 74 CAR 81, where the rule was applied although the burning was carried out by an employee on the employer's directions. The court overlooked the fact that the property was vested in a company; see criticism by G R Sullivan in [1983] Crim.LR 517–518.

It will be attempted deception if a letter is afterwards written to the insurance company making a claim. Whether starting the fire is attempted deception of the insurers depends upon whether the decision in *Robinson* will be followed under the Act of 1981. See § 17.5.

[3] For s. 1(2) see § .7.

[4] S. 10 (2). However, if a bailor at will determines the bailment and retakes the article, even though only momentarily, he cannot thereafter commit criminal damage to it; and similarly if he has agreed to sell the article with payment by instalment and has validly retaken the article for non-payment. See *Judge* (1974) 138 JPN 649 and M Cohen in 142 JPN 721–722.

[5] The law is too feeble to prevent listed buildings being reduced to rubble by unscrupulous developers, when the development value of the land is greater than that of the building. The only way to make the law effective would be to provide for compulsory sale of the land in such cases, even when the demolition is supposed to have been a mistake, the owner being allowed the value of the listed building and the rest of the proceeds being forfeited.

killing a protected wild bird. These offences are trivial in comparison with the spectacular wastes in our society that go uncontrolled and unpunished. Minerals are used when replaceable resources would do as well; they are used and then cast away as garbage so thinly that they will be impossible to recover; if a gas strike at sea goes wrong, although it can be capped it is sometimes left to bubble away, so that gas that has lain in the ground for millions of years runs to waste. The law has not yet caught up with these activities.

Injuring animals can be an offence under the Protection of Animals Act 1911 or one of the other statutes protecting animals, whether or not they belong to the defendant; but the reason of this legislation is, of course, the prevention not of waste but of cruelty.

Although a husband can be guilty of damaging his wife's property, and *vice versa*, a charge requires the consent of the DPP, as for theft.[6]

§ 41.5. THE MENTAL ELEMENT

The mental element is intention or recklessness. We have seen that the requirement of recklessness is interpreted in a semi-subjective, semi-objective sense.[1] The question whether the mental element should be divided between different counts is considered in § .7.

There is no general offence of negligent damage to property, but this is embraced in the offences of negligent driving (Chapter 14), and there are a few limited statutory provisions.[2]

Can the doctrine of transferred intention be applied under the Act?

Almost certainly yes. At common law, the doctrine of transferred intention applies whenever the statute permits it by its wording, provided that the one can find both the *mens rea* and the *actus reus* for the offence charged, though in respect of different property.

The question relates to the meaning of "any such property" in section 1 (1).

- Probably this means "any property belonging to another" (the word "such" referring back to the earlier phrase "belonging to another").[3] If so, the word "any" brings in the doctrine of transferred intention. If the Act had said merely "such property," it would have been pretty clear that the doctrine was excluded.
- An alternative interpretation is that "any such property" means "any property of the same kind." This would involve the courts in inventing numberless classifications of property. What is a thing of the same kind as a watch, apart from another watch? Is a watch the same kind of thing as a car? Is a horse the same as a dog? Not only would such an enquiry result in uncertainty and complexity, but it might mean that intention could be transferred from the defendant's own property to the property of another person—which would be

---

[6] Theft Act 1968 s. 30 (4); § 33.4 at n. 13.

[1] § 5.3.

[2] E.g. Submarine Telegraph Act 1885 s.3 as amended (negligent injury to submarine cables); Post Office Act 1953 ss 59 (*c*), 60 (postal packets and letter boxes); Dogs (Protection of Livestock) Act 1953 s.1 (sheep-worrying by dogs).

[3] Cp. the wording of s.1(2), where "such" is omitted because under that subsection the property need not belong to another.

anomalous. So pretty clearly (1) is the preferable interpretation. "Such property" means not "property of the same kind " but "property belonging to another."[4]

However, the legal transference of intention should not be a reason for increasing punishment. If D tries to break what he knows to be a cheap vase but accidentally (i.e. without intention or recklessness) knocks over a very valuable one, he may be convicted of criminal damage to the expensive vase, but should obviously be sentenced on the basis of his actual intention.[5]

§ 41.6. WITHOUT LAWFUL EXCUSE

Several excuses for damaging the property of another are recognised by the general law. For example, a landowner (or occupier, or probably licensee) may eject trespassing property, notwithstanding that this may inevitably involve some damage to the property (as where he demolishes a shed that has been placed on his land by way of trespass). A person may abate a nuisance by removing any unlawful obstruction to a public or private right of way. Property may be damaged, it is suggested, in a situation of necessity, and of course it may be damaged with the consent of the owner.[1] In addition, a non-exhaustive definition of "lawful excuse" is provided by section 5. Subsection (2) specifies two particular types of lawful excuse for the purpose of the Act; belief in consent and belief in defence. Belief in consent:

> "(*a*) if at the time of the act or acts alleged to constitute the offence he believed that the person or persons whom he believed to been entitled to consent to the destruction of or damage to the property in question had so consented, or would have so consented to it if he or they had known of the destruction or damage and its circumstances."

Belief in defence:

> "(*b*) if he destroyed or damaged . . . the property in question . . . in order to protect property belonging to himself or another or a right or interest in property which was or which he believed to be vested in himself or another, and at the time of the act or acts alleged to constitute the offence he believed—

---

[4] This was clearly the intention of the Law Commission, which said: "The intention or recklessness need not be related to the particular property damaged, provided that it is related to another's property. If, for example, a person throws a stone at a passing motor car intending to damage it, but misses and breaks a shop window, he will have the necessary intention in respect of the damage to the window as he intended to damage the property of another": Law Commission, *Report on Offences of Damage to Property* (Law Com. No. 29 of 1970) para. 45.

[5] Ashworth uses this type of case as part of his argument that the law of transferred intention should be abolished; and I agree with this in respect of criminal damage. See discussion in [1983] CLJ 86–87. Practical instances are in any case rare. There is not the same difficulty for offences against the person, because here the legal distinction between a.b.h. and g.b.h. or death should generally prevent great anomaly arising.

[1] S. 5 (a provision about to be discussed) allows a defence of belief in the owner's consent, but the Act does not think it necessary to say that the owner's actual consent is a defence, evidently because this falls under the general defence of "lawful excuse" in section 1 (1). The CA in *Denton* § .4 n. 2 said that this is "probably" so; but why "probably"? Where the owner consents to the act there is no *actus reus*; and this is true even though the defendant did not know that the owner consented. See J C Smith in [1982] Crim.LR 108.

(i) that the property, right or interest was in immediate need of protection; and

(ii) that the means of protection adopted or proposed to be adopted were or would be reasonable having regard to all the circumstances.

(3) For the purposes of this section it is immaterial whether a belief is justified or not if it is honestly held.

(4) For the purposes of subsection (2) above a right or interest in property includes any right or privilege in or over land, whether created by grant, licence or otherwise.

(5) This section shall not be construed as casting doubt on any defence recognised by law as a defence to criminal charges."

These two paragraphs apply to cases where there is to the defendant's knowledge an actual consent of the owner,[2] or an actual necessity for protecting property, as well as to cases where the defendant makes a mistake as to these matters. It is clear on principle that the burden of negativing the defence rests on the prosecution.

Paragraph (*b*) means, for example, that a sheep-farmer who has shot a marauding dog is not guilty of criminal damage if he believed that this was immediately necessary and reasonable in protection of his sheep. The qualification that the property must be believed to be "in immediate need of protection" is regrettable. Action in defence of property may be necessary and reasonable even though the threat is not immediate. A hill farmer does not live among his sheep, and it may be reasonable for him to kill a marauding dog even though his sheep are safe so long as he is with them. Notwithstanding this restriction in paragraph (*b*), the defendant should have the defence of necessity in such circumstances. It must be said, however, that the decided cases do not give much encouragement to the argument that necessity can supplement the right of private defence.[3]

It is not clear how far anticipatory action is justified when it takes the form of creating static deterrents. A farmer surrounds his field with barbed wire, on which a trespasser tears his clothes. Has the farmer intentionally or recklessly damaged the clothes? On the causation principles studied in Chapter 16 it may perhaps be held that it is not the farmer who has done this, but the trespasser in trying to climb over an obvious danger. Assuming, however, that the court finds a *prima facie* case of criminal damage caused by recklessness, the question is whether the defence under paragraph (*b*) applies. This turns on whether the requirement of immediate danger rules out anticipatory measures by way of static defence. The prosecution may advance the argument that when the anti-trespasser device operates, it is immediately necessary for the protection of the property, because the trespasser is actively trying to get in. The barbed wire does nothing to the trespasser when set, and when it operates it is immediately necessary. But the difficulty is the question of timing. If "the time of the act or acts alleged to constitute the offence" is when the wire is put up, the farmer does not then believe that immediate protection is required. If the time is when the damage is caused to the trespasser, the farmer may then be asleep, and have no belief that his property is "in

---

[2] *Denton*, last note.

[3] See particularly *Workman* v. *Cowper* [1961] 2 QB 143. Smith and Hogan, 4th edn 660, suggest that the criminal courts might now allow a defence by analogy with the defence provided in civil cases by the Animals Act 1971 s.9(3)(*b*), where the dog *has been* worrying livestock. By the Dogs Act 1906 s.3 and the Dogs (Protection of Livestock) Act 1953 s.2(2), a police officer may "seize" stray dogs in certain circumstances, and after a certain time have them destroyed.

immediate need of protection." So, in addition to relying on paragraph (*b*), the farmer would do well to seek to establish a defence of "lawful excuse" as a matter of private defence. The barbed wire is a customary and reasonable form of static defence against trespassers.

Doesn't the ultra-subjectivism of paragraph (b) raise the same problem as in blackmail?

It is true that the paragraph is widely drawn in that it makes the issue depend on whether the defendant himself thought the act reasonable. But the courts will probably hold, as in blackmail, that this means that he must have thought that right-thinking people would regard what he did as reasonable. Of course, the more unreasonable the defendant's conduct was in an objective sense, the less the tribunal is likely to credit his claim that he believed his conduct reasonable. Some of the decisions before the Act took an extremely costive attitude towards the defence of claim of right. The intention of the Act is to remove from the criminal law any damage done under a supposition of right, since such conduct is adequately provided for by the civil law. So the message to the police is: do not prosecute in these circumstances.

Another liberality in the drafting is that paragraph (*b*) applies not only in respect of acts done to protect property but also in respect of those done for the protection of what the defendant believed was "a right or interest in property."[4] It therefore covers not only what is usually called private defence but such matters as abatement of nuisance.

If a person, mistakenly believing that he is entitled to a right of way over another's land, removes what he regards as an obstruction, he is not protecting physical property against attack but regards himself as protecting his right in property, i.e. his incorporeal interest in the land over which he claims a right of way. The paragraph therefore applies. Similarly, the paragraph applies if a person, having or believing that he has an incorporeal interest, does something that he believes to be reasonably necessary to protect the interest even though the law does not authorise the interest to be protected in that way. A person who has sporting rights over the land of another is not entitled to shoot a strange dog that is disturbing the game and spoiling his sport[5]; but if he does so, believing that this is reasonable, he has a defence under the Act.

It should follow that if a person has had a parking space allotted to him, and if he damages a trespassing car in endeavouring to remove it from the space, the defence provided by paragraph (*b*) should apply. It may be that the law gives him the right to take reasonable steps to eject the car (certainly it does if he is a lessee of the parking space, and very likely it does so also if he is a licensee of it[6]); but even if it does not, he has a defence if he believed that his parking right gave him a right or interest in property and that what he did was reasonable. Note that subsection (4) expressly extends protection to licensees. Indeed, even if the defendant did not believe that he was entitled to act on his own account, the paragraph gives him a defence if he believed he was acting to protect the property rights of the owner of the ground. The intention of the paragraph to rest the defence on a subjective basis is clear; all that creates a doubt is the

[4] Cp. subs. (4), reproduced above, which makes doubly sure by repeating the point.
[5] *Gott* v. *Measures* [1948] 1 KB 234.
[6] § 23.6 n. 6.

constant tendency of the courts to distrust subjectively worded defences, and indeed to construe defences narrowly whenever possible.[7]

One restriction has already been imposed by the judges on the defence under paragraph (*b*). The statutory defence is held not to apply where the act (starting a small fire to demonstrate that fire alarms do not work) was done merely to call the attention of the authorities to a present dangerous situation, even though the object of the defendant was to reduce this danger. The defensive act is apparently regarded as not being related sufficiently closely to the avoidance of danger.[7] On the other hand, a Divisional Court in *Jaggard* v. *Dickinson*[8] gave a thoroughly subjectivist interpretation to paragraph (*a*).

The two paragraphs leave out something. A person may destroy property in the honest but mistaken belief that it is his own.

Clearly he would be acquitted on the general issue of *mens rea*. The two paragraphs exemplify cases where *mens rea* is absent but do not preclude a defence for other cases. Under section 1 (1) the defendant must have the required mental element in relation to the property of another. The point was decided, it may be remembered, in *David Smith*.[9] The court proceeded not on the wording of the Act, which was silent on the point, but on "the ordinary principles of *mens rea*."

What if the defendant's belief that he owned the property was the result of a mistake not of fact but of the civil law?

These were the circumstances in *David Smith*, above. The reason why Smith thought the property was his own was that he was the tenant of a flat and had made certain improvements in the flat; but the improvements became the property of the landlord by virtue of the rule of law that things attached to the land become the property of the landowner. (There are exceptions to the principle, but none was relevant.) When quitting the flat Smith damaged the fixtures in removing some of them (which he was not in law entitled to do). On a charge of criminal damage, his defence that he thought the fixtures were his own succeeded; yet his mistake was as to the general law of property in fixtures, not as to a matter of observable fact.

Paragraph (b) provides for damaging property in defence of property, but what about damaging property in defence of the person?

Acts done in defence of the person are generally those causing injury to the person, but you are right: it is perfectly possible to damage property when defending the person, as when one kills an attacking dog. The Act, evidently by oversight, leaves this to fall under the general category of lawful excuse.

This may have two consequences, peculiar in principle but unlikely to cause difficulty in practice.

---

[7] *Hunt* (1977) 66 CAR 105. It has been argued, with some justice, that this decision is out of accord with the subjective nature of the defence given by s.5: M Cohen in 142 JPN 720.

[8] § 21.5 at n. 2.

[9] § 6.2 at n. 6. On the present standing of the decision see § 6.2 at nn. 19–24.

1 Paragraph (*b*) allows a person to protect the property of someone who is a stranger to him. But this applies only if he damages property. If he injures the person of an attacker, he cannot justify at common law on the ground that he was protecting the property of a stranger,[10] unless the doctrine of necessity helps him.

2 The Law Commission, who originated the Criminal Damage Act, took a strongly subjectivist position, and in paragraph (*b*) made the defendant's belief in right a defence. As we saw in § 23.2, the general view of the common law is that belief in the necessity for self-defence must be reasonable; and this applies to damaging property in defence of the person, which the Act leaves to the common law. So if a man strikes at and injures a snarling dog, and is prosecuted for damaging the dog, his belief that it was about to tear his clothes is a defence although the belief was unreasonable, but his belief that the dog was about to bite his leg is a defence only if regarded as reasonable. It is to be hoped that the attitude of the Law Commission will eventually govern the whole law of private defence.

It may be mentioned here that there is a rule of the common law ousting the jurisdiction of magistrates in certain cases involving title to land. The reason for the rule is that title to land may involve complicated questions which are thought not to be suitable for magistrates to determine. All the same, the rule has caused much difficulty, and the Criminal Damage Act solves the problem by excluding it in charges of damage (s. 7 (2)).

§ 41.7. DANGEROUS DAMAGE

This phrase is used here merely as a convenient, though unofficial, abbreviation. The offence is defined in section 1 (2).

> "A person who without lawful excuse destroys or damages any property, whether belonging to himself or another—
> (*a*) intending to destroy or damage any property or being reckless as to whether any property would be destroyed or damaged; and
> (*b*) intending by the destruction or damage to endanger the life of another or being reckless as to whether the life of another would be thereby endangered;
> shall be guilty of an offence."

The offence is similar to what I have called the offence of simple damage, except as follows.

1 It applies where a person damages his own property, as well as where he damages the property of another.

2 It is confined to cases where life is intentionally or recklessly endangered. This element is thought to justify the increase in the maximum punishment to imprisonment for life; and there can be no summary trial (except that the offence is triable only summarily, and the maximum punishment drastically reduced, if the damage does not exceed £200). It should be noticed that the offence can be committed although no one was in fact endangered (as where no one was in fact in the building).

3 Although "lawful excuse" is a defence, the partial definition of "lawful excuse" in section 5 is not applied. Presumably the "lawful excuse" under this subsection must be something that excuses not only the

---

[10] But, as said at n. 6 above, a licensee can probably defend the property at common law against wrongdoers.

damage to the property but the peril to life. The excuses of private defence, duress and (perhaps) necessity can sometimes operate to justify imperilling life.

While the measure was under discussion, the inclusion of this offence was criticised (without avail) as being illogical, because the offence is really an offence against the person and not one against property. If D tampers with the brakes of his own car, which he knows his father is going to use, hoping that his father will be killed or injured, it is strange to treat the case as one of criminal damage. (If D had built a car with bad brakes for the same purpose he could not be said to have damaged the car, and therefore could not be punished under section 1 (2)); yet his purpose and the danger would be the same.)

§ 41.8. ARSON

Section 1 of the Act, after creating the offence of simple damage in subsection (1) and the offence of dangerous damage in subsection (2), provides in subsection (3) as follows.

> "(3) An offence committed under this section by destroying or damaging property by fire shall be charged as arson."

It follows that there are two forms of arson; one under subsection (1) and another under subsection (2), combined in each case with subsection (3).[1] Arson in any form attracts a maximum life sentence, except that arson by way of simple damage is triable summarily, in which case the punishment is limited in the usual way.[2] The difference of substance between what may be called simple arson and dangerous arson (apart from the difference of definition) is that dangerous arson may be committed in respect of one's own property.

Is arson a separate offence or just a way of charging criminal damage?

It seems to be a separate offence. Consequently, an intent to cause damage otherwise than by fire cannot be transferred to make the offender guilty of arson of something else if fire is accidentally caused.[3]

There was an offence of arson at common law, and in the discussion leading to the Act some disagreement emerged as to whether a special offence of damaging by fire was worth preserving. The Law Commission stated the arguments for the view that prevailed (though it was not their own view) as follows.

> "There are two main arguments for treating damage by fire differently from other ways of damaging property. The first is that damage by fire, particularly to buildings and stacks, is an offence which has always been regarded with abhorrence. It is argued that this of itself is a reason for allowing a higher maximum penalty. The second argument, which we find much more persuasive, is that many people who resort to damage by fire are mentally unbalanced and in need of treatment, and yet frequently do not qualify for committal to hospital under section 60 of the Mental Health Act 1959. If damage by burning is punishable by a maximum sentence of life imprisonment, a person so convicted may be kept in detention for psychiatric treatment for as long as proves necessary."[4]

---

[1] The offence should be charged under both subs.(1) and subs.(3), or both subs.(2) and subs.(3): *R* v. *Aylesbury Crown Court* [1972] 3 All ER 574, 56 CAR 818.

[2] § 1.5 at n. 24. The usual legislative principle is that an offence carrying a possible life sentence on indictment is not made triable either way; arson is an exception to this.

[3] See [1983] CLJ 86. *Contra*, Ashworth in *Reshaping the Criminal Law* (ed. Glazebrook 1978) 92.

[4] Law Commission, *Report on Offence of Damage to Property* (Law Com. No. 29) para. 29.

Surely it would not be arson if D lit up someone else's cigarette without his permission?

Technically it would be. The cases on the former offence of arson established that it was committed if the thing were caused to smoulder at red heat, though there were no actual flame[5]; and doubtless the same construction will be applied to the new statutory offence. Doubtless, too, your imaginary case will never come to court.

The availability of charges of serious damage and serious arson means that if the conviction (by verdict or on plea) is only of simple damage or simple arson, the judge in sentencing must assume that the defendant neither intended to endanger life nor was even *Caldwell* reckless as to this—however obvious the risk may appear to the sentencer.[6]
In charging dangerous damage or dangerous arson the courts regard it as important for the prosecutor to charge intention and recklessness in separate counts, not in the alternative in the same count. This chief reason is that, if the two kinds of fault are charged in the alternative in the same count, a conviction on plea will give the judge no guidance on whether the defendant intended to endanger life or acted thoughtlessly (*Caldwell* recklessness). The judge can hear evidence to establish the degree of the defendant's fault, but if he neglects to do this he must sentence on the basis of the smallest degree of fault implied by the plea, i.e. *Caldwell* "not thinking." If there is a trial the theory is that the judge is entitled to form his own judgment on the circumstances, to the extent that he is not given guidance by the verdict or the state of the pleadings; but in practice the Court of Appeal may (irrationally) reduce the sentence on the ground that it is left in doubt as to the factual basis of the verdict. What this court ought to do is to see what evidence was before the trial judge, but apparently it will not do this. The problem will be reduced in scale if there are separate counts.[7] Fortunately, the courts have not desired that separate counts should be used for simple damage or simple arson, although one would have thought that a similar argument applied there.

Notice the parallel offence to dangerous arson created by the Explosive Substances Act 1883 s. 2 (causing an explosion likely to endanger life or cause serious injury to property).

§ 41.9. THREATS

> Section 2. "A person who without lawful excuse makes to another a threat, intending that that other would fear it would be carried out—
> (*a*) to destroy or damage any property belonging to that other or a third person; or
> (*b*) to destroy or damage his own property in a way which he knows is likely to endanger the life of that other or a third person;
> shall be guilty of an offence."

It will be noticed that the threat may be made in any way—e.g. over the telephone.[1] The threat need not be made directly to the victim of the threatened attack, and it need not be a threat of immediate damage.
The partial definition of "lawful excuse" in section 5 applies to an offence

---

[5] *Parker* (1839) 9 C & P 45, 173 ER 733.
[6] *Booker* [1982] Crim.LR 378.
[7] See commentaries by D A Thomas to *Hoof* [1980] Crim.LR 719 and *Hayter* [1981] Crim.LR 344.

[1] See also the offences listed in § 9.9 at nn. 16–22.

under this section (with appropriate modifications) unless the threat is to damage property in a way that the threatener knows is likely to endanger the life of another.

§ 41.10. CUSTODY WITH INTENT

Section 3. "A person who has anything in his custody or under his control intending without lawful excuse to use it or cause or permit another to use it—

(*a*) to destroy or damage any property belonging to some other person; or

(*b*) to destroy or damage his own or the user's property in a way which he knows is likely to endanger the life of some other person;

shall be guilty of an offence."

The effect of this is to create a kind of statutory attempt; it has a wide ambit, because the "thing" may be something quite ordinary, like a tin of aerosol paint, or even a box of matches, and there is no requirement of an intent to use it immediately.[1] The partial definition of "lawful excuse" again applies (with appropriate modifications), unless the defendant intended to damage property in a way that he knew was likely to endanger the life of another.[2]

It may be noticed that there are also offences of possessing explosives in the Explosive Substances Act 1883 ss. 3 and 4.[3]

§ 41.11. TRESPASS

Traditionally, and exceptions apart, trespass upon land is a wrong noticed only by the civil law. The reason is not easy to state. Of course, trespassing on a man's land is not a grave matter in comparison with trespassing on his head, or among his insides; but there are plenty of minor offences, and it is slightly surprising that this does not feature among them.

Not only does the criminal law turn a blind eye to the rambler through farms and woods, but it is not generally an offence to disport oneself in some one else's garden; to "gate-crash" a party by slipping in among the guests (except that the consumption of food or drink by the gate-crasher would be theft or obtaining by deception); to enter a house surreptitiously in order to "bug" it, or to sleep in the best bed; even to intrude into Buckingham Palace, sit on the Queen's bed, and engage her in unwelcome conversation[1]; to creep into a cinema or climb the fence to a football match without paying; to organise a "pop festival" without the landowner's permission; to park one's car in some one else's parking space; for a newspaper

---

[1] *Buckingham* (1976) 63 CAR 159.

[2] S.6 of the Act allows the issue of a search warrant for things that a person has for the purpose of committing an offence under s. 1.

[3] Other inchoate offences are contained in unrepealed sections of the Malicious Damage Act 1861, ss. 35, 36, 47 and 48, relating to the obstruction or endangering of railway engines and shipping.

[1] In July 1982 one Fagan did this, and no charge was brought.

reporter to gain admission to a private house or conference by a "ruse" (i.e. by deception) or by stealth; for a man to wander round a hospital and make a nuisance of himself; for hunt and shooting saboteurs to trespass in order to disturb the sportsmen's quarry; or for demonstrators to invade a football or cricket pitch during a match in order to make a political protest. At one time the anaemic state of the law might have been justified on the ground that these events were too rare to be a serious social evil, but that argument cannot stand examination at the present day, when such forms of lawlessness are commonplace.

The most serious consequence is that the police are led to dissociate themselves from the problems caused by trespasses of almost all kinds. Contributory factors to this attitude of the police are the feeling that they have more serious matters to attend to, doubts as to their powers (or so it is said; but it is notable that the police have no doubts when they contravene the restrictive rules as to arrest and search), and the tendency of people at one end of the political spectrum to support so-called demonstrations, which means that law enforcement becomes mixed with politics.

The police are not without legal reasons for interfering if they feel so disposed. At the least, they can often arrest or at least detain a trespasser for an apprehended breach of the peace,[2] and have him bound over to keep the peace and be of good behaviour. Frequently a charge under section 5 of the Public Order Act[3] would be justified. In serious cases involving a number of people the police may consider charging an unlawful assembly. They can stand by while the occupier ejects the trespasser, and if the trespasser makes forcible resistance they can charge him with assault. It would be more sensible, however, if the police saw him out on the occupier's behalf.

Miscellaneous statutes provide special offences of trespass.

It is an offence to trespass on a railway,[4] a ship,[5] an aircraft,[6] a licenced aerodrome,[7] military lands,[8] a military camp,[9] an explosives factory,[10] the premises of a foreign mission,[11] a bird sanctuary,[12] a cemetery,[13] or a public garden.[14] It is an offence for a trespasser on educational premises to cause (or permit!) nuisance or disturbance[15] (student demonstrators beware!); to interfere with a designated wreck[16]; to abandon litter (including derelict vehicles dumped on land)[17]; or to drive a motor without lawful authority off a road "upon any common land, moor land or other land of whatsoever description"; there is an exception for driving within 15 yards of a road for the purpose of parking.[18] An unauthorised climber of Nelson's column can be convicted under Trafalgar Square Regulations; but the climber on the

---

[2] § 22.2 at nn.10–18.
[3] 9.9 at nn. 19–20.
[4] British Transport Commission Act 1949 s.55.
[5] Merchant Shipping Act 1970 ss. 77 (stowaways), 78 (ships in port).
[6] Air Navigation Order, SI 1974 No. 1114 art. 48 (stowaways).
[7] Civil Aviation Act 1949 s.38.
[8] Military Lands Act 1892 ss.14,17(2).
[9] Manoeuvres Act 1958 s.8.
[10] Explosives Act 1875 s.77.
[11] CLA 1977 s.9. See A M Prichard, *Squatting* (London 1981) 127–130.
[12] Protection of Birds Act 1954 s.3.
[13] Cemeteries Clauses Act 1847 s.58.
[14] Town Gardens Protection Act 1863 s.5.
[15] Local Government (MP) Act 1982 s.40.
[16] Protection of Wrecks Act 1973 s.1.
[17] Refuse Disposal (Amenity) Act 1978 s.3; cp. Litter Acts 1958 and 1971; Control of Pollution Act 1974 s.3.
[18] RTA 1972 s.36. See Wilkinson, *Road Traffic Offences*, 11th ed 375. The penalty is low, and in any case the police do not seem to enforce the section. The Law of Property Act 1925 s.193(4) as amended has a similar provision for certain commons without the parking exemption. For the defective and obscure state of the law on illegal parking see 133 JPN 388. For motor cycle "scrambles" see 138 JPN 103.

dome of St. Paul's or the statue of Eros in Piccadilly Circus appears to commit no specific offence; he is likely, however, to be charged with criminal damage if this can be found, or failing that to be bound over. (Magistrates are given remarkable *carte blanche* in exercising this last power, and from time to time bind over trespassers on the ground of an apprehended breach of the peace which is a mere figment of their imagination.) Occasionally a trespass becomes criminal by reason of the intent, as in the case of trespass in pursuit of game (which can be committed by shooting on a country road),[19] burglarious entry to a building,[20] and trespasses forbidden by section 1 of the Official Secrets Act 1911.[21] It is also forbidden for a trespasser in a building (or on land ancillary to a building) to have with him a weapon of offence,[22] or for a trespasser anywhere to have with him a firearm,[23] or (as we shall presently see) for anyone to seek to enter premises by violence.

One day, no doubt, we shall have some more sensible and general provision for criminal trespass. Other countries have shown the way. The Indian Penal Code makes it an offence to trespass with intent to intimidate or annoy.[24] In the Republic of Ireland and Northern Ireland it has been an offence since 1851 for a trespasser to refuse to leave upon request.[25] The Canadian Criminal Code makes it an offence to loiter at night upon the property of another near a dwelling-house (s. 173), and one of the forms of criminal mischief is obstructing the lawful enjoyment of property (s. 387). Considering the wide scope of modern penal law, there is no obvious reason why such conduct should remain in England largely without notice from our criminal courts.

§ 41.12. TRESPASSORY ENTRY TO A BUILDING

The most serious form of trespass is trespassory entry to a building, and particularly to a dwelling, and even more particularly a cuckoo-like trespass, involving the ouster of the lawful owner or other occupier. Even so, the peaceable invasion of buildings is not an offence.

Here again the police have generally adopted an attitude of studied indifference to the problems of the unfortunate owner.[1] Failing all else the owner must face the costs of a court action—costs that he is unlikely to be able to recover from indigent trespassers. He may sue for an injunction to prevent a threatened occupancy if he can identify the threateners.[2] After the illegal occupancy has taken place he can sue for damages (but this remedy is not likely to be enforceable); more importantly, he may ask for a court order for the recovery of his property. An expeditious summary procedure has been devised, under which an order can be made in a matter of days—even as little as two days.[3] The order will be enforced by the sheriff and his officers (in the case of the High Court) or by the bailiff and his officers (in the case of the county court). The sheriff can call upon the police to assist him under the Sheriffs Act 1887 s. 8 (1). The bailiff is too lowly to be given this right; but under the Criminal Law Act 1977 s. 10 it is an offence to obstruct any court officer enforcing an order for the recovery of

---

[19] *Pratt* (1855) 4 E & B 860, 119 ER 319.
[20] Chap. 38.
[21] As extensively interpreted in *Chandler* § 3.2 at n. 1.
[22] CLA 1977 s.8. See Prichard, *op.cit.* 122–127.
[23] Firearms Act 1968 s.20.
[24] S.441.
[25] [1956] Crim.LR 157. Contrast such a fragmentary provision as that in the Licensing Act 1964 s.174(2), whereby it is an offence for a drunkard etc. to refuse to leave licenced premises.

[1] But even before the passage of the Criminal Law Act 1977 the Metropolitan Police Commissioner undertook to assist the displaced occupier of a furnished residence: 139 JPN 463.
[2] See [1972–1973] JSPTL 254. For practical limitations see A M Prichard, *Squatting* (London 1981) (hereafter "Prichard") 42–45.
[3] Rules of the Supreme Court Or. 113; County Court Rules Ord. 24 rr. 1–7. See generally Prichard Part 2.

premises,[4] and the police, if they can be persuaded to stand by, can arrest offenders and so in effect assist their eviction.

The criminal law does, however, concern itself with *violent* entry into buildings (and land associated with buildings). Before the Criminal Law Act 1977 the prohibition of violence in trespassing depended upon the common law and upon ancient Statutes of Forcible Entry. The Law Commission decided to modernise this antiquated legislation, and as a result the Act of 1977 superseded it by a new summary offence set out in section 6. The offence consists in using violence or the threat of violence to secure entry to a building when there is someone present who is opposed to the entry. (It docs not matter that entrance is not gained.)

Section 6 (1):

"(1) Subject to the following provisions of this section, any person who, without lawful authority, uses or threatens violence for the purpose of securing entry into any premises for himself or for any other person is guilty of an offence, provided that—

(*a*) there is someone present on those premises at the time who is opposed to the entry which the violence is intended to secure; and

(*b*) the person using or threatening the violence knows that that is the case."[5]

But why does the offence require violence? Isn't it just as much of an outrage for squatters to move into another person's house during his temporary absence without violence?

For the framers of the Act, political considerations were paramount. Some squatters receive a measure of public sympathy. Besides, the intruders may not be squatters; they may be workpeople (championed by their trade unions) engaged on a "sit in" or "work in" by way of protest against closure of the factory or against an announcement of redundancies; or they may be students peaceably occupying the administrative block on university premises for political reasons in order to impede the work of the University. So, to reduce opposition, it was felt that the offence had to be confined to cases of violence.

By "violence" does the subsection mean violence against the occupier or violence to the building—smashing windows and suchlike?

Both. Subsection (4): "It is immaterial for the purposes of this section . . .

(*a*) whether the violence in question is directed against the person or against property."

I can't see why the lawful occupiers need protection from this law. If the invaders use violence to an occupier, they are guilty of assault, etc.; and if they smash their way into the building they are guilty of criminal damage.

Yes. Section 6 is of very little use to lawful occupiers. Sometimes it may clarify the position if there has only doubtfully been an assault, and it has

---

[4] The provision does not apply against tenants who hold over. See generally Prichard 130–136.

[5] Prichard Part 3 offers an invaluable commentary on the many intricacies of the legislation.

the advantage that the prosecution can charge a summary offence which carries no right of trial. But anyway, the unlawful invaders who are likely to be encountered will probably not offend against section 6. Squatters and demonstrators sneak into premises when no one is there, or unlawfully stay on after a lawful entry, or fiddle the locks; and in none of these cases will section 6 apply.

Then the section is not much use?

Its chief "use," if that is the right word, is in restraining the owner from forcibly re-entering his building after he has been illegally ousted from it. The Law Commission decided that the owner was (with a certain exception to be mentioned in a moment) to be liable to be charged with the offence just as much as if he were a trespasser. Subsection (2) provides that "the fact that a person has any interest in . . . premises shall not . . . constitute lawful authority . . .". It follows that a university or employer can commit the offence when faced with a sit-in; so can the local authority when it finds its empty buildings overrun with squatters. Unless they employ tactics about to be mentioned, such owners must go to court if they want to get the intruders out. We see, therefore, that subsection (1) is not an enactment primarily motivated by concern for the owner of property invaded. In its practical effect it is a legislative provision for the aid and security of lawbreakers, though of course its purpose is to preserve the peace.

Whether the decision of policy was right may be doubted. There was no evidence of serious disorder arising from evicted owners using reasonable force to give effect to their right to enter. Normally, the evicted owner will go to the courts, whether he is given the option of self-help or not. Although the offence in section 6 (1) was meant to be generally neutral between owners and aggressors, in practice, as we shall see, it works lopsidedly—not lopsidedly against the aggressor but against the owner.

But the Act makes an important exception for the "displaced residential occupier." If you are wrongfully dispossessed of the dwelling house or flat you have been occupying, by someone who entered as a trespasser, you are given the privileged position of a DRO and can smash and fight your way back in to evict the usurper; this right you have at common law,[6] and it is limited only by the requirement that the force you use against the trespassers must be necessary and reasonable.

The following are further details of this complex legislation for those who are interested.

We commence with persons other than the DRO. Taking subsection (2) at its face value (and putting aside certain arguments, to be noticed hereafter, that may be used to deflect it, but have not come before the courts), it means that the owner is allowed to do little more than fight on (using reasonable force) until he is ejected; once he is run out, he must generally accept defeat until the forces of law put him back in. If the owner defies the section and fights

[6] The right was abrogated by the Statutes of Forcible Entry, but has now been revived by the repeal of those statutes.

his way back in, he very likely commits assaults as well as offending against the section,[7] at any rate up to the time when he gets back over the threshhold.

The section covers all buildings and land ancillary thereto. But it does not apply to other land[8]; so a farmer who has been evicted from any part of his acres (say by gypsies making an encampment) can use force to get back in and evict his evicters as at common law.

"Uses or threatens violence." It seems that a threat of violence can be an offence even though it is made some time before the projected entry.[9] The threat may be implied, and if an invading mob seeks to enter premises illegally, its mere numbers may be an implied threat of violence to the occupier in case of resistance. But if a particular invader were prosecuted it would have to be shown, first, that he intended to obtain entry, and secondly, that he intended to threaten violence or was reckless as to such threat being understood.[10]

Although the main object of the Act is to preserve the peace, it does not pursue that aim consistently. It does not prohibit the owner entering peaceably and then using force to turn the squatters out again. The displaced owner may get in by stealth, persuasion or fraud; once in, he can admit his friends, and together they may (so far as subsection (1) is concerned) set upon the intruders.[11] (There may be argument on when the owner can be regarded as having got back in; if he or his friend simply gets a foot inside the door without the use of violence, can he then use violence to expel the usurpers?)

You may suppose from the foregoing that a good plan for the displaced owner would be to collect his friends and at dead of night break a window, get in and join battle. Not so: the prohibition of using "violence" against property in order to get in applies against the ousted owner as much as against trespassers. This is remarkable, since the window is the owner's. The explanation of the anomaly lies in the section's duality of purpose. If the section had created two distinct offences, one of unlawful entry by trespassers and one of the use of force by owners to re-enter, each offence could have been drafted in terms appropriate to it. Instead, those who drafted the legislation decided to get it all in to one offence. They wished to prevent trespassers getting in by breaking windows, and since they had (foolishly) decided to treat owners generally with the same medicine as trespassers, they applied the same rule to owners. No sensible reason can be given for saying that the owner can get back in with his own key but not by breaking his own window.

Another oddity is in speaking of violence against property. One would not call it "violence" if a blacksmith at his anvil hammers a horse shoe. Presumably the word in this context means destructive violence. A distinction may be drawn between the technical force used in unscrewing a lock (which is not violence) and smashing a door or window-pane (which is).[12] Difficult intermediate cases may arise; gently levering a door off its hinges, for instance. But what is the reason for distinguishing? We may offer our own answer: none. Even if one is thinking only of an invasion by trespassers, the lawful inhabitant may be just as frightened when invaders are seen unscrewing his door locks as if they are smashing his windows; in either case their object is clearly to get in. Or the inhabitant may not, at first, be frightened

---

[7] *Contra*, Prichard 62. He points out that section 6 (2) states the rule (extending the offence to owners) only "for the purposes of subs. (1)"; he suggests, therefore, that if the owner forcibly re-enters, although this may be an offence under s.6(1), it is not necessarily an assault. If it is not an assault, he suggests, the trespasser has no right to defend himself against the use of force. I doubt this. Notwithstanding that the Act purports to do no more than to create the offence specified in subs.(1), it makes the forcible repossession unlawful; since the use of the force against the interlopers is unlawful, it should logically follow that the force is an assault. (It is true that under the old law a forcible entry that was unlawful under the Statutes of Forcible Entry was held in *Hemmings* v. *Stoke Poges Golf Club Ltd* [1920] 1 KB 720 not to constitute a tortious assault; but that was an illogical decision and should not now be applied to the Act of 1977, particularly in respect of criminal assaults). Even if the unlawful force is not an assault, it is nevertheless unlawful under the Act of 1977; so on principle the person against whom the force is used can act in self-defence.

[8] S.12(1)(*a*).

[9] For the problems that may arise if the threat is substantially before the entry see Prichard, *op.cit.* 56–60.

[10] See Prichard 72–73.

[11] 129 NLJ 1185.

[12] But Prichard 76 cites a civil case in which sliding a lock back with the use of an instrument was held to be "violent." It is to be hoped that a criminal court would not degrade language in this way.

at all, because he does not know his window is being broken or his door lock unscrewed; he is frightened only when he finds that the trespassers have entered. If they get into the building unlawfully, does it greatly matter how they got there? Legally, it does; but that only shows how easily the law becomes an ass.

Suppose the owner has been pushed or locked out by invaders, but he has an ally left on the premises (for example, his son, or a watchman). Can the owner use violence to get back in? The general answer is again no. The section is evidently intended to enact a precise rule. It does not use vague words like "possession," but says distinctly that no one must use violence to secure entry. So anyone once pushed out cannot legally fight his way back in, merely on the ground that he is the owner and has been ejected.

But the full answer to the question depends upon what is happening inside. If the ally has accepted defeat and is sitting philosophically in a chair, the owner, as has just been said, will commit the offence if he uses violence to re-enter. He can steal in by the back door, because it is still his property. He must not break in. (Except in the unlikely event of the invaders leaving the place unoccupied for a short time; if they make this mistake, the owner can smash his way in—he does not commit the offence of using violence to enter, because no one is inside who is opposing his entry; and he does not commit criminal damage, because it is his own property.)

If on the other hand the ally is fighting on, as he is entitled to, or even if he is continuing to demand that the invaders retreat, then if they use force against him they are guilty of assaulting him, and the owner who perceives this happening may use reasonable force to re-enter in order to protect his ally from attack. The section denies that the owner has lawful authority to enter as owner, but does not deny that he or any one else has lawful authority to enter to prevent an offence being committed inside. It is true that s. 6 (4) (*b*) says that "it is immaterial . . . whether the entry which the violence is intended to secure is for the purpose of acquiring possession of the premises or for any other purpose"; this provision affects the forcible gate-crasher who has no lawful authority to enter, but it should not affect the owner or police officer who is entering in pursuance of a power given to him otherwise than in virtue of ownership of the building, namely, for the purpose of defending another person and of preventing the continuation of offences. He therefore has "lawful authority" to enter. Having got back in, he may himself renew the struggle against the intruders.[13]

The same argument applies if the owner enters in order to prevent any other crime (e.g. the abstraction of electricity, if the trespassers are burning the lights at night).

Another possible gap may be seen in the protection apparently given by section 6 to illegal entrants. At common law the owner of chattels may recapt (retake) them from one who is in unlawful possession of them. It has accordingly been suggested[14] that the displaced owner can use reasonable force to enter his own building to recapt his private papers or any other article that are being unlawfully detained from him; and this right to enter (it may be argued) is not excluded by subsection (2). If the owner enters to recapt, having got his article he may again turn round to expel the intruders. Only invaders in an empty building are safe from an argument along these lines. The argument, if accepted, may reduce subsection (2) to a virtual nullity, but if so it will be a well deserved fate.

Where are the police all this time? Can't they, if they are willing to help, join in on the side of the owner? The answer is yes if (but only if) the intruders have committed an offence for which they can be arrested, or are committing an offence that the police are entitled to put a stop to, or if the police are acting at the request of the owner to assist him in recapting a chattel under the argument set out above. The police are most likely to act if the intruders used violence to gain entry and so offended against the section; the police can arrest them for the offence, and can use force to enter in order to do this.CLA 1967 s.2(6); CLA 1977 s. 11.

When the intruders are arrested the place is naturally cleared.

---

[13] Prichard 150–151 proposes a variation of this argument. The owner, inside his premises, is being attacked by intruders who have already entered. He summons reinforcements from outside, but their entry is opposed by the intruders. The owner's friends do not violate s. 6 in using violence to enter, because the owner's summons gives them lawful authority.

[14] See Prichard 63 ff. I am indebted to him for the elaboration of the general argument for the owner's right to re-enter.

If the intruders got in without violence, and are simply keeping the owner out, then they commit no offence merely by seizing and retaining possession. The owner cannot authorise the police to use violence on his behalf (except as his agent to recapt a chattel, if the owner himself has that right); nor have the police, in general, any other "lawful authority" to act. The owner can bring a civil action, but meanwhile the intruders may be vandalising his property, spreading filth upon it, or prying into the confidential papers in his office. It is true that, as already said, if the police reasonably suspect the commission of an arrestable offence like criminal damage, or abstracting electricity, they may use force to enter in order to make an arrest for that. But, in the case of damage, if there are many trespassers it may not be possible to establish that the damage was caused by any particular one of them, in which case no arrest can lawfully be made unless it can be inferred from the circumstances that all the trespassers had a common purpose to cause such damage.

We now come to the exception for the displaced residential occupier. First of all, notice that the prohibition of violent entry by the owner applies even where squatters occupy a house or flat, if the place was uninhabited because it was for sale or to let, or because it was a holiday home not occupied at the time. So if you find your seaside bungalow (which you have left uninhabited since its last letting) occupied by squatters you must leave them respectfully there until you have taken the right steps. For dwellings of this type the Act is a "squatters' charter," enabling them to live in the house with little fear of being evicted for a period of time dependent on the state of congestion of the local county court and the financial ability of the owner to undertake litigation.

However, no offence is committed if the person who re-enters lived in the dwelling, from which he has been excluded by someone who entered as a trespasser. Such a "displaced residential occupier" is allowed to exercise self-help. Reverting to the seaside bungalow, if the owner was the last resident in it, he would probably be taken to be still occupying it as a residence even during the winter when it is shut up, so he will be a DRO if it is taken over by trespassers in his absence. The force he uses must of course be reasonable, in accordance with principles already studied (see particularly § 23.8).

Section 7 of the Act gives further protection in respect of residential premises. It applies, within certain limits, whenever such premises have been invaded, whether the invasion was accompanied by violence or not. Subsection (1):

> "Subject to the following provisions of this section, any person who is on any premises as a trespasser after having entered as such is guilty of an offence if he fails to leave those premises on being required to do so by or on behalf of—
>
> (*a*) a displaced residential occupier of the premises; or
>
> (*b*) an individual who is a protected intending occupier of the premises by virtue of subs. (2) or subs. (4) below."

The latter expression ("protected intending occupier") is elaborately defined in the Act; roughly, it means a purchaser or a person let in by the local authority, the Housing Corporation or a housing association, bearing written evidence of his claim.[15]

With extraordinary pusillanimity, the section is confined to residential premises. Subsection (7):

> "In any proceedings for an offence under subs. (1) above it shall be a defence for the accused to prove—

---

[15] For the extraordinary problems created by the Act in its ill-considered definition of "protected intending occupier" see [1978] CLJ 11. Note that the PIO is introduced into the legislation only to enable him to activate s.7. He is still not entitled to use force to enter to expel the intruders; that is forbidden by s.6.

(*a*) that the premises in question are or form part of premises used mainly for non-residential purposes; and
(*b*) that he was not on any part of the premises used wholly or mainly for residential purposes."

This definition suited the trade unions and ensured that there would be no political opposition to the measure. It means that workpeople who bar the factory gates against their employer cannot be peremptorily required to leave under section 7, whereas the employer, if he tries to evict them, is liable to be charged under section 6. Similarly, a firm that finds its offices occupied by demonstrators who are busy examining its files is given no protection by section 7, while the demonstrators are again protected by section 6. Even if the premises are residential and the owner is excluded from them, the offence under section 7 is not committed if the owner was not in residence at the time of the invasion. He may, for example, have vacated the house because he was going to let or sell it; here the offence is not committed unless (in the case of a private owner) he has actually sold it,[16] in which case the buyer is a "protected intending occupier." If a prospective buyer is put off by the fact that the house is now in the hands of squatters, and so refuses to buy it, or if the owner has granted a periodic tenancy of it instead of selling it, the trespassers will be immune from the criminal law however long they remain, unless they commit some other offence.

Again, section 7 does not apply to the ordinary trespasser (even one on residential premises) if the owner is not excluded, since such an owner is not a DRO or PIO.[17] Nor does the section apply to a trespasser if, although the owner is excluded, the trespasser did not enter as a trespasser but only became one after entry. So if a man's guest (or son, or mistress) locks him out of his own house, the Act provides him with no remedy. He is not a DRO (because he has not been excluded by someone who entered as a trespasser), and he cannot make a notification under section 7 (because, again, the trespasser did not enter as such).[18]

The advantage of section 7, where it operates, is that, by creating an offence (although only a summary offence) it increases the likelihood of the police bestirring themselves, since they are given power of arrest.[19] If they exercise the power the owner is likely to get his property back without court action. Where the section does not apply the police may quite possibly take no interest in the affair, even to help a bailiff to execute a court order for possession.

Such is the attempt made by the legislature to reconcile the owner's claim with the preservation of the peace. All in all it is of more interest as a social document evidencing the nervelessness of government in the face of social unrest, and political sympathy for illegal action, than as a rational piece of legislation. The law still does not concede any "rights" to squatters, but it leaves them largely free from penal control. Squatters are sometimes in a miserable plight, rendered homeless by a combination of personal misfortune and the inept housing policies of central and local governments. But it is the wrong answer to allow either squatters or demonstrators to take over other people's property with freedom from criminal sanctions. The law enables the owner to get them out in a few days (if he is lucky) by court order, but this will cost him money, and it is hard to see why the police should not be given a general permission to assist the owner in the first place.

SUMMARY

The Criminal Damage Act 1971 creates three offences which may be called simple damage, dangerous damage and arson. § .1

Simple damage involves destroying or damaging something. A thing may be § .2

---

[16] Or granted a lease of it for at least 21 years.

[17] See the definition in s.12(3).

[18] So if a wife locks her husband out he cannot use violence to get back in, even though the dispute is essentially a domestic matter; and a charge against him under s.6 does not require the consent of the DPP, as a charge of theft or damage would. For evidentiary difficulties see 142 JPN 77.

[19] Ss.7(11),11.

damaged by having something added to it, or by being taken to pieces, or, probably, in the case of an animal, by being allowed to escape (or this may be constructive destruction).

The damage or destruction must be in respect of property. Damaging land or a building is included, but not damaging wild mushrooms or the flowers, fruit or foliage of any wild plant. § .3

The property must belong to another; but the offence may be committed in respect of property in the custody of another, or by a person who has custody of the property of another. § .4

The mental element is intention or recklessness. Probably the doctrine of transferred intention can be applied. § .5

The act must be done without lawful excuse. This is defined to include belief in consent (or that consent would be given if the circumstances were known), and belief that property was in immediate need of protection and that the means adopted were reasonable. In the latter case, the act must be done "in order to protect property." The provision covers not only the protection of physical property but the protection of rights in property. The defendant's belief that the property belonged to him could negative *mens rea*, even if it involved a mistake of civil law. Damaging property in order to protect the person is left to the general category of "lawful excuse." § .6

In dangerous damage the property may belong to the defendant, and the defendant must intend to endanger life or be reckless as to this. The statutory partial definition of "lawful excuse" is omitted. § .7

There are two forms of arson, namely where either simple damage or dangerous damage is committed by fire. Dangerous arson may be committed in respect of one's own property. It seems that an intention to commit damage otherwise than by arson cannot be transferred so that it becomes an intention to commit arson. For sentencing reasons, charges for dangerous damage or arson should charge intention and recklessness in separate counts. There is a parallel offence for explosives under the Explosive Substances Act. § .8

The Criminal Damage Act contains an offence of using a threat to cause criminal damage. § .9

It is an offence to have custody of anything intending to use it, or to cause or permit another to use it, to do criminal damage. Possessing an explosive can be an offence under the Explosive Substances Act. § .10

Generally, trespass to land is not a crime, but there are some statutory exceptions. § .11

The most serious form of trespass is a trespassory entry into a building. As with other forms, the victim is generally left to his civil remedy. But under the Criminal Law Act 1977 s. 6 it is a summary offence for a person to use or threaten violence (to person or property) to secure entry to a building (or land associated with a building) if he knows that there is someone inside who is opposed to the entry. The section is of little assistance to lawful occupiers, but it can be invoked against them if they use violence to re-enter after being evicted (even though unlawfully). This is because the Act provides that an interest in premises is not a lawful authority for entering. However, the owner may fight until he is evicted; and even after eviction he may, it is assumed, forcibly re-enter to make a lawful arrest, to prevent a crime, or to recapt a chattel; having entered, he may proceed to turn out the intruders. Police may arrest for the offence of using violence to enter. The offence does not apply to the displaced residential occupier, who is allowed to exercise self-help. Section 7 gives further protection in respect of residential premises; a trespasser on such premises commits an offence if he fails to leave on request by a DRO or protected intending occupier, both these expressions being carefully defined, the definition of the PIO being narrow. Here again the police can arrest. § .12

Part Six

REGULATORY OFFENCES

CHAPTER 42

STRICT LIABILITY

It must needs be that offences come; but woe to that man by whom the offence cometh!

St Matthew 18 : 7

§ 42.1. THE NOTION OF STRICT LIABILITY

IN legal speech an offence of absolute or strict liability means one in which some element does not require proof of fault. As we have seen, an offence may carry strict liability in one respect but not in all.[1]

An unsophisticated lawgiver tends to word offences in absolute terms, but this does not necessarily mean that he wishes them to be construed absolutely. Take the commandment "Thou shalt not kill." Whatever this meant three thousand years ago, the meaning it now conveys to us is that we must not kill intentionally or recklessly, or possibly negligently. An accidental killing is not a breach of it, because no one can help pure accidents.

Unfortunately, there is no fixed rule of interpretation in respect of edicts absolute in their terms. Generally the courts read them straight, so that people who are without fault are convicted. Occasionally, however, the crime (particularly if it is of a grave kind) will be taken to require *mens rea*. In the absence of rule, the legislative and policy question is decided as it arises, uncertainly and expensively, not by our elected legislators but by a few lawyers arguing on supposedly legal grounds before a few judges.

A far better solution of the problem would be to lay down the kind of fault generally required for penal liability, this requirement being implied by law where the particular offence does not specify that a particular kind of fault is required nor yet that no fault is required. This solution could give effect to generally accepted principles of justice. It would give certainty to the law, and would often save the legislature (whether Parliament or Government departments) the complications of drafting involved in specifying required fault elements.

There should be a fixed rule, granted, but is there any need to have a requirement of fault for minor offences? If it helps to repress offences to punish people although they are not proved to have been at fault, why not do so?

Too high a price may be paid for full "efficiency" in the criminal process. Strict liability is apt to create a burning sense of grievance and a loss of confidence in the administration of the law.

---

[1] § 6.11.

Aren't you overstating the position? It would take up too much time if magistrates' courts had to go into the question of fault on minor charges. Besides, one may shrewdly suspect that the defendant has been negligent even though this cannot be proved.

Magistrates must go into the question of fault, even on a charge involving strict liability, if the defendant wants to show that he was not at fault in order to mitigate punishment.

There are, it is true, some types of case, though they are few, where proof of negligence would in practice be impossible, even though negligence is very likely. When driving at night one sees quite a number of vehicles running on only one sidelight, or with tail lamps extinguished; many of these drivers may have been negligent in maintaining their vehicles, but the possibility cannot be excluded that some of the lamps will have only just burnt out. A fixed penalty of minor amount can be justified on the ground that separating the sheep from the goats would be impossible; but even in this type of case liability is best imposed merely by way of a "ticket" fine.

It isn't only a question of magistrates' time. Where offences are very numerous a requirement that the prosecutor should prove fault would impose a burden upon the resources of law-enforcement out of proportion to the end to be achieved. It might mean that the police, or inspectors of health and safety at work, or traffic examiners, or trading standards officers, would have to possess a larger investigative staff than they do now.

This is an argument used by the enforcing officers; but it needs to be viewed with suspicion, particularly since every professional class tends to aggrandise itself. It is always pleasanter to be uncontrolled. But the law enforcers cannot charge every minor offence. They have to be selective, and naturally charge offences when they believe the offender has been at fault. If the prosecutor must consider evidence of negligence before instituting proceedings, why should he not produce the evidence for the consideration of the court?

There is an important distinction between civil and criminal law in relation to strict liability. The law of tort is concerned with cases where a loss or damage has occurred and the question is who should bear it. Occasionally it is thought right that the burden should be placed on the shoulders of a person, usually an entrepreneur of some kind, who is made to act as a sort of compulsory insurer of the public against risk—e.g. someone who brings a collection of dangerous things on his land. The object of the criminal law, on the other hand, is to secure compliance with rules of behaviour, primarily through the threat of punishment if they are broken; and it seems logically to follow that punishment should not be imposed upon a person who has no criminal mind, at any rate if he is not even negligent, unless there are compelling administrative reasons for excluding the trial of fault in very trivial cases. Criminal punishment is not a transfer of a loss that has already occurred: it is an evil deliberately created by the law for imposition upon offenders, and normally has no rational foundation (it may be argued) if the offence could not have been avoided.

Early law, which was briefly discussed in § 3.1, recognised something very near to absolute criminal responsibility. Its disappearance or submergence was due to the influence of the Church and the increasing awareness of moral ideas. By the first half of the 19th century one could say that crime required not merely fault in general but some kind of *mens rea*. (There were exceptions, which still, very largely, survive: a few crimes, such as manslaughter, can be committed by negligence without a positive wrongful mental state, and five other crimes carry strict liability in some respects.[2]) Even when Parliament created a new offence without inserting an express requirement of *mens rea*, the courts generally held that the offence could be committed only by one who knew the relevant facts, since the requirement of *mens rea* was, in the words of Cockburn CJ, "the foundation of all criminal justice."[3] "Acts of Parliament," said Coke CJ "are to be so construed as no man that is innocent, or free from injury or wrong, be by a literal construction punished or endamaged."[4]

This beautiful sentiment, reaffirmed in *Tolson* in 1889,[5] was already in doubt towards the close of the century, when the courts began to edge away from the *mens rea* doctrine. Parliament had commenced a trickle of social legislation which has since become a flood. This protects consumers from sharp practices, safeguards public health and safety, gives special protection to workpeople, tenants, and others deemed to be in need of it, and regulates economic activities in a myriad ways. The regular practice in such legislation is to state the prohibited act without bothering to specify a fault element. In these circumstances, the mind of Parliament might be read in either of two ways. It might be assumed that Parliament intended to create strict liability; and this assumption is confirmed by the fact that when the courts interpret the legislation in this way, Parliament (which in effect means the Government) frequently leaves the Act unamended. Or it might be assumed that Parliament meant the courts to interpret the statute in the light of general principles of law, including a requirement of *mens rea*, and this assumption is in turn confirmed by the fact that on the rare occasions when the courts do this Parliament never makes the legislation more severe, while when the courts fail to do it Parliament frequently amends the legislation to allow a defence of absence of knowledge or absence of negligence. The second assumption would have the practical advantage of leaving the point for Parliament to clarify, thus clearing the judges of the reproach that they have themselves abandoned a principle of justice.[6] Moreover, if the courts insisted upon a requirement of fault this would almost certainly influence Parliament in the same direction, while the ready concession of liability without fault by the judges naturally has the effect of devaluing the principle of justice.

As things have worked out, it is a fairly regular practice, on the part of both legislature and judges, to exclude or qualify a requirement of *mens rea* for statutory offences. Sometimes it is abandoned entirely, as in *Larsonneur*.[7] Usually a mental element is partly retained in the statutory

---

[2] These five, not treated at large in this book, have been said to be exceptions to the general requirement of *mens rea* at common law; but how far this is true has never been altogether clear. *Blasphemy* and *obscenity* are of strict liability in respect of the judgment of what is blasphemous or obscene, but the judgment is very close to being a value-judgment rather than a question of fact. See § 6.11. It is arguable that *criminal libel* requires *mens rea*, except in respect of the judgment of what is defamatory, and except also that an employer is attributively liable for a publication by his employee. See Smith and Hogan, 4th edn 795. Libel has been turned by statute into a crime of negligence in some cases. *Contempt of court* was perhaps a crime of strict liability in certain respects at common law (Smith and Hogan, 744–745); this rule is affirmed, with modifications, in the Contempt of Court Act 1981 ss. 1–7; see Bailey in 45 MLR 304; Lowe in 131 NLJ 1167; Welsh, *ibid.* 1270; Miller in [1982] Crim.LR 71. *Public nuisance* can apparently be committed by negligence, and is a crime of strict liability to the extent that it carries attributive liability, which it does in at least some cases (Smith and Hogan 767–768); but it has lost much of its importance because indictments are now uncommon. The common law crime has been replaced by statutory offences, which continue strict liability.

[3] *Sleep* (1861) 8 Cox at 477.

[4] Quoted in *Margate Pier Co.* v. *Hannam* (1819) 3 B & Ald. at 270, 106 ER at 663.

[5] § 6.7 at n. 1.

[6] The Law Commission, in the Draft Bill annexed to its *Report on the Mental Element in Crime*, clause 5 (Law Com. No 89), proposed that offences should require intention, knowledge or recklessness unless the legislation made a contrary intention clear. Unfortunately the Commission proposed that this measure should apply only to Acts passed subsequently. See the criticism by Hogan in [1978] Crim.LR 596. The draft Bill could well have been made retrospective if it had excepted (1) offences not punishable by imprisonment on first conviction and not expressly or impliedly requiring a mental element, which should in future carry a no-negligence defence, and (2) a scheduled list of other offences, which should either be defined with a specified mental element or carry a no-negligence defence.

[7] § 7.6 at n. 4.

offence, but it may be abandoned in respect of some element where *mens rea* would be difficult to prove. When the legislature, in creating a minor offence of a regulatory character, has not made express reference to a mental element (as by using the word "wilfully" or "knowingly"), the courts generally take the view that the statute is to be read literally in some respect, thus creating strict liability. Even when statutes create serious crimes and explicitly require a mental element, the courts may attach the mental element to something less than the full crime, unless the statutory words are strong enough to prevent this: in other words they may create crimes of half *mens rea*.[8]

Perhaps it was this development that was in Gilbert's mind when he wrote a celebrated parody of judicial reasoning. To a defence that the accused persons had no idea and knew nothing about it and were not there, the Mikado replies;

> "That's the pathetic part of it. Unfortunately, the fool of an Act says 'Compassing the death of the heir apparent.' There's not a word about a mistake, or not knowing, or having no notion, or not being there. There should be, of course, but there isn't. That's the slovenly way in which these Acts are always drawn."

Gilbert had been called to the Bar, and *The Mikado* was first performed in 1885, 10 years after the severe decision in *Prince*, which was discussed earlier.[9]

Granted that a mental element should be required for grave crimes, aren't the courts justified in regarding it as inappropriate to minor offences? Offences like selling impure milk are offences of negligence, not of knowledge.

You are right in saying that there should be a larger place for negligence in relation to minor offences than the courts allow as a matter of common law. In practice they assume that there is nothing between a requirement of *mens rea* and strict liability: every offence must fall into one class or the other unless legislation has expressly introduced a question of negligence. The judges reason thus: the statute does not expressly require a mental element; to find the requirement by implication would narrow the offence too much; therefore it is an absolute offence (an offence of strict liability); therefore no fault is required. But the reasoning is fallacious. One does not establish that negligence is not required by establishing that *mens rea* is not required.

Anyway, one can surely say that in practice a defendant who is held to be strictly liable will have been at least negligent.

Often, but not necessarily so. Consider (to take a single illustration) the case of *Parker* v. *Alder*.[10]

---

[8] Examples are *Mowatt* § 9.3 at n. 7, the dictum in *Phekoo* § 6.2 at n. 19, and *Prince* § 9.12 at n. 12 (though the statute in the last case did not explicitly require a mental element).

[9] See last note.

[10] [1899] 1 QB 20; cp. *Watson* v. *Coupland* [1945] 1 All ER 217. The effect of the decision in *Parker* v. *Alder* is reinforced by the Food and Drugs Act 1955 s. 32 (6).

A farmer (Alder) despatched milk by rail to a purchaser. Some unknown person meddled with the churns, and added water, presumably after abstracting some milk. Alder was convicted of selling an article of food not of the nature, substance and quality demanded, since it was held that the property in the milk did not pass until it reached its destination, and so the milk was adulterated at the point of sale.

This case shows the great difference between an absolute offence and an offence of negligence. To make a man responsible for negligence the prosecution must point to some feature of his conduct that was negligent; they must suggest some step that he could reasonably have taken which would have avoided the evil result. If the defendant is convicted he will know that in similar circumstances in future he can avoid legal proceedings by taking the step thus pointed out to him. But the only certain way for the suppliers of milk to avoid the fine imposed upon Alder would be to give up supplying milk. They might be able to minimise the risk if they could put tamper-proof locks on milk churns. However, a suggestion like this would invite consideration of the question whether such an expenditure was worthwhile, having regard to the smallness of the risk and the very small social harm resulting from the watering down of a single churn of milk. In commercial matters the taking of precautions costs money, and if perfection were really insisted upon the cost of the product would rise substantially, without compensating advantage to the consumer.

It is, in a way, only a minor evil that a farmer should be made to pay a fine of a few pounds, which he can well afford, for the adulteration of milk, even though he could not help it.[11] However, if this is an evil it has the characteristic of being an unnecessary one, since there is generally no compelling need to have strict liability in crime. Careless breaches of regulatory offences abound, and prosecutions for these are usually sufficient to be a standing warning to people to obey the law. Little purpose is served by adding to the large numbers of truly guilty defendants the small number of persons who are morally innocent. The social argument is all the other way. For whereas natural evils can often be accepted as part of the price of living, a man-made evil may be strongly and even bitterly resented because it is felt to be unjust.

A fine imposed upon a business concern irrespective of fault is not so much an affront as is a fine imposed upon an individual. But even if the defendant is a trading concern, the result of a rule disregarding fault may be that business men come to regard fines as part of their overhead costs, as unavoidable and unpredictable as the English weather. The attitude of indifference thus engendered towards the criminal process through inflation of the law may well spread to other offences, where an element of fault is present. Often it is cheaper to run the risk of an occasional small fine than to make the alterations in business arrangements necessary to avoid it. If the trader becomes habituated to the atmosphere of the criminal court, and is taught to regard the criminal process as something that has no connection with responsibility and fault, he may adopt a cynical and self-interested attitude on many of the questions to which legal regulations are directed. The ultimate result may actually be a decrease in the preventive effect of the law.[12]

---

[11] The injustice may sometimes be alleviated if the faultless defendant is allowed a civil action to recover his fine and costs from a person who was at fault. Whether this is permissible is doubtful; see Wasik in [1982] Crim.LR 567. But such an action, even if allowable and practicable, would not salve the grievance of being unjustly convicted.

[12] For an extended discussion see Sanford H Kadish in 30 U of Chicago LRev. 440–444.

But come back to the milk churns. How do you know that Alder was telling the truth when he said that he put the milk on rail in a pure state? Perhaps he had adulterated it himself. Strict liability prevents people getting away with dishonest defences.

- It was found by the magistrate as a fact that the milk was pure when put on rail.
- If dishonest defences are thought to be a problem, this could be eased by shifting the burden of proof. The defendant need not be convicted if he positively proves that he is not at fault. Alternatively, it may be enough to put an evidential burden on the defendant.
- Strict liability exempts the prosecution from having to prove fault, but not from having to prove the act done in breach of statute. Suppose that in *Parker* v. *Alder* the buyer had transferred the milk from Alder's churns to his own, and had only later discovered water in it. Alder asserts that the milk in his churns was pure, and that the adulteration must have occurred after the transfer. The buyer says that the adulteration did not occur after the transfer, so it must have been Alder's fault. In these circumstances the burden would be on the prosecution to show that Alder had violated the statute by supplying watered milk, and he would be entitled to the benefit of a doubt. So the law does not say that, on a charge of an offence of strict liability, the defendant's word is always to be disregarded.
- It seems improbable that the deterrent effect of the law would be weakened greatly or at all if the occasional defendant escaped with a dishonest defence. He would be very unlikely to get away with it often.

We must now say something more on the history of the subject. The way in which strict liability has evolved may be illustrated by the construction of the Food and Drugs Acts which first came on to the statute book in the 19th century and are now represented by the Food and Drugs Act 1955. Section 2 makes it an offence to sell to the prejudice of the purchaser any food that is not of the nature, substance or quality demanded. (It was under the predecessor of this section that Alder was convicted.)[13] The purchaser is deemed to demand an article as it is expressly or impliedly represented by the seller to be,[14] and sellers are taken to represent impliedly that their wares are pure. So the offence is committed if, for example, a nail is found in a bun, a mouse in a meat roll, or water in milk, or if a sausage is deficient in meat content. As we have just seen, the offence is held not to require *mens rea* or negligence (subject to statutory exceptions which we are leaving aside for the moment[15]). The earlier decisions were rested upon a critical examination of the words of the statute and a comparison of one section with another, leading to the conclusion that Parliament must have intended to dispense with *mens rea* for the particular offence although there were no express words in the

[13] Drugs now have their own provision in the Medicines Act 1968 s. 64.

[14] *Per* Lord Diplock in *Smedleys Ltd* v. *Breed* [1974] AC at 857–858.

[15] See Chap. 44. In these cases the burden of proof is placed on the defendant to show that he was not at fault.

statute to that effect. Later the judges became bolder, and placed their decisions not on the language of the statute but on broad social grounds, saying that the purpose of the legislation would be defeated if it were held necessary for the prosecution to prove *mens rea*. (No one has suggested that the law of theft or assault is "defeated" by this necessity, and anyway the question is whether the prosecution should not at least have to prove negligence.)

§ 42.2. EXTENSION OF THE DOCTRINE

Once the notion of justice had been jettisoned in favour of *raison d'État*, strict liability could readily be extended to penal legislation in general, at any rate when the offence was not of a particularly serious character. So it was read into Acts relating to the sale of intoxicants, Acts governing weights and measures, Acts regulating the relation of employer and employee (such as hours of work and rates of pay), various provisions of the Road Traffic Acts,[1] and other legislation too diverse to been enumerated.

The theory that strict liability results from the will of Parliament rather than the predilection of the judges rings particularly hollow when one discovers instances of strict liability being construed even where the legislature has used words indicating a requirement of dishonesty or other fault.

Suppose that you and I were arguing, and I told you that your conclusion was false. This might not be impolite, because the word "false" in that context would simply mean "not true." But if I told you that you were making false statements, you would understandably regard my words as offensive, because in that context the word "false" would generally carry a charge of lying. To avoid misunderstanding one must say that one's opponent is "mistaken," not that he is uttering falsities. Therefore, it might be thought that an Act of Parliament penalising the making of a "false" statement would be construed in favour of the defendant as impliedly requiring *mens rea*—knowledge that the statement is false, or recklessness whether it is true or false. But it has been held that a number of offences worded in this way carry strict liability.[2]

A regulation requiring the brakes of a vehicle to be "maintained" in good and efficient working order might be thought to be satisfied if there has in fact been proper maintenance. Not a bit of it: however good your maintenance is, if your brakes fail, even quite unforeseeably, you will be liable under the regulation.[3] This construction makes the regulation equivalent to one requiring the brakes at all times to *be* in good and efficient order. But if the legislature had meant that, why did it refer to maintenance?[4]

A statute requires a bankrupt to give a satisfactory explanation of the manner in which a loss occurred. It is held that he commits an offence even if he uses all due diligence to give an explanation, if the explanation is not satisfactory.[5] In other words, the bankrupt is legally obliged to do more than can reasonably be expected of him!

---

[1] § 14.7.

[2] E.g. *Laird* v. *Dobell* [1906] 1 KB 131; *Cummerson* [1968] 2 QB 534. But, as regards the second decision, Parliament intervened and added the word "knowingly" to the offence: RTA 1972 s. 170. Whatever view may be taken of these cases in general, the interpretation is reasonable where (as in the case of the Trade Descriptions Act) a prohibition of making a false statement is accompanied by a defence of no negligence; here the word "false" obviously carries an objective meaning, and applies to honest false statements: see e.g. *Taylor* v. *Smith* [1974] RTR 190, Crim.LR 200.

[3] *Hawkins* v. *Holmes* [1974] RTR 436, Crim.LR 370.

[4] But see the civil case of *Haydon* v. *Kent CC* [1978] QB 343, where a statutory duty to maintain a highway was held to involve the question of negligence.

[5] *Salter* [1968] 2 QB 793.

The Construction and Use Regulations require a load to be so secured that danger is not "likely to be caused." Held, that if a load falls owing to a defect in the pallet on which it stands, without the negligence of the owner, the owner is liable; the pallet being defective, danger is "likely to be caused" by it, even though no one could have perceived the danger.[6] This decision shows a misunderstanding of the nature of likelihood. Deterministically speaking, everything that happens is bound to happen. One can speak of the mere possibility, or likelihood, of a consequence only from the standpoint of the imperfect knowledge of some observer. A supernatural observer who can look into solid objects and has a complete knowledge of the properties of matter may foresee the collapse of the pallet not as a likelihood but as a certainty, but the regulations self-evidently do not refer to such an observer.

Even where a statute expressly requires *mens rea*, the courts may cut down the requirement to the minimum that grammar allows. So where the offence was *knowingly* selling intoxicating liquor to a child under 14, "excepting such intoxicating liquors as are sold in corked and sealed vessels," the court thought it was not obliged to read the requirement of knowledge as applying to the words of exception. Naturally, therefore, it did not so read it. The seller was held to commit the offence of knowingly selling although he did not know that the bottle was uncorked and unsealed.[7]

A statutory requirement of knowledge is blatantly disregarded in the "licensee" cases, to be studied later. The holder of a liquor licence commits various offences if he knowingly permits certain acts. It is held that he commits these offences even though he does not knowingly permit the acts, if his delegate does so.[8]

§ 42.3. PRINCIPLES OF CONSTRUCTION

In general, the authorities on strict liability are so conflicting that it is impossible to abstract any coherent principle on when this form of liability arises and when it does not. A particular proposition affirming strict liability can almost always be matched by its contradictory affirming fault liability. The result is that in the absence of express words in the statute judges can generally attach any fault element to it that they please, or refuse to attach any fault element; and they can always find some apparent authority or argument for what they propose to do. Take *Reynolds* v. *G H Austin & Sons Ltd.*[1]

> The defendant company operated motor coaches, but were allowed to carry private parties only, not members of the public in general. A women's guild organised an outing, and the company agreed to provide a coach. The organiser of the outing, without the knowledge of the company, advertised the outing to the public, and some members of the public were therefore included in it. The result was that this particular use of the coach was not covered by the company's licence. The company was charged with the statutory offence of using a vehicle without a road service licence. In view of the many authorities on strict liability the prosecution doubtless thought they had an open and shut case, but the Divisional Court directed an acquittal. Lord Goddard CJ said: "This is not to throw any doubt on the well established principle that if there is an absolute prohibition and the prohibited act is done a penalty is incurred, but hitherto that doctrine has never been applied to a case where the prohibited act was

---

[6] *Cornish* v. *Ferry Masters Ltd.* [1975] RTR 292, Crim.LR 241; cp. *Dent* v. *Coleman* [1977] Crim.LR 753. *Cornish's* case is difficult to reconcile with *Gosney* [1971] 2 QB 674, where it was held that the offence of dangerous driving (now abolished) implied a requirement of negligence.

[7] *Brooks* v. *Mason* [1902] 2 KB 743; but see 2 Leg.Stud. 239–240. The statute in question is now repealed.

[8] § 43.3.

[1] [1951] 2 KB 135. The earlier decision in *Strutt* v. *Clift* [1911] 1 KB 1 is irreconcilable with *Reynolds* v. *Austin* on principle, and the latter is greatly preferable.

not that of the defendant, but of some person over whom he had no control and for whom he had no responsibility."

I think that was an untenable reason. The prohibited act was not advertising the outing to the public; it was using a vehicle without a road service licence, which the company did.

Yes, it was a Homeric nod on Lord Goddard's part, I fear. There was indeed an act by another person, but, as you say, the act charged was that of the defendant company.

Another criticism is that Lord Goddard overlooked *Parker* v. *Alder* (§ .1), and the two decisions stand in opposition to each other. Austin & Sons had committed the act forbidden by statute; they had used a vehicle without having the proper licence covering the use. In the same way, Alder had committed the forbidden act; he had sold goods not of the nature, substance or quality demanded. In both cases no breach would have taken place but for the unauthorised act of another person who was not the defendant's employee. If this was an excuse for Austin & Sons it should have been an excuse for Alder.

A distinction between the two cases is that the actual offender in *Alder* was unknown and presumably unascertainable, whereas the actual offender in *Austin & Sons* was known or traceable. But this fact should have made no difference to the liability of the defendant.

There are other cases in which the court has intimated that although the defendant was in general strictly liable, he might perhaps escape liability by showing that the default occurred by the act of a third party.[2] Half a loaf is proverbially better than no bread, but all the same the restriction of a no-fault defence to cases where there has been an act of a third party is illogical. As J C Smith has commented:

> "If the event is unforeseeable, the defendant is no more responsible for its occurrence when it is brought about by some natural phenomenon than when it is brought about by the intervention of a third party. The only explanation would seem to be that there is an assumption [by the courts] that *someone* must be responsible—the intervening third party if there is one, the defendant if there is not."[3]

The judges frequently claim that the absence of the word "knowingly" in a statute is evidence that Parliament meant the offence to carry strict liability, but this is obviously a *non sequitur*. Parliament may have left out "knowingly" because it was not bothering itself about the fault element (and sometimes this is held to be the case[4]); or Parliament may have meant that the offence can be committed knowingly or recklessly; or it may have meant that the offence can be committed negligently. To say: "This offence does not require knowledge; therefore it is of absolute liability; therefore it does not require negligence" exhibits the fallacy of ambiguous middle. It is high time that the judges made up their minds upon what absolute or strict liability means.

As another example of contradiction: in *Harding* v. *Price*[5] it was held that a driver could not be convicted under statute of failing to stop after an

---

[2] *Alphacell* v. *Woodward* § .4 at n. 11; *Strowger* v. *John* [1974] RTR 124; cp. *per* Parker J in *James & Son Ltd* v. *Smee* [1955] 1 QB at 91.

[3] [1974] Crim.LR 124.

[4] See Devlin J's celebrated statement (or rather, alas, over-statement) that "all that the word 'knowingly' does is to say expressly what is normally implied" (*Roper* v. *Taylor's Central Garage* [1951] 2 TLR at 288; see Smith and Hogan, 4th edn 82–83).

[5] [1948] 1 KB 695; principle applied in *Hampson* v. *Powell* [1970] 1 All ER 929; *Bentley* v. *Dickinson* [1983] Crim.LR 403.

accident if he was not aware of the accident. This might suggest the proposition that offences of omission depend on the defendant having knowledge of the facts that create the duty to act. Until one knows the facts one is not galvanised into action. But, like *Reynolds* v. *Austin, Harding* v. *Price* represents only a brief lucid internal in an irrational part of the law. Other offences of omission have been interpreted to involve no consideration of justice.

> The parents of a girl who played truant from school were held guilty of an offence under the Education Act although they had no knowledge of her absences.[6]
>
> A company employed men to remove lagging from steel beams. The lagging contained asbestos, but the company did not know and had no reason to know this. It was held liable for failing to adopt the precautions enjoined by the Asbestos Regulations.[7] These regulations were intended to apply to firms working with asbestos. In the ordinary use of language the defendant company did not work with asbestos, and it did not know that asbestos was involved even in a minor degree.

Can't one say that strict liability applies to purely technical offences?

This idea is sometimes advanced, for example by Lord Reid in *Sweet* v. *Parsley*.[8] Strict liability is said to be imposed where the offence is the result of modern legislative policy and not of traditional morality, or in other words where it is a matter of *malum prohibitum* rather than *malum in se*. *Mala prohibita* are sometimes called "quasi-criminal offences"—offences that are regarded as "not criminal in any real sense, but acts which in the public interest are prohibited under penalty."[9] They are also called "public welfare offences" or "regulatory offences."

The difficulty with trying to establish a category of this kind is to say exactly what it means. All offences are, in a sense, public welfare offences, and all result from legal regulation. The so–called quasi-criminal offences are followed by the same procedure for prosecution as other offences. One might have thought it impossible for any judge to hold that an offence carrying a possible prison sentence is "not criminal in any real sense," but three law lords felt no incongruity in saying so.[10] People have in fact languished in jail for offending without proof of fault.

Perhaps the argument is that a person's reputation is not lowered because he is found guilty of a technical offence, and in such a case people are not interested to know whether he committed the offence knowingly or not. One can indeed make a broad distinction between technical offences and particularly disgraceful acts, but it is a matter of degree. If the principle is that strict liability applies only to technical offences, the courts have an idiosyncratic idea of what constitutes such an offence. Strict liability has been read by the courts into various offences that many people would regard as involving odium, including:

---

[6] *Crump* v. *Gilmore* (1969) 68 LGR 56, [1970] Crim.LR 28. See the editorial comment in the latter place.

[7] *Atkinson* v. *Sir Alfred McAlpine & Sons Ltd* [1974] Crim.LR 668, 16 Knight's Ind.R 220.

[8] [1970] AC at 839.

[9] Wright J, subsequently quoted on several occasions, e.g. by Lord Reid, last note, and in *Alphacell*, next note.

[10] Lords Dilhorne, Pearson and Salmon in *Alphacell* v. *Woodward* [1972] AC at 839G, 844C, 848E, where the offence was punishable by imprisonment when committed a second time by an individual. See, further, § .7.

- the sale of diseased meat;
- the unlawful possession of fictitious insurance stamps[11] or controlled drugs;
- making a false statement;
- sexual offences and abduction (in respect of the age of a young person)[12]
- a serious offence under the Firearms Act[13]; and
- obscenity.[14]

The truth is that judges have an open-ended list of reasons for imposing strict liability, and the fact that the offence is technical is only one of them. If the offence is technical, that will be a reason for dispensing with proof of fault[15]; if it is a serious offence involving odium, it must threaten "danger to the community," which will be another reason for reaching the same conclusion. In other words, following a familiar pattern of judicial thinking, the legal reasoning is biased in one direction: in favour of the prosecution. However, isolated instances of benevolent interpretation occur.[16]

If the doctrine of quasi-criminal offences is taken seriously, it should mean that these offences should be punishable only as "contraventions" by a small or moderate fine, enforced not by the police or (primarily) the courts but by enforcement agencies, with recourse to the courts only on appeal.[17] But this would need wide-ranging legislation, for which Parliament has no time. The best that can be hoped for is that, if a change of attitude can be brought about, gradual progress may be made towards this goal as new offences are created.

It has been pointed out before that strict liability does not apply to inchoate offences[18] or to accessoryship.[19] To be guilty as attempter or accessory, the defendant must know the relevant facts.

§ 42.4. USING AND CAUSING

Three verbs occurring in a subsection of the road traffic legislation have been the subject of much judicial labour. By a provision now in the Road Traffic Act 1972 s. 40 (5), offences are created in respect of the Motor Vehicles (Construction and Use) Regulations[1] in the following words.

> "A person who . . . (*b*) uses on a road a motor vehicle . . . which does not comply with any such regulations or causes or permits a vehicle to be so used, shall be guilty of an offence."[2]

Each of the three verbs "uses," "causes" and "permits" has been held to create a separate offence. "Uses" is understood to create strict liability, in the sense that one need not know the quality of the thing one uses.[3] So

---

[11] *Winkle* v. *Wiltshire* [1951] 1 KB 684.
[12] *Prince* § 9.12 at n. 12.
[13] *Howells* [1977] QB 614.
[14] § 6.11.
[15] As in *Strowger* v. *John* [1974] RTR 124.
[16] E.g. *Cain* v. *Campbell* [1978] Crim.LR 292 ("taking"). It is instructive to compare two cases of low authority on the Medicines Act 1968. On a charge under a section where the defendant could demonstrably not ensure that no violation could occur, a circuit judge applied the presumption that *mens rea* was required: *Pharmaceutical Society* v. *Harwood* [1981] Crim.LR 255. But on a charge before another judge under another section where a contravention could normally be avoided by due care, and where in fact the defendant could have avoided it in a way suggested by the court, it was ruled that the offence was absolute: *Pharmaceutical Society* v. *Logan* [1982] Crim.LR 443. Why did the judge in the second case not say merely that negligence was sufficient?
[17] See "Justice," *Breaking the Rules* (London 1980); § 1.2.
[18] § 17.4.
[19] § 15.12.

[1] At present the Regulations of 1978.
[2] The offence itself is specified in s. 177 and the Schedule.
[3] *Green* v. *Burnett* [1955] 1 QB 78 (defective brakes); *Gifford* v. *Whittaker* [1942] 1 KB 501 (insecure load). But see, as to disqualification, § 14.7 n. 15.

if a vehicle is used by an employee on his employer's business, and the vehicle does not comply with the regulations (though without fault on anybody's part), the prosecutor's clear course if he decides to bring a charge is to frame it against the employer (and also the employee, if he wishes) in terms of using the vehicle in breach of regulations.[4]

A prosecutor who charges the employer with having "permitted" the use will face a solid body of authority to the effect that an offence of "permitting," "suffering" or "allowing" anything can be committed only by one who knows the facts (or, perhaps, the possibility of the facts) that he is supposed to have permitted, suffered or allowed.[5] This verb, therefore, imports a requirement of *mens rea*.

The courts have placed a curiously restrictive interpretation upon the word "causes" in the Construction and Use Regulations. It is held that the verb in this context implies the giving of an order or direction to use the vehicle.

> When, therefore, a motor mechanic negligently carried out work on a van so that it contravened the regulations, his employer was held not liable when the owner subsequently drove the van on a road[6]; and it follows that the mechanic would not have been liable either.

Here the criminal liability is placed solely on the unfortunate van-owner, who takes his van on the road believing that it has been put in order by the repairer. The courts thus achieve a double failure of justice. On causal principles it is the negligent repairer who has caused the violation, since he caused the owner to believe that the work had been properly done; and on a rational view of the law the owner should be regarded as free from blame.

Suppose D tells his son to go to the railway station in D's car to pick up a parcel. Unknown to D the car has defective brakes. Does D cause the use of the car?

It has been held that a person does not cause the use of a vehicle by another person in breach of the regulations unless he knows the facts, and it does not matter whether the person he directs to drive the vehicle is his employee or not. "Causes" is interpreted to carry the same *mens rea* requirement as the word "permits."[7]

Strictly speaking, if the autonomy principle of *novus actus*[8] were applied it should be held

---

[4] See §§ 43.5, 6. Note that in some contexts the verb "use" does not bring in a subordinate employee: § 15.15 n. 14.

[5] For the only important exception, see § 6.4.

[6] *Shave* v. *Rosner* [1954] 2 QB 113.

[7] So held in *Ross Hillman Ltd* v. *Bond* [1974] QB 435, a notable rejection of strict liability. The actual decision was on the "causes or permits" section relating to the Construction and Use Regulations, but it was said that the same construction applied to statutes that only used "causes." Strangely, but perhaps fortunately, the decision in the *Alphacell* case, n. 11 below, was not considered.

The only exception is that a publican or other licensee who delegates to a manager in the way explained later (§ 43.3) can be convicted of causing his manager to commit an offence although he himself does not know the facts: see *Sopp* v. *Long* [1970] 1 QB 518 as interpreted in *Ross Hillman Ltd* v. *Bond*. This, as we shall see, results from the exceptional rules relating to licensees.

[8] § 16.9.

that a person does not commit an offence of "causing" a result if the causing is immediately by another free agent. The responsibility, if any, of the remote causer should be either as perpetrator when he comes within the statutory verb (as when he is held to "use" something[9]) or as accessory to the immediate causer, and liability as accessory should carry the usual requirement of knowledge.[10] So when an employee uses a vehicle in breach of the Construction and Use Regulations, the fault being his, a charge against the employer should be of using, not of causing the use. But it is understandable that the courts should overlook this technicality and convict the employer of an offence of causing where he too knows the facts.

A person who causes an event other than an act may be held to be strictly liable.

So in *Alphacell Ltd,* v. *Woodward*[11] the House of Lords upheld the conviction of a company of "causing" polluted matter to enter a river, without the need for either *mens rea* or negligence. Their lordships reserved the question whether the company would have been liable if the result had been brought about by the act of a stranger or of God.[12]

- Where an event other than an act (an event such as injury, or danger of injury) is factually caused by two persons acting independently, the courts are likely to find that the person who was negligent was the cause of the event in law, not the person who took due care.[13] This may be regarded as an application of the reasonable foresight principle in causation.[14]

§ 42.5. OFFENCES OF POSSESSION

Some offences are worded in terms of "possessing" a forbidden object (such objects being here called contraband).[1] Examples are the offences of unlawfully possessing explosives, firearms and controlled drugs (which in general are the drugs capable of affecting consciousness and behaviour). Other statutes use different language having much the same effect, for instance "keeping" a dangerous wild animal without a licence,[2] receiving" stolen goods (one form of handling), and the offence where a person "has with him" an offensive weapon. (But "has with him" refers to immediate personal possession,[3] whereas a person can be guilty of an ordinary possession offence if he entrusts the contraband to another person for safe keeping on his behalf.[4]

---

[9] § 43.5.

[10] § 15.12.

[11] [1972] AC 824. See comments in [1973] Crim.LR 41, [1974] *ibid*. 123.

[12] This is an unusual incursion of the notion of act of God into the criminal law. For its use in the law of tort, see, e.g. Clerk and Lindsell, *Torts*, 15th ed. § 1–27.

[13] See *Sever* v. *Duffy* § 14.7 at n. 18, which is especially noteworthy because the person at fault was not in breach of the regulation.

[14] § 16.8.

[1] See § 19.6.

[2] Dangerous Wild Animals Act 1976.

[3] It can, however, extend to possession of articles in a parked vehicle: § 38.7 n. 1.

[4] *Kelt* [1977] 1 WLR 1365; *Sullivan* v. *Earl of Caithness* [1976] 2 WLR 361. Cp. Lord Pearce in *Warner* [1969] 2 AC at 305; Misuse of Drugs Act 1971 s. 37 (3). The person so entrusted (employee or bailee) possesses also: *per* Lord Pearce, *loc. cit.; DPP* v. *Brooks* [1974] AC 862; *Woodage* v. *Moss* [1974] Crim.LR 104.

According to the theory of possession, this concept involves both a physical and a mental component: the corpus and animus of possession. The corpus is supposed to be the capacity to control the thing in question. We need not go into the theory of this in detail, beyond observing that it can have importance in contraband offences.

> The employee of a company was the holder of a liquor licence for premises belonging to the company. Measuring instruments at the bar, which were owned and maintained by a brewery company under contract, were found to give false measures. The House of Lords held that the employee licence-holder was not responsible for the defects; the instruments were not "in his possession" for legal purposes, because he had no control over them.[5]

Some possession offences specifically require knowledge, the most prominent example being receiving stolen goods.[6] Where the statute creating an offence of possession does not specifically require knowledge, the present tendency is to say that it imposes strict liability, and this even though the offence is a serious one with a potentially severe penalty. The point will be developed in connection with drug and firearms offences.

§ 42.6. THE POSSESSION OF CONTROLLED DRUGS

The law relating to drug ofences is now largely settled by the Misuse of Drugs Act 1971 section 28 (3). This makes liability depend, for the most part, on knowledge by the defendant that he has the thing, or negligence in not ascertaining what he has. The subsection, omitting non-essentials, runs as follows.

> "Where it is necessary for the prosecution to prove that some substance was [a] controlled drug, and it is proved that the substance in question was that controlled drug, the accused shall be acquitted—
> (i) if he proves that he neither believed nor suspected nor had reason to suspect[1] that the substance was a controlled drug, or
> (ii) if he proves that he believed the substance to be a controlled drug such that, if it had in fact been that controlled drug, he would not have been committing any offence to which this section applies."

Paragraph (i) provides a defence of no negligence when the defendant did not know he had a controlled drug. Paragraph (ii) allows a very limited defence if the defendant thought he had a different controlled drug: the facts must be such that if it had been that drug he would have committed no offence. He must show, for example, that he had a prescription for the drug he believed it to be. Otherwise he can be punished as for possessing

[5] *Bellerby* v. *Carle* (1983) The Times, March 19.

[6] We have seen that the alternative of belief merely refers to wilful blindness, which would be equivalent to knowledge in any case: § 39.6.

[1] A similar phrase to "had reason to suspect" was indulgently construed in a semi-subjective sense in other legislation: *Hudson* [1966] 1 QB 448. On its face, however, it seems to import liability for negligence.

the drug he in fact has. So he can be punished for possessing a packet of heroin when he reasonably believed that he was committing the much less serious offence of possessing cannabis resin.

However, the Act is spatchcocked on to the existing case-law, which draws complicated distinctions in relation to the doctrine of possession. These would now be of small practical importance were it not for the fact that they can still affect the technical correctness of a summing-up, and can therefore lead to acquittals, merited or otherwise. This means that the common law must be set out if the law is to be fully stated; but, to mark our displeasure with its irrationality, it will be reduced to small print.

Under the legislation before 1971, unauthorised possession of a controlled drug was declared to be an offence in unqualified terms, and the courts held that the offence carried strict liability. This was finally settled by the decision of the House of Lords in *Warner*.[2]

> Warner was found with a box containing 20,000 amphetamine tablets; he first said that the box contained rubbish, and then said that he thought it contained scent. His story as to his belief was evidently highly suspect; but the trial judge told the jury that his belief was irrelevant to guilt, so that the appellate courts were faced with the alternative of either agreeing that the offence was of strict liability or upsetting the conviction. In these circumstances their lordships had every temptation to agree with the trial judge, which they did. Lord Reid vigorously dissented, holding, in accordance with *Tolson*, that although the legislation then in force was silent on the mental element, *mens rea* was impliedly required. The offences carried stiff penalties and could be said to belong to the realm of traditional morality since they would incur moral disapproval from many people; they could not be dismissed as relating to mere matters of convenience.[3] The majority of the lords, however, were moved by what they regarded as the social importance of closing loopholes in the anti-drug legislation. Their speculation of what Parliament probably intended was perhaps partly falsified by the Act of 1971, which provides the no-negligence defence already mentioned, the burden of establishing which is placed on the defendant.

A person who read section 28 (3) by itself would understand that if he is charged with unlawfully possessing, say, cannabis, and he did not know he had a controlled drug, he must prove that he was not at fault. But the position is more complicated. Such proof would indeed be a defence; but the need for the no-negligence defence arises only if the defendant is proved to have been in possession of the drug, and the doctrine of possession at common law contains ingredients that can work to his advantage.

To explain: it might be supposed that in an offence of possession the *actus reus* consists in the physical control of the contraband; and if the Misuse of Drugs Act had enacted that proposition we should have been saved much agonising. But it did not; it left the law of possession as it was settled in *Warner*. In that case the House of Lords, having thrown the notion of fault out of the offence, with mistaken ingenuity put a bit of it back in again via the doctrine of possession. They were able to do this because it has always been accepted that possession involves a mental element, known as the *animus possidendi*, the intention to possess.[4]

In relation to the law of theft, we have seen that *animus possidendi* on the part of the victim

---

[2] *Warner* v. *Metropolitan Police Commissioner* [1969] 2 AC 256.

[3] Lord Reid swung his colleagues round to his general approach the next year: *Sweet* v. *Parsley* [1970] AC 132. This turned on another section of the Act then in force which is now represented by s. 8 of the Act of 1971: see below at n. 22. The facts were far more favourable to the defendant than those in *Warner*; indeed, the imposition of liability would plainly have been unjust; and that, no doubt, helped the decision. See Spencer in [1982] Crim.LR 269. S. 8 now accepts and enacts the view taken in *Sweet* for the type of case there in issue. The latter decision at first raised a flicker of hope that the House of Lords might repent of its attitude in *Warner* on the general question of strict liability; but the hope was snuffed out by their lordships' subsequent decisions in *Alphacell* § .4 n. 11 and *Smedleys* § 44.5 n. 5.

[4] For details, reference may be made to the specialised literature, particularly Pollock and Wright, *An Essay on Possession in that Common Law* (Oxford 1888).

is very readily found. Since possession is ownership as against wrongdoers, theft and criminal damage may be committed against possessors. And, for this purpose, a person can be credited with possession of a thing although he does not know of its identity, or even of its existence, as in the container cases.[5] Being in possession of a house, conveyance, bureau or other container, he is deemed to intend to possess all the contents, unless they are in the immediate possession of someone else. Everybody, except perhaps thieves, would agree that this is reasonable doctrine. The mental element required of a victim for the purpose of protecting him in his possession is therefore minimal.

It is otherwise with the possession of contraband. Where the alleged possessor is not the complainant in the witness box but the defendant in the dock, he cannot, in general, be convicted of possessing a forbidden object, according to the House of Lords, unless he is in some tenuous way aware of it. However, the concession so made is extremely limited. It is held that a person can be held to possess contraband in three cases, even when he is unaware of what precisely he has. Three rules may be stated.

First, where a person invites contraband to be delivered to him, he is guilty of unlawfully possessing it the moment it arrives on his premises, even though at that moment he does not know it has come. So the tenant of a house in multiple occupation is guilty of possessing cannabis he has ordered as soon as it drops through the letter-box addressed to him.[6] This was decided by the Court of Appeal after the decision in *Warner*, showing that that case has not exhausted the ingenuity of the courts in creating new rules on this subject.

Secondly, the fair inference from the opinions expressed in *Warner* is that a person who is morally irreproachable when he comes into possession of a contraband object has a reasonable, though short, time to examine the thing to find whether it is contraband, and, if it is, to purge himself of its pollution.[7] This view is supported by their lordships' acceptance of the proposition that substantial possession must be established, not momentary control.

While *Warner* appears to give the defendant a short period of grace to examine what he has, it does not allow him to make a mistake. If he thinks he has sweets and so does not bother to examine the contents of a box, he possesses the contents whatever they are. If, realising that he does not know what he has, he conscientiously examines the contents and erroneously comes to the conclusion that they are sweets, he is again deemed to be in possession of the contents.

The Misuse of Drugs Act[8] explains when a person may lawfully acquire what he knows is (or suspects may be) a controlled drug. The defendant may prove:

> "(*a*) that, knowing or suspecting it to be a controlled drug, he took possession of it for the purpose of preventing another from committing or continuing to commit an offence in connection with that drug and that as soon as possible after taking possession of it he took all such steps as were reasonably open to him to destroy the drug or to deliver it into the custody of a person lawfully entitled to take custody of it; or
> (*b*) that, knowing or suspecting it to be a controlled drug, he took possession of it for the purpose of delivering it[9] into the custody of a person lawfully entitled to take custody of it and that as soon as possible after taking possession of it he took all such steps as were reasonably open to him to deliver it into the custody of such a person."

It will be observed that the subsection does not give the defendant a defence merely because on ascertaining the illegal nature of the drug he threw it away or gave it back to the transferor. But either of these facts may perhaps induce the court to hold that the defendant did not have a sufficiently substantial relation to the thing to be accounted possession.[10]

---

[5] §§ 33.5.

[6] *Peastol* (1978) 69 CAR 203.

[7] *Wright* (1976) 62 CAR 169 endorses the view that the defendant has a reasonable time to examine a container, but states that this is so only when he does not suspect and has no reason to suspect that it contains controlled drugs. It would seem harsh if a person who accepts a box doubtfully, suspecting that it may contain contraband and intending to examine it immediately, with a view to turning it over to the police if it is contraband, is guilty of possessing contraband.

[8] S. 5 (4). Cp. § 7.4 n. 3.

[9] The words "should it be a controlled drug" are evidently to be implied.

[10] See *Wright*, n. 7 above. See, however, *Murphy* [1971] NI at 200, where the Northern Ireland CCA said, *obiter*, that a person who finds a pistol on the road and picks it up to throw it into a river would be guilty of unlawful possession, though he might lawfully pick it up to hand it to the police.

Thirdly, a person is held to be in possession of uninvited objects (even though he neither knows nor suspects them to be contraband) according to certain rules which we are to study, the minimum requirement being that he must know that he possesses *something*. Everyone who knows he has *something* must immediately examine what it is, on pain of otherwise being held to be in possession of contraband if it is in fact contraband.

This rule, that the defendant must know he has something, may sound an extraordinarily anaemic requirement, as indeed it is, but at least it has the effect that if the article has been delivered into the hands of the defendant's employee, or into his building, or put into his handbag or car, he does not acquire possession of it if he does not know that anything has been so delivered or put. The House of Lords, by affirming this rule in *Warner*, gave tepid support to the idea that contraband offences should require some mental state; but instead of expressing the rule in terms of a basic fault element (which would have been open to the objection that it would have let Warner off), their lordships concealed the mental requirement under a refinement of the doctrine of possession, applicable only to contraband offences.

Although *Warner* was decided before the Act of 1971, and although the technicalities thus introduced into the doctrine of possession became unnecessary after that Act allowed a no-fault defence, the decision has been followed since.[11]

> Suppose that the defendant charged with possession of a controlled drug knew that a box had been delivered to his house, and believed it to be empty, but in fact it contained cannabis. Assuming that the defendant has not ordered cannabis, he cannot be convicted (even apart from section 28 (3)) of unlawfully possessing cannabis. The trial judge must direct the jury (or the clerk must advise magistrates) that the burden is on the prosecution to prove that the defendant was in possession of the cannabis, which means that it must be proved he knew there was X in the box. The judge must not tell the jury that the defendant can be convicted if he "had reason to suspect that X was in the box." This "objective" formula, under the Misuse of Drugs Act, applies only when the defendant is in possession of the contraband, and at present we are considering whether he *is* in possession of it.

What (you will want to know) is this mysterious algebraical quantity that has suddenly entered the discussion? The defendant is charged with possessing cannabis; must it not be shown that he knew he possessed cannabis? No. What must be proved we do not precisely know; and that is why I inserted the symbol in the previous paragraph. As a partial definition, it means "something additional to the contents that the defendant does not dispute he knew were there." Consequently, he is not liable in what may be called the "planting" cases.

> He may know that there are many small items in his car, but is not guilty of an offence if a cannabis cigarette has been put there by someone else without his knowledge.[12]
>
> He may know that he has a bottle of stomach pills, but is not guilty of an offence if an amphetamine tablet (a controlled drug) has been introduced among those pills without his knowledge.[13]
>
> He may know that he has a knife, but is not guilty of an offence if traces of cannabis resin are found on it, and he did not put them there and did not know they were there.[14]

It will be seen that the law is, to use the kindest possible adjective, extremely subtle. It supposes that a man can possess the six sides of a box without possessing what is inside. The defendant possesses the container or other article, and also any known contents or adherents, but not (for the purpose of a contraband offence) the unknown contents or adherents. In general, he can be guilty of a contraband offence only in respect of the contents or adherents that he knows are there.

This brings me to the question that I am sure is trembling on your lips. When we speak of "the contents that the defendant knows are there," do we postulate that he knows the nature of those contents? Suppose he knows that he has a packet of cigarettes; he thinks they are

---

[11] *Ashton-Rickardt* [1978] 1 WLR 37, 1 All ER 173, 65 CAR 67; cp. *Fernandez* [1970] Crim.LR 277. An evidential burden rests on the defendant to negative knowledge: see Lord Wilberforce in *Warner* [1969] 2 AC at 312 and Lord Diplock in *Sweet* v. *Parsley* [1970] AC 132.

[12] *Ashton-Rickardt*, last note.

[13] *Irving* [1970] Crim.LR 642.

[14] *Marriott* [1971] 1 WLR 187, 1 All ER 595; *Colyer* [1974] Crim.LR 243. Cp. § 26.11 at n. 15.

tobacco, but in fact they are cannabis. He knows he has a bottle of pills; he thinks they are all his wife's stomach pills, but in fact they are his son's amphetamine tablets—the whole lot of them. He knows there is something brown on his knife; he thinks it is toffee, but in fact it is cannabis. Does he know that the thing in question is there?

This was the problem considered by the House of Lords in *Warner*. The majority (having an eye to Warner and his unconvincing defence) regarded a person's mistake as to the "qualities" of the thing as not preventing him from being in possession of it. In all the instances just given the defendant would be held to be in possession of the contraband. If he knows he has the substance, he possesses it, even though he mistakes its nature.[15] It has been held, for example, that if the defendant knows he has a cigarette he possesses it, even though it contains cannabis and not, as he thinks, tobacco.[16]

But the line drawn by the law is so fine that sometimes common sense disappears.

> (1) A man knows that he has a packet of 20 cigarettes. He thinks they are all tobacco, but they are all cannabis. Conclusion; he possesses the cannabis.
>
> (2) The same, except that only one of the 20 is cannabis. The law seems to be (though one cannot be sure) that this is essentially the same as in case (1), so that the man *is* in unlawful possession of the one reefer. He knows he has 20 cigarettes, and this is one of them. But:
>
> (3) if he only knew that he had an indeterminate number of cigarettes, and this one had got among them without his knowledge, he would not be in possession of it.[17]

It seems strange that so much should depend on whether the defendant knows the total number. And is it not crazy that a person's criminality should depend on whether he thinks he has a clean knife or whether he thinks he has a knife with a little toffee on the blade?

It will be seen that the rule in *Warner* is an abstruse and irrational compromise between liability for fault and strict liability. As the cases on theft show, it is not an essential part of the notion of possession that a person should know of the existence of the thing that is under his control. The only reason for insisting on knowledge when the question of possession arises

---

[15] In *Warner* the defendant thought he had scent (or so he said); in fact the box contained cannabis, and the House of Lords held that the defendant was in possession of the cannabis. Lord Pearce, whose speech appears in effect to state the *ratio decidendi* of the majority, said (at 305): "I think that the term 'possession' is satisfied by a knowledge only of the existence of the thing itself and not its qualities, and that ignorance or mistake as to its qualities is not an excuse. This would comply with the general understanding of the word 'possess.' Though I reasonably believe the tablets which I possess to be aspirin, yet if they turn out to be heroin I am in possession of heroin tablets. This would be so I think even if I believed them to be sweets. It would be otherwise if I believed them to be something of a wholly different nature. At this point a question of degree arises as to when a difference in qualities amounts to a difference in kind. That is a matter for a jury who would probably decide it sensibly in favour of the genuinely innocent but against the guilty." His lordship is struggling valiantly to state a rule that may seem to make sense and yet will save Warner's conviction, but there is a conflict between the first part of this statement and the last, for if a mistake as to the kind of object is a defence, then surely aspirin or sweets and heroin are different in kind; and similarly scent and cannabis are different in kind, so that Warner should have heen acquitted. It seems that in practice the courts do not apply the latter part of Lord Pearce's dictum, and that a mistake as to the kind of object does not negative possession of it. See *Marriott* [1971] 1 WLR at 190D; Teff in 34 MLR 582.

Two other confusing questions are whether the decision in *Warner* applies where the thing is not obtained in suspicious circumstances, and whether it applies only to things in containers. In *Fernandez* [1970] Crim.LR 277 the CA assumed that the strict rule applied only when the defendant came by the thing in suspicious circumstances. But the later cases seem to give up this qualification, which was not expressed by Lord Pearce in the passage just referred to. The opinion of Lord Pearce also indicates a negative answer to the second question. On the one hand, a mistake as to the thing possessed does not negative possession, whether the thing is in a container or not. On the other hand, if the defendant does not know he has the thing he does not possess it, even if it is not in a container (as *Marriott*, n. 14 above, shows). So containers are irrelevant to the question of knowledge of possession of contraband (apart from the "right to open" point, to be discussed presently).

[16] *Searle* v. *Randolph* [1972] Crim.LR 779.

[17] *Irving*, n. 13 above.

in contraband cases is the feeling that it is unfair to the defendant to convict him if he does not know that he possesses the thing. This was made plain by Lord Pearce, who became the architect of the law by the accidental fact that he held the balance between two law lords who would have supported a more stringent liability and two who were more lenient. Lord Pearce avowedly used the notion of *animus possidendi* as a substitute, though an imperfect substitute, for *mens rea*.[18] But if fairness is the issue, it is surely unfair to convict the defendant of possessing a controlled drug when he believes that what he has is something totally different, like a bottle of scent. To distinguish between the defendant who believes he has an empty box and the defendant who believes he has a box containing scent, when in fact in both instances the box contains cannabis, is to reduce the law to complete artificiality. The beauty of the distinction in *Warner* (as it appeared to their lordships) was that it ensured that Warner stayed convicted; but that was an ephemeral advantage, and now we are lumbered with absurd law for the indefinite future.

However, the rule in *Warner* is important only on the issue of possession. The Misuse of Drugs Act leaves untouched the conceptual mess of *Warner* but sits on top of it the new statutory defence of section 28 (3).[19] So, even if the defendant is found to be in possession of the drug, he now gets off (by virtue of the subsection) if he did not know or suspect and had no reason to suspect that it was a controlled drug that he was not supposed to have. The upshot is that, under the Act, a person is not guilty of illegally possessing the drug if there was nothing to put him on enquiry as to its being a controlled drug.

> The awkward consequence may be illustrated. The defendant is found to have a cigarette containing cannabis in his car, and his defence is that he did not know it was there and that it must have been placed there by someone else. The judge must direct the jury, first, that the burden rests on the prosecution to satisfy them so that they feel sure that the defendant knew he had the cigarette, that is to say he knew he had something, and that something was the cigarette.[20] (Goodness knows if the jury will understand it.) If they find in the affirmative, then the burden rests on the defendant under section 28 (3) to establish on the balance of probability that he did not know or suspect or have reason to suspect that the something was or included cannabis.

This is an entirely artificial separation of the issues. The substantial question is not whether the defendant knew he had a tobacco cigarette (the possession of which is no offence) but whether he knew (or, since the Act says so, had reason to suspect) he had a reefer; and in common sense the issue should be confined to that, and should be a single issue carrying a single burden of proof.

Having spoken of things in boxes (and the same remarks apply to things that are wrapped up so that the contents of the wrapping are invisible), we must now consider the case where the possessor of the box or parcel has no right to open it. Suppose a man is given a box for safe keeping, or to give to someone else. He knows there is something inside it, but he believes this to be innocent, like sweets. Actually it is a controlled drug. It seems unfair to make him guilty, if he had no right to open the box.

The House of Lords invented a special rule for this situation in *Warner*.[21] The majority view appears to have been that the defendant possesses a thing if he:

- knows that he possesses something, and
- has an opportunity to ascertain what it is, and
- either has a right to ascertain what it is (e.g. by opening the container) or came by the thing in suspicious circumstances.

The above was specifically the view of Lord Pearce, who, as said before, expressed the highest common factor of opinion in favour of liability.

It need not be observed that this complex rule cannot be deduced from any theory of possession. It is judicial legislation pure and simple, the object being to give a defence to apparently honest people but not to those who evoke suspicion (an object that it achieves only

---

[18] See his remark on "planting" in [1969] 2 AC at 306G.

[19] See the criticism by Goodhart in 84 LQR 393–394.

[20] This is the result of *Warner*, which survives the enactment of s. 28 (3). See *Ashton-Rickhardt*, above n. 11.

[21] See J C Smith in [1968] Crim.LR 381.

very imperfectly). The fact that the defendant is an employee or bailee who had no right to open the box entrusted to him is no defence, either under the rule in *Warner* or under the Act, if he came by the box in suspicious circumstances—which presumably means, if he ought to have suspected the truth.

The rule does not operate against the defendant if he did not know that he had anything (as if he thought he was being entrusted with an empty box, when in fact it was full of controlled drugs). However stupid he was, and however suspicious the circumstances, he cannot be convicted of possessing the drugs. But if he knew there was *something* in the box, like aspirins, he can be convicted if the box contained controlled drugs and if he came into possession in objectively suspicious circumstances.

The rule in *Warner* means, further, that if the defendant comes into possession of a box for safe custody otherwise than in suspicious circumstances, believing the box to contain scent, then he is not guilty although it actually contains cannabis, because he has no right to open the box.

A final question relating to the possession of drugs is the liability of the occupier of premises where drugs are consumed. Is it, for example, an offence to allow your guest to use drugs at a party? Section 8 of the Act provides the answer.

> "A person commits an offence if, being the occupier or concerned in the management of any premises, he knowingly permits or suffers any of the following activities to take place on those premises, that is to say—
>
> (*a*) producing or attempting to produce a controlled drug in contravention of section 4 (1) of this Act;
>
> (*b*) supplying or attempting to supply a controlled drug to another in contravention of section 4 (1) of this Act, or offering to supply a controlled drug to another in contravention of section 4(1);
>
> (*c*) preparing opium for smoking;
>
> (*d*) smoking cannabis, cannabis resin or prepared opium."

This section requires *mens rea*. It applies not only to occupiers but to the landladies of lodging houses, and, presumably, to universities and colleges in respect of the activities of students. (A student who lives in a college hostel is himself an "occupier" of his room within the meaning of the section,[22] even though the college would seem to be an occupier as well. A similar remark applies to a lodger.)

§ 42.7. THE POSSESSION OF FIREARMS

The unauthorised possession of firearms is an offence under the Firearms Act 1968. Problems arise particularly with regard to antique and toy guns, some of which are firearms within the Act while others are not. If a prosecution is brought, it will be for the jury, under the direction of the judge, to decide whether the particular gun comes within the definition in

---

[22] *Tao* [1977] QB 141.

the Act. Suppose, then, that a person possesses a gun which he believes to be an antique or toy falling outside the Act, but the jury (or magistrates on summary trial) find that it is a prohibited firearm. Has an offence been committed?

The sensible (though not the law's) answer to this question would be that although the police can seize and forfeit the prohibited weapon, the defendant is not necessarily guilty of an offence in possessing it. His mistake may be either one of fact or one of law. He may mistakenly believe that the gun has a particular attribute (that there is some fact relating to the gun); and this attribute may be one that if true would take the gun out of the class of prohibited firearms. Or the defendant may not make a mistake of fact but simply be ignorant of the statutory definition of a firearm, or apply it wrongly (i.e. in a way that the jury or magistrates do not apply it). Here his mistake may be said to be one of law.[1] On *mens rea* principles, the mistake of fact should be a defence, but not the mistake of law.

The courts apparently do not distinguish between the two situations: they hold that the defendant is liable either way. In two decisions on the subject, on a supposed antique and a supposed toy respectively,[2] the court said that the offence of possessing firearms is "absolute," and quoted *Warner*.[3] The distinction from *Tolson*[4] (and other similar decisions) was stated to be, principally, "the danger to the community resulting from the possession of lethal weapons." It is to be observed, however, that in both cases the defendant knew he had a gun of some sort. What if he did not know that he had a gun at all? Suppose, for example, that he thought that what he had in a particular box (inherited from his grandmother) was a power drill. If *Warner* is applied he will be liable even then.

The discussion of *Warner* in the last section was reduced to small print because in respect of controlled drugs, with which it was concerned, the decision has been greatly reduced in importance by the no-fault defence in the Misuse of Drugs Act. Perhaps, properly speaking, the discussion should now reappear in large print in the present section, because the Firearms Act does not give a no-fault defence, so that the rule in *Warner*, if it applies, has much more practical importance. Two hypotheticals will illustrate the consequences if the courts finally decide to let the horrors of this case loose on the law relating to firearms.

(1) D was found with a gun in his car; he had no gun licence; and his defence is that the gun (wrapped in brown paper) was planted on him: he did not know that the parcel or any gun was there. The gun was something additional to the objects that he knew were in the car. On the doctrine of *Warner*, if this defence cannot be disproved, D was not in possession of the gun.

(2) As before, but D admits that he saw a brown paper parcel in his

---

[1] Although this distinction may seem clear in theory, it can raise subtle problems. As an example from a different context, see *Champ* [1982] Crim.LR 109.

[2] *Howells* [1977] QB 614; *Hussain* [1981] 1 WLR 416; cp. *Pierre* [1963] Crim.LR 15.

[3] § .6 n. 2.

[4] § 6.7 n. 1.

car, which he says he assumed to contain a constructional toy belonging to his small son. According to *Warner* (if that case is applied to firearms) D is strictly liable for possessing the gun.

The *Warner* distinctions have not yet been specifically applied to firearms, and we may hope that in view of their manifest absurdity and injustice they will not be imported into this new field. It has been held without qualification that a person cannot be convicted of "having with him an offensive weapon" if he did not know he had it,[5] and the same rule should be applied to firearms. It is regrettable, but must now be accepted, that if a person knows that he has a gun of any kind he takes the risk of its coming within the Act, even though he reasonably believes that the gun falls outside it.

§ 42.8. PRACTICAL ALLEVIATIONS OF STRICT LIABILITY

In offences of strict liability the police and government inspectors do not come down like a wolf on the fold. They generally consider the question of fault when deciding whether to prosecute,[1] and are adjured to do this by the courts.[2]

Certainly it is desirable, as things are, that prosecutors should exercise a discretion along these lines. But while this alleviation of strict liability is better than nothing, it is a *pis aller* because, as one commentator observes, it "delegates the problem of fault to the enforcer."[3] The enforcer is left not only to decide what sort of fault should be looked for but to try the question of fact whether the suspect was guilty of that kind of fault, without any agreed guidelines or procedural safeguards. The real trial takes place in the prosecutor's office, or in the police station or at the roadside, without the safeguards of a proper trial, and perhaps without the suspect even being fully heard. If the prosecutor decides to go forward, the courts simply rubber-stamp his decision and convict. Where prosecutions are brought by the police there is no assurance that consistent policies will be adopted.

Even when an offence of strict liability is charged the defendant may produce evidence of no *mens rea* or no negligence, by way of mitigation. Viscount Dilhorne said:

> "In cases where it is apparent that a prosecution does not serve the general interests of consumers, the justices may think fit, if they find that the Act has been contravened, to grant an absolute discharge."[4]

Although it is almost always open to the courts to make the sentence a nominal one, in the past they have sometimes sentenced quite severely on the basis of strict liability. Offenders who were not proved to have been at fault, at any rate by the verdict of the jury, have been ordered to be imprisoned or (when an alien) deported.[5] It has happened, and still happens,

---

[5] *Cugullere* [1961] 1 WLR 858, 2 All ER 343, 45 CAR 108. Cp. *Murphy* [1971] NI 193, where the NI court refused to appply *Warner* to a firearm offence, holding that possession for this purpose requires knowledge that the thing is a firearm.

[1] See, however, §44.7.
[2] *E.g.* by Viscount Dilhorne in *Smedleys Ltd* v. *Breed* [1974] AC at 856G.
[3] D A Thomas in *Reshaping the Criminal Law*, ed. Glazebrook (London 1978) 30.
[4] [1974] AC at 857 B.
[5] *The General Part*, 2nd ed § 89; *Prince* § 9.12 at n. 12.

that an offender has been imprisoned although the court expressly found that he made a mistake of fact.[6] What useful purpose is served by the sentence is not explained. But usually a severe sentence is to be explained by the fact that the judge, who has himself been able to assess the evidence, sentences with regard to the degree of fault that he attributes to the defendant. It would seem highly desirable in such a case that he should indicate, with reasons, what this fault is.

Recently the courts have become more concerned with the question of fault in sentencing. It is now established that if a defendant pleads guilty to an offence of strict liability, the judge may sentence in accordance with his own opinion that the facts indicate *mens rea* or negligence; but in such a case he must indicate that a particular question is relevant, so that the parties can call evidence upon it.[7] Presumably the same rule applies where the defendant is convicted after a plea of not guilty.

It will be observed that what may well be the most important issue in the case is removed from the jury and left for sole decision by the judge. It will be observed, further, that our courts have not yet attained the degree of sensitivity of the American courts, which hold that a sentence of imprisonment for an offence of imputed liability (or, presumably, for any offence where fault has not been proved) violates "due process," so that only a fine is permissible.[8]

SUMMARY

The courts generally decline to imply a requirement of fault in minor offences, §.1
and they have also declined to do so in various more serious ones.

Statutes have been read to create strict liability even though the words used §.2
would naturally indicate a fault element.

There are no fixed principles of statutory interpretation on this subject. §.3
Practically every case affirming a particular principle can be matched by one denying it.

The word "use" in the Construction and Use Regulations is understood to create §.4
strict liability. So does the word "cause," except that if D's conduct causes another person to commit the *actus reus* without D's knowledge he will be held not to have caused it.

Some offences of unlawful possession have also been held to carry strict liability; §.5
but the requirement of *corpus possessionis* means that a person does not possess a thing if the law does not consider him as being in control of it.

As regards the unlawful possession of controlled drugs, the Misuse of Drugs Act §.6
1971 s. 28 (3) requires knowledge or negligence for liability (the burden of disproof being placed on the defendant). However, the pre-Act case of *Warner* is still

---

[6] In *Lawrence* (1978) 142 JPN 401 a man of 20 was sentenced to one year's imprisonment, upheld on appeal, for sexual intercourse with a girl of 12, although he found her unexpectedly in his bunk and (as the court was prepared to find) genuinely believed her to be at least 14½. It is true that the defendant had *mens rea* as to intercourse with a girl under 16, and therefore was to blame; but he was subjected to an unexpected, uninvited and irresistible temptation. The court sentenced him on the basis that the girl was in fact under 13, though there was no *mens rea* as to that; had the girl been 13 with the facts otherwise the same, it is unlikely that such a prison sentence would have been passed for the under-16 offence. Sentences like this show that the courts cannot be trusted with their present degree of discretion in sentencing for offences of strict liability and sexual offences.

[7] *Lester* (1975) 63 CAR 144. See note, [1975] Crim.LR 144. If the prosecution wish to take the initiative in giving evidence of fault, they should, on a trial on indictment, give advance notice of it: cp. *Robinson* (1969) 53 CAR 314. If the judge takes a view adverse to the defendant without evidence, an appeal lies: *Hearne* [1976] Crim.LR 753. The judge may take into consideration the fact that the defendant has not set up a statutory defence of no negligence: *Hammerton Cars Ltd.* [1976] Crim.LR 755. It seems that he may also take account of a view of the facts indicated by the jury (*Jama* (1968) 52 CAR 498), or may ask them to retire to consider the point (*Warner* [1967] 1 WLR at 1213–1214); in neither of these cases, however, was the propriety of the judge's action decided on appeal. J C Smith points out that a judge who asks the jury such a question should direct them as to the burden of proof of fault ([1967] Crim.LR 530).

[8] *Commonwealth* v. *Koczwara* (1959) 397 Pa. 575, 155 A 2d 825.

important, because it shows that the prosecution must prove the possession, which requires (according to the House of Lords) a certain mental element. A person does not possess a contraband article unless he knows he has it; but this principle is heavily qualified. (1) He possesses the contraband as soon as it is delivered to him if he has invited contraband to be sent to him. (2) The Misuse of Drugs Act allows the defendant to prove by way of defence that, knowing or suspecting the object to be a controlled drug, he took possession of it in order to prevent another from committing an offence or in order to deliver it into lawful custody. (3) According to *Warner*, a person who *de facto* receives a controlled drug will be guilty of possessing it (although he does not know precisely what he has) if he knows of the thing in question as being *something* he has. It is no defence that he thought it was an innocent article. If the thing is wrapped up or in a container he is not regarded as possessing it if he does not know what it is unless (*a*) he has the right to examine it or (*b*) he came by it in suspicious circumstances. By the Act, the occupier or manager of premises is liable for certain drug offences committed on the premises if he knowingly permits them.

If a person knows that he has a gun, but believes it is a toy or an antique, when §.7
in law it is regarded as a firearm, he can be convicted of unlawfully possessing a firearm. The cases go further and say that it is an offence of strict liability to possess a firearm without authority, and assume that the rule in *Warner* applies; but perhaps this is not yet finally settled.

Judges have sometimes criticised the bringing of charges where there is no fault. §.8
On conviction of an offence of strict liability the judge may sentence in accordance with his own opinion on whether the defendant was at fault, but he must first indicate to the parties that a particular question is relevant. There are still instances of judges passing sentences of imprisonment on persons who, owing to a mistake of fact, did not realise that they were committing the particular offence.

Chapter 43

ATTRIBUTED ACTS

Qui peccat per alium peccat per se is not a maxim of criminal law.

Lord Diplock ([1972] AC at 199)

§ 43.1. STRICT LIABILITY WITHOUT AN ACT BY THE DEFENDANT

Some cases of strict liability require at least a physical act by the defendant in violation of law. But, as was observed in § 27.6, there are also "situational" or "status" offences carrying strict liability.

> Thus, to take a case that has been given before, the parents of a girl who truanted were held guilty of an offence under a statute providing that in such circumstances "the parent of the child shall be guilty of an offence," although they did not know, and quite possibly had no reason to know, of their daughter's misbehaviour.[1]

The most prominent instances of situational and strict liability are the offences of unlawful possession already studied.[2] Nowadays, legislation that *prima facie* creates situational liability frequently (though by no means always) allows a defence of no negligence, of greater or lesser ambit. One example is the defence allowed by the Misuse of Drugs Act.[3] Another example is the Prevention of Oil Pollution Act 1971. This provides, in section 1 (1), that where:

> "any oil . . . is discharged from a ship . . . the owner or master of the ship[4] shall . . . be guilty of an offence,"

but the Act goes on, commendably, to allow a no-negligence defence.[5]

In the typical situational offences the external element is defined simply in terms of an event occurring, it being immaterial whether the event results from the defendant's act. The event may be defined without reference to human beings (oil is discharged from a ship), or it may be defined as the conduct of a human being (one's child is absent from school).

It may tempting to categorise some cases of the last type, where the conduct of another person is involved, as "vicarious liability," an expression properly belonging to the law of tort, which does not sit well in the criminal law. The civil courts hold that if an employee

---

[1] *Crump* v. *Gilmore* § 42.3 at n. 6. Cp. *Thomson* v. *NCB* (1977) The Times, August 3, a civil case where it was held that an offence was committed in respect of a person "employed" in certain work although he had not been employed to do it but had done it without the employer's knowledge; and it was also held that "the notion of foreseeability had no place."

[2] § 42.5–7.

[3] S. 28 (3), discussed in § 42. 6 at n. 1.

[4] Both can be convicted: *Federal SN Co. Ltd* [1974] 1 WLR 505, 2 All ER 97, 59 CAR 131.

[5] See s. 5. There is a parallel offence in s. 2. See the discussion by Dickens in 37 MLR 297. See more below § 44.3 n. 6.

commits a tort in the course of his employment the employer, as well as the employee, is liable for it. This vicarious liability is difficult (I do not say impossible) to support if considered in terms of justice; but one of the objects of the law of tort is to compensate the victim of the wrong, and it is thought that the object is best effected by giving him a remedy against the employer, who is more likely to satisfy the judgment than the employee, and who can, after all, insure against his liability.

The reasoning does not apply in criminal law, the chief object of which is deterrence. Here it would seem to be an elementary principle both of justice and of utility that one man should not be held accountable for the wrong of another. For the utilitarian, punishment can be justified only by reason of its useful effect for the future. In general there is no utility, any more than there is justice, in imposing punishment on a person who did not do the act and could not have prevented it by any reasonable precaution.

The notion of justice seems so instinctive that it is hard to imagine any society so callous as to punish people severely for the crimes of others; yet examples abound. In the earliest extant code of law, the Code of Hammurabi (dating from the second millenium BC), one section provided that if a builder built a house so poorly that it fell upon the owner's son and killed him, the builder's son should be put to death.[6] In the Old Testament, too, group responsibility was accepted, though the prophets Jeremiah and Ezekiel protested against it. By the time of the New Testament, the personal, atomistic conception of duty had become fully established in religious thought.[7] Even then it did not completely permeate secular systems of law among Christian peoples. In medieval England, men of the hundred were fined for murders and robberies committed in the locality, and not so long ago the collective punishment of towns and villages was used as a means of colonial rule.

Notwithstanding that the criminal courts do not apply a wide general principle on this subject, something like vicarious liability is still recognised for certain minor criminal offences, the object being to induce the defendant to exercise control over others. One instance occurs in relation to juveniles. The court must order that fines, compensation and costs awarded against a child or young person shall be paid by his parent or guardian unless, in the circumstances, the court thinks it would be unreasonable to make them pay.[8] Again, the registered owner of a vehicle is liable by statute in respect of certain fixed-penalty offences and excess parking charges, even though the fault was that of some other person (not being a person in possession of the vehicle without the owner's consent).[9] This provision was found to be necessary because it was too burdensome for the police to trace the actual offender, when offences were so numerous and so trivial.[10]

There are various other examples of criminal liability for the act of another (particularly of employees) which we are now to study. It is sometimes argued, in favour of this liability, that if an employer is fined for his underling's contraventions he is likely to discipline his staff better in future. But much the same result could be achieved if the employer were allowed a no-negligence defence. He would still be under considerable pressure to supervise those under his control, because otherwise he would fail in the defence.

§ 43.2. THE ATTRIBUTION OF ACTS

Some statutes that on their face seem to refer to the defendant's conduct are interpreted to impose situational liability. This arises because the

---

[6] Kocourek and Wigmore, *Sources of Ancient and Primitive Law* (Boston, Mass. 1915) 433 s. 230.

[7] Sturt and Hobling, *Practical Ethics* (London 1949) 56.

[8] CJA 1982 ss. 26,27. Social workers have strong reservations about the utility of this legislation: see Harriet Wilson in 21 Howard Jrnl 23 and 146 JPN 436. The parent or guardian may be required to enter into a recognisance: see s. 28. A local authority that is responsible for a juvenile under a care order does not come within these provisions: *Leeds City Council* v. *W. Yorks. Metropolitan Police* [1982] 2 WLR 186, 1 All ER 274, 74 CAR 336.

[9] RTA 1974 ss. 1–5 as amended.

[10] There would also be a good case for making a parliamentary candidate liable for illegal fly-posting by enthusiastic party workers unless he produces evidence as to the actual offender. See 138 JPN 399.

courts in interpreting these particular statutes deem the act of some person other than the defendant (generally his employee,[1] or a person closely similar to an employee) to be the act of the defendant.

> An example of a statute encouraging such interpretation is the Licensing Act 1964 s. 163, which provides that "a person shall not, either himself or by his servant or agent," do certain things. The section shrinks from saying anything so barbarous as that A shall be liable for the offence of B. The wording might perhaps have been understood by the MPs who passed it to apply only when the employer ordered the commission of the offence; but in fact it was doubtless intended to make the employer punishable also for the unauthorised act of his employee in the course of the employment; and this is how the courts interpret it. So here we have a situational offence masquerading as an ordinary offence by personal act.[2]

The reason for legislation of this kind rests largely on difficulties of proof. The employer will frequently have been guilty of negligence in failing to prevent the offence, even though negligence cannot be proved by the prosecution from its own hand, so to speak—particularly when no one is obliged to answer questions. Situational responsibility enables a conviction to be registered and the employing firm to be mulcted in a monetary penalty. This penalty may persuade the firm to discipline its employees, even to the extent of dismissing them when this seems to be the only way of preventing a repetition.

To a large extent, of course, the purpose of the law could be satisfied by making the employer liable for negligence, the burden of establishing absence of fault being placed on him. But the argument in favour of a severe rule is the same as that for strict liability. It is said that the penalties for these offences are light, and that the prosecutor ought not to be put to the trouble of investigating too closely what the employer has done. Whether this is a convincing answer must be a matter of opinion. As was pointed out before, the issue of fault may arise on the question of penalty, so that the prosecutor cannot avoid the issue if the defendant wishes to raise it.

This type of penal liability differs from vicarious liability in tort in the fact that the provisions creating it are only fragmentary, depending upon particular statutes or their interpretation.[3] Vicarious liability in tort, on the other hand, is a general principle of law. Further, the theory is different. The theory of the criminal law in these cases of pseudo-personal liability is not that the employee commits a crime for which the employer is made liable but that in certain cases the employer is debited with the *act* of the employee (or certain other persons) more or less as though it were his own act. These practical and conceptual differences from the law of tort make it desirable to give the criminal doctrine a distinctive name, for which reason it will here be called "the doctrine of attributed acts." It may also be called, for convenience, "attributive liability," but only on the understanding that in legal theory what is attributed to the defendant is not the offence of another (since the other person need not have perpetrated an offence) but the other's act or default.[4]

§ 43.3. IMPLIED ATTRIBUTION; THE LICENSEE CASES

The courts frequently hold that acts may be attributed to another person

---

[1] The traditional expressions are "master" and "servant"; these have largely gone out of use because they belong to an antiquated social order (though the second survives honourably for "civil servants").

[2] For an even more remarkable example see *Lindsay* v. *Vickers Ltd* [1978] Crim.LR 55.

[3] There were three crimes at common law in which something like vicarious liability is or was recognised: criminal libel, nuisance and contempt of court. See § 42.1 n. 2. The instances of attributed acts discussed in this chapter rest on the judicial interpretation of certain statutes.

[4] I am indebted to P R Glazebrook for suggesting this expression. See his criticism of the use of the term "vicarious liability" in *Reshaping the Criminal Law* 108.

without express words in the legislation to suggest it; but many doubts exist.

As was said before, there is no general principle whereby a person is held criminally liable merely because a criminal act is committed by his employee in the course of his employment. The courts often seem to be pressing towards such a principle, but have not yet reached it. The basic stance of the criminal law is therefore the opposite of the law of tort, and to that extent the dictum of Lord Diplock quoted at the head of this chapter is clearly correct. A defendant to a criminal charge is liable only if he falls within the words of the statute, as interpreted by the courts—except that in the licensee cases, to be noticed in a moment, the courts have interpreted the statutory words so strangely that they have in reality created an exception to the principle. The point to be understood is that the courts often find that the defendant does fall within the words of the statute because of what has been physically done by his employee or agent. This will become clearer as we proceed.

The cases come from different dates, and there has been a notable shift in judicial interpretation; even the modern authorities do not state a completely coherent doctrine. However, we may perhaps perceive two main principles which explain most of them. One concerns public licences; the other concerns the construction of statutory verbs.

The defendant may have a licence from a public authority to do something that would otherwise be forbidden, and the statute providing for the licence may contain special offences capable of being committed by the licensee. This is certainly the case with the licence to sell intoxicating liquor. In interpreting the offences, the courts hold that the licensee is responsible for the acts of his manager or other delegate[1] committed in his absence.

For example, the Licensing Act 1964 makes it an offence for the holder of a justices' licence to permit drunkenness on the premises.[2] The word "permit" is generally read as a *mens rea* word, i.e. as presupposing the defendant's knowledge of what is happening.[3] Suppose that the licensee has installed a manager who knowingly permits drunkenness on the premises. Paradoxically, it is impossible to convict as perpetrator the manager who is the real offender, because the Act strikes only at the licensee. If the licensee could not be convicted as perpetrator then the manager could not be convicted as accessory,[4] so the legislation would wholly fail of effect in these circumstances.

One way of dealing with the situation, and the most sensible and obvious way, would be for the judges to acquit the licensee for lack of *mens rea*, and to call the attention of the Home Secretary to the "slovenly way in which the Act was drawn." If the policy of the legislation were frustrated in this way, Parliament could be expected to try again and do better. It could easily amend the section to apply to the manager or person who actually serves the drinks. But, knowing the tardiness of Parliament in these matters, the courts have decided to change their function from that of applying the law to that of rescuing Parliament from its own ineptitude. They declare that when the publican "delegates" the management of the

---

[1] Including a partner or co-licensee: *Linnett* v. *MPC* [1946] KB 290.
[2] See s. 172 (1) of the Act of 1964, repeating earlier legislation.
[3] § 6.4.
[4] § 15.16 at n. 1.

premises he can be convicted of the act of his manager. Even when the statute expressly requires *mens rea*, as when it punishes a licensee who "knowingly allows" prostitutes to resort to the premises, the licensee is liable on account of his manager's knowledge, though he himself has none.[5] Thus the doctrine of delegation allows a person to be convicted of violating the statute when he quite clearly does not come within its terms. Since the licensee can be convicted as perpetrator, the manager can be convicted as accessory.

Parliament, we must suppose, is well pleased with this solution; at any rate it has re-enacted the defective provisions in identical terms in consolidating Acts, leaving the courts to continue to wrench the meaning of the language to make practical sense of it. From this short history we see that neither the judges nor Parliament, nor of course the Government, care a straw that they are making a piggery of the criminal law.

But if you forget academic purism, isn't the delegation doctrine really a good wheeze?

In a way. But one may ask whether it is proper for the courts to convict people in contradiction of the words of a statute. When the draftsman of an Act has confined an offence to one who knowingly allows, the draftsman must have considered and rejected (or been instructed to reject) the possibility of extending the scope of the offence to include one who negligently fails to prevent. No self-respecting Parliamentary counsel would use the phrase "knowingly allows" if he meant to include negligence in failing to prevent an occurrence that is not known; yet that is how the courts read the phrase in the licensee cases. Indeed, the interpretation favoured by the courts not only takes in negligence but enables a publican who could not have discovered the facts to be punished, if his manager knew. The publican may end up with an array of convictions for what purport to be *mens rea* offences, and when he applies to the justices for the renewal of his licence these convictions may count against him. No one will know from the record that he was not at fault. Is it right to convict people on a fictitious basis?

To add to the anomaly of the present law, the courts hold that if the publican has not delegated the management of the premises but is personally present, he is not responsible for the act of his barman or other employee when the offence requires personal knowledge.

> If, for example, the licensee is charged with "permitting" drunkenness, and the permitting was by his employee without his knowledge, but he himself was personally present, he will not be liable, because "permitting" requires knowledge.[6]

---

[5] *Allen* v. *Whitehead* [1930] 1 KB 211; the relevant provision is now in the Licensing Act 1964 s. 175 (1). The licensee is also liable for an offence of "causing": § 42.4 n. 7. According to the weight of authority the delegation principle is limited to offences requiring *mens rea*, but it is only in these cases that it is required. See Pace in [1982] Crim.LR 628–629.

[6] *Somerset* v. *Wade* [1894] 1 QB 574. Even if the employee commits an offence of strict liability the licensee will not be liable as accessory in the absence of knowledge. This is because of the rule in *Callow* v. *Tillstone* § 15.12 n. 1. Cp. *Ferguson* v. *Weaving* [1951] 1 KB 814.

The effect of the rule that the licensee's responsibility depends on delegation means that his responsibility varies inversely with the possibility of control. Take two contrasting situations.

> (1) A barman allows prostitutes to resort almost under the publican's nose, but without the publican's knowledge. The publican genuinely does not know what is going on, because he is busy with something else at the time, though he has not delegated control of the premises. Here he cannot be convicted of the statutory offence of knowingly allowing the licensed premises to be the habitual resort of reputed prostitutes.
> (2) The barman tolerates prostitutes as before, but the publican is on holiday in Majorca, and has installed the barman as a responsible manager whom he has chosen with care. Here the rule is that the publican can be convicted, because he has delegated authority.

Yet it is obvious that in case (2) the publican is if anything less able to control the situation than he is in case (1). So the result of this judge-made rule is that the less control the publican has in fact, the more likely he is to be penalised. The anomaly is the result of illegitimately introducing into the criminal law the concept of general agency developed in the civil law, where it admits of altogether different justification.

But if the publican were present it would almost always be possible to find that he knew of the prostitutes or drunks on his premises, or was wilfully blind to their presence, so there would be no difficulty in convicting him.

Even if this assumption is invariably true for offences of permitting prostitutes and drunks to be on the premises (which may be doubted), there are other offences where the publican's awareness is by no means a necessary inference. Take the facts of *Vane* v. *Yiannopoullos*.[7]

> By a provision now in the Licensing Act 1964 s. 161 (1), "if the holder of a justices' on-licence knowingly sells or supplies intoxicating liquor to persons to whom he is not permitted by the conditions of the licence to sell or supply it he shall be guilty of an offence." The licensee of a restaurant was allowed by the conditions of his licence to serve drinks only with meals. His waitress, contrary to his instructions, served drinks without a meal, while he was in another part of the restaurant. The House of Lords held that the licensee could not be convicted of the offence. Lord Donovan expressed the position succinctly when he said; "If a decision that 'knowingly' means 'knowingly' will make the provision difficult to enforce, the remedy lies with the legislature."[8]

The speeches in the House of Lords left undecided the question whether their lordships would be prepared to overrule the decisions making the publican liable for the *mens rea* of his manager in case of delegation. However, the Divisional Courts have not shared these doubts,[9] and have

---

[7] [1965] AC 486.
[8] For a discussion see Pace in [1982] Crim.LR 628–625.
[9] Save that Bristow J in *Howker*, next note, expressed the hope that the delegation principle might be overturned by the House of Lords.

continued to apply the traditional rule that a licensee is liable when he delegates—a matter that depends almost exclusively on the question whether he is present or absent.[10]

How far away must the publican be to be "absent"?

At one time it was thought that "absence" meant complete absence from the premises; but a Divisional Court has now stretched the law still further by holding that a licensee who himself happens to be in a different room can be found to have delegated the management of the room in which the offence takes place.[11] A waitress can therefore become a "manager" for the purpose of the rule as soon as the licensee goes into the next room. This is impossible to reconcile with *Vane* v. *Yiannopoullous,* where the licensee who was on a different floor from that on which the offence was committed was held not to have delegated his authority.[12] The licensee who is on a different floor is likely to be more remote than one who is merely in a different room. Why should the law distinguish between a different floor and a different room in the same building; and if it does distinguish, should it not be the other way round? The truth seems to be that the intermediate appellate courts find the decision of the House of Lords unpalatable, and will not apply it if they can by any means distinguish it.

If only the licensee can commit the offence as perpetrator, and if on the facts he has not delegated but his employee commits the forbidden act, then, on principle, no one can be convicted. For instance, in *Vane* v. *Yiannopoullous*[13] the waitress knew all the facts that made what she did a *de facto* breach of the conditions other employer's licence. Although the waitress was morally an offender, it has never been suggested that she could be convicted as accessory to a non-existent offence of the licensee. It is only when the delegation doctrine applies, and the licensee can be convicted, that the employee who does the actual selling can be convicted as accessory. If it were always possible to convict the employee who commits the offence in fact, so to speak, it is unlikely that the courts would have felt obliged to convict the licensee, in defiance of the statute requiring the licensee to have *mens rea*. This is a strong argument against the validity of the dictum in *Cogan*.[14]

It seems that where the offence requires knowledge the licensee's delegate must know the facts. If he does not, the licensee is not liable. Also, the doctrine applies only to the acts of the delegate manager, not to those of his assistant[15]; but there is at least one difficult decision on this.[16]

A minor point has caused no trouble in practice. Liquor licences are not usually granted to companies, so a brewery company has to arrange for the licence to be issued to an employee who is the manager of the licensed premises. This manager is not the employer of the barman, since both are employees of the company. Nevertheless the manager is held liable for the acts of a barman to whom he delegates.[17] The decision is contrary to the rule

---

[10] *Howker* v. *Robinson* [1973] 1 QB 178. This case shows that the licensee is vicariously liable even when the statute expressly provides for the liability of "the holder of the licence or his servant." See note in [1977] Crim.LR 482. But if the statute by its terms imposes liability on the barman alone, the licensee will not normally be vicariously liable for him. The licensee can be liable as accessory, but only if he knows the facts (above n. 6).

[11] *Howker* v. *Robinson,* last note. See Pace in [1982] Crim.LR 636–638.

[12] See note, [1972] Crim.LR 378, and Pace in [1982] Crim.LR 633–634.

[13] Above n. 7.

[14] § 15.16 at n. 12.

[15] Cp. *Rowlands* v. *Gee* [1977] Crim.LR 481.

[16] In *Winson* [1969] 1 QB 371 an absent licensee was held guilty of an offence requiring knowledge when it was committed by his assistant manager without his knowledge, although the full manager was on the premises. See criticism by Pace in [1982] Crim.LR 633–634.

[17] *Goodfellow* v. *Johnson* [1966] 1 QB 83.

of the civil law that a superior servant is not the master of an inferior servant. The foreman is not the master of the workman who digs the trench. Ordinary legal principles, including the principle of strict construction of penal legislation, go by the board in this branch of the law.[18]

The doctrine of delegation is not necessarily confined to liquor cases, but may be applied to other statutes with licencing provisions.[19] One may hope that the courts will call a halt at this point and not extend it outside offences by licensees, though from time to time there are threatening signs that this may be done.[20]

In general Parliament has passively accepted these judicial extensions of the law. But on one particular point it bestirred itself to action; a publican who is convicted of "knowingly" selling liquor to a person under 18 because his delegate has done so is now, paradoxically, given a no-negligence defence.[21] (How could he prove non-negligence if he has knowingly—as his conviction records—allowed the violation to occur?). Why the publican should not equally be allowed a no-negligence defence when he is convicted of all the other offences under the delegation principle does not appear.

§ 43.4. THE CONSTRUCTION OF STATUTORY VERBS: SALE

The peculiarity of the provisions of the Licensing Act just examined is that in terms they strike only at the licensee who is generally the employer, and are silent as to the employee, who is left to be brought in, if at all, only under the doctrine of accessoryship. Most legislation does the opposite; it strikes at the actual doer, who in matters of trade and industry will often be the employee, and appears on its face to be silent upon the responsibility of the employer. However, the courts have for many years groped for some principle that would bring in the employer.

This represents another effort to get away from *mens rea*. The courts had held, in an indulgent moment, that a person cannot be convicted as accessory without *mens rea*; but it was thought that it should be possible, all the same, to convict an employer where his employee committed an offence of strict liability, without casting on the prosecution the necessity for proving the employer's *mens rea*. To effect this end, the courts had to find that the employer himself perpetrated the offence.

A few cases apply to other statutes the distinction drawn in the licensee cases; has the employer delegated his authority generally? (in which case he is responsible for his delegate) or has he merely appointed the employee to do some specific task? (in which case he is not liable).[1] But this distinction has generally been dropped, except in the licensee cases. It is irrational in the context of the criminal law, because it does not succeed in picking out either those employers who are most likely to have had

---

[18] See, however, *Taylor* v. *Speed* [1979] Crim.LR 114, where it was held that the holder of a liquor licence in respect of certain premises who was totally unconnected with the premises was not liable for an illegal sale of liquor on the premises by persons who were not his employees.

[19] Cp. *United Dairies (London) Ltd.* v. *Beckenham Corpn.* [1963] 1 QB at 446–447; *The General Part*, 2nd edn 272; Pace in [1982] Crim.LR 628–629.

[20] See § .4 n. 1. In *Allen* v. *Whitehead* § .3 n. 4 the doctrine was applied where the offence was confined to persons "who shall have or keep a house," even though not licensed; but there are authorities the other way: *The General Part* 272–273.

[21] CLA 1977 Sched. 12.

[1] E.g. *Barker* v. *Levinson* [1951] 1 KB 342. See § .3 n. 20.

effective control or those who are most likely to have been at fault. Also, it involves an unwarranted exercise of legislative power by the courts.

A certain break-through occurred when the courts discovered (as they thought) that the verbs used in penal statutes can sometimes be interpreted to include the conduct of persons other than the immediate doer. In one context this interpretation is fully justifiable, namely when the verb refers to the creation of a legal relationship. Take again section 2 of the Food and Drugs Act 1955 (re-enacting earlier legislation). This penalises a person who "sells" improper food.[2] In its legal meaning the word "sells" refers to a legal transaction, a sale under a contract of sale. When a person makes a purchase in (say) a department store, the sale in law is by the store company, which owns the goods that are sold, not by the assistant who deals with the customer. Therefore, the store company can be convicted of the offence of improper selling under the Food and Drugs Act,[3] this offence not requiring *mens rea*. The employer, who himself performs no physical act at the time of the sale, is made liable as perpetrator although the sale is physically arranged by his employee, because the employer is regarded in law as making the sale.

Contractual verbs, then, are almost inevitably read to apply to the employer who is the contracting party. The argument for this interpretation is not so strong as applied to factual verbs, which on traditional principles should be read as applying to the actual doer; otherwise vicarious penal liability would be let in by the back door. But the courts have been making ventures in this direction. As one example, they interpret the verb "supply" in an attributive sense. The word appears in the Trade Descriptions Act 1968 s. 1, which penalises a person who in the course of a trade or business "supplies" goods to which a false trade description is applied. The offence is regarded as being committed not when the contract is made but when the seller makes delivery[4]; and it is held to be committed where an employee delivers goods on the employer's behalf. They are the employer's goods, and the employer supplies them by authorising his employee to supply them.

The interpretation is open to the objection already adumbrated. "Supply" is a physical act, and when an employee hands over the goods he is the physical supplier. On the usual principles of complicity, the liability of the employer should be that of a person who has authorised the supply, i.e. as accessory. But that would mean that if the employer is to be convicted he needs *mens rea*, which is undoubtedly out of place in many of these regulatory offences. Moreover, picking on the employee who actually effects the delivery as carrying the liability of a perpetrator would often be arbitrary. So there is practical sense in the judicial interpretation, even though it moves subtly away from classical criminal theory.

Suppose that the employee disregards instructions by the employer when he sells the goods, and therefore violates the statute?

The contract of sale is still binding on the employer (if the employee had a general authority to sell and if the limitation of his authority was not

---

[2] § 42.1 at n. 13.

[3] *Coppen* v. *Moore (No. 2)* [1898] 2 QB 306. So a liquor licensee can be liable for an offence of selling committed by his employee if it is an offence of strict liability, even though he has not delegated management. His liability is not as licensee but on the extensive construction of the verb "sells." On principle, however, he is not liable for an offence of selling that requires *mens rea* unless he has the *mens rea* or has delegated management. See § .3 n. 6.

[4] *Rees* v. *Munday* [1974] 1 WLR 1284, 3 All ER 506. The court added: "or notification that they are available for delivery if they are being collected by the buyer"; *sed quaere*.

known to the buyer), so the employer still commits an offence if the sale is wrongful.[5] But a sale by an employee (like an errand boy) who is not authorised to sell at all does not involve the employer.[6]

What if the sale is not by an employee?

The same principle applies. In the civil law, a person may authorise any other person to make a contract as his agent. The agent need not be his employee. An agent is anyone who is authorised to make a contract on the principal's behalf; he may, for example, be an auctioneer.

If a barman employed by a club sells liquor in breach of law, are the members of the committee liable?

Yes if the offence is one of strict liability and if it is an unincorporated club; the committee members are then the barman's employers.[7] But if the club were incorporated as a registered company the employer would be the company, and not the committee members.

I suppose the employee or other agent who does the actual selling is liable as accessory?

More than this; he is held to be liable as co-perpetrator, so that he is (in the absence of an express statutory defence) strictly responsible (which he could not be if his liability were only as accessory).[8]

The decisions on this point, though clearly settled, are open to challenge on grounds of logic. As we have just seen, the courts have held that the word "sell" in a penal statute refers to a legal relationship. A shop assistant is not a party to that relationship, so his liability should be only as accessory. To say that he is a perpetrator of an improper sale involves reading the statutory word "sells" in two different ways at once: as applying to the creation of a legal relationship (legally sells) and the making of a factual arrangement (physically sells). It is highly unlikely that a Parliamentary draftsman would have intended such a double meaning; if he had wished to bring in both employer and employee as perpetrators he would have done so by appropriate language. Nor is the interpretation necessary in order to place a legal duty on the employee; if he were held liable as accessory he could still be convicted, but only on proof of *mens rea*. The unpersuasive reading of the word "sells" in a double meaning is due simply to the desire of the judges to bring as many people as possible within the net of strict liability.

An even more extensive notion of "selling" has been adopted. To understand this, the scheme of the Sale of Goods Act 1979 must be known. The Act, which is the general code regulating the contract of sale of goods in the civil law, provides (in s. 2 (44)) that an "agreement to sell" turns into a "sale" when the property (ownership) in the goods passes to the buyer. Property may pass at the time of the contract; but sometimes it passes at a later time. When the contract is for the sale of "unascertained goods" no property can pass until the goods are ascertained (s. 16), and they become ascertained when they are "appropriated"

---

[5] *Per cur.* in *Anderton* v. *Rodgers* 145 JP Rep 181, [1981] Crim.LR 404.

[6] *Adams* v. *Camfoni* [1929] 1 KB 95. The same rule applies in respect of other contractual verbs, e.g. "employ": *Portsea Island Co-op. Soc.* v. *Leyland* [1978] ICR 1195, 77 LGR 225.

[7] *Anderton* v. *Rodgers*, n. 5 above.

[8] E.g. *Caldwell* v. *Bethell* [1913] 1 KB 119; *Knapp* v. *Bedwell* (1916) 80 JP 336, 85 LJKB 1507, 115 LT 486, 32 TLR 704. In *Sandford Motor Sales* v. *Habgood* [1962] Crim.LR 487 liability was extended to an auctioneer. (The decision in *Lester* v. *Balfour Williamson (MS) Ltd* [1953] 2 QB 168 is irreconcilable with these cases, though perfectly correct in point of general legal principle.) Contrast the position in the licensee cases. Here the delegate is liable only as accessory; he cannot be liable as perpetrator, lacking the qualification for a perpetrator.

to the contract (designated as being the goods agreed to be sold). Suppose I ring up my coal merchant and order 10 sacks of coal. My order is taken, so that the contract of sale is between myself and the coal merchant. The next morning the coalman employed by the merchant (who took no part in forming the contract) sets out with a full load of sacks. None bears my name, and there is at that time no appropriation. Unknown to the coalman, the sacks contain short weight.The coalman takes 10 sacks off the lorry and delivers them to me with a ticket showing a false weight. This is the point of appropriation, the time when the agreement to sell turns into a "sale" (s. 18 r. 5). The courts held, under legislation preceding the Trade Descriptions Act, that the coalman, by delivering the goods with the false ticket and passing the ownership in the goods under the contract of sale, "sold" them and so could be convicted of selling them with a false trade description.[9] The same result would undoubtedly be reached under the Trade Descriptions Act: it would be held that the coalman "supplies" the goods.[10]

The reasoning is even less convincing than before, because a person whose act happens to pass the ownership in goods cannot reasonably be described as selling. Suppose I sell you a horse on condition that a third person, X, signifies approval of him. When X signifies that the horse is sound, the contract becomes unconditional and the ownership passes; but it would be strange to say that X's approval meant that X "sold" the horse. X's approval is simply an event on the happening of which the contract becomes fully effective. I might sell you the horse on condition that it rained tomorrow, but the rain would not sell the horse. In the same way, the delivery man who appropriates goods to the contract does not sell them in any sensible meaning of the words. What he may do is to assist the sale, but then his liability should depend on *mens rea*.

§ 43.5. "USING" UNDER THE CONSTRUCTION AND USE REGULATIONS

Where the statutory verb refers not to a legal but to a purely factual situation the task of bringing the employer within it is not so easy. The traditional principle, exemplified by 19th-century cases, is that the employer of the doer is not affected. If a statute makes it a crime (for example) to "make" a forgery or to "enter" a building, an employee who "makes" or "enters" does not automatically inculpate his employer, for it is the employee who violates the statutory prohibition, not the employer. It is only the employee who can be convicted of forgery or burglary or other serious crime, unless of course the employer has incited or helped the crime. These cases are still law, because in crimes requiring *mens rea* the employee's intention cannot usually be attributed to the employer. But in regulatory offences, not requiring *mens rea*, the courts have succeeded in interpreting certain statutory verbs in such an extensive sense as to include the employer, even when such verbs do not refer to contracts.

One example is the verb "cause." It was shown in the last chapter that an employer may be held to "cause" a result by employing someone who causes it, though in this case he is not liable if he has no knowledge of the facts.[1]

Much more prominent in the case-law is the verb "use." The Motor

---

[9] *Preston* v. *Albuery* [1964] 2 QB 796.
[10] *Knapp* v. *Bedwell,* above n. 8.

[1] § 42.4 n. 7.

Vehicles (Construction and Use) Regulations require vehicles to be in good order in sundry respects, and, as we have seen, a penalty is imposed upon any person who "uses on a road a motor vehicle or trailer which does not comply with any such regulations or causes or permits a vehicle to be so used." Suppose that A drives a vehicle, B loads goods on it and C rides in it. Common speech allows us to say that all three "use" the vehicle (at least in some circumstances), and so does their employer D if they are acting in the course of the employment. How far should the legal interpretation follow common speech? The question arose in *James & Son Ltd* v. *Smee*[2].

> James & Son Ltd's employee used a motor vehicle in the course of his employment. Unknown to the company's management the brakes were out of order, which was a breach of the Construction and Use Regulations. It was held that the company could not be convicted of permitting the offence, since the defect in the brakes was not known[3]; but the company could have been convicted of "using" the vehicle through its employee, if it had been charged with that, this being an offence of absolute prohibition. Parker J (later Lord Parker CJ) said; "In common parlance a master is using his vehicle if it is being used by his servant on his business."

The reasoning is plausible, and has been accepted ever since[4]; but it is legally fallacious. The orthodox principle is that it is the actual physical doer of the act who is the perpetrator of an offence (apart from the law of innocent agency). Therefore, in an offence of using a thing it should be the person who handles the thing who perpetrates the offence. The employer should not be regarded as perpetrating the offence even if he has expressly ordered it; his liability should be as accessory, and accessorial liability requires *mens rea*. The fact that the employer can be said to use the thing via his employee is nothing to the purpose; Lady Macbeth could be said to have killed Duncan by the hand of her husband, but she was an accessory, not a perpetrator of murder. Nor is it *à propos* that the accessory can be charged as principal; this procedural rule does not affect the substantive law. Moreover, Lord Parker's interpretation is basically inconsistent with the legislation. This distinguishes between using and permitting a use, which suggests that the legislature intended the notion of using to be confined to personal use.

The courts had no sooner established the new rule than they repented of the width of the attributive liability they had created. They realised that in interpreting the notion of using so extensively they were in danger of making nonsense of the statute by depriving the alternative of permitting a use of any practical effect. So they took the commendable course of qualifying the "common parlance" approach and cutting down the doctrine of attribution in this context by holding that the only person who "uses" a vehicle without driving it is the driver's employer.[5] Anyone else is liable only if he can be said to cause or permit the use (or, of course, to abet it). Therefore, the owner of a vehicle who asks a friend to drive it on such

---

[2] [1955] 1 QB at 90.

[3] Cp. § 6.4.

[4] Cp. *Drysdale* v. *Harrison* [1972] Crim.LR 573.

[5] *Bennett* v. *Richardson* [1980] RTR 358, following *Garrett* v. *Hooper* [1973] RTR 1. Cp. *Carmichael & Sons (Worcester) Ltd.* v. *Cottle* [1971] RTR 11, Crim.LR 45; *Howard* v. *G T Jones & Co. Ltd.* [1975] RTR 150, [1974] Crim.LR 606. The owner can of course be charged with causing or permitting the use if he knows of the condition of the vehicle.

owner's business does not use the vehicle[6]; and a person who lets a vehicle on hire does not use it either.

But it might be the owner's fault, not the hirer's, that the van was constructed or maintained badly.

That is the trouble with the wording of the offence, which does not provide for negligence. The owner is liable only for permitting the use by the hirer, and permitting requires knowledge of the defect (or possibly recklessness).

There is no attribution even in respect of the acts of a partner. In the civil law a partner is liable for the acts of his co-partners on the partnership business, and in the criminal law a partner is liable for an offence in connection with a sale or supply by his co-partners, as if they were his employees.[7] The sale or supply by any partner is a sale or supply by each of them. But the same rule does not apply in respect of a partnership "use." A partner in a firm is held not to "use" the vehicle when it is being driven by his co-partner, even when it is being used on the partnership business and even when he is travelling as a passenger.[8] His co-partner is not his employee. The justification for this decision is that it sets relatively clear bounds to the notion of "use." However, a partner "uses" the vehicle when it is being driven by the firm's employee.[9]

Unfortunately, the courts have now qualified their concession and impaired the clarity of their rule by holding that a person can "use" a vehicle in some circumstances when it is being driven by someone other than his employee. This is when the defendant was being driven in the vehicle "directly for his own purposes." In a case where D was being driven in his own car by a friend in order to get him home, he was held to be using the car[10]; so on this point we are back to "common parlance." The exception not only smudges what was thought to be a clear rule but creates anomalies. It is strange that a partner who is being driven on partnership business is not regarded as being driven for his own direct purposes for the purpose of the exception. And does the exception about being driven for one's own direct purposes mean that a bus passenger uses the bus, so as to be liable under the Construction and Use Regulations if the bus's brakes are defective?[11]

Even when the employer can be convicted of an offence of using, the employee who drives the vehicle can also be convicted, and will be strictly liable, notwithstanding that the defect in the vehicle of which complaint is made was not his fault but that of the firm's maintenance department. The law has nothing to do with justice.

Of course, the driver is not likely to be charged; the prosecutor will be gunning for the

---

[6] *Crawford* v. *Haughton* [1972] 1 WLR 572, 1 All ER 535. In the law of tort, a voluntary helper can be an employee, or sufficiently in the position of an employee to inculpate the person helped, at any rate where use is made of the latter's property; but it is right that the criminal law should eschew this nebulous extension of liability.

The position of a wife who gives her husband a hand now and again in his business is doubtful. In *Brandish* v. *Poole* [1968] 1 WLR 544, 2 All ER 31, a wife who helped her husband in his business on one occasion was held not to be his "servant" within the meaning of a statute. This is difficult to reconcile with some criminal cases like *Foulkes* (1875) LR 2 CCR 150, as well as with civil cases. However, since a partner is not liable for a use by his co-partner (below n. 8), it is reasonable that the same exemption should apply to use by a wife.

[7] *Clode* v. *Barnes* [1974] 1 WLR 544, 1 All ER 1166. Cp. *Parsons* v. *Barnes* [1973] Crim.LR 537; *Linnett* v. *MPC*, § .3 n. 1; *Anon*, 138 JPN 644.

[8] *Bennett* v. *Richardson* n. 5 above.

[9] *Passmore* v. *Gibbons* [1978] Crim.LR 498. But the director of a limited company does not use the company's vehicles when driven by employees, because the company, not he, is the employer.

[10] *Cobb* v. *Williams* [1973] RTR 113. The owner was convicted of using the car without insurance (an offence under RTA 1960 s. 201, which again refers to using or causing or permitting another to use); no enquiry was made whether he knew or should have known of the driver's lack of insurance. See also *Bennett* v. *Richardson*, n. 5 above; § .6 at nn. 5–10.

[11] But see, as to disqualification, § 14.7 n. 15. The limitation on Lord Parker's rule apparently does not operate to its full extent when the charge is brought for an offence that is committed only by using (and not by permitting the use) of a vehicle: see next section.

employer. But an unwary prosecutor may perhaps charge the driver with using in order to charge the employer with abetting. In that event, the prosecution, while succeeding against the unfortunate driver, will collapse against the employer unless it can be shown that the employer knew all the facts of the offence.[12] To get home against the employer on the basis of strict liability you must charge him not with "permitting" nor with abetting the offence, but with "using."

Problems may arise where an employee in driving is pursuing his own purposes. The employer's liability will depend on the precise facts.

- Suppose the employee takes out the firm's van in the evening on some private frolic. In that case, obviously, the employer does not "use" the van, since he has not authorised the use in any way.[13]
- The position is not necessarily the same if the employee starts out on an authorised journey but deviates from his round of toil to call on his girl friend. Cases on vicarious liability in tort show that the test then is the degree of deviation. If the employee merely takes a roundabout route (on the outward or return journey) he is still within the general course of his employment and the employer is therefore still "using" the vehicle. If the employee goes off in an entirely wrong direction, that is a frolic of his own. But no precise angle of deviation can be laid down as a way of deciding these cases. One has to make an impressionistic judgment.[14]

The employer cannot escape liability by giving the employee a list of "Don'ts" unless he puts the whole category of conduct in question outside the employee's authority. If a bus *conductor* is told not to drive the bus, he will be acting outside the course of his employment if he drives it.[15] But if the *driver* is told not to drive the bus without first checking the brakes, he will still be acting within the course of his employment if he disregards the order, so that his employer will still in law be "using" the bus. If the law were otherwise, employers would merely instruct their employees not to break the law, and the employers would escape liability even though they made no serious effort to see that the law was obeyed.

An intermediate case is where a driver is instructed to make a certain journey, and he uses not his ordinary vehicle but another vehicle that he is not authorised to drive. Here again it is held that the employer "uses" the unauthorised vehicle. The fact that the vehicle is being used on his business by the employee who is authorised to drive on that journey is decisive.[16] The interpretation of the law is distinctly hard on the employer if the authorised vehicle was well maintained and the unauthorised vehicle was not supposed to be driven at all.

If I "use" the vehicles driven by my employees, do I "use" those driven by a builder whom I employ to build a house?

No. The builder is an independent contractor, not an employee. The general rule of the civil law is that vicarious liability does not extend to independent contractors, and the rule is followed by the criminal courts in cases of the type here being considered. The law would be reduced to absurdity if the employer of a building contractor, or the passenger in a taxi, were deemed to "use" the vehicle in such a way as to make him responsible for its defective brakes.[17]

---

[12] Cp. *John Henshall (Quarries) Ltd.* v. *Harvey* [1965] 2 QB 233. The better view is that, if knowledge is proved, the employer is guilty of abetting the offence even though he could, in the alternative, be charged with permitting it: § 15.7 at n. 15.

[13] Cp. § 32.4 at n. 17.

[14] For a criminal case in which the question arose see *Jack Motors Ltd* v. *Fazackerley* [1962] Crim.LR 486.

[15] For a civil case to this effect see *Iqbal* v. *LTE* (1973) 16 KIR 329.

[16] *Richardson* v. *Baker* [1976] RTR 56, Crim.LR 76.

[17] On the distinction between employees and independent contractors, and the problems that arise when a vehicle is hired along with a driver (or a driver is hired from an agency), see 1st edn 937–940.

§ 43.6. "USING" BY ITSELF

The previous discussion was concerned primarily with legislation in relation to "using or causing or permitting to be used." Where the legislation penalises "using" only, the principles appear to be identical except in one respect. The simple "using" offence has been held to be wider than the "using or permitting" offence because it includes use by independent contractors. However, the authorities are in conflict.

In *F E Charman Ltd* v. *Clow*[1] the defendant company, Charman Ltd, contracted to supply a quantity of ash to V. To fulfil their contract, they ordered the ash from a supplier and engaged the owner-driver of a lorry to deliver it. The lorry did not comply with the Weights and Measures Act 1963 as a cubic measure, so that short measure was delivered. The Act makes it an offence to "use" an article for trade as a cubic measure unless it has been passed by an inspector. It was held by a Divisional Court that Charman Ltd was guilty of the offence, since it "used" the lorry through the contractor. Cases on the Construction and Use Regulations were distinguished, since here the statute did not refer in the alternative to"permitting" the use.

The *ratio decidendi* was that the word "use" was in itself wide enough to cover use through an independent contractor, and that the narrower meaning adopted in relation to "using or permitting" sections was due entirely to the desire to leave an ambit of operation to the alternative of "permitting." The court thought itself constrained by authority[2] to reach this conclusion, but expressed regret that the law should thus be made so complicated (and, it might have added, so flagrantly unjust). The attention of the court was not called to a contrary decision, later in date than the authority on which it relied. This was *United Dairies (London) Ltd* v. *Beckenham Corporation.*[3]

United Dairies, a milk distributing company, supplied bottles to a farmer from whom it bought milk. The farmer filled the bottles with milk and returned them, so filled, to United Dairies. The bottles proved to be dirty. Regulations provide that milk bottles must be thoroughly clean before "use." It was held that "use" referred to filling the bottle; only the farmer filled the bottle, and only he was liable under the regulations.

Certainly the farmer used the bottles by filling them. No doubt it was the practice that he, rather than the milk distributor, should wash the bottles; so it was the farmer who was at fault if the bottles were dirty. These would have been excellent reasons for convicting the farmer. But the food inspector, for some obscure bureaucratic reason, chose to charge the distributor; and the decision in its favour was a matter of common sense. Yet if the view expressed in *Charman Ltd* is accepted, did not the distributor "use" its bottles by having them filled by the farmer as an independent contractor? Filling was simply part of the general use of the bottles for conveying milk to the public, and that use was, on the principle of *Charman Ltd*, a use by the distributor (employer) as well as by the farmer (contractor). Consequently, there seems to be an antinomy between the two decisions, and the result reached in the *United Dairies* case is greatly preferable. To interpret the word "use" to include use through contractors gives it a vast extension; it could mean, for example, that a passenger in a taxi is liable for breach of regulations governing the use of the taxi, when in common sense they are none of his business.

Apart from the question mark hanging over independent contractors, it appears that (as already said) the word "use" is construed in the same way whether or not it appears as an alternative to permitting a use. Perhaps the commonest situation in which the question arises is where a vehicle is taken without authority and a passenger is charged with using the vehicle without insurance.[4] If he was a party to the unlawful taking he is clearly guilty as an accessory

---

[1] [1974] 1 WLR 1384, 3 All ER 341.
[2] *Quality Dairies (York) Ltd.* v. *Pedley* [1952] 1 KB 275.
[3] [1963] 1 QB 434. For another restrictive interpretation of the same verb in a different context see § 15.15 n. 14.
[4] RTA 1972 s. 143.

to the unlawful taking of a conveyance,[5] and as an accessory to the uninsured use,[6] and he can therefore be convicted of the unlawful taking and uninsured use.[7] If he was not a party to the unlawful taking but knew at the beginning of the ride that the vehicle had been unlawfully taken, he is guilty of allowing himself to be carried on the vehicle,[8] but not (at least generally) of using the vehicle without insurance (even as an accessory).[9] This seems to be an application of the principle discussed in § .5: he is not the driver or the driver's employer, and has not commissioned the use. Perhaps if he commissioned the use of the vehicle (though after it had been unlawfully taken) he would be guilty of using it on the "direct purposes" rule.[10]

§ 43.7. "PERSONAL" VERBS

In the instances studied in this chapter offences of strict liability have been extended to include employers by construing a verb attributively, to cover someone other than the immediate doer. How far the courts will go with this practice of attribution remains in doubt, but certainly there are some verbs that cannot be construed attributively but only "personally."

An important instance is the verb "drives." The owner of a lorry might say that he "used" it for a journey to Manchester even though he was not in it; but he would never say that he "drove" it to Manchester unless he were at the wheel. As was pointed out before,[1] the notion of driving strongly connotes the physical act of controlling the vehicle in motion. Besides, to hold that an employer drives through his employee would have absurd results. It would mean that the millionaire who has never learnt to drive, lounging in the back of his limousine, could be convicted of driving without a licence, although the actual driving was done by his chauffeur who had a licence. If the millionaire were being driven back from a good dinner he might be convicted of driving under the influence of drink. Even millionaires do not deserve to be treated so unjustly. Statutes referring to driving can sensibly only be understood as referring to the actual driving; and that is how they are construed.

What if the millionaire tells his chauffeur to drive at 60 in a built-up area?

Then, of course, the millionaire would be an accessory to the offence (of reckless driving, or of exceeding the speed limit) committed by the chauffeur.

It may be suggested that another instance of a personal verb is "demanding." An employer does not make a demand if it is made by his employee without his authority.[2]

In one case[3] an employer was held to have been rightly convicted of wilfully obstructing the highway by reason of an act of his employee which he had not authorised; but this is clearly wrong. In the first place the offence in question was one of wilfulness, which (this not being

---

[5] § 32.4 at n. 8.

[6] *Ross* v. *Rivenall* [1959] 1 WLR 713, 2 All ER 376; *per cur.* in *Boldizsar* v. *Knight* [1980] Crim.LR 653.

[7] *Ross* v. *Rivenall*, last note; this on the rule stated in § 15.2 at n. 8.

[8] See n. 5 above.

[9] *D (an infant)* v. *Parsons* [1960] 2 All ER 493. *A fortiori* if he only came to know of the unlawfulness during the ride: *Boldizsar*, n. 6 above.

[10] § .5 at n. 10.

[1] § 15.16 at n. 8.

[2] Cp. *Barker* v. *Levinson* [1951] 1 KB 342.

[3] *C. Gabriel Ltd* v. *Enfield LBC* [1971] RTR 265, Crim.LR 363.

a licensee case) should not have carried attributive liability. In the second place, it is not the law that an employer is to be regarded as doing everything that his employee does. The *Tesco* case, which is to be dealt with in § 44.2, is full of remarks by the law lords to the effect that the concept of vicarious liability has no general application in criminal law.[4] If employers are to be made vicariously responsible for offences of this kind it should be done by specific legislation.

§ 43.8. MENS REA

On principle and on the clear balance of authority, legislation requiring *mens rea* does not saddle the employer with the mental state of his employee. The construction of some statutory verbs in an attributive sense settles the question of the employer's liability in strict liability offences; but if the offence requires fault the employer will not be liable if the only fault is that of an employee. This is expressed or implied in various of the licensee cases and cases on corporate liability, which recognise that *mens rea* cannot be attributed to the employer outside the special liability attached by those cases.[1] Similarly with negligence.[2] One or two decisions go the other way,[3] but they are out of the current of authority.

The following well-established rules may be listed in support of this view; all of them show that the *mens rea* of the employee is not automatically transferred to the employer.

- Even a licensee is not liable for a *mens rea* offence committed by an employee if he does not delegate to that employee: *Vane* v. *Yiannopoullos*.[4]
- Since "permitting" or "causing" a person to do something requires *mens rea*, an employer is not liable for permitting or causing an employee to do something if he has no *mens rea*.[5]
- Even where a corporation is identified with the state of mind of its controller (§ 44.2), it is not identified with (or liable for) the states of mind of its other employees.[6]
- Even where an employer is attributively liable for an offence of strict liability directly committed by his employee, he is not liable for the employee's attempt to commit it, because an attempt requires *mens rea* in the defendant, and the *mens rea* of his employee is not sufficient.[7]
- Even where an employer is attributively liable for an offence of strict liability committed by his employee, he cannot be convicted without proof of *mens rea* if he is charged with abetting the offence.[8]

SUMMARY

Situational offences frequently carry strict liability, so that the defendant is liable §.1

---

[4] See also *Ross Hillman Ltd.* v. *Bond*, § 42.4 n. 7.

[1] The principle was reaffirmed in *Coupe* v. *Guyett* § 44.6 n. 18; *Essondon Engineering Co. Ltd* v. *Maile* [1982] Crim.LR 510. It may be suggested that even if the offence in the latter case had not required a mental element, the employer should still not have been regarded as "issuing" a test certificate by the hand of its employee, except as accessory.

[2] *Tesco* § 44.2 n. 11.

[3] *C Gabriel Ltd.* v. *Enfield LBC*, § .7 n. 3, and *Mousell Bros Ltd* v. *L. & NW Rly* [1917] 2 KB 836. It seems from the speech of Lord Evershed in *Vane* v. *Yiannopoullos* § .3 n. 7 that *Mousell Bros Ltd* is to be restrictively interpreted, and is no authority for saying that every employer is vicariously liable for his employee's offence involving *mens rea*.

[4] § .3 n. 7.

[5] §§ 6.4, 42.4 n. 7, 44.4 n. 1.

[6] § 44.2.

[7] § 17.4.

[8] §§ .3 n. 6, .5 n. 13.

although he was not at fault and did not act or culpably omit. However, a no-negligence defence is occasionally allowed. Some statutes impose liability for the act or omission of another: parents can be made to pay a juvenile's fine, and liability for ticket offences can also involve liability for another's wrong.

Some statutes, either expressly or by judicial interpretation, allow the act of an employee to be attributed to the employer almost as though it were the employer's own. In this way, what is essentially situational liability masquerades as personal liability. §.2

The licensee cases are an important example. Where a person has a public licence (e.g. to sell intoxicating liquor) and delegates the management of his business in his absence to a manager, he is liable as licensee for offences committed by the manager even though the statute requires knowledge on his part, provided that the manager has that knowledge. In *Vane* v. *Yiannopoullos* the House of Lords held that a licensee who was on another floor of the premises when the contravention occurred and did not know of it was not liable for an offence of knowledge, since he was not absent; yet a Divisional Court subsequently held that a licensee was liable where he was merely in a different room, on the ground that he was then absent. The delegation doctrine does not make the licensee liable for the acts of his manager's assistant, unless perhaps it is an assistant manager and not a menial assistant. §.3

Where a statute makes it an ofence to "sell" in certain circumstances, a sale by an employee is held to involve the employer, provided that the employee has general authority to sell. Similarly with the verb "supply." The employee who makes the contract for his employer is also held to sell, and so does an employee who delivers the goods sold and thereby passes the property in them. §.4

It is an offence for a person to use on a road a motor vehicle not complying with the Construction and Use Regulations, or for him to cause or permit a vehicle to be so used. An employer is held to "use" a vehicle through his employee (provided that the employee is acting within the course of his employment). In general, the only other person who is regarded as using a vehicle is the driver. So the owner of a vehicle does not use it if it is driven by a friend, even on the owner's business, or if it is driven by his partner or by an independent contractor. But to this rule again there is an exception: a person uses his own vehicle when he is being driven in it for his own "direct" purposes. §.5

Where the word "use" appears in a statute without the alternatives of causing or permitting the use, the interpretation appears to be the same, except that, according to one decision, use by an independent contractor may be covered; but there is another decision the other way. §.6

It seems clear that the verb "drive" will be construed only as being "personal"; and no verb should be construed in an attributive sense unless there are strong legal arguments for this. §.7

Except in the licensee cases, a requirement of fault requires fault by the defendant; fault by his employee is insufficient. §.8

Chapter 44

CORPORATIONS; EXCEPTIONS TO STRICT LIABILITY

"I'm Lingley of Lingley Ltd. Not one of you can touch me. I turned myself into a company years ago."

Sutton Vane, *Outward Bound*

§ 44.1. CORPORATIONS

Sutton Vane's unpleasant business man had grasped a certain truth in regard to the civil law of corporations, but directors of companies are by no means immune in the criminal courts.

What is the difference between a company and a corporation?

The strict technical term at common law was "corporation." A "company" may be an unincorporated firm (partnership). But when we speak of a company we usually mean an incorporated company, a corporation, and that is what "company" will mean in this chapter. A group of people may have been incorporated

- — by royal charter (e.g. a University, or an Oxford or Cambridge college),
- — by special statute (e.g. public corporations), or
- — by registration under the Companies Act 1967 or its predecessors (by far the commonest way). This is the ordinary trading company (though there are also registered companies not engaged in trade, e.g. some charities).

What is the difference between a company registered under the Companies Act and a company that is a partnership?

A partnership ("John Brown & Co.") is not recognised in the criminal law, and receives only limited recognition in the civil law. The same applies to other unincorporated associations like a club. When a member of a members's club "buys" a drink in the bar, there is in law no "sale" or "supply" to him for the purpose of (say) the Trade Descriptions Act, because in law he is already the beneficial owner of all the property of the club, in common with the other members.[1] If the club were registered as a company, then the company would own the property and there would be a sale. The point about a registered company ("John Brown & Co. Ltd") is that it is a corporation, i.e. a notional entity, a ghostly person—what lawyers call a "legal person." It is based upon but distinct from a number of human beings who sign the memorandum of association and so bring the

[1] *John* v. *Matthews* [1970] 2 QB 443.

company into existence; these human beings may afterwards die without affecting the existence of the company. What needs to be understood is that when John Brown and his wife "turn themselves" into a limited company, they have between them given birth to a new person in law, which may hold property and make contracts on its own account, and that these are not the contracts and property of John Brown and his wife.

What is the point of saying that a company is a person in law?

The independent legal existence of the company is useful because individual shareholders may come and go; and it has the great advantage of creating limited liability. Only the company is liable for its debts. If the company is insolvent, creditors cannot go against the private property of the shareholders. The shareholders are responsible only to the extent of their shares, and when their shares are fully paid up they are not liable at all. Few people would invest in a large company if they were liable without limit for the debts of the company if things went wrong.

Do you mean that a man can commit crimes under the disguise of a company?

The law recognises corporate liability, but the device of incorporation is not a bolt-hole for people who commit offences. A company can act only through human beings, and a human being who commits an offence on account of or for the benefit of a company will be responsible for that offence himself, just as any employee committing an offence for a human employer is liable. The importance of incorporation is that it makes the company itself liable in certain circumstances for offences, as well as the human beings. Corporate liability was slowly developed by the judges, with some help from statute on the procedural side.[2]

§ 44.2. IDENTIFICATION

Companies are liable in two ways; either (1) attributively, or (2) by virtue of a special kind of legal attribution known as the identification doctrine.

(1) They are liable for the misdeeds of their employees to the same extent as a human employer would be. We have seen that attributive liability does not (except in the licensee cases) apply to offences requiring *mens rea*, and the same limitation applies to companies, in so far as their liability is based upon ordinary rules of attribution for rank-and-file employees.[1]

(2) However, the identification doctrine goes a step beyond this. A company is identified with its controlling officers. The doctrine owes its origin to a civil case, where it was held that, for the purpose of a statute

---

[2] See *The General Part*, 2nd edn § 278.

[1] See, e.g. *Ross Hillman Ltd* v. *Bond* [1974] QB at 440.

referring to "actual fault or privity," the privity of the manager was that of the company. Viscount Haldane LC said:

> "My lords, a corporation is an abstraction. It has no mind of its own any more than it has a body of its own; its active and directing will must consequently be sought in the person of somebody who for some purposes may be called an agent, but who is really the directing mind and will of the corporation, the very ego and centre of the personality of the corporation."[2]

In other words, those who control or manage the affairs of the company are regarded in a sense as the company itself. Whenever they are acting in their capacity of controlling officers, the company is identified with both
— their acts, even in respect of verbs that would not be read attributively for a human employer, and also
— their states of mind.
In this way, the company can become liable for an offence requiring *mens rea*, even in circumstances where a human employer would not be liable.

> The leading case on the criminal side is *ICR Haulage Ltd*,[3] where a company, its managing director, and others were indicted for conspiracy to defraud. The Court of Criminal Appeal upheld the indictment. Although the crime charged required a state of mind, and although a corporation has no mind of its own, yet the state of mind of its managing director is imputed to it, so that his fraud is its fraud.

Notice that other persons besides the company and the one director were involved in the conspiracy; if there had not been, there could have been no conviction. A company, through its director, may conspire with another person. But a director who does something illegal on behalf of the company cannot be convicted on that account of conspiring with the company, because then there is only one mind at work, whereas conspiracy needs two.[4]

Where a company is liable under the identification doctrine, the director or other controlling officer will almost always be a co-perpetrator of or accessory in the offence, or commit one of the special statutory offences for company officers.[5]

The doctrine of identification applies not only to private companies but to public corporations like local authorities and public utilities. But a corporation that is an "emanation of the Crown" can be protected by the Crown's general immunity from statutes.[6]

You speak of the controlling officers, but isn't it impossible to draw a sharp line between the top brass and the lower ranks in a large company? Even a workman who is sent out with his mate to do a routine maintenance job is invested with a certain discretion.

The law provides no clear principle for deciding who is a controller. According to Lord Reid in *Tesco Supermarkets Ltd* v. *Nattrass*[7]:

---

[2] *Lennard's Carrying Co. Ltd* v. *Asiatic Petroleum Co. Ltd* [1915] AC at 713.
[3] [1944] KB 551.
[4] *McDonnell* [1966] 1 QB 233.
[5] §15.19.
[6] §28.1.
[7] [1972] AC at 170, 173.

"It must be a question of law whether, once the facts have been ascertained, a person in doing particular things is to be regarded as the company, or merely as the company's servant or agent . . . .The judge must direct the jury that if they find certain facts proved then as a matter of law they must find that the criminal act of the officer, servant or agent including his state of mind, intention, knowledge or belief is the act of the company."

Unfortunately, the decision does not make it clear what are these facts to which the judge must direct the jury's attention.[8] It can certainly be said that the directors are controllers, but the company manager or even secretary[9] will join the select circle if he has an important say. Denning LJ in a civil case described the distinction as being between the "brain" of the company and its "hands,"[10] but that is no more than a metaphor.

In the *Tesco* case[11] (the full facts of which will be given later), the question arose whether the branch manager of a supermarket firm was sufficiently in control of the company's affairs to have his negligence attributed to the company as the personal fault of the company. The House of Lords held not. Lord Reid restated the general principle as follows. "Normally the board of directors, the managing director and perhaps other superior officers of a company carry out the functions of management and speak and act as the company. Their subordinates do not. They carry out orders from above and it can make no difference that they are given some measure of discretion. But the board of directors may delegate some part of their functions of management giving to their delegate full discretion to act independently of instructions from them. I see no difficulty in holding that they have thereby put such a delegate in their place so that within the scope of the delegation he can act as the company. It may not always be easy to draw the line but there are cases in which the line must be drawn." Lord Reid made it plain that the liability of a company for its controllers is equivalent to the personal liability of a human being. "There is no question of the company being vicariously liable."

Although it is now clear that a branch manager is not necessarily to be regarded as a member of the top echelon with which the company is identified, the actual decision was helped by the fact that Tesco branch managers were tightly controlled by visiting branch inspectors and above them by area inspectors. But it seems that even without this fact the branch manager would not have had sufficient administrative powers to be identified with the corporation. Lord Pearson said:

"In the present case the company has some hundreds of retail shops, and it would be far from reasonable to say that every one of its shop managers is the same person as the company . . . .Supervision of the details of operations is not normally a function of higher management;

---

[8] For the resulting difficulty, see *Andrews-Weatherfoil Ltd.* [1972] 1 WLR 118, 1 All ER 65.

[9] *Moore* v. *I Bresler Ltd* [1944] 2 All ER 515. In *Kent and Sussex Contractors Ltd* [1944] KB 146 the company's transport manager was included, but that decision may perhaps be reconsidered since *Tesco*.

[10] *H L Bolton (Engineering) Co. Ltd* v. *T J Graham & Sons Ltd* [1957] 1 QB at 172.

[11] [1972] AC 153. Cp. *Magna Plant* v. *Mitchell* [1966] Crim.LR 394 (depot engineer).

> it is normally carried out by employees at the level of foreman, chargehands, overlookers, floor managers and 'shop' managers (in the factory sense of 'shop')."[12]

I find it strange if the number of retail shops is a factor. Is it the law that a company with two retail shops is identified with branch managers, while a giant company with hundreds of shops has its brain located entirely at HQ? Why should such a line be drawn?

Lord Pearson's remark was probably no more than rhetoric. We have no reason to suppose that the matter depends upon the number of branches.

More generally, it can only be said that the identification doctrine is a compromise on a difficult question of policy. On the one hand, it would be possible to say that every company employee is identified with the company, in which case the company would be liable for a *mens rea* offence committed by the lowliest workman. This would make a remarkable contrast with the rule for human employers. At the other extreme it would be possible to say that the company is never liable except for an offence of strict liability. But then it could not be liable for an inchoate offence (even one committed for the purpose of committing an offence of strict liability), nor could it be liable as accessory, even to an offence of strict liability. Both inchoate offences and accessoryship require *mens rea*. A company could not even be liable for an offence of negligence; and since the present legislative tendency is to turn strict liability into negligence liability, this might eventually exclude corporate liability altogether.

If it be accepted that a compromise is necessary, the view may still be taken that the "voices of infallibility" drew the line too tightly in the *Tesco* case. There is no absolute right and wrong about this, but the practical effect of *Tesco* appears to be to confine the identification doctrine to the behaviour of a few men meeting, say, in London, when the activities of the corporation are country-wide or even world-wide. It would seem on the whole to have been more sensible to have extended identification to cover the person or persons in control of local branches.

In crimes requiring *mens rea* it does not greatly matter if the range of persons inculpating the company is restricted, since the purposes of deterrence are generally best served by prosecuting those who are responsible. It is in offences of negligence that the limitation of liability imposed in *Tesco* is most injurious. That a company should not be liable for an offence of negligence committed by its branch manager, who after all represents the company in the particular locality, is a considerable defect in the law. (The importance of negligence in these offences will appear presently.) What is evidently needed is a statutory redefinition of the officers whose acts and mental states implicate the company.[13]

What if a controller of a company commits an offence for his own fell purposes?

It has been held that the acts of a controller are attributed to the company even when the controller is acting in fraud of the company.[14] This is the sort of reasoning that has been characterised as "mechanical jurisprudence." There is little sense in punishing the company by a fine when the act was directed against the company and therefore against the shareholders.

---

[12] Cp. *per* Lord Diplock at 199–200, attaching importance to the person empowered by the articles of association of the company.

[13] For example, the proposed United States Federal Criminal Code includes among these officers "an executive officer or any other agent in a position of comparable authority with respect to the formulation of corporate policy or the supervision in a managerial capacity of subordinary employees." A minor employee of the company does not become a controller merely because the sole director is absent: *Essondon Engineering Co. Ltd* v. *Maile* [1982] Crim.LR 510.

[14] *Moore* v. *I Bresler Ltd* [1944] 2 All ER 515. But see *Belmont Finance Corpn Ltd* v. *Williams Furniture Ltd* [1979] Ch. 250, a much more sensible decision of a civil court.

The identification doctrine can be important not only when a company is the defendant but when it is the victim of an offence. The knowledge of a controller, and the consent of a controller if given with his powers,[15] is a defence to the same extent as that of a human victim. But, of course, it is no answer to a charge based on deception committed against an honest director to say that a dishonest director knew the truth.[16]

Although authority is lacking, it can be argued that identification applies only in respect of acts done on company business, not in the manager's private concerns, and that it applies only in respect of acts done in a managerial or directorial capacity.

> For example, suppose that the managing director of a London-based company drives to Oxford to see a branch manager, and in the course of driving is guilty of gross negligence causing the death of a pedestrian. A corporation can in an appropriate case be held guilty of manslaughter; but it is probably not guilty here, since the act of the director, though within the course of his employment for the purpose of the law of tort, is not what may be called a managerial act. It is not an exercise of the corporate powers, or a decision relating to the corporate activities.[17]

Is there any kind of legal trouble that a company cannot get into?

Virtually none. Since a company cannot be put behind bars, the only possible penalty is a fine, apart from any forfeitute of property or cancellation of licence that may be allowable by law on conviction of the offence in question. But all offences except murder, treason and some forms of piracy are now finable.

A company cannot perpetrate perjury and similar false statements on oath, because no one has tried to put a corporation on oath; but there is no reason why a company should not be convicted as accessory to perjury.

§ 44.3. THE POLICY OF CORPORATE LIABILITY

The liability of corporations, like strict liability, exemplifies utilitarian theory in the criminal law. It is based not on the theory of justice but upon the need for deterrence.

I can see that slapping a large fine on a company may cause it to pull up its corporate socks. But surely criminal responsibility should be human, because in the last resort only human beings can be punished. Why not simply convict the directors or other persons responsible for the offence within the corporate organization?

That is an important question. The main answer is that prosecuting

---

[15] *Pearlberg* § 35.3 at n. 2.

[16] *Buono* [1970] Crim.LR 154.

[17] Such a case is put by Welsh in 62 LQR 360.

solicitors report that companies generally fight quite hard to avoid conviction, even when only a modest fine is involved—and sometimes the fine is far from modest. Those responsible for the affairs of the company dislike the possibility of adverse publicity involved in a conviction, because they have been trying to build up the fair name of the company in the minds of the public. So it seems that corporate responsibility in crime has social utility in promoting obedience to law.

Two other points may be made.

(1) If a statute creates an offence of omission—say, requiring the corporation to make a return of information—there may be no "person" to convict of failure to do the act other than the company itself. For the duty is imposed only on the company. (Parliament may impose it also on the officers, but generally it does not do so.) Similarly, if a statute imposes a duty upon the owner or occupier of property, there would be difficulty in convicting anyone but a company as perpetrator of the offence where it is the company that owns or occupies the property in question. And unless the company can be convicted as perpetrator the directors cannot be convicted as accessories.[1]

(2) If there is social justification for bringing the name of the company before the public when it is involved in an offence of strict liability, then with much stronger reason it should be possible to bring in the company when there has been negligence or wilful misbehaviour by its controlling officers.

Your answer speaks mainly of besmirching the company's image. But what about the fine? The reality of a fine imposed on a company is that it is imposed upon the shareholders, whose assets are depleted by that amount. Or, if the company is insolvent, the fine falls upon the creditors. Perhaps the employees may be affected, because if the company is impoverished their jobs may be in peril. But the shareholders, the creditors and the employees are probably, for the most part, innocent of the offence. Where is the justice in punishing them?

I think we must leave the creditors out of it. Whenever anyone is fined, his creditors may be affected.

As to the others, one answer is that the fine has not the same effect upon the shareholders and employees as if it were imposed on them directly. A shareholder does not feel the punishment in his body or reputation. He suffers it only in his bank account—and perhaps imperceptibly at that. Employees are unlikely to be affected unless the fine has a crippling effect upon the company.[2]

The company itself is a legal figment. Its physical embodiment is only a piece of paper—in the case of a registered company, the memorandum of association. It has no feelings. It can hardly be said to be convicted "justly" or "unjustly." Upon being convicted it never becomes neurotic, or spends the rest of its life writing letters to the Lord Chancellor complaining of having been unjustly dealt with. So any analogy with a human being is inapt. Whether a company should be liable to conviction depends entirely on whether this subserves the general good of society.

To say that a company can commit virtually any crime does not mean that it always makes

---

[1] This is subject, however, to the possible effect of *Cogan*, § 15.16 at n. 12.

[2] In a case concerning one of Lord Kagan's companies, the judge fined the company £375,000 and intimated that it would have been higher but for the risk of causing unemployment (The Times, December 13, 1980).

sense to prosecute the company. Where directors commit a *mens rea* offence, it may be better policy to concentrate upon them, and some prosecuting counsel take this view.[3] Success in the prosecution depends, generally, upon proving that the directors (1) perpetrated the offence or (2) were accessories to it, knowing the facts,[4] or (3) were guilty of what we may call a "company officer's offence." We have seen that it is now common form in statutes creating new offences relating to trade etc. to provide that when an offence under the statute is committed by a company, any director, manager or other officer with whose consent or connivance (or even by whose negligence) the offence is committed becomes implicated in it.[5]

One difficulty in confining liability to the human perpetrator is that it may not always be possible to identify the individual within the company who was at fault. Even when he is found, he may have been blatantly "leaned on" or subtly influenced by pressures from his superiors, which makes it unjust to treat him as solely responsible. William Whyte's book *The Organization Man* shows how the vast business corporation tends to produce a subculture, an environment in which individuality becomes submerged, exacting complete conformity to the organization's norms as the price of financial security. In these circumstances it may be necessary to punish not only the offending individual but the organisation as a whole, in order to compel a change of behaviour in the group. The fine may help to call down upon the offender the displeasure of his equals or superiors, or it may cause the officers of the company to change their policy.

Instead of talking about punishment, wouldn't it be more sensible to justify fines upon a company as a way of compensating the community for the breach of law?

Sometimes that may be so, as when a shipping company is fined for illegally discharging oil at sea.[6] Or the fine may make the company disgorge ill-gotten gains, as when it trades without obtaining the licence that is legally required. But the company can generally be fined a really large sum only if the offence is indictable and is tried on indictment (magistrates are limited in their power to fine, and cannot commit a company to the Crown Court for sentence). Moreover, in so far as the penal law pays attention to questions of fault it is inappropriate for cases where a large illegal profit has been made without fault. This difficulty has become particularly acute since *Tesco*; if a Tesco-type branch manager commits a *mens rea* offence to make a big profit for his company, the company, since it cannot be convicted, cannot be fined in order to claw back the gain. What is obviously needed, apart from other reforms, is a civil proceeding for compensation on behalf of the public where illegal profits have been made with or without fault.

It may be mentioned in conclusion that an effective civil sanction for use

---

[3] The danger that corporate liability can shield guilty individuals is again illustrated by the *Kagan* case, where the directors of the company, under Kagan's influence, wished to cause the company to plead guilty to a charge of fraud arising out of Kagan's machinations, in order to shift to the shareholders part of the fine that would otherwise fall upon Kagan. A High Court injunction was issued on behalf of minority shareholders to forbid the plea.

[4] *Love* [1955] Crim.LR 250; § 15.11–12.

[5] § 15.19.

[6] For this the owner or master can be fined up to £50,000 on summary conviction and an unlimited amount on indictment: Prevention of Oil Pollution Act 1971. See Bernard M Dickens in 37 MLR 297, and the important judgment of a circuit judge in 144 JPN 703. When it is desired to compensate the public in this way the prosecution must be brought against the employer, not merely against the employee who was at fault, because a person cannot be fined beyond his ability to pay. See Dickens *op. cit.* at 301. For a discussion of the relative public advantages of criminal and civil proceedings see *ibid.* 306, and for defects in the machinery for enforcing fines see Thomas in [1979] Crim.LR 796.

against a company that is given to fraudulent trading is to have it wound up.[7] The Secretary of State for Trade may petition for this, and often acts at the instigation of the police.[8]

§ 44.4. HUMAN EMPLOYERS AND IDENTIFICATION

The notion of identification is not applied to human employers, or at any rate it never has been.

In the *Tesco* case, Lord Reid disapproved a dictum of Lord Parker CJ that a human employer would be liable if his manager was "a person to whom delegation in the true sense of the delegation of management has been passed."[1] On the other hand Lord Pearson, speaking specifically with regard to the defence of "no negligence" under section 24 of the Trade Descriptions Act (to be considered later), said:

> "Section 24 requires a dividing line to be drawn between the master and any other person. The defendant cannot disclaim liability for an act or omission of his *ego* or his *alter ego*.[2] In the case of an individual defendant, his *ego* is simply himself, but he may have an *alter ego*. For instance, if he has only one shop and he appoints a manager of that shop with full discretion to manage it as he thinks fit, the manager is doing what the employer would normally do and may be held to be the employer's *alter ego*. But if the defendant has hundreds of shops, he could not be expected personally to manage each one of them and the manager of one of his shops cannot in the absence of exceptional circumstances be considered his *alter ego*."[3]

This opinion, that the identification doctrine applies to human employers, was not voiced by the other law lords, and was evidently a minority view of Lord Pearson's.

But why shouldn't the identification doctrine be extended to non-corporate employers? If the big shots in a company are identified with the company, why shouldn't a manager employed by a partnership be identified with the partners?

The delegation rule for companies is a response to the difficulty that otherwise no company could be convicted of an offence requiring *mens rea*. This difficulty does not arise in the case of a sole trader or a partnership, because here the human beings carrying on the business can have *mens rea*.

If William Smith trades as the Superfood Co. (even an individual may call himself "Co." if he wishes), and through his negligence unfit food is exposed for sale, a prosecution will not name the Superfood Co. as a defendant. Nor will it do so if Smith is trading in partnership. Neither an individual business name nor a partnership name is regarded by the criminal law. Smith (and any partner of his) will be charged personally, though the public may of course gather from the report that the fault was associated with the Superfood stores.

Perhaps the law should be altered to allow a business to be charged under its trading name, and to make the owner liable for his manager to the same extent as a limited company would

---

[7] § 40.11 n. 4.

[8] For valuable discussions of corporate liability see Fisse in 6 Adel.LR 361; Leigh in 9 Ottawa LRev. 247. For legislative proposals see Law Com. No. 44 and comment by Andrews in [1973] Crim.LR 91.

[1] [1972] AC at 173.

[2] "Other self."

[3] [1972] AC at 192–193.

be. But the point is important chiefly for chain stores, and few chain-store businesses are unincorporated; moreover, as we have seen, corporate liability is rather ineffective for branch activities. For human defendants the question of justice is paramount. Even if the business in the hypothetical above could be charged under its name, a conviction would still, in law, be a conviction of Smith (and any partner of his) personally; and it would be wrong to convict them of an offence requiring fault if they have not been at fault.

Can a trade union be prosecuted?

If members of the union's executive council authorise the commission of a crime they can be charged as individuals, and the trade union can also be charged,[4] though there is no instance of this being done.

§ 44.5. THE DEFENCE OF NO NEGLIGENCE

We must now return to the general problem of strict liability. The English courts (unlike the High Court of Australia and Supreme Court of Canada) having failed to develop a no-negligence defence to charges involving strict liability, the Government, through Parliament, has to some extent stepped in. What precisely has moved them to re-activate the issue of fault is not clear. Offences under the Licensing Act and the Road Traffic Act (for example) retain full strict liability. The common characteristic of these two statutes, which the modern changes have passed by, is that they are administered not by special inspectors but by the police; but there is no obvious reason why this fact should deny the defendant a no-negligence defence.

When a no-negligence defence is allowed, the language varies. Sometimes the defence is expressed broadly, as in the following examples.

> Offices, Shops and Railway Premises Act 1963 s. 67: "It shall be a defence for a person charged with a contravention of a provision of this Act or of regulations thereunder to prove that he used all due diligence to secure compliance with that provision."
>
> Trade Descriptions Act 1968 s. 24 (3): "In any proceedings for an offence under this Act of supplying or offering to supply goods to which a false trade description is applied it shall be a defence for the person charged to prove that he did not know, and could not with reasonable diligence have ascertained, that the goods did not conform to the description or that the description had been applied to the goods."[1]

These are defences of no negligence, since "diligence" in law is the opposite of negligence and the equivalent of care.[2]

Even when a defence is given in these wide terms, the Divisional Court will not allow magistrates to dismiss a charge by lightly assuming that the defendant has taken care. It is insufficient, for instance, for the seller of dangerous goods to say that he imported them and

---

[4] Trade Union and Labour Relations Act 1974 s. 2 (1) (*d*); *per* Lord Denning MR in *Gouriet* v. *Union of Post Office Workers* [1977] QB at 755B.

[1] See also Consumer Protection Act 1961 s. 3 (2B), as amended by CPA 1971 s. 1; Fire Precautions Act 1971 s. 25; Prevention of Oil Pollution Act 1971 s. 5 (2); Consumer Safety Act 1978 ss. 2 (6), 3 (3).

[2] *Per* Lord Diplock in *Tesco Supermarkets Ltd* v. *Nattrass* [1972] AC at 199. Cp. *J H Dewhurst Ltd* v. *Coventry Corpn* [1970] 1 QB at 26D.

that he relied on the certificate of the foreign seller that the goods complied with English law.[3] He must test samples to satisfy himself that they do comply. The questions, as always on an issue of negligence, are: What precautions could the defendant have taken to comply with the law? Was it reasonable to expect him to take those precautions? If so, did he take them? Where the fault is that of the defendant's employee, the defendant, to disprove his own negligence, must show what steps he took to train, instruct, and control his employee.

In other legislation the language is more restricted, in one way or another, than that instanced above. The Health and Safety at Work etc. Act 1974 is an example of a statute allowing a defence of absence of fault on the wording of some but not all offences. It contains sections imposing duties only "so far as is reasonably practicable," as to which the burden of proof is placed on the defendant.[4]

Sometimes the courts restrict no-negligence defences even further by interpretation. Section 3 (3) of the Food and Drugs Act 1955 provides:

> "In proceedings under section 2 of this Act in respect of any food . . . containing some extraneous matter, it shall be a defence for the defendant to prove that the presence of that matter was an unavoidable consequence of the process of collection or preparation."

However, the House of Lords has virtually construhed this defence out of existence.

> In *Smedleys Ltd* v. *Breed*,[5] the customer of a supermarket found a caterpillar in a tin of Smedley's peas bought from the supermarket. In proceedings against Smedleys it was proved on their behalf that their factory had canned 3,500,000 tins of peas in a season of seven weeks, with only four complaints. There was an efficient and up-to-date inspection system which missed the caterpillar only because it was almost the same density, diameter, weight and colour as the peas. The caterpillar had been sterilised by being cooked and was certainly harmless and probably nutritious. Notwithstanding this evidence, which the House of Lords accepted, it was held that the presence of the caterpillar was not unavoidable.

Lord Diplock expressed the decision caustically by saying:

> "A majority of your lordships are of opinion that the presence of 'extraneous matter' in an article of food which is the product of a process of preparation can only be the 'consequence' of that process if every article of food produced by it contains similar extraneous matter . . . In the result no one has been able to think of any circumstances in which the defence under s. 3 (3) could be applicable. So local authorities and magistrates can in practice ignore the subsection altogether. This has the merit of simplicity."[6]

In addition to the arguments against this decision based on grounds of fairness and reasonable statutory interpretation, there are arguments based on cost-benefit and important environmental considerations to which their lordships paid no heed. Getting rid of the minute risk left after all the precautions the company took would cost money, and would quite possibly add a penny or two to the price of the can. Is the consumer so scared of finding one tiny caterpillar in perhaps half a million cans that he is prepared to pay extra on each can to avoid it? And would he not prefer to have the very occasional caterpillar than to have pesticide in his food? It is common knowledge that, as the Royal Commission on Environmental Pollution pointed out, the use of pesticides involves some risks for people and for wildlife. Referring particularly to the decision in *Smedley*, the Commission said:

> "The Food and Drugs Act as now interpreted bears more heavily on processed fruits and vegetables; modern marketing methods are leading to an increasing quantity of our produce being processed (packaged, frozen or tinned). Thus the pressures for an absolutely pest-free crop are applying to an increasing area of land, with a consequent increase in pollution risks."[7]

---

[3] *Taylor* v. *Lawrence Fraser Ltd* [1978] Crim.LR 43.

[4] See s. 40. In judging what is reasonably practicable the degree of risk must be weighed against the sacrifice involved: *per* Lord Reid in *Marshall* v. *Gotham Co. Ltd* [1954] AC at 373. See Holgate in 153 NLJ 549.

[5] [1974] AC 839.

[6] The decision was perforce followed by a Divisional Court in *Greater Manchester Council* v. *Lockwood Foods Ltd* [1979] Crim.LR 593, the court saying: "the case demonstrates that a defence under s. 3 (3) is virtually a dead letter."

[7] Seventh Report, Cmnd 7644 of 1979, para. 3.86.

With this consideration in mind, the Commission proposed an amendment to the Act to reverse the effect of the decision in *Smedleys*.

§ 44.6. BLAMING A THIRD PERSON

The drawback of a general defence of no negligence from the enforcer's point of view is that the defendant may be able to establish the defence without revealing the identity of the person who was really at fault, which is what the enforcer wants to know. For this reason many defences of no negligence under statute specifically require the defendant to make this disclosure. Some adopt what is called a third-party procedure, while some (the more modern) merely include a provision for the giving of notice.

Under the third-party procedure the defendant is not allowed a defence of no negligence unless he lays an information against the person who he alleges was really the person at fault.

This third-party procedure (or "passing on" defence) is a timid, over-rigid, and generally inadequate alleviation of strict liability, and is no longer used in new legislation though it is still found in some statutes. The procedure provides that when a charge is brought under the statute the defendant may bring in any other person (e.g. a supplier) to whose act or default he alleges that the contravention was due, and shift the blame to him. The most important examples are in the Shops Act 1950 (s. 71 (6)), the Food and Drugs Act 1955 (s. 113), and the Medicines Act 1968 (s. 121) (this Act replacing the provisions of the 1955 Act with regard to drugs). Here is the Food and Drugs Act s. 113 (1).[1]

> "A person against whom proceedings are brought under this Act shall, upon information duly laid by him . . . , be entitled to have any person to whose act or default he alleges that the contravention of the provisions in question was due brought before the court in the proceedings[2]; and if, after the contravention has been proved, the original defendant proves that the contravention was due to the act or default of that other person, that other person may be convicted of the offence, and, if the original defendant further proves that he has used all due diligence to secure that the provisions in question were complied with, he shall be acquitted of the offence."

The new defendant may in his turn blame someone else. Any number can play: the retailer of goods who is prosecuted may bring in the wholesaler, who in turn brings in the manufacturer, who brings in the supplier of a particular component.[3]

It will be noticed that even if the original defendant can establish that the offence was due to the act or default of another person, he is liable if he cannot also prove that he took reasonable care. The result may well be that the prosecution get convictions against both the original defendant and the third party.

The third party who did it is in the same position as the original defendant. Initially, he is strictly liable ("act or default" in the section does not imply a requirement of negligence).[4]

---

[1] Although this Act does not give a general no-negligence defence outside the third-party procedure, it allows a "warranty" defence which has something of the same effect in certain cases. See *Rochdale MBC* v. *FMC (Meat) Ltd* [1980] 1 WLR 461, 2 All ER 303.

[2] All that the defendant need do as regards the third party is to lay an information against him. He will then have the defence of no negligence even though the summons cannot be served because the third party cannot be found: *Malcolm* v. *Cheek* [1948] 1 KB 400. It has even been held, with commendable fairness, that the laying of the information validates the defence though it is out of time: *R* v. *Bicester JJ, ex p. Unigate Ltd* [1975] 1 WLR 207, 1 All ER 449.

[3] *British Fermentation Products Ltd* v. *British Italian Trading Co. Ltd* [1942] 2 KB 145.

[4] *Lindley* v. *George W Horner & Co. Ltd* [1950] 1 All ER 234, WN 48; *Lamb* v. *Sunderland & District Creamery* [1951] 1 All ER 923. In a rare mood of indulgence the court let off a broker who negotiated a contract of sale but did not have physical possession or the opportunity of taking physical possession of the goods: *Lester* v. *Balfour Williamson* § 43.4 n. 4. But the third party's act must be wrongful in some sense: see n. 20.

The only way he can escape is by bringing in a fourth party and proving that that fourth party was also causally responsible while he himself used all due diligence. So the prosecution is bound to succeed against somebody, and that somebody need not have been at fault. It follows that this type of provision is only a half-hearted departure from the general rule of strict liability.[5]

When a third-party procedure is established, the Act usually adds that the prosecution can if they wish "short-circuit" proceedings by charging the third party directly, leaving untouched the person who was directly responsible under the penal section. This is sometimes called the "bypass procedure".

An illustration is *Smedleys Ltd* v. *Breed,* the affair of the canned caterpillar.[6] The customer who bought the can and found the offending but innocuous larva reported it to the local authority whose inspector brought a charge under the Food and Drugs Act 1955 s. 2. However, he brought it not against the supermarket but against Smedleys who had canned the peas, using the bypass procedure allowed by the Act.

Other statutes are more generous to defendants. They do not adopt the third-party procedure but achieve its general purpose by allowing a defence of no negligence with a provision for informing the prosecutor of the identity of the person alleged to have been at fault. This is better for the defendant because he need not lay an information against the alleged culprit. It is also better for the third party, who is himself allowed the no-negligence defence; so strict liability disappears almost entirely. Defences using third-party procedure are no longer inserted in statutes, except consolidating statutes; in their place we simply have notice provisions. What has evidently happened is that Parliament, having made its first cautious sally in the direction of giving a no-fault defence by establishing the third-party procedure, has now mustered up the courage to go further.[7]

In some modern statutes the "notice" type of defence appears in simple and satisfactory terms,[8] but in earlier versions Parliament had adopted an involved, obscure and unjust form typified by section 24 (1) and (2) of the Trade Descriptions Act 1968, which is still in force. I reproduce it slightly trimmed.[9]

"(1) It shall be a defence for the person charged to prove—
(*a*) that the commission of the offence was due to a mistake or to reliance on information supplied to him or to the act or default of another person, an accident or some other cause beyond his control; and
(*b*) that he took all reasonable precautions and exercised all due diligence to avoid the commission of such an offence by himself or any person under his control.

(2) If the defence involves the allegation that the commission of the offence was due to the act or default of another person, the person charged shall not, without leave of the court, be entitled to rely on that defence unless he has served on the prosecutor a notice in writing giving such information identifying or assisting in the identification of that other person as was then in his possession."

The defendant need not bring in the third party. All he does is to explain how the event occurred without his fault, while helping the prosecutor to charge any third party whom he

---

[5] For various procedural problems, see Nuttall in 141 JPN 266.

[6] § 44.5 at n. 6.

[7] A sign of the movement towards greater liberality is the Weights and Measures Act. The third-party procedure previously included in the Act is now replaced by a new s. 26 giving a simple no-negligence defence: see the Act of 1979, s. 26 and Sched. 5.

[8] e.g. Consumer Safety Act 1978 s. 2 (6).

[9] Broadly similar defences of no negligence are contained in the Highways Act 1971 s. 31 (6), (7), the Fair Trading Act 1973 s. 25, and the Consumer Credit Act 1974 s. 168.

blames. The prosecutor then knows the facts, and can charge the real culprit directly, if he so wishes. This is another advantage of the notice procedure. When third-party procedure applies, the defendant can and must drag in the third party whether the prosecuting inspector likes it or not; and the inspector may not like it if the third party is a humble employee, because then the inspector may not wish to incur the odium of proceeding against him. The notice procedure avoids this difficulty, because it leaves the prosecutor with his usual discretion in deciding whether to go on against the third party.

Section 24 (1) has occasioned problems of interpretion. The following account goes beyond the needs and interests of most students of the general principles of the criminal law, but may assist practitioners.

No vicarious liability for negligence of employees.—Contrary to what may appear at first sight, paragraph (*b*) does not make an employer liable for the negligence of "any person under his control." The defendant must have used due diligence to avoid the commission of an offence by his employees, but he is liable only for his own negligence, not for that of his employees.

For many years the courts took the opposite view. They held that sections exempting the non-negligent defendant did not operate to exempt him where his employee was negligent.[10] The present interpretation of the law was settled by *Tesco Supermarkets Ltd.* v. *Nattrass,*[11] with the satisfactory result that vicarious responsibility is excluded.

> A branch of Tesco displayed a sign to the effect that a brand of washing powder was being sold at a reduced price. An old-age pensioner tried to buy a packet but was offered only a packet at the full price. He accordingly complained to an inspector of weights and measures who brought a charge against Tesco under the Trade Descriptions Act 1968 s. 11 (2). Tesco gave notice that they blamed their store manager, who had failed to see that the reduced-price packs were on sale. Tesco also gave detailed evidence of the control they exercised over their managers. Their defence under section 24 of the Trade Descriptions Act was upheld by the House of Lords. The branch manager was a mere employee, not a controller with whom the company was identified; consequently, the company was not liable. Lord Diplock said: "If considerations of cost and business practicability did not play a part in determining what employers carrying on such business could reasonably be expected to do to prevent the commission of an offence under the Act, the price to the public of the protection afforded to a minority of consumers might well be an increase in the cost of goods and services to consumers generally."[12]

Where the House of Lords was open to criticism was in its extremely restrictive approach

---

[10] The trouble arose from the atrocious wording of subsection (1). The *omnium gatherum* of paragraph (*a*) ends with the words "or some other cause beyond his control"; and the word "other" may seem to suggest that the previous causes are only such causes as are beyond the defendant's control. But this interpretation is not grammatically compulsory; and to hold that "the act or default of another person" excludes the acts of employees (who are supposed to be within the defendant's control) would mean that the concluding words of (*b*) are deprived of effect. This is because (*b*) seems to say that the defendant is quit if he took care to control his employee, and it would be odd if he were nevertheless liable because the act of his employee did not come within the list in (*a*). The only reasonable conclusion is that the words "beyond his control" in (*a*) are surplusage, being a muddle-headed anticipation of what is to be said in (*b*).

Notwithstanding the obfuscation of para. (*a*), it seems that if the defendant points to any causation that did not involve his own negligence, he points to a "cause beyond his control," which is obviously the right rule. See, for example, *Bibby-Cheshire* v. *Golden Wonder Ltd* [1972] Crim.LR 657, [1973] *ibid.* 71.

[11] [1972] AC 153.

[12] The rule in *Tesco* obviously applies not only to the Trade Descriptions Act but to other statutes containing a similar provision. Yet in *Pickover* v. *Smith* [1975] Crim.LR 529 one of the bad old cases was followed in relation to the Weights and Measures Act, notwithstanding that it was clearly inconsistent with *Tesco,* which was not considered.

Before *Tesco,* in *Beckett* v. *Kingston Bros. (Butchers) Ltd* [1970] 1 QB 606, the court distinguished between two cases. (1) Where the local manager commits the contravention himself; here the company can plead s. 24 (1) and escape liability. (2) Where the local manager is negligent in supervising an assistant; here it is "proper to regard the manager as representing his employers in a supervisory capacity." The latter rule must now be regarded as inconsistent with the *ratio decidendi* of *Tesco,* even though the facts of *Tesco* perhaps fell within proposition (1).

to the identification doctrine; a point that has already been made. It is an extraordinary state of affairs when a firm like Smedleys, where every responsible member of the organisation took consummate care, is convicted, while Tesco is acquitted notwithstanding the admitted negligence of its branch manager. On a reasonable view, their lordships were wrong both times: in *Smedley*, because the defendants should have been acquitted of negligence on the facts, and in *Tesco*, because the defendants should have been identified with their branch manager.

The purpose of paragraph (*a*) is not apparent on its face. Presumably Parliament meant to require the defendant to go a certain way towards identifying the cause of the contravention, to the extent of bringing the cause within one of the categories mentioned. If the defendant has no idea how the lapse came about, or if he cannot establish how it probably came about, he may be convicted, even if he brings himself within(*b*)[13]—which is unjust.

Defendant must do everything reasonable to ascertain the person responsible.—On the plain reading of the subsection, the defendant escapes liability if he establishes one of the exempting causes listed in (*a*) and in addition establishes (*b*). This should mean that, under (*a*), it is enough that he proves that the offence was caused by one of a number of other persons, even though he fails to establish which person. However, Lord Diplock in *Tesco* proposed a more stringent rule. He said:

> "It is for the principal [the employer] to identify the other person or persons (if any) to whose act or default the offence was actually due and to pass to the prosecutor the available identificatory information. If the principal is not able to do this, it shows a defect in the system which he has laid down for allocating among his servants the duty of taking precautions to avoid the commission of offences under the Act. There is no injustice in requiring him to lay down a reasonably effective system and in treating any failure to do so as a criminal offence. If, on the other hand, the principal is able to identify a person to whose act or default the offence was actually due, he still has to show that he himself exercised due diligence to devise an effective system to avoid such acts or defaults on the part of his servants and to satisfy himself that such system was being observed."[14]

The reason given by his lordship in his second sentence for the general proposition in the first sentence does not go the whole length of the proposition that it is supposed to support. For one thing, the reason applies only where the "other persons" are the defendant's employees; it does not indicate that he must make a positive identification among "other persons" over whom he has no control. For another, the question whether the defendant was at fault in failing to avoid the offence is surely distinct from the question whether he is at fault in failing to identify the offender; and the latter question can arise only if the defendant is under a duty to identify the offender. Parliament has not said that he is.

It seems that Lord Diplock's narrow view of the defence will not be wholly adopted by the courts. After *Tesco,* the Divisional Court laid down the law in more muted terms. The rule stated was that the defendant cannot avail himself of the statutory defence unless he has done all that can reasonably be expected of him to investigate how the offence occurred and who was responsible.[15] This suggests that the defendant can clear himself if he makes every reasonable investigation to find who was to blame. "I do not believe," said Watkins J "that a defendant who has done all else that can be expected of him fails merely because he cannot identify the precise person responsible for the act or default." But even this rule, requiring the defendant to exert himself to trace the person at fault, though eminently justifiable as a matter of legislative policy, runs counter to the Act. The Divisional Court's rule imposes upon the defendant a duty to gather evidence after the occurrence of the offence, as to which the Act is silent. The intention of Parliament is emphasised by section 24 (2) (above), which requires the defendant to give advance notice of "such information as was then in his possession," but does not impose on him a duty to make enquiries after the offence. In placing the latter duty on the defendant, the court restricted the defence in a way not provided for by Parliament.

---

[13] *Moore* v. *Ray* [1951] 1 KB 98.

[14] [1972] AC at 197.

[15] *McGuire* v. *Sittingbourne Co-op. Soc. Ltd* 140 JP Rep. 306, [1976] Crim.LR 268, criticised in 140 JPN 108.

The defence of act or default of another person overrides the other defences.—A defect in the draftsmanship of section 24 (1) is that the specified excuses overlap. The reasonable interpretation, in order to give effect to the policy of the subsection, is to say that if the defence involves a reference to the act or default of another person (the last word including a person who is the defendant's employee), then the notification provision appplies. So a mistake by the defendant's employee (it has been held) is a defence of act or default of another, not a defence of mistake.[16] On principle, the same rule applies to the defences of information supplied and accident; if they involve attributing responsibility to another person, the notification procedure should apply.

> Consider a case where A sells an article to B with a false trade description, and B (not knowing the falsity) sells the article to C with the same trade description. B is charged with an an offence under the Act. When these facts arose, it was held that B had the defence of information supplied,[17] but the present question was not considered. In order to avoid stultifying the statutory scheme, the defence should be regarded as "the act or default of another person," which will not succeed without the statutory notification being given as to the person blamed.)

Bypass procedure under the Trade Descriptions Act.—One other question may have occurred to the attentive reader. On the facts of *Tesco*, could Tesco's branch manager have been convicted? The answer is yes. Acts giving a restricted no-negligence defence of the type now being considered accompany this by a provision enabling the prosecution to be brought against the person actually responsible. The Trade Descriptions Act effects this by section 23.

> "Where the commission by any person of an offence under this Act is due to the act or default of some other person that other person shall be guilty of the offence, and a person may be charged with and convicted of the offence by virtue of this section whether or not proceedings are taken against the first-mentioned person."

But, it may be said, Tesco did not commit an offence, so that section could not apply. This is a reasonable objection at first sight. The section, which is common form in this type of legislation, contains a mistake in drafting. However, the opening words are construed to refer not only to "the commission by any person of an offence" but to "an act that would be an offence by a person if it were not for the defence provided by s. 24."[18] Consequently, Tesco's branch manager could have been convicted under section 23.

Use of the bypass procedure against non-traders.—Another difficulty in the drafting of section 23 is that whereas the main offence-creating sections of the TDA are limited to persons who act in the course of a trade or business, section 23 contains no such express limitation. So it may seem that a non-trader, an amateur seller, who sells to a dealer, and who could not be made liable for misdescription under section 1 of the Act if the prosecution were against him initially, is liable under section 23 if the prosecution is first brought against the dealer who in good faith repeats the misdescription when he resells.

> Suppose that A, the private owner of a car, "clocks" it and sells it to B, a dealer. A is guilty of obtaining money from B by deception, but, not being a dealer, he is not guilty of an offences under section 1. B then sells the car to C, the odometer still showing a misleading milage, and when charged under section 1 sets up a defence under section 24 (1) that the offence was due to the act or default of another person, A, and that he himself exercised due diligence. Assuming that B can establish this defence on the facts it is only right that he should be acquitted. Suppose, further, that the prosecutor then charges A under section 23. It would be anomalous if A is liable by reason of the fact that the proceedings were first commenced against B, when he would not have been liable under the Act if the proceedings had been against him initially. So the reasonable view is that the case should be regarded as one of "act or default of another" for the

---

[16] *Birkenhead Co-op. Soc.* v. *Roberts* [1970] 3 All ER 391; *Butler* v. *Keenway Supermarkets Ltd* [1974] Crim.LR 560.

[17] *Simmons* v. *Potter* [1975] RTR 347, Crim.LR 354. It may be observed that in some other statutes (like the Food and Drugs Act 1955 s. 113 (1), set out at n. 1 above), the statutory defence contains only the "act or default" provision and not the "information supplied" provision, and here the courts construe "act or default of another" to include "information supplied." See R G Lawson in 140 JPN 217

[18] *Coupe* v. *Guyett* [1973] 1 WLR 669, 2 All ER 1058. *Aliter* if such a person would have had a defence *apart* from s. 24.

purpose of a defence under section 24, but not for the purpose of a charge under section 23.

The authorities bearing on this are not easy to reconcile. It has been held that the act or default that makes a person liable under section 23 means a wrongful act or default—not in the sense that it requires proof of *mens rea* or negligence, since liability under section 23, when it arises, is strict,[19] but in the sense that there must be something more than an act that leads to the offence committed by the first defendant (B) as a matter of purely factual causation.[20] Perhaps a fair interpretation of the actual decisions would be to say that the act or default must be itself a breach of the Trade Descriptions Act (or must be, at least, an act or default of an employee of a person who would be in breach of the Act[21]), apart from the statutory defence. This would leave it open to the courts to hold that the amateur seller is not liable under section 23 merely because he factually contributed to what is (apart from a statutory defence) an offence under section 24. There are powerful arguments, both in reason and on authority, in favour of this view.[22] The main obstacle in the way of the solution is an *obiter dictum* of Lord Diplock in *Tesco*. He said that section 23

> "makes guilty of the offence created by some other section of the Act persons, such as servants or agents, who do not fall within the description cntained in that other section of the person by whom the offence can be committed. " 'act' is wide enough to include any physical act which is causative of the offence."[23]

However, this dictum was obiter, since it was spoken in a case turning on section 24, not section 23; and there is no legal impossibility in the phrase bearing a different meaning in the two sections.[24] As applied to section 23 it cannot be reconciled with subsequent decisions of the Divisional Courts,[25] So the question awaits final determination. In the meantime, trading standards officers, who wish to extend their powers under the Act, are obtaining convictions against amateurs under section 23 in magistrates' courts, and are awaiting a case on "strong facts" (i.e. facts that are likely to predispose the Divisional Court in their favour) before taking a test case on appeal.[26]

§44. 7. PROSECUTORIAL DISCRETION

It is worth mentioning certain studies of the way in which prosecutors exercise their discretion in cases of presumptively strict liability.

The earliest English study was, creditably, made by two undergraduates of the University of Kent who sent a questionnaire to about 200 Food and Drugs Authorities.[1] They found great discrepancy of practice and also of opinion among the 149 chief inspectors who replied. Many offences were

---

[19] See particularly *Lamb* v. *Sunderland Creamery* [1951] 1 All ER 923.

[20] In *Lill Holdings Ltd* v. *White* [1979] RTR 120 the defendants zeroed an odometer and sold the car with a disclaimer; this sale was perfectly lawful, and it was therefore held that the defendants were not liable under section 23 in respect of a resale of the car with its misleading odometer. "It would be a strange situation," said the court in the earlier case of *Tarleton Engineering Co. Ltd* v. *Nattrass* [1973] 1 WLR at 1270, 3 All ER at 706–707, if A were guilty of no offence when he sold to B, owing to the terms of the contract of sale, yet guilty under section 23. See Newsome in 143 JPN 606. Cp. *Noss Farm Products Ltd* v. *Lilico* [1945] 2 All ER 609, 45 WN 179, where it was held, under the Food and Drugs Act, that conduct is not the act or default of another when it becomes wrongful subsequently by reason of a change in the law. The law when so changed is not retroactive. Other judicial statements can be found that the act or default under both the TDA and the Food and Drugs Act must be wrongful: see Newsome, *op.cit.*

[21] The bracketed qualification is necessary in view of the decision in *Tesco* and particularly the remarks of Lord Diplock in that case ([1972] AC at 196).

[22] See the important articles by J Edmondson in 144 JPN 594, 670.

[23] [1972] AC at 196.

[24] In *Tesco* at Viscount Dilhorne said of the words "act or default" in s. 24 (1): "In that subsection, whatever they mean in s. 23, they must be given their literal meaning."

[25] Such as *Lill Holdings Ltd*, n. 20 above.

[26] See the letter by a Chief Inspector in 144 JPN 694.

[1] Miles Smith and Anthony Pearson in [1969] Crim.LR 5.

not prosecuted for one reason or another, sometimes because the defendant was not at fault; yet of the prosecutions that were brought, about 25 per cent were against defendants who were known not to have been at fault.

So strict liability is a social reality. Fifty-two per cent of the inspectors thought that strict liability was useful to them in their work of protecting the public. This is not surprising, since strict liability obviously lightened their work and minimised the risk of failure of prosecutions—no prosecuting official likes to fail in a case that he has undertaken, because failure indicates some lack of prevision on his part, if only in bringing the case. What is perhaps more significant is that no fewer than 42 per cent. of the inspectors thought that strict liability was not useful.

Subsequent studies have revealed in more detail the criteria used by inspectors in prosecuting. Generally they use the velvet glove, advising, warning and persuading, and turning to the criminal courts only as a last resort. In deciding whether to prosecute, an important consideration is the number of previous offences and the warnings that have been issued, as well as the strength of the efforts made by the firm to improve its standards. Sometimes, when the inspectors would not prosecute on their own volition, they nevertheless did so on complaint by an aggrieved person.[2]

The no-negligence defence, where Parliament allows it, reminds enforcement officers of the need to ascertain fault. So the defence has a wider importance than the comparatively small number of cases in which it is successfully raised. This, it may be surmised, is why Tesco bore the considerable expense of appealing to the House of Lords in order to shift the liability to pay a small fine from themselves to their branch manager. The effect of their lordships' decision was likely to be that in future, in similar circumstances, the prosecution would be against their manager personally, and would not involve the fair name of Tesco. If it is not socially desirable that a firm should be able to shield itself from adverse local publicity on such facts, that is an indication that the House of Lords construed the identification doctrine too narrowly. When a company has several branches, the law should recognise in every branch some person with sufficient authority in the company's affairs to implicate the company in his mismanagement.

SUMMARY

A company, or corporation, is a legal person distinct from the human corporators who constitute its framework. § .1

It is attributively liable for its employees to the extent that a human employer is. § .2 In addition, it is identified with its controlling officers, whose acts and states of mind are imputed to it. In the case of a trading company the controllers are the directors and other person (such as the manager or secretary) to whom they delegate wide discretion to act on their behalf. But a branch manager who is tightly controlled by higher officers is not himself a controller: *Tesco Supermarkets Ltd* v. *Nattrass*. The company is identified with its controller even though he acts in fraud of the company, but it seems probable that identification takes place only in respect of acts done on company business.

The main justification for this corporate liability is that it may help to keep the § .3

---

[2] Law Commission, *Published Working Paper No. 30* (*Strict Liability and the Enforcement of the Factories Act 1961*); Bernard M Dickens in [1970] Crim.LR 624–633; Stephen White in 142 JPN 622; and particularly W G Carson in 33 MLR 396.

company up to the mark. Liability without fault does not create the same problems of justice as with human defendants. Fines may also compel errant companies to give up illegal profits.

The notion of identification has not been applied to human employers, who are prosecuted in their own names and not in a firm name. § .4

Some penal statutes provide a defence of due diligence, i.e. of no negligence. § .5

A stricter form of this defence is one incorporating the third party procedure, as in the Food and Drugs Act 1955 s. 13 (1). The original defendant lays an information against some other person to whose act or default he claims that the contravention was due. The original defendant will be acquitted if he proves this and proves that he himself used all due diligence. The third party can similarly bring in other parties, and so escape liability, but unless he does so he is strictly liable. The prosecution are usually allowed to short-circuit proceedings by charging the third party directly. More recent statutes, in place of the third-party procedure, achieve the same broad purpose by giving a defence of no negligence on condition that the defendant gives due notice of any third party to whose act or default he alleges the contravention was due. The defence may be in broad terms, or qualified as in the Trade Descriptions Act 1968 s. 24 (1). This requires the defendant, under (*a*), to prove that the contravention was due to (1) a mistake, (2) reliance on information supplied, (3) the act or default of another person, (4) an accident, or (5) some other cause beyond his control. The last words do not mean that the earlier items must be beyond the defendant's control; in particular, "the act or default of another person" includes that of his employee: the *Tesco* case. It has been held that under (3) the defendant must do everything reasonable to identify the offender. Under (*b*) the defendant must prove due diligence. Although the subsection does not require the defendant to bring the third party before the court, the prosecution may charge him directly, and they may do this without charging the person who contravened the Act. § .6

Studies of prosecution practices show that charges are often brought against persons who are known not to have been at fault. § .7

INDEX